CHICAGO PUBLIC LIBRARY
BUSINESS / SCIENCE / TECHNOLOGY
400 S. STATE ST.   60605

HF
5415
.0974
2000

HWBI

The Oxford Textbook of Marketing

Chicago Public Library

Form 178 rev. 1-94

CHICAGO PUBLIC LIBRARY
BUSINESS / SCIENCE / TECHNOLOGY
400 S. STATE ST.   60605

The Oxford Textbook of
Marketing

Edited by
Keith Blois

OXFORD
UNIVERSITY PRESS

OXFORD
UNIVERSITY PRESS

Oxford University Press, Great Clarendon Street, Oxford OX2 6DP
Oxford University Press is a department of the University of Oxford,
It furthers the University's objective of excellence in research, scholarship,
and education by publishing worldwide in

Oxford New York

Athens Auckland Bangkok Bogotá Bombay Buenos Aires
Calcutta Cape Town Chennai Dar es Salaam Delhi Florence Hong Kong
Istanbul Karachi Kuala Lumpur Madrid Melbourne Mexico City Mumbai
Nairobi Paris São Paulo Singapore Taipei Tokyo Toronto Warsaw
and associated companies in
Berlin Ibadan

Oxford is a registered trade mark of Oxford University Press
in the UK and in certain other countries

Published in the United States
by Oxford University Press Inc., New York

© Oxford University Press 2000
Database right Oxford University Press (maker)

First published 2000

All rights reserved. No part of this publication may be reproduced,
stored in a retrieval system, or transmitted, in any form or by any means,
without the prior permission in writing of Oxford University Press,
or as expressly permitted by law, or under terms agreed with the appropriate
reprographics rights organizations. Enquiries concerning reproduction
outside the scope of the above should be sent to the Rights Department,
Oxford University Press, at the address above

Your must not circulate this book in any other binding or cover
and you must impose the same condition on any acquirer

British Library Cataloguing in Publication Data
Data available

Library of Congress Cataloging in Publication Data
Data available

ISBN 0-19-877576-8

1 3 5 7 9 10 8 6 4 2

Typeset by Best-set Typesetter Ltd., Hong Kong
Printed and bound in Italy by
Giunti Industrie Grafiche, Florence

Acknowledgements

CHICAGO PUBLIC LIBRARY
BUSINESS / SCIENCE / TECHNOLOGY
400 S. STATE ST.   60605
R0173608878

BRENDAN George of OUP who was the person who originally conceived the idea of a marketing textbook created out of a number of chapters written by individual subject experts. In that sense the book is his creation. Ruth Marshall, also of OUP, who with patience and good humour managed the detailed transformation of the book from the manuscript through to its final format. Hilary Walford whose copy editing both greatly improved the presentation of the material and in many cases made it more accessible to the reader. Hilary personifies the falsity of the claim that 'Consistency is the plague of small minds' which, as she would correctly point out, is a misquote of 'A foolish consistency is the hobgoblin of little minds'.

For permission to make use of copyright material the kindness of the following is acknowledged:

The *Financial Times* in pp. 378–9; *Journal of General Management* in Section 5 of Chapter 17; Malcolm McDonald and *Insight* in pp. 473–4.

The generosity of those advertising agencies that agreed to the reproduction of their material is noted, together with the names of the staff involved, on the pages concerned.

CHICAGO PUBLIC LIBRARY
BUSINESS SCIENCE TECHNOLOGY
400 S. STATE ST. 60605

Contents

Contributors

Sönke Albers, Christian-Albrechts University, Kiel

Gerrit Antonides, Erasmus University, Rotterdam

George Avlonitis, Department of Management Science and Marketing, Athens University of Economics and Business

Keith Blois, Templeton College, University of Oxford

Roderick Brodie, Department of Marketing, University of Auckland

Richard Brookes, Department of Marketing, University of Auckland

Katia Campo, Department of Business Economics, University Faculties St Ignatius, Antwerp

David Carson, University of Ulster

Bernard Cova, EAP, Paris

Nicole Coviello, Faculty of Management, University of Calgary

Tevfik Dalgic, Faculteit Economie en Management, Hogeschool van Utrecht

Ulrike de Brentani, Concordia University, Montreal

Sally Dibb, Warwick Business School, University of Warwick

Sean Ennis, Department of Marketing, University of Strathclyde

Martin Evans, Bristol Business School, University of the West of England

Els Gijsbrechts, Department of Business Economics, University Faculties St Ignatius, Antwerp

Alan Griffiths, Anglia Business School, Anglia Polytechnic University, Cambridge

Christian Grönroos, CERS Center for Relationship Marketing and Service Management, Hanken Swedish School of Economics, Finland

Klaus Grunert, Aarhus School of Business, Aarhus

Graham Hankinson, Thames Valley University, Slough

Pannapachr Itthiopassagul, Department of Marketing, Thammasat University, Bangkok

Mary Lambkin, Graduate School of Business, University College, Dublin

Peter Leeflang, Department of Economics, University of Groningen

Malcolm McDonald, Cranfield School of Management, Cranfield University

Shiv Mathur, City Business School, City University, London

Gustav Puth, Department of Marketing and Communication Management, University of Pretoria

Jonathan Reynolds, Templeton College, University of Oxford

Robert Salle, Ecole de Management, Lyon

Adrian Sargeant, Henley Management College, Henley

Susan Shaw, Department of Marketing, University of Strathclyde

W. Fred van Raaij, Rotterdam School of Management, Erasmus University

Walter van Waterschoot, Department of Business Economics, University Faculties St Ignatius, Antwerp

Dave Wilson, Smeal College of Business Administration, Pennsylvania State University

Abbreviations

ABC	activity-based accounting
ACORN	A Classification of Residential Neighbourhoods
AMT	advanced manufacturing technologies
APEC	Association of petroleum Exporting Countries
ATM	automated teller machine
A–T–R	awareness, trial, and repeat purchase
Benelux	Belgium, the Netherlands, and Luxembourg
BRAD	*British Rates and Data*
CAD/CAM	computer-aided design and manufacturing
CAS	computer-aided selling
CATI	computer aided telephone interviewing
CCM	computer controlled manufacturing
CD	consumer durable
CEO	chief executive officer
CIS	Commonwealth of Independent States
CM	category management
CMO	chief marketing officer
CPM	cost per thousand
DFI	direct foreign investment
DMU	decision-making unit
DPM	directional policy matrix
DRPA	direct response press advertising
DRTV	direct response television advertising
DUGGING	data under the guise of research
ECR	efficient consumer response
ECSC	European Coal and Steel Community
EDI	electronic data interchange
EDLP	every day low pricing
EFT	electronic funds transfer
EFTPOS	electronic fund transfer at point of sale
EMU	European Monetary Union
EPOS	electronic point of sale
EU	European Union
Euratom	European Atopic Energy Community
FDI	foreign direct investment
FMCG	fast-moving consumer goods
FMS	flexible manufacturing systems
f.o.b.	free on board
FTC Act	Federal Trade Commission Act
GATT	General Agreement on Tariffs and Trade
GDP	gross domestic product
GFCF	gross fixed capital formation
GIS	geographical information systems
GM	General Motors
GP	general practitioner
Hi-Lo	high–low [pricing]
IBC	International Brand Company
IDV	International Distillers and Vintners
IM	internal marketing
IMC	integrated marketing communication
IMF	International Monetary Fund
IMP	Industrial Marketing and Purchasing
IP	intellectual property
ISO	International Organization for Standardization
IT	information technology
JIT	just in time
LSM	Living Standards Measures
LTV	lifetime value
M&As	mergers and acquisitions
MDS	multidimensional scaling
MEAL	*Media Expenditure Analysis*
MGM	member-get-member
MkIS	marketing information system
MNE	multinational enterprise
NAFTA	North American Free Trade Area
NAPM	National Association of Purchasing Management
NIC	newly industrializing country
NMC	National Marketing Company
NPV	net present value
NTB	non-tariff barrier
OECD	Organization for Economic Cooperation and Development
OTS	opportunity to see
Oxfam	Oxford Committee for Famine Relief
PC	personal computer
PDI	purchase decision influencers
PDM	purchase decision-maker
P/E	price/earnings
PLC	product life cycle
POP	point of purchase

POS	point of sale
PSC	Pierre Smirnoff Company
R&D	research and development
RFM	recency, frequency, and monetary value
RFQ	request for quotation(s)
ROI	return on investment
RONA	rate of return on net assets
ROS	return on sale
SBO	sales-based ordering
SBU	strategic business unit
SCU	sales coverage units
SIC	Standard Industrial Code
SKU	stock-keeping unit
SME	small to medium-sized enterprise
SMP	single market programme
SUGGING	selling under the guise of research
SWOT	strengths, weaknesses, opportunities, and threats
TFP	total factor productivity
TGI	*Target Group Index*
TMC	total material control
TQM	total quality management
VAL	Value and Lifestyles
VANS	value-added network services
VAT	valued-added tax
WTO	World Trade Organization

How to use this book

This book contains a number of devices which it is hoped will assist readers to gain the maximum benefit from using it:

Billions Unless otherwise specified a billion is 'a thousand million'.

Figures and Tables Each Figure and Table has a clear heading indicating the main message or content of the Figure or Table.

Objectives and Summaries Each chapter starts with a list of objectives and ends with a brief summary. This enables the reader, before starting to read, to be aware of what material the chapter will cover and at the end of the chapter to be provided with a brief review of the material which has been covered.

Reading In addition to the references to further work given within each chapter there is a short list of Further Reading to be found at the end of each chapter.

Discussion questions A number of discussion questions are provided at the end of each chapter. Some of these enable the reader to check understanding of the material in the chapter while others provide a base for thinking more broadly about the material.

Cases Apart from the first five chapters, every chapter concludes with a Case Study. Some of these are designed to provide the basis for discussion of the 'what should be done?' type. Others provide descriptions of situations which can be used to further illustrate the chapter's contents. Longer cases are provided at the end of each of the book's five sections.

Boxes and Inserts Throughout the text Boxes and Inserts are to be found. These provide practical examples of the issues considered within each chapter. The text can be followed without reading this material but it is hoped that it will be useful and illuminating. The passing of time between the book being written and its publication has meant that the fortunes of some companies mentioned in these Boxes and Inserts (e.g. Marks and Spencer) have changed. However, where this has happened this acts as a useful reminder of the speed at which companies' fortunes can change in the modern world.

Chapter Links One of the interesting features of marketing is the complex interlinking of issues. So although it is necessary to have a chapter dealing with, say, Branding, the topic of branding is mentioned at various other points in the book. In many cases these links are obvious, such as when in the Product Management chapter branding is briefly discussed. However, some of the other links are less obvious and the purpose of the Chapter Links is to indicate some of the other less obvious places in the book to which the topic under discussion is related. Given the large number of possible links only some of the more important ones are noted.

Glossary The definitions of a number of terms which will not be known to readers new to Marketing are given in a Glossary at the end of the book.

Abbreviations At the front of the book is an explanation of the abbreviations used within the book.

Supplements

The main text of the *Oxford Textbook of Marketing* is accompanied by a supplementary pack, available free to all adopters of the text. An Instructor's Manual contains lecture outlines summarizing the main themes in each chapter, and provides suggestions for activities and discussion points suitable for both small-group teaching and individual study. This is accompanied by a set of PowerPoint slides.

More information on the text and supplements is available through the Internet on the web page http://www.oup.co.uk/best.textbooks/business/blois.

You can access further information about other Oxford University Press textbooks and products from the site: www.oup.com.

Part One
Customers, Markets, and Marketing

Chapter 1
Introduction: What is Marketing About?

Keith Blois

Objectives

The objectives of this chapter are:

1 to explain why marketing exists in a modern society;

2 to demonstrate the role of marketing in a modern society;

3 to introduce a number of key marketing ideas that will be considered in greater depth in later chapters of the book.

1 Where does it all start?

You need a pair of sandals—what do you do? You go to a shoe shop, where you are able to examine several different styles of sandals within a range of prices. If you find a pair you like and can then afford them, you purchase them, paying in one of a variety of ways, such as with cash, a credit card, electronic fund transfer, and so on.

What you, as a member of a modern society, are incapable of doing is providing sandals from the natural resources at your disposal. You do not know which of the naturally available materials are suitable; neither, even if you were given appropriate materials, do you have the skills needed to create a sandal. Compare this situation with that of the few remaining, so-called primitive societies where people live in small self-sufficient groups. For example, many Australian aborigines lived in such a way until the second half of the twentieth century, and the organization of their lives was a constant trade-off, as they divided their time between obtaining sufficient food from their natural environment, moving on to other areas when the resources in a locality became depleted, and taking time to provide for their minimal material needs (see Insert). So if one of their group needed some sandals, then the group would decide when to give this matter priority over other activities, and, once this was agreed,

Shoes or food?

'The talk about the activities for the day goes on for a long time. . . . The men have decided to hunt emu, so the discussion centres on what the women will do. Nyurapaya has decided that her bark sandals are worn out and need to be replaced. During the day the sand becomes too hot to walk around on comfortably barefoot, so these sandals (called *playkanpa*) get lots of use. Sandals are made from the green bark of *taliwanti*, a plant that grows in the sandhills. Nyurapaya knows where to find some of these plants, but the place lies in a different direction from the area where the women have been lately looking for edible plants. Should they take a chance that they will come across some edible seeds or fruit on the way to the taliwanti-place? Or should they stick with a sure thing and manage with their worn-out sandals for another day?'

Source: Gould (1969:16).

could produce the sandals from naturally available materials. There was no need to rely on anybody outside the group.

In fact, by the time modern people have got up in the morning and left home for work, we have consumed or used a great many goods and services. These would include food, clothing, and the shelter provided by our homes; there is also a subconscious sense of security arising from the fact that our property is insured, and that, in the event of an accident, the fire, ambulance, and police services are available. What is striking about those of us who live in 'advanced societies' is not only that we consume so much and such a variety of products but that we are incapable of producing the vast majority of these items ourselves. We are, therefore, dependent for our style of living on others producing these items and making them available to us, either by direct purchase with our own funds, or indirectly through public provision paid for through the taxation system or as gifts.

Of course even such a simple activity as making a pair of sandals available for sale in a shop involves a great many organizations trading with each other. Amongst these would be firms supplying the various raw materials (leather, plastic, metal, etc.); converting the raw materials into different forms; cutting up sheets of plastics or leather and assembling the sandals; supplying the packaging; transporting the packaged sandals to warehouses or retail outlets; insuring the products while in transit; and so on. Altogether, to produce even such a basic product involves an immensely complex set of exchanges between many different organizations. At its simplest the subject of marketing is concerned with how such firms decide what they should offer to make and sell and what form their products (be they goods or services) should take. Yet the apparent simplicity of these questions is deceptive and there are numerous and complex factors that need to be taken into account by a firm when deciding what the answers to them should be. To illustrate this Section 2 will consider the problem confronted by a firm as it seeks to decide what it should be making and offering on the market.

2 Factors that influence demand for a product

IMAGINE a small firm producing only one type of product (it could be a physical product or a service), which it sells directly to individual consumers; this firm finds itself in the happy position of having enough customers to be able to run at a profit. This satisfactory situation is illustrated in Fig. 1.1, where the demand from the market is shown as equal to the level of output that the firm needs to achieve to cover its costs.

However, it would be a foolish manager who decided that such a situation was unlikely to change, for the nature of modern markets is that demand seldom remains constant and indeed that changes are often dramatic and disruptive. Most changes in demand derive from a complex interaction of a large number of factors and for simplicity it helps initially to think of these as divided into five broad categories: population; tastes and fashions; economic conditions; technology; and politics and regulations. In reality the demand for most products is affected by a combination of each

Figure 1.1 **The firm with a product meeting a market demand**

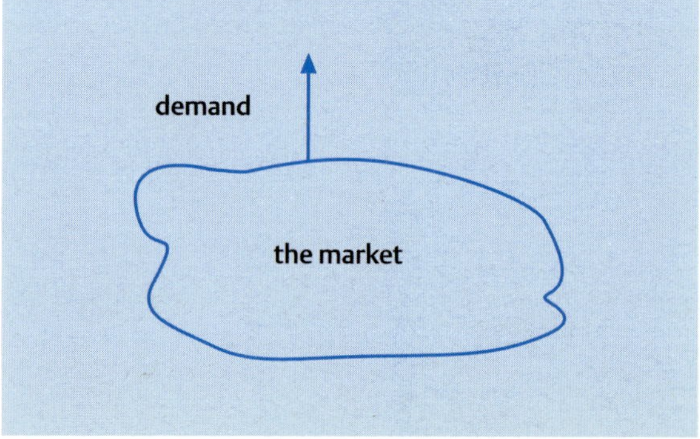

of these factors, though some products are more directly influenced by one factor than by the others. So the demand for some products is influenced by population change more than by technology, while for others the opposite may be the case. For ease of understanding, therefore, each of the factors will first be considered independently and examples of their impact given from different industries. Then an illustration will be given of the way the demand for a product is influenced by the interaction of these factors. These five categories are indicated in Fig. 1.2, with the question mark at the end of the time arrow acting as a reminder that the nature and volume of future demand are uncertain.

2.1 Population

The population in a given geographic market changes in two ways: first, in terms of its size, and, secondly, in terms of its age distribution. Although these are interconnected, they will initially be considered independently.

2.1.1 Population size

In most countries the size of the population is steadily rising and the effect of this is that there is an ever-increasing demand for products such as food, shelter, and so on. Even so, the demand for individual food items varies and it may be that, even in a country with a rapidly rising population, the demand for a particular type of food may fall, owing, say, to changes in consumer tastes (see

below). Assuming that the growth in population does not lead to a reduction in the per capita wealth of the country, then the demand for many non-basic needs will also rise as the population increases. Unless the increase in the population is the result of mass immigration, there are many products for which the demand will be slow to react to any such change in the population. If, for example, the increase—as it most typically will be—is mainly the result of a rise in the birth rate, then the firms most immediately affected will be those concerned with the needs of pregnant mothers and of babies. But other firms will see little if any change in demand for their products for several years as a result of such an increase, even those firms supplying toys for 4–5 year olds will see little effect for a few years after an increase in the birth rate.

2.1.2 Age distribution

The second population effect is the age distribution, for, other than in those countries that have been involved in major wars, the split between male and female normally remains fairly steady. There are many products whose demand is mainly derived from members of specific age groups. For example, the demand for chiropody is primarily related to the number of older people in the population. Although the proportion of people in various age groups changes relatively rapidly (see Table 1.1), the numbers in each age group except for the youngest one are predictable well in advance. So, unless the demand for a firm's product is related to the number of babies in the population, the number of people in its target age group may change but will be predictable well in advance.

There is, of course, a link between the age distribution of a population and its size. Clearly the number of births relative to the number of deaths determines the size of the population. The number of births is related to the number of women in the childbearing age groups, though this link is complex because whether or not a woman wishes to have children is determined by a combined set of factors that fall within the other four broad categories of change discussed in this section. The number of deaths, assuming no famine or major epidemics, is predictable with a high degree of accuracy in Western Europe and is primarily determined by the number of people over the age of 70.

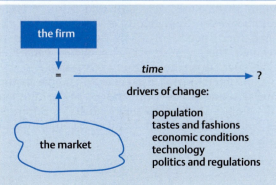

Figure 1.2 **The firm with uncertain future market demand**

the firm

time ?

drivers of change:

population
tastes and fashions
economic conditions
technology
politics and regulations

the market

Table 1.1	**Age distribution of the UK resident population, 1951–2001**										
Age	**1951**		**1961**		**1971**		**1981**		**1991**		**2001**[a]	
	Nos. (000s)	%	Nos. (000s)	%	Nos. (000s)	%	Nos. (000s)	%	Nos. (000s)	%	Nos. (000s)	%
0–4	4,326	8.6	4,272	8.1	4,553	8.1	3,455	6.1	3,886	6.7	3,593	6.0
5–19	10,354	20.5	11,833	22.4	12,778	22.8	12,882	22.9	10,914	18.9	11,424	19.2
20–44	18,279	36.3	17,099	32.3	17,765	31.8	19,069	33.8	21,519	37.2	21,127	35.5
45–64	11,980	23.8	13,393	25.4	13,424	24.0	12,475	22.1	12,388	21.4	14,080	23.7
65+	5,463	10.8	6,208	11.8	7,409	13.3	8,472	15.0	9,099	15.7	9,247	15.5
TOTAL	50,402		52,805		55,925		56,353		57,806		59,471	

[a] Mid-year estimate.

2.2 Tastes and fashions

A significant feature of affluent economies has been the extension of the concept of 'fashions' to a wider and wider range of goods and activities. Fashion in clothing has been accepted for centuries, but it is only in the latter part of the twentieth century that there have been annual changes in what is regarded as being 'in fashion'. Also since the 1980s the concept of 'being fashionable' has extended to an even wider range of items of clothing and other items. For example, people buying new swimming costumes each year is a relatively new phenomenon. It is based not on a need to replace worn-out costumes, as modern materials mean that costumes last much longer than they used to, but from a desire to wear costumes of the latest shape and colour. Similarly the concept of there being fashions in watches is relatively new. The complexity of this is illustrated by the views of the founder of Swatch (see Insert), who believes that Swatch satisfies a desire to identify with a culture of change. The source of new fashions is clearly more often than not an attempt by various industries to create a demand for replacement products. However, from time to time consumers do reject the 'latest fashion': sometimes because they simply do not like it, on other occasions because they cannot afford to replace items that still have a useful life, even if they are no longer fashionable.

> **A personal culture on offer**
>
> To Nicolas Hayek, originator of the Swatch, vision is the basis of Swatch's success. 'To him this success is not simply because Swatch is a fashion item, but lies in the fact that, "we are offering our personal culture. If it were just a fashion item, it could be easily copied, but Swatch have tapped deep into the roots of change, to respond to the feelings of wanting to be identified with what you do."'
>
> *Source:* Irons (1994: 71).

Fashions also arise in markets not associated with clothing. For example, the skateboard craze that hit many European countries in the 1970s turned out to be quite short lived. While in the 1990s skateboards were still sold in quite large numbers, the tremendous enthusiasm that existed for a period of about two years when it seemed that almost every teenager wanted a skateboard dissipated within a few years.

Consumers' tastes also seem to change in the literal sense of the word 'taste', as exemplified by changes in demand for products as different as coffee, whisky, wine (see Insert), and foreign cuisines.

| A substitute for Viagra?

Consumption of Western-style wines—particularly red wine—is rising fast in the more prosperous and cosmopolitan cities of China. Although part of the reason is that the Chinese government has been discouraging consumption of spirits and beer (because their production uses staples such as grain), the main reason seems to be a belief that red wine is good for your health and in particular for your virility.

2.3 Economic conditions

The state of a country's economy obviously has a direct effect on the demand for many products. However, the population's *perception* of the state of the economy and its implications for their personal financial security is probably more important in the short term than its actual state. When people feel confident about their economic situation, they will not only spend the money they have more readily, but will also be more willing to borrow money. So, as members of a population perceive their economic situation to be more secure, their expenditure will increase. The pattern of their expenditure will also change, and typically they will begin to purchase more items that they might previously have classified as luxuries and not felt able to afford. Their changed pattern of purchasing will also include some substitution effects, with, for example, a reduction in purchases of cheaper foods and the substitution of more expensive items—say, steak instead of sausages.

However, what is difficult to understand is how people's perception of their economic well-being relates to actual economic conditions. This is obviously very complex. For example, people may be very aware of the price increase on one product that they purchase, but they may not reflect on the other items they purchase on which there have been no increases. Consumers' perceptions can also be influenced by the topics on which the press decides to concentrate. There is also the complication that, just because people buy an item when they feel better off, it does not follow that they will cease to buy that item if harder economic times return. For example, a family may decide that it is now affluent enough to be able to own a car. If, later, the family perceives that their economic situation is becoming less secure, it is unlikely that

it will immediately dispose of the car. The experience of owning the car will have resulted in changes in the family's behaviour, and the family may now place a lower relative value on items that, when it was previously less well off, would have been seen as too important to do without.

2.4 Technology

The impact of technology on the demand for products is particularly complex because it has three aspects. Technology developments result in: changed production methods, improved existing products, and the introduction of new products. The lay person often remains totally oblivious to the effects of the first of these categories, and may not notice many of those of the second.

2.4.1 Production methods

Engineers are constantly seeking to improve the efficiency of the plant that they run. Similarly, managers in service organizations try to improve the efficiency of their operations. However, the customer often remains unaware of this, even when quite dramatic improvements are achieved. For example, a new method of mixing two or more solids together resulted in the 1970s in a reduction in the number of batches that failed the stringent quality tests in the pharmaceutical industry (where it is critically important to create an even mix, as the active components of some tablets are less than 0.05 per cent of their weight). The tablets reaching the market were no better or worse than before, but the cost of manufacturing the tablets was reduced because of the reduction in the number of tablets failing quality-control tests. In these circumstances the manufacturers were then able to reduce their prices, which could equally have led to an increase in demand. In other industries an improvement in production technology and service delivery organization has led either to a visible reduction in prices or at least to price increases at less than the rate of inflation. The result of this has been a maintenance or even an increase in demand over that which would have been achieved without these improvements in efficiency (see Insert overleaf).

2.4.2 Improved existing products

The nature of competitive markets is such that each firm is constantly seeking to improve its product offering in an attempt at least to keep up

Faster photos

A modern Kodachrome film processor is rather large (occupying 1,000 square metres), costs £750,000, and requires ten staff to operate it. However, a recent development means that in future machines will fit into a space of only 60 square metres, cost about £75,000, and require only one operator. This will mean that, instead of having to send a Kodachrome film away for processing and then waiting some time for it to be developed and returned, it will in future be possible to get it developed at a local store. Even if this is done at the existing price, it is expected that the reduction in inconvenience will result in a growth in demand for this type of film.

Source: The Economist, 15 Feb. 1997, 79–80.

with, and ideally to keep ahead of, its competitors. It follows that few products remain the same over any period of time, for their suppliers are constantly trying to find ways of making improvements, which they believe will be appreciated by the customers.

In many cases the customers are well aware of and do appreciate these improvements. For example, the reduction in the size of mobile phones is both visible to and valued by the majority of their users. In other cases customers do not notice improvements, often because, in spite of the advertising claims of some manufacturers that their product now has a 'new formula', the changes are so marginal and started from an already high standard. Alternatively, the product may be used so infrequently that the customer cannot make a valid comparison between the old and the improved product.

The impact of product improvements on the demand for many products is often not very dramatic (at least compared with the effect of the introduction of a new product—see below). However, in some cases they do have an effect both on the demand for the product itself and also on the demand for other products. For example, the improvement in the quality of house paint has led to both a decrease in the demand for the services of professional decorators and an increase in the demand for paint. These effects have arisen because modern paints can easily be applied by a householder, who then can save money by not employing a professional decorator. Then, although modern paints last longer, the householder per-

ceives repainting as being less expensive and is consequently prepared to redecorate rooms more frequently than before.

2.4.3 New products

While it is sometimes difficult to differentiate between improved products and new products, there are many products that, when they were first introduced to the market, were regarded as genuinely new (see Chapter 24). These would have included CDs, videos, and telephone banking. Clearly, if people do start to purchase a product that is newly arrived on the market, they will have to adjust their expenditure to pay for it. Sometimes these adjustments have a dramatic effect on the demand for other industries: when you started to buy CDs, you probably reduced your purchases of cassette tapes. In other cases, the changes in expenditure are not obvious: if you buy a mobile phone, you do not usually give up your traditional landline phone, though you will probably use it less. It is, however, difficult to predict on what items expenditure will be reduced.

2.5 Politics and regulations

Politics with both a small and a large 'P' affect the demand for many products, and, although many regulations are based on political decisions, there are also many that are not. For example, many professional organizations have regulations that their members must obey if they wish to retain their membership. These regulations are seldom codified in the country's laws, but they can nevertheless exercise great influence over the members' behaviour.

New laws may create markets, expand markets, destroy markets, or make the product unnecessary. The Australian market for bicycle crash helmets, was created by the passing of laws that made wearing them compulsory. The decision reached by many governments to make seat belts in cars compulsory caused the rapid expansion of an existing but small market. In comparison, the decision of the UK Government to ban the ownership of handguns by the public has effectively destroyed the market for these weapons within the UK. The UK Government's ruling that it was unnecessary for cars to show lights when parked on a lit road after dark meant that the market for clip-on parking lights was effectively destroyed. In this case, while it was not illegal to show lights, the demand for clip-on parking lights disappeared almost immediately because most people had purchased them only because of the legal requirement to show lights.

Political decisions may particularly affect market demand through their impact on prices. In some cases governments use increased taxation as a method of raising the prices of products and services whose consumption they believe should be reduced. So taxes on tobacco have been progressively increased in many countries in an attempt to reduce the amount of smoking. In other cases, governments seek to encourage demand for a product by reducing its price through reducing taxes payable on the product or by offering subsidies. For example the Government of Queensland has offered financial incentives to households to encourage them to purchase solar-energy systems.

Political decisions can also affect the supply of raw materials and consequentially their price. For example, the Arab Oil States' decision to quadruple the price of oil in the period 1973–5 was unequivocally a political one. Other countries that control the supply of other strategically important raw materials (such as nickel) have also used their monopoly or near-monopoly power to influence their prices and thus exercise political influence.

Regulations other than those created by governments are also very influential. For example, in England and Wales the market for pocket calculators was transformed when the National School Examination Boards (which are independent of the Government) decided to allow students to take calculators into examinations. Before this happened, many teachers and parents had discouraged schoolchildren from purchasing calculators, because they feared that, if they did become accustomed to using them, they would lose the facility to do calculations without them and thus would have been disadvantaged in examinations.

2.6 Combined effects

As was suggested above, in reality all five of these factors can influence the demand for a product. To use the pocket-calculator example again, the rapid increase in demand for these items in England and Wales was not only affected by the changed examination regulations. Other important factors were that, at the time of the changed regulations, the number of young people in secondary schools was increasing. In addition, the price of calculators was falling, and their capabilities were being extended as a result of improvements in production technologies and product improvements. The economic situation at the time was relatively positive, so both schools and individuals felt able to afford the purchase of these new items, and to some extent young people (who often seem to be the most fashion-conscious sector of the population) saw a calculator as a prestige item to own.

2.7 Second-order effects

It is important to recognize that the effects of these five factors on demand can often have an impact on organizations far removed from the consumer. This can be illustrated by examining developments in the cosmetics market, where concern about and interest in the ingredients used in cosmetics have forced the cosmetic manufacturers to develop products that use a much greater proportion of natural products. The cosmetic manufacturers purchase their ingredients from chemical suppliers, and so this change in consumer preferences has had an effect on these chemical-processing firms—remote as they at first seem to be from the consumer of cosmetics (see Insert).

Natural raw materials are 'in'

Karl Raabe, a Product Management Director at Henkel, a firm that, amongst other things, manufactures cosmetic ingredients, stated: 'In Germany there is a strong trend toward natural ingredients, such as plant extracts used as active components, or surfactants based on natural raw materials such as cocoa nut or palm oil. Petrochemical-free ingredients are also in vogue. In general, the industry is moving towards animal free vegetable-based ingredients. There is also a trend to use ocean-derived products in ingredients such as seaweed, chitin from shrimp shells, or fish oils.'

Source: Gain (1996: 35).

The arrival of new products on the market can also lead to the decline—sometimes to the point of extinction—in the demand for particular products. The development of the market for pocket calculators has led to the near extinction of at least two other products. The first is the slide rule and the second is log tables, both of which enabled students, engineers, etc. to carry out a range of calculations. However, both have been displaced by the calculator, which not only can carry out more functions than either slide rules or log tables, but also is much easier to use and more accurate than either of them. Indeed, it is now difficult to purchase a slide rule in Europe, because there are almost no suppliers left.

3 Factors that influence the way a product is produced

IT is also the case that, even if an organization's own market is not changing, the manner in which it can be most efficiently organized is altered by the need to respond to the changing environment. Indeed the five factors that influence demand also influence the organization of the supply of goods and services. Thus developments in production technologies can obviously impact very considerably on a manufacturing firm, and new advanced manufacturing technologies make it possible for firms to offer quite different product mixes—often at lower costs than previously. Changes in governmental and other regulations can impact on the supplying firm in a variety of ways. Thus firms with a large proportion of female staff have had to re-examine their methods of operation because of the need to absorb increased costs following the implementation of the equal-opportunity regulations being introduced in most European countries. It is also obvious that economic conditions have an impact on a great many decisions that firms make. Clearly, when there is too much economic uncertainty, firms are reluctant to make new investments, and decisions as to whether or not to launch a new product may be influenced by the management's expectation of the level of future economic activity.

Population changes too can have an impact on organizations. In the period 1981–91 the numbers of young people in the 15–19-year-old group (roughly covering the school-leaving age group) in the UK fell by about 970,000. If the severe economic recession that hit the UK during those ten years had not occurred, those organizations whose employment practices had assumed a steady supply of school-leavers enter-

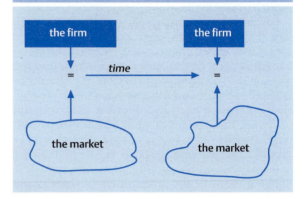

Figure 1.3 **The firm adapted to changes in market demand**

ing the labour market would have faced severe problems.

Thus, as shown in Fig. 1.3, both the market and the supplying organization can be seen changing over time as a result of the influence of these five factors.

The above discussion has centred around the problems faced by a single-product firm. In reality there are very few single-product firms and most of these are very small. Most firms market a number of different products and therefore a significant decision is how many different products to offer and what, if any, their relationship should be. These questions are discussed in Chapters 14 and 15, but the essential issues for each individual product are those raised above. This is true even where the differences between the products are no more fundamental than, say, their size or their colour.

4 Demand and supply in organizational markets

THE discussion in Sections 2 and 3 considered a firm selling directly to the consumer market (i.e. a market made up of individuals making purchases for their own use or the use of the households to which they belong). An identical discussion could be applied to the problem faced by a firm selling to other firms. Indeed, the brief comment in Section 2.7 on second-order effects implicitly touched on this, as it referred to cosmetic firms purchasing from chemical firms. It is, however, very important to recognize that in a modern economy the majority of firms are involved in selling to other organizations.

Some firms, because of the nature of their products, sell only to organizations. For example, the market for multi-spindle lathes consists of manufacturing organizations, for, while there is nothing to stop a rich individual from buying such a machine, there can be few if any individuals who would wish to buy one. Even a keen amateur machinist would not want a multi-spindle lathe. There is also a group of firms that sell both to individuals and to organizations. Thus car manufacturers sell the same car (though by using a totally different marketing mix—see Chapter 9) to individuals and also to organizations, such as hire car companies, which have fleets of cars. A third category of firms that sell to organizations consists of those that need to do so through other organizations if they are to get efficient access to individual consumers. Examples of such organizations are those in the food-processing industry and those in the domestic-appliance industries. Given the structure of the retailing industry, such firms need to sell through the retail chains, for, unless these organizations purchase their products, access to the mass consumer market would be very costly (see Chapters 4 and 11).

The same patterns of behaviour can be observed in business-to-business markets as in consumer markets. For example, when an organization feels financially confident, it will be more ready to consider replacing old equipment, spending on 'luxuries' like replacing the carpets in its offices, investing in new computer systems, and so on. Then, again like an individual, when a firm becomes economically less assured, it does not reverse these behaviours, but cuts back on other items of expenditure. This happens because, like an individual, the relative value the firm places on the items it purchases has been changed by the experience of purchasing and using new items.

In business markets fashions and management fads also rise and fade (see Insert). For example, after a period when any firm that was not re-engineering was, in the opinion of some commentators, destined for the scrap heap, the enthusiasm for re-engineering was by 1997 on the decline. This was partially, but not entirely, because the creator of the concept was signalling by his creation of another management technique that re-

'I promote fads'

'I and other management consultants continue to promote fads despite frequent derision from users of our services. Experience shows time and again that clients are more willing to buy the latest fad than a rational bespoke improvement programme based on careful analysis of the organization's position, environment and aspirations.'

Source: Letter to *The Economist*, 8 Feb. 1997.

engineering was 'old hat'. So consultants who had been advising their clients on the benefits of re-engineering found the demand for their services declining.

5 Management's matching problem

As Fig. 1.3 shows, developments in the environment mean that, over time, both market demand and the nature of the supplying organization change. Management's problem is to determine how best to respond to such developments. There are three possible approaches or orientations that an organization might pursue as it seeks to respond. As is discussed in Chapter 2, these are a production orientation, a sales orientation, and a market orientation.

Most modern organizations are now committed to attempting to pursue a market orientation. Underpinning such an approach is the marketing concept that was described by a successful business executive as 'to make the firm do what is in the interests of the customer and not make the customer do what is in the firm's interest' (McKitterick 1957: 79).

However, in practice interpreting this concept and working out its implications in the context of a specific organization are far from easy. First, it is not always clear what the 'interests of the customer' are. Secondly, customers' perceptions of their wants—especially future wants—are often limited. Thirdly, organizations are made up of a bundle of assets into which considerable investments have been made. Fourthly, few organizations do not face competition in some form. The presence of competitors is shown in Fig. 1.4 and Chapters 18 and 19 consider various aspects of the

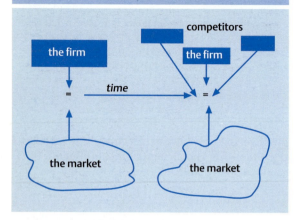

Figure 1.4 The firm facing competitive activity

impact of competition on a firm's marketing strategies.

6 The interests of the customer

THERE is certainly a particular difficulty for organizations that believe that they understand the 'interests of the customer' if the customer is unaware of what might be considered their best interests. For example, car seat belts were marketed in most European countries years before wearing them was made legally obligatory. However, many car-owners apparently did not recognize that it would be in their interest to fit and use these items, and sales remained relatively low until their use was made a legal requirement. Arguably the problem is that consumers themselves often do not know what their best interests are and also regard advertising as little more than a cynical attempt to manipulate them. Certainly with regard to the use of seat belts, even after government-backed campaigns to encourage their use and legislation to make wearing them legally obligatory, many people remained unconvinced that seat belts were necessary. Some continued to believe that wearing them could increase the risk of injury in an accident. Again, sometimes consumers receive so much advice—much of which appears to be contradictory—that they are unable to determine what action is in their own best interests.

For example, with regard to the issue of healthy eating, the steady flow of advice from a wide range of experts leaves many consumers muddled about what is and what is not 'healthy eating and drinking' (see Insert).

People tend to exaggerate their virtuousness

'For a good cautionary tale about how you can't trust everything your customers say, look no further than the recent forays of several fast-food restaurants into diet cuisine. McDonald's McLean, KFC's skinless fried chicken, and Pizza Hut's low-cal pizza all have the dubious distinction of being responses to customers and also flops. For all the millions and marketing savvy expended, the companies failed to see that, when it comes to diet, people tend to exaggerate their virtuousness. A 1993 study by the National Restaurant Association found a gross disparity between what people intend to eat (fresh fruit, bran muffins) and what they really eat (whole lotta burgers).

People asked for diet burgers, but a greasy one still holds the allure. Sales of McDonald's McLean have been, well, lean.'

Source: Martin (1995: 85).

Consumers' perceptions of their future wants are also usually very poor. There are innumerable examples of new products that have been successes even though consumer research had indicated that consumers would not buy them. There are also many examples of changes being made to existing successful products that have resulted in a dramatic fall in sales even though consumer research had indicated apparent enthusiasm for the changes. There are also examples of new-product failures where consumer research had clearly indicated that the new product would sell well. Unfortunately many people use such examples to assert that consumer research is a waste of time. However, as will be discussed, the term 'consumer research' covers a wide range of activities and sometimes the research on which decisions have been made was inappropriate.

Consumers are also 'poor' at predicting the uses to which they may put new technologies. It is also the case that the originators of these technologies often fail to predict how they will be used. For example, digital cameras, which store their pictures on disks or in computer-type memories (see Insert), cannot yet produce the same quality of picture as film-based cameras. Therefore over several

The market that the industry did not know existed

A snazzy new camera is always welcome in the photographic industry, but the digital camera seems to be creating a new market for 'temporary imaging' that the industry never knew existed. Suddenly business people who have never needed a camera at work have found room for one. Many commercial web sites are now assembled with the help of pictures taken directly by digital cameras. Other business people, such as estate agents and insurance assessors, still use film cameras when they want to produce detailed (or especially alluring) pictures. But they have become big users of digital cameras in order to obtain instant pictures.

Source: The Economist, 30 Aug. 1997, 49–50.

Box 1.1 **'Post-it' notes**

The adhesive used in Post-its was discovered accidentally by Dr Spencer Silver, a 3M's scientist trying to produce an adhesive with the opposite characteristics (i.e. a super strong adhesive). Art Fry, another research scientist, was a member of a church choir who was fed up with the fact that the markers he put into his hymn book were constantly falling out, so he tried making up a set of bookmarkers using the 'failed' adhesive; in so doing he 'came across the heart of the idea. It wasn't a bookmarker at all, but a note. These notes were a systematic approach to communicating because the means of attachment and removal were built in. This was the insight.'

Although the samples that Fry created and passed around the firm were praised and people requested further supplies, there remained a reluctance to launch the product on the market. Indeed, it is said that Post-its failed when formally test marketed. In particular it became apparent that the only way to get people to use the product was to provide them with samples, as once people used them they ordered more—though they 'still couldn't talk intelligently about the product'. The product was initially seen as a not-very-adhesive adhesive that replaced paper clips, staples and glue—all things used to stick two pieces of paper together. Such a description did not indicate their true value, but users, while not able to articulate their approval, were prepared to prove it by repurchasing the product.

Source: Kucmarski (1988).

years they have not been much of a threat to the traditional camera. However, the demand for these cameras is suddenly booming with the development of a new market for 'temporary imaging'. This is the use of these cameras by business people to create an image that can be put onto a computer display, a website, and so on.

The use of e-mail is another illustration of this phenomenon. In 1997 it was still very difficult for the average householder to give much of a response to questions about his or her likely use of e-mail in 2000. Most simply would not have known what e-mail was, what it could do at the time, and what it was anticipated it would be capable of doing by 2000. Even those that had some knowledge of what e-mail could do would have tended to regard it as a method of communication suitable for businesses rather than for personal communications. This inability to respond is partly a matter of the consumer lacking the technical knowledge to determine the product's capabilities and what it offers. It is also the conservatism that consumers (both individuals and firms) show. This was pointed out by a Motorola executive who said 'Our biggest competitor, by the way, isn't IBM or Sony. It's the way in which people currently do things.'

What is evident is that listening naïvely to what consumers say may produce information that can lead to wrong decisions (see Box 1.1). It has been suggested that an alternative approach is: 'Ignore what your customers say; pay attention to what they do.' However, such an approach needs careful handling, as, where a really radical innovation is being considered, it has to be recognized that what consumers do is determined by the technologies currently available to them. The essential thing is to 'pay attention to what consumers do' and then try to understand 'the want' they are satisfying through that action. Once that has been identified, then an innovator will be in a position to evaluate his product with respect to that want.

Organizations may be convinced that they know what is in the consumer's interests but are unable to persuade consumers to purchase the product. For example, there can be little doubt that it is in the interest of a married person with young children to ensure that his or her partner is adequately insured against premature death. However, the insurance companies have not found it easy to market such products. First, as with many insurance products, there is a problem in making people aware of the likelihood of 'unpleasant' incidents occurring. Secondly, even if people accept that there is a risk, the financial consequences of which can be reduced by an insurance policy, many regard the price (i.e. the cost of the insurance premium) as beyond their means.

However, some organizations exist primarily to help consumers to understand what their best interests are. For example, many professional service organizations and charities would maintain that their role is to offer advice to their customers (and the fact they usually describe those who use their services as 'clients' rather than 'customers' is an indicator of their perception that their relationship is different). A lawyer, for example, will explain to a client what their legal rights and responsibilities are and, if legal action is a possibility, which approach is most likely to be successful. A charity's objective might be to make people more environmentally aware, believing that access to such knowledge will encourage its clients to act in a manner that the founders of the charity believe is in the consumer's interests.

7 The firm's investments in its assets

THE marketing concept does not mean that a change in consumers' requirements should be blindly followed. There will be occasions when it is inappropriate to do this, for a successful organization will have made a considerable investment into its asset base.

As Fig. 1.3 showed, market demand changes over time because of developments in the environment, and so does the nature of the supplying organization. Management's problem is to find ways of ensuring that there is a 'match' between its organization's capabilities and the market's needs—a match that will enable it to achieve its objectives (see Chapter 15). The challenge is to strike a balance between the apparent advantage of adapting to market developments and the need to exploit as fully as possible investments made in its asset base. Consequently, as Davidson stated, successful marketing

involves balancing the company's need for profit against the benefits required by consumers so as to maximize long-term earnings per share. There is a continuing tug of war between the firm's need for efficiency and the customer's needs for unique benefits. Getting the balance right is not easy. It requires a thorough knowledge of a company's assets and an ability to relate these to profitable opportunities in the market place. (Davidson 1998)

(Davidson's statement was made in the context of a book discussing marketing within the profit-making sector of the economy. In the case of not-for-profit organizations like charities, whose financial objectives are often merely to cover their costs, then this statement is not appropriate. Here the following adaptation of Davidson's definition might be helpful: 'marketing involves balancing the organization's need to cover its costs against the benefits required by clients so as to maximize the probability of achieving its objectives. There is a continuing tug of war between the organization's need for efficiency and the client's needs for unique benefits. Getting the balance right is not easy. It requires a thorough knowledge of the organization's capabilities and an ability to relate these to the needs of its clients.')

It is important to recognize that an organization's asset base is much more than its physical assets—significant though these often are. An organization's asset base will include, not only its physical assets, but also its reputation, its brand names, its staff—their knowledge and attitudes—its business links, its patents and licences, and so on. Such features will have become assets as a result of careful and continuous activity by the firm's employees over lengthy periods of time. For example, a really strong brand name (see Chapter 20) is created not just by clever advertising and promotion (though these are required) but through the identification of appropriate specifications for the product and the consistent delivery to the customers of products of that specification. Such consistent delivery is achieved only through the expenditure of substantial sums of money on a wide range of activities, such as training staff, supplier development, quality control, product development, development of manufacturing processes, control of distribution and distributors, and so on.

Sometimes as a market develops and changes it is relatively easy for the management of an organization to ensure that its capabilities evolve in such a way that it can continue to put a product on the market that satisfies customers' requirements. This might require some retraining of existing staff or some additions to its production facilities, but overall nothing very dramatic or expensive. However, a difficult problem arises when the change in the market demand is so dramatic that the organization has to question whether it can follow the market because the changes that it will need to make to do so are so radical. For example, to follow the market it might need to invest in new technologies that are totally outside its existing range of expertise.

A good illustration of this type of problem arose within Great Britain with the switch from the use of aluminium to plastic frames for domestic double glazing. Originally, domestic double glazing used aluminium frames and therefore the firms that marketed double-glazing were expert extruders of aluminium. (At first plastic frames were not a success, as they tended to warp and discolour in warm weather.) However, once the market found plastic frames more acceptable, the challenge for the companies was which of the four policies to pursue:

■ invest in plastic-moulding technology—to them a totally new and very different technology—and continue to use their existing sales force to sell double glazing; at the same time find another market in which their expertise with aluminium would be valued and develop a new and additional sales force with skills appropriate to that market;
■ invest in plastic moulding technology and continue to use their existing sales force, but divest themselves of their aluminium capability;
■ find another market in which their expertise with aluminium would be valued and retrain their sales force with skills appropriate to that market;
■ find another market in which their expertise with aluminium would be valued and replace the existing sales force with one that had the skills appropriate to that market.

Each of these alternatives presented different difficulties, challenges, risks, and costs. Furthermore, each of the several companies that faced this dilemma made their decision as to which to pursue on the basis of a different assessment of the importance of each of these factors.

It is very important to recognize that the development of any asset incurs considerable expenditures. For example, Heinz Beans is a powerful brand name that is a major asset. However, it has been created by expenditure on a wide range of activities, including: the continuous and careful improvement of Heinz's recipe for baked beans; the maintenance of quality standards in all aspects of the purchasing, manufacturing, and distribution of the product; developments in appropriate processing technologies. Heinz used to have an advertisement in Great Britain stating 'A million people every day say "beans means Heinz"'—the implication being that at least a million people consume Heinz beans each day and the consequence being that the maintenance of the Heinz brand name requires the consistent delivery of a quality product to at least a million people a day. This can only be achieved through the development and implementation of advanced manufacturing, distribution, and management systems, all of which are costly. If this is true for a 'simple' product like baked beans, it is obviously even more of a challenge for complex items such as personal computers.

The term 'asset-based marketing' has sometimes been used to describe this approach of taking account of the organization's asset base when making marketing decisions. Davidson's view was quoted above; Webster has stated: 'It is often unreasonably constraining to define a firm's distinctive competence in terms of the customer need satisfied. The firm's unique competence, especially for an industrial marketer, may be defined more appropriately by its internal strengths, and especially its technical competence, rather than its market relationships' (Webster 1979: 256). Many marketing academics and professionals are ill at ease with this approach because they foresee the danger of companies that follow this approach slipping back into a product orientation, but 'companies have to be production-oriented to be market-oriented' (Ford 1998: 47). However, all that is being asserted is that marketing creates value by utilizing the activities of other parts of the organization. As one commentator suggested, marketing takes devices made in the factory and converts them into products that satisfy customers. Furthermore, it is being suggested that circumstances external to the organization will determine the appropriate emphasis to give to the creation of value by marketing as against other parts of the organization.

8 What does it mean to have 'enough customers'?

THE idea of having 'enough customers' (a phrase used above (see Section 2)) sounds simple but in fact needs careful examination. If a firm is to be profitable, it needs to have customers who place sufficient value on the product it offers them for them to feel it is worth paying a price that is higher than the costs the firm incurs in supplying them. However, the costs of supplying the product will, in most cases, be related to the total volume of sales, and so the numbers of customers together with the amount that they each purchase are also important. In other words, the customers have to be willing to pay a price per unit and to purchase enough units to provide the firm with sufficient income to cover the costs of supplying that number of units. Obviously, if a firm finds that it is not covering its costs at its current level of sales, and raises its prices, there is a danger that sales will fall and actually exacerbate the situation. On the other hand, if a firm lowers it prices, it may turn out that its sales increase but still do not provide sufficient revenue to enable the firm to cover its costs.

This balancing of costs and prices is a complex managerial problem, and it is not just a matter of juggling prices around to achieve a profitable volume of sales, as other elements of the company's products also affect sales levels—indeed some non-price factors may have a greater impact on sales levels than do price changes. Moreover, making changes to the product usually means that the supplier will incur extra costs, and so the process of attempting to balance the numbers of units sold at a given price relative to the price of supplying those products begins all over again.

9 Customers' needs and wants

CUSTOMERS make purchases to satisfy their needs and wants, but people living in a modern economy who are themselves capable of pro-

viding even their basic needs are rare indeed. Most people, therefore, have to resort to paying others to provide them with even those goods and services needed to meet their basic physiological needs.

There is, of course, in principle a difference between a need and a want, but in practice there is often a difficulty in making the distinction. The usual distinction is that a *need* is a generic condition—for example, 'I need a drink because I am thirsty'—and a *want* is the specific form of satisfaction that the individual is seeking—for example, 'I need a drink and I want to satisfy that need with a Coke.' However, it is not possible to classify items unequivocally as either 'need satisfying' or 'want satisfying'. For example, while people will often say that they need a 'Big Mac and a Coke', from the point of view of the human body's essential needs, all that is needed is a sufficient and regular supply of food and potable liquid. Thus for most people it is impossible to claim that beer satisfies a need, for clearly for most people beer satisfies 'wants' and not 'needs' (even though people may state 'I'm dying for a beer!'). However, alcoholics do need alcohol or they can become unwell, and thus for them any beer may satisfy a need.

The distinction between needs and wants gets even more complex as one considers those needs other than the basic physiological ones. To try to argue that a person *needs* a Walkman would seem, in a world where so many do not have even their nutritional needs met, to trivialize the concept of need. Yet, in the so-called developed world, to be the only child in a school class who does not own a Sony Walkman can, to a child who already lacks self-esteem (and having a sense of one's worth is surely a need), mean that for that child owning a Walkman, and specifically a Sony, comes close to being a need.

However, in some societies there are products that individuals do need but that they do not provide for themselves or purchase directly; instead, these are provided by the state as a public good. Such products typically include the police, ambulance, and fire services. Of course, the public, as a whole, do 'pay' for such services through the tax system. But it is important to remember that it is not always the nature of the product itself that determines whether or not it is provided by the state, but each society's view, as expressed through its political system, as to what the state's responsibilities should be.

National security is a public good, so in most

countries the state determines what size the army should be and the members of the armed forces are employees of the state directly answerable to the government. However, if, instead of national security, the case of health services is considered, then a different picture emerges. For example, in Eastern Europe before the collapse of the communist state system the state was the sole provider of health services. Yet in other societies mixed systems exist in which many people rely totally on state-run hospitals, state provision of dental care, and so on, but in which it is also legal for all those citizens who so wish and who can afford it to pay to be treated outside the state system. The same situation exists with regard to education. An in-between situation can also exist where the public pay for a service through the tax system but the authorities contract for its provision with a profit-making organization rather than provide it from within their own resources. This is illustrated by the example of Falck in Denmark (see Insert).

A private fire service?

Falck Redningskorps A/S, Copenhagen, was founded in 1906, being owned by the original family until 1985. It is something of an anomaly in Denmark—a country of strong social-democratic traditions—because it is the major provider of fire and ambulance services. Indeed it is responsible for the fire services in 60 per cent of the local municipalities, and ambulance services to 90 per cent of the Danish population. Falck also provides other services such as road breakdown and rescue, emergency and alarm control, and security.

Some eighteen Danish insurance companies now hold the majority of its shares. The company in 1992 made a profit of Dkr. 34 million on a turnover of Dkr. 1,900 million. Over 80 per cent of the Danes have indicated that they are satisfied with the services that it offers.

Source: Irons (1994).

---

10 Marketing defined

WHAT then is marketing? It is useful to define both 'marketing' and 'marketing management' for, although they are interconnected, they are different.

10.1 Marketing

Marketing is *the exchange process that occurs between individuals; between an organization and individuals; or between organizations as they seek to satisfy their needs and wants.* It does not, however, deal with exchanges of all types of needs and wants. Indeed, most people who practise or teach about marketing would not seek to apply it to exchanges related to what Maslow (1954) called 'social needs' (see Fig. 1.5). In other words, though it would be legitimate to study how a marriage guidance service is marketed, it would be a step too far to argue that marketing has anything to say about the process of marriage guidance.

Both parties to an exchange have something to offer and while, from the point of view of marketing, it is the supplier's offering that is the dominant concern, the customer's 'offering' is also critically important. For example, individual customers do not just offer to pay for an item—they can offer to pay in different ways, each of which has a different degree of attraction for the seller. Thus a bottle of wine can be purchased with cash, with a credit or charge card, by using electronic fund transfer at point of sale (EFTPOS), by having

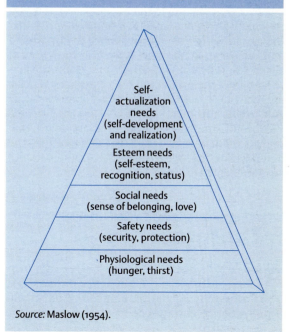

Figure 1.5 **Maslow's hierarchy of needs**

Source: Maslow (1954).

it charged to an account, and so on. These alternatives are not all equally attractive to either the customer or the shop. So some customers are more attractive to the shopkeeper than others and indeed some customers (perhaps those asking for credit) may not be wanted at all—unless they can be persuaded to adapt their behaviour. Similarly in business markets a customer may also offer a range of benefits to a potential supplier. For example, as well as offering to pay in a variety of ways, a customer might offer the supplier the status of being associated with a well-respected customer, technical insights, and so on.

So, while it is obvious that from a particular customer's point of view not all potential suppliers are equally attractive, it is also essential to recognize that not all customers are equally attractive to a particular supplier. Indeed, a central marketing concept is that a supplier should determine which customers it prefers to deal with (which in the case of organizational marks can mean the identification of individual customers).

10.2 Marketing management

Marketing management is *the function that, by assessing customer needs and initiating research and development to meet them, has a major role in determining the form that an organization's goods and services should take to secure optimal acceptance by customers.* It is also the major influence in determining the price and the quantities of the good or service that is offered to the market. In addition, it decides the forms of advertising and publicity that will support the presentation of the product to the customers and the mechanism by which the product is made available to the customer.

A useful summary statement about marketing management is that its role is to ensure that the organization identifies, anticipates, and satisfies customers' wants profitably.

11 The future

ARGUABLY the distinctive contribution that marketing has made to the conduct of business has been constantly to reiterate and remind organizations of the importance of the customer. It is too easy for any organization—especially large ones—to forget that the only justification for its existence is that it has customers who place sufficient value on what it produces to pay a price that provides enough revenue for the organization to keep running. It is easy because in a big organization too many employees have no direct contact with the customers. Marketing should always be listening to the customers. It should always be seeking to ensure that everybody in the firm recognizes the centrality of satisfying customers if the firm is to be successful.

Through the short period of time that marketing has been identified as a separate function there have been several occasions when it has been necessary to remind both academic and business marketers of the centrality of the customer. Thus in a 1981 paper Webster bemoaned the way in which an overemphasis on strategic issues had led firms to forget the customer. In 1998 the same anxiety was still evident and other authors were still finding it necessary to reiterate that 'All companies which show robust growth focus consistently on solving customer problems—they are customer led rather than financially led' (Doyle 1998: 259). Without doubt, human nature being what it is, this need will recur. For example, it is too easy to allow the exciting and challenging developments in information technology (IT) and its associated developments to distract people from the acceptance that IT is merely a tool. Certainly IT is a tool of immense value, but it is only a tool whose development is not necessarily totally beneficial and to which negative reactions do occur if it is used inappropriately when dealing with customers. A simple example is the irritation of many customers when confronted with a customer call centre (sometimes light-heartedly called a customer service centre) that uses an automated answering system.

New technologies, both in IT and elsewhere, will without doubt transform the processes by which firms both keep close to the customer and meet the customer's needs. Marketing's role will continue to be to ensure that this legitimate concentration on efficient processes does not distract from the purpose of the process that is no more and no less than understanding the customer's need. Drucker's (1968: 52) comment will remain its credo: 'There is only one valid definition of business purpose: to create a satisfied customer.'

Further reading

Coviello, N. E., Brodie, R. J., and Munro, H. J. (1997), 'Understanding Contemporary Marketing: Development of a Classification Scheme', *Journal of Marketing Management*, 13/6: 501–22.

Doyle, P. (1995), 'Marketing in the New Millennium', *European Journal of Marketing*, 29/13: 23–41.

Lehman, D. R., and Jocz, K. E. (1997) (eds.), *Reflections of the Futures of Marketing* (Cambridge, Mass.: Marketing Science Institute).

Lilien, G. L., and Rangaswamy, A. (1998), *Marketing Engineering* (Reading, Mass.: Addison-Wesley).

Rayport, J. F., and Sviokla, J. J. (1994), 'Managing in the Marketspace', *Harvard Business Review*, 72 (Nov.–Dec.), 141–50.

Webster, F. E. (1988) 'The Rediscovery of the Marketing Concept', *Business Horizons*, 31 (May–June), 29–39.

Discussion questions

1 What are the fundamental features of modern lifestyles that make exchanges such an important subject of study?

2 Critically evaluate Townsend's view that: ' "Marketing Departments"—like planning departments, personnel departments, management development departments, advertising departments, and public relations departments—are usually camouflage designed to cover up for lazy worn-out executives. Marketing, in the fullest sense of the word, is the name of the game. So it had better be handled by the boss and his line, not by staff hecklers' (Townsend 1971: 96).

3 Is it the case that management has become obsessed with efficiently producing products at just the time when customers are prepared to pay more for products that meet their needs more effectively?

4 What lessons can be learnt from the fact that many products, such as Post-its and the Sony Walkman, that are now recognized as successes were initially in great danger of being rejected by the companies that developed them because of a lack of consumer interest?

5 Are changes in fashions predictable and/or manageable?

6 If your company's business was (legally) printing bank notes, identify the factors that have influenced the demand for your product over the last twenty years.

7 What are the problems in using the idea of 'exchange' as a basis for a definition of 'marketing'?

8 What would you say to a group of managers in a high-technology firm who asked you to explain the benefits that would accrue to their firm if they tried to implement a marketing orientation?

Chapter 2
Market Orientation and its Implications

Tevfik Dalgic

Objectives

The objectives of this chapter are:

1 to define the term 'market orientation';

2 to describe the development of the concept of market orientation;

3 to explain why European organizations were slower than those in America to accept the concept;

4 to set out the characteristics of organizations that are market orientated;

5 to consider how a market orientation can be implanted in an organization.

1 Market orientation: A definition

THE short story in Box 2.1 portrays a case of a 'niche' marketer—a small business organization that has discovered a 'niche', a tiny segment or segment of a segment, in the market that had been ignored by the big companies in the same industry. It is a highly flexible, lean, and mean organization, operating very closely to its customers and supplying its customers with the best beds in every form they may require to suit their different needs. In return, it may charge a premium price, but customers do not mind this because they believe they are getting value for their money. They have flexibility of choice, flexible delivery time, and prompt response from the shopkeepers. In this shop are stored different types of beds, in different colours, shapes, and types, including plastic ones, orthopaedic ones, ones with springs, and so on. The owner of the Bed Centre keeps a list of his customers and keeps them informed about new stocks, sales, etc. He asks what types of beds they require and he has close connections with several bed manufacturers in both Ireland and the UK. They can deliver his requests without delay. A niche marketer applies the marketing concept by operating very closely to its customers and taking the customers to the centre of its operations. It is also classified as a market-oriented business.

Market orientation has been classified in different ways by several researchers. The following are the most frequently used classifications:

- a corporate philosophy;
- the implementation of the marketing concept;
- an ideal;
- a policy statement;
- a corporate state of mind;
- a faith;
- an organizational culture;
- a concept of periods or stages of development and degree of maturity of an organization that parallels the economic development of the national market within which it operates.

The author wishes to thank P. Blackhurst and M. Leuw (Henley Doctoral Fellows) for their assistance.

Box 2.1 **The price of a good night's sleep**

Mr Tony Johnson had got a new job in an international service company with its European Head Office in Dublin, the capital city of the Irish Republic. Together with his wife, Mr Johnson found a lovely house in the south of Dublin at a small town called Dun Laoghaire. It takes fifteen minutes to drive to his office, which is situated in the industrial district of Tallaght. Resettlement problems were solved without any hustle and the family travelled from Amsterdam by plane, leaving some old furniture there. They wanted to buy household durables, etc., new in Ireland. They had even found an international school for their son Jim. The school is called St Andrews College, is situated not far from their new house, and has a good reputation in Ireland among both local and expatriate communities.

Everything went well until Mr Johnson started to look for an orthopaedic bed for his back problem. He and his wife visited almost all the department stores in Dublin but they could not find a high-quality orthopaedic bed.

Although some of the stores displayed good-quality beds, they did not have good-quality orthopaedic ones. Even if the Johnsons were to choose one of those displayed beds, department stores asked for at least a week for delivery, and he needed one as soon as possible. One day, after they had spent hours in the shops, they were returning to their home when they saw a shop in Dun Laoghaire, on the main street, with a sign 'Bed Centre'. Mr Johnson pulled up his car and they went into the shop. This was a small shop displaying beds of different types, colours, and shapes, including good orthopaedic ones. They were delighted with this discovery so close to their home. Mr Johnson asked for the delivery time; the shopkeeper said 'I can deliver tonight'. So the sale was completed easily, although the price was over £400. Mr Johnson was ready to pay a premium for the good-quality product and prompt service. At last he had a restful night in Ireland.

Despite these seemingly different classifications of market orientation, we may conclude that all of the above labels hold true. Market orientation can be a business philosophy held by the management of an organization (McGee and Spiro 1988), or the implementation of the marketing concept (McCarthy and Perreault 1997). Market orientation can also be described as a form of organizational culture that:

- places the highest priority on the profitable creation and maintenance of superior customer value while considering the interests of other key stakeholders;
- provides norms for behaviour regarding the organizational development of and responsiveness to market information.

As Day (1994: 43) puts it: 'A market driven culture supports the value of thorough market intelligence and the necessity of functionally coordinated actions directed at gaining a competitive advantage.' Essentially the market-oriented culture is externally oriented.

Business organizations may be classified according to their tendencies or orientations. In business, some companies are described as production or sales oriented, while others may come under the category of market oriented. The first two descriptions indicate an emphasis on production and sales, while the latter indicates an emphasis on the marketplace, indicating that such companies are directed towards or centred around their customers. Some authors add more orientations. For example, Payne (1988) argues that most organizations have a range of conflicting orientations and associated attitudes. Similarly, other authors, such as Levitt (1960), argue that many organizations do not serve their markets satisfactorily because of the fact that their managers are product oriented. Different orientations that may possibly exist in business organizations are given in Box 2.2.

2 Market orientation: A historical analysis

MARKET orientation has also been defined as a stage of development of an organization, or as a level that reflects an organizational maturity that parallels with the development of a national economy, from a historical point of view. Several authors, including Baker (1991), Dalgic (1992), Cannon (1996), and Kotler *et al.* (1996), subscribe to

Box 2.2 **Different orientations of businesses**

Product orientation. We sell what we can make. The quality of our products speaks itself and our products sell themselves. They should be glad we exist.

Cost orientation. By reducing our production and marketing costs we can improve the profits of our business.

Capacity orientation. The bigger the production of our company, the more profitable it becomes.

No-commitment orientation. We cannot plan the future in our industry. No one knows what will happen from today to tomorrow.

Competitor orientation. We observe and understand the strengths and weaknesses and the strategies and capabilities of the current and potential competitors.

Market orientation. We make what we can sell. We make our profit by creating opportunities to satisfy our customers' needs more effectively within the constraints of our resource and skill limitations.

Sources: Aaker (1988); Day and Wensley (1988); McCarthy and Perreault (1997).

of the greatest importance in the West. Companies were manufacturing/production oriented, and 'marketing' was limited to taking orders and shipping goods. In such a situation, with excess demand needing to be satisfied, companies were usually not very interested in customers' desires and wishes. This was clearly illustrated in Eastern Europe under the communist regimes, where demand for most products exceeded supply and as a result customers were treated in a dismissive manner (see Insert).

The lucky Bulgarian customer

'Lucky customers are those who, on reaching the front of the queue, find that the product on offer is not so defective as to be beyond their capability of repairing it.'

Source: Bulgarian sales manager, 1989.

During this period companies grew in size and this began to put distance between executive decision-making and the customer. However, this had little impact on corporate performance at the time, as the prevailing shortages meant that it was easy for entrepreneurs to find markets for their goods. Raw materials, capital, technology, and labour were viewed as scarce resources; customers were not.

According to some authors this so-called production era began in the early part of the twentieth century (Pride and Ferrell 1989), and according to some others with the Industrial Revolution, which focused on plant efficiency and quantitative output, and operated on principles of scientific management (F.W. Taylor 1947; Skinner 1990). Jobs were broken down into discrete parts and labour was specialized in order to become highly efficient in the execution of a small, repetitive part of the whole. Henry Ford's production line was the physical manifestation of the principle of scientific management. Production-line operatives, often paid by piecework rates, became detached from the holistic nature of work. Individual and departmental objectives and reward systems became inconsistent with satisfying the needs of the final customer (see Insert overleaf). In retrospect, this gave rise to disenchanted, demotivated employees, satisficing behaviour (that is, behaviour that seeks a satisfactory rather than optimal outcome), and low-quality output.

this definition. They see a market orientation as the ultimate stage of development of a business organization, and draw a parallel with the economic development of a country by accepting the fact that a market orientation develops through stages or eras of business orientations. These economic development stages are production orientation, sales orientation, and market orientation. This approach tries to explain the enabling macro-environmental factors, mainly supply and demand relationships and competitive conditions, that are thought to have influenced the progression of firms through these different orientation stages.

In this view, market orientation has been a natural progression from the practice of selling towards the understanding of customers, their problems, and needs, and it works towards a solution and satisfaction of those needs. At first the emphasis was on producing. After the Industrial Revolution, mass production, assembly lines, and division of labour made it possible to manufacture products more efficiently and cheaply. As a result of new technology, new ways of using labour, and an increasing demand for goods, production was

The risks of adopting a production orientation

'The scarcity of a particular item puts the producer into a privileged position vis-à-vis the consumer. And so we get the rule of the producer under which contact is lost with the demands of the consumer and society.

But when the producer rules, absolutely everything is done the wrong way round. The factory sees it as more profitable to increase the output, to mass produce . . .

The producer's main aim is to get rid of his output. Out of sight—out of mind. How and where the product will be used and how long it will work are not the producer's worry.'

Source: Ganbegyan (1989: 43).

It is interesting to debate whether Henry Ford, in setting up his River Rouge plant in the 1920s, was a production-oriented man who satisfied a huge demand in a market, or, in fact, a perceptive marketer who saw the enormous need in the market for a car that the working man could afford. His own words suggest the latter, in which case the man credited with the initial application of the production line should be seen not only as someone in the vanguard of production technology but also as an early mass marketer, for whom that production-line technology made possible the creation of the product that the market wanted: a no-nonsense one-colour car that was affordable ($500) to the working man. In Baker's (1985: 46) words, 'when Henry Ford first produced the Model T, he was exactly in tune with the needs of his market, and . . . his failing, if such it was, was not seeing that the basic demand for cars had become saturated and that the demand needed to be stimulated through the provision of a differentiated product'. As Levitt (1960: 51) states, 'Mass production was the result not the cause of his low prices.'

In time, of course, 'any colour they like as long as it's black' began to sound arrogant, and, when Alfred P. Sloan at General Motors (GM) began to offer cars in a variety of colours, many customers moved to GM. These two examples help us to illustrate another complexity in marketing, and thus business in general: that the competitive environment is always changing. Different industries may exhibit different characteristics regarding the rate of change, but it is true in all industries that what works today, in terms of satisfying customers, may not work tomorrow, and most likely will not work in the long term. The implication for market orientation is the necessity to monitor, share, and respond to changes in the market that arise both from the supply side (competitors and suppliers) and from the demand side (consumer demands, changes in the needs of buyers).

The production orientation raises another debate over whether marketing is required in shortage or monopoly situations. One view holds that marketing is an expensive luxury to exercise unless competitive forces demand its application. The opposing view says that marketing is not necessarily more expensive and that any organization that is perceived to survive by exploiting a monopoly position rather than by creating customer satisfaction has not customers but hostages. Sooner or later, particularly in the late-twentieth-century era of deregulation and increased global competition, an alternative supplier will materialize and then the customers will desert. There can be (but do not have to be) aspects of cost in market orientation, such as in providing variety or enhanced customer service, but these should be accepted only if they are offset by increased, or more profitable, business (Houston 1986). If we take another look at the Ford/GM example above, Ford held an early monopoly at the price level that it established (the $500 car). At this point, by displaying superior (to currently competing car manufacturers) understanding of customer needs and responding to them, Ford was displaying a high degree of market orientation. When it entered the market, GM would have incurred higher costs than Ford, by offering multiple colours. However, because of its superior (compared to Ford) understanding of the needs of the market at that time, GM was able to gain a price premium and increased its business at the expense of Ford. It did this by offering something to which the customer attributed a value greater than the price of the car, which itself was greater than GM's cost. To the extent that market orientation takes into account profitability and core competencies in order to supply goods/services that the market will value at a price that is more than they will cost to supply, market orientation, like quality, is free.

Key words in marketing are 'matching', 'appropriateness', and 'suitability'. A common misunderstanding concerning the application of marketing is that 'more is better'. Any company that indiscriminately loads its market offering with services, variety, and options without taking account of whether the target market needs, values, and hence will pay for those additional services is not market oriented and is not applying the marketing concept. A market orientation is the degree to which a business unit obtains and uses customer information, develops a strategy that will meet customer needs, and implements that strategy by being responsive to customer needs and wants. Marketing is choosing and understanding a certain part of the market very well, and using company strengths and its core competence to satisfy the needs of that market segment with a suitable, appropriate, matching product.

If the segment that the company chooses to serve requires low-price, low-service, standard products, then the company that delivers that, reliably and to an acceptable (or better) standard of quality, can rightly be described as market oriented. The degree of market orientation in the firm cannot be measured by what it spends on advertising, or the number of its salesmen or product lines. These attributes are easy to measure but, without a situational context, are meaningless. Market orientation must be approached by asking questions about how well the company's offers 'fit' the target market's needs, how closely the company monitors changes in those needs, and how prepared the company is to change in order to satisfy new or modified needs.

Bartels (1962), in his book about the history of marketing thought, reveals that in the late 1950s there was a growing need for problem-solving salesmen who could understand the customers' needs and offer solutions. This need created the practice of customer problem-solving, which required a new approach to be adopted by the salesmen. They were expected to be closer to their customers in order to understand their needs and problems. This was simply a customer-oriented approach rather than a company-oriented 'sales-only' approach. Earlier, when the issue was simply sales only, it was expected that salesmen should be familiar with customers' buying motives; now it was assumed that they should have some familiarity with the idea that selling and all other business functions logically begin with an understanding of the customers and their needs and the interpretation of this understanding into all activities of the business. This was, of course, the manifestation of a new business philosophy, the 'marketing concept'.

3 Market orientation in the USA and Europe

3.1 Market orientation and the USA

In the USA, by the early 1950s, living standards were relatively high, discretionary income became available, and, by definition, the consumer was able to make choices regarding the way that such money was spent. In the academic world, textbooks that featured a marketing management perspective began to appear (McCarthy 1960), and the ground-breaking article by Levitt (1960) on marketing myopia helped enormously in raising marketing consciousness among the US businessmen. Some of the larger US firms began to establish marketing departments (admittedly, mainly to coordinate sales and advertising) by the 1950s and by the end of that decade many academic articles had begun to appear. At this stage, some of them were already seeking to follow the pure 'ideology' that marketing puts the customer first and involves the entire organization in the creation of customer value (Levitt 1960).

3.2 Market orientation and Europe

The European experience on this matter, however, showed a different pattern. If we look at the growth of marketing as a distinct aspect of business management, it was stimulated at the beginning of the 1960s because of the prevailing climate of goods and services shortage on the Continent. There was not a single united economy in Europe, as was the case in the USA, where one economy embraced the whole continent as a unified, single, internal market. As early as 1959 the US authors Myers and Smalley had suggested that the evolutionary course of the future European Common Market might be more accurately predicted if the development of marketing in the USA were better understood. What they were saying was that the interstate trade barriers that did exist in the USA were threatening US economic development in its earlier phases. Some other authors called these interstate barriers the 'Balkanization of America' —the division of the US market into small economic-warring sectors (Hollander and LaFrancis 1993). This was similar to the case of Europe between the two world wars and was reflecting the reality after the Second World War.

Historically, in Europe, a real Balkanization took place. Several smaller markets were formed as a consequence of the turbulent European history and they exhibited different patterns of economic development, from very early industrialization levels to mass-production stages. This may lead us to the conclusion that market orientation in Europe showed differing levels of practical application depending upon each national economy's own environments. However, despite these national differences of application levels and moderating factors, it may be claimed that Europe in general was later in applying market orientation than the USA. Again, we may claim that, in general, there were European-wide causes that delayed a similar economic development for the whole of Europe and consequently hampered the development of market orientation by European business organizations. The obvious conclusion of this is that market orientation did not take place in European markets at the same time as in the US market. There are several reasons for this late development of marketing in Europe.

3.2.1 Two world wars

Two world wars destroyed not only the material wealth and production facilities in Europe, but also human resources such as design and manufacturing engineers, scientists, and qualified production workers. It took two decades after the Second World War to return to a level where basic production needs were satisfied. This may have delayed the European economies in general reaching a level of excess supply where competition could have forced the companies to adopt a market orientation. Indeed, since the Second World War, the economic conditions have been such that there has been a seller's market most of the time. The most acute problems have been those associated with meeting promised delivery dates and other more production oriented difficulties.

3.2.2 Delayed market integration

Old rivalries, cultural bias, and political problems meant that there was very little intergovernmental cooperation among the European states after the war. This delayed the creation of a larger European market, that in turn could have created a larger European economy. However, the Marshall Plan, and then the establishment of Benelux (Belgium, the Netherlands, and Luxembourg), the Organization for Economic Cooperation and Development (OECD), the Council of Europe, the European Coal and Steel Community (ECSC), the European Economic Community (EEC), and the European Atomic Energy Community (Euratom) gave many European countries the impetus to increase their production ability and capacity.

3.2.3 Heavy regulations

Although almost all West European countries had theoretically free market economies and multiparty democracies as their common goals, in many parts real competition did not exist. The reason for this could be attributed to heavy regulatory practices governing business life in several parts of Europe. Even in 1999 some broadcasting, telecommunications, and transport systems as well as utilities were in the hands of the public sector.

3.2.4 Public sector involvement

During the post-war period, governments interfered with the markets by establishing companies that were owned and run by the public sector. This practice was particularly dominant in the countries in the Soviet-led Eastern bloc that were run on communist principles based on a one-party and state-owned economic system, and continued until the early 1990s. In addition to that practice, many West European countries had formed companies owned solely by their governments. These practices delayed the establishment and development of private companies based on profit motivation. At the end of the twentieth century many European countries still had several nationalized or renationalized companies—the so-called state-owned enterprises. This European public-sector tradition is in contradiction to the US business traditions.

3.2.5 National markets

Strong national identities and nationalist thoughts in terms of business practices did little to support a unified European market but rather accelerated a tendency towards more fragmentation. Products would be labelled as made in a specific country, and until the 1990s it was not possible to find products with the label 'Made in Europe'. This fragmentation of Europe into smaller markets did not help West European countries develop the conditions necessary to achieve economies of scale in many production areas.

3.2.6 Protectionist tendencies

In several European national markets, import substitution was a national economic policy for many years. This practice hampered the development of a bigger European market and helped the further fragmentation into many industries with smaller production capacity. Consequently, it took a long time to develop global, standard European products that can compete in global markets.

3.2.7 Language differences

Strong feelings supporting the maintenance of national languages and regional diversities have influenced the economic and political agenda of many European states over the centuries. This supported the fragmentation tendencies and prevented the development of a common European business language, though English is becoming the language of both European and global business, perhaps because of the influence of the US companies in international markets (Dalgic 1992).

3.2.8 Local business traditions and practices

In many European markets some companies were kept going despite the fact that they were not economically as sound as they could be. Several forms of government subsidies and government contracts were used to keep many non-economic entities working. In the end, many European companies have had to rely on continued government support in order to continue to exist in the face of competition. This practice, which is characterized by lack of competition and protection by various means, has delayed many West European markets from reaching the level of the sales era and from proceeding on to the era of market orientation.

3.2.9 Dilatory approach to marketing education

Marketing was seen as an unimportant activity in many European universities until the 1970s. Even at the end of the twentieth century some old European universities still retained this tradition. This might have led to the late entrance of European researchers into the field of marketing as compared to their North American colleagues. In many European universities, marketing as an independent area of study was introduced only in the late 1960s or early 1970s. According to a European practitioner, Europeans should blame themselves for this lack of interest. A European marketing author, Grönroos (1989: 53), points out that marketing mix and the other basic ideas of marketing were developed in North America and are widely accepted in the Western world, and admits: 'We have no European marketing theory or model geared to European conditions.' He also blames the European researchers as the cause for this development.

However, these views do not seem to be justified in the light of the reasons discussed. It is neither a matter of laziness nor a lack of vision of European scholars but a cultural, historical, political, and economic reality of Europe and its macroenvironmental factors. Even in the late 1990s, differing opinions among the EU nations about the interpretation and application of articles of the Maastricht Treaty and enlargement issues were perceived to be a reflection of the past, which could explain some of the reasons why Europeans did not develop coherent Euromarket and Euromarketing models.

After studying 436 organizations in the Netherlands, Bamossy (1988) concluded: 'Marketing has a bad image. At best, marketing was seen as equal to advertising, and at worst marketing was associated with aggressive attempts to stimulate demand for and increase the market share of commercial goods. Potential contribution of marketing management concept is not well understood.'

Piercy (1985, 1989) and Piercy and Morgan (1989) reported several research studies from the UK about the state of marketing as a function, marketing as a department, and marketing as a guiding principle among UK companies. They concluded that a great majority of the UK firms that were the subject of those surveys had had problems understanding and handling their marketing activities. Another European author, Baker (1991: 5), in explaining the state of market orientation in the UK, concluded that the Americans 'appreciated this in the 1950s, the West

Germans and Japanese in the 1960s, the British belatedly in the late 1970s (up until the mid-1970s nearly all our commercial heroes were sales people, not marketers)'.

Much of the literature since 1970 concerns itself with a renaissance of the original marketing concept. The number of theoretical papers published since 1974 in the *Journal of Marketing* and the *European Journal of Marketing* has steadily increased following a period of neglect in the early 1970s (Howard *et al.* 1991). The Marketing Science Institute in the USA added weight to these investigations by declaring the understanding of customer-oriented organizations 'as one of four ... highest priority research topics' (Marketing Science Institute 1990: 4).

4 Organizational and managerial characteristics of market-oriented companies

ORGANIZATIONAL and managerial characteristics of market-oriented companies and the antecedents of this orientation in terms of managerial implementation issues have been covered in various conceptual and practical studies. In two separate empirical studies by different researchers, similar or very close conclusions were reached about the definitions and constructs of market orientation. Kohli and Jaworski (1990: 2) define market orientation as the organization-wide generation of market intelligence pertaining to:

- current and future customer needs;
- Dissemination of the information across departments;
- Organization-wide responsiveness to it.

In another study aiming at the exploration of the correlation between the market orientation and business profitability, Narver and Slater (1990*a*: 21) stated that the three hypothesized behavioural components of a market orientation comprised the activities of:

- market information acquisition;
- dissemination;
- the coordinated creation of customer value.

A careful analysis between these two conclusions will reveal the following three common constructs that underline a market orientation:

- organization-wide acquisition/generation of market intelligence/information pertaining to current and future customer needs;
- dissemination of market intelligence/information across departments within the organization;
- organization-wide responsiveness/coordinated creation of customer value.

The authors of these studies consider market intelligence (market information) as the primary activity and as a starting point for market orientation, while, Kohli and Jaworksi (1990) consider the following as market information:

- exogenous forces that affect the needs and preferences of end-users and distributors—e.g. competition, regulation, etc.;
- current as well as future needs of customers.

These researchers posit that each company may be evaluated as to whether or not it has those antecedent characteristics. As stated by Webster (1992: 14), 'marketing can no longer be the sole responsibility of a few specialists.'

Peter Drucker (1954) argues convincingly that creating a satisfied customer is the only definition of business purpose, or, as McKenna (1991) succinctly states, 'Marketing is everything.' Intuitively, and sometimes explicitly, successful entrepreneurs and traders have always accepted as a fundamental truth the fact that creating customer satisfaction is the only way to long-term business success.

The principles of marketing have been applied for many thousands of years. No company, or trader, would ever have existed without supplying a product or service that, at one time, was the best available solution to certain needs of the customer. Traders would perceive needs, develop offerings to meet those needs, and communicate that such solutions to those needs were available. Products would be priced, or bartered at a rate, such that both buyer and seller shared in the value created, the seller by means of a profit and the buyer by means of utility of some kind. This notion is central in the justification of free enterprise capitalism as a social and political system. As Houston (1986) points out, 'Customer focus clearly existed when the king ordered boots from the bootmaker.'

Many small companies still operate on the principles of customer intimacy, where the proprietor is literally 'very close to the customer'. Inside growing firms, such customer intimacy is hard to maintain, and that increasing distance is often the beginning of the end of a market orientation. Dalgic and Maarten (1994) link this closeness with the concept of niche marketing and argue that start-ups are closer to their customers and this closeness may create a niche for them.

☞ 'The personal-contact network will be used by the entrepreneur owner manager to seek out sales opportunities and to glean actual sales on the back of wider information exchanges.' (Chapter 25, p. 578)

The word 'profit' or 'profitability' is often included in definitions of marketing, and, in Narver and Slater's (1990a) words, profit (together with 'long-term') provides a decision criterion for market orientation. How then does a company price its products in order to share the value created equitably with the customer? On the cost side, certain products that a firm may offer will have a very low relative cost/potentially high margin and are probably exploiting company core competencies to the maximum. Other products may be 'service lines', perhaps bought in to complete the product range offering, and will be relatively high cost/low, if any, margin. Should the company cross-subsidize products, should it maximize margins on the low-cost products by benchmarking prices against competition, or should it price at the halfway point between the value to the customer and the cost price—perhaps a 'fair' share of reward? One thing is evident among these interesting questions: it may not be possible simultaneously to maximize customer satisfaction and profits, but we can, and we should, attempt to exceed customer expectations. If, as seems likely, customer expectations are based largely on competitive offerings, then we are reinforcing the importance of competitor and customer intelligence as the basis for price setting and hence (when compared to value created) determining the level of customer satisfaction. For this reason, competitor intelligence must feature in our definition of market-oriented behaviour, either in the context of 'additional forces in a market' (Lusch and Laczniak, 1987; Jaworski and Kohli 1993), or as a focus in its own right (Day and Wensley 1988; Narver and Slater 1990a).

Also, if we accept the reasonable point that every customer has a unique set of needs, then we must also assume that maximizing customer satisfaction must imply a unique, tailored solution for every customer. Clearly, some organizations, large and small, are specifically designed to perform such bespoke work, from tailors in Bangkok or Hong Kong to many management consultants, and, with the increasing power of information technology (IT) some manufacturing companies are moving towards mass customization. However, for many companies who currently target a diverse market with a range of 'standard' products, competitively superior (but not maximal) levels of customer satisfaction, consistent with profit objectives, must be the realistic goal.

The way that these companies can achieve a better fit between a standard product offering and variable customer needs is by empowering front-line staff to vary the service component of the offer, and to provide unbundled pricing options. This way, the full-service/premium-price buyer can, for example, have product, delivery, installation, training, credit, etc., whilst the budget buyer can opt for the core product and collect it himself. Customers in the middle ground can 'customize' their own product package to suit their price range and resources. This is entirely consistent with the marketing concept and is a contributor to the third element of market orientation, as we have defined it: organization-wide responsiveness/coordinated creation of customer value.

☞ 'A large number of contact employees interacting with the customers create value for them in various service processes . . .' (Chapter 21, p. 505)

According to the shareholder value maximization view (Rappaport 1986; McTaggart et al. 1994), no company can create wealth for its shareholders without having very satisfied and loyal customers, yet it is quite possible to do the opposite and to achieve high levels of customer satisfaction and be unable to translate this seeming advantage into adequate returns to shareholders. McTaggart et al. (1994) conclude that the limits to customer satisfaction should be determined as follows:

As long as management invests in higher levels of customer satisfaction that will enable shareholders to earn an adequate return on their investment, there is no conflict between maximizing shareholder value and maximizing customer satisfaction. If, however, there is insufficient financial benefit to shareholders from attempts to increase customer satisfaction, the conflict should be resolved to avoid diminishing both the financial health and long-term competitiveness of the business.

4.1 Company response and innovation

There seems to be a dilemma between satisfying customers' needs and desires and the new levels of technology and innovations. Technological innovations take place gradually and many new technologies are so different from previous offerings on the market that customers may not recognize their need for them before they are marketed. How can the customer know what the customer does not know? As Hamel and Prahalad put it in 1994:

> Customers are notoriously lacking in foresight. Ten or 15 years ago, how many of us were asking for cellular telephones, fax machines and copiers at home, 24-hour discount brokerage accounts, multivalve automobile engines, compact disk players, cars with on-board navigation systems, MTV or the Home Shopping Network? . . . if the goal is getting to the future first, rather than merely preserving share in existing businesses, a company must be much more than customer-led.

As we have discussed, being market oriented is more than being customer led. American business magazine *Fortune* in an article of 1 May 1995 followed this theme and concluded, '. . . if a company truly understands its customers' needs, it can in good conscience disregard what they claim to want'.

The term 'customer intimacy' is sometimes used to describe this closeness to the customer, and market orientation must depend upon an expanded definition of customer needs to include latent needs. Customer needs are evident but not yet obvious, and successful managers will need superior skill in understanding customers in order to identify and satisfy these unidentified, yet significant, needs (Day 1990). Information processing (the major process exhibited in market orientation) is again shown to be the key to satisfying customers, whilst respecting competitive pressures and value-creation constraints. In many situations, of course, the value-maximizing response may well be no response—that is, 'market oriented' does not carry the same reactive obligations as 'market led'.

4.2 Two distinct organizational types of market orientation

The marketing literature appears to disagree regarding what is the impetus to the adoption of a market orientation in companies. There seem to be two distinct organization types regarding their market orientation; one group can be labelled as Type A, the other as Type B.

A-type firms exhibit a purer form of market orientation, and embody a genuine philosophy that generating satisfied customers and satisfactory profits are not mutually incompatible goals and that, in fact, they are the only long-term goals that make business sense. They are 'learning organization', as Slater and Narver (1995) put it. A-type firms are likely to be small and growing, to have strong leadership and culture, to be innovative, lean, and flexible. As Peters and Waterman (1982) describe, these firms may be identified by the kinds of myths and heroes that the company celebrates. A-type firms focus on customer satisfaction, customer loyalty, focus on relationships, and the lifetime value of the customer.

B-type firms view market orientation as a 'magic bullet' solution to external pressures, particularly increased competition, a more expensive *modus operandi* to be used only when necessary and in order to stay one step ahead of the competition. This group of firms regards market orientation as a corporate stage of evolution, brought about by external pressures, particularly competition. The B-type firm is driven by cost considerations and by competitor analysis. It is likely to be large, bureaucratic, and reactive.

B-type firms are obsessed with benchmarking their offerings against competitors, whilst A-type firms attempt to satisfy their customers to the point where a loyalty exists and the company effectively eliminates competitors by domesticating (Arndt 1979) the relevant market, so that the price-driven microeconomic paradigm no longer applies. This (A-type/B-type) distinction may account for the two schools of thought regarding the definitions of market orientation: one (Day and Wensley 1988; Narver and Slater 1990*a*) includes 'focus on competitors' explicitly; the other (Kohli and Jaworski 1990; Jaworski and Kohli 1993) does not include separate reference to the competitor in the list of attributes or exhibited processes in the market-oriented firm, but rather includes competitor intelligence in a broader category of market intelligence including competitors, customers, and other stakeholders. These two organization types of market orientation are compared in Box 2.3.

Marketing strategy can be viewed as a continuum, but it is not wise for a business continuously to attempt to adjust the magnitude of its market orientation in relation to various moderators (Dalgic and van der Weijden 1994). This is the challenge for most mature companies. For existing A-type firms, the challenge is to avoid becoming a B-type as the company grows. The challenge for B-type companies is how to become more like the A-type, and, as the literature on corporate culture shows (Kotter and Heskett 1992), it is much more difficult to change an existing culture than it is to establish an appropriate culture in a new company.

If the link between market orientation and performance can be shown to be robust across all in-

dustries and environments, then the B-type firm has no reason to accept a limited amount of market orientation at a minimum cost. The message for all companies will be to adopt a full market orientation to achieve superior and sustained business performance.

4.3 Management and market orientation

In the management of the company top managers play a critical role in encouraging the employees to act in harmony with the norms and values of market orientation (Kohli and Jaworski 1990). The emphasis of top management on market orientation will encourage personnel to be sensitive for market developments, to share this information with colleagues, and to respond on this information accordingly (see Insert).

> **Talk to your customers if you wish to be profitable**
>
> The Chairman of Marks & Spencer spends sixteen hours out of his 70–80 hour working week in shops talking with customers and staff. By doing so he keeps in touch with the customers and motivates staff to do the same. He says about using his time in this way, 'It is more profitable than cosying up to the City.'
>
> *Source: Marketing Business* (1998).

We can rephrase this relationship with the following conclusions. The greater the top-management emphasis on market orientation, the greater the

- market-intelligence generation,
- intelligence dissemination, and
- responsiveness of the organization.

Responsiveness to the market developments often encompasses the courage to invest in new products and services without knowing beforehand if these investments will yield the expected results. Jaworski and Kohli (1993: 55) found several factors as important antecedents of the implementation of a market orientation. These factors are:

- top management emphasis on market orientation;

Box 2.3 Two types of organization for market orientation

A type	B type
Genuine market customer-orientation philosophy	Customer orientation accepted when market forces require it
Belief that profits come from satisfied customers	Emphasis on cost cutting and profit maximization
Learning organization	Learning only when competitors make it necessary
Customers/competitors/stakeholders/technology-based market information generation	Competitor-based market information generation
Lean, mean, flexible	Large, bureaucratic
Strong leadership and organization culture for customer care	Change in organization culture
Innovative	Imitative
Long-term focus	Short-term focus

- calculated risk-taking and willingness to accept occasional failures of new products and services by top management;
- the development of interdepartmental dynamics and connectedness, and the elimination of interdepartmental conflicts;
- the installation of a market-based rewards system; and
- less centralization, formalization, and departmentalization within the company.

A willingness of top management to take risks is, therefore, crucial for a market-oriented company. We may then reach the following conclusion: the greater the risk aversion of top management, the lower the market-intelligence generation, the intelligence dissemination, and the responsiveness of the organization.

Another point of importance is the quality of the interdepartmental cooperation. A certain amount of interdepartmental conflict will affect the sharing and the responsiveness of relevant market information. Thus the following conclusion may be reached: the greater the interdepartmental conflict, the lower the intelligence dissemination, and the responsiveness of the organization.

Closely related to the former point is the measure of formal and informal contact between departments. The greater the extent to which employees through different departments are connected, the more information will be shared and will be responded on. As a consequence, the greater the interdepartmental connectedness, the greater the market-intelligence dissemination, and the responsiveness of the organization.

Market orientation is directed at innovation and risk-taking. Formal and centralized decision-making is essentially conservative in character. Therefore, it seems likely that formalization and centralization are inversely related to information generation, dissemination, and design of responsive programmes of action. A market orientation stimulates innovative behaviour. Innovative behaviour consists of an initiation stage and an implementation stage. Formalization and centralization may hinder the initiation stage where creativity and flexibility are much needed. In the actual implementation stage, however, where the organization and management of the (production of) the innovation are decisive, it is likely that formalization and centralization actually facilitate the implementation. So, the greater the formaliza-

tion, the lower the intelligence generation, dissemination and response design, and the greater the response implementation.

It also seems likely that, if managers are evaluated and rewarded by market-related factors, this will have a positive influence on a market orientation. This means that, the greater the reliance on market-based factors for evaluating and rewarding managers, the greater (1) the market-intelligence generation, (2) the intelligence dissemination, and (3) the responsiveness of the organization.

Researchers Kohli, Jaworksi, and Kumar (1993) have developed an instrument to measure market orientation of the organizations. This instrument is called Markor. It is in fact, a diagnosing questionnaire and consists of one general market-orientation factor, one factor for intelligence generation, one factor for dissemination and responsiveness, one marketing-informant factor, and one non-marketing-informant factor. Markor has been accepted as a valuable instrument to measure market orientation and, is therefore, used as a point of departure for the research to be undertaken in this field by several researchers.

A developing stream of empirical research has found a strong relationship between market orientation and several measures of business performance, including profitability, customer retention, sales growth, and new-product success. Day (1994) stresses the role of capabilities in creating a market-oriented organization. He observes, 'Capabilities are complex bundles of skills and collective learning, exercised through organizational processes that ensure superior co-ordination of the functional activities. I propose that organizations can become more market oriented by identifying and building the special capabilities that set market-driven organizations apart' (1994: 38). According to Day (1994) market-driven organizations are superior in their market-sensing and customer-linking capabilities.

Slater and Narver (1995: 65) state: 'presumably, learning facilitates behaviour change that leads to improved performance.' It therefore seems most likely that a committed learning organization will perform better than one that is not so committed. Organizations that are able to adapt to, and perhaps even create, their environments, that learn from the behaviour of their customers, and that know how to improve their skills and knowledge continuously must somehow be more successful than their counterparts. Indeed, especially in knowledge-based industries. This may be the only basis on which to build a sustainable competitive advantage.

Some authors have written on the role of the environment for the market orientation–business performance link. In the Jaworski and Kohli (1993) study the following three moderators are found to influence market orientation–business performance (they are three of the four environmental characteristics mentioned above): market turbulence, technological turbulence, and competitive intensity. The performance of the economy appeared to be too complex to measure, so this variable was not included. Kohli and Jaworski consider market turbulence as the rate of change in the composition of customers and their preferences. If an organization operates in a turbulent market, it has to modify its products and services more often than when it operates in a stable market. It therefore seems likely that firms operating in turbulent markets have a greater need to be market oriented and committed to learning than those operating in relatively stable markets. They have to monitor and respond quickly to evolving customer preferences. This leads us to the next conclusion, which is that, the greater the market turbulence, the stronger the relationship between market orientation and business performance.

If competition is low, it does not seem to be difficult for an organization to be profitable. The need to be a market-oriented or learning organization is low, as customers will buy the company's products and services anyhow. If a business meets high competition, customers can walk away to the competition at any moment. Therefore, under these circumstances it seems worthwhile to be highly market oriented and to make a commitment to learning so as to be able constantly to satisfy the customers' needs and wants. This leads to the conclusion that the greater the competitive intensity, the stronger the relationship between market orientation and business performance.

Technological turbulence or the rate of technological change may influence the market orientation and learning–performance link negatively. Organizations that work with nascent technologies that are undergoing rapid change may be able to obtain a competitive advantage through technological innovation, thereby diminishing—but not eliminating—the importance of a market orientation. By contrast, organizations that work with stable (mature) technologies are relatively poorly positioned to leverage technology for gaining a competitive advantage and must rely on market orientation to a greater extent (Jaworski and Kohli 1993). The same will be the case for the need to be a learning organization. It is likely that the need to learn from the customers is conversely related to the degree of a technologically driven strategy: this can be stated as: the greater the technological turbulence, the weaker the relationship between market orientation and business performance.

4.4 The relationship between market orientation and the learning organization

Learning organizations have the collective capacity to learn as entire organizations. They learn from their environment, they learn from their clients, they learn from their competitors, and one part of the organization can learn from the mistakes of another part. So essentially a market orientation and the learning organization seem to have much in common. For instance, market-orientation theorists stress intelligence generation and intelligence dissemination, while the learning-organization scholars mention open-minded enquiry and synergistic information distribution. Slater and Narver (1995) support this notion. Their argument is that a market orientation (complemented by an entrepreneurial drive) is beneficial for the performance of the company. However, this will be the case only if it is accompanied 'by an appropriate climate to produce a learning organization'. This climate must entail generative learning. According to Slater and Narver (1995), learning organizations consist of five critical components:

- market orientation;
- entrepreneurship;
- facilitative leadership;
- organic and open structures;
- a decentralized approach to planning.

Only when all of these five characteristics are present will superior performance be produced.

There is a leak between a market orientation and the learning organization from the viewpoint of the relationship between market information processing and organizational learning. In successful organizations market information is first acquired, secondly distributed, thirdly interpreted, and fourthly stored for future use in the organizational memory. This describes a sound way of market information processing that is typical for both a learning and a market-oriented organization.

As Day (1994: 43) puts it, 'learning is more than simply "taking in information". The learning process must include the ability of managers to ask the right questions at the right time, absorb the answers into their mental model of how the market behaves, share the understanding with others in the management team, and act decisively.' In his paper on market-driven firms—which could also be called market-oriented firms—Day (1994) investigates the learning processes in this kind of company. He states that learning processes in market-driven firms are distinguished by:

- open-minded enquiry, based on the belief that all decisions are made from the market back;
- widespread information distribution that assures relevant facts are available when needed;
- mutually informed mental models that guide interpretation and ensure everyone pays attention to the essence and potential of the information;
- an accessible memory of what has been learned so the knowledge can continue to be used.

So, for Day (1994), market-driven or market-oriented organizations are characterized by learning processes.

5 Implanting market orientation in organizations

WHILE the theoretical arguments in favour of following a marketing orientation are clear in practice, it seems extremely difficult to implant such an approach in an organization. What is required is a strong and decisive lead from top management.

5.1 A strategic vision and long-term commitment

Market orientation is a continuous, strategic commitment. The decision to implant a market orien-

tation into an existing or a start-up business requires the support of the entire organization. For this reason, it must be decided and implemented by the top management team led by the Chief Executive Officer (CEO) of the company on a long-term basis (see Insert). Ansoff (1987: 61) stresses the importance of this long-term view, commenting:

> **Marketing matters too much to be left to everybody**
>
> Kodak's Chief Marketing Officer, Carl Gustin, explains why marketing still matters.
>
> 'We've seen all the articles predicting the death of the marketing organization. Some say marketing should be embedded throughout the organization, eliminating any need for the marketing department. Others note that the classical organizational structures have collapsed, leaving marketing teams without any useful function. Many say that since the Internet is changing everything, it won't be long before people make their major purchases on-line. This, of course, will eliminate sales people, drive retailers out of business, kill newspapers and magazines, and so on.
>
> At Kodak we think marketing matters more than ever; that's why we formed the office of CMO (viz. Chief Marketing Officer) over two years ago. To achieve corporate growth (in volumes, margins, and share), you must enjoy and intimate relationship with your customers and end-users.'
>
> Source: MSI Review (1997).

Exclusive concern with proximate profitability would be almost certain to leave the firm run down at the end of the period. Total emphasis would be on current products and markets; on advertising, promotion, sales force, productivity of the manufacturing organization. But to remain profitable into the long-term, the firm must continue to renew itself; new resources must be brought in and new products and markets must be developed. Many key phases of this self-renewal activity have long lead times. Therefore, during the proximate period resource commitments must be made to such long-term needs as research and development, management training and new plant and equipment.

Levitt in 1983 saw marketing as a lifetime commitment, like a marriage: 'The era of the one-night stand is gone. Marriage is both necessary and convenient. Products are too complicated, repeat negotiations too much of a hassle and too costly. Under these conditions, success in

Box 2.4 **Customer types and customer relationship strategies**

Customer type	Customer relationship strategy
Past	Regain
Existing	Retain
Potential	Gain

Source: Dalgic (1998).

marketing is transformed into the inescapability of a relationship. Interface becomes interdependence.' This interdependence should be reflected in a lifetime commitment to good quality, adaptation to the customers' changing needs, and the establishment of ongoing relationships with the customers. Not only existing customers, but those who have already left the company, must be taken into account, and every effort should be made to regain their support. An outline for applying different customer-relationship strategies for different customer groups is given in Box 2.4.

These strategies may require conscientious efforts, carefully detailed analysis, well-planned, realistically timetabled, and sensitively applied and controlled methods. It may be concluded that a solid reputation in the minds of the customers is essential to be successful as a marketer (see Insert).

Making dedication to customers an obsession

Hewlett Packard successfully combines a dedication to customers with an obsession with measurements. The performance of every employee is evaluated against a scorecard and every scorecard includes some customer-led measures.

5.2 Managing the change for market orientation

To implant a market-orientation strategy may require several changes within an organization. On this matter, Lichtenthal and Wilson (1992) conclude 'to change, a firm must analyze the current system and then prepare a detailed plan to create the norm structure that will support the degree of market orientation it needs to implement its market strategy'. It is clear that analysing the current system and behaviour and preparing a detailed plan for the norm structure that will support the degree of market orientation require changes in the planning and execution of firms' strategic marketing activities. These changes should be planned and implemented. Management should develop methods to influence the behaviour of the people by rewarding the good ones. Top-management commitment and exemplary behaviour support the emergence of new norms because they reinforce the transmission of norms between individuals: stories, rituals, and symbols. With managerial skills and exemplary behaviour, managers must inspire employees and channel their energy, abilities, and qualifications, and they must also exhibit a strong support for the plan for executing the policy (Robbins 1992).

Next to exemplary management behaviour, a well-aimed reward system, and the power structure, the level of delegation and the communication system play an important role in institutionalizing a culture (Ansoff 1990). The job descriptions and policy statements must reflect a market view (Lichtenthal and Wilson 1992). The support of the entire organization in general and employees in particular is vital for a market orientation; as the same authors conclude, 'we might require a majority of the members of the organization to possess a market orientation for it to become normative'. Here internal marketing may offer a better chance of success.

5.3 A guideline for implanting market orientation

As a guideline for implanting a market orientation, the following points may be followed:

■ Put the CEO and the top management team in charge of the process.

■ Ensure that the reason for change towards market orientation is clearly communicated to every individual in the firm by every means of communication.

■ Create an internal environment for consultation and feedback.

■ Take time to finish the total change process including the feedback stage.

■ Involve employees and give them freedom to work out the change for their own functional areas.

■ Provide training in new values, work methods, and customer understanding and service quality improvement.

■ Acknowledge and reward the successful employees.

5.4 Action plan for implementation

The following is a guideline towards achieving the changes in the organizational culture required to implant a market orientation:

■ establishing a market intelligence system and its related departments equipped with human, physical, and financial resources, directed to the market environment to collect information;

■ developing and implementing a method of information dissemination that will be responsible for the distribution and interpretation of the market intelligence;

■ creating an informal, flexible, active communication system between and among departments in a supportive manner, reducing the bureaucracy within the company, supporting bottom-up information flows as well as top-down ones;

■ establishing market-based reward and payment systems, as well as internal communication systems;

■ abolishing formal structures and establishing market-based departments and project teams;

■ planning for an internal marketing system to present the market-orientation strategy to the company personnel;

■ planning company-based training programmes aimed at creating customer sensitivity, service quality improvement programmes, and customer understanding strategies;

■ establishing a customer-retention philosophy within the company;

■ preparing for a relationship marketing strategy, depending upon the size of the company;

■ adopting of one-to-one marketing with big customers, and building niches around customers;

■ applying total quality management and periodical service quality surveys among management and customers;

■ setting up customer help lines;

■ undertaking customer satisfaction surveys about both goods and services and action upon the results.

6 The future

IN order to develop more accurate, well-developed, and fine-tuned management methods and marketing decision-making tools, we need more research in the market-orientation field. This field will help many companies to operate successfully and eliminate failures. We need comparative research between service companies, inter-industry and intra-industry surveys in similar and dissimilar business fields. In addition to studies only in the marketing area, we need cross-fertilization among other fields of study: organization theory, sociology, psychology, social psychology, finance, history, economics, IT, and strategic management. Many marketing issues require multidisciplinary approaches. There are also several issues that need to be investigated. For example:

■ Are market-oriented companies in national markets also market oriented in foreign markets?

■ What is the impact of national culture on market orientation?

■ How long does it take a company to increase its market orientation?

■ What is the relationship between market orientation and entrepreneurship?

Further reading

Dalgic, T. (1994*b*), 'International Marketing and Market Orientation—An Early Attempt at Integration', *Advances in International Marketing*, 6: 69–82.

——(1998), ' "Niche" Marketing Principles—Guerrillas vs. Gorillas', *Journal of Segmentation in Marketing*, 2/1: 5–16.

Day, G. S. (1994), 'The Capabilities of Market-Driven Organizations', *Journal of Marketing*, 58/4: 37–52.

Kohli, A., Jaworski, J., and Kumar, A. (1993), 'MARKOR: A Measure of Market Orientation', *Journal of Marketing Research* (Nov.), 467–78.

Lichtenthal, J. D., and Wilson, D. T. (1992), 'Becoming Market Oriented', *Journal of Business Research*, 24: 191–207.

Slater, F. S., and Narver, C. J. (1995), 'Market Orientation and Learning Organization', *Journal of Marketing*, 59/3: 63–75.

Ruckert, R. W. (1992), 'Developing a Market Orientation: An Organizational Strategy Perspective', *International Journal of Research in Marketing*, 9: 225–45.

Discussion questions

1 Try to identify those shops that adopt market orientation in your neighbourhood shopping mall or shopping centre.

2 Why is market orientation not a once-off activity, but a long-term commitment?

3 Critically examine the contention that 'Marketing is the least developed activity in an underdeveloped country'.

4 'Marketing is the management of life-time relationships with the customers.' Do you agree? Why is managing a relationship with customers so important?

5 Try to find at least five niche marketers in your country.

6 'Today's market-oriented companies may turn out to be production oriented if they do not follow the changes in the market place.' Do you agree? Explain why.

Chapter 3
The Consumer in the European Union

W. Fred van Raaij,
Peter Leeflang,
and Gerrit Antonides

Objectives

The objectives of this chapter are:

1 to give an overview and insights into developments in consumer behaviour at a macro level in the nations of the European Union;
2 to suggest how economic, demographic, and cultural developments and changes in consumer behaviour will evolve.

1 Introduction

CHANGES in consumer behaviour create opportunities and threats for the marketing managers of firms that produce consumer goods and services. These changes in behaviour derive from a combination of economic, demographic, and cultural developments. These developments are discussed in this chapter. The picture that will be presented is that there are striking similarities between the nations of Europe, as well as interesting differences, based upon their history and geographical location. Furthermore even within these individual nations there are large differences, as, for instance, between the north and south of Italy. However, it is suggested that there is more convergence than divergence between the nations, owing, in part, to the EU policy of stimulating economic development in the same direction.

The economic, demographic, cultural, and consumer-behaviour developments are discussed. Using data from the European Union (EU), fifteen propositions are presented.

2 Economic developments

THE economic developments that affect consumer behaviour can be described by data on household income, inflation, unemployment, and gross domestic product (GDP).

2.1 Household income

Proposition 1. Household income is becoming more unevenly distributed and is creating a two-tier population of wealthy and poor consumers.

Average income has gone up in most EU nations since the early 1990s, but the income distribution has become less equal in most cases. Income polarization and a two-tier population of the rich and the poor are reported in Belgium, France, Italy, the Netherlands, and the UK. In some countries—for example, the Netherlands—the lowering of the highest rates of tax has contributed to this development. It is generally accepted that this uneven distribution is likely to remain a feature of the EU.

Well-off consumers will expect to have access to luxury products and prestigious brands, while poorer consumers need access to less expensive goods and second-hand products. In general these two target groups are becoming more clearly separated.

2.2 Inflation

Proposition 2. **Most EU nations, especially the EMU members, have inflation rates under control.**

Much of the income increase apparently achieved in Belgium, Germany, Denmark, Greece, the Netherlands, Portugal, and Spain was destroyed in the 1980s by inflation. During the last two decades of the twentieth century, Greece had the highest inflation rate in the EU, with especially high rates during the first half of the 1980s. However, after 1985 the inflation rate decreased. Factors such as the increase in price competition in the single European market, cost reductions caused by abolishing intra-EU trade barriers, relatively small increases in labour costs, and the general increase in cost consciousness all combined to generate lower labour costs (Leeflang and Pahud de Mortanges 1993). Most EU countries reduced their inflation rates to below 3 per cent so that they could meet the criteria for admission to the European Monetary Union (EMU) and the single European currency (the 'Euro'). However, of those countries seeking admission to the EMU, only Greece did not meet these criteria and was not admitted. The belief in the late 1990s is that most EU nations, especially the EMU members, have inflation rates under control.

2.3 Unemployment

Proposition 3. **Although the unemployment has gone down, the level of unemployment is still high in many EU nations.**

Unemployment rose at the beginning of the 1980s, but returned to the 1980 level in the latter part of the decade. Unemployment, however, remains a major feature of the macro-marketing environment. Table 3.1 sets out the unemployment figures for the EU nations and shows that, although in most nations the unemployment rate decreased after 1988 but increased a little in 1991–3, in the period 1993–6 for most countries little change

Table 3.1 Unemployment rates, European Union, 1993–1996 (%)

Country	1993	1994	1995	1996
Austria	4.0	3.8	3.9	4.4
Belgium	8.9	10.0	9.9	9.8
Denmark	10.1	8.2	7.2	6.9
Finland	17.5	17.9	16.6	15.7
France	11.7	12.3	11.7	12.4
Germany	7.9	8.4	8.2	9.0
Greece	8.6	8.9	9.2	9.6
Italy	10.3	11.4	11.9	12.0
Ireland	15.6	14.3	12.3	11.8
Luxembourg	2.7	3.2	2.9	3.3
Portugal	5.7	7.0	7.3	7.3
Spain	22.8	24.1	22.9	22.1
Sweden	9.5	9.8	9.2	10.0
The Netherlands	6.6	7.1	6.9	6.3
United Kingdom	10.4	9.6	9.2	10.0
European Union	10.7	11.1	10.8	10.9

Source: Eurostat (1997b).

was recorded. Exceptionally high rates existed through the 1990s in Finland, Ireland, Spain, and the south of Italy, while Austria and Luxembourg had the lowest rates. Especially worrying have been the high levels of unemployment among the young and the immigrant communities in many EU nations.

Except for Greece, Spain, and Ireland, where relatively few women have entered the labour force, the numbers of women entering the labour market increased in the 1990s and led to an increase in demand for part-time jobs. While the EU average of female participation in the labour market in 1995 was 39 per cent, in Spain the figure was only 32 per cent (in comparison, the figure in Denmark was 46 per cent).

2.4 Gross domestic product

Proposition 4. **GDP in most EU nations gradually increases over time.**

The changes in gross domestic product (GDP) of the EU nations at current prices are shown in

Table 3.2 **GDP of nations, European Union, 1992–1995 (1990 ecu. bn)**				
Country	**1992**	**1993**	**1994**	**1995**
Austria	130.90	131.38	135.39	137.86
Belgium	157.63	155.50	159.14	162.22
Denmark	103.31	104.90	109.34	112.24
Finland	95.16	94.04	98.32	102.71
France	959.86	947.09	973.86	994.15
Germany	1,367.96	1,352.57	1,391.31	1,418.14
Greece	67.56	67.72	69.21	70.61
Italy	875.88	865.76	884.55	910.54
Ireland	38.53	39.94	42.87	47.47
Luxembourg	8.84	9.20	9.55	9.86
Portugal	55.37	54.79	55.18	56.20
Spain	399.00	394.22	402.58	413.76
Sweden	176.26	172.35	178.10	184.46
The Netherlands	233.11	234.89	242.85	248.05
United Kingdom	752.89	768.49	797.97	817.84
European Union	**5,422.27**	**5,392.84**	**5,550.21**	**5,686.13**

Source: Eurostat (1997*b*).

Table 3.2. Slow growth and some decline in GDP can be observed in 1993, but some acceleration in growth was present in 1994 and 1995. The period previous to 1992 was one of recession in most EU countries. In Denmark, Greece, and Italy, the informal or black economy grew considerably during this period. The informal economy is where people have jobs that they do not register (and they therefore pay no tax, etc., on their earnings and may indeed still be registered as unemployed). The GDP is thus understated and unemployment is overstated where this occurs. Consumer reaction to a recession and the threat of unemployment is usually to curtail expenditure in various ways—luxury goods in particular are affected by a decrease in demand (van Raaij and Eilander 1983).

Economic and political developments are inevitably closely related. By the end of 1998 most EU nations had made a political decision to implement economic policies that would enable them to reach the criteria for entry to the EMU. In 1998 it was decided to admit Austria, Belgium, Finland, France, Germany, Ireland, Italy, Luxembourg, Portugal, Spain, and the Netherlands to the EMU. Greece did not meet the criteria, and Denmark, Sweden, and the UK decided not to join the EMU at that time.

3 Demographic developments

DEMOGRAPHIC developments refer to such matters as population growth, ageing, number of households and household size, education, and immigration. Overall, the EU population increased at a net rate of 3.6 per cent over the 1990s, with the highest growth rates being found in France, Germany, Luxembourg, the Netherlands, and the south of Italy.

3.1 Population growth

In the late 1990s it was forecast that in the year 2000 the total EU population would be 375 million, but the expectation was that it would decline to 337 million by 2050. In 1998 the GDP per capita in the EU was 15,000 ecus and this makes the market much larger than that of the USA (265 million inhabitants and a per capita GDP of 19,000 ecus) or Japan (125 million inhabitants and a per capita GDP of 20,000 ecus). India (945 million inhabitants) and China (1,225 million inhabitants) have much larger populations but smaller per capita GDPs—these being 550 and 430 ecus, respectively.

3.2 Ageing

Proposition 5. In the age distribution of the population, the proportion of elderly people is expected to increase ('greying') and the proportion of young people to decrease.

In all of the EU countries, the average age is rising, as the population 'greys' while the proportion of young people decreases. As women tend on average to live longer than men do, the proportion of females is relatively high amongst senior citizens. It is estimated that, by 2000, 21.6 per cent of the EU population will be over 60 and 23.4 per cent under 20. As Table 3.3 shows, by the year 2020 the figures will be 26.7 and 20.4 per cent respectively. Germany has the widest spread of ages and Ireland has a considerably younger population than other EU nations.

The greying trend has enormous implications for pension plans and social-security schemes. Many marketing opportunities will also arise in the fields of health care and recreation products and services directed at the needs of older people.

Table 3.3 **Greying of the population, European Union, 1960–2020 (%)**				
Age	1960	1980	2000	2020
0–19	31.8	30.0	23.4	20.4
20–59	52.7	52.2	55.0	52.9
>60	15.5	17.8	21.6	26.7

Source: Eurostat (1992).

3.3 Number of households and household size

Proposition 6. Household size is gradually decreasing in all EU nations.

The expectation is that the number of households in the EU will increase to 150 million by 2000. Furthermore, because of the decreasing birth rate, young adults leaving home, older people remaining single after divorce, more widows and widowers who remain single, and more people living on their own, the average household size is decreasing throughout the EU. The proportions of one-person and two-person households in the EU had risen to 26 and 30 per cent respectively by 1998; the smallest households were found in Denmark (2.0 persons) and the largest in Spain (3.6 persons). It is predicted that by 2000 the average household size in the EU will be 2.6 persons.

☞ 'Marketers who understand how family situation affects consumers' buying requirements can capitalize by designing marketing mixes to appeal to these differences.' (Chapter 16, p. 386)

The trend towards smaller households is most noticeable in Northern Europe (except for Ireland), but in Greece, Spain, and the south of Italy more households are larger than the EU average. Some of the marketing implications of this development are a change in the type of housing required and an increase per head of population in the number of brown durables (such as television sets and VCRs) and white durables (such as washing machines and deep freezers) required.

3.4 Education

Proposition 7. The education level of the population is gradually increasing.

The level of education, as measured by length of time spent in education, has increased in all EU countries, though at different rates in different countries. In the Nordic countries and Germany over 57 per cent of the population continues education beyond the age of 18. In Spain, Switzerland, and the UK a smaller proportion has continued beyond that age, as indicated in Table 3.4.

Table 3.4 Population continuing education beyond the age of 18, European Union, 1991 (%)

Denmark	71
Norway	68
Sweden	63
(West) Germany	59
Finland	57
Belgium	54
Netherlands	53
Greece	46
Austria	44
Luxembourg	43
France	41
Ireland	34
Italy	34
Portugal	29
Spain	28
Switzerland	27
UK	24

Source: Eurobarometer (1994).

Table 3.5 Foreign population, European Union, 1994 (%)

Country	Non-EU foreigners	EU foreigners
Austria[a]	5.6	1.0
Belgium	3.7	5.4
Denmark	2.8	0.8
Finland	0.8	0.2
France[a]	3.9	2.3
Germany	6.3	2.2
Greece	1.0	0.4
Ireland	0.3	2.0
Italy	0.9	0.2
Luxembourg	3.0	28.8
Netherlands	3.8	1.3
Portugal	1.2	0.4
Spain	0.6	0.5
Sweden	3.7	2.1
United Kingdom	2.1	1.4
European Union	3.2	1.5

[a] In 1992.

Source: Eurostat (1996).

3.5 Immigration

Proposition 8. The proportion of non-EU immigrants is increasing. They form a considerable part of the population in most EU nations, especially in the large cities.

There is a considerable amount of immigration from Eastern Europe, North Africa, Turkey, and the former colonies of the individual EU nations, with the largest proportion of non-EU immigrants coming from Turkey (23.5 per cent). As Table 3.5 shows, these non-EU immigrants live especially in Austria, Belgium, Germany, France, the Netherlands, and Sweden. The immigrant communities in Germany, the UK, and other countries typically live in large cities, where they add to cultural diversity and are considered as new targets for marketing management (see Insert). Austria and Germany have the largest proportion of non-EU and EU foreigners, while Luxembourg and Belgium have the largest proportion of EU foreigners (because of the EU and NATO offices).

Will the appeal of the East reach the European High Street?

In 1998 the London Research Centre estimated that London's ethnic minorities would grow by 40 per cent in the next fifteen years. In addition, there is a mixture of cultures by marriage, with a fifth of Asian males living in the UK having partners from outside their ethnic group.

4 Cultural developments

CULTURAL developments will, for historical, geographical, and linguistic reasons, differ between the EU nations. However, there are still several striking similarities in the cultural development of the EU nations relating to the liberalization of women, concern for health and the environment, changes in values, and consumer expectations.

4.1 Liberalization of women

Proposition 9. The liberalization of women leads to more women with a paid job outside the home.

The feminist movement and the greater acceptance of working women (especially mothers) together with new gender role patterns have been very noticeable in the EU, though the lead seems to have been taken by the northern nations. Opinions about the role of women are still quite conservative, as is shown in Table 3.6. Many people still indicate that a woman's role is to be a housewife. They still support family values (Antonides and van Raaij 1998). Nevertheless, as indicated earlier, there is a trend towards women participating more fully in the labour market and for women to have a work-based career. The liberalization of women is more accepted in the Nordic countries than it is elsewhere in Europe, especially southern Europe.

Table 3.6 **Opinions on role patterns in the European Union**

Survey statements	Percentage agreeing
A working mother can establish just as warm and secure a relationship with her children as a mother who does not work.	68.5
A pre-school child is likely to suffer if his or her mother works.	60.7
A job is alright, but what most women really want is a home and children	55.4
Being a housewife is just as fulfilling as working for pay.	60.6
Having a job is the best way for a woman to be an independent person.	71.0
Both the husband and wife should contribute to household income.	73.6
Sharing household chores is very important for a successful marriage.	20.1

Source: World Values Study Group (1990).

4.2 Health and environmental concerns

Proposition 10. Health and environmental concerns are increasing in all EU nations.

As Table 3.7 shows, there is a clear trend towards a greater concern about both health and environmental issues with 'health' including physical fitness and general physical condition. Apart from Portugal, concern about environmental issues was high throughout the EU in the period 1986–95. This concern seemed to increase between 1986 and 1992, and, although it has decreased a little since 1992, it still remains high relative to 1986.

☞ 'In 1994 total sales of medicines within the EU were 51,850 ecus, which accounted for nearly 25 per cent of world output.' (Chapter 5, p. 93)

4.3 Changes in values

Proposition 11. In the EU there is a gradual shift from materialistic to post-materialistic values.

Between 1981 and 1990 there was a gradual shift from materialistic to post-materialistic values that is a change from a concern about ownership of products to a concern about the quality of life (see Table 3.8). Such issues as 'maintaining law and order' and 'fighting rising prices' are materialistic issues, while 'giving people more say in government decisions' and 'protecting freedom of speech' reflect post-materialistic values. People with post-materialistic values tend to emphasize experience more than 'ownership', and for them sports activities, recreation, and holiday trips become more important than product ownership and those durables that are purchased are bought for their fun and expressive value rather than for their technical characteristics. Most post-materialistic consumers nevertheless own many products, but these may be of a different type from those owned by a materialistic consumer.

4.4 Consumer expectations

Proposition 12. Consumer expectations in the EU nations are quite diverse.

There is a macro and a micro aspect to consumer expectations. The macro aspect is the consumers'

Table 3.7 Indicators of environmental concern, European Union, 1986–1995

Indicator	1986	1988	1992	1995
Protection of the environment and suppression of environmental pollution is an immediate and urgent problem (% agree)	74	76	87	83
Concern about (4 = highly concerned):				
extinction of plants	3.2	3.2	3.5	3.4
exhaustion of national resources	3.0	3.1	3.5	3.3
global warming	3.0	3.2	3.5	3.4
pollution of rivers and lakes	3.2	3.2	3.5	3.4
pollution of seas and coast	3.3	3.3	3.6	3.3
air pollution	3.1	3.2	3.5	3.4
industrial waste	3.2	3.3	3.6	3.4

Source: European Commission (1995).

Table 3.8 Materialistic versus postmaterialistic values, European Union, 1981 and 1990 (% agreeing)

What is most important?	1981	1990
Maintaining order in the nation	63.7	51.4
Fighting rising prices	48.0	45.2
Giving people more say in important government decisions	41.0	46.3
Protecting freedom of speech	35.8	48.6

Source: World Values Study Group (1990).

confidence in the economic development of their nation—its economic growth, its inflation, and its unemployment rates. The micro aspect relates to the conditions of household and individual consumers and includes household income, value of savings, and job security. The macro expectations influence micro expectations (van Everdingen and van Raaij 1998), but both aspects can be summarized in the Index of Consumer Sentiment. A positive score on the Index indicates that

positive expectations prevail, which should lead to more discretionary expenditure on durables, luxury services, and holidays. A negative score indicates that pessimistic expectations are dominant, which would be expected to result in lower expenditure on luxury items and durables together with the taking of less credit and an increase in savings. There were significant differences between the EU nations in this scale during the period 1993–7. The Danes have been optimistic since 1994, while the Dutch and Irish became optimistic in 1995 and since then their levels of optimism have continued to rise. The most pessimistic were the Greeks and to a lesser extent the French, Italians, Portuguese, and Spaniards—though in recent years the Portuguese and the Spaniards have become less pessimistic. Although the trend for the EU as a whole is towards less pessimistic expectations, only the UK switched from a pessimistic to an optimistic score during the 1990s (see Table 3.9).

Consumer expectations are related to life satisfaction (*Eurobarometer* 1994). Here in 1993 the Danes, Dutch, and Irish scored highest on life satisfaction with scores of 63, 40, and 41 per cent very satisfied. The lowest satisfaction scores were in East Germany, Greece, Italy, and Portugal, with 10, 15, 17, and 5 per cent very satisfied respectively.

Table 3.9 **Consumer expectations, European Union, 1993–1997**

Country	1993	1994	1995	1996	1997	Average 1988–1997
Belgium	−26	−15	−14	−23	−22	−13
Denmark	−5	+8	+9	+4	+9	0
France	−25	−17	−17	−28	−20	−19
Germany	−28	−15	−9	−21	−19	−13
Greece	−27	−22	−31	−27	−26	−25
Ireland	−14	−1	+4	+11	+18	−4
Italy	−32	−21	−21	−25	−22	−18
Netherlands	−17	−7	+4	+3	+17	−1
Portugal	−24	−26	−20	−18	−10	−12
Spain	−34	−25	−20	−14	−3	−14
United Kingdom	−13	−12	−10	−5	+4	−12
European Union	−25	−17	−13	−17	−11	−14

Note: The figures are the net result of the proportions of positive (optimistic) minus negative (pessimistic) expectations. A negative score means that negative expectations are dominant. A positive score means that positive expectations prevail.
Source: Eurostat (1998).

5 Changes in consumer behaviour

THE economic, demographic, and cultural developments cause changes in consumer behaviour that result in changes in the balance of demands for different goods and services.

Proposition 13. The consumption of services is increasing at the expense of durables.

☞ 'Understanding cultural differences is, therefore, an important task in international consumer-goods marketing.' (Chapter 6, p. 127)

Economic, demographic, and cultural developments cause changes in consumer behaviour. Marketing managers have to be flexible to respond to these developments. Although total expenditure on durables continues to increase, expenditure on services, including energy, holidays, leisure, tourism, travel, and medical services, is increasing at a faster rate. In Denmark, Ireland, and the UK consumer expenditure on medical services remains low because of the existence of the National Health Service or similar institutions (Saunders and Saker 1994).

The consumption figures of the EU nations in 1994 are compared in Table 3.10. The table shows large differences in expenditure between nations on specific product categories. In nearly every case the expenditure on services was at that time higher than on durable consumption.

Proposition 14. The demand for health and green or ecological products is increasing.

A growth in the demand for health-related product is apparent in all countries (see Insert). European consumers are also very concerned about the nutritional content of food. This is in line with

Healthier eating

Sales of organic food in the UK grew from £100 million in 1993 to over £350 million in 1998. The expectation of supermarkets is that this growth will accelerate and they forecast sales of £1,100 million by 2002.

Table 3.10 **Consumption of households in categories of goods and services, European Union, 1994 (%)**

Country	Food	Rent, fuel and power	Transport and communication	Furniture	Entertainment and culture	Medical care and health expenses	Clothing and footware
Austria	14.1	18.8	15.9	7.9	4.0	6.7	8.1
Belgium	13.4	18.0	13.0	10.0	1.6	12.3	7.2
Denmark	14.1	27.5	17.7	6.1	3.1	2.1	5.3
Finland	15.7	25.0	14.9	5.8	3.7	5.4	4.5
France	14.1	21.0	16.2	7.4	2.1	10.1	5.6
Germany	10.6	20.4	15.2	8.3	—	15.6	6.7
Greece[a]	28.3	13.5	14.7	7.4	1.9	4.2	7.7
Ireland	17.3	12.0	13.6	6.5	2.4	4.1	6.6
Italy	16.6	17.5	11.9	9.2	2.6	6.9	9.1
Luxembourg	10.9[b]	19.8[c]	19.9[c]	10.8[c]	—	7.3[c]	5.7[c]
Netherlands	11.1	19.5	12.9	6.6	3.2	12.9	6.3
Portugal	23.6[b]	7.0[c]	14.9[c]	8.3[c]	—	4.5[c]	9.3[c]
Spain	15.2[c]	13.1	15.7	6.2	1.6[c]	4.7	7.8
Sweden[a]	14.4	32.9	15.7	6.6	3.5	2.3	5.8
UK	10.6	19.6	17.4	6.6	3.2	1.7	5.9
EU	14.6[b]	18.0[c]	16.1[c]	7.8[c]	—	8.4[c]	7.3[c]

[a] In 1993. [b] In 1991. [c] In 1992.
Source: Eurostat (1996).

the high level of environmental concern, which reached its highest level in many countries in 1992 (see Table 3.7). After 1992 concern about environmental issues decreased a little, mainly because of an increased concern with matters such as criminality and safety.

The increasing concerns of consumers regarding ecological issues explain the demand for green products. These are products whose production, distribution, and/or consumption cause less environmental damage and often use 'sustainable' resources. There are even green saving schemes that guarantee that savings are not invested in environmentally harmful activities.

Within the food budget, expenditure on red meat, coffee, tobacco, and alcoholic drinks fell in the 1990s and the demand for low calorie, light and diet dishes and drinks increased. All these changes are a reflection of increased health consciousness, as is an increasing demand for private medicine and hospitals, products for body care,

and pharmaceutical products. Sports goods, together with health and sports centres, also benefit from this trend.

Proposition 15. The demand for luxury, convenience, and fun products and services is increasing.

In many EU countries the demand for luxury goods grew during the 1990s, as did the demand for goods at discounted prices. This polarization effect is also reflected in the structure of the retail trade, where there has been an increase in the number of discount stores. Examples of luxury or fun goods are gourmet, exotic, and ethnic foods (especially popular in Germany and Denmark), expensive motor vehicles such as four-wheel-drive off-roaders and moderately priced two-seaters, and the strength of expensive international brands (e.g. Porsche, Rolex, Cartier). The trends in demand suggest that European consumers behave more similarly with regard to expensive products than with regard to more everyday products. However, the same brands are increasingly appearing in everyday shopping baskets all across the EU, even though differences in national tastes are still very considerable.

Proposition 16. **Price sensitivity and price consciousness are increasing among European consumers.**

The trend towards increasing price sensitivity still exists throughout the EU and the interest in discounted products has become stronger. Consumers continue to show an increasing price consciousness and sensitivity with regard to a wide range of goods such as food products, cosmetics, books, furniture, and clothing (see Insert). In part this trend can be explained by the increased demand for luxury goods as purchasing products at lower prices creates room in consumers' budgets for the acquisition of luxury products. The increased price sensitivity and consciousness are not restricted to lower-income groups: 'Poor people need low prices; rich people love them.' Furthermore, curtailment of expenditure on non-luxury products is reflected in tendencies to buy less, to buy lower quality, to buy private label brands, or not to buy some goods at all (van Raaij and Eilander 1983).

Discount junkies?

American studies have found that consumers exposed to repeated price cuts learn to ignore the 'usual' price and wait for the next discount and then stockpile the product. They also require bigger and bigger discounts to stimulate them to buy at all.

However, these sentiments are not identified in all of the EU countries by the Index of Consumer Sentiment. Consumers in some nations (e.g. Denmark) are more optimistic than other consumers (e.g. the southern European nations). Furthermore, income distribution is becoming less equal, and not all consumers, especially the disabled and the unemployed, obtain a share in the favourable economic development. Some low-income groups have to curtail their expenditure on essentials. Inflation and interest rates are relatively low. Trust in the economy is generally high and both saving and credit are stimulated by government activity.

Demographic developments in the EU point towards more diversity and variety amongst consumers: smaller household sizes, higher education levels, and higher proportions of immigrants. The traditional family structure of husband, wife, and children is becoming less common. Ethnic and racial variety is increasing. The proportion of older people is increasing, while the proportion of younger people is decreasing.

Cultural developments show that consumers are becoming more individualistic and experience orientated ('kicks' and 'thrills'). The acceptance of the equality of men and women is becoming very apparent—especially in the Nordic countries. Environmental concerns stay at a high level and peoples' health concerns appear to grow. Post-materialistic values seem to be replacing materialistic values. Optimism about the future appears to be strong.

The major categories of change in consumer behaviour comprise an increasing expenditure on services, health, luxury, and fun items and increasing price sensitivity. Most consumers expect and want 'more for less'—high-quality products for a low price.

6 Conclusions

ALTHOUGH at the end of the twentieth century there were considerable cross-national differences in consumption patterns within the EU, some common trends were clearly present. These trends have been outlined for economic, demographic, and cultural aspects of consumer behaviour.

The economic developments in the EU are in general positive. Income for most consumers is increasing, creating more discretionary income.

7 The future

A number of propositions have been put forward in this chapter. Some will without doubt turn out not to be correct, for the factors that determine what actually happens in the EU are numerous and interconnected in a complex manner. For example, how will the move for greater political unification within the EU proceed? At the end of the 1990s, some parts of the EU were pressing for more unification while others were uncertain and some were opposed. Many aspects of the well-being of European consumers will be determined by how this matter will be resolved. Similarly, whether or not to extend the EU to include some or all of the East European states has not yet been determined.

However, some aspects of the future seem clear. There will be further deregulation of industry (for example, in telecommunications and airlines), so that competition in a number of industries will increase. As, in general, increased competition leads to lower prices, better service, and more product development, then increased demand can be foreseen for such industries' products and services. Yet one of the most difficult aspects to forecast is a feature that might disrupt many predictions. This is the risk of the continued growth of a type of 'underclass' in the EU, made up of the long-term unemployed people. Nobody seems to see a solution to this problem and the risk of social unrest arising from it is a matter of great concern. It is not, as a consequence, perhaps too cynical to suggest that one certain growth market is that for security services, and demand for its products will surely continue to increase.

Further reading

Antonides, G., and van Raaij, W. F. (1998), *Consumer Behaviour: A European Perspective* (Chichester: John Wiley & Sons).

'The Changing Consumer in the European Union', *International Journal of Research in Marketing*, 12/5 (Dec. 1995). This special issue contains eight papers.

'A Single Currency in Europe', *Journal of Economic Psychology*, 19/6 (Dec. 1998). This special issue contains seven papers.

Discussion questions

1 What are the factors that are causing an increase in the demand for customized services?

2 It has been suggested that for the segment of a community for whom 'time is money' a rational approach to purchasing is to accept that it is cheaper to make the wrong purchase than spend time on making the correct one. What are the implications of this for consumption expenditure?

3 For which categories of consumer goods are demands likely to be strongly affected by the predicted changes in the age structure of the population?

4 Does the increased consumption of convenience foods represent a threat or an opportunity to manufacturers of domestic appliances?

5 In what ways would you predict that the falling size of the average household will impact on the demand for housing?

6 Some of the member countries of the EU have relatively low GDPs per head of population. As these countries 'catch up', which categories of consumer products would you expect to benefit most?

7 Will the growth in the number of 'house-husbands' impact on consumer consumption patterns?

Chapter 4
Intermediaries

Jonathan Reynolds

Objectives

The objectives of this chapter are:

1 to demonstrate the importance of intermediaries in all types of markets;

2 to explain the role of intermediaries in the marketing process;

3 to discuss the changing structure of the 'intermediary' industries;

4 to consider the factors that have and are influencing the development of these industries.

1 Introduction

THE changing nature of intermediaries—those organizations that lie between producers and consumers or customers—and the implications for the markets in which they act have long been a neglected aspect of marketing. Indeed, academics have often been guilty of treating the decisions of intermediaries—be they retailers, wholesalers, brokers, or industrial distributors—as a wholly downstream consequence of decisions made by manufacturers and suppliers. Whilst this is still true to some extent in some markets, both sectoral and geographical, it is by no means true of all. The structure of intermediaries themselves and their unarguable closeness to the final consumer means that this treatment represents a description, which is at best incomplete and at worst incorrect, of the contemporary marketing scene. 'The middleman is not a hired link in a chain forged by a manufacturer, but rather an independent market, the focus of a large group of customers for whom he buys' (McVey 1960: 64). Many marketing textbooks written since McVey's seminal observations on the roles of intermediaries in 1960—particularly those written from a US perspective—tend to offer his observations as a fop to critics. They nevertheless then relegate discussions of such actors within the marketing channel to the very end of their texts, often buried within considerations of aspects of the marketing mix. In effect, they perpetuate the view that certain channel alignments are somehow '"right" or "customary"' (McVey 1960: 61). This chapter serves to position intermediaries alongside consumers and producers in deserving a similar degree of attention and discussion.

In particular, this chapter seeks to describe the changing structure of the intermediary 'industry' in relation to the consumer as well as the industrial and business-to-business markets. The chapter considers the evolution of intermediary markets and reviews the factors that have influenced these developments. It reviews the consequences for the distribution of power within channels that have accompanied these changes and describes how intermediaries have increasingly sought to manage marketing channels. Whilst the retailing industry plays a significant role in this discussion and therefore features largely in this chapter, it is not the only major player. Industrial distribution in the USA was a $1.6 trillion industry in 1996, for example, over 63 per cent of which was accounted for by merchant wholesalers. It has also been suggested that distribution channels have become a major strategic battleground for financial-service providers in recent years, where the debate about the use of brokers or intermediaries vis-à-vis direct marketing of products and services has been extensive (Easingwood and Storey 1996). Nevertheless, it is retailers who are consistently extending their activities into new fields on a continuing basis, through such activities as product-range extension, internationalization, or the use of strategic alliances. Indeed, some European alliances active in the late 1990s between food retailers were larger than the largest food-supplier companies.

☞ '... the traditional power base in many product areas has resided with the manufacturers. However, since about 1980, in the USA and Western Europe, this has swung dramatically to large retailer businesses, whose scale of purchasing has given them considerable power over other channel members.' (Chapter 11, p. 252)

Related to this evolution is the natural question of whether intermediaries possess distinctive needs when it comes to interpreting and applying generic marketing concepts and frameworks. This chapter seeks to answer this question by considering some selected examples of the marketing activities of retail intermediaries, before finally reviewing the future for intermediaries.

2 The evolution of intermediaries

INTERMEDIARIES are often seen as ciphers in the distribution channel, 'smoothing the flow of goods and services' between suppliers and consumers. In practice, not only are they often more active agents in their own right within the supply chain than the literature would sometimes seem to suggest, but they have also come to represent a significant proportion of a mature economy's gross domestic product (GDP) and employment base. For example, retailing and wholesaling comprised some 33 per cent of the European Union's enter-

Table 4.1 **The contribution of retailing to selected economies**

Country	Enterprises (%)	GVA/GDP (%)	Persons employed (m.)
France	21.4	13.2[a]	2.09
Germany	19.0	10.1[a]	2.35
Italy	30.3	15.8[a]	2.41
UK	19.4	12.8[a]	3.03
USA	n.a.	8.73	21.87

[a] GVA.

Note: GVA = gross value added; n.a. = not available.
Source: Eurostat (1993); US Department of Commerce.

prises and employed 17 per cent of the EU's labour force in 1993. The European distributive trades accounted for some 13 per cent of EU countries' GDP in 1992, according to *Eurostat* (Table 4.1).

The growth of the sophisticated mix of intermediaries with which we are confronted at the beginning of the twenty-first century can nevertheless be traced back in developed economies only some 150 years and is the consequence of well-documented industrialization processes, as described by schema such as that proposed by Jeffreys (1954) (see Box 4.1). Many of the well-known retail brands have their origins in the second phase: in the UK, the first Woolworth stores were developed in the late 1880s, for example, those of Marks & Spencer in the 1920s. Likewise, in other developed economies, similar origins can be discerned: for the French group Printemps in the early 1930s and for the Australian department-store chain Coles Myer in 1914. In the USA, well-known operators such as Sears (mail order 1887; stores 1925), Bloomingdales (1872), and Macy's (1858) grew up during a similar period. Such merchants were nearly always wholly subordinate to manufacturers and suppliers.

The third phase in Jeffreys's schema is one of consolidation and it is here that the first indications of the nascent power of intermediaries can be detected. Whilst still dominated by the influence of suppliers, larger firms were clearly emerging, driven by the need to achieve economies of scale and scope and the eagerness with which

Box 4.1 Retailing change in the UK, 1850–1950

Period	Phase	Characteristics
Pre-1850	Pre-industrial	Small-scale retailing, guild and skill oriented, importance of markets
1850–1914	Industrialization	Urbanization, increasing reliance upon industrialized products, growth of commerce and large-scale retailing
1914–1950	Consolidation	Growth in importance of the large retailer, still subordinate to manufacturer control

Source: Jeffreys (1954).

Figure 4.1 Decline in UK store numbers

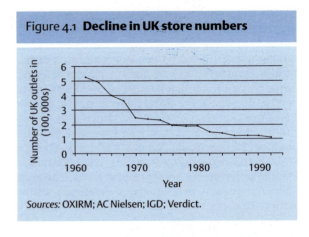

Sources: OXIRM; AC Nielsen; IGD; Verdict.

Table 4.2 Concentration in European retailing, 1993

Country	Food market share of top five retailers (%)
France	40
Germany	41
Italy	20
Netherlands	44
UK	45

Source: SECODIP.

their new modern formats were being received in provincial towns and cities. Such consolidation began to take place at the expense of the smaller, independent intermediary, leading to a reduction of store numbers (see Fig. 4.1).

'Growing retail power is a relatively recent phenomenon, whether it be automobile megadealers, consumer electronics outlets, grocery supermarket chains, home furnishing depots, or toy warehouses.' (Chapter 22, p. 529)

The period from 1950 to the beginning of the twenty-first century has witnessed substantial further concentration of market power in the hands of retail intermediaries worldwide, although local incidence varies, largely for reasons of regulation. The reasons for this growth are discussed in some detail below. As a result, 13 per cent of sales in the major global retail markets in 1996 (estimated to be in the order of $11 trillion, growing at an annual rate in the order of 3 per cent) were thought to be in the hands of the top 100 retailers. These top retailers themselves were growing at a faster rate, in the order of 7 per cent on average per annum (O'Connor 1997). When individual sec-

A buyer's market?

In one quarter of 1998 North American food retailing saw almost $30 billion of mergers. The impetus seems to have been a response to Wal-Mart's decision to enter the food market by opening 150 Supercentre grocery stores per year.

tors and national markets are considered (Tables 4.2–4.4), levels of concentration appear considerably higher.

The increasing concentration occurring within certain sectors and certain national markets has worked to limit the potential for growth of many

Table 4.3 Concentration in US retailing, 1993–1996

Factor	1993	1994	1995	1996	CAGR 1993–6
Top thirty retailers as % of total US retail sales	27.8	29.1	30.4	32.9	10.8
All other retailers as % of total US sales	72.2	70.9	69.6	67.1	2.4

Note: CAGR = compound annual growth rate.
Source: US Census of Retailing.

Table 4.4 UK Grocers' market shares, 1997 (%)

Grocer	Market share
Tesco	16.8
Sainsbury	13.3
Asda	8.8
Safeway	8.1
Co-op	5.5

Source: Independent, 23 Sept. 1998.

retail intermediaries within their domestic markets. There has been a limited amount of internationalization activity by retail intermediaries since the mid-nineteenth century: some of the earliest and most prominent of the internationalists were US companies. Woolworth came to the UK in 1909, although it is not now American owned; British Home Stores (now BhS) was incorporated in 1928 by two Americans, who were also subsequently bought out; Safeway came to Britain at the later time of 1963, but again was taken over by Argyll, who have now become Safeway plc. However, the last thirty years of the twentieth century witnessed substantial and significant attempts by the larger or more innovative businesses to grow outside their home markets.

Davies and Finney (1997) describe four different types of global activity.

■ *The hypermarket companies of France and the powerful Dutch and German food retailers.* Carrefour now trades in fifteen countries, ranging from Brazil to Korea and Portugal to Taiwan. Promodès trades in eleven countries and Auchan in eight (the latter has plans to open in Hungary, Argentina, and Thailand). Metro, the biggest of all the European companies, trades in seventeen countries, including Greece, China, and Romania. Ahold trades in twelve countries, including China, Malaysia, and Thailand.

■ *The large-scale deep-ranged specialist formats (often referred to as 'power retailers').* These emanate mainly, but not exclusively, from the USA. The leading players are IKEA (from Sweden), trading in twenty-eight countries, and Toys R Us, trading in twenty-seven.

■ *The smaller-format specialist niche retailers.* These are particularly prominent in the UK. The Body Shop trades in forty-six countries, Tie Rack in thirty, and HMV in nine. Many of the niche retailers have expanded rapidly through franchising.

■ *The international fashion houses.* These are drawn principally from the USA and Western Europe. International fashion has a distinguished history, but during the 1970s and 1980s tended to be manifested in the form of concessions outlets in department stores or hotels in the capital cities around the world. In the last few years, however, brands such as Donna Karan and Ralph Lauren have been opening large flagship stores, again in capital cities, which focus upon upmarket fashion rather than *haute couture*. These stores are not judged purely on their local profit contributions (indeed, many flagships are not profitable in themselves), but make a greater contribution to brand awareness in their wider markets.

Davies and Finney (1997) suggest that many retailer intermediaries will continue to be essentially regionally based in their future international activity. For some of these, such as GB Inno (of Belgium), building dominance or concentration within a region through retail diversification will be at the heart of the development strategy. For others, such as the symbol chains (for example, Spar), internationalization will be reflected in a series of alliances. For still others, such as Zara, the fast-growing fashion chain in Spain, so-called border-hopping will continue to be the main form of expansion.

Again, according to Davies and Finney, it is possible to describe four different types of regional activity:

■ *The deep discounter retailers*—Aldi, Lidl and Schwarz (Germany), and Netto (Denmark). Aldi now trades in nine countries of Western Europe and the USA and has a total of 1,460 stores. All three operate 'no-frills' stores, with limited lines and very low prices. All three are very aggressive in their expansion plans, border-hopping through organic growth.

■ *The supermarket companies*—such as Tesco, Edeka (Germany), and Julius Meinl (Austria). Their target for future expansion is likely to continue to be the changing markets of Central Europe (the Czech Republic, Hungary, and Poland). Interestingly, there are effectively no American international supermarket companies now, with the exception of Wal-Mart and Safeway (the latter trades in Canada and Mexico); but A. S. Watson and Dairy Farm will continue to expand in the Far East from their Hong Kong base.

■ *The convenience store retailers*—made up primarily of the symbol chains in Europe and the franchise operations in North America and the Far East.

Whilst these comprise mainly small, traditional stores, there are emerging new chains with what are called 'modern convenience stores'. Some of the UK food retailers are developing rapidly with this concept; Tesco, with its new Metro and Express stores, Safeway with its link to BP oil company, and Alldays, a new regional franchising operation which was opening four stores per week in the late 1990s.

■ *The mail-order companies*—these divide between the traditional large catalogue distributors, such as Otto Versand and Quelle (both from Germany), and the new 'specialogues', such as LL Bean and Racing Green. Whilst some of the mail-order operators are amongst the most traditional of all retail companies, others, of course, are at the forefront of the most modern forms of retailing—namely, teleshopping and shopping on the Internet.

Helfferich *et al.* (1997) categorize the international activity of retail intermediaries using a more holistic and strategic framework (Boxes 4.2 and 4.3). They observe: 'Retailers progressing beyond the "international" status in the narrow sense could develop into any one of the three categories; this is a matter of choice depending in all likelihood on factors such as market opportunities elsewhere and market threats at home, the type of retail institution involved and the vision of senior management' (Helfferich *et al.* 1997: 304).

Not all intermediary markets are so highly concentrated. Industrial distributors, by and large, are much less well consolidated than intermediaries in consumer markets. Herbig and O'Hara (1994)

Box 4.2 **Four categories of international retailing**

	International	Global	Transnational	Multinational
Geographic scope	1 continent	2+ continents	1+ continents	1+ continents
Cultural spread	1 cultural zone	2+ zones	2+ zones	2+ zones
Cultural orientation	Ethnocentric	Mixed	Geocentric	Polycentric
Marketing	Home format expansion or alliances	Minimal adaptation	Medium adaptation	Major adaptation
Management	Domestic HQ	Centralized control	Integrated network	Independent units

Source: Helfferich *et al.* (1997).

Box 4.3 **Examples of retail internationalization**

INTERNATIONAL (beginners/slow developers)	GLOBAL (fast developers/ inimitable niche)	TRANSNATIONAL (accumulators of experience)	MULTINATIONAL (portfolio managers)
Free Record Shop	IKEA	CandA	KBB
Blokker	McDonalds	Body Shop	Vendex
Hunkemoller	Benetton	Marks and Spencer	Ahold
Halfords	Toys R Us	Spar	Tengelmann
Hennes and Mauritz	Shell	Makro	Delhaize 'Le Lion'
	Aldi	Carrefour	
	Louis Vuitton	BATA	
		Schlecker	

Source: Helfferich *et al.* (1997).

report that, in the USA, industrial distributors are still fairly small businesses, often owner managed, and, although they have relatively high levels of expertise, they are often dependent upon manufacturing organizations for managerial support.

However, Arthur Andersen predicts a 15 per cent fall in the number of such industrial distributors in the USA by 2000, and considerable consolidation amongst the remainder, with the larger firms taking some 50 per cent of the market with the emergence of many large national distributors. Cort, Stith, and Lahoti (1997) observe that industrial distribution is undergoing a similar transformation to that which has been seen in retailing, with efficiency improvements and consequent reduction in transaction costs driving a consolidation of the sector.

3 The effect of regulation on the changing role of intermediaries

THE use of public policy instruments in the regulatory environment has been one of the chief constraints acting to prevent high levels of intermediary concentration within particular geo-graphical and sectoral markets. The impact of competition policy and of planning legislation will be discussed.

3.1 Competition policy

Governments at both the national and regional level have sought to regulate the nature and extent of competition within intermediary markets, largely in an attempt to protect established structures dominated by small- and medium-sized businesses and thereby prevent the development of oligopolistic or monopolistic market conditions. Anti-competitive practices by intermediaries (amongst others) were regulated in the USA from 1936 by means of the Robinson Patman Act, subsequently amended by the Clayton Act. In the UK, so-called Resale Price Maintenance dated from 1955, introduced when it became clear that there were significant pressures for concentration within retail intermediary markets. As far as retail intermediaries were concerned, legislation of this kind effectively stifled the ability of the intermediary to negotiate discounted terms that could not be linked to corresponding savings in cost. In the UK such legislation was abolished in 1965 (which can be said to have had the effect of accelerating concentration); similar restrictions remain to varying degrees in other countries. The debate about the efficacy of such interventions centres around the trade-off between a more permissive form of competition policy (which leads in the short term to lower prices, but in the long term to weakened suppliers and supplier brands, more intermediary branding, and fewer intermediaries) against a more restrictive scenario. Here, consumers have the power at least in principle to achieve lowering of prices (by shopping around), but ultimately suppliers have the greater market power through a fragmented distribution structure to raise prices.

We have already suggested that one of the main differences between manufacturers and intermediaries in a marketing sense is their involvement with a physical network. For this reason, monopolies and mergers legislation has been less effective at constraining the growth of intermediary businesses, because of the difficulty of arriving at a measure of what is the relevant market within which the potentially anti-competitive practice is proposed (local, regional, or national?). Sometimes, such interventions have been drafted in a way that regulates the manner in which intermediaries might physically develop: for example, setting out floorspace limits on growth that specifically discriminated against large space users. French and German legislation has been particularly effective in this respect.

Regional governments, such as the Commission of the EU, are still concerned with the promulgation of measures to protect established small- and medium-sized businesses. Within Europe, the Commission's Directorate-General XXIII, whilst unable to intervene in the planning policies of member states, funds training and technological assistance programmes for small businesses within those states considered most vulnerable to increased levels of retail concentration. The Directorate has also sought to monitor the growth of buying and other strategic alliances amongst the major food retail groups of the EU. Critics of this approach suggest that the focus on policy has been upon conserving historic patterns of change, rather than allowing intermediaries to operate more freely in an increasingly turbulent business environment (Dawson 1996).

3.2 Planning legislation

One of the other ways in which the state seeks to regulate intermediary growth and concentration is explicitly geographical, through the application of land-use or zonal planning legislation, seeking to control the location and size of specific categories or units of an intermediary's physical network. This again focuses upon the principle of the local market, and is generally concerned with such matters as defining levels of appropriate provision and avoiding duplication of capacity. However, many components of legislation—such as the UK's Town and Country Planning Acts—seek not to regulate competition as such, but to determine applications for development on their merits. Such controls are, therefore, essentially restrictive; the state is much less good at more positive planning for intermediary development.

During the 1960s, French, German, and UK planning legislation sought to allocate retail development more formally to centres within a notional hierarchy; new concepts (such as hypermarkets or out-of-town shopping centres) were fiercely resisted (Davies 1995). Following short periods of greater *laissez-faire* during the late 1960s and during the 1990s, most European Governments are again exerting much tighter controls over the location of new forms of retail development. Government concern centres around two issues:

■ the impact of large stores on small- and medium-sized retail businesses;

■ the impact of large stores and out-of-town shopping centres on the vitality and viability of traditional urban centres.

France was the first West European country to introduce special legislation to restrict large-store and out-of-town development. Special permission was required for developments of more than 1,500 square metres. In 1996, this threshold was reduced to 300 square metres.

4 Marketing activity by intermediaries

Is the marketing activity conducted by intermediaries especially distinctive in its character? In this section we select three broad examples of where intermediary power expresses itself in distinctive ways: managing the marketing channel, the growth of intermediary branding, and proximity to the customer.

4.1 **Managing the marketing channel**

As the intermediary becomes more sophisticated in its operations and develops a better sense of its own market and of its position in the marketing channel, so it seeks to impose a more efficient and effective way of managing that channel. First, within an increasingly customer-driven organization, the intermediary attempts to achieve a higher level of integration within the supply chain. Secondly, the intermediary tends to seek to re-evaluate the relationships between itself and supplier companies, particularly when it operates within an increasingly concentrated market.

4.1.1 **Supply-chain integration**

Part of the difficulty that intermediaries have in exerting influence over the supply chain is linked to the generally wide supplier base. US retailer Wal-Mart, for example, has over 5,500 suppliers with whom to deal. No one supplier accounts for more than 3.7 per cent of the group's total buying activity. These kinds of ratios are relatively common amongst intermediaries, which have broadened their product ranges in attempts to become 'mass' retailers. Many had difficulty in negotiating with suppliers, since product ranges were not planned or ordered in any systematic or integrated way—with orders often placed on the initiative of individual store managers. Wal-Mart sought to develop integrated marketing, buying, and distribution activities through the construction of thirty-three distribution centres. These support a central buying function and some 85 per cent of the company's products are handled through this integrated system.

☞ 'The ultimate goal of ECR is a responsive, consumer-driven system, in which retailers and suppliers work together as business allies to maximize consumer satisfaction and minimize cost.' (Chapter 14, p. 344)

In a 1994 study dealing with the changing character of retailer and supplier partnerships, it was observed that the move towards so-called efficient consumer response (ECR) (addressing the need to reduce costs and improve profitability along the supply chain by increasing sales and gross mar-

gins) would provide overall benefits estimated at 10–11 per cent of sales turnover at retail prices within three years of implementation in the USA and 2–4 per cent across Europe over a similar period (GEA Consulenti Associata di Gestione Aziendale 1994).

The role of information technology (IT) in achieving these efficiencies is well documented. Wrigley (1988), for example, suggests six technological factors that have assisted retailers in reaching positions of strength within the market:

- introduction of self-service methods;
- economies of scale by merchandising and substituting labour;
- development of automated warehousing;
- computerized stock control;
- unitization of stock replenishment;
- enhanced distribution networks.

4.1.2 **Intermediary–supplier relations**

A tighter focus upon an increasingly integrated supply chain within the context of a more highly concentrated market inevitably leads intermediaries to reconsider the nature and style of their relationships with suppliers. This may involve re-evaluating the size and characteristics of the supplier base. It may also lead to the development of more selective relationships with specific suppliers, perhaps acting as partners (in the sense of style of working rather than in any reference to joint ownership). The move towards a relationship-building model represents a very different approach for many intermediary firms, where the interactions between intermediaries and suppliers have been historically based upon more confrontational models of negotiated selling. This trend has been well documented (Davies 1993), and appears to be firmly established at the macro level. Nevertheless, there are differences geographically, by sector and in terms of extent of influence, that need to be better understood, although we have some indication of retail intermediaries' perceptions of the balance of power in specific areas relevant to marketing (Fig. 4.2).

The style of relationship between retail intermediary and supplier varies enormously internationally (Box 4.4) and both the areas within which partnershipping takes place and as the main issue areas differ substantially between countries. Of course, there is a finite limit to the number of

Figure 4.2 **Balance of power in retail decision-making, UK, 1987**

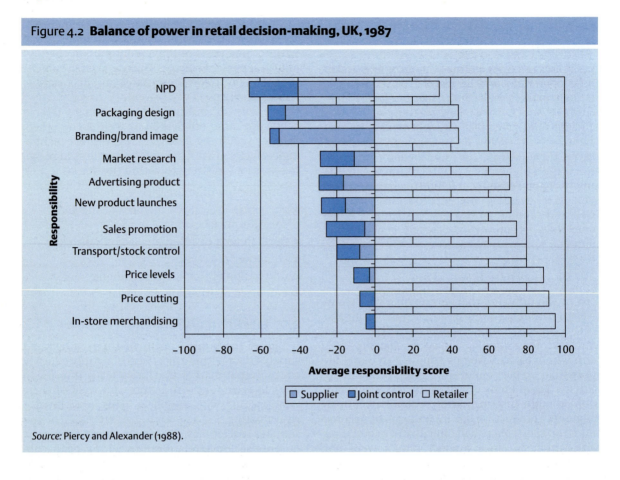

Source: Piercy and Alexander (1988).

Box 4.4 **Variations in retailer–manufacturer relationships, 1997**

Country	Negotiation climate	Partnership areas	Issue areas
France	Competitive	Merchandising supply chain	Price segmentation
Germany	Confrontational	Reusable packaging	Order lead time
Netherlands	Constructive	Category management	Information sharing
UK	Cool (detached)	Supply chain	Private labels

Source: OXIRM.

high-quality relationships an intermediary may develop. In the case of Wal-Mart, the company has selected just 110 suppliers from the base of 5,500 described above with whom to develop explicit partnership arrangements.

Intermediaries may also approach the practice of strategic marketing somewhat differently from suppliers. For example, Corstjens and Corstjens (1995) propose four main sets of contrasts between retailers and manufacturers that may affect their ability to apply segmentation, differentiation, and brand-development strategies (Box 4.5).

Ford creates shock waves

In October 1998 Ford (UK) announced that it would take over its largest dealership. By doing so it would gain control of about 8 per cent of its UK car sales. Analysts expect this to be the forerunner of further consolidation in the car sector, as manufacturers move to take over the independent car dealerships.

One advantage of not using intermediaries

When, in 1998, the bottom dropped out of the Asian market for PCs Dell was left with only a few days inventory compared with those of its competitors that sell through independent distribution outlets.

We should finally note that intermediaries have not always been successful in dominating their respective channels. Seeking to shift consumers away from reliance on intermediaries has been one successful way for some suppliers to differentiate their businesses (see Insert). For example, in markets where consumer confidence and information levels are low, intermediaries have played a role in assisting suppliers with market growth. Personal computing has been one such area. Dell Computers made the deliberate decision to position themselves as direct sales vendors of personal computers (PCs) during the early 1990s, deliberately excluding the sales agents who had conventionally dominated the PC supply market and with whom the leading suppliers had exclusive agreements. Dell explicitly targeted the business end-user audience with price-competitive machines built to order. They judged that the consumption decision by firms no longer required the intervention of an intermediary (see Insert). By 1996 the company ranked seventh in Europe and second in the UK in terms of units shipped.

Marketing opportunities also present themselves for suppliers within markets where intermediaries are poorly regarded, such as motor-vehicle sales, where consumer experience of dealerships has proved, in many countries, to be the most unsatisfactory part of the vehicle-buying experience. In the UK, for example, a Consumers' Association survey in 1996 found car salesmen to be 'lazy, incompetent and even law-breaking' (R.G. Cooper 1996). Daewoo Cars was the fourth Korean car manufacturer to enter the UK market, with models—moreover—based upon former Vauxhall Astra and Cavalier designs. Daewoo's marketing strategy centred on the disillusionment of the British consumer with the conventional buying process. By dealing direct with the consumer, with supplier showrooms with sales staff not on commission, and using direct-marketing techniques, Daewoo generated a 250,000 strong database of disenfranchised consumers. This was successfully converted into a 1 per cent UK market share two years after initial launch and twelve months ahead of the Chairman's target.

Box 4.5 Variations in retailer–manufacturer marketing strategies

Factor	Retailer	Manufacturer	Implications
Physical network	Fixed set of locations	No direct equivalent	Local marketing
Cost structure	Chain or store-level scale advantages	Company-level scale advantages	Critical mass required to be competitive
Financial structure	Delays of payment common; equity poor	Equity rich	Low barriers to entry
Pricing and price perceptions	Larger role	Smaller role	Need constantly to manage price perceptions

Source: Corstjens and Corstjens (1995).

4.2 The growth of intermediary branding

The use of branding has been a major historical source of supplier power. For this reason, it is being suggested that food retailers' investment in 'own-label' or 'private-label' brands represents one of the most dynamic strategic marketing forces within intermediary markets, capitalizing upon the retailer's chain image and manifesting it in product form (Laaksonen and Reynolds 1994). Retailers certainly find own brands an important tool in helping them differentiate themselves more tangibly from competitors and thereby increase their profitability during a period when consumers' attitude to price has been hardening. Examination of the penetration, characteristics, and consequences of the growth in own-label activity therefore provides a second useful perspective on the nature of strategic marketing conducted by retail intermediaries.

☞ 'Large and powerful retailers such as Sainsbury and Carrefour have now acquired brand propositions of their own.' (Chapter 20, p. 492)

For example, amongst retailers the traditional dominance of simplistic 'product-price' announcements has reinforced commentators' views that the sector has been a relatively unprofessional proponent of marketing principles: 'Each store sings the same song . . . "here tomatoes are cheaper". The result is a poor attribution of advertising claims and some lack of credibility.' (Kapferer 1986).

In the late 1990s, in line with increasingly professional and strategic thinking by the leading organizations in the sector worldwide, we witnessed a move to develop an 'image' of good price. So-called every day low pricing (EDLP), first developed by leading US retailers such as Wal-Mart and perpetuated, for example, in the UK through such strap-lines as 'Asda price' and the 'never knowingly undersold' claim of the John Lewis Partnership are examples of positioning seeking to develop a longer-term belief in the price positioning of leading retailers. Retailers have then often sought to shift the debate from price to quality and service differentiators, including the development of own brand.

4.2.1 The penetration of retail intermediary brands

The penetration of own-brand development is very varied between countries (Table 4.5). There appears to be a quite clear geographical distinction within Europe, for example, between Central and north-western Europe, on the one hand, and the Nordic and Mediterranean countries, on the other.

Nevertheless, many of the major European grocery retail intermediaries have already developed, or are planning to do so, sophisticated value-added own-brand ranges. Much of the variation in penetration has to do with the varied stage of development of food retail markets within European countries and with the different sizes of the markets concerned. In many countries, also, wholesalers or manufacturers still exercise significant control over the market place, effectively preventing full-scale own-brand development. Even in countries with higher-than-average own-brand shares, it is the largest retailers who drive own-label growth (Fig. 4.3).

4.2.2 The characteristics of retail intermediary brand development

There have been a number of attempts to model the own-brand development process. Generally own-brand development can be seen to go

Table 4.5 **Varied growth of retail own brands, selected European countries, 1992–1997**

Country	Private label share of grocery sales 1994 (%)	% change 1992–7 (%)
Belgium	19.8	5
France	16.4	7
Germany	18.5	9
Italy	6.8	1.5
Netherlands	16.3	1
Spain	7.7	4.5
Switzerland	41.2	7
UK	37.1	2.7

Source: AC Nielsen.

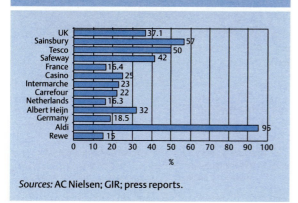

Figure 4.3 **Private-label share of food, country average and major retailers, 1994**

Sources: AC Nielsen; GIR; press reports.

through four stages or generations (Box 4.6). In each generation, the retailer's objectives, as well as the products, required technology, and consumers' motivation to buy are different. The level of sophistication of the products increases from one generation to the next. The first and second generations comprise simple commodities, which are launched in order to increase margins and provide choice in pricing. The third generation of own brands imitates manufacturers' brands whilst still retaining lower pricing. The fourth generation of own brands matches and surpasses manufacturers' brands in quality and innovation in order to differentiate the retailer from the competition.

☞ 'No longer are own-label brands regarded as cheap and cheerful alternatives to manufacturers' brands, but arguably, in many product sectors—for example, chilled foods and dairy products—own-label brands are regarded in the same way as manufacturers' brands.' (Chapter 20, p. 492)

This model may oversimplify reality. In practice, the generations overlap and the development is not always gradual from first to fourth generation. For example, in France evolution of own brands has gradually developed through the various stages, whereas in the UK second-generation own labels existed before first-generation generics. Different countries are also in different stages of the evolutionary process, but they are generally moving in the same direction. The move towards higher sophistication is driven by both retailers

and consumers, the first wanting to increase their profitability and the latter wanting better value for money, wider choice of products, and increased convenience.

Consumers' attitudes towards own brands across Europe have also changed over time. Until the early 1980s own labels were generally seen as cheaper alternatives to manufacturers' brands. Initially, consumers purchased own labels as a reaction to the perceived high price of manufacturers' brands. Later in the 1980s, consumers tended to associate generics with recession. Price alone was no longer enough to motivate consumers to buy. In the late 1990s low price appeared to be merely one element of own brands' appeal, but, together with good and consistent quality, own brands offered good value for money. Further, although customers still perceived own brands to be cheaper than manufacturers' brands, they also generally perceived them to be of comparable quality. Moreover, the majority of consumers had as much confidence in own brands as they did in manufacturer brands (Table 4.6). Own brands have the clearest image in Germany. Aldi is the clear champion in the German own-brand market and it has been building its 'high-quality-at-low-prices' image since the early 1960s. Of the five countries, own brands have the weakest image in Italy. Much of this has to do with the fact that manufacturers' brands still dominate the Italian market and there are very few retailers with a strong own-brand range.

4.2.3 The consequences of retail intermediary brand development

Is it possible to detect a set of common marketing consequences of own-brand strategies across Europe? Perhaps the most significant is the discovery that, in several product categories in European countries, the product market is polarizing. Particular markets are becoming divided between leading national or often international manufacturer brands and own brands, whilst secondary brands are gradually being squeezed out. Polarization is especially evident in France (Fig. 4.4), Germany, and in the UK.

In the UK, it is perhaps most pronounced in the markets where own brands have large market shares: these include yoghurts, squash, canned fish, and canned soups. In France, there are several product markets in which secondary manufacturers are under intense pressure from leading

Box 4.6 Evolution of own brands

Brand criteria	1st generation	2nd generation	3rd generation	4th generation
Type of brand	■ generic ■ no name ■ brand free ■ unbranded	■ 'quasi-brand' ■ own label	■ own brand	■ extended own brand, i.e. segmented own brands
Strategy Objective	■ generics ■ increase margins ■ provide choice in pricing	■ cheapest price ■ increase margins ■ reduce manufacturers' power by setting the entry price ■ provide better-value product (quality/price)	■ me-too ■ enhance category margins ■ expand product assortment, i.e. customer choice ■ build retailer's image among consumers	■ value-added ■ increase and retain the client base ■ enhance category margins ■ improve image further ■ differentiation
Product	■ basic and functional products	■ one-off staple lines with a large volume	■ big category products	■ image-forming product groups ■ large number of products with small volume (niche)
Technology	■ simple production process and basic technology lagging behind market leader	■ technology still lagging behind market leaders	■ close to the brand leader	■ innovative technology
Quality/ Image	■ lower quality and inferior image compared to the manufacturers' brands	■ medium quality but still perceived as lower than leading manufacturers' brands ■ secondary brand alongside the leading manufacturer's brand	■ comparable to the brand leaders	■ same or better than brand leader ■ innovative and different products from brand leaders
Approximate pricing	■ 20% or more below the brand leader	■ 10–20% below	■ 5–10% below	■ equal or higher than known brand
Consumers' motivation to buy	■ price is the main criterion for buying	■ price is still important	■ both quality and price, i.e. value for money	■ better and unique products
Supplier	■ national, not specialized	■ national, partly specializing to own label manufacturing	■ national, mostly specializing for own brand manufacturing	■ international, manufacturing mostly own brands

Source: Laaksonen and Reynolds (1994).

Table 4.6 Image of own brands compared to brand leaders (among consumers who were aware of own brands), 1994 (%)

Image regarding	France	Germany	Italy	Spain	UK	All five
Price						
More expensive	2	3	3	2	1	3
As expensive	26	12	29	16	13	19
Less expensive	72	85	68	83	86	78
Quality						
Higher	3	2	7	6	4	5
Same	78	90	71	73	77	78
Lower	19	8	22	21	18	17
Confidence						
More	4	3	10	7	5	6
Same	73	84	66	71	74	74
Less	23	12	24	22	21	21

Sources: Secodip; IGD; Europanel.

Figure 4.4 Brand polarization in France, 1992

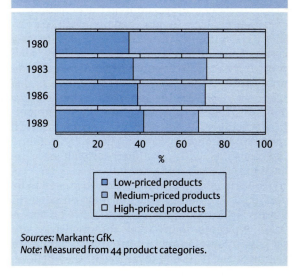

Chips
Syrup
Fruit juice
Meat
Rice
Soft drinks
Chocolate bars
Sausage

0 20 40 60 80 100

% share 1992

□ Top 2 manufacturers
□ Own brand
□ Other

Source: LSA.

Figure 4.5 Polarization of the German food market, 1980–1989

1980
1983
1986
1989

0 20 40 60 80 100

%

□ Low-priced products
□ Medium-priced products
□ High-priced products

Sources: Markant; GfK.
Note: Measured from 44 product categories.

manufacturers' brands and own brands. For example, in markets such as soft drinks, syrup, rice, and chips, little over one-third of the market is left for which secondary brands may compete.

During the 1980s, price polarization was very much evident in Germany (Fig. 4.5). High and low price segments increased consistently at the expense of medium-priced products. The market share of medium-priced products decreased from

38 per cent in 1980 to 26 per cent in 1989. The strongest growth was in the high-price segment, which increased from 35 per cent in 1980 to 42 per cent in 1989, reflecting the increased affluence of German households. Yet the growth of the low-price segment is even more remarkable as a result. The German example in particular clearly shows

that an intermediate 'medium-price' positioning is not viable. It is increasingly vital to position an own-brand range in either the high- or low-price segment.

Not all retailers have fully appreciated the strategic power of own brands within the marketing channel. Used properly as an integral part of a company's marketing strategy, store brands are effective tools of differentiation and promotion. Because of their image and profitability advantages, grocery retailers across Europe are strongly committed to developing their own-brand ranges. Moreover, consumers are increasingly confident own-brand shoppers. However, own-brand growth is to some extent limited by national boundaries and differences. As a consequence, without organic growth abroad and exporting of the whole store format, it often proves difficult to create an international value-added own-brand range.

4.3 Proximity to the customer

From the point of view of the marketer, intermediaries are, by definition, closer to the customer than supplier companies. This has two implications. First, intermediaries are in principle better placed to gather information on the behaviour of consumers and customers than organizations further back in the supply chain. Secondly, and as a consequence of this data-gathering activity, such companies are also therefore better placed to communicate more effectively with consumers. In this section we deal with the first of these implications and consider the growth of so-called customer-loyalty schemes as an attempt by retail intermediaries to consolidate this proximity by building 'relationships' with consumers, as well as to reduce the effects of competition.

Not least amongst the questions that need to be answered is whether the much overused term 'loyalty' is the appropriate behaviour to be understood. However, many retail intermediaries are seeking to develop reward-based programmes to reinforce the trust and loyalty that, they believe, consumers place in them.

4.3.1 Can loyalty be a differentiator?

There are a number of questions that need to be addressed if we are to understand why customer loyalty, as far as the retailer is concerned, has become such a topical subject. First, what have been the drivers for this shift in focus? Secondly, has technology—as has been claimed—played the role

of facilitator of this process? Has it, however, as a result, prevented an effective examination of the true strategic benefit of a loyalty scheme as part of an effectively managed marketing strategy for a retail intermediary? Finally, how well is the consumer likely to respond to the sorts of initiatives that are underway in many developed retail markets in Europe, North America, and Australasia? What kinds of 'relationships' do retail customers really want?

☞ 'The research about marketing practice has shown that the dominant trend in the organizations studied is to develop relationships.' (Chapter 22, p. 525)

Why has loyalty become such an important topic so far as retailers are concerned? Fig. 4.6 shows that there is considerable international interest in developing frequent shopper and reward programmes amongst grocery retail companies. However, many other organizations have been involved with this area of marketing for much longer: suppliers in particular have been experimenting with loyalty schemes and with below-the-line direct-marketing exercises. For retail intermediaries, however, there appear to be four motivators.

4.3.2 The rediscovery of the customer

Retailers, amongst other consumer-service intermediaries, have discovered that the cost of recruiting a new customer is considerably higher than that of retaining an existing customer. Techniques

Figure 4.6 **Extent of frequent shopper programmes in grocery retailing, 1996**

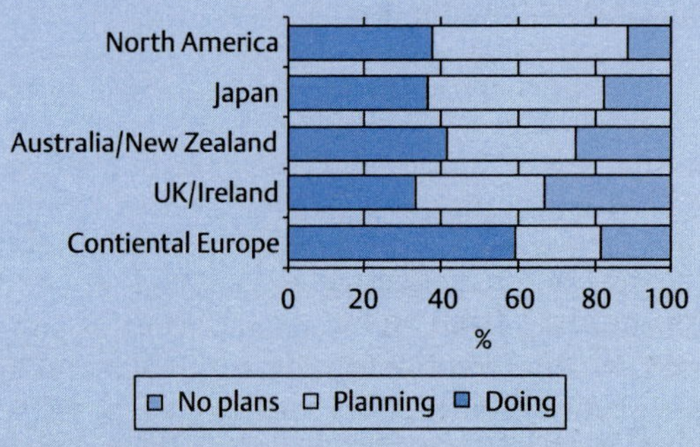

Source: Food Marketing Institute.

such as data mining are now starting to provide stark assessments of the true, lifetime, value of a loyal customer to the business. Marketing efforts have, therefore, been redirected towards strategies that reinforce retention.

4.3.3 Intensification of service-driven competition

Service differentiation is likely to be a consequence of an increasingly mature grocery industry in many developed economies over the early part of the twenty-first century. 'Loyalty' is likely to be one aspect of that competition. In addition to simple product-line extension, retail intermediaries are offering a whole range of additional services such as crèches, post offices, pharmacies, and hairdressers. Nor is this just an aspect of grocery retailing. German cosmetics retailer Douglas offers customers the Douglas-Card, at a price of DM12 per year. In addition to non-cash payments, the card will give customers access to other services, including travel and beauty-farm arrangements, visits to fashion shows, and a telephone booking service for concerts and other events. UK variety store retailer Boots had recruited 9 million holders of its smart-card-based Advantage card by the middle of 1998.

4.3.4 IT as a facilitator

The fall in cost and increase in functionality of database technology has meant that it is much easier and more straightforward, at least on the surface, to develop customer-oriented databases for customer loyalty schemes.

4.3.5 Customer expectations

Customers who are presently purchasing petrol with their smart cards, or receiving frequent-flyer air miles, or making use of affinity cards through various financial services companies are becoming used to these sorts of encounters when they purchase goods or a service.

4.3.6 What is customer loyalty?

Perhaps the most effective definition of customer loyalty comes from an authoritative study undertaken in 1993 by the Coca-Cola Retail Research Group: 'an initiative where a specific mechanism is used to incentivise the customer to give a higher share of his/her grocery spend to a retailer—over and above that warranted by the attractiveness of the retailer's core offering of location, product, service, price, etc.' (Coopers & Lybrand 1993).

There are two features of this definition that are of particular interest. It describes an activity that first seeks to attract new customers into a store and secondly deals with enriching the experience of existing customers above and beyond the basic image and reputation of the organization. It has also been suggested that there are a number of different kinds of loyalty:

- *monopoly loyalty*—where there is often no choice available: in remote rural areas, for example;
- *inertial loyalty*—where consumers do not actively seek out an alternative;
- *price loyalty*—where consumers evaluate alternatives on the basis of price alone through a discount scheme;
- *incentivized loyalty*—where the extent of patronage is converted into points that can be redeemed against gifts;
- *emotional loyalty*—an exceptionally intractable category for those retailers who do not already command it, based upon the intangibles associated with the retail brand.

The majority of the focused loyalty schemes in place across Europe and the US in the late 1990s were in the areas of price and incentivized loyalty.

We can also start to categorize loyalty in terms of its orientation. If we see loyalty schemes and promotional activity as part of an overall marketing strategy, then they can be of two broad types: offensive and defensive, (Fig. 4.7). Offensive

Figure 4.7 **Loyalty-scheme orientation**

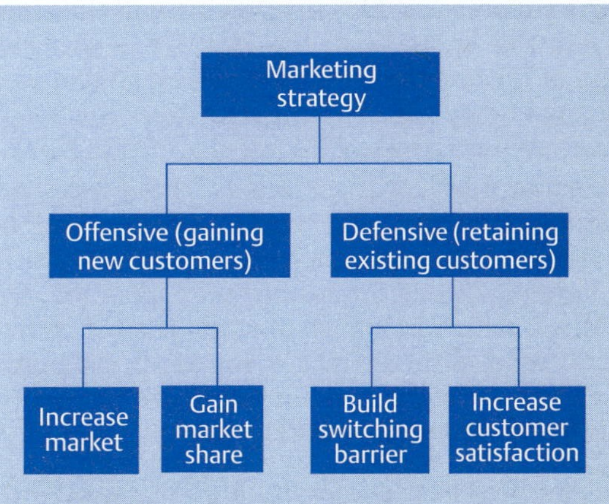

Source: OXIRM.

strategies, aimed at gaining new customers, are perhaps the more difficult, because just like any other kind of initiative in this area, they involve either gaining market share or increasing the overall size of the market by displacing spending from elsewhere. Defensive schemes make up by far the majority of schemes at present. These schemes are aimed at retaining existing customers in the face of increased competition and the blandishments of increasingly differentiated grocery retailers. These take two forms: either they build a switching barrier through the use of such phenomena as club cards, or they seek to increase customer satisfaction in a much more qualitative way. (This latter is typical of the kind of strategy adopted by Superquinn in the Irish Republic—an overall strategic investment in customer care and customer satisfaction driven from the top and not necessarily involving a large amount of technology.)

The 1993 Coca-Cola study (Coopers & Lybrand 1993) came to some quite useful conclusions about loyalty from data analysis of UK grocery retailing. There were four conclusions of particular interest from a study of loyalty characteristics within both Tesco and J. Sainsbury:

- Loyalty is not a fixed quality but a continuum in terms of degree. This has interesting consequences: the most loyal 30 per cent of Sainsbury and Tesco customers, for example, accounted for nearly 65 per cent of the organizations' turnover.
- As a consequence, both Tesco and Sainsbury commanded only a 30 per cent market share of customers, with a major opportunity for 'upgrading' loyalty.
- This continuum of loyalty and non-loyalty exhibits radically different shopping patterns. Any kind of focused loyalty scheme will thus have to come to terms with the mixture of different kind of loyalties expressed by different groups of consumers within a particular store for which there are profound marketing-mix implications.
- For the most loyal customers, this means persuading them to change their total shopping behaviour; for the rest, which represent the majority of individuals but the minority of spending, this means a switch in choice of store. It is, of course, much more difficult to develop loyalty schemes to encourage store switching that are not simply short-term promotional exercises.

We can further position any kind of loyalty on a continuum between the tactical to the more

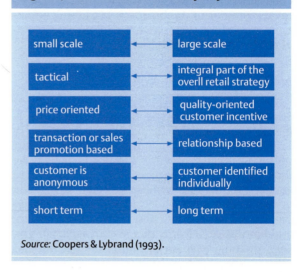

Figure 4.8 **Role of customer loyalty schemes**

small scale	↔	large scale
tactical	↔	integral part of the overll retail strategy
price oriented	↔	quality-oriented customer incentive
transaction or sales promotion based	↔	relationship based
customer is anonymous	↔	customer identified individually
short term	↔	long term

Source: Coopers & Lybrand (1993).

strategic in terms of its actual role (Fig. 4.8). There is considerable rhetoric in this area at present, with many essentially tactical schemes being promoted as being strategic in nature. As a consequence, some of the schemes that are presently in existence may be legitimately criticized in terms of their scale, their degree of strategic orientation, and their service offering, whether they are simply transaction based—offering a coupon or discount at the till—or to do with longer-term development of relationships.

4.3.7 International experience

Some 60 per cent of US food retailers claimed that they would have a 'frequent-shopper' programme in place by the end of 1997. In practice, this meant a very low-cost, low-technology investment in some kind of short-term incentive programme. US retailers were enthusiastic because they were able to see a substantial increase in sales achieved by early adopters (growth rates of between 10 and 20 per cent have been quoted). Such schemes are essentially reliant on a database that is supplier driven rather than retailer driven, with suppliers selling their services to risk-averse retailers.

The USA is rather different from Europe in relation to loyalty schemes for reasons that can be seen by looking at what encourages store switching amongst US consumers. About 25 per cent of US consumers claimed that they had switched

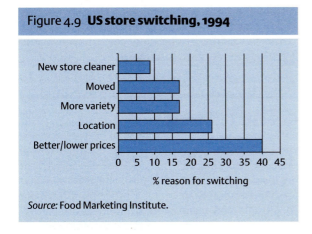

Figure 4.9 **US store switching, 1994**

% reason for switching

Source: Food Marketing Institute.

Figure 4.10 **Store switching across Europe, 1992–1995**

% changing store in previous year

Source: Food Marketing Institute.

stores in 1994. As Fig. 4.9 shows, something like 40 per cent claim that better and lower prices were their main reason for switching. The most promiscuous in the USA tend to be younger people. Those who exhibited above-average switching behaviour were the 18–24 year olds, 25–39 year olds, and those in work. The most loyal consumers tended to be older working men, from Mid-West communities.

What characterizes the best of US experience? In the late 1990s one regarded by competitors as 'one of the most sophisticated in the US' was A and P's Bonus Savings Club with a club card. It acts as a cheque-encashment privilege card. Manufacturers sponsor between 500 and 700 items per week, which are available only for club members in the stores: some exclusivity is available. But little mailing-out is done and there is no extensive database maintained in-house to allow understanding of the buying behaviour of the customer base. One of the reasons for that, of course, is the particularly critical concern that US consumers have about privacy issues, in respect of database marketing. Nevertheless by 1998 A and P had around 70 or 80 per cent of their consumers within their 'Club' and we may legitimately ask how exclusive that is?

This paints a rather simpler picture than the experience within Europe. The reasons for switching in the USA are essentially to do with price. Across Europe, not only do switching rates vary, but the reasons for promiscuity are often very different, although price remains an important factor (Fig. 4.10). For example, two Belgian retail intermediaries, GB-Inno and Delhaize 'Le Lion', take different approaches to customer loyalty. Within Belgium in 1995, these two major supermarket

chains used customer loyalty schemes as a major competitive weapon. Both issued shopping cards. However, GB offered promotions and incentives (such as compact discs) with its 'Advantage' card, with points being converted directly into gift items, whilst the Delhaize 'Plus' card offered a discount equivalent to between 0.8 and 1.6 per cent, again using a points scheme.

Delhaize saw the 'Plus' scheme as a cornerstone of its EDLP strategy. Indeed, the company attributed a greater-than-average rise in retail sales during 1994 (3 per cent as against a 1 per cent national rise in this sector) to this scheme.

In 1994 the scheme held data on over 1 million Belgian householders—one in four of all Belgian households. Data mining, investigating the nature of the existing customer base, produced a number of surprises for the company: defections, at 24 per cent, were much higher than expected; the average shopper visited stores much less frequently than market research had predicted (0.85 times weekly as against the estimated 1.5 times); however, the most loyal customers were visiting stores at 1.96 times per week, and 12 per cent of customers were providing 21 per cent of sales turnover.

These and other findings gave rise to a number of targeted initiatives, some more successful than others:

■ An attempt to recruit new shoppers from a bought-in list of 250,000 names and addresses produced only a 1.3 per cent response, of which only 20 per cent remained loyal.

■ A 'reactivation' effort, by means of a special mailing seeking to bring back lapsed cardholders, drew a 16 per cent response.

A small group of so-called medium spenders in terms of total sales who were 'low' spenders on wines were targeted with mail shots to encourage wine purchase. This was largely unsuccessful and had the further effect of causing resentment amongst customers with higher loyalty who had not received similar offers.

The company estimated that each cardholder cost the company BFr.460 (Ecu 11.5 ecus) per year. Discounts and incentives comprised over half of this figure; mailings a further one-third. Much of the cost of the programme was funded from savings in other areas of the business—from the cancellation of a weekly promotional flier, for example.

In conclusion, when we look at the marketplace as a whole, we see a few retail intermediaries investing in customer loyalty in a strategic way. We see responses from others, who are using it in a largely tactical manner. 'Loyalty schemes are not a substitute for an effective retail marketing strategy' (Coopers & Lybrand 1993).

Retailers have to decide whether they are using loyalty schemes simply as price incentives for particular kinds of customers or are using them to offer exclusivity and a real difference to the most loyal groups of their customers (Fig. 4.11). What is the ultimate willingness of retailers to make long-term investments? The success of these sorts of initiatives and the database marketing that lies behind them rests in better targeting of more sophisticated and demanding individual consumers. This is never likely to be a low-cost solution to differentiation for retail marketers.

5 The future

THE material presented in this chapter would seem to suggest that, whilst a somewhat neglected topic for marketers, the role of intermediaries is likely to become more important for consumers and business customers in the future. This is not least because of the natural growth in control over the supply chain of intermediaries positioned closer to the end-consumer or business purchaser than the originating supplier or producer. At the end of the twentieth century, the growth of retailer power in particular was a phenomenon being observed not just within parts of Europe, but in Australia as well as in the USA. There is no doubt that we shall see intermediaries becoming more important in their own right, with consequent implications for marketing, in the first decade of the twenty-first century.

☞ **'A major phenomenon to be mentioned here are the shifts that may occur over time with regard to the use and suitability of push-versus-pull marketing mix instruments. The relative power of intermediaries represents a major determinant in the choice between a push versus a pull approach.'** (Chapter 9, p. 207)

For example, Dawson suggests that the largest European retail intermediaries will begin operating within much broader-reaching frameworks of corporate strategy. He identifies three distinct approaches (Dawson 1996):

■ *knowledge-based*: more creative ways of running the business are identified and developed;

■ *alliance-based*: Co-operative initiatives between firms seek to generate new or reinforce existing competitive positions;

■ *productivity-based*: assets and resources are focused on key business areas to achieve cost substitutions.

However, whilst we may see the perpetuation of these trends, it is clear that there are likely to be a number of moderating influences on the power

Figure 4.11 **Effectiveness of loyalty schemes**

Source: Brann Direct Marketing.

of intermediaries. Institutional forces, such as strengthening competition policy and, indirectly in the case of retail intermediaries, planning policy, may work to constrain the dominance of intermediaries within the supply chain. Already, the role of the competition directorate within the European Commission can be seen as an increasingly interventionist one, for example.

☞ 'As the Internet matures, shopping on it will become much more interesting than shopping with paper catalogues, because there will be such a diversity of shops and goods.' (Chapter 12, p. 289)

It is also clear that technology will play an inevitably ambiguous role in determining the scale and character of intermediary operations in the future. On the one hand, technological innovation will work to facilitate the effectiveness of the frameworks that Dawson describes. For example, IT used in connection with sales-based ordering (SBO) or ECR will allow traditional retail intermediaries to accrue significant cost reductions and raise barriers to entry. On the other hand, the restructuring of marketing channels to the consumer by means of such phenomena as the Internet may hold the threat of new entrants to conventional markets challenging traditional intermediary niches (Reynolds 1997). This has often been termed 'disintermediation'. However, the reality of channel proliferation and new opportunities for different kinds of organization to add digital value (Rayport and Sviokla 1995) may result in an effective 'reintermediation' of channels with new players and new configurations and networks of actors (Sarker *et al.* 1996).

6 Summary

INTERMEDIARIES lie between producers and consumers, or customers, within marketing channels. The increase in their size, character, and sophistication has made them increasingly relevant to marketers, although they have not always merited the same degree of attention and discussion as have consumers and producers. Intermediary markets worldwide have evolved with implications for the distribution of power within marketing channels. Retail intermediaries have proven to be the most active organizations in this

respect, although financial services and industrial distribution also witnessed changes, to varying degrees, during the twentieth century. The growing power of intermediaries has been increasingly constrained by regulatory measures in such areas as competition and planning policy. However, the consequences of powerful intermediation for marketing can be seen most distinctively through changes in intermediary–supplier relationships, through the growth of intermediary branding in its own right, and through the advantages potentially available (but not always realized) through the intermediary's proximity to the end-consumer or customer. Future challenges to intermediaries revolve around the likely future extent of regulatory control and the role of technology in reintermediating the markets within which traditional organizations presently operate.

Further reading

Collins, A. (1991), *Competitive Retail Marketing* (Maidenhead: McGraw-Hill). A textbook welcomed as 'eminently readable' by practitioners. Collins writes in a popular style in seeking to interpret marketing rhetoric for retail marketing practitioners. Extensive anecdotal and case-study material is provided.

Davies, G. (1993), *Trade Marketing Strategy* (London: Paul Chapman). One of the few books that focuses the reader's attention in an academic way on the marketing challenges facing retailers in their relationships with supplier companies.

de Chernatony, L., and McDonald, M. (1998), *Creating Powerful Brands in Consumer, Service and Industrial Markets* (2nd edn., Oxford: Butterworth-Heinemann). An excellent reader on branding generally, which also undertakes some useful analysis and demonstrates effective insights into branding issues affecting intermediaries.

Fernie, J. (1990) (ed.), *Retail Distribution Management* (London: Kogan Page). A worthwhile collection of readings that combine economic and socio-political perspectives on the development and evolution of the supply chain.

McGoldrick, P. J. (1990), *Retail Marketing* (London: McGraw-Hill). A student textbook that comprehensively reviews the particular environment faced and the tasks and skills required of the retail marketer.

—— (1994) (ed.), *Cases in Retail Management* (London: Pitman). A well-developed collection of cases reviewing the strategic and organizational challenges for the retail business.

Discussion questions

1 Why have intermediaries been a neglected topic for marketers?

2 To what extent can intermediaries within industrial distribution learn from experience within retailing?

3 Do retail marketers face distinctive and unusual challenges in managing the retail marketing mix?

4 Do intermediaries take best advantage from their proximity to the end consumer?

5 What are the challenges of Internetworking technology for traditional intermediary organizations?

Chapter 5

The Structure of EU Industry and Services

Alan Griffiths

Objectives

The objectives of this chapter are:

1 to show that the changing nature of competition in Europe can be appreciated only in the context of the forces of globalization and deindustrialization;

2 to provide a guide to the important factors that partly determine such structural change;

3 to provide an understanding of the nature of EU trade and the effect of the introduction of the single market programme (SMP) on such trade flows;

4 to provide an insight into the dynamics of EU industry and services by discussing the forces that affect industrial structure;

5 to show, by investigating the effect of various trade and structural forces on price margins and price convergence across the EU, how competitiveness is affected by the changes noted above;

6 to explain and clarify the more immediate macro- and corporate-level factors that will determine the EU's future competitiveness.

1 Introduction

FOR many marketing managers economists are an irritant whose main value is to be the source of old and rather weak jokes about their unwillingness to make definitive predictions. However, many marketing managers recognize the value of economics and indeed would agree that 'the use of economics and economic measurement techniques is being increasingly recognized as an important element in marketing and other areas of business analysis. Economic analysis and quantitative techniques allow the major factors affecting market growth and other business issues to be related to each other in a coherent and consistent way and in a form which can be used for the evaluation of marketing plans' (Greenway 1999: 58). Section 2 shows how economic factors determine the nature of the competitive environment within which individual firms have to operate as they market their products. The following sections will consider what determines these economic factors and the pharmaceutical industry will be used as an example.

2 The competitive environment

TWO major influences on the development of the modern competitive environment have been globalization and deindustrialization. These two influences are considered in the following sections.

2.1 Globalization

Over the last two decades of the twentieth century most of the world's nations experienced an acceleration in the pace of economic change. The period saw a convergence of forces that led to a rapid growth of interdependence between countries, while at the same time causing important structural shifts to occur within those same nations. These interrelated changes resulted in a business environment where the only constant factor is change itself. For a fuller understanding of the general trends in the world economy and the way that such underlying factors facilitated economic change in Europe, we need to look more closely at the concepts of globalization and structural change—that is, the international and intranational aspects of economic behaviour.

From a macroeconomic perspective, globalization involves the growing interdependence of countries worldwide, which results in an acceleration in the volume of goods and services transacted internationally. Such movements of goods and services are also accompanied by increased flows of international capital and the rapid diffusion of technology across national boundaries. Therefore, the process of globalization can be seen as a continuous adaptation by firms to the changing global environment. Some firms that serve mainly the domestic market come under pressure from foreign competitors, while other firms react by aiming at worldwide intra-firm division of labour—that is, they become multinational in their production and distribution strategies. In this context it is interesting to note that, if multinational companies aim at worldwide intra-firm operations, this will tend to increase worldwide trade, whilst, if such activity is established within a geographically concentrated area (i.e. within trading blocs such as the EU, NAFTA, or APEC), sometimes known as 'global localization', then this could lead to a fall in international trade. It is the dynamic interaction between macro- and microeconomic forces noted above that often decides the changing pattern of world trade and production.

The pace of globalization trends has been determined to a great extent by the interaction of technological, organizational, and policy changes. First, the progress in computer/communications technology has meant that companies are able to coordinate production activities across international borders in search of low-cost locations. At the same time, the costs of transportation have fallen, making it possible for companies to operate competitively in many areas of the world. These changes have spilled over to financial markets, where the diffusion of telematics and communication technologies have allowed markets to overcome the barriers of space and time, thus affecting the volume of capital transactions. Secondly, there have been significant changes in the organization and operation of many firms. An increasing number of domestic and international companies have become less hierarchical in structure, with decision-making being delegated downwards to often semi-autonomous subunits that are closer to the actual market. Organizational changes such as these, together with communications technology, have also made it possible for companies to distribute R&D and marketing facilities worldwide. Thirdly, no major movement towards globalization can occur without political/policy changes. In this context, the liberalization of flows of trade and services by such organizations as the WTO (GATT), IMF, and OECD has accelerated since the 1970s.

What have been the symptoms of rapid globalization? First, the ratio of world exports to world GDP had reached 24 per cent by 1996, having doubled since 1950, and increased by as much as a quarter over the period 1986–96. Similarly, the average daily turnover in the world's main foreign exchange markets grew from $1,880 billion in 1986 to $1.4 trillion by 1996. The amounts of foreign direct investment (FDI) outflows have increased fivefold over the same period. Obviously, the degree of globalization does differ across the continents. For example, the ratio of exports to GDP for North America in 1996 was 12 per cent, while the figures for Europe (including intra-European trade) was 30 per cent, and for Developing Asia (China and the NICs) the figure rose to 40 per cent.

In the European context, we can look at the process of globalization in two ways: first, at increased trade between the countries of the EU—i.e. intra-EU trade—and, secondly, at increased trade between all EU countries and the outside world—i.e. extra-EU trade. We have seen above that, on the basis of intra-European trade, the whole area has been 'internationalized' for many years. This is also reflected in the share of EU merchandise exports (extra-EU trade) to world exports, which stood at 24 per cent in 1996—indicating the importance of the EU as a major trading bloc.

Growing interdependence between nations and trading blocs is seen as being beneficial for many reasons. It is argued that the integration of global markets via trade and FDI flows will create growth and employment, will act as a vital mechanism for the transmission of new ideas and new production and marketing techniques, and will improve management practices worldwide. In this way, improved benefits are expected for consumers, since goods and services can be produced in the least-cost locations while simultaneously giving more choice to consumers. Also, financial benefits accrue from the growth of a world market for capital, in that countries and firms can raise money on different world financial centres using a greater range of sophisticated financial instruments. On a microeconomic level, globalization will bring competition to the doorstep of domestic companies, forcing them to compete or die. This will significantly increase competition, which, in turn, will increase efficiency in the allocation of resources.

The trend towards the globalization of the economy is, therefore, multidimensional. Despite the trends noted above, it must be remembered that three-quarters of the world's production of goods and services are still consumed within national economies and that world-outward FDI of the advanced countries is only 7 per cent of their domestic fixed investment, which indicates how important domestic savings are in the investment process. Similarly, globalization to date has not involved large international movements in labour, since residents born abroad comprise only between 5 and 10 per cent of the workforce of large industrialized countries. However, to say that these figures prove that integration of global markets is not a real phenomenon is to ignore the important changes that have already occurred over the last decade in particular.

The integration of global markets will heighten competition in markets worldwide. Ironically, it will tend to increase competition between nations in some markets while at the same time making nations cooperate through pooling of knowledge and joint venturing in other markets. Globalization based on the increasing activity of multinational companies will also alter the concept of what national production means. Some writers, such as K. Ohmae (1990), have pointed to the fact that national governments will have to attract investment for the development of their economies independently of the origin of that capital. Similarly, Reich (1991) has pointed to the increasing conceptual problems that arise when trying to distinguish between the competitiveness of nations and that of international companies. For example, the competitiveness of the EU-owned corporations is not the same as EU competitiveness, since foreign companies that undertake production, research, and marketing in the EU may be more competitive than EU companies operating abroad. The factors noted above mean that the future of global competitiveness will have critical repercussions on domestic/regional interests, as national governments organize themselves on a more re-

gional basis to achieve global influence. At the same time, governments have to cope with the increasingly complex task of providing modern economic and industrial policies to provide a suitable domestic economic environment in which both domestic and foreign multinationals can operate. Achieving the correct blend of independence and interdependence will be at the core of national policies for the foreseeable future.

2.2 Deindustrialization and structural change

The increasing integration of the world economy noted above has coincided with a longer-term phenomenon that can also help to shine light on the nature of the competitiveness of nations. This revolves around the continuing structural changes that affect economies as they mature. A brief analysis of this concept will help place competitiveness and structural change in the EU in their proper perspective. Basically, as an economy matures, there is a shift in the sectoral composition of its total output (value added), and employment from the agriculture sector shifts towards manufacturing and then services. For the more advanced countries, the most significant change over the last forty years of the twentieth century involved the continuing shift in the share of output and employment from manufacturing to services as per capita income rose.

When we look at the value added by the manufacturing sector as a percentage of GDP (current prices), we find that there was a fall in the ratio in all major economies after 1960. For example, taking the main industrial countries together, we find that manufacturing comprised 30 per cent of their combined GDP in 1960 but only 20 per cent by 1995, while the share of the service sector rose from 53 to 66 per cent over the same period. For the EU, the share of manufacturing fell from 33 to 23 per cent, and the share of services rose from 47 to 68 per cent in the same period. The greatest change occurred in the USA, where the share of manufacturing fell from 28 to 19 per cent, and the share of services rose from 57 to 72 per cent.

These statistics seem to indicate that the shift from manufacturing to service reflects a shift in the pattern of domestic spending away from manufacturing and towards services. This conclusion seems to be confirmed by sectoral changes in employment, as shown in Figs. 5.1 and 5.2. Here

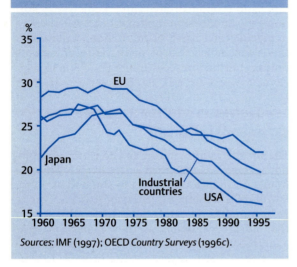

Figure 5.1 **Employment in manufacturing, by sector, as a percentage of total civilian employment**

Sources: IMF (1997); OECD *Country Surveys* (1996c).

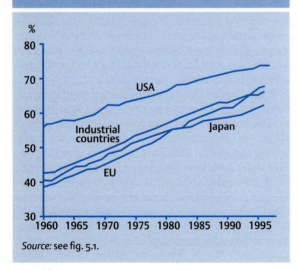

Figure 5.2 **Employment in services, by sector, as a percentage of total civilian employment**

Source: see fig. 5.1.

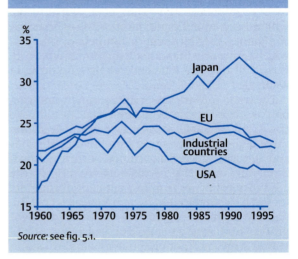

Figure 5.3 **Value added in manufacturing as a percentage of GDP (constant prices)**

Source: see fig. 5.1.

we see that the share of manufacturing employment in total civilian employment fell significantly from 1970, while, conversely, the share of employment in services rose strongly at the same time. These trends seem to follow the pattern for the share of output (value added) discussed above,

and appear to confirm the hypothesis that such shifts probably reflect the changing pattern of domestic spending, as per capita income rises as the more income-elastic services are substituted for manufacturing.

However, this analysis is not wholly correct, as the current value of a given output is composed of the price of each unit of output multiplied by the number of units produced. Therefore, the current value of total output can change from year to year, not only because more units are produced but because the price of each unit has changed. To get a clearer picture of the real changes—that is, whether the number (volume) of units of output has increased—we need to adjust the value figures for changes in prices—that is, calculate output at constant prices. This has been done in Fig. 5.3. This shows us that after 1970 the value added in manufacturing as a share of GDP at constant prices (i.e. volume) did not fall significantly in the industrial countries or in the EU, while there was a somewhat sharper fall in the USA, and even a rise in the ratio for Japan until the early 1990s.

The above analysis indicates that, in volume (i.e. constant prices) terms, there has not been a very significant shift in real expenditure from manufacturing to services either in the major industrial countries or in the EU. The question that naturally arises is why should the shares of manufacturing in money GDP fall (and in services rise), while the shares of manufacturing and services at constant prices do not show the same extreme shifts. The answer is to be found in the changes in the relative movements in the prices of manufacturing and services over the period. In the major industrial countries, the average growth of productivity in services between 1960 and 1996 was only 1.6 per cent per year (EU 1.5 per cent), while that of manufacturing was 3.5 per cent (EU 3.1 per cent). These productivity differences resulted in a relatively high cost/price structure in the less tradeable service sector, while the influence of new technology and global competition was more severe on more tradeable manufacturing, thus bringing costs and prices down relative to those of services. These price changes tended to exaggerate the real structural shifts in value added.

What we can conclude at this stage is, first, that deindustrialization (as measured by value added at constant prices) is a phenomenon that is occurring at a slower rate in the major economies, including the EU, than shown by the money figures alone. However, trends since 1970 do still show a slow decline in the share of real value added in manufacturing. In other words, real expenditure on services has not risen consistently faster than real expenditure on manufacturing. Secondly, that productivity in manufacturing has increased at a rate that is twice that of services. Thirdly, that the significant shifts in employment from manufacturing to services must therefore be due to the difference in productivity between the two sectors. Research by Rowthorn and Ramswamy (1997) indicates that, of the 9.6 per cent drop in the share of manufacturing employment in OECD countries between 1970 and 1994, some 6.3 per cent (i.e. 65 per cent of the drop) was due to higher productivity in manufacturing industry than services.

Despite the picture presented above, it is also true that the pace and timing of the deindustrialization process can differ across the globe, as seen in Fig. 5.3. For example, the share of manufacturing in real value added actually rose in Japan until the early 1990s and fell more rapidly in the USA. The EU experienced only a slow decline. These factors seem to reflect the fact that domestic expenditure seems to have been shifting from services to manufacturing in Japan, while in the USA the shift of expenditure has been the reverse, with the EU's experience showing a more constant pattern. However, the reason for these trends may come from another source. For example, Japan has had a healthy trade surplus in manufactured goods since the 1970s, while the USA has experienced a growing trade deficit in manufactures. This tends to indicate that the pace of deindustrialization may be determined not only by shifts in domestic expenditure within nations but also by the nature and success of manufactures in export markets, which can slow down the deindustrialization process, as in Japan, or accelerate it, as in the USA. Again, the EU has had a relatively steady surplus on trade in manufactured goods, which has helped keep the manufacturing sector's real value added relatively constant.

We can, therefore, see that deindustrialization is not necessarily a symptom of the failure of a nation's or a trading bloc's manufacturing sector, but is a natural outcome of a long-term process of economic development, where productivity in manufacturing rises more rapidly than services, thus leading to a shift of labour to the service sector. The pace of deindustrialization can vary in different countries or blocs for reasons linked to both expenditure and trade patterns. In each country, the weight of various sectors in the economy partly reflects this trend, as seen in Table 5.1. Here, figures for the sectoral share of GDP and employment are shown for the EU, the USA, and Japan. Some countries, such as Belgium, UK, France, Sweden, or Luxembourg, have tended to shift resources towards the services sector somewhat earlier than countries such as Spain, Italy, Portugal, or Finland. The reasons behind the speed of transition are complex and related to a country's stage of development and to specific country-based factors. What is obvious is the fact that the EU is a heterogeneous group of economies bound together within a trading bloc. The convergence of such economies is, by definition, a complex and difficult process.

Comparing the EU with the USA, we find that there are still more resource shifts to be experienced in the EU if it is to follow the US trend, while the discussions on how to manage future deindustrialization or 'hollowing-out' is also a worry for Japan. Such shifts inevitably occur not only in the major industrial countries but also in the newly industrialized economies of East Asia, where the share of labour in total employment began to shift from manufacturing to services in the late 1980s. Another factor revolves around the role of the fast-growing market services (i.e. non-government)

Table 5.1 Sectoral shares of GDP and employment, 1995 (%)

Country	GDP					Employment				
	Agriculture	Industry	(Manufacturing)	Services	(Market services)	Agriculture	Industry	Manufacturing	Services	Market services
Austria	2.2	34.3	(25.1)	63.5	(46.5)	7.2	33.2	32.2	59.6	42.3
Belgium	1.3	28.5	(20.9)	70.2	(53.9)	2.6	27.7	22.6	69.7	42.8
Denmark	3.3	23.9	(18.5)	72.8	(46.5)	5.1	26.8	21.6	68.1	34.0
Finland	3.7	31.4	(24.5)	64.9	(34.3)	8.3	26.8	22.7	64.9	30.9
France	2.4	26.5	(20.4)	71.1	(50.3)	4.9	26.7	21.9	68.4	39.5
Germany	1.1	30.9	(28.6)	68.0	(47.4)	3.3	37.6	32.4	59.1	36.6
Greece	12.7	21.2	(15.8)	66.1	(40.9)	20.8	23.6	23.5	55.6	36.1
Ireland	6.8	35.3	(30.3)	57.9	(41.3)	12.0	27.6	24.7	60.4	32.6
Italy	2.9	31.6	(21.6)	65.5	(49.7)	7.7	32.1	26.2	60.2	34.3
Luxembourg	1.4	33.7	(23.8)	64.9	(51.5)	2.9	30.7	20.4	66.4	52.4
Netherlands	3.4	26.9	(18.0)	69.7	(55.5)	4.0	23.0	17.3	73.0	53.8
Portugal	3.7	33.4	(25.2)	62.9	(44.9)	11.5	32.8	32.2	59.6	42.3
Spain	3.5	32.7	(20.8)	63.8	(44.9)	9.8	30.0	24.8	60.2	33.8
Sweden	2.0	27.5	(21.6)	70.5	(37.2)	3.4	25.0	23.0	71.6	30.7
UK	1.7	27.1	(21.1)	71.2	(49.8)	2.1	27.7	18.6	70.3	50.7
EU[a]	2.7	29.1	(23.8)	68.2	(49.3)	4.4	29.4	24.2	66.2	41.2
USA	1.7	26.2	(18.9)	72.1	(57.8)	2.9	24.0	16.9	73.1	57.3
Japan	2.1	38.3	(27.6)	59.6	(49.5)	5.8	34.0	26.5	60.2	51.8

[a] Weighted average.

Note: Figures are for 1995 or nearest available date.
Sources: OECD (1996*a*; 1997).

sectors, such as distribution services, finance and business services, etc., which will probably be the area of growth if the EU follows the US/Japanese pattern.

It should be noted here that, when we discuss the concept of deindustrialization with its shifts of resources from industry to services, it is necessary to remember that we should not underestimate the interlinkages between the sectors. For example, the faster-growing transport, communication, finance, insurance, and business services all benefit from the purchase of technologically sophisticated intermediate investment goods from manufacturing. It has been calculated that some 25 per cent of the service industry depends directly on manufacturing. For example, the production of goods places increasing demand on services such as R&D, design, marketing, and distribution. Therefore, there is a more sophisticated interlinkage between manufacturing and services than is often imagined.

3 Industrial structure in a European context

THE impact of the processes of globalization and deindustrialization described above has had an important overall effect on the structure of European industries and hence on the nature of industrial competition in the region. To investigate the matter further, it is necessary to examine the different elements that make up the industrial structure of the region. At this stage it is worth pointing out that the EU is by no means a homogeneous entity, as we have already seen in Table 5.1, but for this study we need to concentrate on the common elements that define the region as a whole in order to try to compare its performance with other main players such as the USA and Japan. The most obvious place to begin to understand the dynamics of EU competitiveness would be to investigate the relationship between trade and the degree of production specialization within the EU.

3.1 Trade, specialization, and integration

In terms of intra-EU trade, we see can see from Table 5.2 that some members of the EU tend to be more geared to trading within the EU than others. For example, the trade intensity of economies such as the UK and Germany tend to be less EU centred, while countries such as Spain, the Netherlands, and Portugal tend to be more Euro-centric in their trading habits. Given these differences, an examination of the EU as one bloc shows that exports from EU countries to other members of the Union as a proportion of their total exports of goods and services—that is, total intra-EU exports—increased over the period 1986–93. Although not shown in this table, intra-EU trade in manufacturing rose strongly from 58 to 68 per cent, and services from 45 to 50 per cent over the period). The US share of exports to the EU has remained the same, while an increasing proportion of Japan's total exports has been geared towards the EU. On the import side, we see that imports into EU countries from other EU countries as a proportion of all EU imports have remained steady, as has the proportion of total US and Japanese imports that came from the EU. It might be useful at this stage to enquire whether these figures give us any clue as to whether the single market programme (SMP) has led to a net trade creation for the EU.

Trade creation is the situation where the removal of trade barriers within the EU replaces a country's local production with more efficient imports from within the EU, leading to an increase in overall welfare. Trade diversion occurs when the barriers to trade that still exist between the EU and outside countries lead EU countries to switch their imports from more efficient outside countries to countries within the EU, thus decreasing overall welfare. The idea here is that the lowering

Table 5.2 **Intra-EU trade in goods and services**

Country	Exports			Imports		
	1986	**1992**	**1993**	**1986**	**1992**	**1993**
Belgium	70.1	73.0	71.2	69.4	69.0	71.2
Denmark	43.1	48.3	47.4	51.6	48.3	47.4
France	53.0	58.9	57.0	58.6	58.1	57.0
Germany	48.9	52.6	48.7	50.5	50.8	48.7
Greece	49.5	53.2	53.3	56.4	60.2	53.3
Ireland	69.9	69.6	69.8	70.1	69.0	69.8
Italy	53.3	57.1	53.5	56.9	56.6	53.5
Netherlands	72.0	73.9	71.4	64.0	65.0	71.4
Portugal	64.8	71.8	73.8	58.9	72.9	73.8
Spain	61.0	68.8	66.5	51.4	60.0	65.5
UK	42.7	50.9	47.8	51.3	51.2	47.8
EU	**54.0**	**59.1**	**56.5**	**56.3**	**56.9**	**56.5**
USA	**24.4**	**25.4**	**23.7**	**21.9**	**20.2**	**23.7**
Japan	**14.9**	**18.4**	**15.8**	**12.8**	**13.7**	**15.8**

Note: Intra-EU trade as a % of total trade in goods and services.
Source: European Commission (1996: 51).

of trade barriers within the EU can make the goods of EU countries more attractive to each other, thus resulting in increased trade flows between them. However, the remaining trade barriers between the EU and countries outside might result in some of the trade previously done with countries outside the EU (extra-EU trade) being diverted to countries within the EU. A cursory glance at Table 5.2 shows that between 1986 and 1992 the share of EU imports in total imports did not change within the triad (EU, USA, and Japan)—that is, trade diversion was minimum. At the same time, the figures show that the EU had become more open as a destination for both EU and triad exports—that is, trade creation had taken place. These tentative conclusions are based on the period 1986–92, since the change in statistical reporting after 1993 created difficulties in comparing pre- and post-1993 figures. However, the table seems to indicate that net trade creation appears to have taken place as a result of the SMP.

Although the above analysis has given us an insight into trade flows in general, it has not provided a sectoral analysis of competitive conditions in the EU. To provide this type of information, it is necessary to take the discussion down to the level of the industry concerned. *Inter-industry* trade refers to the situation where some countries within the EU tend to specialize in the production and export of products of industries where they have a comparative advantage (that is, those in which they are relatively more efficient), while importing from other countries the products of different industries in which these countries have a comparative advantage. In simple terms, this type of trade involves an exchange of products from different industries. On the other hand, *intra-industry* trade is based on the exchange, between countries, of products that are classified as being in the same industry; that is, it involves trade in similar products.

Inter-industry trade carries efficiency gains, because each country can specialize in commodities in which it is relatively more efficient—so lowering prices and benefiting consumers. However, this sort of trade may entail redistributive effects, since production may have to close down in less efficient industries, leading to a fall in incomes or unemployment in those sectors. The cost of adjustment is also high for companies, since it may not be easy to shift resources from one industry to another.

Intra-industry trade also carries benefits in that consumers of various countries have a greater variety of products from within a given industry to choose from, as countries continue to exchange a large range of products from within the confines of the same industry. In this case, the redistribution and adjustment costs are less, because resource shifts are not so large, since it is less likely that the whole of an industry will disappear as a result of competition. Also, adjustment costs are lower, since companies are involved in shifting resources to similar products within the industry rather than closing down altogether. A study of the nature of inter/intra-EU trade will, therefore, give a clearer view of the structure and nature of competition in the EU.

Before analysing these trends, it would be beneficial to discuss the forces that determine the nature of EU trade flows and hence the nature of inter- and intra-EU trade. First, as was intimated earlier, trade flows are partly determined by comparative advantage, in that countries with different relative endowments of resources can specialize in certain commodities and then exchange these internationally. Secondly, trade flows are also sensitive to changes in transport costs, since, as transport costs fall, the volume of trade will expand, often affecting the location of such trade. For example, before transport costs fall significantly, production may tend to be located somewhere near the centre of the EU, where the main market lies, but, as costs fall, locating production on the periphery of the EU becomes more feasible. Thirdly, the potential benefits derived from internal economies of scale can stimulate trade flows in those companies whose domestic market may have previously been too small to sustain the outputs necessary to enjoy such economies.

Fourthly, the volume and nature of trade patterns are also determined by technological factors. Countries that tend to have firms that are technology/R&D intensive may become more internationally specialized and thus increase their ability to engage in profitable worldwide exports. A fifth, and increasingly important factor that has a powerful effect on trade is the trend towards product differentiation. As average incomes rise, there is a well-known tendency for consumers to demand a greater range of goods. At the same time, technological progress and increased R&D expenditure mean that firms discover new product specifications that are different from other products even in the same industry.

Some products may be differentiated because of their clearly perceived quality differences, while others may be very similar in quality/price but be differentiated by some other characteristics—for example, colour range, and so on—all designed to meet the increasing demand for variety. Finally, the role of national governments in trade creation should not be forgotten. For example, the opening-up of the EU through the SMP has meant that governments have had to dismantle trade control and decrease other regulatory constraints that previously inhibited trade. The influences of the above factors on the relative growth of inter- and intra-industry trade varies. For example, any growth in the importance of comparative advantage would tend to enhance inter-industry trade, while, the greater the influence of technology/ R&D as incomes rise, the more likely it is that intra-industry trade will be stimulated.

With the above theoretical framework in place, we can now trace the pattern of trade within the EU over the 1990s in order to clarify the competitive forces at work. Table 5.3 shows the shares of

inter- and intra-industry trade in different trade categories in 1994 and the change in the shares between 1987 and 1994. In 1994 inter-industry trade accounted for 38.5 per cent of total trade within the EU, while the share of intra-industry trade in similar or homogeneous products was 19.2 per cent and trade in differentiated products stood at 42.3 per cent.

Table 5.3 indicates that EU inter-industry trade (that is, trade between countries in products of different industries) declined significantly over the 1987–94 period, while intra-industry trade (that is, trade between countries in the products of the same industries) rose. The intra-trade category has been divided into two—homogeneous and differentiated products. The former category includes products of the same industry that are very similar in price and quality, while the latter includes products that are quite different in terms of price and quality. Over the period, both increased their share of EU trade, but particularly the differentiated category. On average, inter-industry trade accounted for more than half the trade mainly, but

Table 5.3 Shares of product types in inter- and intra-EU trade, 1994 (%)

| Country | Inter-industry | | Intra-industry | | | |
| | 1994 | 1987–94 change as a % | homogeneous | | differentiated | |
			1994	1987–94 change as a %	1994	1987–94 change as a %
Belgium/ Luxembourg	34.8	–3.8	23.2	1.6	42.0	2.2
Denmark	60.0	1.1	8.1	–1.1	31.9	0
France	31.6	–6.4	24.1	2.8	44.3	3.6
Germany	32.6	–5.4	20.5	1.9	46.9	3.4
Greece	86.0	–0.2	3.7	0.8	10.3	–0.6
Italy	46.9	–2.8	16.2	5.8	36.9	–3.1
Ireland	57.7	2.2	7.9	–0.9	34.4	–1.3
Netherlands	39.3	–4.8	18.9	–0.3	41.9	5.1
Portugal	68.6	–8.6	7.5	3.9	23.9	4.8
Spain	45.9	12.0	18.9	8.7	35.2	3.3
UK	35.6	–7.0	16.5	–1.9	47.9	8.9
EU 12	38.5	–5.1	19.2	2.0	42.3	3.1

Source: European Commission (1996: 74).

not exclusively, in economies with lower levels of economic development—for example, Greece, Ireland, and Portugal—while intra-industry trade, both in similar and particularly in differentiated products, was higher in the more developed economies of the EU. Although not shown on Table 5.3, it should be noted that inter-EU-industry trade is located mostly in sectors such as food and beverages, mining, non-metallic minerals, and textiles, which account for one-third of manufacturing value added. On the other hand, intra-trade is located mostly in sectors such as electrical and non-electrical machinery, motor vehicles, chemicals, scientific instruments, televisions, video recorders, and so on, and accounts for two-thirds of manufacturing value added.

While the analysis above has pinpointed the importance of inter- and intra-industry trade across the EU, we need to take a closer look at the nature of the products being traded in order to provide us with a clue as to the specialization process in terms of quality products. Table 5.4 shows that in 1993–4 high-price/quality goods represented more than 40 per cent of exports in countries such as Ireland, Germany, Denmark, the UK, and France, while low-price/quality products represented more than 25 per cent of total exports in Portugal,

Greece, Spain, and Italy. The influence of multinational investment in assembly and technology industries in Ireland has been important in placing the country in the high-quality category. If we want to look at which types of products are being traded between nations, rather than what each nation produces, then we should investigate the trade balance in different types of products. The countries with the strongest trade balance in high price/quality goods are Ireland, Germany, and France, whereas the UK, the Netherlands, Benelux, and Denmark tend to have the strongest trade balance in medium price/quality goods. Spain, Greece, Italy, and Portugal appear to have positive trade balances in the low price/quality range.

EU countries also show a tendency to have particular strengths/specializations in the products of certain industries. For example, trade balances tend to show that the UK has strengths in the electrical machinery industry, particularly in the medium- to high-quality range. Portugal has particular strengths in textiles, wood, and paper, especially the medium- and low-quality range. Germany is the only EU country that does not show strong industrial specialization in any one area. Its major strengths are to be found in the

Table 5.4 Price/quality structure of intra-EU trade, 1993–1994

Country	Exports			Imports		
	Low	Medium	High	Low	Medium	High
Belgium/ Luxembourg	18.1	50.0	31.9	19.9	45.2	34.9
Denmark	19.8	38.4	41.7	20.8	32.9	46.3
France	14.9	45.2	39.9	19.2	44.1	36.7
Germany	14.0	38.6	47.4	14.2	46.4	39.4
Greece	31.0	42.3	26.7	21.5	37.0	41.6
Ireland	21.3	24.9	53.8	28.3	30.3	41.4
Italy	28.5	39.4	32.2	15.1	43.7	41.2
Netherlands	15.4	50.9	33.7	19.6	45.2	35.2
Portugal	34.1	39.6	26.3	22.8	41.0	36.2
Spain	28.9	48.0	23.1	23.8	40.4	35.8
UK	20.5	39.1	40.5	21.8	36.7	41.6

Source: European Commission (1996: 76).

products of many industries, most of which are in the high-quality category.

A final point of interest is to investigate whether the development of the SMP has affected the structure of production (value added) in the different countries. In other words, has the structure of manufacturing production and exports tended to converge across EU countries as a result of the freeing of trade from various restrictions? Comparisons of 1985 and 1994 figures tend to show that the structure of value added and exports has become more similar across EU countries, a conclusion that seems to contradict the analysis of Krugman (1995) that the elimination of barriers would lead to more specialization and an increasing dissimilarity in the structures of output and exports. However, it is possible that, after an initial convergence, there might be a move to greater country specialization once more.

3.2 Trade, investment flows, and multinational activity

The trade flows described above are inextricably bound up with international flows of capital between nations. One of the most important forms of capital flow that involves industry and services directly is that designated as foreign direct investment (FDI). FDI is a long-term investment relationship involving significant control by a parent company investor in one country over another enterprise located in another country. Technically speaking, FDI has three components: equity capital, reinvested earnings, and other capital. Figures for FDI include the value of shares held by a home-based 'parent' company in an affiliated foreign enterprise, provided that the value of such shares exceeds 10 per cent of the total value of the voting capital of the affiliate enterprise. FDI also includes any retained profits earned by the affiliated company together with any long- or short-term borrowing between parent and affiliated company. In effect, the direction and character of FDI flows are intimately bound up with the operation and strategies of multinational enterprises (MNEs).

In more practical terms, FDI usually takes the form of a parent company in one country setting up a brand new subsidiary company abroad—that is, a 'greenfield investment'—or a company acquiring, or merging with, a company based in another country. Whichever way the FDI takes place,

it results in substantial changes to the location and strategy of companies and hence the flows of goods and services in a global environment. Historically speaking, the relationship between trade and FDI in the manufacturing sector has been simple, in that companies have usually supplied home markets first, and then, through exports, licensing, and other methods, begun to sell their products abroad. When a firm finds it can extend its market and improve its profits by producing abroad, it will begin to engage in FDI. In this way, FDI becomes a substitute for trade. However, if domestic manufacturing firms are searching for low-cost inputs—for example, labour—they may engage in international production immediately via FDI and thus create new trade.

In both these situations, trade and FDI can be viewed as options for the manufacturing sector. However, it has been more difficult for services to follow the manufacturing pattern—that is, from domestic production to trade, and then on to overseas production. This is because services often need to be delivered to the customer in the locality where it is demanded in the first instance. In other words, services have traditionally been less 'tradeable' across boundaries than goods. This may account for the shift in world FDI stock towards services over the last fifteen years of the twentieth century, as affiliate service companies were set up abroad or through international takeovers and mergers in the service sector. However, it should be noted that the rapid development of information-intensive services in recent years has begun to make some of these services more tradeable. For example, telecommunications and information-technology (IT) developments can mean that service companies in one country can export their services overseas via these links without setting up subsidiary companies abroad through FDI.

The importance of FDI may be gauged by realizing that in 1995 the total outward stock of FDI in the world economy stood at $2,730 billion (Table 5.5). The additions to such a stock—that is, the flows of FDI—grew at a phenomenal rate of 24.7 per cent per annum in 1984-9, before falling to 12.7 per cent per annum in 1990–5 as a result of the slowdown of the world economy in the early 1990s. These growth rates of FDI outstripped the growth of trade in goods and services, which showed yearly growth rates of 14.3 and 3.8 per cent over the same periods. In 1995 the value of the total stock of FDI was equivalent to 48 per cent

Table 5.5 **World foreign direct investment and multinational activity**

	Total outward FDI 1995 ($bn.)	Annual averages 1984–9 ($bn.)		Annual averages 1990–5 ($bn.)		Multinationals (number)	
		Inflow	Outflow	Inflow	Outflow	Parents	Affiliates
Total	2,730,146	115,370	121,630	285,519	237,932	38,747	265,551
Developed countries	2,514,317	93,117	113,995	143,835	209,922	34,199	90,786
Western Europe	1,332,458	39,755	67,961	87,892	121,159	24,609	59,594
EU	1,209,838	37,702	62,641	84,220	112,227	20,609	52,594
UK	319,009	13,545	23,283	19,674	23,910	1,443	3,376
Other Western European	123,620	2,052	5,320	3,054	8,433	4,000	7,000
Central/Eastern Europe	1,377	59	14	4,994	204	400	55,000
Japan		81	20,793	1,359	27,973	3,967	3,290
North America	815,958	48,656	21,511	45,996	56,523	4,578	21,851
Canada	110,388	4,718	4,664	6,222	4,901	1,565	4,708
USA	705,570	43,938	16,847	39,774	51,622	3,013	16,543
Developing countries	214,453	22,195	7,621	64,201	27,807	4,148	119,765
Africa	15,271	2,728	1,031	3,523	766	—	—
South America/Caribbean	24,631	7,739	597	18,880	2,774	1,284	24,390
Asia	174,447	11,540	5,984	41,371	24,264	2,485	89,527
China	17,268	2,282	581	19,635	2,602	379	45,000

Source: UNCTAD (1996).

of the world's gross fixed capital formation (GFCF) and 11 per cent of world GDP for that year.

Table 5.5 also helps to show that the bulk of the world's stock of FDI (92 per cent) is concentrated in the developed countries, and also that, over the period 1984–95, some 91 per cent of the total annual average outflows, and 66 per cent of the total annual average inflows, of the world's FDI came from, or went to, developed countries. In other words, the bulk of the flows involved the developed countries investing in each other. From the context of the EU, we can calculate from the table that this region accounted for 44 per cent of the total world outward stock of FDI in 1995. Between 1984 and 1995 the EU accounted for 32 per cent of the world's average annual inflows, and 51 per cent of the world's average annual outflows, of FDI.

Figures for 1996 show that the total inflow of FDI into the EU was 66,822 million ecus, of which 40,947 million ecus, or 61 per cent came from within the EU and 39 per cent from outside the EU (30 per cent from the USA). These figures help to show the extent of the intra-investment activity in the EU. Of the cumulative FDI inflows between 1984 and 1996, some 65 per cent were in the service sectors, whilst about 30 per cent went to manufacturing. This follows from the dominance of the service sectors in most economies and the fact that, since services are less tradeable, it is not surprising that FDI and multinational activity have often been the only way to supply foreign markets. For example, the impact of the SMP on German outward FDI between 1987 and 1992 was to increase it by ($13.7 billion) or 17.5 per cent. Of this amount, the contribution of distribution ($2.9 billion) and finance and other services ($8.9 billion) have dominated, indicating the importance of such services in intra-EU investment (Pain and Lansbury 1997).

The rationale behind such FDI flows (that is, that firms prefer to produce abroad rather than export) is complex, although the groundwork for such rationale was laid down in the work of Dunning (1995). He indicates that such decisions often depend on three conditions. First, ownership-specific advantages: i.e. a firm may possess assets that are internal to the firm that provide a cost advantage over a local rival in a foreign country (for example, it may have a better processing technique or capital resources). Secondly, locational advantages: a firm may locate a subsidiary overseas in order to overcome trade barriers or to take advantage of cheaper foreign factors of production or foreign markets. Thirdly, internationalization advantages: a firm may prefer to set up a subsidiary abroad to ensure stability of supplies or to protect the quality of service.

These basic ideas have been modified through the 1990s as the nature of economies has changed. For example, ownership-specific advantages have tended to be seen less in terms of traditional assets such as capital and more in terms of 'knowledge-based assets'. This idea revolves around firm-specific activity such as production processes, product innovation, and other activities that involve 'intangible' assets such as marketing, management skills, and R&D. These types of assets are easily transferred back and forth between different locations at little cost and can, therefore, give firms significant advantages. For example, a multi-plant MNE firm need make only a single investment in R&D, which it can spread over many overseas plants, whilst independent firms must make their own R&D investment (see Insert). Such MNEs can enjoy joint input shared across various plants, which gives economies of scale to the firm rather than at the specific plant level. Two other examples of the idea of a knowledge-based firm-specific asset can be seen in a situation where a single multi-plant firm can locate production near a market and, using knowledge-based assets, customize the product to that market with the help of its specific knowledge of computer techniques, brand imaging, etc. Similarly, knowledge-based assets also encourage firms to engage in FDI rather than licensing foreign locals to produce the prod-

uct or service. This is partly because licensing has the risk that quality may not be maintained or that technical secrets may be lost. Interestingly, the level of FDI and its industrial pattern seem to be determined partly by knowledge-based factors such as expenditures on R&D and patents.

The work of Krugman (1995) has pointed out that theories that try to explain the location of FDI and MNE activities in terms of the classical comparative advantage lines need to realize the fact that modern competition occurs within imperfect markets and is based to a great extent on product differentiation. This means that FDI and MNE activities may be more strongly related to the interaction between, on the one hand, the advantages of knowledge-based firm-specific assets that facilitate product differentiation, and the structure of barriers to trade between large blocs such as the EU and NAFTA, on the other. It is interesting that the integration of the EU market has not necessarily led to rapid concentration of production in a smaller number of plants, as has happened in large markets such as the USA. This may be partly due to the activity of knowledge-based MNEs operating in an area such as the EU with its diverse national markets and consumer preferences.

We can see some of the complexity of motives for FDI if we investigate the trends in EU FDI. For example, the location of outward FDI flows from German firms tends to have been influenced by the development of the SMP. German firms have tended to divert FDI towards the EU as a result of the SMP. Within the EU, their location decisions have been more sensitive to cost factors—for example, labour costs and tax burdens. However, investment outside the EU has been determined more by market pull and the existence of specialized products.

Meanwhile, the motivations for Japanese FDI in the EU has been largely due to the existence of EU barriers to outside trade and the strength of its legislation—for example, dumping regulations. Once inside the single market, the Japanese have located according to cost conditions, such as labour flexibility and labour costs. As far as the UK is concerned, it has been successful in attracting labour intensive FDI because of its lower labour costs—especially in the non-manufacturing industry—but poor in attracting capital intensive investment, especially from high-tech. producers for whom labour costs are not as important. This is disappointing, especially when one of the major sources of UK technical progress is FDI.

Spreading R&D costs

One of the reasons why BMW bought the Rover Car Company was so that it could spread the costs of R&D over a bigger market. These costs have been escalating in recent years and sales of the BMW models were no longer large enough to generate enough income to cover these costs. (It was also, of course, a quick way of obtaining an established brand name.)

Finally, it is interesting to note that, despite labour flexibility and low labour costs in the UK, there has been no tendency to exploit economies of scale at home and then increase exports to the EU, instead of investing in other members of the EU. This tends to substantiate the fact that outward investment has an important role to help open up markets, thus allowing the UK to exploit whatever knowledge-based firm-specific benefits it has over local firms abroad. An idea of the major EU companies who engage in multinational activity can be seen by scrutinizing the top twenty EU companies by capitalization, as shown in Table

5.6. Although they are dominated by goods industries, a quarter of the companies shown are in the fast-growing banking and insurance sectors. It would be beneficial at this stage to realize that one important feature of international production through FDI is that of intra-firm trade across international boundaries. In other words, the flows of goods and services between parent firms and their affiliates and vice versa, as well as the export and import between the affiliates themselves, are an important part of a nation's trade flows and determine the structure and competitiveness of their economies.

Table 5.6 Top EU companies by market capitalization, 1996

Company	Country	Sector	Market capitalization ($bn.)[a]	Employees worldwide (000s)[a]
1. Royal Dutch/Shell	Netherlands/UK	Oil/gas	1,353	104
2. British Petroleum	UK	Oil/gas	582	58
3. Glaxo Welcome	UK	Pharmaceuticals	523	52
4. HSBC Holdings	UK	Banking	500	109
5. Unilever plc/NV	Netherlands/UK	Food	431	308
6. ENI	Italy	Oil/gas	410	86
7. Allianz Holding	Germany	Insurance	405	69
8. British Telecom	UK	Communications	353	135
9. SmithKline Beecham	UK	Pharmaceuticals	334	52
10. Lloyds TSB Group	UK	Banking	302	91
11. Siemens	Germany	Electrical	294	376
12. Daimler Benz	Germany	Transport	291	321
13. Bayer	Germany	Chemicals	263	144
14. Veba	Germany	Oil/gas	262	123
15. Astra	Sweden	Pharmaceuticals	259	17
16. Ericcson LM	Sweden	Engineering/electronics	242	80
17. ING Group	Netherlands	Insurance	241	24
18. Deutsche Bank	Germany	Banking	237	67
19. Zeneca	UK	Pharmaceuticals	234	31
20. L'Oreal	France	Pharmaceuticals	231	40

[a] Figures rounded.

Source: Financial Times (1997: 9).

An idea of such MNE activity can be gauged from the latest figures available for the numbers of parent firms and their affiliates worldwide, as seen on Table 5.7. In total there were in 1995 some 38,747 parent companies operating abroad with 265,551 affiliates. The sales of foreign affiliates in 1995 were $6,022 billion which was greater than the world's export of goods and non-factor services at $4,707 billion. The 100 largest MNEs ranked by foreign assets abroad accounted for 33 per cent of global FDI stock and in 1995 employed 12 million or 16 per cent of the 73 million people employed by all MNEs worldwide. An overwhelming 88 per cent of parents originated in the developed regions, while the affiliates were more spread out among the regions of the world. Table 5.7 provides a further breakdown of the FDI/MNE situation in the EU. Here we see the main location of foreign affiliates and the share of total FDI inflows in EU countries. The activity of these multinationals and their effects on different EU economies can be striking. For example, intra-firm exports by MNE's can make up quite a high proportion of total exports of some countries. We can measure this proportion by adding the value of the exports of parent MNE firms based in a country to the exports of any foreign company affiliates also resident in that country. If we compare this figure to the country's total exports then we can have an idea of the role of intra-MNE trade in total trade. The figures for exports are as follows: USA 36%, Sweden 38%, France 34%, and Japan 25%. The figures for imports are 43%, 9%, 18%, and 14% respectively. The main conclusion here is that FDI investment has helped to create powerful trade flows between various sectors of the same company, which has implications for a country's total trade and the competitiveness of its industries and services.

Together with the growth of intra-firm exports, we find that the relationship between different parts of the firm has also changed. For example, the flows between parent and affiliates and vice versa have become less important and the flows between affiliate and affiliate have increased. In other words, the affiliates of large MNEs are forming closer links with each other in certain regions of the world. The most complete insight into this process may be seen by investigating the global trade flows between US parent companies and their affiliates. At the world level we see that the share of affiliate to affiliate trade as a percentage of all intra-firm trade (i.e. parent to affiliates + affiliates to parent + affiliate to affiliate) for US MNEs between 1977 and 1993 rose from 30 to 44 per cent. If we look at US MNEs in the EU, we find that the figures rose slightly from 68 to 71 per cent over the same period. These figures show that the intra-firm trade of US MNEs has been relatively high in Europe, even before the SMP. The intra-firm integration already apparent in the EU is spreading to developing Asia, where the figures in 1977 and 1993 for US MNEs were 23 and 35 per cent respectively. Using the USA as an example, we can see that the general trend will be for more intra-affiliate integration across the MNEs of most major countries.

Interestingly, the above analysis included MNEs in all sectors. The case of intra-firm exporting in manufacturing is more well known, as parts and intermediate products are sent from one affiliate to another for processing or assembling—that is, tradeable flows are created. On the other hand, the parts of the service sector that are relatively

Table 5.7 EU multinational activity: parent firms and affiliates, 1995

Country	Parent firms based in country	Foreign affiliates located in country
Austria	838	2,210
Belgium/ Luxembourg	96	1,121
Denmark	800	1,289
Finland	1,200	1,150
France	2,216	7,097
Germany	7,003	11,396
Greece	—	798
Ireland	39	1,040
Italy	445	1,474
Netherlands	1,608	2,259
Portugal	1,165	7,602
Spain	236	6,232
Sweden	3,520	5,550
UK	1,443	3,376
WORLDWIDE TOTAL	38,747	265,551

Note: 1995 or nearest available year.
Source: UNCTAD (1996: table 1.4).

tradeable are normally produced abroad by setting up identical 'clones' in the other country and the amount of intra-firm division of labour is quite underdeveloped (with the exception of financial services). However, the rapid technological developments in telecommunications and computers may make some services more tradeable—for example, financial services, professional services, consulting and engineering R&D, and information-intensive industries as a whole. This means that, instead of having to engage in FDI to set up affiliates abroad, some of these services can be exported from their home base—that is, become more tradeable. This may create a new set of international flows in services without necessitating any movement of capital or labour.

4 EU mergers, concentration, and size of firm

To understand the linkages between FDI and MNE activity in both a world and an EU context, it is necessary to understand that mergers and acquisitions (M&As) are a popular way for firms to restructure in order to improve their international competitiveness.

☞ '. . . for many years strong brands have been the focus of major takeover bids by international companies. For example, in 1988 the Swiss company Nestlé acquired the British company Rowntree-Mackintosh in order to gain a strong foothold in the European confectionery market. It was recognized that there were significant financial advantages in buying brands such as Kitkat, Rolo, and Quality Street.' (Chapter 20, p. 484)

By selling off divisions/subsidiaries they do not need, and acquiring other subsidiaries, they can often enhance their effectiveness. Such reorganizations are a quick way of acquiring established brand names, supplier networks, and technical expertise. Although the value of FDI and M&As is not identical, they tend to follow each other, since they have one important common element. They both include foreign equity investment, a feature that was discussed above when we defined the

term FDI. While much of the investment flow is designed to set up new production sites abroad, a significant amount is also used to take over foreign companies or merge with them, creating an 'instant' MNE.

4.1 Mergers and acquisitions

M&A activity can be defined in two ways. A merger is usually defined as a situation where two companies agree to join to become one entity. However, the definition of an acquisition is a little more complicated. 'Majority' cross-border acquisitions refer to business combinations where the investor acquires at least 50 per cent of the voting securities of the resulting business, and, in general, this means that the deal has involved a change of ownership. 'Minority' cross-border acquisitions refer to the situation where less than 50 per cent of the voting shares are acquired. The latter often occurs when companies forge links with the aim of diversifying, engaging in loose cooperative activities, or forming joint ventures. The total value of world cross-border (majority plus minority) M&As doubled between 1988 and 1995. By the latter year, the EU accounted for 48 per cent of the world's M&As as compared to 35 per cent for Japan and 30 per cent for the USA.

In 1995, if we take mergers plus majority acquisitions only, the sectoral distribution of the world's M&As were as follows: primary sector (9 per cent), secondary sector (41 per cent), and tertiary sector (50 per cent). Within the secondary sector, the greatest share of world M&A activity was to be found in food, drink, and tobacco (10 per cent) and in chemicals and pharmaceuticals (13 per cent). In the tertiary industries the dominant area for M&A was banking and finance (13 per cent). Between 1988 and 1995 the growth of majority M&As was particularly active in chemical, pharmaceutical, and finance sectors. If we also include figures for minority control in the M&A figures, then sectors such as electrical engineering in the secondary sector, and the utilities and the media in the tertiary sector, become important, reflecting the increasing cooperative activity between enterprises in such sectors.

The share of EU M&A in the worldwide total more than doubled between the mid-1980s (20 per cent) and 1995 (48 per cent), so that many of the world trends shown above are also relevant to the EU case. Of the EU total share of world M&As in 1995 of 48 per cent, 32 per cent were basically intra-EU mergers and 16 per cent extra-EU. During the 1990s, mergers and majority acquisitions accounted for around 60 per cent of total M&A activity in the EU. This figure decreased over the decade, reflecting the growth of minority ownership as the relationship between firms becomes more complex.

Table 5.8 shows the breakdown of M&As across the EU and the nationality of the partners. It also shows those countries whose companies were active acquisitors (bidders) and those countries whose companies were vulnerable to mergers and takeovers (targets). What becomes obvious from this table is that over the period 1986–95 some 70 per cent of all EU M&As were purely domestic occurrences, with such M&As being particularly important in the restructuring in the largest economies such as Germany, France, and the UK. Secondly, the smaller countries on average tended to have a greater proportion of EU-based M&As. Thirdly, the countries most active in M&A activity

with firms outside the EU were the UK, Ireland, Austria, and Sweden, while the larger economies of Germany, France, and Italy were much less involved in such activity. Finally, it is interesting to note that the most aggressive bidders in EU cross-country mergers were the UK, France, and the Netherlands, while the target countries were predominantly Germany, Italy, and Spain.

The sectoral breakdown of M&As shows that up to the late 1980s most restructuring through M&As occurred in the manufacturing sector, while during the first half of the 1990s the service sectors became increasingly more important. In 1995, for example, the total number of M&A operations in services (2,600) exceeded the number in manufacturing (2,300), as the effects of the SMP began to filter down to the less tradeable service sector. Within this sector, the M&A activity in banking and finance comprised some 18 per cent of both national and EU cross-border M&As, while the distribution/hotels section accounted for 8 per

Table 5.8 Mergers and acquisitions in the EU by nationality of partners and by target/bidder (%)

Country	National		Community		International		Target	Bidder
	1990–5	1986–9	1990–5	1986–9	1990–5	1986–9	(1990–5)	
Belgium	60.2	60.4	31.9	34.8	7.9	4.9	5.0	2.9
Denmark	67.0	41.7	22.0	40.6	11.0	17.7	3.9	4.8
Germany	79.5	72.9	12.3	18.7	8.2	8.4	25.5	14.4
Greece	73.1	0.0	19.2	0.0	7.7	100.0	0.4	0.1
Spain	80.9	74.6	11.5	23.9	7.6	1.5	8.1	1.5
France	66.0	60.7	24.5	26.7	9.5	12.6	13.8	18.5
Ireland	36.9	19.9	49.0	58.1	14.1	22.0	0.9	2.9
Italy	77.8	74.9	14.9	18.6	7.3	6.4	6.9	4.3
Luxembourg	2.0	5.3	86.1	89.5	11.9	5.3	0.6	1.0
Netherlands	57.9	57.0	30.5	30.1	11.7	12.9	7.5	9.1
Austria	22.4	30.4	65.7	56.5	11.9	13.0	1.3	1.7
Portugal	64.9	0.0	35.1	100.0	0.0	0.0	1.2	0.1
Finland	78.8	65.8	14.4	23.0	6.8	11.2	3.1	4.0
Sweden	56.8	47.2	29.4	34.9	13.7	17.9	4.5	8.2
UK	73.8	75.1	12.9	9.0	13.3	15.9	17.5	26.5
EU	**70.8**	**70.1**	**18.7**	**15.5**	**10.5**	**14.4**	**100.0**	**100.0**

Source: European Commission (1996: 117, 118).

cent of all national M&As and a more impressive 17 per cent of EU cross-border M&As. However, some 70 per cent of M&A activity in the service sector was primarily domestic as compared to 60 per cent for manufacturing, which may reflect the fact that the SMP changes have been slower to be implemented in services than manufacture. However, buoyant M&A activity in the banking and finance sector tends to show that national and international mergers in services may grow together in the future. For example, since 1989 large national mergers in banking (TSB/Lloyds Bank (UK 1995) and Midland Bank/HSBC Holdings (UK 1992)) and insurance (UAP/Axa (France 1996)) have also been followed by increasing interest in international mergers, as evidenced by the 1997 activities shown between BAT/Zurich and Generalli Assicurazioni/Assurances Générales de France in insurance, and Merita/Nordbanken in banking.

☞ 'Allied to the drive for geographic expansion, whether global or regional, is the increasing incidence of strategic alliances.' (Chapter 18, p. 448)

The rapid change in the market environment brought about by deregulation led to an increasingly more efficient European capital market, with more companies being quoted on the exchanges and more capital available for investment. At the same time, there was a more effective market for corporate control as institutional investors such as pension funds and insurance companies became more dominant. These features allowed companies that wanted to diversify and restructure to take advantage of the more efficient market for corporate restructuring. One such mode of restructuring is external to the firm— that is, through mergers, acquisitions, joint ventures, or equity participation. This activity grew rapidly in the 1990s and the pattern is set to continue in the future.

The natural question that remains is the extent to which the growth of M&As in the EU has gone hand in hand with changes in the structure of various sectors. To investigate this a little further, it would be beneficial to look briefly at the trends in concentration ratios and firm size across the EU and to ask whether these have affected EU competitive environment. This latter proposition will be investigated after we have discussed concentration and firm size.

4.2 Concentration

Concentration ratios are normally defined in terms of a four- or five-firm ratio. In other words, it measures the combined production of either the four (C4EU) or the five (C5EU) largest producers in a specific industry as a share of total EU production of that industry. Statistical tests have shown that the difference in the predictive results obtained from using either of the ratios is small, so that they can be used as alternatives. From an international perspective, comparable data for the manufacturing sector for 1995 show that the C4EU measurement for the EU (21.8) was lower than for the USA (35.7) and Japan (55.4). Given that the US (and to a lesser extent the Japanese) manufacturing sector is roughly comparable to that of the EU, then one might expect EU concentration levels to rise as the EU market becomes more integrated under the SMP movement. Obviously, concentration will differ between different industries, and to measure this it may be beneficial to divide the manufacturing industry into two main categories. The first type of industry (type 1) is where the products are relatively homogeneous and where the influence of scale economies is important. This means that the predominant form of competition is through price (as in shipbuilding, cement, cotton, wood products, etc.). The second type of industry (type 2) is not restricted to the use of price competition as the only competitive weapon. Instead, this type depends more on advertising and/or R&D and uses these as their main competitive weapon. This type may be predominantly advertising intensive (type 2A) (food, confectionery, beer, tobacco, etc.), or predominantly R&D intensive (type 2R) (chemicals, telecommunications equipment, office machinery, electrical machinery, aerospace, etc.), or a mixture of both (type 2AR) (pharmaceuticals, soaps, detergents, radio and television, motor vehicle). As far as EU manufacturing industry is concerned, in 1995 type I covered 52 per cent of manufacturing industry, type 2A 13 per cent, type 2R 25 per cent, and type 2AR 14 per cent of EU manufacturing.

Research on concentration ratios across EU industry has shown that sixteen out of the twenty most concentrated industries (C5EU > 33.3%) are in type 2 industries, indicating the high advertising- and R&D-related costs of product differentiation. This trend is shown when the concentration ratios of the EU are compared with those in the USA (i.e. US C4/EU C4). We find that US/EU concentration ratios are relatively higher for both type 1 (2.08) and types 2 (1.36), but, as can be seen, the gap is smaller for the latter type. In particular, the EU's R&D-intensive industries (type 2R) are the most concentrated/integrated (1.15) as compared to those in the USA, followed by type 2AR (1.27) and type 2A (1.67). However, if, in the future, the EU moves towards the US industrial pattern, the pressure for increases in concentration may come from type 1 and type 2A industries.

Absolute levels of concentration and the growth of concentration in the different types of industries within the EU between 1987 and 1993 are shown in Table 5.9. Here we see that the C4EU ratio was much lower in the type 1 industries than in type 2, with R&D-intensive industries (2R) and advertising and R&D industries (2AR) being more concentrated. The growth in concentration was positive for all types, but particularly so in the R&D-driven (2R) sector. These trends show that, in the industrial sector, the sectors that depend mostly on economies of scale—that is, plant-based economies—are not the most concentrated across Europe, since, as the market grows, the minimum efficient scale becomes smaller relative to the size of the market and so the degree of concentration remains small. However, those sectors that are based on advertising and R&D tend to be more concentrated, partly because their success depends on creating greater product differentiation—that is, either perceived or actual changes in quality. This means that they invest more heavily in advertising and R&D expenditures, which then become strategic weapons in such industries to enable them to improve their market share. The need for large firm-based outlays in such industries tends to contribute to higher levels of concentration in type 2 sectors in the EU (Davies and Lyons 1996).

In terms of services, increased concentration has been experienced in distribution and road freight transport as a result of the SMP, although the highly regulated services such as telecommunications, airlines, or retail banking have experienced less European-wide concentrations although more national concentration.

The industrial restructuring shown by the level and change in industrial concentration shown above is, to some extent, related to the evolution of firm size across the EU. The argument here is that the increase in concentration and size of firms may signify efficiency gains as reflected by the growth in the size of plants (production economies) and/or growth of assets shared by the whole firm (research, financial, or advertising economies). The opening of the EU market will exaggerate these features, as firms are able to benefit from access to specialized knowledge available from other countries of the EU. Firms in the manufacturing sector, as we have seen, where the goods are more tradeable, may grow relatively more as a result of plant-based economies, while firms in the service industry may be more likely to grow as a result of setting up foreign establishments to spread their knowledge and skills abroad.

4.3 Size of firm

On an absolute level, the distribution of firms by size according to turnover/persons per enterprise varies across the EU, as seen in Fig 5.4. Countries can be grouped into three categories. The southern countries, Greece, Spain, Italy, and Portugal, have the smallest average enterprise size in the EU, especially in the retail trade and craft sectors. Germany, Luxembourg, the Netherlands, and Austria have the highest average size of enterprise, twice the size of the southern countries. Belgium, Denmark, France, Ireland, Finland, Sweden, and the UK are in a middle position.

Table 5.9 **Concentration ratios in manufacturing by type of industry (%)**

Industry	C4EU			C4 National (%) Change (1986–92)
	1987	1993	Change	
Conventional (type 1)	13.2	14.4	1.2	−0.3
Advertising intensive (type 2A)	22.3	23.6	1.3	1.3
R&D intensive (type 2R)	32.9	38.9	6.0	−1.9
Advertising and R&D intensive (type 2AR)	30.1	32.4	2.3	1.3

Source: European Commission (1996: 120).

Figure 5.4 Average size of EU enterprise, by country

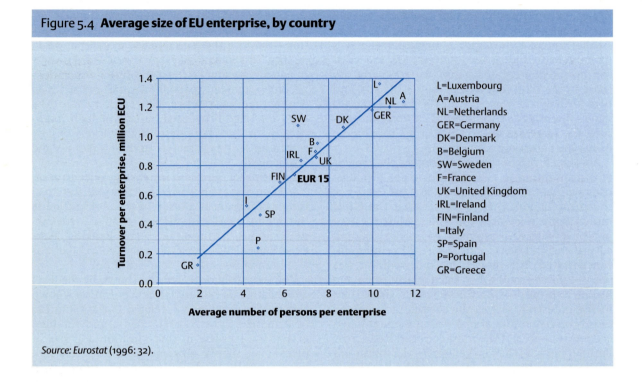

L=Luxembourg
A=Austria
NL=Netherlands
GER=Germany
DK=Denmark
B=Belgium
SW=Sweden
F=France
UK=United Kingdom
IRL=Ireland
FIN=Finland
I=Italy
SP=Spain
P=Portugal
GR=Greece

Source: Eurostat (1996: 32).

If we look at the sectoral distribution of enterprises in the EU (Table 5.10), we find that the larger firms are located in the traditional capital-intensive industries (energy and extraction industries) and also in the manufacturing sectors (chemical and metal manufacturing) and the 'other services' (air transport, banks, and insurance). The smaller size of company is clearly located in the construction sector, and in services such as the trade, hotel, restaurant, and catering sectors.

Within this pattern, there are great differences. For example, in Luxembourg the importance of larger firms in the financial sector exceeds the EU average, while the importance of larger manufacturing firms in German industry exceeds the EU average. In manufacturing, the most significant cross-country difference can be seen by taking the gross value-added (GVA) figures for the average company. In Germany in 1992 the figure was 7.4 million ecus per company, while in France (4.9 million ecus), UK (4.8 million ecus), and Italy (3.3 million ecus) the figure was much less. Over the period 1985–92 the growth in size of German

GVA was 15.4 per cent, similar to Italy (15.4 per cent) but above France (7.7 per cent) and the UK (−0.2 per cent). The difference in the average size of firms has, therefore, remained largely unchanged. The relatively larger size of German firms ranged across the motor-vehicle, chemicals, and engineering industries as well as in the more traditional food, textiles, and clothing. The impact of the SMP has not been great in this area, as those sectors that were more sensitive to the SMP have not registered higher growth of firm size. This means that the changes in the size of firms have been due more to the nature of competition within each sector. For example, the size of firm has increased in the advertising-intensive industries (type 2A) across the main EU countries, as firms hope to gain economies of advertising and product development.

From the above account, one would expect some relationship between concentration data and the evolution of firm size across member states of the EU. Basically speaking, at the EU level, the more concentrated the industry within individual member states and/or the higher the

Table 5.10 **EU enterprises by sector and size, 1992**

Sector	Enterprises		Employment		Turnover		Employment share of SMEs
	000	%	m.	%	ecu (bn.)	%	%
Energy and extraction	55	0.3	2.76	2.7	691	5.9	20.4
Manufacturing industry	2,050	13.0	29.73	29.4	3,364	28.9	55.5
Construction	2,010	12.7	9.53	9.5	730	6.3	85.7
Trade and HoReCa	6,355	40.3	28.28	28.0	5,021	43.1	83.3
Finance and business services	2,407	15.3	13.44	13.3	1,032	8.9	61.6
Other services	2,901	18.4	17.29	17.1	798	6.9	56.7
All sectors	**15,778**	**100.0**	**101.03**	**100.0**	**11,636**	**100.0**	**66.2**

Note: SME = 0–249 employees.
Source: Eurostat (1996: 28).

intra-EU multinationality, then the higher the concentration. In other words, if individual member countries are experiencing an increase in concentration, it is not surprising that the overall EU concentration levels will increase. However, the overall EU concentration level could also increase if more companies operated as multinationals across the EU, since their activity would begin to dominate the EU industry as a whole. At the level of the member state, the concentration level would rise if the mean size of business grew more rapidly than industry size.

Let us now put these ideas into practice. We can see from Table 5.9 that, for the member states, the conventional industries (type 1) and also the technologically intensive industries (type 2R) seemed to experience slower growth in the size of firms than in the size of the industry between 1987 and 1993, since the national concentration ratios tended to fall in these sectors. However, in the advertising-intensive sector (type 2A) we find that the growth of firm size was faster than industry growth, thus leading to an increase in national concentration ratios. However, what is interesting is that, if we look at the European concentration levels (C4EU), we find that the concentration ratios rose slowly for most sectors but very rapidly for the technologically intensive industry.

These facts tend to indicate two things. First, that between 1985 and 1993, the growth of EU concentration ratios in all sectors was generally above the growth of national concentration ratios, indicating a general shift towards concentration on the EU level. This movement was much more pronounced for the technologically intensive sectors, which moved strongly towards concentrative activity at the EU level, probably reflecting cross-border multinational activity in this sector, as suggested in the above analysis.

Secondly, there was a strong growth in the size of firms in the advertising-intensive sectors, with concentration ratios growing positively on both national and EU levels. Again, this relates to a situation where those companies in the advertising- and R&D-intensive sectors seem to be the ones that are sensitive to growth and concentration, possibly reflecting the fact that these sectors have high fixed costs of R&D (spending on new products and processes) and advertising (spending on reputation and brand development). With the increasing openness of the EU market, the main benefits may be for these types of sectors, where competition is very much in terms of product differentiation. They will then invest even more in R&D and advertising across the whole firm in order to gain an increased EU market share. This, in turn, leads to a larger size of company and increased concentration at the EU level.

5 Structural change, competition, and efficiency

THERE seems little doubt that the development of the SMP has provided the platform for an increase in concentrative activity both at the national and the EU levels. However, it can be argued that the growth of companies and the concentrative power that often accompany such power can have two possible effects. First, the SMP may result in the rationalization of firms by allowing them to benefit from plant/firm economies. Secondly, it also opens up the possibility for the abuse of monopoly power as a result of mergers, acquisitions, and concentrative power in general.

There are two main ways of assessing whether the development of the SMP and the structural features noted above have been beneficial in terms of improved efficiency and increased competitiveness. First, we can assess whether the company price–cost margin has changed as a result of the SMP. Price–cost margins are defined as value-added minus labour costs divided by value added (or sales). A second way of confirming improved efficiency and increased competitiveness would be if, other things being equal, there were evidence that prices were converging across the EU. Such evidence would suggest that the implementation of the SMP has helped to create a pan-European market with increased competition.

5.1 Competition and price–cost margins

Evidence of the effect of the SMP on price–cost margins tends to show that EU countries can be placed into three categories: those with high margins (Italy, Belgium), medium margins (France, Netherlands, the UK, and Ireland), and low margins (Germany, Luxembourg, Denmark, and Greece). The cross-country dispersion in margins was not systematic up to 1987, but after that period the dispersion fell, indicating inter-country convergence of margins. In terms of the trends

in the margins themselves, the evidence tends to show that, after 1987, there was an average reduction of 0.25 per cent per year in margins. Those manufacturing sectors where the margins fell were in vehicles, consumer electronics, textiles, and clothing—sectors where there were relatively moderate tariff barriers before the SMP. However, other sectors, such as pharmaceutical products and electrical equipment, which also had some degree of barriers before the SMP, did not show clear margin decreases. Interestingly, advertising- and R&D-intensive industries (types 2A and 2R) did not experience a fall in price–cost margins. This may be because such markets are, as noted previously, in the branded/quality consumer goods sector, where advertising and R&D costs are naturally high, making it necessary for margins and prices to be higher. Interestingly, we noticed earlier that such markets tended to exhibit elements of concentration, and this may also help to explain the tendency for price–cost margins to be higher—a symptom of excess market power.

The experience of services tends to follow that of manufacturing but to a lesser degree, as the SMP has not been as fully effective in services as is the case with manufacture. There have been particular decreases in prices in telecommunications, banking, and airlines, largely because of competition at the national level. For example, the margins in retail banking have fallen with the lower prices of credit cards, etc. Similarly, margins have fallen in the road freight industry, leading to an average of 6 per cent fall in real transportation costs over the 1985–94 period. This change has allowed firms to search across the EU for lower costs of inputs. Some 42 per cent of businesses reported that the decrease in inter-country barriers had been important in accelerating purchases of raw material from other EU markets.

The change in the level of competition, and therefore in price–cost margins as a result of the SMP, can be gauged from Table 5.11. Here we see that firms in manufacturing have been confronted by more competitive pressures than those in the service sectors. Manufacturing tends to have more competition (in terms of number of competitors as well as price and quality competition) from other EU countries than service industry, where the main thrust of competition is predominantly domestic. Nevertheless it should be remembered that the service sector is not homogeneous and that, in areas such as financial intermediation, there seems to have been much more active price

Table 5.11 **Change in competition level on domestic markets, 1995**						
Classification	Manufacturing			Services		
	Increase	No change	Decrease	Increase	No change	Decrease
No. of competitors						
Domestic firms	25	64	11	30	63	7
Other EU-owned firms	39	59	2	21	77	2
Non-EU-owned firms	25	74	2	9	88	2
Price competition						
Domestic firms	44	51	42	37	60	3
Other EU-owned firms	41	55	4	16	81	3
Non-EU-owned firms	29	67	4	9	87	3
Quality competition						
Domestic firms	33	64	3	27	69	4
Other EU-owned firms	29	69	2	14	83	3
Non-EU-owned firms	18	79	3	8	89	3

Note: The *Eurostat* survey shown above refers to the percentage of enterprises expressing opinions on the consequences of the single market.
Source: Eurostat (1997a).

competition from non-EU enterprises, as the global financial competition intensifies.

5.2 Competition and price convergence

It was noted above that, if prices across the EU tended to converge over time in Europe, then this could be taken as an indicator that the EU market had become more open to competition. Despite the fact that price convergence can occur at relatively high levels because of collusive behaviour (when oligopolistic firms come together to agree prices), it is nevertheless true that, on average, the general convergence of prices across national borders can give some general idea as to whether the EU market is becoming more competitive. A study by the DRI (DRI Europe Ltd. 1997) attempts to answer this question by calculating price dispersion coefficients (standard deviation of prices divided by the average) over time for the manufacturing and service sectors and then assessing whether the price movement is converging towards the EU average price.

The conclusions of the survey show, first, that the levels of price dispersion increased as more

member states joined the EU (i.e. EU6, EU9, EU12, and EU15). Secondly, if we take figures for the EU12 between 1980 and 1993, we find that there was a general trend towards price convergence, with price dispersal being lowest among the more tradeable products or services. In general, the consumer and equipment goods industries experienced more convergence than did energy, services, and construction. Finally, of the eighty-six products/services categories for which there was a clear change in price dispersion, some seventy-eight cases showed price convergence, while there were only eight cases where prices diverged. These seventy-eight cases accounted for 60 per cent of total private consumption in the EU.

The pace of such trends depends on the nature of individual economies and their industrial structure, the nature of competition within such industries, and the effect of government policies. For example, it is not surprising that price dispersion increased as more countries joined the EU, since the smaller 'core' EU6/EU9 had more similar economies to begin with, and had had more time to become more integrated. Also, the greater convergence of prices in the consumer and equipment-goods manufacture is mainly due to the fact that they became more tradeable as time progressed. On the other hand, the energy sector did not experience such a decrease in price dispersion, mainly because energy markets are not fully liberalized and they are affected by different levels of taxation in different countries. In the service sector, price dispersion was higher than for more traded goods and decreased more slowly over time. This is partly due to the fact that price levels in services are strongly related to GDP per capita, so that the convergence of service prices is likely to have been slower because of the disparities of per capita GDP levels across the EU.

Price convergence in services is particularly important, given that it has been slower than the goods sector. The price dispersal measure for the EU12 was 33.7 for 1985 and had decreased to 28.6 by 1993. The fact that the figures for durable goods over the same period was 20.8 and 16.4 shows clearly that price disparity and the degree of price convergence partly depend on whether the output of the sector is tradeable or not. Nevertheless, within the service sector, there was stronger price convergence in postal services, banking and insurance, and telephone, telegraph, and telex services, while price convergence was slow in household services, medical services, and pharmaceutical products, for example. The former set of services were more open to internationalization and competition, as seen in the liberalization of telecommunications and the entry of new suppliers. The latter group still have particular factors inhibiting price convergence—for example, national regulations on pharmaceutical standards and medical health care.

A final question to ask would be what general factors tend to affect the movement towards a more competitive situation in the EU with a 'law of one price'. We can divide the explanatory variables into three groups. First, there are structural and policy factors. These include price disparities based on differences in both consumer demand and fiscal policy (e.g. VAT incidence) across the EU. The existence of non-tariff barriers (NTBs) is another structural factor. Secondly, there are the competitive variables in each market—that is, the importance of economies of scale, advertising, and quality factors. These variables often indicate the presence of either homogeneous (type 1 industry) products or vertically differentiated (type 2 industry) products, whose attraction is based on both price and quality. Thirdly, there is the degree of competition in European markets over time,

as illustrated by figures such as intra/extra-EU import penetration, the concentration levels in product markets, and the degree of multinationalization that was discussed earlier in the chapter.

Econometric analysis (DRI Europe Ltd. 1997) has shown that about 30 per cent of the variance in prices across the EU is due to structural and policy factors, with consumer preferences being the dominant reason for price dispersion under this heading. Under the second heading, which covers those products where competition depends mainly on prices (homogeneous products, such as flour, bread, rice, etc.), or on both price and diversity (horizontally differentiated products, such as clothing, footwear, glassware, etc.), the development of the SMP has generally led to increased price convergence. On the other hand, those products that are from markets that are advertising and R&D intensive (vertically differentiated products, such as televisions, electronic equipment, optical instruments, etc.) tend to have high and stable price disparities—that is, no recognizable price convergence. This tends to substantiate the idea suggested previously that firms use these high costs of R&D and advertising as a strategic barrier to entry, thus enabling them to maintain price disparities and prevent convergence. Interestingly, imports in these sectors do not tend to create more competition and hence lower price disparity, because they are in markets where imports are generally of the intra-firm type, a feature that was discussed in Section 3.2.

A final set of conclusions from the econometric analysis shows that product markets that are intensive mainly in R&D only—products such as computers, replacement parts for vehicles, etc.—show a low average price disparity, which tends to suggest that when the large investments needed in such areas are not coupled with high advertising investments, the firms are compelled to adopt pan-European strategies. On the other hand, products that are differentiated primarily because of high advertising costs, which reflect companies' strategy to raise the consumer willingness to pay—products such as food, confectionery, tea, and alcohol—tend to have high price disparities, since these companies use advertising to raise barriers to entry and tend to keep prices high.

Under the third heading, the rate of import penetration and the extent of multinational activity tended to decrease price dispersion, while the degree of concentration exerted a significant positive impact on price disparity. These conclusions provide some information on the effect of these variables (see Section 5.1) on price variables.

What we see from the above analysis is that the competition environment in Europe is sensitive to a range of different factors and that price convergence has, in general, occurred, but the pace of convergence has depended on the sector, the type of product or service within each sector, and the degree of national government regulations. However, even when we allow for further inevitable future decreases in various types of trade barriers and the probable price convergence that such a trend will bring, we may still be left with relative price differentials that are based on the nature and structure of the sector that firms inhabit, as discussed in Section 5.

6 Structure and competition in the pharmaceutical industry: a case study

IN 1994 total sales of medicines within the EU were 51,850 ecus, which accounted for nearly 25 per cent of world output. Some 15 per cent of the medicines were prescribed within hospitals, 74 per cent were prescribed mainly by general practitioners (GPs), and 11 per cent were bought for self-medication by individuals.

On the production side, economies of scale and scope are present in the industry, although, unlike the heavy chemical sector, pharmaceutical output is relatively small and often general-purpose rather then dedicated plant can be used. Research economies are linked to size, since only firms whose annual sales are over 1,000 million ecus are capable of developing new active products. Economies of scope are present in the discovery phase, since research in one area can often give rise to many different products. The sector is marketing intensive, in that patented products sold under brand names are promoted directly to physicians or in the medical press, while only products permitted for self-medication can be advertised to the final consumer. Finally, because the pharmaceutical sector is fragmented, manufacturers distribute their products through specialist wholesalers who sell to retailers, although

hospital medicines and self-medication products often bypass the wholesaler. All in all in 1997, production accounted for some 30–40 per cent of the turnover, R&D 10–15 per cent, and sales and marketing some 15–20 per cent, and the sector is one that is both advertising and R&D intensive.

☞ 'New products fail at a disconcerting rate and companies can incur huge losses, not only in immediate monetary terms when they fail to recover their development and marketing costs, but also in terms of future potential when a new-product failure negatively impacts on the reputation or image of the firm.' (Chapter 24, p. 551)

There were some 2,662 pharmaceutical companies in the EU in 1997, compared to 775 in the USA and 1,556 in Japan, with some half of them located in Germany. However, the forty-eight largest worldwide firms dominated the industry; they produced some 65 per cent of the world market by value, and also accounted for 85 per cent of the world's R&D in the industry. In the EU the pharmaceutical industry was still dominated by some fifteen companies, which had sales of more than 1,000 million ecus, representing a third of the world's total of such firms. Five of the twenty lagest EU companies can be seen in Table 5.6, and if we had included the Swiss companies Roche Holdings and Sandoz in this group, then they would have taken second and sixth positions respectively. The market is relatively fragmented, in that no one individual company had more than 7 per cent of sales within any individual state. On average, the top ten had between 25 and 30 per cent of the retail market and the top twenty-five had between 40 and 50 per cent of the market of member countries. If we take the EU as a whole, no firm had as much as 5 per cent of the market.

In terms of market share by product, the best-selling medicine in any country normally has less than 5 per cent of the market, with the top fifty having 25—35 per cent and the top 100 having 40–50 per cent by value. The major market concentration by products was greatest in the UK in 1994 and least in Germany, although figures for concentration did fall between 1984 and 1994, indicating the entry of generic products. Although the overall level of concentration is low for medicines, it is still possible to have one or two therapeutic areas dominated by a few medicines accounting for a large proportion of sales—as, for example, happened with Zantac/Tagamet for stomach ulcers, before their patents ran out. To summarize, the pharmaceutical industry has been dominated by a few large companies for many years, and, although the national concentration ratios have increased, it has been mainly by the growth of the top seventy-five firms rather than at the top-ten level.

However, despite the lack of a large change in concentration ratios, there has been a degree of M&A activity in recent years. Between 1989 and 1994 some 312 M&As occurred in the EU pharmaceutical sector, with nearly 40 per cent of them between firms of the same country (i.e. national), with Germany, Italy, and the UK undergoing the largest internal rationalization. Some 27 per cent of the M&As were intra-EU mergers, with French, Italian, and German companies being the most frequently targeted. Finally, about 33 per cent of EU M&As involved companies from outside the EU, and here again the main target countries in over 80 per cent of the cases were France, Germany, Italy, and the UK. Apart from the massive SmithKline–Beecham merger, the majority of the acquisitions were below 60 million ecus, which is too small to support genuine innovation. This fits into the growth of concentration but only at the middle to lower end of the size scale and may reflect the fact that many family-controlled firms may be disappearing. Between 1983 and 1993 employment in the pharmaceutical sector rose by only 10 per cent, while labour productivity rose by 54 per cent, partly as a result of rationalization activities through mergers. The rationalization through mergers still continued through to 1997, with the Hoffman–La Roche/Corange, Nycomed/ Amersham International deals, together with the possibility of new relationships between such companies as Zeneca, Astra, Novo Nordisk, Rhone-Poulenc, and Pharma.

👉 'Mergers and acquisitions have proved to be an effective means for a company to expand its product mix.'   (Chapter 14, p. 326)

The role of FDI and of multinational activity in the pharmaceutical industry has been important since before the Second World War as multinational companies have attempted to overcome import barriers by producing locally. The number of companies with plants in the EU but outside their own country of origin remained quite steady between 200 (1984) and 207 (1994). Of the total of 207, some seventy originated from France, Germany, and the UK, and seventy-eight from the USA. Since 1994 the rationale behind the location of pharmaceutical FDI in Europe has varied, and a 1997 study of US companies operating in the EU found that nearness to the size of the local market, the quality of its specific skills, and government incentives, together with past experience, were the main considerations. If we take these criteria, then France, Germany, and the UK appear to be very attractive locations for US multinationals in terms of both production and research. However, it is unlikely that many new 'greenfield' facilities will be built, as growth is more likely to occur through M&As. This strategy is designed to gain some economies of scale and scope, not only in production, but also in marketing and sales. Where R&D is concerned, the great benefit of mergers is to cut out costly duplication of overlapping research.

While the above account has delineated the structure of the pharmaceutical industry, it is also necessary to assess the nature of competition within the sector. To understand this we need to study the components of competitive strength in this sector and then the nature of competition in the different markets. We can assess the first of these aspects by looking at the three main world markets—the EU, the USA, and Japan—and enquiring as to whether there has been a change in the shares of each one in the other's market—that is, a shift in competitive strength. Basically, the distribution of competitive strength has been stable. For example, over the period 1982–93, EU-based companies' share of the EU market fell only slightly from 65.6 to 61.4 per cent. However, EU-based companies' share of the US market increased from 10.1 to 21.9 per cent in the same period, much of this due to the growth of UK companies (their share of the US market rose from 9.4 to 15.1 per cent). EU penetration of the Japanese market is small, as over 80 per cent of that market is served by local producers.

Basically speaking, EU companies have maintained their strength at home and penetrated more of the US market. The lifeblood of the pharmaceutical industry revolves around new innovations and new products. In this respect, 40 per cent of most original and innovative products discovered in the pharmaceutical sector between 1975 and 1994 originated in the EU, with over half of the EU number originating in Germany and the UK. The USA accounted for 26 per cent. If we take the top fifty pharmaceutical products in 1994 worldwide, twenty-four originated in the USA and seventeen in the EU (eleven from the UK).

We have looked at the competitive strength of the sector; it is now relevant to look at the nature of competition in this area. To do this it is necessary to understand that nearly all medicines start off life by being prescription-only medicines and are protected by patents and brand names. These are prescribed by doctors within and outside hospitals, and the cost of such drugs was not always of great consideration. However, once the patent for a successful product has expired, generic copies appear and are often offered at a lower price to overcome the attraction of the originally branded product. This often leads to fierce price warfare. On the other hand, self-medication products can be bought directly by the customer, who pays the full cost, so that such products will be more price sensitive. Despite the growth of generic drugs, there is still intensive advertising undertaken by the owners of branded drugs that moderates the degree of competition.

For those medicines that are still under patent, the competition depends on the ability of companies to innovate rather than on price. This is because the barrier to entry in this area is high, as heavy R&D is needed, which is beyond most of the middle-to-small companies. Competition in the out-of-patent market between originators and generic producers has undoubtedly increased in countries where there is official action, such as pressure on physicians to control their spending on medicines. Finally, competition between self-medication and prescription drugs depends on the range of drugs that can be sold without prescription. In general there was a more lenient attitude towards self-medication in the late 1990s, so that this market will become more important as time progresses. EU legislation in the 1990s effectively allowing patents to be extended through Supplementary Protection Certificates helped the research-orientated companies to the detriment of generic companies. Also the Classification Directive (92/26/EEC), by classifying prescription and non-prescription medicines, may lead to an increase in the market for self-medication products, although the degree of change depends on how each country administers the directive.

Given these aspects of competitive strength and competition, how have prices been determined in the EU and are there any signs of convergence in this sector? Basically, prices of medicines vary widely between EU member countries and are often determined by variations in the national income of countries and the policies of national governments towards expenditure on medicines by their public health-care systems. Manufacturers' prices for medicines that are reimbursed under public health-care systems (i.e. that have been officially approved and reimbursed by the government) are fixed at launch in most EU member countries, and official permission is required for any price rises. Distributors' margins are also controlled in all member countries by setting maximum levels. Discounts to retailers are allowed, although the numbers of such outlets are often regulated. All of this means that, despite EU Transparency Directive (89/105/EEC) to make the situation clearer, the pricing of medicines is still complicated and linked to national government health policies.

The final price of medicines in EU member countries is related to absolute income levels, national government policy, the degree of generic competition, and the degree of parallel imports. All in all, the introduction of new EU directives has not significantly reduced the spread of prices in the EU. Prices in Denmark, Germany, Ireland, the Netherlands, and the UK were consistently above the EU mean in 1997, while prices in France, Italy, Portugal, and Spain tended to be below average.

From a strategic point of view, the pharmaceutical industry is one where the threat of new entrants comes mainly from the generic companies, and the bargaining power is generally with the buyers—the public health-care systems of member states. However, the emergence of generic companies and the parallel trade provided increased power for the suppliers in the late 1990s. Rivalry within the main companies producing new products is still through R&D spending and product differentiation, while, even when their patents have lapsed, they may still aggressively market and promote their products. The generic companies compete in the sector where the barriers to entry are much less than the larger firms, and they compete primarily in terms of cost leadership, although they cannot wholly forget some element of branding, which consumers find is still important.

From the above account it is possible to see that merger and concentration activity, together with the influence of FDI, have all been important in moulding the development of this industry. At the same time, the influence of national standards, government policies, and the per capita income of member states have affected the way in which price and output strategies have been formulated across the EU. The pharmaceutical industry is a particularly important competitor on world markets whose development has and is being influenced by many interacting factors. We will now discuss how these factors influence not just the pharmaceutical industry but the whole EU economy.

7 Structural challenges and outlook

THIS chapter first stressed the importance of globalization and technological change. We saw how such forces affected flows of trade and investment, which, in turn, influenced the pace of structural change in both a world and an EU context. It then discussed the structural components of EU industry such as concentration, mergers, and the size of firm, together with the effects of the opening of the EU market through the SMP on strategic competitive variables such as price, cost margins, and price convergence. This final section will attempt to place the debate in both a macroeconomic and organizational context by investigating the concept of competitiveness in the context of EU manufacturing and services.

7.1 Macroeconomic dimension

In terms of macroeconomic policy, there are three main indicators of the competitiveness of a given nation or trading bloc. First, there should be a relatively buoyant export performance and favourable movements in international cost competitiveness. Secondly, domestic productivity should increase at a steady rate that is similar or higher than that of its rivals. Thirdly, productivity improvements should occur hand in hand with a high level of employment. The underlying factors affecting the 'competitiveness pyramid' and therefore the standard of living of a nation or group of nations is shown in Fig. 5.5. Here we see that, if a nation or a bloc of nations such as the EU is to improve its competitiveness in manufacturing and services, there is a need to address a number of factors that underlay the two main pillars of employment and productivity. On the employment side, the task is to create a labour market that stimulates employment creation while also making labour more skilled and flexible. On the productivity side, it means creating an environment that stimulates R&D and other innovative activity while encouraging business investment and sympathetic government involvement.

To achieve such benefits for one country is difficult enough, but for a whole trading bloc to im-

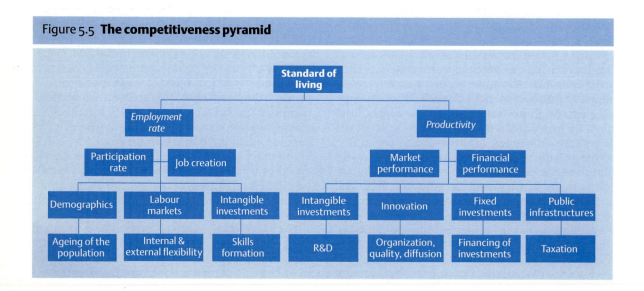

Figure 5.5 **The competitiveness pyramid**

prove its performance is more problematic. The aim of the SMP and the EU structural policies has been to create some degree of uniformity or convergence across the bloc. Given this aim, the main question to ask at this stage is whether the EU as a whole is showing signs of improved competitiveness vis-à-vis other advanced countries. In relation to the first criteria for sustained competitiveness given above, it is clear that the EU has lost export market share since the early 1980s at an average rate of −0.13 per cent per year, with Japan's export market share also declining by an average of −3.3 per cent. On the other hand, the USA has seen its export market share rise by an average of (0.4 per cent per year, while, until their 1997 currency crises, the Asian economies experienced a growth of 3 per cent per year in their market share of world exports over the same period.

In terms of the 'competitiveness pyramid', the performance of the EU on employment and productivity has varied. The employment rate (i.e. the proportion of working population that is employed) has fallen in the EU, while, at the same time, it has increased in Japan and the USA. By 1995 the EU's employment rate was around 60 per cent as compared to rates of 73 per cent and over in the USA and Japan. This underutilization of labour is also to be seen in the unemployment rates, which, since the early 1970s, have been, on average, 35 per cent higher in the EU than the USA and 230 per cent higher than in Japan.

From the productivity side, the EU performance can be measured in terms of the productivity of labour. After the oil shock of the early 1970s there was a deceleration of labour productivity in all industrial countries, but since that time the EU has experienced a steady growth rate of labour productivity of around 2 per cent per year, some three times as fast as the US rate but well under the Japanese rates. However, since the 1990s EU labour productivity rates have been higher than those of both its main industrial competitors. This steady growth of labour productivity over the last two decades of the twentieth century allowed the EU virtually to catch up with the absolute levels of productivity of its competitors. In 1960 the level of GDP per person employed in the EU was only 45 per cent of the US level, but by 1996 this had risen to 83 per cent. The relatively high rate of growth of productivity in the EU has helped to narrow the gap.

From the two aspects of the competitiveness pyramid we can see that the EU has done relatively well on the labour productivity side but that its employment performance has been poor in comparison. This weakness on the employment front is largely due to the interaction between labour productivity and the substitution of capital for labour, on the one hand, and the growth of the economies, on the other. For example, the growth of labour productivity (GDP per person employed) has two determinants. One determinant is technological progress in the form of new innovations, improved labour skills, and more organizational efficiency within firms. This is often called total factor productivity (TFP). Another determinant of labour productivity is the rate at which capital is substituted for labour. This means that GDP per employed can rise because new efficient machinery is capable of producing more output with less labour (see Insert). Table 5.12 provides an insight into the determinants of both labour productivity and GDP in the EU as compared with the USA and Japan. Here we see that the growth of labour productivity was more rapid in the EU than the USA both before and after the oil shock, with its immediate post-oil-shock period experience being equivalent to that of Japan. In the more recent period between 1986 and 1995 the EU's performance on labour productivity was better than that in the USA and equivalent to Japan's.

> **Automated hotels in a country with 12% unemployment**
>
> Why haven't automated hotels sprung up like robotic mushrooms in Canada and the US? It's not because of lack of technology. It's because, on the whole, employing humans is cheaper there. In France, with 12% unemployment, the rationale for automating hotels is not lack of workers. However, the minimum wage is much higher than in North America and payroll taxes are twice the Canadian rate. In addition there are many complex labour laws.
>
> *Source:* McGugan (1997).

When we investigate the reasons for this labour-productivity performance, we find that some 40 per cent of the EU's growth of productivity over the whole period was due to the substitution of capital for labour—a figure similar to that of Japan's but much higher than that of the USA at 16 per cent. Although the substitution of capital for labour does, of course, help increase economic

Table 5.12 **GDP growth and its components, 1961–1995 (%)**

Growth and components	1961–73			1974–85			1986–95		
	EU	USA	Japan	EU	USA	Japan	EU	USA	Japan
1. Technical progress	2.8	1.6	6.3	1.0	0.4	1.1	1.2	0.8	0.9
2. Capital/labour substitution	1.5	0.3	1.8	1.0	0.1	1.6	0.7	0.1	1.1
3. Labour productivity	4.4	1.9	8.2	2.0	0.5	2.7	1.9	0.8	2.0
4. Employment creating growth	0.3	1.9	1.3	0.0	1.8	0.7	0.4	1.7	0.9
5. Actual GDP growth	4.7	3.9	9.7	2.0	2.3	3.4	2.3	2.5	2.9

Note: Figures are related in the following way: (5 = 1 + 2 + 4 or 3 + 4); (4 = 5 − 3); (3 = 1 + 2); (2 = 3 − 1).
Source: European Commission (1997: 57).

growth and the standard of living, it does not address another important problem—that of unemployment. For example, the unemployment rate for the EU during the first half of the 1990s was 11 per cent, while those of the USA (5.4 per cent) and Japan (3.3 per cent) were significantly smaller. In other words, the substitution of capital for labour in the EU is superimposed on an already high level of unused labour resources, while the same is much less true for the USA or Japan.

Two other factors are worth mentioning in this context. First, the rate of economic growth has not been high enough in the EU to create sufficient growth in the number of jobs. This can be seen in row 4 of Table 5.12 which is the difference between the actual growth of GDP (row 5) and the labour productivity (row 3). Here we see that the growth of GDP in the EU was not rapid enough to generate enough overall employment to compensate for job losses resulting from the relatively healthy growth of labour productivity in the EU as compared to that in the USA or Japan. Secondly, this relatively rapid rate of substitution of capital for labour in the EU reflects some inflexibility in the EU labour market in relation to the USA and Japan.

The above analysis means that the dilemma for the EU is to maintain the growth of labour productivity while, at the same time, trying to slow down the rate of substitution of capital for labour so as not to increase the already high level of unemployed. The growth of employment obviously depends in part on keeping average wage cost under control, which the EU has managed to achieve quite successfully. Its growth of wage costs per head and unit labour costs has been slower than inflation, thus allowing industry to increase investment and create more jobs. However, this process has been slow, and the signs from the USA are that not only do average wage costs need to be controlled, but the dispersion of wages—that is, the wage level between the highest and lowest—may need to be wider. This revolves around the finding that the widening of the wage scales tends to increase employment. This argument stems from the fact that, as the forces of globalization and technical change widen labour-productivity differentials between different sectors, there is a need also to widen the wage dispersion to enable more employment to be created at the relatively low productivity end of the economy.

The solutions to the EU labour-market problems cannot be 'imported' from the USA, since the US reliance on market forces with low minimum wages and social benefits would not suit the European model with its relatively high non-wage cost (social-security contributions) in its total wage bill. However, the strategy is aimed at the twin goals of increased growth and employment intensity. To do this, the labour market has to be more flexible through measures to improve education and other labour-skill formation programmes, while at the same time increasing the flexibility of work arrangements within companies and firms.

While the issues above have tended to concentrate on productivity/employment aspects of the competitiveness pyramid, one should not neglect the role of investment, innovation, and investment in public infrastructure, which lies at the base of the productivity pyramid. To maintain employment growth as well as productivity, the EU has to create the capacity for future growth and development. This involves resources being channelled into intangible investments such as R&D and innovation. The EU's total R&D spending is smaller than that in the USA or Japan, with less being generated from the business sector in terms of both financial involvement and research personnel. Similarly, as Table 5.13 shows, the fact that of all the patents taken out in the EU about a half were from within the EU, while the USA and Japan together accounted for a half, indicates that an increase in the innovation rate might also be needed. The striving for improved competitiveness calls for a more effective development of 'immaterial' investment in general—such investments include effort to improve after-sales service, design, reputation, image, etc.—the so-called soft aspects of competitiveness. Finally, the market/financial performance underlying productivity has to include suitable government policies to stimulate growth and technical change.

The outlook for EU industry and services depends very much on the nature of the sector concerned. Table 5.14 shows a sectoral breakdown of the annual productivity change over the 1990–9 period, together with the absolute change in numbers employed. We see that labour productivity in manufacturing and energy rose rapidly in this period as a result of the reorganization and concentration of production in fewer plants, and the reallocation of labour-intensive processes to areas outside the EU. The growth in labour productivity in services was at half the rate of manufacturing,

Table 5.13 Share of total patents, 1994 (%)

Share of patents granted in Europe	
EU	51.0
USA	23.1
Japan	22.8
Share of patents granted in USA	
EU	16.5
USA	55.1
Japan	22.0
Share of patents applications in Japan	
EU	5.3
USA	5.9
Japan	88.3

Source: Eurostat (1997b: 14).

Table 5.14 Change in EU employment and productivity, 1990–1999

Sector	1990–5		1995–9		1999
	Employment (000s)	Productivity (yearly % growth)	Employment (000s)	Productivity (yearly % growth)	Employment share (%)
Agriculture	−299.1	3.5	−40.4	1.7	1.9
Energy	−225.7	5.0	−40.8	1.6	1.4
Manufacturing	−4,004.6	3.5	37.5	2.4	23.5
Construction	−909.4	1.4	145.9	1.7	6.3
Market services	+1,591.2	1.4	1,972.8	1.7	44.5
Government services	463.7	1.7	309.8	0.7	22.4
TOTAL SERVICES	2,054.9	1.5	2,282.6	1.6	66.9
TOTAL (ALL SECTORS)	−3,383.9	2.1	2,381.8	1.7	100.0

Source: Eurostat (1997b: 79, 82, 83).

but was still at a favourable level in relation to past performances in this sector, mainly because of relatively rapid growth of productivity in the transport, distribution, financial, and business sectors. Employment trends during this period show the shake-out of labour from manufacturing and construction as a result of both productivity improvements and the recession of the early 1990s. The growth of employment in market services rose during the period by over 2 millions, with sectors such as distribution, hotels, and restaurants, and 'other market' services such as business services, social services, cultural and recreational service, and personal services, accounting for the bulk of the employment gain.

Labour productivity slowed down overall during the 1995–9 period, as the corporate restructuring and relocation mentioned above decelerates. In terms of employment, there will be a small addition to employment in manufacturing and building, while market services will continue to provide the bulk of employment gains, led by the growth of business services such as market research, advertising, accountancy services, computing, and software services. Also the growth of communication technologies will enable small companies to succeed in markets where previously only large companies dominated. These shifts will mean a change in relationship between the demand for skilled/unskilled workers, as can be seen in Table 5.15.

Here the high-skill sectors are defined as the first three occupation categories, with the other occupations defined as the relatively lower-skilled occupations. At the end of the 1990s the demand for labour was of the skilled kind, whose growth was particularly active in the service industry. In the absence of policies to remedy the skill problems, the EU will find it increasingly difficult to remain competitive and to maintain the desired type and level of employment.

7.2 Corporate dimension

Section 7.1 discussed the macroeconomic adjustments that will be needed for the EU to maintain its competitiveness. However, the key to such improved macro-competitiveness in the future will also be dependent on organizational change at the micro or corporate level in both manufacturing

Table 5.15 Change in EU salaried employment by occupation, 1995–1997

Occupation	Total[a]		Manufacturing		Services	
	Number	% change	Number	% change	Number	% change
Legislators and managers	779.0	10.0	87.1	6.8	668.7	11.0
Professionals	1,484.9	10.1	177.2	10.5	1,265.2	10.0
Technicians	1,438.0	9.7	381.3	14.2	976.7	8.5
Clerks	−298.6	−1.8	−110.6	−3.7	−142.3	−1.1
Service workers	−145.5	−1.0	−63.6	−7.8	−42.1	−0.3
Skilled agricultural workers	−44.9	−2.6	—	—	—	—
Craft and related workers	−110.2	−0.6	−68.8	−0.8	−194.7	−4.3
Plant and machine operators	−342.1	−3.2	−235.8	−4.0	−45.3	−1.1
Elementary occupations	−235.6	−2.1	−129.3	−5.5	−60.0	−0.8
Armed forces	−143.6	−18.4	—	—	−143.6	−18.4
TOTAL	2,381.8	—	37.5	—	2,282.6	—

[a] Includes agriculture, energy, and construction.

Source: European Commission (1997: 92).

and services. The reason for the increasing stress on the corporate level comes from an understanding that competition between individual nations or between blocs of nations such as the EU and NAFTA is different from competition between companies. For example, if companies are unsuccessful, then they can go bankrupt, but nations cannot. Put another way, we should remember that it is companies who compete with one another, not nations or trading blocs (Krugman 1994). Countries or blocs of countries compete only in the sense that some do better than others at delivering rising standards of living to their citizens within an open competitive environment. In order to provide this increase in the standard of living, it is the task of governments to help to nurture the competitive performance of their companies across both manufacturing and services.

The competitiveness debate at the corporate level has also shifted somewhat from the 'hard' factors (corporate planning, financial control, scale economies, R&D, etc.) towards the 'soft' factors (organizational innovation, speed to market, reputation, service, and the management of people, etc.) Successful companies have focused on new flatter decentralized structures, better supplier–customer relationships, improved quality, increased training, multi-skilling, and flexible employment systems. Examples of such improvements in the manufacturing sector can be seen in the cases of the Baxi Partnership (UK, heating appliances) and Brabantia (Netherlands, household consumer goods), and in the service sector in the cases of Karolinska Hospital (Sweden, medical) and Nationale Nederland (Netherlands, insurance) (Eurostat 1997b).

Therefore the winners in the twenty-first century will be those companies that can shift their focus more towards the customer. This will involve companies changing their organizational structures, the location of decision-making, and their concepts of what makes up a competitive enterprise. For example, a Coopers & Lybrand survey (Coopers & Lybrand 1996a) showed that only 41 per cent of EU firms had centralized organization, while the figures for the Americas and Asia-Pacific companies were 56 and 53 per cent respectively. This tends to indicate the EU firms in the latter half of the 1990s had a more responsive structure, in that decision-making was closer to the relevant market. However, American and Asia-Pacific companies indicated that they planned to decentralize rapidly in the twenty-first century, so that less than 40 per cent of their organizations would be centralized, while EU managers did not anticipate any further move to decentralization. The cost of staying still could be large.

A survey of 1,000 business leaders in Germany, France, Italy, and the UK in 1996 by Coopers & Lybrand (1996a) showed that these leaders felt that they had an advantage over other nations in 'industry experience' and 'leading-edge products', while they perceived their rivals' competitive advantage to be in areas such as 'price' and 'scale economies'. In global markets such relative complacency about pricing strategies can be problematic. Other companies can always buy in know-how and create elements of non-price competitiveness, whilst also maintaining their pricing 'edge'. A further study by the accountancy company of 500 companies in 1995 (Coopers & Lybrand 1996b) identified a small number of 'hypergrowth' companies, whose success was very closely related to the level of education of senior executives, team skills training, and the willingness to hire management from bigger companies in different industries. These factors illustrate the importance of companies as 'learning' organizations.

It should be noted that a certain degree of restructuring has occurred in EU manufacturing and services, but the degree of restructuring depends on the dynamics of competition in the specific EU industry concerned and the stage of organizational development of the individual companies concerned. An attempt on a European level to raise awareness of the need to change organizational attitudes to competitiveness was seen in the second half of the 1990s in the 'benchmarking initiative'. At the enterprise level, this is aimed at identifying the manufacturing and managerial processes that a company needs to improve. It then studies a company that is known to perform outstandingly in its sector, and measures how this performance is achieved, and then tries to emulate it. The Commission (Com. (96) 413) suggests that common rules and a European information network would be set up to gather the vital competitive data that would provide the core of the improvement needed to increase the standard of living of people in the EU.

8 Summary

THIS chapter has shown that the structure and operation of the EU's industry and services have been affected by many forces. First, the chapter explained the overriding effect of globalization forces coupled with the trend towards 'deindustrialization' on maturing economies such as the EU. Secondly, the changing nature of inter- and intra-EU trade flows provided an insight into future trends in product demand and the EU's performance in this field vis-à-vis other competitors. Thirdly, the nature of competition in different sectors of EU manufacturing and services was explained through a discussion of the effects of the SMP coupled with structural changes, as evidenced by trends in mergers, concentration ratios, and firm size. Fourthly, the effect of sectoral changes on competition variables such as mark-ups and price convergence were investigated in an attempt to understand the degree of competition in different markets. Finally, the chapter concluded with assessments of the relative macroeconomic performance of EU manufacturing and services in relation to competitors and the importance of corporate-level changes in management organization in such a process. What is clear from the discussion is that competitiveness is an elusive concept, but that concentration on improving the quality of all inputs is an essential ingredient if the EU is to improve the standard of living of its inhabitants.

Further reading

A variety of national and international organizations regularly present reports that make predictions of likely economic developments and also provide interpretations and comment on past macro and microeconomic experience. These include:

- The International Monetary Fund Staff Reports;
- International Monetary Fund, *World Economic Outlook*;
- OECD Economic Surveys (individual countries).

In the UK:

- Bank of England Quarterly Reports;
- National Institute Economic Review published by the National Institute of Economic and Social Research, London.

There are several useful web sites including:

- www.ft.com for the *Financial Times*;
- www.wsj.com for the *Wall Street Journal*;
- www.economist.com for *The Economist*;
- www.nber.org for National (US) Bureau of Economic Research.

Discussion questions

1 If most of the investment, saving, and consumption of nations tends to be domestic in origin, why are such countries worried about the effects of globalization and structural change?

2 Explain how a study of multinational activity helps us to understand that EU competitiveness is not the same thing as the competitiveness of EU companies.

3 Why is it important to distinguish between homogeneous and differentiated products when discussing the nature of competition in the EU?

4 In what ways has the SMP changed the economic landscape of the EU? Why have its effects on the manufacturing sector been different from those on services?

5 Explain why it is essential to study economic activity at both the national and the corporate level if the standard of living of a nation/blocs of nations is to improve.

Case 1
Return

Keith Blois

1 Introduction

John was getting increasingly cross with Peter. Yet again the shop was almost out of stock of doll's houses—the most popular product they sold. Several customers had expressed considerable disappointment at finding that there were no doll's houses in stock and at being told that there was no likelihood of any more being available before Christmas. Furthermore, some other customers, who had previously purchased doll's houses, were surprised to find that the stock of furniture items (designed to fit into the doll's houses) was very limited. John's main responsibility was managing the shop in which RETURN sold the items its workers produced, and he was very aware that it was the wooden items that were the major draw for customers. Although a few did simply purchase cards or flowers, the majority came to the shop to buy items like the doll's houses that were made by the woodworkers and listed in the RETURN catalogue. Then, while there, such people would also usually buy some other items.

Peter's explanation for the lack of supplies was that an increasing proportion of his workers' time was being taken up manufacturing items designed to meet the requirements of specific customers. These covered a wide range of products and had recently included a set of display stands for a local shop; some storage boxes for a play-group; and some garden furniture designed to fit into a gap between a house and a garage. Peter stated that manufacturing these items was of benefit to everybody. He claimed, first, that he was able to make a higher profit on these items than on those listed in the catalogue; secondly, that the work was more stimulating for his workers than the repetitive activities involved in manufacturing items for the catalogue, and, thirdly, that, as well as being more stimulating, it was providing the workers with the opportunity to extend their range of woodworking skills.

John decided that he had to raise this issue with RETURN's marketing committee (which was comprised of the Chairman, the Director, and John). He therefore prepared a note setting out the situation in which he warned that selling RETURN's produce was becoming increasingly difficult and that he believed the lack of a stock of wooden items would exacerbate the situation and result in a serious loss of customers. When the Chairman received his copy of this note, he was busy preparing a document to present to a special meeting of RETURN's Trustees at which the sole topic of discussion was to be what activities RETURN should undertake in the future.

2 RETURN's background

RETURN was established in 1976 in Barchester to meet the needs of people with mental-health problems by providing a different service from that offered by the hospital-based occupational therapy and sheltered workshop units. From its founding RETURN had strong links with the National Heath Service and Barchestershire's Social Services Department, but is still run independently as a registered charity. It has two sites, eleven full-time equivalent staff members (i.e. their total working hours are equivalent to those of eleven full-time staff), and fifty full-time equivalent places for 'workers'. The term 'worker' is applied to the people for whom RETURN's service is created. They are not employees of RETURN but the avoidance of terms such as 'patient' or 'client' is aimed at contributing to the process of rebuilding the workers' sense of self-esteem. Box 1 gives a worker's viewpoint.

RETURN has five work groups offering training in the following skills:

■ Woodwork. This group produces toys and gifts. Special-order items can be produced to the customer's own specifications. All items conform to European safety standards and are decorated with non-toxic paints. All items are made from sustainable forested wood.

■ Screen and hand-press printing. This group creates high-quality hand-screen printed cards, stationery, business cards, and special-order work. Only recycled paper is used.

■ Sales, marketing, and computing. This group is responsible for the shop on the main site and provides training opportunities in retailing, publicity, and customer care, as well as keyboard skills and basic computing.

■ Horticulture. Chemical-free vegetables and flowers are grown and sold in the neighbourhood.

■ Town garden. A range of ornamental shrubs, herbs, and bedding plants suitable for the small domestic gardens typical of the neighbourhood are grown. A range of basketry items is also produced.

In addition to the staff members, there are about twenty people who act as unpaid helpers who are called 'volunteers'. Some of these people have specific skills that they are prepared to use—for example, helping with the

Box 1 A worker's view

'RETURN is an organization where people who have come straight from psychiatric hospitals or mental health day care centres are busy, friendly, sharing experiences and being tolerant of each other. There is a great sense of shared purpose and also one of striving. In the gardens people are digging, weeding, potting up, cutting bunches of flowers, and pricing plants. In the woodwork department they are making doll's houses, children's toys, and special order furniture. In the print room they are designing and printing greetings cards, printing business cards, invitations and letter heads. In the computer room people are being trained in the use of computers, typing, and administration. In the shop they are selling the goods produced by the woodworkers, the printers, and the gardeners and learning to stock take and much more.

This does not mean that there are not pockets of tranquillity as well. Sometimes people have difficulty in concentrating and need short breaks from work, other times people are visibly upset and some people need to work on their own for part of the time. At coffee and lunch breaks there is a hum of conversation and people read newspapers, and play cards or chess.

RETURN has a fundamentally democratic rather than autocratic basis and it believes in worker involvement providing for this in its structure. For example, the workers' monthly meeting is a process for change in RETURN. It is a place where information is shared and where issues are raised and discussed. The topics can range from the cleanliness of the building to fundraising plans to what types of activity the workers feel they need.

Individual workers meet regularly with their staff supervisor and community psychiatric nurse to discuss their progress. At these meetings they set themselves short- and long-term goals and they monitor how well they achieve them. Workers make decisions about themselves and about the workplace—and why not? They are, after all, just adults recovering from bad times. Most of all workers are asking when they come to RETURN for their confidence to the restored.'

Table 1 RETURN's Income and Expenditure, 1996/7 (£)

Income	
Barchestershire Social Services	77,224
National Health Service	87,638
European Social Fund	5,775
Donations from charitable trusts	10,235
Donations from individuals	9,193
Sales	23,582
Events	4,558
Interest	2,082
Miscellaneous	11,725
TOTAL	**223,012**

Expenditure	
Salaries	184,758
Capital purchases	3,400
Raw materials	9,293
Catering	4,197
Administration	7,431
Insurance	2,013
Electricity and water	5,250
Building maintenance	2,678
Utilities	4,801
Miscellaneous	8,589
TOTAL	**232,410**

sources include the European Social Fund; donations from charitable trusts and individuals; and the sale of products produced by the workers in the work units (see Table 1 for the accounts for 1996/7).

The Director is a full-time member of staff responsible for detailed running of the operation and reports to a Management Committee that is made up of elected Trustees (none of whom are employees of RETURN though some are also 'volunteers'). The Management Committee is legally responsible for all major policy decisions; approving contracts with any funding body; overseeing the financial soundness of the organization; dealing with any substantive staff issues such as decisions to recruit additional staff; and so on. Its meetings are attended (except for discussions of sensitive matters such as salary decisions) by representatives of the staff, the volunteers, and the workers. The Management Committee has a series of subcommittees, the members of which include representatives of those involved in RETURN's daily routine.

accounts. Others are simply an additional pair of hands ready to help the staff in any way they can.

Funding comes mainly from statutory bodies and particularly the Health Authority (38 per cent) and the Barchestershire Social Services Department (29 per cent). Other

3 Mission and activities

RETURN's mission statement is as follows:

RETURN aims to help people with mental health problems, through creative work rehabilitation and training, to enter open employment or to receive long-term support within the community.

In pursuit of this mission RETURN is committed to continue to develop an excellent service for its workers, quality products for its customers, and a challenging but supportive environment for its employees and volunteers.

Its three main activities are:

■ Vocational rehabilitation for people who hope to get back to paid employment and/or achieve greater independence in their daily lives; and sheltered work for people with long-term mental-health needs.
■ The provision of products and services including craft goods and horticulture to the local community through direct sales and to the wider community by sales through retailers.
■ Fund-raising to maintain and develop RETURN's existing service.

The number of people in RETURN's catchment area diagnosed as having a depressive disorder is between, 10,000 and 14,000. The number believed to be suffering from a lifetime schizophrenic illness is 3,500. Only a minority of these people would benefit from attending RETURN—some would be too ill, while at the other extreme others can, with medication and the support of families and friends, already cope in the community. Nevertheless, as it is currently the only provider of this service in the area, there is always a waiting list of people wishing to take up places as workers when such places become vacant.

RETURN's 'production' activities require the maintenance of a structured but supportive environment in which the workers, without being stressed, can learn to work with others and respond to the expectations of other members of a team. In addition to the revenue it produces, the sale of RETURN's products has a number of benefits. The shop and the stall (which is set up at local community events such as school fetes), which are run by the workers, with a staff member or a volunteer on hand, provide a public face for RETURN and help to educate the public on the capabilities of people with mental-health problems (see Box 2 for some comments from members of the public). The creation of products for sale also gives the workers considerable pride and confidence in their ability to contribute to RETURN and society. In addition, the shop meets the needs of those members of the local community who like to buy locally grown chemical-free vegetables and locally handmade items.

Box 2 The views of some members of the public before and after visiting RETURN

BEFORE
Visitor 1. 'The fact that RETURN was a rehabilitation centre for the mentally ill made me feel rather uncomfortable and nervous. I pictured RETURN as a kind of hospital but maybe more asylum-like.'
Visitor 2. 'My biggest worry was how to communicate to the people at RETURN; after all I had no idea how ill they were. Would they understand what I was trying to say or would they be so ill that they were "dead to the world?"'
Visitor 3. 'What I expected was that of a very negative view. This was mainly because of how the media portrayed people with mental health problems, such as straight jackets and putting people in confined rooms.'

AFTER
Visitor 1. 'Alice [a schizophrenic who needs regular medication and even so has to spend some time each year in hospital], a worker at RETURN, was the person who really made me understand what these people are like. On the outside Alice looked like a normal person and if she walked past you in the street you would have no idea about her past and how she has come to terms with her problem.'
Visitor 2. 'I learnt that these people were not "thick". Some of these people were studying for degrees when they had their breakdowns. One has a Ph.D.'
Visitor 3. 'I learnt that the people who use RETURN are normal people who have gone through difficulties in their lives which they are admirably trying to sort out.'

4 Current issues

In common with most charities, RETURN is constantly concerned about its financial situation. The Management Committee is aware that its staff are all underpaid and only remain at RETURN through a sense of vocation and commitment. However, attempts to recruit staff—to replace those who have left—have recently become increasingly difficult, with the low salaries clearly causing some applicants not to accept jobs offered to them at RETURN. The staff work under great pressure and, while they seem prepared to accept the stress of dealing with workers whose demands are often considerable and whose behaviour is sometimes unpredictable, they object strongly about two issues. First, the increasing amount of time spent on completing records and other administration. Secondly, the growing pressure, especially from the main funders (see below), to 'move workers on' (i.e. persuade them to leave RETURN), so that politically determined targets are achieved. This pressure means, in their opinion, that they have either to reduce the amount of time workers spend in learning a skill or persuade people to leave who are not fully prepared for life in the community.

RETURN is currently struggling with a number of issues, including (not in any order of importance) the following difficulties.

■ There are problems in finding employment for those ready to leave. Not only has the relatively high level of unemployment created a problem, but the nature of the available work has changed. For example, garden centres are increasingly being supplied with plants already in containers rather than growing items themselves. This means that the demand for employees with basic horticultural skills is falling.

■ As the employment market changes, the need to provide the workers with training in such matters as preparing a c.v. and conduct at interviews is increased. Providing this training is an added cost and reduces the amount of time that workers can spend in their work group. The current staff were recruited for their skills as woodworkers, printers, etc., and—even if they had the time—are, therefore, not equipped to provide professional advice on such matters.

■ The Christmas and greetings cards designed and printed by RETURN's workers and sold in its shop are seen as expensive relative to other charities' cards.

■ The demand for RETURN's simple wooden articles has fallen as other charities—particularly those with overseas links—have started to import similar items made of more exotic woods from lesser developed countries.

The main funders have in the last three years changed their relationship from that of providing a grant to an annual contract. The significance of this is threefold. First, whereas they previously asked to be informed only of the numbers of workers entering RETURN, they now set targets for and require regular reports monitoring the numbers passing through RETURN. Secondly, there is now no guarantee year on year of their continuing to fund RETURN. Thirdly, in spite of their support of RETURN over many years, if a competitor was to be established and applied for funding, they would be obliged to consider the competitor's bid.

5 Discussion question

Would it be appropriate to seek to introduce a marketing orientation to RETURN? If so what would this involve?

Part Two

Understanding and Assessing Buyer Behaviour

Chapter 6
Consumer Behaviour
Klaus Grunert

Objectives

The objectives of this chapter are:

1 to explain why consumer behaviour is a central topic in marketing;

2 to provide some simple tools that can be used for thinking about consumers, speculating about their possible behaviours, analysing marketing problems from a consumer-behaviour perspective, and, most important of all, designing studies that investigate consumer behaviour in a concrete product and market context;

3 to present a simple model of consumer decision-making, and, based on this, to distinguish four basic types of consumer purchases;

4 to consider how consumers learn about products and services from their environment and how they use this information to direct their behaviour;

5 to introduce the concepts of values, lifestyle, and culture.

1 Why study consumer behaviour?

WHY do some companies perform more profitably than others, even though they compete for the same customers, have to pay the same wages, and are subject to the same regulations? One major reason commonly advanced is that some companies are better than others at developing products and services in which their customers see a high value relative to competing products and relative to the price (Day and Wensley 1988). Developing products in which customers will see a high value requires, in turn, a good understanding of customers—what they want, how they buy, what determines whether they will be satisfied with a product or service. A company that continuously tries to understand its customers and uses that knowledge in developing products and services is also said to be *market oriented*. It has been shown that companies that are more market oriented are generally more profitable (Narver and Slater 1990*a*; Jaworski and Kohli 1993).

The customers that companies deal with vary widely in nature. Often, customers are other manufacturing companies, as when a manufacturer of lamps sells them to Volkswagen, which builds them into its cars. In many other cases, the customer is a trading company, as when a Swedish furniture producer sells to an import company on the German market or when a manufacturer of frozen vegetables sells to a large supermarket chain. A few manufacturing companies also sell directly to consumers—for example, by mail order or via the Internet.

Even though most companies do not have consumers as their immediate customers, the analysis of consumer behaviour is a major topic in marketing. The reason is that most products eventually end up in private households, even though they may pass various steps on their way from the producer to the consumer. Volkswagen sells its automobiles to consumers, including the lamps it received from its supplier; the German importer sells the Swedish furniture to a furniture retailer, who sells it to consumers, and the supermarket chain sells the frozen vegetables to consumers. Producers and traders form vertical chains or networks, also called *value chains*, and the consumer

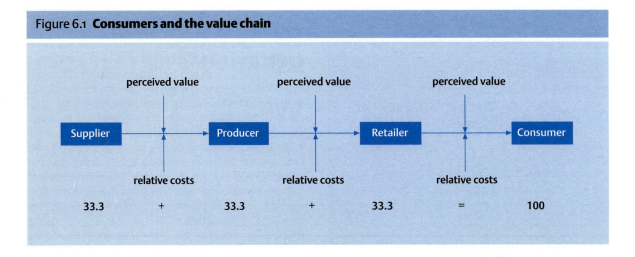

Figure 6.1 **Consumers and the value chain**

appears as an 'end-user'—the one who eventually uses or consumes the products and services. A simple example of a value chain is given in Fig. 6.1.

Understanding consumer behaviour is, therefore, important not only for those who sell to consumers directly, like retail companies, but also for all actors preceding the retailer in the value chain. The value that the consumer perceives in a product sets the limit for what all others in the value chain can get out of their activities: if the consumer is willing to pay £5 or dkr. 50 or DM 12 for a product, this is the amount that is available for distribution among all members of the value chain, as indicated in Fig. 6.1.

Many producers have learnt the importance of understanding consumer behaviour the hard way. In the 1960s a number of industrial bakeries in Denmark started to export a product that became known as *Danish Butter Cookies*—small cookies in colourful tin boxes featuring pictures of the Little Mermaid, the Danish Royal Guard, and the like. The product was an immediate success in markets such as Germany and the UK, because consumers perceived it as a high-value product that could be used, amongst other things, as a gift. Initially, the product was sold from the Danish producers to importers on the export markets, who then resold it to retailers. Later, the Danish producers thought that it might be more profitable to sell the product directly to a retailer, and found amongst others the German discount chain Aldi as a customer. In the ensuing price war, prices dropped and consumer perception of the product changed from a high-value product to a cheap discount item. The Danish producers have repeatedly tried to develop

new products to repeat the earlier success, but little has come out of that. Today, producing butter cookies is a problematic business in Denmark, even though the whole world knows the product.

How could that happen? Part of the explanation is that the producers thought mainly in terms of their immediate customers and not in terms of the end-users—the consumers who end up munching the cookies. Producers did not understand that finding a retail customer is not only a question of getting good deals with high volume, but also a question of positioning the product in the minds of the consumer. And when they tried to develop new products to replace the declining one, they found that they did not know very much about what consumers want when they buy cookies.

This chapter gives an introduction to the analysis of consumer behaviour. This is a broad area, and only the major topics can be mentioned. Advice for additional reading is provided at the end of the chapter.

2 A basic model of consumer decision-making

FIG. 6.2 shows a simple model for analysing a consumer purchase. This model has been widely used throughout the consumer-behaviour

Figure 6.2 **A simple model for analysing a consumer purchase**

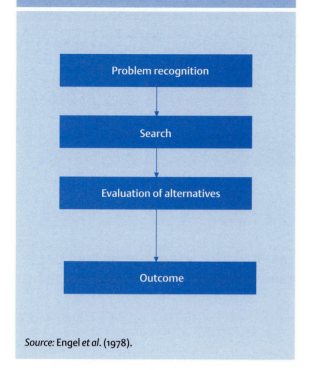

Problem recognition

Search

Evaluation of alternatives

Outcome

Source: Engel *et al.* (1978).

He then buys the beer and hopefully enjoys the outcome.

👉 'The brand, name is a shorthand device for all that the brand stands for. Not only does it serve to identify the brand; it should also trigger the brand proposition in the consumer's mind.' (Chapter 20, p. 487)

This is an example of a very simple buying process. Buying a car or a house is the other extreme. Problem recognition develops over time, as when a buyer starts to perceive the need for a new car. She may then start to look for options, initially guided by criteria such as a maximum price, a need for five doors, and a desire to avoid (or a preference for) French cars. These criteria may change, however, as she collects more information, and over time she may narrow down her choices to two or three options, among which she then makes a decision based on a number of criteria such as price, comfort, looks, fuel economy, and availability of financing. After the purchase, experiencing the outcome is likewise a process extended over a long time.

The four steps in Fig. 6.2 are a framework that we can use to speculate about a buying process, as we have done with the two examples above. We now add a few more specific comments to some of the five steps.

2.1 **Problem recognition**

Generally, a consumer can be said to experience a problem when he or she perceives a discrepancy between an actual state and a desired state: the fridge is empty but should be filled with beer, the car is rusty and old but should instead be shiny and new. Problem recognition can originate inside the consumer, but can also be influenced by outside sources, including marketer-controlled sources such as advertising and product displays.

In analysing problem recognition, the *means–end chain* concept is useful. A means–end chain is an attempt to analyse how consumers relate concrete product characteristics to consequences and ultimately life values relevant to them. They show why consumers perceive that a product may solve a problem, or, put another way, what motivates consumers to buy products (Gutman 1982; Peter *et al.*, in press). Fig. 6.3 shows a bundle of means–end chains for a product that has become more popular in many countries in recent years: alcohol-free beer.

literature, and it is a good start for thinking about consumer behaviour (this model was originally proposed by Engel *et al.* 1978, but has been widely adopted by others since).

The model views the purchase as a process that goes through several steps: problem recognition, search, evaluation of alternatives, purchase, and outcome. A buying process starts with a recognition of some kind of problem, which leads to a search for ways of solving the problem. Possible solutions to the problem are then compared and evaluated, leading to a decision to buy one of them, resulting in some kind of output. In one way or another, all buying decisions can be analysed using these five steps, even though the way they materialize may differ enormously. When a regular beer-drinker buys beer, the problem recognition may be the simple fact that he has run out of beer. He knows how to 'solve the problem': he knows which brand he prefers, and where he can buy it, and remembering this information is the only 'search' that occurs. In the shop, he immediately recognizes his brand, which is the only 'evaluation of alternatives' occurring.

Figure 6.3 Means–end chains for alcohol-free beer

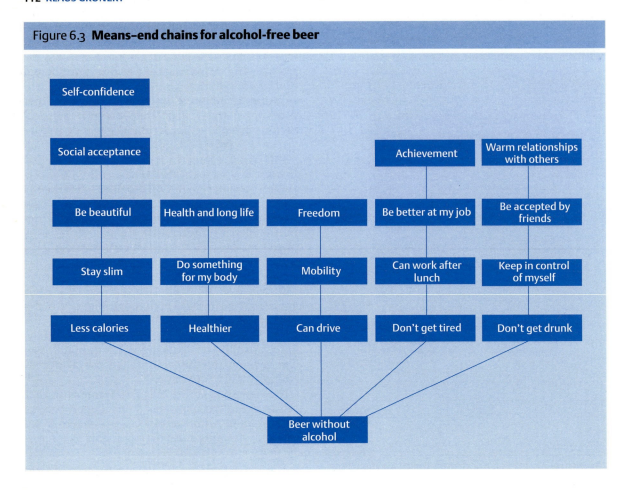

Which 'problem' does alcohol-free beer solve for consumers? As Fig. 6.3 shows, there may be a host of reasons why consumers may choose it: some like the product for health reasons, some for slimming reasons, some because it improves their work performance, some because it gives them the freedom to drive, and still others because they want to remain in control of themselves in social situations. The problem recognition leading to the purchase of alcohol-free beer may start by the consumer thinking about ways, for example, to have a healthier lifestyle, but is certainly also influenced by marketer information about the availability of beer without alcohol.

2.2 Search

When consumers have previous experience with a certain type of purchase, as regular beer-drinkers do with buying beer, then they will already know how to solve the problem—they know the brands available, their different tastes, and where to get them. The only form of search occurring in such situations may, therefore, be *internal search*—retrieving previous experience from memory. *External search* involves acquiring new information about purchase options, their characteristics, and consequences.

Within external search, a further distinction can be made between *active* search and *passive* search. In active search, the consumer takes the initiative to acquire information—by asking a salesperson, obtaining a brochure, asking a friend. This type of search mostly occurs in the context of purchases that have some subjective importance for the consumer. Since many purchases are not of that nature, and sellers nevertheless want to inform consumers about their offerings, they have to find means where the seller takes over the active role and channels information to the consumer, who remains mostly passive. When the consumer is exposed to TV commercials, billboards, and many other forms of advertising, he or she is usually passive—that is, not really interested in the information presented. Getting the consumer's attention is, therefore, a major task in this type of market communication.

2.3 Evaluation of alternatives

In the large majority of purchase situations, consumers have to choose between various options, and therefore have to find ways of making a decision. In the simplest case a previous decision is simply repeated, and remembering what has been bought on earlier occasions is the only mental task involved for the consumer. In other cases, a real comparison between alternatives is involved. This again may be rather simple or rather complex. When buying large-ticket items such as cars, houses, and expensive holidays, many product characteristics will be involved in making the decision. This form of evaluation of alternatives is also called *multi-attribute decision-making* (Lutz and Bettman 1977). In other cases, rules of thumb may be invoked: buying what is cheapest, buying the product with the most well-known brand name, buying a product in a store that one trusts. Such rules of thumb, which characterize many buying decisions, are also called *decision heuristics* (Bettman and Park 1980).

2.4 Outcome

Outcomes are usually characterized by the degree of the consumer's satisfaction or dissatisfaction with the item bought. Satisfaction is commonly regarded as being determined by the discrepancy between expectations and performance: if the product's performance meets or exceeds expectations, satisfaction results, whereas consumers will be dissatisfied when the performance of the product falls short of the expectations (Oliver 1980). Having satisfied customers is one of the main determinants of business success, because it has a major influence on whether the consumer will buy the product again.

Both components of satisfaction—expectations and performance—are influenced by marketers, at least to some degree. Expectations are influenced by advertising, packaging, the store where the product is sold, the price, and the physical appearance of the product. The performance of the product as perceived by the consumer is, of course, affected by the physical characteristics of the product. It is in the interest of marketers that the expectations created do not exceed how the product can be expected to perform once bought and used.

To make things more complicated, both expectations and perceived performance are affected by factors that are not under the marketer's control. Expectations are influenced by what friends and relatives say, and the perceived performance depends on how the product is used.

As mentioned, the step model in Fig. 6.2 is a useful way of thinking about consumer purchases. When a new product is to be developed and marketed, for example, the model immediately leads us to the following questions:

- Will the new product be perceived as solving a problem?
- Will consumers be motivated to search actively for information about the product, or do we have to become active as a seller?
- Which product characteristics will influence consumers' decision to buy the product or not?
- Where will consumers want to buy the product?
- Will they be satisfied? Why or why not?

3 Types of decision-making: involvement and habit formation

WHILE the model in Fig. 6.2 is useful, the discussion in Section 2 shows quite clearly that purchase processes can differ enormously. In this section we discuss two criteria that are useful for distinguishing between different types of purchases: involvement and habit formation.

Involvement is the subjective importance of a purchase to the consumer. Consumers are highly involved with some purchases and less involved with others. The major determinants of degree of involvement are as follows (Laurent and Kapferer 1985):

- *Functional and financial importance*: a washing machine has great functional importance for a family with small children, while it has less functional importance for a bachelor, and the family will therefore be more involved with the purchase of a washing machine than the bachelor; also, the higher the price of a product, the more involved will consumers be.

■ *Perceived risk*: if a purchase is perceived as risky—for example, because considerable variations in product quality are believed to exist and there is, therefore, a good chance of getting a low-quality product—consumers tend to be more involved with the purchase.

■ *Emotional value*: consumers have emotional attachments to some product categories—for example, some consumers really *love* chocolate and are therefore involved when buying it, though the purchase has neither functional nor financial importance nor is it very risky.

■ *Sign value*: many products have social significance—i.e. other people infer something about the person based on the products they use; this is often the case for clothing and for cars; the more sign value a product has, the more involved consumers tend to be with the purchase.

Table 6.1 shows a number of product categories for involvement indices on these four dimensions. The degree of involvement has a major impact especially on the search and evaluation of alterna-

tives phases of the buying process. With high degrees of involvement, consumers tend to engage in active search, and tend to use many product characteristics when making a decision—that is, they engage in multi-attribute decision-making. When involvement is low, there will be no or only passive external search, and evaluation of alternatives will often be based on choice heuristics.

Many consumer decisions are based on habit, and, as habits are formed, the way in which decisions are made changes quite drastically. In a German study, purchase behaviour of young mothers having their first child was studied with regard to baby products (Kaas 1982). From the time when their child was born—when they had to buy these products for the first time—until a year later their purchase behaviour with regard to these products changed in several ways. These changes can be summarized in the following steps:

■ At the beginning, there is little knowledge about the various brands and their characteristics, and therefore only weakly formed opinions about them.

■ Based on active external search (asking doctors and other mothers, reading information on the

Table 6.1 Involvement with a variety of products

Product	Functional and financial importance	Perceived risk	Emotional value	Sign value
Dresses	121	112	147	181
Bras	117	115	106	130
Washing machines	118	109	106	111
TV sets	112	100	122	95
Vacuum cleaners	110	112	70	78
Irons	103	95	72	76
Champagne	109	120	125	125
Oil	89	97	65	92
Yogurt	86	83	106	78
Chocolate	80	89	123	75
Shampoo	96	103	90	81
Toothpaste	95	95	94	105
Facial soap	82	90	114	118
Detergents	79	82	56	63

Source: Laurent and Kapferer (1985).

package), knowledge about the brands available and their differences is being built up.

- Based on this knowledge and experience with different brands, more strongly held opinions about the various brands are formed.

- Eventually, external search declines and the consumer becomes loyal to a certain brand, which she buys regularly.

The habit-formation process in this case ended with the consumers becoming *brand loyal*. Brand loyalty is here the result of a subsequent simplification of an originally complex buying process, as knowledge and experience are being built up and the consumer finds out which product or brand is best suited to her needs.

Buying baby products for your first child is probably a high-involvement purchase, which explains that it is characterized by a high amount of external information search before habit formation sets in and simplifies the buying process. What then about habit formation regarding low-involvement products?

With low-involvement products, even when a product is being bought for the first time and no habit can have been formed, it is unlikely that consumers will engage in large amounts of external information search, as mentioned above. Before habits have been formed, buying decisions will be characterized by the use of simple choice heuristics, and, in some cases, even by decisions that are taken at random or that are pure trial purchases. Two mechanisms that can influence purchase of low-involvement products when no habit has been formed have received special attention. One is called the *mere exposure effect* and refers to the fact that, under low involvement, purchases can be affected by the simple fact that a product appears more familiar than others—because one has seen it on TV, or because it bears a well-known brand name (Janiszewski 1993). The other is called *emotional conditioning*—when a product has been paired many times in advertising with stimuli that elicit positive emotional responses, such as beautiful landscapes or sexy ladies, seeing the product on the shelf may evoke some of these emotional associations, which, in a low-involvement situation, may have an effect on purchase (Kroeber-Riel 1984).

Under low involvement, consumers are usually much less motivated to try out several products and process information until they have found the best product. Since differences between products are not regarded as very relevant anyhow, they may look only for a product that performs in a satisfactory manner. If the product does, the consumer may keep on buying the same product in the future—that means, the consumer has developed a habit of buying the product.

While habitual buying under low involvement looks quite like brand loyalty in a high-involvement situation, it is actually quite different—brand loyalty (under high involvement) is based on considerable experience and product knowledge, and on a strongly held opinion that the brand to which one is loyal is the best. Under low involvement, the product habitually bought has been satisfactory, but there is no strongly held opinion that it is the best, and there will be less knowledge about products. The reason a habit has been formed is mainly that keeping on buying the same product is an easy way of purchasing, because there is no need for a real decision. That is why it has been suggested that this type of habitual buying behaviour under low involvement be called *inertia*.

We can, therefore, distinguish between four types of buying decisions, depending on the degree of involvement and on whether a habit has been formed or not, as shown in Fig. 6.4: complex decisions, brand loyalty, limited decisions, and inertia (the terms and the figure were coined by Assael 1992). Each of these types of buying decisions has quite different marketing implications.

3.1 Complex decisions

We have here a motivated, interested, and probably critical consumer, who will look carefully at products and make a thorough evaluation. It is, therefore, crucial to adapt the quality of the product to what the consumer expects. We can inform about the product's advantages by adopting an informative type of market communication, because the consumer is interested in getting this information and will be willing to obtain and process things like brochures and other forms of product descriptions. Price is only one purchase criterion among others, and there will be a trade-off between quality and price, allowing better products to be priced higher. A well-advertised high-quality product can be distributed selectively, since the consumer will be willing to go for it.

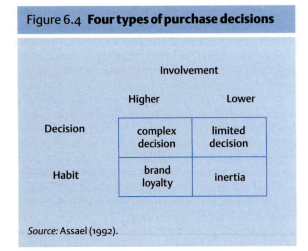

Figure 6.4 Four types of purchase decisions

	Involvement	
	Higher	Lower
Decision	complex decision	limited decision
Habit	brand loyalty	inertia

Source: Assael (1992).

3.2 Brand loyalty

This is the marketer's heaven: consumers who keep on buying our product, and who do so based on a conviction that our product is the best. This gives protection from competition and a degree of freedom on marketing parameters such as price and distribution—consumers will be willing to go for the product, and to pay a price premium.

3.3 Limited decisions

Here we have consumers who are not very interested in our products, and who have not developed habits of buying a particular product. Given the lack of interest, there is not so much point in praising the advantages of the product. But it is important to create awareness of the product by market communication and wide distribution, and to induce trial of the product by shelf placement, merchandising, and sales promotions. The product quality must be satisfactory, but the other marketing parameters have higher importance here compared to the first two types of purchases.

☞ 'Thus the first objective of any marketing communication campaign is to ensure adequate awareness levels amongst the target audience.' (Chapter 12, p. 273)

3.4 Inertia

When consumers have formed a habit of buying our product, it is important to support it, because it is not based on strong opinions. Continuous advertising to remind consumers of the product and broad distribution are ways of doing this (see Insert).

> **Creating awareness for a low-involvement product: Stimorol chewing gum**
>
> Within a few years, Stimorol Chewing Gum (produced by the Danish 'Dandy' company) had become the market leader in the growing Russian market for chewing gum. In 1997 Stimorol chewing gum was airing nation-wide commercials in Russia 5–6 times per day. It sponsored the Russian football league, now called the Stimorol league, the Stimorol brand name was on the players' clothing, the tickets, score boards, and programmes, and commercials were inserted into TV transmissions of the football matches. Stimorol had also sponsored the Russian ice-hockey team and the weather forecast on TV; it had arranged rock concerts and disco evenings at Moscow University.

High-involvement purchases are easier to deal with from a marketer's perspective than low-involvement purchases. It is, therefore, always worth thinking about whether consumer involvement with the product can be increased. Increasing involvement basically means differentiating the product in such a way that the consumer starts seeing important differences between competing products. Products like detergent were typical low-involvement products for most consumers until the late 1990s, when manufacturers found that some consumers become involved when detergents were differentiated with regard to their environmental consequences.

4 Consumer information processing

CONSUMERS are constantly subjected to new information about products, services, shops, and other matters relevant for their buying and consumption behaviour. Much of it is ignored, but some of it influences consumer behaviour. Understanding the processes by which consumers process information from the environment and use it to direct their own behaviour is a very important topic for marketers. We discuss four aspects of consumer information processing: attention and comprehension, storage in and retrieval from the memory, attitude formation, and inference processes and decision-making.

4.1 Attention and comprehension

It is a well-known fact both from psychological research and from everyday experience that attention is selective: of all the things going on around us, we perceive only a small part. In particular, much marketing information is not attended to: we walk past a billboard without noticing it, we are exposed to advertising on buses and in trains without perceiving it, we leaf through a newspaper or watch a TV show without being able, afterwards, to say which advertisements and commercials we have been exposed to. The human mind has mechanisms that prevent us from being overloaded with information, and that screen out most of the information that we are exposed to. Understanding these mechanisms helps when communicating with consumers.

Part of the selection process can be explained by the strength of the sensory impression made: large advertisements are more easily noticed than small ones, coloured ones more than black-and-white ones, loud music more than soft music. But other factors are at work, too. Most consumers remember incidences where their attention seems unconsciously guided by some kind of personal relevance criterion: when you consider buying a new car, for example, and you have narrowed your choice down to two alternatives, say a Nissan Micra and a Fiat Cinquecento, you start noticing Micras and Cinquecentos in the street much more often than before you considered buying them. Of course, their presence in the streets has not increased, and the sensory impression they emanate has not changed either, but somehow the fact that these objects are more relevant for you now increases their likelihood of passing the filter of selective attention.

Thus, two major factors are at work influencing the likelihood of a particular piece of information or a particular object passing the filter of selective attention: strength of the sensory impression and personal relevance. Fig. 6.5 shows a psychological model that integrates these two factors into explaining selective attention (Norman 1968; see also Grunert 1996). Whenever we are exposed to objects in our environment—cars in the street or

pictures in advertisements—the human mind subconsciously tries to link them to concepts in memory. Since we have earlier learned the concept of a Fiat Cinquecento, it is stored as a concept in our memory, and when we are exposed to one, the sensory impression made by the car causes our concept of the Fiat Cinquecento to be activated. This activation is called *external*, because it is caused by being exposed to an object in the environment, and it will be stronger the stronger the sensory impression. But, in addition to that, concepts can also receive *internal* activation, which mirrors the things our mind is preoccupied with at present. When we consider buying a Cinquecento, which is a major purchase, our mind is preoccupied with this purchase, and the concept of a Cinquecento will be internally activated. Selective attention is determined by the sum of both external and internal activation—that means, the stronger the sensory impression from the environment, and the more the sensory impression is related to something our mind is preoccupied with, the higher the chance of attention.

When marketers want to communicate with consumers, they are obviously interested in their information passing the filter of selective attention. The model in Fig. 6.5 suggests the two major ways in which this can be achieved.

First, we can increase the strength of the sensory impression made by our communication. This leads to all the common tricks of the advertising business—using more colours, larger advertisements, surprising gimmicks, and so on.

Secondly, we can try to communicate in such a way that the information will be relevant for the consumer at the time of exposure. One way of doing this is to select the right context. An advertisement for food will not be relevant for most consumers when placed in a newspaper, but will be relevant when placed in a gourmet magazine, since consumers' minds will be preoccupied with food when reading gourmet magazines. Another way is to adjust the content of the message itself. If we believe consumers to be involved with the purchase, there is a chance that the information we give about our product will be perceived as relevant and hence attended. But if consumers are believed to be uninvolved, we need to add other elements to our message that consumers will find relevant, even though they may be unrelated to the product. The use of celebrities in advertising is an attempt to add elements to a message that are relevant to the consumer public and that will,

Figure 6.5 A model of selective attention

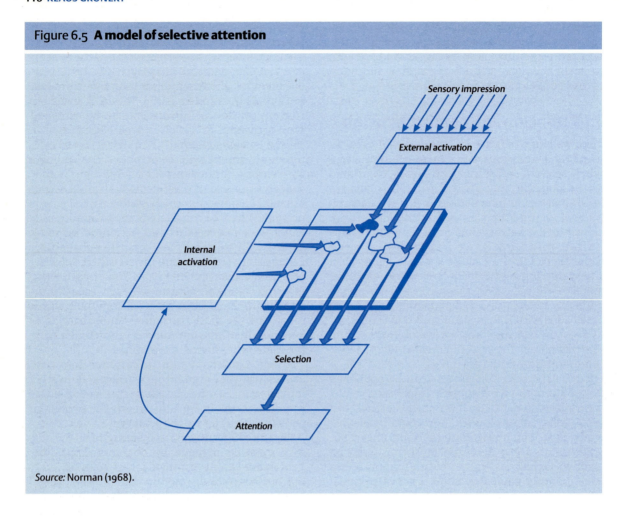

Source: Norman (1968).

therefore, increase the likelihood of the message passing the filter of selective attention (Petty *et al.* 1983).

4.2 Storage in and retrieval from the memory

Information from the environment that has passed the filter of selective attention is stored in the memory, from which it can later be retrieved for directing behaviour, like making a purchase decision. Storage in the memory consists of two interrelated components: comprehension and integration.

Comprehension means making sense of the new information. And in making sense of the new information we have to draw on existing information—that is, on the knowledge already stored in the memory. Most information about new products, for example, would be incomprehensible unless the product category were already known—consumers can tell kitchen tissue from toilet paper, and know its different uses, and therefore market communication does not have to communicate this to them.

This interaction of new and known information affects the way in which new information is integrated into existing knowledge in the memory, which can be called the 'given-new principle' (Clark and Haviland 1974). It basically says that incoming information from the environment—for example, from an advertisement—is dissected into what is already known (given) and what is new, and only what is regarded as new will be stored in the memory. The example in Fig. 6.6(a) will make this clear. Fig. 6.6(a) shows a common way of thinking about how knowledge is organized in the consumer memory—namely, as a network of nodes and links. The figure shows what a typical consumer associates with the concept 'chocolate': that it is brown, sweet, high in calories, and has a typical price range. Information about a new brand of chocolate ('Sweet'n'lite') will then be integrated into this network by storing only how the new brand differs from these com-

mon characteristics of chocolate. If the new brand is advertised as being a low-calorie, non-fattening chocolate with a price that is twice that for normal chocolate, this information will be added to the network, whereas information about brown colour or a sweet taste will not be added, because this is what the consumer commonly expects from chocolate.

What if we changed the positioning of our low-calorie sweet and advertised it not as a chocolate, but as a health food? The given-new principle would result in quite different changes to consumer knowledge. As Fig. 6.7(b) shows, our consumer expects health food to be expensive, have a bad taste, and be low in calories. The new information in this case is thus not the high price or the low calories, but instead the nice sweet taste.

Even though the example is hypothetical, it makes an important point. How consumers perceive our product depends both on our communication and on their previous knowledge and hence expectations about product categories. If we understand consumers' previous knowledge—what they typically associate with a chocolate or a health food—we can position our product relative to consumer expectations and design our product communication accordingly. In the example, we may think about whether a positioning as a chocolate or a health food is more advantageous.

Information that has been stored in the memory is available for retrieval at a later point in time—in principle at least, because, as everybody knows from experience, remembering information previously learned can sometimes be quite difficult. From the marketer's perspective, there is an interest in ensuring that our product and its positive aspects have a higher chance of being remembered in the context of a purchase situation than competing products. Remembering can be supported by 'retrieval cues'—elements or parts of the message originally learned. Logos on packages or in product displays, repeated major elements from advertising such as symbols or figures, or just the shape or name of the product can serve as retrieval cues, resulting in the consumer remembering things learned earlier about the product. This can be a personal experience, both positive and negative, and it can include moods and feelings, like remembering the feeling of sitting in a French street café while sipping a glass of Pernod when seeing the Pernod bottle in the supermarket at home. It can also be

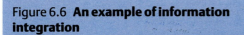

Figure 6.6 **An example of information integration**

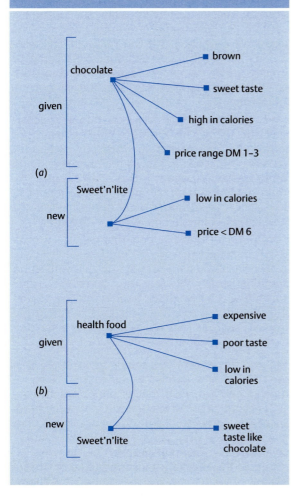

information from advertising, including celebrities, music, and images.

4.3 Attitude formation

Consumers use the information they have about products and services to form evaluations about them and to direct their behaviour towards them—for example, to buy or not to buy them. This relationship between knowing something about things, liking or disliking things, and behaving towards things is captured in the attitude concept. Attitude is one of the most central concepts in social psychology and in consumer behaviour. A common definition of an attitude is 'a learned disposition to react towards an object in a positive or negative manner' (Fishbein and Ajzen 1975).

Usually we assume that what we know about an object, like a product, determines our liking or disliking of the object, which in turn determines our behaviour, like buying or not buying. However, this is not always the case. As we saw above, low-involvement purchase behaviour is often experimental, which means that we might act first and then afterwards build up knowledge and form evaluations, based on experience (which can then determine future behaviour). Alternatively, we may spontaneously like a product and then find reasons for why we like it or not afterwards.

Most commonly in consumer behaviour, attitudes to products or services are explained by the product characteristics the product is perceived to have, and by the evaluation (positive or negative) of these characteristics, as shown in Fig. 6.7. In the example, a food product is perceived as very tasty (very positive evaluation), as moderately healthy (positive evaluation), as expensive (slightly negative evaluation), and as time-consuming to prepare (negative evaluation). The overall attitude towards the product is then explained as an average of the evaluations of these characteristics weighted by their certainty, as shown in the following formula (Fishbein 1963):

$$A_o = \sum_i b_i e_i$$

where:

A_o = attitude towards object o (positive–negative)

b_i = certainty of object o having characteristic i (certain–uncertain)

e_i = evaluation of the characteristic i (positive–negative)

It seems that many cases of attitude formation in a consumer-behaviour context can be described by the above formula (Sheppard *et al.* 1988). In marketing consumer goods, one is usually interested in consumers developing a positive attitude towards that product. By trying to relate consumers' attitude to the characteristics of the product they perceive and the evaluations of these characteristics, we can try to understand the reasons why consumers have a positive or negative attitude. In addition, we can devise ways in which the attitude can be changed into a more positive direction. It seems that there are three basic ways of changing consumer attitude, based on the formula above and the example in Fig. 6.7:

■ We can try to change the perception of the characteristic that is negatively evaluated. In the example in Fig. 6.7, 'time-consuming to prepare' is negatively evaluated. We can redesign the product so that it becomes less time-consuming to prepare, or we can suggest ways to the consumer in which preparation can become less time-consuming.

■ We can try to change the evaluation of the characteristic. Using a lot of time to prepare meals can be negative, but in certain situations it can also have positive aspects of social togetherness, doing things right, and being proud of the result. We could concentrate on communicating these positive aspects of spending time, hoping to change the evaluation into a more positive direction.

■ From the formula, we note that negatively evaluated characteristics can be compensated by positively evaluated characteristics in their impact on overall attitude. We can thus leave the 'time-consuming' characteristic as it is and try to add other, positively evaluated characteristics to the product, such as that the product has been produced organically/ecologically.

Of these three ways of influencing attitude, usually the first is regarded as the easiest. Here we know a characteristic that is important to consumers, and all we have to do is to adapt the product or the perception of the product. We do not have to change what people like or dislike, as we have to in the other two options.

Can we explain why consumers like or dislike certain characteristics of the product? Actually, we have already addressed that question when

Figure 6.7 **Attitude formation for a food product**

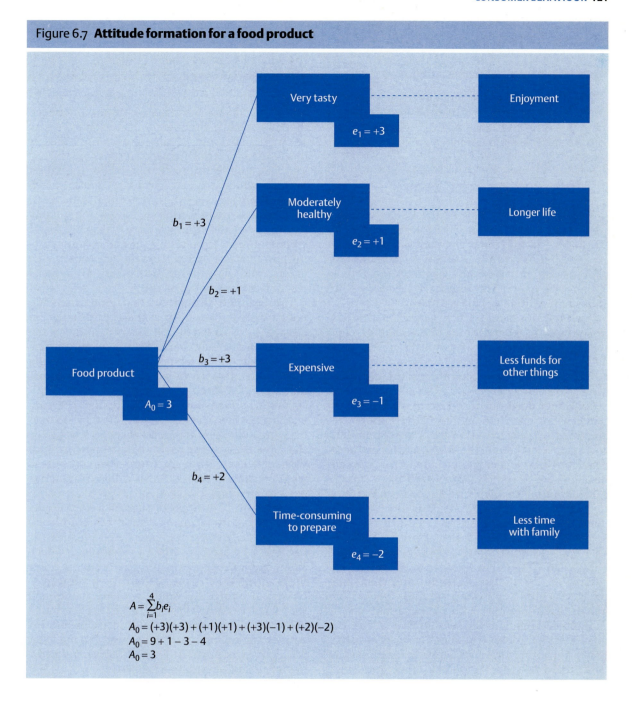

we discussed the means–end-chain concept earlier on in the chapter. There we said that consumers become interested in product characteristics to the extent that they perceive them to lead to self-relevant consequences, which in turn are perceived to help them attain important life values. Fig. 6.7 shows this for the food example: 'time-consuming' is negatively evaluated because it detracts from time spent with the family and consequently attainment of the value of close relationships with others; 'good taste' is positive because it leads to enjoyment and happiness. If we attempt to change the way in which consumers evaluate product characteristics, it will imply that we have to change the way in which they perceive that the product characteristic leads to self-relevant consequences (Peter *et al.*, in press).

4.4 Inference processes and decision-making

When consumers form attitudes, we expect these attitudes to have an impact on their behaviour. We expect a more positive attitude to increase the likelihood of purchase, and, given a set of choice options, we expect the consumer to choose the one where attitude is most positive.

However, this is only a first approximation. As we know from the beginning of the chapter, consumer choices can vary enormously in degree of deliberation, and the attitude concept will play a different role depending on how the decision-making process evolves.

Consumer decisions may extend over a longer time period, when various alternative options are identified, characteristics of them are found out, and knowledge about the implications of these characteristics is being built up. This can go through several rounds (Hayes-Roth 1982). A consumer wanting to buy living-room furniture may start by going to one shop, looking at several options, and being told by a sales clerk that Italian furniture is beautiful but that delivery is unreliable and the finish not always good. With this knowledge he goes to another shop where he ignores all the Italian furniture, and then proceeds to a third shop where he finds a beautiful Italian living-room set with perfect finish and a guaranteed home delivery within two weeks. He now revisits the two first shops to inspect other Italian furniture, stumbles across a Scandinavian living-room set that he thinks looks gorgeous, and orders it without even asking about delivery time.

This consumer identified alternatives, and was helped by a sales clerk in developing relevant choice criteria—namely, looks, delivery time, and finish. He learned to use country of origin as an indicator for all three of them. But this newly built

means–end chain linking 'Italian' to several relevant consequences is shaken by additional experience. He finally sees an option that is so ideal on one of his decision criteria (looks) that he completely ignores the others.

The example shows how consumers try to find indicators for what they really are interested in—that means, finding product characteristics on which to build means–end chains. This is one of the most tricky aspects of consumer behaviour, because consumers, not being specialists in the product area and lacking technical knowledge, often use seemingly irrational indicators. Well-documented examples are inferring reliability of an appliance from country of origin, taste of a piece of meat from visible fat and colour, washing power of a detergent from the presence of blue grains, and beautifying properties of a facial cream from its smell (Cox 1967).

The example also shows that evaluations are not always compensatory, as the attitude model in Section 4.3 assumed (Bettman 1979). In the example, an extraordinary performance on one particular criterion (looks) led to the consumer ignoring the others (this is called disjunctive decision-making). Likewise, it is common that unacceptable performance on a particular criterion leads to not considering the option at all, no matter which quality it has otherwise. This would be the case if a consumer said that any furniture with a delivery time of more than six weeks would be unacceptable (this is called conjunctive decision-making).

The furniture example is a case of a complex decision. As we know, many decisions are not complex, either because they are based on habit or because they are real, but low-involvement decisions. Habitual decisions use the brand or other forms of product identification for making purchases. In limited decisions, we have mentioned that choice heuristics are often used—simple rules that allow people to make decisions fast. Examples are buying what is cheapest, buying what is most well known, buying what a friend buys, buying what the salesman suggests.

Both complex decision-making and limited decision-making based on choice heuristics involve the formation of attitudes towards the products under consideration. However, in addition to own attitude, other factors will have an impact on the choice finally made. Two prominent factors are social factors and control factors.

Social factors refer to the fact that consumer decision-making is affected by others. Many purchase decisions are made in a family context (Kirchler 1995). Some are real joint decisions, whereas in other cases men and women have developed specialized roles where one takes the lead in making decisions in a particular product category. Children can have considerable influence on purchase decisions. With important decisions, the role of various family members in the overall decision process may be quite intricate: a child may take the initiative and make the original suggestion to buy a swimming pool for the garden, other family members indicate their interest, the wife collects information from various suppliers, the man and wife make a decision jointly, and the man finally goes out and buys the pool (Jensen 1991).

With purchases where the result is socially visible, the expected reactions of others such as colleagues and friends will also affect the decision (Brown and Reingen 1987). Such groups of others will serve as reference groups for these decisions. But reference groups may also be groups to which one has no direct social contact, but which serve as a standard or to which one aspires. Professional sports people can serve as reference groups for amateurs buying sports equipment.

Control factors refer to the fact that sometimes our intended behaviour is inhibited by forces beyond our control (Ajzen 1985). My preferred brand of beer is sold out, and therefore I have to buy something else. I really would like to buy a Geo Tracker, but it is not imported into Denmark. I would like to stop smoking, but I do not think it is something that is quite under my own control. I would like to prepare a rabbit for dinner, but I have no idea how to get one or how to prepare it.

Consumers' intentions to buy or not to buy a product or service are thus influenced by a host of factors in addition to their attitude towards the product. Social considerations play a large role, the social embeddedness of the purchase often plays a large role, and there may be factors both in the environment and in the consumer that result in the fact that a purchase basically regarded as desirable is not carried out (see Insert). In addition, buying is a dynamic process, and consumer attitudes may change in the course of the buying process. These factors must be understood in formulating effective marketing strategies.

A case of lack of control: fish for the family

Why don't consumers eat more fish in Central and Northern Europe, even though public authorities have untiringly proclaimed how healthy it is to eat fish? Consumer focus groups have indicated that most people actually have a quite positive attitude towards fish. They realize that it is healthy to eat fish, many consumers actually say that they enjoy the taste of fish, and they regard both the health and the taste as important ingredients for a good family life. Why don't they eat more of it? When analysing what consumers thought about buying and preparing fresh fish, it turned out that a major barrier was that fresh fish was perceived as difficult to get hold of, difficult to prepare, and difficult to eat. Consumers did not like to go to fishmongers, did not know recipes, and thought that preparing fresh fish was complicated and time-consuming. Some companies have picked this up and are starting to develop dishes that contain fresh fish, but have a higher degree of convenience. They sell through supermarkets, have the fish cut into serving-size portions, have them guaranteed boneless, and include quick recipes.

---

5 Values and lifestyle

As we discussed in connection with the means–end-chain concept (Fig. 6.3), we believe that consumers demand product and services because of the self-relevant consequences they believe these products to have for them, which in turn help in the fulfilment of life values. Life values are believed to provide the motivation for buying.

Life value is a central concept in social psychology. Life values have been characterized as desirable end states that motivate and direct behaviour across a broad variety of situations (Schwartz and Bilsky 1987). People's life values are usually characterized by a set of values, which differ in relative importance from person to person. Fig. 6.8 illustrates a system of values that has been shown to be applicable across many nations and cultures (Schwartz 1992). It characterizes people's life values by ten value domains, which can be ordered along two dimensions. One dimension refers to conservatism versus openness to change, whereas the other refers to self-enhancement

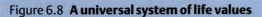

Figure 6.8 A universal system of life values

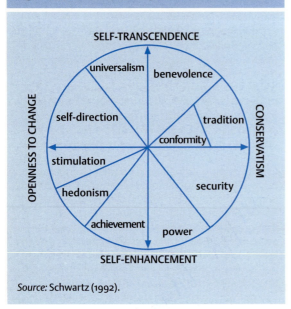

Source: Schwartz (1992).

(mastering others and the environment) versus self-transcendence (living in harmony with others and the environment). People with a high score on a particular value domain—for example, people for whom achievement is very important—also tend to have high scores on adjacent value domains, such as power and hedonism, and low ones on the opposite value domains, such as universalism and benevolence (see the positions on Fig. 6.8).

Because values are so abstract, their impact on consumer behaviour will usually be quite indirect. However, a number of more direct links can also be noted. People with high scores on universalism and benevolence tend to have more interest for products that are produced with care for the environment or for animal welfare (Grunert and Juhl 1995). People with high scores on self-direction and stimulation can be expected to have a more experimental, variety-seeking behaviour, and to be interested in products stimulating creativity. People with high scores on achievement, power, and security can be expected to like products that give them increased control over their lives. Finally, people with high scores on conformity and tradition will favour products adopted by others in the same social group, or that contribute to orderliness and cleanliness.

But the indirect effect of values on consumer behaviour is much more important. Consumers perceive possibilities in the world of goods and services, of shopping and consumption, that help them attain their life values. This goes not so much for individual products, as for consumption areas or broad product categories such as leisure, housing, travelling, eating and drinking, or clothing and beauty. Consumers tend to develop typical patterns in which they use products and services within these areas to attain life values. Consumers with high scores on self-direction and stimulation may attain these values by having a rich set of creative leisure activities, by exotic travelling, by experimental and creative eating and drinking, or by any combination of these. The way in which consumers use products and services in a certain area to attain their life values can also be called consumer lifestyle.

Lifestyle is a widely used concept in understanding consumers, and it is used in widely different ways (Anderson and Golden 1984). Formerly, there was an assumption that lifestyle is heavily affected by external constraints, such as income and working conditions, and that lifestyle is relatively congruent across areas of life and consumption—so that a consumer who is experimental and creative in leisure is equally experimental and creative in eating and drinking, in housing, and in clothing. But the importance of external constraints has diminished in the Western world, and it seems that consumers have less congruent lifestyles across consumption areas now than before.

Box 6.1 shows a classification of consumers based on their lifestyle in the area of food and drink (Brunsø *et al.* 1996). The various types distinguished clearly differ in the importance food has in attaining life values—for some consumers food and drink play a large role in attaining their life values, while other consumers attain their life values by different means. Among those consumers for whom food and drink are important, the life values to which they are supposed to contribute differ considerably, especially on the conservatism–openness to change dimension.

Quite clearly, the different types of consumers in Box 6.1 have to be addressed in different ways. They need different products, different ways of communication, and different ways of distribution. Lifestyle is a useful tool for segmentation that is not linked to individual concrete products, but transcends a class of products.

Box 6.1 Lifestyle-based segmentation in the food sector

Segment name	Segment characteristics	Marketing implications
The uninvolved food consumer	Uninterested in most aspects of food Not interested in quality Does not read product information Convenience important Heavy snacking Little planning Food not a family matter	Unstable shopping behaviour Little brand loyalty Few perceived differences between different food products Price as the major parameter
The careless food consumer	Resembles the uninvolved food consumer Is interested in novel products if they are convenient Buys spontaneously	Possibility for product differentiation by novelty New products should not be demanding Not likely to develop any great loyalty Constant stream of short-lived product variations probably best strategy
The conservative food consumer	Plans shopping and cooking No interest in new products or recipes Freshness and taste important Convenience not important, Take time for cooking Little snacking Food is a woman's task Security by traditional food major purchase motive	Interested in shopping for food Wants predictability and to avoid change Strong preferences for products and shops, difficult to overcome through new products Maintain traditional products
The rational food consumer	High use of product information and speciality shops High degree of planning All quality aspects very important Heavy use of organic food	Most receptive to better-quality food products Easy to inform about product improvements Quality in relation to price Highly critical consumers
The adventurous food consumer	Novelty and looking for new ways very important High involvement with cooking Convenience not important, Cooking is a task for the whole family Self-fulfilment and social aspects of food more important than security	Needs to be stimulated to creativity Must encourage self-expression, creativity, and social togetherness Possibility for experimenting in cooking important Interested in exotic food products, but not exotic pre-cooked meals

Source: Brunsø *et al.* (1996).

6 Culture and cross-cultural differences

Most people working with consumer behaviour agree that it is culturally ingrained. Culture is a somewhat elusive concept used to describe differences between and similarities within groups of people. Such differences and similarities may arise between nations, sometimes also between larger groups, such as language areas or cultures, as when comparing European culture to Asian culture, and sometimes also between groups within nations, as between the north and south of Germany (in the latter case, sometimes the term *subculture* is also used to express that we deal with cultures within a culture).

The term *culture* is used to describe what people within a group have in common (Peter *et al.*, in press). Meanings, attitudes, values, and beliefs shared by a group of people are considered to be a part of culture. For example, cultures can be characterized by the relative importance of the value domains depicted in Fig. 6.8—among other things, it has been shown that Asian cultures tend to have higher scores on value domains related to self-enhancement, whereas European cultures tend to have higher scores on value domains related to self-transcendence. The term *culture* is also used to describe common ways of acting or reacting in certain situations—like the way one greets a stranger, the way one enters a house that is not one's own, the way one deals with one's children. Specific behaviours that have special cultural importance attached to them are also called rites. Rites are, for example, associated with festivities (trimming a Christmas tree, throwing rice after a newly wed couple), but rites also pervade everyday life including consumer behaviour, as we will see below.

Culture is learned, and the process of learning the shared beliefs, values, and behaviours of a culture is called socialization (Kuhlmann 1983). Much of socialization occurs during childhood, and parents, peers, and institutions such as schools and the Church have a major impact on it. However, socialization is considered a lifelong process. Interesting socialization processes occur when people move from one cultural setting to another. Many people do that briefly when going on vacation, and some do it more permanently when emigrating or being posted to a foreign country for a number of years. They find that their own cultural habits are in contrast with the ones of their environment, and they have to balance adapting to the environment with sticking to their own cultural values.

Consumer behaviour is related to culture and cultural differences in several ways. First, major rites usually involve consumption activities. Christmas involves giving presents. It usually involves eating special dishes, which vary from country to country. Children in Germany get their shoes filled with sweets on 5 December, whereas Danish children get 'calendar presents' every Sunday in Advent. Secondly, consumption activities have developed their own rites. A common rite is tasting wine in a restaurant. It is a behavioural sequence where the restaurant demonstrates care for the customer and the customer demonstrates a knowledge of wine and fine living. Very rarely does a customer reject a wine as unsatisfactory, and when he or she does the waiter may be offended because the customer deviates from the rite. Thirdly, many mundane aspects of consumer behaviour, which do not have the symbolic content of rites, nevertheless are quite culturally ingrained. This goes for how people react to advertising, how they shop, how they judge the quality of a product, how they use a product, and how they handle prices.

A few examples will suffice. In a country like Sweden, consumers have become so used to sales promotions that many will not buy anything that is not on sale, whereas consumers in Germany are not used to this and therefore have not developed the same kind of behaviour. But consumers and dealers in Germany find it appropriate to negotiate the price when buying a car, which consumers and car dealers in Denmark find quite inappropriate. A Danish exporter of Danish pastry found that his product is eaten for breakfast in Denmark, with afternoon coffee in France, and as a snack while on the move in the UK. Moreover, he found that French consumers liked the product light and crisp, British consumers liked it doughy and with fruit fillings, and Danish consumers liked it glistening and sweet. British consumers seem to like subtle humour in advertising, French consumers sophistication and puns, and German consumers slice-of-life settings.

Cultural differences in consumer behaviour present obvious hazards for the exporting manufacturer. Taking into consideration economies of scale, and possibly influenced by discussions about global marketing strategies, manufacturers may want to sell the same product both on their domestic market and when exporting, and they may even want to use the same packaging and the same advertising. While this may work for products with a high degree of standardization (hamburgers) or for products aimed at niche markets that can be found internationally (expensive watches), in many other cases it can lead to costly failures.

Understanding cultural differences is, therefore, an important task in international consumer-goods marketing (see Insert). The traditional instrument for understanding cultural differences is ethnographic research—living in the foreign culture for an extended period of time and trying to get an in-depth understanding of that culture. Since this is time-consuming and costly, other ways are used as well. One prominent approach is to study the foreign culture's media, based on the assumption that media are an ex-

pression of culture. Another prominent approach is to do survey research, where consumers in several cultures are asked about, for example, their perceptions of and wants with regard to certain products. Both approaches have the possible pitfall that the cultural framework of the initiator of the study (a manufacturer, a market-research company, a scientist) may form the study and the interpretation of the results. Researchers in ethnography and in cross-cultural psychology have developed methods to avoid this. Some of the simpler ones are conducting such investigations as a collaboration between people rooted in the different cultures.

7 The future

IN marketing practice, people sometimes say that consumers have become increasingly erratic and therefore unpredictable. Consumers say one thing and do another, which makes consumer research, which is largely interview- and survey-based, unreliable.

The diagnosis is at least partly correct. This follows from the fact that in the Western world consumers' discretionary incomes have been rising for decades, giving consumers more freedom in allocating their funds. Also, in many cultures, external pressures towards specific types of consumption, especially status-related consumption, have become less, and this also gives consumers more freedom in allocating their funds.

The conclusion that consumer behaviour cannot be understood or analysed is wrong, however. Just because consumers have both more options and more means does not mean their behaviour is random. For all we know, consumer behaviour is purposeful and goal-directed. But purposes and goals become more diverse, and they no longer correlate as well with, for example, consumers' income, age, profession, and education, as they did in the 1960s.

The conclusion, therefore, should be that understanding consumers requires use of sophistication, in terms of both theories applied and methods used. Just asking consumers whether they are in favour of products produced with due concern for animal welfare, and cross-tabulating the answers with all conceivable demographics, has never been a good way of doing consumer research, but it will be even less appropriate in the

Introducing 'After Eight' to foreign cultures

In the early 1960s After Eight, thin chocolate-covered mints, was introduced by Rowntree (now Nestlé). The product was positioned as a very British product, with advertising themes emphasizing the style of an old English country house, with butler, Rolls Royce, and finely laid tables. Many people have wondered how Rowntree could successfully introduce a product so essentially British to, for example, the French, to whom the combination of chocolate and peppermint as an after-dinner treat was almost sacrilege; or to the Germans, to whom the typical English after-dinner gathering did not mean anything at all. Nestlé decided to use one international advertising agency and its subsidiaries in Europe for the task. Why, one might ask, could the UK commercials not simply be taken as they stood, and dubbed into the local language, thereby saving a considerable amount of money? At the time, the answer was simple. If, in addition to introducing the new habit of having mint chocolate after dinner, the advertising had contained dinner tables or picnics that did not look like the ones that continental consumers were accustomed to, the audiences could not have been expected to identify emotionally with the situations that the commercials presented.

Source: Rijkens (1992).

future. But if we try to understand why some consumers are interested in animal welfare (because they have high scores on self-transcendence values), how they perceive the animal-welfare aspects of existing production methods, and how the animal-welfare aspect trades off with other product characteristics (such as taste, convenience, and price), then we have gained insight that is valuable for the marketer. For this type of sophisticated consumer research, the future demand is likely to rise.

8 **Summary**

THIS chapter has introduced consumer behaviour as an important concern for companies connected with manufacturing consumer goods. We have introduced a simple model of the consumer decision-making process which can be used to analyse all forms of purchases. We have distinguished types of purchases based on the degree of consumer involvement and based on whether purchases are made habitually or not, and discussed the implications these types have for the design of the marketing mix. We then went through the major aspects of consumer information processing—how consumers learn from the environment about products and services, how they store this information in their memory, and how they use this information in attitude formation and decision-making.

We then introduced the concept of life values to understand what motivates consumers to buy one thing and ignore another. We looked at the social context of consumer behaviour and introduced the concept of lifestyle to describe how consumers use their consumption-related activities to attain life values. We closed with a discussion of the cultural determinants of consumer behaviour and means to understand cultural differences.

Further reading

Bettman, J. R. (1979), *An Information Processing Theory of Consumer Choice* (Reading, Mass.: Addison-Wesley).

Bloch, P. H., Sherrell, D. L., and Ridgway, N. M. (1986), 'Consumer Search: An Extended Framework', *Journal of Consumer Research*, 13: 119–26.

East, R. (1993), 'Investment Decisions and the Theory of Planned Behaviour', *Journal of Economic Psychology*, 14: 337–75.

Grunert, S. C., and Juhl, H. J. (1995), 'Values, Environmental Attitudes, and Buying Organic Food', *Journal of Economic Psychology*, 16: 39–62.

Gutman, J. (1982), 'A Means–End Chain Model Based on Consumer Categorization Processes', *Journal of Marketing*, 46/2: 60–72.

Kaas, K. P. (1982), 'Consumer Habit Forming, Information Acquisition, and Buying Behavior', *Journal of Business Research*, 10: 3–15.

Kroeber-Riel, W., and Weinberg, P. (1996), *Konsumentenverhalten* (Munich: Vahlen).

Laurent, G., and Kapferer, J.-N. (1985), 'Measuring Consumer Involvement Profiles', *Journal of Marketing Research*, 22: 41–53.

McCracken, G. (1986), 'Culture and Consumption: A Theoretical Account of the Structure and Movement of the Cultural Meaning of Consumer Goods', *Journal of Consumer Research*, 13: 71–84.

Peter, J. P., Olson, J. C., and Grunert, K. G. (in press), *Consumer Behaviour and Marketing Strategy* (European edn.; Maidenhead: McGraw-Hill).

Solomon, M. R., Askegaard, S., and Bamossy, G. (in press), *Consumer Behaviour* (European edn.; London: Prentice Hall).

Discussion questions

1 Find four examples of consumer-purchase decisions that cover the four types shown in Fig. 6.4, and characterize them in terms of problem recognition, search, evaluation of alternatives, purchase, and outcome.

2 Find a low- and a high-involvement product and speculate about consumers' means–end chains with regard to these products.

3 Do you think there are products where consumers never form habits in buying them? Give some examples and characterize the way in which consumers seek information about these products.

4 Summarize briefly how advertising to involved consumers should differ from advertising to non-involved consumers.

5 Assume a manufacturer finds that consumer decision-making for his product is mainly determined by social factors and control factors, as compared to the buyer's own attitude. What are the implications for marketing strategy?

6 Find examples of products that appeal mainly to the value domains tradition, hedonism, self-stimulation, and benevolence. Give some advice on how to market them.

7 Going back to the butter-cookie example at the beginning of the chapter—what would you recommend the manufacturers do?

SCA Mölnlycke is the Swedish producer of the well-known Libero diapers, Libresse sanitary towels, and o.b. Fleur tampons. In Scandinavia, the company holds a market share of approximately 50 per cent. When it comes to marketing, SCA Mölnlycke prefers to reach its customers with more selective tools than just TV advertising. The company places emphasis on more qualified and personal advice and favours information to and dialogue with its customers. This attitude is reflected in the marketing strategy of their Libero diapers in Scandinavia.

The health-care system is used to get in touch with the target group. For twenty-seven years in a row, SCA Mölnlycke has published a booklet called 'Pregnancy and Birth—the Newborn Boby', which the midwife gives the parents-to-be the first time they attend an antenatal control routine. The booklet contains factual, non-promotional information about pregnancy, birth, and the time immediately afterwards.

Not until halfway through the book does the reader encounter any promotion for the company's products. Even then, SCA Mölnlycke stresses that it does not want to intrude on the readers with its information. Therefore the pages with product information have been sealed. It is then up to the reader to decide whether he or she wants to skip this section or to cut open the pages and read about the products. By showing this lack of importunity, SCA Mölnlycke hopes to obtain an image of credibility.

In the booklet SCA Mölnlycke offers membership of the Libero Baby Club, which sends samples, gifts, and letters with information to the parents as long as the children use diapers. To become a member, the mother needs to fill out a card attached to the book and return it to SCA Mölnlycke. By joining the Club, the parents receive samples of Libero diapers, a bib, a baby mobile, and for the mother a cassette with exercises for the pelvis floor and samples of Libresse sanitary towels. By far the greater part of the mothers-to-be respond to the offer.

The sample package arrives around the time of the birth and SCA Mölnlycke encloses a letter with good advice to the new parents combined with information on Libero's Newborn diapers. It explains how Libero Newborn diapers are designed specifically to meet the characteristics of the newborn baby.

In the letter, SCA Mölnlycke further informs the customer that, having bought a pack of Libero diapers, he or she can cut out a small coupon and send it to the company. In return, the customer gets another booklet about becoming a family or simply a refund. Besides that, SCA Mölnlycke offers a nursing bra and breast pads at favourable prices. Finally, there are some questions to be answered about the customer's satisfaction with the product and probability of repurchase.

If it is the customer's second child, the information material is adjusted to the different situation, addressing the relationship between the parents and their first and now older child. By returning the coupon, the customer receives either a rattle or the booklet 'I Also Want to be a Baby' for the elder child.

From the database of Libero Baby Club members, the company has addresses of their target group which form the basis of later direct mail and analyses of consumer satisfaction. Every now and then, SCA Mölnlycke informs their customers that the average baby will now need to advance to a larger Libero diaper category. Every letter contains both an offer, in the form of toys or a book, which is available in return for a coupon cut out from a pack of diapers, and some questions to be answered concerning satisfaction with Mölnlycke products.

The satisfaction expressed by the customer determines how the communication between SCA Mölnlycke and the customer will continue. If the customer expresses dissatisfaction, the company will respond by advising on what could be the reason for the experienced unsatisfactory product performance. If the answer is positive, the communication will just continue regularly until the child reaches the age of $2^1/_2$ and usually stops using diapers.

Discussion questions

1 Which of the phases of the consumer purchase process does SCA Mölnlycke try to influence by its promotional strategy?

2 Analyse how SCA Mölnlycke tries to overcome the barriers of selective attention and integration.

3 Do you think the promotional strategy employed by SCA Mölnlycke would work in your culture? In which type of culture would you recommend a different strategy?

Chapter 7
Organizational Buying Behaviour

Bernard Cova and Robert Salle

Objectives

The objectives of this chapter are:

1 to describe the organizational buying process and some models of this process;

2 to identify the main influences on organizational buying behaviour;

3 to distinguish the factors influencing organizational buying behaviour;

4 to consider the role of the purchasing function in modern organizations.

1 Introduction

FACED with the challenges presented by competition, the business practices of industrial firms have developed a great deal since 1980. The intervening period of time has seen many changes, among which the following have been of particular importance: the growth of outsourcing, the increasing power enjoyed by purchasing departments within companies, and the importance given to developing partnerships with suppliers. These three factors are sufficient to point out how important it is for a company to understand the decision-making process of industrial organizations in order to define and undertake the relevant marketing actions.

2 The organizational-buying-behaviour process

BUSINESS-TO-BUSINESS marketing is based on the understanding of organizational buying behaviour. Researchers and experts have invested a great deal of effort in this study and they have tried and developed an organizational-buying-behaviour model with the intention of structuring marketing approach. As early as the end of the 1960s and the beginning of the 1970s, various models were developed in the USA (Robinson *et al.* 1967; Webster and Wind 1972; Sheth 1973). They are at the core of the founding models of organizational buying behaviour. They usually include the various phases of the buying process, the members involved, and the decisions made in each phase. These founding models are explained in detail in many marketing textbooks, but their relevance seems to have decreased over time (Cova and Salle 1992). We have, therefore, chosen to refer to them briefly and to point out the recent developments of the organizational buying behaviour.

2.1 Buying decision phases

The founding models (of the 1970s) vary in complexity, but they are nevertheless similar in that they break down the buying process into the five following main phases:

- need recognition;
- specifications definition;
- search for suppliers;
- proposals evaluation;
- supplier selection.

However, these phases no longer seem to express exactly how rich and complex the organizational buying behaviour process has become. The innovations and changes brought by other models developed in the 1980s and 1990s need to be taken into account.

The supplier choice model developed by Woodside and Vyas (1987), based on an analysis of six American factories' buying behaviour with regard to raw materials and components, breaks down the buying process into five updated phases:

- preparation of the request for quotations (RFQ);
- search for potential suppliers;
- evaluation and selection of approved vendors for bidding products;
- analysis of quotes received;
- evaluation and selection of supplier(s).

This model adds the phase, 'Evaluation and selection of approved vendors for bidding products', which leads to the setting-up of the 'approved vendors' list'. This phase has been the focus of many researchers' attention during the 1990s. Thus Jackson and Pride (1986), with a sample of 333 buyers members of the US National Association of Purchasing Management (NAPM), showed that a majority (63.4 per cent) used a bidders' list (also called an approved vendors' list, an approved bidders' list, or an accepted producers' list). Descriptive research both in the USA and in Europe shows that the search for suppliers leads to the development of a shortlist of suitable sources, from which a quotation should be requested.

The Matbuy model (Möller 1986), with a sample of six Finnish computer firms, is based on a survey of the process of selecting components suppliers. It includes the eight following phases:

- purchase initiation;
- evaluation criteria development;
- information search;
- supplier definition for RFQ;
- evaluation of quotations;
- negotiation;
- supplier choice;
- choice implementation.

This model confirms the first phases of the buying process suggested by the supplier choice model and introduces the fourth phase, 'supplier definition for RFQ', which results in the creation of the 'accepted producers' list'. Additionally, it introduces the phase 'negotiation' with the selected suppliers after an evaluation of their proposal. By emphasizing that the final selection is not based solely on the submitted proposals but involves negotiating with one or more tenderers, the Matbuy model confirms Dale and Powley's study (1985). Four out of the five British firms they studied negotiated all the proposals received; the fifth one, a public-sector firm, based its choice only on the written proposals. Likewise, a study based on a sample of fifty-eight buyers, members of the Compagnie des Dirigeants d'Approvisionnements et Acheteurs de France (the Company of Purchasing Managers and Buyers of France), showed that many of them (84 per cent) negotiated after receiving the tenders (Cova and Salle 1992).

The founding models developed in the 1970s can be compared with the updated ones of the 1980s on the basis of their breaking-up the buying process into various phases (Box 7.1).

2.2 The buying centre

Industrial marketers have long been aware that some buying decisions are not made by the purchasing agent alone but occur with the involvement of other members of the customer's organization. Industrial sellers are sometimes informed when such instances occur, or it may become obvious from the actions of the purchasing agent. Often, however, the problem is in knowing when such decisions will be the result of group consensus, the make-up of the group, and whom to target within the group to maximize the effectiveness of the offer (see Insert). The understanding of such group-procurement decisions is the study of buying centres.

The buying centre consists of those people in the organization who are involved either directly or indirectly in the buying process. In the founding models, the roles of the members of the

Box 7.1 **Stages of organizational-buying-behaviour models: A comparison**

Original models (1960s–1970s)	Supplier choice model (1987)	Matbuy model (1986)
Need recognition	—	Purchase initiation
Specifications definition	RFQ preparation	Evaluations criteria formation
Suppliers' search	Potential suppliers' search	Information search
—	Evaluation and selection of approved vendors for bidding product	Supplier definition for RFQ
Proposals evaluation	Analysis of received quotes	Evaluation of quotations
—	—	Negotiations
Supplier selection	Evaluation and selection of supplier(s)	Supplier choice
—	—	Choice implementation

Bringing multiple buying influences together

When Klix tried to sell their new drinks dispensing trolley to hospitals, they found that to have it accepted it was necessary to deal with three distinct buying influences in the hospital. First, there were the hospital catering managers, who calculated that it cost 3p to provide a cup of tea from the traditional teapot while Klix's own figures costed a cup of tea from their trolley at 4.5p. However, the manager in charge of domestic staff, who was responsible for the payroll cost of porters, tea ladies, cleaning staff, etc., found the Klix drinks trolley attractive. This was because using the Klix trolley would reduce costs, as dispensing tea from the trolley was quicker than using a teapot. Finally, the nurses showed some dislike of disposable plastic cups, seeing the traditional teacup as more 'homely' and friendly.

buying centre are those of user, buyer influencer, decider, and gatekeeper (Webster and Wind 1972).

■ *Users* are defined as members of the organization who use the purchased products and services.

■ *Buyers* are those with formal responsibility and authority for contracting with suppliers.

■ *Influencers* are those who influence the decision process directly or indirectly by providing information and criteria to evaluate alternative buying options.

■ *Deciders* are those with authority to choose among alternative buying options.

■ *Gatekeepers* are those who control the flow of information and materials into the buying centre.

Some researchers, however, now add the role of 'initiators' to the previously mentioned ones. The initiator does not always belong to the buying organization, since the organization may not be aware that it has a problem or may be unsure of how to solve it. Companies often rely on the technical knowledge of their suppliers, and, when this is the case, a member of the supplier's organization may initiate the buying process by pointing out a current problem.

This is often the case in project activities. The supplier creates the concept of the project, carries out the feasibility study, gathers the financing package, and identifies the actor that will later become its customer. All this takes place over an extended period of time and includes various actors in a logic of involvement. The project then clearly becomes a technical and social construct initiated by the supplier and raising the interest of the various parties involved inside and outside the buying centre. The buying centre for projects can, therefore, often include participants from outside the organization such as consultants, engineering firms, government officials, etc., that make up a network of actors around the buying organization.

Typically though, participants in the buying process, regardless of their role (user, buyer, influencer, decider, gatekeeper, or initiator), perform their activities as employees of the buying organization. Their actions will therefore be evaluated, and part of all their formal compensation will depend on the outcome of this evaluation process. Purchasing activities are also likely to account for at least some of the informal rewards of the buying-centre participants (Anderson and Chambers 1985). The fact that each individual (especially when they come from different organizational levels) may be evaluated and rewarded according to different performance criteria is a key issue to the functioning of the buying centre. It should be interpreted by a supplier as a major opportunity to use various scenarios to influence the buying centre. Each scenario will depend on the agenda, potential risk, and rewards of the members of the buying centre acting as individuals with sometimes contradictory motives but linked by the same group dynamic of solving a buying problem (Anderson and Chambers 1985).

2.3 Decisions at each phase of the buying process

Organizational buyers are subject to a wide variety and complexity of buying motives and rules of selection. The work of Woodside and Vyas (1987) reveals that the following buying pattern was used by US companies during the 1980s:

- A relatively stable set of selection rules applies, regardless of the product being bought or the firms involved.
- A conjunctive rule is used by the buyer to disqualify any unsuitable supplier at the beginning of the buying process.
- Then, price becomes a major criteria and candidates are disqualified on the basis of a disjunctive rule. The remaining suppliers are typically those whose prices do not exceed the best price offered by more than 6 per cent.
- The number of accepted tenders varies greatly but is always higher than three. It may go up to sixteen.
- Most of the time, the final selection is made just after the analysis of the submitted tenders. Some-

times, however, a negotiation will take place with the suppliers (between two and four candidates) in order to reach the final decision.

Möller (1986) presents the results of a study of the buying pattern used by European companies in the 1980s:

- Buyers try to use stable supplier evaluation criteria. This drive for the use of constant evaluation criteria does not lead through to their mechanistic or uncreative application. Depending on the buying market situation, the application forms and the relative importance of the criteria used can vary considerably.
- In the early phases of the buying process, the technical dimension and quality are critical criteria. They are used in a typically conjunctive sense to divide up potential suppliers into acceptable/non-acceptable sets. A compensatory approach dominates the final supplier choice, so, if other criteria are clearly above the threshold levels, price will be weighted more heavily.
- The buying process is almost always initiated through routinized internal channels. Because of external turbulence, the process is sometimes initiated during the contract term.
- The primary information source is the company buying records and other sources are considerably less important.
- Whenever possible, a testing sample is requested from a new supplier being considered.
- Requests for quotation are seldom sent to more than six potential suppliers, based on the assumption that the evaluation costs would exceed the marginal benefits of a greater group of candidates. Active search for new suppliers is a rare occurrence.

The buying decision-making process appears to be a heuristic exercise in programming. It applies a series of rules to reduce the alternatives to a number the buyer can cope with, and to minimize the element of uncertainty inherent in making a buying decision.

2.4 A global model

The main contribution of the Matbuy model is the dynamic combination of the various phases with the different participants in the decision-making

Box 7.2 **A detailed model of organizational buying behaviour**

Purchase stage	Type of decision	Departments involved[a]	Problem faced and tasks involved
Purchase initiation	Whether or not a purchase is needed to solve problem	Any department in the organization may identify a need for purchase	How to organize for unplanned action
Determination of evaluation criteria	Choosing and weighting the choice criteria and setting threshold values for each	Production; Buying; Finance; R&D	How to integrate the criteria chosen and resolve potential conflicts between criteria
Information search	What sources of information to use and when to terminate the search for more information	Buying; Production; R&D; Finance	How to organize the evaluation of information
Supplier definition for RFQ	How many potential suppliers to invite to quote	Buying; Production; R&D; Finance	How to organize the selection of suppliers from those submitting quotes
Evaluation of quotations	Check quotations against specification and choose supplier(s) with whom to open negotiations	Buying; Production; R&D; Finance	Evaluating whether the choice criteria are adequate
Negotiations	Negotiation procedures and strategy. Who should be involved	Buying	How to organize the negotiations and conflict resolution procedures
Supplier choice	Select supplier(s) and determine quantity to be purchased from each supplier	Buying; Production; and Finance	How to organize the application of selection rules
Choice implementation	Inform those suppliers not accepted	Buying	Organize the monitoring of the delivery of the product

[a] The departments referred to are merely illustrative. The number and names of departments involved in any particular purchase will vary from one organization to another, and also within an organization, depending on the exact type of purchase being considered.

Source: adapted from the MATBUY Model (Möller 1986).

process and with the different criteria and selection rules used in the process (see Box 7.2). In each phase, the Matbuy model includes:

- the type of decision to be made;
- the different departments of the buying firm involved;
- the problems faced and the tasks involved.

This model tries to cover the main problems and conflicts that can potentially emerge during each phase.

It gives marketers a way to focus their efforts on the critical phases knowing *who* is making *what decisions* based on *which criteria.*

3 Risk and uncertainty— the driving forces of organizational buying behaviour

Many studies have pointed out that the level of risk or uncertainty associated with a given buying situation is a factor explaining organizational buying behaviour.

In these studies, two different points of view have been adopted successively. The first one is focused on understanding how a customer comes to a decision and behaves through the concepts of uncertainty or risk. The second one is centred on the actions undertaken by the supplier given the customer's behaviour.

3.1 The importance of the risk factor in organizational buying behaviour

The risk level depends on the characteristics of the buying situation faced by the customer. According to Johnston and Lewin (1994), when the risk level associated with the buying situation faced by a customer increases, the following occurs:

■ The buying centre becomes larger and more complex. Participants from a larger number of different departments become involved. They tend to be more experienced and to come from a more senior organizational level.

■ Price becomes a relatively less important criterion in the decision-making.

■ Members of the buying centre conduct a more extensive information search (especially during the initial phases of the decision-making process).

■ The probability of conflicts occurring between the members of the buying centre increases. The greater importance of the outcomes and the conflict between many participants each with their own motives explain this greater potential for conflict.

■ The negotiation between supplier and customer is collaborative and orientated towards problem-solving. The existence of a relationship between supplier and customer facilitates this problem-solving approach.

In their study, Hakansson, Johanson, and Wootz (1976) focus on the relationship between a decision and the uncertainty associated with it from the customer's point of view. The buying situation faced by a customer can be characterized by the following three combined dimensions of uncertainty:

■ The need uncertainty relates to the difficulty that customers find in expressing exactly the nature of their need. When this type of uncertainty is high, the customers interact with suppliers they know and with which they feel comfortable. They are more involved in their relationship with the supplier and include internal and external experts and specialists in the decision-making process.

■ The market uncertainty results from the existence and nature of the alternative supply sources available to the customer. This type of uncertainty depends on the characteristics of the supply market: the differences between suppliers (market heterogeneity) and the evolution of these differences over time (market dynamic). Faced with a high market uncertainty, the buying firm will have contact with a greater number of suppliers. Decision-makers can also specialize in function of these markets.

■ The transaction uncertainty depends on the customer's ability to anticipate how the transaction will work, mainly the product delivery and the mode of resolution. Different languages, technologies, and cultures in each organization and the existence or not of standardized procedures allowing faster action influence this mode of resolution. When transaction uncertainty is high, the buying firm uses several suppliers, is more sensitive to delivery questions, and more involved with the suppliers before making the final decision.

The supplier can influence the degree of perceived uncertainty by the buyer along the three above-described dimensions and cause certain desired behavioural reactions. The supplier can use the information transmitted to the customer and implement certain actions in order to increase or decrease the degree of uncertainty depending on the chosen tactic.

In order to function, an organization needs to gain access to resources from suppliers. The degree of risk perceived by this organization will depend on the impact of these resources on its activity, and their characteristics, accessibility, and availability on the supply market in the short, medium, and long term. The organization will implement short-, medium-, and long-term actions to control or decrease these risks. The risk perceived by the customer in the short, medium, and long term is, therefore, considered as a driving force of his buying behaviour. By understanding the sources of the perceived risks and how they are reflected in the actions implemented by a customer, a supplier can adapt his own actions (Salle and Silvestre 1992).

3.2 A typology of risks

The risks perceived by the customer result from a combination of the characteristics of various factors: the transaction he is involved in, his relationships with the supplier, and his position *vis-à-vis* the supply market (Fig. 7.1).

A distinction can be made between three kinds of risks. First, there are the risks associated with the characteristics of the transactions. The level of risk perceived by the customer depends on the complexity and potential outcomes of the problem to be solved during these transactions. This type of risk includes various dimensions: the tech-

nical risks, the risks resulting from the availability of the products and services purchased, the risks depending on the customer's ability to use the products and services purchased properly, and the financial risks.

Secondly, the risks associated with the characteristics of the relationship between the customer and the supplier that results from the successive transactions between both parties condition the climate of current and future exchanges between the customer and the supplier and therefore the behaviour of the customer during the transactions. These risks reflect the customer's questions regarding the supplier's ability and willingness to follow up on his offer (products, services, price, logistic) and to adapt it to the changing needs of the customer without infringing on his independence. Some organizations perceive the existence of a tight relationship between customers and suppliers as a situation of dependence, while others see in it a source of security and of progress. There are, therefore, two kinds of risks resulting from the characteristics of the relationship between a customer and a supplier: the risk of becoming dependent and the risk resulting from the supplier's involvement in the relationship.

Thirdly, there are the risks resulting from the customer's position *vis-à-vis* the supply market. The customer will seek to establish, maintain, or improve his position through his purchasing strategy. The customer's objective is to secure and improve his performance *vis-à-vis* the supply market. In order to do so, he will manage in a medium- and long-term perspective relationships with his current and potential suppliers to secure various supply alternatives. The customer's buying behaviour during any transaction will, therefore, be influenced by his purchasing strategy.

👉 '... the role of price in the purchasing process may differ, depending upon the type of product, the repetitive nature of the purchase, and the parties involved (buying group versus individual professional purchaser).' (Chapter 10, p. 221)

The members of the buying centre are aware of the risks associated with the characteristics of the transactions, with the relationship with the supplier, and with the customer's position *vis-à-vis* the supply market. Their perceptions of these risks, though, will depend on their individual characteristics, their position in the organization, their re-

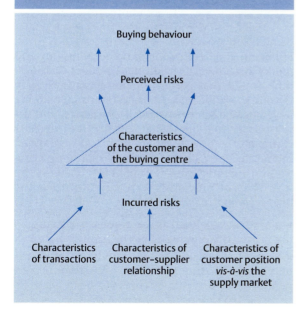

Figure 7.1 The development of the buying behaviour

Buying behaviour

Perceived risks

Characteristics of the customer and the buying centre

Incurred risks

Characteristics of transactions | Characteristics of customer–supplier relationship | Characteristics of customer position *vis-à-vis* the supply market

lationships with the other members of the buying centre, the functioning mode of the organization (for example, types of mission impacted, reward system in place), and the information available to them to reach a decision. The various perceptions of the members of the buying centre affect the type and level of risks they perceive and together make up the customer's buying behaviour.

An outside observer who would ideally have access to all the information associated with the decision (characteristics of the problem to be solved, context of the choice, various alternatives available) could judge this behaviour as lacking rationality and the subsequent decision as not optimized. We refer here again to the idea of the bounded rationality of the actors (Simon 1952). The rationality of a decision-maker depends both on the position effect and on the disposition effect. The position effect of the decision-maker depends on the organizational and social characteristics (rules and procedures in place, balance of power and alliances within an organization) that condition his access to information and therefore his perception and the rationality of his decision. The disposition effect of the decision-maker depends on his mental, cognitive, and affective characteristics, which condition his preferences and perceptions. This explains why, depending on the participants' individual characteristics and on the nature of their involvement in the buying centre, the level and types of risk perceived by the various participants can differ from what the above-mentioned outside observer could ideally identify and evaluate. We, therefore, introduce the idea of risk incurred by the customer. The difference between the incurred risks and perceived risks results from the characteristics and functioning mode of the buying centre.

In order to understand the customer's buying behaviour, a supplier must do two things:

■ On the one hand, he must investigate the characteristics of the transactions, of the customer's relationships with his supplier, and of the customer's position *vis-à-vis* the supply market. This analysis can allow the supplier to assess the level and nature of the risks incurred by the customer. This is particularly true if the supplier has access to extensive information either through the experience accumulated while solving similar problems with other customers or through a long-lasting relationship with the customer.

■ On the other hand, a supplier must also analyse the functioning mode of the customer's organization and, more specifically, of the buying centre. This analysis enables the supplier both to define the targets of his actions and to detect possible gaps between incurred and perceived risks.

The existence of these gaps gives the supplier opportunities to develop actions targeted to the members of the customer's buying centre. These actions can have different objectives. They can stimulate the risks incurred by the customer in order subsequently to reduce them, directly reduce the risks, or do nothing that could generate risks. The supplier can therefore 'play with the risks'.

4 Factors influencing organizational buying behaviour

MANY factors influence organizational buying behaviour. Those that research has shown to be of particular significance are discussed in the next three sections, which consider types of buying situations and situational factors; geographical and cultural factors; and time factors.

4.1 Types of buying situations and situational factors

In addition to identifying the buying activities, Robinson *et al.* (1967) in their founding BuyGrid model discarded the traditional product classification, stated that certain buying situations were far more significant and consistent in explaining buyer behaviour than product variables, and developed a situational scheme called the 'buyclass variable'. The buyclasses are 'new task', 'modified rebuy', and 'straight rebuy'. They represent a continuum ranging from the purchase of items the firm has not previously purchased to items the firm buys routinely:

■ a *new task* is defined as the purchase of items not previously purchased by the firm;

■ a *modified rebuy* is the purchase of items purchased in the past but not recently nor regularly;

■ a *straight rebuy* is defined as the purchase of an item that is purchased frequently and regularly.

This Buygrid model has been widely disseminated in marketing textbooks by Kotler and other authors. In fact, the buyclass model has been, and still is, presented in most textbooks as an excellent predictor of organizational buying behaviour, especially as far as the number, the quality, and the influence of the members of the buying centre are concerned. This assumption is based on the work of several researchers (Robinson *et al.* 1967; Doyle *et al.* 1979). They emphasize the relevance of the buyclass in predicting:

■ the time invested in the organizational-buying-behaviour process (ranging from long for a new task to short for a straight rebuy);

■ the size of the buying centre (ranging from large for a new task to small for a straight rebuy);

■ the role of the purchasing agent in initiating the need to buy (ranging from small for a new task to major in straight rebuy).

This positive conclusion is not always corroborated by practical examples. A study conducted by Bellizzi and McVey (1983) in the construction business shows an overall absence of significance of the buyclass variable as a predictor of organizational buying behaviour. There may be a relationship though between the buyclass and the amount of information sought by a buyer, as well as the number of alternatives a buyer will consider when making his purchase decision.

The marketing literature may, therefore, have overemphasized the role of the buyclass variable in organizational buying behaviour. In their previously mentioned study, Bellizzi and McVey (1983) conclude that the product type (operating supplies, major material, accessory equipment, and capital equipment as far as their study is concerned) is a better predictor of organizational buying behaviour than the buyclass (see Insert). They observe that the influence of top managers increases as the product purchased changes from inexpensive operating supplies to expensive capital goods. They also notice that the involvement of architects and, engineering consultants is greater when purchasing capital goods.

Today, the trend in industrial marketing practices is, therefore, to combine the approach of the buyclass model with others focusing on the prod-

> ### Who buys the notepaper?
>
> Most types of business stationery are purchased by somebody fairly junior in the hierarchy and are bought, as likely as not, on price. However, a senior member of the management team (perhaps even the Managing Director) will choose the company's stationery with its letterhead. Such a person will usually choose from a number of alternative types of paper and letterhead designs and these will usually have been prepared by a graphic designer, who will determine the quality and perhaps even the brand of the paper that should be used for the stationery. Another group who may have some influence are the printers, whose recommendation may be influenced by the paper that they currently have in stock.

uct types. Note that the concept of product types is here much larger than tangible products and includes on a continuum: tangible products, services, systems, and projects. Using this larger definition, Jennings and Plank (1995) have recently proposed an interesting analysis underlining the relationship between the product complexity and the risk perceived by each member of the buying centre. They define complexity along four dimensions: functional complexity, specification complexity, commercial complexity, and political complexity.

A product is functionally complex when it is made up of a large number of parts or systems. The specifications of a product are complex when it requires extensive testing to ensure that the design requirements are met (see Box 7.3). A product is commercially complex when the product transactions involve complicated procedures such as progress payment, penalty clause, and so on. Finally, a product is politically complex when the purchases involve differing factions that could impact the deal.

Most departments in an organization are affected by one or more of the above-described dimensions. Jennings and Plank (1995) recommend formulating the marketing strategy to target the members of the buying centre and offer the following guidelines:

■ address the functional-complexity issues with the purchasing agent alone;

■ address the specification-complexity issues with the purchasing and manufacturing departments;

Box 7.3 **The project-buying process**

A buyer wishing to purchase seven locomotives that will serve on the Portuguese National Railroad enquires about recent developments in technology. For this purpose, he contacts the three European suppliers from whom he had already bought locomotives: one English, one German, and one French. The combination of the data he receives allows him, in the space of four months, to set up a request for proposal. In order to avoid too much variety in his rolling stock, the buyer decides to consult only these three suppliers. The call for tender is sent to all of them with a three-month timespan for the answer. This time is used by each of the three suppliers to visit the buyer and to (re)-create social links with local subcontractors. Each of the three suppliers responds to the bid and their respective offers are analysed by the buyer, who, after two months, invites each of them to negotiate the bid. During the negotiations, the buyer introduces a new demand that is imposed upon him by his State department: the locomotive frames must be manufactured in Portugal by a small subcontractor under a foreign licence. The three suppliers rewrite their respective offers to take account of this new counter-trade demand. After the final round of negotiations, the French supplier wins the bid thanks to a better counter-trade agreement, although quoting the highest price. His counter-trade offer is less risky and more attractive for the buyer and his local network.

Box 7.4 **The project buying behaviour**

1. Need awareness
2. Search for suppliers (including contacts for recommendations)
3. Definition of specifications
4. Drawing-up of list of bidders
5. Request for proposals
6. Exchange of information
7. Analysis of proposals
8. Drawing-up of a short list
9. Negotiations
10. New proposals ⎫
11. Analysis of new proposals ⎬ Possible repeat of steps 9–12
12. Negotiations ⎭
13. Final assessment
14. Final selection
15. Contract

Source: Cova and Holstius (1993).

■ address the commercial-complexity issues with the manufacturing and engineering departments;

■ finally, address the political-complexity issues with top management and the engineering departments.

At the extreme of the continuum previously mentioned, a project is an interesting product type, since it is so specific and complex that it implies a level of sophistication of the organizational buying behaviour not included in the previous models defining the average process (Möller 1986).

The project buying behaviour has the following particularities (Cova and Holstius 1993):

■ a long-lasting, negotiated and interactive process (see Box 7.4)

■ a request for intercompany links;

■ an enlargement of both the buying and the selling centres;

■ a coming-into-play of interpersonal relationships between, on the one hand, the buyers and their networks, and, on the other hand, the suppliers and their networks;

■ a great importance given to the quality of these interpersonal relationships;

■ a large set of choice criteria used during each phase.

4.2 Geographic factors/cultural factors

While European companies use the act of negotiating extensively as an opportunity to interact with their customers or their suppliers throughout the buying process, North American ones avoid it as much as possible, since they dislike the idea of an interaction between a customer and a supplier (Cova and Salle 1991). These are, of course, only generalizations, but research tends to confirm them rather than to disprove them, even if these behaviours tended to become more homogeneous in the late 1990s (see Section 4.3).

Referring to the European surveys quoted above (Dale and Powley 1985; Möller 1986; Cova and Salle 1992), one may wonder if the existence or not of negotiations between suppliers and customers does not depend on the business practices and culture of each region. Europeans, on the whole, seem to negotiate after tenders have been submitted. This negotiation is considered as a phase before the final choice takes place. During this phase, more detailed information about the suppliers' proposals and/or the suppliers themselves is exchanged. This phase seems to be used rarely by North American companies. Johnston and Bonoma (1981) showed that the request for bids is sometimes used to identify the lowest bidders, with whom subsequent negotiations will be conducted. More generally, though, negotiations take place only after and not before a supplier has been chosen, with the objective of finalizing certain points of the contract. In the light of the research carried out by Woodside and Vyas (1987), it appears that North American buyers seem more influenced by a competitive ideology, which leads them to reduce the use of negotiation.

The core of the North American approach to organizational buying is the invitation to bid, not according to the European style with negotiation, leading to the final selection (Möller 1986), but according to the American style, with the final selection occurring as soon as the bids have been received by the buyer. According to Woodside and Vyas (1987), North American buyers believe that negotiating is against their company's policy for the following reasons:

■ vendors quote high prices under negotiating conditions; they quote their best price when price changes are disallowed after bids have been submitted;

■ if suppliers are squeezed too much, their product quality and service will decline;

■ during shortage, suppliers will drop customers whose prices and terms are least attractive; with market competition so intense, suppliers have little room to negotiate and already offer an attractive price.

Some explanations can be found to understand this kind of logic. North Americans seem to be uncomfortable when entering the uncertain and imprecise world of personal relationships in business exchanges. They like to predict the nature and the content of these exchanges. American culture, therefore, favours well-defined contracts that allow customers to compare suppliers on the same items and to negotiate more on price. As a consequence, US buyers do not favour

medium-term, single-partner, and long-term buyer–supplier relationships (Cova and Salle 1991).

4.3 Time factors

During the 1980s and the 1990s, deep changes took place in the relationships between industrial customers and their suppliers initially in Japan and Europe and later in North America (see Insert). The main reason behind these changes was the fact that, to be competitive in the 1990s, a company had not only to obtain the best prices from its suppliers through systematic competition, but also to develop long-term relationships with a limited number of suppliers able to create value and reduce costs.

Changes in the US OBB

'Ten years ago, the Japanese were considered as setting the standard reference when someone spoke about the problem of car manufacturer/suppliers. Today, everyone is talking about Chrysler. Many manufacturers analyse its approach in order either to borrow from it, or to adapt or simply to copy it. Created under pressure—the American number three was fighting for its survival, while its best engineers let it down and its R&D was disappearing—it is now a strategic weapon, which has allowed the group to accelerate the renewal of its range of cars at much reduced costs. Chrysler dramatically lowered its R&D costs, while transferring the major responsibility for complete ranges of components to its suppliers, who had already become its partners. These partnership agreements have implications for the very highest level of the hierarchy—for example, one of the CEOs with true dialogues on strategies. Investments in R&D are now up to 2.6 per cent of its turnover, while its competitors are up to 4 or 5 per cent.'

Source: François Castaing, VP Chrysler, interviewed by Patrick Chabert, in *Les Echos*, 8 Oct. 1997.

☞ 'This change from "a competitive to a cooperative" relationship does not mean that buyers and sellers did not have good personal relationships under the old model. . . . Nevertheless, the basic atmosphere was one of adversarial negotiation when it came to price setting and to gaining concessions on the size of orders and volume.' (Chapter 23, pp. 534–5)

These changes have affected organizational structures and the characteristics of inter-organizational relationships. For example, large industrial companies tend to centralize and coordinate their buying decisions further, pushing suppliers to adapt their approach by using, among other things, key account management. In many areas, the development of new ways to work together and to divide up the activities between the organizations has also increased the complexity of the relationships between customers and suppliers. This has happened in the following areas:

- *Product development.* New products are often co-developed, which results in a very early integration of the suppliers in the technical platforms of their customers. It is the case, for example, when new models are developed in the automotive industry. In some industries, customers transfer the entire management of the complete technical function to the suppliers. They no longer buy components after having defined the required specifications, but rather use sub-systems or systems already developed by their suppliers.

- *Delivery.* Since 1990 time has become an obsession. A product delivery time is considerably reduced by the just-in-time approach and even more so by the location of suppliers on the customer's production site. The example of the new Mercedes plant located in France to build and launch a new car called Smart in 1998 is very interesting. In order to reduce the production time of this new car, seven suppliers are located on the production site.

- *Information.* We could mention here all the recent technical developments that allow a rapid information flow between organization and, more specifically, electronic data interchange (EDI).

These factors result in a very high interdependence between organizations and in a major modification of the customers' decision process, as illustrated by Fig. 7.2, which was presented during a conference by a supplier in the automotive industry.

Figure 7.2 **Evolution of the decision processes and supplier–customer relationship in the automative industry**

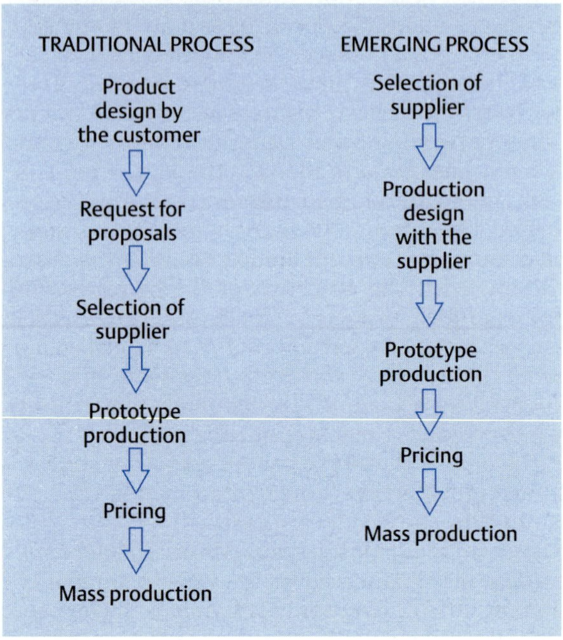

Fig. 7.2 compares the traditional system with the new system currently used in this industry. In the traditional system, the design department defines the characteristics of the vehicle's components, the engineering department defines the process, and the purchasing department invites the suppliers to compete based on the specifications and forecast volume. Suppliers are selected in the light of their ability to manufacture at a given cost. The supplier then builds the prototype and the final price is agreed upon before production starts. In this system, the purchasing department is the sole contact point between the manufacturer and the suppliers. The negotiations are based on the most important criterion: pricing. The purchasing department controls the characteristics of the incoming flows: consistency of the quality and degree of commitment to deadlines. The design department is supposed to be knowledgeable about the products and the technologies of the components. An anecdotal example would be the case of a design department of a French automotive manufacturer in the 1980s, which specified the composition of the rubber to be used for a windscreen wiper.

In the new system, suppliers are selected very early in the process. For example, the decision to launch the Twingo project, a vehicle manufactured by the French automotive manufacturer Renault, had not been finalized by top management when the suppliers had already been selected (Midler 1993). Suppliers are selected, based on their ability to take into account the financial parameters decided by the customer, on their ability to conceive and manufacture a product, on their technological knowledge, and on their ability to become part of the project team managed by the automotive manufacturer. The supplier and the customer work closely together during the conception phase. As the project moves forward, new information is integrated and sub-systems are modified, resulting in the need for various suppliers to adapt and adjust.

The major differences between the two systems are, therefore, the role of the supplier and the characteristics of the interaction between the customer and the supplier throughout the process. The traditional system focuses on the greater autonomy of the customer, while the new system insists on cooperation between the customer and the supplier. Numerous studies underline these changes in various industries. But, even though the managerial and scientific literature focuses on many examples of partnership between suppliers and customers, the industrial buying situation should not be limited to this type of relationship between suppliers and customers. In fact, the variety of existing buying situations and the spectrum of the types of relationships established between suppliers and customers have most probably widened since 1980. This is acknowledged by several scholars (Webster 1992; Möller and Wilson 1995), who offer a classification spreading from 'market transactions' to 'long-term relational exchange'. In the 'market-transactions' situation, market forces determine the terms of the exchange that takes place between independent parties in an atomized market. In the 'long-term relational-exchange' situation, the organizations involved have a long-term orientation and aim at developing the relationship between them.

5 Purchasing strategy

THE role played by the purchasing function in the competitiveness of the modern industrial firm is critical for both economic and strategic reasons. The importance of its economic role stems from the fact that it manages a buying volume amounting to between 50 and 80 per cent of the turnover and that its actions impact on the organization's profitability. Its key position as an intermediary between the organization and the supply market explains its strategic role.

5.1 Development of the purchasing strategy

The characteristics of current and future business lead the organization to secure resources from suppliers for the short, medium, and long term. These resources must meet as closely as possible the needs of the customer at the best price while offering the highest level of reliability. This process is rendered more difficult by the fact that the various resources to be secured have a different impact on an organization's business and that their availability on the supply market differs greatly.

The objective of the methods used to develop a purchasing strategy is to evaluate and classify the various items purchased in order to be able to choose and manage the suppliers accordingly. This classification takes place along the following two dimensions:

- the economic importance of the items to be purchased and their impact on the current and future business of the organization;
- the characteristics of the supply market—in other words, the degree of its technical and commercial complexity (stemming from the number of substitute offers available and from the degree of competitiveness of the market).

All the product families are evaluated according to both dimensions and presented in a matrix (see Fig. 7.3).

- *Strategic items*. These have a great impact and are important for the customer's business. The complexity of the supply market causes the buying decision to be very risky. Strategic items usually justify a lot of follow-up activities on the part of the purchasing department and the development of partnerships with a limited number of suppliers.
- *Critical items*. These also have a great impact and are important for the customer's business, but the level of complexity of the supply market is rather low. In this case, the risk faced by the organization will depend on its ability to use the items purchased properly.
- *Bottleneck items*. These have a low impact and are not very important for the customer's business, but the supply market is complex. From the point

Figure 7.3 Classification of items purchased according to buying situations

		Importance of items purchased	
		Low	High
Characteristics of the supply market	High complexity	bottleneck items	strategic items
	Low complexity	non-critical items	critical items

Source: Krajlic (1983); Marcel and Nassoy (1984).

of view of the purchasing managers, such a situation is not acceptable. It exists, however, when buying energy (electricity, for example, when the market is not yet deregulated) or raw materials, or when suppliers dominate a market.

- *Non-critical items.* These have a low impact on the customer's business and the supply market is not complex. Pricing is a key decision criterion.

A company's objective will be to move an item upwards or downwards and/or to the left when possible, depending on the position originally occupied by this item in the matrix. If not possible, the organization will have to manage the position originally occupied by the item by trying to increase the accessibility and availability of the resources for its business. Sometimes an organization can choose to limit its dependence on outside sources (make or buy decision). However, over the 1990s the trend for most organizations located in the industrialized world was to outsource heavily.

To manage or evolve the position occupied on the matrix by its various items, an organization can use various levers

- to influence the overall supply market by trying to modify its position *vis-à-vis* all the suppliers available for a given item;
- to influence a given supplier by trying to modify the characteristics of its relationship with this supplier;
- to modify its own position *vis-à-vis* the overall supply market or a given supplier through the use of its technology, structure, and procedures.

Such an approach is interesting, since it takes into account the various possible situations and allows differentiation between the types of relationship that can be developed with suppliers. On the other hand, the partnership 'craze' and the tendency to generalize it to all the purchased items can be criticized (Kapoor and Gupta 1997). Indirect purchases (e.g. main frames, advertising frame, office equipment and supply) represent nearly 25 per cent of the expenses of a manufacturing company and can justify aggressive approaches such as the ones suggested by the proponents of 'reverse marketing' (Leenders and Blenkhorn 1988). This type of approach would sometimes lead to a 10–15 per cent decrease in a company's expenses.

The example of Alpha (Box 7.5) will illustrate some of these approaches and the various paths chosen. Note that it is a real case study, but the name of the organization has been changed to ensure confidentiality. The Alpha example underlines the levers used and the manœuvres undertaken by the purchasing department to evolve or secure its position *vis-à-vis* the suppliers.

Four levers can be distinguished:

- the actions undertaken to influence the supply market;
- the nature of the relationship developed with suppliers;
- the organization of the buying activities;
- the procedures developed to work with the suppliers.

5.2 Actions undertaken to influence the supply market

The Alpha example illustrates a set of actions taken to influence the supply market. Given the importance of the product purchased in its business, Alpha tries to acquire a greater control over the resources available from a limited number of suppliers. Such a control can be achieved either through actions aimed at motivating new suppliers to enter the market, or by threatening suppliers if the market is overly concentrated. An example of the latter took place a few years ago when Italian capital was successfully invested in Valéo, a French supplier. Concerned by the potential power of this supplier, a French automotive manufacturer attempted to hinder the process. The purchasing manager of this manufacturer commented that, 'since we spend a few billion

Box 7.5 **Alpha**

Alpha, a subsidiary of a large industrial group, purchases a special plastic film and integrates it in practically all of its products. This film represents an average 30 per cent of the cost of the finished products and conditions the characteristics of the products manufactured. Four suppliers make up the worldwide supply market:

■ Filmus and Plastus are American companies and their market share is respectively 50 and 30 per cent;

■ Japafilm is a Japanese company and has a 10 per cent market share;

■ Filmeuro is a European company and has a 5 per cent market share.

Alpha is a major player in this film market and buys about 20 per cent of the worldwide production. Given its needs, Alpha buys only from the two American suppliers, considering Japafilm and Filmeuro to be too small. Various factors are nevertheless challenged by Alpha's central purchasing department regarding the selection of Filmus and Plastus as suppliers:

■ Filmus and Plastus manufacturing plants are located in the USA;

■ only a limited technical team is based in Europe;

■ the extent of these supplier's collaboration with Alpha is correct but no more;

■ the supply market being rather concentrated, Alpha is quite dependent on these two American suppliers.

To reiterate, the plastic film can be considered a strategic item: it greatly impacts on Alpha's business, and the supply market is complex given its degree of concentration.

Once it had been recognized that the plastic film was a strategic item, various manœuvres were attempted in order to modify Alpha's position *vis-à-vis* the supply market:

■ Alpha tried to develop a partnership—in other words, to become a key account of either Filmus or Plastus because of the potential represented by Alpha. This approach failed. These US suppliers did not want to favour Alpha, in order to avoid similar requests from their other major customers. The approach chosen by Alpha was to develop a tight collaboration through the development of the customer–supplier relationship.

■ Alpha then tried to find European suppliers capable of developing their ability to supply this plastic film, given the potential represented by Alpha. Filmeuro had no interest in further increasing the supply of this product, since it felt its relative size was too small as compared to Filmus and Plastus. Alpha also contacted other companies, but they declined, because they had not mastered the necessary know-how and wanted to avoid impact on other markets. This manœuvre was meant by Alpha to attempt to decrease the complexity of the supply market and to change the balance of power through the entry of additional suppliers.

■ As a result, Alpha decided to study its ability to manufacture the film itself. The studies took nearly ten years and enabled Alpha to cover a quarter of its needs, while acquiring an extensive know-how.

■ Faced with Alpha's production-capacity development, the US suppliers (one of them had, in the meantime, started its own production plant in Europe) changed their attitude towards Alpha and become more open to a potential collaboration. One of the reasons motivating their interest in a collaboration with Alpha was the opportunity to have access to the know-how developed by the latter through its applications.

French francs with Valéo each year, we would like to know the name of its major shareholder'.

In order to modify its position *vis-à-vis* the supply market, the purchasing department can change the definition of the size of the technological or geographical reference market considered. To satisfy the same need, a company can consider either the use of a single technology or the use of various technologies. The greater the number of technologies considered, the larger the technological reference market and the weaker the power of a supplier in the overall market from the customer's perspective.

The geographic location of the potential suppliers considered by a customer is another criterion used to define the reference market. Many medium-size companies purchase their products on a market located in a 100-kilometre radius around their production site. They, as a result, achieve greater flexibility and control over their purchasing activities. At the opposite end of the spectrum is the French upscale cosmetic and perfume industry. Packaging being a crucial element of their marketing strategy, they look for supplies all over the world, hoping to find packaging ideas that will differentiate their products from those of their competitors.

5.3 The nature of the relationship developed with suppliers

Based on the type of items purchased and on its position in the buying matrix (see Fig. 7.3), a company will develop different relationships with its suppliers playing with the following factors: the number of suppliers (sourcing), the suppliers' share, characteristics of selected suppliers, and the nature of customer–supplier relationships.

Number of suppliers (sourcing). There is no ideal rule and the sourcing choices can differ greatly from one company to the next in identical conditions. Through sourcing, the customer attempts to achieve an acceptable level of dependence *vis-à-vis* the suppliers without losing the benefit of their competencies and at a manageable cost. Today, many companies significantly reduce the number of their suppliers without hesitating to work with a sole source (see Insert). In 1997, for example, the US airline company Delta did not hesitate to sign an exclusive contract with Boeing for the purchase of 644 planes over the next twenty years. The European purchasing manager for Case, a US manufacturer of farming equipment and of road-construction material, indicated in 1998 that a

---

A tougher game of musical chairs

'Finding themselves in a more competitive environment, utilities are acutely concerned about containing or even reducing costs. Some are looking for savings through sole-source purchasing. Administrative costs are reduced by dealing with only one supplier, and the higher volume of business given to a single suppler leverages lower prices.

'The situation can be likened to a game of musical chairs. The way the game used to be played, a larger number of utilities spread their business among a larger number of suppliers with smaller purchases and annual contracts. Suppliers that lost one customer could generally expect to gain another. "When the music stopped there were always chairs to be grabbed," says a utility's purchasing manager. "Now there aren't as many chairs and they don't play the music as often because they're going to three to five years. And the contracts are getting huge, making the available chairs harder to fill." '

Source: Interchange (June 1998).

---

sole source was used for the strategic components needing heavy investment costs. The selected supplier benefits from an exclusive contract over a few years, sometimes even over the product's entire lifetime.

Supplier's share. When companies use various sources, most of the time they have one leading supplier covering over 50 per cent of the needs of a given product family. Very frequently a supplier will meet 100 per cent of the needs of a subgroup of items, and the needs of the remaining items are fulfilled by another one.

Characteristics of selected suppliers. Through such a choice, a company tries to achieve a few objectives that are not always compatible: to control its relationship with the supplier, to optimize the use of the resources and competencies of this supplier, and to keep a competitor from developing a relationship with the best suppliers. In order to select its suppliers, a company uses, among others, the following criteria: size, business, and reputation, as well as expertise. They will condition the type of relationship to be established between a customer and its suppliers. What type of business is the supplier in? Should the company choose a specialist in a given product or a supplier offering a wide and varied product mix? The importance of a supplier's reputation and expertise will depend on the items purchased and their impact on the company business. In the aerospace industry, for example, a supplier has a greater chance of being selected if he has experience in high tech. and aerospace, and if he has previously worked with this customer.

Nature of customer–supplier relationships. The complexity of the supply market and the impact of each item on the business will influence the way a customer manages his relationships with the selected suppliers. If the supply market is not very complex and the impact of the product is low (non-critical items), a customer may adopt an opportunistic approach focused on competition. When the complexity of the supply market increases and the impact of the product on the business is high (strategic items), a customer may choose a partnership approach with his suppliers. Purchasing departments are, however, able to manage only a limited number of target suppliers with this approach. A decrease in the number of suppliers used by the purchasing department can, therefore, be interpreted as a willingness to give them a greater volume of business, allowing a stronger collaboration to develop.

5.4 Organizing the buying activities

The organization of buying activities can support the purchasing strategy. Two elements are interesting to mention from the point of view of the resulting actions: the degree of centralization of the buying activities, and the missions and status of the buying function.

Degree of centralization of the buying activities. Industrial concerns often present a high level of organizational complexity, and the decision to buy a given item can take place at different levels within the buying organization: at the group, branch, company, or manufacturing-plant level. The geographic dimension must also be added to these four levels: international, national, regional, or local level. In every case, companies seek to locate the decision-making at the most effective level, in other words at a given hierarchical and geographical level. This choice is based on the following factors:

- usage characteristics of the items: will these items be used in one or more countries, plants, companies, branches?

- geographic characteristics of the supply market: local, regional, national, or international;

- importance of the items in the company business: in some companies, the higher the financial investment, the higher in the hierarchy will the decision be made.

Missions and status of the buying function. These vary considerably from one company to the next. In most industrial groups, the purchasing function has a very important role. Its missions are external and internal. It manages external resources. The purchasing department defines the panel of selected suppliers, keeps it current, and monitors their performance. It manages the relationships with the suppliers and helps them when they need to improve their quality and reduce their costs. The buying department also conducts the commercial negotiations. In certain industries, the purchasing department is involved in restructuring the suppliers' industries with the objective of achieving the most competitive service level and costs internationally.

Internally, the purchasing department helps the technical departments by informing them as soon as possible about the know-how of the selected suppliers, allowing the technical department to standardize as much as possible the parts and components to be purchased. It is also involved in the meetings dealing with product creation and evolution matters and with pricing, quality, and reliability decisions. In the case of a project-type situation involving suppliers, the role of the purchasing function is more complex. Multiple contacts take place between the suppliers and the project team of the customer, increasing the risk of incoherences and confusion. The purchasing department's role is, therefore, to synthesize the information, and it must look for information whenever something happens.

5.5 Procedures established to work with suppliers

The company will adapt its procedures to the type of items purchased and these procedures will exert an influence on the relationships with suppliers. These procedures can encompass numerous dimensions:

- ISO standardization;
- quality insurance;
- need to work with a given CAD/CAM software, as far as the technical dimension is concerned;
- JIT as far as the logistic dimension is concerned;
- terms of payment as far as the financial dimension is concerned;
- types of contracts as far as the legal dimension is concerned;
- EDI as far as the information flow is concerned;
- systematic bidding process.

These procedures can either be specific to a company or common to an entire industry.

6 The future

To answer the question as to how organizational buying behaviour will evolve in the twenty-first century, it is necessary to make some assessment about the evolution of a number of activities. Two of these are the information technologies and the production technologies. For example, it is being predicted that soon much more commercial activity will be conducted by electronic exchanges in a relatively impersonal manner. What effect will this have on the challenges that new suppliers already face as they seek to win business? It is not obvious how companies will in future be able to buy online from suppliers with whom they currently have no contact. As has been commented, 'Trust does not reside in integrated circuits or fiber optic cables. Although it involves an interchange of information, trust is not reducible to information' (Fukuyama 1995: 25), and so how will the confidence necessary for exchanges to occur be created?

The issue of production technologies is important, because developments since the mid-1980s show that the size of the minimum economic batch size is falling very rapidly, which amongst other things makes further moves towards segmentation of existing markets an economic possibility. In addition, the size of production units is also decreasing in many industries, so that small local manufacture becomes a possibility once again. Given the rising costs of congestion in many countries, this may lead to a swing back from the large centralized production facilities of the 1960–80 period and open up the possibilities of an increase in competition, perhaps resulting in a strengthening of the purchasing organization's negotiating position.

7 Summary

THE organizational buying process is very complex. This complexity stems from the very large number of factors internal to the organization and related to the market affecting the buying decision.

Given this complexity and the major changes constantly affecting industrial markets, understanding organizational buying behaviour is not easy. This understanding is, however, a key element in an organization's ability to compete, since it is one of the pillars of the development of a marketing strategy. This is why organizational buying behaviour is a source of interest both in the business and in the academic world.

Further reading

Corey, E. R. (1978), *The Organizational Context of Industrial Buyer Behavior* (Cambridge, Mass.: Marketing Science Institute).

Ford, D. (1997) (ed.), *Understanding Business Markets* (2nd edn., London: Dryden Press).

Johnston, W. J., and Lewin, J. E. (1996), 'Organizational Buying Behavior: Toward an Integrative Framework', *Journal of Business Research*, 35: 1–15.

Monka, R. M., and Trent, R. J. (1995), *Purchasing and Source Strategy: Trends and Implications* (Tempe, Ariz.: Center for Advanced Purchasing Studies).

Discussion questions

1 Is it a fair criticism that a weakness of model of organizational buying behaviour is its failure to suggest criteria by which the identity of those individuals who exercise buying influence can be established?

2 Consider two firms, one of which sells a frequently purchased component and the other an item that is infrequently purchased. What are the challenges each faces with regard to identifying and keeping in contact with members of its customers' buying groups?

3 Can a supplier really understand the risks that a customer perceives as being associated with purchasing its product?

4 If the nature of a product is that its customers purchase it infrequently, is it more appropriate to regard each purchase as 'new task', even in those cases where the customer has purchased that item in the past?

5 Many suppliers develop new products in association with customers. This usually means that they work closely with the customer's technical staff. As the product develops, should they ensure that they have contact with other sections in the customer's organization?

Mini Case
Internet Supplies Ltd.

Having worked in the IT Department of a large organization for many years, Fred is well aware of the difficulty in maintaining an organization's hardware and software standards. The problem is that individual departments can easily order many items of equipment or software without the involvement of either the Purchasing or the IT Department. They can do this, because such items are often relatively inexpensive and can therefore be bought using the department's discretionary budget. Indeed, in some cases these purchases actually do not need to involve the IT Department, as the item purchased would only be used within the department making the purchase. However, there are many occasions when the item purchased needs to match the standards of the existing systems (for example, the company's network), and it is therefore important to ensure that it is compatible with the company's standards.

In addition to the difficulty mentioned above of controlling many of these purchases because they are so inexpensive, there are additional difficulties in imposing company standards in this area of activity. Most departments still seem to have at least one member of staff who considers himself an 'expert' at computing, and frequently, as is so often the case with such people, he creates an 'ideal' solution for his own situation which is unfortunately incompatible with the company's standards. Such 'experts' then take delight in criticizing the IT Department for, in their view, its inappropriate standards—ignoring the fact that IT has to deal with company-wide issues and that sometimes it has to make trade-offs between the economies achievable by working to a common standard and providing people with exactly what they require.

Fred is considering setting up in business as an Internet-based product distributor of computer hardware and software. He recognizes that competition in this field is already quite intense, but he plans to guarantee a twenty-four-hour delivery of any item from a catalogue that he believes is as extensive as any currently available on the Internet. Moreover, he is formulating the idea of providing an ordering system based on passwords that will mean that customers can only purchase items that are on their own company's list of approved items. There seem to Fred to be two approaches to creating such a system. The first would be to let potential purchasers only see those items in the catalogue that their company had approved for purchase. The other would be to let the potential purchasers see the whole catalogue but to inform them which items are approved by their company.

His initial discussions with the IT and Purchasing Departments of a number of companies have been encouraging. It seems that IT Departments would support any procedure that would enable them to impose their standards throughout their company. The interest of the Purchasing Departments was mainly in the possibility of achieving increased volume discounts, which Fred said he would base on the totals of all items that he could identify as being purchased from a company's approved list.

Discussion question

What advice would you give to Fred?

Chapter 8
Market Information and Research

Martin Evans

Objectives

The objectives of this chapter are:

1 to provide an understanding of marketing information systems (MkIS);

2 to examine a variety of secondary and primary data approaches to researching markets;

3 to explore the environmental scanning methods involved with marketing intelligence provision and examples of the dynamic nature of the marketing environment;

4 to extend traditional coverage of market research into the contemporary areas of market productivity analysis and marketing models, as provided and facilitated, especially, by technological developments in marketing, notably the marketing database;

5 to explore some of the emerging ethical issues concerning information and research for marketing.

1 Introduction

THIS chapter provides an overview of how marketing information systems (MkIS) inform marketing decisions and explores some of the related issues. The MkIS can contain many different sources and types of information—internal operational data, market intelligence data, market research data, and external data. As well as the data, there are functional aspects of the MkIS in terms of its role in support of information gathering, evaluation, processing, dissemination, analysis, and control. A helpful model is that of Piercy and Evans (1983), as illustrated in Fig. 8.1. This chapter covers marketing information systems, including marketing research, marketing intelligence, marketing productivity analysis, and marketing modelling.

The first two sections of this chapter cover *marketing research* and *marketing intelligence*. The relatively greater immediacy of marketing research can be seen from Fig. 8.2, in which the 'boxes' provide examples of the more immediate contexts for marketing research. Marketing intelligence, with its methodology of *environmental scanning*, is more concerned with longer-term marketing planning. These less decision-oriented dimensions of marketing intelligence are shown as marketing's various 'environments'. The later sections will discuss *marketing productivity* and *marketing modelling*.

2 Marketing research

MARKETING research is clearly a key element in the MkIS; indeed it is probably the one that springs to mind most readily. What marketing research is specifically concerned with is the provision of information about markets and the reaction of these to various product, price, distribution, and promotion policy actions. It is not, however, concerned with the provision of information *per se*. Marketing researchers tend to fear somewhat a client request 'for information' about a market, an advertising approach, and so on. The problem here is that such vague requests are not decision oriented—they do not help in the selection of WHAT market or advertising information is relevant or WHY it is required. In turn, this creates difficulties in deciding how, when, and from

Figure 8.1 **Marketing information systems**

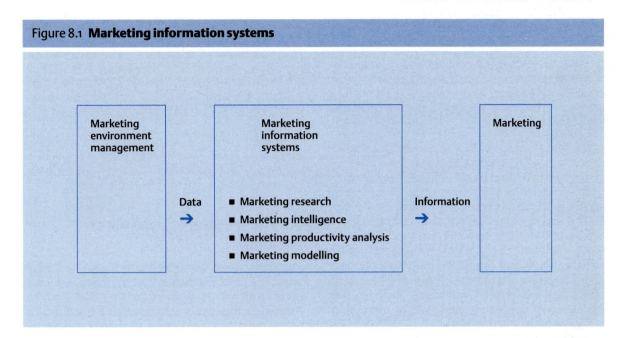

Marketing environment management		Marketing information systems		Marketing
	Data →	■ Marketing research ■ Marketing intelligence ■ Marketing productivity analysis ■ Marketing modelling	Information →	

Figure 8.2 **Marketing Research and Marketing Intelligence**

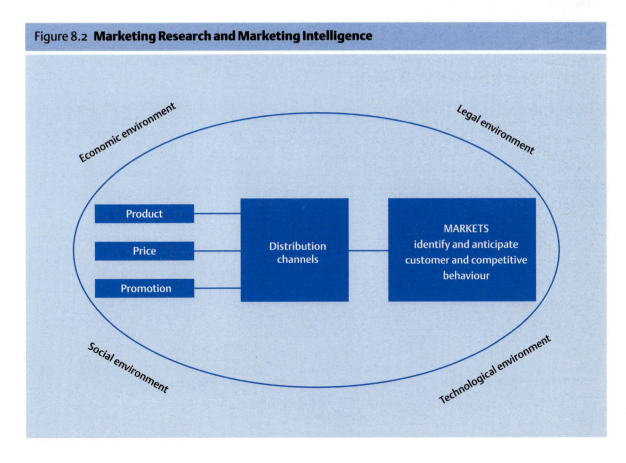

where such information should be collected, and how it should be analysed and interpreted.

☞ 'As with any data-collection exercise, the process must begin with clearly stated research objectives. Marketers must be entirely sure of the underlying reasons for the research.' (Chapter 16, p. 396)

The point is made clearly in numerous standard definitions of marketing research. Few have advanced beyond the classical definition put forward by the American Marketing Association as long ago as 1960: 'The systematic gathering, recording and analyzing of data about problems relating to the marketing of goods and services.' This reinforces the point that marketing research is about specific marketing problems—not the collection of information for its own sake. Marketing research has a relatively 'immediate' focus, in that the decision context is not usually more than several months into the future.

In the same way that marketing is concerned with providing appropriate product, price, distribution, and promotion offerings to target markets, so marketing research includes market research, product research, price research, distribution research, and promotion research, as summarized in Box 8.1. There is, therefore, a distinction between *marketing research* and *market research*—the former being far more inclusive than the latter.

Another significant dimension of definitions of marketing research is that marketing research is systematic and formalized—and this is the point that the following section expands upon.

2.1 The marketing-research process

The implication of marketing research being systematic and formalized is that there is a sequence of research events, from diagnosing marketing information requirements through data collection to data analysis. This leads to the structuring of research programmes around a series of stages in the research process, as shown in Box 8.2. Such

---

Box 8.1 **Types of marketing research**

Types	Examples
Market research	Identifying customer requirements: motivation and attitudinal studies
	Studying customer groupings and market segmentation studies
	Measuring size and potential of markets
	Examining competitive positions and market-share analysis
Product research	New product development programmes
	Concept and product tests
	Test marketing
	Packaging research
	Research over product life cycle
	Brand loyalty and brand switching research
Pricing research	Measuring price awareness of buyers
	Analysing price sensitivity
	Examining brand perceptions and price relationships
Distribution research	Testing the effectiveness of marketing channels
	Measuring buyer behaviour towards manufacturer and retailer branding decisions
	Retail location studies and other retail marketing research
Promotion research	Research to help determine promotional objectives
	Promotional copy testing
	Promotional media research
	Measuring buyer response campaigns.

Box 8.2 **The marketing-research process**

Stage 1. Defining and clarifying the marketing problem and determining what information this requires.
Stage 2. Determining cost effective sources of information.
Stage 3. Determining techniques for collecting information
Stage 4. Data collection
Stage 5. Data processing
Stage 6. Communicating results

Source: Moutinho and Evans (1992).

stages can be of great help in both the planning of research programmes and in the control and evaluation of them.

2.1.1 *Stage 1.* Defining and clarifying the marketing problem

It is suggested here that, of all the stages in the total process, it is often this one, at the beginning of a research programme, that in practice can be riddled with error and bias.

A research programme is manifested in its final research report and it is usually possible, in this, to some extent to be able to evaluate other stages of the process. For example, any questionnaire used should usually appear in an appendix and the reader can scrutinize this. Also, the sample design and size should be explained and again the reader is given the opportunity to evaluate this. The manner in which the data has been analysed and reported can also be studied in the report, but, although the project objectives may appear reasonable to a reader who is not the person responsible for making decisions on the basis of this report, they may actually be wholly inadequate for the actual decision area concerned.

The point, then, is that, although error and bias can occur at any stage of the process, if the first stage is not fully explored and agreed between decision-maker and researcher, the entire programme can waste time and money. A brewery campaign demonstrates a real case in which the first stage was not explored as fully as perhaps it might have been (see Insert).

Other instances of wasted marketing research as a result of faults in problem analysis and the

briefing of researchers are provided by England (1980), and the dangers are generalized by Millward, the joint managing director of the Millward Brown Agency: 'The utility of any research project is critically dependent upon the quality of the original brief ... too often research is neither communicated effectively to the decision takers nor relevant to their decisions ... make sure that the real decision-makers attend key presentations ... the best briefing session is a two-way discussion which both crystallizes and challenges current management thinking' (Millward 1987).

The 'problem-definition' stage should lead naturally to the listing of appropriate informational requirements (the 'data list') in the context of the decision areas concerned.

Exploratory versus conclusive research Developing a clear formulation of the scope and nature of a research problem may be referred to as exploratory research, which explores the parameters of the problem in order to identify what should be measured and how best to undertake a study. Exploratory techniques are usually relatively unstructured, sometimes merely discussions of the problem with knowledgeable people or the study of case histories of similar projects that could suggest a methodology. Group discussions with consumers are popular, as they are not constrained by highly structured questionnaires and enable the problem to be seen from a 'market' perspective. Indeed, in the practical setting exploratory research may provide enough

Who uses the data?

An advertising research programme was commissioned by a brewery to evaluate a poster advertising campaign for a new beer. Levels of awareness were evaluated and attitudes measured using a questionnaire and street interviewing and the results were gratefully received by the brand manager concerned. However, later feedback from the organization revealed that the decision-maker resided in general marketing management and, while the research results were relevant and useful, they had their limitations. The problem materialized as poor communication: while the brand manager had briefed the researchers in line with his perception of the problem, the marketing manager wanted to use the information to decide whether to launch a new lager using, predominantly, a poster campaign. The point is that the initial research problem was broader than could be evaluated in one campaign.

information for the decision-maker's needs (or perhaps all he or she can afford). Certainly, there have been increases in the use of qualitative research, such as the employment of group discussions with small samples without, necessarily, any large-scale follow-up.

In contrast, conclusive research is conducted through the main research design and is aimed at measuring the variables identified from the exploratory exercises. It provides the information, specified on the data list, that management requires.

2.1.2 *Stage 2.* Determining cost-effective sources of information

The list of specific informational requirements (the data list) should have been built up in problem definition, and it is necessary to determine from where the data can be found. There is a popular misconception that marketing research is no more than an interviewer in the street with a questionnaire and a clipboard. While this image is appropriate for some research programmes, there are others where the interviewing is conducted in a hall, or someone's home; others that require no interviewer at all (for example, postal surveys), and some that involve no questioning (such as observation studies); and yet others that rely exclusively on existing reports or other documentation (that is, secondary data sources).

Primary versus secondary data sources The range of data sources can be broadly categorized under the headings of secondary and primary. Secondary sources involve information that already exists, such as company records or previous reports, government statistics, newspaper and journal articles, and commercial market-research agency reports.

Box 8.3 lists some examples of the wealth of information that exists and this point serves to demonstrate that it is always worth exploring the possibilities of using secondary sources—as a *first* resort—before commissioning what would usually be a more expensive and time-consuming programme of collecting 'new' information using 'primary' research methods.

In fact, the major area of search that precedes buying agency research or starting an in-company research project involves secondary data, and, because of the heavy use of such sources, there is a need to adopt a critical perspective in using them.

The researcher determines, first, that secondary sources are impartial—that is, that there is no slant or bias in the information resulting from the provider or compiler attempting to make a case for or against something; secondly, that sources are valid—that is, whether the information is what the researcher wants to know; thirdly, that sources are reliable—that is, whether the information is representative of the group it purports to describe (for instance, a sample of twelve consumers is unlikely to reflect all consumers in a national population); and, fourthly, that sources provide information with internal homogeneity—that is, whether there is consistency in, for example, a set of figures.

Primary sources, on the other hand, involve collecting new information, first hand, for the particular research programme.

Within primary data collection methods there is a distinction between *ad hoc* and continuous research. When the same respondents are observed or interviewed repeatedly over a period, then this is referred to as continuous research, as opposed to an *ad hoc* study that collects data on one occasion only from given respondents.

One version is the consumer panel (not to be confused with a group discussion). Here, respondents—often in the form of 'households'—agree to report on their buying behaviour or media habits over a period of time, perhaps completing a type of diary every week or so and posting this to the research agency concerned.

The Royal Mail operates a panel on this basis to study the receipt of different types of mail, from a variety of sources and in a variety of source categories, including, of course, from direct marketers. Other panels employ technological methods to gather data, such as the electronic recording of television viewing habits (set meters), people-metring of those in the room at the time, and bar-code scanners for panelists to record their purchases.

The retail audit is the other main form of continuous research and operates on a similar principle—a sample of retail outlets allow sales patterns to be analysed and sold. Again, the main benefit is to discover customer activity with respect to competitor stores—and, as with the panel, on a regular, continuous basis. Sales of specific brands are recorded. This used to be by means of physical stock checks by observers at regular intervals, but laser scanning EPoS systems are now commonplace.

Box 8.3 **Secondary data sources**

Many of these are free (either because they are to be found in most public libraries or because they are available free from Government Departments). Even some of the expensive commercial reports can be found in some libraries.

KOMPASS: gives names and addresses of companies (i.e. possible competitors) by country and by product category.

Kelly's Guide: lists industrial, commercial, and professional organizations in UK, giving a description of their main activities and providing their addresses. Listings are alphabetical according to trade description and also according to company name.

Guide to Key British Enterprises: a register of 25,000 top UK companies that provides company name and address and also some basic financial data such as sales, number of employees, and the Standard Industrial Code (SIC).

UK Trade Names: lists trade names and the parent company.

Who Owns Whom: lists firms and their parent organization.

Business Monitor: gives statistics for different products—e.g. numbers of manufacturers, industry sales, and import levels.

Family Expenditure Survey: gives average weekly expenditure on many products and services according to: different regions, size of household, age of head of household, household income levels. Useful for estimating market size and potential sales levels.

Regional Trends: plots population size and structure trends through the regions, together with more on regional income and expenditure.

The Henley Centre: projects future social attitudes, lifestyles, income, and expenditure.

Market Intelligence (Mintel): monthly reports on profile of different markets (both customers and competitors).

Market Assessment: reports on profile of different markets (both customers and competitors).

Key Note: reports on profile of different markets (both customers and competitors).

Retail Business: monthly reports on profile of different retailing markets (both customers and competitors).

The Retail Directory: gives details of retail trade associations and lists retail companies according to type (co-op, multiple, department store, and so on) and according to geography (for example, the retail outlets within many towns are listed).

Target Group Index (TGI): annual profile of most product-markets in terms of who buys what, 34 volumes each year.

National Readership Survey: profile of readers of newspapers and magazines (for advertising media selection); that is, when matched with profile of target market.

BRAD (British Rates and Data): gives costs of advertising in press, radio, poster, cinema, TV, and all other mass media.

MEAL (Media Expenditure Analysis): provides information on competitors' advertising expenditure on specific brands per month. Also gives advertising agency concerned.

Trade associations: usually have information on numbers of competitors, and size of market.

Local Chambers of Trade: have statistics on companies in their trading area and information on trading conditions.

Electoral Register: can be used to help define the catchment areas of retail outlets and the number of potential customers. Also used to draw samples for market research.

Viewdata: general purpose online databases including some market and company information. Others are more specialized: for example, TEXTLINE, which provides a 'key word' search of many newspapers and journals for information and articles on the topic concerned.

Internal databases: these are covered further under marketing productivity analysis and can be used to analyse transactional data in order to understand patterns of buying for individualized targeting.

Internet: continues to offer ever-expanding quantities of data about markets, though the sources and criteria for evaluating the data must be uppermost in the researcher's mind when trawling through some web sites.

Cost effectiveness In terms of determining cost-effective sources, there are practical, but constraining, influences of time and money—and indeed, expertise and politics—and research designs are really based on a compromise of some sort.

Secondary sources are often cheaper and less time-consuming than primary ones—though some are very expensive in absolute terms. If secondary sources provide only exploratory results, or if there are problems due to invalidity and/or reliability, then first-hand data collection is likely to be the next stage, if time and money warrant.

A rule of thumb in assessing cost effectiveness is the extent to which research results provide benefits exceeding their costs, and this approach has been refined by the use of Bayesian Analysis, which helps by using probability theory to estimate the value of decisions made without research information, compared with decisions made with information derived from different types of research design—sample size variations and so on (Fig. 8.3).

The presentation of research alternatives in the form of decision trees is useful to both researcher and research user—and, as discussed earlier, the more the decision-maker is involved in the preliminary stages of research programmes, the more likely is the resulting programme to produce information that is appropriate to the specific decision context.

If additional information is deemed necessary, how can the decision-makers determine the amount of money to allocate to the marketing research unit that will gather it? If marketing research is the only cost associated with decision delay, the marketing manager could, in theory, allocate any amount that does not exceed the estimated profit consequences of a wrong decision. In other words, if additional research data improve the chances for a more profitable decision, then the maximum amount that should be expended for such data is the difference between the expected profit consequences of the decision taken without additional data and the expected profit consequences of the decision taken with additional data. This difference is sometimes referred to as the expected value of added information.

The cost of marketing research is only one cost element in decision delay. Opportunity cost is another. For example, delaying the introduction of a new product pending the results of extensive con-

---

Figure 8.3 Decision trees for launch of product

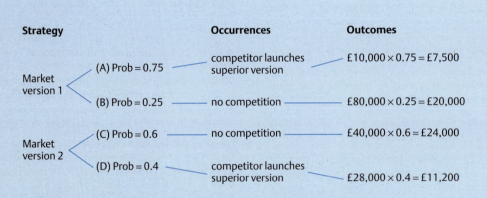

From the outcomes column it can be seen that the expected value of marketing version 1 is £7,500 + £20,000 = £27,500, while the expected value of marketing version 2 is £24,000 + £11,200 = £35,200. Thus marketing version 2 would appear to be the more favourable course of action.

sumer research may improve the chances of making the right decision. However, the expected benefits from such a decision should be compared to the amount of predicted sales revenue that would be lost during the testing period.

Another cost in decision delay stems from the reduction of lead time over competitive counteraction. Less and less frequently do companies enjoy long periods of competitive product advantage. A new product, even when a competitor is caught by surprise, can often be quickly duplicated, or a highly similar product soon introduced. To test a contemplated product in the marketplace over a long period of time will alert competitors. They can analyse the product and produce a similar one while the originator is still seeking additional data for the reduction of uncertainty.

Once it has been determined what information (Stage 1) should be collected, and from where it would be found and indeed whether it should be pursued (Stage 2), it then has to be determined how it should be collected.

2.1.3 *Stage 3.* Determining techniques for collecting information

This stage is concerned with the instruments and procedures for data collection; secondary data have merely to be found, interpreted, and summarized, so the main focus of discussion in this stage is on primary data collection.

Box 8.4 shows that the techniques of observation, interview, and experimentation are more than mere categories and actually fit a continuum in terms of the degree of control the researcher can exert over the variables being researched. Whichever of these techniques are used, decisions also have to be made about the sampling procedures to be used.

Observation In a formalized research programme, observation may be used in an unstructured form to record, for example, general purchasing behaviour, as opposed to the more structured observation of such factors as the sex of purchasers of a specific brand of toothpaste. Indeed, a fairly unstructured observational approach may serve as exploratory research in attempting to explore and clarify the focus that is needed in conclusive research.

It is usually more realistic to observe in actual or real conditions, such as recording the number of people who look at a poster, although this is not always possible. For instance, when evaluating new store layouts, customer flows can be observed using a hall as a simulated store to test alternative designs without disrupting the real stores.

☞ 'Typically a market-research firm rents an area in a shopping mall, where it sets up a drug- or grocery-store aisle. The new product being tested is placed on the shelf in this "simulated" store.' (Chapter 24, p. 561)

Perhaps the greatest potential problem of observation is that of modified behaviour—people who know they are being watched may not act as they would otherwise. For example, some continuous studies record respondents' television viewing habits and record the grocery products they purchase. It has been found that some respondents

---

Box 8.4 **The primary data continuum**

Observation	Interview	Experimentation
Little control over what is being studied. Highly objective because actual behaviour is recorded as opposed to what the researcher thinks is important.	Degrees of control depending on the method used. In group discussions participants can veer off into areas of little interest, whereas more structured surveys restrict the range of answers to what the researcher feels to be the relevant issues.	High levels of control over variables (e.g. different pricing levels) but complicated and expensive experiments required to cover all the factors that might account for the relative success of one variant.

watch different programmes, or buy different products, during the first few weeks of such recording, until reverting to their more normal habits. Box 8.5 demonstrates the problem of modified behaviour graphically.

Various mechanical and electronic devices offer alternatives to a human observer watching an event. The marketer can use checkout EPOS and EFTPOS scanning linked with loyalty cards to record customer purchase behaviour. This is observation research, because no questions are asked of the customer.

For monitoring the television viewing habits of respondents in consumer panels, meters attached to their sets have been used for many years and cable television effectively makes such meters common to all those households receiving cable output. Response levels to advertisements can be matched with time (and TV channel) of viewing such commercials. The set meter records whether the set is on or off at regular intervals, and, if it is 'on', which channel has been selected.

Marketing via the Internet provides related examples of non-human observation of behaviour—in terms of the digital recording of which web sites are visited and by whom.

Mechanical observation techniques may use devices like the psychogalvanometer, or lie detector, one version of which records changes in perspiration rates as a result of emotional reaction to stimuli such as test advertisements. Similarly, the tachistoscope allows an object, such as an advertisement or a product package, to be illuminated for a fraction of a second to test the advertisement or package for initial impact, legibility, recognition, and so on. The marketer can use such techniques to pre-test alternative colour combinations or positions for their brand name, copy headline, and so on. Another machine being used to great effect by the marketer is the eye camera—messages can be checked for how the reader's eye moves over the copy.

The advantage of observation is objectivity, because what *actually* happens is recorded, compared with the subjectivity of questioning approaches, which, as will be shown shortly, by the very nature of question wording and interviewing, can introduce some bias. However, as discussed above, such objectivity is lost if subjects are aware of the observation and modify their behaviour. In practice, the researcher may be unable even to approach the ideal of effective data collection through observation.

Interview survey methods There are various types of interview used in research surveys and typically a distinction is made between personal, telephone, and postal interviews. Further distinctions can be made between structured and unstructured interviews and the personal interview can be of a depth or group type. Indeed, new technology provides another kind of interviewing, where the computer provides a vehicle for asking questions and collecting responses, in some cases using the cable facilities of domestic television sets and via the Internet. Each form of interviewing merits a brief outline, as the basis for a choice of methodology.

Postal questionnaire studies have the obvious advantage over personal interviews of being able to cover a very large geographic area, usually with

---

Box 8.5 Modified behaviour in observation studies

A study of the demand for taxis in a town involved observation of taxi ranks to calculate the average time taxis had to wait before picking up passengers, and the average time that passengers had to wait for a taxi. The taxi-drivers knew that research was to be carried out, with the aim of deciding whether to increase the number of taxi licences in the city. Observers were positioned at all the ranks, including the two most popular. Observers at one main rank were positioned openly and were noticeable to anyone in the vicinity (not by design, but as a result of the topography of the area). Although there were several taxis at this rank at the beginning of the first observation period, within minutes there was a mass influx of taxis—far more than arrived at any other similar length of time over the next fortnight. When the results were later analysed, it was found that the same number of taxis that arrived at the first rank in the first fifteen-minute period had departed from the second main rank. The striking difference was that the observers at the second rank were positioned in a hidden location and it was concluded that, as soon as the observers were themselves seen by the taxi-drivers at the first rank, the drivers contacted their colleagues by radio and called them from the rank which (to the taxi-drivers) appeared not to be under observation.

The rationale was that the drivers did not want the number of licences increased and wanted, therefore, to give the appearance of plenty of taxis!

little increase in postal costs. The major characteristic of postal surveys is the absence of an interviewer, which eliminates interviewer bias but at the same time provides little scope for respondents to query the meaning of the questions. The lack of personal contact also means that, when a questionnaire is sent to an address, there is no guarantee that the respondent is the addressee. The questionnaire may be completed by another member of the family, or another member of the organization.

However, on the positive side, where a survey requires the respondent to consult with others, or with filed information, the postal survey provides the necessary time and freedom, and another result of there being no interviewer is that some respondents may be less inhibited about answering certain questions. On the other hand, without an interviewer, misunderstood questions cannot be explained, open questions cannot be probed, and the non-verbal communication of the respondents (facial expressions, intonation, and the like) cannot be observed.

However, the single most significant problem usual in postal surveys is a low level of response—it is all too easy for the respondent to ignore a postal questionnaire. Without a carefully constructed covering letter, emphasizing such factors as how useful (and confidential) the respondent's replies will be, or without a reminder, response rates can be as low as single figures in percentage terms. Even with these and the obvious enclosures such as stamped addressed return envelopes, response rates may be so low as to be unrepresentative of the selected sample. The point is, of course, that non-response may not be a random factor—the characteristics of those who do respond may be significantly different from the characteristics of these who do not respond—a factor for which survey results should be tested where possible.

Once such limitations have been identified, it may be decided to avoid a postal survey for a particular study. But, despite the important problems, postal surveys are used extensively, perhaps because they are an acceptable compromise between reliability and cost considerations.

Telephone interviews might not be used as much as other interviewing approaches, nor as much in the UK as in the USA, but the telephone interview is becoming more important and merits consideration in research design, as long as the sampling can be restricted to those with telephones. Indeed the Market Research Society (1994) in a major report confirms that most telephone interviewing is just as appropriate as personal interviewing but much more convenient because of the easier and cheaper access to respondents (no waiting in cold and wet streets for the 'right' people to come along when a quota sample is being used, and no more futile multiple call-backs to a name and address when the sample design is random and the interviewing is face to face).

As in the case of postal surveys, there is a geographical advantage, although it is less pronounced than with postal questionnaires because of long-distance telephone rates, time-related call charges, and the inability in many cases to make use of cheap rate times (phoning companies at the weekend or in the evenings promises little success).

Telephone interviews are often appropriate for industrial or organizational surveys because most companies have telephones and the chances of contacting someone from the organization during office hours are reasonably good—although it may be more difficult to contact the relevant respondent within the organization. Once the problems of organizational switchboards are overcome, telephone interviewing can be the quickest of all the interviewing methods, because the interview is made from the researcher's desk so no fieldwork travel is involved, and the replies are immediate. Telephone interviewing can also be used in consumer markets. For example, BT conducts some 13,500 telephone interviews monthly. Interviewees are chosen from those customers who have asked for a service or fault repair, made a request, or filed a complaint.

There can also be a misuse of the telephone for bogus 'research' purposes. Consider the car exhaust and tyre company that made telephone contact with its customers on the basis that they had been recorded in the database as having purchased new tyres/battery or exhaust systems in the last month. The questioning commenced with satisfaction with the service according to a 5-point scale—with no request for further feedback. Soon, however, the questions moved on to cover aspects of car insurance such as renewal dates. The research was clearly an attempt to cross-sell another service, because, when a customer tried to provide reasons for his degree of dissatisfaction, the questioner was very reluctant to pursue this and admitted there was no provision to record such information.

There have been many applications of new

information technology (IT) in marketing research and the link between telephone interviewing and the PC is an obvious one. The computer is used to store the questionnaire, and, as the interviewer goes through the interview over the telephone, the computer can select and display the appropriate questions for each respondent, and the replies can be keyed directly into the computer store, for immediate analysis. This is now common place and is referred to as computer assisted telephone interviewing (CATI).

The more sophisticated interactive TV technology, being interactive, allows questions to be sent down the line to households possessing such a system. The questions are displayed on people's television sets, and their answers can be keyed in via a keypad, or via a home computer keyboard, and sent back along the line to the researcher for analysis. Such systems are as yet in their infancy. However, already tested and used is a compromise between the above approaches, involving the use of a computer visual display unit, presenting the respondent with a self-completion questionnaire. The future is likely to see the Internet being used more as an interviewing vehicle—appropriate respondents can be identified through records of their web-browsing or other lists. They can be 'e-mailed' questionnaires and any responses can be analysed rapidly, because the data is communicated online in an already coded form.

Personal interviewing has the obvious distinguishing feature of face-to-face communication between respondent and interviewer, which poses problems of bias and error, as well as offering flexibility and control. However, it is the fieldwork cost of interviewing that provides the main disadvantage of this type of data collection. In fact, the sample design employed is of some importance here, because different fieldwork problems occur when using different sampling methods. For example, with a quota sample, the interviewer has to select respondents who possess the required characteristics, while with random sampling, the interviewer must contact a specific name and address.

The presence of an interviewer offers the opportunity for varying degrees of structure. For instance, questions might be open-ended to allow the respondent to answer in his own words, without the constraints of predetermined optional answers in closed questions, and the interviewer can ask the respondent to expand on a point with various probing techniques. In unstructured interviewing, there is more of a conversation, because, although certain broad topics are to be explored, there is no set sequence of pre-worded questions. This is sometimes referred to as a depth interview and is an example of qualitative as opposed to quantitative research.

Group discussions (or *focus groups*) are generally unstructured and qualitative. With this method several respondents (possibly between six and ten in number) are brought together (perhaps in a coffee morning in one of the respondents' homes) and the interviewer guides the discussion through relevant topics, leaving most of the talking to members of the group. This method is widely used to pre-test advertisements. While the costs per respondent may be high with group discussion work as a result of the degree of skill required by the interviewer and the time that a group discussion takes, group discussions may still prove cost effective relative to large-scale sample surveys.

> ☞ 'companies can use *focused group discussions* with small groups of customers to gain insights about their likes, dislikes, and attitudes.' (Chapter 24, p. 554)

In the late 1990s the cost of a group discussion could exceed £1,000, which would include screening participants for relevant characteristics, devising the interview schedule, paying group participants, organizing an appropriate venue, recording and transcribing events, and analysing results. Since groups revolve around the sociology of group dynamics, it is not surprising that the interviewer, as group leader, must possess social skills in dealing with such problems as respondents who emerge as group dominators, or who adopt the roles de Almeida (1980) describes for different personas that respondents can adopt and with which moderators must deal (see Box 8.6).

There are a number of commonly cited criticisms of group discussions that must be acknowledged. The method is seen to lend itself to providing evidence to support preconceptions and relies heavily on the moderator's interpretation. Box 8.7 summarizes an example of group discussion methodology.

Omnibus surveys, or shared surveys, are becoming increasingly popular in the UK. The research design of an omnibus survey is constant, but the questions included vary according to which clients 'buy in', thus providing a quick and inexpensive survey approach. As long as the research

Box 8.6 **Respondents' persona**

- The Competing Moderator
- The Rationalizer
- The Choir
- The Super Ego
- The Compiler
- The Conscience
- The Rebel
- The Pseudo-Specialist

design and methods are satisfactory, the advantage is that costs are shared among all clients.

Omnibus surveys vary in the specialization of their samples, different operators offering, for example, samples of 4,000 adults nationally, 1,000 motorists nationally, or 2,500 managers of small businesses. Clearly the operators do not alter their published designs for a single client, but repeat a survey of the same design at regular intervals. Because the research design is the constant, there is a minimum of administration in planning and fieldwork, and it is claimed that the major sources of error and bias will have been removed.

Omnibus surveys can be used in a number of ways. For example, if the same questions are asked in consecutive surveys, the results can either be combined to give a larger sample size, with the aim of reducing sampling error, or analysed to measure change over time. However, this last example should not be equated with continuous research, since the same respondents would not be interviewed in consecutive surveys, in spite of the same sample design being used.

Most of the opinion polls reported in the national media are omnibus surveys, and the clients are normally paying something between £100 and £600 per question, depending on the operator.

Experimentation After observation and interview studies, the third form of data collection is experimentation. A simple example demonstrates the nature of marketing experimentation (see Box 8.7).

A way of improving an experiment is to include a control group—that is, to measure the same dependent variables in the control group in the absence of the experimental variable. This often takes the form of a before–after design (see Table 8.1), where only one group is exposed to the new advertising campaign.

Marketing experiments can use data from consumer panels or retail audits, with the advantage of being able to demonstrate changes over time more effectively than can *ad hoc* research. The test market is the largest marketing experiment, because the whole mix is tested, rather than just one variable. Panel data are particularly useful in test markets, because not just sales, but customer profiles, new and repeat buying levels, attitudes, retail preferences, and so on are analysed over a period.

In *direct* marketing (see Chapter 26) 'experimentation' is usually referred to as 'testing', and there are two general types that can be distinguished: first, when we want to compare the results from different mailing lists (lists of consumers assembled and categorized on the basis of information collected about their lifestyle and/or purchasing behaviour) (Box 8.8 (p. 163)); secondly, when we want to test a direct marketing approach on a small scale in order to predict how it will work in full. The former type is a comparative test and the latter is a predictive test. Direct marketers test response rates to, for example:

- different mailing lists;
- timing of campaigns: whether business–business customers are more likely to spend their budgets at the beginning or end of a financial year;
- different creative treatment: whether different wording for men and women produces different response rates.

Table 8.1 **A before–after design**

	Experimental group	Control group
Before measure (initial sales)	X1	Y1
Experimental variable (new advertising)	YES	NO
After measure (new level of sales)	X2	Y2
Therefore, effect of experimental variable = (X2 − X1) − (Y2 − Y1)		

Box 8.7 **Using group discussions to investigate consumer reactions to supermarket loyalty schemes**

The study described was conducted in the mid-1990s. The choice of a qualitative methodology was predicated on a desire to explore consumers' reactions to loyalty schemes with minimal prompting from the researcher. Six discussion groups were conducted within an exploratory and relatively unstructured framework that was group oriented rather than moderator influenced. A highly structured discussion guide was not used, since the purpose of the group was to use the experience of the respondents themselves. The use of a flexible guide promoted the maintenance of a good rapport with respondents, facilitated interaction between group members, and provided the opportunity to improvise—to explore unexpected but possibly useful lines of thought and questioning. In terms of analysis, emphasis was placed on extensive verbatim quotes from group members, as the objective was to communicate respondents' perspectives in their own words.

By way of introduction, the groups were given a brief scenario dealing with the introduction of a hypothetical supermarket 'loyalty scheme' as a way of initiating discussion. The subsequent agenda was determined largely by respondents, who were encouraged to explore their experiences of the rewards, satisfactions, dissatisfactions, and frustrations of loyalty schemes within a wider context of direct and database marketing. Respondents were recruited by professional recruiters on the basis that they had received some direct marketing communication in the last three months.

The scenario presented was: 'Your local supermarket launches a "loyalty scheme" that will allow you to accumulate points based on how much you spend. These points will then be redeemable in terms of money off future purchases. In order for you to participate in this scheme you are required to fill out an application form regarding your personal details.'

This particular project found that nearly all of the group participants or their partners were members of a retail loyalty scheme. However, the richness of information to come out of group discussions is demonstrated by the comments volunteered by the participants, such as:

- 'If you shop in that store anyway—it's a good idea.'
- 'It's a bit bloody cheeky I think really, they can obviously bring the prices down because they can operate the scheme, so just bring the bloody prices down.'
- 'People shop because of convenience.'
- 'Wouldn't give my personal details—not for a woman on her own.'
- 'Elderly women are worried about others knowing they are on their own.'
- 'There's no guarantee of confidentiality.'
- 'I don't like to give address. In the old days you could trust people—not these days.'
- 'Its a real Big Brother thing.'

So, alongside general participation, there were concerns about the low level of discount; that such schemes do not result in much switching behaviour, and over what happens to personal details. A more structured survey approach to these issues would probably have lacked this richness of comment.

Source: Based on a study conducted by Martin Evans.

Sampling There is an inevitably close relationship between the choice of data-collection method and research instrument, and the selection of respondents or sample design. Actually, the ideal plan would be to include all relevant people in the study, which would make the study a census. Indeed, this is sometimes possible, if the relevant population is small, and perhaps geographically concentrated, as is sometimes the case in industrial markets. It is more usual, however, for populations to be larger, and thus less suitable for a census. In these circumstances, something less than the whole population will be observed or interviewed, and it is necessary to select a sample from the total population. The main choice in sample design is between those samples based on the laws of probability (probability samples) and those based more on subjectivity (non-probability samples).

Random sampling. When a complete list exists of all individuals or elements in the relevant population (i.e. a sampling frame), it is possible to design a sample that gives each a calculable chance of being selected. This principle provides the basis of random sampling. There is a popular misconception that random is something rather vague and haphazard, like interviewing anyone available in the street, while in fact it is extremely precise.

Box 8.8 **Experimentation**

Suppose a marketer believes sales are low because of inefficient advertising, and wants to establish what will happen if some change is made in advertising. A new advertising campaign is developed and launched, and sales are monitored and compared with sales before the new campaign. In terms of experimentation this would be a simple before–after design, in the following manner:

Before measure	YES (initial sales = X_1)
Experimental variable	YES (new advertising)
After measure	YES (new level of sales = X_2)

The difference between the two levels of sales is taken to be the effect of the new campaign. So, if X_1 is 5,000 units per month and X_2 is 6,000 units per month, the organization might conclude the new campaign to be effective. Clearly, this would not necessarily be valid. If, for example competitors' distribution systems delayed delivery of competing products to the shops during the time of this new campaign, the customers may be purchasing the test product, not because of an effective advertising campaign, but because of the lack of availability of alternative brands.

It is clearly impossible to control competitors' marketing activity when conducting marketing experiments, and there are many other uncontrollable variables to take into account when designing and analysing experiments. For example, there might be a general trend of increasing sales; perhaps sales might have been even higher if the old campaign had continued!

There are dangers of simply comparing sales before and after the introduction of an experimental variable. The effect of time has to be considered, and it might be—as, for example, with poster advertising—that the time delay before achieving any influence might be substantial.

Another problem with the experiment above is that the wrong dependent variable (that is, the variable that is measured to judge the effect of the experimental variable) may be selected. Much depends on what the advertising campaign is trying to do, of course, and it may, therefore, be more valid to measure changes in attitudes, or perceptions, rather than sales.

Take a population composed of twelve people: each could be listed and allocated a number between 1 and 12. Then there are two ways that a sample of three can be selected. The first is called *simple random sampling*, where three numbers are selected from a table of random numbers—for example 5, 6, and 8. Items labelled 5, 6, and 8 would then be the sample. The second approach, called *systematic random sampling*, would be particularly appropriate with a large sample. Here the population size would be divided by the sample size to calculate the sampling interval (n) and then every nth item can be selected. In this example the sample interval would be 12/3 = 4 and so every fourth item would be taken: 1, 5, 9; 2, 6, 8; 3, 7, 11; or 4, 8, 12.

When there are subdivisions in a population, there are four ways of designing a random sample. Take, as a common example for all four, a mailing list purchased by a direct mail company. Assume that the company knows that their most relevant customer groupings are within two geodemographic categories—that is, categories based on a classification of geographical areas according to combinations of such measures as household composition, housing type, etc. (e.g. MOSAIC categories 'High Income Families' and 'Stylish Singles'). These categories are included—and coded as such—on the newly acquired list. These groups, within the list, might represent the 10,000 potentially most lucrative customers. 'High Income Families' are further subdivided in the MOSAIC system into 'Clever Capitalists', 'Rising Materialists', 'Corporate Careerists', 'Ageing Professionals', and 'Small Time Business'. 'Stylish Singles' are divided into 'Bedsits and Shop Flats', 'Studio Singles', 'College and Communal', and 'Chattering Classes'. In total the two main MOSAIC groups divide into nine sub-clusters.

Assume that a random sample of 1,000 people is to be taken from the new list. The alternative approaches would be as follows.

The first method would be to select the same number from each of the nine clusters, that is 111 from each. Selection could employ the *systematic* approach described above. This is referred to as *stratified random sampling* using a *uniform sampling fraction*.

A second method would be to select that proportion of the sample from each sub-cluster that reflects the proportion of the cluster that live in each. This is again a *stratified* sample, but this time

Table 8.2 Mailing list profile

Clusters and sub-clusters	Percentage of high income families and and Stylish Singles in each sub-cluster (= sample proportions)	Number in sample in each cluster
High Income Families		
Clever Capitalists	10	100
Rising Materialists	8	80
Corporate Careerists	6	60
Ageing Professionals	20	200
Small Time Business	12	120
Stylish Singles		
Bedsits and Shop Flats	6	60
Studio Singles	8	80
College and Communal	5	50
Chattering Classes	25	250
TOTAL		**1,000**

Box 8.9 Three clusters

*Clever Capitalists
Rising Materialists
Corporate Careerists
*Ageing Professionals
Small Time Business
Bedsits and Shop Flats
*Studio Singles
College and Communal
Chattering Classes

with a *variable sampling fraction*. Thus, to make up the sample, we select from each subgroup the percentages shown in Table 8.2.

However, it is not always essential to include respondents from each subgroup and it may not be convenient if, for example, the study requires personal not postal interviewing and the fieldwork costs of covering nine geographically dispersed areas are high. Then, it is possible randomly to select only some of the clusters and the choice of which to select is itself based on random sampling. It might be decided, for example, to concentrate the fieldwork in just three clusters; Box 8.9 shows how a random selection of three clusters from the nine has been identified. Clever Capitalists, Ageing Professionals, and Studio Singles have been selected by systematic sampling and either 333 people from each would be selected, according to a uniform sampling fraction, or a proportion of each according to a variable sampling fraction. This approach is referred to as *multi-stage sampling* and there can be many more stages than in this example.

Finally, further concentration of fieldwork is possible if only a very few subgroups are selected,

but the sample includes everyone in these subgroups. In the example, if only Ageing Professionals are selected, the sample of 1,000 might be fulfilled by interviewing everyone in this category from the list. This is referred to as *cluster sampling* and can again be implemented through selection at two or more levels, though it is probably better suited to a situation in which the strata are equal in size, since a random selection of very few subgroups producing exactly the desired sample size, is unlikely to occur. The question of how sample size is calculated is not explored here, but relevant references are provided at the end of the chapter.

Quota sampling. With many marketing research programmes no suitable sampling frame exists (for example, there is no complete list of baked beans buyers). Typically, such markets are segmented according to characteristics such as age, sex, and socio-economic groupings, where there is no accessible sampling frame. Quota sampling allows for such factors, as the following example demonstrates.

Assume that a market is segmented according to age and socio-economic group, producing four segments (Box 8.10). Sufficient data are available for marketing regions (for example, ITV areas) to estimate the incidence of these characteristics in regional populations. For example, 70 per cent of an ITV region might be C_2DE, and 67 per cent might be 25 years and older. Assuming that a sample of 500 is required, this type of sample design would produce cells of the relevant sampling characteristics with quotas allocated to each in proportion to their incidence in the population. In this case, because 70 per cent of the population are C_2DE and 67 per cent are 35 years or older, the

Box 8.10 **Quota sampling**

15–34 year olds in socio-economic group ABC₁
15–34 year olds in C₂DE
35 years and older in ABC₁
35 years and older in C₂DE

quota of 35 years and older C₂DEs is 70 per cent of 67 per cent of 500 (the sample size), and this produces a total of 235.

It is then up to the interviewer to select the correct quotas of respondents with each set of characteristics. This would very often be the basis for street interviewing and, hopefully, the misconception (indeed, oxymoron) of selecting people *at random in the street* is now apparent.

2.1.4 *Stage 4.* Data collection

During the fieldwork stage of actually collecting data the main types of error and bias are due to poor interviewing or observation procedures. Kahn and Cannel (1968) propose three conditions necessary for successful interviewing: accessibility of the interviewer to the respondent, and of the information to the respondent (both physically and psychologically); cognition on the respondent's part, in understanding what is required; motivation on the part of the respondent to answer, and to answer accurately. They also describe five symptoms of inadequate response that can occur during interviewing: (*a*) partial response, where the respondent gives a relevant but incomplete answer; (*b*) non-response, which is either refusal to answer or a silent response; (*c*) inaccurate response, which is a biased or distorted answer; (*d*) irrelevant response, where the question asked is not answered; and (*e*) verbalized response problem, where a respondent explains why he or she cannot answer the question.

To encourage respondents to reply more fully and accurately, experienced interviewers develop skills such as using neutral questions, like 'how do you mean?' and 'could you say more about that?'. Sometimes aided recall (indicating some of the possible answers) can be used, as can the explanation of questions to respondents. The danger of explanation, however, is that the interviewer actually changes the meaning of questions, so there is

a thin line between interviewer bias and interviewer help.

Non-verbal behaviour can be exploited during interviews, with interviewers employing 'expectant pauses, glances and nods' to elicit more information. Indeed, non-verbal communication is two way, because respondents' intended meanings can be interpreted through their gestures and intonation. However, interviewers should be aware of the dangers of misinterpreting what respondents are trying to say. For this reason it is usual to require interviewers to record verbatim everything a respondent says.

This last point introduces further interviewing problems, since responses have to be recorded as well as questions asked. Open-ended questions especially create recording difficulties, because each word of sometimes lengthy replies has to be taken down.

Interviewers have to repeat their task with many different respondents, but with the same questionnaire, so the resulting boredom and fatigue should be taken into account when setting the number of interviews, or interviewing time, for each interviewer. The repetition, for example, of asking the same question in the same way over and over again can eventually lead the interviewer to short-cuts by, for example, paraphrasing questions, which provides another source of interviewer bias.

Interviewers have responsibilities beyond asking questions and recording answers—for example, there is the initial task of making contact with appropriate respondents, and the need to gain sufficient cooperation for the interview to proceed. When quota sampling is used, interviewers are provided with a list of the characteristics they must look for in potential respondents, and errors often occur when interviewers become tired of waiting for the 'right' people to come along. Close supervision can go some way to overcoming this problem—for example, by checking up that some of those interviewed do indeed possess appropriate characteristics. This encourages interviewers to select more carefully, and, if a quota cell is difficult to complete, to discuss this with a supervisor rather than attempting to cover up. An alternative interviewing point might be decided upon, or merely a decision to try again later. The same could apply in poor weather, when no one wants to stop to be interviewed.

When a survey is sampled randomly, interviewers will work from a list of names and addresses.

When the named respondent is not at the listed address at the time of call, no one else should normally be interviewed. Up to three callbacks are usually made and, if there is still no success, another respondent may be randomly selected.

For some surveys, especially those using an electoral register sampling frame, some addresses may be out of date, either because the respondent has moved (or died), or, indeed, because the whole street no longer exists. Again, another respondent should be selected from the sampling frame at random (rather than the interviewer choosing the most convenient person).

Often only about a third of the interviewer's time is spent actually interviewing, because of the time needed for travelling to interview points, waiting to contact appropriate people, possibly editing questionnaires at the end of an interviewing period, and certain general administrative functions.

2.1.5 *Stage 5.* **Data processing**

Once the data have been collected, they have to be analysed, edited, and tested, before communication to the decision-maker. It is all too easy for the planning stages of a research programme to revolve around designing samples and questionnaires and little else. When this happens, the researcher will be shaken by the problems of data analysis. Perhaps hundreds of questionnaires have been returned—how should they be analysed? What should happen to open-ended questions—there appear to be as many different ways of answering these as there are respondents?

The key is to plan in advance—indeed this is another reason for this general division of the whole research process into a series of stages.

A valuable discipline is to list all the data-processing requirements in Stage 1, at the time of compiling the data list; it is more likely, then, to be reasonably sure that the data list is accurate.

Space does not permit a discussion of statistical analysis in this chapter, but the Further Reading includes texts that cover this matter.

2.1.6 *Stage 6.* **Communicating results**

In the same way that it was suggested in Stage 1 that communication between decision-maker and researcher is important for the research programmes objectives to be clarified and agreed, so the same applies at the end of the process. Results have to be communicated to the users of research

in such a way that their meaning is not distorted and so that they answer the brief as originally agreed.

3 **Marketing intelligence**

WHEREAS marketing research is concerned with relatively focused aspects of marketing information, the theme of this section is one of 'wider horizons' with the main (though not exclusive) contexts of analysis being both external to the organization and concerned with less immediate decision-making.

The context of analysis is, in some senses, the least tangible one of an MkIS, because, by dealing with the marketing environment through environmental scanning, investigation is less focused than marketing research—what is studied may be totally irrelevant to the organization.

The basis of 'intelligence' informational requirements for marketing is that marketing's environment (Fig. 8.2) provides conditions and influences that impinge or potentially impinge upon marketing. Examples include the effects of government economic policy, changes in technology, legislative changes, and the implications of societal change.

The importance of the environment comes from the nature of marketing itself—for example from the Institute of Marketing's definition of marketing: 'the management process responsible for identifying, anticipating and satisfying customer requirements profitably.'

This importance is based on the word 'anticipate', which requires a degree of forecasting and projection into the future. Merely to 'identify' customer requirements usually involves specific marketing-research programmes, but to anticipate requires a broader perspective—continuously monitoring current trends (not all of which are necessarily obviously relevant) in order to plan ahead.

It is the marketing function in an organization that is primarily responsible for looking outwards. Indeed it is generally the case that this function, being at the interface of the organization and its environment, is at least theoretically in a particularly good position to understand what is happening—and what might happen—outside, in order to initiate appropriate organizational response.

It should be added, however, that marketing's

environment is concerned not only with things external to the organization but also with those influences internal to it but external to the marketing function—such as the organizational position and relative power of the marketing function *vis-à-vis* other functions.

Some influences might directly affect marketing activities: new technology might provide alternative methods of conducting the same activities, or legislation governing these; other influences might cause market behaviour to change: changes in social structure or social attitudes, or changes in lifestyles resulting from technological and/or economic change, might have indirect implications for marketing response.

A further point is the interaction of influences: the combined impact of economic and technological change, for example, might give extra momentum to (say) the home-centred society in certain segments, since in-home entertainment expands with technological development; home working becomes a reality for more people via PCs linked via a modem to their employer; and enforced leisure time expands with high unemployment.

The competitive environment, as a component of the market, can be included, because a greater understanding of the competitive nature of the market environment is probably becoming more important. As Unger (1981) has suggested 'knowing what the consumer wants is often not too helpful if a dozen other companies also know . . . a company must be competitor oriented. It must look for weak points in the positions of its competitors and then launch marketing attacks against these.'

Unethically, there has been an explosion of mechanical observation techniques that come into the category of 'competitor intelligence'—which is sometimes a euphemism for espionage. Equipment can be located in mobile vans parked outside competitors' buildings and record what is being displayed on VDU screens inside—plans for new products, direct marketing creative, databases, and so on. Clearly we do not legitimize this as an example of observation in market research, but it does raise an interesting point about where to draw the line between market intelligence and industrial espionage—and this issue is likely to become more pronounced as more sophisticated technology becomes available. The Market Research Society's Code of Conduct explicitly states that 'any form of espionage' shall not be associated with marketing research.

3.1 Environmental scanning

Scanning has been described concisely by Jain (1981) as 'an early warning system for the environmental forces which may impact a company's products and markets in the future'.

In this way scanning enables an organization to *act* rather than to *react* to opportunities and/or threats. The focus is not on 'the immediate', but rather has a longer-term perspective that is necessary for being in a position to plan ahead. Indeed, the whole effectiveness of organizations is to some extent dependent on their abilities to understand—and to use this understanding of—environmental uncertainty. One key point is that environmental influence is not static but continuously changing, hence the need for continuous monitoring of various influences, both internal and external. A danger of not thinking in this way might be a kind of 'Future Shock'.

Some writers and researchers point to organizational problems in the practical implementation of scanning procedures—as well as in more general aspects of marketing decision-making. Aguilar (1967), for instance, demonstrated that those who most need scanning information (top management) are not those who deal with the collecting and analysing of such data, and this is a problem because there is quite a distortion and loss of information before the data reach the decision-makers.

In smaller companies Aguilar (1967) found that top management were the main scanners, but, whereas this might appear to overcome the above problem, the information they generally scanned was somewhat narrow and too focused in nature to be considered a true environmental scan. That is, management was concerned more with the more immediate state of specific industries and markets than with scanning widely in order to identify longer-term trends and effects.

Three organizational scanning modes were identified by Jain (1981)—that scanning is conducted by:

- line managers;
- planners;
- a specific environmental scanning department.

Cravens *et al.* (1980) suggest that the main commitment to scanning should be on the part of line managers, but this is possibly a rather narrow view. It is probably appropriate for people other than line mangers to scan, because line managers tend to be very, if not too, close to their own spheres, so that broader horizons of perspective can be difficult to achieve. This is certainly the view adopted by Jain (1981).

A related consideration is whether scanning should be conducted centrally or decentrally. Jain (1981) and Johnson and Scholes (1984) point to the importance of being able to scan the environment more globally and therefore more synergistically—something that would be difficult if different environments were scanned by different departments for their own relatively narrow perspectives and uses.

With these problems and dangers in mind, some suggestions are now submitted for how to scan the marketing environment.

3.2 Techniques for scanning

A useful framework integrating the models or stages of the scanning process with specific techniques for conducting the scan has been extended by the writer from the work of Jain (1981), whose empirical research resulted in a systematizing of environmental scanning.

Stage 1. Environmental events are picked up from a continuous literature search (and any other source of information, such as personal contacts and so on). Information collection should be conducted not 'by area' according to specialist departments, but rather by freer-thinking teams (preferably including representation from the decision-making planners).

Stage 2. Relevant trends may be screened using Trend-Impact Analysis. For this DELPHI panels are set up, to identify for each environmental event:

- the desirability of the event;
- the organization's technical feasibility of using or coping with the event;
- the probability of the event occurring;
- the likely time (within the next few years) of the event occurring.

These may be assessed quantitatively, for example from '0' through '0.5' to '1.0'.

The team may also discuss the nature of organizational impact in terms of areas of marketing affected, such as direct implications for advertising or market-research procedures, or implications for changes in market behaviour to which marketing should respond.

Because the problem is essentially to identify change and trends and then to determine their likely impact on the organization in the future, a matrix for evaluating environmental influence (in terms of threats and opportunities) might be useful. This uses two main criteria: the degree of probability of the influence happening at all, and the degree of impact it will have on the organization if it does happen.

Stage 3. This next stage is to analyse the current and future organizational impact of relevant events. This requires more detailed consideration of the selected events—analysing effects 'between' events. Cross-Impact Analysis can help here. A grid plotting events against themselves is constructed, thereby forcing analysis of the interaction of events.

Stage 4. These results can be fed into more conventional SWOT analysis to relate events and their implications to the organization's strengths and weaknesses.

☞ '...it is necessary to summarize the unit's present position in its major markets, in the form of a SWOT analysis for each major segment, product, or business group. The word SWOT derives from the initial letters of the words strengths, weaknesses, opportunities, and threats...' (Chapter 19, p. 461)

Stage 5. The planners may also be involved in the reworking of scenario building for the marketing impact of these events. This was a recommendation made by Aguilar (1967) because of the problem he identified over the information-collectors not being the decision-makers, resulting in poor use and integration of information.

Stage 6. From here there will be further progression as an input to corporate strategy planning. However good the scanning may be, the results should be properly used. In general terms the organization can respond to its environment by: (1) opposition—it can fight the constraints; (2) modification—it can change its market segments or mixes; (3) relocation—it can change to another market.

4 Marketing productivity analysis

IN marketing productivity analysis, the organization uses information already available internally in order to quantify marketing inputs and outputs. In other words, we are concerned here, for example, with examining the level of advertising or sales effort (the inputs) and then measuring the response in terms of numbers of enquiries, orders, and sales revenue—the 'outputs'.

There are many accounting procedures relevant here, especially those based on ratio analysis. Because of the space restriction, these will not be covered (but Chapter 17 and the Further Reading at the end of this chapter point the interested reader to other sources). However, one of the more topical developments will be covered here—namely, the trend towards marketing 'direct', which enables greater use of *productivity analysis* because response rates can more easily be identified and attributed. Much of this has come about because of the impact of information technology (IT) on marketing, notably the database. Indeed, the many studies of MkIS that blossomed after IT became a significant factor, especially during the 1980s and 1990s, are clear evidence of this trend. The mere presence of computer hardware, however, is not evidence of IT's usefulness or appropriateness. Indeed, in a qualitative study, Kench and Evans (1991) found significant differences between 'strategic' versus 'tactical' uses of computer and IT systems. Some of the most sophisticated 'online' database technology is often employed only on a relatively low-level day-to-day tactical basis.

4.1 New 'in-house' sources of data

Examples of sources of data include customer records and results from sales promotion campaigns (coupons, competitions, etc.) and transactional data—the latter being one of the major growth areas for contemporary marketing.

Retailers such as Tesco, Safeway, and Sainsbury are capturing transactional data at point of sale (pos) via loyalty-card schemes. By late 1996 Tesco had analysed its customer database and identified 5,000 different segments—each of which was targeted differently. Its aim at that time was to be literally one-to-one by 1999! The company analysing the Tesco data is DunnHumby, and Clive Humby (1996*b*) describes the interrogation of data and states that it is not worth including 'everything'. There is always the danger of 'paralysis by analysis'. Humby goes on to suggest that 'it is not the detailed transaction data that is of interest, but patterns in transactions, such as an increasing balance over time of the range of products purchased' (Humby 1996*a*).

Such data can also be used to 'score' customers—another emerging measure of 'marketing productivity'. Most items of data are scorable—we shall take just two as examples. We might know from previous campaigns that we have had a greater success rate when marketing to those with the 'Mr' title rather than those with Mrs or Ms, in which case we can give a quantitative weight to 'title'. Postcode is especially revealing, because we can profile geodemographically from this. This allows us to compare with previous success/failure rates and then score the geodemographic cluster and the postcode itself at different levels—for example, do we have more success in Cardiff (CF) or Bristol (BS)? This is an example of scoring from two of the most basic elements of data. By adding lifestyle and transactional data and scoring all those in the database on a weighted index that incorporates all of these variables, we can produce very useful league tables for targeting purposes, and these provide detailed measures of marketing productivity.

Marketing-database data become 'information' when we identify the recency, frequency, and monetary value (RFM) of customer orders.

■ *Recency*: knowing that a customer has purchased from us in the past is important, as we are probably less interested in customers who bought from us in 1984 but not since than in more recent customers, but this information is insufficient.

■ *Frequency*: a one-off purchase may also make a customer less attractive (depending, of course, on the product market in which we operate, so knowing how often customers buy from us is an important measure.

■ *Monetary value*: small orders are usually less attractive than larger ones, so this is yet another measure of significance.

Indeed, marketers are increasingly concentrating on their 'better' customers—those who have the highest monetary value (and frequency) of purchase—and are segmenting on the basis of 'volume' because in this way their actions are more cost effective, because they concentrate on those who bring greater returns. Vilfredo Pareto's theory of income distribution has been transferred and borrowed by direct marketers to support the proposition that 80 per cent of sales come from just 20 per cent of customers; in many markets the ratio can be even more polarized (95:5 is not uncommon). The Pareto principle is often quoted by direct marketers and is certainly relevant to this discussion of RFM analysis. RFM analysis, by the very nature of the variables involved, clearly involves tracking transactional data by the database—actual purchase history is needed.

In addition to leading to the identification of volume segments and best prospects, the RFM information also contributes to the calculation of 'lifetime value'—another of the new cornerstone *productivity* measures. 'Lifetime' is perhaps a little of an overstatement;—it refers not to the lifetime of the customer, but rather to a designated period of time during which he or she has been a customer of your organization. Sometimes we might use a 'lifetime' period of only three years. It would probably be better to refer to longtime value analysis, but, whatever period is relevant, the concept of what that customer is worth to the organization in sales and profit terms over a period of time is a critical marketing-productivity-analysis concept.

This brief overview of some of the emerging measures of internal market information shows how sophisticated databased marketing, in particular, has become. From the days of 'not knowing which half of one's advertising is effective' we now have the capability to measure more precisely marketing inputs and outputs within this area of marketing productivity analysis. The final element of the MkIS takes this a little further. It is concerned with methods of modelling market behaviour and response and many of the emerging approaches are again based on databased marketing.

5 Marketing modelling

SECTION 4 discussed transactional data as being at the heart of many databases. At the end of the 1990s a new development was that of *biographics*—the fusion of profile and transaction data. Fig. 8.4

shows some of the typical sources of data for fusion into biographical profiles. Indeed, the ability to match names, addresses, purchasing behaviour, and lifestyles all together onto one record allows companies to build a model of someone's life—that is, the state of the art with respect to market modelling is not so much 'market' modelling as modelling 'individual' buying behaviour. Database linking occurs on two levels: first, on an industry level—census data, geodemographics, and lifestyle data build up a broad picture of the population—ideal for segmentation purposes; secondly, at the individual company level—matching these data to credit history, actual purchasing behaviour, media response, and the RFM of purchases can potentially describe someone's life.

Often it is very useful to be able to model, geographically, what the database information tells us. The key to this is address and postcode, because from this information there are geographical information systems (GIS) that allow any linked database to produce map overlays. Another application of GIS-linked data is in the citing of posters for direct response advertising, based on the profile of the neighbourhood or even the profile of 'through' traffic. A related approach solution is the calculation drive times as isochrones (the distance one can drive in a given time along roads).

Other dimensions of modelling from database data revolve around data mining, which refers to the digging around in databases in a relatively unstructured way with the aim of discovering links between customer behaviour and almost any vari-

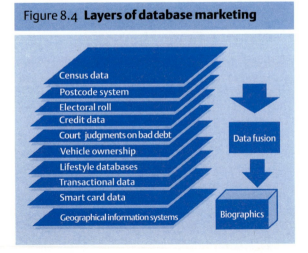

Figure 8.4 **Layers of database marketing**

Census data
Postcode system
Electoral roll
Credit data
Court judgments on bad debt
Vehicle ownership
Lifestyle databases
Transactional data
Smart card data
Geographical information systems

Data fusion

Biographics

able that might potentially be useful. There is a parallel with market research versus environmental scanning, because the former focuses on specific problems and the latter has a wider-ranging brief to identify anything in the marketing environment that might have a relevant impact upon the marketing operation.

Marketers are investigating a variety of marketing-modelling approaches based on their database data. For example, some have examined consumers' individual biorhythms and 'star signs' as predictors of their purchasing patterns and others have linked their transactional and profile data with meteorological databases to predict, perhaps months ahead, what demand there might be for ice cream or woolly sweaters. The psychological characteristics of the 'first born' are also being modelled in the buying context.

Another example is afforded by the linking with a GIS database to target as specifically as a newspaper round. This is usually around 150–200 households, and, by linking transactional data with lifestyle, geodemographics, and panel data, a very accurate picture of individual buying patterns emerges. The newspaper round—or milk round—can be used for door drops or direct mail as well as for local catchment area analysis. This has been formalized by Unigate, which has advertised a doorstep delivery service based on MOSAIC geodemographic profiles at local level. In addition to product delivery, it offered a delivery service for samples and vouchers and a delivery and collection service for questionnaires.

A number of dedicated tools are available for analysing databases. One such 'product' is VIPER—software developed by Brann Software. This tool

Figure 8.5 **VIPER database interrogation**

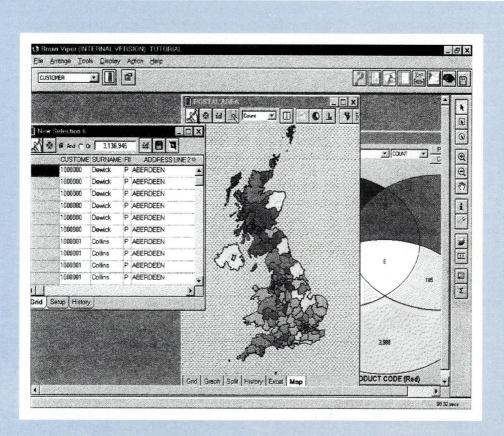

allows very fast linking and analysis of different databases. Fig. 8.5 demonstrates some of the prints-out from VIPER-processed queries on a lifestyle database, linked with a geodemographic database and a GIS. The questions asked might have been: select those (name and address) who claim to be readers of the *Sun*, like to play Bingo, drink above average quantities of lager, and live in South Wales.

The graphical print-out of the model combines data from all of the databases interrogated and shows, in topographical form, where these people live and, in tabular form, the actual names and addresses of the individuals concerned. VIPER is not the only database interrogator on the market but it does reflect the sort of capability that was available in the late 1990s; the speed with which the analysis can be completed is indeed impressive—and on what is now a relatively standard desktop PC.

As a summary of this section, the writer suggests that transactional data, fused with profiling data, will produce the new biographics, and this will be the basis of marketing modelling over the next few years. It will also provide the overwhelming source of data for marketing productivity analysis—and indeed will be the mother lode of all marketing information well into the twenty-first century.

6 The future

IN 1997 the writer and colleagues conducted some market research into consumer attitudes towards direct marketing. In interviews, some of the older women in particular declared that they received substantial quantities of direct mail on behalf of charities. They also said that this was not 'junk mail' because it was of interest to them—the matching of 'causes' with their own interests was very accurate. They were so moved by the direct mailing that they felt it important to donate—and they did just this. As far as the direct marketer is concerned, this 'response' reinforces the donors' status on the database and they will be targeted again—and probably by related charities, who are likely to share lists.

The point that the writer feels important is that in 'research' the women went on to say that they were barely able to afford to donate, but felt they 'had to', and were almost in tears over the issue. The reaction of the direct-marketing industry was

'but it worked'. Such reliance on mechanistic experimentation (testing) at the expense of more insightful research is submitted here as being an issue that the industry would do well to address. Although this targeting might 'work' in the short term, what problems might be being stored up for the future—and not only when the 'targets' decide 'enough is enough' and refuse to donate any more and 'bin' all subsequent mailings or when they merely spread ill will about the charities' direct-marketing approach.

One future issue, then, is that, as marketing moves more and more towards direct and data-based approaches, there is a real danger that interview research as explored in Section 2.1.3 will be displaced by experimentation that in turn relies on behavioural response rather than attitudinal measures. Much database data, such as transactional and profiling data, provide valuable information on who is buying what, when, how, and where, but it is market research that can get beneath the surface even further and discover reasons 'why' behaviour is as it is.

Direct marketing needs to be able to identify individuals. Even if direct marketers do not use the personal details for immediate selling, they are keen to develop databases of personal information—DUGGING (data under the guise of research) (see also Insert). The Market Research Society has long outlawed this practice but has now compromised over the issue by having dual codes of conduct for the two 'reasons' for data collection. These issues are well explored by Fletcher and Peters (1996), and their research revealed practitioners to be reasonably comfortable with the situation. Researchers and sellers were keen to make it clear to their informants the purpose to which personal details might be put. However, Fletcher and Peters show that privacy issues are highly relevant here and have not been resolved.

> **Sugging!**
> An issue is raised by Fletcher and Peters (1996) with respect to the use of market-research data to populate databases for personalized selling. The main problem is one of using marketing research data for selling purposes (selling under the guise of research: SUGGING).

The Market Research Society (1997) Code overcomes the conflict with the instruction: 'members shall only use the term confidential survey research to describe projects which are based upon respondent anonymity and do not involve the divulgence of names or personal details of informants to others except for research purposes.'

The new code excludes, from its 'confidentialresearch' principles, the collecting of personal data for sales or promotional approaches to the informant and for the compilation of databases that will be used for canvassing and fund-raising. In such circumstances the data collector should not claim to be involved in a confidential survey and should make this clear to the informant.

In a variety of empirical research studies (Evans *et al.* 1996) consumers have expressed concerns over the lack of privacy of their personal details; *1984* it may not be, but the privacy issue clearly needs constant vigilance and the writer suggests that this will be an issue for the future as well as for the present.

and therefore provides the ability for marketers to evaluate the effects of different marketing approaches. Extending this analysis, the chapter has also explored some of the contemporary directions that marketing modelling is taking. Specifically, the database is providing marketers with vast amounts of information—even biographical information on specific customers—and this is allowing innovative approaches, based on profile and transactional data, even on biorhythms and astrology!

Some of the emerging issues for the future revolve around the use of technology in the marketing information industry. These are, on the one hand, providing marketers with exciting and cheaper ways of accessing information. On the other hand, they also lead to some ethical concerns over the use of personal (private?) information of consumers and also to unethical methods of collecting competitor intelligence.

7 **Summary**

THIS chapter has reviewed contemporary aspects of market information and research. A model of the marketing information system has been suggested, together with a summary of some of the issues involved with each of its components.

It is clear that modern marketing information is concerned with much more than the image of market-research interviewers with clipboards. Even within marketing research, there is an explosion of data collection via the telephone, post, and 'new' media such as interactive TV and the Internet.

Beyond marketing research, the scanning of marketing's environment is increasingly important in order to stay ahead of the competition, but where do you draw the line between competitive intelligence and industrial espionage? Techniques have been suggested for the collection of marketing intelligence, and the dynamic and interactive nature of environmental trends and factors have been discussed.

Although the traditional aspects of (for example) ratio analysis within marketing productivity analysis have not been covered because of space constraints, the emerging methods of tracking the results of marketing inputs in terms of output effects have been reviewed. These are based, essentially, on the use of databased marketing information, which is increasingly customer specific

Further reading

Marketing Information Systems

Fletcher, K. (1994), 'The Evolution and Use of Information Technology in Marketing', in M. Baker (ed.), *The Marketing Book* (Oxford: Butterworth Heinemann).

—— (1996), *Information Technology and Marketing Management* (Hemel Hempsted: Prentice Hall Ltd.).

O'Connor, J., and Galvin, E. (1997), *Marketing and Information Technology* (London: Pitman).

Piercy, N., and Evans, M. J. (1994), 'Developing Marketing Information Systems', in M. Baker (ed.), *The Marketing Book* (Oxford: Butterworth-Heinemann).

Marketing Research

McDaniel, C., and Gates, R. (1996), *Contemporary Marketing Research*. (St Paul, Min.: West).

Moutinho, L., and Evans, M. J., *Applied Marketing Research* (Reading, Mass.: Addison-Wesley).

Marketing Intelligence

Aguilar, F. J. (1967), *Scanning the Business Environment* (New York: Macmillan).

Brownlie, D. (1994), 'Environmental Scanning', in M. Baker (ed), *The Marketing Book* (Oxford: Butterworth-Heinemann).

Evans, M. J. (1988), 'Scanning the Marketing Environment', *Marketing Intelligence and Planning* (Summer).

Marketing Productivity Analysis

Piercy, N., and Evans, M. J. (1983), *Managing Marketing Information* (Beckenham: Croom Helm).

Wilson, R. M. S. (1981), *Financial Dimensions of Marketing* (London: Macmillan/The Research Foundation of the Institute of Cost and Management Accountants).

Market modelling

Piercy, N., and Evans, M. J. (1983), *Managing Marketing Information* (Beckenham: Croom Helm).

Evans, M. J. (1994), 'Market Segmentation', in M. Baker (ed), *The Marketing Book* (Oxford: Butterworth-Heinemann).

Diamantopoulos, A., and Schlegelmilch, B. (1997), *Taking the Fear out of Data Analysis* (London: Dryden).

Discussion questions

1 What is the relationship between marketing, marketing research, and marketing intelligence?

2 Error and bias can occur at every stage of the research process. Discuss this statement.

3 Go to your business library and extract two pieces of information that you, personally, are intrigued by, from each of the following sources of secondary data: *Who Owns Whom*, *Business Monitor*, *Family Expenditure Survey*, *Regional Trends*, *Social Trends*, *Mintel*, Market Assessment, *Target Group Index*, *Retail Business*, *National Readership Survey*, *BRAD*, *MEAL*.

4 How do consumer panels and retail audits operate and what are their uses?

5 How can the Bayesian approach help determine cost effectiveness of a research programme?

6 Observation is objective, interviewing is subjective. Discuss.

7 How and why are group discussions employed in marketing research?

8 What is the concern over the use of 'testing' rather than 'research' by direct marketers?

9 How would you select a sample of 500 consumers by (*a*) random and (*b*) quota methods?

10 Conduct an environmental scan for a product market of your choice, indicating to which events and trends an organization in that market should respond.

11 How are profiling and transactional data fusing to form biographics? What are the implications for (*a*) marketing productivity analysis and (*b*) marketing modelling?

12 To what extent do you think that the collection and analysis of personal details of consumers is an invasion of personal privacy?

Buy a car—and provide the marketer with a wealth of marketing information

A motor-car dealer has been on a marketing information course and discovered that he has much more information about his customers than he previously realized. Before attending the course he was really rather reactive in his marketing—waiting for customers to book services/repairs for their vehicles and, apart from some cooperative local advertising with his supplying motor manufacturer, generally waiting for people to come into the showroom. Now he realizes that he can be proactive and understand his customers and potential customers much more—and on an individual basis.

He was shown that when a car was purchased he gathered information on the purchaser—name, address, and telephone number. Also, when there was any credit agreement, there was information on the customer's financial and occupational circumstances. As a result of the course he realized that he could send letters (perhaps backed by telephone calls) asking about the new customer's evaluation of how well he or she was treated during the purchase process, thus potentially starting a relationship with that customer. Furthermore, such satisfaction surveys could be used to gather a little bit more information about the customer—perhaps lifestyle details that could help with the targeting of relevant offers.

At regular intervals, he could mail customers to remind them about servicing—and after several 'services' he would know the mileage that customers normally did, thus making the reminders more timely. He could, by checking the purchase date in the log book, also send out a timely reminder about when the MOT is needed. At appropriate intervals he could contact the customer individually with news about new car launches and modifications, thereby creating selling opportunities for his dealership. Wine and cheese evenings could be arranged for selected customers for appropriate launches.

Cross-selling would also be possible, because he could contact the customer with details of car alarm systems and other accessories. The customer's partner could become an important target as well—the second family car might be a 'used' vehicle—and targeting for cross and up-selling could be approached in a similar way. He might also become aware of the ages of the couple's children so that he could target them when they reached the age of 17.

The customer's business address might be useful for targeting a potential fleet market. An analysis of the addresses of customers—geodemographically profiling their postcodes—was helpful in defining his catchment area and in identifying who and where potential customers live. This surprised the dealer, who previously thought he knew his market. Likely targets in this catchment area who are not as yet customers could then be mailed, with invitations to attend launches or other events.

The dealer also now has a 'list', which he sells on to warranty or 'breakdown' companies. He muses over the ethics of doing this—but it **is** a lucrative operation!

He realizes that, with regular contact, a relationship might be developed with some of his customers. He recognizes that, if he were able to retain a customer—and his or her family—over several years, the 'lifetime value' of their business would be quite significant, and at the same time much cheaper than trying to recruit new customers.

Discussion question

This case describes how a manager can use information readily available within his firm to gain a fuller understanding of his market and to identify market opportunities. What inexpensive information available outside the firm might further enhance the value of this information?

Case 2
Newland PLC
Keith Blois

1 Newland's background

In 1999 Newland, a specialist engineering distributor based in North London, was considering its future. The company had a long and complicated history from being a manufacturing concern through to its present position where it now concentrates entirely on the distribution of a standard range of high-quality engineering components. It ceased all manufacturing activities in 1986 and from then concentrated on distributing components purchased from a number of suppliers. It has eleven employees and a turnover of £4.48 million. Mr Burridge, the majority shareholder of Newland, leaves the day-to-day running of the company in the hands of Mr Tyrell, the Managing Director, but takes an active interest in Newland's strategy and particularly its results.

Of the eleven employees, two are responsible for testing every component as it is delivered to Newland to ensure that it conforms with the appropriate British Standard specification. There are two staff who receive phone orders and also deal with customers' enquiries about such matters as prices, technical specifications, deliveries, and complaints. The warehouse supervisor, with two assistants, draws items from stock and packs them ready for delivery. Three staff deal with the accounts and administration. No 'on-the-road' sales staff are employed.

Mr Tyrell oversees the whole operation and, knowing 'everything' about the organization, can, and does when necessary, take over any employee's work. He carries a lot of commercial information in his head. This is not because he wishes to hide information from the employees, but simply because he does not like paperwork and gives matters such as filing, clearing his desk, etc. a very low priority. In fact, he readily shares his knowledge of the business with the other employees when either he sees that they need it or they ask for it.

In spite of this division of labour, the staff have built up a tradition of helping each other if any one is under pressure. Mr Tyrell allowed this situation to develop once he was sure that each employee had sufficient competence to undertake the work of other staff. However he did this only when they were clear about the limitations of their capabilities. For example, the inspection of the products requires special training.

2 Product range

Newland sells inch and metric sizes of a wide range of standard designs of engineering joints for specialized pipe work. There are about 1,100 different items in its catalogue grouped into twelve categories. The selling prices range from about £4 to £100 per item.

In total Newland has about 1,000 different product lines in stock at any one time and on average holds four months' stock. By the standards of the typical engineering distributor, which holds two months' stock, this is very large. However, as Table 1 shows, four months' stock of some items is a very small number in absolute terms. Furthermore, even in the case of those items where the absolute levels of stock are large, occasionally several orders are received close together and this reduces the stock level dramatically. Luckily Newland enjoys very good relationships with its suppliers and a number of them are willing and able to make rush deliveries when this is necessary.

3 The database and order processing

There is one important aspect of Newland's organization that arose from a fortuitous accident. In 1979 the then owner, Mr Meen, was joined by his son, who had a passion for computers. He persuaded his father to invest in what, at the time, was an advanced computer plus some state-of-the-art software for recording sales and inventory as well as handling accounting functions.

No rational analysis would have justified this investment at that time, but, since its installation (and the surprisingly rapid and successful implementation of the system) it has become a major asset. Since the mid-1980s there has been a terminal beside each of the phones used to receive customer enquiries, and this enables the staff to tell customers at once whether or not the required items are in stock. If they are not, the staff can indicate when deliveries are expected from Newland's suppliers. If customers wish to place an order, it is possible to check whether they are an established customer. If they are, then it can be determined whether they have any outstanding items of business with Newland. For example, do they have any unfulfilled orders with Newland or do they owe Newland money? If they are not an established customer, then a display indicates the information required to establish a file for them.

Table 1 **Sales by product group, 1997/8**

Group	No. of items in group	Unit sales
1	47	46,741
2	107	100,089
3	112	72,425
4	164	120,035
5	133	27,678
6	45	244,743
7	64	15,127
8	144	69,735
9	124	80,785
10	112	2,843
11	51	699
12	33	6,385

When an order is placed, the sales clerk enters it through his terminal, asking the customer as he does so what mode of delivery is required. If the item is in stock, Newland guarantees to get it into the hands of the national carrier (e.g. Securicor, DHL, etc.) specified by the customer within twelve hours—except at weekends. The cost of the delivery is added to the invoice without any handling charge. The computer then raises an invoice and adjusts the stock levels.

The use of independent delivery organizations is felt to be beneficial in two ways. First, because it is the customer who specifies the mode of delivery, the risk that Newland can be criticized for late delivery is reduced. Secondly, it enables Newland to supply customers nation-wide without incurring the administrative work of calculating costs of deliveries to different locations and for different levels of guarantees regarding speed of delivery.

One limitation of the database is that, being based on old software, it is inflexible. Although state of the art at the time of its installation it has become dated; unlike modern databases, its field lengths cannot be altered, neither is it possible to amend the lay-out of the record. However, the database holds a lot of very useful information. As well as the customers' names and addresses, the name of the person placing orders and their job title are recorded. In addition, the address of any location to which Newland has been asked to make a delivery is listed, plus a record of the items and volumes purchased. A final piece of information is an industry classification, but unfortunately this is only based on the information given by the customer on the first occasion on which he placed an order. More unfortunate still is that, when Newland

started to collect this information, nobody in the company had heard of the Standard Industrial Classification (SIC), so they invented a simple classification of their own which is not compatible with the SIC.

4 Sales strategy

The sales strategy is essentially a passive one. Mr Tyrell, who has no training as a salesman, does occasionally visit an existing customer, but, as was indicated, Newland does not employ any 'on-the-road' salesmen. It relies on business arising in response to the advertisements that it places in a number of engineering journals and on recommendations from satisfied customers. Most orders are placed over the phone but fax is often used.

Mr Tyrell has a thorough knowledge of the business, but on one issue his knowledge is of particular importance and this is with regard to pricing. Newland has only one price list and officially does not have a discount structure. In the case of customers that require immediate delivery, no extra charge is made for this service other than passing on the delivery company's charge. On the other hand, a small number of the larger customers have bargained with Mr Tyrell and he has agreed that they can make purchases at below list price. These agreements are seldom documented and are rather haphazard in that the size of the 'discount' does not relate in any rational way with anything. It is in fact what Mr Tyrell was able, as he puts it, 'to get away with'. He claims that the sales staff know which customers these special arrangements apply to and what they are. However, they cannot be recorded on the database.

5 The existing market

Because of the variety of situations in which Newland's products are used, its market is complex. The range of industries in which the customers operate is very wide, but, as Table 2 shows, Newland has divided them into five groups, one of which is Distributors. In 1997/8 seven of the twelve customers spending more than £40,000 with Newland were Distributors.

Table 3 shows that Newland has about 3,800 customers on its files, of which about 1,500 had made no purchases in 1997–8. The largest customer purchased £182,200 of goods and the value of the average order placed in 1997 was £382. Only a few of the remaining customers place orders on a regular basis. About twenty customers of various sizes give Newland a forecast of their requirements a few months in advance, but the majority of the customers make irregular demands. Most of these irregular demands are described by the customers as 'urgent', though

Table 2 Sales by customer group, 1997/8

Industry	Sales (£000)
Distributors	1,266.4
Chemical engineering	219.0
Pneumatic & hydraulic equipment	1,021.2
Pumps & compressors manufacturers	170.4
Filter manufacturers	1,803.0

Table 3 Number of customers by sales level, 1997/8

Sales per customer (£000)	No. of customers	Total value of sales (£000)
0	1,477	0
0 < 0.4	1,263	} 372
0.4 < 1.0	283	
1.0 < 2.0	267	348
2.0 < 10.0	383	} 3,740
10.0 < 20.0	58	
20.0 <	41	
TOTAL	3,772	4,480

Table 4 Sales to some of the largest companies, 1996/7–1997/8

Company	Sales (£000)	
	1996/7	1997/8
A	27.0	13.2
B	23.8	36.2
C	11.6	0
D	8.8	0
E	8.6	6.2
F	7.8	8.6
G	6.2	1.8
H	5.8	2.4
I	5.0	2.2
J	4.8	6.0

sometimes these apparently urgent demands are for several hundred units of a particular item. Table 4 shows how the value of the purchases made by some of the larger customers in 1997–8 varied between 1996/7 and 1997/8.

The data do not indicate any pattern in the customers' behaviour. Comparison of two customers of a similar size in the same industry group might typically show that one places regular small orders, while the other places orders in an irregular pattern, both over timing and in the size of the order.

6 Competition and profits

In 1997/8 Newland's gross profit (see Tables 5 and 6) was 60 per cent and was between 50 and 65 per cent on all products—its prices being based on a simple cost-plus formula. Newland believes that its prices are competitive, and one major customer has told Mr Tyrell that this is the case. In addition, Mr Tyrell has seen the price list of a major competitor and this showed Newland's prices to be below this competitor's, but Mr Tyrell was unable to establish what discounts this competitor offered its customers. However, Newland believes that its image with its established customers is that it supplies high-quality products; usually has products available in stock; and offers a quick and efficient delivery.

7 The distributors

During his business career Mr Tyrell has had a lot of contact with engineering firms and distributors. His view is that distributors' customers seldom use them for only one type of purchase and usually purchase a number of different products from a particular distributor. Furthermore, he believes that one of the important roles performed by distributors is the 'breaking of bulk'. Thus customers requiring only small quantities of a particular item buy from a distributor to avoid the need to purchase some minimum quantity, possibly in excess of their immediate needs, or to pay a premium because of the smallness of their order.

One of the largest distributors in the country is one of Newland's largest customers, purchasing £54,600 of goods in 1997/8. Whenever it places an order, it always demands a twenty-four hour delivery. Other distributors place large and small orders more or less at random, requiring some delivered in twenty-four hours and others only within a few days. However, none of the distributors places orders in advance.

Table 5 Balance sheet end of financial year 1997/8 (£000)

		1996/7		1997/8
Fixed assets		655.8		621.8
Current assets				
Cash	1,037.2		940.8	
Stock	1,158.8		1,668.4	
Debtors	834.8	3,030.8	1,503.0	4,112.2
		3,686.6		4,734.0
Current liabilities				
Overdraft			237.0	
Corporation tax	445.8		557.6	
Creditors	415.2	860.0	483.6	1,278.2
Trading Assets		2,826.6		3,455.8
Share capital		200.0		200.0
Retained reserves		2,626.6		3,255.8
Shareholders' funds		2,826.6		3,455.8

Table 6 Profit and loss account, 1997/8 (£000)

		1996/7		1997/8
Sales		3,480.6		4,480.4
Purchases of components		1,351.8		2,039.6
Added value		2,128.8		2,440.8
Direct labour and other costs		200.0		300.2
Gross profit		1,928.8		2,140.6
Overheads				
Prodn/Distn	91.6		156.6	
Sales	109.2		154.8	
Administration	300.6		377.8	
Depreciation	46.8	548.2	70.4	759.6
Operating profit		1,380.6		1,381.0
Bank interest		(113.8)		77.0
Profit before tax		1,266.8		1,458.0
Tax at 25%		316.7		364.5
Earnings		950.1		1,093.5
Dividend		560.0		610.0
Retained earnings		390.1		483.5

8 Industrial customers

Those customers who are not distributors are a mixed group and little is known about why they use Newland or why their demand, as it so often does, fluctuates so much. In some cases it seems that Newland's products are required for replacement or maintenance work in the customer's factory. However, why such customers do not carry adequate stocks to meet emergencies is not known. Other customers, judged by the size of the orders they place for a single product, appear to be using the product for production purposes, yet it is not clear why customers in this category often require these items urgently.

9 Advertising and promotion

The advertising budget is set in a somewhat arbitrary manner. In 1995/6 it was £60,000 but it had fallen to £40,000 in 1996/7. Advertisements are placed in trade directories and an assortment of engineering journals. There is no defined strategy for advertising and promotion, and the current advertisement, which has been used for many years, is a picture of the front cover of Newland's catalogue plus a brief comment on the product range.

Mr Tyrell argues that this approach is satisfactory in that it seems to have generated plenty of business. He claims that, on average, two new customers per day are obtained. However, it has been noted that, of those people who request a catalogue, only a small number are ever identified as subsequently placing an order.

The catalogue is a book of about twenty pages printed on good-quality paper. The cover has a large colour photo of a selection of the company's products overprinted with Newland's name. Immediately inside the front cover are details of the company's location: postal address, phone, and fax numbers are provided. There is also a brief statement to the effect that a fast delivery service is offered and that higher than normal stocks of all items are held. The remaining pages are typical of such catalogues with each one headed by a technical drawing of a particular item with tables below giving part numbers against various combinations of dimensions. No price information is given.

10 The market

It is difficult to assess the size of the market in which Newland operates for four reasons:

- the products are used in a wide variety of industries;
- they are used both for OEM purposes as well as for spares and maintenance;

- the products being a relatively small cost component in most applications, any statistics accumulate them with other products; and,
- many of the known competitors do not have identical product ranges—most selling several additional types of products.

However, the belief is that the British market is worth £260 million annually and, therefore, that Newland has only a 2 per cent market share. Only a small number of competitors have higher turnovers than Newland (none more than £10 million), but all of these sell a wider range of goods than Newland.

11 Capacity

Mr Tyrell says that he does not know what Newland's capacity is. He knows that at certain times, when orders are low, there is not sufficient work to keep all the staff busy. At other times they are hard pressed, even with overtime working, to maintain their delivery promises. There is a visible resource constraint in that the stores, particularly after a supplier has made a delivery, are very congested. Furthermore, it has been noted that, after a period when a large number of orders have been dispatched, some activities, such as sending out invoices, become delayed.

Unfortunately the location and design of Newland's premises make physical expansion impossible, and, because Newland is located in an area of low unemployment, recruitment of additional staff is unlikely to be easy.

Discussion question

Mr Burridge has told Mr Tyrell that he believes the company could make much higher profits. He has asked Mr Tyrell to draw up a plan indicating how this might be done, but has told him that the plan must not involve any substantial expenditure. What should Mr Tyrell do?

Part Three
The Product Offering

Chapter 9
The Marketing Mix as a Creator of Differentiation

Walter van Waterschoot

Objectives

The objectives of this chapter are:

1 to establish the centrality of the concept of the marketing mix;

2 to demonstrate that a marketing mix is an assembly of demand-impinging elements selected from a large number of alternatives;

3 to explain how the individual elements of the marketing mix are sensitive to different effects depending on such factors as the time horizon, different behavioural and mental effects, primary and secondary effects, and positive and negative effects;

4 to provide a way of classifying mix instruments with an eye to analysing and planning their effects;

5 to provide an understanding of the positive and negative interactions between instruments directed at a particular public as well as between instruments directed at different but interacting publics;

6 to understand why the marketing mix is a prime source of competitive differentiation and why successful differentiation relies on stringent conditions.

1 Introduction

IF any single concept of the marketing discipline could be named its most popular and at the same time its most central one, it may well be the marketing-mix concept. Any novice should be and is actually introduced to it. No seasoned practitioner, researcher, or academic can avoid using or mentioning it. This common and widespread understanding and use, however, does not make a formal discussion of the concept superfluous. On the contrary, it is vital that it should be thoroughly defined and analysed, as almost any other aspect of the marketing discipline in one way or another relies on it or interacts with it.

2 The marketing-mix concept

THE expression 'marketing mix' follows from the metaphor of the marketing executive as somebody combining different ingredients to provoke a certain market response (Borden 1964). The mix metaphor suggests the availability of a wide range of possible ingredients, as well as the numerous ways in which these elements can be combined. The mix metaphor also suggests that different amalgamations produce different results and that some of those may be preferable to others (van Waterschoot 1995: 433).

☞ 'Put simply, a business is more likely to be successful if it designs a specific marketing mix for a group of customers with similar needs.' (Chapter 16, p. 382)

This is completely similar to the use of the word 'mix' in expressions such as grill mixes, cake mixes, or alcohol mixes. In a comparable way, the 'marketing mix' refers to the mixture of instruments a marketer may combine to effect demand for his offering. Expressed more precisely, the marketing mix refers to 'the set of controllable demand-impinging instruments that can be combined into a marketing program used by a firm or any other organization to achieve a certain level and type of response from its target market' (van Waterschoot and Van den Bulte 1992: 88).

2.1 The nature of demand-impinging effects

By demand-impinging instruments are meant instruments that influence demand more or less directly to a greater or lesser extent. In accordance with the nature of marketing itself, the underlying idea is that demand is neither certain nor decided upon by the marketer. The marketer, however, has instruments at his disposal that may influence demand to a greater or lesser extent. Examples could be the price that is asked for a product or the way it is advertised. All sorts of price influences on demand could indeed be envisaged. This influence may be greater or smaller, may take place sooner or later, and generally may lead to demand changes for the whole product category and/or for particular offerings. Let us look at a few examples related to energy consumption. Electricity prices, for example, do not influence household demand very strongly in the short run. If prices go up, there is, for instance, no sudden drop in the number of hours of television watching. Neither will washing machines or refrigerators be turned off. Longer-run effects of price changes, however, could be more substantial. Electrical heating, for instance, might compare unfavourably on a cost basis with oil heating, hence make less people prefer the more modern, convenient, and safe electrical heating.

Changes in car petrol prices, on the contrary, may hardly affect long-run driving habits, as people are very much attached to the comfort of driving a private car. Some of them could, however, be very keen on economizing on the everyday cost of driving wherever and whenever possible without substantially changing their driving habits. Take the following example. Different national price agreements on car petrol prices between the government and the industry in Holland and Belgium have led to occasional price differences between the two countries. As a result, small price differences of a few Belgian francs or Dutch guilder cents sometimes cause marked regional shifts in demand in the border regions between the two countries. Small price changes for home heating oil, on the other hand, may provoke marked temporary shifts in demand rather than determining people's longer-term energy preferences. Elderly people, for instance, who are very keen on saving a few pounds, and who at the same time can afford the investment in a few thousand litres of oil, may, in the event of a price decrease, promptly place an order to be prepared for the coming winter. Less prosperous elderly people, however, might not react so promptly, as they have first to save for the order.

Similarly, the influence on demand of advertising may be greater or smaller, may take place sooner or later, and may also lead to demand changes for the whole product category and/or for particular offerings. Major brands of sportswear such as Nike and Adidas rather systematically advertise their products and brand name in important media such as television and magazines. The main aim of these campaigns seems to be the enhancement of their brand image and awareness, perhaps more than immediate sales improvements. In the medium and long run, of course, it is hoped that these advertisements will contribute to actual purchases of the brand. The image building, in other words, mainly prepares for the future. Direct response advertisements, on the other hand, mainly try to induce instant reactions. Travel agencies could, for instance, advertise in magazines, using techniques that allow people to send in a coupon for extra information. Although this type of advertisement will also increase people's awareness of the tour operator and of the specific tourist destination, the prime aim is to elicit an immediate reaction. These examples already indicate the latitude of possible market responses. Let us now be more precise about the possible nature of these reactions.

2.2 Behavioural versus mental responses

Ultimately, most marketing programmes aim at making people act in a way favoured by the marketer. In an economic setting this is mostly buying. This does not conflict, however, with the fact that other sorts of reactions may also be favoured by the marketer and somehow logically fit his marketing programme. It could, for instance, be necessary to create broad brand awareness during an extended period of time before substantial sales are built up. When Philips and Dupont de Nemours created their videotape brand PDM, the creation of brand awareness and of brand recognition was one of the first marketing aims and tasks. One of the chosen means of communication was the sponsoring of a bike racing team, which indeed contributed substantially to the establishment of the name in people's minds.

Very often, some combination of behavioural and mental effects takes place. A television ad for Nike sportswear during the World Championships of Athletics may be an example. Some people might just vaguely notice the ad, but have somehow captured the brand name or be influenced in their attitude towards the brand. Some people who happen to be buying a pair of sports shoes for their holidays in this period could be influenced in their brand choice. Still others, who otherwise would not have bought a pair of sports shoes, might be encouraged to buy a pair and, more in particular, a pair of Nike shoes, although other brands could also profit from the ad because of a phenomenon known as 'response generalization'.

2.3 Instant versus delayed responses

The type of response provoked by marketing-mix instruments may therefore range all the way from invisible, mental changes to visible behaviour. Depending on the case, these changes may be intended to take place in a shorter or longer time period. In the early 1990s Interbrew carried out an intensive four-week advertising campaign on television to inform Belgian beer-drinkers that the Jupiler brand for home consumption was now packed in a new type of crate with a grip. The aim of the campaign was to make 80 per cent of Belgian beer-drinkers aware of the more convenient crate. But the marketing mix may also aim at provoking an immediate, visible response. When a supermarket chain announces a significant price reduction on a popular brand of beer during one week, the goal is to create store traffic in the course of that particular week. The aim is to induce an immediate visible reaction. Sometimes, such a reaction is expected to happen over a long or even very long time period. Banks, for instance, spend a great deal of money on influencing banking preferences of schoolchildren, although the majority of their transactions will come about only many years later.

2.4 Direct versus indirect responses

Closely related to the previous distinctions is the fact that marketing-mix instruments may provoke direct and indirect market responses (see Insert).

> **Michelin Guides were created to increase the demand for tyres not good food**
>
> The famous Michelin Guides were originally introduced with the intention of encouraging French drivers to travel further and thus to use more tyres. They did this by informing car owners of the location of attractive towns, hotels, restaurants, etc.

A direct reaction is one that follows from the use of marketing-mix instruments without any intermediate effect. A good example of a direct reaction is the earlier mentioned stockpiling of oil by elderly people as a result of a price decrease. No intermediate effect, stage, or condition has to be fulfilled for the demand reaction to take place in this case.

2.5 Demand creation versus instrument creation

As was shown above, the range of marketing-mix instruments is extremely broad. Any instrument that might provoke desirable visible behaviour or mental changes like brand awareness, be it immediately or with a shorter or longer time delay, may be considered a marketing-mix instrument. Marketing instruments, however, that only contribute to the creation or fine-tuning of marketing-mix instruments are not marketing-mix instruments themselves. Marketing research, for instance, could lead to better balanced marketing-mix compositions. But, although often a useful marketing instrument, marketing research is not a marketing-mix instrument itself. The same holds for the choice of a skilful advertising agency. The demand-impinging effect of advertising money may differ enormously, depending on the quality of the advertising campaign. The amount of money spent on advertising is a marketing-mix element and so is the quality of the campaign. But the marketing analyst who decides on the optimum amount of money to be spent is not a marketing-mix element and the same goes for the advertising agency that produces the creative campaign. These marketing people and marketing instruments indeed conceive or create marketing-mix elements, but are not marketing-mix elements themselves. Salespeople, however, do belong to the marketing mix, as their way of interacting with the client impacts on demand without any intermediate element intervening anymore.

2.6 Controllable versus uncontrollable demand-impinging elements

The list of possible marketing-mix instruments is a very long one, but still much shorter than the list of demand-impinging elements in general. There is indeed a major difference between the two. To be considered a marketing-mix instrument, the demand-impinging element should be controllable by the marketer. Having control over a variable means being able to establish its value (Van den Bulte 1991: 17). In most instances the price of the product is such a controllable, demand-impinging element, and therefore a marketing-mix instrument. Sometimes price is not a controllable element, as when a third party like the government intervenes in it, which is the case with petroleum prices in Holland and Belgium. Another example would be the countries' birth rate. A high birth rate fosters the sales of baby clothes. The birth rate, however, is not controllable by the marketer and is, therefore, not a marketing-mix instrument. The distinction between controllable and uncontrollable demand-impinging elements, however, is not always self-evident. Moreover, lack of control does not necessarily mean lack of influence. Product sales, for instance, depend more or less strongly on what magazines, newspapers, and media such as radio and television publicize about it. This 'free publicity' generally has a strong effect on the public, as it is perceived to be made up by competent and independent people. Positive publicity, however, is not controllable by the marketer, since it is decided upon by editors and programme directors. The marketer, however, could use controllable commercial elements or in other words marketing-mix instruments to try to elicit positive publicity. Examples of such marketing-mix instruments would be press releases, exclusive stories or interviews, press conferences, bylined articles, and so on.

A basic idea also of the marketing mix is that several instruments are fitted together in such a way that the combined effect is much more positive than the mere sum of elements ever could be. The rationale behind this property is so important that it is explained in Section 7 on marketing-mix functions.

2.7 Desirable demand creation

Marketing aims at creating desirable exchanges and at avoiding undesirable ones. In other words, it aims at creating or maintaining some specific level and type of demand. Most frequently, marketing managers use, as they should, the marketing mix to stimulate demand. It should, however, be emphasized that more generally marketing management implies the task of influencing the level, timing, and composition of demand in such a way that this will help the organization achieve its objectives (Kotler 1997: 15). As a result, the marketing mix should be used to stimulate demand in specific ways and at specific moments and sometimes even to discourage it. Marketing tasks and, more in particular, the use of the marketing mix indeed differ depending on different possible states of demand (Kotler 1973, 1974; Kotler and Levy 1971).

An organization may, for instance, strive for a desirable level of demand and not just for the highest possible level of demand. Some organizations may face a level of demand above the level they can handle. The reputable archaeological site of Pompei, for instance, is visited each year by two million people (De Pauw 1997). This number is too high to safeguard the world-famous archaeological site. Some people show little respect for this historical heritage. They scratch graffiti close to the delicate frescos or try to take away a piece of stone as a souvenir. Out of the many measures that could be taken, some are related to the marketing mix. One possibility would be to start some sort of merchandising programme to bring in money to pay for extra guards and monitoring systems. Another possibility would be to raise money for the site amongst rich Italians and to look for sponsors. One other possible approach would consist of demarketing. Demarketing generally implies the reverse use of marketing-mix instruments, such as raising prices and cutting promotion and services. Higher prices would reduce demand to a manageable level and at the same time—depending on the price elasticity of demand and the cost structure—provide a prospect of a higher profit contribution. Selective demarketing then consists of discouraging specific elements of demand—for example, demand by less cultivated visitors, as their purchases or presence or behaviour may reflect negatively on the product itself as well as on the product image and on purchases by more cultivated customers.

The marketing mix may also contribute towards a more desirable timing of demand. Actual demand may indeed fluctuate on a seasonal, daily, or even hourly basis and as a result pose, for instance, capacity problems. Ferry services, for example, between England and the Continent are confronted with peak moments and off-peak moments. Flexible pricing as well as promotion incentives may help to alleviate this problem.

2.8 Any marketer, any market, any public

The company executive is the most obvious marketer mixing controllable demand-impinging instruments. The most evident market is presumably the market of end-users. But obviously a company addresses itself in many instances to a particular part or segment of this broad market. It is much less obvious though to which segment in particular marketers should turn. It is not surprising, for instance, that the majority of Mercedes S buyers in Belgium belong to the higher-income bracket, own a company, or are professionally active as a chief executive officer (CEO). Yet it is much less evident that 30 per cent are strictly private buyers and that 80 per cent have already bought one or more Mercedes cars before. Also surprising is that more than 77 per cent of those buyers live in Flanders, against only 15 per cent in Brussels and a mere 8 per cent in Wallonia (Dheeden 1996).

It should none the less be stressed that the marketing-mix idea is also at the heart of less visible profit marketing situations like business-to-business-contacts and also of non-profit marketing situations. Take, for example, Oxfam (the Oxford Committee for Famine Relief), which is a privately funded, British-based agency that provides relief and development aid to impoverished or disaster-stricken communities worldwide (McHenry 1993: 28). One of the initiatives taken by Oxfam was the establishment of a network of Oxfam–Third World outlets to sell mainly agricultural and food products from developing countries and to inform people about the origin of these products. Obviously decisions have to be taken such as the location and size of these outlets, their opening hours, the range of products to be sold, their packaging and pricing, and so on. These decisions fully fit the idea of a marketing mix as discussed in this chapter, although the prime objective is not one of generating profits.

In the same vein it should be stressed that a marketing mix can be composed with an eye to any public. In addition to being targeted at end-users, the marketing mix will also be aimed at other groups. The intermediate buyers of a product such as wholesalers or retailers may represent another important target group. They are so important that Section 9 will be devoted to this target group. But other groups like the general public could be approached by means of a marketing mix or at least with the help of some marketing-mix instruments. Greenpeace, for example, aims at several goals such as heightening environmental awareness and leading people to environmentally sound behaviour (van Waterschoot 1995: 435). It also tries to win financial support from ecologically minded individuals. To attain these aims Greenpeace uses instruments that are very similar to commercial marketing mixes. It mainly tries to generate free advertising or publicity. Their—often original, reckless, and spectacular—actions yield them wide exposure. On top of that, their marketing programme towards the general public consists of personal mailings and sales of Greenpeace merchandise. The latter is realized via mail order and via a small set of specialized shops in major cities.

3 Generic and situational marketing-mix functions

MARKETING-MIX instruments are put into operation to create desirable forms of demand or, in other words, to bring about desirable exchanges under some form sooner or later. For that reason the fundamental marketing-mix functions are structurally intertwined with the exchange situation, and in particular correspond with some of the basic conditions for exchange actually to take place. This idea is so important that it will be discussed in some detail. For exchange to be possible at all, some preliminary conditions have to be fulfilled. There must be at least two parties. These two parties must be aware of one another and find it desirable to deal with one another. They must be free to make, accept, or reject an offer. For exchange to be possible, each party must possess something that might be of value to the other. Each of these parties, moreover, must be capable of communication and delivery (Kotler 1972). For exchange not only to be possible but actually to take place, the two parties will also have to communicate in some way or another. They will have to agree on the conditions of exchange. This means that they will have to agree on what each party will have to give up and receive. This logically presupposes that each of them will gain more than they give up. Ultimately they will have to be capable of delivery. The fundamental functions of the marketing mix correspond with these conditions (van Waterschoot and Van den Bulte 1992: 86).

3.1 The generic marketing-mix functions

Logical exchange—or call it demand creation—is not possible if one does not have any object or ser-

vice at one's disposal that might be of value to the other party. The generic marketing-mix functions (see Table 9.1) each reflect this. A first fundamental function of the marketing mix, therefore, consists of configuring something that could be valued by the prospective exchange party. In brief we would call this the *need-fulfilment function* of the marketing mix.

Exchanges are pursued to attain goals decision-makers have put forward or somehow have in mind. The decision-maker gains by attaining these objectives. A logical second function of the marketing mix, therefore, consists of determining the offers and sacrifices that need to be made by the prospective exchange party. In brief, we would call this function the *pricing function* of the marketing mix.

Table 9.1 **Marketing-mix functions—their relative importance**

Marketing-mix functions	Marketing-mix instruments				
	Product instrument	Price instrument	Communication instrument	Distribution instrument	Promotion instrument
Generic functions					
Need-fulfilment function					
Configuration of something valued by the prospective exchange party	XXXXX	X	X	X	X or XXXXX
Pricing function					
Determination of the compensation and sacrifices to be brought by the prospective exchange party	X	XXXXX	X	X	X or XXXXX
Distribution function					
Placing the offer at the disposal of the prospective exchange party	X	X	X	XXXXX	X or XXXXX
Communication function					
Bringing the offer to the attention of the prospective exchange party and influencing its feelings and preferences about it	X	X	XXXXX	X	X or XXXXX
Promotional function					
Inducing immediate, overt behaviour by strengthening the generic functions during relatively short periods of time	X or XXXXX	X or XXXXX	X or XXXXX	X or XXXXX	XXXXX

Source: van Waterschoot and Van den Bulte (1992: 89).

👉 'A similar point of view is expressed in Zeithaml's (1988) price definition: "From the consumer's point of view, price is what is given up or sacrificed to obtain a product".' (Chapter 10, p. 213)

The two previous functions, however, do not suffice for exchange to come about. Both parties should be informed about one another's wishes and requirements. They should be informed about the attractiveness of one another's offering and perhaps even about actually entering into an exchange relationship. A logical third marketing-mix function, therefore, consists of bringing the offer to the attention of the prospective exchange party and influencing its feelings and preferences about it. In brief we would call this function the *communication function* of the marketing mix. But even now exchange would not come about, if both parties were not in a position actually to deliver the object or service they want to exchange. A fourth fundamental marketing-mix function, therefore, consists of placing the offer at the disposal of the prospective exchange party. In brief, we would call this function the *distribution function* of the marketing mix.

These four functions are generic in the sense that they cannot be avoided. They have to be fulfilled for exchange to come about. If any of these functions was not carried out, no exchange would take place. No demand would be created, fulfilled, or maintained (van Waterschoot and Van den Bulte 1992: 86).

3.2 The promotional marketing-mix function

Next to these generic functions, however, there is also a promotional or complementary or situational marketing-mix function (van Waterschoot and Van den Bulte 1992: 88). Whereas the generic marketing functions will lead to exchange 'sooner or later', the promotional marketing-mix function aims at eliciting exchanges 'sooner rather than later'. This promotional function indeed consists of direct inducement or direct provocation, meaning that it leads to immediate exchange or, more generally, to desirable forms of immediate, overt behaviour fitting an immediate exchange in a particular situation. This promotional function consists of inducing potential exchange partners to consummate exchange immediately. It tackles

'barriers to acting' such as physical and psychological inertia barriers, risk barriers, or competitive barriers from close substitutes (Beem and Schaffer 1981: 16–18). Suppose indeed that the customer hesitates to buy and is postponing his purchase. The promotional function might then consist of offering price reductions to make this customer take immediate action. This provocation of immediate exchanges implies that the promotional function is situational in the sense that it is carried out on a non-routine basis during short periods of time. If in the previous example the customer was not convinced that a price reduction is exceptional, it would be unlikely to provoke an immediate purchase.

4 Primary and secondary functions of mix instruments

WITH an eye to theoretical insight and practical application alike, it is worthwhile looking at the marketing-mix functions from the point of view of specific mix instruments. A basic observation concerning any marketing-mix instrument is that it primarily serves one of the four generic functions and/or that it primarily serves the promotional function. That particular function is called its primary function. At the same time it is crucial to observe that any marketing-mix instrument also contributes to a lesser extent to the other functions. The latter functions are called its secondary functions. This idea is summarized on the right-hand side of Table 9.1.

Advertising is a classical communication instrument within the marketing mix, meaning that its primary function is one of bringing the offer to the attention of the prospective exchange party and influencing its feelings and preferences about it. At the same time, however, advertising may add extra need fulfilment to the product—for instance, by providing prestige or the suggestion or belief of power or excellence. The Nike or Adidas advertisements mentioned above are examples. Conversely, advertising may imply a cost and hence influence the pricing function of the marketing mix. Such could be the case if a highly distinguished, favourite brand of wristwatch were featured in a notorious magazine like—

supposedly—*Playboy*. Advertising also contributes to the availability function of the marketing mix—for instance, by informing the public about the available points of sale. Finally, advertising also contributes to the promotion function of the marketing mix, even if theme advertising is concerned, which by definition tries to build a long-term image and to prepare long-term sales. Coca-Cola theme advertisements, for instance, next to establishing and maintaining this picture of young, smart, and joyful people who at crucial moments in their lives never fail to think of Coca-Cola, will also make some people under some circumstances aware of their current thirst, or at least make them search for their favourite thirst-quencher.

☞ **'The most important fact that emerges even from these early pioneering efforts in the field of marketing communication is that it can and should never be seen or managed in isolation from the total marketing context.'** (Chapter 12, p. 274)

Let us look at a second example—the product itself, for which the primary function is obviously one of want fulfilment. The product itself may also contribute to the pricing function. If it has any unwanted features—for instance, your favourite fax machine is available only in white, whereas you wanted a black one—this is clearly the case. The product also communicates. A silver-coloured Rolls Royce will convey a message completely different from one that a tomato-red Seat is conveying. The packaging of a product, next to communicating, may also add to the distribution or availability function. A fruit juice packed in a tetrabrik is much better suited for mass distribution than fruit juices in elegant bottles, and hence packaging affects the availability function. Finally, the product may contribute to the promotion function. Bakery products, for instance, may look so tasty that people are persuaded to buy them on the spot and eat them immediately.

Let us take promotion instruments as a third example to illustrate the multi-functionality of mix instruments. Promotion or sales promotion instruments are demand-impinging instruments that have no power of themselves but can, during relatively short periods of time, complement and sustain the basic instruments of the marketing mix for the purpose of stimulating prospective exchange partners to desirable forms of immediate, visible behaviour (van Waterschoot and Van den Bulte 1992: 89). Promotion instruments by definition primarily contribute to the promotion function next to their primary generic function. Yet these instruments also affect the other generic functions, sometimes in a negative way. Price reductions, for instance, by their very nature primarily influence the pricing function next to the promotion function (see Insert). Price reductions could more specifically limit the bracket of pricing possibilities for the future. If customers' price expectations are reshaped by massive price reductions, it may indeed turn out to be difficult to charge a higher price again afterwards. Promotion instruments may, however, also play a secondary, even undeniable role outside their own strict field of operations. Consumer price discounts may result in, say, retailers spotting massive sales opportunities and therefore grant much more shelf space to the brand than they would have done otherwise. As a result, not only the availability function, but the communication function, may be influenced. More seriously, the impression may be created that a very ordinary brand is involved, available everywhere, with no distinct features except its price. If for that reason the exclusiveness of the product is endangered, this loss of exclusiveness also touches upon the need-fulfilment function of the marketing mix.

Price is an ingredient of a scent

The British Monopolies and Mergers Commission exonerated the fragrance houses of unfairly refusing to supply shops that sold their products at less than the recommended retail price. It accepted the fragrance houses' arguments that 'Fine fragrances are marketed as luxury products and the Commission accepts that the suppliers need to be able to control their distribution in order to protect their brand images.' Thus the Commission accepted that the consumer buys a complex set of attributes that must, at least, not be mutually contradictory. Indeed, note how these are not 'scent manufacturers' but 'fragrance houses'—part of the marketing mix.

5 Classification of marketing-mix instruments

As mix instruments are put into operation to contribute to the execution of marketing-mix functions, it seems sensible to classify those instruments on the basis of the primary marketing-mix function they fulfil (van Waterschoot and Van den Bulte 1992: 86). This primary function can be one of the generic functions and/or the promotional function of the marketing mix. Let us look at the generic marketing-mix functions and their corresponding primary instruments first. They are represented in the four columns of Box 9.1, one of which has three subdivisions.

5.1 A functional classification of the marketing mix

In the first column are grouped instruments that primarily contribute to the need-fulfilment function. This group, which is a sub-mix of the marketing mix in itself, is called the product mix. Instruments primarily contributing to the pricing function of the marketing mix are brought together in the second column in a sub-mix called the price mix. Instruments primarily contributing to the communication function of the marketing mix are brought together in the third column in a sub-mix called the communication mix. This communication mix is further divided up into subclasses, based on two criteria. One criterion is whether the ultimate message is fully under the control of the marketer or not. The first subset of communication instruments obtained in this way is traditionally further divided up according to a second criterion—namely, the personal or the non-personal nature of the communication instruments. Instruments primarily contributing to the availability function of the marketing mix are brought together in the fourth column in a sub-mix called the distribution mix.

Next to the generic functions of the marketing mix, there is also this promotional function. We know that some instruments primarily contribute to this function. For that reason Box 9.1 is divided up vertically into instruments belonging to the basic composition of the marketing mix and into those fulfilling a complementary or situational or promotional role. Mix instruments that in the first place contribute to the promotional function of the marketing mix are represented in the lower half of Box 9.1. Together they form the promotion mix as opposed to the basic elements of the marketing mix, which together form the 'basic mix'. The promotion instruments are spread out over all the major classes of marketing instruments. As a result there is a subset of promotion instruments corresponding with a subset of basic instruments to be found within each of the earlier defined sub-mixes of marketing-mix instruments.

The basic marketing mix contains strategic instruments that remain relatively constant over time or evolve only gradually. The basic mix could, for instance, consist of a high-quality product, sold at a premium price via upscale retail outlets and advertised in highly reputable magazines. Unless drastic strategic changes are called for, gradual changes most typically take place over time, like the addition of more popular versions, a slight lowering of the price while the image is nevertheless maintained, and also an intensification of distribution and communication efforts. The promotion mix contains tactical instruments which most often cannot be planned very long in advance. They aim at sustaining the basic mix in the short run to take advantage of unusual opportunities or to fight unexpected threats. In the early 1990s, for instance, Procter & Gamble Pampers had to cope with the introduction of a major American rival brand in Europe. P&G started a heavy price couponing campaign. As a result, numerous parents stocked up on P&G Pampers and the introduction of the rival brand flopped.

5.2 The four (or more) P's

Although the previous functional classification of mix instruments suffices to describe and analyse most mix applications, it is worthwhile signalling some popular older and more pragmatic typologies. In the development of marketing thought throughout the twentieth century several pragmatic marketing-mix classifications were developed. Known elements, supposedly belonging to the same population, were inventoried and grouped into classes, not so much on the basis of theoretical insight, but rather on the basis of their apparent similarity (van Waterschoot 1995: 438). By far the most popular one of these pragmatic

Box 9.1 A functional classification of the marketing mix

Marketing mix	Product mix	Price mix	Mass communication mix
Basic mix	Basic product mix Instruments that mainly aim at the satisfaction of the prospective exchange party's needs	Basic price mix Instruments that mainly fix the size and the way of payment exchanged for the goods or services	Basic mass communication mix Non-personal communication efforts that mainly aim at announcing the offer or maintaining the awareness and knowledge about it: evoking or maintaining favourable feelings and removing barriers to wanting
	e.g. product characteristics options, assortment, brand name, packaging, quantity, factory guarantee	e.g. list price, usual terms of payment, usual discounts, terms of credit, long-term savings campaigns	e.g. theme advertising in various media, permanent exhibitions, certain forms of sponsoring
Promotion mix	Product promotion mix Supplementary group of instruments that mainly aim at inducing immediate overt behaviour by strengthening the basic product mix during relatively short periods of time	Price promotion mix Supplementary group of instruments that mainly aim at inducing immediate overt behaviour by strengthening the basic price mix during relatively short periods of time	Mass communication promotion mix Supplementary group of instruments that mainly aim at inducing immediate overt behaviour by strengthening the basic mass communication mix during relatively short periods of time.
	e.g. economy packs, 3-for-the-price-of-2 deals; temporary luxury options on a car at the price of its standard model	e.g. exceptionally favourable price, end-of-season sales, exceptionally favourable terms of payment and credit, short-term savings campaigns, temporary discounts, coupons	e.g. action advertising, contests, sweepstakes, samples, premiums, trade shows or exhibitions

Source: van Waterschoot and Van den Bulte (1992: 90).

Communication mix

Personal communication mix	Publicity mix	Distribution mix
Basic personal communication mix Personal communication efforts that mainly aim at announcing the offer or maintaining awareness and knowledge about it; evoking or maintaining favourable feelings and removing barriers to wanting.	*Basic publicity mix* Efforts that aim at inciting a third party (persons and authorities) to favourable communication about the offer	*Basic distribution mix* Instruments that mainly determine the intensity and manner of how the goods or services will be made available
e.g. amount and type of selling, personal remunerations	e.g. press bulletins, press conferences, tours by journalists	e.g. different types of distribution channels, density of the distribution system, trade relation mix (policy of margins, terms of delivery, etc.), merchandising advice
Personal communication promotion mix Supplementary group of instruments that mainly aim at inducing immediate overt behaviour by strengthening the basic personal communication mix during relatively short periods of time.	*Publicity promotion mix* Supplementary group of instruments that mainly aim at inducing immediate overt behaviour by strengthening the basic publicity mix during relatively short periods of time.	*Distribution promotion mix* Supplementary group of instruments that mainly aim at inducing immediate overt behaviour by strengthening the basic distribution mix during relatively short periods of time.
e.g. temporary demonstrations, salesforce promotions such as salesforce contests	e.g. all measures to stimulate positive publicity about a sales promotion action	e.g. extra point of purchase material, trade promotions such as buying allowances, sales contests; temporary increase of the number of distribution points

typologies is McCarthy's (1960: 39–40) classification. This typology has become known as the Four P classification of the marketing mix, since it distinguishes between four classes of instruments under four headings beginning with the letter P: Product, Price, Place, and Promotion. Although McCarthy only labelled those classes and did not define them, the first three of them correspond roughly with the first three generic marketing-mix functions described before. The fourth P, however, in spite of its label, is a hybrid combination of predominantly communication instruments and, only to a lesser extent, of promotion instruments, which are moreover defined as a residual category of instruments not belonging elsewhere. In spite of its conceptual shortcomings, McCarthy's mnemonic has nevertheless contributed enormously to the spectacularly quick acceptance of the marketing-mix metaphor. Indeed, for many the Four P's have even become synonymous with the marketing mix. In the course of the years, however, its shortcomings have become obvious, mainly as promotion instruments became more important in marketing practice.

As a consequence of the enormous popularity of McCarthy's four P classification, however, numerous other marketing authors have considered it useful to extend the mnemonic Four P list as a means of drawing the attention to specific sub-mixes or even to marketing aspects outside the marketing mix. Let us look at two examples out of the many. Sometimes a fifth P has been added to indicate People, Personnel, or Personal selling. This label stresses the importance of all sorts of selling and servicing efforts by all sorts of people throughout the organization. In situations where selling efforts are particularly important—as in service marketing—no fundamental objection can be made against this extension. There is, however, no necessity to do so, as the provision of services belongs to the P of the (service) Product, and sales efforts are part of the communication instruments (van Waterschoot 1995: 443). Also in service marketing, a P has sometimes been added to represent Participants. The Participants in a service marketing situation often significantly influence in a positive or in a negative sense the quality of the execution of the service. From a pedagogical viewpoint, therefore, there is ample reason to stress this aspect. The activities of the personnel carrying out the services, however, primarily belong to the product mix. From a clas-

sificatory point of view, then, there is no reason to add another category. Moreover, in so far as participants are meant to be the client, the addition becomes conceptually incorrect, since the marketing mix groups together controllable demand-impinging elements and not the actual demand-constituting elements (van Waterschoot 1995: 444).

6 Marketing-mix differentiation

ECONOMIC marketing applications most typically imply the pursuit by the marketer of the strongest possible competitive position. But this aim also typifies many non-profit marketing situations. Charitable organizations, for instance, usually like to obtain the largest possible share of potential donor contributions. And universities for their part do not like to see their relative number of students dwindle. The pursuit of the strongest possible competitive position corresponds with the avoidance of competitive pressure, following from the actual or latent presence of substitute offerings. High substitutability follows not only from the number of substitute offerings, but also from their similarity with the organization's offering or even from their relative superiority.

6.1 Minimization of substitutability

Marketers naturally avoid high competitive pressure or, in other words, high substitutability of their offerings. Pure competition, defined in the jargon of economists as a market structure typified by the presence of numerous participants selling an identical offering, is the least of their desires. Indeed, marketers try to create market situations for themselves typified by the presence of as few close substitute offerings as possible. They are in favour of product market selections with the lowest number of participants and the highest degree of positive differentiation of their own offering. They are, thus, in favour of monopolistic power, as this allows them to charge premium prices and hence to gain premium profits as a result. Marketers will naturally take strategic and tactical moves that will yield monopolistic power and/or maintain it. A strategy of differentiation— or of 'differential advantages' or of 'competitive advantages'—is, therefore, at the heart of almost any marketing strategy. The marketing mix is a logical platform to create such differentiation.

The most straightforward and also the most traditional source of differentiation within the marketing mix consists of the elements of its product mix. Differentiation is indeed most traditionally defined as a competitive strategy of offering products and services that are unique or superior to those of competitors (Bradley 1995: 537). Differentiation of the product offering from competition is realized by offering value to the customer in some or other way, perhaps by enhancing the performance, quality, prestige, features, service back-up, reliability, or convenience of the product (Aaker 1995: 7). The core idea is the selection of one or more choice criteria that are used by many buyers in an industry. The marketer uniquely positions himself to meet these criteria so as to give customers a reason to prefer his product over competing ones. As the extra value to customers (e.g. higher performance) often raises costs above the average for the industry, the aim is logically to differentiate in a way that leads to a price premium in excess of the cost of differentiating (Jobber 1995: 527).

6.2 Differentiation of 'anything'

Although differentiation possibilities are primarily and most basically sought in the product mix, a broader interpretation also includes other elements of the marketing mix to set a company's offering apart from competitors' brands: likeable advertising, faster delivery, or some other aspect of the marketing mix other than price. Ultimately, there is a still broader view that extends the differentiation idea to all possible elements of the marketing mix, even to the price elements. In this view, differentiation consists of designing a set of meaningful differences to distinguish the company's offering from competitors' offerings without any restriction as to specific marketing mix elements (Kotler 1997: 282). This has been called the differentiation of 'anything' in a classic article by Theodore Levitt (1980). As a result, the price mix may become a source of differentiation. This is obviously only possible in combination with some other form of differentiation. If the latter was not the case, a situation of 'pure competition' would prevail, assuming the (latent)

presence of many 'players' in the market. If any player raised his price, he would price himself out of the market. If he undercut his colleagues, he would go bankrupt. Provided, however, some differentiation is present in an organization's offering, it can charge a price yielding it a distinct and favourable quality–price relationship. Buyers might indeed be prepared to accept second-best offerings at a lower price (Brassington and Pettitt 1997: 856–7). A typical example is the introduction of me-too products. Following the original launch of a distinctive and superior product by an innovative competitor, an organization introduces a rather close copy, which is offered at a markedly lower and therefore attractive price. The launching of IBM clones may serve as an example.

6.3 Conditions for successful differentiation

For differentiation to be successful, some crucial conditions have to be fulfilled (Kotler 1997: 294–5). By definition the offering should be different from the competition in a superior, even unique way (see Insert). By definition also the differential element must be valued in a positive way by customers. Developing a superior electronic mousetrap makes sense only as long as people value its superior efficiency. Moreover, the appreciation of the superior characteristics should be expressed in actual demand. If this is not the case—for instance, because the differentiated offering remains beyond customers' budgetary means—its strategic value is questionable. Moreover, the differential advantage should be sustainable.

> **Differences must be sustainable!**
>
> Heudebert, a small French biscuit producer, introduced a Swedish *crisp brod*. The Swedishness of the product was mainly vested on the portrait of an attractive Swedish girl figuring on the package. Unfortunately this was not a sustainable differential and within a year several competitors had introduced their own *crisp brod*, just as 'Swedish' as Heudebert's.

The condition of sustainability is closely linked to the condition of communicability of the differential advantage. The aim is to create an edge over rivals, and to have a differentiation package that is sustainable over time. In marketing, this can be 'real' (e.g. a product design feature) or 'imaginary' (a strong brand image or advertising campaign). People really have to believe that there is a difference. In consumer markets there are many interesting examples of how differentiation is communicated. Kotler (1997: 301) cites the example of a lawnmower manufacturer who uses a noisy motor, as buyers think noisy lawnmowers are more powerful. He offers also a related example of car manufacturers making cars with good-slamming doors as many buyers slam the doors in the showroom to check the robustness of the car.

However, also in business-to-business markets the crucial condition of communicability of positive differentiation holds. An example is provided by Bekaert Textiles, a Flemish producer of a range of high-quality wall textiles. Bekaert sold its assortment via a selected network of upscale decorators and home-interior specialists, who also put up the product in the consumer's house. Consumers tend to be fairly unaware of the advantages and disadvantages of wall textiles in comparison with other sorts of wall decoration. They are also rather ignorant about the qualities of specific brands. As a result, the advice and even prescription of dealers is vital in the determination of the ultimate product and brand choice. Bekaert motivates its dealers not only by providing an excellent assortment, but also by granting substantial margins, by maintaining stocks instead of its dealers, and by delivering within twenty-four hours of an order being placed. Following a basic financial rule, the Bekaert arrangement is extremely profitable for its dealers. Indeed, their return on investment is extremely high, as no stock investments—which are traditionally made by dealers in this sector—need to be made and as hardly any other investment is necessary. For that reason, Bekaert management was astonished to learn from an image study by MBA students that dealers perceived the profitability of its range to be inferior to that of its immediate competitors. The explanation was that the dealers—who were fine craftsmen but with limited financial insight—judged profitability solely by the size of the distribution margins. Bekaert's margins—although substantial—were slightly below those of its nearest competitors. As a result of this perceptual issue, the company faced the choice of altering its—expensive—differentiated stock policy or else communicating it more con-vincingly to its dealers. Last but not least, differentiation should indeed be profitable. Otherwise, it should not be carried out. Bekaert's expensive efforts to hold inventories for their distributors may underline this point.

7 The ideal marketing-mix combination

THE marketing mix as a strategic and tactical tool kit of demand-impinging instruments comes to exist in a differentiated or differentiable market—that is, in a market where there is more or less price freedom as a result of more or less monopoly or market power by the marketer. The next question then is which specific combination of marketing-mix instruments should be preferred. This prime issue will be dealt with in this section in two major steps. First, the basic theoretical answer, which is of an economic nature, will be provided. Next, implementation issues will be discussed with regard to this basic economic–theoretical solution. The following basic theoretical framework of marketing-mix optimization takes the stance of a business organization, although many other situations can be modelled in a more or less similar way. In this theoretical framework the assumption is that the marketer pursues one major goal—namely, that of profit maximization—without specifying, however, the exact time horizon that delineates this goal. It presupposes a well-delineated market or market segment. In the most basic representation of this theoretical approach it is also assumed that there is no direct influence of marketing-mix choices by competitors. We call this framework economic as it fits the traditional assumptions of an elementary microeconomic approach. Microeconomics obviously covers hosts of more complicated settings as well. We deem it wise, however, to introduce the basic framework summarized here for two major reasons. First, in spite of the simplicity of the framework and perhaps even thanks to it, the basic underlying allocation principle of the financial means to different marketing-mix instruments is clearly shown. Secondly, the rudimentary nature of the framework allows us to point to missing elements, together with the possibilities and difficulties to make up for them.

7.1 Sales-response functions

The reaction of the market to different marketing-mix possibilities is seen in terms of different quantities that are actually bought or would supposedly be bought as a result of different combinations of the possible elements of the marketing-mix. A sales-response function then forecasts the likely sales volume during a specified time period with different possible levels of marketing-mix elements (Kotler 1997: A-3). A sales-response function is a mathematical representation (see Box 9.2) of the relationship between the sales volume and major classes of marketing-mix variables such as the price charged for the offering, the level of the advertising budget, and the chosen quality level of the product. The actual form of the relationship can vary from a very simple linear one (as in Fig. 9.1: P1 and P2) through to extremely complex forms where the marketing-mix variables are seen to interact with each other.

However, there are two reasons why it is unlikely that a linear presentation of the relationship will be adequate. First because it supposes that demand will keep growing at a constant pace in relationship with, say, advertising expenditures, which is not a realistic assumption. The effect, for instance, of varying levels of the sales force size is often quite well represented by a concave function (Fig. 9.1: P3), for, if a field sales force consisted of only one representative, he would call on the best prospects. A second sales representative would call on the next best prospects and so on, resulting in a gradually diminishing rate of sales increase. Functional forms other than linear ones will, therefore, be more realistic.

Advertising expenses, on the other hand, often provoke buying responses that can be effectively summarized by means of an S-shaped functional form (Fig. 9.1: P6). Kotler argues that small advertising budgets do not buy enough advertising to create more than a minimal brand awareness. Larger budgets can overcome this threshold and ultimately lead to increased purchase responses. However, as there is an upper limit to the potential demand for any product, very large advertising budgets would not produce many additional sales. Moreover, easier sales prospects will have bought first, leaving behind the more difficult ones.

A second reason to doubt that a linear relationship describes reality very well is that it takes no account of the possibility of interaction between the marketing-mix elements. In reality it is unlikely that the effect of advertising on sales would be independent of the level of other marketing variables such as price, or that the effect of product quality on sales would not be influenced by the price set, and so on. The incorporation of these interactions can be represented by more complicated mathematical forms such as that shown in the second part of Box 9.2.

Box 9.2 **Response functions**

(i)   The mathematical representation of a linear response function would be

$Q_i = b - p.P_i + a.A_i + x.X_i$

where
Q_i = sales volume
P_i = price charged for the offering p is the coefficient of sales response to price
A_i = level of the advertising budget a is the coefficient of sales response to advertising
X_i = chosen quality level of the product x is the coefficient of sales response to product quality

(ii)   If it is believed that the individual marketing mix elements interact with each other to produce an effect on the sales level then one way of representing this mathematically is by the formula:

$Q_i = b.P_i^p.A_i^a.X_i^x$

where
b is a scale factor
p; a; x are constant elasticities of the respective values (p is usually assumed to be negative).

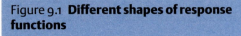

Figure 9.1 **Different shapes of response functions**

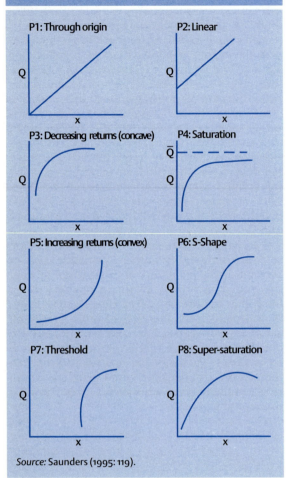

Source: Saunders (1995: 119).

7.2 The cost function

Whereas the sales-response function summarizes the purchase responses corresponding with different marketing-mix combinations, the cost function summarizes the corresponding costs. A certain demand level will go together with the marketing costs that evoked it, but may also cause production or administrative costs, and so on. Some of these costs will vary proportionately with sales. Others will remain unaffected. Still others will evolve stepwise. Advertising costs, for example, will remain constant within certain intervals, whereas the compensation of the sales force will

partly vary directly with the magnitude of the realized sales.

☞ 'Naturally, adjustments in the seller's "total offering" tend to result in variations in the seller's costs structure and profitability. The seller, therefore, must be constantly engaged in creating a "total offering" from all the elements under his or her control, in a way that will give differential advantage and profit.' (Chapter 14, p. 320)

7.3 The profit function

Deduction of the cost function from the sales-response function provides a profit function. It is this function that will be maximized in order to find the optimum level of marketing-mix instruments. This principle is often expressed mathematically, by applying standard calculus. The profit function reaches a maximum when the first-order derivatives are zero and the second-order derivatives are negative. The first-order derivatives are thus equalled to zero. The equations obtained make it possible to express the theoretical optimum values of the different marketing-mix instruments as summarized in Box 9.3. These expressions are called the Dorfman–Steiner theorem, after the scholars who invented them. The Dorfman–Steiner conditions allow us to control whether a proposed or actual marketing-mix combination may be considered optimal. Naert and Leeflang (1978: 132–6) evaluated the profitability of advertising for a well-established, frequently purchased consumer product sold on the Belgian market. They calculated the optimum, marginal revenue product of advertising per 1,000 potential consumers to be BFr.2,545. In comparison with the actual expenditures of BFr.3,440 this result suggested a substantial actual overspending on advertising.

7.4 Criticism on the ideal marketing-mix combination

The basic economic–theoretical model described in Sections 7.2 and 7.3 may be criticized because it is too simplistic. Goals other than profit maximization may and will also determine the ideal marketing-mix combination. Examples would be the pursuit of a target rate of return or the concern of keeping economic risk within reasonable

Box 9.3 **The Dorfman–Steiner conditions**

Let $q = q(p, a, x)$, be demand (q) as a function of price (p), advertising (a), and quality (x).
Let $c = (q, x)$, be variable cost per unit, and FC fixed costs.
Profit Π is:

$$\Pi = pq(p,a,x) - c(q,x)q(p,a,x) - a - FC$$

If the objective is to maximize profit, at optimality we should have

$$-\eta_p = \mu = \eta_x \frac{p}{c} = \frac{1}{w}$$

where $\eta_p = \dfrac{\partial q p}{\partial p q}$ = price elasticity

where $\mu = p\dfrac{\partial q}{\partial a}$ = marginal revenue product of advertising

where $\eta_x = \dfrac{(\partial q / \partial x)/q}{(\partial c / \partial x)/c}$

where $w = \dfrac{p - MC}{p}$ = percentage of gross margin.

Source: Naert and Leeflang (1978: 143–4).

boundaries. Those objectives could indicate divergent and even contradictory solutions. Massive advertising, for instance, could be desirable from a strict profit maximization outlook, but could be too risky actually to implement, as a major commitment to spend a huge and fixed amount of money is concerned. Even if actual sales results were disappointing, this amount of money would be spent anyway or would at least be difficult to cancel on accepted commitments.

The marketer may not only pursue multiple goals. The mixture of goals may, moreover, require different emphases depending on the different time horizons that are envisaged. A marketer should indeed, and in fact often does, keep different time horizons in mind, perhaps even discernible into the immediate, the short, medium, long, and very long term. The immediate or short term could dictate price discounts to dominate the marketing mix, whereas the medium- and long-term interests of the organization could for-

bid this tactical choice, as it would impede a future strategy of asking premium prices.

Marketing-mix optimization also very often needs to take account of all sorts of constraints not taken up in the basic optimization model. Available financial means, current image, current assortment, and current retail network are just a few common examples. These constraints may, moreover, have a different magnitude, character, and importance depending on the time horizon. The basic optimization framework also disregards the (potential) presence of multiple segments and regions.

Closely related to the previous criticism is the fact that a response function summarizes only visible purchase reactions and not invisible reactions. As was stressed in the introductory section, the marketing mix may also provoke other than visible purchase reactions, which may be more or less desirable. An advertising campaign, for instance, may lead to brand awareness, positive feelings towards the brand, and some inclination to buy it one day, without inducing many immediate sales. The previous example already suggests that the marketing-mix implementation may also cause lagged purchase reactions. The well-known French cheese spread 'La vache qui rit', for instance, has been on the market for about a century. Even if its producer stopped all advertising for it, demand would continue for some time as a result of many years of advertising. In other words, today's sales may also be the result of yesteryear's advertising. To summarize this criticism, the theoretical marketing-mix model optimizes the immediate purchase effects of the marketing mix and not the delayed and/or mental effects.

As has already been said, a marketing-mix framework that does not take into account interaction between marketing-mix effects runs the risk of being more or less unrealistic. But also the non-visible and/or delayed effects may interact in some way or other and influence the optimal marketing-mix composition as a consequence. Price discounts, for instance, may lead to faster market penetration, higher price sensitivity, and the need for a more dense distribution network. As a result of the addition of more outlets, however, upmarket retailers may become demotivated to carry the brand any longer, etc. (see Insert) As a result, only downmarket retailers would be left, and the service aspect might deteriorate. Perhaps the producer would need to spend more on consumer advertising to compensate for lingering

It is possible to be too successful for your own good

BMW's British sales rose so fast after 1996 that the company was worried that the famous brand could be devalued to little more than an upmarket version of Ford or Vauxhall. The company, therefore, set a sales limit of 70,000 for 1998, even though it could have sold many more cars than this. 'This is a question of balancing our brand image. We could set a target of twice that number but it would damage our brand,' a spokesman said.

dealer motivation. All sorts of interactions within the marketing mix may lead to a shifting dynamic optimization background instead of a stable and solid static one. This point is so tremendously important that Section 10 will be fully devoted to it.

In addition, response functions are very often not known or only partly known at best. This point is crucial and the situation is worsened by the fact that response functions are not present in an absolute way, but depend on external circumstances, including competitive actions and reactions. In prosperous times car sales can be very sensitive to advertising, but are less so during a depression. In a depression the elasticity of advertising for very cheap cars could in contrast be high—Lada cars used to be a classical example. Both the external circumstances and the way they will influence the response function may be unknown to a greater or smaller extent. Competitive reactions are not the least important amongst those external circumstances.

Finally this critical overview should mention some mathematical issues. The mathematical optimization of the framework that was pictured presupposes metric variables and continuous functions. Marketing-mix 'variables' are not always 'metric', meaning that they cannot always be expressed as elements taking different values with distances between them that can be measured in units. The overall advertising budget, for instance, is a clearly metric element, but media choice is not, and the same holds for the choice of an advertising agency. The example also implies that variables may be composed in turn of a large set of sub-variables, which in turn may be composites of a set of elements, and so on. Moreover response functions need not always be continuous—a precondition to allow mathematical calculus.

7.5 More sophisticated modelling

Some of the conceptual shortcomings of the model set out in Sections 7.1–7.3 can be cured by developing more realistic—mathematical—models. Marketing-mix interaction, lagged effects, competitive reactions, environmental influences, cost constraints, and so on can be taken up in a mathematical model. The same holds for the possible incorporation of multiple segments or regions. But the more complex this model is, the more difficult it will become to estimate and to use it as a forecasting tool and also as a tool for optimization. So, although many of the conceptual shortcomings can be incorporated into a more complex marketing-mix model, they do not make practical marketing-mix choices any easier.

7.6 The limits of historical information

It may be clear that the presence of a good 'marketing-mix model' in the mind of the marketing-mix decision-maker is of prime importance. To arrive at a formal estimation of a 'marketing-mix model', it is possible to rely on existing statistical information. Organizations indeed often have records of past sales, which can be related to marketing-mix compositions prevailing at the corresponding moment in time. Regression analysis, for instance, would make it possible to estimate the effect of different marketing-mix elements on sales. Such an approach, however, presupposes a sufficient number of relevant observations. Historical observations indeed often suffer from one or more of the following shortcomings. To begin with, the number of past observations may be small because the market has only recently been entered or because statistical figures have only been stored on a yearly basis and not on a monthly or quarterly basis.

Moreover, a historical record of sales and of corresponding marketing mixes may reflect a very heterogeneous set, representative neither for the present nor for the future. It could, for instance, consist of old data when the brand was alone on the market and distributed via a limited set of retail outlets, which were paid heavily to push it.

More recent data may reflect a fundamentally different market situation where many competitors have joined the field and where the original brand is heavily advertised to differentiate it from the numerous me-too's. In brief, the historical data may not be comparable and not representative any more. The weeding-out of the irrelevant data may result in the number of 'observations' being too low to allow meaningful statistical analysis.

Optimization on the basis of historical data is also handicapped by a limited range of observations. An organization may have followed a policy that has not given rise to much variation in the magnitude of an instrument. It may have followed an extremely conservative pricing strategy. For example, suppose that, in the past, a public telephone company adapted its prices only to the general index of consumption prices. It would clearly be impossible to derive conclusions from statistical analysis as to the price elasticity of household demand for its services. Suppose this organization now considered much more aggressive pricing, then the past data would be completely insufficient as a base for future choices.

Moreover, data may also give rise to statistical problems as a result of too much intercorrelation. Rising theme-advertising budgets in the past may, for instance, have coincided with rising sales-promotion budgets, making it difficult to determine each instrument's share of the obtained sales increases. Historical data may also be difficult to interpret in terms of cause-and-effect relationships. If, for instance, advertising appropriations are determined in an organization as a fixed percentage of actual past or present or even of expected sales, it becomes difficult to interpret statistically what exactly has caused what.

8 More pragmatic marketing-mix compositions

OFTEN a mathematical model is too complex to allow for optimization. Or else the information is inadequate for estimating the parameters of the model, so that it becomes impossible to estimate it. This section makes some brief suggestions as to more pragmatic approaches, which could—

usually in combination with one another—make up for the impossibility of applying a strictly ideal mix optimization.

8.1 Less sophisticated modelling

Partial mathematical optimization sometimes needs to replace real overall optimization. A focused area of the marketing-mix problem area is isolated, represented in some detail in the form of a mathematical model, and then optimized, assuming everything else stays the same. Reactions of the market to different levels of advertising expenses, for instance, are isolated from the rest of the problem. On the basis of this partial picture, information from alternative sources and methods is taken into account, and, last but not least, managerial approval is sought, and a best budget is agreed.

8.2 Simulation and heuristics

As a model may be too complicated to allow for mathematical optimization, an alternative approach may consist of using the model to simulate the decision situation. Specific alternative marketing-mix 'values' are brought into the model, and a comparative study of the outcomes helps to decide on the 'best' choice of commercial instruments. Many 'business games' for managers and students work this way. Sometimes methods—called heuristics—incorporate their own decision rules to establish automatically a sequence of attempts to try out different solutions in a complex system and to come nearer to a reasonable choice relatively quickly, although this is not the mathematically optimal one.

8.3 Rules of thumb

Very simple substitutes—often far too simplistic—for genuine optimization consist of the use of rules of thumb. Such rules of thumb often imply some reliance on the collective wisdom and/or the majority behaviour of other market participants. It is possible, for instance, to decide on an advertising budget by applying the same percentage of sales competitors tend to use. Or to decide on a price using similar mark-up percentages. Such rules of thumb generally tend to lead to stable competitive situations in the short or medium run. They often imply opportunity costs, as more individual strategic choices would lead to higher profits in the long run. Between strict—often too theoretical—optimization and—often overly simplistic—rules of thumb, ample attention should be given to the managerial alternative of a thorough analysis of the current and future situation, together with the inherent strategic possibilities, and of choosing on the basis of the best fit between resources and objectives. In the following paragraphs an overview will be given of means that may at least partly contribute to such a practical marketing-mix optimization.

8.4 Collection of new information

The drawbacks of lacking or non-representative information may be overcome by collecting new information in one or more of the following ways. Both before and during implementation of such approaches it remains vital, of course, to balance the benefits of the availability of this information against the cost of acquiring it. Experimentation, for instance—by means of laboratory and/or real market tests—may produce information about marketing-mix effects in a relatively accurate way. Surveys, for their part, might also reveal how prospects might react towards different stimuli. This type of information presupposes the fulfilment of several major conditions. Respondents should be identifiable and/or attainable via sampling methods. They should be aware of their own—even hypothetical—reactions and be prepared to disclose this information.

8.5 Explication of implicit historical information

The lack of solid explicit historical information does not exclude the presence of implicit historical information within the organization or the possibility of acquiring it externally. Internal or external expert opinions could be collected, summarized, and even formalized. Reliable historical information or experimentation will be relatively difficult if not impossible to obtain for new markets. The identification and interviewing of knowledgeable people, either alone or in some other situation, perhaps in a small group setting, may be very informative. Sometimes careful questioning may even allow information that at first glance is only present under a vague and sketchy form in the minds of the interviewees to be summarized formally. The shape and parameters of response functions, for instance, can often be reconstructed relatively accurately in this way. Indeed, stepwise questioning of people may make them convey their understanding of the lower and upper limits of such functions. The same holds for the slope of the function in different ranges.

This point already indicates that judgement, guesswork, intuition, sometimes imitation, and perhaps even genius cannot be excluded from the decision process. On the contrary, they represent vital elements (as will be argued in the next sector), but they should be reasonably backed by objective information and analysis. Analysis and judgement are also helped by the use of good checklists of problem areas. Indeed checklists form a basic and handy device to make sure that thought at least is given to the possibly crucial elements in a decision situation. Making a round-up of all primary and secondary effects of a specific marketing-mix choice could serve as an example here.

8.6 Analysis, judgement, and the specification of measurable instrument goals

The analytical aids mentioned in Sections 7.1–7.6 will help to formulate specific goals for the marketing-mix instruments. In turn, the determination of such instrumental goals will contribute to the realism and relevance of the analysis of the situation. It is, indeed, often quite difficult to establish the exact relationship of the quality and magnitude of a marketing-mix element and possible purchase responses. The determination of operational instrumental goals helps to bridge this gap, as these instrumental goals should logically fit one another and the higher strategic aims—for example, market share objectives—as well. Preferably those instrumental goals should be measurable. A good example is the determination of operational distribution objectives by a manufacturer, which may encompass the following specific goals (Bilsen *et al.* 1997: 550).

■ *Specification of the type of distribution channel to be aimed at.* Once it has been decided what type of distribution it is wished to use, the availability of an offering in the channel should be expressed by such operational aims as the degree of distribution, the weighted degree of distribution, and the share of the distributor's product line sales. These objectives can and should be expressed as percentages. They differ markedly depending on the type of product and fit one another logically. Fast-moving consumer goods (FMCG) for instance, call for a high weighted degree of distribution in combination with a low share of the distributor's product line sales—say, for example, 80 and 5 per cent respectively. More exclusive products—luxury cars could be an example—would call for opposite proportions, say 5 and 80 per cent respectively. In both instances these objectives would by definition fit a market-share objective of 4 per cent, as their multiplication equals market share. Next to the latter availability objectives others should be added, like the speed of delivery after an order has been placed.

■ *A specified level of control over retail channels.* Channel alternatives differ in terms of the control a manufacturer has over them. For example, different levels of control will exist between the use of a fully owned network and the use of independent retailers. Therefore, management objectives must be clearly stated so that an evaluation of different channel arrangements can be made.

■ *A specified level of flexibility.* The degree of flexibility in a channel also varies. In itself high flexibility is preferable. The bad thing is that channel alternatives typified by a high control level—such as fully owned networks—tend to be inflexible.

■ *A specified level of profitability.* Alternative channel arrangements are likely to offer different expected revenues and costs and require different levels of investments. Estimates, which must take account of any associated uncertainty, have to be made of the likely level of profitability over a period of time.

■ *The attainment of information feedback.* The ease with which information can be obtained about the levels of activity in the channel differs according to the channel's design. An assessment has to be made of the speed and accuracy with which information can be obtained.

■ *The establishment of a win–win relationship with the retailers and distributors participating in the chain.* A trade-relations mix should be decided upon, together with a determination of conventions and procedures. These should also aim at the medium and long term and therefore be well balanced. This implies that they are advantageous for all parties concerned.

■ *Honest and equal treatment of retailers and distributors.* The treatment of any business associates should obviously be honest. However, equality of treatment is difficult to achieve because the parties involved may have differing perceptions of equality.

8.7 Educational implementation

A wise approach by marketers often consists of gradually implementing a marketing composition allowing the collection of experimental information. A marketing mix is implemented on a limited basis—for instance, in some very familiar regions or segments. Next this mix is revised if necessary and implemented in the original regions and/or in additional regions. This approach gradually extends to additional regions. In this way a full roll-out has, for instance, often been realized in Europe by Unilever. Also many partial customizations of a standard offering by international marketers are of this kind. But it is not only customized marketing-mix compositions that may be adapted as a result of a learning process. Standardized international marketing-mix compositions may also be adjusted as a result of new information and insight during its implementation. As a result, standardized offerings may even become partially customized to a greater or lesser extent, as illustrated by the Buckler–Heineken case in Europe (see Mini Case below).

9 The marketing mix directed at intermediaries

THE discussion of the marketing mix has so far assumed one major target public. This section relaxes this assumption by discussing the use of mix instruments towards more than one public, which, moreover, interact with one another. Marketing indeed touches upon many groups or publics and so does the marketing mix. When it comes to client publics, which are most often of prime concern to an organization, a major distinction arises between intermediate customers and the end-users. Indeed, the end-users of an organization's product are very often reached via intermediaries. For consumer goods in many instances all sorts of agents and/or wholesalers and/or retail organizations usually contribute to bridge the physical and information gap between the source of production and ultimate demand. Also in business-to-business-marketing, although this is more often of a direct nature, intermediaries may carry out the distribution function to a greater or lesser extent. As a result, many organizations face two major sorts of client publics: a public of intermediaries and a public of end-users. In other words, demand can be divided up into intermediate and ultimate demand.

The distinction between intermediate and ultimate demand is crucial to marketing-mix management. Marketing-mix choices have to be made with an eye to stimulating both types of demand, taking into account that those two levels of demand in turn interact. Intermediaries will, for instance, be more strongly motivated to stimulate ultimate demand for brands for which they are offered high margins by their manufacturers. For that reason, the manufacturer could consider offering high margins so as to motivate intermediaries to stimulate ultimate demand. Manufacturers could also decide to stimulate ultimate demand, as this will in turn cause intermediaries to be interested in the generated business opportunity, and will make them eager to carry the item and promote it.

☞ 'For instance, retailers may adapt their service level as a function of the margins granted to them by manufacturers.' (Chapter 10, p. 223)

9.1 Push instruments

The distinction between intermediate and ultimate demand has lead to a distinction between so-called push versus pull marketing-mix instruments and to a similar distinction in terms of marketing-mix strategy. Push instruments fit a 'push strategy', indicating a marketing approach in which both strategic and tactical marketing efforts are mainly focused on the stimulation of intermediate demand, much more than on demand stimulation of ultimate customers. The main goal is to sell the assortment of goods to the nearest level of intermediate demand in the chosen distribution channel, assuming and feeling safe that this level will take the necessary actions to sell it to the next level (if there is one) until finally ultimate demand is stimulated, created, and satisfied. In this way, the assortment is so to speak pushed through the distribution channel—hence

the choice of the metaphor to name the approach. A push approach typically makes much use of a few particular marketing-mix instruments and much less of other instruments. Personal selling—for example, carried out by a manufacturer's sales force—will be of high importance. Trade advertising will be the major kind of impersonal communication that will be considered. Consumer advertising will be of much lesser importance. Sales promotion will consist of trade promotions and sales-force promotions, and not so much of consumer promotions. Much emphasis will be given to margin policy: relatively high margins will be provided to motivate the intermediaries to carry out their push activities. The same holds for all other sorts of remuneration, compensations, and incentives. Very often the degree of distribution is not very high, as the relative monopoly position of the intermediaries should be another element of motivation to stimulate the brand's sales.

9.2 Pull instruments

Pull instruments fit a 'pull strategy', indicating a marketing approach in which both strategic and tactical efforts are focused mainly on demand creation at the level of the ultimate customers and much less on demand creation at the intermediate level. Ultimate demand is created and stimulated so that ultimate customers search for the product or brand at intermediaries. The intermediate level closest to the ultimate customer will in turn order the product or brand at the level above him and so on. A retailer might place an order with a wholesaler, who in turn contacts an importer, and so on. As a result of these successive forces, a process is started up whereby the product is so to speak pulled through the distribution channel—hence the metaphor to denominate this marketing approach. A pull approach also relies predominantly on some marketing-mix instruments, and much less on others. Relatively impersonal communication takes place, which is directed at ultimate customers. Advertising and publicity for that reason are generally important instrument categories. If sales promotion is used, this will be mostly consumer promotions—at least in consumer-goods marketing. The degree of distribution is most typically quite high. Margins and other types of compensations for intermediaries are typically rather low, because of their relatively passive role.

9.3 Cost differences between push and pull instruments

The choice between a push and a pull approach, respectively between the instruments, partly follows from the corresponding cost aspect. In a push approach a large part of the costs is of a variable nature, as a result of the ample use of compensations and incentives to stimulate intermediaries. Fixed costs are typically relatively small, as a result of the absence of major consumer advertising and promotion campaigns. The latter are typically much more substantial in a pull approach, which for that reason is characterized much more by high fixed costs. Variable costs, on the other hand, are typically much smaller in a pull approach, as a result of the much smaller need for all sorts of compensations for intermediaries. As Fig. 9.2 indicates, the cost aspect suggests a dependence of the choice between a push and a pull approach based on the expected turnover. Beyond a certain break-even level a pull approach is cheaper, below it a push approach is preferable.

9.4 Risk differences between push and pull instruments

The cost distinctions, however, should be completed with the risk element of both approaches. Sales forecasts are only estimations, surrounded by a smaller or greater amount of uncertainty. Fixed costs are incurred regardless of the level of sales actually taking place. Advertising campaigns, for instance, will have been started up and the commitments for the rest of the campaign taken. As a result, more or less heavy losses will be incurred if sales expectations are not met. Variable costs are by definition incurred only at the moment sales are closed. If the expected sales level is not reached, no corresponding costs occur. If sales expectations are exceeded, the resultant extra costs are still lower than the extra return. A push strategy, in other words, is much less risky than a pull strategy, even at the break-even point x of Fig. 9.2. For that reason, smaller firms very often stick to push strategies, and will be hesitant to switch over to a pull strategy too quickly.

To the same extent that it would be unrealistic to act as if push–pull choices were not bounded by risk aspects, it would be unrealistic to ignore other limitations. Available financial means, for example, will often prohibit the possibility of a pull approach, even if preferable from other points of view. Actual market positions, on the other hand, may cancel out some possibilities. The presence of a very strong retail level in a certain market may make it necessary to follow a push strategy, as these retailers would otherwise not be prepared to carry the product.

9.5 Marketing-mix dynamics

So far, the marketing mix has been discussed mainly from a static or stable point of view. Finally this chapter will now relax this static assumption by focusing on some dynamic aspects. The previous sections have described major marketing-mix distinctions: primary versus secondary instruments, presence versus absence of differentiation in marketing-mix instruments, and push instruments versus pull instruments. Those distinctions were discussed in a fairly static way—against a stable background. The present section discusses the same distinctions against a changing background, which typifies the marketing environment much more than a stable one. Those dynamics may be the sole result of external forces, but may also result more or less directly from the use of the marketing-mix elements themselves. They may also follow from the interaction between external forces and the choice of particular marketing-mix compositions. The described phenomena represent only a few principal examples out of

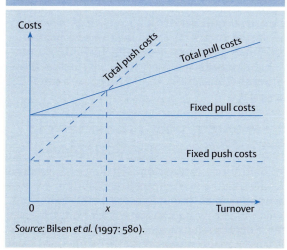

Figure 9.2 **Cost differences between push and pull instruments**

Source: Bilsen et al. (1997: 580).

the many. They nevertheless serve well to underline and illustrate the necessity of not just looking at the immediate effects of marketing-mix compositions but also of looking at least a few steps ahead.

9.6 Isolated versus repetitive exchanges

In many instances a marketer aims not just at one-time exchanges, but rather at repetitive exchanges with the same customers. This is not so much the case in homogeneous markets like those of natural commodities, where the presence of similar offerings would make customers buy on a price basis. As a result of the extreme price sensitivity that marks such markets, investing and spending on repetitive transactions with the very same customers may not be a prime issue. Also if potential customers are seldom the same, this is obviously the case, as in some tourist areas or in the case of selling encyclopaedias. Again, in markets with few players and much monopoly power, repeat buying may not be a prime concern, at least not in the short run. The repetitive exchanges are sought most strongly by marketers in differentiated or differentiable markets. Here repetitive exchanges become vital, as they affect market share, profitability, and the efficiency and composition of the marketing mix. Repetitive transactions presuppose a relatively high degree of customer satisfaction anyway, which most directly follows from high product quality in relation to its price. Depending on the case, other marketing mix instruments may also contribute more or less strongly to this customer satisfaction.

To a large extent customer satisfaction follows from a fine-tuning of the offering to the needs of the customer. This fine-tuning of the product mix, including its service elements, can be partly realized via the communication mix. Direct marketers, for instance, can use their database to reach possible clients at opportune moments of time with relevant specific information. By keeping track of customer characteristics, expressed preferences, and purchase history, both offerings and communications can be fine-tuned. Consequently, the contact with the client may prosper as a result of this personalized communication and develop into the direction of 'relationship' marketing. For more important products and clients, as in many business-to-business situations,

literally personal contacts will play a prime role in the personal-communications mix. Mutual confidence, respect, and honest communication will lead to a clear picture of what the client needs, how his needs are best fulfilled, and which approaches may lead to the benefit of both parties. Both personalized and genuine personal communication used on a permanent basis will lead to a more or less strong personal relationship with the clients, which offers substantial benefits in terms of communication efficiency. The organization need not introduce itself and its offerings over and over again. Moreover, as customers' attitudes normally develop in a positive way, less communication may suffice and the effects may in general be substantially more positive too. As a result, it becomes cheaper to keep clients than to win new ones. Moreover, negative word-of-mouth publicity by previous clients, which is often very damaging, can be avoided. The results of the existence of a relationship, however, stretch out to other elements of the marketing mix as well. This happens not only by implying and allowing customer-oriented adaptations of the product mix, but also through product extensions that become easier to market with those customers. Price advice will be accepted more readily as well, allowing more control over prices to ultimate customers. Scarce retail space will be granted more easily and so on.

☞ 'These traditional views are sometimes referred to as *transaction marketing*, or marketing-mix management.' (Chapter 22, p. 517)

☞ 'While relationship marketing may originally have been more prevalent in industrial and service markets, it is becoming pervasive to all types of businesses, including consumer products. However, the shift to relationship marketing is not at the exclusion of traditional transaction marketing.' (Chapter 22, p. 532)

9.7 From the post-promotion dip to a negative promotion spiral

By definition, promotion instruments are used during relatively short periods of time to lead customers to desirable forms of visible behaviour, which is mostly purchasing. As a result, the sales curve of promoted products shows or should show at least a marked rise above the usual sales level during promotion periods. But immediately afterwards there is a typical low in sales, below the usual sales level, known as the 'post-promotion dip'. The post-promotion dip is mainly the result of stockpiling by intermediate and ultimate customers. If all goes well, this post-promotion dip does not last very long. It is hoped that sales will re-establish themselves at least at the usual level, but hopefully somewhat above it. The expectation is that customer satisfaction following from increased product trials of new buyers will lead to repeat purchases and even brand loyalty. A few less positive developments may, however, endanger this positive scenario.

Customers' stockpiling activities may lead to an erosion of profits. If their financial and technical means allow it, customers may await periods of sales promotions to buy when conditions are most favourable, generally at low prices. If all goes well, the company may sell the same or an even higher quantity than it used to sell before, but at a markedly lower price. The company, moreover, may have condemned itself to selling at lower prices. The risk is indeed real that price expectations by customers have been influenced as a result of the promotion campaign(s), making it difficult ever again to charge higher prices in the future. Moreover, the brand image risks being hurt, as the impression is created that this is a product that must be sold even at a dumping price. So the brand may also become less attractive for middlemen, especially for more upscale ones.

The previous scenario may even become more gloomy. If all does not go well, the sales volume may indeed not even reach the original level after the post-promotion dip. Competitors who have seen some of their customers switch over to promoted brands may become tempted to try to regain them quickly by using similar promotional weapons, and in fact they often do so. This may be the beginning of a promotion spiral. As more and more competitors become involved, the massive use of promotion will typify the sector. The net effect of this may be disastrous in terms of profitability for all parties involved, except for the customers.

9.8 The downward spiral of pull instruments

A major phenomenon to be mentioned here are the shifts that may occur over time with regard to the use and usability of push-versus-pull marketing-mix instruments. The relative power of intermediaries represents a major determinant in the choice between a push versus a pull approach. And if a shift occurs in their power versus that of manufacturers, this bears consequences with regard to the existing policy. The traditional policy for large FMCG manufacturers, for instance, has for years been one of a pull nature. Efforts were concentrated on final consumers, so as to try to create brand preference that would result in market-share gain or at least maintenance. Relatively little marketing effort and money were spent on intermediaries, who were generally prepared to carry many brands without particularly pushing any one of them. As, however, retailers grew much larger and stronger over the years and as their shelf space became more scarce as a result of a growing number of different product (sub)categories, they became more demanding. As a result, manufacturers found themselves obliged to grant them all sorts of allowances, incentives, and remuneration, on top of greater margins. These expenses squeezed the manufacturers' profits, both in a relative and in an absolute sense. At that moment it is very tempting for them to economize on those elements of their policy that offer most opportunity for curtailing, at least at first glance: research and development (R&D) expenses, on the one hand, and advertising expenses, on the other. The result of this trimming will not be felt overnight, but after a while, of course, the results will manifest themselves anyway. In particular, loss of objective product differentiation will result from R&D economies and loss of psychological differentiation will result from curtailing the advertising budget. As a result, brand awareness and brand preference by the ultimate consumers will drop. As a result, the negotiation position of the manufacturer versus the mighty retail chains weakens. Consequently, manufacturers will have to grant still better conditions for their products to remain on the shelves, and so on. In the end a 'downward spiral' will take place. If the manufacturer is still in the market, he will ultimately be following a push strategy instead of the original pull strategy.

9.9 The upward spiral of push instruments

The dynamics of the use of push and pull instruments are also well illustrated by the 'upward spiral'. Suppose that a manufacturer is confronted by very strong retail organizations. By necessity, he will have to invest strongly in push means to be accepted by those major intermediaries. If he is and remains successful, his brand will reach the shelves and remain there. If it is also valued by final customers, brand awareness and also brand preference may gradually develop. To the extent that brand awareness and preference develop favourably, a 'consumer franchise' is established and enjoyed by the manufacturer. At this junction, he may consider economizing gradually on push means and starting spending more on efforts of a pull nature. This type of development occurred, for instance, in West European car dealing. For years, car manufacturers spent heavily on push efforts. One push element was their investment in cars placed in dealer's showrooms. As this push policy resulted in brand loyalty, they gradually started to focus more strongly on ultimate customers. One indication of this shift was the manufacturers' gradual refusal to invest any more in cars standing in their dealers' showrooms. Dealers were now obliged to invest in these stocked cars themselves.

9.10 The commodity trap

The search for differentiation is central to marketing thinking. At the same time, however, market forces such as market entry and imitation tend to neutralize differentiation. They lead to what can be called 'commoditization' (Buisson 1995: 788). The term is derived from 'primary commodities', which are goods in or near their first stage of transformation—products harvested or fished until they have undergone transformation. Since the mid-1990s, commodities have been defined in terms of market dynamics. 'Commodities' have become a synonym of 'homogeneous or undifferentiated products'. Commoditization refers to the tendency for differentiation to be eroded as a result of increasing competition, of me-too products, of the reluctance of customers to pay for features and services accompanying the product, and of pressure on prices and margins in general (Buisson 1995: 788). As commoditization takes place, customers start to perceive the product as a homogeneous one and price becomes the predominant buying criterion. Differentiation with its accompanying price freedom and premium profits, therefore, bears in itself the seeds of imitation and competition. Corstjens and Corstjens (1995: 54) offer the example of a regional French com-

pany called Saint-Hubert. The company capitalized on an idea developed in Japan of using the bifidus bacteria to increase the beneficial health effects in yoghurt. Within a few years, more than twelve comparable offerings had found their way onto the French market, thereby turning the differentiated product into 'a commodity' again. A prime concern for marketers, therefore, is to look for ways to avoid the 'commodity trap'. They can do so by searching for sustainable competitive advantages, not publicizing their high profits, and, last but not least, building up entry barriers against newcomers and taking away exit barriers for those competitors who might consider leaving the market. Falling into the commodity trap is seen as the worst of all evils by marketers. The commodity trap is the opposite of the natural aim of maximum monopoly power, following from maximum differentiation, in which the marketing mix has such an important role to play.

10 The future

FORECASTING is generally a tricky activity, rightly compared with the discouraging task of a blindfolded car driver guided by a co-pilot looking through the rear window. Foretelling future developments concerning the marketing mix is no exception to this pessimistic task interpretation. Moreover, the marketing-mix concept is so fundamental that it covers thousands of specific situations. Related to each of these situations, several interacting developments may take place that could lead to several different scenarios. Nevertheless, a few rather general 'observations' can be made. One rather solid observation is the further rise of professional marketing-mix management as a result of accumulated knowledge, education, expertise, and experience. The better-skilled professional, however, also confronts quicker changes in the environment, especially when technological changes take place. He experiences shorter product life cycles partly following from the still-rising affluence and whimsicality of major market segments. He also meets ever-mounting competition—hypercompetition seems to become the rule rather than the exception—requiring quicker, more efficient, and more original marketing-mix compositions. The latter requirement may be particularly troublesome as thousands of original ideas have already seen daylight—successfully or unsuccessfully. Moreover, creativity is at least as much a gift of nature as an acquired skill. Training and intellectual analysis, however, may serve to distinguish the genius from the would-be genius, the genuinely original and solid plan from the fake one. In the years to come, solid marketing plans are more likely to encompass direct contacts with ultimate buyers following from technological evolutions like the further development of electronic media and of computerized databases. Indirect contacts with ultimate customers, for their part, will increasingly take place via vertical channel arrangements. These arrangements will pose constraints on the freedom of movement of the marketing mix, as instrument choices must fit partnerships. Both direct and indirect contacts, however, will lead to more customized marketing mixes. Database management, new communication techniques, the search for relationships, as well as robotic production techniques will generally lead to more customized offerings. This phenomenon seems so certain that the new term 'mass customization' has already been coined. It occupies a midway position in the classic bipolar distinction between 'custom marketing' and 'mass marketing' (Blois 1978: 575). On the other hand, one may wonder whether hyper-customization may not create opportunities for extremely low-cost standardized offerings. For product categories that may be losing their expressive value as a result of an unprecedented proliferation and that may be brought back to their essential function, like personal computers, back-to-basics opportunities may exist for genuinely low-cost players. Price may, in such instances, paradoxically become the main differentiation-creating element.

11 Summary

IN essence marketing is demand management. The set of instruments the marketer can dispose of to influence demand for his offering is traditionally indicated by the metaphor of the marketing mix. The marketing-mix idea presupposes an actually or potentially differentiated market as opposed to a homogeneous market where the organization is a price-taker. The marketing mix will be the creator of positive differentiation for the individual organization's offering, but may also affect the nature of the overall market. The mix

metaphor indicates the wide range of ingredients that can be combined into numerous combinations that may cause all sorts of effects—favourable as well as unfavourable ones. Individual instruments may provoke all sorts of effects: behavioural versus mental effects, instant versus delayed effects, direct versus indirect effects, effects related to their primary function and secondary functions. The combination of instruments, therefore, may lead to all sorts of combined effects in a positive and negative way in the shorter or longer term. This picture is complicated if several important target publics interact, as is the case with intermediate and final customers. As a result of this complexity, the basic economic marginality principle to determine optimal marketing-mix compositions can only seldom be applied in a straightforward manner. Often optimal solutions can be approached more or less closely only by educated managerial judgement, backed by analytical tools of a diverse nature and kind.

Further reading

Beem, E., and Schaffer, H. (1981), *Triggers to Action: Some Elements in a Theory of Promotional Inducement* (Report No. 81–106, Cambridge, Mass.: Marketing Science Institute). Major theoretical source concerning the nature and delineation of the promotion concept.

Gary, L., and Kotler, P. (1983), '*Marketing Decision Making: A Model Building Approach*' (New York: Harper and Row Publishers). This book, written by authoritative model builders, contains a description of how managerial judgement can be translated in the formal form of a mathematical model. The book concentrates in particular on marketing-mix issues.

Houston, F. S., and Gassenheimer, J. B. (1987), 'Marketing and Exchange', *Journal of Marketing*, 51/4 (Oct.), 3–18. Investigates systematically and thoroughly the interrelationship between marketing and exchange theory.

Kotler, P. (1972), 'A Generic Concept of Marketing', *Journal of Marketing*, 36/2 (Apr.), 46–54. Classic article that clearly delineates the borderlines and core concepts of the marketing discipline.

—— (1973), 'The Major Tasks of Marketing Management', *Journal of Marketing*, 37/4 (Sept.–Oct.), 42–9. Classic article discussing the nature of and rationale behind the discouragement of demand as well as the possible role of the marketing mix.

Kotler, P. (1986), 'Megamarketing', *Harvard Business Review*, 64/2 (Mar.–Apr.), 117–24. Discusses marketing mixes targeted at non-traditional but important parties such as government and labour unions.

—— and Levy, S. (1971), 'Demarketing, Yes, Demarketing', *Harvard Business Review*, 49/6 (Nov.–Dec.), 71–80.

Levitt, T. (1980), 'Marketing Success through Differentiation—of Anything', *Harvard Business Review*, 58/1 (Jan.–Feb.), 83–91. Classic article arguing that differentiation of an offering is not confined to product differentiation but may encompass any element of the marketing mix.

Lilien, G. L., Kotler, P., and Moorthy, K. S. (1992), *Marketing Models* (Englewood Cliffs, NJ: Prentice-Hall). Representative overview of publicized marketing-mix models.

Naert, Ph. N., and Leeflang, P. S. H. (1978), *Building Implementable Marketing Models* (Leiden, Boston: Martinus Nijhoff). Unusually clear, readable, and practical textbook about implementation issues related to marketing-mix models.

Van den Bulte, C. (1991), *The Concept of the Marketing Mix Revisited: A Case Analysis of Metaphor in Marketing Theory and Management* (Ghent: The Vlerick School of Management). Metatheoretical paper containing, amongst other things, a thorough inventory of criticisms on the marketing-mix concept and metaphor.

van Waterschoot, W., and Van den Bulte, C. (1992), 'The 4P Classification of the Marketing Mix Revisited', *Journal of Marketing*, 56/4 (Oct.), 83–93. Analyses the classification problems of the 4Ps and proposes an improved classification.

Discussion questions

1 Could you think of exchanges resulting not from the use of the marketing mix, but from other mechanisms or sources?

2 The marketing mix has been criticized for not fitting into mutual or reciprocal marketing situations. Would you consider this to be a valid criticism?

3 What might be the most typical demand-impinging elements of both a controllable and a non-controllable nature in the case of fund-raising?

4 In which way may price instruments contribute to marketing-mix functions other than the pricing function?

5 Do you see any explanation for the widespread use of sales-promotion instruments in marketing practice in spite of their many long-term dangers?

6 Should a marketing-mix model under all circumstances possess high descriptive, predictive, as well as prescriptive qualities?

7 Is a marketing-mix composition that maximally differentiates an organization's own offering from competing ones always to be preferred over one that rather boosts the sales of the whole product category?

Mini Case
Buckler-Heineken

Heineken is an international brewing company of Dutch origin. In addition to its brand Heineken, which is reputable worldwide, it also produces and markets other well-known brands such as Amstel, Sourcy, and Royal Club, plus a variety of national and regional brands. To cater for the international market, the company relies on exporting, licensing, and also on the acquisition of other breweries. Although local breweries remain relatively autonomous to enable them to exploit local market conditions, certain areas such as policies on finance and technology are centralized. Over time, the marketing function has become more centralized as corporate management has become more strongly committed to standardization of its marketing approach.

In view of the rising importance of non-alcoholic beer, in 1997 Heineken intended to launch a Pan-European brand of non-alcoholic beer that was centrally managed and highly standardized. A working team of production and marketing managers indeed 'instinctively believed that non-alcoholic beer drinkers tended to be the same everywhere'. The consensus, therefore, was that a standard marketing strategy for the newly developed brand Buckler could be used across European countries with only minor changes. When the Executive Board decided to launch the product in late December 1987, Corporate Marketing was surprised to find that only the divisions in France and Spain were interested in introducing the product immediately. Of these two, France was the only one really interested in having an advertising campaign, but Corporate Marketing still wanted to pursue a standardized communications strategy. The product was actually launched in 1988. It was positioned as a beer without alcohol and not as a non-alcoholic adult drink. It would direct itself at consumers between 25 and 40 years of age, as these people were supposedly more concerned about alcohol consumption. In order not to jeopardize the position of its existing brands, a completely new name would be selected for the new non-alcoholic product. After tests in four countries, the new product was called Buckler. It was introduced at a premium price to sustain its image, in spite of the relatively low production price following from scale economies.

As to the advertising programme, a first campaign proposal developed by a Dutch agency was not welcomed whole-heartedly, especially not by the Spanish division, as the campaign focused too much on developing the non-alcoholic beer category instead of specifically developing the Buckler brand. As a result, some adaptations were made for Spain. To develop a second advertising campaign, another advertising agency was selected. The

actual campaign was then tested in the various European countries. If the tests turned out to be positive, the operating companies had to accept it. Otherwise they were allowed to run their own campaign. One year later, in 1989, this second advertising campaign was (still) used by each national division, including Spain, France, the Netherlands, and Ireland. In 1990 the last two operating companies to launch Buckler also started using this campaign. Ultimately, the communications strategy could be considered highly standardized, as indicated in Table 9.2, which also rates the other elements of the marketing mix.

Not only was the standardized part of the marketing mix adapted as a result of the stream of information. The customized part of it was also atuned more closely as a result of new information and/or changing circumstances. In Holland, for example, the Dutch operating company was reluctant to support the Buckler brand, as it had introduced a low-calorie product called Amstel Light only a few months earlier. When Buckler reached a market share of 60 per cent in 1989 without advertising support, the Dutch management quickly established a budget of 13 million guilders for the European advertising campaign. One year later, however, Buckler's market share in Holland was down to 30 per cent because of the success of a new local brand. Bavaria Malt was indeed not only priced 30 per cent below the Buckler brand, but blind tests also consistently attributed a much better taste to it.

Source: Quelch *et al.* (1994).

Table 9.2 Level of standardization for Buckler's marketing-mix elements

Marketing-mix elements	Level of standardization
Brand name	5
Product name	4
Product	5/4
Design	5
Positioning	5
Packaging	4
Pricing	4
Advertising	5/4
Sponsoring	5/4
Sales promotions	3/2
Public relations	3/2
Customer service	2
Expiry date	5/4

Note: 5 = highly standardized, 1 = highly localized.

Chapter 10
Pricing

Els Gijsbrechts and Katia Campo

Objectives

This chapter does not have as its aim the provision of ready-made methods for the assessment of price levels. Its objectives are:

1 to indicate the importance and complexity of price decisions for marketing managers;

2 to consider what is a 'price';

3 to identify the factors internal to the firm that influence price decisions;

4 to identify the factors external to the firm that influence price decisions;

5 to discuss pricing strategies and tactics.

1 Introduction

CONSIDER a Belgian couple contemplating a shopping trip to London during the Christmas period. The cheapest way to cross the Channel would be to take a ticket on the ferry from Oostende to Ramsgate, which would amount to about Bfr. 1,500 per person. While they can afford this from a budgetary viewpoint, taking the boat would mean spending about five hours travelling, which would mean losing almost half of the 'available' weekend to hunt for interesting bargains in the London shopping area. Taking the plane would drastically reduce travelling time, but the air fare of Bfr. 4,900 per person is not overly appealing. Friends recommend that they buy a combined ticket from the Belgian Railways and the Channel (regular price: Bfr. 3,465 per person). This seems to be the most interesting option, but unfortunately no more regular tickets are available for the morning of the Christmas weekend. The price of a first class-Railway/Channel ticket (Bfr. 6,960 per person, including a luxury meal and free drinks) is prohibitive. Ultimately, the couple decides to travel by Hovercraft, at a rate of Bfr. 2,200 per person.

This example illustrates the complexity of consumer choices in the face of a variety of alternatives offered at different prices. The mirror image of this problem is the pricing issue for firms offering the products or services to various types of customers: their pricing problem will be equally multifaceted and complex.

To introduce the nature of the problem and the issues involved, Section 1 elaborates on the meaning of price, and on the importance of price as a marketing-mix instrument.

1.1 The meaning of price

'The price of a product or service is the number of monetary units a customer has to pay to receive one unit of that product or service' (Simon 1989). This was the traditional definition, but in the 1990s a broader interpretation of the price concept became customary. Illustrative of this broader view is Hutt and Speh's observation that 'the cost of an industrial good includes much more than the seller's price' (Hutt and Speh 1998: 441).

This broader interpretation extends the 'traditional' price notion along three dimensions. First, it recognizes the possible discrepancy between *objective* and *perceived* prices. As will be documented in Section 4.1.2, it is unrealistic to assume that all customers have complete information on amounts to be paid for market offerings, and psychological processes may affect how price information is assimilated by customers. Secondly, price need not be specified exclusively in monetary terms at the time the product is acquired. Product usage may entail additional costs of repair, maintenance, and energy consumption that should be accounted for. Also, price in a general sense encompasses non-monetary efforts of product acquisition. A typical example in consumer markets is 'time costs' associated with alternative offerings as a result of travel, shopping, waiting, search, and transaction time involved. To the couple ready to engage in the London shopping adventure, the time needed to reach their destination is of crucial importance. In industrial markets, efforts related to installation, transportation, order handling, and inventory-carrying represent examples of non-monetary efforts. Thirdly, price encompasses not only an 'effort' but also a 'risk' component. Risk associated with product adoption may be functional, such as the risk of product failure or of poor technical and delivery support. It may also be social or psychological in nature, an example being the risk of signalling low social status when driving around in a Lada. These 'recent' views on pricing seem to reiterate Adam Smith's statement in *The Wealth of Nations* (1776) that 'The real price of everything is the toil and trouble of acquiring it' (cited in Keegan 1995), complemented with the perceived effort and risk associated with product use. A similar point of view is expressed in Zeithaml's (1988) price definition: 'From the consumer's point of view, price is what is given up or sacrificed to obtain a product.'

Recognizing the broad implications of pricing is crucial to managers facing the pricing decision. First, decision-makers have to account for eventual disparities between real and perceived prices in targeted customer segments. Also, setting prices may not be restricted to determining the number of monetary units to be paid for one unit of the product at the time of purchase. It may encompass the specification of 'purchase and use conditions' associated with monetary price, over the product's life cycle. In brief, the multidimensional view on prices leads to the recognition that complex pricing schemes may be needed, including a 'system' of prices for different types of customers, product packages, and time periods. This observation is the essence of strategic pricing.

1.2 The importance of price

While the importance of price as a marketing-mix instrument went unquestioned for several decades, the 1990s witnessed an even stronger interest in pricing issues, putting price at the forefront of all marketing actions. Statements like 'Pricing is the moment of truth—all marketing comes to focus in the pricing decision' (Corey, cited in Nagle and Holden 1995) are illustrative of this point of view. Surveys indicate that US as well as West European companies rank pricing as more important than other marketing-mix elements (Phillips *et al.* 1994; Nagle and Holden 1995).

Price distinguishes itself from other marketing-mix instruments in that it captures some of the value created by the firms' other marketing activities by generating 'cash'. As Nagle and Holden (1995) put it: 'If effective product development, promotion, and distribution sow the seeds of business success, effective pricing is the harvest.' Other typical characteristics of price are its *flexibility* (it takes relatively little time to change it), its *speed of effect* (price yields fast reactions from customers and competitors), and the *force and magnitude* of the reactions it entails. These properties have made price a particularly relevant weapon in times of increased competition, fast technological progress and proliferation of new products, and changing economic and legal conditions. Yet, while price may be crucial in coping with these situations, few managers to date know how to price effectively. The situation is well described by Winkler (1990: 18), when he states: 'Price, Product, Promotion. The greatest of them is Price. It is also the least talked about and the least understood. Correct pricing decisions can be a matter of commercial life and death. Yet companies often fail to develop coherent pricing strategies, and too often marketers find themselves at loggerheads with financial colleagues over what price should be.'

The purpose of this chapter is to uncover basic principles underlying prices and pricing. Like most marketing decisions, pricing is an art but also a science. Given the complex and multifaceted nature of prices, and the importance of price as a marketing instrument, a systematic approach to 'strategic' pricing is called for.

2 Strategic pricing

PRICING strategies have to support the firm's objectives and overall strategy. Prices obviously affect revenue per unit directly, but the price is also a component of the marketing mix and therefore impacts on overall sales via its contribution to the consumers' perception of the product's image. It follows that decisions about prices have a significant impact on the company's success.

2.1 The notion of price boundaries

As suggested in the introduction to this chapter, numerous factors affect the 'appropriateness' of price decisions, and a company may have to develop pricing schemes adapted to a variety of situations and market segments simultaneously. This calls for a systematic and well-planned approach to pricing. At the same time, given the multitude of influencing factors, it may be hard to identify the 'best' price for a given product. Moreover, even if it were possible to determine an 'optimal' price in each situation, such a price or set of prices may not be feasible to implement because of its complexity, its non-compliance with legal constraints, or the costliness of administration. These observations place the 'systematic' approach to pricing developed in this chapter in the proper perspective. Instead of pursuing the best price level to be implemented, one may simply attempt to delineate a range of acceptable price levels within which the ultimate price will be situated. Even managers with a 'back-of-the-envelope' approach to pricing have some lower and upper bound on price in mind. The purpose of the 'systematic' approach outlined below is to shed more light on the factors that structurally affect the level of the minimal and maximal acceptable prices, and, given information on these factors, to assist managers in *narrowing down* the feasible price range in their particular situation. The systematic approach thus provides managers with a more reasoned and complete picture of available pricing options depending on the circumstances, and helps them select one or some of these options in view of their priorities or trade-offs.

It is important to note at the outset that strategic pricing is not a 'one-time' exercise. The systematic approach allows managers gradually to improve their picture of acceptable prices in a given situation, without having to go 'all the way' from the start.

2.2 A systematic approach to pricing

Fig. 10.1 outlines a systematic approach to pricing. As can be seen from this figure, pricing encompasses a process with two main stages: analysis of the pricing environment, and price determination. A prerequisite for effective pricing is knowledge of the internal (company) *environment*, where information on overall objectives, strategies, and costs, but also on 'value-creating' marketing-mix activities such as product, communication, and distribution, is crucial. Together with characteristics of the *external environment* (customers, competitors, channel members, and other publics like the government), they shape the possibilities for effective pricing available to the company. *Price determination*, then, comprises the selection of pricing objectives, and the choice of a pricing strategy providing long-term support for these objectives. This strategy needs to be translated into concrete price structures and levels, and supplemented with short-term-oriented, tactical price manipulations. As suggested earlier, pricing is far from a strictly sequential, one-time process that managers go through. Instead, managers may find it fruitful to repeat the stages, gathering supplementary and updated information as they proceed through the stages repeatedly.

The remainder of the chapter is organized around the pricing process depicted in Fig. 10.1. Section 3 concentrates on internal factors affecting pricing. Section 4 discusses major external influences. Given the basic picture obtained from environmental analysis, Section 5 elaborates on the company's pricing objectives. These form a crucial input to the selection of an appropriate pricing strategy, a systematic overview of which is given in Section 6. Section 7 subsequently focuses on the assessment of price structures and levels, and tactical price decisions are dealt with in Section 8. Section 9 illustrates some of these principles in a case study. Section 10, finally, provides a summary of the discussion and conclusions.

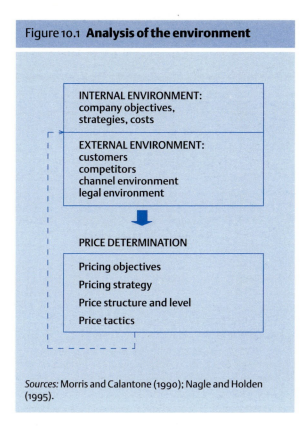

Figure 10.1 **Analysis of the environment**

INTERNAL ENVIRONMENT:
company objectives,
strategies, costs

EXTERNAL ENVIRONMENT:
customers
competitors
channel environment
legal environment

PRICE DETERMINATION

Pricing objectives

Pricing strategy

Price structure and level

Price tactics

Sources: Morris and Calantone (1990); Nagle and Holden (1995).

3 Internal factors affecting pricing

3.1 Company objectives and strategies

An essential ingredient of effective prices is their consistency with company objectives and overall marketing strategy. Company objectives are 'general aspirations toward which all activities in the firm, not only pricing, are directed' (Nagle and Holden 1995: 10). The realization of company objectives necessitates the development of an overall marketing strategy. To be effective and efficient, the company's pricing decisions must fit into this strategy, and be in line with decisions on other marketing-mix elements. Also, prices should not be set as an 'afterthought'. Reflections on appropriate prices should occur at the time the product, communication, and distribution are conceived, because the different instruments of the mix have a 'synergetic' influence on the market. There is ample evidence that the impact of pricing strategies and structures depends on the companies' communication and distribution approach and on the product's characteristics.

Various sources highlight the impact of *communication* strategies on customer price sensitivity. The debate centres around the question whether advertising increases or reduces customers' attention to price. In a special *Marketing Science* issue on empirical generalizations in marketing, Kaul and Wittink (1995) conclude that an increase in non-price advertising leads to lower price sensitivity among consumers. Conversely, increased price advertising leads to higher price sensitivity. Along similar lines, it is well documented that feature advertising or point of purchase (PoP) support significantly increase the impact of price deals (see e.g. Blattberg *et al.* 1995). *Distribution* and price decisions may equally interact in a variety of ways. To illustrate: the service and functions provided by distribution outlets affect what prices customers find acceptable, as do the outlet's image, ambient, and design factors (see e.g. Grewal and Baker 1994). Perhaps the most obvious interactions are those between price and *product characteristics* such as product quality. Not only does quality affect the customers' willingness to pay and price sensitivity; in a number of product categories, price may serve as a quality indicator (see Section 4.1.2).

Some of these issues will be taken up again below. The observation to be made at this point is that managers should be aware of marketing-mix interactions, and exploit them through integrated decisions on communication, distribution, product, and price. According to Nagle and Holden (1995), the failure to do so is one of the major sources of ineffective pricing.

3.2 Costs

Costs have traditionally played a major role in pricing decisions. They constitute a basic ingredient for setting a price floor or lower boundary on acceptable prices. Yet, while costs are an essential ingredient to pricing, their role in the pricing process can be very complex. Costs indeed have many faces, and can be classified along different dimensions.

A first dimension concerns the degree to which costs can be directly attributed to specific products. Hutt and Speh (1998) distinguish between direct traceable, indirect traceable, and general costs. *Direct traceable* costs can be immediately associated with individual products. An example is the cost of raw materials. *Indirect traceable* costs are not directly linked to, but can with some effort be traced back to, individual products. The cost of filling shelves is illustrative of this type. *General* costs, finally, cannot be linked to specific products. A typical example is administrative overhead costs. Assessing direct traceable costs, and attributing indirect traceable costs, are important for pricing.

Equally crucial is the distinction between *variable* and *fixed* costs. Which of these components should enter the pricing decision depends on the company's objective. For profit-maximizing companies, fixed cost may not (immediately) affect optimal prices. Yet, for not-for-profit companies maximizing sales or participation subject to a deficit constraint, fixed cost may have a major effect on feasible outcomes. The company's time horizon also has a fundamental impact on the costs to be considered. Whether costs are fixed or variable depends on the time frame adopted by the company. Also, forward-looking companies may forgo covering fixed costs in view of future possibilities.

This leads us to the discussion of cost dynamics. Short-term costs may differ from long-term cost levels as a result of changes in the scale of company operations, or thanks to accumulated experience. *Economies of scale* arise if the cost per unit decreases with the output level in a given period. This could be the result of the facility to share corporate resources across products, the use of more efficient (large-scale) production facilities, long production runs, access to volume discounts in purchases, or shipment in full carload or truckload lots (Monroe 1990). *Experience effects* are a second major source of declining production (and possibly other) costs. As cumulative production quantity increases, manufacturing procedures become more efficient ('learning by doing', technological improvements), allowing the production of similar output levels at lower unit cost over time. The reduction in costs with accumulated experience is usually represented by means of an experience curve (see Fig. 10.2), displaying unit costs as a function of accumulated production experience (approximated by cumulative production volume). Though experience effects are potentially important, they are not obtained 'automatically'.

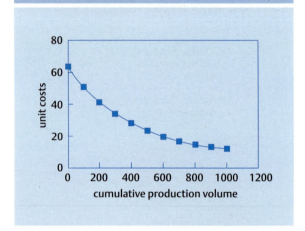

Figure 10.2 **Experience curve**

Why a shirt costing $100 in Alaska will cost $190 in Paris

An OECD study of international parcel delivery found that it costs $90 more to send a shirt from New York to Paris than from New York to Anchorage, Alaska. Given that the shipping distances are similar, this is surprising, but the price difference reflects costs of customs clearance and differences in import duties and national taxes.

A thorough effort may be needed to exploit the benefits of experience. This is especially true in an international setting, where experience effects are conditional upon an efficient transfer of skills and knowledge between strategic business units (SBUs) throughout the world (Phillips *et al.* 1994).

A full appreciation of costs requires attention not just to production activities, but also to the multitude of functions to be performed at various stages in the company and channel. Such additional functions may be transportation (see Insert), assistance in product use, and maintenance. Attention to these functions is particularly relevant in international marketing, where production cost typically represents only one part of the total cost. Keegan (1995: 514) refers to this as the problem of 'price escalation' in international marketing: product prices (costs) may substantially increase as transportation costs (including insurance, special packaging, and warehousing costs), duties, and distribution margins are added

Cost factors	Domestic market	Export market
1. Manufacturer's price	100	100
2. Transportation cost domestic market	10	
3. Shipment, insurance, packaging and warehousing costs for exported product		25
4. Import tariff (20% on landed cost, i.e. on 1 + 3)		25
5. Importer's margin (10% on cost, e.g. on 4)		15
6. Wholesaler's margin (20% on cost, i.e. on 5)		33
7. Retailer margin (33% on (1 + 2) or 6)	36	65
8. VAT (19% on 7)	28	50
Price to end-user	**174**	**313**

Table 10.1 **Example of price escalation in international markets**

to factory prices. Companies engaging in international activities will have to monitor those costs closely, and attempt to reduce them by offshore sourcing or by regular audits of the distribution structure. An illustration of international price escalation is given in Table 10.1. As the table suggests, retail prices abroad can easily amount to three times national ex-factory prices.

Last but not least, in trading off different pricing alternatives, the cost of implementing these alternative pricing schemes should come into play. As indicated below, the cost of administering and implementing a complex pricing programme may be prohibitive, and may induce managers to settle for less involved or more easily controllable pricing options.

As argued above, costs are related to price floors: they typically set a lower bound on prices. The contribution margin for a product equals its price minus its unit variable cost: if negative, selling the product at that price leads to a loss; if positive, at least part of the fixed cost can be recovered. While this principle seems utterly simple, the foregoing discussion illustrates that the determination and quantification of all relevant costs may be far from evident. The notion of costs as a 'price floor' is 'blurred' by product inter-

dependencies, cost dynamics, cost allocation over channel members and company subsidiaries, and the pursuit of multiple company objectives. Yet, knowledge of basic cost components remains a crucial input to the pricing decision, and companies should strive for a complete picture of various cost issues.

4 External influences on price

As well as factors internal to the firm, there are many factors external to the firm that must be taken into account when prices are set. It is useful to consider these in four groups—first the characteristics of the customers themselves and then three aspects of the environment within which the firm operates: the competitive, the channel, and the legal environments.

4.1 Customer characteristics

4.1.1 Price–volume relationship

A core issue in pricing is the impact of price on demand and sales volume. Following classical economic theory, the typical demand function is negatively sloped, indicating that the number of units sold is inversely related to price. The strength of the relationship between demanded volume and price—the customers' price sensitivity—is usually measured by the price elasticity. The price elasticity is the relative change in demand (sales) resulting from a relative change in the unit price of the product. A price elasticity of –2, for instance, indicates that a 1 per cent price increase would reduce the sales volume by 2 per cent of its current value. Price elasticities are generally negative, but their value and even their sign strongly depend on product and market characteristics. In a meta-analysis relating changes in a product's regular price to changes in demand (sales or market share), Tellis (1988: 337) found elasticities for a diversity of consumer products to range between approximately –10 and +2.5, with an average value of –1.76. Similar 'average' elasticity values have been reported in other meta-studies and reviews. While there is some consistency in these 'average' outcomes, empirically measured elasticities cover a wide range of values.

Several reasons can be brought forward for this diversity.

First, measured price sensitivities depend on how 'demand' is quantified: *market-share* changes in response to price are typically larger than *sales* changes. Price sensitivities also vary with the unit of analysis considered (e.g. item, brand, or category); lower levels of aggregation usually entail stronger price responsiveness.

Secondly, the 'nature' of the price change affects elasticity outcomes. Market reactions to a 'regular' price change may be different from response to temporary promotional price cuts. While evidence on the issue is conflicting, there are at least a number of studies reporting price promotion elasticities to be more negative (Blattberg and Neslin 1989). The impact of temporary price offers is further commented upon in Section 8.

Thirdly, as suggested in Section 3.1, the level of price elasticity depends on *distribution* and *communication*, but especially on *product characteristics*. Products or services with a unique brand value are said to be less sensitive to price changes (increases). An example would be the limited price sensitivity within the target segment for Ferrari cars, or Rolex watches. Situations where price comparisons are complex also imply less pronounced reactions to price changes. Examples are insurance packages, and pharmaceutical products that come in various forms and require different daily dosages and usage periods. Price elasticities are typically less negative (and occasionally even positive) in categories where price serves as a quality cue. This is, for instance, the case for beauty creams. Products that involve shared payment exhibit lower price sensitivity. Examples are tax-deductible gifts, or managers' participation in educational programmes partly paid for by the employer. Customers seem less reactive to price changes and willing to pay higher prices for products that they have invested in previously. Typical cases are maintenance products for expensive items, such as high-tech. machinery or leather couches. Similarly, products that are used 'in combination' with others entail less price sensitivity. An example is the choice of wine in a restaurant accompanying a meal: consumers tend to have a higher willingness to pay for wine in those circumstances, compared to in a bar, where only the drink is consumed. Factors that enhance responsiveness to prices are the product's importance in the total budget (for example, phone conversations versus paper clips), its storability (for example, bulky or perishable items), and the availability of substitute products (Nagle and Holden 1995).

Finally, price elasticity changes over the *product life cycle* (PLC). The traditional view is that price sensitivity increases as the product evolves over the life cycle, owing to more intense competition and better customer knowledge. Recent evidence (Simon 1989; Parker and Neelamegham 1997) suggests that in many categories price sensitivity first declines as the product moves from the introduction to the growth and maturity stage, and then increases in the decline phase of the PLC.

☞ 'Gross margins tend to decline in the *saturation* period stage, since prices begin to soften as competitors struggle to obtain market share in a saturated market.' (Chapter 14, p. 332)

So far, we have considered the aggregate (market-level) relationship between demand and price, and discussed general factors affecting the strength and the direction of the association. While these are relevant as a first step, managers determined to utilize pricing strategies to their full potential have to look beyond aggregate demand functions. A first reason is that the overall price–volume relationship reflects the reaction of a 'typical' or average consumer, but conceals considerable variation in individual responses. Secondly, the demand function is a 'black box' that measures how price is ultimately translated into sales, but forgoes all intermediate steps. More specifically, it yields little information on how price is perceived and processed. Recent research points to the importance of insights into individual customers' price reaction processes as a basis for strategic and tactical price decisions. Since these processes may be different for individual consumers and for industrial customers, we elaborate on them separately.

4.1.2 Individual consumers

The traditional microeconomic picture of a consumer who correctly registers all prices and price changes, and acts 'rationally' upon them so as to maximize his utility, has been falsified for quite some time. A myriad of studies on consumer price knowledge, perception, and evaluation uncover that consumers' reactions to price are much less stylized and homogeneous than suggested by traditional microeconomics. Understanding the implications of pricing, therefore, requires consideration not only of factual prices and their sales outcomes, but also of how these prices are perceived and evaluated.

Several studies reveal that, for frequently purchased consumer goods, consumers have low *awareness* of specific item prices. In 1990 Dickson and Sawyer investigated shoppers' price recall immediately after they had selected an item from the shelf. The researchers found that about 20 per cent of the shoppers had no idea of the price of the item just chosen, and only 55 per cent of the respondents provided an estimate within 5 per cent of the exact price. Price knowledge is low not only for regular, but also for promotional prices: about half of the shoppers in the study could not even tell whether the product just bought was on price promotion. Similar results were obtained by other researchers. Reasons for this limited price knowledge could be the complexity of price information, the time pressure, the limited price differences between items in supermarket categories, and the typically low involvement levels in those categories.

The issue of 'price recall' and of limited absolute price knowledge is also related to consumers' *price encoding*. Consumers may internally 'register' or encode prices in different ways. They may store absolute prices, or concentrate on relative prices—whether the product is cheaper or more expensive than other products in the category. Whether consumers encode absolute or relative price information is related to their processing goals. If the information is to be used immediately, and for choice rather than quantity decisions, relative price storage will do. Especially in such situations, managers should worry less about absolute prices, but find it crucial not to be more expensive than relevant competitors.

So far, we have concentrated on price perception of items or brands. Retailers may, in addition, be concerned with the price image of their store or chain as a whole. As price is deemed an important element in consumer store choice, and influences store traffic and performance, *store price image* is a hot topic on the retailer's agenda. Given that a typical supermarket carries about 20,000 stock-keeping units (SKUs) it is impossible for consumers to process complete price information. Instead, they form store price images on the basis of non-price cues such as the store's atmosphere and

design, and on the basis of price information for a subset of products (see e.g. Grewal and Baker 1994). Product categories likely to contribute to store price image are categories with large sales revenues, high visibility, and little product differentiation. Examples of such categories are milk and coke or, in the case of DIY stores, an electric drill.

But consumers do not limit their effort to price encoding. Especially for frequently purchased consumer goods, they also use simple decision rules and procedures for price *evaluation*. Most consumers have a range of acceptable prices, with an *upper* and a *lower price limit* (Lichtenstein *et al.* 1993). The upper limit, commonly referred to as the 'reservation price', corresponds to the maximum amount consumers are able or willing to spend on the product. This maximum level exists because price acts as a 'constraint'—if the price is too high, the consumer cannot afford the product within the confines of his budget, or prefers to spend his money on other products (opportunity cost). Above the upper limit, therefore, no purchase will be made. The lower limit of the consumers' price range originates from the role of price as a 'quality indicator' or an 'asset'. Below this limit, quality is considered suspect, or the product not acceptable because it may signal low social status. Studies on the association between price and perceived quality show that price may be used as a quality cue, depending on the availability of other cues. Consumer characteristics such as risk proneness, product interest, familiarity with the product, and demographics also affect whether price is used as a quality signal. The range of acceptable prices is a crucial starting point for consumer purchase decisions. Products with prices out of this range are discarded as alternatives for adoption. Knowledge of consumers' acceptable price ranges is, therefore, important for managers to assess their own price boundaries.

The range of acceptable prices acts as a preliminary 'device' to rule out a number of products. Next, prices for products within the range are compared with the consumer's 'reference price'. This reference price is a standard or benchmark for evaluation. Actual prices will be perceived more favourably when they are lower or equal to the reference price than when they exceed reference prices. Several empirical studies have demonstrated that the difference between reference and actual prices (the 'transaction utility' (Thaler 1985)) can play an important role in product evaluation. Products are more likely to be chosen by a consumer if the difference between their actual price and his reference price becomes more positive.

Reference prices can be external or internal. *External* reference prices are derived by the consumer from observed stimuli in the purchase environment, such as competitive prices or 'regular' price levels indicated in promotion advertisements. *Internal* reference prices are stored in consumer memory. They reflect the 'normal' or 'fair' price a consumer expects he will have to pay, based on historical prices or expectations (for example, expected seasonal price reductions). When internal reference prices are mainly formed on the basis of past prices, frequent price promotions may lead to a downward adjustment of the reference price, the promotional price becoming the benchmark for price evaluation instead of the (higher) 'regular' price (see e.g. Folkes and Wheat 1995). This has implications for the long-term impact of sales promotions, as will be clarified in Section 7. Whether internal or external reference prices are used in evaluation depends, among other factors, on the 'plausibility' or 'fairness' of externally provided reference prices (e.g. a regular price level used in comparative price advertisements).

Evidence suggests the existence of a region of indifference around the reference price: consumers are insensitive to price differences or do not react to price changes within a certain 'band' around the reference price. This phenomenon is referred to as 'latitude of price acceptance' (see e.g. Kalyanaram and Little 1994). Also, price changes must exceed certain thresholds—referred to as 'just noticeable differences' before they lead to adjustments in internal reference prices. Small price changes initiated by managers may, therefore, go unnoticed or generate little consumer response.

In brief, recent studies point to the importance of reference prices in consumer price evaluation, and provide evidence of the use of simplified decision procedures that are in line with observed limited price knowledge. For manufacturers and retailers, it is fundamental to find out how reference prices are formed and used in the categories they operate in. Based on such insights, they could attempt to 'alter' reference prices in their favour, and anticipate at what price levels their product will survive the consumers' benchmarking against his reference price. Some of these issues will be taken up again in the section on pricing strategies and tactics.

The psychological implications of price endings constitute an additional point of interest. 'Odd pricing', or the practice of ending prices in odd numbers (1,3,5,7,9) and of pricing just below a 0 (.49, .99, . . .), has become widespread in many categories. It is believed that 'odd' price endings may affect price perceptions beyond the monetary price value and may generate higher sales. Recent studies provided factual evidence of this phenomenon (see e.g. Stiving and Winer 1997). The price-ending effect may stem from an *underestimation mechanism*. Psychological factors explaining the underestimation of odd prices are the consumers' tendency to round prices down and to compare prices from left to right. Consumers are also bound to ignore rightmost digits as a result of limited information processing and memory capacity, again leading to underestimation. In addition, an *association mechanism* may be at work. Odd price endings may be perceived as promotional price levels, as they give the impression that original (round) prices have been lowered. This promotional connotation could be an incentive to buy the product. While odd prices may thus imply higher sales, they are not always recommendable. As pointed out by Levy and Weitz (1995), they are not appropriate for products that require thought (e.g. cars) and for products for which an upscale image is pursued. An additional psychological phenomenon affecting consumers' price evaluation relates to the *mental framing* of price offers (see Insert). Price differences between purchase options can be 'framed' as a gain (e.g. you get a 5 per cent discount on the regular furniture price of £1,000 if you arrange transportation yourself) or as a loss (transportation by the seller costs you an extra 5 per cent on the normal price of £950). Following a psychological reasoning called 'prospect

> **Price distortion by euro**
>
> The introduction of the EMU has presented some interesting pricing challenges. In those countries where the euro is worth more than one unit of their existing currencies (e.g. France, Portugal, and Spain) price differences between products have appeared to be compressed. There is some suggestion that one effect of this has been that consumers do not perceive own-label products to be so cheap in comparison with branded products.

theory' (see e.g. Thaler 1985), consumers judge a loss as more painful than they judge a gain of equal size pleasurable. In our example, the second offer would give people a stronger incentive to arrange for their own transportation. Depending on the purchase option they want to stimulate, managers should thus frame their offers in a different manner. A similar phenomenon is that of asymmetric reactions to upward or downward price changes. Price increases (losses) often evoke larger changes in demand than equally sized price reductions (gains). In planning their price structures, managers should anticipate and 'exploit' these differential reactions. Finally, framing affects the consumers' immediate reaction to price changes, but also whether reference prices will be adjusted. Managers should be sensitive to this issue in setting prices.

So far, we have concentrated on general aspects of consumer reactions to prices. An extensive range of studies documents that consumers are *heterogeneous* in their levels of price search, knowledge, and recall accuracy. Consumers also differ in the location of their acceptable price range: they have different upper and lower price limits, different reference price levels, and different latitudes of acceptance around the reference price. A wide range of factors may explain these differences. *Economic factors*, such as perceived price differences, budget restrictions, and income levels, are a first source of heterogeneity. *Search and transaction costs* stemming from time constraints, mobility restrictions, age, household composition, and location, also affect consumer price processing and evaluation. Thirdly, *human-capital* characteristics such as time-management skills and basic knowledge may come into play. Fourthly, the level of price processing depends on the *expected psychosocial returns* from price information collection and product adoption, which are often related to culture and peer group. Finally, *consumer traits* like variety-seeking versus loyalty cause consumers to react differently to prices. As will be argued in subsequent sections, recognition of consumer heterogeneity is crucial for effective pricing: managers should exploit these differences in the development of pricing strategies and tactics.

4.1.3 Industrial customers

The price sensitivity of industrial customers is much less researched and documented than that of individual consumers.

The general product-related determinants of price sensitivity mentioned in Section 4.1.1 also apply to industrial customers, but there may be differences in the relative impact of these determinants. Overall, industrial decision-making is believed to be more 'rational' and based on more complete information. Price would, for example, be less often used as a quality signal in industrial settings. Other factors such as the importance in the total cost of the end product and the importance in the functioning of the end product are deemed more important determinants of the price sensitivity of industrial buyers than of individual consumers. It is also believed that, in a number of industrial exchange settings, customers are not simply price-takers, but have some negotiation power and actively participate in the price-determination process. This is rarely the case in consumer marketing. Apart from these general tendencies, it should be recognized that, even more than consumer-price perception and processing, industrial buyers' reactions to prices are heterogeneous. The importance of price surely depends on the *sector* considered. Price has typically become less crucial in supplier–manufacturer relationships, where long-term partnership, relationship marketing, and single sourcing are now key elements. In contrast, price has become the more dominant issue in manufacturer–retailer interactions—a shift linked to the reallocation of power in classical distribution channels. *Within sectors*, the role of price in the purchasing process may differ, depending on the type of product, the repetitive nature of the purchase, and the parties involved (buying group versus individual professional purchaser). Even *within products and product types*, heterogeneous reactions to prices may prevail. Large-sized customers are, for example, often particularly sensitive to prices. As in consumer markets, the industrial marketer, must, therefore carefully analyse differences in price perception and evaluation in various customer segments, and consider the use of strategies capturing the opportunities set out by these differences.

In brief, insights into price reactions of customers are crucial to the assessment of price boundaries. While the budgetary implications of price for consumers put pressure on the company's maximum price level, price–quality associations and the importance of price as a quality signal contribute to a lower limit on company prices. As has become apparent from the previous discussion, both roles of price (as a constraint, or as an asset) are highly product, customer, and situation dependent; and consequently so will be the company's price boundaries and ultimately chosen price structures and levels.

4.2 Competitive environment

In determining prices, the competitive environment should explicitly be accounted for. The level of demand associated with a given company price strongly depends on prevailing competitive prices. Moreover, in a dynamic setting, not only must current prices of competitors be taken into account, but so should competitive reactions. Competitive retaliation may attenuate pricing effects. It could even provoke price wars where prices of all market players are systematically reduced, possibly to unprofitable levels. In the late 1990s increased competition in the airline market has systematically driven down air fares for all major market players. Careful analysis of competition is, therefore, a prerequisite for effective pricing. Competitors may react with an adaptation of price or other marketing instruments: price actions may stimulate a price response from some, and a non-price response from others (Guiltinan and Gundlach 1996). Both price and non-price reactions of current market players affect the feasibility of a company's own pricing policy, and should be monitored. In addition, the company's pricing activity may attract new competitors or drive current players out of the market; attention to potential and future competition is thus needed.

Competitive price reactions to price changes vary from passive (no reaction), through matching (following price changes), to retaliatory (cutting prices below competitive levels). Leeflang and Wittink (1996), for example, found empirical support for competitive 'overreaction' to promotional price changes, whereas other studies provided evidence of less pronounced competitive reactions (see e.g. Brodie *et al.* 1996). One reason for the divergent findings is that competitive behaviour depends on the nature of the competitive environment: the market structure, the level of market concentration, and the existence of competitive advantages.

Market structure is defined by the number of buyers, the number of sellers, and the degree of product differentiation. Less buyers, more sellers, and less product differentiation lead to higher price

sensitivity of consumers, and to a higher probability of competitive reactions to own prices and price changes. Apart from the overall market structure, the level of *concentration* (distribution of market shares across competitors) affects the likelihood and nature of competitive reactions. Competitors with larger shares and more vested interests in the market often react more strongly to price adjustments. Thirdly, the presence and nature of *competitive advantages* influence the extent to which a company can maintain prices below or above competitive levels, as well as the type and outcome of competitive reactions. Cost advantages occur when the product can be produced or distributed at a lower unit cost than competitive products thanks to superior skills, resources, experience effects, and economies of scale. Unique product value advantages are valid if the company product has tangible or intangible characteristics that differentiate it from those of competitors and are valued by customers. Competitors' pricing strategies are inspired by their strategic positioning. If their competitive advantage is based on product features, prices above competition can be justified; if it is based on cost only, maintaining a low price is essential. Also, competitors tend to respond to actions of other market players by using those marketing variables that are their 'best weapons' (Guiltinan and Gundlach 1996). Companies relying on product-based advantages typically show little price reaction and are less likely to engage in price wars. Companies whose competitive strength is based on cost are bound to react with a price change, may engage in price war, and are more likely to survive it. The sustainability of competitive advantages is a crucial issue, which severely impacts on prices and pricing strategies. At the end of the twentieth century, for instance, retailers had a hard time finding sustainable competitive advantages, which led to more intense price competition and smaller margins.

☞ 'In any case, as differentiation governs the price sensitivity of an offering, it is both a precondition and a source of whatever freedom the seller has in setting prices. The less differentiated the offering is, the less latitude the seller has to set prices.' (Chapter 15, p. 363)

From the foregoing discussion, it becomes clear that anticipating competitive reactions to own prices is crucial for assessing price boundaries and, ultimately, price determination. The threat of competitive reactions and price wars will put upward pressure on lower price boundaries. At the same time, the risk of losing share to competitors, and of attracting new players to the market, pushes prices downward. While crucial for sound decision-making, predicting competitive reactions is utterly difficult. As Guiltinan and Gundlach (1996: 87) put it: 'Competitive conjecturing is (understandably) mediocre or erroneous in many settings.' Anticipation of competitive moves is often based on public statements, signals, rough estimates, and previous reactions. In an international setting, predicting competitive reactions is even more difficult, especially for companies with a multi-domestic strategy (Phillips *et al.* 1994).

4.3 Channel environment

Most companies operate within a marketing channel: they obtain products, components, and/or materials from suppliers; and many pass their products onto intermediaries before they reach the end-users. The characteristics of the channel, and the (associated) reactions of channel members, strongly affect the nature of the pricing problem as well as the effectiveness of alternative pricing strategies, structures, and instruments.

Marketing channels may exhibit different structures. The *channel structure* relates to the flow of products from the manufacturer to the end-user: it depends on the number of levels in the channel, and on the number of players at each level. Channels vary from short (e.g. two levels only: the manufacturer sells directly to the end-user) to very long, and they may have different lengths even within industries. For fast-moving consumer goods (FMCGs), typical channels consist of three levels: manufacturer, retailer, and end-user. In international marketing, it is not uncommon to have as many as five levels. The *nature of competition* at given channel levels also varies: from no competition (only one member, or exclusive distribution) to many competing middlemen. Channels can be further characterized by their level of vertical *integration*, which can range from complete integration (wholly owned subsidiaries), through franchising, to the presence of independent middlemen. Finally, channels differ in the *allocation of leadership* across levels, where the power may rest primarily with manufacturers, retailers, or even end-users.

The impact of channel characteristics on company price decisions has become a topic of great concern. Depending on the channel structure, the level of vertical integration, and the allocation of power, a company may have to set prices for different channel levels simultaneously. An example of such 'multi-tiered' pricing is a manufacturer deciding on the price he will charge to the retailer, and at the same time formulating a 'suggested' retail price for end-consumers. Channel characteristics also determine which price structures and instruments are appropriate, as further illustrated in Sections 6, 7, and 8. The location of power within the channel determines who initiates price changes, as well as who reacts. In a leader–follower framework, one channel member (for example, manufacturer or retailer) decides on price adjustments, and channel members at other levels follow. Alternatively, price decisions at different channel levels may be set in coordination. Just as in the case of competitive interactions, channel members from a different level may react to price changes with changes in other marketing-mix instruments under their control. For instance, retailers may adapt their service level as a function of the margins granted to them by manufacturers. Finally, price actions at one level have an influence on the number of players and intensity of competition at other levels. This often confronts managers facing price decisions with the trade-off between availability and power of middlemen.

While channel interdependencies bear some resemblance to competitive interactions, their impact on pricing is more involved and outspoken. Channel participants at different levels experience rivalry (allocation of profit within the channel), but also perform complementary functions, possess complementary information, and have more shared interests (allocation of profit to the channel) than is true for competitors at the same level. Also, even when the degree of vertical integration is low and channel members are formally independent, parties at different channel levels are likely to engage in negotiations or look for some form of contractual arrangements. This is rarely true for competitors, where such agreements are forbidden by law (see also Section 4.4).

The mid-1990s witnessed an increased attention to the channel implications of pricing strategies. It is now recognized that effective pricing requires consideration of channel interactions and dynamics. Academics as well as practitioners attempt to integrate channel considerations into decisions on pricing strategies, structures, and tactics. Yet, the issue is highly complex, and, although the basic issue has been identified, the analysis of the problem is incomplete. We will come back to some of these principles in the sections below.

4.4 Legal environment

In setting prices, managers must be aware of legal constraints that restrict their decision freedom. In most countries, governments have installed price regulations, the objective of which is to defend consumers and/or preserve competition. In an international setting, additional constraints have been formulated to limit tax evasion or keep cash, employment, and economic activity within country boundaries.

4.4.1 Consumer pricing regulations

In the area of consumer pricing, regulations deal with deceptive pricing, and with direct price controls restricting the range of legally accepted price levels.

Governments can influence final consumer prices indirectly by means of VAT rates. They can also control prices directly by imposing price ceilings or price floors for specific product categories. In many European countries, for example, maximum price levels are valid for basic products such as bread and milk. In addition, 'minimum price laws' may enforce legal price floors upon retailers to discourage 'loss leader pricing', the practice of pricing selected products below cost to increase store traffic or drive small retailers out of the market. Besides imposing restrictions on absolute price levels, governments can limit the freedom of companies to change prices. Examples of such measures are (temporal) price freezes aimed at slowing down inflation; or regulations on sale periods, limiting the period of time during which merchandise can be offered on sale.

In many countries, additional regulations are in effect to provide buyers with correct information about prevailing price levels. Regulations like unit pricing laws, for example, compel retailers to indicate price levels clearly on product units or by means of shop-window lists. Service firms such as restaurants and hairdressers, for instance, are obliged to display prices outside the store using such price lists. In addition, regulations on deceptive pricing aim to protect consumers against misleading price information that can materially

affect their buying decisions. Retailers pursuing a high–low pricing strategy (see Section 6.4) often use comparative advertising to announce price promotions, in which the reduced price is compared to a high regular price. In the USA, the FTC Act, and other guides against deceptive prices, stipulate that such practices are illegal when the indicated reference price is not the 'fair' or 'bona fide' price, a bona fide price being defined as 'the price at which the article was offered to the public on a regular basis for a reasonably substantial period of time' (Kaufman et al. 1994). To US courts, the advertised regular price is a bona fide price when a minimum percentage of total volume has been sold at this 'regular' price, or when the article has been sold at this 'regular' price, or when the article has been offered at this price level during a minimum percentage of the total time it was available.

4.4.2 Restrictions on competitive pricing and channel pricing

Manufacturers' pricing decisions are further restricted by government regulations that aim to preserve competition and avoid monopolies and collusion among firms. In assessing the implications of these regulations for pricing decisions, marketing managers should take into account not only government legislation (legislated law), but also the interpretation of this law by major courts (Nagle and Holden 1995). For many of the regulations discussed below, for example, pricing practices that can be demonstrated to be beneficial to consumers or not to harm competition constitute exceptions that are legally accepted by most courts.

Horizontal price fixing consists of agreements among competitors to fix prices at a certain level. As these agreements may reduce competition and raise consumer prices, they are prohibited by the Sherman Act in the USA and by Article 85 of the Treaty of Rome in the EU. Price agreements between manufacturers and their distributors are also illegal when they enable manufacturers to enforce minimum resale prices (vertical price fixing or resale price maintenance). Manufacturers are, however, allowed to announce recommended resale prices, and to refuse to deal with distributors selling below suggested prices (Nagle and Holden 1995).

Price discrimination refers to the practice of charging different prices for the same product to different customers or segments. It is prohibited by law when it is intended to, or has the effect of, reducing competition. In the USA, price discrimination is regulated by the Robinson–Patman Act. In the EU, similar stipulations are valid (Treaty of Rome, Article 85). US courts generally accept two exceptions to the rule that equal prices should be charged: price differences are accepted if they reflect differences in manufacturing or distribution costs, or if they are needed to adjust to (low prices of) local competitions (Nagle and Holden 1995). In the EU, price discrimination among member states is generally considered to be illegal, except when price differences are a reflection of cost differences.

In the case of *predatory pricing*, price is set at a low, unprofitable level to drive out competition, a practice that is prohibited by the Sherman and Robinson–Patman Act in the USA. Where predatory-pricing cases were previously judged by comparing (marginal or average) costs to prices, courts now increasingly apply a 'rule-of-reason' approach, and concentrate on the expected consequences and feasibility of alleged price predation. Whether pricing is deemed predatory and therefore illegal is assessed by examining whether effective entry barriers could be created and the company would be able to recover lost profits by raising prices after competition has been reduced or eliminated (Nagle and Holden 1995).

Tie-in or sales requirements contracts, finally, oblige buyers of a given product to purchase other products exclusively from the seller. Such (re-)purchase requirements are considered illegal when they have the effect of or are intended to reduce competition. This is true in the USA as well as in the EU.

4.4.3 International setting

In international markets, government regulations can affect prices indirectly through import duties and other import barriers that increase costs. Except when additional import costs are not passed on to consumers but carried by the importing or exporting firm, import duties will result in price differences between domestic and export markets, and possibly among export markets.

Import duties have an impact on the transfer prices a company charges to its foreign subsidiaries: import duties expressed as a percentage of unit value (price) drive transfer prices down. Admissible *transfer-price* levels are further restricted

by government regulations aimed at preventing tax evasion. By charging high transfer prices to subsidiaries located in countries with high tax rates, taxation bills in these countries could be artificially reduced.

Similar to predatory pricing laws, *anti-dumping* regulations prohibit companies from charging unfairly low prices in export markets with the intent of injuring domestic competitors. Whether the exporter's price is 'unfair' is commonly assessed by comparing the dumping price with the exporter's domestic price level or the exporter's production costs.

5 Pricing objectives

ENVIRONMENTAL analysis generates fundamental inputs to pricing objectives. Indeed, pricing objectives should, in line with overall company objectives, strengths, and weaknesses, exploit the possibilities of the marketplace. Pricing objectives can be classified in a number of ways. A typical, and fairly general, classification distinguishes between objectives that are profit oriented, volume oriented, cost oriented, and competition oriented. Examples of each type are displayed in Box 10.1. As these examples demonstrate, pricing objectives may coincide with overall company objectives (e.g. profit maximization), or be directly related to pricing decisions (e.g. price leadership). While profit maximization is the most often-cited company objective, it is seldom the exclusive goal of the company. Most companies do not pursue one single objective, but a series of them, with priorities placed on various sub-objectives, or one criterion to be optimized subject to a 'minimum' performance on other dimensions. In such cases, sub-objectives must be mutually consistent.

Specifying overall pricing objectives is essential. They have a major impact on the location of price boundaries. They also affect whether the company should pick prices near the lower or upper bound of its acceptable price range. Clearly, volume-oriented objectives suggest low prices, while profit orientation requires a trade-off between volume and unit profitability, and therefore requires intermediate prices. Competitive considerations like entry deterrence, or cost objectives such as pursuit of economies of scale and experience effects, push the company towards the low end of

Box 10.1 **Pricing objectives**

Profit oriented	Volume oriented	Cost oriented	Competition oriented
Maximize profit	Sales growth or maintenance	Pursue economies of scale	Price leadership
Reach target return on investment	Market share growth or maintenance	Exploit experience effects	Entry deterrence
Maximize market skimming	Market penetration	Recover investment costs	Market stabilization
	Increase usage, participation, or store traffic		Meet competition

the price range. Overall objectives thus provide general guidance for price decisions.

Yet, effective pricing requires companies to go beyond the overall pricing objectives just mentioned, and to specify what Nagle and Holden (1995) refer to as pricing *goals*. These goals are more concrete, have specific deadlines, refer to specific 'objects' or units, and usually apply to specific activities. The period in which one wants to obtain results crucially affects price decisions: different strategies may be needed to maximize short-term profit (for example, through liquidation of excess inventories) versus long-term profit (for example, through maximizing customer lifetime value). As far as the 'object' or unit of analysis is concerned, several options could be contrasted. Within the confines of the company, results could be pursued for products versus product lines, or actions could be taken that benefit the company versus the decision-maker's own career. From a channel perspective, decisions could stimulate profit for the channel as a whole, or concentrate on one level. Not-for-profit companies could attempt to increase consumer versus total surplus. In international settings, local or global profits could be strived for.

Having specified overall pricing objectives and pricing goals, the next question is how to generate the desired outcomes, and what key issues to address. Interesting insights can be obtained from a classification provided by Tellis (1986). Tellis distinguishes three types of what we refer to as 'derived' objectives. A first would be to exploit consumer heterogeneity and the presence of market segments. Secondly, the company can use its competitive position as a basic 'asset' for pricing. Thirdly, opportunities offered by product-line pricing could be exploited. These derived objectives already suggest means or courses of action to achieve overall pricing objectives and goals. Together with key environmental characteristics, they form a 'bridge' to a taxonomy of pricing strategies, our point of interest in the next section.

6 Pricing strategies

A wide range of pricing strategies have been put forward by academics and practitioners, and different labels have been used to denote them. The appropriateness of a strategy is linked to environmental characteristics—especially those of the target market (Tellis 1986; Nagle and Holden 1995)—and to company objectives. As outlined above, a revealing taxonomy of objectives has been put forward by Tellis, who distinguishes between segment-, competition-, and product-line-based objectives. Coupled with characteristics of the target market, these derived objectives give rise to a matrix with nine generic approaches to strategic pricing (see Fig. 10.3). In Sections 6.1, 6.2, and 6.3 we explain Tellis's classification of pricing strategies, and supplement it with subsequent findings from the marketing literature and practice. Section 6.4 puts the taxonomy into a wider perspective, and comments on the meaning and use of the generic strategies in specific settings.

Figure 10.3 **Taxonomy of pricing strategies**

		OBJECTIVE OF FIRM		
		Vary prices among consumer segments	Exploit competitive position	Balance pricing over product line
CHARACTERISTICS OF CONSUMERS	Some have high search costs	Random discounting	Price signalling	Image pricing
	Some have low reservation price	Periodic discounting	Penetration pricing Experience curve pricing	Price bundling Premium pricing
	All have special transaction costs	Second-market discounting	Geographic pricing	Complementary pricing

Source: Tellis (1986: 148).

6.1 Segmented or differential pricing strategies

Segmented or differential pricing strategies aim to exploit heterogeneity among consumer segments.

In *random discounting*, the company sets the regular price at a high level, but offers temporary price cuts at random points in time. It thus exploits consumer heterogeneity in price knowledge and search costs: knowledgeable consumers search for bargains and buy the product at the low price, while others usually pay the regular price. If some consumers are uninformed and willing to pay more, the random-discounting strategy allows the company to preserve a broad customer base at the same time as charging less knowledgeable and price-sensitive consumers a high price.

Periodic discounting implies that prices systematically change over time to exploit consumers' willingness to pay different prices at different times. A typical example is peak-load pricing, where lower prices are charged in off-season periods. In price skimming, a new product is highly priced in the introduction phase, and gradually becomes cheaper over time. End-of-season sales can also be placed under the heading of periodic discounting.

While, in the previous strategies, differences in prices paid by consumers result from self-selection, *second-market discounting* is a more direct form of price discrimination. This strategy explicitly stipulates that different prices be charged to different consumer segments. Segments could be defined in geographic terms, or based on consumer characteristics other than location. A typical example is dumping, where the same product is offered at a high price in one market (often the country of origin), and at a lower price in other (more price-sensitive) markets. Price discrimination based on consumer identity or membership (e.g. lower rates), and trade discounts offered by manufacturers to distributors performing specific functions, are also illustrations of second-market discounting. Price quantity discounts, aiming to attract heavy users with higher price sensitivity and lower holding costs, can also be seen as a form of second-market discounting. In each of these examples, transaction costs or other barriers prevent consumers from shopping in a cheaper segment.

6.2 Strategies exploiting competitive position

While the foregoing strategies imply that different prices be charged for the same product to different segments, this is not true for the strategies described in this section, the logic behind which is to take advantage of the firm's competitive position in the market.

In *price signalling*, a low-quality product is offered at a high price and targeted at non-knowledgeable consumers. These infer quality from price, possibly because of the positive price–quality relationship of competitive offerings. Following Tellis, a prerequisite for this strategy is that some competitors are 'honest' in the sense that they offer high/low quality at high/low prices, and that some segments of consumers have high search costs. Parker (1995) refers to the products for which price signalling is used as 'sweet lemons'. He posits that sweet lemons can prevail even if there is no link between objective price and quality for any firm—for example, if none of the suppliers is 'honest'. This is true in markets with extreme information asymmetry between the supplier (manufacturer or retailer) and all customers, and where prices are driven up by advertising claims concentrating on certain (irrelevant) quality aspects. Medical care and legal services are examples of such markets. Along the same lines, Alpert *et al.* (1993) stipulate that price signalling is more effective (1) when consumers are able to get information on price more easily than information about quality, (2) when buyers want the high quality enough to risk buying the high-priced product even without certainty of high quality, and (3) when there are a large number of uninformed consumers. The market of skin moisturizers is an illustration of a market satisfying those conditions. Hence, though high-priced moisturizers often show little superiority, they succeed in securing a substantial portion of the market (see Alpert *et al.* 1993).

In *penetration pricing* and *experience curve pricing*, new products are introduced at low prices. The objective is to exploit pioneer advantages: low prices attract and capture the price-sensitive consumer segment, or build up economies of experience before competitive entry occurs. The low prices are thus justified by the presence of a number of price-sensitive customers in the market.

This is also the basis for a recently uncovered strategy that we refer to as 'advertised discounting.' In advertised discounting, the company offers infrequent, irregular promotions on high-quality items, and announces them through advertisements. The strategy may be appropriate when consumers have different reservation prices and price/quality trade-offs. In such markets, high-quality brands enjoy asymmetric promotion effects: they are able to attract more switchers from low-quality brands through promotions than vice

versa. Advertised discounting is thus a competitive strategy: it is used by quality brands against lower-level brands or private labels, to take advantage of their superior competitive position and the resulting asymmetric promotion effects (see also Section 4.1.2 and Section 8). In advertised discounting, price cuts should be sufficiently infrequent and irregular for the long-term equity of the promoted brand not to be harmed.

Geographic pricing, or 'spatial pricing', is a pricing strategy adopted by firms serving different geographic markets, where transportation cost is an important component of transaction cost. Prices to be charged in various regions depend on competitive conditions in those regions and on consumer valuation of transaction costs and prices in various markets. Possible strategies are f.o.b. (customer pays for transportation), uniform delivered (company delivers product in all markets at the same ultimate price and thus incurs transportation cost), or an in-between strategy (zone pricing).

6.3 Product-line pricing strategies

Product-line pricing strategies can be used by multi-product firms, and involve balancing prices over different products in the assortment.

Firms that apply *image pricing* sell an identical product, often under a different name, at a low price (to knowledgeable consumers) and at a high price (to consumers considering price as a quality or 'status' cue). Categories where image pricing is often used are wines and cosmetics.

In *price bundling*, two or more products in a line that constitute 'imperfect substitutes' or complements are sold together at a special price. A bundling strategy can be 'pure', 'mixed', or 'amplified mixed'. In pure bundling, all products have to be purchased together. In a mixed bundling regime, the customer may purchase the whole bundle at a special price, but can still obtain individual products separately at their 'normal' price. In the case of amplified mixed bundling, there is an additional option of buying a subset of the bundle products together at a special rate. Price bundling may be profitable if consumers differ in their willingness to pay for the separate components of the bundle. Venkatesh and Mahajan (1993) point out that customers' reactions to a bundle depend not only on their reservation prices for the separate items, but also on their probable consumption rates of the tied good. An example would be the reaction to season tickets for theatres, where the attractiveness of the season ticket depends on the likelihood of having time to attend several performances. From this perspective, mixed bundling—with higher prices for bundle and for individual items than under pure strategies—may effectively discriminate among frequent and occasional users. The bundle will attract those who expect to have high-use rates, and whose mean reservation prices are higher than the mean prices of the separate items. In a sense, price-quantity discounts, where larger package sizes (bundles) are offered at lower unit prices so that customers are persuaded to purchase and consume more, can be seen as an example of this strategy.

The adoption of *premium pricing* implies that high-quality products in a line are sold at a very high price. This high price level compensates for the loss incurred on low-quality products that are priced below cost. The appropriateness of this strategy depends on the presence of economies of scope, and on differences in consumer reservation prices. Some hotels, for instance, adopt premium pricing: the rate they charge for 'luxury' rooms and suites by far exceeds the regular room rate. A second example is the automobile industry, where high prices for large cars have to compensate for low margins on small cars.

In *complementary pricing*, some products in the line are sold at a low price, but a 'premium' is charged on complementary products in the line that are hopefully bought on subsequent occasions. This strategy is based upon the 'complementary' or 'captive' nature of the market. Having bought the first product, consumers incur transaction costs to switch to other (competitive) product lines. The presence of these transaction costs allows the company to charge more for the second (complementary) product. An example would be a manufacturer charging a low price for computer games' hardware, and high prices for accompanying software. A variant of complementary pricing is 'loss leadership' by retailers (see Section 4.4.1).

6.4 Discussion

The taxonomy developed by Tellis offers a simple integrative scheme for positioning and understanding a wide range of pricing strategies. Yet, being a stylized scheme, Tellis's framework necessarily has some limitations for managers interested in developing concrete pricing strategies.

First, the framework allows only an indirect treatment of price dynamics and multi-tiered price decisions (channel pricing).

Dynamic pricing strategies can, for example, be followed to exploit reference price effects (see e.g. Greenleaf 1995), to obtain insight into consumers' price reactions, or in anticipation of future product improvements in highly innovative markets (see e.g. Padmanabhan and Bass 1993).

Multi-tiered price decisions or *channel pricing* are a particularly complex issue that presents problems and opportunities not accounted for in Tellis's framework. Pricing affects how much profit the channel obtains as a whole, as well as how this profit is allocated within the channel. In independent channels, there often exist conflicts of interest or 'sources of channel miscoordination'. Information asymmetries, for instance, can jeopardize coordination: manufacturer research may characterize the product as a certain winner, but the retailer does not blindly accept this and refuses to carry the product. Another example of channel miscoordination is the problem of 'double marginalization'. When a retailer with some monopoly power sets a high price to maximize his own profit, and the manufacturer also seeks high profit, the margin for the entire channel can become excessive. As a result, consumers that would be profitable clients for the integrated channel may be excluded. Other factors causing channel conflicts are summarized in Gerstner and Hess (1995). In situations where such conflicts are important, improving channel coordination may constitute an alternative or additional pricing objective. Specific pricing strategies may be required to overcome or attenuate these conflicts, and lead to a fair allocation of profit within the channel. For instance, 'targeted pull' strategies, where the manufacturer offers a discount directly to price-sensitive consumers who then ask the retailer for the product, are a way to overcome double marginalization (Gerstner and Hess 1995). Profit-sharing arrangements constitute another example of a conflict-resolving strategy. Additional illustrations of how channel interdependencies affect pricing are discussed in Section 8.

☞ 'Bekaert motivates its dealers not only by providing an excellent assortment, but also by granting substantial margins, by maintaining stocks instead of its dealers, and by delivering within twenty-four hours of an order being placed.' **(Chapter 9, p. 196)**

Another limitation of Tellis's taxonomy is that it presents only generic pricing strategies. These strategies may take different forms depending on the situation; managers should translate the generic principles into a form tailored to their specific situation. More importantly, most real life situations allow for the use of a combination of strategies. For example, two basic approaches to pricing by retailers are every day low pricing (EDLP) versus high–low pricing (Hi-Lo).

An EDLP approach resembles a uniform pricing strategy, where the retailer charges permanently low prices. Following Levy and Weitz (1995), this strategy emphasizes the continuity of prices at a level somewhere between a 'regular non-sale price' and deep discount sale price. It is for this reason also referred to as 'every day stable prices'. The Hi-Lo strategy, in contrast, is characterized by higher regular prices, but which are accompanied by frequent temporary price cuts on selected items. Retailers adopting a Hi-Lo approach (sometimes referred to as promo-stores) often buy their merchandise on deal. According to Lal and Rao (1997), EDLP and Hi-Lo are not merely pricing, but overall positioning strategies. EDLP stores try to secure a sufficiently large customer base through low prices. Promo stores, in turn, offer higher service and larger assortments permanently to attract service-sensitive consumers (with higher time constraint) for all their products. They use the promotions to appeal to cherry-pickers for the promoted items, eventually even convincing them to buy non-promoted merchandise from the store. The Hi-Lo strategy therefore combines principles of *random discounting* (selling promoted items to price sensitive consumers through irregular promotions) and of *complementary pricing* (convincing consumers to buy other items at regular prices once they are in the store).

Various authors have discussed the advantages and disadvantages of EDLP versus Hi-Lo approaches (see e.g. Levy and Weitz 1995). While EDLP leads to reduced price and advertising wars and stockouts as well as to improved inventory management, profit margins, and customer service, Hi-Lo allows for more emphasis on quality and service, creates excitement, and helps move merchandise.

7 Price determination

THE pricing strategy outlines the company's basic approach to pricing. The next step is to develop a *price structure*, which specifies how the characteristics of the product will be priced, and lays the foundation for how price levels will be set (Stern 1986). More specifically, the price structure determines: (1) for which aspects of the product or service prices have to be set, (2) how prices will vary over customer segments or products in the line and (3) the timing and conditions of payment. In this section we start out discussing price structures accompanying the generic pricing strategies described above. Next, we have a look at some price structures used in specific settings.

7.1 Price structure

A company adopting a random-discounting strategy faces decisions on the depth, frequency, and timing of the discounts: how large should the price cut be, how many discounts should be offered per period, and when exactly should promotions occur? Other decisions relate to the choice of promotion instrument (e.g. straight price cut or a rebate), and the way it will be communicated (e.g. using in-store displays or feature advertising). For a multi-product company, the selection of the item(s) to be put on promotion is also primordial.

While the strategic rationale for random discounting is clear-cut, deciding upon the accompanying price structure remains a difficult issue. Each of the aforementioned price-structure decisions has a major effect on company outcomes. A more detailed discussion on the impact of various discount structures is given in Section 8.

In strategies such as penetration pricing, experience curve pricing, and seasonal discounting, an optimal price trajectory needs to be specified.

For penetration and experience curve pricing, the company must decide on the initial price level as well as on the pattern of price adaptations over time. Crucial ingredients in these decisions are the reservation prices for various customers, and the magnitude of loyalty or experience effects. Lowering the initial price implies that the company loses money initially on customers willing to pay more, but this may be made up for by a larger 'loyal' customer base or stronger cost position by the time competitors enter the market.

Seasonal discounting requires, besides specification of the regular price, a decision on when discounts will be offered, and how deep they will be. Contrary to promotions offered in a random-discounting strategy, seasonal discounts occur at regular intervals.

Second-market discounting implies decisions on the definition of the markets where different prices will be charged, and on the depth of the discount offered to the 'second market(s)'. A crucial consideration in delineating markets is the presence of market barriers, such as tariffs, (high) transportation costs, and legal restrictions (see Phillips *et al.* 1994). Low barriers between markets coupled with substantial price differences lead to the advent of 'grey markets'. Grey markets, or 'parallel imports', appear when third parties buy products at the low price in the second market, and resell them at a price below the company's price in the first market. In some sectors, like the pharmaceutical market, grey markets constitute an important problem that is hard to control for or defend against. Another difficulty with second-market discounting is the threat of legal problems related to the price-discrimination aspect of this strategy. Companies should make sure they are able to 'justify' the price advantage offered to specific segments based on cost or competitive conditions.

In geographic pricing, a pricing plan must be specified that links the customers' location to specific price levels. The pricing plan affects the 'market served'—that is, the area from which customers are actually attracted. It also determines the 'amount of surplus' the company retrieves from customers, the idea being to charge customers in different locations a price as close as possible to their reservation price. Extreme cases such as FOB and uniform pricing (see Section 6.2) necessitate only a single price level. In-between strategies like zone pricing require that various prices be associated with pre-specified geographic areas. Companies may also adopt 'menu plans', in which (some) consumers can choose from different options. Menu plans are often a combination of FOB and uniform-delivered prices: consumers within a designated area are offered a uniform-delivered price but get a discount if they transport themselves. Outside the zone, only FOB is possible. In a menu plan, the choice of the geographic area affects both the market served and the market share and margins within that served area (Basu and Mazumdar 1995).

Price bundling requires deciding on the basic bundling approach to be adopted (pure versus mixed bundling), and on the items to be included in the bundle. In addition, prices must be set for individual items (in case of mixed bundling) and for the bundle. As indicated earlier, pricing items and bundles requires insights into different customers' willingness to pay for each product separately, as well as on their probable consumption rate.

In complementary pricing, a company has to select the products involved, and decide upon specific price levels to be charged for the different items. A crucial input here is the degree of complementarity of the products, which is in turn linked to the nature and magnitude of the transaction costs.

Specific settings may require very particular and even more complex price structures because of channel interdependencies (see Section 8.3), the link between price and other contractual arrangements in industrial markets, and specifics of international pricing. For example, two major international pricing strategies adopted by export companies are a standard-price and a price-adaptation strategy. In a standard or global pricing strategy, the same base price is charged in each market. Companies following a price-adaptation or market-differentiated strategy set export prices in accordance with local market conditions, often in a decentralized way (i.e. local managers are allowed to set or adjust prices). In comparison with a global pricing strategy, market-differentiated pricing allows the exploitation of international differences in price sensitivity and the competitive position of the export firm. At the same time, it entails a risk of parallel imports from low to higher price markets (development of 'grey markets'), and is far more difficult to administer. A completely differentiated pricing strategy will, therefore, often not be feasible or profitable. International companies may in that case opt for a 'mixed strategy', allowing for limited adjustments to the base price in view of differences in costs or competitive position. Examples of such strategies are 'dual pricing', where a different price is charged in the home and in the export markets to account for additional export costs, and 'standard formula pricing', where a similar cost-based formula is used to calculate prices to be charged in each of the export markets. International differences in competitive position can be taken into account by setting 'price lines' or 'price patterns' that specify export price levels in relation to the prices charged by local competitors' (see e.g. Dahringer and Mülbacher 1991). Major factors affecting the choice and appropriateness of an international pricing strategy are the degree of variation in price sensitivity, competitive position and/or costs across export markets. Other factors that may influence the choice between a global, differentiated, or 'mixed' pricing strategy are product characteristics (e.g. commodities versus intangibles), government regulations, the length of and degree of control over distribution channels, and the knowledge and experience of the exporting firm (Dahringer and Mühlbacher 1991; Toyne and Walters 1993). In addition, as for retailer pricing strategies, the choice between a global and a differentiated approach is usually not restricted to pricing decisions, but rather represents an overall company strategy that affects pricing as well as other marketing decisions (for example, advertising).

7.2 Determining price levels

Whatever the pricing strategy and structure a company adopts, it ultimately has to arrive at *price levels* for specific items, target markets, and periods. Such prices may be unilaterally specified by the company ('fixed price levels'), or may result from interactions between buyers and sellers. In this section we discuss methods for assessing fixed price levels, the basic principles of price negotiations, competitive bidding, and then leasing.

7.2.1 Fixed levels

To determine price levels, companies often make use of simple decision procedures that focus on one dimension of the pricing problem. We first discuss these simplified methods, and then touch on complex optimization, simulation methods, and price adjustments.

Simplified decision methods Among the simplified decision procedures, cost-based methods are the most widely used approaches to pricing.

Cost-based methods have a common denominator: they start out from information on unit costs for the product, and take this as a 'floor' above which a pre-specified remuneration is charged by the company. In *mark-up pricing*, the company sets a price per unit equal to the cost per unit plus a pre-specified 'mark-up'. Mark-ups are often specified as a percentage of unit cost, and vary widely between sectors and product categories. An alterna-

tive cost-based method is *target return pricing*. Here, the company starts out from a desired return on investment (ROI), and then calculates the premium to be charged over unit cost to realize this ROI. In *break-even pricing*, finally, the company computes the minimum price needed to cover fixed and variable costs (and, eventually, a pre-specified ROI) in view of the forecast demand level. Box 10.2 illustrates the different cost-based pricing principles with a simple example. Cost-plus pricing is used in a wide range of consumer and industrial settings, and is adopted by almost all retailers.

Competition-oriented rules of thumb concentrate on competitive price levels to determine the company's own price. The most simple procedure is that of 'going rate pricing', where the company simply aligns its own prices with those prevailing in the marketplace. A similar procedure is followed by some international companies, which try to maintain a 'global' competitive position by setting prices relative to competitors' price levels in each export market.

Demand-oriented methods take the customers' willingness to pay as the basis for pricing. A popular approach, especially in industrial settings, is *perceived-value* pricing. The basic idea is to set price in such a way that the ratio of perceived value to price for the company's product equals that of competitors. Perceived value can be calculated as a weighted average of the products' perceived attribute scores.

While the simplified pricing methods are extremely popular, they suffer from basic defects. Cost-plus pricing rules forgo the link between price and demand: they start out from estimated volume (and associated unit cost) to set price, but ignore the crucial impact that this price will have on ultimately realized volume. Competition-oriented approaches ignore differences in cost and demand between the company and its competitors. These methods rely upon the 'collective wisdom of the market', and their outcomes depend on the selection of competitors whose prices will be mirrored. Perceived-value pricing resolves some of these problems by allowing differences in perceived value to affect prices, yet it does so in a simplified manner. Multi-product and channel considerations, as well as market heterogeneity and dynamics, are ignored in each of the 'simplified' approaches discussed in this section.

Each of these procedures concentrates on one major environmental factor (cost, demand, competition), and basically ignores the others. As a

Box 10.2 **Illustration of cost-based pricing rules**

A manufacturer of toothbrushes considers the following costs and demand level:

Production costs	Bfr. 1,000,000	fixed costs per month
	Bfr. 20	variable costs per unit
Expected demand	20,000 units	per month

(1) To earn a mark-up (MU) of 20% on price, the following unit price should be charged:

Mark-up price $= AC/(1-MU)$

$$= Bfr. \frac{70}{1-0.20} = Bfr. \ 87.5 \text{ per unit}$$

Average cost, $AC = Bfr. \ 20 + Bfr. \frac{1,000,000}{20,000} = Bfr. \ 70 \text{ per unit}$

In this example, mark-up (MU) is specified as a percentage of the selling price. Alternatively, MU can be defined as the margin by which price exceeds average costs (mark-up price = average cost × (1 + MU)).

(2) A target return of 8% on investments (INV = Bfr. 2,000,000) per month results in the following price level:

Target return price $= AC + \frac{INV \times ROI}{Sales}$

$$= Bfr. \ 70 + \frac{Bfr. \ 2,000,000 \times 0.08}{20,000 \text{ units}} = Bfr. \ 78 \text{ per unit}$$

(3) The break-even price level at which total returns cover total costs, finally, equals:

Break-even price = Total cost/Sales

$$= \frac{Bfr. \ 1,000,000 + Bfr. 20 \times 20,000 \text{ units}}{20,000 \text{ units}}$$

$$= Bfr. \ 70 \text{ per unit}$$

result, each method separately yields only partial insights at best. At the same time, though, the approaches are complementary. Applied in combination, they may provide an indication of the range of acceptable prices within which a specific price has to be selected.

Optimization methods Optimization methods take on a different approach: they try to derive an optimal price level analytically or numerically. Optimization methods start out with the specification and estimation of demand and cost functions. Occasionally, competitive and channel intermediary response functions are also formulated. Next, the pricing objective is identified. In a last step, optimal prices are derived using mathematical techniques. Optimization methods can deal with a variety of complex situations. They can set prices for single products as well as product lines, and for single periods as well as multiple period

sequences (trajectory models and optimal control theory). Competitive reactions and channel interdependencies (game theory) may be explicitly incorporated. Other complicating factors such as demand heterogeneity and uncertainty, asymmetric or limited information, and psychological effects can also be accounted for.

Yet, in order to allow for analytical solutions, many optimization methods rely on simplified models and assumptions. Others pursue numerical optima for less restrictive settings, but necessitate the use of extremely complex optimization routines. In any of these approaches, one is confronted with the problem of a priori model specification. As pointed out by Kalyanam (1996): 'Demand functions are latent constructs whose exact parametric form is unknown. Estimates of price elasticities, profit maximizing prices, etc. are conditional upon the parametric form employed in estimation. In practice, many forms may be found that are not only theoretically plausible, but also consistent with the data, yet lead to different (optimal) pricing implications.' Solutions are currently suggested to reduce the impact of specification error, but none of these is widely applicable yet.

Simulation methods Simulation methods are similar to optimization methods, except that the price recommendations are obtained in a different fashion. No 'optimal' prices, but near-optimal or satisfying prices are derived from a comparison of alternative scenarios. Simulation methods are often used in combination with conjoint analysis, a technique for estimating 'utility' functions for existing or new products. Conjoint Analysis is the basis for simulating demand in various price settings. Combined with cost functions, it can yield overall insights into profit implications of alternative price levels. Simulation may be applied to complex problems and settings. Yet, as for optimization, simulation applied to comprehensive settings may become complex, and necessitate the collection of a large amount of information.

Price adjustments While the previous methods, alone or in combination, help determine the appropriate amount to be charged to consumers, small adaptations may be needed to translate them into price levels. These adaptations are in line with practical requirements and originate from psychological pricing issues. In particular, principles of odd pricing and of price lining (the practice of using a limited number of price points to price products in a line) may be highly relevant here. As indicated earlier, both have psychological as well as practical implications, and therefore deserve managerial attention.

7.2.2 Negotiations

In price negotiation, sellers and buyers make a number of proposals and counter-proposals before a price is agreed upon. Price negotiation is typical in industrial marketing, and especially in complex buying situations. Very often, the negotiations are not limited to price alone, but equally encompass discussions on quality, service, terms of delivery, and maintenance (Reeder *et al.* 1991).

Negotiations can evolve following four bargaining strategies that reflect the relative strength or power of both parties involved. A negotiated strategy occurs if buyer and seller are strong, and strive for a win–win or fair price. In a dictatorial strategy, the seller has the dominant position, and tries to impose a price favourable to him. The reverse holds in a defensive strategy, where a weak seller may have to settle for a price that is more advantageous to the buyer. Finally, if both buyer and seller are weak, a gamesmanship strategy results, in which each party tries not to reveal its position in bargaining for a price (Reeder *et al.* 1991). The relative strength of seller and buyer is a crucial determinant of how the negotiations will proceed. The strength of the buyer typically increases with company size as well as past and expected purchases. Seller power is positively linked to uniqueness and quality of the product and services, delivery, and technical and post-sale service capabilities. Furthermore, whether the negotiation style is competitive rather than cooperative is contingent upon factors such as negotiation expertise, attitude, perceived role, number of issues to be discussed, number of parties present, time pressure, and atmospherics.

Negotiation tactics, or specific manœuvres in the course of the bargaining process, will primarily depend on whether there is an acute, moderate, or marginal need for the buyer to buy, and for the seller to sell the product. The speed of the process overall depends on the urgency of these needs, as does the length of subsequent negotiation stages. Successful negotiation, like all pricing decisions, requires careful analysis of internal and external environmental factors. For each aspect of the 'exchange' between buyer and seller, one has to assess whether it is a non-negotiable, prime-trade-off, or non-value factor. Non-negotiable factors are those for which companies have strict requirements that are not open to debate. Non-value factors are of no importance to the decision. Prime-trade-off factors constitute an in-between; they are a subject of discussion in the course of the negotiations. Not only assessment of the company's own range of acceptable values on each factor, but also anticipation of the desires of the buyer, are crucial inputs for successful bargaining. The discussion on internal and external factors affecting price (see Sections 3 and 4) may prove helpful in identifying those factors and levels.

7.2.3 Competitive bidding

In a number of markets, transactions are based on competitive bidding rather than on the basis of 'established' prices for products. Competitive bidding often occurs for the purchase of tailor-made products or services that do not have a market price, or for complex items with varying levels of specification and quality. Many government agencies and institutions are required to go through a bidding system for all their purchases. In closed competitive bidding, the potential buyer formally invites sellers to submit—before a given date—sealed bids, specifying the characteristics and price of the offer. After the deadline, all bids are reviewed and the most appealing one (often, but not always, the one with the lowest price) selected. In open bidding, which is a more informal process, sellers make a series of subsequent offers before the specified date; open bidding, therefore, closely resembles negotiations.

Sellers operating in a market where competitive bidding prevails should carefully prepare their bids. Traditionally, competitive bidding proceeds in two stages: pre-bid analysis, and bid determination. The pre-bid analysis stage uses information from the internal and external environment, combined with information on pre-specified objectives, to 'screen' the bid opportunities. To decide upon the contracts to bid for, simple scoring procedures may be used. Such procedures first identify 'relevant factors' for bid selection, and their importance weights. Then, bid opportunities are scored on each factor, and the weighted sum of these scores leads to an overall evaluation of each bid. Having selected a limited number of bids, the company moves to the stage of bid determination, in which it is attempted to establish the bid price that maximizes expected profit. Anticipated profit is the product of two components: the probability of winning the bid as a function of price, and the profit obtained when carrying out the contract at that price. While costs constitute a crucial input to the second component, the probability of winning is more difficult to assess. It requires consideration of potential competitors and the characteristics of their offer, coupled with their anticipated price level. Historical data on past bids may serve as a cue in anticipating competitors' bidding actions.

7.2.4 Leasing

In industrial markets, leasing may be an interesting alternative to buying for the acquisition of capital goods. Leasing allows the industrial company to pay for the equipment by periodical instalments. A distinction can be made between two major types of leasing contracts: financial leases, and operating or service leases. Financial leases are typically long-term contracts that are fully amortized and usually include the option to purchase the product at the end of the contract. Operational leases are usually short-term, not fully amortized contracts, directed towards customers that need the equipment only temporarily. Operational leases often include maintenance and service provisions. From the customer's perspective, major advantages of leasing compared to buying consist of tax advantages, piecemeal financing, and the avoidance of interest and operating expenses (Haas 1992). A major disadvantage is that in most cases the customer will have to pay more for the equipment than when it is purchased directly. The difference in overall cost between buying and leasing options depends on the price structure set by the capital-goods company. Besides setting product prices for regular purchase, sellers offering lease contracts have to decide on the amounts and frequency of periodical lease payments, the duration of the lease contract, and the residual price for contracts with purchase option. Through its price structure, the company can encourage leasing, stimulate purchase rather than leasing, or try to achieve a balance between lease and sales rates. Leasing arrangements should be in line with the company's objectives. Sellers aiming at increasing penetration in market segments with limited financial resources, establishing long-term relationships with customers, or meeting competition in markets where leasing is widely used view leasing as an essential instrument in strategic pricing (Haas 1992).

8 Pricing strategy versus tactics

IN the literature, the term 'pricing tactics' is subject to much confusion. In this text, we adhere to the viewpoint of van Waterschoot and Van den Bulte (1992) and Morris and Calantone (1990), which is that pricing strategies determine long-term price structure and levels (regular prices) and their evolution over time in response to long-term environmental changes, while tactics refer to short-term price decisions to realize short-term objectives or respond to short-term environmental changes. Often, the same instruments are used for strategic and tactical purposes. A temporary price cut, for instance, can be part of a random-discounting strategy, or intended to pursue an immediate goal like liquidating excess stocks. For many companies, discounting is 'correctional', in response to sudden changes in consumer demand (taste, weather), trading conditions, and operational inefficiencies. At the same time, the strategic role of short-term price fluctuations is well documented and has been extensively discussed in previous sections of this chapter. In this section we concentrate on empirically observed effects of short-term price reductions or 'price promotions'. As the literature on promotions is extensive, we keep the discussion tractable by studying only price discounts in their purest form. Coupons, or other short-term marketing instruments such as gifts or extra quantities, are not considered here. Also, our discussion is based mainly on studies in the packaged-goods sector, which constitute the bulk of the promotion literature. We therefore analyse consumer and retailer promotions (offered by the manufacturer and retailer, respectively, to consumers), and trade promotions (offered by manufacturers to retailers).

8.1 Consumer and retail promotions

When studying the impact of price promotions, we make a distinction between their effect on the promoted item itself, and the implications for other items. In each case, short-term as well as long-term effects are considered.

8.1.1 Impact on the promoted item

The literature on *short-term* effects for a promoted item is extensive, and yields a number of interesting generalizations and issues for discussion. It is generally accepted that temporary price cuts have a substantial impact on sales, resulting in a short-term sales spike (see Blattberg *et al.* 1995). Some authors conjecture that promotion effects follow the '80, 15, 5 rule', implying that 80 per cent of this sales spike results from brand switching, 15 per cent from changes in purchase acceleration, and 5 per cent from increased purchase quantity or 'stockpiling'. This issue is subject to debate, though, and the source of the sales spike strongly depends on category characteristics (cf. below).

A number of authors report that short-term price cuts have a stronger impact than regular price changes, the difference being explained by the temporary nature of promotions. This temporary character increases stockpiling, acceleration, and consumption, and is associated with a higher transaction utility (see Blattberg and Neslin 1989). Others feel that promotions and regular changes work exactly alike, a statement that probably holds in some categories but not in others.

☞ 'In a country like Sweden, consumers have become so used to sales promotions that many will not buy anything that is not on sale, whereas consumers in Germany are not used to this and therefore have not developed the same kind of behaviour.' (Chapter 6, p. 126)

It is widely accepted that higher-share brands are less 'deal elastic' (see Blattberg *et al.* 1995). At the same time, there is evidence of asymmetric switching: promotions for higher-quality brands attract more buyers from lower-quality brands than promotions for low-quality brands attract high-quality buyers. Finally, as indicated earlier, price discounts are found to interact strongly with other marketing-mix instruments: promotions supported by POP signals or ads yield significantly larger sales spikes.

From a *long-term* perspective, much less is known about promotions. Some argue that promotions may be 'consumer franchise building' or contribute to a positive consumer attitude towards the product (franchise), thereby increasing market share in the long run. However, there is no solid evidence of such effects. In their paper on promotion-effect generalizations, Lal and Padmanabhan (1995) find no relationship between market share and long-run promotional expenditures. For many products, long-run market shares are stationary (i.e. do not increase or decrease). For products where market share exhibits a trend, this cannot be directly attributed to a positive impact of promotion expenditures. Conversely, there are indications of negative promotion effects beyond the promotion period, where purchase acceleration and stock building lead to a post-promotion trough in sales. Evidence on the existence of post-promotion dips is, however, mixed (Blattberg *et al.* 1995). This may result from the difficulty in assessing true incremental sales from promotions based on aggregate data. Post-promotion dips may exist at the individual level, but may be 'masked' by aggregation because of the timing of consumer purchases, retailer and competitive behaviour, low inventory sensitivity, and differences in average purchase rates among consumers (see Blattberg *et al.* 1995).

Academics and practitioners have increasingly recognized the potentially harmful impact of price discounts on product image and price sensitivity. Price promotions may have a negative impact on the buyer's (future) attitude towards the brand, when he starts attributing his purchase motivation to the promotion instead of to a liking for the brand (self-perception theory). Frequent price cuts may also enhance deal-to-deal buying, as consumers learn to anticipate future price cuts (Blattberg and Neslin 1989). Finally, as suggested Section 4.1.2 on psychological pricing, frequent promotions may reduce consumers' willingness to pay through their impact on reference prices (see e.g. Folkes and Wheat 1995).

8.1.2 Implications beyond promoted item

Price cuts clearly have implications beyond the item that is promoted. In the short run, there is overwhelming evidence of switching from other items to the one on promotion. If customers are drawn away from other company items, this results in cannibalization; otherwise sales are 'reaped away' from competitors. Price discounts on one item may also positively affect sales of complementary items. According to Blattberg *et al.* (1995), the magnitude of such cross-effects varies with the product category. The profitability of price promotions for retailers depends on their traffic-building effect (Walters and McKenzie 1988). While it seems logical that advertised promotions can result in increased store traffic and interstore switching, the evidence is mixed and, once again, probably highly category specific (see Blattberg *et al.* 1995). In the long run, price discounts can be used as an entry-deterring device and increase store competitiveness. The impact of price discounts on store image is not unravelled yet. While price discounts may signal low prices overall, they may also harm store credibility and create a cheap image. In their review on price-promotion effects, Blattberg *et al.* (1995) conclude that little is known about how price promotions shape store image.

👉 'Sales promotion is a marketing communication technique where additional incentives beyond the inherent qualities or benefits of the product or service are offered to the target audience, sales force, or distributors. This is achieved by, for instance, temporarily modifying the price relative to that of the competitors.' (Chapter 12, p. 282)

The potential negative effects of price discounts have led some academics and practitioners to believe that promotions have been overused. The return to EDLP strategies by retailers and some manufacturers, as for instance, Proctor & Gamble, could be a response to the less desirable impacts of price promotions just outlined.

In summary, the impact of manufacturer and retailer promotions is complex. Price discounts operate at different levels and in different periods. Their effect depends on many factors. Crucial determinants are product category characteristics, such as category penetration, perishability and ability to stockpile, length of the purchase cycle, and novelty. Consumer characteristics such as variety-seeking tendency, consumer perceptions, economics of time, consumer attitude, and loyalty shape deal proneness. In addition, the competitive promotion environment and a company's own promotion conditions such as promotion frequency, depth, timing, instrument, and way of communication have a major effect on promotion outcomes. For retailers, supply characteristics such as retail margins, depth and frequency of manufacturer deals, retail inventory, and retagging costs further complicate promotion effects and decisions (Tellis and Zufryden 1995).

8.2 Trade promotions

Lal, Little, and Villas-Boas (1996) define trade promotions as 'temporary price reductions offered by manufacturers to retailers for the purpose of stimulating sales'. Following these authors, trade promotional spending has exceeded advertising spending in much of the consumer packaged goods industry. Many reasons have been put forward to explain this phenomenon. While the logic behind trade promotions may be similar to that for consumer and retail promotions (for example, they may appeal to the deal-prone final consumer segment, limit the competitive threat from smaller and private label brands, and so on), it is increasingly believed that a specific explanation of the success of trade deals should take the point of view of the retailers into account. Ultimately, it is they who decide to accept or reject trade deals.

The belief that trade deals cannot be solely justified on the basis of ultimate consumer reactions is supported by observed retailer reactions to trade deals. First, various studies have demonstrated that retailers may forward buy in response to trade promotions, and engage in deal-to-deal buying (see e.g. Blattberg *et al.* 1995; Lal *et al.* 1996). Secondly, having profited from a trade deal, retailers typically pass through less than 100 per cent of the deals (Blattberg *et al.* 1995). As a result, consumer sales usually increase but not as much as retailers forward buy, as can be judged from troughs in manufacturer shipments after the deal (see also Blattberg and Neslin 1989). Lal *et al.* (1996) summarize this as follows: 'Retailers regularly take advantage of trade deals to stock up with extra goods: they engage in forward buying. This leads to decreased margins for manufacturers on large amounts of goods, often not made up for by increased sales to ultimate customers as a result of merchandising. Hence, manufacturers report that many trade deals are not profitable.'

On top of these seemingly limited positive sales effects, offering trade deals implies 'transaction costs' to manufacturers. Costs of preparing and implementing trade deals encompass costs of the sales force promoting the deal to retailers, and of the development of sales support material (Blattberg and Neslin 1989). Also, retailer forward buying creates logistical dysfunctions, which sheds another shadow on the attractiveness of trade deals.

Justifications for trade deals should thus find arguments beyond final consumers' reactions. One argument is that trade deals are needed to appeal to 'warehouse store channels'. These warehouse chains exclusively purchase merchandise on deal, and are in a sense comparable to the deal-prone consumer segment.

Another justification is developed by Lal *et al.* (1996), who argue that managers use trade deals to secure sufficient shelf space and POP support (features, displays) for their products at the retail level. These authors observe that many trade deals are offered with 'performance clauses': the manufacturer offers to reduce wholesale price for a certain period—say, 6 weeks—in return for the retailer running a prespecified kind of merchandising during, say, at least one week of the period. Many manufacturers use trade promotions to obtain displays and features—price is not the whole story. Within this context retailers may or may not accept a trade-deal offer from a manufacturer. If they do not accept, purchases are made at the regular (non-deal) price. If they do accept, they are bound by the Cooperative Purchase Agreement, and receive payment only upon receipt of the certificate of performance by the manufacturer. Once accepted, trade deals usually lead to non-zero pass-through because they make features and displays

more effective (Lal *et al.* 1996). In brief, following this reasoning, manufacturers use trade deals to 'be in the retailers' inventory'. These deals may imply extra sales as a result of the displays, features, and pass-through, but this is not their sole advantage. The authors suggest that, besides the sales-generating effect to ultimate consumers in the given competitive setting, trade deals may imply more favourable competitive environments for manufacturers. This is true because retailers can accept only a limited number of trade deals from manufacturers. The latter cannot offer trade deals all the time because of transaction costs. Following Lal *et al.* (1996), this leads to a system of channel interactions that softens the intensity of competition between manufacturers. Other authors have studied 'optimal' or prevailing retailer reactions in the presence of trade deals empirically. These studies reveal that retailer pass-through depends on deal depth, the normal margin, the response of ultimate customers, and the choice of promotion instrument (see e.g. Greenleaf 1995).

In brief, trade promotions have been increasingly used by manufacturers as a marketing tool. While the rationale behind trade promotions may partly be based on ultimate consumer reactions and the attempt to increase ultimate sales, retailer reactions to trade deals (forward buying, limited pass-through) and the observation that net long-term sales effects remain small have cast some doubt on the effectiveness of this instrument. Despite additional advantages, such as securing shelf space and promotion support, some of this doubt remains in a number of categories. In planning trade promotions, manufacturers should at least take retailer reactions into account, or take appropriate counter-actions to discourage forward buying.

9 The future

BECAUSE of a wide range of factors such as increasing competition, rising costs (putting higher pressure on margins), and better availability of information to consumers, pricing is bound to become an even more important decision in the future.

The polarization typical of many Western societies (where people become more heterogeneous in wealth, education, and availability of time) makes it more and more crucial to account for consumer heterogeneity in reactions to price. Price customization, or charging differential prices to various segments, is gaining way. At the same time, companies should be aware of the risks and costs involved in such customization. Appropriate differential pricing is more costly and difficult to implement and control, and companies should ensure they apply their price strategy systematically. Also, customization requires insights into the price sensitivity of different segments. Measuring this price sensitivity will become even more important than it is at present. This measurement will be facilitated by the availability of external data sources like scanner (panel) information, or necessitate management of customer databases by the company. The challenge becomes, not to find data, but to extract relevant information on price sensitivity from those huge databases.

Technological developments will continue to put their mark on pricing decisions in a variety of ways. Electronic shopping (for example, shopping over the Internet) will increase the accessibility of price information to customers (see Insert). It will also reduce the potential for geographically differentiated prices in a number of product categories. Technological advances are bound to further shorten product life cycles. This enhances the importance of establishing the right price strategy from the start (quick and sound price decisions), but also calls for a long-term perspective, where managers must anticipate the impact of their current prices on future own and competitive product versions.

> ### Price comparisons via the Internet
>
> 'Shopping "agents" such as Netbot's Jango can mimic a megastore by searching across many stand-alone stores for a product at the cheapest price.'
>
> Source: The Economist, 11 Nov. 1997, 100.

Even in settings that are not high tech, dynamics in consumer reactions should be carefully monitored. The long-term implications of price strategies are still under-researched, and managers should be aware of shifts in customer reactions that may result from frequent adoption of certain strategies. Increased use of promotions may enhance customer price sensitivity or lead to more price anticipation. Conversely, consumers may become weary of deals and more alert to potential deception in price promotions. Time-based price strategies other than promotions may trigger similar customer reactions. The attractiveness of these strategies should thus be regularly re-evaluated.

The future is likely to give more attention to channel pricing. Retailers are bound to become more active price-setters vis-à-vis final consumers, and more powerful negotiators in discussions with manufacturers. Issues in retailer pricing that have been neglected—such as the impact of prices on category or store profit as a whole, and the link between prices and store image or store traffic—are likely to become prime areas of attention. At the same time, negotiation skills will become a more important asset to all channel members.

International pricing will also stay a viable research area in the years to come. Markets will continue to open up and more strongly depend on one another; customers will tend to become increasingly 'mobile' and/or better informed about prices in an international setting; legal and trade restrictions are bound to be adapted and regulations made more uniform. It is obvious that these evolutions will affect opportunities for profitable pricing. Companies that 'master' international pricing techniques, and have access to information systems keeping them up to date, have a brighter future ahead of them.

10 Summary

WHILE a company's product, distribution, and advertising decisions are crucial factors determining the product's overall attractiveness, effective pricing is essential to turn these assets into profit. Effective pricing requires a systematic approach, starting with a thorough analysis of the wide variety of environmental factors that may affect a company's pricing decisions and results. Next, strategic pricing objectives and operational pricing goals have to be selected. Pricing objectives need to be in correspondence with overall company objectives and should focus on the possibilities uncovered by the environmental analysis. In this way, pricing objectives set the stage for selection of appropriate pricing strategies. The essence of profitable pricing is indeed to select a pricing strategy that exploits the opportunities offered by customer heterogeneity, competitive position, product characteristics, or a combination of these (Tellis 1986). Successful implementation of the pricing strategy requires selection of an appropriate price structure and regular price levels, and the planning of short-term variations around these levels. Several methods are available that can help to narrow down the range of feasible price levels within which a regular price has to be selected. Yet, as a result of the multitude of influencing factors, imperfect or partial information, and product- and situation-specific effects, the pricing problem is in most cases too complex to derive optimal prices in a single round. Instead, managers should learn to assemble 'bits and pieces' of information and insights to arrive at appropriate prices. More information and better insight into the pricing problem can be acquired gradually, allowing managers to improve their pricing decisions over time. Besides this learning process, the continuously changing environment and evolution in pricing objectives over the PLC require that—even for existing products—prices be evaluated at regular intervals and adjusted if necessary (Keegan 1995).

Further reading

Blattberg, R., and Neslin, S. A. (1990), *Sales Promotion: Concepts, Methods and Strategies* (Englewood Cliffs, NJ: Prentice Hall). This book provides an in-depth discussion of various short-term pricing actions and their implications. Consumer and retailer, as well as trade promotions, are dealt with.

Dolan, R., and Simon, H. (1996), *Power Pricing: How Managing Price Transforms the Bottom Line* (New York: Free Press). This book emphasizes the opportunities offered by strategic pricing. Particular attention is paid to 'price customization', or the adoption of 'demand-oriented' and 'differential' pricing strategies. The book also provides interesting insights in and checklists for the implementation of price decisions.

Gijsbrechts, E. (1993), 'Prices and Pricing Research in Consumer Marketing: Some Recent Developments', *International Journal of Research in Marketing*, 10/2: 115–51. This paper provides a review of developments in the literature on consumer pricing after 1985, and indicates directions for further research.

Monroe, K. (1990), *Pricing: Making Profitable Decisions* (New York: McGraw Hill). This textbook provides a systematic analysis of the different pricing aspects. It is fairly complete and encyclopaedic in nature.

Nagle, T. T., and Holden, R. K. (1995), *The Strategy and Tactics of Pricing: A Guide to Profitable Decision Making* (Englewood Cliffs, NJ: Prentice Hall). This book is not intended as a textbook, but rather as a guide for managers. It is organized around major pricing issues/questions encountered in practice, and illustrates the strategic importance of pricing.

Tellis, G. J. (1986), 'Beyond the Many Faces of Price: An Integration of Pricing Strategies'. *Journal of Marketing*, 50/4 (Oct.), 146–60. This article provides an interesting taxonomy of pricing strategies. It discusses the conditions under which these strategies can be profitable, and provides examples and various forms of the generic strategies.

Discussion questions

1 The contemporary definition of price goes beyond 'the monetary effort to obtain one unit of the product'. How is the price concept broadened, and what are the implications for pricing?

2 Using a systematic approach to pricing allows managers to respond quickly and effectively to environmental changes. Discuss.

3 Discuss the factors that have a major impact on aggregate price–volume relationships, and illustrate with an example.

4 Customer reference prices play a major role in a variety of buying situations. In what way are they relevant for managers in charge of pricing?

5 Why is there less knowledge on price sensitivity in industrial markets than in consumer markets?

6 Competitive interrelationships and channel interactions affect a company's optimal pricing policy. What are the differences and similarities between both types of interactions in view of pricing?

7 The strength and weakness of Tellis's taxonomy is that it discusses and positions *generic* pricing strategies. Discuss.

8 What are the differences between random discounting, second-market discounting, and advertised discounting? Under what conditions will these strategies be profitable?

9 Discuss generic pricing strategies likely to be used by (i) a company operating in an international market, (ii) a retailer, (iii) a not-for-profit company.

10 Complex price structures exploit market opportunities, but they also entail costs. Discuss and illustrate.

11 Short-term price cuts may be part of a pricing strategy, or serve operational purposes. Discuss.

12 In deciding upon their trade promotion activities, manufacturers should anticipate retailer reactions. Discuss.

13 There is no single best method for determining optimal price levels. Instead, managers should use a combination of rules, and qualitative as well as quantitative information, to develop relevant price boundaries. Discuss.

On 12 April 1992, at 9 p.m., Walt Disney Co. opened its Euro Disney theme park in Marne-la-Vallée in France, approximately 30 kilometres east of Paris. Euro Disney—now referred to as Disneyland Paris—was the fourth Disney theme park in the World, next to Disneyland in California, Disneyworld in Florida, and Disneyland Tokyo. Its concept was identical to that of Disney's US theme parks, which create a complete 'fantasy' world where client orientation is of primary importance. The Euro Disney theme park, on its opening day, covered fifty-six hectares of land offering twenty-nine attractions. The total Euro disney resort further comprised golf courses, parks, a camping and entertainment centre, six hotels, thirty-two stores, and twenty-nine food outlets. Total investment was estimated at approximately FFr. 30 billion. The Walt Disney Co. owned 49 per cent of Euro Disney, the remaining capital coming from banks and other investors. Euro Disney planned on starting up the second phase by 1993, during which time Disney-MGM studios would be built. Only minor adaptations were made to adapt the Disney Theme Park to European taste and conditions. The Theme Park personnel—referred to as 'Cast Members'—were required to be multilingual (they should speak English and French, but preferably also other European languages), such that all visitors could be served in their mother tongue. Many of the personnel had been recruited from North European countries. The number of attractions involving language was kept at a minimum, and the fairy tales that were emphasized catered to European tastes and background. The infrastructure was adapted to European weather conditions, and brighter costumes were used to give the park a lively atmosphere even when there was no sun. Euro Disney counted on attracting visitors in all age categories, and—given its accessibility—from a range of European countries. The price for a day ticket was set at FFr. 225 per adult; children between 3 and 11 were charged FFr. 150. The minimum rate for a night at one of Disney's theme hotels amounted to FFr. 450 per person. Despite these premium prices (ticket prices were about two to three times higher than those of other European theme parks), Euro Disney did not fear the competition of other European attraction parks, which were smaller, closed during the winter season, and used a different concept. Convinced that the Disney label would sell itself, the company spent little on advertising, yet counted on 11 million visitors during the first year of operation. About half of these visitors were expected to be French. Foreign visitors were forecast to spend about FFr. 6.6 billion yearly in the theme park.

While there was great enthusiasm in France and throughout Europe, some criticisms emerged even before the park opened its doors. A number of observers postulated that entrance tickets were too expensive, and that Europeans might be less seduced by the overly friendly and humble 'American' style of the cast members. Others emphasized that Euro Disney management had underestimated the seasonal patterns of theme-park attendance in Europe.

12 April to 1 October 1992

After approximately six months of operation, Euro Disney's results were disappointing. The revenues of FFr. 1,501 billion during the first quarter were below expectations, and by 1 October, the end of the fiscal year, a considerable loss (various sources indicated losses ranging from FFr. 188 to 339 million) was recorded. While the number of English and German visitors was in line with the original objectives, attendance by the French was surprisingly low, and accounted for only 29 per cent of all visitors. The target level of 11 million visitors during the first year seemed threatened. Euro Disney management reacted to these results by lowering the ticket prices for the local population from FFr. 225 to FFr. 150. In addition, reduced group rates were offered to the French during the down season. These local price adaptations were accompanied by intense advertising campaigns, and personal selling effort addressed at French schools and companies. Yet, Eisner (the president of the Walt Disney Corporation) emphasized that these price changes were in line with US practices of offering low prices to locals (local inhabitants pay about $20 for a Disneyland ticket in Anaheim), and were by no means an indication that tickets were generally too expensive.

1 October 1992 to 30 March 1993

By March 1993 Euro Disney announced that it had reached the target of 11 million visitors during the first year of operation. Yet, the improved attendance was largely the result of its focus on the French market. This increased local interest, however, created new problems. French visitors were less likely to spend a lot on food and merchandising, and made less use of hotel infrastructure. Also, demand was much more seasonal than expected at first. Both the local recruitment and the seasonal dip translated into poor results. Hotel occupancy rates dropped from 74 per cent in the first six months of operation to less than 40 per cent from October to the end of March. The total number of visitors during the latter period hardly reached 3.3 million, and the return of FFr. 1.79 billion they generated was below expectations. It is estimated that between the beginning of October to the end of March, Euro Disney incurred a loss of FFr. 1.08 billion.

In an attempt to 'turn the tide', managers quickly

responded with a number of marketing changes. First, the price structure was adapted to account for seasonality in demand. One-day ticket prices for the period November to February (excluding Christmas) were reduced to FFr. 175 per adult and FFr. 125 per child. This decrease was compensated for by higher prices for the summer and Christmas periods, during which adults paid FFr. 250 and children were charged FFr. 175 for a one-day passport. In the in-between periods, the original ticket prices of FFr. 225 (adult) and FFr. 150 (child) were sustained. Prices for food and souvenirs were equally reduced. Visitors to the theme park complained that waiting lines were too long (waiting for an hour and a half for one attraction was not exceptional), and that the number of attractions was too limited to justify spending two days or longer at the park. In reaction to this, Disney management offered reduced entrance rates for visitors coming into the park after 5 p.m. It also announced its plans to open up six new attractions in the near future, in order to encourage longer stays or multiple visits. Further in line with this objective, hotel rates were reduced (the cheapest hotel was now available for FFr. 300 per night, and children were allowed to stay for free), and annual passports (covering eleven visits) were offered at lower rates per visit.

An additional problem arose as a result of different eating habits in Europe compared to the USA. While Americans tend to nibble all day, or are prepared to have their meals between 11.30 a.m. and 3 p.m., Europeans want to have lunch between 12 a.m. and 2 p.m. This resulted in long waiting lines at the restaurants, especially since the six classical establishments where one could sit down and eat at ease were less favoured by visitors. Management, therefore, changed the biggest classical restaurant into a fast-food eating location. In addition, Disney's complete ban on alcoholic drinks in the theme park, which was badly received by Europeans, was relieved: from May 1993 visitors could consume French and Californian wines in the restaurants.

Given its tight financial situation, the company also felt compelled to slim down the cost of its operations. Personnel cost was significantly lowered by using more flexible and part-time cast members, and by reducing the number of employees from 19,000 in the peak to 10,000 in the down-season periods. Plans for the second phase of the theme park were put on hold.

1 April 1993 to 30 September 1994

Despite the adaptations in marketing approach, the company did not crawl out of its unsound financial situation. Between 1 April and 30 June 1993 only 3.1 million visitors were attracted, and there was a strong fall in foreign attendance, especially from UK and Italian visitors. According to managers and outside observers, the general recession and the strength of the French franc (compared to the UK pound or Italian lira) partly accounted for this.

Hotel occupancy rates were reasonable (68.5 per cent), but this was probably the result of hotel rate reductions; and the overall return of FFr. 1.456 billion was disappointing. The situation became worse in the months that followed. While the number of visitors still reached 6.7 million from 2 July to 30 September, attendance figures and spending levels per visitor further decreased in the months after. The many changes in marketing approach had not yielded the anticipated success, and Euro Disney had to find a settlement with the Walt Disney Company. With a total debt of FFr. 20.3 billion by the end of 1993, Euro Disney was close to bankruptcy, and a financial restructuring was needed.

Multiple criticisms of Euro Disney's marketing approach appeared in the international press, and Euro Disney was blamed for being 'arrogant' in imposing its own way of doing business on the Europeans. On the distribution side, this resulted in unsatisfactory relationships with European tour operators. Critics also postulated that ticket prices were still too high, especially if repeat visits were to be encouraged—a necessity for becoming profitable. Others suggest that price schemes should become more complex to differentiate between days of the week, and that hotel rates should be further reduced to meet competition from Parisian hotels. Finally, the number of attractions (thirty-five compared to fifty-five in Disneyland California) was still deemed too low to lead to long stays and repeat visits. During the first nine months of 1994, the number of visitors hardly reached 8.2 million, and these visitors kept spending too little and did not return for repeat visits. By the end of September 1994 Euro Disney closed the fiscal year with a loss of FFr. 18 billion, and a total of only 8.8 million visitors. Clearly, the company had seriously to rethink its strategy.

A new Elan

In December 1994 Euro Disney's top manager Philippe Bourguignon announced further revisions of the theme park's pricing scheme. In order to escape from the negative spiral of low visit frequency and spending level of visitors, the company decided (again) drastically to reduce its entrance prices from 1 April 1995 on, and simplify the price structure. In the new pricing scheme, the price for an adult one-day passport dropped from FFr. 250 to FFr. 195 during the peak season (1 April to 30 September), and from FFr. 175 to FFr. 150 in the down season (1 October to 31 March); the in-between season tariff no longer applied. Following Bourguignon's announcement, the price of FFr. 250 constituted a psychological barrier for visitors. Rates for children were adapted accordingly: to FFr. 150 in the peak season, and to FFr. 120 otherwise. Two- and three-day passports were still offered at slightly lower rates, and local inhabitants continued to receive special reductions. As tickets constituted only part of total return, it was estimated that the break-even increase in number of visitors (needed to compensate for the price reductions) came down to only 700,000 visitors.

During the first half of 1995 the number of visitors increased, and returns rose by 7 per cent. The company still incurred a loss, but this was less considerable than had been expected, partly as a result of the financial restructuring during 1994 (reduced royalty payments to the Walt Disney Co., and to postponed interest payments to the banks). By the end of the fiscal year 1994/5, the company finally came out of the 'red figures': a profit of FFr. 114 million was noted.

By July 1995 the company opened up five more attractions, leading to a total of forty attractions in the theme park. Disneyland Paris, as it is now called, was slowly coming out of its disastrous position. From 1 October 1995 to 31 December 1995, losses were kept down to FFr. 57 million (about half the figure for the same period in the previous year). Yet, the company refrained from becoming overly optimistic. The reductions in ticket prices had increased the number of visitors by about 21 per cent, but the returns fell somewhat behind, with an increase of only 10 per cent. A crucial point of concern remained the low spending levels of visitors in the theme park. Also, the evolution of exchange rates was still to Disney's disadvantage.

Epilogue

In 1997 Disneyland Paris celebrated five years' of existence. While it would be an exaggeration to speak of a real upswing, the company was certainly improving its position. The fiscal year 1995/6 ended with a profit of about FFr. 197 million. About 11.7 million visitors visited the theme park during 1996—a million more than the year before. In total, about 50 million visitors had crossed the entrance gate since the opening in April 1992. (While French participation was obviously still dominant, the Benelux countries were now in second position and accounted for 19 per cent of all visitors.) Occupancy rates had also increased, from a level of 68.5 per cent in 1995 to 72 per cent in 1996.

In January 1997 Eric-Paul Dijkhuizen, General Director of Disneyland Paris for the Benelux countries, stated: 'We have made some beginners' mistakes. While the Park was originally conceived as a holiday destination, we now position it as a "trip" comparable to a weekend to London or Paris.' By then waiting times in the park had dropped significantly—for top attractions like the Space Mountain they had been reduced by half (from 1.5 hours down to forty-five minutes) and Euro Disney made sure that its visitors were entertained while waiting. In the course of 1997 the company plans to open up a new cinema complex Gaumont in Disney Village, with eight theatres offering seats for 2,500 visitors. In 1997 Disneyland Paris celebrated its fifth birthday.

Sources: Euro Disney; *De Financieel Economische Tijd*, 28 Apr. 1993, 12 Oct. 1994, 15 Dec. 1994, 13 Mar. 1996; *Financial Times*, 12 Apr. 1992, 9 July 1993; *Gazet van Antwerpen*, 10 May 1997; *Tijdschrift voor Marketing*, Mar. 1992; *Trends*, 9 Jan. 1997.

Question and exercise

Critically examine Disney's pricing strategy in the context of the discussion of 'The meaning of price' in Section 1.1.

Chapter 11
Marketing-Channel Management

Susan Shaw and Sean Ennis

Objectives

This chapter considers the key issues in the management of marketing channels. Its objectives are:

1 to consider the part that supply chains play in delivering value to the end customer;

2 to identify the factors that determine the structure of a supply chain;

3 to discuss the role of the intermediary within the supply chain and the roles that intermediaries may perform in different supply chains;

4 to examine the management issues associated with a particular type of intermediary activity (retailing) and with a particular management structure (franchising).

1 Delivering value to the end-user

THE supply chain from the manufacturer to final users, whether final consumers or industrial customers, must be designed so that it achieves a level of value to the customer that creates a sustainable competitive advantage for the chain. Value is what customers are prepared to pay for the product/service and this is the combined value of all the activities carried out by the chain. The value chain (Porter 1985) represents the linkages and interdependencies between suppliers and intermediaries. This chapter concentrates on the part of the value chain that is normally called the *marketing channel*: 'an organized network of agencies and institutions which, in combination, perform all the activities required to link producers with users to accomplish the marketing task' (Bennett 1988).

Most of the examples in the chapter are from channels leading to the final consumer, but the same principles govern industrial channels between manufacturers.

Value takes many different forms depending on the requirements of the customer. As well as the product itself, value includes the attractiveness of the purchasing environment to the consumer, convenience of access to the product in terms of geographical location and/or sales systems, and the level of service offered in support of the product. The relationship between the value of the product and the shopping experience is particularly important and the skill of the value chain is in the positioning of the total offer for the consumer in a profitable way. There is no single positioning. This will depend on the target market. This is shown in Fig. 11.1, which shows the different marketing positions adopted by different European clothing retailers.

2 Supply-chain management functions

THE supply chain is made up of an array of interdependent functions:

Figure 11.1 **Market positioning of European clothing retailers**

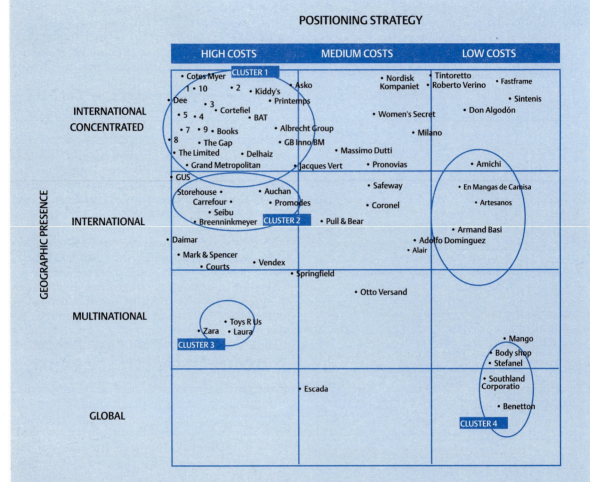

POSITIONING STRATEGY

Notes: Cluster 1: mature; Cluster 2: multinational; Cluster 3: aggressive; Cluster 4: global
1. Ashold N. V.; 2. Sears, Roebuck; 3. J. Sainsbury; 4. John Menzies; 5. Tenglemann; 6. Docks de France; 7. Dixons; 8. W. H. Smith; 9. Ward White; 10. Ratners.

■ *Demand analysis and forecasting.* This involves identifying the requirements of consumers that can be met profitably and forecasting the future pattern of demand from day to day and week to week and over the production and planning cycle.

■ *Product production.* This is the creation, design, and manufacture of the products that demand analysis has identified.

■ *Inventory management.* Stockholding is necessary in warehouses to match the imbalances between demand and production. Inventory management is concerned with reordering—deciding how much and when to reorder, controlling out-of-stock situations, maintaining the quality of the product from manufacture through to the final sale, etc.

■ *Order processing.* This is the preparation of orders, their transmission, product receipt, and sorting.

Sorting involves a variety of activities (Alderson 1954):

■ *Sorting out*. Heterogeneous stocks have to be broken down into separate homogeneous stocks.

■ *Accumulation*. Similar stocks have to be brought together from a number of sources to create a larger homogeneous supply.

■ *Allocation*. Large homogeneous lots of products have to be broken into smaller lot sizes.

■ *Assorting*. Assortments of products have to be brought together for resale in customer convenient groups.

■ *Transportation*. Goods have to be loaded and transported from the point of manufacture to the point of sale, delivered and unloaded, and presented in a form and way that is attractive to the consumer. This includes shelf-space allocation and positioning, displays, demonstrations, etc.

■ *Returned goods*. Processes have to be set up to deal with goods returned by consumers and for product servicing, when necessary.

■ *Marketing communication*. Consumers have to be told about the product and persuaded to buy.

In order for the chain to operate efficiently and to be responsive to demand, additional activities have to be carried out:

■ *Information transmission*. There has to be a flow of information up and down the supply chain to trigger activities. This can be carried out by hard copy (computer links, paper exchange, telephone, fax, e-mail, etc., as well as by direct personal communication. Since the 1970s, information technology (IT) has greatly contributed to reducing costs and achieving efficiencies in this area.

■ *Financing of activities*. Flows of product in the channel also require financing: both finance to allow the activities of the channel to take place before sales revenue is received and money to allow buyers to finance their purchases. This may be provided by the channel itself from past earnings or provided as credit by agencies such as banks and other financial institutions.

■ *Negotiation*. Trading partners negotiate price, selling terms, delivery dates, and functions to be performed.

■ *Changes of title*. Ownership of goods changes as trading partners make exchanges of finance for the performance of particular functions.

A flow of the activities in a supply chain can be seen in Fig. 11.2.

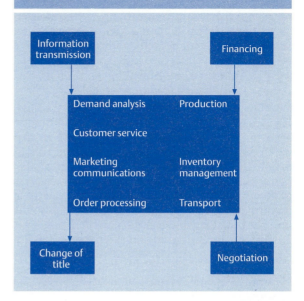

Figure 11.2 **Supply chain functions and support**

3 Roles in the marketing channel

THE marketing channel has to fulfil a number of roles. Each type of channel fulfils these roles in different ways and with different degrees of effectiveness and efficiency. It is, therefore, necessary to be clear what these roles are.

3.1 Gaps between production and consumption

The role of the marketing channel is to fill a number of gaps between production and consumption; these were defined by Alderson (1954) as:

■ *Time gaps*. These occur because final consumers typically purchase items at discrete intervals (e.g. daily or weekly food shopping, monthly clothing purchases, etc.), while manufacturers produce products to schedules that are most efficient for them and that are often continuous.

■ *Space gaps*. Manufacturing usually takes place in one or a relatively small number of locations, depending on the most efficient size of operations.

Manufacturing location does not match with the places where final consumers live and wish to buy.

■ *Quantity gaps.* Manufacturers produce in larger quantities than the individual consumer wishes to buy. A means has to be found of breaking bulk by dividing the product up into smaller consignments for the final consumer.

■ *Variety gaps.* Typically the product ranges of a manufacturer are narrower than the product assortment desired by customers. Product ranges have to be made available to consumers in the width and depth which they require, and this is handled in many different ways. Some retailers, for instance, offer wide assortments of a variety of products. The typical large supermarket carries a product range of over 20,000 items. At the same time, a specialist cheese shop may carry only one product range: it depends on the benefits sought by the consumer. These are increasingly varied in an affluent society. This is reflected both in growing product assortments and in the growing variety of ways in which products are made available to consumers for purchase.

3.2 Intermediaries

Intermediaries perform various functions to bridge Alderson's gaps between the manufacturer and the customer. They can reduce time and expenditure by reducing the number of contacts required. Fig. 11.3 shows the number of required contacts with and without intermediaries. Intermediaries can re-sort product ranges from the narrow ranges of a single manufacturer to the wider assortments that may be required by consumers. They can use their knowledge of markets to create and design products for consumers that they subsequently work with the manufacturer to

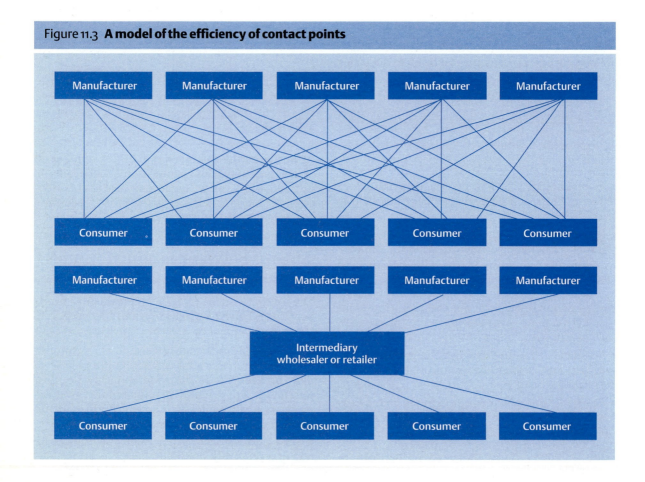

Figure 11.3 **A model of the efficiency of contact points**

produce. They can communicate with the customer through displays and other marketing activities.

There are many different types of intermediary but they can be grouped broadly into two categories: retailing and wholesaling.

Retailing consists of those business activities involved in the sale of goods and services to consumers for personal, family, or household use. It is the final stage in the distribution process and includes not only store-related activities but also non-store purchases such as vending machines, direct selling, catalogue sales, and mail-order sales. Section 9.2 considers retailing in more detail.

Wholesaling involves the buying or handling of goods and subsequent resale to organizational users, retailers, and/or other wholesalers, but, unlike retailing, not to the final consumer. Wholesaling takes many forms. Wholesalers can provide wide product ranges from many manufacturers, which are delivered to retailers and others. Other wholesalers operate cash-and-carry outlets to which retail customers come to buy. An example is the food wholesaler, Makro, which has a cash-and-carry operation selling to retailers and the food service sector. In these cases, wholesalers buy products from manufacturers, which they resell. Some wholesalers act as distributors for limited product ranges only, either buying those product ranges from manufacturers or selling on commission as agents of the manufacturer. In these cases they often have exclusive rights to handle these products within their sales areas, in return for not simultaneously selling the products of competitors.

Retailers and wholesalers are not necessarily—or indeed typically—responsible for all the functions that supply chains are required to perform. Also playing an important role in the functioning of the supply chain are third-party logistics companies as well as other facilitators.

Third party logistics companies are businesses that carry out combinations of warehousing and transport functions on behalf of members of the channel but are not themselves usually involved in the creation, sale, or marketing of products (see Insert). Retailers, wholesalers, and manufacturers can choose from a variety of options that range from contracting out the whole of operations to a third party to hiring equipment and drivers for some activities. Because of specialization in these activities, third-party logistics companies may be

> **Third party is big business**
>
> P&O European Transport Services is one of the market leaders in the provision of integrated distribution and transport services throughout Europe. Its turnover in 1996 was £883.4 million and in 1996 its largest new contract was a £27 million contract to handle distribution for a firm in the automobile sector.

able to offer a more cost-effective alternative to company-owned and managed operations for large companies. They are also attractive to smaller retailers and/or manufacturers who do not have sufficient volume of product to justify the creation of dedicated facilities. Similar arguments apply when the product is seasonal or has great fluctuations in volumes demanded or supplied for other reasons. Multi-user facilities have become more attractive as information technology has allowed for more efficient scheduling and use. Even retailers or manufacturers who otherwise have total control of their supply networks are likely to make at least some use of third parties. Wincanton Logistics, part of Unigate plc, is the second largest third-party logistics contractor in the UK. Its client list spans many industries, including food, drink, pharmaceuticals, cosmetics, and hardware. It offers a range of services from warehouse space, drivers, and contract hire to client fleet management.

Other facilitators include banks, who offer financial services to the channel, and telecommunications companies, who support computer systems, as has already been mentioned. Other businesses provide services such as systems design, advertising and marketing, product design, packaging design, and so on.

4 The operation of supply chains

4.1 Integration

Together the businesses described above create a network to deliver the product and service benefits required by the end-user. This network is required to operate in an integrated way because of the need to:

- coordinate the product specifications of retailers and the manufacture of those products;

- match in-store product availability with demand and manufacturing schedules, which depends on the alignment of the transport and stockholding systems throughout the chain;

- handle the product in a consistent way so that it reaches the consumer in the best condition—for example, for fresh foods to reach the consumer in optimal condition consistent temperature control is required throughout the supply chain;

- coordinate promotional campaigns by retailers and/or manufacturers to match consumer demand and product availability.

Production/ordering cycles became shorter in the 1990s, and as a result margins of error are smaller, so more accurate coordination is required. Increasingly, therefore, supply chains should be viewed not as a set of discrete stages but as an integrated system. If the channel is not organized in this way, the channel will lose out to other better organized channels. Fox example, the Birds Eye Walls' (a food manufacturer) view of its supply chain contrasts with a traditional view where each organization carries out activities separately and members of the chain meet only to bargain and negotiate (Fig. 11.4)

4.2 Requirements for a successful operation

To operate as an integrated system requires members of the chain to operate as a team (Buzzell and Ortmeyer 1995). Ways have to be found of ensuring that any conflicting objectives of individual members of the channel are reconciled with the interests of the operation of the channel as a whole.

Magrath and Hardy (1987) identify a number of strategies employed by companies that can create conflict in the channel:

- *bypassing channels*: skipping established channels and selling direct to the customer;

- *over-saturation*: appointing too many resellers in a designated area, which, whilst achieving the object of coverage for the manufacturer, can restrict sales opportunities for individual dealers or franchisees;

- *new channels*: developing innovative channels that pose a threat to established channel partici-

pants, although they may be necessary to develop a competitive advantage or simply to keep up with the competition;

- *Cost-cutting*: utilizing wholesalers that are viewed as 'discounters' by established wholesalers and that, as a consequence, could damage the image of product lines;

- *inconsistency*: treating some intermediaries or manufacturers more favourably than others and generally behaving in an arbitrary manner, thus provoking confusion and ill-feeling among channel members.

A company that engages in some of these procedures over time succeeds only in perpetuating an adversarial relationship. This is not a happy situation for its partners in the marketing channel.

It can, however, be argued that constructive conflict is a healthy phenomenon in channel relationships: it can keep other members of the channel 'on their toes', knowing that a drop in performance might lead to a change in the channel arrangements. Thus a correct balance needs to be achieved between a healthy competitive atmosphere and an unduly authoritarian, restrictive, and damaging approach.

4.3 Resolving conflict

It is too simplistic to assume that conflict can be eliminated in any channel relationship. Rather, it is more realistic to adopt a policy of conflict minimization. Since the end of the 1980s the formulation of manufacturer–intermediary partnerships has emerged as a significant trend in marketing-channel relationships (Michman 1990; Joseph et al. 1995). Such partnership-style arrangements are characterized by a high degree of coordinated effort and planning, and full sharing of information.

Narus and Anderson (1987) suggest that intermediaries and manufacturers need to follow certain guidelines in order to improve the quality of the working relationship.

- Reach consensus on the role of each party in the marketing channel. This requires both parties accepting that the overall objective of the channel should be to minimize the total cost and/or to maximize the total value associated with moving goods from point of purchase to point of consumption. This involves both parties engaging in

Figure 11.4 **Supply-chain integration**

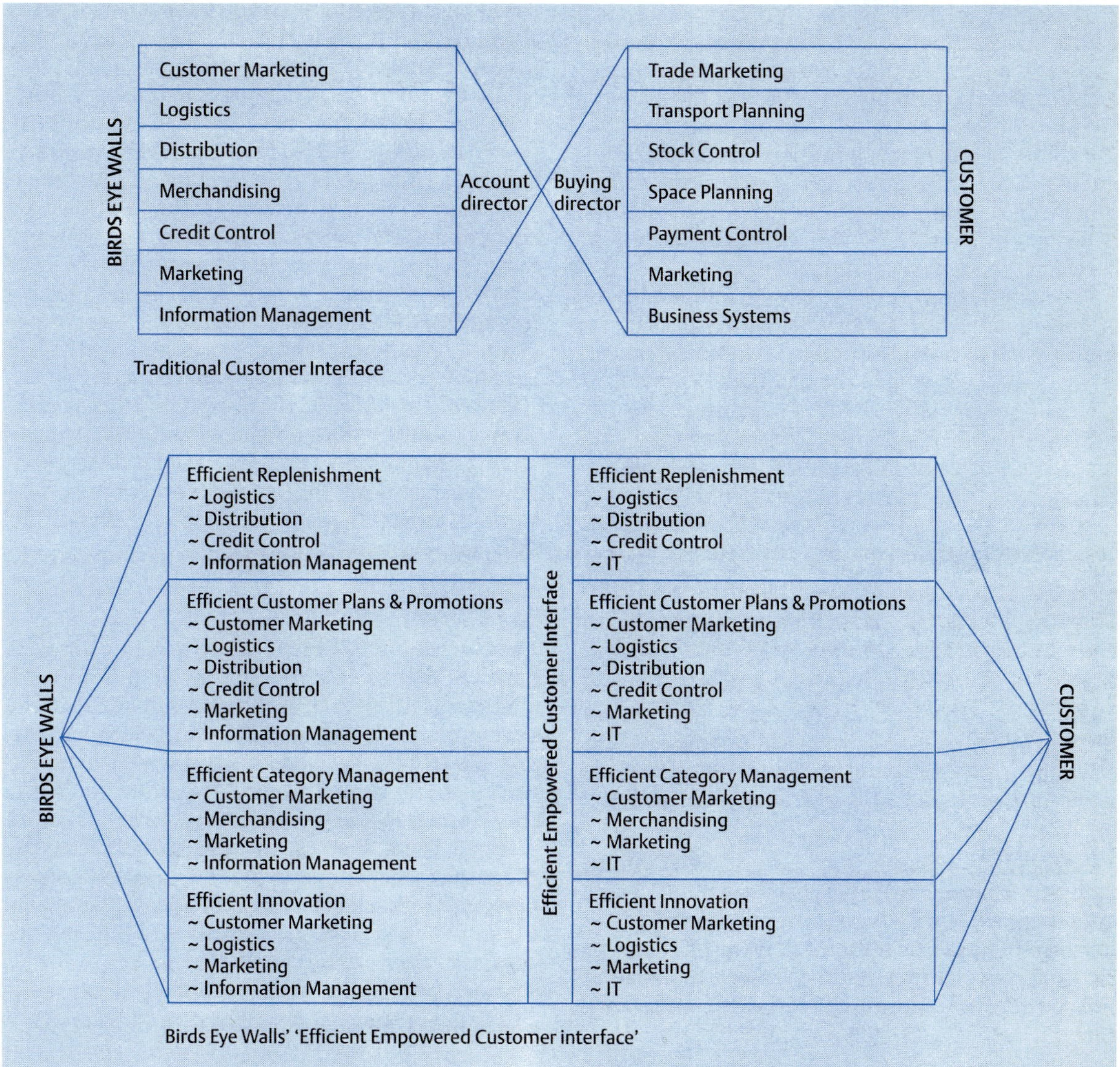

BIRDS EYE WALLS		Account director	Buying director		CUSTOMER
	Customer Marketing			Trade Marketing	
	Logistics			Transport Planning	
	Distribution			Stock Control	
	Merchandising			Space Planning	
	Credit Control			Payment Control	
	Marketing			Marketing	
	Information Management			Business Systems	

Traditional Customer Interface

Efficient Replenishment
~ Logistics
~ Distribution
~ Credit Control
~ Information Management

Efficient Customer Plans & Promotions
~ Customer Marketing
~ Logistics
~ Distribution
~ Credit Control
~ Marketing
~ Information Management

Efficient Category Management
~ Customer Marketing
~ Merchandising
~ Marketing
~ Information Management

Efficient Innovation
~ Customer Marketing
~ Logistics
~ Marketing
~ Information Management

Efficient Replenishment
~ Logistics
~ Distribution
~ Credit Control
~ IT

Efficient Customer Plans & Promotions
~ Customer Marketing
~ Logistics
~ Distribution
~ Credit Control
~ Marketing
~ IT

Efficient Category Management
~ Customer Marketing
~ Merchandising
~ Marketing
~ IT

Efficient Innovation
~ Customer Marketing
~ Logistics
~ Marketing
~ IT

BIRDS EYE WALLS

Efficient Empowered Customer Interface

CUSTOMER

Birds Eye Walls' 'Efficient Empowered Customer interface'

market research and operating on a policy of 'open-line' communication.

■ Appreciate each channel member's requirements. By visiting the manufacturer's plant and observing such activities as ordering procedures and quality management activities, the intermediary can gain a clearer picture of the potential difficulties that can occur in terms of getting a product delivered on time. Likewise, by making joint visits to trade fairs and to customers, and sharing infor-

mation, both parties can achieve a more harmonious working relationship.

■ Fulfil commitments. Given that most channel members will look for evidence that partners should be proficient in a number of areas such as prompt payment of bills, financial stability, market knowledge, and so on, the onus is on all channel members to examine performance levels in these areas and seek improvement where possible.

4.4 **Managing power in the marketing channel**

A further potential source of conflict is the role played by power—although power, if properly exercised, can also be a positive force in the smooth operation of the channel. Using power refers to the ability of one party to influence other channel members and ultimately get them to do something that they might not otherwise have done. It is heavily influenced by the level of dependency between the various channel members.

In this respect, it is fair to say that all members of the channel are interdependent, so that, to some extent at least, the potential for using power resides with everyone in the channel. However, as the channel structure evolves over time, and becomes established, a channel leader emerges, and that leader or captain can wield considerable influence over other parties in the channel.

There are different bases upon which power can be achieved and subsequently utilized:

- *reward*: if a channel member performs a specific function effectively, something of value will be given as a form of reward, e.g. discounts;
- *coercion*: the 'stick' approach, where a channel member can threaten another into performing certain roles or tasks by withdrawing certain privileges or terminating an agreement if expectations are not met, e.g. a franchising arrangement;
- *legitimization*: based on an understanding that one channel member has a right to exert influence on other channel members; this may stem from patent or trademark laws, or from the fact that one channel member is well established and power has traditionally resided with that party;
- *referent*: where the source of power is the deference shown by one channel member to another; it is particularly evident when one channel member has achieved a brand franchise and where intermediaries take a certain pride in stocking that brand, or when retailers have particularly distinctive retail brands;
- *expert*: where a channel member has access to a more cost-effective supply base or retains more detailed and accurate industry information than other channel members.

In practice, it is unlikely that any channel leader will rely on one single basis for achieving power. A combination of the various bases is more realistic, and the precise manner in which they are used is based on the specific situation facing the company at a particular point in time. It is also dangerous to assume that, once the power base has been established by a particular channel member, it cannot then be altered. We have seen many shifts in power in different industry sectors. For instance, the traditional power base in many product areas has resided with the manufacturers. However, since about the 1980s, in the USA and Western Europe, this has swung dramatically to large retailer businesses, whose scale of purchasing has given them considerable power over other channel members. This is discussed further in Section 7 and was also discussed in Chapter 4.

If used correctly and in the right balance, a company can drive more efficiency and effectiveness among channel members. However, if the focus of power is based on unduly harsh or negative measures, it creates a potential recipe for dissatisfaction and, ultimately, conflict.

4.5 **Partnerships**

The careful management of the relationship with partners is thus essential for the system to work effectively. An outline of the stages involved in the development of partnerships can be seen in Fig. 11.5. Clearly the social context in which such networks operate cannot be underestimated. While the contact between different parties is often referred to as that of business to business, the practical reality suggests that it is driven by interpersonal contact between individuals. Thus *relationship management* is central to the overall administration of the channel.

To achieve this in turn requires:

- synchronization of business philosophies and strategies;
- commitment of senior management;
- maximizing the potential of modern information technology and communications;
- high levels of information-sharing;
- culture and attitudes within businesses that favour cooperation;
- performance indicators and company structures that reflect the need for cooperation.

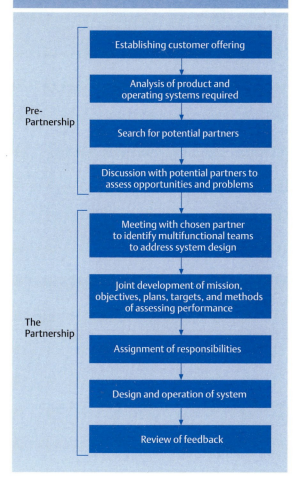

Figure 11.5 **Developing supply-chain partnerships**

Pre-Partnership

- Establishing customer offering
- Analysis of product and operating systems required
- Search for potential partners
- Discussion with potential partners to assess opportunities and problems

The Partnership

- Meeting with chosen partner to identify multifunctional teams to address system design
- Joint development of mission, objectives, plans, targets, and methods of assessing performance
- Assignment of responsibilities
- Design and operation of system
- Review of feedback

5 Efficient consumer response

THE most exciting recent development in the management of supply chains, particularly for fast moving consumer goods (FMCG) such as food and clothing is *efficient consumer response* (ECR), which has been defined as 'a total system to eliminate all activities that do not give value to the end consumer and to encourage all those that do' (Mitchell 1997). To achieve this aim ECR focuses on fourteen ECR improvement concepts in three

strands (Fig. 11.6). Some explanations of the strands and concepts are necessary.

☞ 'By jointly focusing on the efficiency of the total grocery supply system, rather than the efficiency of individual components, retailers and suppliers are reducing total system costs, inventories, and physical assets, while improving the consumer's choice of high-quality, fresh grocery products.' (Chapter 14, p. 344)

5.1 Category management

Category management originated in retailing with a desire to improve retail management. A category is a distinct, manageable group of products/services that consumers believe to be interrelated and/or substitutable in meeting a consumer need (Lamey 1996). In category management a group of cross-functional retail managers is assigned to a category group. This approach recognizes that marketing, in-store product management, allocation of shelf space, sourcing, and logistics cannot be considered separately. Within retailing, this has led to reorganization of activities into groups with category rather than functional responsibilities. These are replacing retail marketing, merchandising, and buying departments, which traditionally had a broader focus across products but were less integrated within the category. An example of a category might be women's coats or canned soups. The aim is to ensure the right mix of products, reduce the number of failed product launches, and ensure that all promotions of product are in line with plans for the category as a whole. These plans are built up after an examination of the market opportunities for the category and the levels of customer satisfaction with products in the category, and a comparison with other categories to ensure that products are not mixed up or duplicated. Today this is greatly facilitated by the large amounts of data that retainers collect from electronic point of sale (EPOS) systems.

Retail category management plans are then linked with functions being performed by other members of the supply chain, particularly manufacturers but including the third-party logistics companies.

Figure 11.6 **The fourteen core ECR concepts**

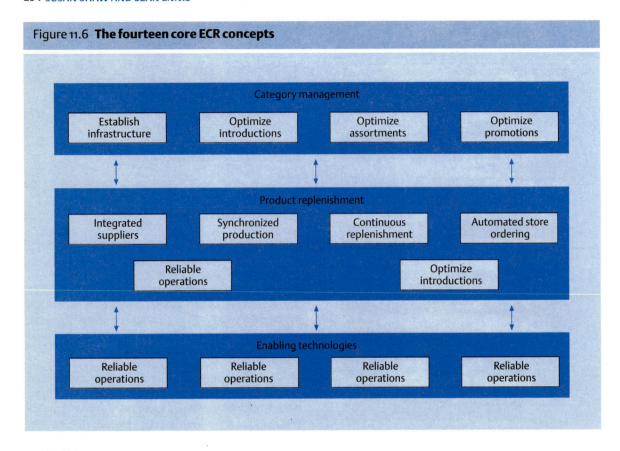

5.2 **Electronic data interchange systems**

ECR is facilitated by electronic data interchange systems (EDI). EDI is the exchange of information and documentation between two or more trading partners sent electronically between two computers. Since trading partners often have different hardware and software, many companies use services offered by telecommunications companies called value-added network services (VANS), which can reconfigure data to ensure that messages in one format can be understood in another. The use of EDI is critical to the success of ECR, because it allows businesses to eliminate large amounts of labour-intensive but non-value-added work, such as rekeying paper documents, and to speed up response times.

The activities in EDI implementation include:

- aligning data throughout the chain;
- sending and receiving orders;
- exchanging invoices;

- exchanging prices and other terms of business;
- stipulating product details such as item codes, details of packing (e.g. number of items per case, cases per pallet), etc.;
- creating delivery notes, receipt notes, order confirmations, credit notes, inventory details.

5.3 **Electronic funds transfer**

Linked to EDI is electronic funds transfer (EFT), which means that orders automatically generate the payments to support them. Invoicing is based on received and accepted goods, which immediately generates the appropriate EDI payment scheme.

5.4 **Activity-based costing**

Activity-based costing is the modern approach to costing in the supply chain. It identifies all costs associated with a particular activity across functions and businesses in the value chain.

By establishing what is spent on different activities in an accurate and detailed way, this allows the supply chain to question expenditure and why the activity is undertaken, leading to a continuous process of improvement.

These concepts are new. By the mid-1990s, the USA was the most advanced user of EDI (Lamey 1996). Mitchell (1997) reports a survey conducted by Kurt Salmon in the USA in 1994 that suggested that 85 per cent of retailers and 83 per cent of manufacturers were committed to ECR. Within Europe the use of ECR is patchy. In Europe it is suggested that the average level of usage among European manufacturers is 35 per cent for retailers and 38 per cent for manufacturers. This conceals considerable variations between countries, with the fastest progress among the supply systems of large retailers in the UK. For example, Tesco, the largest UK food retailer, is linked to over 13,000 suppliers through EDI. This network is used for data exchanges, forecasting, transactions, order requests, delivery notes, and invoices. There is no doubt that ECR approaches are demanding in management time, capital investment, and cultural change. Equally, early results suggest that this will in time become a common approach. Mitchell (1997) suggests benefits worth 10 per cent or more on the supply side and profitability gains of 30 per cent on the demand side.

6 Designing supply chains

THE functions of supply chains have been described above, as have some general characteristics of retailing and wholesaling intermediaries. The step from this, however, to the design of a channel structure is not a straightforward one. According to Kotler the question is not whether these (channel) functions need to be performed but rather who is to perform them. All the functions use up scarce resources and can often be better performed through specialization, but they are also shiftable among channel members.

Responsibility shifts from one party to another, depending on the nature of the product market being addressed. Roles that are traditionally performed by one party in the chain may be passed on to another intermediary, back to the manufacturer, or indeed on to a new channel intermediary.

For example, many of the traditional functions performed by travel agents may now be handled by the web page of an airline, as customers will increasingly be in a position to purchase tickets directly over the Internet. This concept of shiftability has significant implications for channel design because it highlights the dynamic and constantly changing nature of channel structures.

Whichever member of the supply chain performs a function, its costs are likely to go up as a result, so that the issue as to who should carry out various functions is one of relative efficiency and effectiveness. Stern et al. (1993) focus on designing a strategy that is based on the needs and demands of the customer in areas such as:

- order size;
- location;
- convenience;
- delivery time;
- product variety;
- after-sales service.

Such a scheme also recognizes that there are likely to be multiple requirements from the customer base. Customers have to be segmented on the basis of their distribution needs and requirements. This is particularly so in business-to-business markets, where the impact of order size and company size can dramatically affect the level of customer service demanded of the manufacturer or supplier.

For these reasons, supply chains are characterized by enormous variety. At this point we return to the very important distinction that must be made between the actors with ownership or transactions roles in the channel (retailers and wholesalers) and the use of third-party logistics companies.

6.1 Ownership and transactions structures

Key issues in the design of marketing-channel structures are illustrated through the example of different marketing channels for a gourmet food in the UK (Fig. 11.7). The shortest channels are those where the manufacturer performs all functions and deals directly with the consumer. At a small scale, this can happen when the manufacturer sells directly to consumers through factory outlets or shops owned by the business. Thus our

Figure 11.7 **Contrasting marketing-channel structures**

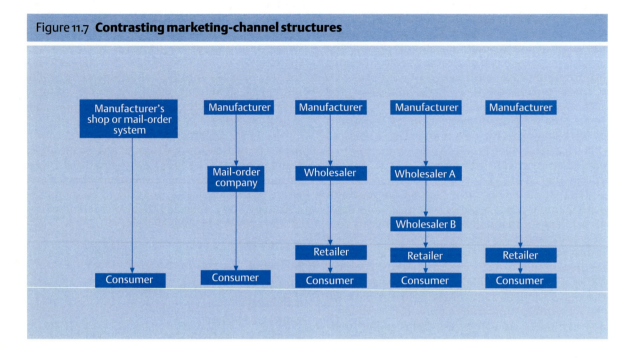

gourmet food manufacturer runs a shop on site, where visitors can purchase products. More commonly, manufacturers who wish to reach consumers directly can do so through mail order and catalogue sales. In this case we will assume that our manufacturer advertises the speciality food in magazines. Consumers place orders directly with the manufacturer by phone, fax, and so on, and the manufacturer in due course dispatches the product (although it may use a third-party distributor to transport and deliver the product). The manufacturer also sells the product to specialist mail-order companies, who act as marketers of the product as well.

The manufacturer operates in longer channels by selling the product to wholesalers, who in turn supply a range of retailers in the UK and elsewhere in Europe. Sometimes there may be two wholesale stages involved in international business transactions, although this is now relatively rare within the UK itself.

The manufacturer also sells large volumes of the product directly to major UK retailers, for sale both under its own brand name and under retailer brand names (see Chapter 20). In this case also there may be outside facilitators because the retailer may use a third-party operator to manage warehousing and logistics (see Section 6.2).

A major factor in decisions on channel structures is the nature and size of the market and the costs of reaching it by different routes. Manufacturers who can attract adequate numbers of customers to their own retail outlets may prefer the enhanced control and the opportunity to earn profit from all value-adding activities by operating facilities themselves. They need to be skilled retailers as well as manufacturers for this option to be successful. Some manufacturers successfully manage this combination. The Swiss shoe manufacturer Bally has operated successfully on this basis for many years. By contrast, the troubled British clothing and furniture retailer and manufacturer Laura Ashley is divesting itself of much of its manufacturing facilities because of an inability to manage them in a manner that allows it to supply its retail outlets in a customer-responsive, flexible, and cost-competitive manner.

Mail-order sales are attractive to those consumers who prefer to choose products without the need for shopping trips. The more specialist the product and the narrower the market, the more difficult it may be to persuade retailers to stock it, so that mail order can be a means of ensuring more widespread availability than possible with retailer distribution.

Traditionally—at least in the UK until the 1970s

and this was still the case in many countries in the 1990s—manufacturers sold to national or regionally based wholesalers, who in turn sold product to retailers. The dominant motive for the use of this longer channel relates to the structure of retailing. Where retailing is in the hands of large numbers of independent businesses, it would be neither efficient nor effective for the manufacturer to deal directly with them. The imbalance between the pattern of orders of the individual retailer and the manufacturer is too great for this to be a cost-effective solution. Therefore, the wholesaler buys in bulk from the manufacturer and breaks bulk to sell to individual retailers. This is still the main route for sales to small retail businesses and this is why the gourmet food manufacturer sells to regional wholesalers, who in turn sell to small specialist retail delicatessens. Traditionally the wholesaler would also carry out a number of other functions such as transport and warehousing through internal ownership of transport fleets and storage facilities. This still occurs but became less common in the 1990s because of the development of third-party logistics.

The gourmet food manufacturer also sells direct to retailers. By the end of the twentieth century in many European countries, shorter channels had become the dominant supply route to consumers for many different types of product, with direct dealing between the manufacturer and the retailer. This change had been driven by the changing retail structures discussed earlier. The scale of ordering by the retailer had obviated the need to deal with wholesalers, and direct purchases from manufacturers had been a source of savings in logistics costs. It had also been a means of securing improved information transmission because of the smaller number of links. Intermediaries might still be used by large retailers in some cases for sourcing of smaller volumes of product internationally, but the norm was for direct dealing with manufacturers and other producers globally for products of significance to the retailer. The developments in and availability of third-party logistics companies had facilitated this.

6.2 Logistics networks and the role of warehousing

Regardless of ownership structures, all operators must find the optimal sites for warehouses and the optimum numbers of warehouses in relation to the physical transport of goods. How many facilities are needed and where should they be located?

We return to earlier discussion of the functions carried out by the channel. Functions that can be carried out in distribution centres and warehouses are:

- *stockholding*: to balance the mismatch between production and demand;
- *consolidation and mixing*: to consolidate lot sizes to take advantages of bulk transport rates, to sort goods, and to convert homogeneous lots into heterogeneous lots in response to customer orders;
- *breaking bulk and transshipment*: to create assortments from large input loads.

Key consideration's in decisions on structure are:

- product volumes to be handled;
- mix of products and order sizes;
- network source and destination links and flows;
- transportation rates for different lot sizes and to different locations inbound and outbound from warehouses;
- warehouse operating costs for warehouses of different sizes and in different locations;
- product handling requirements and shelf life;
- customer service levels demanded and acceptable order cycle times.

Every logistics network involves a trade-off of the cost of different activities against each other (Fig. 11.8). The greater the number of warehouse facilities, the greater the cost of holding stock. A greater number of distribution centres increases market coverage but at the cost of increased stockholding and transportation costs. The challenge is to provide the required market coverage and service level at the lowest possible overall costs.

Retailing and manufacturing logistics have become increasingly controlled and centralized by retailers and manufacturers. Improvements in technology are also leading to reductions in the levels of stocks that have to be carried and increases in the speed of replenishment. The

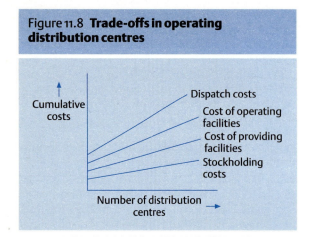

Figure 11.8 **Trade-offs in operating distribution centres**

speed of FMCGs through the warehouse has been increased through *cross-docking techniques* that transfer the product directly from inbound to outbound transport. As a consequence, warehouses and distribution centres are growing in size but falling in number. They are usually located close to major transport routes. Because of the dominance of road transport, this is usually close to major motorways in the UK. Four different types of warehouse can be found (Lamey 1996):

- *small storage facilities*: for buffer stocks;

- *manufacturer storage facilities*: for storing the product after manufacture and before entry into the channel;

- *local warehouses*: to service local markets, although small numbers of warehouses may serve large areas; Safeway, the retailer, distributes to its 129 stores in Scotland through one large warehouse in Scotland and one national distribution point in England;

- *central/national distribution centres*: to serve national markets.

Again, it is worth remembering the distinction between the physical distribution channel, which may/or may not be owned by the manufacturer, wholesaler, or retailer, and the transaction channel. The example of a parallel system with the use of third-party logistics companies can be seen in Fig. 11.9. When the retailer or manufacturer is considering whether to own or subcontract logistics,

there are key components for analysis. The advantages of dedicated facilities are:

- clear focus;
- no compromises on requirements;
- economies of scale for large operations;
- shorter information chain;
- less likelihood of inter-functional conflict;
- less inter-business conflict.

The advantages of third-party facilities are:

- more efficient use of facilities through higher utilization rates and a larger scale of operations;
- reduced risk and capital investment;
- activity handled by specialist.

7 Choosing partners— the retailer decision

SECTIONS 7 and 8 address the choice of channel partner. Given that the structure of the channel has been decided, who should be the partners? What does a business look for in the choice of the appropriate partner?

All members of the channel consider this question. We look first at the issues from the point of view of the retailer or wholesaler, who must examine the following:

- products sought and match of manufacturer with retail quality position;
- ability to meet orders;
- scale of operations;
- ability to grow product volumes with market development;
- lead times;
- efficient information systems;
- attitude and business culture of suppliers;
- willingness to work in an integrated manner;
- willingness to change;
- potential profit margins;
- marketing support from suppliers.

The mix will vary with the market position of the retailer. A retailer demanding high-quality prod-

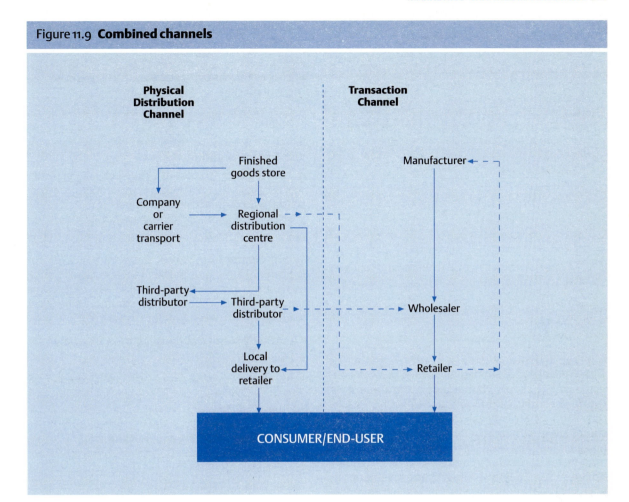

Figure 11.9 **Combined channels**

ucts for high-income consumers may well make different choices from those of a discount retailer mainly concerned to obtain low base prices and low operating costs.

Retailers are consolidating the number of their suppliers. Consolidation of the supplier base enables a retailer to reduce costs and simplify the supply chain through less documentation and more efficient organization of deliveries (see Insert overleaf). It becomes ever more important for the supplier to work with the retailers in the integrated way to keep them as customers.

Customers today demand higher quality at lower cost, rapid response, and immediate avail-

ability at the time of procurement and use (Gopal and Cypress 1993; Hanmer-Lloyd 1993). Retailers and others dealing directly with consumers evaluate suppliers not only on the basis of their products but also on other factors. The ability to deliver just in time, in small lots, and with great frequency is becoming increasingly important. Ability to package material for ease of use is also relevant, so that the total system from manufacturer to retailer is designed to minimize handling costs. Ability to preserve product quality to the final point at which the consumer buys is also essential and complex, particularly for fragile products with a short shelf life.

The power shift towards retailers

'The route to higher profit margins for retailers lies in . . . a power shift from manufacture to retailer. Before, retailers bought from their suppliers and had to wait for the customer to buy up the inventory. Today, with a demand-driven supply chain, the store demands that its suppliers manage product replenishment by assessing how quickly those products are selling.'

Source: Johnston (1998).

☞ 'As, however, retailers grew much larger and stronger over the years and as their shelf space became more scarce as a result of a growing number of different product (sub)categories, they became more demanding.' (Chapter 9, p. 207)

In the 1990s large retail businesses in the UK with considerable buying power sought more control over the supply chain. They sought a greater role in the products and product assortments that they sold. Their key position close to the consumer allowed them to take a much greater role in product creation and specification, which was manifested particularly in the rise of retail brands (Chapter 20). They also sought improvements in in-store product availability and general reductions in costs to be competitive with other retailers. As a result they needed to work in more closely integrated channels (see Insert, right). It is not surprising that retailer requirements have been one of the major pressures behind the development of ECR systems.

8 Choosing partners: the manufacturer's decision

First, the manufacturer must identify the objectives and relevant issues to be considered (Morden 1987), which are likely to be:

- how to gain access to the market;
- how to gain appropriate and adequate distribution coverage;

- how to build market share;
- how to achieve cost-effectiveness in gaining access;
- how to maximize revenue returns from the intermediaries;
- how to develop programmes that will *motivate* resellers;
- how to achieve the most cost-effective physical distribution of products;
- how to present a cost-effective level of customer service that will, at the same time, maximize potential for competitive advantage;
- how to achieve consistency with other elements of the marketing mix.

While channel objectives must be specified for traditional financial performance measures such as volume, market share, profitability, and return on investment, operational channel objectives should also be developed for:

- market coverage and distribution intensity;
- channel control;
- flexibility.

Stores help with new product launch

In advance of the launch of its new product Fuse, Cadbury held seventy one-to-one briefings with key trade customers. As a result it secured orders for instore displays and merchandising ahead of the launch date and was able to make its first national launch for twenty years.

Source: Archer (1998: 54).

8.1 Market coverage and distribution intensity

Whether a manufacturer pursues an intensive, selective, or exclusive distribution strategy depends, to a large degree, on its overall strategic corporate objectives. For example, if a volume-maximizing strategy is adopted, an intensive approach will be used with many intermediaries and channels to get widespread coverage. A selective strategy, on the other hand, uses a limited number of intermediaries, who may be given exclusive rights within their sales areas. The latter may be more appropriate if a company adopts a differentiation strategy, because a selective range of intermediaries has a bigger incentive to promote quality and image. Exclusive distribution can also be relevant to a product that requires major input from intermediaries in terms of selling and promotional effort.

8.2 Channel control

The more intermediaries and tiers of distribution that exist, the smaller the likelihood that the manufacturer can maintain maximum control over its products and associated services. This will be particularly the case in areas such as pricing, determination of margins, the type of selling effort required, and the maintenance of a consistent product image and quality. It is important that manufacturers achieve a balance between market coverage and control objectives. In this respect, intensive distribution would be inconsistent, with a strong desire on the part of the company to retain as much control as possible.

☞ '. . . manufacturer research may characterize the product as a certain winner, but the retailer does not blindly accept this and refuses to carry the product.' (Chapter 10, p. 229)

In many markets suppliers face a situation where a small number of organizations dominate the distribution channels. This is clearly the case in the market for groceries, where in the UK a small number of very large retail chains dominate the market. In such situations the supplier may find that any demand that large customers make can be very difficult to resist, because they represent such a proportion of the available market. To manage the relationships with such large customers, it is now common to appoint key-account managers, who have overall responsibility for the relationship between the supplier and perhaps only one customer.

☞ 'Very often, key-account managers have already negotiated with the retailers' procurement managers whether a certain brand will be stocked by supermarkets or not.' (Chapter 13, p. 299)

8.3 Flexibility

It can be dangerous for manufacturers to lock into a rigid approach in their relationships with intermediaries, given that most markets and environments are dynamic. Existing channel arrangements will have to be modified or changed entirely in order to counteract changes in customer preference, for example. The car industry provides an interesting example of the need to respond to a new business environment (*Financial Times* 1998). A significant development in the last two decades of the twentieth century occurred in the design of cars. Japanese car-makers dramatically reduced the time and costs of designing and assembling a new model, cutting the process from about six to two years. By the end of the twentieth century product developments in both Europe and the USA began to reach Japanese standards, as had a cost-cutting and quality-improving assault on assembly. This was evidenced by the concept of lean manufacturing and was driven by much closer control over the components bought in from suppliers.

The car dealers represented the next revolutionary change. Distribution accounts for 20–30 per cent of the value added of a car and represented a large area of waste in distribution. Achieving changes in this area has proved to be more difficult because car dealers are mostly independent firms and therefore the car-makers have had less control over them than over components suppliers.

The main challenge still remaining at the turn of the century was to reduce the 'order-to-delivery' time. In the 1990s, a long period elapsed between the time a customer ordered a vehicle and the time it was sent from the factory to the dealer. Often the car sat expensively in large parks near the factory. Car-makers believe that this time factor can only be reduced by working much more closely with the dealer, so that they can integrate what the customers order more closely with what they themselves make. This will also allow them to meet the customer's specification, rather than some alternative from the dealer's lot—thus reducing the need for discounting.

Up to the mid-1990s, car-makers had worked on the principle of bombarding geographic areas with dealers in an attempt to maximize profits and market shares. Hence, many countries had (and at the turn of the century) continued to have too many small dealers, often with unskilled staff. In the mid-1990s France and Germany had one dealer per 3,000 people but the USA had one per 5,000.

However, consumer behaviour is changing. At

the end of the twentieth century more people owned cars, which meant that consumers were willing to travel further to shop. Saturation ownership in mature markets had cut the rate of growth in new car sales, leading to lower profits for dealers. Declining brand loyalties, linked partly to the arrival of new marques, had reinforced the reassessment of established sales networks. And cars' greater safety and reliability had cut dealer's profits from repairs and servicing—two areas that had formerly compensated for lower margins on sales.

The expectation is that early in the twenty first century bigger dealerships will be the order of the day—with more expensive staff and premises, leading to greater economies of scale in advertising and the back office. The model for this is General Motor's Saturn subsidiary, where by the end of the 1990s showrooms were well appointed, bright staff were salaried, and every dealership sold cars at a fixed price, with no haggling or high pressure pitches.

Daewoo of South Korea, in its UK operations, eschewed conventional dealers in favour of direct sales to customers. Its approach, like that of Saturn, has been designed to take the pain out of purchasing by using trained, salaried staff to sell at fixed prices.

Saturn had the advantage of starting from scratch. Revitalizing existing networks is more difficult and consolidation is critical.

In the USA, three companies, Republic Industries, CarMax, and Auto Nation, have revolutionized used-car sales by creating nation-wide chains working to high standards. In the mid-1990s Republic bought out Auto Nation and moved into the new-car sales area by buying and merging family-owned dealerships.

In the UK it may prove to be easier to implement change, given the number of well-capitalized, professionally run dealer chains such as Reg Vardy and Evans Halshaw. These chains are likely to be more keen to entertain ideas such as swapping territories than family firms.

Ford has been the busiest of all. It has redrawn its dealership network in the UK into 112 new areas based on changing demographic and consumer patterns. About 60 per cent of sales are going through reorganized zones. This model is likely to be replicated in continental Europe and the USA. Its immediate goal is to cut costs and improve dealers' returns. Its long-term aim is to turn dealers into 'antennae', reporting market trends to the factory directly by computer. This should allow for better forecasting and lead to reduced waste in manufacturing. Components can be ordered just when required and a massive reduction in the traditional stockpiling, associated with traditional supply chains in the car industry, can be achieved. Ford at the end of the 1990s was investing $400 million in its UK dealers and European plants to implement this scheme and aimed to cut the 'order-to-delivery' time to only fifteen days from six weeks, as was the case in 1992.

8.4 Selecting intermediaries

There are several important issues that can help a manufacturer to assess the relative merits of potential partners:

- financial position;
- depth and width of product lines carried;
- whether competitive lines are carried;
- evidence of marketing, sales, and promotional ability;
- approach to order processing and fulfilment;
- capability and or/willingness to invest in IT (e.g. EDI);
- reputation within the industry;
- reputation in local, national, and international markets;
- willingness to share data;
- capability in technical and support servicing (if relevant).

Not surprisingly, these are very similar to the comparable list of intermediary requirements for their partners that were listed earlier.

A number of methods can be devised for evaluating potential channel partners, in terms of their likely contribution. One method for selecting wholesale representatives has been developed by Marshall and Siegler (1993) and is outlined in Box 11.1. The exercise is not easy. While it may be possible to obtain a relatively accurate picture of an intermediary's financial position, it becomes more difficult to judge such factors as enthusiasm, managerial capability, or willingness to upgrade existing facilities. Judgement has to be used in interpreting results.

Box 11.1 **Independent wholesale representative checklist**

Does the independent representative

1. Have an internal customer service or telemarketing staff to work as a team, with its field sales people?
(up to 15 points)

2. Clearly understand the time needed properly to develop account relationships? (up to 10 points)

3. Initiate lead follow-up internally (rather than using field sales) to gain more information about needs rather than focusing on immediately offering a quote or making a sale? (up to 5 points)

4. Use the lead opportunity to sell synergistically rather than going for a one-product, one-shot approach? (up to 5 points)

5. Use leads as a way to search for information on new accounts as they build the relationship?
(up to 10 points)

6. Offer related high-quality products/services and have a good, long-term sales history?
(up to 5 points)

7. Follow up all leads the same week they are received and report back to you within three weeks as to the status of those leads? (up to 10 points)

8. Receive leads with enthusiasm and constantly ask for more? (up to 5 points)

9. Have automated account management systems for accurate and up-to-date record-keeping?
(up to 15 points)

10. Integrate its telemarketing efforts with field sales reps through a well-managed team effort and by sharing software and hardware? (up to 10 points)

Total Score

Maximum Score 100 points

Scoring

80–100 points: these are the cream of the crop; send a contact to them before a competitor does.

60–80 points: good firms that could move to the top-ranked group if you have a good lead management programme to help them achieve their full potential.

50–60 points: check their growth plans: they may be ready to add some tools that will take them to the top level.

Below 50 points: keep looking; and don't forget: there are thousands of organizations out there to choose from. You deserve the best—especially if you have invested the time, effort, and money to design a lead generation programme that will support your rep firm.

Source: Marshall and Siegler (1993: 83)

9 Retailing

In Sections 9 and 10, we turn to two specialist examples: retailing and franchising. The position of retailing as the closest link in the supply chain to the final consumer gives it some distinctive characteristics that are different from those of manufacturing firms and different in emphasis from other intermediaries. These differences are best understood by exploring the elements of positioning that were introduced earlier. There are four interrelated elements that define retail positioning (Harris and Walters 1992): merchandising decisions, trading format, customer service, and customer communications (see Box 11.2).

9.1 The retail elements and their relationships

Retailers take *merchandising decisions* on the basis of the intrinsic characteristics of the products and on the way in which products can link together in an assortment to maximize profitability. The retailer wishes to know, when introducing a new product range, whether the range can make more profit for the shelf space that it occupies than the products that it replaces. The elements of retail profit on a product line are a combination of:

■ *margins per unit*—the differences between buying prices, costs of the retailer in making the product available in store, and selling prices;

■ *volume of sales*—speed of turnover of product for given shelf space;

Box 11.2 **Elements in retail positioning**

Merchandising decisions
- key product groups
- merchandise width—the different lines of products for sale
- merchandise depth or assortment—the selection within any product line
- merchandise quality
- branding strategy (e.g. manufacturer brand ranges, retail brand ranges)
- Price points

Trading format
- the location, size, and number of outlets
- convenience of access
- external design and facilities
- in-store design
- display themes

Customer service
- advice
- credit services
- delivery services
- after-sales service
- the transactions process

Customer communications
- in store
- media and creative approach—themes, media choice, spend
- public relations—national, local

■ *impact on sales of other products*—will the presence of this item in store bring more customers to the shop and hence increase sales of other products?

Format decisions are based on the type of internal and external shopping environment that will attract customers. Location decisions are based on a variety of factors.

■ *Accessibility*. This needs to be considered for car-borne passengers, and for those who arrive on foot or by other transport, and in relation to other shops.

■ *Convenience of shopping environment*. Externally this covers matters such as car parking and covered access. Internally it covers all aspects of store design including aisle layout, lighting, display systems, and so on.

■ *Costs of land*. If lower site development costs enable the retailer to charge lower prices, this can attract consumers to such locations. They can also justify larger assortments, if they reduce the margins required so that lower margins or slower moving goods can be sold.

■ *Competition*. This has two aspects. Some types of retailers may not wish to be geographically too close to their competitors because they fear there will be excessive competition. For example, out-of-town superstores are anxious to obtain sites well away from their competitors. Other types of retailers believe there are benefits in being close to competitors, as this creates 'a centre' to which customers are attracted because of the choice it provides. Thus jewellery shops are often close together.

Decisions on *communications* and *customer service* reflect and complement decisions made on *merchandising* and *trading format*, but can also be very important features in competitive success. For instance, the success of the retailer Vision Express is built on service differentiation through fast provision of spectacles.

All the elements are, in any case, inextricably related. Decisions on *merchandising* are closely interrelated with decisions on *trading format*. At one extreme, specialist shops retailing very narrow lines such as—say—watches and limited amounts of jewellery (Watches of Switzerland) rely on the consumer's willingness to visit that trading format for that item alone. At the other extreme, larger stores such as Sainsburys that sell very large numbers of food and non-food items rely on the ranges as a major competitive advantage, because the consumer wishes to purchase a large selection of these items during a single shopping trip. Willingness to visit a shop in turn depends on the relationship between the merchandising assortment and the physical location of the shop. For example, a specialist limited-line snack store such as a sandwich shop may survive well on a busy high street because it is in an area to which many people have easy access. Such shops would not survive well if longer special trips had to be made to visit, because customers would not consider it worth the effort or time for a relatively minor item. By contrast, a small specialist women's clothing shop carrying major brands could survive in a less dense location, because its customers would be willing to make a special effort to visit. Customers are willing to drive considerable distances to food supermarkets that may be remote from other shops—but only because the large assortment of goods justifies the trip.

Customer-service strategy is also closely linked to *merchandising decisions*. Consumers have an expectation of the type of service they will receive for particular levels and qualities of goods—for instance, the role and quality of advice available can reinforce the confidence of consumers in the products available, as does willingness to handle faulty purchases in a customer-friendly way. Media used for *communication strategy* will reflect the target markets, and the messages used in the advertising and public relations of the retailer should reflect the core product values of the *merchandising decisions*.

9.2 Shopping and store selection

To design the appropriate coordinated strategy for all these elements requires an understanding of consumer product preferences and of shopping motivation. Fig. 11.10 shows how consumers' preferences influence shopping activity.

9.3 Outcomes: retail position and store type

The combination of products and different shopping motivations gives rise to a wide variety of retail formats. Fig. 11.1 showed format variety along a price–quality spectrum in the retail clothing sector. A small number of other examples can be seen in Box 11.3—but it should be stressed that the variety of different store formats and locations is much greater than can be indicated here.

10 Franchising

The second specialist example is of a management system: franchising.

Franchising has been one of the most popular mechanisms for expanding the distribution network since the 1980s (Hoy 1994). The typical franchise relationship involves satellite enterprises (run by franchisees) operating under the trade name and business format of a larger organization (the franchisor) in exchange for a continuing service fee and (usually) a front-end payment. The

franchisee sets up his or her business along standards specified by the franchisor. The main advantage to the franchisor is that it allows the company to achieve national and/or global coverage quickly and without the costs of leasing or buying premises that are associated with other forms of business expansion. Most of the capital is put up by the franchisee. The latter benefits from getting the chance to run a business that has been proven to work in the marketplace and gets the further benefit of advice and a broad range of support services from the franchisor. Table 11.1 provides some statistical evidence on the popularity of franchising in Europe.

The nature of the franchise relationship can be viewed from two extremes. Rubin (1978) argues that the franchised enterprise is, in reality, a managed outlet featuring in the larger marketing pattern of another truly independent business—that of the franchisor. Stanworth (1995) observes that this distribution strategy has certain advantages for the larger enterprise, but, just because the manager of the outlet has a capital stake in the business, that is no reason to confuse a franchise outlet with a genuinely independent business. He notes that the franchised small business may be viewed as an emerging form of independent small

Table 11.1 **European franchising, 1997**		
Country employed	Franchises (no.)	Outlets (no.)
Austria	210	3,000
Belgium	170	3,500
Denmark	98	2,000
France	470	25,750
Germany	530	22,000
Hungary	220	5,000
Italy	436	21,390
Netherlands	345	11,910
Portugal	220	2,000
Spain	288	13,161
Sweden	230	9,150
UK	474	25,700
TOTAL	3,691	144,561

Source: European Franchise Association, European Franchise Survey (Aug. 1997).

Figure 11.10 **Shopping attitudes and store selection**

Store selection and purchasing decision process	Task oriented (convenience dominated)	Pleasure oriented (environment dominated)
Pre-purchase Search Comparison	Convenient location Ample parking Close to other task-oriented stores Relevant merchandise selection	Exclusive store merchandise Wide choice Prestigious image
During purchase Product augmentation	High availability	Ambience and excitement Visual merchandising
Transactions Facilities	Competitive prices Rapid cash-handling	In-store facilities Product-service centres Credit facilities
Post-purchase Delivery Installation Use extension Evaluation Repeat visits	Product displays and customer advice areas	Theme displays and customer advice areas

business in advanced industrial societies which has as a distinguishing characteristic its overt and close relationship with another, usually larger, enterprise.

Franchising is more developed in the USA than in Europe. The significance of its contribution to the US economy cannot be underestimated. Stanworth (1995) lists the following statistics about franchising in the USA in 1990:

- franchising accounted for 35 per cent of all retail sales in the USA;
- franchising accounted for 10 per cent of Gross National Product;
- franchising expanded by around 300 per cent between 1975 and 1990.

A number of factors have been identified by Stanworth that suggest that growth in franchising within Europe can be expected. They can be summarized as follows:

- worldwide decline in traditional manufacturing industry and its replacement by service-sector activities;
- growth in the overall popularity of self-employment;
- increasing female participation in the workforce and rising numbers of dual-career and dual-income families will result in an increase in home service franchises;
- demands of an ageing population—special needs in the fields of leisure and care.

Stanworth notes that it does not appear that franchise operations will substantially displace conventional small business. When challenges to this sector occur, it is mainly because franchise acts as a new force in the field.

Porter and Renforth (1978) point to typical problems that can arise and that lead to litigation between the franchisor and franchisees. These

Box 11.3 **Retail formats: some examples**

Format	Consumer requirements	Merchandise	Store format	Example
Discount store	Low prices	Wide product range with few lines, variable to low quality	Relatively large, suburban, secondary high street	Aldi What Everyone Wants
Convenience store	Time/convenience	Premium prices, wide ranges, few lines, usually leading brands	Small suburban sites or major traffic routes	7 Eleven Tesco Metro
Superstore	Time/convenience	Wide ranges, good quality at competitive prices	Out of town high quality environment	Tesco main format
Style shop	Design/originality exclusivity	Premium prices, narrow product ranges, few lines, high quality	High street, shopping centre, exclusive format	Bally Gucci
Specialist store	Choice	Narrow ranges but great depth	Varies	Tie Rack Sports Connection
Department store	Wide and deep ranges	Town centres and shopping centres	Format varies with positioning on quality/style dimensions	Debenhams John Lewis

typically occur over issues such as advertising costs, inspection and evaluation, performance requirements, and fees for support services. Global franchisors such as Benetton and the Body Shop have encountered problems and conflict with their franchisees over issues such as territory allocations and a refusal to take back unsold stock.

Part of the conflict is also due to the nature of the relationship between the franchisor and the franchisee. On the one hand, the franchisee may like to be perceived as an entrepreneur: someone who is willing to take risks and who likes to be independent, try out new ideas, and generally be in charge of things. On the other hand, a typical franchise arrangement is predicated on the basis of regulations, procedures, and a tightly drawn-up contractual agreement. This may be at odds with

what the typical entrepreneur might expect from a business enterprise and poses major managerial problems for the franchisor in terms of ensuring that consistent standards are maintained across the franchise base. There is a great need for more substantive research in this area before general guidelines and principles can be put forward.

11 **The future**

The single biggest development that we are likely to witness in the first decade of the twenty-first century is the increasing attempt on the part of manufacturers to utilize electronic commerce. Some of the advantages are clearly demonstrated in the case study on Dell Direct (see Box 11.4).

Box 11.4 Dell direct and the Internet: the shape of things to come?

Dell Computer Corporation was founded by Michael Dell in 1983 and is now one of the biggest computer systems manufacturers in the world. In its 1997 financial year its net sales income increased 91 per cent to $518 million on revenues up 47 per cent to $7.8 billion. In its European operations, sales for 1997 topped $2 billion for the first time.

Dell attributes its success to the direct relationship model it has pioneered since the mid 1980s. This is based on the principle that delivering PCs custom built to specific customer orders provides the most relevant solution to end-user needs.

As a further stage in the evolution of the Dell Direct model, the corporation launched www.dell.com/uk in May 1997. As of March 1998, this new channel accounted for 10 per cent of its overall sales.

Worldwide, sales from Dell's web sites reached $4 million per day by March 1998—making Dell by far the biggest online computer vendor and one of the top five electronic traders in any industry.

Dell's view is that the Internet offers a better customer experience and allows it to get truly close to the customer in an interactive way. By clicking on the Buy a Dell icon on the web page, customers can select various options and generate instant price quotes. The 'Configurator' is Dell's online configuration system, which allows customers to tailor their own systems, with inbuilt controls to ensure that all configurations selected are legitimate. Customers can select a purchase button to submit a secure order electronically with a choice of online payments.

This has a number of key advantages for Dell:

- It produces to order, not to inventory. Only seven days' stock is carried in its plants and no finished stock is maintained at all.

- Any cost reductions achieved by Dell can be passed on

in the form of revised price quotations in a matter of three hours (the time it takes to update the web-site page). Contrast this with the four to five weeks it would take to book space and generate copy for print advertising.

- Every PC is built individually within five days from receipt of order to receipt of goods for small customers, forty-eight hours for larger corporate customers

- Every customer who has bought a PC is known. Great datamining can be carried out as a consequence. For instance, someone who bought a PC two years ago could benefit substantially from a communication from Dell. In future, as the Internet develops further, Dell can contact the customer by electronic means to give this information. Any number of products or services, upgrades, technical fixes, etc. can be offered because of the detailed personal profile the Web gives Dell.

- Unnecessary mark-ups can be eliminated because there are no resellers.

- 850 intra-web pages have been developed for companies. This allows the individual company to order direct from Dell via its own web page, and for centralized purchasing facilities to be operated. It allows customers to browse or order products—thus taking them through the purchase process. If they don't have the confidence to order via the Internet, they can phone in their order under the conventional DD model.

In 1998 Dell was selling $8 million per week in Europe via the Internet. It was experiencing a conversion rate of 23 per cent on callers to the site. It aims to improve this to a 33 per cent conversion rate by 2001. Likewise, Dell expects 50 per cent of its business to be carried out over the Internet in the same period.

Source: Hubbard, (1998).

The adoption of tools such as the Internet will speed up the process of 'disintermediation'—where many traditional intermediaries will either disappear or will reinvent themselves as new roles and responsibilities emerge. The attractions to the manufacturers of replacing or dispensing with intermediaries are obvious: economies of scale, greater control, and greater scope for passing on margins saved to the end-user or for investing back into the supply chains. As the Internet becomes more widely available to customers via the television set, we can anticipate more companies going the 'direct' route. As key retail players such

as Marks & Spencer follow this path, the competitors will quickly follow suit.

☞ 'In October 1994 Daewoo took the motor industry by storm with its announcement that it would take control of the distribution chain and deal direct with customers, eliminating dealers from the equation.' (Chapter 20, p. 487)

It is difficult to pinpoint with any accuracy how quickly and what percentage of consumers, for instance, will engage in direct shopping, as opposed to the traditional method of visiting stores. A study carried out by Coopers & Lybrand (1996*b*) suggested that only 5 per cent of food would go to new modes of shopping by the year 2005. However, this 5 per cent would still be worth $33 billion at 1994 prices—a sizeable opportunity.

Street (1998) identifies a number of anticipated impacts that arise from these new channels, such as the Internet, interactive shopping, and E-commerce. They are summarized as follows:

■ Consumer access will be increasingly multi-channel—it will be a case of selecting a portfolio of channels through which to compete.

■ Channels will increasingly be tailored to international and narrow bands that address the needs of a thin slice of the population in many countries rather than a wide slice of the population in one.

■ Multi-layering will become more common. For instance, the Royal Bank of Scotland has an arrangement whereby it accesses customers through Sainsbury in support of the retailer's loyalty card. This is likely to become more common in other sectors as people unbundle the value chain and reconfigure it, to dominate just one part—the area in which they can add value. This will place considerable pressure on companies to seek the right kind of alliances in accessing the customer effectively.

■ The classic position-based economics of retailing will be undermined. The appeal of direct home shopping is likely to be with the same high-value urban consumers that currently frequent the edge of town superstores, supermarkets, and hypermarkets across Europe. There is a big opportunity for rival operators to service these customers economically and undermine the economics of existing retailers.

12 Summary

The aims of the supply chain to the consumer are to provide an offer that the consumer will value and buy in preference to alternatives. This value is created by products and by the way in which time gaps, space gaps, quantity gaps, and variety gaps are bridged. These functions are performed by various combinations of manufacturers, and retail and wholesale intermediaries, with considerable structural variations between channels depending on the characteristics of products and markets. Valuable functions are also performed by third-party logistics companies, which organize transport and storage.

Supply chains have been changing as a result of the emergence of large powerful retail businesses that have wished to take more control over the operation of the supply chain, but changes have been greatly facilitated by developments in IT. For this reason, channel management requires an understanding of the way in which supply-chain functions can be integrated and coordinated among members. Marketing channels will continue to be dynamic and rapidly changing, because of the continuing impact of new information technologies.

Further reading

Buzzell, R. D., and Ortmeyer, G. (1995), 'Channel Partnerships Streamline Distribution', *Sloan Management Review*, 36 (Spring), 85–96.

Gattorna, J. L., and Walters, D. W. (1996), *Managing the Supply Chain: A Strategic Perspective* (London: Macmillan Business Books).

Gopal, C., and Cypress, H. (1993), *Integrated Distribution Management* (Homewood, Ill.: Business One Irwin).

Discussion questions

1 Describe additional retail formats to those listed in Fig. 11.5. Explain the existence of these formats in terms of the relationship between merchandising ranges and shopping motivations.

2 Why is the presence of third-party logistics companies one of the reasons for the emergence of shorter channels? Why is it not the main reason?

3 Is the role in the supply chain of the manufacturer of manufacturer brands likely to be different from that of the manufacturers of retail brands?

4 Considering the requirements for successful partnerships and the problems in building partnerships, how would you advise a retailer to persuade a new supplier to join in EDI?

5 Why do we shop? Why is electronic shopping unlikely ever to replace shops completely?

Arthur and company

Arthur and Company have developed a new product for use on machine tools. This product is available from two other established firms in the industry and they distribute their products in two ways. First, direct to final users in the case of large customers, and, secondly, through wholesalers who deal with the smaller users.

The management of Arthur is discussing the best way to distribute its product and feel that there are three possibilities:

■ that they should sell only direct to wholesalers;

■ that they should sell only direct to final users;

■ that they should imitate the two major competitors.

Mr Smith, the Marketing Manager, is preparing a paper setting out the merits of each of these courses of action and has so far gathered the following information:

■ Of those wholesalers who claim to stock this type of product, 95 per cent are already selling one of the two leading brands and 60 per cent are selling both the leading brands.

■ The sales force of the larger of the two competitors does not call at the established clients of any of its wholesalers, while those of the second competitor do make such calls but pass orders of whatever size back to the wholesaler in whose territory the customer falls.

■ Arthur's range of products is less extensive than either of the competitors', but an independent article in a trade journal had described Arthur's products as the best available for any given application.

With this information in mind Mr Smith is trying to decide which of the three distribution policies offers the best opportunities.

Source: Blois and Cowell (1973).

Chapter 12
Marketing Communi-cations
Gustav Puth

Objectives

This chapter considers the role and nature of marketing communications. Its objectives are:

1 to set out marketing communication's context;

2 to describe some marketing communication objectives;

3 to describe the marketing communication process;

4 to discuss how a marketing communication plan is developed;

5 to consider the nature of marketing communication research.

1 Introduction

ALTHOUGH there is a proliferation of books, journals, newspapers, and magazines dealing specifically with the various aspects and elements of marketing communication, it is still somewhat disconcerting to see that there is not necessarily an equal degree of clarity in the terminology used in the field. Textbooks invariably have one or more of the terms 'promotion', 'advertising', 'marketing', 'communication', and 'management' in their titles. In the 1990s the term 'integrated', or even 'holistic', also crept into the titles. However, there seems to be very little consistency in the use of these terms, and they are often used interchangeably, as the following extract from the preface of a widely used textbook indicates: 'Nearly everyone in the modern world is influenced to some degree by *advertising* and *other forms of promotion*. Organizations . . . have learned that the ability to *communicate* effectively and efficiently . . . is critical to their success. *Advertising* and *other types of promotional messages* are used' (Belch and Belch, 1995; emphasis added).

Even a cursory inspection of the literature will, however, reveal that the two terms 'advertising' and 'promotion' are used most frequently to describe and explain the theory and practice of marketing communication. It may be useful, therefore, to return to the root meanings of these terms to discover what they represent. Both of these terms are derived from Latin, and are constituted by a prefix and a verb. The word 'promotion' is constituted by the prefix *pro*, which means 'forward', and the verb *movere*, which means 'to move' or 'to push'. Thus, promotion, in a literal sense, means to push forward. The word 'advertising' similarly comes from the prefix *ad*, which means 'towards', and the verb *verto*, which means 'to turn'. The root meaning of advertising is, therefore, to turn towards. It does not take too much thought to realize that marketing communication entails pushing forward the product or service, and turning the consumer towards the product or service. Once these two essential elements of the marketing communication process meet, there is the chance of a sale.

Naturally, the art and science of marketing communication have developed far beyond the rudimentary beginnings embedded in these original root forms of the terms. However, although advertising and promotion most naturally come to mind when we think of marketing communication, it also includes other important elements of the marketing communication mix, such as personal selling, sales promotion, publicity, direct marketing, and, more recently, cybermarketing. In this chapter, the term 'marketing communication' is used to encapsulate and encompass all of these vital elements.

☞ 'A firm, therefore, has actively to search for applicants through different channels. These may consist of advertisements in newspapers, enticing salespeople away from competitors, looking for prospective candidates in its own company who are not currently in sales positions, and providing internships for college students.' (Chapter 13, p. 301)

2 The marketing communication process

As is the case with most communication contexts, the marketing communication process can be very complex. It also exhibits the same universal components that are found in most forms of communication: a sender or source who encodes a message, the message, receivers or an audience who decode the message, and a medium or media that carry the message. In most communication processes there is some form of feedback. Underlying most forms of communication, including marketing communication, is the aim of sharing the same meaning.

However, this universal process needs to be contextualized to present a clear picture of the marketing communication process.

2.1 Components of the marketing communication process

The following components of the marketing communication process can be distinguished:

The source. The advertiser that generates the idea is the *source* of the communication. Although this function is in reality mostly performed by an advertising agency, most of the receivers in the marketing communication process would probably identify the producer of the product or service as the source.

The communication object. The communication object, or the topic of communication, is that which the message is about. In general communication, it may be an object, a person, an idea, an abstract concept, or a complex combination of any number of these. In the case of marketing communication, the product or service, labelled by its brand name, is the communication object.

The message. The idea to be communicated is the *message*, and the source encodes the *message*, translating it into symbols such as words or advertising copy, or images, such as graphic or photographic pictures, that can be understood by the audience, the people, or consumers to whom the message is directed.

The media. The medium or *media* carry the encoded message to the audience. In marketing communication, the media are traditionally divided into printed media—newspapers, magazines and trade publications, electronic media—television and radio, outdoor media—billboards, bus shelters, and posters—and transit media—bus panels and other message-carrying vehicles. There are also other important types of media, such as the cinema, packaging, direct mail, and, more recently, the Internet.

The receivers. The *receivers* or audience of marketing communication—current and prospective consumers of the product or service—play a vital role in the communication process by decoding and interpreting the message before deciding whether to act on it or not. The reaction to the message is seldom in the form of immediate action, although the advertisement may elicit immediate evaluation of the message and its content. In most instances, buying behaviour comes only later when the consumer is in the purchasing situation where recall of the core message of the advertisement may or may not take place, and the consumer may or may not be influenced by it.

Feedback. In the unidirectional kind of mainly mass communication such as marketing communication, *feedback* from the audience is seldom spontaneous, and has to be induced in some way. This is mostly achieved by conducting marketing communication research, either before or after the formal launching of the campaign of messages directed at the audience.

2.2 Marketing communication effects

In most instances of marketing communication, a specific communication campaign will have a very specific communication purpose or purposes. Over the years there have been various ideas about all of the possible communication purposes, mostly expressed in the form of a formula or an acronym. One of the oldest and best-known approaches is the AIDA formula—representing the four stages of attention, interest, desire, and action. But in the 1990s there was a realization that consumer decision-making processes are rather more complex than is implied by such simplistic recipes. A comprehensive discussion of the latest thinking on and knowledge of consumer behaviour can be found in Chapter 6. However, to provide some idea of the possible objectives of marketing communication in relation to the way in which the audience may react to the messages, the original *hierarchy of communication effects*—represented by the four phases of awareness, comprehension or understanding, evaluation, and behaviour or action—still serves as a useful way to decide on the purposes of a marketing communication campaign.

☞ 'It is a well-known fact both from psychological research and from everyday experience that attention is selective: of all the things going on around us, we perceive only a small part. In particular, much marketing information is not attended to.' (Chapter 6, p. 117)

Phase 1: Awareness. It should be obvious that there is no possibility for any consumer who is unaware of the product or service to react to it in the form of buying behaviour. Thus, the first objective of any marketing communication campaign is to ensure adequate awareness levels amongst the target audience. This is particularly critical where a new product or service is being launched, or where an existing product or service is being introduced into a new market or segment.

Phase 2: Comprehension. Not all consumers who are aware of the product or service will necessarily understand its features or benefits. Therefore some marketing communication campaigns may be specifically aimed at ensuring and increasing consumers' comprehension of the advantages to be derived from the product or service, and how it may benefit them in particular. This phase be-

comes more challenging in the case of complex or technologically advanced products or services.

Phase 3: Evaluation. After becoming aware of the product or service, and understanding its potential benefits, prospective consumers can decide whether it will meet their specific and personal needs. In this phase it is likely that they will weigh up a particular branded product and compare it with those of competitive brands in the market, and then decide whether to show further interest or not.

Phase 4: Action. During this phase, which may involve several steps and stretch over a considerable time, the consumer either purchases or does not purchase the advertised product or service. This is not a once-only kind of occurrence, and the consumer may go through this phase of the hierarchy each time there is a need to acquire an item or service in the particular product or service category. On every such occasion, the marketing communication, both for the particular brand and all others in the category, that the consumer has been exposed to in the preceding time may have a determining influence on buying behaviour.

3 The marketing context of marketing communication

MARKETING communication is and should undoubtedly be the most visible element of the marketing mix. It is a pervasive force in society, and appeals to people from every conceivable description or classification. Although it still functions on the assumption of the consumer's free choice to be exposed to it, it can be accepted that every consumer in the developed economies in the world today will have a daily encounter with some form of marketing communication.

Over the years, marketing communication has come to be known and accepted as one of the elements of what is generally described as the marketing mix, which is the topic of Chapter 9 of this book.

What is a marketing decision variable? Philip Kotler formulated the following definition: 'A marketing decision variable (or marketing instrument, marketing tool) is any factor under the control of the firm that may be used to stimulate company sales' (Kotler, 1967). In further elaborating on the context of marketing, Kotler also dealt with aspects such as *marketing effort*, *marketing allocation*, and *market response*. All of these terms were still considered in the late 1990s and dealt with in general marketing and marketing communication strategy, albeit in some instances in a modified form or description.

The most important fact that emerges even from these early pioneering efforts in the field of marketing communication is that it can and should never be seen or managed in isolation from the total marketing context.

3.1 The marketing planning process

Because there are often vast differences in the strategies of different products and services, not all marketing plans will have the same mix of marketing elements. Fast-moving consumer goods (FMCG), that are used and consumed on a daily basis in the market, will naturally be approached differently from expensive durable products, such as automobiles and computer equipment.

It is essential, therefore, to conduct a thorough situation analysis, including factors such as opportunity analysis, competitive analysis, environmental analysis, and target-market analysis. However, as the marketing plan is dealt with extensively in Chapters 18 and 19, it will not be discussed in too much detail here.

3.1.1 Communication as part of the marketing plan

As clearly implied by the early pioneers of the study and application of marketing communication referred to above, marketing communication is only one of many components of any marketing plan. (See Chapters 18 and 19 for comprehensive discussions of Strategic Marketing and of Marketing Planning and Control.) A marketing programme is intended to plan how products or services are taken from the point of production to the point of consumption in such a way as to develop a positive relationship between consumers and the producer that will foster additional or repeat usage.

From this point of view, the marketing communication plan should be aligned with and supportive of both the short-term and long-term objectives of the wider marketing plan. The marketing plan should, therefore, spell out the marketing strategies and tactics that will be implemented to achieve these objectives.

3.1.2 The marketing communication plan

Together with all of the issues, strategies, and plans regarding the other marketing decision variables, the marketing communication plan is a crucial element of the marketing mix. Depending on the type of product or service, or the life-cycle stage of the product or service, the importance of the marketing communication plan may vary considerably in relation to the other elements of the marketing mix. For example, in business-to-business marketing where there may be a narrow and clearly defined market, marketing communication is often not as prominent as in the case of FMCGs aimed at large segments of the total population.

3.1.3 Steps in the marketing communication plan

The essential objective of the marketing communication plan is to contribute, with the plans for the other elements of the marketing mix, to the successful execution of the marketing strategy. In this context, the marketing communication plan will in most instances consist of a series of decisions about the components of the communication process.

Setting marketing communication objectives. The first step in the marketing communication plan is to establish marketing communication *objectives* for the particular communication campaign. The objectives will give direction to every single aspect of the compilation and execution of the marketing communication plan. In many respects, the objectives also serve as a checklist for controlling purposes and to ensure that the execution of the various actions contained in the plan are still on track.

Determining a marketing communication budget. The second important step in the marketing communication plan is to allocate a *budget* for the execution of the plan. In this regard, marketing communication literally has to compete with the other elements of the marketing mix for an appropriate and viable proportion of the total budget allocated for the marketing plan.

Identifying the target audience. The third step in the marketing communication plan is clearly to affirm the *target audience* for the campaign through rigorous market segmentation. Although this may already have been done as part of the wider marketing plan, it is essential that clarity and finalization be reached in this regard, as it will have a direct impact on the rest of the marketing communication plan. Corporate advertising (see Insert) is often an example of poor target audience selection.

Puffed up

Corporate advertising's audience is much broader than for normal consumer-goods advertising. It is usually aimed at three constituencies: business customers, opinion formers (investors, politicians, activists, media) who can influence share prices, and employees. Ultimately, though, the main reason for corporate advertising is usually the directors' ego.

Determining the marketing communication mix. Once the budget has been appropriated and there is clarity with regard to the target audience, decisions can be made on an appropriate blend of the *marketing communication mix*. It is often too easy to think of marketing communication only in terms of the elements of advertising and promotion. However, careful consideration needs to be given to the appropriateness and use of publicity, personal selling, direct marketing, and cybermarketing.

Adopting a creative approach. The next important step in the marketing communication plan is to make decisions about *creative* aspects of the content and structure of the messages to be conveyed to the target audience. Such decisions will obviously be affected by all of the preceding steps in the marketing communication plan.

Compiling a media plan. Once the message decisions have been taken, the planners are in a position to determine the most appropriate *media* to carry the messages to the target audience. Today there are many more media available than could conceivably be used in any particular marketing communication campaign, and media planning has advanced to a state of being a science in its own right.

Conducting communication research. Undergirding all of the above steps of decision-making in the marketing communication planning process is the essential element of marketing communication *research*. Although research is mentioned last in this discussion of the planning process, it can be conducted early in the process with a view to assisting in planning and decision-making, as well as after implementation of the plan for evaluation and adaptation purposes.

It should finally be pointed out that, although some order has been implied above in discussing the elements in the marketing communication plan, it does not always occur as a neatly ordered linear process. The planning process can, in fact, be prompted by any of the above-mentioned elements. It is entirely possible, for example, that the total process can be prompted and directed by an unexpected media opportunity, or a glaring gap suddenly emerging in a particular segment of the market. These interdependent, rather than strictly linear, relationships between the elements of the marketing communication plan should be borne in mind in considering the more comprehensive discussion of the elements below.

4 Marketing communication objectives

IT has been pointed out earlier that marketing communication objectives should be aligned with the objectives of the overall marketing strategy for the product or service. This clearly implies that there may be a difference between overall marketing objectives and marketing communication objectives. In essence, these two sets of objectives merely operate on different levels of the total planning process. It should be equally clear, however, that they will be closely linked, and that the marketing communication objectives should be derived from the marketing objectives.

4.1 Distinguishing between marketing objectives and communication objectives

The distinction between marketing objectives and marketing communication objectives can be formulated as follows:

Marketing objectives refer to what is to be accomplished by the overall marketing programme. They are often stated in terms of marketing variables such as sales, market share, or profitability. Communication objectives refer to what the marketer seeks to accomplish with its marketing communication plan. They are often stated in terms of the nature of the message to be communicated or what specific communication effects are to be accomplished. Marketing communication objectives may include creating awareness or knowledge about a product and its attributes and benefits; creating an image; or developing favourable attitudes, preferences, or purchase intentions. (Belch and Belch 1995)

From the above distinction it can be seen that, although marketing communication objectives are clearly intended to contribute to the attainment of marketing objectives, there is not necessarily a direct cause-and-effect relationship between the two sets of objectives. Short-term sales, for example, may not provide a reliable indication of the effects of marketing communication strategies. In the first instance, marketing communication is usually only one of many factors influencing sales, and, secondly, the impact of marketing communication often occurs primarily over the long term (Batra *et al.* 1996).

4.2 **Four crucial questions**

It is generally advocated that marketing communication objectives should be considered and formulated in terms of four basic variables of the communication process (Britt 1969). These four aspects can also be formulated as four general questions.

Who is the target audience? This is probably the single most important decision the marketing communication planner has to make. Virtually all of the other communication decisions flow from this basic decision. Is the budget sufficient? Is the media mix appropriate? Does the creative execution address the stated objectives? All of these questions are evaluated in view of the target audience's size, characteristics, and behaviour.

What are the intended effects of the marketing communication? It is vital that the behavioural decisions or actions that marketing communication is attempting to influence be analysed and explicitly stated. Such analyses can be based on any one of the communication-effects models referred to earlier in this chapter, and would provide guidelines in terms of desired effects such as awareness, knowledge, liking, preference, conviction, and purchase.

What message structure and content will lead to the intended effects? The third question related to the clarification and determination of marketing communication objectives should lead to a clear description of the competitive attributes and consumer benefits to be focused on in the message.

How will the success of the communication campaign be measured? Sound marketing communication objectives should ideally be measurable. This implies that the method of measurement, and an appropriate budgetary allocation for measurement, be included in the overall marketing communication plan. Measurement of objectives enhances accountability in the communication process, and incorporates research as an integral part of the planning process.

4.3 **Statement of marketing communication objectives**

Marketing communication objectives are essentially statements describing and specifying what needs to be accomplished in order to capitalize on opportunities and to overcome problems during the communication planning period. It is advisable literally to write down such descriptions to formulate an overall statement of marketing communication objectives. The following are some guidelines to consider in the formulation of a statement of marketing communication objectives:

☞ 'At this stage [the growth stage of the product life cycle] . . . promotion should shift the emphasis from building product awareness to nuturing product preference.' (Chapter 14, p. 335)

Overall alignment. Like all other marketing-mix objectives, marketing communication objectives should be aligned with overall marketing and corporate objectives. The objectives should be in writing and should be clearly understood and supported by everyone involved in the marketing communication planning, development, and implementation. The objectives should also be set out in a specified time frame.

Internal consistency. The marketing communication objectives should be internally consistent. This simply means that there should be a logical relationship between the target audience, the message, and the intended effects of the communication. The measurement methods suggested should be appropriate to the stated objectives and be able to generate data to evaluate the success of the communication campaign.

Underlying assumptions. It is important to realize that the formulation of marketing communication objectives, being at the beginning of the planning process, will always be based on a number of explicit or implicit, assumptions. Examples are assumptions about the adequacy of the budget appropriation, the relevance and impact of the creative execution, the effectiveness of the media plan, and related competitor activities.

Subjective judgement. Despite the clarity of set objectives, and the measurability and quantification thereof, judgement and intuition will and should always play a role in the evaluation of the success of marketing communication. It has often been stated that marketing communication is both an art and a science, and this also applies to the evaluation of how successful communication objectives are achieved.

☞ '. . . when marketing proposes to introduce a new advertising campaign, the accountant can, on the basis of past experience, accurately estimate the costs that will be incurred. In comparison, the marketing manager's estimate of the benefits of the campaign will necessarily be less precise.' (Chapter 17, p. 424)

5 Budgeting decisions

ONCE the marketing communication objectives have been determined, the focus moves to the communication budget. Two questions emerge at this point: What will the marketing communication programme cost? How will these funds be allocated? Ideally, the amount a company needs to spend on marketing communication should be determined by what has to be done to accomplish its communication objectives. However, in the real world of marketing communication budgets are sadly often determined through much more simplistic methods, such as how much money is available at a given time, or by calculating an arbitrary percentage of the company's or the brand's sales revenue. It should be pointed out that the determination of the marketing communication budget and decisions about the marketing communication mix are often totally interdependent, and that they are separated in this chapter for purposes of clarity. In reality, the budget may not be finalized before specific communication-mix strategies have been determined.

The various approaches or techniques used in determining the marketing communication budget are often divided into two groups referred to as top-down approaches and bottom-up approaches.

5.1 Top-down budgeting methods

In top-down approaches a budgetary amount is usually established at executive level in the company, and the allocated figure then passed on to the marketing or marketing communication department. The budgets that result from this approach are in essence determined before consideration of any of the dynamics of the marketing and communication planning processes. Top-down methods include the affordable method, arbitrary allocation, percentage of sales, and competitive parity.

The affordable method. Companies following the affordable method often determine and allocate all the other expenditures related to its operations, such as production, procurement, and research and development, and then allocate the remaining funds to promotion and advertising. This amount is considered as the most that they can afford to spend on marketing communication. In this approach, the tasks to be performed by marketing communication are not taken into account. This means that the chances of under- or over-spending are quite high, because there are no criteria to measure the effectiveness or appropriateness of allocated budgets. In spite of its glaring shortcomings, this approach is still followed, especially by small and medium-sized enterprises.

Arbitrary allocation. If the 'what-we-can-afford' method seems subjective and without objective references, this applies even more in the case of the arbitrary allocation of funds as a method of marketing communication budgeting. In colloquial language, it could be said that, in arbitrary allocation, the budget is set on the basis of what can at best be described as a 'gut feeling'. In effect, management determines the marketing communication budget solely on the basis of what is felt to be necessary. There are no apparent advantages in this approach, as it takes absolutely no cognizance of the communication objectives to be reached, or the cost of tasks needed to reach such objectives. However, despite the obvious folly of this approach, there are many instances where budgets continue to be set in this way.

Percentage of sales. The percentage-of-sales approach is probably one of the most popular ways of establishing the marketing communication budget, particularly in larger companies. In this approach, the communication budget is defined as a predetermined percentage of either past or expected sales. For instance, if the sales for the coming year are expected to be $100 million, and the communication budget is set at 7 per cent of sales, $7 million is allocated for marketing communication. The major reasons for the popularity of this method is its simplicity and the fact that it neutralizes much of the wrangling and differences of opinion often associated with some of the other methods. It also has some distinct disadvantages, which include possibly spending too much (on big sellers that may not necessarily need that much advertising) or spending too little (on products that may need a marketing communication boost) (Bovée *et al.* 1995). A more serious shortcoming, however, is that the percentage-of-sales method fails to take account of extraneous factors, such as what marketing communication actions the competition might be undertaking in the market. Finally, there is no clear-cut indication of what percentage of past of projected sales should be allocated to marketing communication, and in most instances this figure is determined purely arbitrarily.

Competitive parity. In contrast to the percentage-of-sales method, which takes little or no account of the competition's actions, the competitive-parity approach is almost entirely driven by perceptions of the competition. In this approach, companies simply try to match what the competition is doing. As the marketing communication expenditures in any market are often readily available, this method is relatively simple. If, for instance, general trade figures indicate that, on average, companies in your industry spend a certain absolute amount or even a certain percentage of sales on marketing communication, your budget is simply determined along similar lines. Other measures sometimes used in this approach are industry figures representing market share or share of voice. The obvious shortcoming of this method is that marketing communication is determined by what the competition does, rather than by strategies that are relevant and appropriate to your own circumstances and objectives. Underlying all of this, there is the implicit assumption that the competition knows what it is doing, and that we simply follow its lead. In essence then, this method is reactive rather than proactive.

5.2 Bottom-up budgeting approaches

One of the major problems with top-down approaches to marketing communication budgeting is that it is predominantly prejudgemental, leading to predetermined budget allocations that are not necessarily appropriate for the set objectives and the strategies to reach them. It should be clear that budgetary approaches that are led by marketing communication objectives and by the expenditures needed for strategies to reach those objectives will result in much more realistic appropriations. The most important bottom-up approaches to marketing communication budgeting are the objective and task method, payout planning, and a range of quantitative models.

Objective and task method. Starting with the marketing communication objectives, the objective and task method first identifies the tasks that need to be performed to meet the objectives. The marketing communication budget is determined by simply calculating the cost of all the tasks needed to be accomplished to attain the objectives. The most apparent and biggest advantage of the objective and task method is that it is objectives driven. All of the funds allocated and expenditures incurred are related to performing specific tasks and meeting predetermined objectives. This approach enables and enhances both implementation and financial accountability. Where money is spent on specific actions, it is entirely possible to measure the effectiveness of such expenditures. There are, however, also some potential disadvantages. The major disadvantage of the objective and task method is that it may not necessarily take account of the affordability of the required expenditures. In addition, it is entirely dependent on the appropriateness and relevance of the identified objectives and tasks, and, where these may be misdirected, major financial losses may result.

Payout planning. In the payout-planning approach to marketing communication budgeting, which is typically for the introduction of new products into the market, the planning period is often extended for longer than a single financial year. In most instances it covers three years, although, in the case of a product that may move exceptionally slowly through the product life cycle, the planning period may even be extended to cover a five-year term. The payout-planning approach typically consists of five stages:

- estimation of market-share objectives;
- assessment of needed trade inventories;
- determination of needed expenditures;
- determination of payout period;
- evaluation.

Although space does not permit a detailed discussion of these phases, the approach is essentially driven by a projection of desired market share for the product (step 1), leading to a calculation of the number of units necessary to meet both customer and trade demands (step 2). These two factors will determine the estimation of needed expenditures (step 3) as well as the payout period (step 4). In the evaluation of the payout plan (step 5), consideration is given to aspects such as achieved market share, sustainable profit margins, and current net cash flow value in determining the investment value of the expenditures for the period.

Quantitative models. Although a number of attempts have been made to design and apply standardized quantitative methods of marketing communication budgeting, it has generally met with limited success. Most of such endeavours are based on computer-simulation models employing statistical techniques such as regression analysis, and, more recently, neural network applications. In general terms, it seems as if such methods may be regarded as too theoretical or too complicated to be relevant in the reality of marketing communication planning. However, despite its apparent lack of success when compared to other methods and approaches, quantitative methods may yet gain acceptance, as specialized computer software and more user-friendly statistical modelling applications gain a foothold in the day-to-day management of the marketing communication process.

5.3 **Summary**

It should be clear from the preceding general discussion of approaches and methods that there is no universally accepted norm when it comes to marketing communication budgeting. While a particular method may seem totally unacceptable in one situation, it may be quite appropriate in another context. However, what does emerge from marketing communication practice is the growing use of the objective and task method, with a decline in the less sophisticated and somewhat expedient approaches to marketing communication budgeting. At the same time, a slow increase in the use of the payout-planning approach can be detected. It seems inevitable that, in concert with higher levels of computer literacy and user-friendly statistical application packages, we may see significant advances in the use of quantitative budgeting models.

6 **Target-audience decisions**

TARGET marketing can be seen as a logical extension of the marketing concept, which Philip Kotler defines as 'a management orientation that holds the key to achieving organizational goals [and which] consists of the organization's determining the needs and wants of target markets and adapting itself to delivering the desired satisfactions more effectively and efficiently than its competitors'.

In many respects, making the decisions concerning which groups of consumers to target for a marketing communication campaign is the most important step in the marketing communication process. Virtually all the other marketing communication decisions flow from this crucial decision. Is the budget sufficient to reach the target audience effectively? Is the media mix appropriate to the target-market characteristics? Does the creative execution represent the way in which the target audience thinks and feels about the product? All of these questions should be considered and assessed in view of the variable attributes and emotional and behavioural characteristics of the target audience.

The process of defining the target audience for a particular marketing communication campaign in terms of its collective characteristics and attributes is widely known as market segmentation. This topic is specifically dealt with in Chapter 16, and will be discussed here only in the most general terms.

The definition of a target audience should, first,

be based on a clear and concise statement of its key demographic characteristics, such as age, gender, income, occupation, and family size. However, these characteristics are not sufficient to provide a clear understanding and insight into the latent factors that motivate consumers in relation to their preferences and usage patterns. To gain insight beyond that which is perceivable from the face-value information of demographic data, it is essential to turn to lifestyle and psychographic segmentation. A wide range of psychographic and lifestyle typologies, such as Value and Lifestyles programme (VAL) in the USA, SocioMonitor and Living Standards Measures (LSM) in South Africa, were developed in the mid-1990s in attempts to capture consumers' attitudes, needs, and beliefs. The LSM index encompasses eight groupings described in the following way:

- LSM 1—The Traditional Have Nots;
- LSM 2—Self-Centred Non-Earners;
- LSM 3—Transitional Rurals;
- LSM 4—Urbanized Singles;
- LSM 5—Young Aspirers;
- LSM 6—Emerging Market;
- LSM 7—Established Affluents;
- LSM 8—Influential Affluents.

Each of the eight LSM groupings is defined in terms of products, finance, large appliances, media, shopping habits, and lifestyle. Adding such data to the descriptive demographic definition of the target audience provides a deeper and more comprehensive understanding of how a particular target audience may react to the marketing communication campaign, and how the campaign should be planned and executed to be optimally aligned with these latent characteristics and motivations of the target audience.

Any target-audience definition based on product consumption must also take into consideration that there may be a difference between the person responsible for the purchase of the product and the person who actually uses the product. The primary purchasers of products such as breakfast cereal or peanut butter are mothers with children, but the primary consumers are the children themselves. It is imperative, therefore, clearly to identify the Purchase Decision-Makers (PDMs), as well as the extremely important Purchase Decision Influencers (PDIs), for a particular product. Few consumers take decisions in isolation, and

there are many forces at play within the target audience that influence the individual's decision to purchase. In the case of the breakfast cereal, the influence of the child on the mother's decision is of paramount importance and considerable marketing communication effort is directed at giving impetus to this skirt-tugging phenomenon.

6.1 Steps in defining the target audience

In a certain sense, each individual could almost be described as a distinct target audience, as no two people are exactly alike in their motivations, needs, decision processes, and buying behaviour. However, it is obviously not feasible to tailor a specific marketing mix to every single individual (see Insert), although the trend at the end of the 1990s of moving from macro-marketing to micro-marketing was certainly approximating such an approach. Even then, the objective is to identify groups within the broader target market that are sufficiently similar in needs and responses to marketing communication to warrant a focused communication campaign. More specifically, this process of defining the target audience requires five steps, which are listed below.

A new life for an old medium?

'Posters are part of our lives. At their best, they are a powerful medium of communication, compelling and persuasive. The originator of the poster (individual, institution, business or organization) has a message to sell; the target audience must be persuaded to buy it. The interchange takes place in the public domain. Arguably as other media fragment into niche markets, the pervasiveness of the poster may give it more importance.'

Source: The Power of the Poster Exhibition, Victoria and Albert Musuem, London, 1998.

Step 1: Identifying the needs structure of the target audience at the individual level. This is usually done by selecting a sample from the total potential market and identifying individual consumer needs as they relate to the particular product or service. This will result in many need profiles that represent the diverse needs of the total potential market.

Step 2: Grouping the consumers into homogeneous segments based on their needs profile. In this step, the objective is to form groups of consumers that are clearly homogeneous within the groups in terms of needs and clearly heterogeneous across the groups. This can be done with the use of standardized methods of statistical clustering. This step should clearly distinguish between the needs of the different groups—for example, those consumers in the automobile market who are primarily focused on safety and those for whom economy may be the prime concern.

Step 3: Identifying factors related to the various needs-based subgroups. These relationships may include variables such as demographic, geographic, lifestyle, and consumption patterns. Care should be taken to focus on the underlying needs here, and not only on the variables that correlate with the needs. It is the needs that form the segment, and the descriptive variables that allow the marketing communication access to the segment.

Step 4: Selection of the target audience(s). This step entails the selection of the target audience or audiences for which a specific marketing communication programme will be developed. The selected target audience(s) are those that offer the greatest opportunity for profitability under a given set of market and competitive conditions.

Step 5: Developing a positioning for the product or service within the target audience. Positioning addresses the issue of how consumers in the selected target audience are supposed or desired to perceive the particular branded product or service as compared to those of the competitors.

👉 'However, fundamentally a brand's positioning is established in the minds of targeted customers through marketing communications and promotional activity.' (Chapter 16, p. 401)

6.2 Communication-mix decisions

In keeping with the earlier discussed root meanings of the two traditionally dominant forms of marketing communication, advertising and promotion, these two elements of the marketing communication mix, as well as the other elements that will be discussed below, all have the underlying intention of setting up channels of communication with a view to selling products or goods or to promoting an idea. In order to achieve this goal, it is necessary to select an appropriate mix of all of the marketing communication methods available

to the marketer. The particular selection employed for a specific marketing communication campaign is known as the marketing communication mix. The importance and significance of each element of the marketing communication mix may vary depending on the product type, the target-audience characteristics, and other factors in the marketing communication process. It should be equally obvious that even companies in the same industry will have different marketing communication mixes depending on the size of the company, its competitive and managerial strengths and weaknesses, and the positioning of the product or service in relation to its competitors. The marketing communication mix can consist of any one or a combination of the following marketing communication methods: advertising, direct marketing, sales promotion, personal selling, and publicity and public relations.

6.3 Advertising

Advertising is traditionally defined as any paid form of non-personal communication about a product, a service, or a company with the intention to sell the product or service or to influence opinions on and attitudes towards the product, service, or company. Each of the elements in this definition merits a brief explanation. Most advertising has to be paid for, first in terms of the media space or time needed to carry the advertisement, but, secondly, also for the production of the advertising message. The reason that advertising is described as non-personal can be attributed to the fact that advertising usually involves one or more of the mass media that enable the advertiser to convey the message simultaneously to large groups of individuals. This has the implication that there is generally no opportunity for the target audience to provide direct feedback to the advertising message.

6.4 Direct marketing

Direct marketing refers to marketing communication techniques, which will enable the marketer to communicate directly with the target audience with a view to prompting immediate or direct reaction in the form of purchase behaviour or asking for more information. Direct marketing has not traditionally been regarded as an element of the marketing communication mix. In recent years it has, however, become such an integral and important element of the overall marketing communication strategy of many companies that it often merits a substantial portion of the total budgetary appropriation, and an extensive separate strategy. Over the past fifteen years large international advertising agencies have set up their own direct-response divisions, or purchased existing direct-marketing agencies.

In line with its very strong technology-based nature, the key underlying assumption of direct marketing is that it is not only possible, but essential, to acquire and use precise knowledge in order to identify and directly to communicate to increasingly segmented and specialized target audiences. In essence, direct marketing subscribes to the idea of forging interactive and long-term relationships between the company and its customers. The unique characteristics of direct marketing make it ideal for the needs of both consumers and companies. Consumers use it for its convenience and the wide choice of products and services available. It is a 'fun' way of buying for working women, older people, and all in search of a labour-saving source of products and services. Direct marketing also offers marketers audience selectivity, since they can select those whom they wish to reach and observe the responses. It therefore proves very acceptable to companies in search of greater effectiveness and profitability. This topic is discussed in greater detail in Chapter 26.

6.5 Sales promotion

Sales promotion is a marketing communication technique where additional incentives beyond the inherent qualities or benefits of the product or service are offered to the target audience, sales force, or distributors. This is achieved by, for instance, temporarily modifying the price relative to that of the competitors. Sales-promotion efforts are implemented in the context of either the consumer or the trade and sales force. The first invariably leads to a pull strategy of stimulating consumer demand for the brand, while the latter results in a strong push strategy. Consumer-oriented sales promotion is aimed at creating immediate short-term consumer demand and makes use of a wide range of communication techniques and incentives, such as coupons (see Insert), sampling, premiums, rebates, contests, sweepstakes, and a variety of point-of-purchase materials. Trade-oriented sales promotion is aimed at encouraging

> **Couponing still the most popular promotional technique**
>
> The 19th US Annual Survey of Promotional Practices (1996) indicated that coupons influence where shoppers go (56 per cent) and which brands they choose (43 per cent). The two most common sources of coupons were colour leaflets and the Sunday newspaper, with a significantly smaller number of respondents stating that they received them in the shopping mall.
>
> *Source:* Ray (1997).

trade and sales-force intermediaries to stock and promote the company's products and services, and can be in the form of promotional and merchandising allowances, price deals, sales competitions, and trade shows. The major benefits of sales promotions are that they can stimulate sales that would not necessarily have taken place under normal conditions, and, as a result of short-term price cutting, immediate consumer response is stimulated. Sales-promotion programmes are also easily measurable in terms of short-term consumer behaviour during the sales-promotion campaign.

6.6 Personal selling

Personal selling is exactly what it says—a form of person-to-person marketing communication in which the seller attempts to persuade the consumer to buy the company's product or service. Personal selling is particularly appropriate and effective in situations where customers are in the process of developing a personal preference for the product, where they are in search of specific information or knowledge on the product, or when they are in the final stage of deciding whether to buy the product or service. However, comparatively speaking, personal selling is also probably the most expensive form of marketing communication. It requires highly trained sales professionals to engage in personal interaction with individual consumers, which pushes the unit cost per sales call far beyond the individual costs of advertising, direct marketing, or sales promotion. For this reason personal selling should be used very selectively, based on a careful comparison and weighing against other forms of marketing communication.

6.7 Publicity and public relations

Similar to advertising, publicity can be described as a non-personal form of marketing communication regarding an organization, its product or services, or an idea. It also makes use of the mass media in reaching a large audience at the same time. However, in contrast to advertising, publicity is not directly paid for nor directly published under the identified auspices of the organization. Rather, it mostly appears in the form of editorial content about the company's activities, products, or services, or any other aspect of its operations. Specific techniques include news releases, press conferences, feature articles, photographs, films, and video programmes.

Public relations, in contrast to publicity, generally has a wider aim, and is broadly directed at getting and keeping the goodwill of all of the company's stakeholder groups and publics. Publicity can be and often is used as a technique in public relations. Public relations is far more than a communication technique, and can be regarded as a strategic management function in its own right. Although it serves an essential purpose within the context of integrated marketing communication, its domain clearly transcends the narrower focus on the consumers as the main public of marketing communication. In its supportive role of working with the other forms of marketing communication within the limited marketing context, public relations uses a variety of tools and techniques, including special publications, participation in community activities, fund-raising, sponsorships, and various other public-affairs activities. In its wider strategic scope, public relations serves as an environmental scanning function, filtering and processing issues and cues from the company's operating and strategic environment, and translating the information into usable strategic guidelines, which may have a significant impact on the formulation of marketing strategies.

☞ 'Apart from advertising and sales promotion, successful contributions to brand building and brand maintenance have been achieved through the use of sponsorship.' (Chapter 20, p. 486)

6.8 Creative decisions

Probably regarded by most people as the really dynamic and exciting aspect of marketing communication, creative strategy decisions and implementation are naturally the most visible part of the total communication process. The various marketing communication media are filled with all types of commercials and advertisements aimed at persuading the consumer to support our brand and purchase our product or service. Creative decisions have to be made with regard to the copy of the messages, the format and visualization of graphic and photographic material, and all of the production elements that contribute to and determine the eventual marketing communication message. Each of these aspects can be dealt with only briefly in this chapter.

It should be clear that creative strategy occurs relatively late in the wider process of marketing communication strategy. It follows strategic decisions on the marketing communication objectives, the target audience, the marketing communication mix, and the media to be used. Although this apparently linear order may not necessarily occur in all situations, it is unlikely that appropriate and effective creative decisions could be made without at least some information on these elements of the marketing communication process. It could be said that the purpose of developing a creative strategy is to make the marketing communication more effective by channelling the efforts of creativity in the most productive marketing communication direction. In practice, creative people in the marketing communication field mostly create the messages on the basis of a creative brief, which is derived from all of the preceding strategic decisions. In this regard, there is an old adage that states that the creation can only be as good as the brief is. It is essential, therefore, to ensure absolutely that creative people know exactly what is expected in terms of the intended outcomes of the marketing communication strategy, as well as the constituent elements of the communication process, such as the identity and characteristics of the target audience and the media. All of these elements need to be included in a written creative brief or strategy.

Once the creative brief has been clearly communicated and discussed by everyone concerned, the creative people should be allowed to work on the execution. Most marketers generally rely on advertising agencies, as creative specialists, to develop, prepare, and execute their creative strategies. The creative specialists are responsible for developing an effective and appropriate way of communicating the marketer's message to the consumer. It is essential, therefore, that individuals on both the client and the agency sides work with the creative team to develop, implement, and evaluate the creative strategy. This phase may require writers, artists, and various other creative specialists to come up with fresh, unique, and appropriate ideas that can be used as ways to communicate to the consumer. An important part of the creative process is to develop a major selling idea or key benefit that will become the central theme or platform of the campaign.

Once the creative strategy that will guide the marketing communication campaign has been determined, the attention turns to the question of the appropriate communication appeal and execution format. The appeal refers to the way in which the message is formulated and conveyed to elicit specific responses from the consumers or to influence their thinking, feelings, or behaviour. The various appeals can broadly be categorized as being either rational or emotional. Rational appeals are focused on the consumer's practical, functional, or utilitarian needs for the product or service, while emotional appeals are aimed at social or psychological reasons for purchasing the product or service. Numerous types of appeals—such as rational appeals based on comfort, convenience affordability, and value for money, or emotional appeals based on humour, fear, status, and sexual attractiveness—are available to the marketer (Belch and Belch 1995).

After the creative team has developed some tentative executions, these endeavours need to be considered and evaluated against the strategic objectives for the campaign. It has to be decided whether the execution is consistent with all of the other elements in the marketing communication strategy, whether it clearly conveys the brand personality and the core consumer benefit in such a way that it is compatible with the relevant characteristics of the target audience. Objective copy testing may be used at this stage to evaluate the target audience's reactions to the rough creative concepts. Once sufficient validation has been found for a particular execution, final creative refinement and production of the campaign follows, after which the final artwork is provided to the media for placement. Further ongoing research is conducted after exposure to ensure that the campaign is still on track and either to make needed adjustments or to withdraw the campaign once it has served its purpose and needs to be replaced by a new campaign.

6.9 Media decisions

Once the market has been analysed and the marketing communication budget established, two major expenditure factors become relevant. The first, that of creating and producing the marketing communication message, has been dealt with in Section 6.7. The second major expenditure concerns the development and implementation of a media strategy. One of the most widely used definitions of media planning describes it as: the development of a specific and detailed process of reaching the right number of appropriate people, the right number of times, in the right environment at minimum cost, to achieve the brand's marketing objectives.

Marketing communicators can use a variety of media to convey the message to the selected target audiences. Three major forms of media can be distinguished:

- media classes—e.g. print, electronic and out-of-home;
- media types—e.g. radio, television, magazines, newspapers;
- media vehicles—e.g. ITV, CNN, *Le Figaro*, *Washington Post*, *The Economist*, *Time Magazine*.

Four predominant traditional media classes can be distinguished: printed media, electronic media, out-of-home media, and all other media. More recently, the Internet and its various cyber-applications have emerged as a new media class. Each of these broad media classes represents a number of specific media types, of which radio and television are the most frequently used electronic media, and newspapers and magazines the predominant printed media. In addition, there are many different vehicles within each media category, such as specific radio stations and television channels or specific magazine or newspaper titles, that can be used to convey the message. Thus, one of the crucial decisions in marketing communication is to determine the most appropriate combination of media vehicles to convey the message to the target audience.

The media plan starts with developing media objectives that are in line with and supportive of the marketing objectives and strategy. As with most of the other variables in the marketing communication process, there is no set formula for creating media objectives. Media objectives are often formulated in terms of reach and frequency—that is, the percentage of potential consumers in the target audience to be reached and the frequency with which they need to be exposed to the message. In general terms, the following questions will provide guidelines for the development of a media plan.

- What target audience should be reached?
- What are the budget parameters for the campaign?
- Which geographic areas need to be covered?
- How far into the target audience can the media plan reach within the budget constraints?
- What message frequency is desired?
- At what times should the message reach the target audience?
- Which media types provide the best fit between the intended market and the actual audience?
- Which support functions will best ensure the effective performance of the selected media plan?

6.10 Media dispersion

Although the task of buying media time and space for conveying a marketing communication message to the target audience may seem straightforward, it is not. The media plan is complicated by a number of factors, ranging from the size and dispersion of the target audience to the increasing number and variety of available media. The degree of potential media fragmentation caused by such scope and variety poses both benefits and problems to media buyers and marketers.

6.11 Media costs

The relative costs of the various media types need to be considered in view of the budget allocated for the specific campaign (see Insert). Two types of costs should be considered: the costs of the time or space purchased in the selected media vehicles, and the relative costs of the various media vehicles in reaching each member of the specified target audience. For example, television may have a high cost, but, because of its mass reach, the relative cost per member of the target audience can be lower than that of a media type with a lower absolute cost.

6.12 Reach

Reach refers to the percentage of the target market that is exposed to the marketing communication message within a specific time period. As is the case with frequency, media reach is subjected to and determined by budget constraints. The question of reach can be determined somewhere between a wide reach, allowing as many prospective consumers as possible to receive at least one message, and a narrow reach, exposing a small number of prospects to multiple repetitions of the same message.

6.13 Message frequency

A further challenge is presented by the question of how many times a message needs to be repeated before an adequate impression, awareness, or learning occurs. This question is complicated by the possibility that effective frequency may vary widely between product categories and audience types. As the media environment becomes more cluttered and it becomes increasingly difficult to capture the attention of potential consumers, marketing communication relies even more on increasing the frequency with which the target audiences are exposed to messages. There is still little verified knowledge, however, to indicate the optimal level of message exposures. A generally applied guideline is that three exposures are necessary as a minimum, and ten as a maximum.

6.14 Media and target-audience mix

It should be clear that media decisions cannot be made in isolation of the inherent characteristics and qualities of the various media types or even individual media. Such media source effects associated with the atmosphere and technical aspects of the medium or media type can have a significant effect on the appropriate strategic fit between the product or service and the media audience. Marketing communicators should, therefore,

How many bus shelters equal one TV advert?

In 1998 the cost of buying thirty seconds of prime TV advertising time was £60,000, while, in comparison, to buy the space for an advertisement on a bus shelter for two weeks worked out at about £90. So the cost of one thirty-second slot equalled 666 bus shelters for two weeks.

carefully consider the media choices at their disposal in developing a media plan. The media types and categories should clearly be compatible with the overall marketing objectives, but should also be compatible with both the brand and audience characteristics.

6.15 Timing and continuity

The old adage that timing is of the essence applies particularly in the context of media planning. The nature and usage of the product or service may often largely determine the decision of where and when the target audience should be exposed to the marketing communication message. Some products and services are in demand throughout the year, while others may face varying demands at different seasonal periods. Despite the fact that there are many quantitative measures to assist in media planning and decision-making, the timing and scheduling of marketing communication messages often call for a measure of subjectivity. Media planning is essentially about where best to place the marketing communication message to maximize its effectiveness and the efficiency of the media expenditure.

6.16 Appropriate support functions

In many instances a media plan needs to be complemented by a number of appropriate support functions to ensure that it will meet the determined objectives. Examples of such support functions are direct response techniques, such as return coupons, toll-free numbers, and free sample redemption vouchers. These techniques not only complement the media plan, but also offer the possibility of constant control of marketing communication effects and consequent modification of media plans where appropriate.

6.17 Summary

Media decisions are a vital step in the marketing communication process. At the end of the 1990s the traditional experiential steps and procedures developed over time by media planners and buyers were rapidly being replaced by technology-based computer applications of media planning and purchasing. Furthermore, the digital revolution will see the emergence of yet unknown media vehicles, of which the Internet may be only the beginning. Recent trends in global marketing and micro-segmentation will certainly pose exciting and daunting challenges to media decision-making. Whatever changes may emerge, the ultimate objective will still be one of finding an optimal strategic fit between the media and the target audience.

7 Marketing communications research

IT should be pointed out that marketing communication research falls within the wider scope of marketing research, which is the topic of a more comprehensive discussion in Chapter 8. This section will, therefore, deal specifically and briefly only with the communication-research aspect of marketing research, and will be limited to a general discussion of the role of research rather than dealing with detailed methodological and research technique issues.

7.1 Ensuring the value of marketing communication expenditures

If one considers the vast amounts of money spent on marketing communication throughout the world, it is not surprising that there is a constant and ongoing demand for the effectiveness of marketing communication to be scrutinized through appropriate research. At the same time, it should be clear that, with these substantial expenditures, it seems futile to ask only after the implementation of a campaign whether it has worked. During the 1990s much more research was conducted to ensure that marketing communication would work, rather than only retrospectively measuring the outcomes thereof. If the marketing communication programme does not achieve its objectives, both the money spent and the potential gains that could have been realized from an effective campaign may be lost.

At the same time, these two stages of conducting research in the marketing communication process represent the broad distinction between planning research and evaluative research, also traditionally known as pre-testing and post-testing. These two research applications are primarily concerned with the marketing communication message and the anticipated or real reactions of the target audience.

7.2 Pre-testing

Pre-testing is aimed at gathering relevant information before the actual transmittal of the message, such that it will allow for final modification of the message before it goes to media. The objective is not to find an ultimate and final measurement or assurance of success, but rather to provide a general indication whether the marketing communication message will be comprehended, and whether it will result in the desired responses from the target audience. Although pre-testing may not be a foolproof assurance of the success of marketing communication, it nevertheless substantially lowers the risk of failure. At the least, proper pre-testing will differentiate a poor message from a good one. In essence, pre-testing entails probing for answers to two questions: what to say (communication theme, copy platform), and how to say it (copy, creative execution).

7.3 Post-testing

Post-testing is widely used to establish the effectiveness of a marketing communication campaign after it has been launched and carried by the media. Post-testing is designed to perform two roles: first, to determine whether the campaign is accomplishing the desired goals and outcomes, and, secondly, to provide input for an analysis of the situation for continuing the programme. General measures used in post-testing are recognition and recall (whether members of the target market are aware of the campaign and have been exposed to it), retention (whether they remember what was said or conveyed), liking (whether the message had a positive appeal and caused the target audience to like the message, product, or brand), and propensity to buy (whether the message induced the target audience to consider buying the product). More specific content and reaction research can naturally be done at this stage if it is required and would contribute to better decisions for continuation or even termination of the campaign.

7.4 The testing process

As pointed out earlier, testing may occur at various stages in the marketing communication process and throughout its development. Research may be conducted during the concept generation phase, at the stage of rough and pre-finished artwork or copy, once the artwork and copy are finished, but before publication thereof, or after the launch and implementation of the campaign. Each of these contexts is characterized by a number of specific research techniques, which may vary significantly between different countries. The detailed discussion of such techniques and their methodological implications are beyond the scope of the current chapter, and students are advised to consult more comprehensive literature on marketing communication and marketing and advertising research (see Further Reading).

7.5 Summary

All marketing managers want to know whether their marketing communication programmes are working and whether the specified results and outcomes are achieved. The information gained from marketing communication research, at whatever stage of the communication process, provides vital information for adaptation, continuation, or termination of certain elements or even the total campaign.

8 The future of marketing communication

I⊤ has become an accepted adage that change is the only certainty today. This truism also applies to the world of marketing communication (see Insert overleaf). Most of the existing textbooks on marketing communication, including this current chapter, are predominantly representative of an endangered, if not almost extinct, paradigm of marketing communication. Alvin Toffler's assertion that companies that are unable or unwilling to change will become 'exhibits in the museum of corporate dinosaurs' may very well apply to marketing communication executives and

'I think I shall never see, a billboard as lovely as a tree'?

There has been a revolution in the quality and ingenuity of outdoor displays. Famous architects such as Britain's Sir Norman Foster are designing arty bus shelters and kiosks with backlit displays. Movement and sound is now possible too and a Smirnoff advert made a spider appear to crawl up a man's back while a Disney advert emitted the sounds of puppies barking.

practitioners. This section provides a somewhat speculative, and hopefully provocative, overview of current trends, and new and future technologies that already affect and will in future impact on marketing communication as we know it now.

It should be clear that many of the traditional variables and dynamics in the marketing communication process are currently changing so rapidly that it can be said that the 'good old days' are gone forever. The following were some of the trends affecting marketing communication at the end of the 1990s:

Vastly increased consumer options. In most developed countries of the world, there is an increasing and almost never-ending proliferation of new products. This simply means that the consumer now has a much greater selection to choose from than only a few years ago. Competition is much fiercer, and the marketing communication clutter requires revolutionary new approaches to vie for consumer attention, interest, and support.

Increase in mass-distribution outlets. There is an increasing trend towards mass merchandising, with a concurrent discounting for bulk purchasing by the end consumer. Bulk discounters, such as Makro in South Africa and Wal-Mart in the USA, are rapidly redefining the position and role, even the very existence, of smaller retail operators.

Changes in consumer motivation and buying behaviour. Significant changes took place with regard to the way in which consumers decide and buy during the last three decades of the twentieth century. Consumers generally show less involvement now than in the past, with the result that less time is spent on evaluating alternative products or brands. Products are, in fact, increasingly viewed as functional commodities, resulting in price as the predominant decision factor in many instances. An inevitable result is that brand loyalty has been eroded throughout a broad range of products and services.

Individualized marketing. The non-differentiated mass markets of the past decades are rapidly disappearing, and many marketers have now to come to grips with the requirements of individualized marketing that recognizes, acknowledges, and serves the needs of narrowly selected groups of consumers whose individual identities need to be established by the marketer. This requirement has lead to a significant increase in database marketing or micro-marketing, often using a combination of marketing and other database technologies and the mapping technology of geographic information systems (GIS).

Integrated marketing communication (IMC). The almost seamless symbiosis between the various stakeholder groups of any particular marketing company makes the integrating of all its communication endeavours an imperative rather than another strategic option.

8.1 Digital technology

It should be clear by now that the three dominant elements of the digital era—computing, telecommunications, and television—are set to bring about fundamental changes to the marketing communication process and the industry in general. Television's original analogue signal conventions were technically incompatible with the digital systems of the computing and telecommunications. The developments that make it possible for television to speak the same digital language as the other two will have enormous implications for marketing communication. The following are some of the results of this fusion that were already in place in the late 1990s and were affecting marketing communication to some degree:

■ Yellow Pages and Talking Pages, and the use of touch-tone telephones to navigate multiple information offerings;

■ premium channels on satellite television (75 per cent of BSkyB subscribers in the UK buy them);

■ home banking and remote access financial services;

■ tele-shopping services;

■ on-screen information services like Teletext, which generates and handles 14 million requests on a weekly basis;

■ interactive advertising, such as CD-i-based interactive commercials in Finland, which have been attracting audiences 50 per cent higher than the programmes that preceded them.

These trends are clear indicators that on-demand information will dominate digital life. Consumers will ask explicitly and implicitly for what they want, when they want it. This will require a radical rethinking of advertiser-supported programming. In future digital media, there will be more pay-per-views, not just on an all-or-nothing basis, but more like newspapers and magazines, where the cost is shared with advertisers. In some cases the consumer may have the option to receive programme material without advertising, but at a higher cost. In other cases the marketing communication may be so personalized that it will be indistinguishable from the news. In fact, to that individual it will be news.

As far as computer networks are concerned, the increasing capability for selling on the Internet and its interlinks with television may cause Internet shopping and marketing communication to become the most familiar aspect of the Net with the mass public. By 1998 almost $100 billion worth of goods were already bought through more conventional direct marketing channels in the USA alone. As the Internet matures, shopping on it will become much more interesting than shopping with paper catalogues, because there will be such a great diversity of shops and goods. The consumer will be able to explore the world and shop around for the best products and prices. The creation of Internet shopping malls will require a whole new set of marketing communication skills: a combination of the computer skills of the hackers and the communication skills of Madison Avenue.

8.2 Summary

The preceding few thoughts merely scratch the surface of the submerged iceberg of the new marketing communication awakening. The traditional approaches and well-known practices will certainly remain for some time yet. At the same time, the rapid rate of change introducing new and yet unknown marketing communication paradigms may not only take some marketers and practitioners by surprise, but could in fact render them irrelevant. This seemingly stern warning, once again, applies equally to this chapter and the entire book. Who knows what it may look like if it were to be reconsidered in a few years?

9 Summary

MARKETING communication is as old as the history of mankind. Long before there ever was any awareness of marketing as a practice or as an academic discipline, people used communication to trade and barter and to provide each other's consumer needs. During the twentieth century, both the mother discipline of marketing and the art and science of marketing communication made great strides. Practical experience and scientific study and research have greatly clarified and systemised the subdiscipline and the application of marketing communication principles and procedures. There are established and proven principles and guidelines for developing marketing plans, for identifying and profiling the target audience, and for reaching decisions on the marketing communication budget. Decisions about the marketing communication mix, creating the message, and selecting appropriate media can be based on well-developed marketing communication research techniques and methodologies.

However, concurrent with the dawn of a new millennium, it is certain that marketing and marketing communication will undergo significant changes. Moving from the information era to a digital society, and increasingly conducting business in cyberspace, require that marketing communication scientists and practitioners should be prepared critically to reconsider their current way of thinking about marketing communication. Even without these inevitable changes, marketing communication is one of the most exciting and challenging fields to study and to work in. There is no doubt that the excitement and challenges will only become bigger and better in the future.

Further reading

Corstjens, J. (1990), *Strategic Advertising: A Practitioners Handbook* (Oxford; Heinemann Professional Publishing).

De Mooij, M. (1994), *Advertising Worldwide* (New York: Prentice Hall Inc.).

Ehrenburg, A., Barnard, N., and Scrive, N. (1997), 'Justifying our Advertising Budgets', *Marketing and Research Today* (Feb.), 38–44.

Fill, C. (1995), *Marketing Communications: Frameworks, Theories and Applications* (Englewood Cliffs, Ill: Prentice-Hall Inc.)

Hart, N. (1993), *Industrial Marketing Communications* (London: Kogan Paul).

O'Harra, B., Palumbo, F., and Herbig, P. (1993), 'Industrial Trade Shows Abroad', *Industrial Marketing Management*, 22: 233–7.

Schultz, D. E., Tannenbaum, S. I., and Lauterborn, R. F. (1992), *Integrated Marketing Communication* (Chicago, Ill.: NTC Publishing).

Discussion questions

1 Why is marketing communication described as a process? What are the components of this process, and how do these components interact with each other?

2 Marketing communication is not necessarily a linear process. Do you agree with this statement? What does it mean? How would you explain it to a person who has no marketing background?

3 Identify and briefly discuss the elements of the marketing communication plan.

4 What are the differences between marketing objectives and communication objectives? Name examples of each.

5 Write one descriptive paragraph for each of the following terms so that a person without marketing background knowledge will understand what they mean:

- target-audience decisions;
- communication mix decisions;
- creative decisions;
- media decisions;
- marketing communication research.

Good Stuff is a fairly small delicatessen chain operating in Perth and the larger towns of Western Australia. Its customer base comes mainly from the upper-middle- and upper-class shoppers who are typically discriminating buyers of up-market gourmet food products. An interesting trend is that the same group of consumers also seem to be the primary consumers of above-average-priced wine labels. However, with the advent of speciality food sections in large department stores, such as Myers, and the isolation of dedicated gourmet merchandising areas in general grocery stores, such as Coles and Woolworths, *Good Stuff's* traditional customer base has come under threat. It seems that the offering of the same or similar brands by these other stores may now weaken the strong degree of customer loyalty that it has managed to build up.

 Good Stuff's management are naturally extremely concerned about the situation, and would consider accepting and following any strategy that would stem the attack on their customer loyalty base. In essence, they not only want to retain their current customers, but want to be more aggressive in the marketplace to be able to cope with increasing competition. They are not sure, however, as to whether they should tackle the competition head on, or whether they should use a more subtle strategy to retain and expand their position in the market.

Discussion questions

1 Develop a marketing strategy and specific measurable marketing objectives for *Good Stuff* that would accomplish their objectives.

2 Write a concise profile of the primary target audience in this case.

3 Formulate three specific marketing communication objectives that are in line with the marketing objectives in your answer to Question 1.

4 Which budgeting approach would you suggest to the management of *Good Stuff*? What reasons would you give to justify your recommendation?

5 What combination of the marketing communication mix would be appropriate in this case? Why?

6 What would be an appropriate selection of media types to accomplish the marketing communication objectives?

7 Write a single sentence statement expressing the main copy platform that you would suggest as the core of the marketing communication message in this case.

Chapter 13
Sales-force Management

Sönke Albers

Objectives

The objectives of this chapter are:

1 to consider the role of selling in modern organizations, whether it is selling to consumers, to resellers, or to businesses;

2 to identify the tasks that salespeople must fulfil;

3 to consider how a firm can identify the best salespeople;

4 to recommend ways of managing and motivating a salesforce;

5 to consider appropriate compensation plans and the setting of quotas for salespeople;

6 to discuss how to set up a sales organization and the best way to design sales territories.

1 The role of the salesperson

1.1 Image

Although selling is of utmost importance for Western economies with free markets, people performing the task of selling still have a bad image in society (Mason 1965). This may be because people build their image on experiences in situations where a salesperson tries to persuade consumers at the door to buy goods such as encyclopaedias, magazines, or insurance policies. Because many people feel uncomfortable with this kind of hard selling, they hesitate to become a salesperson. However, apart from this type of direct selling, there are quite different selling jobs in the business-to-business sector, where a salesperson communicates the specific advantages of the firm's products and services to another business that depends on purchasing raw materials, half-ready components, or machinery tools. This selling job does not involve door-to-door selling but visits to customers upon appointment. Communication about products, in particular about high-tech products or complex financial arrangements, has become more and more difficult, so that the selling job demands more and more technical or economic expertise. Given the high-income opportunities, the job of a salesperson offers very attractive prospects. This is especially true for women, who are, in general, believed to be better in listening to and taking care of a customer, which, today, is considered the most important success factor in selling.

1.2 Tasks

Often, people tend to think that a salesperson spends most of his or her time calling on customers. In reality, he or she has to perform many other tasks, such that the percentage of calling time is only about 33 per cent (Krafft 1995). The following tasks have to be carried out in order to be able to call on customers. First, potential customers have to be identified from databases. The salesperson has to plan on which customer—for industrial firms these are called 'accounts'—he or she should call, and with which priority and frequency. Then, the salesperson has to decide how to approach a customer. For many calls a sales

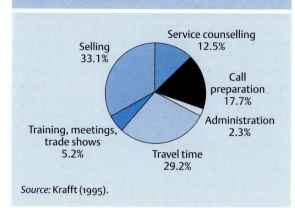

Figure 13.1 Time requirements of the task of a salesperson

Selling 33.1%
Service counselling 12.5%
Call preparation 17.7%
Administration 2.3%
Travel time 29.2%
Training, meetings, trade shows 5.2%

Source: Krafft (1995).

presentation has to be prepared. In the case of a repeat visit the salesperson has to gather all the information a customer has asked for during the last visit. Also, salespeople have to be trained to deal with their customers' counter-arguments and to close a sale. Later on, he or she has to prepare written offers. Each visit requires a substantial amount of time for travel and sometimes for entertaining the customer. After the customer has placed his order the salesperson must administer this order, offer after-sales service by helping with installation, train the customer to use the product, advise him about the profitable use of the product, and handle any complaints or warranty problems. In addition, the salesperson's firm will request administrative work such as providing all kinds of data on customers, reporting activities, participating in sales meetings and conferences, and visiting trade shows. In order constantly to improve his or her competence, the salesperson has to take part in product as well as sales training. Fig. 13.1 shows what percentage of working time a salesperson spends on the various activities according to a survey of German companies.

2 Selling to customers

For many people, successful selling can be reduced to recipes for the interaction with the customer; of course, *how to sell* is of importance to the ultimate success. However, it is just as important to be good at managing one's own *selling effort*.

Know-how for both aspects of the job is therefore, presented in Section 2. Section 3 describes how both activities can be supported by sales information systems and planning software as well as the use of powerful electronic media.

2.1 Art of selling

In bookstores readers will find bestsellers with titles such as '99 Golden Rules for Successful Selling' or '20 Lessons to Become Rich with Selling'. Such books give the impression that selling can easily be learned by following certain recipes. Of course, this cannot be true. Otherwise, one would find many rich people who had benefited from such recipes. In this section we discuss two key concepts of selling.

2.1.1 Adaptive versus canned selling

A lot of effort has been devoted to finding profiles of salespeople and selling techniques that are particularly successful. In consequence, many sales training programmes consist of teaching a standardized behaviour towards a customer involving canned presentations and the like. In the long run, these programmes have not proved to be successful, because personal selling that is implemented in a standardized form offers hardly any advantage over other less costly communication forms such as advertising, direct mail, or tele-marketing.

'However, comparatively speaking, personal selling is also probably the most expensive form of marketing communication.' (Chapter 12, p. 282)

Rather, the advantage of personal selling is that it allows a salesperson to communicate individually with a customer, answer all of his questions, and deal with all of his concerns. A key to success, therefore, lies in the ability and willingness of the salesperson to listen carefully to the customer and to adapt the products and services to the customer's needs. This also means that potentially all people can become successful salespeople if they really are customer oriented and try to solve their problems. Therefore, adaptive selling must be superior to any kind of canned presentation or standardized interaction. Saxe and Weitz (1982) have provided the SOCO (sale orientation–customer orientation) scale by which the degree of industrial salespeople's customer orientation can be measured.

2.1.2 Soft versus hard selling

In the past, some salespeople have successfully used certain influence techniques to persuade customers to buy products that they did not really want. This technique turned out to be particularly successful in door-to-door selling, because there is potentially a high conflict between salesperson and consumer and no future interaction is likely. As pointed out, this behaviour may have contributed to the poor image of salespeople. In order to protect the consumer, the law has been changed in Germany, for example, to allow a consumer to cancel any house-door contract (order) within seven days without justification. In industrial selling the situation is generally different, because a firm and a customer are involved in a long-term relationship where any hard selling entails the risk of losing the customer. However, even in industry settings this kind of behaviour has been observed. This is mainly because of incentives rewarding short-term behaviour at the expense of long-term advantages. Hard selling then becomes understandable if a salesperson remains in his or her position only for a certain time and therefore has a shorter planning horizon than the firm. However, a firm is better off encouraging its salespeople to engage in long-term behaviour and to avoid any high-pressure or hard selling. Otherwise, it cannot establish long-term relationships with its customers. Thus, it is more advantageous to listen to the customer, carefully to analyse his needs, and to sell him a solution to his problem. This kind of behaviour is termed soft selling and entails the salesperson becoming a consultant to the customer. If a customer gets a solution to his problem, he will increase his commitment, accept a higher reservation price, and exhibit more patience towards any kind of delays. With the exception of some businesses where future interactions are not likely, it is, therefore, always better to apply soft-selling methods (Chu et al. 1995).

2.2 Managing selling effort

If a firm works with a reasonable number of salespeople, it will generally not be possible—or, if possible, not profitable—for a salesperson to call on every customer as often as necessary to achieve maximum sales. Rather, the salesperson has to allocate his or her scarce resource of working time across customers. In general, customers differ with respect to their response to sales calls.

First of all, we can distinguish between existing customers (accounts) and potential customers (prospects). Secondly, customers of each group have a different buying volume and show different propensities to buy. In addition, accounts are dispersed over a certain territory and to call on them requires different travel times as well as travel cost. If a salesperson's success is measured in terms of achieved sales or profit contribution, he or she faces the problem of determining which accounts to call on and how often.

2.2.1 Allocation of time or calls

Allocating the effort with which accounts are served is a difficult task. Accounts exhibit different sizes with respect to their potential buying volumes. In many companies accounts are, therefore, classified into A, B, and C accounts according to their sales volume. Then, for example, salespeople are asked to call on A accounts once every other week, B accounts once a month, and C accounts once a quarter. Very often, this classification is too simple. Because of their sales volumes, the accounts of the three groups receive different conditions, leading to different gross margins. There may be other classification criteria that provide account groups with different responsiveness to calling effort. Last but not least, accounts may differ in the attractiveness of their locations and thus in the profitability of a visit. The effective use of one's working time for selling is, therefore, critical for the success of a salesperson.

Since the task of allocating calling effort is very difficult to accomplish intuitively, Lodish (1971) has developed a computerized decision support system, called CALLPLAN (see Box 13.1). As input the model requires a functional relationship between sales and calling effort, operationalized as calling time, for each single account or account group (comprising similar accounts). Lodish uses the following functional form:

$$(1) \quad S_i = S_i^{\min} + (S_i^{\max} - S_i^{\min}) \cdot \frac{t_i^{\delta}}{\gamma + t_i^{\delta}}$$

where:

S_i = sales volume of the ith account,
$S_i^{\min}$ = base sales volume that can be achieved without calling time,
$S_i^{\max}$ = saturation level of the sales volume of the ith account,
t_i = calling time for the ith account,
γ and δ = parameter values.

Box 13.1 Increasing the sales force's sales by over 8 per cent

CALLPLAN was evaluated in a field experiment at United Airlines in 1975. Ten pairs of salesmen (eight passenger and two cargo), five in New York and five in San Francisco, were matched by local management according to personal characteristics, compatibility of territory size, revenue, and account mix, such that each member of the pair would be equally likely to have a similar sales increase in 1975. Ten salesmen were chosen randomly, one from each pair, to use CALLPLAN, while the others were told only that they were participating in an experiment in order to control for the 'Hawthorn effect'. After six months, the average CALLPLAN salesperson had 8.1 per cent higher sales than his matched counterpart. The probability that such a large increase could occur by chance is less than 2.5 per cent. The actual dollar sales improvement compared to the control for just those ten people was well into seven figures. One participant said: 'The best thing about CALLPLAN is the opportunity I have to express my knowledge of my accounts, and then ultimately to see this develop into an overall program that aids me in planning my workday, workweek, and beyond, perhaps a full year. . . . The plan that I'm working with today I'm not just comfortable with, I'm enthusiastic regarding its precision and potential.'

Source: Fudge and Lodish (1977).

Figure 13.2 Sales response function in CALLPLAN

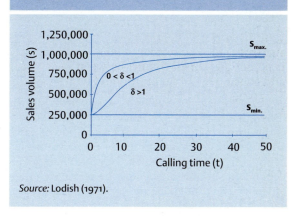

Source: Lodish (1971).

- What sales do you expect as saturation level at a very high calling time? This gives the value of the saturation level S_i^{max}.
- What sales do you expect as minimum level that will be achieved without any calling time? This gives the value of S_i^{min}.
- What sales do you expect at current calling time? This is often current sales.
- What sales do you expect if calling time was increased by 50 per cent.

The answers to the last two questions form a system of two equations that can be solved for the two unknowns γ and δ. This has to be repeated for each account.

CALLPLAN (see Box 13.1) asks for the division of a salesperson's territory into subareas. The underlying assumption is that visits to accounts within one subarea can be combined into a tour. This allows for calculation of travel time and the cost of a tour from the salesperson's office into a subarea. The model determines the optimal number of calls per account by maximizing profit contribution from sales summed up over all accounts minus travel cost summed up over all tours subject to the constraint that the resulting total calling time plus travel time does not exceed the available working time. As the exact travel time and cost depend on the sequencing of calls, which results in a rather complex problem, Lodish works with the approximation that travel time and cost depend only on the number of tours to the various subareas. The number of tours itself is assumed to be equal to the maximum number of calls on one

Depending on the value of δ, this function can exhibit either a concave ($\delta < 1$) or an S-shaped ($\delta > 1$) relationship (see Fig. 13.2). It is a general economic principle that the outcome of selling effort diminishes with increasing effort, hence the concave shape. Sometimes, effort must pass a threshold before becoming effective and only then shows decreasing marginal response, hence an S-shape. Note that sales response functions of a group of accounts must always be concave, because the salesperson can allocate his or her time optimally within the group.

In order to solve the allocation problem, the parameter values of this function have to be estimated for each account or account group. In general, one knows only one point of this function—namely, current sales at current effort. Therefore, Lodish asks for subjective calibration of the functions through answering the following questions for each account:

of the accounts per subarea. An application of a similar approach, including the determination of an optimal pricing policy, is described by Albers (1996b).

In practice, it can be tedious to estimate all the response functions, apart from the problem of whether these estimates are at all reliable. Therefore, salespeople often follow a policy of allocating their calls to accounts in proportion to the previous or planned sales volume. It has been shown theoretically (Albers 1997) that this is optimal only if the gross margins and the elasticities of sales with respect to calling time are equal across accounts. An elasticity gives the relative change of a dependent variable divided by the relative change of the causing independent variable. In our case, the elasticity of sales with respect to changes of selling time can be computed as follows:

$$(2) \quad \beta = \frac{\text{Relative change of sales in \%}}{\text{Relative change of selling time in \%}}.$$

If a salesperson has increased his or her calling time by 10 per cent and sales have increased by 3 per cent, then the elasticity is 0.3, which is a very realistic value for many sales forces. Furthermore, the above-mentioned practice is suboptimal if travel time is not equal across accounts. It is unusual for all three requirements to be fulfilled. If one, nevertheless, wants to work with a heuristic, then it is near-optimal to allocate selling time according to equation 3.

$$(3) \quad t_i \cdot (1 + r_i) = \frac{g_i \beta_i S_i}{\sum g_j \beta_j S_j} \cdot T$$

where:
- j = total number of accounts,
- g_i = gross margin of the ith account,
- S_i = sales volume of the ith account,
- β_i = elasticity of sales of the ith account with respect to changes of calling-time,
- r_i = travel time as average multiple of calling time,
- t_i = selling time for the ith account,
- T = total selling time of a salesperson.

Of course, this formula can be applied only if the salesperson feels able to give a subjective estimate of the elasticities.

Equation (3) also answers the often-posed question whether it is better to call on each customer with a rather low frequency than to call only on high-potential customers but with a higher frequency. This is of particular relevance for pharmaceutical salespeople, who operate in markets where the complete set of customers is explicitly known. They have lists of all physicians they can call on in their territory and have to decide what share they should visit (coverage) for how many times (frequency). Equation (3) states that it is profitable to visit any physician as long as the optimal selling time is longer than the time required for just one visit.

2.2.2 Old versus new accounts

A special allocation problem arises if a salesperson has to serve established accounts and at the same time convert prospects into new accounts. In general, both groups differ with respect to their loyalty as well as the effort that has to be invested until the salesperson can achieve sales. This has the following implications.

If a customer is treated carefully and offered good solutions for his problems, the probability is very high that he will stay with his supplier. Compared to the high effort of converting a prospect into a customer, it is generally better to hold a customer than to take actions that involve the risk of losing certain customers. A more detailed evaluation is possible by determining customer equity. This implies a calculation of the average profit contribution that can be expected from a customer during the period he is loyal. Depending on this value, it can be decided which actions are profitable and what amount of money should be spent for holding such a customer. The profit contribution of such actions can also be compared to the effort and actions necessary to gain one new customer. Very often, salespeople experience a rate of 3–20 trials to convert prospects into new customers before being successful once (Krafft 1995).

On the other hand, the value of new customers is often underestimated because the acquisition of new accounts involves a high level of effort and investment in the short run but pays off only in the long run. This makes prospecting unattractive to salespeople who are short-term oriented because they expect to stay in their position for only a few years or because they are evaluated or even paid according to current sales. However, in the long run it is very important not to neglect the effort for new account acquisition. Losing some customers after a while is inevitable, so there is a constant need for new customers. In order to motivate salespeople to invest in this prospecting activity despite its short-term unattractiveness, firms often pay a bonus for each acquired new customer or run contests with this objective in addition to sales-related financial incentives. As already discussed, a customer-equity analysis is also advantageous for prospects. Then, one can assess the long-run profit of a prospect per required unit of effort and compare it to the profit of established accounts.

Once a salesperson has decided to try to convert a prospect into a customer, he or she has to decide how many times to visit this prospect before giving up. This decision can be supported by information on the probability of successfully converting a prospect into a new account after having visited him a certain number of times. Then, it is worth making an additional call only if the long-run profit multiplied by the probability of converting him, given that the previous visits have not led to a sale, is higher than the profit from visiting an established account.

In many instances, suppliers have to write offers in which the technical solution and the price have to be provided. Very often, the costs for preparing such offers are as high as 5 per cent of the expected sales volume. If the firm experiences a rate of 8–15 offers per one successful sale, then it is necessary to plan the effort per offer. It is, therefore, profitable to prepare the offers with a different degree of detail. Depending on the success probability and expected profitability of the contract. Vague enquiries should be answered only with standard offers that can be easily generated with the help of a computer. In contrast, in cases where the firm forecasts a high probability of gaining the sale, an offer should be provided with a detailed technical solution.

2.2.3 Tour planning

We have already seen the importance of travel times in the allocation of a salesperson's selling time. This leads to the question of how the salesperson should plan tours of visits to minimize travel time and cost. In Operations Research, the problem of determining the cost-minimizing tour through a set of locations is called a 'travelling-salesman problem'. Note that, despite its name, this sequencing problem is often not relevant for

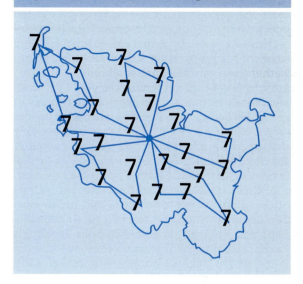

Figure 13.3 Cloverleaf tours as good heuristic

our salesperson. Rather, he or she has to plan tours combining several accounts to be visited on one day and then schedule tours over time such that the number of visits per customer is met, the available time per day is not exceeded, and the travel time is minimized. This results in a complex mathematical programming problem for which software is available only for special cases (Hall and Partyka 1997). Without computer support, the following heuristic is recommended. The salespeople should cluster accounts into regions such that the accounts of one region can be called on in one day. Then, the tours from the salesprson's location in circles through the accounts of one region and back to the salesperson's location will look like a cloverleaf (see Fig. 13.3).

2.3 Computer-aided selling

Based on the typical remuneration of salespeople and their average times for calls and travel, one can calculate the cost of one visit to a customer. In the early 1990s this amount varied from DM200 to DM500, depending on the industry (Krafft 1995). These very high expenses have led to two consequences: first, in some accounts, the profit contribution of which does not justify the cost of a visit, communication has been changed to telephone and fax. Secondly, the need to increase the effectiveness of the use of time has been realized. Substantial improvements have been achieved by computer-aided selling (CAS), where sophisticated information technology (IT) supports each activity of the salesperson. CAS can be used for the selling stages of call preparation, call execution, and call analysis (Link and Hildebrand 1993).

An effective *call preparation* requires retrieval of all kinds of information about the customer to be visited. Rather than working with often incomplete account files on paper, salespeople are now supported by a centrally maintained customer database. It usually contains such data as the addresses of customers, names of contact persons and their telephone numbers, current selling price conditions (e.g. discounts), and the interaction history with respect to sales, profit contribution, and number of previous calls. Ideally, it should also provide information on the current status of the negotiation (e.g. number of calls, probability to buy). In addition, salespeople can access a product database that provides all necessary information on the products sold by the company. This includes technical specifications, selling arguments, comparisons to competitive products, and price conditions. In some cases, firms have extended the information offered to their salespeople to a sales strategy information system. It contains recommendations as to which products should be emphasized in selling, what kind of special offers exist, and whether there are any shortages of products for delivery. It is important to note that, besides the better information available through such sales information systems, salespeople can access these centrally maintained databases and information systems from their home or even on the road via telecommunication, and are thus much more flexible than in the old days.

In addition to providing customer and product information, firms usually equip their salespeople with software that supports the generation of professional sales presentations (e.g. Power Point), the writing of letters and documents (e.g. Word), the analysis of their business with spreadsheet software (e.g. Excel), and the management of their time (time planner). In some cases, salespeople can also use software for supporting their planning task. There are programs that give recommendations on when to terminate further visits based on overall experience (see Section 2.2.2). Other programs suggest the number of calls per account (see Section 2.2.1) or even the accounts to

be visited. If call frequencies and the locations of accounts are specified, the process of scheduling calling tours can be assisted by appropriate software (see Section 2.2.3).

When it comes to *call execution*, computer programs may also aid selling. Customers want to obtain detailed and valid information on the products of the company. If an electronic product catalogue exists, the salespeople can access the central computer of his or her headquarters and show the product features and other product-related information online on the screen. This guarantees reliable and complete information, avoids written enquiries to the headquarters, and reduces the time from the first contact to the final order. In the case of selling computer systems and other complex machinery tools, special software can support the configuration of these systems from parts or modules of the supplier according to the needs of the purchaser. Such an early known system was the expert system XSEL/XCON by Digital Equipment. The functionality of such programs can be viewed and tried by everybody on the Internet when ordering a computer by Dell (www.dell.com). Nowadays, a variety of programs exist. Most of them offer computer-aided design such that complex systems can be designed interactively with the customer during a call. Some programs already have the capability of determining the optimal product for a customer. Financial service companies offer programs where the optimal insurance policy or the optimal combinations of loans and mortgages are determined based on the individual circumstances holding for a customer. Later on, the preparation of an offer can be supported by the same systems. It may be complemented by a know-how databank that offers access to all previous offers, to all previous technical solutions, and standard text modules for writing the offer.

A database is also invaluable in *call analysis*. At the same time as providing data *for* its salespeople, the firm also asks for data *from* its salespeople. Salespeople have to provide all the necessary information for the customer database. This enables the firm to perform analyses about the efficiency of selling by calculating ratios like the number of visits necessary to convert prospects, of contracts per offer, of sales per visit, of visits per salesperson, of sales potential, and many more. By comparing these figures across salespeople, a firm can carry out an evaluation of performance but also provide benchmarks for its salespeople.

3 Managing a sales force

3.1 Performance measurement

Salespeople are on the road most of their time, making it impossible to observe and hence to evaluate their real effort and the appropriateness of their behaviour. At the same time, there is no other group of employees in a company for which the outcome of work (sales volume) depends so strongly on individual effort and effectiveness. As a consequence, it is a widely accepted practice to use the achieved sales volume as a measure of salespeople's performance and to tie financial incentives to it. However, in addition to individual effort, there are many other exogenous factors that influence sales, and, depending on the nature of these factors, firms have adopted one of the following systems for performance measurement.

If sales depend only weakly on effort, salespeople are evaluated on the basis of inputs. This is common practice, especially in sales forces selling consumer products to retailers. Very often, key-account managers have already negotiated with the retailers' procurement managers whether a certain brand will be stocked by supermarkets or not. This decision is based mainly on an analysis of the strength of a brand in a market and the conditions influencing its profitability. Now, the salesperson can support a high sales volume only by good merchandising. This includes making sure that the products are arranged attractively on the shelves, that products with overdue expiry dates are sorted out, that displays are properly erected, and so on. In this case, the evaluation of salespeople relies either on *quantitative* measures, such as the number of visits to a retailer's outlets, the number of displays set up, or the number of stores with goods actually stocked, or on *qualitative* measures, such as the salesperson's actual behaviour. While the quantitative measures do not provide a full picture of the effort of salespeople, the qualitative measures suffer from all kinds of subjectivity and non-comparability. Salespeople located far away from headquarters can be evaluated only by first-line sales managers. Now, it is well known that some of them give very good evaluations for exactly the same situation, while others tend to be very critical. Companies like IBM have, therefore, normalized the evaluations such that the average judgement is equal across all subunits. However,

this turns the evaluation into a 'tournament' in which it is important to be better than the other members of a subgroup within the salesforce rather than to try to increase the effort and efficiency level of the whole subunit. In consequence, salespeople will no longer be cooperative, although team behaviour might be more beneficial to the success of the firm.

☞ 'A push approach typically makes much use of a few particular marketing-mix instruments and much less of other instruments. Personal selling—for example, carried out by a manufacturer's sales force—will be of high importance.' (Chapter 9, p. 204)

If sales depend on effort, salespeople are evaluated on sales volume as their outcome. However, the firm then faces the problem of equity across salespeople. It is well known from empirical studies that salespeople who feel that they are not treated fairly are demotivated and are not willing to devote their best effort to their selling task. More precisely, the performance evaluation or financial incentives must meet the equity-condition that the same input leads to the same evaluation or reward across all salespeople. As a consequence, firms have to control for all exogenous factors influencing a salesperson's outcome. This can be done by creating equal starting conditions mostly by designing territories with equal potential. However, we will show in Section 4.4 that this does not involve an equal workload. In general, it is not possible to provide both for equal potential and an equal workload.

Because of this impossibility, it is recommended that the company controls all exogenous factors by quantifying their impact and correcting the sales volume for it. This can be done by estimating a sales response function at the territory level, where sales depend on the salesperson's effort and all quantifiable exogenous factors. Box 13.2 provides a list of potentially relevant factors. It shows that exogenous factors come from four different sources (Albers 1989).

First of all, sales territories differ in their sales potential and the conditions for its realization. Sales potential can be operationalized by the number of companies in the respective territory or by their purchasing volume. However, this alone does not say anything about whether it is possible to reach this potential. If in one territory the customers are geographically dispersed and in the other one they are condensed in one big city, then

Box 13.2 **Factors influencing the sales in a territory**

Factors controlled by the salesperson	Exogenous factors not controlled by the salesperson

1. Effort of the salesperson
  ■ Number of calls
  ■ Calling time
2. Characteristics of the salesperson
  ■ Experience
  ■ Attitudes
  ■ Aptitudes (selling skills)
  ■ Education
	3. Effect of sales management
	  ■ Span of control
	  ■ Type of supervision
	  ■ Experience of managers
	4. Marketing effort of the firm
	  ■ Advertising budgets in areas
	  ■ Promotion activities
	5. Characteristics of territory
	  ■ Potential
	  ■ Realization conditions
	  ■ Concentration of customers
	  ■ Dispersion
	  ■ Workload
	6. Level of competitive intensity

In a situation where data on individual efforts are not available, we can regress sales on exogenous factors only and assume that the unexplained variance is due to differences in effort and effectiveness. In this equation the coefficients β_k to be estimated represent elasticities. If this regression has been carried out for the data on all territories, then equation (4) represents the sales volume that an average salesperson can achieve under the specific conditions in a certain territory.

Given the conditions in a specific territory, it is possible to calculate what sales volume an average salesperson should have achieved. This can be compared to his or her actual sales. If actual sales are higher, then the salesperson is either working harder or is smarter or both than the average salesperson. This method can be used very effectively for performance assessment. The case of German Disco GmbH (see Box 13.3) illustrates the different conclusions drawn from sales volume alone, and from a thorough analysis of the impact of exogenous factors and a correction of sales by this impact.

it is easier because of lower travel time to utilize the potential in the big city. In addition, territories may exhibit different levels of competitive activity. In the German building society market there are some very strong regional companies, so the national companies face very different competitive conditions across Germany. Finally, if the company supports the selling process by sales promotions or advertising, the level of which varies across territories, these differences have to be taken into account when controlling for the real performance. Having identified possible exogenous factors, we can estimate their impact on sales by regressing past sales volumes of all territories against individual effort and levels of exogenous factors. A prerequisite is that data are available on the factors and that they vary across territories. This can be done through the following equation:

$$(4) \quad S_j = \alpha \cdot \prod_{k \in K} x_{jk}^{\beta_k}$$

where:
x_{jk} = level of kth influencing factor in the jth sales territory,
β_k = elasticity of sales with respect to changes of the kth influencing factor.

3.2 Selection and training of salespeople

When the ability and effectiveness of its salespeople are critical to the success of a company, then it is of great importance to select the best people for this job and to train them for high performance. The costs to a company of hiring poor-performing salespeople are very high. They include costs for recruiting—for example, placing advertisements, possibly using an employment agency, and screening potential job candidates—costs for selection—for example, opportunity cost for time spent on interviewing and assessing potential candidates as well as travel expense reimbursements—and finally the costs of training. This amounts to a considerable sum, even without taking into account any lost present and future sales due to an ineffective salesperson. Furthermore, the probability of choosing the right person just by intuition is very low. In the face of the aforementioned costs, this calls for a discussion of how the selection process can be supported by scientific methods to obtain better results.

Recruitment and selection of salespeople involve two different types of decisions:

Box 13.3 A reappraisal of a sales-force's effectiveness

German Disco GmbH (GeDi) is a Frankfurt-based subsidiary of an internationally operating company producing and selling music discs. The German subsidiary employs twenty salespeople, who call on retail outlets to sell the GeDi collection. The retailers are visited regularly in order to present the respective novelties. Each of the twenty salespeople operates in a specified territory. In order to motivate the salespeople, remuneration is by salary and a commission on achieved sales. In order to stimulate the salesperson's motivation even further, the management posts a ranking list of the twenty salespeople with their sales on an information display in the headquarters' main building every month. However, some salespeople opposed this practice, because they felt they had received less attractive territories and therefore considered a tournament on unadjusted sales to be unfair. Because of the resulting motivational problems, the management hired a consultant of ASCON Analytical Sales Consulting GmbH, Kiel, to come up with a resolution for this conflict. First, with the help of regression analysis, the consultant analysed whether and by how much sales volume depended on characteristics of the respective territories. He found out that sales did, indeed, depend on such factors as wholesalers' sales volume of electrical goods (ELECGOODS—indicating the size of the wholesalers and retailers), the number of retailers (NRETAILERS), and the rate of urban popula-

tion (URBANPOP). These three factors explain 74 per cent of the variance. The data on sales and the explaining variables are displayed in Table 13.1. In order to respect confidentiality, the sales data have been linearly transformed such that they are structurally but not actually valid.

The regression led to the following equation:

$$(5) \quad \text{Sales}_j = 5.70 \cdot \text{ELECGOODS}_j^{0.124} \cdot \text{NRETAILERS}_j^{0.4} \cdot \text{URBANPOP}_j^{1.994}.$$

Inserting the values for the three variables into this equation gives the sales volume that can be achieved under the conditions of a certain territory by an average salesperson. This sales quota is also displayed in Table 13.1. Since the sales quota is entirely determined by exogenous factors, the difference between actual sales and quota represents individual performance. The consultant recommended this measure was used to evaluate performance instead of unadjusted sales. The management was surprised, because under the new measure some of the salespeople turned out to be high performing with below-average sales because they were operating in difficult territories, while others with high sales were benefiting from the quality of their territories and were really low-performing employees. This led to a new evaluation procedure and increased motivation.

■ Which type of channel provides the applications promising the best qualification/cost ratio?

■ What is the best method to select salespeople from a set of applicants?

Especially for sales positions, it is not easy to obtain a sufficient number of applicants. This is true in particular for insurance companies that experience a turnover rate as high as 50 per cent and thus have to replace half of their salesforce each year. A firm, therefore, has actively to search for applicants through different channels. These may consist of advertisements in newspapers, enticing salespeople away from competitors, looking for prospective candidates in its own company who are not currently in sales positions, and providing internships for college students. These channels may differ in their effectiveness. It is, therefore, advantageous systematically to record the costs of

recruiting per channel and to conduct a longitudinal study of how many candidates from which channel have ultimately proved to be high performers on the job. On this basis, the firm can calculate the cost of recruiting and selecting *one* successful salesperson per channel. This can be used either to improve the effectiveness of poorly performing channels or to allocate higher budgets to the more effective channels.

The selection of salespeople is done on the basis of a variety of methods. They range from graphology over interviewing to psychological testing. Although many people have strong confidence in one of these methods, its predictability has proved to be questionable. The most widely used method is the interview, which has been found to have insufficient reliability and validity for use in personnel selection. The problem is that it is often misused, in that the first five minutes is spent making a decision and the rest of the time is spent

Table 13.1 Sales of German Disco GmbH explained by exogenous factors

Sales area	Sales volume	Rank (sales)	Wholesalers' sales volumes for electric goods	Rate of urban population	No. of retailers	Estimated sales volume for average salesperson	Performance = sales volume difference	Rank (performance)
1	3,600	11	600	1.000	81	3,861	−261	15
2	3,436	13	912	0.733	106	3,225	211	7
3	4,656	4	1,817	0.790	166	4,564	92	10
4	3,391	15	1,808	0.674	172	3,889	−498	18
5	3,104	17	773	0.747	111	3,286	−182	14
6	3,680	10	771	0.709	97	2,939	741	2
7	3,598	12	1,345	0.773	101	3,519	79	11
8	3,145	16	545	0.794	85	3,022	123	9
9	5,082	1	1,222	0.916	135	4,702	380	4
10	3,416	14	2,267	0.822	96	3,935	−519	19
11	2,663	20	985	0.673	121	3,127	−464	17
12	3,967	8	2,469	0.874	99	4,306	−339	16
13	4,985	2	2,525	0.780	127	4,212	773	1
14	2,754	19	913	0.799	108	3,571	−817	20
15	4,253	6	2,361	0.849	116	4,420	−167	13
16	4,950	3	1,402	0.899	128	4,587	363	5
17	4,379	5	1,343	0.784	109	3,684	695	3
18	3,730	9	1,189	0.741	114	3,473	257	6
19	4,012	7	1,421	0.764	130	3,870	142	8
20	2,768	18	403	0.714	107	2,842	−74	12

in supporting this decision. Many companies use tests for measuring personality and intellectual capabilities. However, as firms are mostly unable to pinpoint the characteristics necessary for successful salespeople, selection on the basis of these tests has not shown a high validity. The results with respect to bio-data are mixed. Items such as individual family responsibility, having dependent children, and being committed to financial obligations are indicators for successful salespeople. All other indicators such as sex, age, education, and leisure activities do not seem to have much predictive power. Graphology appears not to have any validity at all. By far the best results to date have been achieved with assessment centres. The idea is to observe the behaviour of applicants in a simulated environment that is as close as possible to the real selling situation. The tasks often consist of role-playing games, administration of telephone calls while answering mail, leaderless

group discussion, and so on. The danger is that the applicants gain experience with this kind of test, train their behaviour, and thus do not provide data on their true abilities. As with every prediction, the quality of the selection method can be increased by combining methods. This calls for a careful analysis of the data obtained from the biography, a psychological test, an interview, and, last but not least, an assessment centre.

The use of several methods for prediction offers the additional advantage of having data for the evaluation of the best selection method. The firm should constantly evaluate its selection procedure by measuring the performance of its salespeople and comparing the results with the predictions obtained from the various selection methods applied when hiring the salesperson.

Once a salesperson has been hired, it is important to provide training such that he or she has the necessary knowledge and skills to perform well. In particular, the performance evaluation of new salespeople may point out that they need further sales training. An empirical study by Ingram, Schwepker, and Hutson (1992) has revealed the six most important reasons why salespeople fail:

- poor listening skills;
- failure to concentrate on top priorities;
- lack of sufficient effort;
- inability to determine customer needs;
- lack of planning for sales presentations;
- inadequate product/service knowledge.

This shows that failures are not merely due to a lack of knowledge of influencing techniques, but are also the result of a failure to apply the adaptive selling philosophy. Thus, training is necessary for improving product knowledge and adaptability. Currently, there are about 6,000 sales trainers offering their services in Germany. They train according to more than 100 completely different approaches and all of them claim success (e.g. Munkelt 1992). In the face of these numbers it is very hard to believe that only certain training approaches will provide success. Rather, the success may be due to the 'Hawthorne effect'—namely, that somebody cares about the salespeople, motivates them afresh, and therefore achieves success. Hence, it is no surprise that, as in soccer, new coaches can stimulate a sales team irrespective of the method for a while, until the effect wears out and a new person (not so much a different approach) has to bring new motivation into the team.

3.3 Motivation

Many employees have an intrinsic motivation to do a good job because they love their work and get enough rewards from doing interesting activities. This intrinsic motivation is often low for salespeople, because it is common to fail several times before making one successful sale. These failures are combined with a low prestige in society. Therefore, it is necessary to create extrinsic motivation through incentives that can be of non-monetary as well as monetary nature. In the following, we discuss the advantages and disadvantages of alternative incentives. In particular, the suitable combination of financial rewards in the form of compensation plans is investigated. In order to deal with heterogeneity across salespeople we also discuss quota systems.

3.3.1 Non-monetary incentives

Extrinsic motivation is created through rewards. These rewards can be related to income, but can be also related to the status of the salesperson within the firm and society. To increase a salesperson's status, firms can use either career or recognition programmes to reward high-performing salespeople.

Advancements in their career are often as important to salespeople as a good compensation. In general, a career within a firm is only possible through management positions. However, a high-performing salesperson need not necessarily be a good manager. In order to allow for the career of such people, firms have created two different career paths. One is the classical management career with responsibility for personnel, while the other one provides advancements to a salesperson by assigning more and more important selling responsibilities such as key accounts.

Besides career opportunities, a firm can work with a recognition programme that makes public the fact that some salespeople belong to the group of high-performers. This is often achieved through so-called 100%-clubs, the members of which have fulfilled their goal. Salespeople that have achieved specific goals or have exceeded their quota become members of this exclusive club and gain a reputation within the firm. This was very popular at IBM in the 1960s and 1970s.

Because of the low prestige of salespeople, firms have given them better-sounding titles, such as district director, territory delegate, and so on. In addition, salespeople are provided with high-prestige cars to support their standing in the public eye.

Moreover, it is important to give salespeople responsibilities such that they can make offers without asking the management for permission. However, it is questionable whether salespeople should be given complete pricing authority. Salespeople often tend to offer unnecessary rebates in order not to risk a sale. As a consequence, it is more profitable to let them fix prices within narrow limits (Stephenson *et al.* 1979).

3.3.2 Monetary incentives

Monetary incentives to enhance extrinsic motivation can be provided in four different forms:

- fixed salary;
- commission rates;

- bonuses;
- prizes for winning sales contests.

The expressions 'commissions' and 'bonuses' are often used in a confusing way. Therefore, we define commissions as incentives that are paid on a regular basis, mostly based on sales volume or profit contribution, while bonuses are paid from time to time for the achievement of certain goals (Albers 1989). Bonuses on the achievement of sales quotas are something of a hybrid: they are paid regularly but the goal may change over time. Prizes for winning sales contests also represent some kind of bonus. The difference is that prizes are related to the achievement of relative goals (e.g. being the first among all salespeople), while bonuses are paid in the case of absolute achievement of a goal (like a quota). These four forms of incentives offer the following advantages and disadvantages (disadvantages are not listed if they correspond to advantages of other incentive forms) (Albers 1989).

The advantage of fixed salaries is that they provide some financial stability, giving the salesperson the patience to persist in closing difficult sales. With a salary one can compensate tasks that do not immediately lead to sales (e.g. counselling). Of course, salaries can be adjusted over time and thus provide incentives, too. Salespeople receiving a relatively high fixed salary tend to be more loyal than salespeople with very variable income. Salaries do not imply restrictions for changing territories or recalculating quotas. Finally, salaries represent fixed costs that lead to decreasing selling costs per unit with increasing sales volume. However, in the case of decreasing sales, salaries are disadvantageous with respect to costs per unit.

☞ 'However, the pursuit of commission may lead some sales staff to neglect parts of their job, such as giving technical advice to customers.' (Chapter 17, p. 418)

Commissions that depend on outcome are assumed to be strong motivators. The differentiation of commission rates across products and/or customers enables the firm to direct its sales force towards certain activities. With commissions a firm transfers a part of the selling risk to the salesperson. On the other hand, commissions may lead to myopic behaviour such that salespeople sell only when they are rewarded with commissions immediately, but neglect any effort that might result in future sales. Moreover, salespeople may overreact by ruining their health or engaging in unethical behaviour.

Bonuses provided the company with a certain flexibility, because the company can change the goals for getting bonuses as the selling conditions change. With bonuses it is possible to motivate salespeople for a specific behaviour, such as the conversion of prospects into new accounts or emphasizing sales of a specific product that is below the target. In some cases, bonuses serve as a repair for any disfunctionality of commissions. Bonuses can be given for the achievement of outcome goals as well as for providing a certain input like a certain number of visits to customers.

Finally, prizes for winning sales contests are controversial incentives. High prizes that can be won by only a few salespeople provide a strong incentive and increase motivation. However, this holds only if it is not always the same salespeople who are winning the prizes. At the same time, contests create conditions comparable to a tournament, turning the salespeople into competitors. In this case, salespeople no longer cooperate with each other, which can make the working climate worse and, as a result, lead to lower motivation.

3.3.3 Design of compensation plans

The financial incentives outlined above have to be combined into compensation plans. This requires the following major decisions:

- How large should the expected income for the salespeople be?
- Which components should be used in the compensation package?
- How large should the respective components be in terms of percentage of total income?

Typically, companies take these decisions based on common practice. In most countries there are consulting firms that offer surveys on these issues—for example, Kienbaum in Germany or Dartnell Corporation in the USA. Krafft (1995) has also conducted a survey to provide data on usual practices in Germany. The results he obtained in 1994 in respect of the incomes of salespeople, differentiated across industries, are shown in Fig. 13.4. Now, a firm can take these results either to provide an average income level or to follow a more competitive policy of offering higher

Figure 13.4 **Incomes of salespeople in different industries in Germany, 1994**

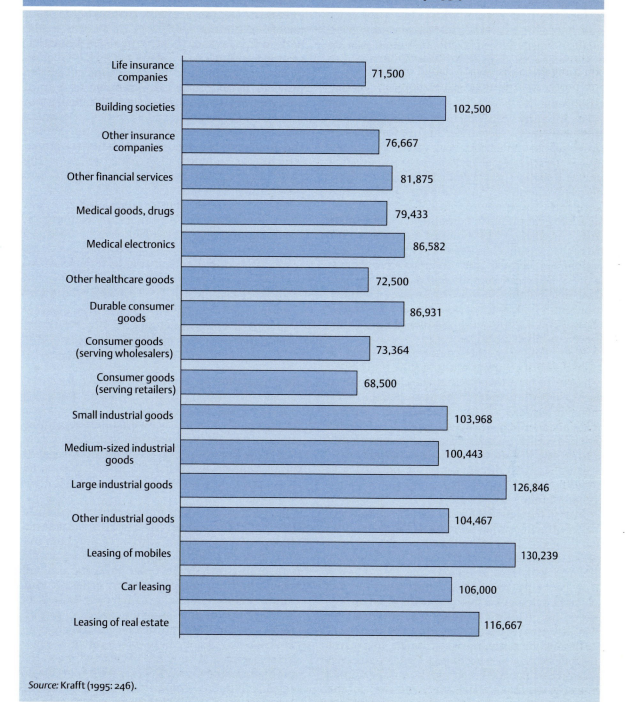

Life insurance companies	71,500
Building societies	102,500
Other insurance companies	76,667
Other financial services	81,875
Medical goods, drugs	79,433
Medical electronics	86,582
Other healthcare goods	72,500
Durable consumer goods	86,931
Consumer goods (serving wholesalers)	73,364
Consumer goods (serving retailers)	68,500
Small industrial goods	103,968
Medium-sized industrial goods	100,443
Large industrial goods	126,846
Other industrial goods	104,467
Leasing of mobiles	130,239
Car leasing	106,000
Leasing of real estate	116,667

Source: Krafft (1995: 246).

income opportunities. IBM has followed the latter policy for a long time and justified it by the ability to hire the best people, who achieve a higher contribution than average salespeople. Moreover, small and medium-sized companies often provide higher compensation than average in order to attract salespeople from larger companies because they lack the facilities to train prospering salespeople.

The intensity with which the various components of financial incentives are used in practice varies across industries. Very often, companies follow an average behaviour, because this has proved to be the practice of companies that have survived. The survey by Krafft (1955) shows that companies rarely choose just one component. Most of them prefer to combine at least a salary with commissions or bonuses and very often make use of all components. This is also recommended because the different components address different issues of control, and only with their combination may a firm reach a complete solution. In particular, bonuses are a flexible instrument to tailor the compensation to the specific needs of a company.

When designing the compensation plan in more detail, it is important to decide on the percentages of total income that should come from the various components. The main decision is on the split between the fixed and the variable part of the income. Many firms are guided by industry practice, which differs substantially across industries, as Fig. 13.5 shows. Apart from industry practice, we want to discuss what the optimal split between fixed and variable components of the compensation plan should be. This question is addressed by agency theory. It deals with the optimal contract between a principal, here the firm, and an agent, here the salesperson, in situations where the agent has a different objective from the principal. This is exactly the case here. A firm generally maximizes profit contribution, while the salesperson maximizes his or her utility, consisting of utility from income corrected for disutility from working time. In addition, both parties exhibit different risk attitudes. In general, the salesperson is considered to be more risk averse than the firm, because he or she cannot diversify the risk, while the firm can do this across all salespeople. Now, this goal conflict is realigned by using financial incentives that are compatible with the company's goals, such that the salesperson is highly motivated to devote

sufficient effort to selling. Moreover, with the split between fixed and variable components, the firm offers a certain mode of risk sharing to the salespeople. With the help of a theoretical model derived from agency theory it has been found that working with a salary is profitable only in cases of high uncertainty, because it is then cheaper to provide the necessary risk premium as a fixed amount (Albers 1996a). However, this model is not developed far enough actually to help determine the optimal level of commission rates. Rather, the model has provided insights into the optimal structure of compensation plans and how the structure depends on exogenous factors like uncertainty.

Apart from risk consideration, research has found the following formula for the commission rate to be optimal (Albers 1986):

$$(6) \quad c = g * \beta / \eta$$

where:
g = gross margin,
β = elasticity of sales with respect to changes in time devoted to selling,
η = elasticity of disutility with respect to changes in the time devoted to selling.

The estimation of the sales elasticity β can be carried out as described in Section 2.2.1. The disutility elasticity η can be estimated by giving salespeople a set of profiles with different combinations of income and required selling time that they have to rank order. η can be interpreted as the percentage by which the income has to increase until a salesperson is willing to work 1 per cent longer.

In equation (6) the common constant commission rate is assumed. However, a substantial number of firms operate with increasing commission rates in order to motivate the salespeople even more strongly. In order to avoid windfall income by the salespeople, firms generally constrain the commission rate to an upper limit or let the commission rate function increase degressively. While it is not controversial that increasing commissions can increase the level of a salesperson's effort, it remains unclear whether the cost of obtaining more sales is so high that it is no longer profitable. Commission rates increasing with sales may also lead to gaming behaviour on the side of the salesperson, who may try to postpone sales from one period to the next in order to maximize income from commissions.

Figure 13.5 Variable part of salespeople's income in different industries in Germany

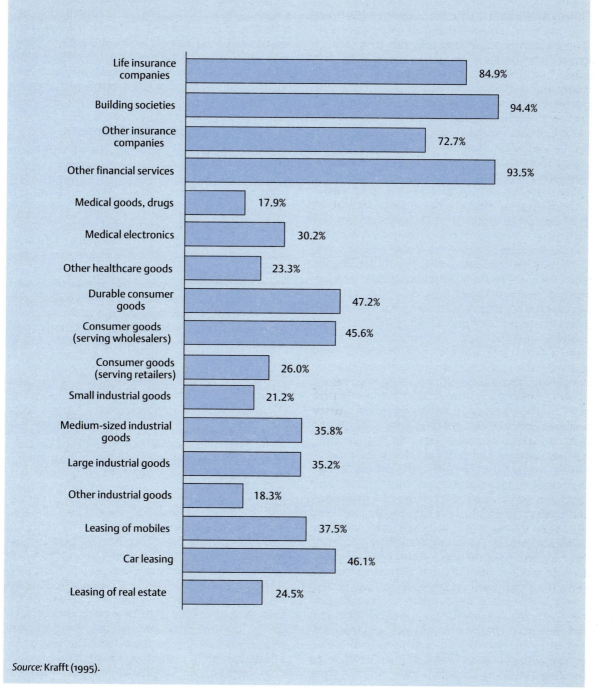

Source: Krafft (1995).

3.3.4 Quotas

Commission rates can be considered as an unspe-
cific motivation to do the best, leaving open what
that really is. From psychology we know that
humans may be motivated better by giving them
explicit targets such as sales quotas. Then, the
relative achievement of this quota is used for
either the performance evaluation of the salespeople or the determination of the bonus level.
Quotas also offer the opportunity to reflect different conditions in the territories, as discussed in
Section 3.1. According to the survey by Krafft
(1995), more than 90 per cent of firms work with
some kind of quota.

The determination of quotas is not an easy task.
Generally, it is agreed that quotas should be
high enough to represent real challenges but low
enough for them really to be reached. Otherwise,
the salesperson may become frustrated and will
perform even worse than without quotas. A good
procedure is, first, to ensure that quotas are equitable across territories and, secondly, to have
quotas that are highly motivating but also as realistic as possible. Such quotas can be determined as
follows.

In a first step, a response function of sales
volumes of an average salesperson depending on
exogenous factors should be estimated, as described in Section 3.1. Inserting the respective values for the exogenous factors as given in the
various territories, we get sales quotas that represent the sales that can be expected from an average salesperson under the specific conditions in
the various territories. These sales quotas are fair
because they are equitable across territories. However, the quotas may not represent challenging
targets. In particular, some fair quotas may even
be below the currently achieved sales volumes.
Thus, these quotas are unrealistic and cannot be
used for other planning purposes, such as adjusting the number of back-office personnel and determining the production capacity. In a second
step, it is, therefore, necessary to ask the salespeople themselves for challenging targets. The firm
can then offer a bonus for a higher quota that is accepted by the salesperson, and punish the salesperson who falls short of this target. The firm can
then offer a bonus if a salesperson offers to work
to a higher quota than the firm itself would have
set him or her. However, should the salesperson
then fail to achieve his or her own target, he or she
is penalized by receiving a lower bonus. An example of IBM's use of such a scheme is given by Gonik
(1978). This system was originally developed in the
former Soviet Union to motivate managers to accept high targets. After realizing that, under such
a system, it is indeed in a salesperson's best interest to accept the highest achievable sales volume,
IBM later adopted this system in Brazil (Gonik
1978). We also know of several medium-sized
firms in Germany applying similar quota-setting
systems.

3.3.5 Directing salespeople's effort

The previous sections were concerned with overall motivation to devote as much effort to selling
as possible; here we discuss opportunities to use
financial incentives to control the allocation of
salespeople's efforts across products and/or customers. Taking into account that products generally exhibit different gross margins, a firm is
interested in directing the effort of its salespeople
to the more profitable products. In a pioneering
article, Farley (1964) proved that commission rates
proportional to gross margins are incentive compatible—that is, that they will direct the salespeople to allocate his or her selling effort in the same
way that the firm would have done it. However,
it later turned out that this result is valid only
as long as allocation of effort is concerned. If the
commission rates also influence total effort
devoted to selling, then this recommendation is
no longer optimal; the same is true for any other
simple rule. However, from equation (7) one can
deduce that a differentiation of commission rates
c_i across products proportional to the gross margin
g_i multiplied by the elasticity of sales volume with
respect to changes of selling effort β_i is near-
optimal:

$$(7) \quad c_i = \lambda \cdot g_i \cdot \beta_i.$$

In some countries like Germany, the introduction
of new compensation plans is legally possible only
if the works council has given its approval. Even if
there are no such laws, firms get acceptance from
their salesforce only if the new plan is not inferior
to the old one. This means that the new plan
should provide at least the same total income for
all salespeople (on the basis of the current sales
volumes) as under the old plan. This is called a cost
neutral change in compensation just to improve
effort allocation decisions. If a firm has operated
with a constant commission rate on sales of all
products and wants to switch to commission rates

meeting this cost neutral condition, it can calculate the scaling factor λ in equation (7) for the new commission rates as follows:

$$(8) \quad \lambda = \frac{c^E \cdot \sum_{i \in I} S_i}{\sum_{i \in I} g_i \cdot \beta_i \cdot S_i}$$

where:
  c^E = equal commission rate for the sales volumes of all products,
  S_i = current sales volume of the ith product.

However, it should be noted that there may be situations in which a new system of commission rates might enable salespeople to achieve a certain income level while reducing their overall effort, which would lead to a less profitable solution for the firm. This can occur in particular when the salesperson has a very high elasticity of disutility with respect to changes of selling time, which is an indicator for saturated salespeople (Albers 1989).

4 Organizing a sales force

IF a selling task requires more than one person, the firm faces decisions as to the type and size of its sales force. The type determines the degree of controllability while the size has profit implications. If it operates with a large sales force, sales management has to decide about the kind of specialization and coordination to use. Specialization can be implemented by making salespeople responsible for specific products, customer segments, or geographic territories. The first two possibilities call for an optimum between the advantages of specialization and the costs of coordination. The latter involves trading off the advantages of specialization against the avoidance of travel time and travel cost.

4.1 Sales-force type

A company can work with salespeople that are either employees, independent sales representatives, or franchisees. Employees are characterized by receiving substantial parts of their income through a fixed salary. Independent sales representatives, called reps in the following discussion, run their own business but sell in the name of the company. Their activities are in general remunerated through commissions on sales, but sometimes they also receive a fixed allowance as a reimbursement for organizational purposes. Reps can sell multiple products from several distinct companies. This offers the advantage to each single company that they can benefit from spillover effects across the whole assortment and that even products with little sales can be sold. In very rare cases companies sell through franchisees. A good example is Eismann, a company that offers a delivery service for frozen goods in Germany and elsewhere in Europe. Their salespeople have to pay a fixed franchise fee for getting the right to sell Eismann products in a certain territory. In addition they have to rent the truck with which they distribute the goods. They purchase the goods they have on their truck at an attractive price such that their income is generated from the difference between selling and purchase price. The purchase price is still substantially higher than the production cost and thus also offers profit to the company.

The choice between employed salespeople and reps has for a long time been discussed in the light of the advantages and disadvantages of fixed versus variable components of the compensation. In general, a fixed salary bears the risk that it is not paid off by the profit contribution from sales. However, if a company grows and the employed salespeople are able to sell more and more, then the additional cost of compensation is lower for employed salespeople than for reps, who are paid on a variable basis only. Therefore, a lot of companies switch from reps to employees once they exceed a certain size.

There are also other considerations that influence the choice between employees and reps. Employed salespeople are generally more loyal and have better product knowledge. Their behaviour can also be controlled more tightly. This is not the case for reps, who can decide on their own how to sell. However, they show a more entrepreneurial behaviour leading to higher sales. Selling through a franchise system is a hybrid solution between employed salespeople who can be tightly controlled and reps with lower risk aversion and possibly stronger motivation.

4.2 Sales-force size

The sales-force size is very often determined by the sales management according to the budget it has received from the company's CEO. In general, the budget is divided by the average remuneration costs of a salesperson plus the average selling expenses associated with his or her activity. Although very easy, this method does not answer the question of what budget level is optimal for the firm.

Nowadays, the downsizing of many sales forces creates the impression that general management has clear ideas on how to determine the optimal sales-force size. However, in many cases the downsizing has been justified only by a need to cut costs. This leads to the question why the size has not been reduced to zero, since then costs would also be zero. Obviously, salespeople incur costs, on the one hand, but generate profit contribution from their sales, on the other hand. If one can quantify the functional relationship between sales volume and number of salespeople, it is possible to derive the optimal number of salespeople with the following approach.

Given are the average gross margin g, the costs of one salesperson C, and the response function of sales volume $S(n)$ depending on the number of salespeople n. Then, profit contribution π is given by:

(9) $\pi = g \cdot S(n) - n \cdot C \Rightarrow$ Max!

Differentiating this function with respect to n, setting the first derivative to zero and solving for n, leads to the optimality condition (10), expressed in terms of the elasticity of sales with respect to selling costs μ, which is defined as in (11):

(10) $\dfrac{n \cdot C}{g \cdot S(n)} = \mu;$

(11) $\mu = \dfrac{\text{Relative change of sales volume in \%}}{\text{Relative change of number of salespeople in \%}}.$

Empirical investigations (Krafft 1995) point to a value for this elasticity of 0.3, which is also a very common ratio of selling expenses (nominator in equation 10) to profit contribution before selling costs (denominator in 10). This is a very helpful equation because a firm can use its own data to check whether it operates near the optimum.

Although many firms think that determining its sales-force size is a very important decision, this is not true. Rather, when plotting the profit contribution of (9) as a function of sales-force size n, one can see that the profit contribution exhibits a

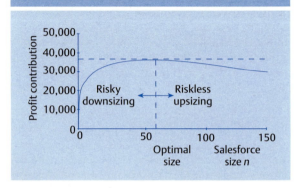

Figure 13.6 **Flat maximum of sales-force sizes**

flat shape around the optimum such that many other values of n are near optimal (see Fig. 13.6). This implies that it is less risky to have an oversized sales force than to have one that is too small. This, in turn, means that many decisions to achieve 'lean' sales forces are questionable. If salespeople have an effect, then the size is not important. Only if they do not have an effect, can a lean policy lead to positive results. However, then a sales training of the existing sales force would be more helpful.

4.3 Sales-force specialization

One of the most important decisions is whether salespeople should specialize and, if so, along which aspect. In markets for insurance policies or other financial services (such as leasing or building society contracts) the principle is often found that every salesperson can contact any customer. This creates conflicts and may prove advantageous only if the contact is crucial and not the subsequent interaction with the customer. In contrast, assigning salespeople exclusively to certain customers results in a long-term-oriented interaction with the customer where the salesperson is motivated to give his or her best because he or she can harvest later from the invested effort.

In the case of fixed assignments, it is profitable to specialize one's sales force. Specialization makes it possible to offer better solutions to the customer, and constitutes a more efficient way of dealing with customers, thus leading to increased profit contribution. However, the advantages of specialization come at the cost of coordination. If, for example, several salespeople from one company, each specializing in different products, call on the same customer, there is the risk that the customer will not get a comprehensive solution. Either this leads to less profit, or the firm has to employ additional people to coordinate all efforts. In general, it is recommended to specialize along the dimension that offers the highest profit improvements after accounting for coordination costs. The degree of specialization should be increased as long as its marginal profit is higher than the marginal cost of coordination.

Specialization has been discussed mainly with respect to products, customer groups, and geography. When firms sell a multitude of different products that require different know-how, they form separate sales forces for the respective product groups. This can lead to negative effects when one customer is served by many salespeople whose efforts are not coordinated. Therefore, Xerox, for example, has switched back to a geographically organized sales force, where the salesperson is responsible for all affairs related to the customer but can order more detailed know-how from headquarters to answer all specific questions by the customer (T. C. Taylor 1985). This also offers the advantage of less travel time and travel cost. Very often different solutions for different industries—such as machinery tools, insurance, banks, services, and so on—have to be developed. Then, it pays off to specialize along these lines. If the sales force is large enough, more than one specialization criterion may be applied hierarchically. For example, the company may divide its sales force into four units specialized in product groups, while in each unit the salespeople are assigned to geographically defined territories.

If the coordination of activities related to one customer is more important than product specialization, as in selling to large retailers, it is worthwhile to install a key-account management. These managers are mostly experienced salespeople who are given some kind of promotion within the company without responsibility for personnel.

Nowadays, companies are reorganizing their activities in a process-oriented way. The implication for sales forces is that the whole process from acquisition, order taking, order processing, after-sales service, and ordering of parts, to selling product extensions and modifications is organized in such a way that there is no longer a strict division between salespeople and back-office employees. If these tasks cannot be carried out by just one person, firms build teams that are as a whole responsible for the complete process with respect

to specific customers. This implements the principle of one face to the customer.

4.4 Sales-force territory design

If a firm wants to minimize travel costs by applying geographical specialization, it has to establish sales territories that are assigned to individual salespeople. In general, a country or sales region can be divided into small sales coverage units (SCUs) that may represent counties, communities, or postal areas. Firms then assign the SCUs to the various territories such that they are as equal as possible. The criterion for equality is either sales potential or workload. The idea is that equal potential or workload provides a fair territory design, because every salesperson has been given the same chance. However, equal potential is generally not associated with equal workload unless potential is equally distributed over space. Moreover, equal workload may not result in equal sales if the response of customers is heterogeneous. In addition, attempts to design territories that are as equal as possible often result in solutions that are associated with rather high travel time and cost. It has already been pointed out that equal sales opportunities are not necessary if one controls for heterogeneity by determining individual sales quotas per territory and compensate according to the relative achievement of the quotas. Under these circumstances, the goal of equal territories is questionable and should be replaced by territories that maximize profit contribution.

Creating profit contribution maximizing territories involves two subproblems. Once certain SCUs have been assigned to a territory, we are interested in the profit that can be achieved in this territory. It is determined by the response functions of sales per SCU depending on the salesperson's selling time, the travel times from the salesperson's location to the various SCUs, and the allocation of the total available working time across SCUs. From Section 2.2.1 we already know that it is optimal to allocate selling time proportional to current sales multiplied by its elasticity. This principle is used for determining the profit implications of reassigning SCUs from one territory to another. Note that the optimal solution is not characterized by equal marginal profits across all SCUs as assumed in literature but by equal marginal profit only across the SCUs assigned to a certain territory. On the basis of these ideas, Skiera and Albers (1998) have developed the computer program COSTA, which provides profit contribution maximizing territories on the basis of response functions of sales per SCU and travel times as well as costs from salespeople's locations to all SCUs.

4.4.1 Reallocating sales territories

Hansen & Petersen AG, based in Hamburg, was a mid-sized German company selling gifts to businesses. Traditionally, it served the market almost exclusively by mail order. In order to increase its growth Hansen & Petersen planned to build up a sales force better able to serve its large accounts. In 1995 Hansen & Petersen hired ten salespeople within a few months and immediately assigned them to sales territories as shown in Fig. 13.7(a). These territories were demarcated on the basis of the ninety-five two-digit postal areas in Germany. The salespeople's locations are marked in Fig. 13.7(a) by the position of the number of the respective territories. Having analysed the existing sales

volumes and profit contributions, the company noticed rather high differences across its territories. Since it had heard about the software COSTA, it hired a consultant of ASCON GmbH to suggest a better territory design. He had to take into account that the two SCUs in the vicinity of the headquarters should continue to be served by back-office personnel, and that for internal reasons territory 10 should remain unchanged.

In order to calculate the profit contribution consequences of different territory alignments, the consultant set up a response function of sales depending on potential and calling time. He operationalized the potential as number of businesses in a territory. Since there were no data available from which such a relationship could be estimated statistically, he asked the management to estimate subjectively the elasticities of sales with respect to potential and selling time. After long discussions and plausibility checks, management agreed on response function (12) for the rth SCU when assigned to the jth territory:

Figure 13.7 Territory design of Hansen & Petersen

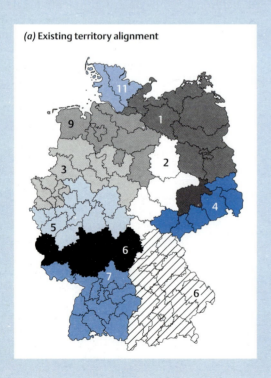

(a) Existing territory alignment

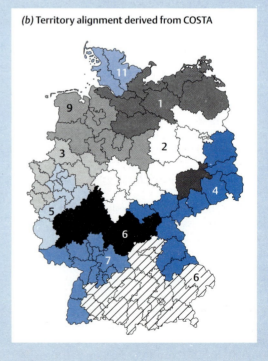

(b) Territory alignment derived from COSTA

Table 13.2 **Characteristics of current and recommended territory design**								
Territory	Current design				Design recommended by COSTA			
	Profit contribution (DM)	Potential (number of accounts)	Number of calls	Marginal profit of time	Profit contribution (in DEM)	Potential (number of accounts)	Number of calls	Marginal profit of time
1	510,042	2,543	715	537	410,172	1,803	816	458
2	73,784	604	710	216	431,168	2,132	701	484
3	799,294	4,394	668	745	533,234	2,598	733	554
4	198,798	950	794	304	341,028	1,661	717	414
5	651,040	3,232	728	635	686,541	3,179	812	658
6	609,833	3,164	689	613	573,065	2,890	708	585
7	807,281	4,242	715	748	732,975	3,585	764	693
8	726,205	3,723	726	697	853,954	4,583	721	791
9	354,816	1,637	743	418	448,094	2,058	755	486
10	120,414	448	973	208	120,414	448	973	208
(11)	—	385	—	—	—	385	—	—
Total	4,851,508	25,322	7,462	—	5,130,646	25,322	7,701	—

(12) $$\text{Sales}_{j,r} = 1350 \cdot (\text{Potential}_{j,r})^{0.625} \cdot (\text{CallingTimeFraction}_{j,r})^{0.375} \cdot (\text{SellingTime}_{j,r})^{0.375}.$$

Note that the ratio of calling time to selling time depends on the territory and thereby on the location of the salesperson to whom the SCU is assigned. This ratio can be calculated from the respective travel times from each salesperson's location to each SCU and those between accounts in a SCU. These travel times can be determined in a computer-based way with the help of systems such as DISTANCE supplied by ptv in Germany or AutoRoute offered by NextBase in the UK.

After applying COSTA the consultant recommended the solution displayed in Fig. 13.7(b). As can be seen from Table 13.2 the solution from COSTA increased profit contribution by 5.8 per cent, which amounted to DM 1.4 million over five years. Although the solution was much more balanced than before, the marginal profits of selling time varied substantially across territories. The solution was found very useful by the management.

5 The future

THE future way of selling will be determined heavily by technological advancements of electronic media and telecommunication (Anderson 1996). Personal visits may be replaced by telecommunication via telephone, fax, or videophone. The use of these media avoids the direct costs of travel as well as the opportunity costs of travel time. Videophones will enable salespeople to communicate as in personal face-to-face conversations, with the possibility of showing documents or products to the other party. There is already software available that allows two parties to look at the same computer program from two different locations. With the diminishing importance of locations, it will be possible to reach more customers and in more distant locations than before. This creates more opportunities, but at the same time also more competition. Furthermore, all geographical aspects discussed in particular in the sections on selling time allocation, tour planning, and territory design will lose importance.

This kind of telecommunication may be supplemented by the use of the Internet. First of all, firms use the Internet for internal purposes as Intranet. The provision of customer, product, and know-how databases can be realized more effectively through the Internet if it is restricted to its own employees. The Internet is also a good medium for providing all kinds of information to potential customers. It may answer any question with respect to products or the maintenance of products. However, communication through the Internet can never replace personal interaction. Although the communication can be designed to be as interactive as possible, it is the potential customer who has to take the initiative to interact with the firm. In contrast, salespeople can initiate contacts such that the Internet will never represent more than a supplement although a rather effective one. This development reveals that effective selling consists of effective information management. Focusing on salespeople's tasks, it becomes clear that selling can be reduced to the acquisition, processing, and provision of information. Therefore, many firms are now analysing this entire process of information handling. In consequence, the efficient handling of interfaces—for example, between sales- and back-office people or the computer department—is becoming more important. Since the results are less and less attributable to a single person, firms are now forming teams to perform the entire process, hoping that the team members are organizing themselves more effectively than is possible by any standardized direction from management.

6 Summary

SALES-FORCE management involves three different tasks. First, the firm has to provide its salespeople with suitable methods for selling to customers and managing a sales territory. We have found that there are no golden recipes for this task. Rather than following canned selling techniques, it is more important to engage in adaptive selling by carefully listening to a customer's needs, which usually involves applying soft- rather than hard-selling methods. A good territory management includes the optimal allocation of calling time across accounts and prospects. This is achieved by selling times that are proportional to profit contribution multiplied by the respective sales elasticity. In addition, we describe

how the process of selling can be supported by computer-aided selling.

Secondly, salespeople have to be supervised by management. This includes a valid performance measurement. Rather than relying on sales alone, firms should adjust for exogenous factors whose effects can be estimated via regression analysis. High-performing salespeople can best be selected from a combination of biographical data, a psychological test, an interview and, most important, an assessment centre. Salespeople can be motivated through either non-financial incentives such as career advancements or financial incentives such as a salary, commissions, bonuses, and prizes for contests. Each element offers specific advantages, and the best overall result can be achieved through a balanced combination. Sales quotas represent a way to motivate salespeople directly to achieve certain goals. Quotas should be fair, equitable, and challenging, all at the same time. Fairness and equity can be achieved by an approach similiar to the one used for performance measurement. In addition, we describe a scheme by which a salesperson can get the highest bonus by accepting the highest achievable quota. In the case of heterogeneous products we show that salespeople can be directed in their effort by offering commissions proportional to gross margins multiplied by sales elasticities.

Thirdly, we have discussed how to set up a sales organization. We show that the size of a sales force should be determined in such a way that the expenses for personnel divided by the profit contribution before marketing cost should be equal to the sales elasticity. A company can operate with either employed salespeople or independent sales representatives or franchisees. The choice depends on the firm's size as well as on a trade-off of control costs versus entrepreneurial motivation. Sales forces can be specialized with respect to products, type of customer, or geography. Each type of specialization causes coordination costs that have to be traded off against the marginal profit of specialization. If salespeople are responsible for territories, then the well-known practice of creating almost equal territories with respect to potential or workload is inferior to directly applying a profit contribution maximizing territory alignment procedure as provided by the computer program COSTA.

Finally, we have discussed future developments. Technological advancements of electronic media and telecommunication will to some extent replace personal visits. Information can be provided much more effectively through the Internet. Moreover, it will be necessary to reorganize the whole process of information handling.

Further reading

Albers, S. (1996), 'Optimization Models for Salesforce Compensation', *European Journal of Operational Research*, 89: 1–17.

Anderson, E. (1985), 'The Salesperson as Outside Agent or Employee: A Transaction Cost Analysis', *Marketing Science*, 4: 234–54.

Basu, A. K., Lal, R., Srinivasan, V., and Staelin, R. (1985), 'Salesforce Compensation Plans: An Agency Theoretic Perspective', *Marketing Science*, 4: 267–91.

Churchill, G. A., Ford, N. M., and Walker, O. C. (1997), *Salesforce Management: Planning, Implementation, and Control* (5th edn., Homewood, Ill.: Irwin).

———— Hartley, St. W., and Walker, O. C. (1985), 'The Determinants of Salesperson Performance: A Meta-Analysis', *Journal of Marketing Research*, 22: 103–18.

Darmon, R. Y. (1992), *Effective Human Resource Management in the Sales Force* (Westport, Conn.: Quorum Books).

Ingram, T. N., LaForge, R. W., and Schwepker, G. H. (1997), *Sales Management: Analysis and Decision Making* (3rd edn., Fort Worth: Dryden Press).

Lodish, L. M. (1971), 'CALLPLAN: An Interactive Salesman's Call Planning System', *Management Science*, 18: P25–P40.

—— (1980), 'A User-Oriented Model for Sales Force Size, Product and Market Allocation Decisions', *Journal of Marketing*, 44 (Summer), 70–8.

—— Curtis, E., Ness, M., and Simpson, M. K. (1988), 'Sales Force Sizing and Deployment Using a Decision Calculus Model at Syntex Laboratories', *Interfaces*, 18/1: 5–20.

Mantrala, M., Sinha, P., and Zoltners, A. A. (1994), 'Structuring a Multiproduct Sales Quota-Bonus Plan for a Heterogeneous Salesforce: A Practical Approach', *Marketing Science*, 13: 121–44.

Rangaswamy, A., Sinha, P., and Zoltners, A. (1990), 'An Integrated Model-Based Approach for Sales Force Structuring', *Marketing Science*, 9: 279–98.

Skiera, B., and Albers, S. (1998), 'COSTA: Contribution Optimizing Sales Territory Alignment', *Marketing Science*, 17/3: 196–213.

Discussion questions

1 What are the advantages and disadvantages of the communication instruments of personal selling, advertising, direct mail, and the World Wide Web?

2 Why is it not profitable to call on accounts proportional to their current sales?

3 Why is it not fair to allocate an increase in a company's sales target as additional sales quotas proportional to the sales in the respective territories?

4 How can a company find out which selection method or training method is the best one?

5 Why do the percentages of salary and commission income to total income represent different strategies of risk sharing between a company and its salespeople?

6 Why do managers consider bonuses as a repair mechanism for misallocation problems of commissions?

7 Why is it unprofitable to offer commission rates proportional to sales or profit contribution?

8 What purposes are served by sales quotas?

9 Why are pharmaceutical firms operating exclusively with employed salespeople, while insurance companies work often with independent sales representatives?

10 Should an insurance trust like Allianz sell its insurance policies for life, health, car collision, and house through different sales forces or all products through one single sales force?

11 Why is it impossible to design sales territories that are really equal?

Waldemar Behn GmbH & Co. KG is a mid-sized company, based in Eckernförde (Germany), producing and selling the fancy liquor brands 'Küstennebel' (translated: coastal mist, named to associate anis taste) and 'Kleiner Feigling' (translated: 'Little Coward', composed of vodka and fig, the latter being the same word as 'cowardly' in German). They operate with some fifty independent sales representatives (reps) who are each responsible for a certain territory. At the time of the introduction of 'Kleiner Feigling', the reps were remunerated through a constant and equal commission rate on the sales of all brands. Chief executive officer (CEO) Rüdiger Behn was not satisfied with this compensation, because the reps were receiving windfall commissions from large retailing chains. Sales with these chains are mainly determined by the negotiations of the key-account managers with the chains, rather than the reps. Moreover, these chains operate with just a few large warehouses, to which the sales are invoiced, and only those reps in whose territory one of these warehouses is located were receiving the high commission. At the same time, the reps were not calling on inns, bars, and restaurants (IBR), because these outlets buy through other distribution channels. Behn considered that effort devoted to IBRs was of high importance for the further diffusion of his products, because their sales created pull effects to the retailers.

Behn asked a team of the University of Kiel to recommend the best type of salespeople for this task and to design a new compensation system that would avoid windfall commissions and motivate the salespeople to call on IBRs. It turned out that reps did not like calling on IBRs. Therefore, Behn supported the launch of 'Kleiner Feigling' with a leasing sales force that made initial calls to IBRs for a quarter. However, a leasing sales force may be not as loyal in the long run as reps or employed salespeople. Employed salespeople offer the advantage that they can be instructed to call on certain outlets and thus on IBRs. However, Behn felt that his reps were more entrepreneurial, less risky, and more effective because they were carrying complementing products from other companies and could profitably call on more accounts than salespeople offering only the Behn assortment. As a consequence, Behn wanted to continue working with his reps.

Since the warehouses of large retail chains supply outlets in many sales districts, a team solution was investigated in which the reps of four super-districts should form teams for the channel of large retail chains only. The commissions on all sales in these super-districts should be pooled across the respective reps and allocated to them according to their share of calls on IBRs. In order to create a cooperative climate it is necessary to design rewards in such a way that an increase of calls by one rep does not lead to a smaller reward for the other reps. This is the case if the commission pool benefits more from an additional call than the individual salesperson through his increased share. This proposal solved both problems: avoiding windfall commissions and stimulating calls on IBRs. Unfortunately, it turned out that, according to German law, this is possible only if an individual rep gets the right to control the figures on sales and the number of calls to IBRs of all other reps. As the reps would not accept a disclosure of figures to others, the team from the University of Kiel had to search for an alternative solution.

As a new solution it was proposed to differentiate the commission rates of the reps according to the channel and the meeting of a quota on calls on IBRs. In order to avoid windfall commissions, it was recommended that the commission rate for sales with retail chains should be set at a very low level compared to the current one (see Table 13.5). A commission rate of zero was not possible because German law requires that sales with all channels of a given territory have to be remunerated with commissions. In order to motivate the reps to call on IBRs, the commission rates were split into a basic (and not very attractive) level and an advanced level that could be achieved only if the reps could prove they had visited a certain quota of restaurants. A deeper analysis showed that the response of different distribution channels such as retail chains, beverage wholesalers, cash and carry markets, and IBRs is very different. The management subjectively estimated the response of these channels to number of calls. Since restaurants only have an indirect effect on sales, the response functions incorporated an interaction term of the following form:

$$(13) \quad S_i = M_i \cdot \left(1 - e^{-(a_i + b_i \cdot t_i + c_i \cdot TG)} \right)$$

where:

S_i	= sales with i-th distribution channel,
M_i	= sales potential of i-th distribution channel,
T_i	= selling time for i-th distribution channel,
TG	= selling time for IBRs,
a_i, b_i, c_i	= parameters.

These advanced commission rate levels were optimized with the Add-In-Function Solver in the spreadsheet software Microsoft Excel. In more detail, profit contribution from sales was maximized subject to the constraint that all reps in total receive a certain amount of commission income. The new levels of the commission rates are shown in Table 13.3. The CEO then notified all reps of the cancellation of the current contracts, and offered new contracts. All reps agreed and the management was satisfied with the new structure.

Table 13.3 **Current and new commission rates for Behn reps (%)**				
Distribution Channel	**Commission rates**			
	Current	**New: Basic**	**New**	
			if quota on calls on IBRs is met	Increase per 5% more sales
Retail chains	4.0	1.0	1.0	—
Cash & carry markets	5.0	4.0	7.5	0.5
Beverage wholesalers	7.0	6.0	11.5	0.5
Department stores	5.0	4.0	5.0	—
Rest	5.0	4.0	4.0	—

Discussion question

1 Identify the features of the new compensation plan that were crucial to its acceptance by the sales force.

2 Was there any other way that the CEO could have achieved his aims without using the approach described here?

Chapter 14

Product Management

George Avlonitis

Objectives

The objectives of this chapter are:

1 to place the product variable and its significance in a historical perspective;

2 to discuss the various types of product decisions;

3 to examine the influence of the product variable in the development of the marketing strategy;

4 to provide empirical evidence to aid the navigation of students and marketing managers through the often unfamiliar territory of deleting existing products.

1 Introduction

THE product is the *raison d'être* of the company, its *sine qua non*. Even more fundamentally, all economic activity centres around the product. It is the culmination of efforts by the seller to match his resources with the requirements of the market. While many factors contribute to long-run success or failure, a high degree of accuracy in this matching process is fundamental.

A product has been described as an arrangement of attributes or properties; it enters the economic stream when its properties are desired by others. The more desirable the product, the greater the demand (the matching process again).

The product is the starting point for the majority of planning activities; it is impossible to price, to plan promotions, or to choose channels of distribution until the identity and nature of each product are determined and product policies are established. In the long run, all strategies and tactics in marketing revolve around the product, because it is the basic tool with which the marketing manager bargains for revenue.

The fact that a product is not wheat, or apples, or nails—common examples of classical economics—over which the seller has no control, but something that can be adapted, differentiated, introduced, modified, or eliminated for profit-making purposes is the theme of this chapter.

2 The product as economic variable

IF one were to review the history of economic activity, it would become apparent that the idea that the product itself was not a given but a variable that could be planned and whose sales could be administered by the seller is of quite recent origin. This idea is rooted to the concept of differential (competitive) advantage, which in turn—being the belief of a consumer that one seller's offering possesses more want-satisfaction ability than other sellers' offerings—is rooted in the competition and in the varied needs and wants that exist in the marketplace.

The concept of differential (competitive) advantage in terms of 'product' is absent in the literature of Economics up to the 1930s. Under the assumption of homogeneity on both demand and supply side, made by the classical and marginalist economists, the price is the basis for competition in the economic system and the consumer has no choice preference for different products. These assumptions were partially valid until the end of the nineteenth century. By virtue of the mass production techniques brought by the Industrial Revolution, product homogeneity was probably more of a reality in the eighteenth and nineteenth centuries, when producers had to compete on the basis of price, emphasizing quantity rather than quality or choice.

By the early years of the twentieth century these assumptions were no longer valid. A number of changes took place in the economic system that brought different bases for competition: variety both in materials and in the means of production had started to be introduced at an increasing rate; improved forms of transportation had largely eliminated the security of locational monopolies and had broadened market opportunities that would support more sophisticated production systems; improved means of communication with the market dispersed information about the sellers' products and also provided strong incentives for the inclusion of the product in the sellers 'total offering' (marketing programme).

These concurrent revolutions in production, communication, and transportation, plus the fact that the supply of products was concentrated in the hands of a relatively few sellers, and therefore that industries had become oligopolistic, brought forward bases of competition other than pricing. By the early years of the twentieth century the more percipient economists had recognized that such changes had taken place and that product differentiation was more typically the basis of competition than was price. In the early 1930s this view was crystallized in two famous contributions by Robinson and also Chamberlin (1933). Both authors abandoned the assumptions of a homogeneous product and developed the theory of 'monopolistic competition' under which the seller's sales are limited and defined by two more variables in addition to price: namely, the nature of the product and advertising outlays.

In Chamberlin's monopolistic competition theory the product (defined as a 'bundle of utilities' in which the physical offering is but one element) becomes the basis on which a seller can differentiate his offering from that of his competitors. Chamberlin (1957) asserts that 'Anything which makes buyers prefer one seller to another, be it personality, reputation, convenient location, or the tone of his shop, differentiates the thing purchased to that degree, for what is bought is really a "bundle of utilities" of which these things are a part.'

Chamberlin's assertion that buyers in the market have a real freedom to differentiate, distinguish, or have specific preferences among the competing outputs of the sellers, led to the development of the differential advantage concept, one of the most important concepts in the marketing theory.

Marketers, such as Alderson, have attempted to provide the link between the concept of differential advantage and the economy as it actually exists. Alderson has noted that differentiation in a product's characteristics gives a seller control over the product with that exact identity and configuration, supporting the view that 'the seller offering a product different from others actually does occupy a monopoly position in that limited sense'. However, product differentiation can take various forms. According to Alderson, 'it may be based upon certain characteristics of the product itself; patented features, trademarks, trade names, peculiarities of the package or container, singularity in quality, design, colour or style. Product differentiation may also exist with respect to the conditions surrounding its sale. Examples of this are convenience of the seller and various other links that attach the customers to the seller' (Alderson 1965).

It is, however, the existence of varied wants and needs in the marketplace that allows competition through product differentiation and a policy of differential advantage to be pursued. Alderson asserts that, behind the acceptance of differentiation, are differences in tastes, desires, income, location of buyers, and the uses of commodities. Smith (1956) also notes that lack of homogeneity on the demand side may be based upon different customs, desires for variety, or desire for exclusiveness, or may arise from basic differences in user needs. According to Smith, the seller pursues a policy of differential advantage in general, and product differentiation in particular, in order to meet both competitive activities and the various wants and needs in the marketplace. The seller can pursue a policy of product differentiation in two ways. First, he can offer the same product throughout the whole market and secure a measure of control over the product's demand by advertising and promoting differences between his or her product and the products of competing sellers. Secondly, he can view the market as a number of small homogeneous markets (market segments), each having different product differences, and adjust the product and the elements surrounding its sale according to the requirements of each market segment. The seller who adopts the latter method in pursuing a policy of product differentiation is actually simultaneously pursuing a policy of market segmentation.

However, a policy of differential advantage through product differentiation and/or market segmentation must be dynamic in nature, since the seller must continually adjust his or her 'total offering', (i.e. the product and the elements surrounding its sale) to match the ever-changing competitive activities and customers' 'motivation mixes' in the marketplace. Naturally, adjustments in the seller's 'total offering' tend to result in variations in the seller's cost structure and profitability. The seller, therefore, must be constantly engaged in creating a 'total offering' from all the elements under his or her control, in a way that will give differential advantage and profitability. This 'axiom' has led to the development of the marketing-mix concept, which was discussed in Chapter 9.

The importance of the product variable is evidenced by the use of the product management system by many consumer and industrial goods companies. The product management system evolved from a general awareness of the need for some degree of specialized management to ensure that individual products or product lines were receiving comprehensive and adequate attention (Buell 1975; RaStaschs 1975).

As management became more cognizant during the 1990s of the importance of the product variable, so it realized that, to sustain the product variable as actively as possible, it needed continuously to monitor the normal process and development in the marketplace—the new trends that affect social habits, particularly technological changes, and the new approaches introduced by competitors to meet market needs—and incorporate all these changes into its own products. It follows, therefore, that management is continuously engaged in making product decisions, and it is to the type and nature of such decisions that we now turn our attention.

3 Type and nature of product decisions

Any conscious change in the company's product offering as viewed by the buyer is defined as a product decision.

There are a great variety of possible changes in the company's product offering and consequently a great variety of product decisions. At one extreme are such things as a minor modification of the label or colour of the package. At the other extreme are such things as diversification into new business fields either through internal R&D or through mergers and acquisitions.

Fig. 14.1 depicts a classification scheme in which product decisions are classified into three broad categories: changes in the product types offered, changes in the tangible physical product, and changes in the intangible/augmented product, depending on the nature of changes in the company's product offering.

3.1 Changes in the product types offered

Changes in the product types offered represent the most critical decisions in determining the future of a company. The management must first decide what products to offer in the marketplace, before other intelligent product decisions pertaining to the product's physical attributes—packaging, branding, and so on—can be made.

There are two distinct levels at which such changes take place—namely, the product-mix level and the product-line level. The Committee on Definitions of the American Marketing Association has defined product mix as 'the composite of products offered for sale by a firm or business unit'. The same committee has defined product line as 'a group of products that are closely related because they satisfy a class of need, are used together, are sold to the same customer groups, are marketed through the same type of outlet or fall within a given price range' (Alexander 1980).

Changes at the product-mix level represent the highest-order decisions made in the company, constraining all the subsequent lower-order decisions and identifying the business that the company operates.

Product decisions at the product-mix level tend

Figure 14.1 **Classification of product decisions**

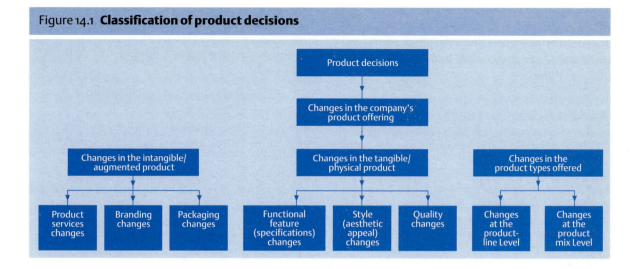

to determine the width of a company's product mix. Product-mix width is the number of product lines offered by a company. For example, General Foods offers several product lines, including desserts, coffees, cereals, pet foods, beverages, and household products. Likewise, Procter & Gamble has several product lines, including laundry detergents, toothpastes, bar soaps, deodorants, and shampoos.

The basic product-policy/strategy issues at the product-mix level cluster around the following questions:

■ What types of products should we offer? Will we function primarily as a supplier of materials and components or as a manufacturer of end products?

■ What are the groups and classes of customers which our products are intended to serve?

■ Do we seek to serve our markets as full-line suppliers or limited-line specialists? Closely allied to this is the degree of custom manufacturing to meet the needs of individual buyers versus quantity production of a limited range of product types.

■ Will we attempt to take a position of technical leadership or will we achieve greater success as a follower?

■ What are the business characteristics (criteria) such as target rate of profit, payback period on investment, minimum sales volume, etc., that each product line must meet in order to be included in the product-mix portfolio?

The answers to the foregoing questions tend to form the company's general product policy which will guide management in making decisions pertaining to the addition or elimination of product lines from the company's product mix. In adding new product lines management has to decide about the type and the nature of the product lines as well as the ways that these lines should be added to the mix (see Insert). The decision to add new product lines to the mix is ordinarily described as 'diversification', and it can be achieved through internal R&D, licensing, merger and acquisitions, joint ventures, or alliances.

Friend or foe?

The digital camera does not seem to be cannibalizing the market for either the traditional compact cameras or the single-lens reflex cameras, because it has created a new market for 'temporary imaging' that the camera industry did not know existed. However, the APS system is cannibalizing the market for traditional compact cameras. In 1996, APS's first full year on the market, 4.2 million APS cameras were sold, while the sales of traditional compact cameras fell by 4.5 million to 22.9 million.

We may distinguish between related and unrelated diversification (Aaker 1992). Related diversification provides the potential to obtain synergies by the exchange or sharing of skills or resources associated with any functional area such as marketing, production, or R&D. Delta, a large Greek dairy-products company, successfully introduced a new line of beverages exploiting synergies in distribution, marketing, brand-name recognition, and image.

Unrelated diversification lacks commonality in markets, distribution channels, production technology, or R&D. The objectives are, therefore, mainly financial: to manage and allocate cash flow, to generate profit streams that are either larger, less uncertain, or more stable than they would otherwise be. For example, tobacco firms such as Philip Morris and Reynold's have used their cash flows to buy firms such as General Foods, Nabisco, and Del Monte, in order to provide alternative core earning areas in case the tobacco industry is crippled by effective anti-smoking programmes.

However, companies are also involved in contracting their product mixes through the elimination of product lines. Decisions are made about identifying, evaluating, and specifying which product lines are to be removed from the market. If a company continues to devote time, money, and effort to a product line that no longer satisfies customers, then the productive operations of marketing are not as efficient and effective as they should be. The procedure of eliminating product lines from the company's product mix is called 'divestment' or 'divestiture' and, unlike the addition of product lines (diversification), is final with no alternatives. However, there are various ways that a product line can be eliminated. For instance, a company may decide to harvest (run-out) the product line by cutting back all support costs to the minimum level that will optimize the product-line performance over its foreseeable limited life, it may decide to continue manufacturing the product line but contract other companies to market it, it may sell or license the product line to someone else, or it may abandon it completely.

Important and complex decisions are also made at the product-line level that tend to determine the depth of a company's product mix. The depth of a product mix is measured by the number of different products offered in each product line. For instance, General Food's coffee line consists of Maxim, Sanka, Maxwell House, Brim, and General Foods International Coffees, while its Household Products include SOS, Satina, and Tulfy. Similarly, Procter & Gamble has a deep laundry detergents line, with a large number of products/brands, which include Tide, Bold, and Ariel, and a rela-

tively shallow toothpaste line with two major products/brands—namely, Crest and Gleem.

The basic product policy-strategy issues at the product-line level cluster around the following questions:

■ What are the boundaries beyond which no product should be added?

■ What is the number of different products to be offered in the line and to what extent should they be differentiated?

■ What is the number of different versions (models) to be offered for each product in the line?

■ What are the business characteristics (criteria) such as minimum profitability, minimum sales volume, and market share that each product must meet in order to be included in the line?

■ In how many segments should we compete in order to maintain a secure overall cost and market position *vis-à-vis* competitors in business?

■ Should we keep in the line products that cannot be made to produce a profit in order to keep a customer happy or should we let the competitors have the losers?

Closely allied to the company's general product-line policy governing the answers to the foregoing questions is the company's design policy. The formulation of a design policy may aim at:

■ giving attention to innovation, high quality, and reliable performance, to allow each product in the line to be differentiated from its competitors;

■ making the products compatible with the needs, emotional and rational, of the customer;

■ achieving variety reduction of the range of product types in the line, and a simplification of the design and construction, to secure reduction in overheads and inventories;

■ replacing expensive materials and those production processes requiring skilled labour to bring about savings in production costs.

The number and the types of products that comprise a product line are the result of changes at this particular level that are guided by the company's product-line and design policy. Changes at the product-line level imply either the extension of the line through the addition of new products, or the contraction of the line through the elimination of products, or the replacement of existing products with new and improved ones. The products that are added, eliminated, or replaced in the product line might be either versions of existing products—models, sizes, and the like—or product types that make up the product line.

👉 'The process of developing a range of products under the banner of one brand name is called brand stretching.' (Chapter 20, p. 490)

RCA cut down its colour television sets from 69 to 44 models. A chemical company cut down its products from 217 to the 93 with the largest volume, the largest contribution to profits, and the greatest long-term potential. In 1996 Lever brothers and Procter & Gamble (see Insert) announced that they were going to reduce the number of their sub-brands in order to simplify the choices faced by customers.

> **Too many Crests?**
>
> Until the late 1990s Procter & Gamble was selling thirty-five variations of Crest toothpaste. The result of reducing this number has been an increase in market share and a reduction in costs—particularly production costs—as manufacturing reliability has risen.

Indeed, product-line decisions tend to be complex and the maintenance of a balanced-optimum product mix is of paramount importance for the well-being of a company. For this reason it is worth turning our attention to the factors influencing the formation of a company's optimum product mix.

3.1.1 Factors influencing a company's product mix

Having too many products increases the company's cost of doing business and having too few permits market opportunities to slip away and results in excess capacity. Both extremes are costly and affect profit adversely. Companies tend to extend their product lines either on the grounds that they can achieve economies of scale or in response to marketing-department pressures. Product lines tend to mushroom and mature and weak products remain in the line regardless of their position in the life cycle because of management attention to new products.

However, there are economic trade-off points beyond which any extension achieves disecon-

omies rather than economies of scale, since an increase in the company's product line is always accomplished at some cost. Product overpopulation spreads a company's productive, financial, and marketing resources too thinly. This in turn leads to further problems. Forecasting becomes more difficult and even the mechanics of product-pricing become complex and time-consuming. Also the use of informative advertising as a means of persuasion, particularly by the companies manufacturing shopping goods and industrial goods, may be made difficult where an extensive product line is being promoted. Moreover, an excess of products in the line not only creates internal competition among the company's own products but also creates confusion in the minds of customers, since differences among individual products usually diminish as more products are added to a given line.

Planning and controlling a large number of products likewise present serious problems. For instance, management must contend with mutual supply characteristics when planning production schedules, allocating production costs to products, and purchasing additional production equipment. Also as management attempts to spread its efforts over a wide and varied product mix, its ability to coordinate and control the mix is weakened. When a company has only a few products, its management can scrutinize and control each product's problems as they arise. For instance, a technical fault in the functioning of the product can be quickly rectified thus enhancing the customer loyalty. Let us now discuss some of the most important factors influencing the company's product mix.

Company mission How a company chooses to define its mission determines the products and services it will offer now and in the future and provides guidelines for managing the company's product mix. Drucker (1968) was the first author to note the importance of answering the question 'What business are we in'. He then proceeds to suggest that this question can be answered only by looking at the business from the point of view of the customer and the market: 'What is our business is not determined by the producer but by the consumer. It is not defined by the company's name, statutes or articles of incorporation but by the want the customer satisfies when he buys a product or a service.'

It follows, therefore, from the Drucker axiom

that to be effective the definition of the company's mission should be made in terms of the consumer needs and wants that the product is designed to satisfy. The extremely important distinction between customer orientation and product orientation in defining a company's mission has been pointed out by Levitt in his provocative article 'Marketing Myopia' (Levitt 1960) (see Insert). The point Levitt is making is that a company's mission and consequently products must be defined in terms of more basic consumer needs. What is required is a definition that will enable the company to survive profitably in the long run regardless of the vicissitudes that befall any one product or range of products in the present.

Marketing myopia

Marketing myopia 'defines an industry, or a product, or a cluster of knowhow so narrowly as to guarantee its premature senescence. When we mention "railroads", we should make sure we mean "transportation" ' (Levitt 1960: 46). It is a view that would lead a firm printing bank notes to fail to understand that it is actually creating a payment system.

Company capabilities A key factor influencing the formation of an optimum product mix is the extent to which this mix is compatible with the company's financial, manufacturing, and distribution capabilities.

A classic example is a record-breaking RCA write-off of its general purpose computer operation. RCA's attempt to reach into neighbouring fields did not result in added profits and, when faced with the need to invest $500 million more in its line of computers, RCA's management decided to discontinue computer manufacturing operations at a loss of $250 million after tax. The price of continuing an operation that was not compatible with the company's 'know-how', in the words of one executive, 'was simply too high for RCA'. Any attempt to revitalize the computer operations resulted in greater losses.

Corporate image For many companies the corporate image not only dictates the continuance and discontinuance of their products, but also governs most of their activities. A company that is highly respected by the public for its high quality cannot afford to launch or retain products whose quality is not compatible with the rest of its products. In fact, this is the risk that a company that embarks upon a policy of trading down undertakes. When trading down, the new product may hurt the company's reputation and image and its established high-quality product line. An example in this case is the A-Class model of the Mercedes Benz, which ran into design problems, temporarily hurting the company's image.

Company objectives *Sales growth.* One objective emphasized by many companies is growing sales through time. A company's sales growth is determined by a wide range of variables, the product mix being the predominant one.

Since the mix of products offered for sale by a company determines its capacity to grow, it follows that the rate of sales growth depends upon where various products in the company's product mix are in their respective life cycles. However, the determination of the life-cycle positions of all the company's major products that might guide a company to formulate its sales-growth objective as well as its product mix to reach the growth objectives can be difficult.

A simple approach that might assist a company to anticipate its future sales growth is to divide a company's product mix into six categories, each representing different growth rates (a proxy for stage in the product life cycle). The potential of a company's future sales growth is revealed through the proportions of its products in each of these six categories, which include:

■ tomorrow's breadwinners—new products or today's breadwinners modified and improved;

■ today's breadwinners—the innovations of yesterday;

■ products capable of becoming net contributors if something drastic is done;

■ yesterday's breadwinners—typically products with high volume but badly fragmented into 'specials', small orders, and the like;

■ the 'also rans'—typically the high hope of yesterday that, while they did not work out well, nevertheless did not become outright failures;

■ the failures.

The point Drucker is trying to make through this classification is that, if a company neglects either the new product development or the product elimination function or both, it will find itself with a very unbalanced and unhealthy product mix that will jeopardize the growth potentials.

Sales Stability. One objective that is particularly concerned with the ability of the company to survive in the long run is that of sales stability. Unstable sales can be quite costly both economically and socially. They tend to place an additional burden on the operating budget, since the company would find itself needing more men, material, and money at certain times of the year than at others. This, in turn, will force the company to lay off employees and pay more interest on its money, because of its lessened ability to cover its interest payments, in periods of low sales. Unstable sales also tend to make planning more difficult, because sales are more difficult to forecast.

A company could, therefore, consider how alternative adjustments of its mix would be likely to affect the stability of sales and develop a balanced product mix in which

■ declining or low-growth products are offset by new growing lines, and
■ products achieve sales complementarity such that the peaks and troughs in the sales of one product are offset by those of another product.

The sales stability objective is of paramount importance to the capital equipment industry, where the different demands made by orders on the range of 'mix' of company capabilities and resources can have serious unbalancing consequences. Some types of capital-goods work—for example, shipbuilding, civil engineering, large-scale engineering, and so on—may take so long to evolve from the order being taken to its final execution that the demand for different types of company capabilities may be very uneven unless some attempt is made to maintain a flow of orders to strike a balance.

However, while it is obvious that a company's product mix determines its sales stability, it is also obvious that the sales-stability objective can, and does, dictate the composition of a company's product mix, as it imposes certain constraints on which products might be added or eliminated from the product mix. For instance, in evaluating a number of products as possible additions to its product mix, a company that is tailoring its mix towards stable sales will select those products whose sales are negatively correlated with current total sales. In this way the company will decrease its overall sales variability. A company that fails to consider the impact of a new product on the variance of sales might find itself subsequently handicapped by excessive sales volatility. Of course, sales stability may force a company to sacrifice its sales growth and it is up to the management to decide the trade-off point between sales growth and sales stability.

Profit. Regardless of the way that a company measures its profits, the amount of profit that it can realize depends ultimately upon its product mix. As Kotler (1997) has observed 'the firm's product-mix tends to set the upper limits for the company's potential profitability while the quality of its marketing program tends to determine how closely this upper limit is reached'.

The company must, therefore, ensure that it has a mix of products that does not just generate sales or achieve a certain market share but rather produces profitable sales and a profitable market share. A typical company's product mix contains products that range along a spectrum from very high-profit products to low-profit products and often to products that contribute no profit at all—though they make a valued contribution to overheads.

It is well known that a limited part of the mix (15–30 per cent) is often responsible for a more than proportionate part of profits (65–85 per cent). This relationship, also known as the 20/80 rule, is very common in industry and has at least two important implications for product-mix decisions. The first implication is that the company has to devote a major part of its effort and marketing resources to protecting and enhancing the market position of the products that largely determine total profits. The second implication is that the company may be able to increase its average level of profits by eliminating some of its products that do not perform satisfactorily, especially those that absorb a great amount of management time and company resources in relation to the profits they generate.

Competition Competition is another important factor that may dictate the formation of a company's product mix. Competition may stem from a variety of sources, such as new designs, new and better raw materials and components, better and more extensive promotional devices, more efficient distributive networks, price reductions, and increased number of competitors. Evaluating competitors should uncover the strengths and weaknesses of the company's products *vis-à-vis* those of competitors and assist management in determining the best course of action to be followed *vis-à-vis* its product mix. Indeed, when competition hits a company at the cash register, there are only three things to do: meet it, whip it, or go out.

Technology Technology is a powerful force in all economies, as it exerts a strong influence on all their micro-units—that is, business organizations and customers. Its contribution to the growth of companies and the economy as a whole is obvious and needs no further explanation. It was, among other things, the principal agent in the birth, growth, decline, and death of innumerable products in the second half of the twentieth century. Companies usually develop new products in the hope of serving their customers more satisfactorily, stealing customers away from competitors, stimulating sales growth, penetrating additional segments, or any combination of these marketing objectives. As technology advances, new products multiply and are often improved, thus rendering other products obsolete—that is, outdated, outmoded, less efficient, and less useful. Products that bear any of these characteristics should be removed, since competition, be it internal or external, is likely to result in a shifting of customers away from obsolete products to new or improved ones.

Mergers and acquisitions Mergers and acquisitions have proved to be an effective means for a company to expand its product mix. However, when a company merges with or acquires another company, it often faces the problem of harmonizing the newly acquired products with its own product offerings.

Some newly acquired products may fall totally outside the scope of the acquirer's present product lines with respect to their production and/or distribution requirements. If the acquirer is ill equipped to handle such products adequately, it would, perhaps, be preferable to eliminate them. On the other hand, some of the newly acquired products may be closely related to the acquiring company's products. What is called for in this case is the determination of the nature and extent of the interrelationship between all products in the expanded mix, the retention of the most promising products, and the elimination of those products whose continued presence in the mix may be inimical to the sales performance and profitability of other products.

3.2 Changes in the tangible product (changes in the product's physical configuration)

Changes in the product types offered at the product-mix and product-line levels mainly involve the addition or elimination of products, and represent, as we have already seen, the most extreme and complex types of product decisions.

However, companies are also engaged in relatively less complex changes that involve the addition, elimination, and modification of the products' specifications and physical attributes.

Since products have a multitude of specifications and physical attributes, there is an almost unlimited number of ways that products can be changed. Nevertheless, quality, functional features, and style are the typical dimensions along which changes occur. These types of product changes may result in new and improved products, which either are added to the product line, or replace existing products in the line, and consequently they are intimately tied up with product-line decisions.

Changes in the product's quality, functional features, and style are guided by the company's product-quality policy, design policy, and induced obsolescence policy. In formulating a product-quality policy, management must answer the following questions:

- What level of quality should the company offer compared with what is offered by competitors?
- How wide a range of quality should be represented by the company's offerings?
- How frequently and under what circumstances should the quality of a product (line) be altered?
- How much emphasis should the company place on the quality in its sales promotion?
- How much risk of product failure should the company take in order to be first with some basic improvements in product quality?

Quality stems from manufacture, design, or processing, and its basic dimensions are reliability and durability. Both reliability and durability can be varied by the company by altering the materials of which the product is made and/or changing the way the materials are configured. A company may feel that it can make a real gain on its competitor by increasing the quality of its product and launching the new and improved product.

Changes to a higher quality may also be linked to a policy of trading-up.

However, an increase in the quality usually means higher costs, and, although the relationship between level of quality and cost can usually be reflected in the company's cost function, the explicit relationship between demand and quality is far more elusive. The estimation of the elasticity of demand with respect to quality is a difficult exercise. In addition, the more durable the product is, the longer the time before it must be replaced.

The importance of the replacement market has suggested to some companies the intentional design and manufacturing of less durable products. In this instance, a company decreases the quality of the product so that it will wear out physically (physical obsolescence) within a reasonably short period of time. It follows, therefore, that a company's product-quality policy is clearly related to its design and induced-obsolescence policies.

Alternatively, a product can be modified by changing its functional capacity. This involves the addition or alteration of functional features that can make the product more attractive to customers. The modification of functional features has several competitive advantages and may assist the company, among other things, to find new applications for its product.

The selection of functional features depends very much on the company's design policy, which should give answers to the following questions:

■ What specific product features should be developed and made ready for the next product?

■ Which of our competitors' product changes should we copy?

■ Should we hold back certain new product features—and which ones—for possible slowdown in sales?

■ What product features should our company emphasize?

The rate at which new functional features are adopted depends on the ability of the customer to discern differences in performance as well as on the company's induced-obsolescence policy. Significant improvements as measured by technical standards create functional or technological obsolescence.

Finally, another way to change a product's physical configuration is through style changes that aim to improve the aesthetic appeal of the product rather than its functional performance. Changes in the style may render a product 'different' in terms of its functional capacity and quality level. Style changes again depend on the company's design and induced-obsolescence policies. Frequent changes in the style can make a product out of date and thus increase the replacement market. This is called style or psychological obsolescence and is intended to make a person feel out of date if he/she continues to use it. However, despite the fact that style changes can be extremely effective for a company, they contain a significant element of risk. To start with, style changes are usually thoroughgoing; companies tend to eliminate the old style in introducing the new one and therefore they risk losing some of the customers who liked the old style in the hope of gaining a large number of customers who like the new one. Moreover, styling is usually not as flexible as functional features. Style changes can be adopted or dropped quickly, but they usually cannot be made optional as easily as functional features. With functional features, it is often possible to fit features to satisfy the requirements of specific market segments; with styling, it is usually more difficult to predict what kind of people will prefer the new style.

3.3 Changes in the intangible/augmented product

Customers usually seek more from a product than the performance of some specific tangible function. The tendency to attach a lot of emphasis to the physical product as a basis for customer appeal might have severe consequences for the manufacturer. Management has become more cognizant of the fact that the distinction between the physical characteristics of competing products and their performance efficiency has diminished, and the period of exclusive advantage in the product's physical qualities has been shortened, and so seeks to develop innovations in areas external to the physical product. The recognition of the fact that characteristics other than the physical ones assist a company to gain a comparative advantage led to the development of the 'augmented-product' concept. Augmented product is the physical product along with the whole cluster of services that accompany it. Put another way: is the totality of benefits that the buyer receives or experiences in obtaining the physical product. It is more the development of the right augmented product rather than the development of the right physical product that distinguishes a company's product from those of competitors. According to Levitt (1969), the competition of product augmentation is not competition between what companies produce in their factories but between what they add to their factory output in the form of packaging, services, advertising, customer advice, financing, delivery arrangements, and other things that people value.

In the same context, Blois (1991: 29) argues that 'in an attempt to ensure that their product is not regarded as a "commodity" undifferentiated from their competitors' products, firms will seek ways of augmenting their product—that is adding goods or services to the product over and above what the customer had come to expect'.

👉 'This search for differentiation is central to marketing thinking.'
(Chapter 9, p. 208)

As far as the product variable is concerned, the key characteristics external to the physical product that offer a company means of achieving a competitive plus are: (*a*) branding, (*b*) packaging, and (*c*) product services. Changes in these characteristics are the result of important product decisions.

3.3.1 Branding

A brand is a name, sign, symbol, or design or a combination of them that is intended to identify the goods or services of one manufacturer or group of manufacturers and to differentiate them from those of competitors. The more the products in the market have reached a plateau of similarity, the greater the need for branding to achieve distinction; this applies equally to both industrial and consumer goods.

Branding gives the seller several advantages. According to Kotler (1997) these are:

■ The Brand name makes it easier for the seller to process orders and track down problems.

■ The seller's brand name and trademark provide legal protection of unique product features, which competitors would otherwise be likely to copy.

■ Branding gives the seller the opportunity to attract a loyal and profitable set of customers.

■ Brand loyalty gives sellers some protection from competition and greater control in planning their marketing programme.

■ Branding helps the seller to segment markets. Instead of Procter and Gamble selling a simple detergent, it can offer eight detergent brands, each formulated differently and aimed at specific benefit-seeking segments.

■ Strong brands help build the corporate image, making it easier to launch new brands and gain acceptance by distributors and consumers.

Issues to be considered by management about brands include choosing the brand name, selecting the brand symbol, registering the brand, and measuring brand acceptance, loyalty, and equity. However, before considering these issues, management makes some more fundamental policy decisions pertaining to branding. Some of the questions to be answered in formulating a branding policy include:

■ Should we establish our own brand names or should we engage exclusively in reseller brands (private branding or own-label brands).

■ Should we make products for reseller brands similar to those bearing our own brand?

■ Should we establish a family brand (multi-product brands) over all types of products offered or should we create a special brand for each type of product (multi-brand products)?

■ Should we establish a single brand or multiple brands for a product type?

■ Should we use our existing brand name to introduce additional items in the same product category (line extensions) or a new product category (brand extensions)?

■ Should we use a new brand name for launching products in a new category?

Branding decisions are intimately tied up with the product-quality decisions. For instance, a company deciding about the range of quality to be represented by its product offering should specify the quality level that will be adhered to under the brand. Any quality claim made for a branded product will give the brand an expectation connotation in the mind of the customer. For example, Seiko has established different brand names for its higher-priced (Seiko Lasalle) and lower-priced (Pulsar) watches.

The execution of the company's quality policy is the main determinant of customer satisfaction with branded products. Branding decisions are also tied up with product-line decisions. For instance, if a company wishes to test a new product it might do so under a new brand name. Should the product receive customer approval it could be added quickly to the regular product line. If it does not satisfy many customers, it could either be dropped or continued under the separate brand name. Branding may also be used as a method of market segmentation that enables the company to produce a basic product with variations to suit identifiable segments of the market. Such segmentation usually requires the use of different brand names for each segment.

3.3.2 Packaging

Packaging is often the key element in assisting mainly consumer-goods companies to achieve a comparative advantage. The critical decisions that must be made on the package are concerned with the functions the product pack will perform as well as with the mix of packaging components best able to perform in different degrees, the particular functions of the packaging. The functions of packaging can be grouped into six categories:

■ *Containment and Protection*: concerns the state of goods on arrival with the customer.

■ *Transportation and distribution*: has to do with efficiency in handling at all stages in the marketing channel and covers utilization and pack size.

■ *Management*: refers to efficiency in stocklisting, pricing, and ordering and covers some aspects of labelling (e.g. bar codes).

■ *Sale*: covers the aesthetic value and sales power to the consumer as well as labelling for recognition, information, and product description.

■ *Use*: concerns transportation, storage, opening, and possible reshutting by the customer as well as unit size.

■ *Disposal*: refers to the positive or negative restvalue of the packaging after its content has been used.

It is obvious that management expects a package to perform different functions and meet diverse requirements. Whenever a single element has so many functions to perform and demands to meet, the possibility of conflict emerges. However, the conflict that emerges in packaging becomes obvious at the time management has to decide about the packaging components that perform the packaging functions. The packaging components that perform the packaging function and are subject to changes each time management makes decisions about packaging are: (*a*) packaging materials, (*b*) package size, (*c*) package shape, (*d*) package colour, texture, and graphic art, and (*e*) other packaging components such as 'ease of opening', 'ease of use', 'reusability', and so on, that are incorporated into the package design.

One of the most important decisions pertaining to packaging components is the package-size decision, which is ultimately tied up with the product-line decisions. Changes in the size of the package may create an illusion of a new product. Companies tend to add in their lines either 'king' or 'giant economy' package sizes or small package sizes. The packaging-size decision evolves from appraisals of several factors, but the most important are the consuming unit and the rate of consumption. So important is the package-size–consumption-rate relationship that a major base for market segmentation is that of product usage, which, of course, has special meaning for package size. For instance, companies tend to segment markets on the basis of heavy-, moderate-, and light-user characteristics, and to develop package sizes accordingly.

Generally, packaging can be a powerful competitive tool as well as a major component of a marketing strategy. A better box or wrapper, a secondary-use package, a unique closure, or a more convenient container size may give a company a competitive advantage.

However, in designing their packaging companies should also pay attention to the growing environmental and safety concerns. Yet, while some companies that practise green marketing design packages that are more friendly to the environment, the responses on the part of the consumers are not always positive. It appears that, for some consumers, the lack of convenience could well be a barrier in actually purchasing an environmentally friendly packaged product. Indeed, a recent study found that convenience and environmental friendliness are the two underlying cognitive dimensions in the consumer evaluation of packaged products and that both dimensions exert an influence in preference formation (van Dam and van Trijp 1993). This implies that attempts to change consumer behaviour in the direction of product packaging that is more environmental friendly will be more effective if these two dimensions are taken into account more explicitly.

3.3.3 **Product services**

Finally, one more intangible characteristic through which a company may achieve a comparative advantage is product services. Product services tend to expand a product's utility and the buyers associate them with the physical product when considering alternative offers. For many industrial products, service policies are indispensable; for some consumer products, they are important elements in marketing programmes. However, companies do, and can, offer an almost infinite range of services. However, the product-connected services are rather limited and can be classified, using the type of value they add to the product as a basis for classification, into product performance enhancing services, product life prolonging services, and product risk reducing services.

The *product performance enhancing services* are more important for industrial goods and include installation, application engineering, and the training of operators.

The *product life prolonging services* are equally important for both consumer and industrial products and intend to keep the product operating satisfactorily for a long period of time, and, therefore, increase the customer's satisfaction. This type of service is primarily concerned with maintenance and repair.

The *product risk reducing services* aim to reduce the risk associated with the uncertainty about a product and include product warranties. A warranty whether expressed or implied represents a seller's obligation for certain services such as free repair, full and partial refund of the purchase price, or replacement of the product.

However, since every type of service is associated with different cost structures and customer perception, a company should combine services into a total 'service offering' in such a way as to minimize cost, on the one hand, and maximize favourable customer responses, on the other. This means that each time a company changes its product service policies, such change (product decision) should lead towards an 'optimum' product service offering. This, of course, presupposes that the company knows very well the services that customers value most and their relative importance.

4 The product and the company's marketing strategy

SINCE the marketing mix is the key dimension of marketing strategy, the optimum integration of the marketing variables is the continuing and overriding concern of marketing management. The integration of marketing variables is important because of the interaction that exists between and among marketing variables; if it is performed, it creates a synergistics effect for a company's 'offering', since the impact of an integrated mix is assumed to be greater than the summed impact of separately implemented marketing variables.

Two product-related marketing models provide a useful framework that can be used to ascertain the appropriate marketing mix. One such model tends to classify products in such a way that a meaningful marketing mix and strategy proceed from this classification. The other model recognizes the existence of distinct stages in the sales history of a product and meaningful marketing mix and strategy proceed by identifying the stage that a product is in or may be headed towards.

4.1 Marketing strategy as a function of product classification

Typically products are classified as consumer versus industrial and durable versus non-durable on the basis of 'who buys it' and 'how durable it is' respectively. Since the strategies associated with these dichotomies are at best appropriations of the marketing efforts that tend to be suitable for the respective product categories, other classification schemes have been developed in the literature in the hope that products may be classified in such a way that rational marketing strategy decisions may proceed from such classification. A thorough review of the pertinent literature by Murphy and Enis (1986) revealed eighteen such classification schemes.

Historically, one of the most widely accepted classifications of products was proposed by Copeland (1923). He proposed a trichotomy: 'convenience goods, shopping goods and specialty goods', based on consumer buying habits. Although his concern was with consumer goods, his scheme may be easily generalized to include industrial goods as well.

Convenience goods are those for which the consumer will not spend much money or time in purchasing nor does he/she perceive significant levels of risk in making a selection. Examples of consumer goods that fall into the convenience category include fresh produce and grocery staples, umbrellas, gum, and batteries. Supplies and raw materials that are commodities could be classified as convenience items for industrial buyers.

Shopping goods, as the name implies, are those for which the buyers are willing to spend a significant amount of time and money in searching for and evaluating. Increased levels of risk are also perceived for these high-involvement products. Examples of shopping goods are automobiles, clothing, and furniture for end consumers, and equipment and component parts for industrial users.

Speciality goods are 'unique' in some regard and require special effort in terms of both money and time for their acquisition. Comments such as [I would] 'wait for weeks', or 'not settle for anything else', are good indicators of the time effort that distinguishes speciality products. Examples of speciality products include vintage imported wines, expensive sports cars, and paintings by well-known artists. In the industrial sector, installations (buildings) would be speciality products because their location, cost, and furnishings require great organizational effort and risk.

Holbrook and Howard (1976) made a major contribution to the study of goods classification by proposing a fourth category, *preference goods*, which involve low shopping effort and low ego involvement, but high brand preference. This four-product category classification was adopted by Murphy and Enis (1986). Building on the works of Copeland, and Holbrook and Howard, they developed an integrated product classification scheme consisting of the four aforementioned product categories defined in terms of the effort and risk dimensions of price as perceived by both organizational and ultimate consumers. According to the authors, their proposed product classification scheme provides a managerial road map for strategy development: buyer's perception of price, buyer's behaviour, marketer's objectives and basic strategy, and specific strategies for each element of the marketing mix. Box 14.1 presents the marketing implications of the scheme proposed by Murphy and Enis.

The product classification schemes suggested in the literature, and the one discussed here, indicate that the classification of products can form the foundation for building a meaningful marketing strategy. However, the managers who attempt to devise a workable marketing strategy as a function of product classification should be aware of certain deficiencies inherent in this approach.

First, neither every product nor every marketing variable fits precisely into the suggested framework, since the classification of products in the suggested groups will vary between different individual customers, groups of customers, and even geographical markets. This indicates how important it is to analyse market opportunities and target markets before developing a marketing strategy to appeal to that particular market. Secondly, the classification of products is, like all marketing, dynamic and, therefore, a product once considered in a particular group may not stay in that group indefinitely. This is because of changes that occur in the buyer economic environment and habits, in the performance of basic marketing variables, and in other environmental conditions. These changes in turn affect the market demand of the product as well as the composition of the marketing mix that supports it.

The fact that the product's position, and even its concept, can be expected to change over time led to the development of the product life-cycle model as a framework for the selection of meaningful marketing strategies.

4.2 The product life cycle and marketing strategy

One of the widely used frames of reference for product as well as for marketing strategy decisions is the product life-cycle (PLC) model.

Most discussions of the PLC portray the sales history of a typical product as following the form of a time-dependent S-shaped sales curve, as illustrated in Fig. 14.2. This curve is typically divided into four successive stages: introduction, growth, maturity, and decline. However, a number of authors view 'saturation' as a distinct stage between the maturity and decline stages.

During the *introduction* stage of the PLC the product is relatively unknown, sales volume rises slowly, but the expenses involved in communicating the availability of the product as well as the expenses of establishing channels of distribution

Box 14.1 **Managerial implications of classifying products strategically**

Managerial focus	Product category			
	Convenience	Preference	Shopping	Speciality
Buyer's perception of price	Low effort, low risk	Low effort, medium risk	High effort, medium risk	High effort, high risk
Buyer behaviour	Impulse or habit (auto reorder)	Routine (straight rebuy)	Limited (modified rebuy)	Extensive (new task)
Marketer's objective	Move to preference or shopping, or dominate via low cost	Brand loyalty	Source or store loyalty	Absolute (source and brand) loyalty
Marketer's basic strategy	High volume, cost minimization, or move product	High volume, brand identity, differentiation	High volume or high margin, segmentation	High margin, limited volume, market 'niche'
Product strategy	Standard grades and quantities, quality control, innovations copied quickly	Standard grades and quantities, quality control, some R&D	Standard base, many options, much R&D, warranties	Custom design, much R&D, warranties, personalized service
Price strategy *monetary*	Market	Market	Bundled or negotiated	Negotiated
non-monetary	Minimize time and risk	Minimize time, warrant risk	Accommodate time, warrant risk	Pamper for time and risk
Place strategy	Saturation distribution	Intensive distribution	Selective distribution	Exclusive distribution
Promotion strategy	Point-of purchase, some sales promotion	Mass advertising, sales promotion, some personal selling	Personal selling, some advertising	Publicity, personal selling, testimony

Source: Murphy and Enis (1986: 24–42).

are high and consequently few or no profits are realized, despite the fact that the price is on the high side. If the product gains acceptance, it moves into a stage of more rapid sales, known as the *growth* stage, because of the cumulative effect of introductory promotion, distribution, and word-of-mouth influence. During this stage, the company's profits increase. If the product has achieved the market acceptance associated with the growth stage, it might be expected that competition would enter the market. If price was not crucial at the beginning, the advent of competition would lead to a reduction of prices. During the *maturity* stage sales cease to grow exponentially and they tend to stabilize and the gross margin may be reduced.

When a high proportion of the potential buyers of the product have purchased it and sales settle at a rate governed by the replacement purchases of satisfied buyers, the market may be said to be saturated. Gross margins tend to decline in the *saturation* stage, since prices begin to soften as competitors struggle to obtain market share in a saturated market. Finally, the product reaches the stage of *decline*, during which it ceases to be profitable. This may occur because technologically advanced products have become available and/or because of changes in the buyer's economic environment and habits.

It is important to note, however, that, while both the product's sales volume curve and its total profit curve are similar in configuration, there is

Figure 14.2 **The product life-cycle curve**

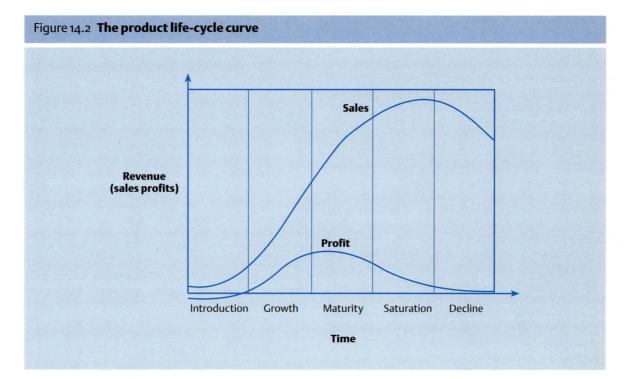

a dissimilarity in timing. During the latter part of the growth stage and the early part of the maturity stage, the product produces more revenue, as an increasing number of units are sold, but total profit decreases as a result of price reductions. Although a greater number of units are sold to produce a higher sales volume, the product's total profit actually declines. Consequently, as the product's sales peak and turn down in the saturation stage, its profits fall more rapidly. The implication for this 'dissimilarity' in timing is that, since the objective of long-range profit maximization is consistent with both business and consumer welfare, it is more appropriate for business companies to plan their marketing strategies (products) around the profitability function than the sales function. In fact, marketing management should think and plan in terms of profit life cycle rather than product life cycle.

However, the length of life cycles for different products varies widely. The different lengths of cycles are usually governed by factors such as the rate of technological change, the introduction of superior products, the market acceptance of products and the ease of entry of competitive products. In plotting life cycles, however, it is important to distinguish between the industry life cycle (generic group of products that constitute the total market also known as product-class life cycle), a company's product-line life cycle (also known as product-form life cycle), and a company's product/model life cycle (also known as brand life cycle). The industry life cycle reflects changes in aggregate market demand and consequently is longer than the product-line life cycle and certainly longer than the model life cycle and can be expected to exhibit a 'maturity' for an indefinite period. The company's product-line and product/model life cycles, on the other hand, tend to reflect the company's competitive strength and consequently they seem to exhibit the standard PLC histories more faithfully than the industry life cycle.

However, what are the basic implications of the PLC model for marketing management? First, it is possible to highlight gaps in the product mix that could arise in the future owing to the predictable reduction in profit margins, as products enter the maturity, saturation, and decline stages. R&D resources can be specifically directed towards either formulating new products or redesigning existing ones that will generate the revenues and profits at the required time in the future and compensate for the anticipated decline arising from current products.

Secondly, it highlights the need to shift the relative levels and emphasis given to price, promotion, and other marketing strategies as products move from one stage to another, owing to the distinct opportunities and problems with respect to marketing strategy and profit potential that each stage of the cycle offers.

However, the utility of the PLC model has been questioned by a number of authors in the literature who regard it as vacuous, empty of empirical generality, and positively dangerous if used as a guide for action. Their main criticisms (Kraushar 1972; Fildes and Lofthouse 1975; Dhalla and Yuspeh 1976; Doyle 1976) can be summarized as follows:

▪ Year to year variations make it difficult to predict when the next stage will appear, how long it will last, and what levels the sales will reach.

▪ One cannot often judge with accuracy in which stage of the life cycle the product is.

▪ The major stages do not divide themselves into clear-cut compartments. At certain points a product may appear to have attained maturity when actually it has only reached a temporary plateau in the growth stage prior to its next big upsurge.

▪ Not all products pass through the idealized S-shaped product life cycle that may be described as a simple parabola (polynomial of the second degree) represented by the equation $Y = a + bx + cx^2$. Even an advocate of the PLC identifies no less than nine variants of the idealized shape: (a) the high learning product life cycle, (b) the missing link and other low-learning substantive product life cycles, (c) the straight fads, (d) the fads with significant residual market, (e) the instant busts, (f) the market speciality, (g) the pyramided cycle, (h) the aborted introduction, (i) the fashion cycle (Wasson 1971).

▪ The time-dependent PLC model is insufficient for two reasons. First, the PLC is partly endogen-

ous—the long-term pattern of sales is determined by the strategic decisions of management. Secondly, exogenous factors are not adequately modelled as random errors around the time-dependent PLC.

Studies pertaining to both consumer and industrial products have shown that the PLC model holds up well for these types of products and market situations (Buzzell 1966; Cunningham 1969; Polli and Cook 1969). The main conclusion of these studies was that, when tested in an explicit form for given categories of goods, the PLC can be a useful model for planning the launching of new products, establishing price policies, planning the timed use of the marketing mix, and undertaking cash flow and financial-investment appraisal.

However, the PLC model is mainly useful as a framework for developing effective marketing strategies in different stages of the PLC, and some leading experts who view the PLC model as the foundation of marketing strategy have made a number of suggestions regarding the marketing implications that each stage has for marketing action (Levitt 1965; Smallwood 1973; Kotler 1997). Their suggestions for each stage can be summarized as follows:

Introduction stage. In introducing a new product (line), marketing management should offer a limited number of models with modular design to permit flexible addition of variants to satisfy new segments as soon as identified. Quality and quality control are highly important during this stage. If price and promotion are considered together, management has to select between four alternative strategies at this stage: (a) a high-profile strategy that consists of introducing a new product with a high price and a high promotion level, (b) a low-profile strategy that consists of introducing the new product with a low price and low level of promotion, (c) a selective penetration strategy that consists of a high price and low promotion, and (d) a pre-emptive penetration strategy that consists of low price and heavy promotion. The basic factors that management has to consider in selecting any of these four strategies are: (a) the market size, (b) the market awareness about the product, (c) the degree of price sensitiveness in the market, (d) the type and nature of competition, and (e) the company's cost structure. As far as distribution is concerned, it should be intensive and extensive with introductory deals and logistics weighted heavily towards customer service and heavy inventories at all levels.

Growth stage. At this stage management should focus on best-selling versions, the addition of few related models, the improvement of the product and the elimination of unnecessary specifications with little market appeal. As far as pricing is concerned management should focus on the market broadening and promotional pricing opportunities. Promotion should shift the emphasis from building product awareness to nurturing product preference. Distribution should be intensive and extensive with the addition of new distribution channels to gain additional product exposure.

Maturity stage. During this stage, which lasts much longer than previous stages, management is facing the most formidable challenges. Most products are in the maturity stage of the life cycle and most of the product decisions (changes in the product's physical configuration and in the augmented product) discussed in the previous section are made at this stage. Management should try to break out of a stagnant sales picture by initiating changes in the product's tangible and intangible characteristics that will attract new users and/or more usage from the current users. Attention should be paid to possibilities for product improvement and cost reduction through changes in the quality features and style of the product. Proliferation of packages, private brands, and product services could also bring positive results for the company at this stage.

Price should be reduced as a way of drawing new segments into the market as well as attracting customers of competitive products. Management should also search for incremental pricing opportunities, including private branding contracts. Promotion should maintain consumer and trade loyalty, and a search for new and brilliant advertising appeal that wins the consumer's attention and favour should be pursued. Another way to attract the consumer's attention at this stage is through heavy incentives programmes and many short-term promotions, deals, and contests. Distribution should be intensive and extensive, as in the previous stages.

Decline stage. As the sales of the product decline at this stage, management should either eliminate the product or, in the case that it is offered in a number of versions, sizes, and models, it should eliminate those items that are not returning a direct profit. However, there are a number of strategies that marketing management could follow to eliminate the product. For instance, management could adopt a concentration strategy, in which case it would concentrate its resources in the strongest markets, while phasing out promotional and distribution activities as they become marginal, and maintaining profit-level pricing with complete disregard of any effect on market share. Management could follow a milking strategy, in which case it sharply reduces its marketing expenses to increase its current profits, knowing that this will accelerate the rate of sales decline and the ultimate demise of the product. If a hard-core loyalty remains strong enough at this stage, the product may be marketed at the old or even a higher price, which means good profits.

Most of the previously mentioned marketing strategies are concerned with consumer goods. Wasson (1976), a leading expert in this area, has made a number of suggestions regarding the marketing implications that each stage has for marketing action in the industrial field. According to Wasson, the strategy objective for each stage of the PLC should be as follows:

- *Introduction (market development) stage*: minimize learning requirements, develop widespread brand awareness.
- *Rapid growth stage*: establish strong market position.
- *Competitive turbulence stage*: maintain/strengthen market niche.
- *Saturation (maturity) stage*: defend position against competition.
- *Decline stage*: milk the product of all possible profits.

However, one comment should be made about the suggested marketing strategies for the decline stage. The emphasis given on the product-elimination decision as the appropriate strategy for the decline stage has led many marketing scholars to believe that management should consider the elimination decision only when the product has reached its decline stage. However, as will become obvious in the following section, age is a poor criterion for deleting products: not all old products are ready for elimination, nor are elimination candidates only those that have been around for a long time.

5 The product-deletion decision

HISTORICALLY, the major consideration given to product-line management by practitioners and scholars has focused on the development of new products. In contrast to the new-product-development area, the product-elimination decision has received comparatively little attention. Recent years, however, have witnessed an interest in product elimination, and a number of studies using various theoretical constructs have investigated various aspects of this important area of product-line management (Avlonitis 1985, 1987).

☞ 'A shrewd decision to retain or divest, and skilful timing of a divestment, can add much value to a competitive strategy that had been adopted earlier.' (Chapter 15, p. 375)

Much of the literature on product elimination either explicitly or implicitly assumes that product elimination is a strategy for declining products—that is, for those products that have moved through the various stages of the conventional life cycle and have reached their decline stage. In other words, much of the literature assumes that the basic problem situation that evokes the elimination of a product is its weak performance, measured usually in terms of sales and profits.

However, to assume, as the bulk of the pertinent literature does, that the product-elimination decision arises only when a product reaches the decline stage of its life cycle, and is not performing satisfactorily with respect to a company's sales, profit, and/or market-share objectives, is no doubt an oversimplification.

Recent studies have shown that not all 'poor old heavyweights' are ready for elimination, nor are elimination candidates only those that have been around for a long time and show signs of low profitability and declining sales; the various problem situations that result in the elimination decision are not always easy to detect, and in a number of cases a company depends on outside forces to form the 'lead' in its elimination decision.

In major research recently conducted by the author, 156 discontinued products were studied. More than half of these products were not dropped at the decline stage, which is usually associated with the product-elimination decision. About 20 per cent of the products were dropped before they even reached the maturity stage (Avlonitis 1990).

The study also identified the problem situations or precipitating circumstances triggering the product-elimination decision of the various stages of the PLC. According to our findings, operational problems (e.g. production, marketing) experienced by a product and its poor sales performance are likely to initiate the elimination decision at the introduction stage of the PLC. These findings are consistent with research by Calantone and Cooper (1979), who have shown that two major causes of new-product failure are technical problems, implying manufacturing and marketing deficiencies, and lack of understanding of customers' needs, which is reflected in the product's poor sales performance. The study also showed that an uncontrollable factor—namely, a policy decision made by the parent organization—may also evoke the product-elimination decision at the introduction stage of the PLC.

With respect to the growth stage of the PLC, a product's poor quality/design, in addition to its operational problems, might trigger an elimination decision.

Two precipitating circumstances—namely, competitive activity and decline in market potential—are most likely to initiate the product-elimination decision at the maturity and decline stages of the PLC. The elimination decision at the decline stage of the PLC may also be evoked by two more precipitating circumstances—namely, development of a variety reduction policy and poor sales performance, which are strongly associated with this particular stage of the PLC.

5.1 The product-revitalization/ deletion process

The focus of this section is on the product-revitalization and product-deletion decision process. These decisions are interrelated. Product deletion, for example, cannot be made in isolation from consideration of other options, such as changes in product specifications or marketing strategy. Indeed, these two decisions—revitalization or deletion—represent the two key alternative courses of action a company can undertake in response to either current or projected unsatisfactory product performance. Also, both of these decisions require a routine performance evaluation of the product portfolio, designed to identify products that exhibit unacceptable performance and that, unless they have a realistic chance of being restored to strength (product revitalization), should be dropped (product elimination). A number of approaches to the routine evaluation of the product portfolio for the identification of weak products have been proposed in the literature. These approaches can be grouped into three major categories. The first category includes those approaches that advocate a systematic and periodic review of the product line, in which every product is subject to performance evaluation on a number of key performance dimensions/criteria—namely, sales volume, profitability, market share, share of company's sales, and so on. The second category includes those approaches in which the routine evaluation of product performance on a number of key dimensions/criteria is summarized into a single overall performance index. Finally, the third category includes those approaches that advocate the joint consideration of a number of key product performance dimensions, which leads to the development of a product portfolio classification/matrix scheme. For a review of the approaches to the routine evaluation of the product portfolio, see Avlonitis (1986).

The product-revitalization/deletion decision can be conceptualized as a multiple-stage sequential process, as shown in Fig. 14.3. The process begins with a 'diagnostic' routine, which makes up the first stage. The overall intention of the 'diagnostic' routine is to define the causes of the product's unsatisfactory performance and generate alternative corrective actions, which are considered and evaluated by management at the second and third stages of the process respectively.

When management decides that a corrective action has a good possibility of making the product competitive again, then it proceeds to implement this particular action. If, on the other hand, management decides that no corrective action is feasible, then the next logical step is to undertake a detailed investigation to determine whether elimination is, indeed, indicated. If it is decided to eliminate the product, then management proceeds to implement the decision and determines the most opportune time and method of its disposal to minimize the elimination's effects on customers and the company's profit structure.

In the following paragraphs we will be concerned mainly with the presentation of some empirical evidence pertaining to the policies and practices of manufacturing companies at the various stages of the product-revitalization/deletion process (see Fig. 14.3). This evidence is based on extensive studies conducted by the author in this area.

5.1.1 Diagnosis

If a product's performance deviates from the established norms on the various performance measures used by the company—for example, profitability, sales volume, and so on—then some form of diagnosis takes place. This diagnostic routine generally starts with knowledge, based on the management's experience and judgement, about the sources that have caused the deviation in the product's performance. The sources of deviation that management generally considers and investigates include:

- production methods;
- competitive activities;
- product's cost structure;
- product's design;
- customer requirements;
- product's market price;
- product's market share.

The identification of the sources of deviation is followed by an investigation within these sources to define the causes of deviation. Usually in-house studies and research are conducted by the accounting and/or engineering departments, aiming at:

- measuring the total costs associated with the product;
- analysing the product's design and manufacturing methods;
- making recommendations regarding the feasibility of reducing the product's costs.

In certain cases in-house meetings also take place during which the opinions of the sales force (sales representatives, sales engineers, product/marketing engineers) are sought regarding the weak performance of the product.

The investigation into the sources of deviation is followed by the preparation of memos or reports stating the causes of the product's poor performance. These documents are generally studied during 'general management' or 'product

Figure 14.3 **The product revitalization/deletion process**

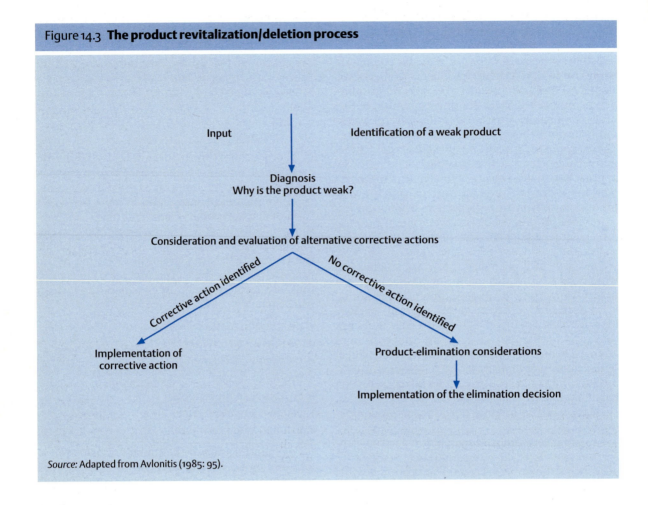

Input Identification of a weak product

Diagnosis
Why is the product weak?

Consideration and evaluation of alternative corrective actions

Corrective action identified No corrective action identified

Implementation of corrective action Product-elimination considerations

Implementation of the elimination decision

Source: Adapted from Avlonitis (1985: 95).

planning' meetings, where decisions regarding corrective actions are taken.

5.1.2 Consideration and evaluation of corrective actions

Hart (1989) uncovered eighteen courses of corrective action generally considered by manufacturing companies in revitalizing weak products. These corrective actions, in descending order of importance, are:

■ *Increasing sales-force effort*. An increase in effort by the sales force can be achieved through higher incentive, sales competitions, or a period of retraining to establish the 'selling proposition' of the product in question in the salespeople's minds. However, despite the popularity of this corrective measure, it can be somewhat short term in its ap-

proach, especially if incentives are part of a larger promotional deal.

■ *Cost reduction*. A second popular method of revitalization was a cost reduction, which could be undertaken, either to prepare for a price cut without a loss in profits or to increase the profit margin on a product. A cost reduction was described by the participating companies in a number of ways: altering the mix of parts of ingredients in the product, altering the source or quality of parts or ingredients, reducing the numbers of parts or components, reinvesting in more productive plant, or withdrawing promotional support.

■ *Product modification*. Rather than a short-term approach, some companies, where appropriate, might try product modification as a way of altering the sales or profit trends of a particular product. This differs from 'cost reduction' in that it represents an attempt to add value or variety to the product, which, although it *can* result in a lower price, is not done specifically to achieve a lower price.

■ *Production efficiency improvements.* In a similar vein, production efficiency improvements were cited by some companies as ways of reducing costs. This usually means that, where demand justified it, production batch sizes were increased to achieve lower unit costs, which could be passed on to customers by a price reduction.

■ *Price decrease.* This tactic was adopted, either to meet a competitive price promotion or to attempt to resuscitate sales in the longer term. However, no company would reduce price if the product in question became, as a result, loss-making. Decreasing the price of a product is also used to run down finished stocks of a product that is being replaced by a new one.

A number of companies were reluctant to use price as a tool for avoiding low sales, for a number of reasons. First, price cuts lower profits and can encourage the competition to follow suit, leaving lowered profits without a competitive advantage. Secondly, cutting the price on some of the company's brands can stimulate 'cannibalization'.

In some situations, price cuts do not actually increase sales of a product, they merely change the date of purchase. Cuts can also undermine the confidence of the distribution.

■ *Quality improvements.* A branch of 'product modification' important enough to warrant separate treatment is quality improvements, which were usually considered where quality was known to be inferior and unsatisfactory. Frequently, where product quality could not be improved, the product was phased out.

■ *Increase in sales promotion.* Also reserved for short-term use was an increase in sales promotion. This meant attending trade shows, increasing and revamping sales brochures and literature as well as incentives for the distributive trade.

■ *Development of new markets.* Two improvement options suggested by the participating companies related to the marketplace. The first is to extend the product to new markets to enhance sales performance. A similar option in this connection is for the company to export the product, thereby increasing its sales base.

■ *Product range reduction.* Product range reduction was seen to help the problems of managing extended product ranges, eliminating the dispropor-tionately high costs of manufacturing and stocking slow-moving items.

■ *Product range extension.* This option allows the company to compete with a wider choice of products for potential customers, with little physical or functional difference among the products: an altered feature or form perhaps, or trimming, or slightly cheaper version. While this response was not necessarily specific to a particular problem product, for companies using it it might help rekindle interest in the range generally.

■ *Market concentration.* This involves withdrawing a product from those markets or segments where its performance is sluggish.

■ *Packaging changes.* Not unrelated to 'product modification' are packaging changes, which can be used to reduce the cost, without actually impinging on product quality, to alter the image of the product in the mind of the customer, or to differentiate it from competitive products.

■ *Distribution improvements.* Distribution improvements attempt to improve display or shelf space given to a product by the distributive trade. A number of companies underlined the importance of shelf space to the sales of their products; all were consumer goods companies. The marketing director of a relatively small manufacturer of fresh foods explains that, as the retail chains became bigger and accounted for a larger share of consumer purchase, and as their allocation of shelf space became more and more centralized, 'it became as crucial to negotiate the "number of facings" given to a product as it was to negotiate entry to the store itself'. Accordingly, an increase in shelf space could greatly enhance sales of the product.

■ *Factoring or sourcing.* This 'corrective' measure amounts to a psychological elimination of the product. Deciding to buy the product rather than make it, or sourcing it, allows a company to market the product without having the production headaches that accompany a product in decline.

■ *Price increase.* While a price increase could often increase the speed of an ailing product's demise, this was not always the case. Where declining markets were involved, companies increased the price of products to increase the yield of the products in those markets.

■ *Greater use of print-media advertising.* Increased advertising was also reported to mobilize customers' support. The marketing director of a large company manufacturing domestic appliances commented that 'as a consumer goods manufacturer you often have to turn up the volume through advertising and promotion'. The advertising response was popular in, but not exclusive to, the consumer goods companies. However, some respondents were of the firm opinion that promotional activity was very much a short-term answer, especially where mature products were concerned.

■ *Change in channels of distribution.* This option was feasible only where a few key wholesalers and retailers did not account for a large proportion of sales. Companies attempting to improve sales performance by a change in channels of distribution were involved in exporting through agents.

■ *Guarantee extension.* An alternative way of enhancing product quality reported by the respondent companies was the extension of warranties and guarantees.

However, in selecting or rejecting a particular corrective action, management tends to rely predominantly on judgement and past experience. Our studies revealed that in most cases management tends to judge in some qualitative way the nature of the consequences given the implementation of a particular corrective action. The kind of corrective actions that management actually selects and implements is found to be determined by the product's position on the life-cycle curve. Table 14.1 shows the corrective actions that were considered, evaluated, selected, and implemented by management over a product's life cycle in a sample of seventeen industrial products.

This leads us to propose that the weak product-revitalization decision in the industrial field is very much a hierarchical process. At the early stages of a product's life cycle, acceptable solutions for the product's problems are generally sought in immediately accessible and familiar areas and product modifications and improvement are the main courses of corrective actions actually selected and implemented. Failure of these corrective actions to make the product competitively healthy again, brings the product under elimination review and solutions for the product's problems are generally sought in less familiar areas such as the product's marketing strategy. However, it is not very likely that the corrective actions considered at this stage and which usually involve changes in the product's price and promotion will be actually selected and implemented.

Table 14.1 Corrective actions over a product's life cycle (n = 17)

Corrective actions considered/ evaluated	No. of cases	Corrective actions selected/ implemented
		Early stages of the PLC n = 11
Product modifications	7	Product modifications
Product improvement	3	Product improvement
Price reduction	1	Price reduction
Increased promotional expenditure	1	Increased promotional expenditure
Changed channels of distribution	1	Changed channels of distribution
		Late stages of the PLC n = 15
Price increases	5	Price increases
Product modifications	5	—
Price reduction	3	Price reduction
Product improvement	3	Product improvement
Increased promotional expenditure	2	Increased promotional expenditure
Increased effort by the sales force	1	—

Source: Avlonitis (1985: 102).

5.1.3 Product-elimination considerations—evaluation and decision-making

If management realizes that no corrective action is feasible, then the managerial attention shifts from the product itself to the impact on the entire company of eliminating the product. With respect to this stage of the process, the normative views see a weak product as entering a detailed, formalized procedure, in which all relevant considerations are tabulated with numerical weights and ratings. At the termination of this procedure an 'index' is obtained indicating the degree of prod-

Oh little one
if I had known
it was to be
our last day together
I would have
done it all
differently.
I would have taken you
to the beach
to hear the waves
and to the mountains
to feel the snow.
I would have shown you
rainbows and
Christmas trees
and ferris wheels.
Or maybe
I would have done
exactly what I did.
Sing you to sleep
tuck you in with Teddy
and whisper
goodnight.

Debbie Gemmill

COT DEATH DEVASTATES ONE FAMILY A WEEK IN SCOTLAND. PLEASE GIVE MONEY FOR RESEARCH TO: SCOTTISH COT DEATH TRUST, YORKHILL CHILDREN'S HOSPITAL, GLASGOW.

Scottish Cot Death Trust
MARR Associates, 46 The Shore, Leith, Edinburgh EH6 6QU
Art Director: Martin Lambley *Copywriter:* John Cooke *Creative Director:* Colin Marr

A powerful message whose stark presentation is entirely appropriate for the topic. This advertisement was voted the best regional press advertisement in its year.

Will you be as fortunate finding a second career?

Heaven knows, you are going to need a second career more than this gentleman.

Compulsory retirement at 55 is on its way.

No matter how long your service, no matter how high your position, you could be out of a job, come your 55th birthday.

The company car will disappear.

The expense account will disappear.

The private health insurance will disappear.

Sadly, your mortgage won't. You may well find yourself repaying that until you are 60 or 65.

Civil servants should be alright. They have indexed-linked pensions, courtesy of the poor old taxpayer.

Members of trade unions should make out too. They often have an army of negotiators to battle on their behalf.

No, it's the private sector business-man who will be in trouble.

His retirement age is going down, but his life expectancy is on the up and up. Today's 40 year olds can expect to reach 80. You could easily be faced with 25 years in retirement.

How will you manage?

That fixed company pension that looked oh-so-generous ten years ago, won't be worth much in another ten year's time, never mind twenty or thirty.

State pensions aren't famous for keeping up with inflation either.

Of course, with the two added together, you may just have enough to survive.

But is that all you want to do? Survive?

Wouldn't you prefer to do some-thing positive with the second half of your adult life?

Albany Life and the Inland Revenue can help you.

Start salting away a regular sum each month. £15, £50, whatever you can spare.

We will bump up your contributions by claiming back from the taxman every last penny of tax relief we can.

We will then invest the total amount on your behalf.

We receive what is arguably the best investment advice there is. We retain Warburg Investment Management Ltd., a subsidiary of S. G. Warburg & Co Ltd., the merchant bank.

Start saving in your thirties or forties and you will amass a considerable sum, well before your 55th birthday.

When you are pensioned off, you will have a wad of tax-free money to cushion the blow.

Enough to set up shop in some sleepy Devon village.

Enough to pursue some half-forgotten craft, like working with cane or stained glass.

Enough to buy you a stake in some successful small business near your home.

Whatever you decide to do, you'll be better off mentally as well as financially. People vegetate if they have nothing but the garden to occupy their minds.

There is no reason why you shouldn't be active and working at 73, like Mr. Reagan here.

Though hopefully you won't have to carry the worries of the world on your shoulders.

To learn more about our plans send this coupon to Peter Kelly, Albany Life Assurance, FREEPOST, Potters Bar EN6 1BR.

Name _____

Address _____

Tel: _____

Name of your Life Assurance Broker, if any

Albany Life

Albany Life

Lowe Howard-Spink, 68–114 Knightsbridge, London, SW1X 7LT

Writer: Alfredo Marcantonio *Art Director:* David Christensen

An advert that gets attention through the use of a combination of humour and a well-known public figure—Ronald Reagan at the time being President of the United States.

WE STOLE THEIR LAND, THEIR BUFFALO AND THEIR WOMEN.

THEN WE WENT BACK FOR THEIR SHOES.

Timberland

Timberland

Legas Delaney Partnership Ltd., 233 Shaftesbury Avenue, London WC2H 8EL

Writer: Tim Delaney *Art Director:* Steve Dunn

Timberland used the '1–2–3–wallop' headline structure to gain attention.

Four Corners

Legas Delaney Partnership Ltd., 233 Shaftesbury Avenue, London WC2H 8EL

Writer: Paul Marshall *Art Director:* Gary Marshall

The *Four Corners* advertisement for British Airways' Four Corners Travel Shops used a *double entendre* to gain attention.

If you can collect every bit of data relevant to your business, you don't need us.

You could spend every waking hour chasing the information your business needs to stay ahead.

Or you could switch on your PC and get Reuters on the case.

With the Reuters Business Briefing service, you get the world's most powerful business database delivered online to your desktop. So you can draw on 10 years' archived information from over 2,000 publications, on every subject under the sun.

For good measure, Reuters Business Briefing also brings you up-to-the-minute news from over 1,900 journalists. There's financial data on 24,000 companies. Plus prices for all major currencies, and stock market indices from around the world.

To find out what Reuters Business Briefing could do for you, the next step is to visit http://www.bizinfo.reuters.com or get in touch with Reuters on 0171 542 9029.

With business information like this at your fingertips, you'll soon be feeling on top of the world.

REUTERS BUSINESS BRIEFING. If you've got it, you've got it. REUTERS

REUTERS and the dotted logo and sphere logos are the house trademarks of REUTERS Limited. REUTERS is a registered trademark in more than 25 countries worldwide.

Reuters
Warman Bannister, 40 Marsh Wall, London E14 9TP
Writer: Philip Tetley-Jones *Art Director:* Steve Smith

A business-to-business advertisement which uses an engaging personification that has been placed in international media such as *The Economist* and the *Financial Times*.

Born 1963.

Still kicking, 1998.

David Bailey, Nicholas Barker, Bob Brooks, Rod Butcher, Julian Cottrell, Hugh Laurie, Richard Loncraine, Squid, Charles Sturridge.

James Garrett

James Garrett & Partners, 8 Great Titchfield Street, London W1P 7AA

An advertisement created solely for inclusion in the Special Edition to celebrate *Campaign*'s 30th 'Birthday'. *Campaign* is a weekly newspaper read widely by the UK advertising and media community.

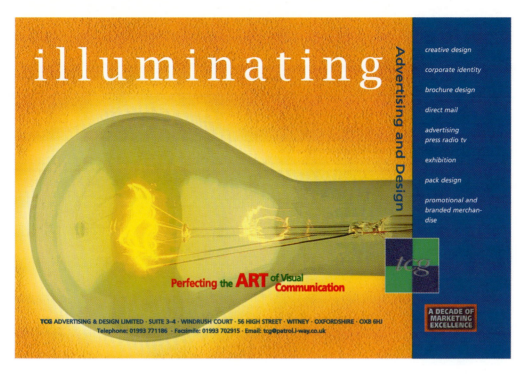

TCG Advertising and Design Ltd
Windrush Court, Witney,
Oxfordshire OX8 6HJ

Hot Air
The Hot House, Hurst Street,
Oxford OX4 1EZ

Two examples of the high quality
of advertising which small local
agencies are capable of creating.

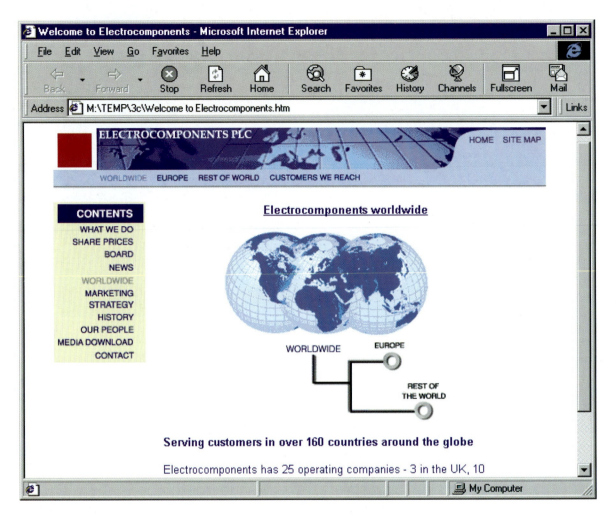

www.electrocomponents.com

Electrocomponents Plc, International Management Centre, 5000 Oxford Business Park South, Oxford OX4 2BH

It is estimated that advertising spending on the internet will rise from $3.3 billion in 1999 to $33 billion by 2004.

uct desirability and thus assisting management to make a decision as to whether or not to drop the product. However, there was no evidence in our studies to suggest that a formalized procedure was in operation. This lack of formal procedures for the elimination/retention decision, however, is not to be thought of as being necessarily synonymous with a lack of systematic thinking. The participating companies appeared to develop more or less clear perceptions of what factors need investigation in evaluating a weak product and in making the elimination/retention decision.

Nineteen evaluation factors are generally considered by management in manufacturing industry in order to make the product-elimination/retention decision. These factors, which cut across industry boundaries and represent facets of all the major functions of a manufacturing company—that is, marketing, accounting/finance, production, R&D, etc.—can in fact be subsumed into categories that represent the critical dimensions (considerations) of the weak-product evaluation process. At least six such dimensions (considerations) are necessary to describe an appropriate framework within which a weak product may be evaluated in manufacturing industry:

■ *Implications for company resources*. This dimension contains evaluation factors that are concerned with the implications of the product's removal upon company resources, including the capacity utilization issue.

■ *Market reaction*. This dimension is composed of evaluation factors that are concerned with the company's image and the possible reactions of competitors and customers *vis-à-vis* a product's deletion.

■ *Financial implications*. This dimension is composed of evaluation factors examining the financial implications of a product's removal and particularly the issue of recovery of overheads.

■ *New product potential*. This dimension portrays management's desire to consider the development of a new replacement product that will provide customers with a satisfactory alternative.

■ *Alternative opportunities considerations*. This dimension is composed of evaluation factors that are concerned with the exploration of the possibility of using the funds, transferable facilities, and executive abilities freed by eliminating the product in other ventures promising better returns.

■ *Product range policy considerations*. This dimension is composed of evolution factors that are concerned with the assessment of the product's removal upon the company's 'pull-range' policy and the sales and profits of the other products in the range.

During the weak-product evaluation process, some of these dimensions/factors are more relevant than others, depending not only on the particular situation that the product faces at the time of the decision, but also on the company's certain contextual organizational, managerial, and environmental conditions (Avlonitis 1993).

5.1.4 Implementation of the elimination decision

Once a decision to eliminate a product has been reached, its departure should be systematically planned and coordinated. At this stage management faces further strategic choices that have to do with the speed with which the product is removed and the amount of support that it is to be given during the removal stage. It should be stated, however, that the elimination strategy might have been largely determined at an earlier stage of the product-elimination process, when management made a judgement on whether or not it could prolong the life of the product on the market by changing its design and/or its marketing mix. This point is exemplified by the following statement made by the sales manager of a large manufacturer of automatic controls: 'When we become aware of the difficulty of expanding a product's market or fighting for a larger market share, we generally consider three basic options: (1) make it obsolete; (2) kill it by pricing; (3) selling it out to another manufacturer.' In this section we focus on the elimination strategies used by manufacturing companies to implement the elimination decision and the factors that influence the phase-out tactics and timing.

Five elimination strategies were detected in our studies:

■ *Drop immediately*. This strategy implies the immediate departure of the product and implies no further production, selling of inventory, and redirection of investment.

■ *Phase out immediately*. This strategy is a modification of the drop-immediately strategy and involves the rundown of the product's inventory by satisfying the customers' orders received up to the decision day and/or other contractual agreements. No one appreciates perfunctory treatment, including those on whom the company depends for sustenance.

■ *Phase out slowly*. This strategy is somewhat similar to the 'milk', 'run-out', and 'harvest' strategies suggested in the literature, which involve changes in the product's marketing strategy (for example, price changes, reduction in marketing promotion) to capitalize upon the remaining strength of the product and any hard-core customer support. Some of the companies that showed a definite preference for this strategy provided evidence that they consider changes on the product's marketing strategy during the phase-out period. These companies indicated that in certain cases they raised the price of the product and made some money out of it, knowing that this action would accelerate the rate of sales decline and the ultimate demise of the product. Other companies used this strategy mainly as a means of buying some extra time until the replacement product approached readiness for launching or the customers located adequate substitutes.

■ *Sell out*. The selling of a weak product to another manufacturer is an elimination option often considered by management. A variation of this strategy is to offer the discontinued product to another manufacturer through licensing arrangements. One of the companies studied was able to interest a foreign manufacturer in producing and marketing a weak (eliminated) product through a licensing agreement; in this case, movable equipment, parts, and supplies were also sold to the licensee for a profit.

■ *Drop the product from the standard range and reintroduce it as a special*. This strategy, which is unique in the industrial field, implies that, if some residual demand exists after the product's discontinuation, it can be manufactured and marketed again. Elimination in this case means that the product will no longer be manufactured as a standard, but will, if demanded by a customer, be produced as a 'special', at a premium price. The existence of this kind of elimination strategy, which tends to reduce the gravity of the elimination decision, was indicated by the following kinds of responses. The marketing director of a small manufacturer of heavy machine tools: 'Our elimination decision is not a lasting decision; a customer can still ask for the discontinued product provided that he is willing to pay a premium price to cover the additional costs involved in the production.' The marketing director of a medium-sized manufacturer of boilers: 'If we receive an order for the discontinued product which cannot convert into an order for the new one, then we will manufacture it as a special charging a higher price.'

The foregoing discussion clearly indicates that variation exists as to the way in which managements handle the implementation stage of the product-elimination process. However, one basic factor that was found to influence the selection of a particular elimination strategy is the problem situation that initiated the product's elimination in the first place. The specific product case histories conducted indicated that, if the rationale behind the elimination of a product is either the decline in its market potential or a variety reduction policy developed by the company, then the 'phase-out-immediately' strategy is generally used. If, on the other hand, the rationale behind the elimination of a product is the development of a new one, then the 'phase-out-slowly' strategy is generally preferred. When a product is dropped because of its poor financial, commercial, and/or technical performance, then either of these two alternative elimination strategies may be used, depending on just how unprofitable the product is and/or whether a new product is being developed to replace it.

Of the 156 products studied, 65 (42 per cent) were phased out immediately, 45 (29 per cent) were phased out slowly, 18 (12 per cent) were dropped immediately, 19 (12 per cent) were dropped from the standard range, and 9 (5 per cent) were sold out.

However, the implementation of the elimination decision can be as complex a process as product introduction and requires the same thorough planning and programming. Indeed, the duration of this stage varied in our research from two months to over three years (the median is about one year). Consequently, the complexity of the implementation process, which stems from the need to coordinate and synchronize a large number of management people and activities respectively, and the major importance of timing, point to the need for the establishment of a systematic deletion implementation system to ensure efficiency in product phase out. To provide some guidance in this area, we have developed an empirically based product-elimination implementation model, shown in Fig. 14.4. Certainly, as the current

Figure 14.4 A sequential flow diagram for the Implementation of the product-elimination decision

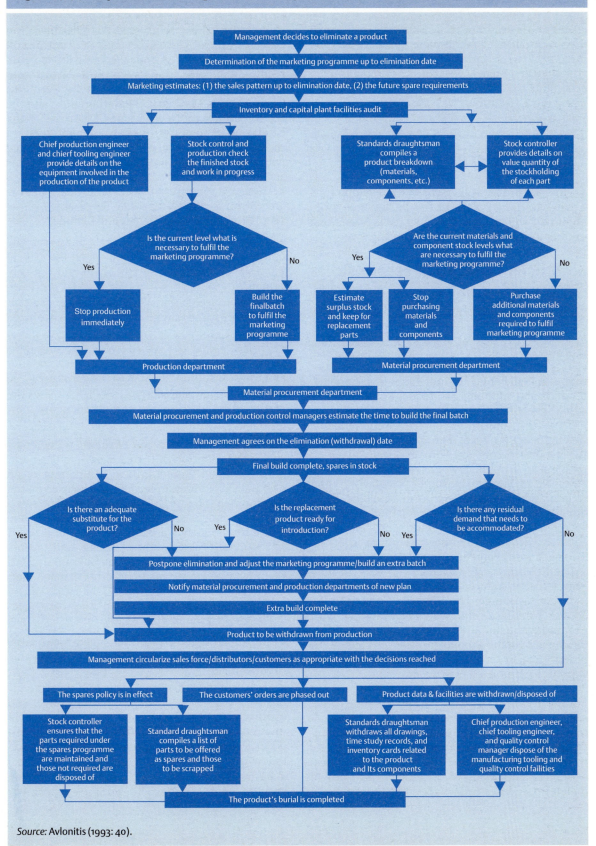

Source: Avlonitis (1993: 40).

economic environment has shifted the decision to drop unprofitable and obsolete products from an important to a critical position in corporate strategy, the actual disposal of such products in an economic and efficient way will, undoubtedly, demand more attention.

6 The future

IN this section we will discuss two developments that have taken place in the business environment that will influence product decision-making in consumer and industrial fields respectively.

6.1 Efficient consumer response

One recent development in the grocery industry is efficient consumer response (ECR), defined as a strategy in which retailers and suppliers are working closely together to bring better value to the grocery consumer. By jointly focusing on the efficiency of the total grocery supply system, rather than the efficiency of individual components, retailers and suppliers are reducing total system costs, inventories, and physical assets, while improving the consumer's choice of high-quality, fresh grocery products. The ultimate goal of ECR is a responsive, consumer-driven system, in which retailers and suppliers work together as business allies to maximize consumer satisfaction and minimize cost. Accurate information and high-quality products flow through a paperless system between manufacturing line and check-out counter, with minimum degradation or interruption both within and between trading partners.

The ECR initiative started in the USA. In mid-1992 grocery industry leaders created a joint-industry task force, the Efficient Consumer Response Working Group, which was charged with examining the supply chain and its trade practices to identify potential opportunities for changes in practices or in technology that would make the supply chain more competitive.

In 1994 ECR Europe was formed to provide European consumers with the best possible value, service, and variety of products through collaborative action to improve the supply chain. Among the companies participating in ECR Europe are, from the industry side, Behlen (Germany), Coca-Cola (France), Mars (UK), Procter & Gamble (Belgium), and Nestlé (Switzerland), and, from the

trade side, Albert Heijn (the Netherlands), Promodes (France), Tesco (UK), and KG Dorthmund (Germany). Several European countries have already established their own ECR boards and formal organizations, including Italy, Germany, Spain, Greece, Denmark, the Netherlands, and the UK. According to 'Newsletter ECR Europe' at the beginning of 1996 twenty-nine companies with a combined turnover of $500 billion were participating in forty ECR projects and operating trials across Europe.

There are four areas in which ECR participants are working closely together. These areas represent the major ECR strategies and include:

■ *Efficient store assortments*, which addresses the optimum use of store and shelf space, the critical interface between the supply chain and the consumer.

■ *Efficient replenishment*, which links the consumer, retail store, and supplier into a synchronized system.

■ *Efficient promotion*, which refocuses suppliers' promotion activities from selling-in to the retailer and towards selling-through to the consumer.

■ *Efficient product introduction*, which addresses the processes of developing and introducing new products.

However, the realization of these strategies requires the adoption of the category management (CM) concept. CM is a critical component of an overall ECR strategy. Indeed, ECR is focused on the development of internal CM capabilities and selective joint efforts between trading partners to enhance the efficiency and effectiveness of product introductions, assortment planning, and promotions. At the heart of CM are fundamental shifts in the way retailers and manufacturers manage their product portfolio with an increased emphasis on category-based thinking.

The general themes of CM are:

■ the implementation of a changed focus away from buying to selling products that provide value to consumers;

■ an acceptance of the need to rely on strategic business units to achieve company objectives and satisfy consumer needs (that is, a move away from micromanaging at the brand or stock keeping unit (SKU) level to managing a category of products that consumers perceive to meet their needs);

■ the reliance on strategic partnership between retailers and suppliers to optimize consumer value while meeting trading partners' company objectives (CM is the framework for linking retail and supplier processes to focus on selling to consumers);

■ the achievement of a change in organizational structure, responsibilities, and reward systems from a traditional departmental to an integrated process structure—for retailers this may mean the merging of buying, merchandising, pricing, promotion, and inventory management departments into one CM function responsible for sales and profits; for suppliers this may also mean new job titles and revised job descriptions as we move from brand management to category management and from the traditional salesperson to advanced salesperson, category sales manager, trusted adviser, and finally strategic alliance partner;

■ recognition that CM is a fact-based discipline relying on information technology and scan data to support product decision-making and business processes.

The implications of CM for product decision-making are far-reaching. When it comes to store assortment optimization, the CM concept focuses on:

■ understanding the role of the category within the retailer or manufacturer's portfolio;

■ ensuring that the assortment reflects the retailer and manufacturer strategy;

■ eliminating poorly performing SKUs;

■ improving the shelf presentation of each category.

While retailers and manufacturers can do much to optimize their assortment alone, true assortment optimization often requires a free flow of information between trading partners.

With respect to product introductions, the CM focuses on

■ the need for manufacturers, retailers, and partnerships to develop an improved understanding of consumer needs and desires to avoid launch failures;

■ ways of eliminating complexity and reducing time/costs associated with new product introduction.

It is true, however, that product introductions optimization is the most difficult ECR strategy to be implemented, because of:

■ difficulty of assessing product success ahead of launching;

■ traditional friction between trading partners;

■ the fear of branded launches being copied into private label;

■ chronic lack of trust.

One retail company that has adopted the CM concept is Albert Heijn in the Netherlands. In 1996 the company integrated CM and logistics into one cohesive commercial organization creating a unit management structure. Seven unit managers were responsible for thirty category managers and fifteen logistics managers. It was a radical reform, which brought together under each unit manager CM elements such as space management, product innovation, and private label development, as well as the information systems and physical replenishment activities of the supply chain.

According to Harry Bruijniks, Vice-President of the company

the major benefits of this approach are a much more flexible and rapid response to local market changes and the ability to assess and determine strategic options for products and categories based on all the costs and methods involved in getting products from suppliers to customers. This resultant clarity of category and product priorities also provides the platform for a more informed and professional partnership with selected suppliers who share those priorities and the belief that a new level of cooperation can be achieved, based on mutual trust and total openness, with direct communication between the relevant disciplines.   (Bruijniks 1996)

It is true that ECR favours the big supermarket players and manufacturers. However, change always has two faces—opportunity and danger. ECR will have such profound changes on supply-chain economics, and therefore on the competitive position of individual participants, that those companies who adopt ECR early will gain a significant competitive advantage over other companies. ECR allies will pass through much of the supply-chain savings to consumers, gaining market share from companies who fail to adopt the ECR strategies.

6.2 The Internet

Despite its short history, the Internet proliferates in the area of industrial organizations of exponential rates. Its wide adoption by the business-to-business companies may be largely attributed to its enhanced communication capabilities. Through the commercial use of the Internet, organizations may enhance their performance and efficiency and explore effectively new marketing opportunities.

It has been argued that, since the Internet can be used commercially as both a distribution channel and an interactive communication tool, it tends to affect organizational effectiveness by enhancing sales and interorganizational relationships.

The Internet's capabilities for achieving industrial sales is beyond any doubt. According to the Forrester Research (1997), $66 billion in business-to-business commerce would be conducted on the Internet by the year 2000, with the number of businesses connected in the Net rising from 4 per cent in 1997 to 33 per cent. Such growth rates indicate that the commercial use of the Internet has already reached the critical mass of business-to-business organizations.

The capabilities of the Internet to enhance the interorganizational relationships and cooperation have also been noted. A number of authors in the literature (Glazer 1991; Sashittal and Wilemon 1994; Hoffman and Novak 1996; Quelch and Klein 1996) argue that this interactive technology:

- helps organizations to enhance their cooperation efforts with their market actors (suppliers, customers, even competitors) in order to customize their products successfully to the ever-changing customer needs and market trends and in a faster and more effective mode, than through traditional marketing;

- drives marketing to a new paradigm, where differentiated products are sold in differentiated markets;

- leads to a radical shift in the role of the firm, from being a provider of goods and services to being a partner in the creation of goods and services;

- leads to increased information exchanges between organizations, thus promoting the faster discovery of customer needs and acceleration in the rates of the development of innovations and the elimination of mature products, thus resulting in faster PLCs;

- allows networking between autonomous firms to be even more important so that it becomes the normal way of conducting new product development;

- creates interdependencies for the participating companies in their value chains—for example, joint high-tech R&D programmes, joint market research.

The impact of the Internet on product management in business-to-business organizations was studied by Avlonitis and Karayianni (1996). In a sample of seventy-eight American and European companies the use of the Internet was found to affect product management activities and to lead to the acceleration of innovations and greater product customization. It appears that companies that utilize the Internet do so in all the activities pertaining to successful commercialization of new products. In addition, they involve their sales departments with the Internet, mainly with the aim of facilitating the crucial tasks of market segmentation and targeting and the discovery of sales leads.

It is obvious, therefore, that, as in the case of the ECR initiative for grocery products, the Internet is a competitive weapon that is going to revolutionize marketing transactions in the industrial field. Consequently, those industrial-goods companies that adopt the Internet early enough as both a communication tool and a distribution channel will gain a distinct advantage over their competitors.

7 Summary

In this chapter an attempt has been made to place the product variable in a historical perspective, to discuss the various types of product decisions, to examine the influence of the product variable in the development of marketing strategy, and finally to shed some light on the product elimination decision, one of the most neglected areas in the literature on product management.

Following Robinson's (1933) and Chamberlin's (1933) development of the theory of monopolistic competition, which introduced the product as an economic variable in the literature of Economics in the early 1930s, marketing writers recognized the crucial importance of the product variable not only as a competitive weapon but also as a basis for the development of comprehensive competitive marketing strategies. Indeed, apart from the classical PLC model, which was used as a framework for the selection of meaningful marketing strategies, product classification schemes have been proposed in the literature to form the foundation for building workable marketing strategies. The most recent classification scheme classifies products as convenience, preference, shopping, and speciality, and suggests pertinent marketing strategies.

However, to remain competitive, the product variable and the company's product offering should continuously incorporate the changes that take place in the business environment.

There is a great variety of possible changes in the company's product offering and consequently a great variety of product decisions. Product decisions can be classified into three broad categories depending on the nature of the changes in the company's product offering:

■ changes in the product types offered, which involve the addition, replacement, and deletion of products and product lines;

■ changes in the tangible, physical product, incorporating change in the product's quality, functional features, or style, which result in new and improved products that either are added to the product line or replace existing products in the line;

■ changes in the intangible/'augmented' product involving important product decisions pertaining to branding, packaging, and product services.

However, one product decision that has received very little attention is product deletion. In this chapter we presented a product-elimination process that incorporated the product revitalization decision. Indeed, these decisions are interrelated, since a decision about product elimination cannot be made in isolation from consideration of other options that could revitalize a weak product and that include changes in product specifications and in the elements of the product's marketing mix.

Failure of these corrective actions to make the product 'healthy' again brings the product under elimination review and a detailed investigation takes place to determine whether elimination is indeed indicated. Nineteen evaluation factors are generally considered by management in manufacturing industry in order to make the product retention/deletion decision. These factors can be subsumed into six categories that represent the critical considerations of the weak product evaluation process: implications for company resources; market reaction; financial implications; new product potential; alternative opportunities considerations; product range policy considerations.

Once a decision to eliminate a product has been reached, its departure should be systematically planned and coordinated. To provide some guidance in this area, we have developed an empirically based product-elimination implementation model and we have discussed the five alternative product elimination strategies faced by management at this stage—namely, drop immediately, phase-out immediately, phase-out slowly (milk), selling-out, and drop the product from the standard range and reintroduce it as a 'special'.

Two recent developments that have taken place in the business environment—namely, the ECR initiative in the grocery industry and the extensive use of the Internet by business-to-business organizations—are going to have a pronounced effect on product decision-making in the consumer and industrial fields respectively.

Further reading

Aaker, David A., *Managing Brand Equity* (New York: Free Press, 1991).

Avlonitis, George J., 'Effective Product Decision-Making in the Industrial Environment', in A. G. Woodside (ed.), *Advances in Business Marketing and Purchasing* (6th edn., Greenwich: T. Jai Press 1994), 83–139.

Doyle, Peter, *Marketing Management and Strategy* (London: Prentice Hall, 1994).

Levitt, Theodore, 'Marketing Intangible Products and Product Intangibles', *Harvard Business Review* (May–June 1981), 94–102.

Swan, John E., and Rink, David R., 'Fitting Market Strategy to Varying Product Life Cycles', *Business Horizons* (Jan.–Feb. 1982), 72–6.

Wind, Yoram J., *Product Policy: Concepts Methods and Strategy* (Reading, Mass.: Addison-Wesley, 1982).

Discussion questions

1 Why was price the main instrument of competition in the nineteenth century while the product is the primary competitive weapon in the twentieth century?

2 What is the relationship between product differentiation and market segmentation?

3 What is your definition of a product decision?

4 Which are the product decisions involving changes in (*a*) the product types offered, (*b*) the tangible/physical product, and (*c*) the intangible 'augmented' product?

5 Why is the 'augmented' product increasingly important when determining a competitive advantage?

6 Which are the brand strategies followed by major grocery manufacturers?

7 In your opinion, which are the major problems faced by those who attempt to estimate brand equity?

8 Identify the characteristics distinguishing convenience, preference, shopping, and speciality products. Give examples of each.

9 Why is the PLC concept important for marketing managers?

10 What are some typical pricing, promotion, and distribution strategies during each stage of the PLC?

11 What guidelines would you suggest for the revitalization of a weak product?

12 What are the major factors that management should consider in determining whether or not to delete a product?

SBM in the cat-litter business

Ms Sonia Ruiz and Mr Kriton Anavlavis under the guidance of Professor George J. Avlonitis

SBM Co. was created in 1934 in a southern Mediterranean country. With sales of $US63 million in 1997, SBM Co. was one of the largest European mining companies producing bauxite, bentonite, and perlite, among other industrial minerals.

As far as the bentonite mineral is concerned, SBM Co. has been present in the market for the last thirty-five years. Bentonite is mined and processed in a Mediterranean island and then shipped in bulk from the company-owned port facilities to different destinations worldwide. In 1996 SBM Co. exported nearly 600,000 million tons of processed bentonite, which makes it the largest exporter of bentonite in the world and the largest producer in the European Union.

SBM Co. bentonite product portfolio is mainly addressed to industrial markets. The company is market leader in the European iron ore pelletizing market and the civil engineering market, and is a minor player in the foundry industry. Nevertheless, SMB Co. bentonite is not a major presence in the consumer markets other than being a bulk material supplier to the cat-litter business.

Cat litter is one of the most important markets for the absorbent clays industry. In 1997 the European cat-litter market was about 1 million tons, consisting mainly of lightweight (70 per cent of the total) and heavyweight clays (30 per cent). Traditionally, cat-litter products have been produced from minerals such as attalpugite and sepiolite, the so-called light weight (LW) materials. However, bentonite—the heavyweight (HW) material—has been gaining ground in recent years, following the trend that appeared in the USA some years ago. In the bentonite cat litter, the refuse forms a convenient clump that is easy to scoop away, contributing to a better odour control and leaving the remaining clean cat litter for further use. Thanks to these significant advantages over the LW materials, bentonite tonnage for the cat-litter business presents a growth of 3–6 per cent per year.

The UK, the Netherlands, the Scandinavian countries, and Germany are the main markets for HW cat litter, with 84 per cent of the total volume. Market characteristics vary from country to country. Each of them presents different product and distribution segmentation as well as different competitor structure with diverging competitor strategies. Consequently, in order to compete successfully at pan-European level, a company should have an extensive distribution network that would allow proximity to the market, a wide product range to cover all possible segments, and aggressive and high-class consumer marketing skills to reach sophisticated and demanding consumers.

SBM Co. first attempted to enter the European cat-litter business in 1990, through a joint venture established in the UK. The main aim of this venture was to match SBM Co. strong core competences in the upstream sector (this is the extraction, primary processing, and shipping of bulk bentonite) with a company that could provide access to the downstream sector (bagging, distribution, and marketing of the final product). The venture would provide SBM Co. with a sales and bagging operation capable of serving the European cat-litter market. However, the venture soon ran into problems. Most major cat-litter customers were 'tied' to established UK and European suppliers, limiting the venture's sales opportunity. Moreover, downstream cost disadvantages and no product differentiation or branding further restricted market penetration. In continental Europe, the venture had even fewer opportunities for bagged sales, owing to complex and cost-inefficient logistics as well as market dominance from a few vertically integrated companies, baggers, and wholesalers. In 1992 the venture was terminated; since then efforts for bagged product sales have been conducted only in the local market. Sales of bulk product to the European market via an intermediary accounted for 10 per cent of the European HW cat litter in 1997.

Aware of the HW litter market potential, SBM Co. Managing Director has called the marketing team into his office for the elaboration of a new strategy at pan-European level.

The marketing team has to return with a proposal as soon as possible.

Discussion questions

1 Analyse the reasons why the UK venture failed to penetrate the European cat-litter market.

2 Propose a strategy for the European cat-litter market.

Case 3
Chinese Business Service Centre

Pannapachr Itthiopassagul

1 Introduction

At the end of the 1990s China was one of Thailand's most important trading partners, and the expectation is that this trading relationship will continue to grow. Indeed, the CP Group (a Bangkok-based company) is one of the largest foreign investors in mainland China. As Table 1 shows, there was a rapid increase in trade between the two countries during the 1990s, though Thailand exports substantially less to China than it imports. A trade agreement between Thailand and China and a Committee on Economic Cooperation was set up in 1996 between Thailand and China, with the Thai Deputy Prime Minister leading the Thai delegation and the Chinese Minister of Economic Cooperation and Trade leading the Chinese delegation.

Several Thai banks have taken advantage of the Chinese Government's rules that allow foreign banks to operate in its country in the form of representative offices, branch offices, or joint ventures with Chinese companies. These are T.M. International Bank (jointly owned by M. Thai Group, CP Group, and Thai Farmers Bank), the Bangkok Bank, the Krung Thai Bank, and the Thai Farmers Bank. In addition,

Table 1 **Thai trade with China (Baht m.)**		
Year	Exports	Imports
1991	8,554	29,327
1992	9,800	30,979
1993	13,636	27,609
1994	23,366	34,895
1995	40,867	52,187
1996	47,369	49,499
1997	55,495	69,467
1998 (Jan.–July)	43,325	44,382

the number of Thai organizations active in China increased from 133 in 1990 to 1,401 in 1993, and there is every indication that this number has continued to rise. This is both because Thai businessmen are constantly seeking out new markets and because the Chinese Government is trying to demonstrate that it has an open-door policy with regard to trade so that it can gain membership of the World Trade Organization (WTO).

2 Background to the proposal

This growth in trade with China has led to indications of interest within Thailand for courses in both the Chinese language and Chinese business practices. This was noted by a group of five young business people, who were studying together on an evening course at Thammasat University. They recognized that this growth in trade created a business opportunity. To establish an organization to run courses in Chinese and Chinese business for middle and senior managers from Thai industry and commerce.

They conducted a survey to identify whether or not there was a demand for such a service, and, if so, what it would be expected to provide. They used structured interviews to collect information from the staff of firms in each of the following three groups: banks; large companies; and small and medium-sized companies. (Box 1 gives details of the status of the personnel interviewed.) Half the firms in the sample had not yet traded with China and it was found useful to divide those that were trading with China into two groups: those with limited experience (taken arbitrarily to be less than five years' experience); and those with more than five years' experience. A considerable amount of information was gathered from this market survey and the following is a summary of the main results.

2.1 Language problems

The firms that had not yet traded with China expected language to be a problem and were unsure how they would overcome it. Those firms with less than five years' experience in China seemed to feel that this was a big problem but had done little about it. The companies with more than five years' experience stated that their lack of Chinese language skills was a problem. However, they had overcome it to a limited extent by employing Chinese nationals. It was recognized by all respondents that there was a shortage of Chinese nationals who could speak Thai. Also it was realized that, even if a Thai manager's Chinese was inadequate for use in business dialogues, it was a great advantage if he could speak sufficient Chinese to engage in some social conversation.

Box 1 **Respondents in market survey**

Large companies

Company A	Vice President of Business Development
	Vice President of China Department
Company B	Technical Manager
Company C	Training Manager
Company D	Foreign Affairs Manager
Company E	Training Manager
Company F	International Trade Manager
Company G	Managing Director
Company H	Vice President
Company I	Managing Director
	Export Manager

Small and medium-sized companies

Company J	Managing Director (Furniture)
Company K	Export Manager (Electronics)
Company L	Export Manager (Steel)
Company M	Export Manager (Chemicals)
Company N	General Manager (Chemicals)
Company O	General Manager (Shipping)
Company P	Managing Director (Shipping)

Banks

Bank A	Head of Educational and Scholarship Department
Bank B	Foreign Affairs Manager
	Head of Regional Investment Research Department
Bank C	Training Manager
	Head of China Business Affairs Department
Bank D	Human Resources Manager

2.2 Culture

Understanding Chinese culture (which included matters such as traditional approaches to negotiation, gift-giving, frankness in discussions, matters relating to 'face' and gaunxi, and so on, all of which differ from those of Thai culture in often subtle but significant ways) had created problems for those companies that had done business in China. The banks seemed least worried about the issue of culture, but did not ignore its importance. However, they maintained that their negotiations did not involve them in as much direct personal contact with Chinese clients as was found necessary by the other groups in the sample. It was noted that the problem of being responsive to Chinese culture was acccentuated by the fact that there are differences in the cultures in different regions of China.

Companies that had not traded with China were aware that there were cultural differences between Thailand and China. They were, however, less worried about them as those companies that had experience of trading in China.

2.3 Chinese law

Although some of the banks had identified people in Thailand who could give them advice on Chinese law, it was recognized that there were very few such people available. As a consequence, it had been necessary to rely heavily on Chinese personnel and/or on Thai employees who had undertaken some training in China. Those firms that were active in China mostly sought to overcome the problems of understanding and working within a very different legal system by employing Chinese staff either full-time or on a consultancy basis.

2.4 Trade and market information

The group of companies that was already doing business in China claimed to have overcome the problem of lack of trade and market information. However, it was clear from the solutions used (mostly making many business trips and employing extra Chinese staff) that it continued to create problems for them. Those considering doing business were already well aware that the lack of information would create problems.

3 The potential market and the competition

When asked about their reaction to the creation of an organization that would provide Chinese language training, training in and information about Chinese business practice, and possibly study tours of China, the respondents indicated considerable interest—subject to a number of conditions. These conditions included ensuring that the lecturers and instructors were of the highest quality and that the training was offered in appropriate locations. With regard to the latter point, it was felt that, in the case of senior executives, given the pressures on their time and the need for frequent regular sessions, it would be essential to offer individual language tuition at a time and place of their choosing.

Having identified these problems, the group decided to investigate whether any courses designed to help firms overcome these difficulties existed in Thailand. Their investigations soon indicated that there were a number of bodies offering training in the Chinese language. As well as a large number of private individuals and a number of small private firms, some of the major universities offered courses for both undergraduates and postgraduates but also 'occasional' students. The Taiwan Association offered some courses, but the major player in the market was the Oriental Culture Academy, which is financially supported by the Thai–Chinese Educational Association. The courses offered ranged from those for people with an elementary level of competence in spoken Chinese to those for speakers of an intermediate level. None of the courses appeared to be designed with the needs of businessmen in mind, either in the type of vocabulary they introduced or where and when the course was run.

There were also a number of organizations running management courses (though few of these specifically considered the issue of the Chinese market). These included some private organizations, but they were mostly trade associations such as the Thai Management Association, the Marketing Association of Thailand, the Personnel Management Association of Thailand, and so on.

There was no organization that offered both Chinese language training and training in Chinese business behaviour. The one that got closest to this was the Chinese Studies Centre, based in one of Bangkok's universities, whose courses covered many areas of business such as economics, social sciences, language, art, culture, and an information service. However, this centre was not run in a flexible manner, would not adopt its programme to meet other people's requirements, and lacked the type of service-oriented environment that would appeal to businessmen. (See Box 2 for some information, which was collected through observation, informal contacts, and comments made during the survey, about the courses offered and market share.)

There therefore did not appear to be any organization that would:

- offer tuition in the Chinese language with an orientation towards business requirements; and
- run courses on various aspects of Chinese business practice.

In addition, none of the organizations took account of businesses' special requirements with regard to such matters as the location and the timing of the training or the quality of the staff.

4 The marketing proposal

The group needed finance if they were to enter this market and they therefore prepared a proposal with regard to their marketing of the Chinese Business Service Centre, which was the name they had decided to give to the organization that they wished to create. (The proposal also included a detailed financial analysis that is not attached here.)

4.1 The target market

The centre would provide courses for the senior executives of Thai companies that were either already doing business with or in China or expected to do so. It would also provide courses for those at the managerial or supervisory level in such organizations.

4.2 The product

The centre would offer four services:

- seminars;
- language programmes;
- a business information service about China;
- translators and advisors to accompany business visits to China (if requested the Centre will plan all details of such visits).

The Centre would be positioned as offering a high-quality service that was sensitive to the needs and expectations of senior businessmen, with regard especially to such matters as the flexibility and quality of the services offered.

The seminar programme would include the following courses:

- trade negotiation between Thailand and China;
- Chinese market and consumer analysis;
- negotiation techniques;
- investment analysis;

Box 2 **Language courses offered by potential competitors**

Organization	Target market	Image	Market share[a] (%)
Oriental Culture Academy	Working people University students Children	Reasonable price Practical teaching	60
Major universities	Working people University students	Price leader	30
Taiwan Association	International students	Teaching quality very high	6

[a] Qualitative estimate made using secondary data.

- cultural management;
- import–export procedures;
- Chinese law.

The market survey had indicated that each of the three categories of companies that had been interviewed had expressed differing views as to the importance of each of these topics. This information would be utilized when planning the advertising of each programme.

'Trade Negotiation between Thailand and China' would be designed to be the centre's most prestigious programme. It would be the first programme the centre would run, and would be marketed only to senior executives. The centre would seek out prominent keynote speakers from business, commerce, government, and the civil service.

Initially all these seminars would be run in five-star hotels in the centre of Bangkok. The intent was to identify a hotel with excellent conference facilities and sufficient parking, located in the centre of the city, and to develop a relationship with that hotel. However, once the centre had established itself, the plan was to rent space where conferences could be run—a factor that would need to be taken into account when choosing the location of the centre's offices.

The Chinese language courses would be offered in the centre's own premises (which would include a language laboratory). A number of courses at various levels from basic Chinese through to advanced Chinese would be offered on a regular basis and be open to the general public as well as to business people. However, should a firm have a group of employees who required training in Chinese, then either such a course could be run on the firm's own premises, or the group could come to the centre and the course would be run there at a time convenient to them. In addition, the centre would offer individual tuition in Chinese in the offices of interested executives—such sessions being arranged to suite the executives' own timetable.

The business information service about China would bring together, collate, and interpret information available from a variety of sources such as government offices, the major universities in Beijing and Bangkok, the Thai–Chinese Chamber of Commerce, the Thai Management Association, and so on.

Business visits to China would be arranged to help Thai businessmen gain an understanding of China and the issues involved in doing business there. Such visits could be of any of the following types:

- those where the centre provided translators and advisers to accompany a visit planned and organized by a firm or group of firms;

- those where the centre planned and organized a visit at the request of a firm or group of firms and provided translators and advisers to accompany the visit;

- those where the centre planned and organized a visit that it then advertised to the Thai business community.

4.3 Price

The market survey had indicated that the demand for the proposed training courses (other than in Chinese) was not very price sensitive for two reasons. First, firms were aware that they needed such courses. Secondly, there was currently nobody providing such courses. The survey had indicated that the banks regarded price as unimportant relative to other factors such as the quality of the lecturers.

It appeared that the prices of language courses currently available ranged from Baht 40 per hour to Baht 70 per hour per student. In 1997 the average annual wage of monthly paid employees in Bangkok was Baht 111,500. In view of the existing large number of suppliers of Chinese language courses, it would be difficult to achieve a high price in this part of the centre's activities. However, the market research supported the view that, if the centre offered a professional service and was willing to provide tuition at the times that business people find convenient, then it would be possible to charge prices of between Baht 100 per hour and Baht 200 per hour per student—the price of Baht 200 being for individual tuition at a location and time chosen by the student.

The prices of seminars would vary a great deal according to topic and length. A general management training seminar would cost between Baht 1,000 and Baht 3,500 per day per participant. However, the top-level high-profile courses with prominent outside speakers would be Baht 10,000 a day. Some information on the costs of existing language and business courses is provided in Table 2.

The price of business trips would be dependent on the length, destination, and purpose of the trip.

Table 2 Price ranges (per hour) of existing training courses offered by potential competitors (Baht)

Basic computer training	80–100
Technology and advanced computer training	200–300
Management training	200–300
General training	60–100
Language training	100–200

Consideration would be given to the idea of creating a category of Corporate Member of the Centre. Corporate Members would pay an annual fee in return for which they would receive certain services such as priority booking for popular seminars, quarterly newsletters, and so on. These would either be services available to anybody but 'free' only to Corporate Members, or only available to Corporate Members but for which a charge might be made.

4.4 Location

The survey had indicated that, while overall half the respondents would be willing to attend courses in the centre's own premises, about 40 per cent would wish the courses to be held in their own offices. Of this 40 per cent, a significant number were the more senior executives. As some of the language tuition would be offered in the centre's own premises, it was essential that these were to be in the centre of the city, with access to good parking. The main reason for this is that Bangkok's traffic problems are notorious and even a short journey can unexpectedly take a great deal of time and people would therefore be loath to travel long distances to the centre. Another reason why it must be centrally located is that the Centre's staff would need to be able to reach the hotel in which any seminars were to be run without excessive journey times. The concern with travel times arises from the fact that within Bangkok a journey covering even a short distance can take a long time to complete, and, more importantly, how long it will take is quite unpredictable. For courses being run in a firm's premises, a central location would also be advantageous.

4.5 Promotion

The promotion plans had four elements: public relations, direct sales, advertising in newspapers, and direct mail. The public-relations activity would be especially important when the centre commenced activity and the expectation was that a good PR campaign would obtain substantial TV and newspaper coverage. As has been indicated, the intent was that the first seminar would be 'Trade Negotiation between Thailand and China', and, on the first occasion that this was run, invitations to attend would be sent to all those who had been interviewed in the market survey. A dinner to celebrate the launch of the centre would follow the seminar.

The direct-sales approach would involve personal approaches to the training managers of all firms known to be interested in the Chinese market. A special price reduction would be offered on the first booking that any firm made for a course run by the centre.

Advertisements would be placed in the *Nation* and the *Bangkok Post* (both English-language newspapers) and Thai-language newspapers. These would be both advertisements for the centre as a whole and, when appropriate, for specific activities such as special seminars.

Direct mail would be used at the launch and then at regular times throughout the year. These communications would be sent to all senior Thai managers and executives of firms believed to be interested in trade with China.

5 Respondents' decision criteria

The three industry groups used very similar criteria to evaluate the management training currently on offer by the centre's potential competitors. However, there were some differences between the groups in the emphasis that they placed on these criteria (see Table 3).

6 A weakness in the proposal?

One of the five managers who had originated the idea was explaining the proposal to a friend who had substantial marketing experience. The friend expressed concern that any attempt to position the centre as 'offering a high-quality service that is sensitive to the needs and expectations of senior businessmen' might be compromised by the suggestion that the centre would also offer courses for junior employees and courses open to the public. He suggested that, as the centre would inevitably initially be a small organization, their plan contained contradictions in terms of such matters as the quality of staff employed, the types of advertisements used, the appropriate facilities and materials, and so on.

Table 3 Criteria for evaluating courses

Criteria	Banks	Large companies	Small and medium-sized companies
Reputation of the institution	3.6	3.7	3.5
Course topics	4.8	4.4	5.0
Appropriate time	3.2	3.2	3.6
Reputation of lecturers	3.6	4.1	4.1
Location	2.8	3.3	3.5
Facilities	2.4	2.9	3.5
Price	2.2	3.2	3.4

Part Four
Formulating and Implementing Marketing Strategy

Chapter 15
Offerings and Markets: The Main Elements of Strategic Marketing Decisions

Shiv Mathur

Objectives

The objectives of this chapter are:

1 to clarify the purpose and objective of a business;

2 to define the role of strategic marketing in meeting that objective;

3 to show that strategic marketing decisions are fundamentally about offerings and markets;

4 to explain precisely what competes for the choices of customers—i.e. the idea of the offering;

5 to identify where competition takes place—i.e. the idea of the market;

6 to describe how offerings compete—i.e. competitive positioning and its two dimensions: differentiation and price;

7 to illustrate the 'scissors' technique of matching attractive positions with competition-beating resources, for selecting each of tomorrow's offerings, and thus each *competitive strategy*;

8 to emphasize the importance of *corporate strategy*—selecting a value-building cluster of offerings—and the critical role of divestments in cluster decisions.

1 Introduction

THIS chapter examines two of the most fundamental ideas of marketing. First, it examines *what* it is that competes to be chosen by customers. This is the 'product' or 'service', which here we call the *offering*. Secondly, it examines *where* competition takes place: this is the *market*.

Offerings and markets are central to the theory and practice of marketing. Market research, for instance, collects and analyses information to decide what offerings to sell in the future, and in which markets. What selling persuades customers to purchase is again offerings. The central purpose of distribution is to make offerings accessible to customers. Advertising and promotion shape the attractiveness of offerings in their markets. Pricing decides what to charge for offerings in changing markets. There is no aspect of marketing that does not use these two ideas.

All these marketing activities are carried out every day, often without very great clarity about just what precisely is meant by an offering or a market. There is, however, an area of marketing where clarity about these ideas is absolutely essential. This is the task of deciding what the company should sell tomorrow and where—what we call *strategic marketing*. This strategic stage is usually the decisive one. Once an unsuitable offering is on the market, it will make losses. If so, it is usually too late to take more than cost-cutting or other fire-fighting actions, which may improve results only marginally and for a short time. The crucial choices are made at the design and planning stage.

Strategic marketing, like microeconomics, analyses the competitive process. Many of the analytical tools and concepts are, therefore, common to both disciplines. On the other hand, economics tends to take the offerings as given, and to ask (*a*) how prices are determined under various conditions, and (*b*) what the effects of those conditions are on public welfare. It does not primarily

Discussions with Axel Johne and Paul Raimond have been most helpful in writing this chapter. Tarun Mathur has helped with the *Get WithIt* illustration. I am indebted to Alfred Kenyon for many ideas and his detailed comments. I have drawn on my earlier writing, much of it with Alfred Kenyon, in preparing this chapter. In particular I have greatly relied on the paperback edition of our book *Creating Value: Shaping Tomorrow's Business* (Butterworth-Heinemann, 1998).

examine the competitive process from the point of view of the business, whose biggest decision is what to offer. The difference lies in the fact that strategic marketing treats the offering as something to be designed and planned, not as something given.

This chapter begins by outlining the objective of business and the key role of strategic marketing—the choice of tomorrow's offerings and markets—in meeting that objective. It then clarifies the nature of offerings and markets. It finally shows how clarity about these two ideas can help a particular company frame its key strategic decisions and thereby move towards its objective.

2 The financial objective of business and strategic marketing

THE purpose of a business is to create long-term financial value: to earn more than its cost of capital. It is that purpose of creating financial value that distinguishes businesses from charities and not-for-profit organizations. In a free market economy a business goes to the wall, or is taken over, if it fails to earn its cost of capital. To be successful, a business has to be financially successful, or what we shall sometimes refer to as 'profitable'.

There are those who disagree with this financial objective (e.g. Kay 1996). They claim that the objective is to serve not just the investors and lenders, but also other stakeholders such as employees, customers, suppliers, the wider community, and the environment. Over a wide field of business decisions, there is no conflict between these two views. A business that leaves these groups dissatisfied will court disaffection, incur extra costs, and forgo financial value. However, beyond that point, any business must put its own survival first. Once it fails to exist as an independent entity, its managers cannot any longer look after its employees or any other stakeholder.

2.1 The source of financial success

Where, on what battleground, must a business beat the cost of capital? It normally does that in competitive markets. Success in financial markets

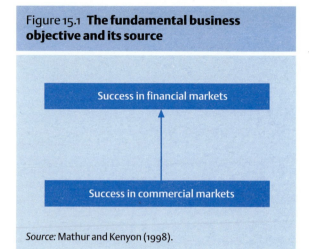

Figure 15.1 **The fundamental business objective and its source**

Success in financial markets

↑

Success in commercial markets

Source: Mathur and Kenyon (1998).

is the reward for success in commercial markets: the winning of profitable customers. For these customers, the business provides better value than competing substitutes. Better value of what? Of the products or services, here called *offerings*, that the business offers to customers. Business success, therefore, involves two different types of markets: commercial and financial. Fig. 15.1 shows the relationship between the two.

2.2 Strategic marketing: competitive and corporate strategy

Strategic marketing must, therefore, look at a business as a collection of offerings. It is this imperative that puts an understanding of markets and offerings at the heart of both the theory and the practice of business strategy—the task of shaping tomorrow's business.

Business strategy seems to seek the answer to two different basic questions:

- What are the top management skills and qualities that make companies successful?
- What should the company sell tomorrow?

The second of these is the focus of what is here called strategic marketing. It consists of competitive and corporate strategy. *Competitive strategy*, as here defined, determines tomorrow's position of an individual offering in the eyes of its customers and relative to its competitors, so as to generate fi-

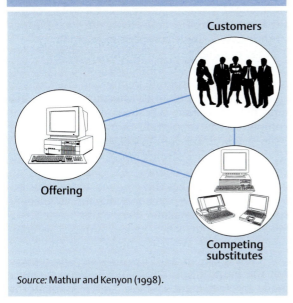

Figure 15.2 **Competitive positioning: the triangular relationship**

Customers

Offering

Competing substitutes

Source: Mathur and Kenyon (1998).

nancial value. *Corporate strategy* manages tomorrow's cluster of offerings for greater financial value: in other words, it decides which offerings to add, retain, or divest.

2.3 The nature of competitive strategy

We must now state the essential task of competitive strategy. How an offering competes depends on how its customers see it positioned relative to its substitutes. It is this triangular relationship (see Fig. 15.2) that constitutes the *competitive position* of an offering in its market. An offering must be so positioned relative to its competitors as to be attractive to customers. Ohmae (1983a: 91) highlighted this triangular relationship, but without stressing the offering. Since competitive strategy decides how an offering is to compete tomorrow, it positions a single offering in a triangular relationship with tomorrow's customers and tomorrow's competitors. A competitive strategy is required for each of tomorrow's offerings.

That brings us to a critical issue that is sometimes overlooked by those who focus exclusively on customer choices. Though a competitive position and strategy are defined solely in terms of how an offering is positioned, its selection by a company requires a careful review of its own distinctive resources. As we shall see in Section 5, attractive positioning is necessary, but not enough to justify a strategy to launch a particular offering. The investment in an offering must be profitable enough to recover its cost of capital. The offering must, therefore, be protected from competitive attempts at encroachment, so that it remains a money-maker long enough to attain that goal. To achieve that, the company must have a resource advantage over its potential rivals. The aim of strategic marketing must be to have profitable offerings, not merely attractive ones.

2.4 Offerings and markets: the two central elements

So what exactly is meant by the terms 'offering' and 'market'?

There is wide agreement in marketing that a product (offering) is any good, service, or idea (Dibb *et al.* 1997: 11) that is offered to customers 'for attention, acquisition, use or consumption and that might satisfy a want or need' (Kotler *et al.* 1996: 545). However, we need to go beyond merely describing what is sold if we are to assist practising and aspiring managers to make strategic decisions. The manager needs to know more than what kind of things are offerings: he or she has to identify each separate offering in order to answer the question 'What are, and what should be, *my* offerings?' The next section, therefore, looks more closely at offerings.

The term 'market', on the other hand, 'has several senses' (O'Shaughnessy 1995: 190). Many marketers (e.g. Dibb *et al.* 1997: 200) use the term to mean 'the set of all actual and potential buyers of a product or service' (Kotler *et al.* 1996: 232). Definitions like these describe a market quite adequately, but shed little light on the practical difficulty of defining its boundaries. This is because they draw attention to buyers and away from sellers. After all, a market is where buyers and sellers come together and arrive at prices. We shall, therefore, in Section 4, join others (e.g. Day *et al.* 1979) and the economists in defining markets in terms of both buyers and sellers—i.e. customers and competing substitutes. Such an approach helps us in answering the manager's question 'Which are, and which should be, *my* markets?'

Once we have sharpened these two ideas, we will illustrate how a particular company could use them to make its strategic marketing decisions.

3 What competes for customer choices?

3.1 Offerings, not companies

The first issue that strategic marketing must address is 'What is it that competes to be chosen by customers?'

Marketing has always helpfully concentrated on competition in customer markets—that is, on competition to be chosen by customers. It does not focus on competition in resource markets. That kind of competition occurs when Marks & Spencer is after the same high-flying graduates as the Bank of England, or when Barclays Bank and McDonald's are rivals for the same prime site in a high street. We shall see in Section 5 that such winning resources play an important role in the framing of a competitive strategy, but competition for resources is not what marketing people mean by 'competition'.

Marketing's intense focus on customers has one clear advantage. It highlights the pitfalls of seeing competition as if it took place at the level of companies, multi-offering 'firms', strategic business units (SBUS), divisions, or profit centres. PepsiCo and Coca-Cola are usually termed competitors. That is certainly valid usage if one thinks of the companies' cola offerings; customers choose between them. However, PepsiCo also sells fast food, for which Cola-Cola offers no significant substitutes; there they are not in competition. Customers choose between offerings, not between companies: the offering alone is the unit of choice (see Insert). It makes no sense to speak of PepsiCo, the company, as competing or as having a competitive strategy: the collectivity of its offerings cannot have a single competitive position.

Many of a company's offerings, perhaps even all of them, may benefit from a corporate reputation or brand. This corporate reputation may add to the attractiveness of all its offerings, but this still does not imply that it is the company itself that competes. The reputation of Yves Saint Laurent plays a significant role in helping its wide diversity of offerings—from men's belts to ladies cosmetics and perfumes—to compete. Yet in commercial markets the competition is still between offerings. A man looking for an elegant suit would not consider Yves Saint Laurent together with the other makes unless the company sells suits. What customers may choose or not choose is an offering bearing the brand, not the brand itself. The choice is between suits made by Yves Saint Laurent and suits made by other companies; not between Yves Saint Laurent itself or even its parent Sonafi and other brands or companies.

☞ 'There are broadly two approaches to corporate branding. The first is what is referred to as the monolithic approach, in which the corporate name is used across a range of several different product sectors or market segments . . . The alternative to a monolithic approach is the endorsement approach, which allows a more market related approach to branding' . . . (Chapter 20, p. 493)

The point that it is not the company that competes for customer choice can be illustrated by extending the Yves Saint Laurent example. Several of the company's offerings are in mutual competition. For example, its Paris and Opium perfumes compete against each other for the preferences of customers. Nor is this example in any way exceptional. Diageo sells several competing brands of Scotch whisky such as Bell's, Dimple, Johnnie Walker, Haig, White Horse, and Vat 69. Many models of Electrolux refrigerators compete with Zanussi models—owned by the same company. Unilever sells competing brands of detergents, such as Persil and Surf, which may share production resources and are probably even part of the same division. Often the hottest competition is be-

---

Disc players compete with cameras

'The role of other consumer products was important because some of them competed for the same segment of the consumer's disposable income. For example, consumer research had shown that many consumers were trying to choose between buying a compact disc player or a compact camera. Therefore "Olympus" viewed compact disc players as competitive products.'

Source: R. Cooper (1995).

tween sister offerings of the same company. Of course, as we shall see in Section 5, companies would be ill-advised to include such rival offerings in their cluster unless that inclusion generated extra value. However, all this serves only to reinforce the point being made here: it is offerings that compete to be chosen, not companies or divisions or profit centres.

Therefore any model of competition or competitive strategy that takes the multi-offering company—the 'firm'—or any of its organizational subunits as the unit of analysis is unlikely to portray the reality of customer choice.

3.2 Identifying the single offering

If the offering is the unit of competition, then it becomes vital to be clear about what exactly constitutes an individual offering. It may seem obvious that the Paris and Opium perfumes are separate offerings, but is a 30 ml. bottle of Opium perfume a separate offering from a 100 ml. bottle? How do we resolve such borderline cases between offerings sold by the same company?

By a *single offering* we mean an offering that has a *single competitive position* in relation to its specific set of competitors and customers. The test of whether two items are one offering or two is a simple one: is price determined in a common and inseparable process? If yes, then they are one offering.

It is instructive to apply this test to the two bottles of Opium perfume. If the label itself is the decisive determinant of customer choice, then the two bottles are such close competitors that their unit prices are determined in a single process and in relation to an identical list of customers and competitors. If, on the other hand, size is what matters to choosing customers, then they will compare the 30 ml. bottle with many other competing brands of similar size, or maybe even with non-perfumes before they consider the 100 ml. bottle. The two different-sized bottles would in that case have distinct competitive positions, separate price-determining processes, and would thus be separate offerings.

Sometimes what may look like a collection of many offerings may actually be a single offering. For example, a supermarket may sell a variety of goods besides food: it may sell cosmetics and flowers and tobacco. However, if the predominant group of customers see it as a one-stop shopping facility and regard rival supermarkets rather than

independent florists and tobacconists as its immediate competitors, then the whole range of goods may be so complementary as to constitute a single offering. In that case the price—in this instance the mark-up margins—that the supermarket can charge will be far more influenced by the pricing of other supermarkets than by the prices of specialist shops. The rival supermarkets are much more central to the price-determining process.

In real life there is rarely much difficulty in identifying the distinct offerings of a company. Borderline cases, such as those just illustrated, are, however, of two kinds:

- where customers see two offerings as either fairly close or very close substitutes;
- where customers see them as so complementary as to make it uncertain whether they are separate or not.

This definition of a single offering in terms of a single competitive position clarifies a number of cases that are not on the borderline at all, but that can still be confusing. It clarifies them because the *competitive position* is what identifies an offering: physical similarities, sharing properties such as the same production line or the same workforce, or any other intrinsic commonalties do not achieve this at all.

It is easy to illustrate this. A Ford Fiesta model intended for sale in India may be completely identical with one intended for the UK, but that is not enough to classify the two as a single offering. Car buyers in India would face different competing substitutes—many of them unknown outside India—and would therefore have different maps of preferences. The two sets of cars may be physically identical, but they would have distinct competitive positions. They would be separate offerings and would require different competitive strategies. It is not even necessary for two such distinct offerings to have different competitors. A French Fiesta may face exactly the same list of rivals as its UK counterpart, but it may be seen in a different competitive position by French customers with a flag preference for French manufactured goods; that difference in their configurations would be enough to separate the offerings and require different competitive strategies. In the case of malt whiskies, the preference map may well be different in Scotland and England, let alone Singapore and Malta.

It may now be clearer why the word 'offering' is preferred to 'product' to describe what it is that competes for customers. The Ford Fiesta may be thought of as one 'product', but it is in fact several *offerings* in different parts of the world, each with a different competitive position.

3.3 Outputs compete, not inputs

When customers choose between offerings, what counts are those attributes of each offering that the choosing customer considers. Therefore, for a full understanding of positioning we need to make a vital distinction between the *outputs* and *inputs* of an offering.

Those components and characteristics of an offering that—consciously or subconsciously—influence customers' choices are its *outputs*. Customers' buying decisions rest entirely on them. By contrast, all those components and characteristics that do not enter the customer's selection process are its *inputs*. In so far as efforts or resources characterize or shape an offering without, however, themselves affecting the choices of customers, they are inputs.

If customers take picture quality into account when choosing television sets, then picture quality is an output. On the other hand, the R&D, the precision plant, the highly skilled workforce, and the quality-assurance programme that produce a better picture are in our illustration invisible to customers and are therefore inputs. If customers take the country of origin of an item into account, then the location of the plant, which would in other circumstances be merely an input, also becomes an output. Charles Revlon implicitly had this input/output distinction in mind when he said, 'In the factory, we make cosmetics. In the store we sell hope' (Levitt 1983*b*: 128).

It is therefore outputs, not inputs, that position an offering in customers' eyes. Market positions are determined solely by the outputs of competing substitutes. If all perfumes offer hope, then the question is: how does Perfume X's hope differ from its competitors' hope? Does it offer more hope? Or is it a different hope: more romantic, or more career-promoting, or more 'independent', or more environmentally conscious? Or is it the same hope at a lower price?

None of this in any way negates the vital role of inputs. Inputs play a critical part in shaping outputs. Our TV receivers will not have a better picture quality until we have the necessary expertise in production and quality control. We shall not have the right country of origin if we do not set up our factory there. If our airline is to be known for offering an outstanding in-flight service, we may have to spend substantial sums on equipment and staff training. If the new model of our car is to have special safety features, then the assembly and the production process must be redesigned to achieve that. If our perfume is to signify independence, we must mount an appropriate advertising campaign. There is never any point in selecting a competitive position that we lack the means—the inputs—to attain.

3.4 Differentiation and price as the dimensions of competitive positioning

We are now ready to examine more closely the important idea of *competitive positioning*, which defines an offering. From the customers' perspective there are two attractive ways in which an offering can be positioned relative to its competitors. It can either have distinctive non-price outputs that customers find preferable, or it can be cheaper, or even both. Therefore the two dimensions of positioning are differentiation and price.

Differentiation Differentiation is here defined as the difference (price apart) that draws choosing customers to a particular offering and away from its rivals. The purpose of differentiation is to reduce customers' interest in price comparisons. The measure of differentiation, however, must always be the perceptions of customers, not the intrinsic properties of the offering. In other words, differentiation implies distinctive and valuable non-price outputs. 'Differentiation' describes both the act of differentiating and its result.

Differentiation can be along a single attribute, as when one hotel has better rooms than others. It can also take a multi-attribute form if one hotel has more attractive rooms while the other has a superior location. It is too simple to see differentiation as merely 'better' in some overall sense—as if there was a single scale of 'quality'. Nor is quality necessarily a matter of 'more' or 'better' inputs. For example, a restaurant with an abundance of waiters may deprive customers of some privacy, whereas inelegant furniture and menus scrawled on cheap paper may impart 'atmosphere'. Often less is more.

Price The other dimension along which an offering can be positioned is price. Price is what determines customers' choices to the extent that they do not see offerings as differentiated.

Just as differentiation is a matter of subjective customer perceptions, so price can occasionally be a subjective impression rather than an objective fact. For example, customers may believe that a nationwide plumbing business, with liveried vans that can be instantly summoned, would charge a lot more than the local handyman who responds at his leisure. Yet the nationwide business may be the cheaper of the two.

3.5 Differentiation is more fundamental than price

To the practitioner of strategic marketing, differentiation is more fundamental than price for two reasons. First, price can usually be changed at very short notice: price normally plays a merely tactical role. Differentiation, on the other hand, concerns output features, which usually take time to change—sometimes a lot of time. Differentiation, therefore, needs to be planned ahead, and is invariably strategic.

The second reason is that, though a higher price can in some special cases be used to differentiate an offering, the relationship normally works the other way round. The seller can charge a price premium for the differentiating features. In any case, as differentiation governs the price sensitivity of an offering, it is both a precondition and a source of whatever freedom the seller has in setting prices. The less differentiated the offering is, the less latitude the seller has to set prices.

☞ '... the presence and nature of *competitive advantages* influence the extent to which a company can maintain prices below or above competitive levels ...' (Chapter 10, p. 222)

Differentiation is therefore the dominant dimension of positioning. In many situations differentiation policy is so much more important than price policy that differentiation and positioning can be regarded as virtually interchangeable terms—a practice we adopt, whenever appropriate, in this chapter.

4 Where does competition take place? The anatomy of markets

As stated in the Introduction, this chapter focuses on two fundamental concepts of strategic marketing. The first, the *single offering*, is the answer to the question '*what* competes for the choice of customers?' This has been discussed above. We now turn to the arena of competition—that is, the *market* in which each offering competes. This second concept is the answer to the question '*where* does competition occur?'

4.1 The definition of a market

A market is a communication system in which buyers and sellers can determine the prices of competing offerings. In practice we regard a market as containing those offerings that have a significant actual or potential influence on one another's prices. It contains all actual and potential competitors with that much influence, and no others. A market and its offerings can, therefore, best be identified by the list of significant substitutes—those that customers regard as effectively competing.

Why only those with a 'significant' influence on prices? Because that is the most sensible point for drawing the line. Ultimately all offerings in the entire economy are substitutes to some degree—poor pensioners may choose between food and heating. However, the manager is concerned with profit, and it is only substitutes with a significant influence on prices that appreciably affect the profitability of the offering.

On the other hand, a market includes potential as well as actual competitors. Competitors who do not at present, but might in the future, try to capture our customers can significantly influence prices long before that attempt actually occurs. For example, in the English Channel the ferry companies took the threatened entry of Eurotunnel into account for some years before the event. The market is said to be 'contestable' by these potential competitors (Baumol, *et al.* 1982). Those who have the required skills, capabilities, and resources are well placed to contest our market.

4.2 Models of a market: public and private

The most common assumption made by practitioners and writers alike is that competition takes place in a market or industry. The concept of an industry is examined in greater detail below. For the moment we merely note that in this context it is assumed that the 'industry' is itself a kind of market—that is, a group of suppliers of competing substitutes.

This usage of 'industry' in the sense of 'market' illustrates that the market was traditionally visualized as a closed set of substitutes, in which each offering competes with all the others, but with none outside that set. We can think of such a market, portrayed in Fig. 15.3, as the model of pure competition. In that model all the offerings are homogeneous, so that there can only be one equilibrium price that clears the market. However, that traditional model of a market could accommodate a modest degree of differentiation. It must be so modest that customers (a) treat all members of the set as effective competitors and (b) have no cause to compare the offerings with substitutes outside the group. With such modest differentiation, the group will have not a single equilibrium price, but a varied set of prices at which marginal customers find the offerings equally attractive, equal value for money.

This model, illustrated in Fig. 15.3, can be called the *public market*. Public markets are assumed to be:

- *publicly visible*: all participants know the competing substitutes and the interested customer groups, so that the boundaries of the market are known as an objective fact;
- *all-inclusive*: each member is a close enough substitute for every other member;
- *exclusive*: no member competes with non-members, with no competition across the boundaries of the group.

This model of the public market does sometimes portray reality. The market in uranium may be an example, and so might the market in a particular type of high-density computer disks. It can characterize backward economies like the former Soviet Union: offerings were drably uniform.

However, in the more common case where offerings are more than modestly differentiated, the three conditions of public visibility, inclusivity, and exclusivity do not hold. Can we speak of a public market in bar soaps? That would require inclusivity—that is, all bar soaps are in mutual competition irrespective of whether they are carbolic or presentation tablets. Furthermore it would require exclusivity, with none of the bar soaps competing with shampoos, gels, soap powders, or perfumes. The same difficulty applies to the 'market' in wristwatches. A Rolex Oyster Lady-Datejust encrusted with jewels does not compete with the cheap timekeepers sold at service stations, but it may compete with a lady's diamond necklace. What about a public market in aircraft or hotels in London? A glider does not compete with a Cessna executive jet or with a Boeing 747, but may compete with a four-wheel drive recreational vehicle. Nor does the luxury Savoy hotel in London's West End compete for the tourist trade with a one-star hotel in Earl's Court, but it may compete with service flats in Mayfair.

In other words, the model of the public market is not compatible with significantly differentiated offerings that predominate in advanced economies. Each differentiated offering has its own set of competitors, its own *private market*. That set and that private market are not exactly shared with any competing substitutes, although there may be considerable overlaps among neighbouring private markets. Offerings in one market are also to be found in neighbouring markets, but in varying combinations and relationships.

Though the publicly defined market can in some rare cases fit reality, it is of limited usefulness to the strategist. An offering can only be posi-

Figure 15.3 Public market of offerings A, B, C, D, and E

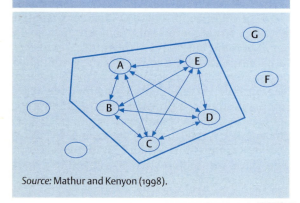

Source: Mathur and Kenyon (1998).

tioned where it competes, and that is usually a private market. The private market is illustrated in Fig. 15.4. In Fig. 15.3 each of the offerings A–E is in competition with all four of the others. Fig. 15.3 therefore describes a public market. By contrast, in Fig. 15.4 A–E is A's market: A competes with all the other four, but with no others. E's market, on the other hand, contains A, D, F, and G, F and G are outside A's market, and B and C are outside E's, but not A's. B's market contains A and C plus two unlettered competitors, but B does not compete with D or E. Every offering has its own market, private to itself. Where there is differentiation, offerings and markets are in one-to-one relationships.

We can illustrate this model by reference to the car 'market' or 'industry'. This is widely defined as including everything from the Rolls-Royce Silver Seraph to the Lada Riva. However, these two cars are not mutual substitutes. Some customers may regard the Mercedes 600 or the Bentley or the Jaguar as a substitute for the Rolls-Royce, but not the Toyota Camry. Some customers may choose between the Camry and the Jaguar, others between the Camry and the Range Rover, but not the Ford Escort. The Escort may or may not be seen as a serious substitute for the Lada, but it certainly is for the Volkswagen Golf. And of course, the Rolls-Royce—unlike the Jaguar—may compete with a yacht, and the Lada with a motorcycle. Each offering has its *private* list of substitutes: there is no common list, no group that includes all competitors and excludes all non-competitors.

In the model of the private market, when an offering is shifted, so usually is its market; it becomes a new offering with a new market. Either the competitors or their configuration—as seen by customers—shift. If a car manufacturer decides to upgrade its offering, tomorrow's competitors may be Jaguar and Rolls-Royce, whereas today's were Jaguar and Range Rover. Shift it further still and it is perfectly possible that it competes more with works of art than with cars.

4.3 The clumps and the galaxy

Figs. 15.5 and 15.6 show the public and private market models as global systems. Fig. 15.5 shows a world in which all markets are public. Offerings and their markets show up as a discontinuous pattern of clumps of offerings and ditches or gaps between the clumps. Within each clump all offerings are close substitutes: it is inclusive. At the

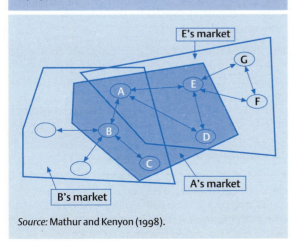

Figure 15.4 **Private market of offerings A, B, and E**

Source: Mathur and Kenyon (1998).

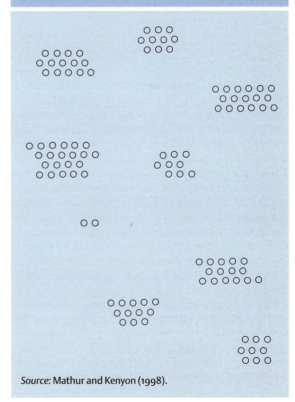

Figure 15.5 **Clumps of offerings: public markets, e.g. industries**

Source: Mathur and Kenyon (1998).

Figure 15.6 **The galaxy of offerings: a composition of private markets**

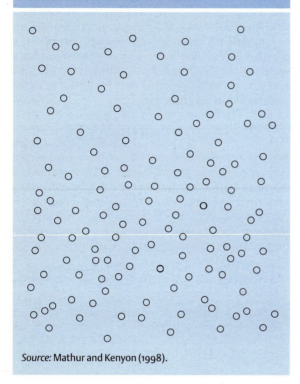

Source: Mathur and Kenyon (1998).

4.4 Industries and markets

There is a very influential belief that competitive strategy should use as its main tool a process called 'industry analysis', which is widely associated with Porter's (1980) famous five-forces model.

There are broadly two possible grounds for advocating an analysis of the industry as an aid to the formulation of competitive strategy. One is that members of the same 'industry' may have similar skills, assets, capabilities, competences, or other resources and may need watching for that reason. Even if such members were unlikely future competitors, observing them might still give insights. The other possible case for industry analysis is the assumption that the industry is the market in which competition for customers takes place. That is being scrutinized in this chapter. To the extent that the 'industry' is found to be a poor representation or even proxy of the market in which an offering competes for customers, the case for industry analysis is weakened.

☞ 'Marketers...try to create market situations for themselves typified by the presence of as few close substitute offerings as possible. They are in favour of product market selections with the lowest number of participants and the highest degree of positive differentiation of their own offering.' (Chapter 9, p. 194)

The concept of competition for customers taking place in industries runs into two major difficulties:

- the fact that an industry could at best be a public, not a private market;
- the ambiguities caused by the multiple meanings of 'industry'.

The first of these difficulties is probably enough to make the industry a poor model of the modern competitive environment. This difficulty has already been discussed.

The second difficulty is that the terminology breeds ambiguity. The word 'industry' is widely used in a variety of meanings, of which 'market' is only one. Common examples are:

- a group of suppliers of whatever is bought by a class of customers, irrespective of whether the items are competing substitutes or not (thus the common characteristic of the defence industry is that it has the armed forces as customers);

same time its members have no substitutes in other clumps: it is also exclusive. At least two of the three features that make up the conventional public image of an 'industry' or a 'market' are, therefore, confirmed. Fig. 15.6, by contrast, shows a world in which all offerings are differentiated. The picture is that of a galaxy with a continuum of offerings. Any one offering has competing neighbours, but each such neighbour has a partly different competing group. It is a continuum in the sense that there is no particular discontinuity in this pattern, just infinite variety. And, of course, each offering has its own market, unmarked in the Figure. Those markets overlap and interlock in the continuum.

Figs. 15.5 and 15.6 depict contrasting models in which either no offerings or all offerings are differentiated. In the real world of the advanced economies, differentiated offerings tend to predominate; however, undifferentiated ones do occur. To that extent the real world therefore presents a mixed picture.

- a group of suppliers of offerings using a common discipline, such as the engineering or chemical industries;
- a group of suppliers using a common raw material, like the plastics industry.

The defence industry cannot be of competitive significance, as ground-to-air missiles do not compete for customer choices with grenades. Nor can the chemical industry: explosives do not compete with pesticides or fertilizers. Nor can the plastics industry: cable insulation is no substitute for shopping bags or telephone receiver casings.

Words such as 'industry', or even 'market', are often employed to convey some broad and useful commonality. This usage is clearly of practical value. It is helpful even for marketing people to be able to talk about 'safety in the British nuclear industry' or 'the effect of the peace dividend on the defence industry' or 'credit control in the market for domestic appliances'. However, such vague usage must never be assumed to refer to a group of offerings that compete for customers' choices. In strategic marketing the term 'market' needs to be used with much greater precision.

4.5 The value of 'industry' and 'industry analysis'

For our purposes in this chapter the industry is little more than a commonly used version of the public market. It is not therefore surprising that both practitioners and researchers in business strategy have come up against difficulties in using the industry concept. Managers found that their competitors included non-members of the industry, and excluded some of its members. Researchers (Rumelt 1991) have empirically confirmed what has long been suspected (Triffin 1940)—that competitive features or performance were not uniform within an industry.

The first reaction was to look for smaller groups, on the hypothesis that the industry was not an accurate enough proxy for a market. An early device of this kind was the market or industry 'segment', which Grant (1995) describes. By the mid-1970s writers turned to the *strategic group* as a subset of the 'industry', consisting of industry members with similar competitive strategies (Caves and Porter 1977; Porter, 1980). Strategic groups were said to be protected by 'mobility barriers' instead of 'entry barriers'. However, Rumelt

had in 1984 made a case for dispensing with groups altogether, at least in principle. There is certainly increasing discontent with the idea of the industry as the arena for competition (e.g. Prahalad and Hamel 1994).

The real problem was the group concept, the public market itself, not the size of the group analysed. The concept of differentiation is by definition incompatible with a group concept like that of an industry, or even the smaller 'strategic group'. The essence of differentiation is diversity, that of the group sameness. The whole point of differentiation is to escape groups, not to join them.

Some exceptional cases apart, neither the industry nor industry analysis can greatly assist managers to formulate competitive strategies. It is worth listing four of the shortcomings that have dogged industry analysis.

- First, a single industry often contains so much diversity of offerings that it cannot be even a public market. For example, white goods are recognized as an industry. However, within this 'industry' washing machines, cookers, freezers, dishwashers, and refrigerators cannot possibly be in competition with each other.
- Secondly, even in a less diverse 'industry', the tidy concept of a public market founders on the hard rock of untidy reality. The automobile industry's various actual private markets shade into each other, all the way from the Lada to the Rolls-Royce: inclusivity and exclusivity are not found for the 'industry' as a whole, nor for any of its parts.
- Thirdly, the contradictions of this usage are compounded when analysts focus on multi-offering 'firms' in such an amorphous 'industry'—for example, if they take Sainsbury and Tesco to compete as companies, and not just with their grocery outlets: Sainsbury, the company, also owns DIY stores.
- Finally, the very process of industry analysis invites a static approach that takes even a competitively defined market as given. Some of the most rewarding competitive strategies aim at destabilizing and reconfiguring markets. This dynamic concept is more fully described immediately below, but an example is the personal computer 'industry', which may appear mature and static. Yet a particular voice-operated offering might well split off from it a profitable and growing private market.

4.6 Dynamic positioning: markets can be destabilized and reshaped

This chapter has repeatedly stressed that what a competitive strategy plans is tomorrow's offering and its triangular relationship is tomorrow *vis-à-vis* competitors and customers. That account may give a relatively sedate picture of what a company would be doing. It looks at the present configuration of the target space in the galaxy, adjusts this for forecast changes including competitive retaliation, and then positions the new offering profitably in that target space.

The tacit assumption is that the arrival of the new offering will *rearrange*, but not radically transform, the target neighbourhood. The landscape will not change very much, customers will not face a dramatically different set of choices. Many competitors may lose some customers, but most of them will survive. The newcomer is either not close enough to them, or not important enough, or not sufficiently novel to transform the neighbourhood. The key continuity here is the map of customers' choices and preferences.

However, a new offering can cause a much greater disturbance in its own environment. The arrival of an offering can explosively *transform* the configuration of markets in its part of the galaxy (see Insert). It can destabilize and reshape the markets of its neighbours, perhaps beyond recognition. Customers come to see their choices in an entirely new light. Preferences are awakened for which no seller had previously catered. The strategy is a *transformer* rather than a *rearranger* of its part of the galaxy.

A differentiated offering that destabilizes the preferences in its part of the galaxy may blur some distinctions and make others obsolete. The new offering may detach some preferences from the rest and thereby split off a profitable private market in which competition is less intense. As the new offering catches on, its market grows, possibly causing the decline of others. The best way to compete can be to compete as little as possible—that is, to differentiate. The first competitor to market a 'green' cosmetic attempted precisely that, as did Direct Line, the first UK insurer to offer motor insurance cover by telephone (see Box 15.1).

In some cases the separation into new private markets will not be complete; in those cases the new offering will still be seen as a substitute, though a distant one, for the other offerings in a radically redefined private market. In other cases, however, the separation may be so complete that a radically new private market is fashioned, remote from the others.

A market can, of course, be destabilized by price as well as by differentiation. Japanese motorcycles destabilized markets in the 1960s more by their lower prices than by their differentiated outputs. Heavy discounting in cigarettes forced Philip Morris in 1993 to slash the price of its Marlboro brand so as to regain some lost volume. However, differentiation is a much more common destabilizer than price. This is what the compact disc did to vinyl discs, and word processing to typewriters.

If a rearranger strategy is one of differentiation, then it often—but by no means invariably—targets a narrower group of customers and a smaller volume of sales, but at higher margins. More differentiation seldom means more sales for the rearranger. The transformer, on the other hand, in rare cases achieves a high volume of sales, scale economies, and an attractive cost position in a completely realigned and reconfigured environment.

Even the most established market system can be totally reshaped by a well-positioned offering. Good examples of market transformation are

- Mars's transformation of the humble choc ice into the ice-cream bar in 1989;
- Häagen-Dazs's introduction of the premium 'adult' ice cream;
- Body Shop's introduction of 'green' cosmetics.

The trick is to outmanœuvre competitors by destabilizing a part of the galaxy in your own favour. That means defining and shaping a private market to suit yourselves, and being prepared to do this as quickly and as often as required. Even when the

---

King of 'off the road'?

'If you are a Japanese maker of fashion-heavy 4 × 4's, you will be dreading this moment. People who like your cars probably like the idea of a Land Rover, but the real thing is too big or too expensive, so they buy the toy version instead. Trouble is Land Rover has now come up with a toy version of its own.

The Land Rover Freelander is compact, car-like in its driving feel, more thoroughly engineered than any Land Rover before it, and it proudly displays that famous badge on nose and tail. Land Rover, maker of the original, copies the copies and makes it better. Result? Full circle, and a new original.'

Source: Independent, 15 Nov. 1997.

Box 15.1 **Direct Line**

Direct Line Insurance Plc sold its first motor insurance policy by telephone in April 1985. Within a few years it had transformed the way motor insurance was bought and sold in the UK.

Prior to the advent of Direct Line, the motor-insurance business in the UK was dominated by the British composite insurers, who traditionally sold their policies through independent insurance brokers. Direct Line's revolutionary approach was to bypass the broker and establish a direct contact with customers primarily via the telephone. It aimed to provide customers with high-quality cover as well as a high level of personal attention and service, all at a lower price. The lower price was made possible not only by eliminating the insurance brokers but also by the innovative use of technology.

An outstanding television advertising campaign that featured a red telephone on wheels encouraged customers to use the telephone to obtain insurance cover. Sophisticated technology and trained operators at the receiving end ensured that customers received fast, competent, and courteous attention. Proposal forms could be completed on the telephone; quotations based on updated underwriting experience could then be generated. If the quotation was accepted, immediate cover could be provided to the customer. Claims too were handled on the telephone, the aim being to settle rapidly and to make the whole process as painless to the customer as possible. In 1990 Direct Line was one of only three companies given the highest rating for claims handling by the consumer magazine *Which?*

By 1992 Direct Line had grown dramatically: it had about 700,000 policies in force, a significant and growing share of those issued in the UK. The company had also done well financially. It was, however, facing increasing competitive pressures. Some composite insurers had retaliated by strengthening their links with brokers—a few going so far as to acquire holdings in leading brokers. However, there was also more direct competition. One of the co-founders of Direct Line had left to start a very similar operation—Churchill Insurance—which was later acquired by one of the leading Swiss insurers. Three composite insurers had established their own direct operations between 1988 and 1990. These initiatives were not always wholeheartedly promoted, for fear that they might jeopardize the traditional broker-based operations.

On 30 January 1996 the *Guardian* reported that by 1994 Direct Line had 1.9 million policies in force. It mentioned that Britannic Assurance had decided to pull out of motor insurance, as the business was no longer worth its while, and commented: 'The move highlights the rapidly changing nature of the UK motor insurance market, which has been fundamentally altered by the new-style direct telephone insurers, notably market leader Direct Line.'

Source: Channon (1996).

present configuration of markets suits you, you may still wish to destabilize the area again, if only to maintain and increase your lead by pre-empting or wrong-footing competitors. Customers can move away from offerings of their own accord, but much more often they are attracted away by nimbler competitors who reshape markets, merging some and splitting others.

Moreover, the transformer holds the initiative. If its vision of the fallout is correct, it will have a profitable and prolonged advantage. This is because competitors have a process of mental adjustment to go through as well as the physical and financial logistics of mounting an effective response. In the UK Häagen-Dazs had few close competitors for several years. The threat from Ben & Jerry, for example, came after five years of dominance by Häagen-Dazs.

The notion of destabilizing and reshaping markets requires a new way of thinking about the concept of the market. It goes beyond the usual model in which a market is regarded as an inert black box with unchangeable boundaries. The important lesson for managers is to regard markets as inherently pliable or even fragile. Virtually all market systems can be destabilized by competitors trying to shape a private market to suit themselves. There is an aggressive as well as a defensive lesson.

5 Strategic marketing decisions: competitive strategy

STRATEGIC marketing decisions are amongst the most important decisions that managers make, for they shape tomorrow's business. Strategic marketing, as we have said, can be subdivided into competitive and corporate strategy. We shall now show that the concepts of offerings and markets are fundamental in both cases.

5.1 Competitive strategy: the financial criteria for selection

A competitive strategy has to be designed for each of tomorrow's offerings: some of these may be successors to those we have today, others may be entirely new. In any case, if we decide to reposition today's offering, then the very act of repositioning creates a new competitive position: in other words, a new offering. Thus in this strict way of thinking the repositioning of an offering has to be treated as its removal and replacement by another. Besides, as we shall argue in the next section, some of today's offerings may best be removed altogether.

The reason for selecting an offering, and thus a competitive strategy, must be that it is expected to add to the financial value of the company, or, more precisely, that the company will be more valuable with it than without it. Competitive strategies that are unlikely to add financial value must be rejected.

The relevant value of an offering is the amount by which it will raise the value of the whole company. It depends not only on its own cash flows, but also on its impact on cash flows elsewhere in the company. For example, adding a service station may boost the sales of our supermarket. On the other hand, adding a detergent with a new brand name may bite into the sales of our existing brand. Yet that may well be the better move if by cannibalizing ourselves we avoid annihilation by an invader (see Box 15.2).

5.2 The scissors: what makes an offering profitable

Competitive strategy asks how an offering should compete tomorrow for tomorrow's customers

---

Box 15.2 Get WithIt

Onyx Breweries was the dominant of two brewers on the island of Maybee. Its beers had long been popular and commanded a loyal following. The owner-managers of the company had prospered through their ancestors' foresight in building an exceptional distribution system and a very successful Onyx brand. They had expected their success to last.

Recently, however, there had been some cause for concern. Television broadcasts from the neighbouring islands had carried advertisements for a new alcoholic drink incorporating tropical fruit juices called 'alcotrops'. Some customers there, especially young ones, had been drawn away from the more traditional alcoholic drinks. Yesterday had brought the news that the other local brewer had obtained a licence to make and sell the drink in Maybee. The owners of Onyx were considering their response to this threat. They debated three options:

- The first option was to do nothing, and allow the rival's new offering to bite into the sales of their beers. They estimated that under this option their total sales next year would drop from £5 million to £4 million. More importantly, the net present value (NPV) of their cluster of beers, and consequently of their business, would drop from £3 million to £2 million.

- Another option was to sell alcotrops of their own, but under a new brand—WithIt. Such a move would reduce the sales of their beers still further, for they would now not only be attacked by the alcotrops of the rival brewer, but also cannibalized by their own. Sales of beers would drop to £3.3 m., though the new offering would add sales of £1.2 m. by using the efficient distribution system. After accounting for the investment in the new WithIt offering, the NPV of the proposed cluster of drinks was estimated at £2.5 m.

- The final option was to market alcotrops, but under the Onyx label. Under that label alcotrop sales would rise to £1.4 m. However, there was another consideration. The Onyx label might be devalued in the community, which had long considered it a symbol of tradition. If prices were maintained, such a move would reduce the sales of beers to £2.9 m. When this consideration had been factored in, the NPV of the whole proposed cluster of drinks was estimated at £2.3 m.

None of the options available to the owners would make the company as valuable as it had been in a world without alcotrops. However, this was not an option: choices could only be made between future scenarios. Moreover, it was clearly better to cannibalize the existing cluster of drinks rather than to try and safeguard their sales. The best alternative seemed to be to market the new drink under the WithIt label. The company is better off with WithIt than without it.

against tomorrow's competitors. However, attractive positioning is not enough to launch a given offering. The offering has above all to recover its cost of capital. It therefore needs sufficient cash flows for that end to be achieved. If the offering is to remain a moneymaker long enough to achieve its objective, it must be protected from competitive attempts at aping it and thus encroaching on its market. That protection requires a sustainable resource advantage over its rivals.

It is perfectly possible to identify a competitive position that would be attractive to customers yet is either unattainable or unprofitable for the company. For example, a given prime high-street location might attract customers to our fast-food outlet. However, that site might not be for sale at all, or only at an uneconomic cost—for example, because a bank is bidding against us. Again, if a competitor could encroach on our market by acquiring an adjacent location or by providing a home-delivery service without a high-street location, the offering would cease to add value before we had recovered our cost of capital.

In other words, attractive outputs are not enough to meet the financial objective. For that, the offering also needs winning inputs and resources that cannot be poached, duplicated, or bypassed by competitors before we have attained our goal. Before we can select a new offering, we must be sure that we have the necessary competition-beating inputs or resources.

A company should therefore select an offering only if it simultaneously exploits:

- a competitive position that attracts profitable customers, and
- the company's own distinctive winning resources and other inputs that give that offering a durable edge over competitors.

An offering will not build value unless these two requirements, like the blades of a pair of scissors, as illustrated in Fig. 15.7, are simultaneously met. We shall now examine each of these blades in turn.

5.3 Blade 1: attractive market position

What are the various possible types of competitive positioning for an offering in its triangular relationship with customers and competitors? In practical terms, how can an offering be differentiated so as to be attractive to targeted profitable customers? The answer to that question will effectively give us a classification of competitive strategies.

There are two dimensions along which an

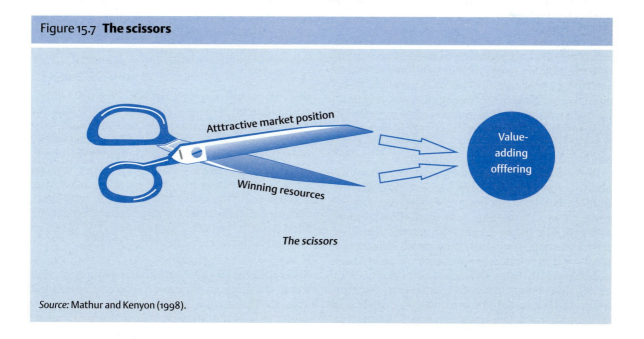

Figure 15.7 **The scissors**

The scissors

Source: Mathur and Kenyon (1998).

offering can be differentiated. We call these the merchandise and support dimensions. Those differentiating features that customers regard as helping them in choosing, obtaining, and then using the offering constitute its *support* dimension. All other differentiating features belong to its *merchandise* dimension.

An automobile's merchandise features would include the colour, shape, size, performance characteristics, facia board, and in-car entertainment equipment; its support features would include the test drive, instruction manual, promptness of delivery, servicing arrangements, and the service agent network.

A restaurant's merchandise features could include the waiter service and the quality and presentation of the food, drink and accommodation, whereas its support dimension might cover the ease of booking a table, the car park, help with interpreting the menu, and credit and debit card facilities. Similarly, a new motor insurance policy's merchandise would include the extent and features of the cover provided, while its support dimension might include the ease with which the cover and assistance with claims can be obtained.

The distinction is mainly practical. What matters is not the precise borderline between merchandise and support. It is not critical whether we think of the provision of a courtesy car while the damaged one is being repaired as merchandise or support. What matters is that we do not neglect either dimension when deciding how to position our offering.

Support features may in some cases be technical; if so, they might consist of process and application assistance, help with design, procurement, and subsequent use. Such help is as likely to be supplied in cosmetics as in engineering. It cannot be overstressed that all merchandise or support features are by definition outputs, not input features and efforts. Input features are those that do not influence the choosing customer.

In each of these two dimensions, merchandise and support, we can select a high or low degree of differentiation. That choice is in fact very significant. It gives us the four base cases illustrated in Fig. 15.8. The figure labels four generic forms of differentiation. They show how an offering can be positioned in relation to substitutes. If an offering is bought with little awareness of differences in either dimension, it is a *commodity-buy*; if highly differentiated in both dimensions, a *system-buy*. If differentiation is low in merchandise, but high in

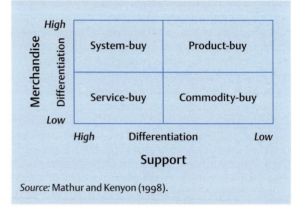

Figure 15.8 **Four main competitive strategies**

Source: Mathur and Kenyon (1998).

support, it is a *service-buy*, and in the reverse case a *product-buy*.

The unfamiliar suffix '-buy' in each case is a reminder that differentiation exists only in the eyes of the *choosing buyer*. The four generic cases thus show four different forms of the triangular competitive positioning of outputs illustrated in Fig. 15.2. Their labels denote an output perspective: they are *output* terms. Strategic marketing decisions will benefit from a language that encourages managers to think in these terms.

These four generic forms of differentiation should not be thought of as peculiar to this trade or that. Any item—tangible or intangible—can be transacted in any of the four ways. For example, a domestic burglar alarm for a standard three-bedroom house can be offered in all four ways:

- *Burglar alarm as system-buy*: the offering is differentiated in both the merchandise and the support dimension. The highly specialized supplier analyses the distinctive features of the customer's premises, such as any special threats in the neighbourhood, discusses with the customer options such as connection to a police station or security service, or extra sensors just inside the front door, recommends the most appropriate configuration, then designs, installs, and maintains the specified configuration as part of a unique package.

- *Burglar alarm as product-buy*: here the offering is differentiated in the merchandise dimension, but not in the support dimension. The equipment has special features and robust quality. To the customer it is differentiated by way of merchandise, but undifferentiated as regards any individual support from the supplier.

- *Burglar alarm as service-buy*: here the offering is differentiated as regards support, but not merchandise. The supplier acts as adviser, analysing the customer's requirements and specifying the installation from a range of standard equipment. The supplier specifies, installs, and maintains the recommended configuration.

- *Burglar alarm as commodity-buy*: the offering is indistinguishable from that of many competitors. Help given by the supplier may well be significant, but is no different from help given by competitors. The customer chooses whatever is cheapest to buy and use. Cost alone governs the buyer's decision.

Differentiation is a matter of degree. In the limiting cases, the degree of differentiation is either zero or infinite. Where it is zero—that is, in the bottom-right corner of Fig. 15.8—the offerings are homogeneous, and the slightest price difference would shift customer choices. Where it is infinite—that is, in the top-left corner—the offerings are hardly substitutes at all and virtually no price difference would shift choices. In the intermediate cases the seller can charge a price premium for the differentiating features. At any given level of differentiation the seller must aim for a price/volume combination that adds financial value. It is in this manner that, for the strategist, differentiation policy governs price policy.

Each of the four competitive strategies—system-buy, service-buy, product-buy, and commodity-buy—is potentially profitable. There may be uncrowded areas in the galaxy where an offering with the required degree and kind of differentiation would be attractive to a sufficient number of customers. Perhaps an innovative offering may be able to destabilize customer preferences and so shape an attractive private market for itself. Even a commodity-buy strategy can be rewarding if the company has a durable cost advantage and the capacity—not necessarily exercised—to attract customers by undercutting competitors.

5.4 Blade 2: winning resources

An offering, no matter how attractive to customers, must have cash inflows that enable it to recover its cost of capital. It must, therefore, be protected from competitive attempts at encroachment till that end is achieved. That protection comes from resource advantages over rivals: these

provide barriers to encroachment. These winning resources are the other blade of the scissors. Resources in this context need to be widely interpreted: structures, culture, alliances, supplier networks, and routines such as those helpful to close relationships with customers are included in the means of competing.

Perhaps the company has inimitable resources that put an attractive way of differentiating within its reach and outside the reach of others; or perhaps its advantage lies in its unique ability to undercut their costs. It is these superior supply-side endowments that protect our company's offering from competitive attempts to ape its success and erode the very process that builds financial value.

The quality of our resources can be tested by asking some searching questions (Peteraf 1993, adapted by Mathur and Kenyon 1998).

- Are they *diverse* enough? If competitors can easily access similar resources, ours may offer little protection. Our ability to attract brilliant MBAs may be called a 'key success factor', but it is of little or no advantage if other management consultancies can do the same.

- Can the resources be easily copied or bypassed? If our resources are not *matchless*, then once again they offer little protection. We may decide to equip our vacuum cleaners with specially designed bags that collect dust more effectively. However, the advantage may be too short-lived if our competitors can easily acquire the technology to copy us, or introduce alternative cleaning systems that dispense with the need for bags altogether.

- Will the NPV of the resource to the company exceed its acquisition or opportunity cost? In other words is the resource *felicitous*? If not, it cannot add value. We may wish to acquire a prime site for our restaurant, but the acquisition costs may be bid up to such a level by competitors who have the same idea that it would no longer add value to the company. Even if we already own such a site, we may be better off selling it than building on it, if it will fetch more than its NPV to us.

- Is the resource *inseparable*? Or can the resource or its value be prised away from us? We may think that our bond trader is a real gem. However, she may be so much more valuable to a rival company that she could renegotiate her terms with us to such a level that we would be better off without her.

In short, a competitive strategy will not normally add value unless it uses *winning* resources: those that can pass these stringent tests. These tests are not often passed by tangible resources, nor by intangible resources located in individual people. Individuals are easily poached by competitors. The most promising category of winning resources is collective intangible ones such as team knowledge, team skills, corporate capabilities, networks, and competences (Nelson and Winter 1982).

Winning resources can enable a company to sustain its differentiation or lower costs long enough for the offering to become a value-builder. In fact, an exceptional advantage may enable the company to accomplish the rare task of producing an offering that is not only better, but also cheaper to produce.

5.5 Which blade comes first?

Fig. 15.7 illustrates that the quest for a value-adding offering is like the two blades of a pair of scissors. One blade searches for supply-side advantages and the other for demand-side ones. The demand-side blade looks for an attractive position in tomorrow's market configuration that would exploit the company's winning resources. This positioning task requires imagination, competitor analysis, and customer intelligence. The supply-side blade looks for resources that would safeguard an attractive market position. The task requires internal analysis to identify those resources that could keep competitors at bay. Neither blade on its own is enough. The demand and supply sides must both be explored for a suitable match.

It is, therefore, important that managers who make strategic marketing decisions do not ignore either blade. It is far too easy to overstress the importance of either blade. Fashionable market-led strategies, which focus primarily on the demand side, may fail to pay sufficient attention to the supply side. On the other hand, resource-based strategies that overlook the demand side miss the point that resources are valuable only if they exploit an attractive market opportunity.

There is no general rule about which blade should be used first. If a company's winning resources are easier to identify, then the resources blade is the better starting point. It often is. However, it is not impossible that a company has a flair for positioning, or that the company's winning resources are not clearly visible, or that they could be mustered. In these cases the positioning blade is the better starting point.

6 Strategic marketing decisions: corporate strategy

THIS chapter has several times referred to corporate strategy as a strategy for creating and maintaining a value-optimizing cluster of offerings. There are those who see something wider than an individual offering as the unit of competitive strategy, and discuss the choice of clusters in terms of such units. This chapter has argued for adopting the individual offering as the unit for competitive strategy.

It is unusual for a business to have just one offering; even a small commercial business is usually a cluster of offerings. The way to shape tomorrow's business is to ask: what should be tomorrow's cluster of offerings and their markets?

Proponents of strategy frameworks such as 'business portfolios' asked a similar question, but about clusters of strategic business units (SBUs) rather than offerings. The objective in the case of the Boston Consulting Group matrix—the most popular version of the portfolio frameworks in the 1970s and 1980s—was to achieve a cluster that matched cash-generating SBUs with cash-absorbing ones, so that the company could finance its growth internally. Modern financial theory questions the validity of that objective. In any case, such frameworks did not ask whether or not there were any links between the members of a cluster. The current trend in corporate strategy favours *related* clusters, for, if there are no value-boosting links between an offering and the remainder of the company, then there is no justification for putting them together.

The decisions of corporate strategy concern which offerings should be added to the cluster, which retained, and which divested.

In the selection of new offerings the tasks of competitive and corporate strategy overlap, as the Get WithIt example illustrated. Moreover, though customers are won by the outputs of a single offering, inputs, if there are economies of scale, are economic only if they are shared by a number of offerings. A winning set of resources can be the result of a well-chosen cluster of offerings. There is an asymmetry here: on the demand side, a single offering competes for customer choices; on the supply side, a single resource, often within a profit centre, can serve several offerings. Life would be so much simpler for both strategists and writers on strategy if the profit centre could be treated as the unit for competition. However, that would not portray the reality of how customers choose: they choose between offerings, not profit centres.

Corporate and competitive strategies can also add value to each other in other ways than by sharing resources (Mathur and Kenyon 1998). For example, one offering can add to the attractiveness of another. Another way is that of increasing market power. For example, the only radio station in a remote community may acquire the only local newspaper so as to exercise a greater degree of monopoly in the setting of local advertising rates.

The most distinctive function of corporate strategy is the continual review of existing offerings or parts of the cluster, if some offerings must be considered together. An offering may, for example, be past its peak; it may no longer have a positive net present value from now on. A shrewd decision to retain or divest, and skilful timing of a divestment, can add much value to a competitive strategy that had been adopted earlier. This pruning function can add a lot of value in its own right.

The importance of the divestment task needs to be stressed. Much value is lost when offerings are retained beyond their 'dispose-by' date. Weak offerings can do much to damage a company's reputation (Kotler 1965). They also often require a disproportionate amount of management attention. However, managers are often reluctant to let go of offerings that have long been part of a company's history, or on which jobs depend.

This failure to let go is not invariably psychological. It often results from unclear thinking about the purpose of a business. Once size or turnover or even 'market share' is incorrectly substituted for financial value as the objective of business, phasing out offerings seems like a retrograde step. However, when managers correctly focus on financial value as the objective of business, it can make financial sense to divest even very successful offerings. For example, if a commercially viable and, on the face of it, financially value-generating hotel in our national chain can be sold at a price that far exceeds its greatest possible net present value to us, then its disposal would build financial value even though it may reduce turnover, physical size, and 'market share'.

7 The changing nature of strategic marketing

MAKING money for investors, or shareholder value, acquired a new importance in businesses all over the world in the second half of the 1990s. This long overdue change in sentiment probably had many causes. The prosperity and vigour of US businesses, which have been more prone to accept this philosophy, is one of them. It may also have been prompted by the collapse of communism and the setbacks in the economies of 'communitarian' countries such as Japan, South Korea, France, and Germany. This has made managers and investors even in these countries re-examine the purpose of business. Certainly the questions raised about the social value of loss-making state enterprises, first in the UK and now in countries as politically different as India and China, have had a part to play. The penny has taken a long time to drop.

Strategic marketing has not been immune to this change. Strategic marketing has always brought to the theory and practice of business management a most useful focus on the customer. There has, however, in the past, been some tendency for its advocates to go overboard and see customer satisfaction in itself as the guiding principle of business. The 1990s have restored a sense of balance. There is now considerable agreement that customers are very important but not all-important: a business must above all be profitable.

The new emphasis on financial value has coincided with a clearer understanding of the central role of the company's resources in achieving it. It is now also much clearer what exactly characterizes winning resources. Marketing has begun to pay more careful attention to supply-side topics (Hunt and Morgan 1995). Editions of leading textbooks in marketing in the 1990s increased their coverage of such matters, thus going well beyond techniques such as SWOT analysis. Much work remains to be done, but we are beginning to see much sharper emphasis on the need to align inputs and outputs (Day 1997). The practical and theoretical challenge lies in incorporating these supply-side ideas without letting go of marketing's great insight about the unit of competition: that what customers choose is offerings, not the organizational units that contain those resources. Otherwise there is some danger of going overboard on the supply side.

This focus on customers is likely to prove of increasing importance as competition intensifies, as so-called industries merge and competitors come from all parts of the globe. Hotter competition in a world of offerings of increasing diversity is already forcing companies to be choosy. They are learning to focus on and develop offerings they are good at, and to divest the rest: pruning decisions are rightly becoming central to strategic marketing. To make these choices managers need a firm grasp of the twin concepts of offerings and markets.

8 Summary

THIS chapter has examined two of the most fundamental ideas of marketing, those of offerings and markets. It has defined an offering—the thing that competes—and has described how it competes for customer choice. It has gone on to suggest that offerings compete predominantly by differentiation, especially in advanced economies, and to set out the meaning and nature of that concept. In such a differentiated world the arena of competition—the market—is private to each offering. In other words, it has a set of customers and competitors that is not wholly shared by any other offering.

These insights, it is suggested, are vital to strategic marketing: to the setting of competitive and corporate strategies. A competitive strategy will create value only if an offering is both favourably positioned, and exploits adequately protected, company-specific winning resources. Corporate strategy puts together valuable clusters of offerings that are more valuable together than apart, and watches for offerings that are ripe for divestment or replacement.

Further reading

Goold, M., Campbell, A., and Alexander, M. (1994), *Corporate-Level Strategy* (New York: Wiley). One of the few available books on corporate strategy. Discusses the logic of corporate strategy and the kind of clusters that are valid. The fact that poor corporate strategy is a great destroyer of value makes this an important book.

Grant, R. M. (1995), *Contemporary Strategy Analysis* (2nd edn.; Oxford: Blackwell). Probably the best textbook on business strategy. A useful description of the key ideas and techniques of the subject and a helpful critique of them. Good on resources. The emphasis is on competitive strategy. However, the book focuses on the industry rather than customer choice.

Hamel, G., and Prahalad, C. K. (1994b), *Competing for the Future* (Boston: Harvard Business School Press). Questions the industry. Does not take markets as given. Emphasizes the value of resources and competition for them. Definitely worth reading.

Kay, J. (1993), *Foundations of Corporate Success* (Oxford: Oxford University Press). An insightful book, which, unlike the author's later writings, focuses on the attainment of financial value and the importance of aligning positioning and winning resources. The underlying framework is valuable, and, unlike many other books on business strategy, it is not based on the industry. Well worth reading.

Kotler, P. (1997), *Marketing Management* (9th edn.; Englewood Cliffs, NJ: Prentice Hall). A widely used textbook that provides a comprehensive coverage of marketing topics. Leaves nothing important out but neither does it provide a decision-making framework for the strategist. Like most marketing texts, it does not give much attention to resources.

Mathur, S. S., and Kenyon, A. (1998), *Creating Value: Shaping Tomorrow's Business* (paperback edn.; Oxford: Butterworth-Heinemann). This book presents a comprehensive framework for business strategy. It covers competitive strategy, resources, and corporate strategy. The present chapter is based on the customer-focused approach developed in this book.

McKenna, R. (1991), 'Marketing is Everything', *Harvard Business Review*, 69/1 (Jan.–Feb.), 65–79. Stirring and uplifting stuff by a believer.

Peteraf, M. A. (1993), 'The Cornerstones of Competitive Advantage: A Resource-Based View', *Strategic Management Journal*, 14/3: 179–91. An excellent, but demanding integrating framework that identifies the characteristics of winning resources.

Porter, M. (1980), *Competitive Strategy* (New York: Free Press). A seminal book that sets out the key questions of competitive strategy. Porter focuses competitive strategy on the relationship with customers and competitors but remains within the constraints of the 'industry'. The book is also less than specific on the unit of competition. It is, however, essential reading for those hoping to understand the recent development of the subject.

Porter, M. E. (1987), 'From Competitive Advantage to Corporate Strategy', *Harvard Business Review* (May–June), 43–59. A seminal paper that examines the logic of corporate strategy.

Rumelt, R. P. (1984), 'Towards a Strategic Theory of the Firm' in R. B. Lamb (ed.), *Competitive Strategic Management* (Englewood Cliffs, NJ: Prentice Hall) 556–70. A seminal piece of work on competitive strategy that questions the value of groups (such as the industry) and highlights the importance of winning resources. Written by an economist and could be difficult for the lay reader.

repositioned in an attempt to improve its profitability,

(*b*) the considerations that would justify abandoning it;

(*c*) what information is required, and how would you use it to decide what should be done.

6 You are asked by the Chief Financial Officer of a South Korean company, 'What is strategic marketing? Why does it matter? Does it apply equally to companies selling goods and services? How should it be adapted for businesses operating in the emerging economies?' What is your reply?

Discussion questions

1 Take any company that you are familiar with.

(*a*) Identify a number of separate offerings.

(*b*) Select one of these offerings and give your reasons for believing it to be a single offering.

(*c*) Then:

  (i) Specify how the offering competes today.

  (ii) Suggest how its successor offering should compete tomorrow. In other words, specify its competitive strategy.

  (iii) Justify the suggested competitive strategy.

2 You are asked by a marketing colleague 'Which industry does Unilever (or the company that you have chosen for analysis in question 1) compete in? 'What is your response? Select two or more of its offerings to illustrate your answer.

3 Are countries markets? Illustrate your answer by using the example of companies you know that sell their offerings internationally.

4 Assume that your favourite hairdresser, bookshop, restaurant, and dentist have really one offering each. Specify (*a*) the industry and (*b*) the private market in which each competes.

5 Suppose your company produces a software package suitable for small businesses. It sells the package directly from the UK to customers in an Asian country. Recently competitors have introduced very similar offerings. Write a memorandum to your Managing Director explaining:

(*a*) the ways in which your offering could be

Sandwiches filled with imagination

Mad Merv is not, of course, mad—in spite of the manic nature of his business, which often sounds as though it is the trading floor of London Metal Exchange rather than a sandwich bar in Manchester called Melia's.

The most visible sign of its popularity is the queue of people stretching out of the door across the wide pavement of John Dalton Street between noon and 2 p.m. each weekday. Inside the shop there is hubhub, as the head of the queue shuffles and jostles with people waiting for special orders. One couple even met and married through bumping into each other in Melia's every day.

'Mad Merv's Madras Express'—a roast beef sandwich topped with a cabbage and peppers salad and dressed with curried mayonnaise—is one of the sought-after products.

Its inventor is a chef named Mervin Hershon and he rejoices in his nickname of Mad Merv, which he feels conveys something of the ambience of his business and what makes it different.

With seven competitors within 300 yards, it has to be. However, the permanent queue outside and bustle inside are potent testimonials. He could have reduced the crowding by taking the shop next door but decided against because the cramped area of only 450 sq. ft in which the business operates is another ingredient in its appeal.

Within that space is cramped an L-shaped front counter, cold drinks cabinets, microwave and baked potato convection ovens, a hot meat pie cabinet and the back kitchen where the food is prepared. Somehow, seven full-timers and two part-timers also squeeze in to work there.

They are needed to shift a queue, which, if it has forty-five people in it, reaches the tree halfway across the pavement outside. Hershon's research has shown that anyone joining it then can expect to be served within three minutes.

This is done through shifting the most popular sandwiches from a constantly replenished buffer stock on the counter and shouting orders to the back kitchen for anything else, such as fillings in baked potatoes.

Usually, all four women on the counter are shouting at once, creating the trading-floor atmosphere. Customers shout back what they want as they cross the threshold into the shop. Mad Merv moves between front and back, preventing bottlenecks.

As any production engineer would instantly realize, it is the customers who are being processed, not the food—and with great success. Since he bought the business four years ago, Hershon has trebled the turnover to more than £6,000 a week.

He learned hotel catering management from seven years around the world with Hilton International, four of them in Australia. His feeling for what makes a good snack came from supplying the airlines, notably Qantas.

It was his idea to serve local 'ethnic' snacks to the Queen on all the hops during an Australasian tour in 1968. He was 22 at the time. Qantas later sent him around the Pacific to extend the principle to its general menus.

Back in Britain, Hershon became a taxi driver in Manchester, then started a betting shop. He nearly went bankrupt on his first weekend when Red Rum, the favourite, won the Grand National for the second time. It took him a few days to pay everybody out, but he survived to open two more shops.

Melia's attracted him because it was well placed and seemed always to be busy without offering anything out of the ordinary. 'I had always wanted to open an American-style sandwich bar offering something different from anyone else, but I never had the capital,' he says. 'Suddenly I realized I could do it.'

He sold his betting shops and borrowed £14,000 from Barclays to buy the business for £59,000. Having succeeded in one small business, he then combined the lessons learned with his training as a chef and caterer.

Within two years turnover had doubled and he had spent £28,000 to refurbish the shop and put some high technology into its management.

By computerizing his two tills, he has been able to keep track of trends in sandwich tastes. This means that, even though Melia's sells an average of 1,430 items to 930 customers who spend £1.32 each every day, he can predict total sales to within ten sandwiches, ordering ingredients and bread from local suppliers the preceding day so that everything is fresh.

The real secret of Hershon's success lies in what he sells. His is the designer sandwich. There are seventeen individual fillings. 'People think that running a sandwich bar is about putting a piece of ham between two pieces of bread. We have tried to create a range of unique fillings that you cannot buy anywhere else,' he says.

His 'tuna special' carries a money-back guarantee, and sales are now approaching 750,000 in four years. The tuna, onions, and salad seem obvious, but the special piquancy comes from the blend of herbs and mayonnaise that is one of his trade secrets.

He gives his sandwiches names and then markets them as brands with posters in the front windows and menus distributed around the city. For example, 'Andy's Avocado Surprise' is named after Andrea, his wife, with the surprise coming from the tasty mixture of avocado, prawns, apple, peach, and nuts.

'Wendy's Wonder' is called after one of the staff and combines beef, ham, and turkey with apple and peaches. 'We nearly called it The Titanic because it goes down so well,' Hershon jokes.

'Debbie's Delight' adds coleslaw to a Tuna Special, 'Beef Wellington a l'Espagnol' combines roast beef and Brussels pate with a Spanish salad, and the 'Orient Express' club sandwich comes in three decks, with turkey, salami, bacon, and salad, the meat alone totalling five ounces.

Meanwhile, 'New York! New York!' is pastrami on rye, with dill pickle, cucumber, mustard, and mayonnaise, in three decks to two, hot or cold.

He is now bursting into expansion. His buffet and party service is growing. He keeps a section of the kitchen for kosher food. He is taking on a partner, Ian Benson, opening another shop in central Manchester and yet another in Bolton.

'New York! New York! So good they named it twice' has been wired up to play whenever one of the eponymous sandwiches is sold in Bolton.

He has also attracted the attention of the local financial and professional community. His seemingly unique concept of how to make and market sandwiches is considered franchisable because it should add at least 50 per cent to the turnover of any normal sandwich bar. The Bolton venture will test the idea.

Have any of Manchester's growing army of merchant bankers spotted his potential? Hershon looked puzzled. 'What's a merchant banker?' he asked.

Source: Financial Times, 14 Apr. 1990.

Discussion Questions

1 What is Melia's main offering, and how is it positioned and in which market?

2 What are the company's winning resources? Justify your selection.

3 Use your answers to questions 1 and 2 to apply the scissors approach explained in this chapter. Then comment on the financial implications of the decision to adopt the offering.

4 Extend the scissors approach to Melia's expansion plans—i.e. to its growing buffet and party service and to its proposed shops in other cities. Based on this analysis prepare a brief note for Mervin Hershon outlining your strategic marketing recommendations.

Chapter 16
Market Segmentation

Sally Dibb

Objectives

The objectives of this chapter are:

1 to understand market segmentation and consider why it is used;

2 to examine how companies segment markets;

3 to explore different targeting strategies;

4 to learn about the role and process of positioning in segmentation strategies;

5 to consider how marketers can achieve the most from market segmentation.

1 Introduction

THE chapter begins by reviewing the underlying rationale and business benefits of market segmentation. Next, the three stages of the market-segmentation process are considered. Segmenting—the grouping of customers with similar needs—is dealt with first. This begins with a review of consumer and business-to-business segmentation variables and concludes by considering the role of statistical analyses in segmentation research. The targeting stage, which is looked at next, involves an examination of alternative targeting strategies and a review of the factors that must be considered by businesses making targeting choices. Positioning, the final stage to be examined, comprises an explanation of the underlying rationale, followed by a review of the process of positioning and repositioning. The chapter concludes by emphasizing the need for effective segmentation. The resources that businesses devote to implementing and reviewing their market segmentation are enormous. There is an implicit assumption that this investment is justified. Possible reasons for implementation problems are highlighted and guidance offered on how to get the best out of market segmentation.

In the mobile phone market, the products and marketing programmes must be carefully designed to appeal to the needs of different customer groups. Box 16.1 shows how important it is for cellular operators to identify customer needs and use this understanding to develop suitable marketing mixes. Vodafone, Cellnet, Orange, and Mercury know that the needs of different customers vary. A business user who travels all over Europe, making several hours of calls each day, will not have the same requirements as an elderly couple who keep a phone in their car for emergencies. Different tariffs, hardware, and insurance schemes are needed to meet these diverse needs. To achieve customer satisfaction, cellular operators identify and single out customer groups at which to direct some or all of their marketing activity. In marketing terms these businesses have adopted a market-segmentation approach, tailoring their products to meet the needs of different, specific customer groups.

Box 16.1 **Booming phones**

The market for cellular phones enjoyed a global boom in the late 1990s. In 1996 the overall UK expenditure on telephone and telecommunications exceeded £8,000 million. A growing proportion of this spend was on calls from mobile phones. When mobile telephone technology was first introduced, its use was restricted primarily to the business domain. Today, there are packages to suit every pocket and situation. There were three distinct phases to this market growth. During the first, it was business people and sales representatives who used the technology to keep 'in touch' with the office. In the second phase, tradespeople such as electricians, plumbers, and heating engineers adopted mobile phones so that they could respond to emergency and other calls. During the third phase, vulnerable and isolated groups, such as women travelling alone, were targeted. In 1996 with more than five million UK subscriptions, there was a mobile phone package for everyone.

Cellular operators such as Vodafone, Cellnet, Mercury One-2-One, and Orange developed product offers that reflected the varying requirements of different customer groups. Heavy users, often business customers, could opt to pay higher monthly tariffs in exchange for free 'talk time'. For an additional charge, international call capability was offered on certain networks. Low tariffs and 'pay-as-you-go' options were available for light users or those on a budget. Each operator prioritized particular customer groups and emphasized those aspects of its service that it believed would appeal. For example, Vodafone made much of its international call capability, which made it popular with certain business users. Orange, meanwhile, became well known to consumers for its combination of clear targeting, novel branding, and innovative service packages. The company launched the first ever mobile phone loyalty scheme, offering free air time in exchange for every 60 seconds of calls.

Table 16.1 **Cellular telephony—retail calls**

Companies	Retail calls	
	Minutes (m.)	Subscriptions (000s)
Vodafone	1,711	2,444
Cellnet	1,387	2,391
Mercury 121	1,573	412
Orange	308	489

Notes: Local, national, and international calls, including calls from abroad (cellular phones). Total PSTN minutes from residential lines were 75,365 million.
Source: OFTEL Annual Report 1995/6.

gramme is used to attract all customers, is rarely appropriate. At the beginning of the twentieth century, Henry Ford's customers were happy to be offered his Model T 'in any colour so long as it is black'. In today's markets, with increasingly varied customer needs and ever more sophisticated marketing techniques, there are few situations in which a mass-marketing approach is feasible. Ford's current product range is evidence that customers expect their diverse requirements and buying behaviour to be met with an array of offerings. For example, the Scorpio for executives, the Mondeo aimed at fleet buyers, the Escort for family use, and the Maverick for customers desiring 4 × 4 off-road capability. Moving away from mass marketing towards a market-segmentation approach is a common way of dealing with diverse customer needs (Dibb and Simkin 1996).

'...The seller can pursue a policy of product differentiation...by viewing the market as a number of small homogeneous markets (market segments)...' (Chapter 14, p. 319)

Although marketers recognize the breadth of customer needs, it is often unrealistic to customize products for individual customers. Businesses usually have neither the resources nor the inclination to deal with customers on an individual basis. To be competitive, they must accumulate customers into groups to reduce costs. They must then target the most attractive groups to

2 The market-segmentation concept

THE underlying principle of market segmentation is that individual customers have different product and service needs. The mass-marketing approach, in which a single marketing pro-

enhance effectiveness. Market segmentation is the process by which this accumulation of customers is achieved, grouping those with similar needs and buying behaviour. If the process has worked properly, customers within a particular segment should have homogeneous product needs and consumption patterns that are distinct from those customers in other segments.

Many companies believe that marketing success is linked to how effectively their customer base is segmented. This is because market segmentation helps companies to satisfy diverse customer needs while maintaining certain scale economies (Dibb and Simkin 1996).

2.1 The economic rationale

Market segmentation is a key decision area for businesses undertaking marketing and strategic planning (McDonald 1995). The underlying rationale is that groups of customers that have been aggregated on the basis of similar needs and buying behaviour are likely to demonstrate a more homogeneous response to marketing programmes. Put simply, a business is more likely to be successful if it designs a specific marketing mix for a group of customers with similar needs. This assumption applies to businesses of all types, from confectionery manufacturers that promote their product ranges on the basis of the occasion on which they are consumed, to hotel groups that organize their property portfolios into sites geared to business or tourist occupancy.

The origins of market segmentation are in economic pricing theory, which indicates that profits can be maximized when pricing levels discriminate between segments (Frank *et al.* 1972). Segmentation allows businesses to deal with diverse customer needs by focusing resources on particular customer groups with relatively homogeneous requirements (Choffray and Lilien 1978). Organizations that apply segmentation to their business are, therefore, better able to fine-tune their customer offerings than those adopting a mass-marketing approach (Blattberg and Sen 1976; Beane and Ennis 1987).

2.2 The business benefits

Businesses use segmentation because they believe it will improve their marketing effectiveness and enhance their ability to capitalize on market opportunities. Some marketers disagree, arguing that, because of measurement difficulties, it is impossible to identify a direct link between segmentation and business success (Esslemont 1996). However, enthusiasts point to many years of segmentation application, which, they say, provides powerful qualitative evidence that companies with segmentation skills perform better (Sharp 1995). Segmentation, they argue, leads to more satisfied customers, fewer direct confrontations with competitors, and better-designed marketing programmes. They attribute various business benefits to a segmentation approach:

■ *Customer analysis.* Segmentation encourages businesses more precisely to define customer needs, expectations, and characteristics. Managers improve their understanding of how, why, and what influences customer buying. Being more closely in touch with customers increases their responsiveness to changing requirements, allowing more finely tuned marketing programmes.

☞ 'Segmented or differential pricing strategies aim to exploit heterogeneity among consumer segments.' (Chapter 10, p. 227)

■ *Competitor analysis.* Analysis of the competitive environment is an essential part of the segmentation process. Businesses applying a segmentation approach must make targeting decisions about the attractiveness of particular segments. They must decide on how to position products within these segments and consider the nature of competitive advantage. Informed decisions on these matters can be taken only following careful competitor analysis.

☞ 'The key is to choose those segments first that are the most likely to adopt the new product quickly . . .' (Chapter 24, p. 562)

■ *Resource allocation.* The financial and other resources that marketers have at their disposal are finite. It is rarely realistic to target an entire market. Segmentation helps businesses allocate their resources effectively, by selecting the most attractive parts of the market on which to focus.

■ *Strengths and weaknesses.* Through the customer and competitor analysis, segmentation encourages marketers to take a realistic view of company strengths and weaknesses. This permits a more balanced appraisal of marketing opportunities.

■ *Marketing planning.* Segmentation allows businesses to gear their planning towards the particular requirements of different customer

Asymmetric ticketing

The Dutch airline KLM has discovered that many passengers fly to the USA in Economy Class but return by Business Class, this arrangement apparently helping them to cope with jet lag. KLM has, therefore, developed a product offering to meet this need.

Box 16.2 **The STP stages of market segmentation**

SEGMENTATION
- Choose variables for segmenting market
- Build a profile of segments
- Validate emerging segments

TARGETING
- Decide on targeting strategy
- Identify which and how many segments should be targeted

POSITIONING
- Understand consumer perceptions
- Position products in the mind of the consumer
- Design appropriate marketing mix to communicate positioning

Source: Dibb *et al.* (1997: 205).

groups. Different plans can be developed for each of the target segments. This allows marketers to be more responsive to the varying requirements of customers (see Insert). Thus a clothing manufacturer may need to revise its plan for the fashion-conscious teenage segment more frequently than in other segments.

3 The market segmentation process

THE underlying principle of the market-segmentation process is that similar customers are grouped together. The process is generally considered to consist of three stages: segmentation, targeting, and positioning. During the segmentation stage, customers are grouped into segments using one or a combination of variables. The aim is to collect together those with similar needs and buying behaviour. For example, the market for magazines can be segmented using the gender and age of consumers. There are titles targeting pre-school children, teenage girls, 20–35-year-old males, and the over 50s. Next, marketers choose the segment(s) on which to target marketing resources. The final stage, positioning, involves the design of marketing programmes that will match the requirements of customers in the segments chosen. The marketing programmes should position the product or service directly at the targeted customers. Box 16.2 illustrates the three stages of the market-segmentation process.

4 Segmentation variables

THE first stage of the segmentation process involves the selection of suitable variables for grouping customers. Sometimes called base vari-

ables, or the segmentation basis, the key to suitability for these variables is in the extent to which homogeneous customer groups are identified. The large number of variables sometimes causes problems for marketers, especially as there is rarely one best way to segment a particular market. Marketers must try different combinations of one or more variables to find the most effective way to group customers. Sometimes moving away from traditionally popular segmentation bases towards more creative approaches can reap benefits for businesses. For example, the First Direct telephone banking operation was set up on the basis that certain consumers' banking needs were not being met by traditional high-street banks and building societies. In building a clearer view of the personal characteristics, lifestyles, and banking needs of these consumers, it was possible for First Direct to tailor-make a new kind of service.

In some circumstances more than one variable can be used to segment a particular market. Marketers must decide whether a single or multivariable approach is the most suitable for their particular business. Single variable segmentation, which involves the use of a single variable, is undoubtedly the simplest to achieve. A soft-drinks manufacturer, which divides its market on the basis of the region in which consumers are located, is using this approach. Difficulties can arise if a single variable approach fails to reveal distinctive and homogeneous customer groupings. For example, the soft-drinks manufacturer may discover that, while the territory-based segmentation is meaningful in terms of the requirement for different package design, the needs of consumers within each region are also diverse. The result is that using a single variable segmentation does not allow sufficient differentiation of consumers. By combining the territory-based approach with benefit segmentation, the organization is better able to cater for this diversity. The result might be that product variants are designed for dieters, fitness enthusiasts, families, travellers segments, the health conscious, and families. Combining variables in this way is known as multivariable segmentation. Although it may be more complex to implement, this approach allows marketers more

precisely to define marketing programmes to suit the target segments.

4.1 Segmentation variables for consumers

Many different base variables can be used to segment a market. A simple classification scheme organizes these variables into two categories. The first contains variables that describe the characteristics of consumers. Demographic variables such as age, sex, race, and religion and socio-economic factors such as occupation, education, and income, are examples of these characteristics. Variables such as these are widely used by companies attempting to segment their market, because information about them is easy to obtain and they

---

Box 16.3 Consumer segmentation variables

Basic consumer characteristics

Demographics
   Age
   Gender
   Race
   Religion
   Family life cycle

Socio-Economics
   Income
   Occupation
   Education
   Social Class

Geographic
   Country
   Region
   Type of urban area (conurbation/village)
   Type of housing (affluent suburbs/inner city)
   Geodemographics

Personality and lifestyle
   Holiday companies often use lifestyle to segment the market. Club Med, for example, concentrates on young singles, while other tour operators cater especially for senior citizens or young families.

Behavioural characteristics

Purchase behaviour
   Customers for frozen ready meals may be highly brand loyal to Findus or Birds Eye or may shop purely on the basis of price.

Purchase and usage occasion
   A motorist making an emergency purchase of a replacement tyre while on a trip far from home is less likely to haggle about price than the customer who has a chance to shop around.

Benefits sought
   When customers buy washing powder or fabric conditioner, they seek different benefits. For some, cleaning power and softness are essential, whereas for others a product's environmental friendliness is the key. Ecover products try to cater for this latter group.

User status and consumption behaviour
   Examining consumption patterns can indicate where companies should be concentrating their efforts. Light or non-users are often neglected.

Product attitudes
   Different customers have different perceptions of and preferences for products offered. Concern about environmental issues has altered many consumers' perceptions of household cleaning products and has resulted in a host of so-called environmentally friendly products.

Source: Dibb *et al.* (1997: 207).

are relatively simple to apply. The second category consists of behavioural variables relating to how consumers buy and use products. Purchase occasion, consumption behaviour, and attitudes towards the product are examples of this type. Although these variables are more difficult to measure and apply than simple consumer characteristics, they can provide detailed insights into product use and purchase behaviour. Box 16.3 illustrates the two groups of variables in more detail.

4.1.1 Demographic segmentation

For businesses looking for ways to segment their customers, demographic variables are very easy to use. Age, sex, family, race, and religion are all widely deployed to group consumers. For example, publishers of children's books and magazines are keenly aware that their offerings must match the needs, wants, and aspirations of particular age groups. At the other end of the scale, an ageing European population is providing a host of new marketing opportunities for the elderly. Fashion, cosmetics, holidays, insurance, and housing are just a few of the product areas that specifically target the older consumer.

In view of the widespread use of demographic variables such as these when segmenting markets, it is not surprising that marketers closely monitor population statistics and trends. Taking an objective view of changes in the population profile allows businesses to assess the attractiveness of the segments they wish to target in the longer term. For example, statistics show that towards the end of the 1990s the proportion of children in the UK will be higher than anywhere else in Europe. This has obvious implications for clothing retailers, toy manufacturers, holiday companies, and leisure operators, which might wish to take advantage of this opportunity. Sales of other products, such as breakfast cereal, freezer foods, and soft drinks, where children are known to influence purchase choice, will also be affected (Sellers 1989). Table 16.2 illustrates the projected

Table 16.2 Population forecasts, 1998–2020 (000)

Country	1998	2000	2005	2010	2015	2020
Austria	8,075	8,137	8,215	8,267	8,305	8,331
Belgium	10,192	10,229	10,297	10,328	10,336	10,338
Denmark	5,295	5,323	5,387	5,451	5,487	5,523
Finland	5,147[a]	5,180	5,218	5,256	—	5,293
France	58,722	59,412	60,642	61,721	62,648	63,453
Germany	82,012[a]	82,182	81,777	81,036	79,864	78,445
Greece	10,486[a]	10,578	10,719	10,791	10,843	10,828
Ireland	3,661[a]	3,618	3,650	3,702	3,757	3,795
Italy	57,461[a]	58,194	57,962	57,135	55,753	54,062
Luxembourg	424[a]	426	443	459	—	488
Netherlands	15,566	15,881	16,349	16,696	—	17,148
Norway	4,418	4,459	4,579	4,648	4,762	5,043
Portugal	9,946[a]	10,595	10,684	10,725	10,704	10,623
Spain	39,371	39,466	39,691	39,799	39,652	39,289
Sweden	8,847	8,894	8,970	9,043	—	9,222
Switzerland	7,097	7,244	7,390	7,443	—	7,553
Turkey	63,747	69,694	79,420	—	—	—
UK	59,009	59,473	60,159	60,798	61,469	62,127

[a] Figure is for 1997.

Source: European Marketing Pocket Book (1999: 12).

demographic profile for Europe. The information in the table also shows how the gender profile is changing. Clothing and cosmetics manufacturers, which operate in markets that might be affected, would do well to ensure that such changes are taken into consideration in future planning.

Demand for many products and services is influenced by marital status and the age and number of children. A young married couple with pre-school age children will spend much of their income on housing, food, and clothing. Their priorities will be to maximize their spending power and they will probably be very concerned with value for money. Older parents, whose children have left home, will be better able to indulge their desire for holidays, leisure activities, and luxury items. Price may not be a key consideration when purchasing certain items. Marketers who understand how the family situation affects consumers' buy-

ing requirements can capitalize by designing marketing mixes to appeal to these differences. For example, large packs of frozen foods, such as oven chips and chicken burgers, provide young families with the value for money they seek, while chilled gourmet meals for two allow older couples to indulge themselves.

The family life cycle concept is designed to take the changing priorities of different households into consideration. The concept is based upon a combination of demographic variables such as age, marital status, and family structure. Various approaches for breaking down the family life cycle have been developed. Perhaps the best known is the scheme described by Wells and Gubar (1966). A modified version of this approach is shown in Box 16.4.

As European trade opens up, race and religion are becoming increasingly important segmenta-

Box 16.4 Stages of the family life cycle

Stage	Financial circumstances and purchasing characteristics
Bachelor stage Young, single, not living at parental home	Few financial burdens, recreation oriented; holiday, entertainment outside home
Newly wed Young couples, no children	Better off financially, two incomes; purchase home, some consumer durables
Full nest I Youngest child under 6	Home-purchasing peak; increasing financial pressures, may have only one income-earner; purchase of household 'necessities'
Full nest II Youngest child over 6	Financial position improving; some working spouses
Full nest III Older married couples with dependent children	Financial position better still; update household products and furnishings
Empty nest I Older married couples, no children at home	Home-ownership peak; renewed interest in travel and leisure activities; buy luxuries
Empty nest II Older couples, no children at home, retired	Drastic cut in income; medical services bought
Solitary survivor Still in labour force	Income good but likely to sell home
Solitary survivor Retired	Special needs for medical care, affection, and security

Source: Hooley and Saunders (1993).

tion variables and marketers are looking for new ways to capitalize on these opportunities. It is interesting to note that the treatment of ethnicity as a segmentation variable differs around the world. In countries where ethnic groups make up a large proportion of the population, businesses often build their marketing programmes around this type of variable. Ethnic marketing is well developed in the USA, where more than a quarter of the population comes from ethnic groups. Companies producing a wide range of products and services actively use ethnicity to target their offerings. For example, the US Hispanic population, comprising those of Central and South American, Cuban, Mexican, and Puerto Rican origins, is very important in a marketing sense. Businesses as diverse as AT&T, Nabisco, and Procter & Gamble have bespoke marketing programmes for this group.

In the UK, where ethnic minorities made up around 5 per cent of the population at the end of the 1990s the use of ethnic marketing is less well developed. However, with the ethnic community expected to double over the next two decades, more direct efforts to target these groups seem likely. Recent Office of National Statistics figures indicate that the buying power of ethnic groups is also set to increase (Clegg 1996; Lyons 1996). For example, by the mid-1990s the UK Pakistani community represented a sizeable marketing opportunity. With around 60 per cent of Pakistani customers under the age of 25, over half of whom occupy managerial or professional positions, the buying power of this group will increase further (Dibb *et al.* 1997).

For companies seeking to capitalize on UK ethnic marketing opportunities, some barriers remain. Ethnic groups are more integrated into the population than in some other countries. This adds complexity to the process of pinpointing particular minorities. Marketers are also concerned that deliberate attempts to target ethnic groups might lead to accusations of racism. However, despite these difficulties, an increase in ethnic marketing seems inevitable, as businesses strive to adapt their offerings to the changing population profile (Dibb *et al.* 1997).

4.1.2 Geographic segmentation

The geographic location of consumers is a widely used segmentation variable. This involves dividing the market into countries, states, regions, counties, cities, towns, or neighbourhoods. There are many circumstances in which location factors affect consumer needs and behaviour. Variations in climate, local terrain, population density, language, and natural resources can all shape consumer requirements. By dividing markets into areas with different needs, businesses can decide on the best combination of regions in which to operate.

Marketing opportunities presented by the EU have increased the use of geographic variables. The use of different languages in different countries clearly affects the marketing of products and services. Businesses such as Coca-Cola and McDonald's design packaging and promotional material to reflect these differences. For manufacturers of other products, climatic variations are important in shaping consumer lifestyle and buying habits. For example, kitchen-appliance manufacturers such as Bosch and Hotpoint must consider the impact of local weather upon product needs throughout Europe. In sunny Portugal and Spain the need for machines with tumble-drying functions is negligible. Washing machine spin speeds are also lower than in the wetter climates of the UK, Belgium, and Germany, where the sale of tumble dryers is higher than ever. Other markets affected by climatic differences include food and beverages, clothing, sports and leisure products, building supplies, and cooling/heating products.

Geographic variables, which help marketers to pinpoint the number of potential customers within a particular area, play an important part in segmenting some markets. When opening new outlets, retailers such as Marks & Spencer, Tesco, and Sainsbury take many geographic factors into consideration. Careful studies of the number of potential consumers within an area, the transport network, and local amenities such as other retailers, offices, schools, and leisure attractions help to ensure that stores are located in areas where consumers will be attracted to shop. Retailers must also consider the likely impact on their other stores within a particular geographic area. One fast-food operator, which will not site branches of its restaurant in cities of less than 100,000 people, also avoids opening a new outlet within five miles of an existing one.

Market density is another useful geographic segmentation variable. This is a measure of the number of potential consumers occupying a particular area of land. For example, in a certain London postal district the proportion of Asian ethnic groups is 40 per cent higher than in a neighbouring district. For businesses trading in Asian food products, this has ramifications for the style of promotional activities and distribution. These activities may be fundamentally different from those adopted in low-density areas.

4.1.3 Geodemographic segmentation

Geodemographic segmentation combines the use of location and demographic variables. Simply defined, *geodemographics* is 'the analysis of people by where they live', sometimes referred to as *locality marketing* (Sleight 1997: 16). This type of segmentation uses census data to develop a neighbourhood classification system. The approach is popular with marketers because it can be easily applied. Geodemographics are attached to a consumer's postcode through the neighbourhood classification. This is attractive, because it tells marketers what their target consumers are like and where to find them. Not surprisingly, the use of geodemographic segmentation is becoming much more widespread. For example, estimates of the value of the British geodemographics market suggest a 70 per cent awareness of leading suppliers and a quadrupling of market value since 1992 (Sleight 1997).

CACI developed the first widely used geodemographic classification system, ACORN (A Classification of Residential Neighbourhoods) groups consumers using census data on location, socioeconomics, and culture. The seventy-nine variables that are used include household size, family structure, occupation, and car ownership. In the UK ACORN identifies six categories of consumers, which can be further subdivided into seventeen groups and fifty-four types. ACORN uses home-address postcodes to classify consumers into one of the types shown in Table 16.3. For example, Expanding (category B) splits into affluent executives, family areas, and well-off workers, family areas.

Other classification systems based on geodemographic data include MOSAIC (from Experien), SuperProfiles (from CDMS), and DEFINE (from Equifax). These systems use between 87 and 150 census variables in combination with additional information such as credit data, employment statistics, insurance ratings, and access to retail outlets. Recently, the use of geodemographic databases has been combined with lifestyle databases to provide an enhanced picture of consumers and the lives they lead. Lifestyle databases contain in-

formation about how individuals live and spend their time. Leisure and sporting activities, musical interests and socializing, house and car ownership, holiday preferences, and food choices are

Table 16.3 Consumer categories in ACORN

Categories	Groups	% Pop.
A Thriving	1 Wealthy achievers, suburban areas	15.1
	2 Affluent greys, rural communities	2.3
	3 Prosperous pensioners, retirement areas	2.3
B Expanding	4 Affluent executives, family areas	3.7
	5 Well-off workers, family areas	7.8
C Rising	6 Affluent urbanites, town and city areas	2.2
	7 Prosperous professionals, metropolitan areas	2.1
	8 Better-off executives, inner-city areas	3.2
D Settling	9 Comfortable middle-agers, mature home-owning areas	13.4
	10 Skilled workers, home-owning areas	10.7
E Aspiring	11 New home-owners, mature communities	9.8
	12 White-collar workers, better-off multi-ethnic areas	4.0
F Striving	13 Older people, less prosperous areas	3.6
	14 Council-estate residents, better-off homes	11.6
	15 Council-estate residents, high unemployment	2.7
	16 Council-estate residents, greatest hardship	2.8
	17 People in multi-ethnic, low-income areas	2.1
Unclassified		0.5

Note: ACORN is a registered trademark of CACI Limited.
Source: CACI Ltd. (1993).

just some of the lifestyle issues that might be included. By combining data on individuals with geodemographic neighbourhoods, a much fuller understanding of consumers is possible.

4.1.4 Socio-economic segmentation

A combination of income, occupation, education, possessions, and ethnic group provides a measure of an individual's socio-economic status. In some markets socio-economic variables have been shown to relate closely to consumers' needs and buying behaviour. This makes segmentation using one or a combination of socio-economic factors popular with many marketers. For example, editorial teams at newspapers and periodicals know that readership is closely linked to socio-economic groupings. In building a profile of readers, it is possible carefully to tailor a publication's content, distribution, pricing, and promotion to appeal to the socio-economic make-up of target consumers. Table 16.4 illustrates the socio-economic classification used by the National Readership Survey.

Sometimes socio-economic status is expressed in terms of an individual's social class. A social class is a group of individuals with similar social rank. The variables used for grouping individuals into social class vary in different parts of the world. For example, in the UK, wealth and income play a greater role in determining a person's class than in Russia, where education and occupation are more valued.

The link between income level and consumer needs is self-evident. Box 16.5 describes how Waterford has developed a lower-priced range of crystal aimed at lower-income consumers. In addition to affecting an individual's ability to buy, a change in income level also alters lifestyle expectations. The aspirations of students graduating from university and beginning full-time employment change rapidly. Their new-found spending power may be reflected in the purchase of a car or in their choice of clothes, food, and luxury goods. An individual's occupation and income level are closely related, so it is not surprising that both affect housing status and, for owner-occupiers, size and location of property. A consumer's occupation also strongly affects their choice of leisure and sporting activities. Social-trends research suggests that professionals are proportionally more likely to spend their leisure time swimming and cycling than skilled manual workers, who prefer snooker, pool, and billiards (*Social Trends* 1996). This makes occupation an obvious segmentation variable for health and sports clubs and leisurewear manufacturers.

4.1.5 Personality and lifestyle segmentation

In some markets personality has proved to be an effective segmentation variable (Weinstein 1994).

Table 16.4 **National readership survey socio-economic groups**

Social grade	Social status	All adults 15+(%)	Occupation
A	Upper middle class	2.9	Higher managerial, administrative or professional
B	Middle class	18.5	Intermediate managerial, administrative or professional
C1	Lower middle class	27.5	Supervisory or clerical, and professional, junior managerial, or administrative
C2	Skilled working class	22.5	Skilled manual workers
D	Working class	16.9	Semi and unskilled manual workers
E	Those at lowest level of subsistence	11.6	State pensioners or widows (no other earner) casual or lowest grade workers
Total		100.0	

Source: Sleight (1997).

Box 16.5 New segment for Waterford crystal

Irish crystal manufacturer Waterford Glass Group acquired the famous chinaware manufacturer Josiah Wedgwood in 1986. The china division became profitable, but the crystal operation suffered a 73 per cent drop in profits. Gradually, there has been an overall recovery, and Waterford Wedgwood is now the world's leading manufacturer of high quality china and glassware. The company is particularly strong in North America, with expanding markets in Japan and Europe. Its products, premium priced giftware, are bought for special occasions or as notable gifts—emotional purchases supported by its strong, reputable brand names. The declining fortunes for the company in the late 1980s/early 1990s forced the company to re-examine its ranges and price levels.

With its new Marquis line targeted at the North American market, the venerable crystal maker has taken a new approach to manufacturing and marketing. Waterford has moved its production into Europe and scaled down its price points, which now start at $30 for smaller pieces, on average 30 per cent cheaper than traditional Waterford lines. Seen by some observers as risky, this new line for 'the less well heeled', manufactured in Germany, Portugal, and parts of the former Yugoslavia, has led to labour unease at Waterford's Irish plants.

In the USA, where Waterford has 28 per cent of the luxury crystal market, 'Marquis by Waterford Crystal' is positioned in the $30–$40 niche (although larger platters and bowls retail at $135) in order to compete more directly with crystal suppliers Mikasa, Lenox, Miller Rogasks, and Gorham. The 1991 launch into thirty stores proved immediately profitable; the question now is how the range can be taken into other territories. Marquis is a huge gamble; it moves the company away from the 'finest hand-crafted Irish' traditions and the Waterford brand heritage, which in the USA and Japan puts it alongside names such as Rolls-Royce and Rolex.

The traditional Wedgwood and Waterford ranges are not generally intended to be day-to-day functional lines. They are premium priced and intended as 'special', lasting purchases. This is an image well cultivated by the company's advertising and public relations and its refusal to become involved in discounting and retailer promotions. Carefully controlled distribution through only leading china/crystal showrooms and department stores further enhances the exclusive branding.

Waterford is striving to build on its roots, while taking its wares into more countries and to a wider audience with its new ranges and lower pricing. In each segment, customers have specific needs and expectations, not always matched by the premium-priced Waterford products. To expand the appeal and sales of a deluxe product without alienating the core target market is no easy task, particularly for such an emotive product as crystal.

Source: Dibb et al. (1997).

The sale of fashion products, make-up, and pop music is all influenced by this variable. However, marketers wishing to use personality as a basis for segmentation must overcome certain difficulties. Complexities, which can be encountered when attempting to measure personality, make it difficult to demonstrate a direct link between this variable and consumer purchase behaviour. Marketers have used a range of personality inventories, such as the Cattell 16-Personality Factor Inventory and the Edwards Person Preference Schedule, to assist with the measurement problem. However, these techniques are taken from the study of psychology and do not work well in marketing applications. The development of more sophisticated measurement instruments, which are specifically tailored to segmentation problems, should help overcome this problem (Lastovicka and Joachimsthaler 1988).

'Lifestyle is a useful tool for segmentation that is not linked to individual concrete products, but transcends a class of products.' (Chapter 6, p. 124)

Lifestyle segmentation, which involves grouping consumers in terms of how they live their lives and spend their time, uses many personality variables (see Insert). For example, the 1997 launch by

Lifestyles influence choice of cars

Research shows that Japanese consumers are increasingly choosing their cars according to their lifestyles. Honda, for example, launched in 1996, amongst others, separate models targeted at women, the elderly, and the rich in their late thirties and forties.

United Distillers of Tony's Freezer Cocktails clearly identified the 'fun girls' night in' as a new opportunity. The drinks business developed an entirely new type of product: different varieties of ready-made cocktails in foil packets designed to freeze. Tony's Freezer Cocktails are designed to appeal to 21–35-year-old women enjoying an evening at home together. The £1.4 million campaign budget devoted to the launch had three objectives: to demonstrate how to use the product, to show when it might be consumed, and to develop a fun brand personality (*Marketing*, 25 Sept. 1997).

Lifestyle segmentation has been developed in order to make personality variables more relevant to marketing. The technique used to measure both lifestyle and personality is known as psychographics. Lifestyle analysis is based on three groups of variables. The first group concerns an individual's activities: work and professional activities, travel and holidays, shopping and housework, family and community activities, leisure and sporting pursuits, and education and religious activities. Interests form the second group of variables. These may relate to a person's job or achievements, home life, family, leisure activities, food, or fashion. The third group concerns an individual's opinions about a variety of areas including moral, social, environmental, political, economic, education, cultural, and other issues (Plummer 1974).

Questionnaires, which are used to measure lifestyle, contain a wide range of questions on these issues. Statistical analysis of the questionnaires can then be used to segment consumers. The underlying logic is that consumers who spend their time in the same ways and share similar opinions will demonstrate similar product needs and buying behaviour. For example, lifestyle segmentation has been successfully applied in the shampoo market. The launch during the 1980s of combined shampoo and conditioner products was clearly targeted at consumers with busy lives, wishing to minimize the time spent washing their hair. The success of this launch is clear from the size of the sector that has developed.

4.1.6 Segmenting using behavioural variables

Many marketers believe that behavioural variables are particularly effective for identifying segments. Segmenting using behavioural variables involves grouping consumers according to how they buy, use, and feel about products. For example,

ample, research into tea consumption has revealed that most consumers no longer prepare the beverage in a teapot. Instead, they place a single teabag directly into their cup and add hot water. Unfortunately, these consumers often find that the teabags drip when taken out of the cup. Now manufacturer Tetley has devised a new teabag design to appeal directly to these consumers. The bag features two drawstrings that are meant to ensure that when it is removed the liquid all drains into the cup.

4.1.7 Purchase behaviour

Marketers can distinguish between consumers on the basis of purchase behaviour. The loyalty status of consumers is a particularly important aspect of purchase behaviour. Different shoppers can be grouped in terms of their loyalty status. Analysis of shopping panel data indicates that consumers vary in their level of loyalty for different products. While some individuals are totally loyal to a particular brand, others are less so, switching among a number of different brands. This is important for marketers to understand, because brand-loyal consumers may require a different treatment from brand-switchers.

Many businesses attempt to increase consumer loyalty, because this helps to stabilize their sales over time. This is achieved by specifically targeting consumers with marketing programmes that are designed to encourage loyalty. Fashion brands Planet and Alexon reward loyal consumers with discounts off future purchases. In recent years the popularity of loyalty schemes has increased. Many food retailers, department stores, and fashion brands have launched programmes to encourage consumer loyalty. Tesco's loyalty card is typical. Consumers present their card to be swiped when paying for their shopping. The higher the spend, the greater the number of points awarded. The system retains a tally of the collected points, and consumers are mailed with money-off vouchers on a quarterly basis.

Some loyalty schemes attempt to build relationships with consumers, going beyond the programmes based on a simple reward system. For example, manufacturers of fine china and porcelain, such as Doulton and Wedgewood, run collectors' clubs. In addition to product discounts, special events are organized for members and there are opportunities to buy limited-edition items not on offer to the general public. Manufacturers believe that schemes that emphasize the relationship aspects are more likely to be enduring. This helps deal with concerns that the effectiveness of reward-based systems is difficult to maintain in the long term.

4.1.8 Purchase and usage occasion

The occasion on which a consumer decides to make a purchase, buys, or uses a product is a widely used segmentation variable. Emergency plumbers and electricians who provide a twenty-four-hour call-out facility are able to charge a premium price because consumers who use them have an urgent problem needing attention. A householder suffering the mess and disruption of a burst water pipe is unlikely to haggle about price. The primary concern is to get the pipe fixed as quickly as possible. By contrast, the same householder having a new central heating system fitted may invest considerable time and effort seeking the most competitively priced offer.

The creative use of purchase-occasion segmentation can help businesses identify market-development opportunities. Breakfast cereal and ice cream are just two products that have particular usage connotations. Yet, in both cases, the use of creative marketing has broadened the usage of these products. The advertising of Kellogg's has emphasized that cornflakes can be consumed throughout the day, not just for breakfast. Ice-cream manufacturers such as Häagen-Dazs have developed consumer perceptions and consumption behaviour. The enjoyment of ice cream is no longer confined to families enjoying hot weather and holidays. Instead, the product represents an indulgence for all ages, to be consumed at any time of the day, in a variety of circumstances, throughout the year. Supermarket freezers are crammed with a range of brands offering the latest delicious flavours.

The usage occasion for a product or service can also provide a powerful means of segmentation because it often has a significant impact on the benefits and features that consumers require. For example, drinks and some food products are specifically packaged to be suitable for the situation in which they will be consumed. SmithKline Beecham offers its Ribena product for sale in a range of formats: consumers can buy various types of ready-to-drink Ribena in small cans, cartons, or bottles. The original concentrated version of the drink is still available in large glass or plastic bottles. Consumers select the Ribena package to match their usage situation.

4.1.9 Benefit segmentation

Many businesses use the benefits that consumers seek from products as the basis for their segmentation approach. As shown in Box 16.6, this segmentation approach was first applied in the toothpaste market, where it was used to identify four consumer segments, each seeking a distinctive range of benefits (Haley 1968, 1984). For example, the *sociables*, a group dominated by teenagers and young

---

Box 16.6 Benefit segmentation in the toothpaste market

Segment name	The sensory segment	The sociables	The worriers	The independent segment
Principal benefit	Flavour, product appearance	Brightness of teeth	Decay prevention	Price
Demographics	Children	Teens, young people	Large families	Men
Favoured brands	Colgate, Stripe	Macleans, Plus White, Ultra Brite	Crest	Brands on sale
Personality	High self-involvement	High sociability	High hypochondria	High autonomy
Lifestyle	Hedonistic	Active	Conservative	Value oriented
Behavioural characteristics	Users of spearmint flavour	Smokers	Heavy users	Heavy users

Source: Haley (1968).

people, were primarily concerned with the brightness of their teeth. This highly sociable and active segment contained a relatively high proportion of smokers, who preferred brands such as Ultrabrite, which emphasized bright, white teeth.

Marketers who use this segmentation approach must be able to identify the key benefits that consumers seek from a particular product type and understand which of these consumers require which benefits. Marketing research may be needed to build the in-depth understanding that underlies this approach.

4.1.10 User status and consumption behaviour

Markets are sometimes segmented on the basis of user status. For example, Nestlé is able to group consumers according to their user status for Nescafé Gold Blend. Individuals can be grouped into regular users, occasional users, first-time users, ex-users, potential users, or non-users. The business may then decide to develop bespoke marketing programmes for one or more of these segments. The loyalty of regular users may be reinforced with a television advertising campaign, which re-establishes the coffee's brand values. Occasional and potential users might be encouraged through on-pack sales promotions. Further information may be sought on non-users. This might help Nestlé to separate users of other brands from those who simply do not drink coffee.

User status is connected to consumers' consumption patterns for products. Consumers can be grouped into heavy, medium, or light users. For marketers, the attractiveness of these different groups will vary. A marketing programme that entices a small number of heavy users away from a competing brand may be more attractive than one that converts a larger number of light users. For this reason, consumption behaviour may be an important segmentation factor in some markets.

Different marketing programmes may be needed for heavy, medium, or light users. For example, consumers become accustomed to discounts for heavy usage of a particular product. Competitively priced family packs are among the products geared to such households. During the 1980s, consumer demand for family-sized value packs reached a point where many of the packages of cleaning consumables were unwieldy and difficult to handle. The industry responded with new 'micro' products, which took up less space and could be contained in smaller pack sizes than previously. A new generation of micro washing powders and floor cleaners, including brands such as Persil Micro and Jif Micro liquid, was born.

4.1.11 Product attitudes

Consumers' attitudes play an important role in shaping purchase and consumption behaviour. Manufacturers striving to stay in touch with consumer priorities increasingly use product-attitude segmentation. The rising power of the consumer movement (individuals, groups, and organizations seeking to protect consumer rights) has been an important contributory factor. Adverse publicity about environmental damage and intensive factory farming are two areas where changing consumer attitudes have yielded marketing opportunities.

The BSE crisis in the 1990s in cattle raised consumer concerns about food safety. Manufacturers and retail outlets have responded by offering shoppers a wide range of organic and free-range products from which to choose. For example, consumers can elect to buy organic carrots and potatoes to accompany their free-range roast pork. Although some of these products command a price premium, the increasing selection on offer suggests that many shoppers are prepared to pay the extra. Anchor butter has recently been promoted on the basis that the milk from which it is made comes from cows that are allowed to graze freely.

It is difficult to predict changes in consumer attitudes. Public concern about alcopops, the fur trade, and passive smoking have each resulted in changing consumer behaviour. Businesses remaining in touch with consumer feeling are more likely to respond quickly to such changes.

4.2 Segmentation variables for business-to-business customers

The principles of segmentation are equally applicable in organizational or business-to-business markets (Wind and Cardozo 1974). As in consumer markets, the choice of segmentation variables is diverse (see Insert overleaf). Some of these variables are the same as for consumer markets—others are specific to the business-to-business context. A car component manufacturer, for example, may subdivide the garages that make up its customer base in terms of demographic factors, such as size and geographic locations; situational

Segmenting the haulage market

One large UK based haulage company initially segments its market in the following way:

- rental (short term);
- contract hire (where the vehicle is painted with the customer's name, etc., but the company provides the driver, maintenance, etc.);
- haulage;
- service (maintenance, rescue, etc., for other companies' vehicles).

It then cross categories these segments by the customer's industry—e.g. fresh food, furniture, etc.

☞ 'Customers have to be segmented on the basis of their distribution needs and requirements. This is particularly so in business-to-business markets, where the impact of order size and company size can dramatically affect the level of customer service demanded of the manufacturer or supplier.'   (Chapter 11, p. 255)

issues, such as the purchase urgency or order size; or even the characteristics of their buying behaviour. Just as in consumer markets, the approach adopted should result in customer groups that demonstrate homogeneous needs and buying requirements. In some circumstances it makes sense to use a combination of segmentation variables. For example, a construction-equipment manufacturer divides its customers first on the basis of country, then in terms of industry area, and finally on the basis of required product type. Thus German civil engineers buying mini-excavators would be one segment.

As in consumer markets, some segmentation bases are easier to use than others (Bonoma and Shapiro 1983). For example, demographic factors, such as company size, location, and industry code (SIC), can be objectively pinpointed and measured with ease. For example, when Loctite developed a new industrial adhesive applicator that would improve operators' working conditions, it knew which industries used industrial adhesives and therefore which companies were potential purchasers. However, only a number of the firms in these industries were likely to be sufficiently concerned with their employees' welfare to incur the cost of buying the new applicator. There was no easy and inexpensive way of identifying which of these firms would fall into this category of 'caring employers'. Attempting to assess the characteristics of buying behaviour of customers is altogether more difficult to do. Not surprisingly, variables that are easiest to apply tend to be widely used. In Box 16.7, which illustrates the sorts of variables that can be used, the variables at

Box 16.7 Segmentation variables for business markets

Personal characteristics
Demographics, personality, and lifestyle of buying centre, buyer–seller similarity, attitudes to risk, loyalty to suppliers

Situational factors
Purchase urgency, order size, product application

Purchasing approach
Buying centre structure (centralized/decentralized), buying policies (sealed bidding, service contracts, leasing), nature of existing relationships (focus on new or existing customers), balance of power among decision-makers, buying criteria (quality, delivery, service, price, product range, innovation)

Operating variables
Technologies used, user status (heavy, medium, light), customer capabilities

Demographics
Business age, location, industry (SIC code) size

Source: Dibb *et al.* (1997), see also Bonoma and Shapiro (1983).

the base of the steps are the easiest to use, while those at the top are the most difficult.

4.2.1 Business demographics

It is no surprise that segmentation variables such as business type, industry, size, and geographic location are among the most widely used in organizational markets. They are simple to understand and relatively easy to quantify, and, in many cases, data are readily available.

The Standard Industrial Classification (SIC) system categorizes businesses according to industry area. The UK system, which is administered by the Central Statistics Office, groups businesses into ten categories (Box 16.8). Each category is further divided into classes, groups, and activity headings. These provide a useful categorization for businesses seeking to segment customers on the basis of type of product or service handled. For example, a regional accountancy company segments its customers into several groups: hotels, farms, coach operators, and construction companies. The company is able to tailor the service offered to suit the requirement of clients within each group.

Business size affects the approach to purchasing, as well as the quantity and characteristics of products required. A hairdresser who visits clients in their own homes buys a relatively small amount of hair-care products on an informal basis. All aspects of the purchasing decision rest with the hairdresser herself. By contrast, an international hairdressing chain, such as Vidal Sassoon, has a much more structured buying approach. A group

---

Box 16.8 UK Standard Industrial Classification (SIC)

0 Agriculture, forestry, and fishing
1 Energy and water-supply industries
2 Extraction of minerals and ores (excluding fuels); manufacture of metals, mineral products, and chemicals
3 Metal goods, engineering, and vehicles
4 Other manufacturing industries
5 Construction
6 Distribution, hotels/catering; repairs
7 Transport and communication
8 Banking, finance, insurance, business services, and leasing
9 Other services

---

of individuals is involved in the purchase of a large amount of different product types.

Geographic segmentation sometimes develops in response to regional concentration of industries. For example, some businesses are reliant upon natural resources. Thus manufacturers of oil-extraction equipment must structure their sales force to reflect the location of world oil reserves. This is reflected in the structure of their sales force. Other businesses, such as computer manufacture, shipbuilding, car manufacture, and banking, require workforces with specialist skills. This skill requirement often leads to regional concentration of these businesses. For example, London and Zurich are associated with banking, the West Midlands with car manufacture, and the Rühr Valley with heavy industry.

4.2.2 Operating variables

Segmentation approaches that use operating variables are based on differences in usage rate, customer capability, or technology applied. How a business uses products directly affects the type of purchases made. Chemical manufacturer DuPont sells large quantities of titanium dioxide to customers whose uses of the product are diverse. These differences in product usage provide a segmentation opportunity, with DuPont modifying the product specification to suit the varying customer needs.

A white powder little known by most consumers appears as a core ingredient in all paints, inks, and most plastics: TiO_2 or titanium dioxide, produced from ilmenite and synthetic rutile. With plants focused primarily in North America, Europe, Australia, and Southern Africa, the market is dominated by America's DuPont. For this commodity product used in the production process for so many materials, continuity of supply and purity of the pigment are important considerations. Customers are quite diverse, ranging from international masterbatch companies requiring long production runs (perhaps producing packaging or film products) to PVC and linoleum flooring manufacturers, marine engineers producing boat mouldings, the paint giants ICI Dulux and Crown, and the manufacturers of road marking paints! The task facing DuPont varies according to which type of customer the company is dealing with. The key customer needs in such a market will vary and may include product consistency over time and through production runs, guarantee of supply, and long-term supplier relationships with reputable companies (Coeyman 1994; Fairly 1995; Shearer 1995; Dibb *et al.*, 1997: 161–2).

4.2.3 Purchasing approach

Appraising a customer's purchasing approach is difficult to achieve, yet this may be a rewarding route for businesses that persevere. Purchasing policies, structure/characteristics of the buying centre, and buying criteria can all affect customers' product requirements. For example, a manufacturer of computer components seeking new customers must establish whether buying is centralized or decentralized. It must find out where the buying power lies in the organization and whether the business favours relationships with existing suppliers. Each of these variables can influence the customers' buying needs and behaviour and may therefore be an appropriate segmentation basis.

An organization's purchasing criteria can be a powerful segmentation approach. Quality, delivery, service, price, product range, and innovation can each form the basis of a segmentation approach. For example, providers of courier services such as DHL, TNT, and Federal Express have segmentation strategies that focus on customers' delivery requirements. A standard service, taking 48 hours or more is usually available for businesses requiring competitively priced routine delivery. In circumstances where overnight delivery is essential, customers are often prepared to pay a premium price.

4.2.4 Situational factors

It is sometimes appropriate to segment business customers in terms of situational factors such as urgency or order size. As the following example shows, urgency can have a significant impact upon the importance that customers attach to particular product or service features.

An example for segmenting by situational variables comes from the field of information retrieval. This is a highly complex industry in which users differ sharply in regard to the kind of information needed and in regard to the speed with which they need it delivered. Military and medical specialists are two groups that seek instant information. When lives are at stake, every second is crucial. In contrast, archivists are content with information delivered a few days late (Gross *et al.* 1993: 209).

4.2.5 Personal characteristics

Although their effects will not be as great as in consumer markets, the personal characteristics of those involved in buying do impact upon purchase choice. For instance, the demographic profile, lifestyle, and personality of catering staff will affect the selection of menus for a work's canteen. In such cases it is particularly important to establish where the power in the buying centre lies. Thus, if much of the buying power rests with a vegetarian manager, it is likely that consideration for non-meat eaters will be high.

5 Segmentation analysis

SEGMENTATION analysis requires a range of data about a market, customers buying products within it, and competitors who vie for their business. Marketers use research to collect this kind of data. Research therefore plays an important role in developing segments. The data used in segmentation analysis originate from a mix of in-company and external sources. For example, company sales and service records are common sources of internal data. In some circumstances businesses do not have access to all of the data they need. Sometimes additional market information is acquired from specialist agencies. In other cases marketing research will be used to fill information gaps. Businesses undertaking research may choose either to carry it out by themselves or to engage a consultancy with specialist research expertise.

Whether a company undertakes its own research or uses a specialist consultancy, segmentation analysis involves a series of stages (Maier and Saunders 1990). As with any data-collection exercise, the process must begin with clearly stated research objectives. Marketers must be entirely sure of the underlying reasons for the research. Once these objectives have been set, decisions about the research approach and data required must be taken. A combination of qualitative and quantitative data is often used. Qualitative research is often used to build a detailed understanding of customers' attitudes, motives, and behaviour. Depth interviews, involving a detailed one-to-one discussion between interviewer and respondent, are commonly used. Focus groups, in which between eight and ten customers have a discussion structured by a moderator, are also frequently used. Quantitative research may also be used: a larger sample is employed to examine the most important customer characteristics and requirements. A research instrument, such as a questionnaire, will be developed that is more structured than any used in qualitative research. Personal or mail interviews will typically be used to administer the questionnaire.

Analysis follows the data-collection stage. Various statistical approaches can be used to analyse data and identify segments. Factor analysis, cluster analysis, and conjoint analysis are just a few of the more commonly used techniques. Multidimensional scaling (MDS), as explained later, is widely adopted in product-positioning studies. Although it is beyond the scope of this chapter to provide a detailed review of suitable statistical approaches for segmentation analysis, marketers need to approach this area with caution. Complex multivariate techniques, such as cluster analysis, are best handled by statistical experts. Inexperienced users may be unfamiliar with the rules and tests that must be applied if reliable and rigorous results are to be produced. For instance, cluster analysis will produce a solution containing segments irrespective of whether any really exist (Aldenderfer and Blashfield 1984). Special tests can be used to ensure that the segments identified are genuine.

The widespread availability of computer software offers easy access to statistical analysis. However, unskilled researchers should be wary of packages promising instant segmentation solutions. Considerable investment may be made on the basis of segmentation analysis, with businesses deciding which customers to target and allocating marketing resources. If the rigour of the segmentation analysis is in doubt, the risks being taken can be substantial. Despite these problems, there are considerable benefits for marketers who learn about these approaches. Diamantopoulos and Schlegelmilch (1997) provide an excellent introduction to statistical analysis that is ideal for the uninitiated. Wind's (1978) review of segmentation research is still regarded as a classic.

6 Targeting

TARGETING decisions involve a business making choices about the segment(s) on which re-

sources are to be focused. Most organizations do not have the resources, products, or inclination to target lots of segments. There are three major targeting strategies that can be followed: the undifferentiated strategy, the concentrated strategy, and the differentiated strategy. Fig. 16.1 illustrates the three approaches. The choice of strategy must be made with care. Businesses that select segments covering only a small part of the market may not reach their sales and profitability targets. Those choosing segments covering too great a part of the market may not have the resources to serve them adequately.

The process of targeting involves taking a balanced view of company resources and capabilities. This will help determine the number of segments to which the business should commit resources. The selection of segments to target must also be based on a careful assessment of current and potential attractiveness. Thus, in the market for instant coffee, the low number of competitors offering decaffeinated brands could make health-conscious consumers requiring these products an attractive segment to target.

Targeting also means making conscious decisions not to seek business from certain segments, as to do so may distract the company from offering the very best product to those segments it has chosen to target (see Insert). This does not usually mean that potential customers from other segments are rejected but that no particular effort is made to attract them. There are even companies that will not take customers who do not fall within their specified segments as they fear that their presence may negatively influence the

---

'There's nothing wrong with kiddies clubs but . . .'

When asked why he did not offer discounts or special services for children, a package tour company's boss replied: 'We've decided that what we are selling is vacations for grown-ups—good, simple tour packages for individuals or couples. Children's clubs don't fit into that strategy. I don't care about all the families with children who pass us by, as long as we've decided that we want to do business with another category of customer and are willing to go the extra mile for them.'

Source: Carlzon (1987).

Figure 16.1 **Targeting strategies**

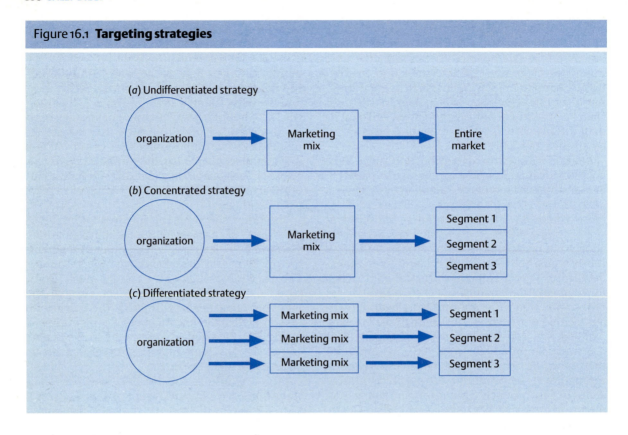

6.1 Strategies for targeting

6.1.1 Undifferentiated strategy

Businesses adopting an undifferentiated targeting strategy have decided to target an entire market with a single marketing mix (see Fig. 16.1(a)). There may be a number of reasons for adopting such a strategy. The business may consider that customers' differences in product needs and buying behaviour are relatively insignificant and that a standard marketing mix can readily satisfy potential customers. In such cases marketers will attempt to develop an offering that is close to the requirements of most of the market's customers. An alternative argument, though one that is difficult to justify, is that the business has sufficient resources to sustain only one marketing mix. In such circumstances, savings in production, R&D, personnel, and marketing costs may be achieved.

Despite the short-term cost savings an undifferentiated strategy may bring, marketers are increasingly dubious about this approach. Most accept that the diversity of customer needs, wants, and expectations means that very few markets can be served satisfactorily with a single product offering. Even in traditionally undifferentiated markets, it is difficult to develop a product and marketing programme that satisfies most customers. The development of a product like cook-

company's image. Thus a number of scent manufacturers will not sell their products to supermarkets that specialize in price-cutting, as they fear that having their product sold in shops with cut-price images will destroy the élite image they have created for their product.

ing oil is a good example. During the 1970s consumers were offered quite a constrained choice of oils for frying. In the health-conscious 1990s, supermarket shelves entice shoppers with oils derived from corn, sunflower, oil-seed rape, olive, and grape seed as well as a host of mixed vegetable oils. What has happened to bring about this change? The answer is that consumer requirements have moved on. The public has become aware of the benefits of a low-fat diet and food preparation practices have changed. The demand for low-cholesterol products has increased, hence the wide variety of products available.

The cooking-oil example demonstrates how the success of an undifferentiated strategy is affected by the product life cycle. As markets mature, customer needs become more diverse and the number of competitors increases. In such circumstances an undifferentiated strategy would mean the neglect of certain customers' needs. Thus market segmentation can be used to help increase customer satisfaction, by shrewdly honing a marketing-mix programme to the needs and expectations of a separate homogeneous group of customers, or several separate marketing mixes to several targeted segments.

6.1.2 Concentrated strategy

With a concentrated strategy, a business directs its marketing effort towards a single segment (see Fig. 16.1(*b*)). The business is able to specialize, to design its product and marketing effort specifically for customers within this chosen segment. The emphasis on a single group of customers allows the business to invest its entire resources in building an excellent understanding of the segment. Marketing programmes can then be fine-tuned to match closely the needs and wants of these customers. For prestige names, such as Chanel, Harrods, and Rolls-Royce, a concentration strategy ensures that the brand positioning is absolutely clear. Customers expect to pay the premium prices associated with these brands, because they reflect the quality and image they are purchasing. These high-income customers would probably be unhappy to see the launch of a cut-price range of Chanel clothing, just as they would not expect Rolls-Royce to advertise in tabloid newspapers. The success that these companies enjoy illustrates that sufficient sales volume is sometimes available to businesses focusing on a

single segment. This concentration of marketing effort may allow a company to avoid the attention of larger competitors operating in other segments. This also explains why a concentration strategy is sometimes used to gain access to new markets. New businesses without the resources to take on larger competitors often find this is a particularly effective route.

By definition, a concentration strategy encourages businesses to focus their resources, yet in some circumstances such an approach is risky. A period of low sales, due perhaps to increased competition or the decline of a segment, can have devastating financial repercussions. Successful concentration can also lead to intransigence. Businesses may become too familiar with their specialization and avoid developing other areas of expertise. This short-sighted approach can leave a business ill-prepared for market changes. Marketers engaged in a concentration strategy, no matter how attractive the segment appears, should always ensure that the business has other opportunities and is ready to act swiftly if a segment's fortunes change.

6.1.3 Differentiated (multi-segment) strategy

An organization that adopts a differentiated strategy (see Fig. 16.1(*c*)) targets its marketing effort at two or more segments, developing a separate marketing mix for each. For some businesses a differentiated strategy develops naturally from an effective concentration strategy. For example, the energy drink Lucozade originally targeted consumers who were unwell and needed a pick-me-up. Targeting sportsmen and women, who also needed a quick energy boost, was a natural progression. In some cases, businesses have excess production capacity that can usefully be used by moving into new segments.

A differentiated strategy is attractive because it gives businesses access to a greater number of customers. This often leads to a rise in sales. For example, business travellers are vital to airlines such as British Airways, Virgin Atlantic, and Lufthansa. They travel business/club class, take regular trips, and may become loyal to a particular airline. In order to encourage loyalty, major airlines have set up business travel clubs. Members collect points each time they travel, which can subsequently be exchanged for free travel and merchandise. Some airlines also offer members special lounge facilities at major airports. Although business people who travel regularly are an attractive segment for the airlines, holiday travellers are also an important target. These customers may not travel as frequently as business travellers and may be more concerned about price, seeking good-value economy flights or packaged deals. The different requirements of these two customer groups mean that separate marketing programmes are needed for each.

From a resource viewpoint, a differentiated strategy is more expensive than a concentrated approach. Serving more than one segment increases the costs of R&D, production, sales, and marketing activities. Thus, when Lucozade moved into the sports-drink segment, investment was required in developing the drink's appearance, packaging, taste, and ingredients. Production costs (processes, material, and people) also increased. Marketing costs have risen to reflect the new promotional and distribution requirements.

6.2 Selecting target segments

Businesses choosing either a concentrated or a differentiated targeting strategy must engage in a process of segment selection. During this process the business must balance its resources and capabilities against the attractiveness of different segments. Nintendo and Sega are able to exploit new computer-game opportunities because they have the necessary technological expertise and financial resources to invest. For smaller competitors without this specialist know-how and financial backing, even the most attractive new segments are not accessible.

Segment attractiveness involves an assessment of which market segments offer the best potential for the business. Measures of segment size, growth rate, and profit potential should all be considered (Doyle 1995; Proctor 1996). Increasing car ownership might indicate that petrol retailing is an attractive market to enter. However, small independent companies are being driven out of business because low margins hit their profitability. The level of within-segment competition also affects attractiveness. Marketers should undertake careful competitor analysis to reveal the size and aggressiveness of this threat. This should focus on both existing and potential competitors. The rapid entry of Daewoo into the UK car market starkly illustrates the dangers of considering current competitors alone. It is important to consider also the impact that substitute products might have upon segment potential. The popularity of Tamagotchi cyber pets at the end of 1997 affected sales of other kinds of hand-held computer games. Environmental factors, such as legal restrictions and regulations, are another important consideration in determining segment attractiveness. The recent ban on cigarette advertising at sports events has constrained the promotional flexibility of tobacco companies. There is a real possibility that sales of tobacco will suffer as a result.

An assessment of business capabilities and resources helps establish whether there is a good fit between a company and the segments it wishes to target. This involves a business reviewing its exploitable marketing assets (e.g. brand name, marketing skills, sales force), managerial capabilities and commitment, cost advantages and technological edge. Such a review can help a business make tough decisions about which of the attractive segments to enter and which to ignore. For example, marketers may reject a segment because it does not fit with the long-term objectives of the business. In other companies, marketers may make deliberate decisions to pursue new kinds of opportunity. British Gas, Tesco, and Virgin are all examples of businesses that are currently diversifying into new markets. British Gas is attempting to take advantage of changes in the electricity market by repositioning itself as an energy company that sells both gas and electricity. The company, in common with Tesco and Virgin, is also moving into the crowded financial-services market. Which of these businesses enjoy success in their new ventures will depend on a mix of factors. Brand strength and flexibility are essential. Virgin has already successfully made the transition from record labels to airline and cola-maker. British Gas, so closely associated in consumers' minds with the supply of gas, may find the switch into electricity sales reasonably straightforward. The move into financial services may be more difficult to achieve. As a general rule, businesses are more likely to be successful when moving into segments that are close to their existing brands or area of expertise. Thus the move by Mars into the ice-cream market was considerably assisted by the company's existing profile as a confectionery provider, with established channels of distribution already in place.

Fig. 16.2 provides a simple checklist of issues

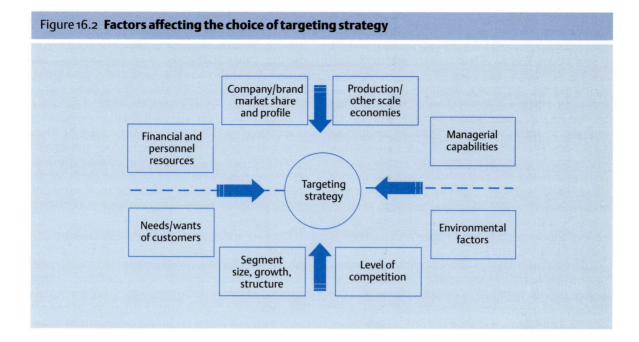

Figure 16.2 **Factors affecting the choice of targeting strategy**

that marketers should consider when making targeting decisions. A comprehensive summary of this issue can be found in Hooley and Saunders (1993).

7 Positioning

THE positioning stage of market segmentation follows logically from the segmentation and targeting components (see Box 16.2). Once segments have been identified and targeting decisions made, a company must position its product, service, or idea to the target segment. Positioning is the place that the target group of customers perceive the product occupying in the market, relative to its competition. Customer perceptions about the product are central to its positioning (Ries and Trout 1986; Trout and Rivkin 1996). It is also about how the product compares, in the customer's mind, with competing offerings. For instance, Rolex watches epitomize expense and quality, Timex timepieces offer value for money, and Swatch watches are vibrant fashion accessories. Each watch brand stands apart.

Positioning provides a link between the target marketing strategy and the marketing mix that is developed. It represents the image or perception that the business will communicate to customers. American Express has developed a clear positioning for its range of charge and credit cards. Consumers understand that the Amex Gold Card is aimed at a different segment from the standard card. An unambiguous marketing communications programme has clarified these consumer perceptions.

Positioning is not confined to tangible products; it can be related to a service, organization, individual, or institution. The process begins with the product, then creates a position that communicates the image of the product in the customers' minds. The image will be backed up by a combination of product name, packaging, design, styling, price, promotion, and distribution. However, fundamentally a brand's positioning is established in the minds of targeted customers through marketing communications and promotional activity. For example, Unilever has recently agreed a sponsorship deal with Sky TV designed to reinforce the positioning of Persil. The deal will see the Persil brand sponsoring the latest series of the popular medical drama ER. A Unilever spokeswoman said 'the programme's theme of outstanding performance and care are totally in keeping with Persil's brand values. We will also be able to communicate with a key target audience of younger viewers' (*Marketing*, 23 Oct. 1997). Positioning is also affected by customer perceptions of the company behind the product. Mercedes has had to act quickly to stem consumer disquiet following safety concerns about its new A Class supermini. Product tests revealed a propensity for the supermini to roll over. Production was temporarily suspended and vehicles recalled so that the problem could be dealt with. The company will need to monitor customer perceptions to measure the extent of the damage to the brand (*Coventry Evening Telegraph*, 25 Nov. 1997).

The position that a product occupies is shaped by existing brands in the market. It is widely accepted that customers first assign a position to the best-known or market-leading brand. This position is usually the standard against which other brands are compared. For example, in the market for fast food, perceptions tend to be orientated around McDonald's. Businesses need to be aware that customers compare brands when making buying decisions and that marketing activity must reflect this. According to Dibb and Simkin (1996: 17), 'product positioning centres on the decision and activities used to create and maintain a firm's product concept in the customers' minds. Market positioning is arranging for a product to occupy a clear, distinctive and desirable place—relative to competing products—in the minds of target customers.'

To summarize, effective positioning means ensuring that the product or service satisfies key customer requirements and that this is clearly communicated to customers. The product's positioning in relation to competing brands must also be readily apparent. A brand must be differentiated and stand out *vis-à-vis* rival's products or services in the eyes of targeted customers.

7.1 Using perceptual mapping

Perceptual mapping is a tool that helps marketers to understand customer perceptions of different products or brands in the market. The approach combines a range of statistical and psychological techniques to generate visual maps that illustrate customer perceptions. Positioning maps provide useful guidance for marketers involved in developing products and marketing programmes. The market image that they reveal can help with positioning decisions for new products or with repositioning existing brands. Both the number and nature of the dimensions used in the positioning map will vary. The choice of dimensions will be influenced by the key requirements of potential customers. In their simplest format, positioning maps have two dimensions. Thus sales of furniture are strongly affected by pricing and quality issues. In this market, a basic positioning map with dimensions relating to price (high versus low) and quality (good versus not so good) might give a perfectly acceptable overview of consumer perceptions.

The two-dimensional map provides a simplistic view of a market. Although this may be appropriate for simple, low-involvement purchases, more complex buying decisions will involve a large number of issues being considered. For example, a family involved in buying a car must consider a wide range of issues including price, rate of depreciation, service, running and insurance costs, size, number of doors, colour, body shape, additional features, safety features, security, brand image, and so on. A statistical technique called multidimensional scaling can be used to generate perceptual maps with many dimensions (Davies and Brooks 1989). Compare the hypothetical two- and multidimensional maps for medium-size family saloon cars in Figs. 16.3 and 16.4.

7.2 Steps in determining positioning

Because positioning is determined by customer perceptions, businesses do not have total control over it. However, businesses with realistic expectations can and should take an active role in shaping these all-important perceptions. The mystique that sometimes surrounds positioning is misplaced. Planning a positioning requires a combination of honesty, common sense, and a clear process. A simple step-by-step approach can be used to develop a clear positioning for a product (Dibb *et al.* 1997).

■ *Step 1.* Define the segments in the market under consideration. A combination of existing information and marketing research will help determine how the segments are defined. A new coach operator seeking to enter the travel market might decide to segment on the basis of reason for

Figure 16.3 **Two-dimensional map**

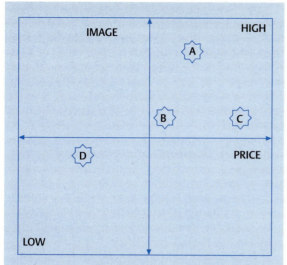

Cars A, B, C, and D are positioned on the map according to consumer perceptions of their relative price and image

Figure 16.4 **Multidimensional map**

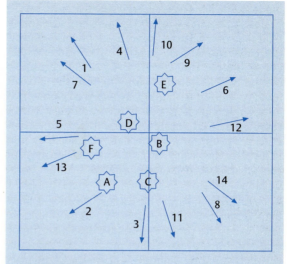

1 Good value
2 Trendy brand image
3 Low depreciation
4 Low service costs
5 Low running costs
6 Good security
7 Good safety features
8 Poor value
9 Untrendy brand image
10 High depreciation
11 High service costs
12 High running costs
13 Poor security
14 Poor safety features

travel (for example, work, shopping, holiday, day trips).

■ *Step 2.* Decide which segment or combination of segments to target. Targeting decisions must be based on a careful analysis of company resources/capabilities and segment attractiveness. Analysing the current and future potential of segments is particularly important. The coach operator described in Step 1 may decide that the 'day-trip' segment offers the best potential.

■ *Step 3.* Develop a clear understanding of the needs and expectations of target customers. It will be necessary to understand the key product needs and benefits that customers seek from the product in question. For instance, for the coach operator the key customer needs may be location of stations/pick-up points, range of routes, and price.

■ *Step 4.* Ensure that the product matches the needs and expectations identified. Marketing research plays an important role in ensuring a fit between new or modified products and customer requirements. Thus the coach operator would need to investigate the sorts of locations that 'day-trip' customers might like to visit.

■ *Step 5.* Evaluate the positioning and images, as perceived by the targeted customers, of competing products in the selected market segment or segments. A positioning map can be developed as a visual aid. The dimensions of the map should correspond with key customer needs identified in Step 3. This would require the coach operator to evaluate the offerings of competing providers, remembering that competitors might also include train operators, taxi companies, and privately owned vehicles.

■ *Step 6.* Select an image that sets the product (or products) apart from the competing products, thus ensuring that the chosen image matches the aspirations of the target customers. To achieve this, the business must decide upon its positioning strategy. This might involve positioning on the basis of one of the following: product attributes, benefits, competitors, product application, product class association, user profiles (Aaker 1982). For instance, the coach operator might use a competitor-based positioning, where the flexibility of travelling with a locally based company providing many pick-up points is compared with the more restricted service offered by national rail and coach operators. Alternatively, benefits may be used as the basis, with the company promoting the affordable relaxation offered by one of its outings.

■ *Step 7*. Inform target customers about the product. While this is primarily a communications task, using the promotional mix, it is also important to ensure that the product is available through suitable channels, and at the right price for target customers. Businesses often use positioning statements (sometimes called strap lines) to communicate with customers. Tesco's 'Every little helps . . .' and British Airways 'The world's favourite airline' are familiar examples.

First, the business must identify a basis for competing. This should relate to any one or a combination of attributes that the business offers and that customers value highly. Ideally, the basis for competing should also give the business a differential advantage over rival companies. This means that the highly valued attribute on which the positioning is based is not matched by rival companies. For instance, a courier company offering the fastest delivery of a package would have a differential advantage, which might help build success in the longer term. A business with a patented package design—as long as it is seen as desirable by customers—may have a differential advantage to stress over its rivals' offers.

7.3 Repositioning existing brands

When the existing positioning of a brand is inappropriate, there are various options that can be followed. A business may decide to introduce a new brand, change the existing brand, alter beliefs about the existing brand, alter beliefs about competing brands, alter attribute importance rates, introduce new or neglected attributes, or

find a new market segment (Doyle 1994). These options are illustrated in Box 16.9.

BMW is responding to changes in the European motor industry that are threatening the exclusive arrangements that manufacturers have with their dealers. In order to deal with these changes BMW is altering its brands and customer beliefs.

Box 16.9 Options for repositioning

■ *Introduce new brand.* After the declining price of personal computers in the 1990s threatened to oust IBM's high-priced machines from the market, the company introduced its own cheap 'clone' under the Ambra brand name and sourced from the Far East. The objective was to maintain a foothold in the booming mass and economy markets.

■ *Change existing brand.* Alternatively a company may change its cost and utility combination to make it more appealing. In contrast to IBM, Compaq tried to solve the problem by cutting its prices and simplifying the features offered to hold onto a position in the mass market.

■ *Alter beliefs about the brand.* Chivas Regal Scotch whisky achieved some success in repositioning itself from the mass market to the premium segment, thus rationalizing its higher price.

■ *Alter beliefs about competitive brands.* The Body Shop retail group succeeded in implying that the beauty and personal-care products of competitors were not environmentally friendly.

■ *Alter attribute importance rates.* Volvo raised the importance of safety as an attribute in choosing a car, thus enhancing the value of its differentiation.

■ *Introduce new or neglected attributes.* Unilever successfully introduced Radion, a new detergent that eliminated odours—a benefit previously not considered important by consumers.

■ *Find a new market segment.* When Dunhill diversified away from smoking accessories into the men's clothing market, rather than enter the already highly competitive segments, it created a new luxury segment of very expensive, high-quality ready-to-wear suits. As the only 'typically British' competitor in this segment, it brought a unique brand with a strong appeal to affluent executives (especially the Japanese!).

Source: Doyle (1994: 80–1).

Changes in the law look set to allow new businesses into the market, while existing dealerships will be able to sell a range of different car brands. BMW believes that repositioning itself as a service brand will help prepare the business for these market changes. Although the business is not planning to move away from its existing dealership network, a more flexible approach to retailing seems inevitable. BMW will look at ways of building on its new positioning, perhaps through the extension of its car financing operation. BMW GB Managing Director, Kevin Gaskell, explained the initiative: 'the way forward is not for BMW to compare itself with others in our industry, it is to be compared with the best in any industry. My objective is to define a culture which aims to be amongst the most respected and admired service organizations in any country' (Barrett 1997: 7). Box 16.10 illustrates how alcopops manufacturer Bass

has repositioned Hooper's Hooch by changing the brand and consumer beliefs about it.

7.4 Positioning problems

Problems with positioning arise for a number of reasons. Sometimes businesses are simply unrealistic about what can be achieved. The company's image and positioning of the existing product range are important factors to consider. When Toyota launched its luxury Lexus car, marketers knew that credibility of the new brand relied on positioning away from the mass-market appeal of the company's other marques. Toyota achieved this by badging the car only as Lexus, then selling it from mini-dealerships within existing Toyota dealers. This encouraged customer perceptions of the Lexus that were not influenced by the Toyota brand.

Once decisions about positioning have been made, consistent and clear customer communication is vital. The most powerful positioning messages are those that are enforced over time through an appropriate marketing mix. For international businesses this presents a particular challenge, as some promotion and advertising may be carried out locally. In such cases it is vital to maintain some central control over product positioning. Furniture retailer IKEA's success is built upon a positioning of good-value Swedish style. Although there is some regional variation in the furniture stocked in different parts of the world, the core offering remains the same. For example, although stores located in heavily populated parts of the Far East offer more small furniture, the majority of the items stocked and the underlying style are consistent with IKEA stores in Europe. IKEA's positioning is deliberately uniform around the world, and is carefully controlled from its Swedish base.

Poor information about customer perceptions is another cause of ineffective positioning. All too often businesses develop positioning maps without collecting real data from customers. Marketers use their own impressions about customer perceptions. Such approaches are dangerous, leading to inaccurate assumptions about key customer needs and brand perceptions. Inappropriate or unsubstantiated product positioning is a common outcome.

Difficulties sometimes arise when businesses attempt to change their product positioning. Although such changes are possible, they are often

---

Box 16.10 Repositioning alcopops

Following the 1995 launch, the runaway success of alcopops (alcoholic soft drinks) took many brewers and cider-makers by surprise. Soon after the launch, a survey showed an 80 per cent awareness of the sector among 18–24 year olds. Products such as Hooper's Hooch (Bass), Two Dogs (Merrydown), and Lemonheads (Carlsberg-Tetley) were taking the market by storm.

Shortly after the introduction of this new drinks category, consumer concern was raised that the new products and their marketing were too appealing to under-age drinkers. Following considerable political pressure, the brewers acted quickly to modify their marketing in a major effort to reposition their brands. Manufacturers such as Bass, makers of market-leading Hooper's Hooch (with 70 per cent market share), responded by redesigning packages, labelling, and marketing programmes to target clearly the adult market.

Sponsorship of adult comedies on UK television's Channel 5 in 1997 was part of the repositioning exercise. Bass agreed a six-month deal to sponsor an hour of comedy, between 10 p.m. and 11 p.m. on Monday nights. According to a Bass spokesperson, 'an adult comedy slot seemed an ideal fit with Hooch's new positioning as a fun drink for responsible adults'.

Source: Benady (1996).

difficult and expensive to achieve. As a general rule, the greater the change required, the harder and more expensive it is to achieve. Sometimes drastic measures are needed. In the early 1990s, following a joint venture with Sumitomo, digger manufacturer JCB launched a new range of crawler excavators. The launch was hampered by poor customer perceptions of JCB's previous excavator range. The company wished to combine the launch with a repositioning exercise. In order to achieve the required perception change, the company stopped selling its previous range six months before the new launch (Dibb 1997).

8 Getting the most out of market segmentation

DESPITE the widespread acceptance of segmentation principles, organizations often encounter difficulties trying to implement it in practice (see Insert) (Waldo 1973; Littler 1992; McDonald and Dunbar 1995). These difficulties can occur at any point in the process (Dibb and Simkin 1997). For example, lack of data, an inappropriate choice of base variables or poor analytical skills, can disrupt the segmentation stage. Targeting problems can arise if businesses have too short term a focus or attempt to use too complex a list of selection criteria. Positioning problems can be caused by poor-quality customer or competitor information.

The essence of segmenatation

'In essence, segmentation can be viewed as a means of imposing a structure on the market in order to simplify the formulation and implementation of marketing strategies. Whether or not there exist clearly defined categories that emerge from the process of segmentation followed is in fact irrelevant as long as it leads to the practical end results desired—namely, the identification of customers whose requirements are unfulfilled, the securing of a competitive advantage by developing and marketing offerings that are perceived in some way as superior by selected customers, and the providing of a focus for and direction to marketing efforts. Market segmentation is then essentially creative and utilitarian; nothing more, nothing less.'

Source: Littler (1992).

Segmentation difficulties arise for a number of reasons. Some marketers believe that segmentation experts do too little to focus on implementation issues (Hooley 1980; Piercy and Morgan 1993). Others suggest that managers have a poor understanding of segmentation principles (Doyle *et al.* 1986). Operational constraints, such as whether a new segmentation approach is compatible with the company's existing distribution system, have also been blamed (Plank 1985). Managers are quick to point out that the planning and execution of segmentation are constrained by a range of operational considerations. For example, an engine manufacturer that conducted a segmentation review discovered that its existing distribution system was failing an important segment of customers. However, it was unrealistic for the manufacturer to scrap its existing distribution system and begin again. Instead, a series of changes was implemented to ensure that distributor personnel were better trained to meet the needs of these customers.

Whatever the underlying reasons for segmentation disruption, there is a universal need for guidance to help marketers achieve effective results. Whether dealing with consumer goods, services, or industrial products, marketers who apply the process in real-world situations often ask what they can do to ensure segmentation success. Box 16.11 lists some of the questions that are commonly asked. The diversity of the questions shows that marketers who put segmentation principles into practice are anxious for the process to be handled properly. Research demonstrates that haphazard implementation may result in ineffective market segmentation, causing missed opportunities and wasted resources.

Using these segmentation questions as a checklist, it seems that marketers need help at three points in the segmentation process. *Before* the project begins, they must try to understand what factors contribute to a successful outcome. *During* the analysis, marketers need to think about what qualities the segments should exhibit. *After* the segmentation output has been finalized, guidance is needed about how to appraise the attractiveness of different segments. For example, a manufacturer of animal feed looking for new ways to segment its customers needs to know which managers to involve in the process. Once the process is underway, the business needs help checking the appropriateness of the segments. Guidance is also needed to ensure that the right

Box 16.11 **Questions that marketers ask about doing segmentation**

Key segmentation questions:

- Is there a segmentation process that can be followed?
- Where should the process start?
- What information or data are needed in the process?
- Who should be involved in the process?
- What variables should be used to segment the market?
- How is it possible to tell if the correct variables have been used?
- How is it possible to test whether or not the segments that emerge are robust?
- What should be done with the segments that result?
- How can the usefulness and effectiveness of segmentation be tested?

criteria are used to identify the most attractive segments.

Help for marketers at the start of their segmentation experience is surprisingly limited. Guidance on segmentation success factors is particularly desired, yet research in this area remains at an early stage. This is primarily due to difficulties proving a quantifiable link between segmentation usage and business success. The sheer number of variables impacting upon business performance makes it virtually impossible to set up a controlled experiment where the effect of just one—segmentation—is tested. Yet, given the high costs associated with putting a segmentation scheme into practice, businesses might reasonably question the likely financial returns.

Success factors of a more qualitative nature have been proposed. Well-designed planning, senior-management commitment and involvement, creative thinking and readiness to respond to market change are just a few of the factors proposed (Engel *et al.* 1972; Coles and Culley 1986; Weinstein 1987; Brown *et al.* 1989). Haley (1984: 170) offers a particularly comprehensive list: clearly defined objectives, careful organization (usually involving a multifunctional project team), considerable up-front work (examining past re-

search, promotion, and marketing trends), a three-phase research design (including a second phase centred on developing sensitive and reliable attitude measures), and implementation plans (including testing and tracking studies).

The most widely recognized guidance for businesses *during* the segmentation process is in the form of a series of recommended segment 'qualities'. These are sometimes termed segmentation criteria and are generally attributed to Kotler (1984), who states that segments should be measurable, substantial, accessible, and actionable. Since the criteria were first proposed, other authors have added to the list. The first requirement is that in the market under review the needs of customers for the product or service must be *heterogeneous*. This concept of diversity in customer needs and buying behaviour is the key prerequisite for segmentation. There is little point in segmenting a homogeneous market. Once this requirement has been satisfied, segmentation can proceed. However, the segments identified must be:

- *Measurable*: it must be possible to identify and measure the segments; once a variable has been used to group consumers or businesses into segments, marketers must be able to predict their likely size and potential;
- *substantial*: from a resource viewpoint, segments must be sufficiently sizeable to justify the design and implementation of a tailored marketing mix;
- *accessible*: it must be possible for the consumers in the segments to be reached and served with a particular marketing mix;
- *actionable*: customers in the segments must be able to be served effectively with a marketing programme.
- *stable*: segment stability is crucial if businesses are to invest resources into a particular segmentation scheme; it may only be possible to justify investing resource into segment-specific marketing programmes when there is some certainty about the longevity of those segments.

Help appraising the attractiveness of different segments *after* the segmentation process is complete is readily available. During the targeting process, marketers consider a range of criteria to help them balance the business's resources and capabilities against the attractiveness of different segments. For marketers carrying out segmentation, it is important to consider a mix of internal organizational dimensions and external market issues. The most commonly used criteria include exploitable marketing assets, managerial resources, cost advantages, segment size, growth rate, and profit potential. A more detailed review can be found in the portfolio planning literature, where market attractiveness and business position receive extensive coverage (Porter 1985; Morrison and Wensley 1991; McDonald 1995).

For those pursuing a segmentation approach, help is primarily focused upon the output of the process. Guidance concerning the business conditions that bring about successful segmentation is much harder to find. Although problems quantifying the link between segmentation and success are likely to remain, it is to be hoped that this area will become a priority for future research. Whatever the progress of such research, it is clear that making segmentation work in practice may not be as straightforward as theory implies. To improve their chances of segmentation success, businesses must carefully consider the planning and execution of the segmentation process, making the most of *before*, *during*, and *after* implementation guidance. In general, it seems that, while the benefits of market segmentation are well established, businesses must be vigilant of the potential pitfalls, doing what they can to ensure that these are avoided through careful segmentation planning, execution, and implementation.

9 Market segmentation: the future

COMPETITIVE and technological forces are changing the way in which marketers think about and implement segmentation in the marketplace. The impact of the competitive environment is felt as the combined effects of growing international trade and maturing domestic markets have led to increasing competitiveness in many industries. The relaxation of trade barriers in Europe and further afield has exacerbated this competitive intensity. An important outcome of these changes has been a rise in the level of customer choice, with more businesses competing for a share of existing markets. This, in turn, has led to increasing segmentation of these markets and a rise in the number of niche players.

Information-technology (IT) improvements are helping managers to develop and apply segmentation strategies in these increasingly competitive markets. Marketing managers have access to a wider range of analytical software packages than ever before. Much of this software is available in PC format, covering the full range of market analysis, planning, and strategy development. Managers now have easy access to a wide range of multivariate approaches such as cluster and conjoint analysis. Many of these managers have been exposed to the principles of market segmentation either in business-school degree programmes or in-company training schemes. This means that more managers than ever before are sufficiently comfortable with segmentation theory and with the use of IT to attempt some segmentation analysis of their own. For those who are more reluctant to become directly involved in data manipulation, an array of 'off-the-shelf' or tailored segmentation approaches are offered by companies specializing in customer profiling. Some of these, including the well-known ACORN and MOSAIC systems, have already been explored in this chapter. Whatever the source of these analytical tools, their use in developing segmentation strategy is becoming increasingly routine. The outcome is increasingly sophisticated segmentation and targeting strategies which focus on more precisely defined customer groups than ever before.

The effects of competitive changes and IT developments are being felt right across the spectrum of products and services on offer to businesses and consumers. For example, recent retail banking research has highlighted a growing conviction that the banks must target the so-called segment of one. The underlying notion is that improvements in customer information and higher levels of competitiveness are forcing service providers to focus on the *individual* needs and requirements of their customers. At a time when consumers have more choice than ever before about how and where they bank, there has been an associated rise in service-level expectations. The banks have responded to these changes by improving customer databases. This has been achieved through more frequent customer contact, the collection of more detailed data, and the integration of systems so that better-quality customer profiles are available. Such profiles now commonly combine demographic and socio-economic information, psychographic and attitudinal data, and transaction-based information. Marketers in the banks can use this information to help them identify key 'life events', such as a house move or the birth of a child, that may trigger the need for additional banking services.

The ongoing changes in retail banking are consistent with the findings of a Mintel report which emphasizes the growing importance of one-to-one marketing. In its examination of tomorrow's consumer, the report signals a possible decline in the effectiveness of mass-market television advertising and a rise in the importance of targeted niche marketing, using direct mail, sponsorship, and the Internet (Bainbridge 1998; Mintel International Group 1998). The report continues by suggesting that, in the future, marketers will be under greater pressure than ever before to offer a portfolio of products that are tailored to specific and shifting demographics, such as age, ethnicity, income, sex, shopping habits, education, and eating patterns. The implications of these changes are that it will no longer be appropriate for marketers simply to devise a mass-market marketing campaign and then modify it for a specific group. Instead, it is suggested that marketers will need to devise campaigns for specific target segments from scratch.

Whatever the future for segmentation, the underlying need for marketers carefully to identify and then to match the needs of target customers will remain a priority. No amount of sophisticated data manipulation can obscure the fundamental importance of staying in touch with what the customer wants, nor can it obviate the need for businesses to develop products and services for profitable segments.

10 Summary

THE underlying principle of market segmentation is that the product and services needs of individual customers differ. The mass-marketing approach, common at the start of the twentieth century, where a single marketing programme is designed for all, is no longer appropriate in most markets. Market segmentation involves grouping together customers with similar needs and buying behaviour; it allows businesses to cater for the breadth of customer wants while maintaining certain scale economies. The rationale is that these segments are likely to demonstrate a more homogeneous response to marketing programmes. Enthusiasts of market segmentation believe that

it leads to more satisfied customers, fewer direct confrontations with competitors, and better-designed marketing programmes.

The market segmentation process consists of three stages: segmentation, targeting, and positioning. During the segmentation stage, one or more base variables are used to group customers. In consumer markets, variables fall into one of two categories, relating to consumer characteristics (demographics, socio-economics, geographic, or personality/lifestyle) or behavioural characteristics (purchase behaviour, purchase and usage occasion, benefits sought, user status and consumption behaviour, product attitudes). In business-to-business markets, the variables used include demographics, operating factors, purchasing approach, situational factors, and personal characteristics of buyers. There is rarely one correct way to segment a market. Which variables are appropriate depends on the market and the business situation. Once segments have been identified, it is necessary to validate them (check they are genuine) and profile them (build a clear picture of segment membership). Marketers undertaking segmentation have at their disposal a range of statistical techniques, which must be used with care.

During the targeting stage, marketers decide on which segment(s) to focus their marketing resources. There are three major targeting strategies: the undifferentiated strategy, the concentrated strategy and the differentiated strategy. The strategy choice must be made carefully, to ensure that the business does not overstretch its resources, but covers a sufficiently large part of the market to be profitable. An undifferentiated strategy involves targeting the entire market with a single marketing mix. Businesses adopting a concentrated strategy direct their marketing effort towards a single segment. A differentiated (multi-segment) strategy occurs when market effort is targeted at two or more segments. Businesses selecting either a concentrated or differentiated targeting strategy must engage in a process of segment selection. During this process the business must balance its resources and capabilities against the attractiveness of different segments.

The final stage, positioning, involves the design of marketing programmes that will match the requirements of customers in the segments chosen. The marketing programmes should position the product or service in the minds of targeted customers. Customer perceptions about the product or service, which are shaped by existing market brands, are central to its positioning. Perceptual mapping is a tool that helps marketers to understand customer perceptions of different products or brands in the market. These maps use dimensions that are influenced by key requirements of potential customers.

A simple step-by-step approach can be used to develop a clear positioning for a product: (1) define the segments in the market; (2) decide which segments to target; (3) develop a clear understanding of the needs of target customers; (4) ensure that the product matches the needs identified; (5) evaluate the positioning and images that target customers have of competing products; (6) select an image that sets the product apart from competing products; (7) inform target customers about the product. Sometimes businesses need to reposition products or brands. Providing a realistic approach is adopted, information about customer perceptions is reliable, and resources are available, this is usually possible.

Despite the widespread acceptance of segmentation principles, poor understanding, lack of data, and operational constraints can create implementation problems. Marketers embarking on market-segmentation analysis have many questions about the way to ensure segmentation success. This is not surprising in view of the size of investment decisions that can rest on segmentation analysis. Yet more research is needed which considers the link between segmentation and success. To improve their chances of segmentation success, businesses need advice at three points in the process: *before* the project begins, *during* the analysis, and *after* the segmentation output has been finalized. There is currently a particular shortage of help on segmentation success factors, which would be particularly useful for marketers at the start of the process. In general, although the benefits that market segmentation offers seem well established, businesses must also be aware of the potential pitfalls, doing what they can to ensure that their segmentation planning avoids them.

Further reading

Dibb, S., and Simkin, L. (1996), *The Market Segmentation Workbook: Target Marketing for Marketing Managers* (London: ITBP).

————, Pride, W., and Ferrell, O. C. (1997), *Marketing: Concepts and Strategies* (Boston, Mass.: Houghton Mifflin).

Hooley, G. J., and Saunders, J. (1993), *Competitive Positioning: The Key to Market Success* (Hemel Hempstead: Prentice Hall).

McDonald, M., and Dunbar, I. (1995), *Market Segmentation* (Basingstoke: Macmillan Press).

Trout, J., and Rivkin, S. (1996), *The New Positioning: The Latest on the World's Number 1 Business Strategy* (New York: McGraw Hill).

Wind, Y. (1995), 'Market segmentation', in M. J. Baker (ed.), *Companion Encyclopaedia of Marketing* (London: Routledge).

Discussion questions

1 Explain how market segmentation allows a business to satisfy its customer needs more closely. What other business benefits does market segmentation offer?

2 Coca-Cola used to produce just one version of its world-famous drink. Explain why the company now markets a range of different formulations. What might you expect to happen in the future?

3 Market segmentation is often said to consist of three stages. Using an example of your choice, briefly describe the key aspects of these stages.

4 A national chain of hotels is considering segmenting its market in an attempt to deal with increasing competition. How can segmentation help businesses such as this become more competitive? Which variables might be appropriate to use in this case?

5 An industrial paint manufacturer sells its products to a wide range of customer types. How could market segmentation be used to help the business organize its marketing effort?

6 Outline the advantages and disadvantages of undifferentiated, concentrated, and differentiated targeting strategies. For each strategy, give an example of a business that has pursued such a targeting approach.

7 How do marketers decide which segments to target in a market? What factors must a shampoo manufacturer consider when deciding whether or not to enter a new segment?

8 Describe the positioning process that a magazine publisher should go through when launching a new publication. What role does information play in the process?

9 A confectionery manufacturer has encountered a number of problems with the positioning of one of its ranges. What might be the causes of these positioning problems? How might they be overcome?

10 Major investment decisions often rest on the outcome of market segmentation studies. Briefly outline the kinds of effectiveness advice that are available for businesses becoming involved in segmentation. What can a business do to try and maximize the usefulness of segmentation study *before* the analysis is started?

11 What criteria must a segmentation solution satisfy before a business should plan for its implementation?

12 Discuss the difficulties likely to be faced by a business striving to develop a new segmentation scheme.

The electric vehicle market

In 1996 the UK Government's Green Paper *Transport: The Way Ahead* indicated a projected growth in traffic of up to 80 per cent by 2025. With increasing use of vehicles and increasing journey length, the problem is not confined to increasing numbers of cars, vans, and lorries. The associated environmental costs are considerable. A combination of rising levels of carbon dioxide, nitrogen dioxide, and sulphur dioxide have already caused acid-rain and global-warming problems as well as spurring an increase in respiratory disease. The scale of the problem alarms environmentalists. In 1994 over one hundred million tonnes of carbon dioxide emissions were recorded. A recent study suggests that this will rise to 150 million tonnes by 2010.

A variety of UK and European legislation has drawn attention to the environmental difficulties associated with road-usage trends. This includes directives which require new petrol-driven cars to be fitted with catalytic converters and the reduction in emission levels of motor vehicles of all types. The 'European Commission Auto Oil Package' has focused attention on air-quality standards, demanding considerable reductions in vehicle emissions. The expectation is that the future will bring increasingly stringent national and European legislation.

It is possible that European moves to reduce vehicle emissions will follow a similar pattern to that seen in California, USA. There, strict environmental legislation requires that, by 2003, 10 per cent of all new vehicles (some 800,000) must be zero emission. Not surprisingly, car manufacturers have invested heavily in developing a range of alternative fuel technologies in their drive towards more environmentally friendly vehicles. Currently, only battery-powered electric vehicles are able to achieve zero emissions. Other fuels under investigation include the use of alcohol, compressed natural gas, hydrogen, liquefied petroleum gas, coal-derived liquid fuels, and fuels derived from biological materials such as soya beans. Chrysler, Ford, General Motors, Honda, Nissan, and Toyota are just some of the manufacturers that have actively developed vehicles for this market. For instance, Ford's Ecostar, a two-passenger electric delivery van, has attracted considerable interest in the press. Since 1993, a demonstration programme involving around 100 of these vehicles has been running in the USA, Canada, and Europe. Running from a high temperature sodium-sulphur battery, the delivery van has a top speed of 70 m.p.h. and a range of around 100 miles before recharging is necessary.

In Europe too, the move towards more environmentally friendly vehicles continues. Nissan's electric-powered concept car the Hypermini, exhibited at the Tokyo Motor Show, is a typical example. Designed for minimal environmental impact, the two-seater vehicle uses a lithium-ion battery pack to achieve a range of 80 miles and top speed of 62 m.p.h. Other features include deformable front and rear body zones, twin airbags, and anti-lock brakes. The exterior measurements of the car are as small as possible to minimize parking difficulties. All this is achieved at a running cost of only a penny per mile. Meanwhile, PSA Peugeot/Citroen has been a major player in the 'Coventry Electric Vehicle Project'. This £400,000 joint initiative with the Energy Saving Trust involves a partnership between five fleet operators and aims to increase electric-vehicle awareness. The five fleet operators involved are Coventry City Council, East Midlands Electricity, Peugeot, PowerGen, and the Royal Mail. Under the twelve-month scheme the fleet operators have tested fourteen electric-powered Peugeot 106 cars and vans. Peugeot's involvement in electric vehicle development is, of course, long established. Following early developments of technology in 1968, the company became the first European car manufacturer to offer electric vehicles to its customers. Now the company is looking to establish the electric 106 through its dealer network. This fits with PSA Peugeot/Citroen's long-term strategy to introduce the electric Peugeot 106 and the Citroen AX throughout Europe.

Industry observers suggest that interest in electric vehicles is also providing a catalyst for the development of other low-emission technologies. For example, Mercedes Benz is investing considerable resources in the development of fuel-cell technology. These fuel cells operate using pure hydrogen or hydrogen-rich fuels (methanol, ethanol, natural gas, or petrol). This technology is attractive because, like battery-driven vehicles, it offers the possibility of zero emissions and is about twice as efficient as petrol internal-combustion engines. Fuel-cell powered vehicles, which are seen by many as the natural successor to those powered by batteries, have the added advantage of being able to match the range offered by petrol-driven cars. Although some difficulties remain, industry experts indicate that fuel-cell technology will be commercially available within the next five years.

Despite the ecological benefits of these innovative vehicles, many consumers remain unconvinced. Images of milk floats and the Sinclair C5 are commonly associated with electric cars. Alternative fuels also provide relatively small amounts of energy when compared with petrol. The result is a negative effect on performance and the requirement for frequent refilling or recharging. Despite vehicle tests that demonstrate the excellent performance of many of the prototypes and the fact that recent technology improvements have extended the range of today's electric vehicles and cut recharging time, consumer perception problems remain. Research highlights a host of consumer concerns about the range, speed, performance, and recharging of electric vehicles. Some consumers also express anxiety about the physical characteristics of some of the vehicles. Despite the attractions of low running costs, the relatively high cost of replacement batteries is also offputting for some people. In order to tackle these perception problems many car manufacturers are undertaking consumer and fleet buyer research, The manufacturers hope that such research will help to establish the main needs and concerns of potential buyers. It will also help to identify the characteristics of these buyers so that the most attractive target markets can be identified.

Sources: hgp:ll@lwww.fordcom'electricvehiclelqvm.html (Ford's electric vehicle site); Haywood (1997).

Discussion questions

1 What base variables can be used to determine market segments in the new-car market?

2 In an evolving market such as electric vehicles, why is shrewd targeting of customers important?

3 Explain whether it is likely that new fuel technologies will appeal to tightly defined ups.

4 Will the positioning of an electric version of the Peugeot 106 be any different from that of the petrol-powered Peugeot 106? Why is this the case?

Chapter 17
Inter-departmental Interfaces

Keith Blois

Objectives

The objectives of this chapter are:

1 to explore why it is important for marketing to have good relationships with other departments in the firm;

2 to indicate the difficulties that marketing has in working with other parts of the firm;

3 to consider how these difficulties might be overcome.

1 Introduction

IN the preceding chapters reference has been made to the way in which decisions regarding marketing strategies and tactics are affected by and themselves affect the activity of other departments in the organization. This chapter will explore the links that must be established and nurtured between marketing and other departments in an organization. It will explain how other departments' activities can impinge on marketing activities and thus point to the need for the organization's management to integrate decisions made in other departments with its marketing plans. It will also point out that the firm's marketing policies impinge on other departments. Consideration will be given as to why there can be conflicts between marketing and other departments when in theory they should be cooperating. In particular, the relationships between marketing and the research and development (R&D) department, the production department, and the accounting function will be discussed.

2 The problem

IN any organization, but clearly particularly in larger ones, there is a difficulty in ensuring that the various parts of the organization know what the others are doing. Failure to do this can create all sorts of inefficiencies and at worst cause real damage to the business.

The cutting-tool illustration in Box 17.1 shows how the failure of one department to keep other departments informed as it went about the process of fulfilling its objectives led to the development of a new product that the firm could not actually produce. Apart from the cost to the company of the resources committed to developing the product, there was also the cost of the failure to develop a new product that could actually be placed on the market. The company was left with a set of dated products.

It is important for separate departments to keep each other informed of their activities, but it is also vital for employees to gain a clear picture of how their work relates to the organization's overall activity. One problem is that many employees' work is distant (sometimes literally so in a geo-

Box 17.1 **The wonder product that was never produced**

Summitt, like most firms manufacturing cutting tools for use on machine tools, invested heavily in developing new ceramic coatings to extend its tools' life. This is technically a complex process, and a particular problem was to avoid infringing any patents. The R&D Department was, therefore, delighted when a new ceramic coating that they had been working on over a prolonged period showed every sign of being 'a winner'. A customer who had agreed to test a prototype had confirmed the results of laboratory tests.

At this stage, therefore, the R&D Department invited the Marketing Department to discuss the market opportunity that the new coating created. The Marketing Department had been aware that new coatings were being investigated but did not receive a briefing on this specific development until after the prototype had been tested. However, Marketing was very impressed with R&D's results and even at the meeting began to make estimates of the size of the market opportunity.

The Marketing staff just wanted to see the results of the trials and were not concerned with the formula of the new ceramic, but they had learnt that tungsten carbide was a crucial constituent of the new coating. Later that week the Marketing Manager, while chatting informally with the Purchasing Manager, mentioned that tungsten carbide was a vital constituent of the new coating. The Purchasing Manager indicated that he knew nothing about the new product but a week later the Purchasing Manager announced: 'There is a world shortage of tungsten carbide. All known sources of supply are tied up in long-term contracts.'

Two years later Summitt, having at last obtained a secure supply of tungsten carbide, was ready to start production of tools with the new coating. By then, however, one of its competitors had produced a coating with a performance that exceeded theirs by a considerable margin.

graphical sense) from the final product and the customer. This can make it difficult for them to see how what they do, which might be concerned with the manufacture of some small subcomponent or part, contributes to customer satisfaction and thus the organization's success. A second type of difficulty is that those employees whose work is not directly related to the production of the or-

ganization's product or service may feel that they could do the same job in any one of a number of organizations. For example, the manager in a salary department could fulfil an almost identical role in a number of organizations, each in quite different industries. However, it is now recognized that there are considerable benefits to be obtained from keeping all staff, no matter how little contact they have with the customer, fully informed about the organization's activities—particularly its marketing activities.

However, putting mechanisms into place that will ensure that employees are kept informed about these matters is not sufficient. It is also critically important that the planning and control mechanisms of all the departments in the organization take account of the company's marketing policies. Unfortunately, as will become apparent, this is easier to discuss than to do. All too frequently conflicts arise between marketing and other departments. For example, a marketing manager may believe that sales could be increased if more product variants were offered. If the production manager knows or believes that his department's efficiency is judged by the cost per unit achieved by his department, then he will not be enthusiastic about marketing's proposal. He knows that the introduction of another variant would cause his unit costs to go up—especially if the nature of the production technology were such that machines would need resetting every time there was a change in the variant being produced. As this simple example shows, the basis of the conflict is quite understandable, often after only a little investigation; unfortunately the solution to such conflicts is seldom as obvious.

The way in which employees can become committed to the marketing orientation has been discussed in Chapter 2. This chapter will, therefore, concentrate on the difficulties that arise between departments. Clearly some of these will revolve around the behaviour of individuals at all levels in the department, for in a modern organization even a junior employee's inappropriate behaviour can be as costly in the short term as managerial incompetence. However, no matter how willing the individuals are to cooperate with their colleagues in other departments, if the organization's structure and control mechanisms make this difficult it is unlikely that they will have much success in working together. In Section 3 the organizational behaviour problems that can impede interdepartmental cooperation will be identified and suggestions made as to how these might be minimized. Then Sections 4–6 will consider the relationships that exist between marketing and three other departments and illustrate how the improvements in these relationships might improve an organization's effectiveness.

3 Impediments to interorganizational cooperation

THERE are four categories of barriers to effective interdepartmental cooperation: territory problems, interpretation barriers, communication barriers, and conflicting performance measures. As is the case with most management issues, the effects of these barriers interact, and quite often the interaction has a greater impact than the sum of each one individually.

3.1 Territory problems

Organizations, other than those that are very small, are normally divided into subunits that are typically called departments. The basis of such divisions is the belief by the management that there are benefits to be gained by grouping employees together on one of a number of bases. For example, employees who have a particular expertise might be placed in a group. There are several reasons why this might be done. It might be believed that, by working together, they would build up and extend their expertise. Alternatively it could be thought that grouping these employees together would produce 'economies of scale', so that, for example, fewer lawyers might be employed if there was a group law department than if there was one in each of several subsidiaries. Other bases for grouping employees together include geographical location, knowledge of specific products and/or applications, and on the basis of a function (e.g. the personnel function) to be fulfilled.

Each group will normally have somebody placed 'in charge' of it. Furthermore, the organization will assess each group's performance using a variety of measures. A unit may be a cost or a profit centre, but in addition it may also be assessed against non-financial measures—a buying

department may not only have to operate within certain cost limits but may also have as a target the reduction in the number of suppliers used. These control measures produce problems of interdepartmental cooperation, which are discussed below.

It appears that for most people the group within which they work becomes important to them in a variety of ways, not least in relation to their self-esteem. There are many benefits that are derived from this sense of group loyalty and arguably those people who have never been part of a cohesive team have missed one of life's great experiences. However, from the organization's and, indeed, society's point of view, the problem is that such groups usually strongly resist any actions that seem to reduce their power and influence. Indeed, more often than not groups actually seek to increase their power over and influence on other parts of the organization. Even more problematical is that any threat to a group results in an increase in the group members' sense of identity with each other (Franwick *et al.* 1994). The difficulties that this causes in achieving interdepartmental coordination are numerous. For example, in many engineering firms, the consequence of the increased importance being accorded to the service element of the product has been the diminution of the importance of other functions, such as manufacturing, which are associated only with the production of the physical part of the product. It must be stressed that in absolute terms the physical elements are no less important than in the past, but the increased awareness of the importance of the service element has led to a relative reduction in manufacturing's importance. As a consequence, budget allocations may be less favourable to manufacturing, and senior management may give manufacturing less attention. In such circumstances it can be predicted that personnel in the manufacturing department will, at best, cooperate reluctantly with the service function but at worst may be antagonistic towards the development of the service element of the product.

3.2 Interpretation barriers

The intent of forming units or departments is to create a focus of some kind—professional, functional, and so on (Dougherty 1992). Unfortunately this focus may produce a view of the world that is often particular to that department and quite disconnected from that of other units with which it is expected to work. At a certain level this is desirable, but the views of each unit must be kept within the perspective of the organization's overall goal. The enthusiasm of the R&D staff is vital to the development of new products. However, their view of what the significant features of a new product are may well differ from that of the marketing department. They may get very excited about some scientific matter that is crucial to the product's development. But marketing's interest will be in asking what is its significance to the customer, and, more often than not, there is no need for customers to be aware of the science incorporated into the product at all. This divergence of interests is illustrated in the electronic speckle pattern interferometer example (see Insert).

The electronic speckled pattern interferometer

As part of the development of the electronic speckled pattern interferometer by Loughborough Consultants, it was necessary to design a series of ingenious combinations of mirrors, lenses, and lasers—some of which were patentable. Even though the customers for this equipment were scientists, they had no need to know how the equipment worked, and most remained oblivious of the very clever science within it. During the market research carried out to determine the product's final specification, the development scientists were continuously irritated by the market researchers' lack of interest in their 'mirrors'. In addition, their enthusiasm for undertaking development work on the more mundane parts of the project was limited because this was not innovative work. For the scientists, the science was the excitement and the natural centre of their concern. What was significant to them was the development of new technology. The market researchers' measure of significance was what the technology would deliver in terms of product attributes and not the technology itself.

3.3 Communication barriers

As well as having a different focus of attention, units often develop a shared language that reflects the way that their members think and interpret what goes on around them and particularly which issues should be given the highest priority (Work-

man 1995). It is very difficult for a manager or a group of staff whose highest priority for some long period has been, say, cost reduction not to judge any new proposal other than in the light of its expected impact on costs (see Insert). Such a focus can happen in any established group. The inclusiveness that develops within groups is demonstrated when an outsider finds that there are certain in-jokes and sayings that they cannot understand when they have contact with a group. However, in the business context, it is not just jokes but important understandings about what is significant and about interpretations of what is happening in the business that may be difficult to follow.

Well intentioned but wrong?

'David Lieberman, marketing director at GVO, a Palo Alto innovation consulting firm, tells the story of a company "known by 3 initials" whose creative types had come up with a great idea for a new product. Just about everybody loved it. But it was shot down at the last minute by a high-ranking manufacturing executive. "A new color?" the executive exploded. "Do you have any idea of the spare parts problem that will create?" This was no dimwit exasperated at having to build a few new storage racks at the warehouse. "He'd been hearing for years about cost cutting, lean inventory, and 'focus'," says Lieberman; "good concepts, but not always good for innovation."'

Source: O'Reilly (1997).

3.4 Conflicting performance measures

Most departments have formal measures against which their performance is assessed. Members of departments also have their own performance judged against some measures and some of these measures will be linked with those applied to the department. This is most obvious in the case of the person in charge of a unit, for the measures against which their performance is judged will frequently include those applied to the department as a whole. For example departmental heads are likely to be judged on the performance of their department. However, measures of their personal performance are in addition likely to include assessment of aspects of personal behaviour such as, in the case of a manager, leadership capabilities.

The problems in setting appropriate measures are considerable, and unfortunately the effect of performance measures can be to cause disagreements both between individuals within a department and between departments. Of course, even when they are not subject to formal assessment, staff will usually assume that their performance is being informally evaluated by their managers and will therefore adjust their behaviour to take account of what they assume the assessment criteria to be.

The issue of the measures used to determine sales-staff remuneration is an example of how problems can arise within a department. Thus in many organizations sales-staff remuneration is based in part on a commission scheme related in some way to the orders received. However, the pursuit of commission may lead some sales staff to neglect parts of their job, such as giving technical advice to customers. Their neglect may lead to other sales staff who take the time to give good technical advice, and consequently get less commission, feeling resentful about their colleagues' behaviour. (Of course, a good sales manager will be aware that those sales staff who do give advice are of greater value to the firm, because their actions are more likely to build a longer-term relationship with the customers.)

Interdepartmental conflicts arise because the assessment measures used in different departments may cause them to pursue policies that are not supportive of each other. As was mentioned above, the marketing department might be convinced that it could increase revenue if new variants were added to an existing product line. Marketing may be assessed in part by the volume of sales, but, if the production department is assessed on the basis of the unit cost of production, then there is the potential for conflict. The problem is that producing added variants might well increase machine-down time, because of the need to reset the production machinery.

A more subtle issue is the growth of jealousy or resentment resulting from the praise and attention that is given to a department for some achievement or action. Sometimes the members of another department will feel that it was they that made the major contribution, and the resentment caused by not receiving the praise they felt was due can cause severe problems of morale.

3.5 How can these barriers be overcome?

Clearly marketing departments do not themselves have the authority to instruct other departments to change their policies and procedures. There are, though, actions that they can take that will lessen the impact of existing barriers and also help to find ways of reducing the effects of those that cannot be removed. However, it is not within marketing's power to alter such issues, for example, as the way in which another department's performance is assessed. All that it can do is find a suitable forum and then draw attention to those cases where it believes the way in which a department's performance is being measured make it more difficult for the organization to implement its marketing strategy. Nevertheless, unless the senior management is committed to implementing a marketing orientation, there can be little possibility that others in the organization will commit themselves to policies such as cooperating with other departments—it seems that cooperation between departments is not something that is automatically pursued (Souder 1988). It often requires senior management to give a strong lead and particularly to set a clear example by the way they behave amongst themselves to make it happen.

Some of the actions that can develop coordination are simple and obvious, but this does not mean they will not be helpful—sophistication, as such, adds little to most actions. First, it is necessary to recognize that marketing has a particularly complex role within an organization in that its activities impinge on and are affected by a large number of other departments. Marketing probably has more interdepartmental connections within the firm than most other departments, and its ability to achieve its objectives is often dependent upon the cooperation of several other departments. The products it markets are a bundle of attributes whose creation has depended upon contributions from several departments in the organization. As the cutting-tool example (see Box 16.1) shows, other departments' concentration on those issues that they regard to be their immediate concern may lead to unfortunate failures to see the picture as a whole.

Furthermore, marketing has a particular problem with regard to the quality of the information and data that it is accustomed to use. Although it is a broad generalization, much marketing information is perceived by other departments to be less well defined than that produced by them. This is unfortunate and mixes up two factors. First, marketing frequently has necessarily to work with estimates and these estimates often have a high degree of error attached to them. Thus, forecasting the sales of a genuinely new product is always going to be difficult. Secondly, the data available from other departments is not always as accurate as it might appear. The accounting analysis that gives costs to the nearest penny makes all sorts of assumptions about allocation of costs, and consequently the accuracy of these cost estimates is often not much greater than that of marketing's forecasts of sales. However, because the money has been 'spent', while the forecast is yet to happen, it seems that some people feel that the cost data are more sound.

Research indicates (Kanter 1989) that successful managers develop a network of interpersonal relationships within their organization. This presents marketing staff with a considerable problem, for the nature of their task means that they are primarily concerned with the world outside the organization. Also, their 'view of the world' is customer dominated. So it seems perverse that they should be encouraged to spend more time inside their organization. However, a manager can use interpersonal networks for a variety of purposes but particularly to communicate with other departments. So, if marketing personnel are to be able to communicate effectively with their colleagues, they must take time to build up such networks—at least until a trust relationship has been developed between them and these colleagues. They must also seek to understand the issues that concern other departments and the problems they face, at least to the extent that they can, whenever possible, take account of these issues when asking for these departments' cooperation.

An ideal way to help develop these networks is to invite non-marketing personnel—especially from those departments where the interdependence between them and marketing is very intense—to spend time with marketing and sales personnel and ideally for them to visit some customers. These visits should be reciprocated, with marketing personnel spending time in the other departments. Such exchanges are clearly time-consuming and not always feasible, but where they are they have two effects. First, the people involved obtain a direct insight into the other department's way of working and the problems that are of major concern to it. Secondly, they help build personal bonds between the staff involved. One of the great advantages that smaller organizations have is that much of the interaction that creates understanding and cooperation between departments happens quite naturally, with staff from various functions meeting over coffee, at lunch, or in the sports club. Unfortunately, in bigger organizations the marketing staff may be based at a considerable distance from some of the other departments. What is worse, their work may not naturally cause them to visit, say, their organization's manufacturing unit—some marketing people never do make such visits. Where this is the case, an apparently imperious demand faxed by a faceless member of the marketing department requiring action that involves, say, a change in the production schedule is unlikely to produce a warm response from a production manager.

4 Accounting and marketing

'They're enemies,' said a senior partner in an international firm of consultants when asked about the relationship between the marketing and accounting functions. Certainly, there has traditionally been conflict (Barwise *et al.* 1989) between marketing managers and accountants, with marketers viewing accountants as 'bean-counters' or 'score-keepers' and accountants viewing marketing personnel as 'big spenders' and 'too intuitive'. Such views may be a slight exaggeration, but, even where personal relationships between members of these two departments are quite good, it is not at all uncommon to find that their business relations are a little brittle.

One of the difficulties is that the accounting function in a firm fulfils a number of roles. In particular, there is the financial accounting role and the management accounting role. The former is particularly concerned with collecting and processing information for such bodies as the tax authorities and the preparation of the balance sheet and profit and loss accounts for inclusion in the company's Annual Report. The management accounting function is, in comparison, concerned with providing managers with the information that they need for decision-making and not with collecting data to be made available to the public.

Financial accounting necessarily requires the careful interpretation of rules and is almost entirely concerned with information that can be expressed in monetary terms. It is as a consequence of this that managers from time to time find accountants' activities involve them in irritating and time-consuming processes that are not seen as adding value to the company's activities. Even at the level of reimbursing expenses, the accounting department may impose rules requiring supporting evidence of expenditure that can take quite a time to assemble in the stipulated format. Such requirements can cause considerable irritation. Thus when a salesman returns from a demanding overseas visit with a brief case full of possible orders, etc., it is perhaps understandable that he becomes annoyed at having to spend time filling in expense sheets and assembling hotel bills, and so on, to support his claims.

👉 'As consumer product markets become more competitive, managers are being challenged to accept that an emphasis on a limited range of financial measures is now inadequate as a means of determining the overall well-being of a company and its brands.' (Chapter 22, p. 527)

In large organizations a different group from the one having responsibility for management accounting normally carries out the financial accounting function. Unfortunately, in a small firm both functions may have to be carried out by *the* accountant or *the* accounting department. Consequently, because of the mandatory nature of much of what a financial accountant does, the 'bean-counting' and rule-dependency aspect of accounting has to dominate, and consequently accounting's monitoring role becomes its most public face.

However, in those organizations (and there are many where this is true) where the management accountants understand both the business and the challenges and problems of the individual functions, they provide substantial assistance, help, and insight into the most effective way of running the organization. Where a management accountant does not fulfil this role, it may be as much the result of the behaviour of the managers in other functions as of the accountant's attitudes. In the context of this chapter there are two particular reasons why accounting may not be as helpful as it might be hoped for. First, the accounting function

has, like any function, limited resources at its disposal. So, if marketing feels it needs substantial additional help from the accounting function, it may need to support a request for extra resources for the accounting function. Secondly, very often the accounting function is unaware of the ways in which it could help marketing, or, if aware, is unwilling to expend energy on it until it is convinced that marketing will value the work involved. It is too often the case that accountants, having set up new procedures, find that the information obtained and the results of the subsequent analysis are being ignored. Unfortunately, there are cases where managers follow the precept 'my mind's made up—don't bother me with the facts!', and, even where they had asked for an analysis to be carried out, will, when it is found not to support their preconceived opinions, ignore the results. However, such people are quite willing, when the analysis is supportive of their position, to present it as evidence of the good sense of their intuition.

4.1 An illustration

The following illustration shows how information available to accountants can help guide marketing staff into actions that will increase profitability. Table 17.1 shows some accounting information relating to a particular customer's (let it be called Jones) performance. The picture that this information provides is one where sales are increasing steadily but gross profits are falling and profit contribution is falling even faster. Clearly part of the problem is that marketing costs have doubled while sales revenue has risen by only 14 per cent. Of course, sales by volume may be rising more

Table 17.1 Jones plc cost of sales

	1995	1996	1997
Sales (£)	350,000	380,000	400,000
Cost of goods sold (£)	262,000	296,000	320,000
Gross profit (£)	88,000	84,000	80,000
Gross profit %	25	22	20
Marketing costs (£)	8,000	12,100	16,200
Profit contribution (£)	80,000	71,900	63,800
Profit contribution %	23	19	16

rapidly than sales by value—prices might be under pressure or the nature of the orders being placed might mean that the customer is gaining bigger discounts than in the past. It may, for example, be placing fewer but individually larger orders. There would be information available that would indicate whether or not either of these cases applied.

However, if the accountants were asked for, or on their own initiative provided the marketing personnel with, information about inventory-carrying costs and accounts receivable, then marketing might see more clearly why less profit was being made than in the past. Table 17.2 provides this information. These figures indicate that the customer has been paying bills more slowly than in the past and the result has been that the cost of providing credit to the customer has nearly doubled while sales have increased by only 14 per cent. Similarly, the cost of financing the stock held for this customer has risen disproportionately. Once the company is aware of this situation, marketing can consider several actions to take to try to improve the profitability of this account. It could, if it has not already done so, introduce a prompt-payment discount and also look carefully at any discounts it has that are related to the size of order. It may be that by using various forms of quantity discount it can encourage the customer to change the size of its orders. This simple illustration demonstrates how careful analysis of appropriate cost data can help a firm to understand why its profitability is falling and more positively point the way to possible responses that may, if not reverse the trend, at least slow it.

However, as with all simple illustrations, there is a catch in this one: to be able to provide the above information, the accountant has to be able to identify costs with customers. In this case the firm is portrayed as having only one customer. Consider now what would happen if a second customer, Smith, had been obtained in 1997. As long as the product that Smith purchases can be produced entirely separately from that for Jones, then there is no problem in producing the cost information above. However, what if both firms purchased the same product—how then could, for example, the inventory costs be realistically allocated between them?

For example, if in 1997 the firm sold Smith £300,000 worth of goods and that the volume of sales was 350 tons and 280 tons to Jones and Smith respectively (see Table 17.3). If the accountant determined that the total inventory-holding cost for 1997 was £50,000, then, if an attempt is to be made to understand the profitability of both customers, this cost has to be split between them. There are several ways this could be done, each of which would lead to a different profit figure for each of the customers, as is shown in Table 17.3. However, not only do these figures differ from each other, but they also underestimate the costs that would have been allocated to Jones if Smith had not arrived. If the figure of £30,000 is accepted

Table 17.2 Jones plc identification of customer cost

	1995	1996	1997
Sales	350,000	380,000	400,000
Gross profit	88,000	84,000	80,000
Marketing costs	8,000	12,100	16,200
Profit contribution	80,000	71,900	63,800
Account receivable @ 20%[a]	12,000	20,000	30,000
Inventory costs @ 30%[b]	15,750	19,500	30,000
Residual income	52,250	32,400	3,800
Residual income %	15	8	1
[a] Customer's average balance outstanding	60,000	100,000	150,000
[b] Customer's average inventory holding	52,500	65,000	100,000

Table 17.3 **Illustration of inventory cost allocation (£)**			
Alternative cost allocations	Jones	Smith	Total
Split in proportion to value of sales	28,570	21,430	50,000
Split in proportion to volume of sales	27,780	22,220	50,000

as appropriate to allocate to Jones, then Smith with 43 per cent of the company's turnover would bear only 40 per cent of the inventory costs (i.e. £20,000) rather than either £21,430 or £22,220, because Jones's behaviour is causing inventories to increase in size. The choice of method of allocating such joint costs is, therefore, of great importance, because it can change management's view of the profitability of a particular customer. Because of this, and particularly because of the increased concentration in size in so many markets, marketing personnel are beginning to ask accountants to split out costs by customer. However, to be able to do this effectively often requires a substantial revision of the methods employed to allocate costs, with activity-based accounting (ABC) being a method that has attracted a great deal of attention and not a little controversy (Kaplan and Norton 1992; Hilton 1994).

☞ 'The differentiation of commission rates across products and/or customers enables the firm to direct its sales force towards certain activities.'   (Chapter 13, p. 304)

4.2 Activity based accounting

ABC essentially tries to allocate costs in relation to the activities that occur in a firm. In doing so it may use several different ways of splitting overhead or common costs. When a salesman obtains an order, this triggers a series of activities that could include: the purchase of additional raw materials, various activities in the factory, a lot of administrative activity, physical movement of the product from the point of manufacture to the customer, servicing activities at the customer's plant, and so on. What an ABC system attempts to do is measure and track the costs of such activities through time. The aim of ABC is to assign the costs of significant activities to the products and customers that caused those costs to be incurred. Ac-

tivities are, of course, the events that preoccupy employees throughout the organization, and any activity that results in costs being incurred is a cost driver. There are, though, many activities that do not incur substantial costs, and ABC, like any costing system, concerns itself only with significant costs.

In ABC a two-stage allocation process is used. In the first stage overhead costs are assigned to a number of cost pools that represent the most significant activities in the organization. After assigning costs to these pools, cost drivers are identified that are appropriate for each cost pool. Then the overhead costs are allocated from each activity cost pool to each customer in proportion to the amount of activity consumed by that customer.

For example, a cost pool might be the group of staff that receives incoming orders and initially checks them for inaccuracies or omissions before forwarding them to another section. What is necessary is to determine the best cost driver to use to apply to this cost pool. If it was decided to use the number of orders as the cost driver, then the costs of running this section would be allocated to each customer in proportion to the number of orders placed. However, other cost drivers might also be used, as is indicated below.

There are three criteria that are important if the introduction of an ABC system is to be worthwhile. First, can the correlation between a cost driver and a customer or a product (depending on whether a customer or a product profitability analysis is being carried out) be identified? For example, assume that a sales clerk's time has been identified as an activity cost pool, then two potential cost drivers come to mind: the number of orders that the clerk deals with within a specified period, and the time taken to process an order. If the time taken to process orders varies very little between the customers placing orders, then the number of orders is an appropriate measure. However, if the time to process an order can vary a great deal according to which customer it comes from (the documentation for some customers may require much more detailed checking than that for others; some customers may order only a few items but others may usually order a large number). In such circumstances, recording the number of orders will not accurately portray the way the clerk's time is consumed in response to individual customers' activities. It would, then, be necessary for the clerk to record the time spent on each order.

The second criterion is that the costs of setting up an ABC system must clearly be balanced against its benefits. It can be very tempting to establish a large number of activity cost pools in a firm, because by doing so the accuracy of the cost assignment will be greater, but clearly the greater the number of cost pools, the higher the costs of data collection. It is also important to recognize that, in choosing which cost drivers to work with, a balance has to be struck between the cost of data collecting and the benefits. For example, in the case of the sales clerk, collecting data about the number of orders processed is likely to be much less costly than measuring how much time is spent on each order. So, especially if the cost of the clerk's time is very small compared to the total cost of the product (if say the firm was selling PCs rather than clothing by mail order), then it is likely that the cheaper though less accurate cost driver would be appropriate.

Thirdly, all information systems have behavioural effects and, as far as possible given the natural perversity of human nature, attempts must be made to foresee how people will react to various measures that might be used. If, in the case of the sales clerks, it is decided to use number of orders as the cost driver, is there a risk that the clerks may tend to rush the work to impress managers with their productivity?

Possible activity areas/cost drivers for a distributor of consumer goods are shown in Box 17.2. However, others might provide more useful information, depending upon exactly what type of operation is being run. The point is that identifying the appropriate cost pools and the best cost drivers must involve both accountants and people who understand the various activities being dealt with. It is no criticism of accountants to say that they are often not in a position to 'see' activities and therefore to understand how costs arise and how personnel behaviour may be affected by imposing certain cost measures. There is certainly

Box 17.2 **Illustration of cost drivers in an order taking function**	
Activity area	**Cost driver**
Order processing	Number of orders
Line item ordering	Number of line items
Store delivery	Number of store deliveries
Cartons shipped at store	Number of cartons shipped to a store per delivery
Shelf stacking at customer store	Number of hours shelf stacking

a strong case for arguing that multidisciplinary teams provide the best basis for designing and gathering information for an ABC system. There are really two reasons for this. The first, as indicated, is that accountants cannot be expected fully to understand either all the facets of an organization's activities or the likely behaviour of quite disparate groups of employees. Therefore they need to work with the managers of each department so that they can gain an understanding of how it works. The second reason is that, if a department's staff are involved in the process, they are much more likely to give the resulting analyses credibility.

4.3 Interpreting an ABC analysis

The interpretation of ABC analyses also needs a multidisciplinary approach. Identifying that supplying a particular customer is currently unprofitable should not mean that steps will automatically be taken no longer to supply it. There are at least four reasons why an 'unprofitable' customer may be retained:

■ This may be a new customer that is currently being nurtured for the future. The costs of dealing with it may therefore be high relative to its current purchases, but there is a potential for future larger orders.

■ Being known as a supplier to a particular customer may have a status that is of value in itself. For example, being known as an authorized supplier to a customer whose reputation for high quality is publicly recognized might be worthwhile in terms of image.

- The customer may be the first client that the supplier has in a new market and is regarded as a stepping stone into that market. In such a situation, therefore, high initial costs are likely to be incurred.
- The resources released by dropping the customer cannot be redeployed (i.e. there is no alternative use for them that generates at least as much income as the current activity) and if they are not redeployed their costs will simply have to be absorbed elsewhere. It may be better to have some income to set against such costs until the resources can be either redeployed or disposed of.

Decisions as to whether any of these circumstances are relevant are not those that accountants are in a position to make on their own. Clearly, marketing and sales personnel should be involved in such an assessment. However, equally clearly, it is important that the accountants are able to press sales and marketing staff for justification of any decision to continue to supply an unprofitable customer. It may, after all, be the case that the sales manager and the customer's purchasing manager are close friends, making the sales manager, because of his personal relationship, reluctant to sever the business relationship. The argument that 'I'm sure that they will give us a big order next year' needs probing by somebody.

Where ABC can be very useful is in identifying actions that the supplier can take to make a customer more profitable. A useful technique is to take pairs of customers that seem similar in the value, number, and types of orders that they place and compare the costs allocated to each line by line. It may be that the costs attributed for, say, technical advice to one customer in a pair is higher than those attributed to the other one. It does not follow that the technical service offered to the customer with the higher cost should be cut. It may be that offering more technical advice to the customer currently receiving the lower level of service would result in a higher level of sales.

Consider the following example of two customers similar in the value, number, and types of orders they place. Technical advice and delivery costs for A are disproportionately low compared with those for B (see Table 17.4). This should lead to questions such as whether or not the sales representatives are spending enough time with A. Could it be that, if the sales staff knew customer A better, they would be able to obtain higher prices?

Table 17.4 **Disparity of costs between two similar customers**

Costs	Customer A	Customer B
Costs:		
Sales representatives	60	100
Delivery	50	80
Profit	1,000	1,300

The disparity in the delivery charges might result in questions being asked about the use of discounts to encourage B to take fewer deliveries. The important issue is to recognize that identifying a disproportionately low cost may indicate either some efficiency that can be achieved with other customers *or* a need to increase spending on that item for that customer. Once again, such an interpretation should be made only by a team of people who understand the activities and the nature of the business being reviewed.

Finally, one factor that marketing managers, even when working with a sympathetic accountant, have to recognize is that accountants often have historic data that enable them to make accurate estimates of the costs of future decisions—certainly much more accurate than estimates marketing staff can make of the results of some of their activities (say, the expected revenues from a new marketing initiative). For example, when marketing proposes to introduce a new advertising campaign, the accountant can, on the basis of past experience, accurately estimate the costs that will be incurred. In comparison, the marketing manager's estimate of the benefits of the campaign will necessarily be less precise.

5 Manufacturing and marketing

5.1 Marketing strategy

In spite of the forceful arguments by a range of observers, the role of the manufacturing function in providing a company with a basis on which to develop a distinctive competence receives little attention (Hill *et al.* 1997), yet changes in production/manufacturing technologies can have several effects. They can reduce the manufacturing costs of existing products, they can improve the quality of existing products, and they can make possible the introduction of new products. Perhaps manufacturing receives relatively little attention because it is only the new products that the customer really notices. However, it will be argued here that, when discussing a company's marketing strategy, at the very least an understanding of its manufacturing capabilities is required, but that, especially in industries where dramatic changes in manufacturing technology are being introduced, failure to integrate manufacturing and marketing strategies can lead to lost opportunities.

There are four generic marketing strategies open to firms, those based upon:

- cost competitiveness;
- product differentiation;
- focus (based on cost or product differentiation);
- vertical linkage.

The successful pursuit of any of these strategies requires the development of an appropriate organization and particularly makes demands on the firm's manufacturing technologies. Thus a firm pursuing a marketing strategy based upon the achievement of cost competitiveness will look to manufacturing to use those processes that make possible the efficient manufacture of the type of product mix demanded by the market.

However, the historic pattern of the development of manufacturing technology has been for improvements to occur along a small number (often one) of dimensions at any one time. Indeed, until the development of advanced manufacturing technologies (AMT), one of the problems with the new manufacturing technologies was that increases in automation often meant less flexibility. Thus the response to the demands of marketing strategy has generally been direct and uncomplicated. For example, if the marketing strategy was based upon focusing on a particular market requiring a limited range of choice, then manufacturing sought to create facilities that met the need to produce a limited range of products economically. Manufacturing then sought to improve the efficiency of this facility by reducing set-up times, the machine time for each product manufactured, and so on. In the past such improvements were at-

tainable in isolation from each other. In comparison, one of the distinctive features of manufacturing technologies such as flexible manufacturing systems (FMS) and computer aided design and manufacturing (CAD/CAM) is that they simultaneously provide improvements along several dimensions of manufacturing capability.

5.2 Manufacturing capabilities and marketing strategies

AMTs are to be found in a variety of industries and applications, but the following seem to be the effects that are associated with their introduction in most circumstances:

- reduction in unit costs;
- reduction in manufacturing lead times;
- flexibility of batch size;
- flexibility of product specification;
- better quality control;
- better managerial control.

What then are the links between a firm's manufacturing capabilities and the four generic marketing strategies? Fig. 17.1 sets out the four generic marketing strategies on the horizontal axis while the vertical axis lists six categories of effects that are associated with the introduction of AMT. Some of these are most obviously directly supportive of one of the four marketing strategies. Indeed, investment in AMT has often been made with the intention of exploiting just one of these attributes in support of a particular marketing strategy. However, each of these attributes can support more than one of these marketing strategies and this fact emphasizes the need, when investing in AMT, to reappraise the firm's strategies.

Failure to do so will, at best, lead to lost opportunities; at worst it may place the firm at a competitive disadvantage relative to any competitor that has understood the benefits that AMT offers.

5.2.1 Reduction in unit costs

There are numerous well-documented cases of firms using AMT and thus achieving considerable reductions in unit manufacturing costs. For example, Lucas Electrical reported reducing the manufacturing costs of many components by two-thirds through the use of an FMS. When AMT provides such cost savings, a decision must be made as to how this saving should be used.

Figure 17.1 Generic strategies and manufacturing capabilities

Marketing strategies

AMT Attributes	A Cost competitiveness	B Product differentiation	C Focus	D Control over supply or distribution
Reduction in unit costs				
Reduction in manufacturing lead times				
Flexibility of batch size				
Flexibility of product specification				
Better quality control				
Better managerial control				

☞ 'But, increasingly, new products must be developed and brought to market quickly in order to meet customer wants in a timely manner and to stay ahead of competition. To this end, CAD . . . has made tremendous contributions both in reducing costs and in speeding up the design process . . .' (Chapter 24, p. 559)

Where Strategy A is being pursued, it may initially seem appropriate to use some or all of the cost reductions to finance the lowering of prices. However, the reduction in costs could be used to finance some form of Strategy B. For example, it might be decided to maintain prices but improve the quality of service back-up by, say, holding higher stocks of spares. Such an action would differentiate the product offering from that of competitors. Alternatively, where Strategy C is being followed, the reduced manufacturing costs might be used to cover the costs that marketing to several small segments inevitably incurs—for example, high distribution costs.

Thus the choice of which marketing strategy to pursue will determine the way in which this cost saving is utilized. However, in those industries where manufacturing costs are not a major proportion of the price, a reduction in manufacturing costs can have only a small effect upon prices. In such cases, especially if the price elasticity in the markets served is low, it is almost certainly best to use the cost reductions to support Strategy B.

5.2.2 Reduction in manufacturing lead times

The use of AMT reduces the delays between the placing of an order by a customer and the delivery of the product. Thus the introduction of FMS by Cessna Fluid Power produced a reduction of twenty days (from thirty) in the time required to manufacture aluminium plates and bodies. Other facilities regarded as part of AMT, such as CAD, have also produced reductions in lead times, as is illustrated by Ford, where the time required to design a simple flange around a car windscreen has been reduced from four days to less than half a day.

Such reductions in lead times are supportive of Strategy B, as they enable the firm to differentiate its product offering ('product' being interpreted in the sense of the bundle of benefits a customer obtains) by providing a more rapid response to customers' demands. If Strategy C is being followed, then for particular segments—say, spares demand—the reduction in lead time may be valuable as a mechanism for offering a superior service without holding costly stocks.

It is, however, possible that the reduction in manufacturing lead time can be best exploited by making cost economies elsewhere in the organization rather than by improving delivery times to customers. Many companies, for example, use flexible and therefore expensive distribution systems because they need to move their products to customers as soon as they are produced. Where this is the case, then it may be that the shorter lead times could be used to maintain existing delivery lead times but by using less expensive distribution schemes, thus providing a cost saving that could be utilized under Strategy A. Alternatively, the lower costs could be used to finance the provision of a better service to customers, thus supporting Strategy D with its intent of strengthening links between the firm and its customers.

It is, in addition, the case that these shorter manufacturing lead times create substantial cost reductions in their own right: Anderson Strathclyde claimed a saving of £1 million per annum on stockholding costs resulting from the faster throughput achieved with AMT. Where cost savings of this sort are achieved, it has to be decided how to use them, as discussed above.

The firm's marketing strategy will indicate how these improvements in manufacturing lead times can best be utilized. Yet, whether they are passed on to the customers or absorbed within the firm, the fact that customers may be prepared to pay a higher price for quicker delivery must be included in the decision-making process.

5.2.3 Flexibility of batch size

The capability of AMT to produce small batches with little, if any, cost penalties in comparison with large batches is now well established. A typical illustration of this was found in Cessna Fluid Power, where the introduction of AMT made possible the economic production of batches anywhere in the range of 25 to 400 units. Previously the minimum economic batch was 100.

As was the case with reduced lead times, many companies have regarded this attribute as supportive of Strategy B, and thus it has been seen as a reason for investing in AMT. Certainly, customers view the willingness of a supplier to accept small orders, without imposing penalties, as a form of product differentiation. Indeed, many suppliers not only charge higher prices on small batches but in various other ways discourage customers from ordering in small quantities. For example, delivery times for small batches are sometimes longer than for big batches. Again, attempts are sometimes made to persuade customers, who only place small orders, to deal with distributors. Therefore the ability to manufacture economically in small batches may be viewed by customers as a significant form of product differentiation.

When Strategy C is being followed, this ability to manufacture small batches economically and without large cost penalties makes possible segmentation based on product differentiation without excessive manufacturing costs being incurred. Alternatively, it might be beneficial to use these savings in manufacturing costs to finance the development of a direct supply to all customers instead of using distributors. Such an action would be supportive of Strategy D.

5.2.4 Flexibility of product specification

The capability of AMT to offer a wide range of variations within a product family without cost penalties is obviously supportive of Strategy B. The ability to do this without long lead times may well enable a supplier to distinguish itself from competitors. Again, though, the price at which this improved service should be offered must be considered with care. It may be that the improved service will be valued by a customer to such an extent that existing prices may be maintained or even raised. In either case, decisions then have to be taken as to how to use the increased profits.

5.2.5 Better quality control

One of the benefits of AMT is the consistently high quality of the products it produces and the speed at which it is able to identify the source of quality deviations. The Westinghouse Electric Corporation estimated that, prior to a campaign to improve it, the cost of poor quality represented 15–20 per cent of its sales. Thus, it is clear that improvements in quality can produce significant cost savings and thus could support Strategy A. However, if competitors are not also improving quality, then Strategy B could be pursued. Furthermore, given the problems created for customers by poor quality, it is also possible that customer loyalty would be increased by the provision of a consistently good quality supply. This would provide an opportunity to exercise considerable influence, if not control, over customers and thus support Strategy D. Indeed, in some industries distributors compete to become recognized suppliers for Japanese firms *because* of their product quality.

5.2.6 Better managerial control

The ability to handle very large volumes of data very fast but at a very low cost is at the heart of the development of AMT. Moreover, in addition to handling data, the ability to transmit it rapidly at low cost has also developed, and this is leading to changes in internal organizational structures and organizational relationships in firms using AMT. This is an important development, for, although most discussions of AMT logically consider it as a system, this does not mean that all the elements must be in one factory or indeed in one firm. In other words, if a manufacturer uses a CAD/CAM system, it could use the system's output within its own organization or send it to another organization that possesses manufacturing equipment that can accept that output. Indeed, much of the need to maintain all aspects of design and manufacture in one organization ceases to exist if it is possible to specify parts in a language that are acceptable to automated facilities.

Developments in AMT and information transfer now mean that firms that do not possess equipment that is compatible with their customers' may be unable to remain as suppliers. For example, Rover, whose cars are built with at least 60 per cent of the items coming from outside suppliers, has found that, for the company to have a fully integrated system, its vendors had to be included in the Rover policy of computer-integrated engineering. It therefore became essential that its suppliers had to adopt similar manufacturing methods to those at Rover, using only numerically controlled machine tools to produce components, so that the finished product was traceable directly to the database, uncorrupted by manual intervention.

The benefits to a customer of being able to build up such a relationship with its suppliers are that it is assured of a consistent quality of supply at a controlled price. Such a situation obviously supports

it in manufacturing an economic but high-quality product and helps Strategy A or B. These benefits also strengthen the links between a firm and its suppliers by forcing the suppliers to invest in machinery and procedures that are appropriate to the particular customer. From the customer's point of view, the creation of such links with reliable suppliers is a considerable competitive advantage and supports Strategy D.

These, then, are some of the possible links between marketing and manufacturing strategies that are relevant in the context of AMT. In some cases the decision to invest in AMT arises because it is seen as a way of meeting the requirements of an established marketing strategy. In other cases the investment is made on the basis of a manufacturing goal of lowering costs. In either case, an investment in AMT opens up possibilities for a marketing strategy that may not have been foreseen. However, this is only possible if marketing management

- fully understands the AMT's capabilities;
- is prepared to make changes in marketing strategy initiated in response to changes in the company's resource base;
- is able to identify any changes required in non-manufacturing and marketing functions if the AMT's capabilities are to be fully exploited.

5.3 The implications for marketing strategy

Therefore, although a firm may invest in AMT in its pursuit of an existing marketing strategy, the set of manufacturing capabilities will often be broader than that which is required for the existing strategy. This can make the pursuit of alternative marketing strategies possible. This difference in approach is compared in Figs. 17.2 and 17.3. In Fig. 17.2 the pursuit of a marketing strategy based on cost differentiation leads to pressure for a reduction in manufacturing costs using conventional manufacturing techniques. The pursuit of this strategy might lead to an investment in new manufacturing plant, and achievement of this reduction in costs supports the marketing policy, as indicated by the arrow.

In Fig. 17.3, pursuit of the same marketing strategy leads to an investment in AMT because of its cost-reduction capabilities. However, an investment in AMT simultaneously brings other attributes such as a reduction in lead times, greater flexibility, improved quality, and, particularly, the cost-versus-variety trade-off inherent in traditional manufacturing technologies. Together, this

Figure 17.2 **Manufacturing strategy as a response to marketing strategy**

new set of capabilities makes possible the pursuit of any of the four generic marketing strategies—for example, the low cost of producing small batches may now make a focus strategy possible. This is indicated by the replacement of the arrow by four alternative routes.

Thus, the introduction of AMT raises questions as to whether or not the new manufacturing capabilities provide the base for a change in marketing strategy? Yet it is apparent that firms can fail to recognize the opportunities that AMT offers for a variety of reasons. In the context of this discussion two common reasons are:

■ a preoccupation with a particular strategy because of market conditions that have remained unchanged over long periods of time—for example, over capacity in the industry leading to severe price competition;

■ a commitment to a strategy that, while appropriate at one time, has involved large investments of both effort and money, which have led to a reluctance to accept change.

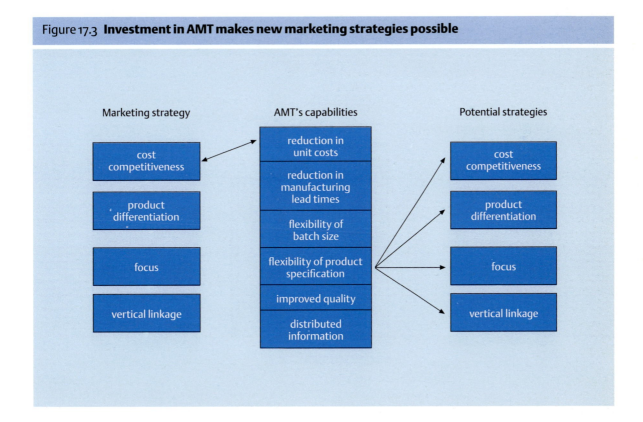

Figure 17.3 **Investment in AMT makes new marketing strategies possible**

5.4 The response of non-manufacturing departments

A full exploitation of AMT requires a flexible organizational design that allows quick responses to take advantage of the capabilities of the technology. This is because AMT heightens the complexity and interdependence within the firm.

An additional issue is that, when introducing an AMT, whatever marketing strategy is followed, changes are required to functions in addition to marketing and manufacturing. No matter which marketing strategy is pursued (indeed even if the investment in AMT does not lead to a change in marketing strategy), the increased efficiency offered by AMT can all too easily be dissipated within the firm itself by a failure to make the necessary adjustments to the operation of other non-manufacturing functions. For example, if it is decided to exploit the AMT's ability to offer greater flexibility of batch size, then this will make quite different demands on departments such as purchasing, finished stocks, accounts, and so on than if the previous strategy had been on cost reduction. So, unless these and other activities within the firm are reorganized, much of the potential benefit of the investments made in an AMT may be lost or 'filtered out' within the firm and will not improve the firm's marketing offering (see Fig. 17.4). The need to recognize that the introduction of AMT will have an effect on most parts of the firm is perhaps illustrated by the research results that assert that 'Existing cost accounting and management control practices are unlikely to provide useful indicators for managing contemporary firm's manufacturing operations' (Jaikumar 1986). Further, this research also established that the selection of an internal accounting system must be made simultaneously with the choice of the firm's corporate and manufacturing strategy. Such views supporting the argument above that accounts and marketing must work together.

5.5 Managerial implications

Developments in the production technologies of a number of industries in the 1990s were dramatic. They provide those firms that invest in them with

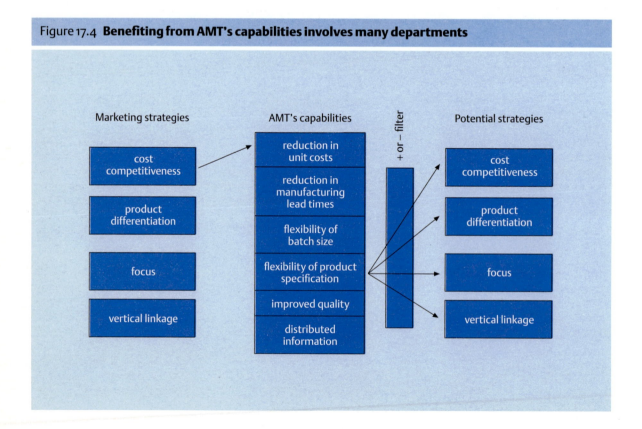

Figure 17.4 **Benefiting from AMT's capabilities involves many departments**

the opportunity of creating a capability gap between their standards of performance and those of their competitors. However, the existence of such a capability gap does not automatically provide a distinctive competence, for this gap must be used to create product/delivery attributes that are a key buying criterion for the market.

There are few parts of the firm that are unaffected by the introduction of AMT. However, there are four issues that stand out as requiring particular attention. First, there is the need for marketing knowledge as distinct from market knowledge in the sense that the latter provides only a description of the market as it is and has been, while marketing knowledge provides an understanding of the factors that determine the nature of market demand. To obtain marketing knowledge requires constant probing of the customers' needs (and thus an understanding of their marketing position) so that what would ideally satisfy the customers is known even if currently it cannot be supplied.

Secondly, management needs to realize that investment in machinery and systems provides only the opportunity to create a competitive advantage, and competitive advantage is obtained through investment in AMT only if management works hard to create it. Just as obtaining a reduction in costs through increasing cumulative output is obtained only by management driving hard to achieve experience-curve effects, so too AMT's benefits do not occur automatically but through changes in management attitudes.

Thirdly, changes in managerial relationships must be planned for; otherwise, at best tensions will arise, while at worst chaos will ensue.

Fourthly, far greater understanding of the concept of flexibility is required. Those managers not closely involved with AMT have been encouraged to expect an extraordinary degree of flexibility. However, the experience of many companies has shown that flexibility at one level may reduce it at another.

Finally, management must consider what is the appropriate costing system for their firm once they have invested in AMT. In so far as prices are related to costs, failure to do so will lead to inappropriate pricing.

5.6 Conclusion

The need to match a firm's assets with market opportunities is a fundamental requirement of strategy formulation. In what have been called 'market-dominated' companies the needs of the market have led developments in manufacturing expertise and technology. However, the introduction of AMT to a firm offers such a radical change in capabilities that a thorough review and possibly a revision of this matching process are required. The successful implementation of the decisions resulting from such a review may require an extensive reorganization of many functions in the firm in addition to those of manufacturing and marketing. If this is not done, then the natural inclination of both marketing and manufacturing personnel to remain preoccupied with their own functional responsibilities will lead to a failure to gain the full benefits of the investment into AMT. Marketing managers must not regard manufacturing as 'not their problem', and manufacturing managers must not regard marketing simply as a source of orders.

6 Research and development and marketing

THE most obvious link between research and development (R&D) and marketing is with regard to new product development. The effective management of the relationship between these two parts of a firm has been identified as a major factor in enabling firms to produce a steady supply of successful new products. However, the management of this interface is far from easy, and, while it is tempting to state that the root of the difficulty is one of communication, the use of such a term hides, in this context, more than it explains. Effective communication between these two activities is clearly important, but what 'effective' means is complex (Moenaert and Souder 1996). In particular, it is clear that for effective collaboration to occur, more than structural solutions, such as ensuring that these departments exchange reports and regularly hold meetings, is required. What is more important is for there to be a behavioural change based upon a greater understanding and respect for each department's competence and expertise.

👉 '... there is at least one essential factor that has consistently been found to have an overriding impact on new-product success and that has to do with how the development process is organized and managed within the firm. Making certain that the right people are involved at the right time and the right way will significantly affect the speed and the effectiveness of the process.' (Chapter 24, p. 562)

Fundamentally the typical member of an R&D department will have a quite different education, training, and business experience from a member of a marketing department. These different backgrounds mean that the way they organize their thinking and actions—interpretative schema—about product development can lead to the creation of a barrier to collaborative working (Dougherty 1992). Members of a department share these schemata, which provide assumptions about reality, the identification of important issues, and their structuring of the environment.

6.1 Differing world views

These interpretative schemata mean that each department has a different view of the world, which leads them to focus on different aspects of the technological/marketing information relating to a new product. To some extent this is a matter of what each group understands, for it is difficult to assimilate information about things that fall outside our technological knowledge. However, even where there is a common understanding, differing emphases will be placed on the same information according to the recipient's interests and knowledge. It is, therefore, not surprising that the information that the various functional groups in an organization understand about a particular customer or a market will differ a great deal. Indeed, left to themselves each department will tend to define an issue from their own perspective and focus on only those parts of the new product process that are their direct concern. This can lead them to dismiss as unimportant the interests, concerns, and contributions of other departments.

These different views of the world are based upon each department's knowledge base and the way that the departments obtain that knowledge and then gain understanding of it. The consequential difference in focus is increased rather than reduced by the different organizational routines. For example, an R&D department is less likely than a marketing department to be constantly respond-

ing to short-term pressures. This is not to suggest that R&D departments are islands of tranquillity, but that in general they are buffered from the day-to-day competitive pressures that buffet and thus tend to preoccupy many marketing departments. As a consequence, they do not need to be organized to deal with such pressures.

People with differing 'thought worlds' find it difficult to share ideas because of their different knowledge bases and their different approaches to the interpretation of knowledge. What is worse, it is not uncommon for such people to view what others perceive to be the central issue as at best unimportant and at worst irrelevant. This does not always lead to conflict, because, in a sense, the participants in this situation tend to talk past each other. The result in the case of R&D and marketing though can be the development of technical solutions that do not match the market's requirements.

This means that, to achieve successful interaction between two groups with differing thought worlds, it is necessary

■ to build on and use the unique insights of both groups;
■ to develop collaborative mechanisms that deal directly with the interpretative as well as the structural barriers to joint action;
■ to develop an organizational context for collective action that assists in the achievement of the two above points.

Nobody wanted the Sony Walkman

'Nobody openly laughed at me... Everybody gave me a hard time. It seemed as though nobody liked the idea... I do not think that any amount of market research could have told us that the Sony Walkman would be successful' (Morita 1987).

In reading this statement by Morita (boss of Sony at the time of the Walkman's development), it is vital to recall that what became the Walkman started as Sony's successful small cassette recorder (called 'Pressman') with its recording circuit and the speaker stripped out and replaced with a stereo amplifier plus newly developed very lightweight headphones. Interestingly the idea for the Walkman came from Morita observing a colleague's attempt to listen to music without disturbing others. This involved using one of Sony's portable stereo tape recorders together with a pair of standard-size headphones—a contraption that he found too heavy and large to carry around.

These problems are particularly acute in high-tech industries, for here technologists are often dismissive of the role of marketing and also of the concept of market research producing anything of value. Indeed, the Sony Walkman tale, with various embellishments, is told with great glee by many R&D staff as evidence of the 'uselessness' of market research (see Insert, pervious page).

There are two themes that underpin the scientists' view. These are that 'customers don't know what they want' and that all that the customers are capable of doing is 'extending the past into the future'. This is a criticism that challenges market researchers. It is indeed clear that customers do have great difficulty understanding new product concepts (which are sometimes not descriptions but can take the form of prototypes) and then visualizing what they might do with them (see Insert). It is also inevitable that most customers do little more than extrapolate from ideas and concepts with which they are familiar—and some cannot even do that.

Fascinating but . . . ?

A number of scientists were interviewed as part of a survey to determine the demand for a technical service that would use a new technology to provide surface analyses of the type only required in high-tech manufacturing operations such as electronic chip manufacturing. After hearing a description of the new technology and the analyses that it could provide, the scientist stated: 'It's fascinating technology and I'll certainly want to try it, but at present I haven't a clue what I would do with the results of the analysis. I therefore can't indicate what use I might make of the service you are thinking of offering.'

6.2 The precision of scientific knowledge

A further issue is that scientific knowledge is very different in form from market and marketing knowledge. Precision of measurement and particularly careful replication of experiments are central features of science, but this can hardly be said to be true of marketing. Although some laboratory-style experiments are carried out, most experiments in the field of marketing inevitably produce results with large error terms. Furthermore, replicating marketing experiments is difficult because they are nearly all conducted in a rapidly changing economic environment that means that the values of many of the relevant variables are constantly changing.

6.3 Technical impossibility

A third level of difficulty between marketing and R&D is that marketing is often seen to be asking for a specification that is impossible in technical terms. For example, marketing may call for certain specifications at a cost that is, in the scientists' view, unattainable. However, there are two ways out of this situation. First, marketing can be asked what the effect would be if the cost were not achieved? Secondly, it can be asked what would happen if the cost target was achieved but one or other of the target specifications was not. The answer in both cases might be that sales would be less than predicted, but the issue is then whether or not strategically the firm should proceed with the proposal:

- at the specified cost but with a changed specification;
- at a higher cost but with the requested specification;
- with some mixture of the two.

The scientist's role in all this is to inform the decision-makers of the probability of their achieving marketing's requirements.

The criticisms made by scientists essentially imply that marketing people lack the expertise to translate what customers say they want into technological terms. But this view would seem to be expecting marketing to 'do' the scientists' job, for, while marketing should be skilled in establishing the needs that customer's perceive they have and will have, it is not its role to propose technical solutions. Marketing's role should be to identify customer's current needs and the value propositions to which they will respond. This is a very demanding challenge, as the 'Post-it' story described in Chapter 1 illustrated. (Post-its failed when formally test-marketed. Eventually it became apparent that the only way to get people to use the product was to provide them with samples, as once people had used them they ordered more—though they 'still couldn't talk intelligently about the product'.)

6.4 Differing time horizons

A fourth difficulty is that R&D considers that marketing's time horizon is too short. Marketing is viewed as providing information on what customers want today and on what competitors are currently doing, rather than looking ahead. This criticism is similar to the first one, but differs in that it is saying that marketing, at best, translates what customers say today into information relevant to the current level of products and not the next generation's products. Again this would seem to be an unfair criticism, as it presumes that marketing personnel are equipped to perceive what the next generation of products will be like technologically.

Against scientists' critical views of marketing (Gupta and Wilemon 1988) must be set marketing's views of scientists. Typically, marketing personnel complain that scientists lack perspective and concentrate on a narrow aspect of a problem—being fascinated by the science or technology involved. A consequence, in marketing's view, is that R&D fails to appreciate the customers' needs or expectations of a product, such that it may develop a product to an unnecessarily high and/or uneconomic level of specification. A second complaint is that scientists are inclined to prioritize their activities in terms of the degree of interest of the science and not in terms of customer benefits. The third complaint is that scientists get impatient with the problem of the customers' prior investments, as when a customer prefers to accept a less technically advanced product that is compatible with its existing equipment rather than purchase the latest technology, which would require extra work to install because of its incompatibility with existing equipment. In all this, the scientist seeks 'the best', which he equates with 'the most advanced', while for the customer the best is a trade-off between many things, such as price and compatibility with existing equipment and specifications.

6.5 How then can the R&D–marketing interface be improved?

First, the quality of the information that marketing provides for R&D should be improved. Various studies (e.g. Gupta and Wilemon 1988; Moenaert and Souder 1996) have indicated that R&D managers see this as a critical issue, with complaints being made that

- marketing does not consider the product design trade-offs;

- marketing is ignorant of the product's technology;
- the information marketing provides is inaccurate;
- the information marketing provides is too frequently subject to revision.

The problem with such views is that, while without doubt marketing managers should try to take account of these complaints, what is being demonstrated is R&D's lack of understanding of the difficulties with which marketing works. Indeed, the complaints made by marketing staff about R&D are almost the mirror image of R&D's complaints about marketing.

There are no neat answers to this dilemma. Nevertheless, although a marketing text can hardly give an unbiased view of this matter, it is arguably the case, given that the problem in most firms is to achieve a better marketing orientation and a stronger customer focus, that what is needed is less for marketing to move towards R&D than for R&D to move towards marketing. To take the first complaint as an example: if a marketing specification always takes account of existing technology, any new product specification it develops will tend to be as a result of technological developments and not developments in market needs. Ultimately, if marketing was always to respond to R&D's lead, then it would end up with clever technological developments for which no need existed.

In fact a marketing department may identify a need in the marketplace and pass to R&D the problem of evolving a commercially viable solution. However, it is equally possible for R&D, having evolved a new technique, process, or product, to ask marketing if it can identify any need that would be satisfied by the development. Of course, marketing will sometimes identify needs for which R&D cannot find a solution at the present or one that is economically viable. Equally, R&D may find that marketing is unable to identify a need which their development can satisfy. In a less than perfect world, both R&D and marketing will sometimes fail to recognize certain possibilities. It must also be accepted that sometimes there is no potential use at a particular time for a new idea evolved in R&D, though it may be fascinating technically and scientifically. Marketing must also recognize that at the present stage of technical knowledge certain identifiable needs have no solutions or none that is commercially viable.

It has to be accepted that there have been many successful new products that have evolved not from marketing research or analyses of customer needs but from ideas and opportunities developed within the organization. One of the most often quoted examples is 3M's 'Post-its' (see Chapter 1). What is interesting in this case is that it took the commitment of a small number of managers (who were working in an organization that deliberately sought to create an atmosphere where staff could 'do their own thing' with a proportion of their time) several years to create this success. However, it is essential that marketing should not adopt a 'not-invented-here' approach to new product ideas that arise within R&D quite independently of marketing's own search for ideas.

7 Summary

A NUMBER of highly successful firms deliberately seek to encourage interdepartmental cooperation. Various approaches are followed. Some firms, like the Mars Group (see Insert), rotate staff at all levels between departments on a regular basis. Others, such as Procter & Gamble, always include somebody from the production and the financial side of the organization when forming new product teams. Both Mars and P&G are, of course, companies that have been committed to pursuing a marketing orientation for many years and they recognize that rotating staff and having mixed project teams are not sufficient to achieve effective coordination between departments. In addition, it is necessary to ensure that the way in which both individuals and departments are evaluated does not discourage cooperative activity.

Interfunctional mobility

'But to progress as a manager you must broaden your experience, look beyond functional barriers and develop an understanding of the whole business. Graduates joining us with a finance background might, therefore, find themselves in manufacturing, or an engineer might have a marketing assignment.'

Source: Mars Group Recruitment Literature (1997).

8 The future

TECHNOLOGICAL developments centring around CAD seem likely to continue to make significant changes to the way in which product development occurs. Not only is product development being speeded up; there is also an ability to draw on the expertise of people all around the world (without actually physically bringing them together). Thus design teams can be assembled and dispersed at great speed because there is now no need for their physical involvement. Thus the benefits of these CAD developments are being extended because of developments in information transmission. Now more thought is being given to the transmission of the complete designs to the point of manufacture perhaps presaging the end of the era of large manufacturing plants from which complex distribution chains have to be developed and replacing them with a larger number of smaller units placed close to the physical location required by the customer.

At a trivial level, if it is now possible for a consumer to mix half a litre of paint to the exact colour required in a local shop, why cannot that be done for yogurts, jams, soups, etc.? The challenge for marketers in the future will be to keep up with the opportunities offered by the new technologies.

Further reading

Fisher, R. J., Maltz, E., and Jaworski, B. J. (1997), 'Enhancing Communication between Marketing and Engineering', *Journal of Marketing*, 61/3: 54–70.

Griffin, A., and Hauser, J. R. (1996), 'Integrating R&D and Marketing', *Journal of Product Innovation Management*, 13/3: 191–215.

Lefebvre, L. A., Lefebvre, E., and Harvey, J. (1996), 'Intangible Assets as Determinants of Advanced Manufacturing Technology Adoption in SMEs', *IEEE Transactions on Engineering Management*, 43/3: 307–22.

Lei, D., Hitt, M. A., and Goldhar, J. D. (1996), 'Advanced Manufacturing Technology: Organizational Design and Strategic Flexibility', *Organization Studies*, 17/3: 501–23.

Lewis, R. J. (1993), *Activity-Based Costing for Marketing and Manufacturing* (Westport, Conn.: Quorum Books).

Sanchez, R. (1995), 'Strategic Flexibility in Product Competition', *Strategic Management Journal*, 16 (summer special issue), 135–59.

Smith, M., and Dikolli, S. (1995), 'Customer Profitablity Analysis: An Activity-Based Costing Approach', *Managerial Auditing Journal*, 10/7: 3–7.

Song, X. M., Montoya-Weiss, M. M., and Schmidt, J. B. (1997), 'Antecedents and Consequences of Cross-Functional Cooperation: A Comparison of R&D, Manufacturing and Marketing Perspectives', *Journal of Product Innovation Management*, 14/1: 35–47.

Tzokas, N., Saren, M., and Brownlie, D. (1997), 'Generating Marketing Resources by Means of R&D Activities in High Technology Firms', *Industrial Marketing Management*, 26/4: 331–40.

Discussion questions

1 How best could a marketing manager go about making a case for their firm to develop an ABC system?

2 Given that market research for 'Post-its' indicated a lack of consumer interest, what would your reaction be if market research for a new product that you had developed showed no consumer interest?

3 Is the argument that the development of ABC has been inhibited by the complexity of many manufacturing and distribution processes reasonable?

4 In many markets, where products have become commoditized, there has been a proliferation of product variants. Where this has happened, what challenges will it have presented to the company's manufacturing departments?

5 How can marketing personnel convince their colleagues in R&D that they respect their expertise while at the same time recognizing that the customer is interested only in a solution to their needs?

any case Fred was required to work on an existing project for the next three months.

Discussion question

What communication problems does this situation demonstrate and how might they be overcome?

After making regular visits to Zedoc over a couple of years, Jon Flint, a salesman at Andecs, was delighted to be invited to quote for a piece of business. He felt this was at last confirmation of his assessment of the opportunity that Zedoc offered his firm—an assessment that had been criticized as naïvely optimistic by his superiors. Zedoc had informed him that they were designing a new machine that would require a number of specially designed components of the type that Andecs manufactured.

Flint spent some time examining the documents that Zedoc had supplied, which set out the specifications for the components. However, although he was a competent engineer, he soon began to realize that there were aspects of the component design that were beyond his capabilities. He therefore requested Fred Scofield (a friend who was a member of Andecs's Technical Department) to 'do him a favour' and take a quick look at the documents. This Fred did and stated that it was a fascinating technical problem, but his view was that to sort out the issues in an effective way he would need to visit Zedoc. Flint therefore formally requested that Fred should be allowed to visit Zedoc to discuss the matter. Permission was granted, but only after Flint's superior had agreed with the Head of the Technical Department that Fred's time on the visit should be charged to the Sales Department, and also that the time he had 'unofficially' spent on the matter should also be charged. Flint's boss was very unhappy about this latter point, but reluctantly agreed.

Fred made a visit with Flint to Zedoc, after which he told Flint that Zedoc's requirements presented a really interesting and unusual technical problem that he was sure he could solve. More importantly, he believed his proposed solution was sufficiently technically distinctive as to make a very good impression on Zedoc's management. However, it would take quite a bit of his time and he reminded Flint that his time was now being charged to the Sales Department for any work he did on Zedoc's requirements. Flint informed his superiors of Fred's views and the fact that he recognized that this order was not big enough to be profitable in its own right. However, he believed that, subject to Andecs proving its technical competence and general commitment to Zedoc, further more profitable opportunities were almost certain to come. Flint's boss, who was not totally convinced by Flint's arguments, was then approached by Fred's superiors, who stated that they believed that there was a simpler solution to the problem, which, while not ideal, would be 'satisfactory', and that in

Chapter 18
Strategic Marketing in a Modern Economy

Mary Lambkin

Objectives

The objectives of this chapter are:

1 to describe the concept of strategy and its role in competitive success;

2 to distinguish the different levels of strategy—namely, corporate, business, and functional;

3 to explain the distinct but interdependent roles of strategy formulation and implementation;

4 to identify generic marketing strategies that are commonplace in Western economies;

5 to consider how to evaluate strategic performance.

1 The concept of strategy

DESPITE the enormous amount of literature on the subject of strategy, including numerous books and articles, the nature and role of marketing strategy are often rather vague and incompletely specified. It is in the interests of marketers and students alike that this ambiguity is addressed in a manner that gives us a clearer view of our role and contribution within organizations. The objective of this chapter is to present the general principles of strategic management and to explain the particular role of marketing in the development and implementation of successful competitive strategies.

From a historical perspective, we owe the term 'strategy' to the ancient Greeks and its fundamental principles derive from military strategy. Phrases such as 'mission statements' and 'strategic manœuvres' have been borrowed and incorporated into everyday business language. But to what extent can military strategy be applied in today's business context? In fact, a little thought readily identifies many ways in which the precepts of military strategy might help business organizations. For example, this way of thinking can

- force a long-term view;
- precipitate the consideration of strategic choices;
- highlight resource allocation trade-offs;
- provide systematic methods to aid decision making;
- provide a communication and coordination system;
- help an organization cope with change.

In modern-day business terms, strategy refers to the matching of the activities of an organization to the environment in which it operates and to its own resource capabilities. In its ideal form, it is presented as a unified, comprehensive plan that relates the strategic advantages of the firm to the opportunities in the environment. It is designed to ensure that the basic objectives of the firm are achieved through proper execution.

Strategy is most often considered as a very deliberate action involving the analysis of environments and abilities, resulting in detailed plans and strategies. In reality, however, research evidence often demonstrates that firms tend to evolve their strategies in a more opportunistic way, feeling their way along as events unfold in the market-place and the competitive environment. Under these conditions, marketing strategy is called an *emergent strategy*, because of the way that it tends to emerge despite the absence of overt structures within which to plan and develop (Mintzberg and Waters 1985). In practice, the actual strategy pursued is a result of both deliberate and emergent decisions that occur within the unique context of each business organization.

1.1 A hierarchical view of strategy

In our analysis of marketing strategy we will adopt a hierarchical view of strategy formulation, implementation, and evaluation. The three most widely accepted levels of strategic planning are as follows:

■ corporate-level strategies, the highest level of the firm, relating to the overall thrust of the corporation's business;
■ business-level strategies, focusing on the strategic business units (SBUs) within the corporate portfolio, in their search for a sustainable competitive advantage;
■ functional strategies, including marketing strategies as well as strategies in each of the other core functions of the business such as operations, human resources, and finance. Marketing strategies typically focus on individual product lines and brands, with an emphasis on issues such as positioning, segmentation, communication, and innovation issues.

Most authors do differentiate between the different roles of strategy at the various levels of the hierarchy. Yet they often fail to translate that into the practical implications for marketing strategy. Marketing has a different input at each level of the organization, and recognizing this is the key to any real understanding of the marketing function (see Fig. 18.1).

1.1.1 The role of marketing within corporate level strategy

This level of the business relates to the long-term viability of the organization and, as such, is the main concern of the chief executive officer. It involves the broad choice of mission, the setting of objectives, and the commitment of resources to major investments such as mergers and acquisi-

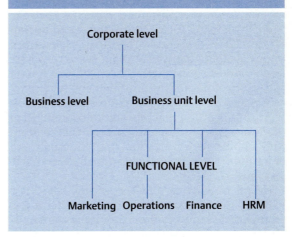

Figure 18.1 **The strategic hierarchy**

'I'll have a double merger, please.'

For years the market shares of Guinness plc and Grand Metropolitan plc had lagged in the market. However, since they merged, the combined companies have a market share in the liquor market of more than double its nearest rival and rank as the world's seventh largest food company.

tions (see Insert), overseas development, or large research and development (R&D) programmes. Typically, this level of strategy is seen as financially driven—that is, the task of general management is primarily to manage a portfolio of investments so as to give the best possible return to the investors.

Doyle (1994) has suggested that two types of leaders may be distinguished at corporate level. A *right-handed* leader is one concerned with matters of finance rather than marketing. They were bred in the recessions of the 1970s and, as a result, are most concerned with cost reductions and keeping their company's finances in check. Conversely, a *left-handed* leader is one with ambitious market-share objectives. The driving force in their lives is the desire to understand the customers' needs, often at the expense of short-term financial gain.

The implied assumption is that the more progressive firms, which recognize that marketing has a role at corporate level, make better long-term decisions, more attuned to trends in the marketplace, which gives them a stronger foundation on which to build and maintain their competitive position. As marketers, we may act as advocates for the consumer, ensuring that the company remains focused upon the one thing that is essential to its success—the client. As described by one leading American author, 'At the corporate level, marketing managers have a critical role to play as advocates for the customer and for a set of values and beliefs that put the consumer first in the firm's decision making, and to communicate the value proposition as part of that culture throughout the organization, both internally and in its multiple relationships and alliances' (Webster 1992: 11).

This is similar to another widely held view which is that marketing (in the sense that it recommends closeness to the customer) is too fundamental to be considered a separate function; rather, we must use it as a corporate philosophy to guide our actions and intentions.

1.1.2 The role of marketing within business level strategy

The SBU is the level at which businesses compete directly in a competitive arena defined by a particular product category. The main concern of the managers running individual business units is how to maintain and expand their overall market share in the face of often tough competition. This is the realm of business strategy, which is concerned with identifying a competitive position that builds on the key strengths of the business so as to give it a unique position in the marketplace that provides a sustainable competitive advantage.

In practical terms, this usually involves managing a product line to ensure that it is correctly positioned in the marketplace relative to competitive offerings, and to make regular adjustments to take account of changing consumer tastes and changes in the competitive environment. The impact of technological innovation in both products and processes is also a very real issue requiring active management for most businesses operating in the intensely competitive environment that existed at the end of the 1990s (see Insert).

☞ 'Changes in the product types offered represent the most critical decisions in determining the future of a company.' (Chapter 14, p. 320)

Ericsson's leap

L. M. Ericsson, the Swedish electronics giant, is facing the crucial challenge of preserving its technological edge in the race with companies such as Motorola and Nokia. With the telecommunications and computer industries converging, they are in a race to develop advanced networks to help the world's phone companies provide the next generation of multimedia services from video conferences to speedy net surfing over cellular phones. The challenge for Ericsson's will be to evolve into a systems and software provider from its traditional role as a hardware supplier.

The issues involved in devising strategy at business level extend well beyond marketing, and probably include an input from all of the main functional areas, including operations, finance, and human resources. In fact, it is at this level that the interface between marketing and the other functions is most evident. Marketing practitioners would like to think that it is they who provide the leadership in the formulation of business strategy, given the well-worn adage that companies should be market led and not production driven, but, in practice, the dominant influence probably depends on the product type and the personalities involved.

1.1.3 Marketing strategy

The most direct application of marketing strategy occurs at the functional level, where marketing personnel are involved in the detailed management of individual brands and the interrelations between brands. This area includes basic decisions on issues such as market segmentation, targeting, and positioning. We will also see, later in this chapter, how the design of the marketing mix is an integral part of marketing strategy.

Some people might be tempted to argue that such concerns are tactical or operational rather than strategic, but it is important to remind ourselves that many of the world's leading companies have been built on the strength of a single brand and it was the creative marketing of that brand that built up the enormous assets that are evident today. Think of Coca-Cola, Nike (see Insert overleaf), Mercedes, Guinness, and IBM, to name but a few. Therefore, it follows that the micro-level strategy supporting individual brands is as important as the macro-level strategy guiding large multilayered organizations.

2 Formulation of marketing strategy

THE formulation of marketing strategy is generally thought of as a planning process, and the topic of marketing planning and control is dealt with in detail in Chapter 19 of this text. We will not repeat that discussion here, other than to say that we are assuming that well-managed companies do generally try to follow best practice by adopting a fairly formal process of planning in their approach to strategy at every level. In other words, they follow some well-accepted planning procedure, such as the one shown in Fig. 18.2 which involves the setting of objectives informed by a careful analysis of the company's situation. No matter at what level of the hierarchy the strategy is being developed, there are two main areas of analysis: external and internal. The most common output of external analysis is the identification of opportunities and threats facing the organization, both present and potential. Through innovative strategic moves, the most successful companies are the ones that are able to turn threats into opportunities for growth.

Most often, external analysis occurs at the SBU level; however, it is useful for it to be conducted at the three levels of the organization. External analysis results in a keen focus on the market and therefore on the changing face of competition. This is the power of strategic marketing at high levels of the organization—being constantly focused on the changing elements of demand and supply rather than merely on internal aspects of finance and costs.

Internal analysis (or self-analysis) looks to the elements of the organization that influence the success of the company. Here we are concerned with the performance of the firm with respect to customer satisfaction and the key determinants of strategy such as the main strengths and weaknesses of the organization.

Neither the external nor the internal elements of strategy are particularly meaningful on their

---

Nike a step ahead

Nike raced ahead of competitors such as Adidas, Reebock, and Puma by exploiting its brand power to move from athletics footwear into athletic clothing, turning itself into a symbol of fitness and well-being. It then went several steps further, positioning itself as an athletic lifestyle company that, by using celebrities such as Michael Jordan and golfer Tiger Woods to endorse its products, enabled customers to identify with their sporting heroes.

Figure 18.2 Andrews's model of the strategy formulation process

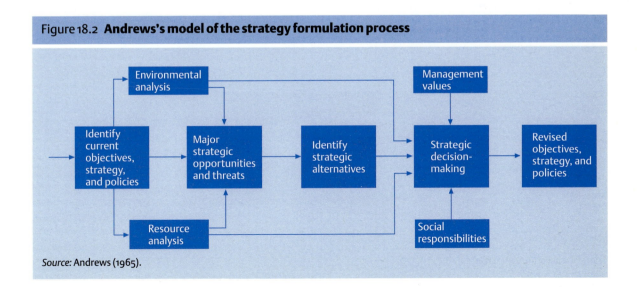

Source: Andrews (1965).

own; the most successful companies are those that learn to combine them in a way that provides true competitive advantage.

2.1 External analysis

Aaker (1995) suggests four main types for external analyses: customer, competitor, market, industry, and environmental (see Fig. 18.3). We will consider strategy formulation within each of these areas.

2.1.1 Customer analysis

As we have noted, customer analysis is often the most influential aspect of strategic marketing at the corporate level of the organization. It is the point at which the marketing department may act as advocate for the needs of the customer and hence impact upon corporate strategy. Thorough analysis of the needs and wants of the market must first occur before we can determine their impact upon strategy. At this stage we must identify existing segments, customer motivations, unmet needs, and the scale of these unmet needs. The conclusions from this analysis will have a fundamental impact upon the investment of capital at future points in the strategy of the firm.

This analysis commonly occurs at the SBU level, with its outcome influencing corporate strategy

Figure 18.3 **External analysis**

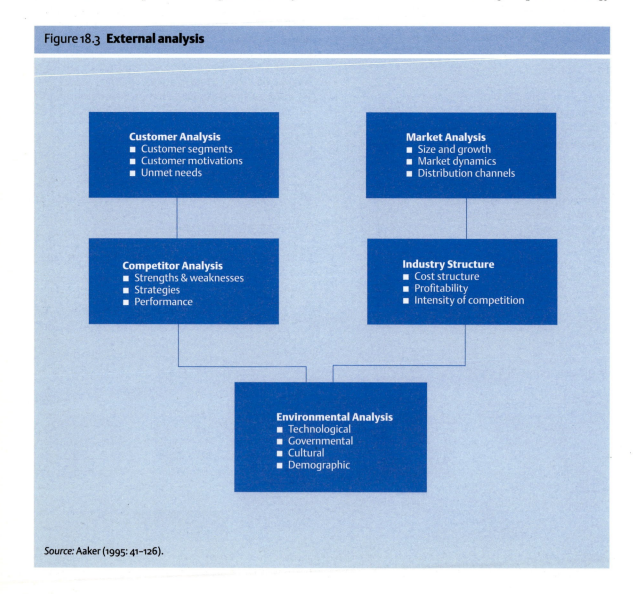

Source: Aaker (1995: 41–126).

decisions further up the hierarchy and tactical decisions further down. In this way, it is the people who are aware of market conditions who are performing the analysis rather than staff who are at a distance from the information on specific markets.

2.1.2 Competitor analysis

Competitor analysis most often occurs at the SBU level, with its results finding application at stages further up and down the hierarchy. Crucial to the analysis is the identification of current and potential competitors. This must be performed in a creative manner, so as to analyse not just current competitors' strategies and performance, but also competitors that are likely to attack segments in the future. As with the other types of analysis, it is important that the vision of the analysis is not narrowly focused, but rather is creative and innovative in its definitions.

The secret to success in competitor analysis is to be able to identify the barriers to entry and turn them into gateways for entry. Marketing has a particularly powerful role in these circumstances. It remains focused on the external market and, combined with an innovative strategy, has the power to overcome many of these barriers.

2.1.3 Market analysis

The attractiveness of a market depends not only on customer characteristics and behaviour but also on the number of customers and their propensity to purchase at various price points. Thus, a very important part of the analysis concerns the current and potential size of the market and its profit potential for the suppliers in the market. Also important is the degree of customer loyalty to individual brands and their likelihood of switching in response to changed incentives. The ideal situation, of course, is to have very loyal customers who are not easily swayed by competitors' offerings, but that is an unrealistic scenario for the majority of companies. It is important, however, to try to understand the precise dynamics of the marketplace, including the structure of distribution channels, that indicate the potential for increasing or losing market share.

2.1.4 Industry analysis

The nature of competition within industries varies a great deal and is strongly influenced by the number and size of firms that operate within the industry. Thus two industries may be made up of similar numbers of firms, but, if the size distribution is different between them, then it is likely that the nature of competition will be quite different between the two industries. Another important feature of industry structure is the cost structure of the industry. For example, do strong economies of scale exist within the industry? If they do, then the bigger firms may have a substantial advantage over their smaller competitors.

2.1.5 Environmental analysis

No market operates in a vacuum solely influenced by the forces of the internal market. There are trends within the environment that also have dramatic effects upon the marketplace. Four forces in particular have been noted as having important influence upon market operations: technological, governmental, cultural, and demographic.

2.2 Internal analysis

While many dimensions of a corporation's structure and functions are of strategic importance, we must remain true to our focus on strategic marketing by looking particularly at the aspects of marketing operations that are of strategic importance. This means that we look to 'soft' or non-financial aspects of the company such as: customer satisfaction, brand equity, product/service quality, firm reputation, and new product potential. Additionally, it is useful to analyse the product portfolio of the company, considering the strengths and the performance of each of the products in the line and any possible synergies available among them. We must also look at general trends and characteristics of the company's history. These relate to strengths and weaknesses inherent in the structure of the organization often related to its history as well as its current strategic direction, capabilities, and constraints. Internal variables that can confer a strategic advantage include age and size. Age is an indication of timing of entry into a market end. Research shows that first movers typically retain a competitive advantage over time.

Company size can be either an advantage or a disadvantage depending on circumstances. Large size can correlate with economies of scale and access to large resources that can provide an unassailable competitive advantage in some industries. Examples include steel, aircraft manufacture, and petro-chemicals. However, large size can sometimes be a disadvantage if the key success factor in the market is innovation and speed of change, because large firms have a tendency to become staid and unwieldy, which inhibits their speed of response.

Small and young companies often have advantages that may be overlooked in internal analysis. While they may not have superior skills and resources relative to incumbents in a market, they are often equipped with the latest technologies that may be incorporated into improvements in their products. Through innovative marketing they may attack niche areas before the dominant competitors react. As they have not invested heavily in specific areas, the young companies are fleet-footed relative to larger companies who have years of investment to support. Also, new entrants can utilize marketing strategy in order to deliver better value to the customer, particularly through innovation in the distribution channels.

2.3 SWOT analysis

The secret of insightful strategy analysis is to be able to bring together the results of both the external and internal analysis so as to provide a clear focus for the company's future direction. The accepted way to do this is through a SWOT analysis. This acronym stands for strengths, weaknesses, opportunities, and threats, and the idea is to find the point at which the strengths of the firm coincide with the best opportunities in the marketplace. That point can then suggest alternatives for action in the final strategy-making phase.

The identification of strategic alternatives is the most creative part of the strategic planning process and is limited only by the imagination and ingenuity of the people involved. In fact, current opinion in the literature on strategy suggests that this is the most critical aspect of strategy. Highly respected strategy writers such as Hamel and Prahalad (1994*b*) refer to the need for innovation and creativity as the foundations of strategy in the late 1990s.

To help generate the initial list of alternatives, it is sometimes helpful to use a checklist or schema, such as shown in Fig. 18.4. This simple matrix is very popular because it manages to summarize a wide range of obvious possibilities in a simple,

Figure 18.4 **Strategic alternatives**

	Existing	New
Existing	Market penetration	Product development
New	Market development	Diversification

Source: Ansoff (1965: 109).

usable way. The first alternative is 'market penetration', which might equally be called a 'growth strategy'. It implies that the potential for sales and profit growth with existing products and/or existing markets served has not yet been fully exhausted and should remain the main focus of attention. This is likely to be the best alternative for companies operating in young, high-growth markets and which have strong brands that are capable of holding or expanding their share of the market.

The second alternative is 'market development', which means the cultivation of new market segments in the geographic region already served, or perhaps the pursuit of an export drive to open up markets for your product in other parts of the world. An example of the former would be mobile phone suppliers targeting personal users as well as business users.

The third alternative is 'product development', which suggests that a company either creates or acquires new products or brands to allow it to generate additional sales from its existing market base. An example would be banks offering insurance services or retailers offering financial services to get a greater level of sales through their branch networks.

The fourth and most adventurous strategic alternative comes under the broad heading of 'diversification'. This suggests that the company pursue new products in new markets, whether through internal efforts or, more frequently, through acquisition. The relentless development of the Virgin Company into new areas, from airlines to entertainment to financial services and beverages, is a much-cited case of a diversification strategy.

In fact, strategy alternatives portrayed in Ansoff's model have an increasing degree of risk according to the distance one moves away from the core business of the firm. A risk line might be plotted on the diagonal from the top-left corner down to the bottom-right corner with diversification being the riskiest direction to pursue. The general advice that accompanies this model is that companies should consider the easier and less risky alternatives first and explore the higher risk options only when there is no other course of action available. Peters and Waterman (1982) famously coined the term 'stick to the knitting', which is still considered the best advice in view of considerable research evidence that conglomerates of unrelated businesses do not perform well over time and much anecdotal evidence of companies coming unstuck with ventures into areas that they did not properly understand.

Another general assumption underlying Ansoff's model is that all strategic alternatives involve growth and, it must be said, that in the business world growth is seen as a normal and regular expectation. This does not acknowledge, however, that companies or parts of companies can sometimes decline and that appropriate strategy alternatives may be either 'turnaround' or orderly 'withdrawal'. These specific alternatives will be considered in more detail in Section 3.

Once the analysis has been done to suggest a general strategic direction for the company, specific objectives must be set to provide benchmarks for measuring progress and to provide a timetable to guide and motivate the necessary work. The objectives and strategy that are eventually arrived at must be simple, clear, and achievable in order to assist implementation.

3 The content of marketing strategy

CLEAR objectives and strategic direction are a good first step but cannot guarantee competitive success. The key to surviving and prospering in a competitive environment is to be able to identify and create a position in the market based on a demonstrable and sustainable competitive advantage.

3.1 Porter's model

A fundamental premiss of strategic planning is that, to survive, a business must do something uniquely well so as to secure its position in the competitive marketplace. The bases on which a competitive advantage can be built are limitless, but, to assist the analytical process, various models have been proposed to summarize the main types of options. The best known of these is Porter's (1980) model of generic strategies, shown in Fig. 18.5. Porter defined three types of competitive strategy: cost leadership, differentiation, and focus. He originally suggested that these strategic options were mutually exclusive and that businesses would have to opt for one or other so as to avoid becoming 'stuck in the middle', which has negative performance implications.

☞ 'Though a competitive position and strategy are defined solely in terms of how an offering is positioned, its selection by a company requires a careful review of its own distinctive resources.' (Chapter 15, p. 359)

3.1.1 Cost leadership

The logic of this strategy is that a firm with lower than average costs, but commanding about average prices, will earn above average profits. Furthermore, since the presence of more than one low-cost competitor is likely to lead to rivalry over market share and consequent price cutting, Porter

Figure 18.5 **Generic business strategies**

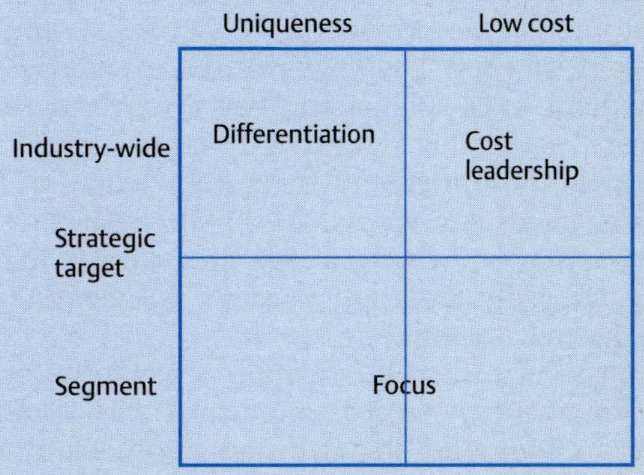

Source: Porter (1980).

argues that the cost leader must be not merely a low-cost producer, but the lowest cost producer in its industry.

Low costs in this sense may result from one of several sources, including a no-frills product or service, economies of scale, experience curve effects, production/operations efficiency, product design, a labour cost advantage, low-cost distribution, or a government subsidiary. Most of these factors are associated with production/operations efficiency and are less likely to occur within the domain of marketing. However, it may also be argued that low cost is a legitimate marketing strategy if it can be translated into lower prices or higher value for the consumer. Companies such as Marks & Spencer retailers, Toyota cars, and Dell computers would seem to be good examples of successful cost-leadership strategies.

The cost-leadership strategy has fallen out of favour in recent years, for several reasons. First, customers may not be impressed by low costs, particularly if they are not passed on through low prices, resulting in a low level of loyalty and a high propensity to switch to competitors' products. Secondly, a price based on a cost advantage is easily replicated by competitors and therefore does not result in an enduring competitive advantage.

3.1.2 Differentiation strategy

Differentiation is defined as uniqueness in some dimension important to buyers across the industry that is recognized as such. When a company is able to make its offering different from those of its competitors in the eyes of the customer, along a dimension that is valued by the customer, then it will have achieved a differentiated strategy. In order to be successful, the strategy must generate customer value, provide perceived value, and be difficult to copy. The power of the marketing department over such a strategy is obvious. Marketers, with their traditionally close interaction with the customer and their knowledge of customer needs and wants, are in the best place to advise on what perceived customer value is. In this way the differentiation strategy is essentially a marketing strategy.

In the 1990s two broad approaches to differentiation strategy were distinguished: the 'quality' approach and the 'strong-brand' approach (Aaker 1995). The quality approach to differentiation has been made popular through Japanese management techniques such as 'zero defects' and 'total quality management' (TQM). It is a team-based approach to manufacturing that strives to have zero defects at any stage of production and hence total satisfaction for customers. This aim of customer satisfaction is one that is facilitated by the marketing department, through research and customer involvement.

Quality in this sense also means a high level of attention to customer service. In fact, the measurement of service quality in all its aspects has become one of the key preoccupations of marketing personnel in recent years. The example of TNT Express Delivery Services is a good illustration of how a company can use service quality as a basis for competitive advantage (see Insert).

> ### A passion for serving the customer
>
> There is no doubt that customer care requires passion. And TNT Express Delivery Services possesses passion in spades. From tea ladies to truck drivers, all 4,800 employees understand that customers count. With over 4,000 parcel courier services operating in the UK, customer focus has become the vital differentiator.

The building of strong brands is another possible way to differentiate a product from that of its competitors. The idea of 'brand equity' has gained much acceptance in recent decades. This indicates that ownership of a strong brand is a valuable asset in the financial sense, often far surpassing the value of conventional assets such as buildings and plant and equipment. The acknowledgement of the importance of brand equity has heightened the perceived importance of investing to grow and nurture brands as perhaps the most important task to ensure a prosperous future for one's company. Given that brand development and brand management are the critical skills of marketing people, it follows that the marketing function has a central product differentiation as a basis for competitive advantage.

3.1.3 Focus strategy

Focus strategies involve choosing a particular market segment with distinctive needs and on configuring the firm's activities to meet those needs. The focus may be based on either low cost or differentiation depending on the character of the individual market segment. A focus strategy allows the firm to compete with limited resources and, sometimes, to bypass larger, more experienced competitors. Additionally, it ensures that the company is not distracted by other strategic alternatives. However, a focus strategy does leave itself open to the obvious danger of the focused segment or product line becoming obsolete and as a result to the loss of market share.

3.2 Are there really three generic strategies?

Porter's generic strategy model was developed at a time when the USA was the dominant world manufacturer. Since then we have seen the success of the Japanese in several industries, including cars and electronics, by what seems to be a combination of differentiation with low cost. The point is that the Japanese have learnt to combine differentiation, low-cost, and focus strategies into a single strategy without getting 'stuck in the middle'. The philosophy of TQM has enhanced this with the elimination of weaknesses from the manufacturing system. This has been achieved through complex networks and value-chain systems that ensure an extremely high level of internal service within the manufacturing system. Now competition is occurring between these chains rather than between firms; marketers and marketing strategy must learn to adapt to this new face of business.

It seems to be generally accepted by now that the idea of a simple matrix of generic strategies cannot adequately capture the diversity of the strategy combinations that companies may pursue, particularly with the extent of technological innovation that is breaking down traditional boundaries across industries as well as up and down the production–distribution chain.

3.3 Alternative sources of competitive advantage

George Day, another leading marketing academic, has provided a useful model to help us to consider the multiple factors that may, jointly, contribute to competitive advantage, as shown in Fig. 18.6

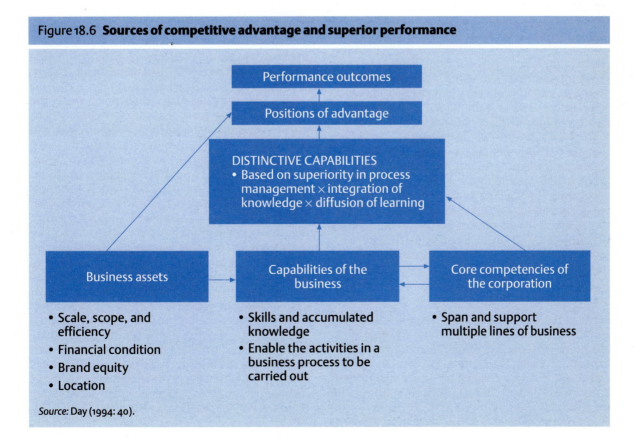

Figure 18.6 **Sources of competitive advantage and superior performance**

Source: Day (1994: 40).

(Day 1994). In sum, he suggests that the competitive advantage of the modern firm derives from a combination of the assets that it already has together with its core competencies, which are the skills and systems it has accumulated over time. The unique configuration that results for each firm defines its distinctive capabilities and these, in turn, facilitate and constrain its position of competitive advantage.

3.4 Other strategic challenges

General strategy frameworks such as those just described are useful diagnostic tools for analysing competitive position and for identifying opportunities and imperatives for the future, but there are a number of specific challenges that many companies around the world are wrestling with currently and that, therefore, deserve special mention. They include timing issues, globalization, strategic alliances, and turnaround situations.

3.4.1 Timing issues

Economists have long recognized that there are advantages to being the first mover in introducing a new product or service and research evidence from many industries tends to bear this out. In the strategy literature, this is often referred to as a pre-emptive strategy, in which a company deliberately sets out to pioneer a new market ahead of competitors so as to build up scale and customer loyalty, which are the benefits of being first.

The very rapid rate of technological innovation that we are experiencing these days gives even greater importance to this type of strategy, so much so that contemporary writers in strategy are advocating time pacing as a key element of strategy formulation. The essence of this idea is that companies need to plan proactively for regular, rhythmic innovation to keep up with and even move ahead of their competitors in fast-changing, high-technology markets.

3.4.2 Globalization

Perhaps the most talked-about issue in the 1990s was the apparently relentless trend towards globalization, with the world's largest multinationals expanding their reach into all corners of the world. An article by Theodore Levitt (1983c) first articulated the logic for globalization. The main justification appears to be the desire for ever-greater economies of scale in all aspects of operations including production, distribution, and marketing. Indeed, the most visible examples of globalization tend to be the leading consumer product companies such as Coca-Cola, McDonald's, Nike, and Sony, in which cases the scale economies are more likely to be in marketing than in production.

Obviously, globalization is only an issue for the largest companies in the world and at the highest level of corporate strategy. In reality, however, most marketing strategists are concerned with a single national territory or geographical region and need only a general awareness of the bigger global context in which their parent company operates.

3.4.3 Strategic alliance

Allied to the drive for geographic expansion, whether global or regional, is the increasing incidence of strategic alliances. One can hardly open a business publication these days without seeing yet another report of a major merger or contractual alliance between companies that are major players in their own right. Recent examples take in almost every major industry, including brewing/distilling (Guinness and Grand Metropolitan), cars (Ford acquiring Jaguar and BMW acquiring Rover), banking (Swiss Bank merging with the Union Bank of Switzerland), pharmaceuticals (Glaxo merging with Wellcome), and so on.

The logic driving such alliances is much the same as the logic for globalization—an ambitious growth objective coupled with a perceived opportunity to leverage their individual strengths—as a basis for enhancing their joint competitive advantage. For example, Grand Metropolitan has a distribution strength in the USA, which Guinness lacked, while Guinness has a strong portfolio of beer brands, which Grand Metropolitan needs to fill out its product line.

This trend towards ever-increasing industry concentration seems set to continue and even to accelerate into the twenty first century. The commercial logic of larger economies of scale seems undeniable, but what is not clear yet is whether the enormous size of some of these newly created organizations will bring new problems for management—how to coordinate and motivate such large groups of employees spread across the globe. History shows that every organization form brings its own dynamic that poses new and often unanticipated challenges for management.

3.4.4 Turnaround situations

All of the discussion so far has assumed an objective of growth from an already healthy competitive position. This is probably a reasonable premiss to reflect the typical competitive situation, but, of course, alongside competitive success there are always some failures, companies that for one reason or another find themselves in a weak competitive position or trading unprofitably. Occasionally, these problems may reflect a decline in the market, whether temporary or permanent, but more often they are casualties of intense competition and of poor strategic decisions in the past.

To come upon a company in a weak competitive position or even in bankruptcy can, in the right hands, be an opportunity. There are abundant stories in the business press about people who took over very weak, unpromising companies and turned them around spectacularly. The most critical requirement is often just fresh thinking, which usually comes with new owners or managers. There may also be a need for some other strategic inputs, whether new product design, marketing skills, access to distribution, or financial investment.

The takeover of Rover Cars by BMW is an interesting case in point. BMW's acknowledged skill in design and engineering has clearly brought an important new dimension to Rover, which, hopefully, will launch it onto a new growth trajectory.

3.5 Market-level strategies

Whatever a company's grand strategy, the execution requires that all of the functional strategies and tactics are carefully coordinated and consistent with the core objectives. For the marketing function, this means that the marketing mix must be managed in a way that correctly interprets and applies the intended strategy for the business.

☞ 'In any organization, but clearly particularly in larger ones, there is a difficulty in ensuring that the various parts of the organization know what the others are doing. Failure to do this can create all sorts of inefficiencies and at worst cause real damage to the business.' (Chapter 17, p. 141)

If the broad strategy is differentiation, then it is the job of the marketing function to translate this into the presentation and communication of the product or service, so as to realize the precise type of differentiation that is intended. For example, if the intention is to position a product at the top end of the market, as a luxury, then the design, appearance, and packaging must all suggest exclusivity, the price must be at a premium to competitors, the advertising must be suitably stylish and sophisticated, and the distribution must be selective and appropriate.

Such features sound rather self-evident, but it is surprising how difficult it is to achieve the right balance or the brilliant advertising idea. We can all recognize the perfect mix when we see it witnessed in very successful brands, but to create such a marketing campaign before the fact is not only difficult but requires a lot of creativity and, ultimately, a leap of faith. For example, who would have thought that the image of a polo pony would be able to underpin a brand that has achieved success all around the world—the Ralph Lauren clothing line? In that case, though, we can see product differentiation at its best, with a stylish product line, beautifully displayed and advertised, all with a consistent theme and presentation, based on an image that captures the imagination of young and old.

Thus, we must acknowledge the key role that marketing plays in the execution of strategy, and recall the discussion of the marketing mix in Chapter 9.

4 Implementation of marketing strategy

I⊤ is essential for any strategy that it is supported by the right people, culture, and structures. While companies may achieve success in the short term, they will not be able to compete in the long term unless they have a structure that is capable of what the Japanese call *kaizen* (the art of continuous improvement). Companies must always face the market and attempt to anticipate the underlying trends at work. Similarly, a strategy will not be implemented successfully unless it is truly supported by the people within the organization. Again, as with the other areas of this chapter, we must take a strictly marketing viewpoint in our analysis of strategy implementation. Services marketing and its influence through human-resource management have much to contribute to this area.

4.1 Implementing strategy through people

For the implementation of strategy, we do not look at the lofty ideals of the corporation or business unit heads, as they are often at a distance from the detail of the implementation process. Instead, we must look at the reality of the strategy delivery—where the staff meet with the customer and the customer operations. Whilst writers in the area of human-resources management have always considered a tight fit between strategy and human-resource policy to be essential for efficiency and productivity, it was only in the 1990s that the marketing function admitted that the task of achieving staff involvement was of central importance in the implementation of marketing strategy.

The concept of internal marketing attracted much interest among marketing academics and practitioners in the 1990s as a response to the recognized need for employee involvement. Internal marketing (IM) has the aim of ensuring that the aims of the employees are congruent with the aims of the organization and its philosophies. This is achieved through the communication of the corporate, business unit, and market strategies to their employees and the involvement within the strategic formulation process. This means applying the philosophy and practices of marketing to people who serve the external customer so that the best people are employed and retained, and they will do the best possible work (Berry 1981).

To achieve this purpose we must ensure the interaction of departments and that organizational staff work together towards the organizational objectives and strategy. We must sell the message of the organization to its internal audience to ensure their full involvement with the corporation's aims and strategies. If we can ensure that staff are motivated and fully involved in the corporate strategy, we will gain satisfaction, motivation, and loyalty from those delivering external quality, satisfaction, and customer care.

5 Evaluation of marketing strategy

STRATEGY is not a once-off exercise; it is an ongoing dynamic for driving a business forward and ensuring continuing success. To proceed in this way relies on regular review and readjustment, what some textbooks would call a 'feedback loop'. The most usual method of performance evaluation is financial, with variables such as sales revenue, profit margins, return on investment (ROI), and price/earnings (P/E) ratios being closely monitored. In contrast, marketing people tend to place more emphasis on variables such as sales volume and value and market share as their way of monitoring progress towards the company's objectives.

In reality, these are complementary perspectives, each of which has an important place in performance measurement. A problem arises only if the financial view and marketing view are not brought together, because the trade-offs between these objectives ought to be actively managed. For example, it is often possible to increase sales volume by reducing price or offering discounts, but either of these options would have a negative effect on profitability.

In our evaluation of marketing strategy we must also pay attention to the less concrete elements of the mix—namely, the long-term brand-building issues of positioning and differentiation. We must not simply measure what is convenient to measure; it is in fact more beneficial for the long-term role of strategic marketing if we learn to measure the less clear inputs of marketing, particularly the perceptions of the brand. Input costs such as promotion expenditure, research costs, and staff costs must be compared, not only with the output results of sales volume and profitability, but also with brand loyalty and other 'soft' measures of consumer satisfaction. This is the only true method of evaluating the effectiveness of strategy.

An annual survey of the best managed companies in the UK, carried out by *Management Today*, uses nine variables to identify the best-run companies. Only three of these variables are financial:

- financial soundness;
- value as a long-term investment,
- use of corporate assets.

The remainder are:

- quality of management;
- quality of goods and services;
- capacity to innovate;
- quality of marketing;
- ability to retain top talent;
- community responsibility

This seems like a well-rounded view of business success and a worthy model to be kept in mind when trying to evaluate strategy.

6 The future

IN the past a significant number of the major developments in strategic thinking have arisen from the work of consultants. The nature of a competitive industry like consulting means that firms will develop new products in an attempt to make or maintain their distinctiveness. However, it is also the nature of a service industry like consulting that any successful new product will be imitated. It follows that one prediction for the future that can be made with reasonable certainty is that new concepts and models will be developed, but what cannot be so certain is the validity of any of these models. It also seems certain that moves to make strategic marketing more rigorous will continue, but most of the moves seem likely to equate rigour with quantitative studies, while it is arguable that greater rigour in defining terms and developing concepts should first be undertaken.

The impact of the information technologies seems certain to create significant challenges to companies' existing strategies. For example, the decision merely to experiment with selling through a web page may provoke such a strong response from existing traditional intermediaries that a strategic decision has to be made, before the experiment has been completed, whether or not to commit yourself to go with the web page or to stick with the existing distribution system. Finally, the development of knowledge-based firms will create a demand for some really original new strategic thinking, if, as many commentators suggest, the traditional economic paradigm cannot be applied to knowledge.

Further reading

Arthur, W. (1996), 'Increasing Returns and the New World of Business', *Harvard Business Review* (July–Aug.), 100–9.

Davidson, H. (1998), *Even More Offensive Marketing* (London: Penguin Books).

Leith, A., and Riley, N. (1998), 'Understanding Need States and their Role in Developing Successful Marketing Strategies', *Journal of the Market Research Society*, 40/1: 25–32.

Piercy, N. F. (1998), 'Marketing Implementation: The Implications of Marketing Paradigm Weakness for the Strategy Execution Process', *Journal of the Academy of Marketing Science*, 26/3: 22–236.

Thompson, H. (1998), 'Marketing Strategies: What do your Customers Really Want?', *Journal of Business Strategy*, 19/4: 16–22.

Discussion questions

1 What contribution can economic analysis contribute to strategic thinking?

2 Do you agree that one of the problems of strategic thinking is that the customer gets overlooked in grandiose discussions of markets and competition?

3 Should you start a SWOT analysis with a definition of the market within which you compete or should you start a definition of the market within which you compete with a SWOT analysis?

4 'Timing issues' are usually taken to refer to whether or not to be first into a market. What other aspects of timing are strategically important?

5 It has been stated that developing a distinctive view of the future is a crucial element in developing strategies ahead of competitors. How would you define 'a distinctive view'?

6 One highly successful US company maintains that part of its success is the requirement that all of its marketing strategies have 'an exit route'. What do you think the term 'exit route' means and why should exit routes be planned before a strategy has even started to be implemented?

Mini Case
Glibbs

Reinsurance broking is a very specialized form of activity, with a modest number of quite small firms, such as Glibbs, handling in total a worldwide turnover of billions of pounds. When the activity known as reinsurance started is not clear, but in 1746 the British Government passed an Act setting conditions under which marine reinsurance could be conducted, so it must be assumed that it was a well-recognized activity by that time.

The need for reinsurance arises when insurers feel that their financial exposure to certain risks is too great and so they seek to find ways of reducing this exposure. So, just as a bookmaker lays off or hedges his bets, an insurance company will lay off some of the risks it is insuring.

For example, the owners of a large factory might decide to insure it for £100 million. The insurance company agreeing to accept this risk might worry that, if a large claim were made, their financial situation would be very stretched. So they would seek to reinsure this risk. This could be done in many ways. For example, another firm might agree for a fee to cover 50 per cent of any claim arising from a fire at the factory up to a specified sum (this might be any figure up to £100 million). Alternatively, there might be a firm that is willing, if a claim arose exceeding a prespecified figure, say £60 million, to meet the rest of the claim up to a maximum of £40 million. An alternative configuration might be to ask another firm to assume 50 per cent of the risk of any claim up to, say, £70 million but assume 60 per cent of any element of a claim over £70 million. There are, in fact, innumerable configurations of reinsurance. Which one an insurer prefers is particularly dependent on its own financial situation and the state of the reinsurance market.

The role of the reinsurance broker was originally simply to help the insurance company find people and other firms who were prepared to share the risks that they had contracted to bear. This process, known as 'placing the business', is complex, because reinsurance companies too do not wish to be exposed to too much risk from any one source or any one type. So, a reinsurance broker usually has to build up the amount of reinsurance cover its client is seeking by approaching several reinsurance companies. For example, if the insurance company in the example above has decided that it will meet the first £60 million of any claim itself but wishes to lay off the risk associated with the remaining £40 million, a reinsurance broker will probably find it necessary to approach several reinsurance companies. One may agree to cover £1 million but another only £0.5 million and so the reinsurance broker tries to place all the £40 million by assembling offers from several reinsurance companies. The reinsurance companies offer to cover the risk on the basis of their being paid a percentage of the sum they are reinsuring. The actual percentage charged is determined by their assessment of the riskiness of the business and the state of the reinsurance market at the time.

Traditionally the reinsurance broker's fee is a fixed percentage of the value of the business that he places. However, over time reinsurance brokers have extended their services to clients in a number of ways. For example, through the knowledge they have built up of the reinsurance companies and the state of the reinsurance market, they began to offer advice to their clients about the different costs likely to be incurred in placing reinsurance in the market in the various forms available to them. They also offer to act as an intermediary in collecting payments when a claim is made. Thus, if the factory in the example above did have a fire, the reinsurance broker would immediately inform those companies that had offered reinsurance and collect their payment for onward transmission to the insurer. In recent years the reinsurance brokers have also started to offer their clients technical advice, such as sophisticated financial models of the risks the insurers are bearing according to the forms of reinsurance they might buy. All of these and other services have been added to the core product of placing the reinsurance 'free' of charge as a part of the total service offered for the fee.

However, an important point is that the income of reinsurance brokers fluctuates quite rapidly according to the state of the reinsurance market. Thus, if there is a major catastrophe and the whole insurance and reinsurance market is affected (as with the loss in 1988 of the Piper Alpha Oil Platform in the North Sea, when 167 people died and the estimated costs of the loss were £1,400 million) because large sums of money have to be paid out in claims, the insurers and the reinsurers will raise their premiums to rebuild their reserves. Then the reinsurance broker's income rises. However, if there are several years without a major claim, then the premiums fall and the reinsurance broker's income decreases, though he may be doing roughly the same amount of work.

Recently Glibbs has recruited a small team of financial analysts, who have developed some sophisticated financial models of the risks that the insurers are bearing according to the forms of reinsurance they might buy. These models can demonstrate the impact on an insurer's balance sheet and profit and loss account of potential insurance claims of different sizes according to the type of reinsurance purchased. Given that the commission paid to reinsurance brokers is directly related to the size of the business handled, plus the fact that this small team is already overloaded with work, it is felt within Glibbs that they must charge smaller clients for this added service. This would be the first time that what in Glibbs is described as 'their full service' would be offered only to selected customers. This suggestion had led to some acrimonious discussions within Glibbs, with one senior manager maintaining that splitting the service offered in this way would only encourage other clients to seek to 'cherry pick' parts of Glibbs's services. The manager stated that, as Glibbs knew only its revenue and not its costs by customer, it was moving onto dangerous ground. Furthermore, one small client, who had somehow heard of this suggestion was very upset that he might be asked to pay for an element of Glibbs' service when other clients would receive it for no charge.

The situation is complicated by the fact that recently a number of Glibbs's clients have started to indicate that they are interested in discussing changing the method by which reinsurance brokers are remunerated. They are suggesting that they do not wish to continue paying the reinsurance brokers a fee based on a percentage of the premiums involved and would prefer to receive a quotation for a fee to perform specific tasks. Furthermore, one insurer that has never used Glibbs as a broker (because it has a reinsurance broker within its own group) has asked Glibbs how much it would charge for the new group of financial analysts to do some work for it.

Discussion questions

1 Should Glibbs sell the services of this new group to its existing small clients and yet continue to provide this free to larger clients?

2 Should Glibbs sell the services of this new group to firms that are going to purchase only that service and not its broking capacity?

3 What should Glibbs do about the change in the method of remuneration being proposed by some of its customers?

Chapter 19
Marketing Planning

Malcolm McDonald

Objectives

The objectives of this chapter are:

1 to define marketing planning;

2 to clarify the difference between strategic and tactical marketing planning;

3 to consider how it fits in with planning for other functions;

4 to explain why it is necessary;

5 to advise where to start;

6 to set out the contents of a strategic marketing plan;

7 to consider how to move from the strategic marketing plan to the tactical marketing plan.

1 Introduction

ALTHOUGH marketing planning would appear to be a simple, step-by-step process, in reality it is a multifaceted, complex, cross-functional activity that touches every aspect of organizational life. This chapter explains and explores some of these pan company issues by focusing on the process of marketing planning. It is not an attempt to suggest that the model outlined here is the only one that can be implemented. Indeed, other models are discussed. However, the one we select to concentrate on is the one that is most widely used and accepted by both academics and practitioners.

2 What is marketing planning?

MARKETING planning is a logical sequence and a series of activities leading to the setting of marketing objectives and the formulation of plans for achieving them. It is a management *process*. Formalized planning by means of a planning system is, *per se*, little more than a structured way of identifying a range of options, making them explicit in writing, formulating marketing objectives that are consistent with the organization's overall objectives, and scheduling and costing out the specific activities most likely to bring about the achievement of the objectives.

3 Strategic and tactical marketing planning

INHERENT in the above is the concept of *time*. Strategy is about doing the right things. Tactics are about doing things in the right way. In the 1990s more managers came to appreciate the real significance between a *strategic* marketing plan and a *tactical* marketing plan.

The reason is that the successes enjoyed in the past were often the result of the easy marketability of products, and during periods of high economic prosperity there was little pressure on companies to do anything other than solve operational problems as they arose. Careful planning for the future seemed unnecessary. However, in the 1990s most companies experienced difficulties precisely because of this lack of planning and there was a growing realization that survival and success in the future would come only from patient and meticulous planning and market preparation. This entails making a commitment to the future, as the environment of the early twenty-first century is much more competitive, complex, fast moving, and abrasive. Marketing's contribution to success in manufacturing and service businesses lies in its commitment to a detailed analysis of future opportunities to meet changing customer needs and a wholly professional approach to selling to well-defined segments those products and services that deliver the sought-after benefits. Such a commitment must not be mistaken for short-term budgets, forecasts, and action plans, for these we have always had. Put simply, the process of strategic marketing planning is concerned with identifying what and to whom and how sales are going to be made in the longer term to give revenue budgets and sales forecasting any chance of achievement.

This point is expanded on in Fig. 19.1, which shows a matrix in which the horizontal axis represents strategy as a continuum from ineffective to effective. The vertical axis represents tactics on a continuum from inefficient to efficient. Those firms with an effective strategy (top left) continue to thrive (see Insert). Those with an effective strategy but inefficient tactics (bottom left) have merely survived. Those firms to the right of the

> **Excellence that wasn't excellence**
>
> According to Richard Pascale (1990), of the forty-three excellent companies in Peters and Waterman (1982), *In Search of Excellence*, there were only six that would have been considered excellent eight years later.
>
> In the UK, during the period 1979–90, according to *Management Today*, most of the UK's top performing companies in terms of return on investment in each year were either sold or collapsed. The list included MFI, Bejam, Polly Peck, Atlantic Computers, Jaguar, and Blue Arrow.

matrix are destined to die, as too much emphasis is placed on tactics, so avoiding the underlying strategic issues surrounding changing market needs. Any organization doing the wrong things more efficiently (top right) is destined to die more quickly than its less efficient counterparts. It is a bit like making a stupid manager work harder, thus doubling the chaos and probably offending twice as many people. It is clear that, whilst both strategic and tactical marketing planning are important, the tactical plan will only be as good as the underlying strategic plan allows it to be. Hence, the main emphasis in this chapter will be on the preparation of strategic marketing plans.

4 How marketing planning fits in with other functions

FIRST of all, it is necessary to position marketing planning firmly within the context of strategic planning generally.

Strategic decisions are concerned with:

- the long-term direction of the organization, as opposed to day-to-day management issues;
- defining the scope of the organization's activities in terms of what it will and will not do;
- matching the activities of the organization to the environment in which it operates, so that it optimizes opportunities and minimizes threats;
- matching the organization's activities to its resource capacity, be it finance, manpower, technology, or skill levels.

Figure 19.1 The strategy–tactics matrix

Tactics		Strategy	
		Effective	Ineffective
Efficient		Thrive **1**	Die (quickly) **3**
Inefficient		Survive **2**	Die (slowly) **4**

Strategic management is characteristically deal-ing with an uncertain future and new initiatives. As a result of this, it is often the harbinger of change. Organizations build their business strate-gies in a number of different ways. There are six accepted strategy-forming models (Bailey and Johnson 1994).

■ *A planning model*. Strategic decisions are reached by use of a sequential, planned search for opti-mum solutions to defined problems. This process is highly rational and is fuelled by concrete data.

■ *An interpretative model*. The organization is re-garded as a collection of associations, sharing similar values, beliefs, and perceptions. These 'frames of reference' enable the stakeholders to interpret the organization and the environment in which it operates, cultivating the emergence of an organizational culture particular to that com-pany. Strategy thus becomes the product, not of defined aims and objectives, but of the prevailing values, attitudes, and ideas in the organization.

■ *A political model*. Strategy is not chosen directly, but emerges through compromise, conflict, and consensus-seeking among interested stake-holders. Since the strategy is the outcome of nego-tiation, bargaining, and confrontation, those with the most power have the greatest influence.

■ *A logical incremental model*. Strategies emerge from 'strategic subsystems', each concerned with a different type of strategic issue. Strategic goals are based on an awareness of needs, rather than the highly structured analytical process of the planning model. Often, because of a lack of neces-sary information, such goals can be vague, gen-eral, and non-rigid in nature until such a time when events unfold and more information be-comes known.

■ *An ecological model*. In this perspective, the envir-onment impinges on the organization in such a way that strategies are virtually prescribed and there is little or no free choice. In this model, the organization that adapts most successfully to its environment will survive in a way that mirrors Darwin's natural selection.

■ *A visionary leadership model*. Strategy emerges as a result of the leader's vision, enforced by commit-ment to it, personal credibility, and how he or she articulates it to others.

It is unlikely that an organization will use a pure version of any of these models. In all probability, its strategic decision-making model will be a hy-brid of some of them. However, it is possible that one or two of these will predominate and thereby give strategic decision-making a distinct 'flavour'.

Whilst academics cannot seem to agree on a sin-gle, best approach, company executives have to get on with strategy formulation as best they can, using a combination of experience, intuition, and hope. One of the earliest Ph.D.'s in the domain of marketing planning (McDonald 1982) came to the conclusion that the process they go through is some sort of logical sequence leading to the set-ting of objectives and the formulation of strate-gies and tactics for achieving them, together with the associated financial consequences. The formality of this process will be a function of the degree of product/market complexity, organiza-tional size, and the degree of environmental tur-bulence. In other words, the degree of formality will be driven in part by the dominant decision-making model in the organization.

Strategic marketing planning obviously cannot be discussed in isolation from the above strategic planning modes, and it is likely that the way in which an organization's marketing planning is carried out will be a microcosm of the principal mode of the total process.

Whilst marketing planning is based on markets, customers, and products, business planning in-volves other corporate resources, which will have a bearing on the identified markets. Corporate planning usually involves applying business plan-ning to several different units of the business aggregate.

Box 19.1 depicts marketing planning and its place in the corporate cycle. If marketing is a major activity in an organization, as in the case of consumer-goods companies and many service or-ganizations, it is usual to have a separate strategy and tactical marketing plan. In other cases, the marketing elements are incorporated into busi-ness plans for all other organizational functions, at the same time as marketing objectives and strate-gies are set. Often, these business plans are inte-grated into a corporate plan, which will contain long-range corporate objectives, strategies, plans, profit and loss accounts, and balance sheets.

One of the main purposes of a corporate plan is to provide a long-term vision of what the company is striving to become, taking account of share-holder expectations, environmental, resource-market, and consumption-market trends, and the distinctive competence of the company, as re-vealed by the management audit. This means in practice that the corporate plan will contain the following elements:

Box 19.1 Marketing planning and its place in the corporate planning cycle

Step 1	Step 2 Management audit	Step 3 Objective and strategy setting	Step 4 Plans	Step 5 Corporate plans
	Marketing audit Marketing	Marketing objectives, strategies	Marketing plan	
	Distribution audit Stocks and control; transportation; warehousing	Distribution objectives, strategies	Distribution plan	Issue of corporate plan, to include corporate objectives and strategies; production objectives and strategies, etc., long-range profit and loss accounts; balance sheets
Corporate financial objectives	*Production audit* Value analysis; engineering development; work study; quality control; labour; materials, plant, and space utilization; production planning; factories	Production objectives, strategies	Production plan	
	Financial audit Credit, debt, cash flow, and budgetary control; resource allocation; capital expenditure; long-term finance	Financial objectives, strategies	Financial plan	
	Personnel audit Management, technical, and administrative ability, etc.	Personnel objectives, strategies		

- desired level of profitability
- business boundaries:
  - which products will be sold to which markets (marketing);
  - what facilities will be developed (production and distribution);
  - the size and character of the labour force (personnel);
  - funding (finance);
- other corporate objectives, such as social responsibility, corporate image, etc.

A corporate plan, containing projected profit and loss accounts and balance sheets, resulting from the above process, is more likely to provide long-term stability for a company than plans based on a more intuitive process, containing forecasts that are largely extrapolations of previous trends and sales forecasts, in which the really key strategic is-sues, relating to products and markets, are lost in an edifice of numbers.

In summary, strategic and tactical marketing planning makes a vital contribution to an organization's long-term financial health.

5 Why is marketing planning necessary?

THERE are three basic reasons why market planning is necessary. First, there is the issue of different types of market, each of which needs a consciously different approach. Secondly, but related to this first reason, is the fact that margins and levels of sales differ between product and markets. Thirdly, there is a need for managers to structure their responses to fast-moving environments.

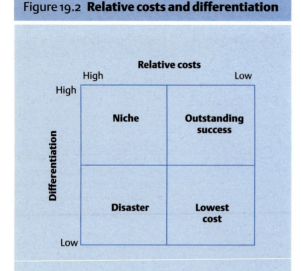

Figure 19.2 **Relative costs and differentiation**

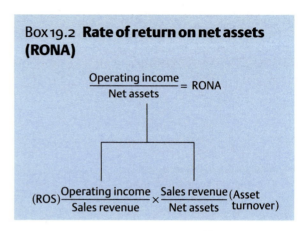

Box 19.2 **Rate of return on net assets (RONA)**

$$\frac{\text{Operating income}}{\text{Net assets}} = \text{RONA}$$

$$(\text{ROS})\frac{\text{Operating income}}{\text{Sales revenue}} \times \frac{\text{Sales revenue}}{\text{Net assets}}(\text{Asset turnover})$$

5.1 The mix of market types

Fig. 19.2 shows a version of Michael Porter's generic strategies matrix (Porter 1980). The matrix shows that some markets are inherently more prone to lack of differentiation in products and services. It is obvious that products such as flat glass, chlorine, car insurance policies, and the like are harder to differentiate than, say, perfume, beer, clothes, and the like. In which case, the attainment of low costs must be a corporate goal, otherwise lack of adequate margins may result. Equally, if an organization's products or services are subsequently different from another's, costs are rarely the driving force.

In reality, in their different ways, most organizations have a mix of products or services that can be classified in all four boxes. All organizations have some 'disaster' products, some 'lowest-cost' products, some 'niche' products, and some 'outstanding-success' products (see Insert). More-

Why sell unprofitable products?

Even though it made little or no profit on these items, Canada Dry in the early 1990s used to have to sell 'pop' products, such as large bottles of lemonade, in order to have a full line of soft drinks, even though it made its profits on 'mixer' drinks such as tonic water and ginger ale. It was a requirement to have a full line in order to be a serious player in the market.

over, whilst it is tempting for accountants to want to delist products that fail to achieve their individual financial targets, it is essential to understand the role they play in making profits. Consequently, it is the role of the strategic marketing plan to spell out at least three years in advance what the mix will be between products and services in each of the four boxes in Fig. 19.2.

'If . . . management decides that no corrective action is feasible, then the next logical step is to undertake a detailed investigation to determine whether elimination is, indeed, indicated.' (Chapter 14, p. 337)

5.2 The mix of margins and sales

Box 19.2 shows the make-up of rate of return on net assets (RONA) and it is clear from this that profit occurs because of a mix of different margin products and different levels of turnover for each of these products. It is the purpose of the marketing plan to spell out at least three years in advance of it happening what the desired mix is of low-margin/high-turnover, high-margin/high-turnover products and all variations in between. It is not enough just to do the accounts at the end of the fiscal year and hope the right net profit occurs.

5.3 Managerial reasons for the need for a marketing plan

Finally, apart from the need to cope with increasing turbulence, environmental complexity, more intense competitive pressures, and the sheer speed of technological and market change, a strategic marketing plan is useful:

- *for managers*: to help identify sources of competitive advantage;
- *for superiors*: to force an organized approach;
- *for non-marketing functions*: to develop specificity;
- *for subordinates*:
  - to ensure consistent relationships;
  - to inform;
  - to get resources;
  - to get support;
  - to gain commitment;
  - to set objectives and strategies.

6 Strategic marketing planning: where to start?

6.1 Understanding the variables

Fig. 19.3 illustrates what is commonly referred to as the 'gap' analysis. Essentially, what it says is that, if the corporate sales and financial objectives are greater than the current long-range trends and forecasts, there is a gap that has to be filled.

This gap can be filled in six ways:

- improved productivity;
- market penetration;
- new products;
- new markets;
- a combination of new products and markets;
- new strategies.

The calculations necessary to decide where to put the emphasis are best done in two separate steps. Step one should be completed for sales revenue only and step two should consider the costs and profit implications of the revenue-generating strategies.

Put simply, each of the six ways listed above has a number of components. For example, improved productivity can include price increases, a better product mix, a better customer/market mix, charging for deliveries, and so on. Market penetration consists of market growth and increasing market share. New products or services can be developed for existing markets. Existing products or services can be sold into new markets, and there is, of course, a combination of these last two strategies, although clearly the risk is highest here. Finally, if the gap is still not filled, the only remaining option is new strategies, often in the form of acquisitions, joint venture, licensing, and so on.

Fig. 19.4 is the Ansoff matrix (Ansoff 1965), on which the above strategies are based. All of this is summarized in Fig. 19.5.

None the less, whilst this exercise is a valuable overview of the levers that can be pulled to achieve corporate objectives, it is not a marketing plan. So we now need to turn our attention to the preparation of the strategic marketing plan, starting with the contents.

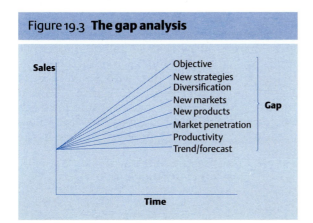

Figure 19.3 **The gap analysis**

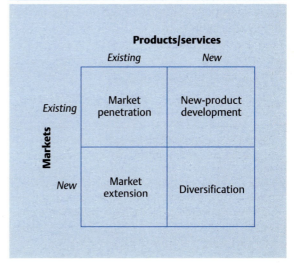

Figure 19.4 **Products and markets**

7 The contents of a strategic marketing plan

7.1 The time span of the plan

First, a strategic marketing plan usually covers a period of three years, although some companies still plan for five years. Basically, an organization should plan for longer than one year and as far ahead as it needs to in order to be sure of ongoing income streams for its shareholders. As it is difficult to forecast for longer than three years ahead, this is what the majority of organizations do.

7.2 The contents

It is generally accepted that the contents of a strategic plan are as shown in Box 19.3.

7.2.1 Mission statement

The purpose of the mission statement is to state clearly (see Insert) the *raison d'être* of the unit and should briefly cover the following points:

- role or contribution of the unit—e.g. profit generator, service department, opportunity seeker;
- definition of business—e.g. the needs the unit satisfies or the benefits provided, without being too specific or general;
- distinctive competence of the unit—a statement that could equally apply to any competitor is unsatisfactory;
- considerations for future direction—e.g. move into a new segment.

The generic mission statement

It is important to avoid crass and meaningless statements like the following, which can be found in most organizations across the world. (Goodness knows what the organizations think they are achieving.)

'Our organization's primary mission is to protect and increase the value of its owner's investments while efficiently and fairly serving the needs of its customers. [Organization name] seeks to accomplish this in a manner that contributes to the development and growth of its employees, and to the goals of countries and communities in which it operates.'

Box 19.3 Strategic plan

- mission statement
- financial summary
- market overview
    - market structures
    - market trends
    - key market segments
    - gap analysis
- strengths, weaknesses, opportunities, threats, and issues to be addressed
    - by product
    - by segment
    - overall business groups
- portfolio summary
- assumptions
- marketing objectives
    - strategic focus
    - target customer groups
    - market extension/penetration
    - product development/deletion/mix
- marketing strategies (4xPs)
    - product
    - price
    - promotion
    - place
- resource requirements
    - budget

7.2.2 Financial summary

This gives an overall view of the unit's total marketing activities, within the context of financial performance. Volume/turnover, gross profit, and gross margin, in percentage and absolute value terms, should be stated for each of the three preceding accounting periods, with a summary of reasons for good or bad performance. Constant revenue ($t - 1$) should be used to ensure meaningful comparisons, and the same base-year values used in any projections provided further in the plan.

Figure 19.5 **Sources of profit improvement**

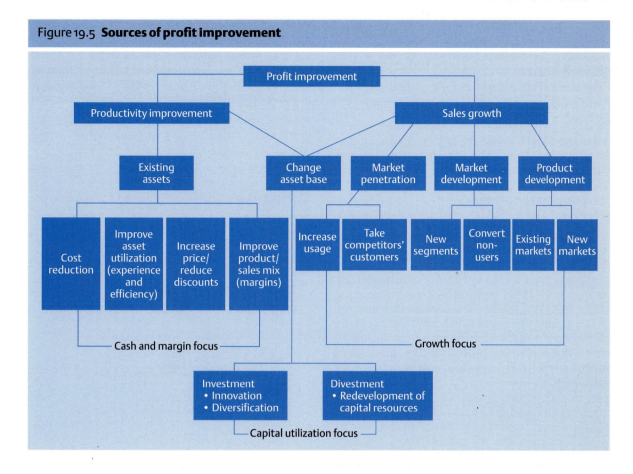

7.2.3 Market overview

Based on a comprehensive audit of the market environment, competitors, the market, products, and the company itself, this section provides a condensed view of the market (size, structure, and dynamics), prior to a detailed analysis of individual market segments, which form the heart of the marketing plan.

The process is based upon market segmentation—that is, homogeneous groups of customers with characteristics that can be exploited in marketing terms. This approach is taken because it is the one that is most useful for managers in developing their businesses. The alternative product-oriented approach is rarely appropriate, given the varying requirements of the different customer groups in the market in which most organizations compete.

A market overview should summarize what are considered to be the key market movements, and include the following:

■ What is the market and how does it work?

■ Which major markets or segments, and products are likely to provide suitable business opportunities?

Much of this information should be presented graphically (e.g. market maps/bar/pie charts, product life cycles), to facilitate easy understanding.

7.2.4 Strengths, weaknesses, opportunities, and threats: issues to be addressed

Before deciding future marketing objectives and strategies, it is necessary to summarize the unit's present position in its major markets, in the form of a SWOT analysis for each major market segment, product, or business group. The word SWOT derives from the initial letters of the words strengths, weaknesses, opportunities, and threats, and simply outlines:

- the unit's differential strengths and weaknesses, *vis-à-vis* competitors which would influence the buying behaviour of the target customers;
- the market opportunities for exploitation;
- the present and future threats to the unit's business in each segment.

From the SWOT analyses, key issues that must be addressed should be clearly identified and summarized.

7.2.5 Portfolio summary

This pulls together the information from the SWOT analyses, to demonstrate the overall competitive position, and indicate the relative importance of each product/market segment. A four-by-four matrix, as in Fig. 19.6, illustrates the position most effectively. Table 19.1 is an example of how market attractiveness can be calculated for each segment. Table 19.2 shows how the strengths and weaknesses for each segment can be calculated. These are transferred to the directional policy matrix (DPM) and show how the circles are positioned.

In Fig. 19.6, the horizontal axis reflects the scores in the strengths and weaknesses analysis and the vertical axis quantifies the attractiveness, to the organization, of each of the important

segments contained in the plan. The circle sizes are relative to the current turnover in each. The darker circles indicate forecast sales in three years' time. From this graphical representation of a portfolio of products or range of segments, a number of marketing options present themselves.

- In the top-left box, where strengths are high and markets are attractive, the probable option would

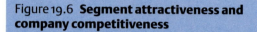

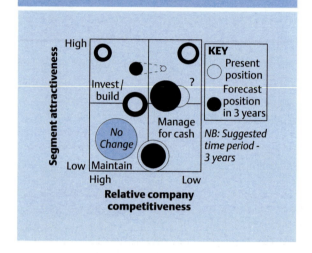

Figure 19.6 **Segment attractiveness and company competitiveness**

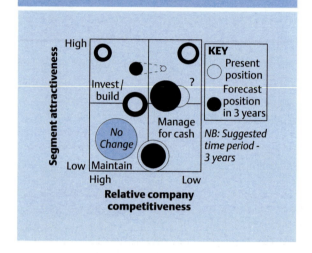

Table 19.1 **Establishing how attractive each segment is to your business. Market: XYZ**

Attractiveness	Weight	Segment 1		Segment 2		Segment 3	
		Score	Total	Score	Total	Score	Total
Growth	25	6	1.5	5	1.25	10	2.5
Profitability	25	9	2.25	8	2.0	7	1.75
Size	15	6	0.9	5	0.75	8	1.2
Vulnerability	15	5	0.75	6	0.9	6	0.9
Competition	10	8	0.8	8	0.8	4	0.4
Cyclicality	10	2.5	0.25	3	0.3	2.5	0.25
Total	*100*		*6.45*		*6.0*		*7.0*

Note: This could be calculated for Year 0 and Year 3, though it is easier and quicker to carry out only the calculations for the final year.

Table 19.2 Scoring your company and your competitors. Market: XYZ Segment: A

Competitive success factors	Weight	Your company		Competitor A		Competitor B	
		Score	Total	Score	Total	Score	Total
1. Price	50	5	2.5	6	3.0	4	2.0
2. Product	25	6	1.5	8	2.0	10	2.5
3. Service	15	8	1.2	4	0.6	6	0.9
4. Image	10	6	0.6	5	0.5	3	0.3
Total	*100*		*5.8*		*6.1*		*5.7*

Note: Calculations are first made for Year 0, as this enables you to establish a fixed position on the portfolio matrix for your company in each segment, against which the forecast outcome of alternative strategies and assumptions for the planning period can be seen when plotted onto the DPM.

be to invest heavily in these markets and increase market share.

■ In the bottom-left box, where strengths are high but markets are less attractive, a likely aim would be to maintain market share and manage for sustained earnings.

■ In the top-right box, low strengths, combined with an attractive market, indicate a probable policy of selective investment, to improve competitive position.

■ Finally, in the bottom-right box, low strengths allied to poor market attractiveness point to a management for profits, or even withdrawal.

Fig. 19.7 shows an actual DPM for a European agricultural company. Completing this analysis enabled the firm to allocate its scarce resources more effectively and helped it to become one of the world's most profitable players in the fertilizer market. This matrix gives a clear indication of the marketing objectives and strategies that should be set for each segment or product shown.

7.2.6 Assumptions

Before any objectives or strategies are set, assumptions about conditions affecting the business, which are critical to the fulfilment of the planned marketing objectives and strategies, should be made explicit.

Key planning assumptions deal with anticipated external changes, which may significantly influence the achievement of marketing objectives. They should be few in number, relate only to key issues identified in the SWOT analyses, and include, for example, market growth rate forecasts, interest rates, government policy, and so on.

☞ 'Apart from the overall market structure, the level of *concentration* affects the likelihood and nature of competitive reactions.' (Chapter 10, p. 222)

7.2.7 Marketing objectives

The preceding steps will have facilitated the process of setting marketing objectives, which are a realistic statement of corporate aims as a result of market-centred analysis. As in the case of objective setting for other functional areas of the business, this is the most important step in the whole process, and constitutes a commitment, on a unit-wide basis, to a particular course of action and determines the scheduling and costing of subsequent actions.

An objective is what the unit wants to achieve. A strategy is how it plans to achieve it. Objectives and strategies operate at all levels, from strategic corporate to tactical functional, such as distribution and advertising. Marketing objectives, however, focus only on products and markets, since it is only by selling to someone that financial goals

Figure 19.7 **Segment attractiveness and business strengths**

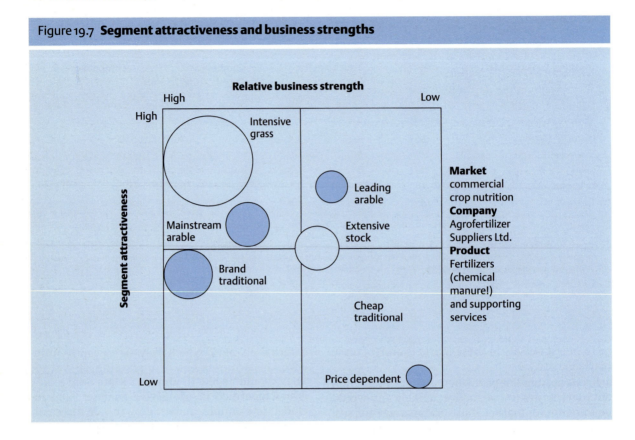

can be achieved. Elements of the marketing mix are the means (strategies) by which the unit can achieve marketing objectives, and therefore sub-objectives for pricing, sales promotion, and so on should not be confused with marketing objectives.

👉 '. . . not all marketing plans will have the same mix of marketing elements.' (Chapter 12, p. 274)

Where possible, marketing objectives should be quantified and expressed in terms of values, volumes, and market shares. General directional terms such as 'maximize' and 'penetrate' should be avoided unless also quantified.

Marketing objectives should be accompanied by broad strategies and revenue/cost projections, all for the full three-year period. Specific objectives for the first year of the three-year planning cycle together with corresponding strategies, should be stated.

7.2.8 Marketing strategies

These should state in broad terms how the marketing objectives are to be achieved:

- product policies (range, technical specifications, additions, deletions):
  - change product design, performance, quality or features;
  - consolidate product line;
  - standardize design, consolidate production, change sourcing;
- pricing policies for product groups in particular market segments:
  - change unit price;
  - improve manufacturing productivity;
- customer-service-level policies provided for specific market segments:

- change delivery or distribution;
- change service levels/maintenance support;
- improve administrative productivity;
- consolidate distribution;
- customer communication policies, including direct sales, advertising, etc.;
  - change advertising or sales promotion, etc.;
  - improve marketing productivity (e.g. improve the sales mix);
  - acquisition of products and markets and withdrawal from markets.

7.2.9 Resource requirements: the budget

Financial projections for the full planning period, under all the standard revenue and cost headings, are stated in the budget. The clear definition of objectives makes the setting of budgets not only much easier, but more realistic, and related to what the whole company wants to achieve rather than just one functional department (see Insert).

The most appropriate method justifying marketing expenditure is from a zero base, annually, against the objectives to be achieved. This is possible if the above procedures are followed, as a hierarchy of objectives is built up in such a way that every item of budgeted expenditure can be related

back directly to the initial corporate financial objectives.

This ensures not only that every item of expenditure is fully accounted for as part of a rational, objective, and task approach, but also that changes can be made with minimal impact on the long-term objectives.

A company must use its discretion as to the allocation of some costs: packaging, inventory, distribution, and customer service expenses can all be considered as marketing or production/operation costs. Only common sense will reveal workable solutions to such issues.

Any form of discounting that reduces the expected gross income, such as promotional and quantity discounts, sales commission, and sales debts, should be categorized as incremental marketing expenses. Other incremental marketing expenses will include advertising, sales salaries and expenses, direct mail, and so on.

The level of expenditure should only be what is required to take the company towards its goals, in a zero-based budgeting approach.

8 Moving from the strategic marketing plan to the tactical marketing plan

ONCE the strategic marketing plan has been signed off, managers can now focus on implementing only the first year of the plan. This means that a tactical marketing plan needs to be prepared.

8.1 Contents of a tactical marketing plan

A tactical marketing plan should state the following.

- Objectives and strategies:
  - *overall objectives*: relating to sales volume/value and gross margins for previous year, current year estimate and budget for next year, together with any relevant commentary;
  - *overall strategies*: e.g. new customers, new products, promotion, pricing, etc.

Avoid the following at all costs

Critiques of over 200 strategic plans from multinationals all over the world by the Cranfield Marketing Planning Centre revealed the following most frequent mistakes in strategic marketing plans:

- voluminous, directionless market overviews;
- no or poor segmentation;
- ignorance of competitor activity;
- SWOTs that are woolly, vague, and far too general;
- failure to describe the value required by customers;
- failure to describe the organization's distinctive competence;
- failure to prioritize marketing objectives;
- confusion between marketing objectives and strategies;
- failure to link the budget to the plan.

- Sub-objectives
  - sub-objectives: more detail on products, markets, segments, and key customers, as appropriate;
  - *strategies*: to achieve the sub-objectives;
  - *tactics*: details, plus scheduling, responsibilities and costs.
- Summary of marketing activities and costs.
- Contingency plan; this should address the following questions:
  - What are the critical assumptions on which the one year plan is based?
  - What would be the financial effect if these assumptions proved false?
  - How will these assumptions be managed?
  - How can any adverse financial effects of incorrect assumptions be mitigated, to ensure profit forecasts are met? Risk assessment, measuring negative or downside risk, evaluates the likelihood and cost of significant change in an assumption.
- Operating result and financial costs, to include:
  - net revenue;
  - gross margin;
  - adjustments;
  - marketing costs;
  - administration costs;
  - interest;
  - operating result;
  - return on sales (ROS);
  - return on investment (ROI).
- Key activity schedule; to assist in the progress monitoring of the annual plan.
- Other information; such as detailed sales call plans.

9 Key analytical tools in marketing planning

Fig. 19.8 shows the contents of the strategic marketing plan broken down into phases (on the left of the diagram). On the right of the diagram are the key analytical tools and techniques considered to be appropriate for producing the relevant outputs on the left. It is not the purpose of this chapter to explain these techniques. (For a full review, see McDonald 1997.)

10 The marketing planning process

10.1 The process

Fig. 19.9 depicts the relationship between the marketing planing process and the output—the strategic and tactical marketing plans. This process can also be drawn as a circular process, so indicating the ongoing nature of the marketing planning process and the link between strategic and tactical marketing plans.

10.2 Marketing planning systems

The degree to which organizations need formalized systems for marketing planning depends on their size and complexity.

In small companies, top management tends to have an in-depth knowledge of the market, and a clear view of comparative strengths and weaknesses. Often, there is also a shared understanding between top and middle management of the logical framework of ideas within which they are all working.

In large organizations and in those operating in complex product and market situations, a more formalized approach via operating manuals, procedures, and processes is necessary, because of the sheer size and complexity.

☞ 'Increasingly firms are using more sophisticated decision models, where both the criteria and the weights used are based on actual research-based evidence . . .' (Chapter 24. p. 555)

Research, however, has shown that the process is universally applicable, with the degree of formality of the systematization being the variant.

11 Barriers to effective marketing planning

It has been pointed out that, in environmental and competitive circumstances that are directly comparable, companies with complete marketing planning systems will be more successful than those without. However, there is a significant gap

Figure 19.8 **The marketing planning process**

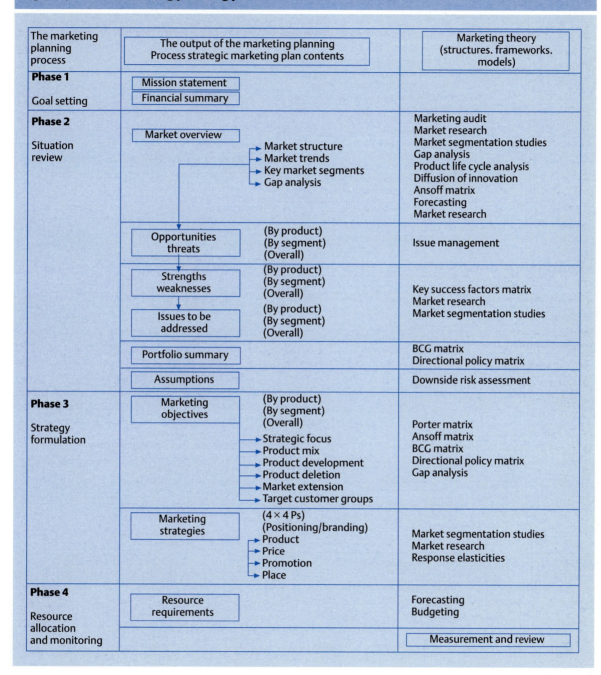

between theory and practice, in that few companies seem to implement marketing planning successfully, so some obvious contradictions are apparent, and it is clear that there are many barriers to the implementation of effective marketing planning. Notwithstanding the importance of marketing planning and its universal acceptance by scholars as being central to the profit-making

Figure 19.9 The marketing planning process: a typical timetable

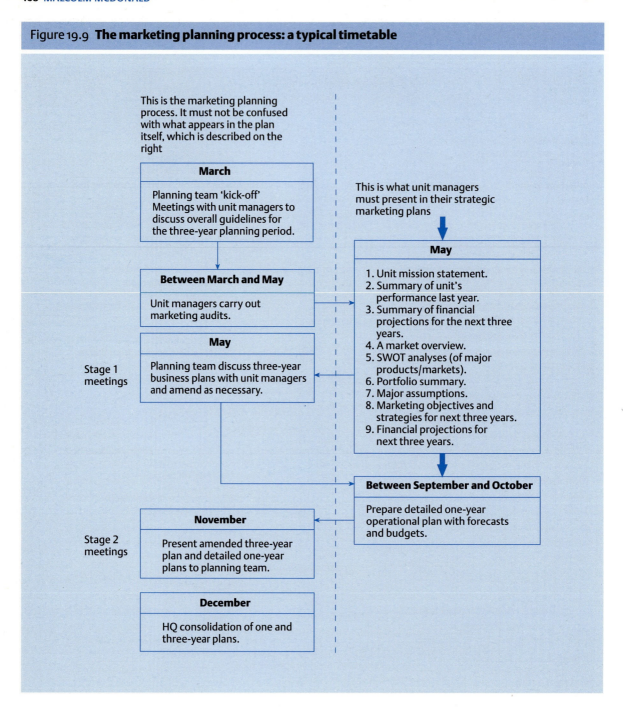

process, little research has been carried out to find out why it appears to be poorly understood and badly executed by a large number of companies on both sides of the Atlantic.

Table 19.3 summarizes what little research has been carried out in this domain. There seems to be wide agreement in the literature that the two biggest barriers are:

Table 19.3 **Marketing planning barriers**

Barriers	Research studies										
	1	2	3	4	5	6	7	8	9	10	11
Roles people play											
B1 Lack of chief executive/senior management involvement	*	*	*	*	—	—	*	*	*	—	—
B2 Lack of cross-functional involvement	*	*	*	*	—	—	*	*	*	*	—
B3 Lack of top management support	*	*	—	—	—	—	*	*	*	—	—
Cognitive											
B4 Knowledge and skills	*	—	—	—	—	*	*	—	—	—	—
B5 Lack of innovation/non-recognition of alternatives	—	*	*	—	—	—	*	—	—	*	—
Systems and procedures											
B6 Lack of care in marketing planning introduction	*	—	—	—	*	—	—	—	—	*	—
B7 Forecasts without documentation of intervention	*	—	*	—	—	—	*	—	—	—	—
B8 Inflexible application of textbook process	*	—	*	—	*	—	—	—	—	*	—
B9 Lack of follow-through to tactics	*	—	*	—	—	—	—	—	—	—	—
B10 Too much detail	*	—	*	—	—	—	*	—	*	—	—
Resources											
B11 Lack of time (elapsed and/or effort)	*	*	—	—	—	—	—	—	*	*	—
B12 Lack of money (for market research, etc.)	*	—	—	—	—	—	—	—	—	*	—
Organizational environment/culture											
B13 Organizational structure inappropriate	*	—	*	—	—	*	*	*	—	—	—
B14 Stage of organizational development	—	—	—	—	*	—	—	—	—	—	—
B15 Corporate politics	—	*	*	—	—	—	*	*	—	—	—
B16 Short-term-oriented reward systems	*	—	—	—	—	—	—	—	—	—	—
B17 Culture-stifling idea generation/openness	—	—	*	*	*	—	—	—	—	*	—
Data											
B18 Lack of information	*	*	*	*	—	*	—	—	*	—	—
Environmental											
B19 Difficulty of forecasting in times of turbulence and inflation	—	*	—	—	—	—	—	—	—	—	—

* The study explicitly claims to have derived the barrier from empirical data with a clearly described and plausible research method.

Sources: studies used as follows: 1: McDonald (1982); 2: Hopkins (1981); 3: Ames (1968); 4: Stasch and Lanktree (1980); 5: Leppard (1987); 6: Hooley (1984); 7: Liander (1967); 8: Saddick (1966); 9: Ringbakk (1971); 10: Camillus (1975); 11: Weichmann and Pringle (1979).

- *cultural/political*: lack of a belief in marketing planning and/or the need to change;
- *cognitive*: lack of knowledge and skills.

At the end of the 1990s, much attention was paid to these two factors as key determinants of strategic marketing planning success, and it is clear that, for marketing planning to be effective, the following conditions have to be met.

- The process must be driven from the top down by the board.
- Marketing planning should be a cross-functional team process.
- There should be no confusion between the strategic marketing planning process and the tactical, one-year operational plan.
- The necessary marketing skills must be acquired by relevant marketing staff.
- There have to be well-understood processes in place for marketing planning.
- Appropriate resources have to be made available.
- The organizational culture must be supportive of marketing planning.
- Measurement and reward systems must be linked to the critical success factors identified in the marketing plan.
- It has to be a creative/innovative process.

12 Final thoughts

IN this chapter, whilst we have concentrated solely on marketing planning, we must point out that there is no intention of implying that non-planning companies are inefficient. Indeed, over the years, some of the most profitable companies have been non-planning, pioneering organizations in their creative evolutionary phase.

Like a stream, as organizations become bigger, wider, or deeper, they become quite different in nature. What sustained company life and made it successful at one stage will certainly be outgrown as it matures.

Our research set out to throw some further light on why marketing planning has been adopted by such a relatively small number of companies. How we chose to define marketing planning was more or less a consensus view of those who have worked in this area. However, because this plan-

Support from the top

A well-known global energy company introduced strategic marketing planning via a series of workshops across Europe during 1993 and 1994. Marketing planning manuals were designed and distributed, but, in spite of all the goodwill generated by the process, very few benefits were delivered. This was because the directors were still driven by financial husbandry and were blocking the new market-driven initiatives.

Then, in 1996, the European Board was introduced to strategic marketing planning at a day-long seminar. After that, marketing planning became the main driving force in the organization. More progress was made in three months with the understanding, support, and participation of the directors than had been made in three years. Profits are the best in the industry and morale is high. This is now a market-driven organization.

ning process embraces a number of implied assumptions and normative values, we found that an organization had to be reasonably sophisticated and mature if it was to use the process to its advantage (see Insert).

It can be hypothesized that, in a manner similar to that in which the three primary colours can, in various proportions, combine to form all other colours, so might all shades and hues of planning approaches be possible. Our intention here was to explore the logical/rational 'territory', for that is where marketing planning (as most have defined it) sits.

It would appear that the more we believe we know about marketing planning, the more we discover there is to learn.

13 The future

THE process of marketing planning will remain the same as it has always been, because—given the multicultural, multi-market, multi-sector, multi-segment, multifunctional, multi-product nature of commerce—some kind of rational process has to be used to cope with the complexity. The complexity itself, however, will increase, as the world becomes increasingly more international in scope and as customers gain more power and choice in an oversupplied world. Furthermore, this level of turbulence will increase with the acceleration of technological advances, which continue to reduce the window of opportunity for the commercialization of innovation.

Customer power has also thrown into sharp relief the pivotal importance of key account planning, as fewer customers account for a larger proportion of total sales. With a growing number of truly international customers, strategic marketing planning will only be as good as the strategic planning that occurs at the individual customer level. This, in turn, will make strategic marketing planning more international, as global key accounts demand seamless service internationally.

Finally, the complexity of strategic marketing planning will intensify as the trend towards supply-chain management grows.

A problem that was endemic to most industries at the end of the 1990s was that of correct market definition. The days of neat markets, constrained by SIC codes, had all but disappeared. A typical example of this is the automotive industry and its impact on all associated value chains. The industry is being driven by more complex technology, stricter environmental legislation, mature markets, more sophisticated customers, and globalization. This has led to the need to become less vertically integrated in order to become leaner, leading in turn to partnerships with a small number of tier-one suppliers. These tier-one suppliers are no longer just component manufacturers, but are truly systems and integrated module suppliers, servicing their clients seamlessly on a global basis through alliances, joint ventures, and acquisitions.

This leaves a massive question mark over the future direction of major corporations like SKF. Does an organization like this become a tier-two, or even a tier-three supplier? The same issues face organizations like British Telecom, for the trends indicate the possibility of their becoming a second-tier supplier to service organizations capable of forming alliances in the value chain to deal with the totality of the communications problems of major companies.

Everywhere one looks, one sees such massive challenges spilling over into erstwhile relatively placid domains such as key account management.

There is little doubt that all of the above will make strategic marketing planning even more important to organizational success. Let us stress once again, however, that the processes outlined in this chapter will remain essentially unchanged.

14 Summary

THE purpose of marketing planning is the identification and creation of sustainable competitive advantage.

It is a logical sequence of activities leading to the setting of marketing objectives and the formulation of strategies and tactics for achieving them, together with associated financial consequences.

It is necessary because of the complexity caused by many external and internal factors that affect an organization's ability to achieve its objectives. There are two outputs from the process of marketing planning:

■ *the strategic marketing plan*: covering a period of between three and five years, outlining a unit's position in its market, relative to competitors, and defining market needs, company objectives and strategies, and the resources required to achieve the desired results;

■ *the tactical marketing plan*: covering a twelve-month period, detailing the schedule and costs of specific actions necessary to achieve the first year's objectives in the strategic marketing plan.

The marketing planning process starts with financial objectives and then proceeds to marketing objectives and strategies for the stated period. At this stage, managers throughout the organization are involved, to ensure that the plan can be resourced effectively, with the final output being tactical marketing plans. Headquarters will often consolidate these into corporate plans. At the start of the organization's fiscal year, the tactical marketing plan is implemented and measured throughout the year, until the whole process starts again.

The degree of normalization of the process depends on an organization's size and complexity, but the process is universally applicable, irrespective of circumstances.

Discussion questions

1 Describe in your own words the difference between strategic and tactical marketing planning.

2 Describe in your own words why strategic marketing planning became more important during the 1990s.

3 What would you say is the main purpose of marketing planning?

4 What are the main components of a strategic marketing plan?

5 Do you believe these have to be written down? Whatever your answer, please justify it.

6 What are the main differences between budgeting and strategic marketing planning and why do you think that, even though the latter is more useful than the former, many organizations still have difficulty doing it?

7 Should marketing planning be a formalized process? Please justify your answer.

8 If an organization introduces strategic marketing planning, what are the factors that might prevent it from being effective?

The dynamic manager

I am Mark Etting, the Business Manager for CRANSERVE, a semi-speciality range of contract and one-off cleaning services used in a wide range of industries, including agrochemicals, paint, plastics, and pharmaceuticals. I was appointed six months ago following a successful career as an account manager in Europe. Today our business is under pressure from increased East European and Far East competition. The CRANSERVE products are well known globally. We are known for our technical competence and ability to offer technical solutions by offering service variations to meet special customer needs. We hold 17 per cent market share in Europe (estimated 9 per cent market share globally.) Our depots are old but efficient and we have invested in new technology to keep operations cost effective. My challenge is to revitalize the service range, stop the decline in sales and margins, and achieve 20 per cent market share in Europe by 2001. I have already started by revising the service mix. As usual, 25 per cent of our services contribute 80 per cent of the margin. I have trimmed minor services that were not generating the minimum return.

Time is short, however; our technical sales team send me daily messages for better prices; just take a look at this, 'Mark, we need your best price on the CRANSERVE bid for our old friend Schwarz Paint Industries in Hamburg. Our bid at DM215k is too expensive—please respond soonest, Manfred Schmidt—Technical Sales.' I need to examine this.

I have spent two months preparing our marketing plan. The SWOT analysis shows that our strengths are in research, leading technology, and the new demand for CRANSERVE in Biochemicals. We are working on ways to compensate for weaknesses in customer service, and to combat the new competitive service, Comserve 230 from Compo. Sales reports show that our competitor, Compo Services, is offering discounts of around 5 per cent below our prices to gain market share.

We have a very good picture of the market and have clearly identified key segments for us, as the DPM shows (see Fig. 19.10). Unfortunately our sales force are finding the key segments difficult to penetrate.

I have sent out two revisions to our price list now and we have looked at our logistics and customer service offer and we are revising systems to provide an improved service to our customers. We are monitoring our service performance and this is improving steadily.

Last month I visited all of our major accounts in Germany, France, Scandinavia, and Italy. This showed that re-

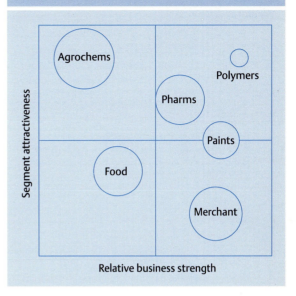

Figure 19.10 **CRANSERVE's segment attractiveness and business strength**

lationships with key customers could be improved, and two of the major customers have already called me direct to discuss the market situation. In the current situation, I have encouraged them to get the latest picture on prices of the CRANSERVE range. Next week I am travelling to Malaysia and Japan to get a full picture of demand in the Far East. I expect it will be the same message to the local sales force—get selling and set some realistic sales targets. I have stressed that all our customers will be under pressure and that we should put maximum effort at all accounts NOW.

I remember the excellent 'Features, Advantages and Benefits' analysis tool and I have sent out a comprehensive list of benefits to the sales force. That should give them all the 'ammunition' they need to convince our customers to buy from CRANSERVE. I just hope they understand what a benefit is.

I have prepared a gap analysis (see Fig. 19.11) and I believe this shows the way forward. If we can just get sales up, then all should be well.

The monthly operations meetings are useful to see how we match sales to our targets. The Operations Manager is doing an excellent job. Often we have to ask the sales force to work after hours and there is a strong customer awareness in the depots. Unfortunately, one of the most expensive areas of our business is high-tech, specialized service, and we have had to make some economies here. I believe we will have to make further cuts here if we are to achieve our budgets for 1996.

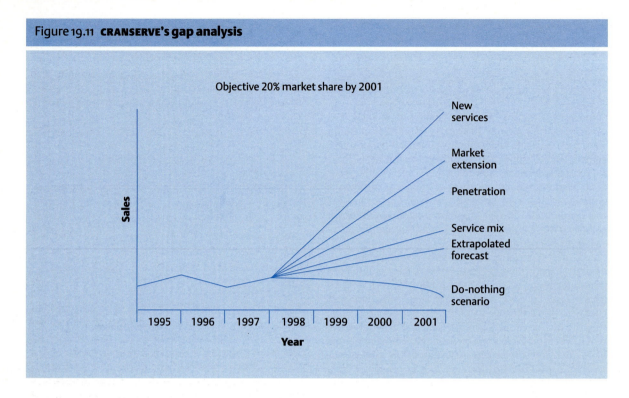

Figure 19.11 **CRANSERVE's gap analysis**

'Ring . . . ring, ring . . . ring,' the telephone called out insistently. 'Now, who is it this time I wonder?'

'Mark?' the voice spoke out, 'Mark, it is Andre from Brussels—we need your support at Lafitte SA . . . they say they can get the service package for BFr.210.'

Discussion question

As Mark's boss, you have seen some of his activities in the three months since joining the business. You have been impressed by some of his work but can see some areas for improvement. What ten items can you identify where Mark has demonstrated good work and what ten items would you like to see improved? Consider this question from the perspective of the process of marketing planning outlined in this chapter.

Case 4
The Peerless Saw Company

Keith Blois

The Peerless Saw Company was founded in 1931 in Ohio to supply band-saw blades to the Ford Motor Company. It grew steadily and reasonably successfully over the years and the number of customers increased so that it was soon not so dependent upon Ford.

The product range contained about 4,000 standard items, which were also offered by most of its competitors. In fact the product had almost all the characteristics of a commodity with comparable prices and delivery being offered by most firms. There was a limited demand for 'non-standard' blades—that is blades that were of unusual external dimensions, that required unusual spacing of teeth, or that were manufactured from special materials. However, it was not known whether this low demand was due to a genuine lack of need or the consequence of customers finding it easier, because of the higher prices and long delivery times that were associated with such items, to adapt their requirements and to purchase standard items.

By 1995 Peerless was finding that it was losing sales even from its established customers, its costs were rising, and its manufacturing equipment was becoming less reliable. Indeed Peerless was facing very strong competition from a number of US-based companies and several foreign firms—many of whom had more modern plant than Peerless. There was overcapacity in the industry, but, in spite of this, foreign firms were still entering the American market. Prices had and were continuing to fall as a result of the increased competition and consequently profit margins were being squeezed. The constant pressure from customers was for further price reductions on both standard and non-standard blades.

Peerless set its prices on a cost-plus basis, but, in this highly competitive market, it had found that trying to maintain its target profit margin on each item sold only led to loss of business from even its long-standing customers. Indeed it had seen its market share fall over the previous few years (see Table 1).

In desperation, Ted Montague (the owner of Peerless) was considering a number of alternatives. He rejected the idea of merging with a competitor or becoming a captive supplier of a major customer. His view was that the best strategy was to find technical improvements that would improve the quality, costs, and most importantly lead times of his manufacturing process. Eventually he purchased a 700-W laser cutter plus extensive ancillary equipment and hardware. In addition, he had a software package written so that the cutter could be programmed off-line by a menu driven protocol that his current operators could be expected to handle.

After months of debugging the software, by October 1996 the laser had been ready to go into operation, with all 4,000 saw patterns having been put into the system. By early 1997 Peerless saw a number of improvements in its operations and some significant changes in customer demand. In 1995 it had had a twelve-week delivery period for most standard blades and at least fifteen weeks for non-standard items (both these delivery periods being fairly similar to those of their competitors). However, with the introduction of the laser cutter this had been reduced to an average of four weeks for both standard and non-standard items and two of these weeks were due to heat treatment (a process not affected by the introduction of the laser technology). However, there was a wide variation around this average figure—though this variation did not appear to be clearly associated with any particular type of blades. Indeed, investigations into these variations indicated that they often resulted from shortages of raw materials, which had delayed the start of the manufacturing process, but that sometimes finished items had got misplaced either on the factory floor or in the stores prior to dispatch.

By the end of the 1997 Peerless was running the system for two full shifts five days a week. (Peerless's sales and market data at this point are given in Table 1 with the financial data being provided in Tables 2, 3, and 4.) Although Peerless was not now making any blades that it could not previously have made it found that its product mix was changing. In 1996 it had mostly made saw blades of 8, 10,

Table 1 Sales and market data, 1994–1997 (current prices)

Year	Sales ($ m.)	Market share (%)
1994	27.73	24
1995	30.78	21
1996	32.91	20
1997	42.07	27

Table 2 Contribution income statement ($000)

	1996			1997		
Sales			32,910			42,070
Less variable expenses:						
Direct materials		10,900			14,720	
Direct labour		6,580			8,410	
Variable indirect manufacturing (Schedule 1)	1,540			2,110		
Total manufacturing cost of goods sold	19,020			25,240		
Variable selling expenses (Schedule 3)	1,690			2,100		
Variable administration expenses (Schedule 4)	160			210		
Total variable expenses		20,870			27,550	
Contribution margin			12,040			14,520
Less fixed expenses:						
Manufacturing (Schedule 2)		4,560			6,300	
Selling (Schedule 3)		2,980			4,200	
Administrative (Schedule 4)		1,540			1,910	
			9,080			12,410
Operating income			2,960			2,110

Table 3 Schedules of indirect manufacturing costs ($000)

	1996			1997		
Schedule 1: variable costs						
Supplies (steel, lubricants, coolants, etc.)	220			320		
Indirect labour		1,070			1,470	
Repairs		180			210	
Power		70			110	
			1,540			2,110
Schedule 2: fixed costs						
Salaries		1,850			1,910	
Training		180			190	
Depreciation		2,140			3,790	
Property taxes and insurance	390			420		
			4,560			6,300
Total indirect manufacturing costs			6,100			8,420

12, and 14 inches. However, now it was making a much wider range of blades. Indeed, it was now primarily making the more complex blades and these at a lower cost than in the past. For example, with the laser cutter it now took one-seventh the amount of time to cut a blade that it had previously and one-eighth the number of machine operations. The resulting average cost saving (on labour, materials, and variable overheads) was 5–10 per cent per blade, but as high as 45 per cent on some non-standard blades. However, selling and administration costs were rising, partly because during 1997 the sales force had been increased in size to cope with the extra business and also because the sales force's customer call rate was falling. Furthermore, sales administration staff, whose numbers had not been increased, were having to work more overtime to deal with the extra orders.

Table 4 Schedules of selling and administration expenses ($000)					
		1996			**1997**
Schedule 3: selling expenses					
Variable					
sales commission		1,200		1,470	
delivery costs	490		630		
		1,690			2,100
Fixed					
advertising		1,100		1,470	
sales salaries		1,390		2,100	
other		490		630	
		2,980			4,200
Total selling expenses		4,670			6,300
Schedule 4: administrative expenses					
Variable					
clerical wages		160		210	
Fixed					
office salaries	460		630		
depreciation of office equipment		230		210	
auditing fees	230		290		
other	620		780		
Total administrative expenses		1,700			2,100

By the end of 1997 Peerless's market share had grown to 27 per cent and it had become clear that the mix of sales of standard and non-standard blades had changed dramatically, with non-standard blades now representing 35 per cent of sales. However, in spite of this, there were no signs of the company's profits improving.

Discussion Questions

1 How has this situation arisen?

2 What actions should be taken to rectify the situation?

Part Five
Issues in Implementing Marketing Strategies

Chapter 20
Brand Management

Graham Hankinson

Objectives

The objectives of this chapter are:

1 to define what is meant by 'a brand';

2 to consider why brands are so important in marketing strategy;

3 to examine what has been the key to the long-term success of some brands;

4 to discuss why it is that brands and branding are most frequently associated with consumer goods and services;

5 to explain how to apply the branding process in the context of both consumer and non-consumer goods and services;

6 to investigate how the international dimensions of branding open up new business opportunities that transcend national frontiers.

1 Historical perspective

BRANDS have been around for decades but they have been a particular feature of the marketing landscape during the 1980s and the 1990s. For various reasons, which we will examine later, brands have become a major focus not only of a company's marketing strategy but also of its financial strategy, as brands have become recognized as part of the key assets that a company owns. The process of brand building has, therefore, become a feature of marketing activities not only in the consumer-goods and services sector but in non-consumer areas as well. Many of the best-known brands go back a long time. Brands such as Coca-Cola, Mercedes, Colgate, Heinz, and American Express have been household names since the beginning of the twentieth century, despite significant changes to the products and a considerable widening in the product mix. But there are also well-known and well-established brands in non-consumer markets as well. Brands such as IBM, Rank Xerox, and ICI have also been around for over half a century. However, it was not until the 1950s that branding became a major marketing activity and the concept of brand management became established. More will be said about the management of brands later in this chapter. First we must define our terms.

2 The concept of a brand

THERE is no one accepted definition of a brand, only a set of perspectives that share a significant degree of agreement. However, each view adds something to our notion of what a brand is and therefore what the task of brand management needs to focus on. We will first review these differing perspectives and then formulate our own working definition. The different perspectives can be grouped into six categories:

- visual/verbal approaches
- positioning approaches
- brand image approaches
- added value approaches
- perceptual appeal approaches
- personality approaches

2.1 Visual/verbal approaches

In our examples of well-known brands above we noted that it was the name that lived on and not the products. Similarly, some brands are instantly recognizable by their packaging—for example, Silk Cut cigarettes. Others are instantly recognized by their symbol—for example, Mercedes. For these reasons some writers emphasize the importance of the name and visual presentation. For example, Aaker (1991) defines a brand as: 'a distinguishing name and/or symbol (such as a logo, trademark, or packaging design) intended to identify the goods or services of either one seller or a group of sellers, and to differentiate those goods or services from those of competitors'.

Clearly, these aspects of a brand are important, particularly for the purposes of recognition. They are also important for legal purposes, as they can be registered, in most countries, on a trademark register to prevent copying by other companies. Companies go to great lengths to protect their brand through registration, taking advantage of trademark legislation wherever it exists.

2.2 Positioning approaches

Other commentators (e.g. Ries and Trout 1986) focus on the need to establish a unique position in the consumer's mind that distinguishes a brand from the competition. The essence of this approach is to use the marketing mix to establish a reputation or position as the number one in a market. The success of this approach depends upon the identification of a gap in the market that allows a brand to claim the number one position. This is a more holistic approach, which focuses the whole marketing mix on the effective communication of the distinctive features of the brand to an identifiable market segment.

2.3 Brand-image approaches

The building of an image is frequently regarded as the main purpose of branding. In this approach, it is the symbolic aspects of the brand that come to the fore. To quote one writer, 'the effort to differentiate the brand is psychologically rather than physically based' (Frazer 1983).

The need to build a relationship between the consumer and the brand is at the heart of this approach. To be successful, the brand's image must be based on a clear understanding of the thoughts and feelings of the target consumer. In so doing, of course, the brand may alienate some consumers in the process of winning others. However, this approach can lead to insufficient attention being paid to the need for a product or service to deliver the functional benefits that consumers have paid for and have a right to expect.

2.4 Added-value approaches

This neglect of the need to meet consumers' expectations is reflected in the value-added approach, which is based upon the notion of a brand as 'an identifiable product, service, person or place, augmented in such a way that the buyer or user perceives relevant unique added values which match their needs most closely' (De Chernatony 1992). Apart from expanding the idea of branding to include people and places, this approach underlines the importance of value in what the brand has to offer, value that is represented in the unique relevance of the offer to the needs of the consumer.

2.5 Perceptual appeal approaches

Other approaches to brands distinguish different aspects or components of a brand, each offering a different sort of appeal. Proponents of this approach suggest that 'there are three sorts of appeal; they are all interrelated and each brand has a different blend of the three—an appeal to the senses, an appeal to reason and an appeal to the emotion' (Doyle *et al.* 1974).

This disaggregated approach allows a more precise examination of a brand's anatomy. If the constituent parts of a brand's appeal can be identified, then it may be possible to build a brand that more closely meets the needs of the target consumer.

2.6 Personality-based approaches

Since the 1980s, the concept of image has been replaced by the concept of brand personality. Just like people, brands are imbued with personalities that go beyond the more simple concept of an image by taking a multidimensional approach based upon appropriate personality attributes taken from market-research findings. The brand personality has been described as 'a shorthand way of describing the nature and quality of the consumer response to a brand' (Gordon 1991). For example, the personality of Coke has been carefully built to represent youth, internationality, and fun, as well as being a refreshing drink—a personality that appeals to a large, identifiable global market segment with similar needs and lifestyles, transcending different cultures and income groups.

2.7 So what do we mean by a brand?

From these different approaches, is it possible to synthesize a definition that embraces the essence of them all? The following may serve as a working definition for the purposes of this chapter: 'A brand is a product or service made distinctive by its positioning relative to the competition, and by its personality in the context of the target market' (Hankinson and Cowking 1993).

Note, however, that we will define positioning in relation to the brand's point of reference to the competition only in respect of price or product usage. This is a more precise (and measurable) definition of positioning than the definition described above and distinguishes positioning from the brand personality, which represents a unique combination of functional attributes and symbolic values. Functional attributes describe extrinsic, tangible properties (in which we include appeals to both the senses and to reason). They include attributes such as 'hard wearing', 'portability', and 'cost effectiveness'. Symbolic values include intrinsic, intangible properties such as 'fun', 'caring', and 'internationality'. Some brands are mainly characterized by functional attributes—for example, Bold, the 'all-in-one detergent and fabric softener'—while other brands are largely characterized by symbolic values—for example, Smirnoff Vodka, 'Pure thrill'. However, the brand personality may not be enough to differentiate one brand from another. For example, Gucci shoes may be described as 'well made' (a functional benefit) and 'stylish' (a symbolic value), but the same might be said of Bally shoes. What distinguishes Gucci from Bally is price positioning, with Gucci at the top and Bally somewhere towards the top end of the medium price segment. Similarly, Muller yogurt may be described as 'wholesome' and 'delicious tasting' (functional attributes), and 'natural' and 'portraying a life style' (symbolic values), but the same might be said of Ski yogurts. What distinguishes these two

Figure 20.1 **The anatomy of a brand**

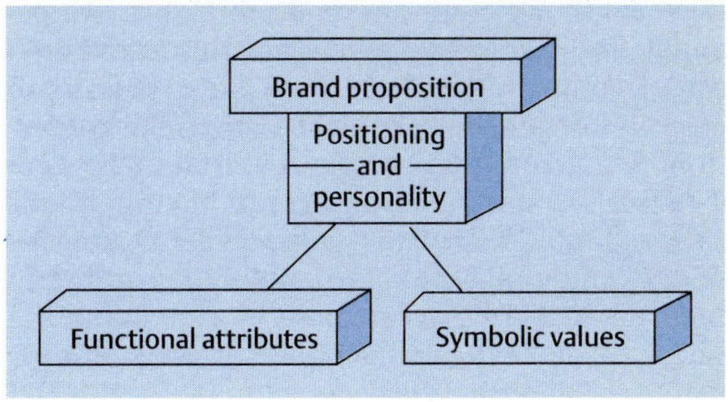

brands, however, is positioning by usage. Muller can be perceived as a breakfast food, in competition with Kelloggs breakfast cereals, and so on, while Ski can mainly be seen as a dessert for children, in competition with Wall's ice cream or Rowntree's jelly. Positioning, therefore, is distinct from personality, as we have defined it.

Fig. 20.1 sets out in diagrammatic form the constituent parts of a brand as we have defined them. These components, positioning and personality (which includes functional attributes and symbolic values), together form the brand proposition.

3 Why are brands so important?

MILLIONS of pounds each year are spent on advertising and promoting brands, but why? There is no doubt that strong brands help a company to maintain market share in the face of a changing competitive environment. Most markets are dominated by two or three well-known brands. It has been shown that, in turn, a strong market share is associated with above-average profits. Research based on studies of over 600 businesses over a long period of time, the well-known PIMS research (Buzzell and Gale 1987), showed that the percentage return on investment increases as market share increases. In this study, brands and businesses with only 10 per cent of the market were likely to have only slightly over 10 per cent return on investment, whereas those with a 30 per cent share or more were on average likely to yield 25 per cent return.

It is probably for this reason that, for many years, strong brands have been the focus of major takeover bids by international companies. For example, in 1988 the Swiss company Nestlé acquired the UK company Rowntree-Mackintosh in order to gain a stronger foothold in the European confectionery market. It was recognized that there were significant financial advantages in buying brands such as KitKat, Rolo, and Quality Street as a means of expanding market share rather than trying to increase Nestlé's market share by expanding the sales of its existing confectionery brands. In 1997 two large multinational companies, Grand Met and Guinness, announced plans to merge in order to obtain what was seen as the critical mass necessary to compete in future international markets. The fundamental reason for this continuing trend of mergers and acquisitions is the belief that it is more cost effective to grow sales from a known brand than to develop new brands. Thus modern brands have become assets in their own right. But what do these assets represent?

First of all, they represent low-risk opportunities for the manufacturer or service operator. The establishment of a successful brand requires sustained investment over a prolonged period of time if the brand proposition is to be embraced by the consumer. The problem intensifies when the traditional route to the marketplace is through a distribution chain, as it becomes increasingly more difficult to obtain distribution for new products without evidence that considerable promotional muscle will be used to move the products from the distributor's shelf to the consumer. Furthermore, as we have already observed, many markets are now dominated by a limited number of major brands, which makes it almost impossible for new entrants to gain a foothold. This is particularly true in static markets in which there is not a lot of scope for product innovation. As a result, as we have noted, many European and US companies have sought to reduce the risks of entering new markets by capitalizing on the reputations of existing brands wherever possible.

Secondly, established brands represent a reduced risk for the consumer, particularly the first-time buyer. An established brand, by virtue of its existing level of awareness in the marketplace, offers the opportunity for new products under the same brand banner to achieve high levels of awareness more rapidly. The use of an established brand name on a new product helps recognition, thereby reducing the marketing communication cost by capitalizing on the heavy level of advertising and promotion devoted to the establishment of the parent brand.

4 Brand loyalty

IT is said that brands offer the opportunity to build consumer loyalty. What do we mean by this? Brand loyalty is about the propensity of a consumer to purchase a brand again. It is usually measured, therefore, in terms of repeat purchase. Consumers are said to be relatively loyal if they tend, on average, to purchase the same brand more frequently than competing brands. Clearly a brand that inspires loyalty in these terms represents a likely income stream for the future, which is the essential requirement of an asset. There are several levels of loyalty, however, which makes the estimation of the value of the future income difficult, a point to which we will return later. These levels of loyalty are represented in the form of a pyramid in Fig. 20.2.

☞ 'Eventually, external search declines and the consumer becomes loyal to a certain brand, which she buys regularly.' (Chapter 6, p. 115)

At the bottom of the pyramid are the consumers who exhibit no loyalty at all, the promiscuous

Figure 20.2 **The five loyalty profiles**

The committed

Active loyalist

Habitual buyer

Constrained switcher

Promiscuous switcher

switchers. For various reasons they regularly switch between a wide range of brands. Perhaps they purchase solely on the basis of price, choosing the best brand offer at the time, or perhaps they are convenience shoppers, buying on the basis of availability. The latter could, of course, look like brand loyalty, if the consumer always buys from the same store. In reality, of course, it would be store loyalty—the two can be difficult to disentangle, as research has shown (Uncles and Ellis 1989). The second level of loyalty is represented by the constrained switchers. These are the consumers who have a limited set of brands from which they will choose depending upon circumstances and the occasion. For example, the brand(s) chosen for general everyday use may be different from the brand(s) chosen as a present. The next level up are the consumers who buy the same brand out of habit and have no reason to change—the habitual buyers. These are, of course, vulnerable consumers from the company's point of view, as they have no reason for their loyalty; it is passive rather than active. The fourth level are the active loyalists. These consumers have a reason to be loyal. The reason may be economic, in so far as they cannot afford the more expensive brands, or it may be functional, in so far as no other brand offers the same functional benefit, or it may be emotional, in so far as the brand offers the symbolic values that match the consumer's own profile. The top level of loyalty is the committed. These consumers will buy no other brand. They are, if you like, the extreme activists. They are also very rare.

In reality, most consumers choose from a short list of brands, depending upon availability, promotional offers, the desire to change for the sake of change, and so on. The marketing implications of this fact are very important. It underlines the need to know what makes up the competitive sets. In terms of our definition of a brand, it means being clear about the brand's positioning and pursuing marketing strategies that firmly establish the brand in the consumer's choice set, accepting that total commitment to the brand is unachievable.

---

5 The branding cycle

BRAND building, as the responsibility of brand management, is a continuous cycle of research, planning, implementation, and control.

As Fig. 20.3 illustrates, creating a new brand begins with research and ends its first cycle with the consumer. Thereafter, the cycle begins again, this time focusing on monitoring research as part of the control process to ensure that the brand continues to meet consumers' needs.

5.1 Research

Research is needed to identify the needs of the target market, both physical and psychological, that are relevant to the product in order to help develop an appropriate brand personality in terms of the physical attributes and symbolic values that match those physical and psychological needs. The research will also explore product usage as well as the consumer's perceptions of competitive brands, their personalities, and positionings in order to define a unique proposition for the new brand in terms of a combination of these components.

5.2 Planning the brand proposition

Crucial to the establishment of a successful brand is consistency in the planning and execution of each element of the mix, in terms both of the positioning relative to the rest of the competitive set, and of the two components of the personality, the functional attributes and the symbolic values, in the context of the target market. It is necessary, therefore, to define simply and precisely what these are before the marketing strategy is defined. As one writer has put it, 'To stand out, you need to have a simple proposition which is easy to understand . . . Brand propositions which are complicated or inconsistent will have no chance' (Davidson 1972).

It is helpful to express the proposition in terms of statements that encapsulate the brand's central features. For example, for the Sony brand this may consist of the following brand proposition statements:

- a brand with technological superiority—*a functional attribute*;
- a brand that is reliable—*a functional benefit*;
- a quality brand—*a symbolic value*;
- a brand that is young and fashionable—*a target market parameter*;
- a brand at the top end of the medium-priced sector—*a positioning parameter*.

Figure 20.3 **The branding cycle**

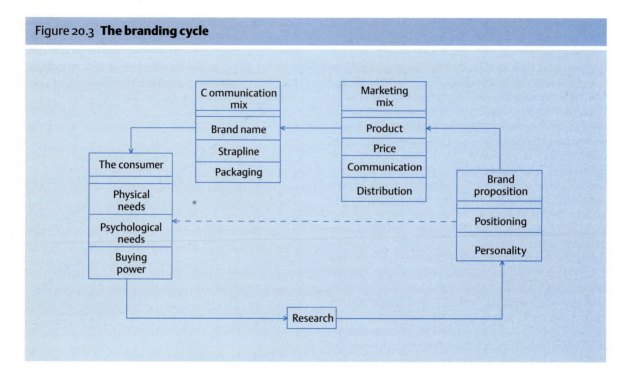

Once these statements have been set down, they become the common criteria against which all subsequent strategy is tested. They also become the elements that help to unite the team of professionals involved in putting the strategy together. Unless there is agreement about the key elements of the proposition, then the consumer is likely to be given confusing messages.

5.3 Implementation—the marketing mix

Successful branding also depends upon defining the correct combination of all elements of the marketing mix. These need to work together in order to present the target consumer with a consistent proposition in terms of the personality and the positioning. Other chapters of this book focus upon elements of the marketing mix. In this chapter we will focus on communications, noting, first, that it takes more than the communication mix to build a successful brand, and, secondly, that successful brands are those that not only communicate consistently but also consistently deliver the

proposition that is offered. Failure to deliver will lead to the demise of the brand, irrespective of how good the communication is.

5.4 Implementation—the communication mix

An essential part of the implementation stage is the communication of the key features of this unique proposition, through the elements of the communication mix. Apart from advertising and sales promotion, successful contributions to brand building and brand maintenance have been achieved through the use of sponsorship, as illustrated by the example of PowerGen (see Insert).

Direct marketing has also been used to help build a new brand. The Daewoo example (see Box 20.1) provides an excellent example of the use of direct marketing, not only to build a new brand, but also to break new ground in terms of the product category, in that new car marques had never hitherto been launched by using direct-marketing methods as a key variable in the communications mix.

PowerGen—building awareness through sponsorship

In September 1989 PowerGen, the largest electricity generator in the UK, signed a contract for just under £2 million for a year's sponsorship of ITV's networked weather forecasts. As a soon-to-be-privatized company, created from the old nationalized Central Electricity Generating Board, the PowerGen corporate brand was unknown to the general public as well as to many large prospective industrial and commercial buyers of electricity. By sponsoring the weather forecast, it not only reached these audiences, but also began to build its personality as a provider of energy to offset the extremes of weather.

Important also was the establishment of a distinct and professional brand personality for PowerGen prior to its flotation on the UK stockmarket in February 1991 through its association with the professionalism of the weather broadcasters.

By March 1990 spontaneous awareness had risen from 3 to 37 per cent and prompted awareness from 39 to 59 per cent.

Branding is ultimately about communicating the whole of the brand proposition as economically as possible. Ideally, this means reducing the message to a series of stimuli or triggers. There are certain key factors that provide the triggers to the communication process. These are the brand name itself, the slogan or strapline, and the packaging.

5.4.1 The brand name

The brand name is a shorthand device for all that the brand stands for. Not only does it serve to identify the brand; it should also trigger the brand proposition in the consumer's mind. There are three alternative naming strategies. The stand-alone strategy, in which the name bears absolutely no connection with the product. Examples include Persil and Mercedes. The advantage is that they are absolutely neutral and therefore can rarely become a limiting factor as the brand franchise grows. For example, the brand name British Telecom was changed to BT in

---

Box 20.1 **Daewoo—a driving force**

Daewoo Cars Ltd is the subsidiary of the huge south Korean Daewoo Group—the world's 30th biggest industrial corporation. The UK business was established in May 1994, with the task of bringing a range of Daewoo cars to the UK market in spring 1995. The Marketing Director, Pat Farrell, proved his mettle from the start and used the company's early anonymity to good effect—the pre-launch campaign focused on 'the biggest car company you've never heard of'. Daewoo thus began to make a major impact long before its UK launch.

The new management team were faced with a number of challenges. One, the company and its cars were an unknown quantity. Two, there was no service infrastructure. And, three, they had been set the target of capturing 1 per cent of the UK car market by 1997. But, armed with a blank sheet of paper (literally—the radical new strategy came out of a four-day brainstorming with the agencies), they developed a strategy that turned these apparent weaknesses into an opportunity.

In October 1994 Daewoo took the motor industry by storm with its announcement that it would take control of the distribution chain and deal direct with customers, eliminating dealers from the equation. Its unique selling proposition was to be the most customer-focused brand in the car market. As part of a pre-launch campaign, it launched a major survey into car buyers' attitudes.

More than 200,000 people responded to the survey, 200 of whom got a free car to drive for a year. The survey not only supported Daewoo's feeling that customers begrudge the traditional high-pressure showroom environment and pushy salesmen; it also threw up new ideas that the company could build into its marketing philosophy. In addition to the huge publicity, it created a massive database of prospective customers.

A further building block in its marketing strategy was the pioneering partnership with Halfords, the components retailer, which provided an instant national service network.

With a range of two models and a fledgling retail network, Daewoo sold 13,169 cars in nine months in 1995. By the end of 1996 they had achieved the target 1 per cent market share with 35,000 cars.

The strategy, its execution, and Daewoo's spectacular success earned the company the accolade 'Brand of the Year' in the UK, and Farrell the highly coveted 'Marketer of the Year' award in 1996 from the Marketing Society. Farrell was also judged 'UK direct marketer of the year' by UK-Direct, and Daewoo scooped the Gold Award in the DMA/Royal Mail Direct Marketing Awards.

Goldfish—a new stand-alone brand name

The Goldfish credit card was launched by Goldbrand Developments, a joint-venture company owned by the unlikely alliance of the British Gas holding company Centrica and the US-based HFC Bank in October 1996. The distinctive functional attributes of this new credit-card brand included savings on (you guessed it) gas bills, BT telephone calls, shopping at the supermarket, Asda, and the television licence. Its symbolic values include a fresh image and an absence of the stuffiness associated with some of its rivals. Twelve months after its launch it had gained 75 per cent awareness amongst consumers and had become the fastest growing credit card in the UK market. Like Virgin, which is yet another example of a successful stand-alone brand name in recent years, Centrica, the owners of Goldfish, plan to stretch the brand outside its current product field into non-financial services markets.

order to enable the company to extend its franchise globally and to avoid the parochial associations of the word British. A more recent example of a stand-alone brand name is Goldfish, the credit card, launched in the UK in 1996 (see Insert).

The second alternative is an associative strategy, in which the name is chosen because it contributes in some way to the brand proposition. Examples include Wash and Go the shampoo, and Readybrek the breakfast cereal. The use of such names can sometimes help to distinguish the brand in the face of a myriad of competing brands. In both these examples the names help to establish the usage positioning of the brands.

The third alternative is the completely descriptive name, such as Do It All or Super Glue. It is interesting to note that there is research (Vanden Bergh *et al.* 1987) to suggest that it is only these purely descriptive or so-called semantic-fit names that have any effect on the success of the brand. The success is largely in terms of their aid in recall through their clear linkage to product usage.

5.4.2 The strapline or slogan

The power of the strapline is evidenced by the familiarity of the following examples of famous straplines:

- *Duracell*, the longer lasting battery;
- A *Mars* a day helps you work, rest and play;
- *Coke* is it;
- Have a break have a *Kit Kat*;
- *Heineken* refreshes the parts other beers can't reach.

In their own way each of these straplines or slogans evoked the proposition of the brand and, in so doing, helped to summarize and reinforce the more extended messages that formed the overall brand-building or maintenance campaigns.

5.4.3 Packaging

Packaging is also one of the ways in which the brand proposition is kept in the forefront of the consumer's mind. Examples such as Silk Cut and Benson and Hedges cigarettes show how the use of a distinctive packaging colour can be so closely identified with a brand that its mere display on a poster without the brand name triggers instant recognition and recall.

5.5 The consumer

From time to time, particularly because of changes in consumers needs and buying power, it may be necessary to change elements of the mix in order to ensure that the brand continues to be up to date in terms of what it delivers to the consumer and also in terms of how it is presented to the consumer. This requires a programme of research to monitor the changing attitudes to the brand and its competitors. However, any changes must, first of all, be gradual and, secondly, still conform to the key elements of the brand proposition. The case of Lucozade (see Box 20.2) shows what can happen if the communication strategy is neglected for too long. In this case the brand had totally lost touch with changes in the marketing environment and consumers' attitudes to the extent that the personality required a complete transformation from its old associations with illness to a modern, and more positive association with health.

The branding cycle, if rigorously and continuously applied, should lead to the clear recognition by the consumer that the functional attributes and symbolic values of the brand as communicated via the marketing mix communication mix continuously match their physical needs and psychological needs. Building and maintaining this relationship over time is the key to the brand's acceptance and continued success.

Box 20.2 **Lucozade—a brand reborn**

Fifty years ago Lucozade was positioned as a sparkling glucose drink to be taken as an 'aid to recovery'. As such, its competitive set was 'over-the-counter' tonics and medicines sold through a chemist. Its personality was sickness related, targeted towards children and by implication for occasional use only. To halt declining sales, a strategic decision was taken to reposition the brand as a source of energy for the more health-conscious consumers of the 1980s, a shift from 'health' to 'healthy'. The competitive set hence changed to include other refreshing drinks. Its point of distinction, however, was maintained through its personality, which retained the functional attribute of 'energy' provided through its glucose ingredient. The first television commercial featured a housewife getting through her busy day with Lucozade. Follow-up commercials featured Daley Thompson, the athlete, as a machismo, a symbol of energy. Then the brand was 'taken onto the streets' with the introduction of 330 ml. cans, a range of flavour vari-

ants, and a poster campaign that featured the word 'energy' as a set of brain-teasing letters:

N
R
G

The next development was to promote Lucozade as a drink for 'anyone', as research indicated that the Daley Thompson endorsement was projecting a male bias. There followed the 'Energy for the Human Race' campaign featured on posters and in the women's press.

Progressively, advertising was used to communicate a changing brand more in tune with today's consumer and today's lifestyle, while at the same time retaining the core energy-giving values that remain at the heart of the Lucozade brand personality. As a result, Lucozade in the 1990s was perceived as a healthy, energetic, fun-loving drink which all consumers can enjoy.

Source: Hankinson and Cowking (1993).

6 The brand franchise

ONCE a brand has been established, it becomes the strategic launchpad for growth. This is frequently referred to as a process of building what is called the brand franchise. A brand's franchise consists of the markets in which it is sold and the range of products and services that are sold under its name. It is represented graphically in Fig. 20.4 in the form of a matrix. The brand franchise matrix is defined by two dimensions, product development (or what we refer to below as brand stretching) and market development.

Along the product-development dimension, the brand is *stretched* first to include minor product variations. For example, in the case of a brand of soup this might mean a new flavour. Beyond the introduction of a new flavour, product development might also include a new form, such as Cuppa Soups, which were launched successfully by Batchelor's many years ago. Moving further along this dimension, a brand may then be stretched to embrace related new products. An example of this from the 1990s was the launch of a range of ice creams by Mars. This was so successful that it was soon followed by ice-cream versions of other confectionery brands, such as Crunchie, Twix, and Snickers.

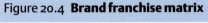

Figure 20.4 **Brand franchise matrix**

Along the market-development dimension, the brand is launched, first, into new market segments and then into entirely new markets either at home or overseas. Brands such as Bacardi, Smirnoff, and Tia Maria are examples of brands that have increased their franchises largely, but not exclusively, through entry into new markets rather than product development. As a result, they are now globally distributed brands. In reality, there are very few single-product brands, but there does seem to be a concentration of them in the alcoholic drinks industry. In most cases, however, the widening of the brand franchise is achieved through a combination of both product and market development, as represented by the diagonal arrow in Fig. 20.4. For example, Dunhill, one of the world's leading luxury-product brands, gradually extended its franchise along the market-development dimension while at the same time extending its product range from cigarettes to other smoking-related products (e.g. lighters) and then completely new products such as clothing and male accessories and cosmetics. This type of growth is also characteristic of the growth of Japanese brands. Yamaha, for example, has successfully extended its brand from motorbikes to musical instruments.

7 Brand stretching

THE process of developing a range of products under the banner of one brand name is called brand stretching. There are certain advantages in this approach to new product launches. First and foremost, brand stretching enables a new product to take advantage of the already established functional attributes and symbolic values that make up the personality of the parent brand, whether that be product specific or corporate. Clearly, the intended personality of the parent brand should be appropriate to the new product. Secondly, brand stretching can, if done successfully, enhance the reputation and sales of the parent brand. An example of this is provided by the toiletries brand Nivea (see Box 20.3).

Brand stretching is, however, not without its critics. It is sometimes argued that stretching a brand can adversely affect its health (Aaker 1991). Brand stretching the original brand proposition can result in cannibalization of the original product's sales by the brand extension(s). It can also dilute the brand proposition such that consumers are confused by what becomes a more complex personality. However, there are probably as many examples of brand-stretching successes as there are failures. The important point is to ensure that the original brand is nurtured. This means, as we have said, periodic reviews of its saliency and relevance to the marketplace. Brands can quickly become old-fashioned and lose their sparkle. The case of Nivea is not all success. In the 1970s this brand had to undergo a radical relaunch aimed at attracting new, younger users, while not alienating the existing ones. This was a necessary prerequisite to the subsequent brand-stretching programme.

Box 20.3 **Nivea—the skincare brand**

Nivea, the largest toiletries brand in the world, began life in Germany as a soap manufacturer in 1906. For a long time, however, its reputation, in the rest of Europe in particular, was based upon the skin formulation, Nivea Cream. The successful stretching of the brand was based on the careful selection of new products that matched the brand's original personality both in Germany and the rest of Europe. This was used to evaluate potential product developments. The essential attributes and values used as the benchmark were as follows:

- other care and protection;
- be simple and uncomplicated;
- be mild;
- have natural active ingredients;
- have a subtle perfume;
- be of high quality;
- give value for money;
- be blue and white (the colours of the parent brand).

Maintaining this personality enabled Nivea successfully to launch a range of sun-care products that were number two in the UK market in the late 1990s. Meanwhile, in Germany, Nivea successfully launched a range of hair-care products. This was followed by a range of Nivea products for men. All these developments were a significant step away from the original product. With the exception of the UK, the sales of the original soap have benefited from these extensions to the range. In the UK, however, Nivea soap was a late entrant into an already crowded market and the benefits of these extensions were less significant.

'Many of a company's offerings, perhaps even all of them, may benefit from
a corporate reputation or brand.' (Chapter 15,
p. 360)

8 Brands as financial assets

BRANDS are valuable strategic assets representing substantial investment, which, over the
years can yield significant income. However, this
does not necessarily mean that they can be treated
in the same way as other corporate assets. There
has been considerable debate about how far it
is possible to place an economic value on a company's brands that could then be recorded in published financial statements. The debate has been a
very British affair, but it raises some interesting issues. We can take the debate in two parts.

The first issue relates to brands acquired
through takeover. There is no doubt that the reason for some takeovers, as we have noted, has
been to acquire strategically valuable brands. The
cost of these acquisitions has frequently been substantial. As a result of this, companies have tried
to find ways of placing a value on these brands for
balance-sheet purposes in order to ensure that the
full benefits of the acquisition are added to the net
worth of the company.

Those companies that have done this (and they
include companies such as Reckitt and Coleman
and Grand Met) have claimed brands to be assets,
which can be clearly distinguished from the more
general goodwill that has been acquired and
which can be given a 'fair value' in line with UK
accounting regulations. If this claim had not
been made, then the brands could not have been
treated any differently from the acquisition of
goodwill and would therefore have had to be immediately written off to reserves, with a consequent weakening of the post-takeover balance
sheet. Treating the brands as separable assets
enabled the cost of the brands to be amortized
against future profits, leaving the balance sheet
unaffected.

The second issue relates to home-grown brands.
The debate here was set alight by RHM (Rank,
Hovis, McDougall) the leading UK flour and foods
company, which in 1988 valued all its brands, both

acquired and home grown, for balance-sheet purposes. This practice was later followed by Guinness, United Biscuits, and Lonrho. Unlike acquired
brands, this was an area in which there were
no definitive accounting regulations, although
the principle of separably identifiable assets still
held. A subsequent enquiry into the practice of
brand valuations for balance-sheet purposes, conducted on behalf of the accounting profession by
the London Business School, came out against the
practice (Barwise *et al.* 1989). At the end of the
twentieth century this issue had yet to be
resolved.

9 Brand Equity

NEVERTHELESS, the concept of establishing a financial value for a brand, in other words its
equity value, remains an attractive one. Notwithstanding the accounting debate, it is useful for
those responsible for brands to be able to place a
value on their brands for several reasons.

■ It focuses management's orientation away
from short-term financial goals towards the
development of a true sustainable competitive
advantage.

■ It enables an objective choice to be made between alternative options for the investment of
limited resources.

■ It helps management to place a value on
potential licensing and merchandising deals.

■ It facilitates the evaluation of the potential
return on the investment of strategic options such
as brand extensions.

The value of a brand has been defined as the balance of both the assets and the liabilities that can
be directly associated with it. On the assets side we
might include such factors as:

■ the extent of brand loyalty;
■ the perceived quality of the brand;
■ the brand's market share;
■ the extent of the brand's leadership compared
to the number in the market;
■ long-term trends in the market;
■ the existence and extent of patents and other
legal protection;

- the susceptibility of the brand to competition, technological change, etc.;
- average profitability.

☞ 'It is widely accepted that higher-share brands are less "deal elastic"' (Chapter 10, p. 236)

On the liabilities side we might include all the costs of maintaining the brand's competitive position. These can include:

- average annual advertising and promotional costs;
- legal costs associated with the protection of patents, trade names, etc.;
- the costs of legislative changes—e.g. on packaging;
- directly attributable staff costs.

The major problem with all these eminently sensible assets and liabilities is, of course, the problem of measurement. All the variables listed above contain, to varying degrees, an element of subjectivity in their assessment. The fact remains, however, that, without some form of systematic approach, decisions on the allocation of funds will be subject to hunch and personal bias. It is not surprising, therefore, that the topic of brand equity and how to measure it has become a focus for research, particularly in the USA.

10 The growth in own-label brands

WITH some exceptions, such as Boots, Sainsbury, and Marks & Spencer, so-called own-label brands have been a feature of retail shopping only since about the 1970s. Own-label brands, however, include not only retail grocery brands such as these but also building societies and banks like Nationwide and Barclays that sell their own products such as life assurance and mortgages. The phenomenon of own label is not, however, confined to the retail sector. Wholesalers such as Nurdin and Peacock and symbol groups such as Mace and Spa also sell their own brands. Traditionally, own-label brands have focused on the functional attributes of the brand, offering inferior performance at lower prices. More recently,

however, own-label brands have begun to acquire symbolic values. As such they have, in many cases, become the 'lookalikes' of manufacturers' brands or 'me-too's'. In most European countries, the power of the grocery retailers has become concentrated among a handful of major players, which has added to the problems faced by manufacturer's brands. Large and powerful retailers such as Sainsbury and Carrefour have now acquired brand propositions of their own. No longer are own-label brands regarded as cheap and cheerful alternatives to manufacturers' brands, but arguably, in many product sectors—for example, chilled foods and dairy products—own-label brands are regarded in the same way as manufacturers' brands.

The typical own-label brand, however, does not enjoy the same level of promotional support as its major manufacturer competitors. The brand personality of the retail product brand has, in contrast, been built up through the development of the corporate brand. This has been achieved through massive store redevelopment programmes providing a quality environment matched by quality service. In a sense it has been a focus on the retailer's core product itself, the shopping experience, which has built the corporate brands of the retailers and provided the means to endorse own-label brands with a balanced personality, embracing both symbolic values as well as functional benefits. Such has been the success of this strategy that, not only are some own-label brands more expensive than their manufacturer equivalents but, as we have noted, some retailers have now launched their own product brands. For example, Sainsbury's have launched their own washing powder, Novon, while Boots, the chemists, has its own very successful range of Natural Collection toiletries.

The growth in the market shares of the own-label brands is in itself evidence of the commercial power of branding. In this instance, this has been the result of a focus on the development of the corporate rather than a product brand, which has enabled the retailers to reap the benefits.

11 Corporate brands

IN the case of the retailers, it is the company that has become the brand. Similarly, companies such as Bosch, Heinz, IBM, and Christian Dior have focused their brand building on their corporate name and used it across a wide range of products and services. The promotion of corporate brands increased in the second half of the 1990s, a trend that seems likely to continue. This trend has been evidenced in the growth in the amount of money devoted to corporate advertising rather than product or service advertising. There are two major reasons why corporate brands have become more prominent. The first is in response to the pressure on companies to behave in a socially responsible way. The UK company ICI provides an example of a company trying to present a caring image to the world by adopting a slogan 'world problems, world solutions, ICI, world class'. Secondly, there have been pressures from stock markets around the world that have forced companies with significant brand portfolios to raise their profiles as the owners of these brands. The UK company Hanson found it prudent to undertake a series of TV advertising campaigns during the 1980s in order, first, to fend off corporate predators and, secondly, to raise awareness of its success when bidding for another significant brand owner, Imperial Group.

There are broadly two approaches to corporate branding. The first is what is referred to as the monolithic approach, in which the corporate name is used across a range of several different product sectors or market segments. Thus, Christian Dior covers products ranging from cosmetics to clothing. In other cases, IBM uses its name on all its products from mainframe computers to stand-alone desktop machines. The most successful implementers of this strategy include Japanese companies such as Yamaha and Mitsubishi, which have successfully stretched their corporate brand names from pianos to motor bikes in the case of the former and TVs to cars in the case of the latter. The weakness of the monolithic approach, however, is that it can stretch the credibility of the brand beyond belief, as we have already noted. This, of course, flies in the face of the experiences of the companies we have just mentioned and must therefore be seen as a point of view rather than a generalizable conclusion.

The alternative to a monolithic approach is the endorsement approach, which allows a more market-related approach to branding, while at the same time providing the advantages associated with the use of an established brand name. This approach has been adopted by Nestlé, which uses its corporate brand name to endorse all its products. Corporate brand endorsement is, as we have noted, a form of brand stretching, which is particularly advantageous in the case of new product or service launches, providing, as it does, a head start in the establishment of awareness and a consequent saving in launch costs.

12 Global brands

WHAT is a global brand? In brief, it might be said to be a brand with a global reputation. Certainly, awareness is fundamental to the claim to be a global brand. But that merely addresses the notion of 'globalness' and not necessarily the meaning of branding in a global context. Our definition of a brand as 'a product or service made distinctive by its positioning relative to the competition, and by its personality in the context of the target market', needs to be transposed into a global context. To be truly global a brand needs more than just awareness; it needs to offer consumers across the world a consistent (i.e. standardized) proposition, including the same product formulation or service characteristics. If we adopt this as a working definition, then we must recognize that it is an ideal rather than something that can ever be fully implemented. Even Coca-Cola varies its recipe in some areas of the world, but it nevertheless comes pretty close to our definition. Other brands that come close are Marlboro, Chanel, Gucci, Smirnoff, and Bennetton. These companies have adopted a fully global strategy, attempting to provide a common personality and positioning in every region of the world.

The growth in global brands as a way of developing the brand franchise has been stimulated by improvements in communications and the growth in international travel, which has resulted in the emergence of market segments with similar demographic characteristics across the world, such as business travellers. We have also seen the emergence of market segments with similar cultural preferences manifested in, for example, the Green movement, fast food, rock music, and fashion. Not all marketing authorities have supported the trend towards globalization. Some have argued that the fully global brand is a move back towards product orientation, sacrificing the marketing philosophy of consumer first for the benefits of standardization that accrue to the supplier rather than the consumer (Levitt 1983c). There is no doubt that many advantages do benefit the supplier. Global branding makes it possible to sell the same product in several countries and this makes it possible for manufacturing economies of scale to be realized. Similar economies arise from sharing the costs of R&D across a larger sales volume. In particular, there is evidence to suggest that industrial products, consumer durables, and high-tech products are more likely to provide benefits from such standardization (Rosen *et al.* 1989). However, it is, of course, possible to obtain these economies without the establishment of a global brand. A standardized product sold under different brand names could achieve the same economies.

There are also economies in marketing costs associated with global branding. As long ago as 1983, British Airways ran the same advertising campaign in four different countries in six languages. This was followed up by other similar campaigns, which have extended into the late 1990s. Campaigns like this must appeal to demands and desires that extend beyond national frontiers. Coca-Cola is another example that illustrates this property. It may be said to symbolize 'youth', 'fun', and 'refreshment' through a common communication strategy across the world. However, in contrast to British Airways, this is not based on a single global advertising campaign, demonstrating that it is possible for global brands to be established and maintained through a variety of different media and promotional executions, provided the brand proposition is adhered to in a consistent way.

The fact remains, however, that most brands do not conform to our ideal of a global brand. Most brands with significant international awareness pursue alternative strategies to the fully global one that we have described. Hankinson and Cowking (1996) suggest that there are basically four strategic alternatives. These alternatives are represented in a matrix in Fig. 20.5. A fully global strategy would use exactly the same marketing mix throughout the world. There are, in fact, few if any consumer products that follow this strategy, for there are nearly always at least small adaptations to local matters. For example, it may be necessary to be sensitive to the religious culture when considering advertising content. Price is often also adjusted to take account of local levels of prosperity.

For most companies, the process of 'going global' is a gradual one. The three alternative strategies represent starting points in the process of establishing some form of global brand that offers an element of consistency to a well-defined international market segment. Note that they are not discrete categories but rather represent a strategic continuum. As we have said, the ideal is to offer all consumers the same proposition across the world. In many cases, such a standardized strategy may not be possible, as has been pointed out.

Figure 20.5 **The global brand strategy matrix**

Brand proposition	Product: Standardized	Product: Adapted
Standardized	Fully global strategy	Product-adaptive strategy
Adapted	Proposition-adaptive strategy	Fully adaptive strategy

12.1 The product-adaptive strategy

One solution to this may be to modify the product (or service) formulation that forms part of the functional benefits of the brand in order to cater for the requirements of different international regions. Examples of such product-adaptive strategies are oil companies such as Shell that offer different octanes of petrol to meet local differences in usage. This may be said to be relatively simple to achieve, particularly with a product like petrol whose consumption is totally invisible. A more complicated example is the case of the Land Rover Discovery, which is offered in different specifications in different parts of the world. For example, in the Middle East, the market need for greater power required the addition of a 3.5 litre V8 engine together with more masculine styling features such as bull bars and side runners. The fact that the product formulation differences were visible meant that there was a very self-evident departure from the consistency in product formulation or functional benefits associated with the ideal of the fully global brand.

12.2 The proposition-adaptive strategy

Alternatively, it may be appropriate to modify other aspects of the brand proposition in order to meet a different marketing environment while maintaining a standardized product formulation. For example, in Europe, where there is a relatively short list of branded jeans, Levi jeans occupies a high price positioning, has a fashionware product-usage positioning, and a 'sophisticated' personality. In the USA, however, Levis are positioned as a medium-priced brand with a less well distinguished personality in a much more crowded market. Nestlé operates a proposition adaptive strategy as regards its Nescafé brand of instant coffee. It has different products on offer in different countries as well as different brand propositions. In the UK, for example, it has been associated with a fast-moving lifestyle (and similarly in France), while in Spain it is associated with its taste and aroma. The proposition-adaptive strategy is frequently a more significant deviation from the global brand ideal, as it results in different functional attributes and symbolic values in different regions of the globe. This inevitably prohibits some of the benefits of standardization referred to earlier.

12.3 The fully adaptive strategy

The final strategic approach is to adapt any aspect of the brand, be it product or proposition related. The brand name may, however, be retained. In this case market conditions vary so much that the benefits of a country-by-country or region-by-region approach outweigh any advantages from standardization. In other cases, the strategy may reflect historical circumstances. Companies that have grown by acquisition frequently find themselves with a portfolio of local brands and choose not to impose a standardized global identity but rather to preserve the strengths that their local brands have in local markets. An example of this approach is H. J. Heinz, which, despite being an internationally recognized brand, nevertheless reports that 65 per cent of its sales come from products that do not carry the Heinz label. Some companies are now beginning to move away from the fully adaptive strategy. An example is again provided by Nestlé, which has attempted to establish a global brand through universal endorsement of all its acquired brands with the Nestlé label.

13 Brand management and the future

As we said at the outset of this chapter, brands have been around for a very long time. As long ago as the end of the nineteenth century brands were becoming established as part of the commercial landscape. At this time brand building was usually the responsibility of the owner entrepreneurs. Brands such as Coca-Cola, Gillette, Rolls-Royce, Cadbury, and Heinz were being promoted in this way—the personal influence of the 'man at the top'. These brands flourished because of the energy and enthusiasm and status of their owner-entrepreneurs. As the brands became successful and their companies became more complex, the responsibility for the brands became more fragmented and 'slipped a notch' in the hierarchy. The role of the owner-entrepreneur was taken over by a team of 'functional specialists' occupying middle and upper-middle management positions (Low and Fullerton 1994). They behaved quite differently from the one-man 'brand champions' of the earlier period, relying more on teamwork than vision and entrepreneurship. It was not until the late 1950s that the concept of a brand champion returned and what we now call the brand-management system began to develop. However, even this now well-established system is coming under attack.

In companies for which brands are a central part of their business, the way in which they are managed is a crucial issue. What we have said so far about brands and brand building has largely ignored the managerial dimension, yet people are at the centre of a brand's success or failure. The way in which they are organized is of crucial importance to the continuing growth in the brand's franchise and its value as an asset. It is worth spending some time, therefore, on the issue of brand management.

The perceived advantages of the so-called brand-management system were that it represented a return to the concept of a brand champion whose role was to lead and coordinate all aspects of the brand-building strategy. The problem with the management of brands by functional specialists was that, while specialists gave their attention to a range of brands, no one had overall responsibility. Moreover, no one had a clear vision of what each brand stood for—that is, the brand proposition. Under the brand-manager system, the brand manager, in contrast, was the guardian of the brand proposition and could, therefore, ensure that the advertising agency, the market-research agency, and all the other necessary inputs into a successful brand-building programme worked together to nurture and grow the brand franchise. However, this system also came under attack in the second half of the 1990s.

Research indicates that in the 1990s the management of brands, at least in the UK, fell short of the original concept of the brand-manager role as brand champion and the focus of corporate resources (Hankinson and Cowking 1997). The indications were that the management of brands had again become a fragmented process involving a range of individual experts rather than focused around one person. What seemed to be happening was that new areas of marketing such as trade marketing and database marketing had developed, and the management of these functions had been the responsibility of functional specialists who were operating at arm's length from those responsible for the management of the company's brands.

In future, the nature of brand management is likely to become more fragmented. In order to ensure the continued success of a brand, it will be necessary for those with brand-management responsibility to have a greater understanding of the newer areas of marketing and to participate in teams as guardians of the brand proposition. The way in which brands are managed will continue to change, but the essence of a brand will not. The centrality of a simple, consistent brand proposition will remain the key to a brand's continued success.

Brand management is changing in other ways as well. First, as we have noted, there is a trend towards corporate branding driven by globalization and the need for large corporations to publicize the extent of their brand portfolios to the financial markets. This will require a greater cohesion between the various levels in the brand-management hierarchy. The development of corporate brands will inevitably move the responsibility for brands towards the top of the organization. Secondly, the continued growth in global brands is likely to increase the need for greater integration of brand-management responsibilities and greater coordination in order to secure a consistent execution of an agreed global strategy. This may once again require changes to the organizational structures to underpin this, as the Smirnoff case study illustrates.

14 Summary

BRANDS are now a central feature of consumer marketing to the extent that they have become assets in their own right, which has made them the focus of financial takeovers and corporate growth. In this chapter we have explored what we mean when we talk of a brand. Although different authors differ in their emphasis, successful brands are perceived by consumers as distinctive and different from their competitors through their personality (a mixture of functional benefits and symbolic values) and/or through their positioning in terms of price or usage. Together these form the brand proposition. In short, brands are about building a long-term relationship with the consumer, irrespective of the type of market. While much attention has been given to consumer brands, it is important not to forget that branding is equally important to the building of reputations in all other markets including services and industrial products. During the last two decades of the twentieth century the principles of branding were successfully applied to the transformation of some own labels into retailer brands as well as the development of other corporate as opposed to product brands. Investing in a brand builds consumer confidence and loyalty and allows the company to stretch the brand-proposition cost effectively to other products and services.

Successful brand building requires a consistent and sustained strategy over the long term. The branding cycle begins with a clear statement of the brand proposition, which can be communicated through the marketing mix. The brand proposition is also used by successive members of the brand-management team to maintain and develop the brand franchise by extending the range of both the products and the services as well as the markets over which the brand is recognized. Some brands have managed to extend their franchise globally, but this is not always the most appropriate strategy. Despite the emergence of similar market segments across the globe, there are very few truly global brands. Clearly the more standardized the marketing and production of a brand, the greater are the economic benefits. However, most internationally recognized brands have found it necessary to modify their offering or their proposition in response to local conditions in order to be successful.

A much-debated aspect of brand management has been the topic of brand equity or the value of brands. It has not been possible to explore this debate fully in this chapter and the reader is therefore referred to the list of further reading. Suffice it to say that the debate is not merely about whether it is appropriate to value brands for balance-sheet purposes; indeed this is to some extent a very British issue. More important is the value to be placed on brands for marketing purposes. Which brands should be invested in, which should be divested? How much do we charge to a company wishing to market the brand under licence? The notion of brand equity remains an area of marketing controversy.

Finally, what about the future? The marketing environment of the future is likely to become more international and dominated by large multinational organizations. This is likely to impact upon the management of brands in two ways. First, we are already seeing the growth in international brands, both through companies acquiring other companies and their brands, and through the development of common advertising and promotional campaigns across international frontiers. Secondly, we are seeing the growth in corporate brands, both as a means of linking different product brands under a corporate umbrella and as a means of stretching the brand franchise. A further development has been the impact of new areas of marketing such as trade marketing and databased marketing, which have grown largely outside the remit of the average brand manager. These trends are provoking widespread discussion about the way in which brands should be managed. What is likely to emerge is difficult to predict in detail, but one development is certain and that is the raising of brand-management responsibility to a more senior level in most organizations.

Further reading

de Chernatony, L., and McDonald, M. (1998), *Creating Powerful Brands* (2nd edn; Oxford: Butterworth-Heinemann).

Ind, R. (1997), *The Corporate Brand* (London: Macmillan).

Kapferer, J.-N. (1997), *Strategic Brand Management* (2nd edn; London: Kogan Page).

MacRae, C. (1996), *Brand Chartering* (Harlow: Addison Wesley Longman).

Pearson, S. (1996), *Building Brands Directly* (Basingstoke: Macmillan).

Discussion questions

The following questions are intended to help you think through the material in this chapter. To test your understanding, you might find it helpful to answer the questions in the context of the Rover case study below. The questions are intended to encourage this.

1 Do you agree with the definition of a brand used in this chapter? Try and analyse the component parts of the Rover marque/brand proposition in terms of this definition or your preferred definition.

2 Think of some strong, successful corporate brand. How are its brand propositions communicated? Is Rover a product or a corporate brand? If you have difficulty with this, have a look at Ind (1997).

3 Do you agree that there are very few truly global brands? How far can Rover be described as a global brand?

4 Japanese companies, such as Yamaha, provide some of the best examples of brand stretching. Why do you think this is? Do you think the Rover brand could be stretched?

5 Can successful brands be developed other than by advertising? What other factors were instrumental in the successful relaunch of the Rover marque?

The Rebirth of Rover Cars

'When Austin Rover became Rover Cars on 4 September 1988, it was most definitely not a cosmetic name change but the culmination of a total marketing strategy.' So said the then Marketing Director of the Rover Group in a speech shortly afterwards.

The company's philosophy hitherto had been biased towards producing cars they wanted to build, that fitted their financial and industrial plans. There was no clear insight into the marketing opportunities of the company or how to focus all the efforts of the company in the right direction.

All this changed to some extent during the early part of the decade, but took on a major impetus with the appointment of Sir Graham Day as Chairman of the Rover Group in May 1986. With a Chairman committed to marketing, the process of moving from a product orientation towards a consumer orientation took on real meaning. Indeed, one of Sir Graham's favourite expressions was 'if you love the consumer to death, you can't go far wrong'. Clearly in a company where the chief executive officer is not fully committed to marketing, effecting significant change quickly enough becomes almost impossible.

At Rover, a fundamental change in strategy was developed, known internally as 'Roverization'. The key to developing a new strategic approach was to develop a full understanding of how consumers purchase cars—establishing the complex relationships between marque and model. A buyer behavioural model was developed that, in its most simplistic form, showed the two crucial stages in purchasing a car: getting on the short list and final product evaluation. Typically, consumers shortlist a number of cars by first considering the desirability and imagery of the marque and then by looking at the car's brand image—what does the car say about the person who drives it?

Some of the basic information that was used in developing the strategy was obtained through extensive consumer research, as summarized below.

Marques and brands

The first findings in 1987 related to brands. The company had a confused image—a schizophrenic blend of Austin and Rover, saying nothing particularly well to consumers individually or together.

Austin was seen as an essentially negative badge and acted in reality as a barrier to purchase. Consumers saw it as being dull and uninteresting, overtly practical and functional, with the virtues of space and economy, but unreliable and for older drivers—aged 55 or more. Not a particularly dynamic base to work from.

Rover, on the other hand, had some genuine qualities. It was seen as prestigious, a quality car, traditional, and original. However, it was also seen as being unreliable, uneconomic, and for older drivers, and, of course, its associations with Austin also had an undesirable effect on its own image. The position was worse when you consider that four of the six models at that time were badged Austin and accounted for around 90 per cent of sales.

So, at the end of the day, Austin Rover products were less likely to get on the shortlist because of the poor marque image and poor brand image. No matter how good the product was in reality, Austin Rover cars were less likely to be chosen than those of the major competitors. For example, the Montego was, in reality, a superior product to the Cavalier and Sierra: it accelerated faster, had a better top speed, was better equipped, and had superior handling. But in the consumer's mind it was just a car from Austin, in the medium price sector, that did not rank alongside the others.

In general, marques could be divided into two main types: first, those with a strong reputation for reliability, technology, and, engineering excellence, seen as being quality marques; and secondly, the higher volume marques, not known for their quality and reliability and seen more as managerial marques, in a fleet context.

Amongst the quality marques, some offered both emotional and rational reassurances. These marques were seen as having high status at low risk and typically included BMW, Mercedes, and Saab. If, however, a quality marque was overtly practical and low on emotional support, it was seen as being low risk, but this time with lower status. This was best exemplified by Volvo.

Looking at the managerial marques, those that offered practical strengths were seen as lower status but with low risk. These included Ford and, to a lesser extent, Vauxhall.

Marques with high emotional and limited rational appeal were seen as high status, but a high risk. In 1987 Rover was seen to be in this category, together with the French and Italian executive cars.

The process of Roverization

The company's first steps were to address the gap between perceptions and reality on the Montego, introducing changes to the product that were in line with what customers wanted and communicating this with high-quality, vibrant advertising on TV, in the national press, and at the dealer level. Next, plans for future products were reviewed to ensure new models in the pipeline were truly worthy of the Rover name—that they would meet and exceed customers' expectations. The results became evident in brands such as the Rover 200 and 400, which commanded the high ground in the medium-car sectors.

Image-building niche vehicles were added to the range—for example, the Rover 220 GTi sports flagship, a Cabriolet (applauded as the best convertible in this market segment), and, in late 1992, the Rover 200 Coupé.

Other successes followed. The Rover Metro, launched in 1990, achieved the accolade of the 'best small car in the world'. Customer research showed that the new Rover 800, launched in 1991 to complete the portfolio of new Rover brands, raised owner satisfaction to new highs and was a fundamental step in the next phase of Roverization—to continue to build the Rover marque values. Reintroduction of the Rover grille, the essence of the company's heritage, played a key role in establishing the Rover 800 as the flagship for the Rover marque. The Rover 800 Coupé, yet another new product, not only competed further upmarket than any previous Rover, but also raised the profile of the whole company. The result was to get customers who would never previously have considered a Rover of any type to take the marque seriously.

Source: Hankinson and Cowking (1993).

Chapter 21
The Marketing of Services
Christian Grönroos

Objectives

The objectives of this chapter are:

1 to explain why service marketing has become a centre of attention in recent years;

2 to identify the characteristics of services that are important from the marketing point of view;

3 to discuss the service marketing process;

4 to discuss the service quality model;

5 to consider some of the managerial challenges of services marketing.

1 The background and focus of service marketing

BEFORE the 1970s no books on the marketing of services had been published and a very limited number of journal articles existed about this topic. In the 1970s an interest in the characteristics of marketing in the service sector emerged in Europe as well as in North America. In 1972 Aubrey Wilson's book on the marketing of professional services (Wilson 1972) was published in the UK and two years later John Rathmell's book on marketing problems in the service sector (Rathmell 1974) was published in the USA. In the latter part of that decade two books on service marketing were published in Scandinavia and Finland, one on professional services by Evert Gummesson (1977) and one on consumer services by Christian Grönroos (1979). These were probably the first books that took a managerial approach to the marketing challenges in service contexts, where not only characteristics of services and existing marketing problems were discussed, but the first steps towards the development of a service marketing theory were taken. In these books was laid the foundation of what was later to be internationally labelled the Nordic School of service research (see Berry and Parasuraman 1993). In the 1970s a growing number of articles appeared in scientific journals, the most influential article being Lynn Shostack's 'Breaking Free from Product Marketing', published in 1977 in the *Journal of Marketing*, and the first ever international workshop in this field was arranged in France in 1977.

☞ '. . . taking the main industrial countries together, we find that manufacturing comprised 30 per cent of their combined GDP in 1960 but only 20 per cent by 1995, while the share of the service sector rose from 53 per cent to 66 per cent over the same period.' (Chapter 5, p. 71)

In the next decade the number of books, scientific articles, and research reports on service marketing grew rapidly (see the analysis of service-marketing publications in Fisk *et al.* 1993).

A major driver of the exponentially increasing interest in the field was the series of special conferences on service marketing initiated by the American Marketing Association in 1980, as well as some well-publicized turnaround processes in service firms, such as the one by SAS Airline (see Carlzon 1987).

In this chapter the special challenges for marketing in service contexts are discussed. External marketing issues such as traditional marketing communications and pricing are not covered, because they do not distinguish marketing in service contexts to any considerable degree from the marketing of physical products. The differences that do exist are not differences in nature. Instead, aspects of service marketing where such differences exist are covered in this context. This includes the nature of service consumption, the marketing object in service contexts, and the quality of services, the marketing effects of the buyer–seller interactions or the service encounters, and internal marketing. This chapter is mainly based on the Nordic School view of service marketing, according to which marketing is viewed more as market-oriented management than as just a specialist function. A cornerstone of the Nordic School of Service Marketing has been the recognition that contacts between service providers and their customers is the basis of a process of building relationships. Therefore, the term *service management* has often been used instead of service marketing, so that the overall management of the process of relationship building in service contexts is emphasized. In the present chapter the older term *service marketing* is used, however, with the understanding that the market-oriented management nature and relationship-process characteristic of services form the foundation for service-marketing theory.

☞ '... services *are* different from goods, and, by taking these differences into account, we can improve our performance in the marketplace ... This too was an important finding in a major Canadian study of new-service development.' (Chapter 24, p. 564)

Service marketing does not only apply to what is traditionally called the service sector. Firms in the manufacturing sector provide a large number of services as well, such as installing, repairing, and maintaining machines and equipment, providing spare-part service, and training customers to use machines that have been delivered. For many firms these services may mount to up to half and more of their billing. In many cases, these and other services are increasingly of vital importance to the competitive advantage of firms in situations where the physical product components of the offering to the market do not distinguish one firm from another. In such situations, which have been characterized as *service competition* (Grönroos 1990a), managing services and understanding how to market the service components of the offering are a key to success on the marketplace. Because of this, any statistics of the size of the service sector, in terms of both gross national product impact and employment, are unreliable and a major underestimation of the real importance of services.

☞ 'The service sector now dominates Western and other developing economies, and the service component of consumer products is increasingly used as the key point of differentiation or competitive advantage.' (Chapter 22, p. 526)

2 Characteristics of services: process, consumption, and the lack of a pre-produced product

THE underlying reasons for the development of service marketing as a separate field was spelled out by Rathmell in 1974, when he observed that the consumption of services cannot be separated from the process by which the service emerges as a solution to customers' problems. For this process the terms 'service production process' or 'service production and delivery process' are traditionally used. In the present context the term 'service process' is used instead, because services are normally neither produced nor delivered in the same way that physical products are. Hence, the product-oriented terms 'production' and 'delivery' are misleading and give wrong associations. It follows that marketing seen as a separate function therefore looks awkward and insufficient for service contexts. Because of this, the nature of service consumption is different from the type of consumption traditional product-oriented marketing models are based on. And, moreover, the scope of marketing is more diverse in service contexts.

In Fig. 21.1 the relationship between the consumption of physical products and the consumption of services, and the process where physical products and services respectively are emerging (goods production process and service process, respectively), are illustrated in a schematic way. In the upper part of Fig. 21.1, the situation for physical products is depicted. As can be seen from the figure, production and consumption follow each other in a sequence, with an empty space on the time axis between the two processes. The role of marketing as a function is to build a bridge over the gap between production and consumption. Marketing gathers information about needs and future consumption patterns and feeds this information into the product development, design, and production processes. When the product or physical good is produced, marketing builds and implements a marketing programme to promote, distribute, and price the product so that potential customers choose the product over those of the competitors. Marketing clearly becomes a fairly well-delineated specialist function between production and consumption.

In the lower part of Fig. 21.1 the relationship between the service process (service production process) and service consumption is illustrated. Some part of the service process, such as the preparation of food in a restaurant kitchen, may take place before the consumption process starts, and the consumption process may sometimes continue to some extent after the service process has ended. However, in the service context the service process and the consumption process parallel each other and cannot be separated. Hence there is a bridge in time between these two processes. The role of marketing is not as straightforward as in the case of physical products. When production and consumption, instead of being sequential processes, are parallel processes, the foundation for marketing changes compared to what we are used to from traditional marketing models. Such models are based on the assumption that customers consume the *outcome* of a production process, where a marketing programme can be developed around a pre-produced outcome or product. The marketing-mix management perspective that was developed for physical goods, especially for consumer goods, is based on *outcome consumption*—that is, on a situation where the customer gets in contact with and consumes the product, not the production process.

In service contexts customers consume the process itself, where the service is simultaneously emerging in an interaction between the customer, possible fellow customers and employees, physical resources, technologies, and systems that are managed by the service provider (buyer–seller interactions or service encounters). Even if the service process naturally must lead to an outcome—for example, withdrawal of money from an automated teller machine (ATM), the arrival of an airline passenger at a flight destination, or the completion of a telephone call—the consumption of services can basically be characterized as *process consumption* (Grönroos 1998). The customer consumes the process and not only its outcome. Moreover, although the customers' perception of the outcome is often considered the most important quality-related factor, it can be viewed as a prerequisite for a good service. Once the outcome is considered satisfactory, various aspects of the ser-

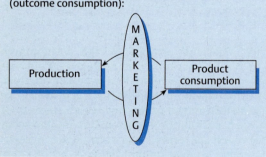

Figure 21.1 **Production and consumption processes in physical-product and service contexts**

Production and consumption of physical products (outcome consumption):

Production — MARKETING — Product consumption

The service (production) process and service consumption (process consumption):

Service process
Service consumption

MARKETING???

Loan arranger

Loanadata Inc. has developed a kiosk that allows car buyers to get approval for car loans with no involvement by the car dealer. A kiosk is available in the car showroom, where, in private, a prospective customer can browse through the different car models available at that dealers, choose the options required, and evaluate the loans that different lenders are prepared to make.

Apart from speeding up the process of obtaining approval for a loan from days to minutes, it saves customers the embarrassment of choosing a car and then finding they cannot obtain the finance with which to purchase it.

vice process are critical to the customer's satisfaction with a service (see Insert).

From the discussion above, three fundamental characteristics of services emerge. First, services are processes, not outcomes of a production process. This is probably the most fundamental characteristic of services. Secondly, because services are processes, the consumption process parallels the service process and cannot be separated from that process, because the service is emerging in interactions between the customer and various resources of the service provider. Thirdly, the consumer takes part in the service process and thus has an impact on the development and outcome of that process.

These characteristics of services change the nature and scope of marketing in a fundamental way. Two main consequences for marketing emerge. First, marketing cannot take the role just of a bridge between production and consumption, as in traditional marketing models. Because the objective of marketing is to find potential customers, make customers buy, and create repeat purchases, the role of marketing in service contexts is much more multifaceted and diverse. Secondly, because services are basically processes, the object of marketing is related to the service process, not only to the outcome of that process. Hence, service providers do not have any pre-produced outcomes that can be readily transferred to its customers. Thus, they have no products as pre-produced objects of marketing around which the marketing programme can be developed. They have processes that can be expected to lead to a given outcome. In service contexts, mar-

keting is related to giving promises about these processes and their expected outcomes as well as to the management and execution of these very processes in such a way that the customers feel satisfied and the likelihood that they will return is increased.

3 Service marketing processes

IN this section the scope of service marketing is first compared with traditional marketing models of product marketing. Then the various functions or rather sub-processes of service marketing are outlined. As a means of illustrating the scope of service marketing and product marketing, respectively, we use the *marketing triangle*. This way of illustrating the field of marketing is adapted from Kotler (1991), who uses it to illustrate the holistic concept of marketing suggested by the Nordic School approach to service research.

In Fig. 21.2 three key parties of marketing in a physical product context are depicted. These are the firm, represented by a marketing and/or sales department, the market, and the product. Normally, marketing (including sales) is the responsibility of a department (or departments) of specialists or full-time marketers (and salespeople). Customers are viewed in terms of markets of more or less anonymous individuals. The market offering is a pre-produced physical product, consisting of a set of features that have been bundled in a factory. Along the sides of the triangle three key functions of marketing are displayed—namely, *giving promises, keeping promises*, and *enabling promises*. Calonius (1988) has suggested that the promise concept, and marketing's role in giving and keeping promises, should be given a central position in marketing models. Bitner (1995) added the expression 'enabling promises' in the context of internal marketing. Promises are normally given through external mass marketing and in some contexts through direct marketing and sales. Promises are kept through a number of product features and enabled through the process of continuous product development based on market research performed by full-time marketers and on technological capabilities of the firm. Marketing is very much directed towards giving

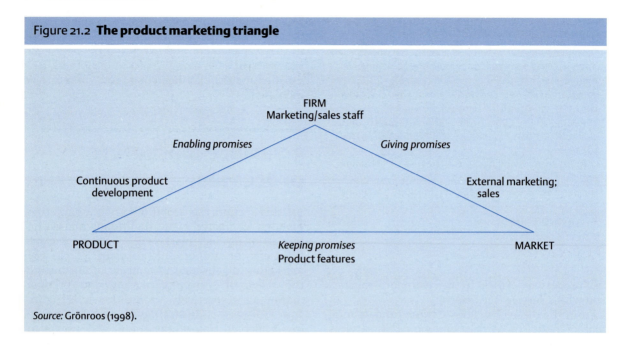

Figure 21.2 **The product marketing triangle**

FIRM
Marketing/sales staff

Enabling promises   *Giving promises*

Continuous product   External marketing;
development   sales

PRODUCT   *Keeping promises*   MARKET
Product features

Source: Grönroos (1998).

promises through external marketing campaigns. The value customers are looking for is guaranteed by appropriate product features, and the existence of a product with the appropriate features will make sure that promises are also kept.

For a service provider the scope and content of marketing become more complicated. The notion of a pre-produced product with features that customers are looking for is too limited to be useful. In many cases it is not known at the beginning of the service process (service production process) what the customer wants and expects in detail, and consequently what resources should be used and to what extent and in what configuration they should be used. For example, the service requirements of a machine that has been delivered to a customer may vary, or the desires of a customer during a train trip may change or new desires suddenly occur. Thus the firm has to adjust its resources and its ways of using its resources accordingly.

In Fig. 21.3, the service marketing triangle, marketing in a service context is illustrated in the same way as product marketing was in Fig. 21.2. From Fig. 21.3 the three marketing sub-processes of service marketing and their goals can be distinguished:

■ *external marketing* (and sales): giving promises to customers that are accepted by them;

■ *interactive marketing*: keeping promises that have been given so that the customers are satisfied with the perceived quality of the service;

■ *internal marketing*: enabling promises by preparing the organization to keep promises (motivating employees to perform as part-time marketers and investing in customer-oriented physical resources and systems).

A closer look at the figure reveals that most elements are different compared to the product marketing triangle in Fig. 21.2. The most important change is the fact that no pre-produced bundle of features that constitutes a product exists (Grönroos 1998). Only preparations for a service process can be made beforehand and partly prepared services can exist. In many service contexts, such as fast-food restaurants or car rental services, physical product elements with specific features are also present as integral parts of the service process. These product elements are sometimes pre-produced, as in the case of car rental, and sometimes partly pre-produced, partly made to order, as in the case of the hamburger in a fast-food operation. However, such physical products have no meaning as such, unless they fit the service process. They become one type of resource among many other types that have to be integrated into a functioning service process. A bun-

Figure 21.3 The service marketing triangle

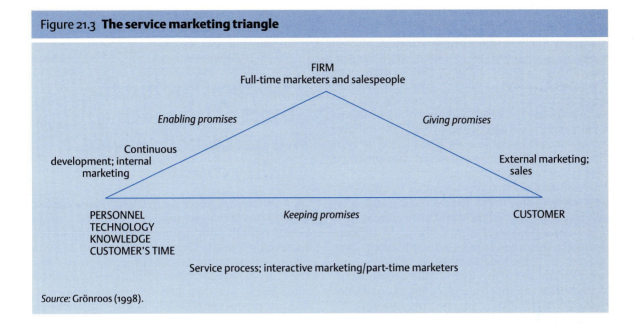

FIRM
Full-time marketers and salespeople

Enabling promises   *Giving promises*

Continuous
development; internal
marketing

External marketing;
sales

PERSONNEL
TECHNOLOGY
KNOWLEDGE
CUSTOMER'S TIME

Keeping promises   CUSTOMER

Service process; interactive marketing/part-time marketers

Source: Grönroos (1998).

dle of different types of resoures creates value for the customers when these resources are used in their presence and in interaction with them. Even if service firms try to create products out of the resources available, they only come up with a relatively standardized plan that guides the ways of using existing resources in the service process and consumption process that parallel each other. No products in the product marketing sense of the term emerge. Customer-perceived value follows from a successful and customer-oriented management of resources relative to customer sacrifice, not from a pre-produced bundle of features.

The firm may still have a centralized marketing and sales staff who are full-time marketers, but they do not represent all the marketers and salespeople of the firm. The marketers and salespeople are mainly responsible for market research and the external marketing activities of the firm, such as mass-marketing communications, direct marketing, sales, and pricing. In most cases the service firm has direct contacts with its customers, and information about each and every customer can be obtained on an individual basis. Moreover, in many cases customers—organizational customers and individual consumers and households alike—like to be treated much more individually than in the past. In principle, no customer should remain anonymous to the firm, provided this can be justi-

Responsive mops and buckets

ISS, a Danish service company in the commercial cleaning business, expects all its staff to be both technically efficient and responsive to customers. Commercial cleaning involves far more than just running a Hoover over a carpet. To serve clients well employees must do their jobs efficiently, which can be difficult enough in an ordinary office suite, but in a hospital or a food processing company is very complex. In addition, ISS staff must learn to spot the idiosyncrasies of their customers and deal with them.

fied from an economic or practical standpoint (see Peppers and Rogers 1993) and the customer does not want to stay anonymous. Contrary to the experience of marketers of consumer goods, almost all service firms have naturally occurring contacts with their customers and thus the possibility to learn to know them without extra efforts to identify and reach them (see Insert).

In Fig. 21.3 the resources of a firm are divided into five groups: personnel, technology, knowledge and information, customer's time, and the customer. A large number of contact employees interacting with customers create value for them in various service processes and some of them are directly engaged in sales and cross-sales activities.

Thus, they are involved in marketing as *part-time marketers*, to use an expression coined by Gummesson (1991). He observes that, in service businesses, the part-time marketers typically outnumber the full-time marketers of the marketing and sales departments several times over. Furthermore, he concludes that 'marketing and sales departments (the full-time marketers) are not able to handle more than a limited portion of the marketing *as their staff cannot be at the right place at the right time with the right customer contacts*' (Gummesson 1990: 13; emphasis in original).

In addition to the part-time marketers, other types of resources influence the quality and value perceived by the customer and hence are important from a marketing perspective as well. Technologies, the knowledge that employees have and that is embedded in physical resources and systems, and the firm's way of managing the customer's time are such resources. Physical product elements in the service process can, for example, be viewed as technological resources. Moreover, the customers themselves often become a value-generating resource. The impact of customers on the final development or design of a technical solution or on the timeliness of a service activity may be critical to the value perceived by them.

In summary, from the customers' point of view, in process consumption the solutions to their problems are formed by a set of resources needed to create a good customer-perceived service quality and value. In addition, the firm must have competencies to acquire and/or develop the resources needed and to manage and implement the service process in a way that creates value for each customer. Thus, a governing system is needed for the integration of the various types of resources and for the management of the service process (Grönroos 1998).

Promises given by sales and external marketing are fulfilled through the use of the various types of resources. This is termed interactive marketing (see Fig. 21.3)—a term introduced in the 1970s—because this part of service marketing takes place in interactions between the customer and contact employees and other resources of the firm. In order to prepare an appropriate set of resources, continuous product development in its traditional form is not enough, because the service process encompasses a large part of the activities of the service firm. Instead, *internal marketing* as well as a continuous development from a customer-oriented perspective of the competencies and of the resource structure (technologies, physical resources, and systems) of the firm are needed.

4 Understanding the object of marketing: the perceived service quality model

As service providers do not have pre-produced and pre-packaged bundles of benefits or products to offer to their customers and around which to develop a marketing programme, but instead processes including a number of resources and the customers, the object of marketing must be understood and managed differently from that used in product marketing with its traditions in consumer-goods contexts.

The characteristics of services—for example, their process nature and the inseparability of consumption from the service process where the service emerges—make it difficult to conceptualize the object of marketing—that is, the equivalence of a physical product in a service context. In physical product contexts, the appropriateness of a solution to customers' problems is often analysed in terms of the quality of the product. Paralleling this, around 1980 in the research tradition of the Nordic School the question. 'How is the quality of a solution to problems or needs perceived by consumers or users of services?' was addressed. By taking such a customer-oriented approach, the conceptualization of the service process could be achieved and the missing product of service firms replaced by a genuinely service-based, and moreover, customer-oriented construct.

Based on some previously suggested aspects of the quality of services (Gummesson 1977) and on perspectives from cognitive psychology (see Bettman 1979), the concept of perceived service quality was developed as a conceptualization of the marketing object of service providers (Grönroos 1982a, 1984). Fig. 21.4 shows the basic perceived service quality model. The original perceived service quality model from 1982 is shown to the left in the figure (*a*); to the right (*b*) is illustrated the extended model (Grönroos 1990a) where the quality dimensions and the disconfirmation notion of the model are put into their mar-

Figure 21.4 **The perceived service quality model**

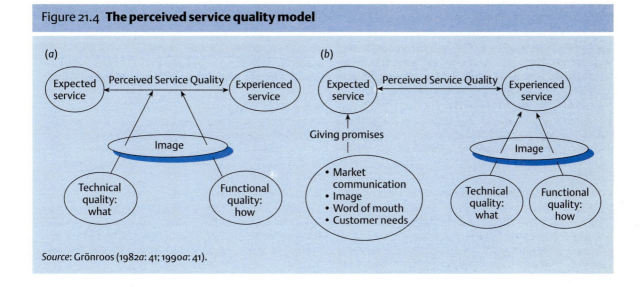

Source: Grönroos (1982*a*: 41; 1990*a*: 41).

keting context. The extended model includes the same phenomena as the 'giving promises' and 'keeping promises' sides of the service marketing triangle in Fig. 21.3.

The customers' perceptions of the service process are divided into two dimensions: the process dimension, or how the service process functions, and the outcome dimension, or what the process leads to for the customer as a result of the process. The two quality dimensions are termed technical quality (what the service process leads to for the customer in a 'technical' sense) and functional quality (how the process functions). Customers perceive the quality of the service in these two dimensions, what they get and how they get it. Technical quality is a prerequisite for good perceived quality, but it is seldom enough. In addition, functional-quality aspects of a service must be on an acceptable level. Moreover, frequently the technical-quality aspect of a service becomes transparent for customers as soon as it is good enough, and after that the functional-quality aspects determine the level of the perceived quality of a service in their minds.

Image, on a company and/or local level, serves as a filter that influences the quality perception favourably, neutrally, or unfavourably depending on whether the customer considers the service provider good, neutral, or bad. As the image changes over time—for example, depending on the quality perceptions of a given user of a service—the image component adds a dynamic

aspect to the model, which in other respects is static.

The disconfirmation concept of the model indicates not only that the perceived service quality is a function of the experiences of the customer, but also that the expectations of customers have an impact on the perception of quality. Hence, the quality perception of a service is the result of a comparison between the expectations and perceptions of a customer. It is, however, difficult to measure how the expectations influence experiences and quality perceptions, so there are clear indications that perceived service quality can perhaps best be assessed through direct measurements of quality experiences (e.g. Cronin and Taylor 1994; Liljander 1995).

However, expectations do have an impact on the perceived service quality, although it is difficult to measure how their impact works. Hence, service marketers have to be careful when giving promises to the market, so that unrealistic expectations are not created in the minds of customers. As is shown in Fig. 21.4, expectations are mainly created through external marketing, including sales. However, word of mouth and the image of the service provider, as well as the needs of the customers, also influence the level of expectations.

The list of six criteria of good service (Grönroos 1990*a*), based on a large number of studies of how customers perceive the quality of a service, offers a fairly good summary (Box 21.1). One of the six

Box 21.1 **The six criteria of good service**

- *Professionalism and skills.* The customers realize that the service provider, its employees, operational systems, and physical resources have the knowledge and skills required to solve their problems in a professional way (outcome-related criteria).

- *Attitudes and behaviour.* The customers feel that the service employees (contact persons) are concerned about them and interested in solving their problems in a friendly and spontaneous way (process-related criteria).

- *Accessibility and flexibility.* The customers feel that the service provider, its location, operating hours, employees, and operational systems are designed and operate so that it is easy to get access to the service and so that they are prepared to adjust to the demands and wishes of the customer in a flexible way (process-related criteria).

- *Reliability and trustworthiness.* The customers know that, whatever takes place or has been agreed upon,

they can rely on the service provider, its employees and systems, to keep promises and perform with the best interest of the customers at heart (process-related criteria).

- *Recovery.* The customers realize that, whenever, something goes wrong or something unpredictable unexpectedly happens, the service provider will immediately and actively take actions to keep them in control of the situation and find a new, acceptable solution (process-related criteria).

- *Reputation and credibility.* The customers believe that the operations of the service provider can be trusted and give adequate value for money, and that it stands for good performance and values that can be shared by customers and the service provider (image-related criteria).

Source: Grönroos (1990a: 47).

criteria, professionalism and skills, is outcome related and thus a technical-quality dimension. Another criterion, reputation and credibility, is image related, thus fulfilling a filtering function. However, the major part of the criteria—attitudes and behaviour, accessibility and flexibility, reliability and trustworthiness, and recovery—are clearly process related and thus represent the functional-quality dimension. In several studies of perceived service quality the reliability criteria surface as the most important process-related quality aspect (Berry and Parasuraman 1995).

The purpose of the perceived service quality model is to provide a conceptual model of services as objects of marketing viewed with the eyes of the customers that makes it possible for the marketer (1) to develop interactive marketing resources and activities and (2) to plan external marketing activities. Customers' satisfaction with the quality of a service should be measured in similar ways to those in which their satisfaction with the quality of a physical product is measured.

As was observed earlier, the way the service process and the resources of that process—employees as part-time marketers, technology, knowledge, customers, and how service providers manage their time—is developed and managed forms the interactive marketing process. At the same time, customers' perceptions of the service

process and of the way the above-mentioned resources are used form their view of the quality of the service. Hence, managing perceived quality and managing interactive marketing are two sides of the same coin. By managing the perceived quality of a service well, the marketer also simultaneously manages the interactive marketing process, and thus keeps the promises given by external marketing activities.

As external marketing is not different in nature in service contexts, that part of marketing is not discussed in this chapter. In the next sections, two models of planning the interactive marketing process are discussed—namely, the augmented service offering model and the gap analysis model.

5 Planning interactive marketing: the augmented service offering

THE augmented service offering model is a model of how to manage the service process so that both the technical-quality aspects and functional-quality aspects of the process and its outcome are taken into account (Grönroos 1990*a*). Thus, the whole interactive marketing process is included in the model.

The model is divided into three phases:

- developing a *service concept*, which should guide the development of the other elements of the model;
- developing a *basic service package*, including service elements that are required to make sure that an acceptable outcome (technical quality) is reached and the basis for a good functional quality of the process is laid;
- *augmentation of the offering*, which covers the process dimension of the offering to make sure that a satisfactorily functioning process (functional quality) is created.

The service concept determines the intentions of the service provider. Based on this concept, the offerings can be developed. For example, a car rental company formulated its service concept in the following way: to provide immediately accessible solutions to temporarily occurring transportation problems. This formulation defines the nature of the problems for which the service provider should develop solutions (temporarily occurring transportation problems), as well as how such solutions should be developed and offered (immediately accessible solutions). When the service concept is defined, the service provider should know what resources and service elements are required, how these resources should be managed, as well as when and for whom.

The next phase is to determine which service elements are needed in order to fulfil the requirements of the service concept. These service elements form the basic service package. In the literature, the service package has frequently been divided into two groups—namely, core services and peripherals (e.g. Eiglier and Langeard 1981; Lehtinen 1983; Normann 1984). Because peripheral services are used for different reasons, in the augmented service offering model they are divided into two groups. Thus, the basic service package includes three groups of services:

- the *core service*, which is the reason for being on the market;
- *facilitating services* (and goods), which are needed so that the core service can be used;
- *supporting services* (and goods), which are not required for the use of the core service but which

help distinguish the service package from those of the competitors.

For example, for a car rental company the *core service* is to provide a means of transportation and for a hotel it is lodging. A company may also have several core services. For example, an airline may offer a shuttle service as well as long-distance transportation.

In order for the customer to make, for example, an overnight stay at a hotel, reception and check-out services are needed. For air transportation, check-in services and baggage handling are required. Such additional services are *facilitating services*. Some facilitating goods are also required, such as a bank card to operate an ATM.

Supporting services and goods fulfil another function. They do not facilitate the use of a core service, but are used to increase the value and/or to differentiate the service from those of the competitors. Hotel restaurants and a range of in-flight services related to air transportation are examples of supporting services.

The distinction between facilitating and supporting services is not always clear. Most facilitating services can be used to enhance the value of the offering and distinguish it from competing offerings, much in the same way as supporting services. The difference is, however, that facilitating services as such are a necessity, regardless of whether they are used to distinguish the offering from other offerings or not, whereas purely supporting services can be omitted without making it impossible for customers to consume the core service. However, the total service package may be less attractive and perhaps less competitive.

Although facilitating services may often serve the same purpose as supporting services, from a managerial point of view it is important to make a distinction between these two types of services (and goods). Facilitating services are mandatory. If they are left out, the service package collapses. The supporting services (and goods) are, however, used only as a means of competition.

The basic service package is not equivalent to the whole service that customers perceive. This package corresponds mainly to the technical-quality dimension of the total perceived service quality. The elements of the package determine *what* customers receive. They do not say anything about *how* the process is perceived, which in the final analysis is an integral part of the total offering customers experience and evaluate.

In the next phase the core service package must be augmented to a functioning process. Owing to the characteristics of services, three key elements of the augmentation process can be distinguished:

■ *making the service accessible*, so that the service package can be easily consumed or used;

■ *developing interactions* between the consumer or user and the resources of the service provider, such as front-line employees (part-time marketers), technologies, systems, and fellow customers;

■ *enabling customer participation* in the service process.

The augmented service offering model is illustrated in Fig. 21.5.

The *accessibility* of a service depends on the amount, mix, and competence of resources used in the service process—such as, for example, the number and skills of employees, customer-orientation of technologies and systems, timetables and office hours, as well as the number of customers in the service process. A service package should be accessible enough, so that the customer perception of the quality of the service is good enough.

The *interactions* between the customer and the service provider's resources also have an impact on the customer's perception of a service and its quality. The more customer-oriented are the interactions, the better is the quality of the service. It should be noted that customers interact not only with front-line employees of the service provider but with all types of resources needed in the service process, including fellow customers.

Customer participation means that the customer himself or herself has an impact on the service process and on the perceived service quality. For example, if a patient is not able to give correct information about his or her problems, the physician will not be able to make a correct diagnosis. The cure may, therefore, be wrong or less effective than otherwise. The service rendered by the physician is damaged. And if a customer does not know how to operate a vending machine, he or she cannot create a satisfactory solution. Depending on how well a customer is prepared to give correct information, fill out documents correctly, and, use machines and other types of technologies in the service process, he or she will improve the service, and vice versa.

Of course, what one customer considers good accessibility and customer-oriented interactions may be perceived differently by another customer. Also, customers want to participate in different ways in the service process in order to consider the service good.

In Fig. 21.5 the accessibility, interaction, and customer-participation concepts indicate how the basic service package can be augmented so that the functional-quality dimension of the service process is fully accounted for. Only when the service package is augmented in this way has the process been incorporated into the service offering, and both the outcome and the process dimensions of the service been planned.

If the augmented service offering functions well and leads to a good perceived service quality, the service process is customer oriented and creates a good interactive marketing impact. If the process meets the needs and desires of the customer and promises given by external marketing activities, the augmented service offering fulfils promises that have been given. Marketing as a whole is successful.

Figure 21.5 **The augmented service offering**

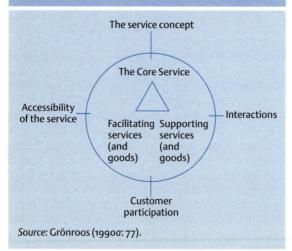

Source: Grönroos (1990a: 77).

6 Planning interactive marketing: the gap analysis model

BERRY and his colleagues have developed the so-called gap analysis model, which is intended to be used for analysing sources of quality problems and for helping managers understand how service quality can be improved (Parasuraman *et al.* 1985; Zeithaml *et al.* 1988). Thus, it helps the marketer to develop a better interactive marketing impact. The model is illustrated in Fig. 21.6.

First of all, the model shows how service quality emerges. The upper part of the model includes phenomena related to the customer, the lower part demonstrates phenomena related to the

service provider. As in the original perceived service quality model, the quality of a service is a function of the expected service and the perceived service (Gap 5 in Fig. 21.6). The expected service depends on the customer's past experiences, personal needs, and word-of-mouth communication, as well as on external marketing communications by the service provider.

The perceived service is the result of a process

Figure 21.6 **The gap analysis model**

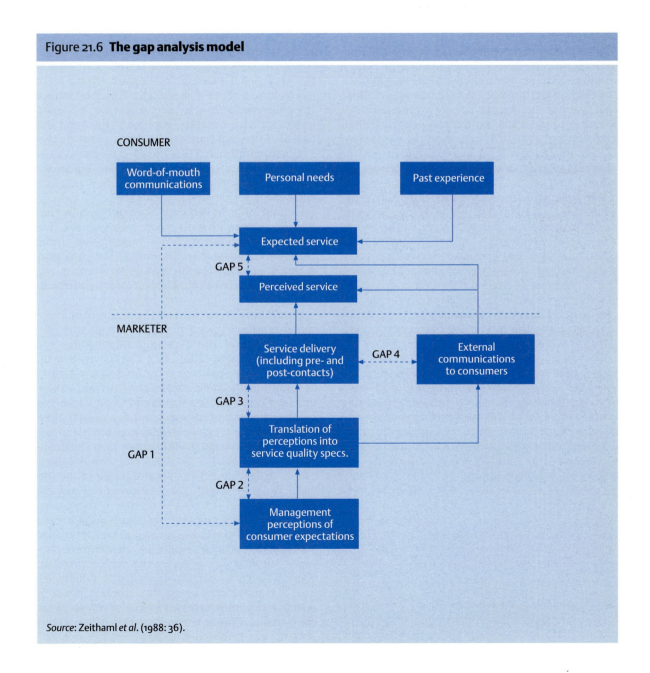

Source: Zeithaml *et al.* (1988: 36).

that starts with market research and the understanding of the needs and desires of the customer. Management perception of customer expectations guides decisions about service quality specifications. Gap 1 occurs if the customers' expectations are not understood correctly, which is mainly a market-research gap. If the quality specifications that guide the service process do not match customer expectations, Gap 2 emerges. This is mainly a planning gap. If there is a discrepancy between the service process (in this model termed service delivery) and the quality specifications for the service process, Gap 3 occurs. This is mainly an internal communication, internal marketing, and process management gap. Gap 4 develops if the service provider's external marketing communication message creates expectations that are not met by the service process. This is mainly a marketing communication gap. All four gaps add up to the fifth gap, which is a perceived service quality gap. This gap emerges when the expected service and the perceived service do not fit.

The basic structure of the model demonstrates where the roots of quality problems may be found and how problems may accumulate. The model also shows which steps have to be considered when analysing and planning service quality. At the same time, it indicates what types of corrective actions may be needed if the perceived quality is to be improved. If the perceived service quality can be developed so that it is considered good by the customers, the interactive marketing impact of the service process is also good.

The augmented service offering model is a model that connects elements that are required for a favourable interactive marketing process. The gap analysis model is rather a planning process model that indicates how to analyse and develop the process from understanding customer expectations and the factors that influence them to the way the service process functions and affects the perceived service.

7 Service marketing in a time perspective: the customer relationship life cycle

FOR too many organizations customers are viewed as an abstract phenomenon or a mass that can always be reached and persuaded to buy its products or services. When someone stopped being a customer, there were always potential new customers to take his or her place, at least if the traditional external marketing efforts were effective and persuasive enough. This is no longer the case, and definitely not for service providers. In most service contexts someone in the organization sees the customer personally, and meets and interacts with him or her. Hence, it is wise to view customers *not as customers or clients only, but as customer relationships*. However, customer relationships are not just there; they have to be earned. Customer relationships are earned through continuous marketing efforts throughout the ongoing interactions with customers over time. However, the type of marketing efforts and marketing resources vary, depending on where in the ongoing interactive process the customer relationship is.

Hence, it is useful to view the progress of a customer relationship as a life cycle (Grönroos 1982b). The concept of the customer relationship life cycle is illustrated in Fig. 21.7. The life cycle is divided into three basic stages or phases. A potential customer is *made interested* in the firm and its service and is drawn into the initial stage of the life cycle. If this potential customer has a need that he or she feels the service provider may be able to satisfy in a desired way, the customer may start considering the solution offered by a given provider. The customer enters the second phase of the life cycle, the purchasing process. During this process the customer evaluates the service in relation to what he or she is looking for and is prepared to pay for in relation to competing options. If the outcome of this process is positive, the customer accepts the promises given by the service provider about how his or her problems can be taken care of. A first purchase is made. This can be characterized as a trial purchase, where the customer gives the organization a chance to prove that it can

Figure 21.7 **The customer relationship life cycle**

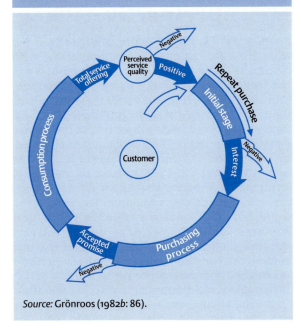

Source: Grönroos (1982b: 86).

Box 21.2 **Marketing objectives and efforts in the three stages of the customer relationship life cycle**

Phase	Objective of marketing	Dominating marketing process
Initial stage	To create interest	Traditional external marketing
Purchasing process	To turn the general interest into sales (first purchase; giving promises)	Traditional external marketing and sales supported by interactive marketing efforts
Consumption process	To create re-sales, cross-sales and enduring customer relationships (keeping promises)	Interactive marketing efforts

Source: Grönroos (1990a: 143).

fulfil the promises which have been given to the customer.

Then the third stages of the customer relationship life cycle starts. This is the consumption process (or usage process, which may be a more adequate term in a business-to-business context). During this process the customer interacts with front-line employees, physical resources, technologies, and systems of the service provider, and often with fellow consumers as well. The total augmented service offering is created and simultaneously consumed. The perceived service quality is emerging for the customer. Depending on how well the total offering fits the needs and expectations of the customer and the promises that he or she perceives have been given, service quality is considered to be various degrees of good or bad. If the perceived service quality is good enough for the customer, the likelihood that the relationship will continue and the service provider will get repeat business increases. How high the likelihood for repeat business is depends on a number of reasons. However, it seems clear that customers who are *very* satisfied with the perceived service quality are considerably more loyal to the service provider than customers that are only satisfied.

If marketing is to be successful, a customer-oriented approach to managing the relationship must continue from the initial stage, over the purchasing process, and throughout the consumption or usage process. In the marketing of physical products, the features of the product take care of most of the marketing impact during consumption. However, as was demonstrated by the service marketing triangle in Fig. 21.3, in service contexts the situation is different. The objectives and types of marketing efforts during the three stages of the customer relationship life cycle are summarized in Box 21.2.

In the initial stage of the life cycle, where the marketing objective is to create an interest in the service provider and its offerings, traditional external marketing, including advertising, direct marketing, and price offers, are responsible for the success of marketing.

In the purchasing process, where the interest should be turned to sales, the goal is to get promises about the provider's offerings accepted so that the customer makes a trial purchase. Here the same external marketing efforts, sometimes including sales by sales representatives, are used. In some situations—for example, when buying an inclusive tour from a tour operator or deciding to go for lunch to a restaurant, or purchasing services from a consultant—the customer may also interact with the front-line employees, the part-time marketers, of the organization, and even with systems and technologies of the firm.

In the consumption or usage process, the goal is to provide the customer with such a total service offering that he or she is satisfied with the perceived service quality. To reach this marketing goal the interactive marketing process including all resources in the interactions with the provider and the customer, has to function in a customer-oriented manner. The impact of part-time marketers and of the other resources of the service process is fundamental here. Traditional external marketing resources, such as advertising and sales, have a marginal effect only. They cannot in the long run compensate for negative marketing effects caused by the interactive marketing process.

In conclusion, successful marketing of services requires that the marketing orientation of all resources and activities perceived by customers in the various stages of the customer relationship life cycle is maintained throughout the life cycle. Interactive marketing as well as traditional external marketing must function well and be integrated, so that promises that are given are fulfilled. Finally, the better the interactive marketing process functions, the less external marketing efforts are needed, unless the firm introduces new services or expands to new markets. Customers that are satisfied enough return with considerable likelihood, and through positive word-of-mouth communication new customers are attracted to the firm. If such a positive circle can be achieved, unnecessary external marketing efforts can be avoided. And, according to a generally accepted rule of thumb, it is almost always more expensive to get new customers than to make satisfied customers buy again. However, it may not be enough for customers to be satisfied with the quality of the service; they may have to be *very* satisfied.

8 Internal marketing

As has been noted, the role of the part-time marketers is imperative to successful marketing in a service organization. These employees are not part of a marketing department, nor are they in-

clined to think about themselves as persons who have an influence on the buying behaviour of customers. However, although their main duties are not related to marketing but to doing their job in the service process in a correct and effective manner, the way they take care of their tasks, and what they are saying and communicating with customers, have a profound marketing impact in the interactive marketing process. In addition, they sometimes get re-sales and cross-sales opportunities. The service provider has to prepare them for these aspects of their job as well. In the service marketing literature this is called *internal marketing* (Eiglier and Langeard 1976; Berry 1981; George 1986; Crompton *et al.* 1987), because the personnel forms a first, internal market for the service (cf. the service marketing triangle in Fig. 21.3). If the strategies, goals, quality specifications, physical resources, and technologies as well as external marketing efforts cannot be marketed to this market, the part-time marketers will not perform as intended and total marketing will fail.

The objectives of internal marketing are, thus, to get the commitment of the employees to the strategies and tactics of the firm and to create an environment where they feel motivated for a customer-oriented and marketing-like performance. Internal marketing is not a project but an ongoing process, which can of course include specific projects, such as training programmes, the development of supportive technologies in the service process, and so on. However, internal marketing is part of human resource management and, thus, has a continuous focus.

Target groups for internal marketing include not only the front-line employees but also back-office employees, supervisors, middle-level managers, and top management. If any of the other groups are left outside, the front-line employees will not be properly supported in their part-time marketing efforts. On the contrary, such efforts by them may be counteracted by back-office performance, supervisors, and even top-management behaviour, if these groups do not understand and appreciate the utmost importance to successful marketing of the part-time marketers and the interactive marketing process.

9 **Where is service marketing going?**

U**NDERSTANDING** the nature of service marketing will of course remain a key issue for firms in the service sector. However, manufacturers of physical goods are realizing that it is becoming more and more difficult to differentiate the products from those of the competitors, and they have to look for new sources of competitive advantage. If a sustainable cost advantage or technical advantage cannot be achieved or maintained, services offer a possibility to create a strong competitive position. Manufacturers can and should emphasize service elements as parts of their offerings in their customer relationships. In this respect every firm is becoming a service business, because it is not the product components in a manufacturer's offering that makes the difference on the marketplace but the service elements (Webster 1994).

☞ '. . . in many engineering firms, the consequence of the increased importance being accorded to the service element of the product has been the diminution of the importance of other functions . . .' (Chapter 17, p. 416)

In this situation, understanding service marketing becomes important for every organization, regardless of whether the core of the offering is a service or a physical product. The perspective of a relationship marketing strategy, which relies heavily on the interaction and customer relationship concepts from service marketing as well as from network theory in industrial marketing, is developing into a new heavily service-based marketing approach.

Further reading

Bateson, J. (1995), *Managing Services Marketing* (Orlando, Fla.: Dryden Press).

Gabbott, M., and Hogg, G. (1997), *Services Marketing Management: A Reader* (Orlando, Fla.: Dryden Press).

Grönroos, C. (1998), 'Marketing Services: A Case of a Missing Product', *Journal of Business and Industrial Marketing*, 13/4.

Lovelock, C. (1992), *Managing Services* (Englewood Cliffs, NJ: Prentice Hall Inc.).

Peppers, D., and Rogers, M. (1993), *One-to-One Future: Building Relationships One Customer at a Time* (New York: Currency/Doubleday).

Discussion questions

1 What are the difficulties in measuring productivity in the service sector?

2 What features would a service need to have to make it appropriate to be run as a franchising operation?

3 How would you define a service? Test your definition against a range of consumer services such as insurance, hairdressing, medical advice, a fast-food restaurant, and so on.

4 It has been suggested that in many markets there is now so little to distinguish between competing goods that the only truly competitive element is the services associated with the goods. Do you agree and if you do what are the implications of this situation?

5 How would you go about defining the quality of a garage's service?

Mini Case
Bridson and Greaves Solicitors

Leslie is a partner in a medium-sized firm of solicitors based in Cambridge. He specializes in non-contentious intellectual-property (IP) matters with a particular interest in trademarks and software licensing. His interest in this activity has been stimulated because the local university's activities have led to some high-technology products being developed and a number of start-up organizations being set up in association with university staff. Because of his wife's new job, Leslie knew that he would soon have to move to the East Midlands. However, he was aware that both Nottingham University and Loughborough University of Technology had established reputations for exploiting their research commercially and that Leicester University was also moving along a similar path. In addition a number of software houses and research institutes had been established in close proximity to these universities because of their reputations in specific fields of science and technology.

Leslie therefore felt sure that there was a demand for advice on IP matters in the East Midlands but did not know how such a demand was currently being met. So, when, by chance, he met Jones, a partner in Bridson and Greaves based in Loughborough, he sounded him out about the nature of Bridson and Greaves's practice and found that they did not have anybody who specialized in IP work but that their Commercial Department dealt with those trademark issues that, from time to time, did arise from the firm's clients. However, Jones (who often advised one of the universities on employment matters) stated that he had been asked for IP advice on a number of occasions but had referred the enquiries to a Leeds firm that he knew specialized in this field.

Later Leslie, on reflection, approached Jones with the suggestion that Bridson and Greaves would benefit from the addition of his expertise to their existing portfolio. He argued that the demand for IP is expanding fast and that in general universities have still not fully come to terms with the idea of restricting the flow of knowledge that they produced and were therefore often missing opportunities to safeguard their IP. He believed, on the basis of his time in Cambridge, that he was able to overcome academics' traditional reluctance to protect, or commercially exploit, their ideas and that he would rapidly develop a practice. He also argued, again on the basis of his experience in Cambridge, that he would be able to cross-sell other services offered by Bridson and Greaves. For example, once IP rights had been registered, clients usually wished to develop, license, or assign them.

Leslie believed that his relationship with a number of his existing clients was such that they would follow him when he left Cambridge. Furthermore, he had undertaken work in Cambridge in connection with research contracts placed there by British Gas and he knew that the British Gas manager with whom he had had particular dealings was about to be appointed to the British Gas Research Institute on Loughborough University's campus.

Jones took Leslie's idea to the next partners' meeting. At the time Bridson and Greaves had ten partners, twenty-one fee-earners, and forty-three support staff, and worked from an old-fashioned set of offices in the centre of Loughborough. It was a general and commercial practice. The firm was rather proud of the fact that it had a business plan. This plan was for the firm to grow, not by entering any new field of work, but by gaining additional business in those fields in which it already had expertise and a reputation.

Discussion question

You are a partner in Bridson and Greaves.

1 What further questions would you ask before agreeing to Leslie being offered a position in the firm?

2 On the information that you already have, are you favourably disposed to making Leslie an offer to join the firm?

Chapter 22

Relationship Marketing in Consumer Markets

Roderick Brodie,
Richard Brookes,
and Nicole Coviello

Objectives

The objectives of this chapter are:

1 to examine the nature of relationship marketing and its relevance to consumer products;

2 to suggest that relationship marketing is becoming pervasive to all types of businesses;

3 to discuss how relationship marketing as practised varies in different contexts;

4 to discuss five future trends that are making the focus on managing relationships important to all businesses.

1 Challenges to the traditional view of marketing

WITH the arrival of the post-industrial era, major changes are occurring within both the marketing environment and business organizations. Markets are more global and technologically sophisticated, competition is more intense, and consumers are more demanding. These changes are leading firms to place a greater emphasis on the service aspects of products as a way of competing. Also information and communication are becoming increasingly important to all businesses, and the traditional boundaries between industries are becoming less relevant. For example, the boundaries between established industries such as banking, insurance, and financial services are no longer as clearly defined (Chakravarthy 1997). Related to this, new types of business organizations based on partnerships, alliances, and networks are replacing hierarchical organizational structures (Achrol 1991; Webster 1992).

Accompanying environmental and structural change is a shift in the way marketing is being organized and practised, and this in turn is challenging the traditional views of the discipline (George *et al.* 1994; Doyle 1995).

The traditional view of marketing is summarized in the American Marketing Association's 1960 definition as follows: 'Marketing is the process of planning and executing the conception, pricing, promotion, and distribution of ideas, goods and services to create and satisfy individual and organizational objectives.' The UK's Chartered Institute of Marketing provided a similar but more concise definition in 1996: 'Marketing is the management process of planning, anticipating and satisfying customer requirements profitably.' These traditional views are sometimes referred to as *transaction marketing*, or marketing-mix management. This is due to the focus on managing the marketing-mix decision variables of product, price, promotion, and place in order to generate a transaction (i.e. attract customers).

The *transaction* approach has been a dominant theme in marketing education since the 1960s. McCarthy and Perreault (1997), Kotler (1997), and Stanton (1997) reflect this in the North American textbooks. Still in wide use, the first editions of these textbooks were published in the 1960s, and focused mainly on mass marketing of branded consumer products. This focus reflected the steady increase in demand in rapidly expanding consumer markets. Under these market conditions, mass advertising and other forms of promotion activity were appropriate. The textbooks paid far less attention to the marketing of services and industrial products, let alone attention to customers at the individual level. While textbooks of the 1990s have been modified to accommodate the service and industrial markets, it is argued by some that they still fail fully to embrace a modern view of marketing and focus too much on transactions rather than relationships (Gummesson 1987; Möller 1992; Grönroos 1994).

These authors challenge the traditional transaction view of marketing as being overly clinical and outdated. It is argued that it is more important to focus on the development and management of relationships—relationships that may extend beyond customers to include suppliers, channel intermediaries, and other market contacts. Often referred to as *relationship marketing*, this view has received increasing support in the literature, with a number of special journal issues appearing on the topic, and a number of useful books becoming available (e.g. Sheth *et al.* 1988; Grönroos 1990a; Christopher *et al.* 1991; Houston *et al.* 1992).

Some proponents of relationship marketing suggest that it is perhaps more important for industrial and service markets while others suggest it is equally important for consumer products. This chapter examines these different views. Section 2 discusses how relationship marketing has been defined and how it differs from the traditional transactional view of marketing. In Section 3 evidence about how marketing is currently practised, particularly by consumer product organizations, is presented. The final section examines how marketing practice is likely to change in the future and why relationship marketing is likely to become increasingly important to consumer product marketing.

2 Concepts and definitions

2.1 Defining relationship marketing

One of the strongest advocates of relationship marketing is Christian Grönroos (1990a,b; 1994); he defines relationship marketing as follows: 'to identify and establish, maintain and enhance and terminate relationships with customers and other stakeholders, at a profit, so that the objectives of all parties involved are met. This is done by a mutual exchange and fulfillment of promises.' It is, however, important to emphasize that the relationship marketing perspective excludes neither the marketing decision-making activities associated with attracting customers, nor the processes that lead to innovation and new product development (Grönroos 1990b). Rather, it recognizes that these types of marketing activity need to be balanced with activities associated with the building of ongoing customer relationships.

The relationship marketing perspective provides a broader and a longer-term view of the role of marketing in an organization. In doing so, it leads to integration of other aspects of management, so that the division between what is 'relationship marketing' and what is 'relationship management' becomes somewhat arbitrary. This broader perspective is recognized by Christopher, Payne, and Ballantyne (1991), who define relationship marketing as 'a synthesis of marketing, customer service and quality management'. Similarly, Sheth (1994) talks even more broadly by defining relationship marketing as 'the understanding, explanation, and management of ongoing collaborative business relationships between suppliers and customers'. And Morgan and Hunt (1994) define it as 'all marketing activities directed towards establishing and maintaining successful relational exchanges'.

These broad perspectives span cross-traditional sectors and functional boundaries, and they also suggest that the relationship is as much between the buyers and the sellers as between sellers and buyers. In some situations, relationships can even become 'partnerships' (Wilkinson and Young 1994). Further, it is recognized that it is not only the relationships between sellers and buyers that are important, but also a network of other relationships both within the organization and external to the organization. For example, Buttle (1996) identifies four such groups of partnerships or relationships:

- supplier partnerships (with goods and services suppliers);
- lateral partnerships (with competitors, government, and other organizations);
- internal partnerships (between business units, employees, and departments);
- buyer partnerships (with intermediate and final customers).

A similar classification was developed by Christopher *et al.* (1991), who identify six 'markets' with which organizations have relationships:

- customer market;
- referral market;
- supplier market;
- employee market;
- influence market;
- internal market.

According to Christopher *et al.* (1991), the traditional *customer* market is where the emphasis is on developing relationships to attract and retain customers. Secondly, the *referral* market includes all organizational contacts that have the potential to act as advocates for the firm, providing word-of-mouth support for the organization. Christopher *et al.* give the example of banks, where referral groups include insurance companies, property brokers, accountants, solicitors, surveyors and valuers, and other banks, as well as existing customers. The third group is the *Supplier* market, where the need is to foster cooperative buyer–supplier relationships—relationships that reflect a 'win–win' situation rather than the traditional and somewhat adversarial focus on getting the lowest price from suppliers. Thus the emphasis shifts to achieving reliability, quality, on-time delivery, flexibility in delivery, lowering of costs, and so on.

The fourth group is the *employee* market. This recognizes the vital role people play in an organization, and hence the success of the organization depends on attracting a sufficient number of suitably motivated and trained employees. The fifth group is the *influence* market—a market that includes parties that may influence the business

environment in which the organization operates. These parties include government policy-makers, the media, environmental and other lobbyists, and the general public. The final group is referred to as the *internal* market. This market explicitly recognizes employees as internal customers, and the importance of developing strong relationships with them. Consistent with this is the view that, in every firm, marketing is becoming everyone's job (McKenna 1991).

Moving from a discussion of 'who' relationships might be with, Bitner (1995) describes three 'types' of marketing activity in the context of 'promises'. Drawing from Grönroos (1990*a*), she suggests that the external, rather traditional and transactional approach between the organization and its customers is about 'making promises'. Secondly, internal interaction occurs within the organization, and this is referred to as 'enabling promises'. Finally, the interaction between employees and customers is described as 'keeping promises'. Organizations that have a relational perspective will focus also on internal and interactive marketing activity as well as on external marketing. These interactions are expressed in Fig. 22.1.

Gummesson (1995) has developed a more elaborate classification of relationship types. After two decades of studying marketing organizations, he identified thirty generic types of relationships, relationships that can be categorized into five groups:

- *mega relationships*: relationships on levels above the market proper—e.g. political and economic alliances between countries;

Figure 22.1 **Three types of marketing**

■ *inter-organizational relationships*, such as alliances between companies;

■ *mass relationships*, such as communications with different segments of a market;

■ *individual relationships*;

■ *nano ('dwarf') relationships*, such as relationships within an organization.

Gummesson emphasizes that to understand and manage these relationships it is important not to focus on simple dyads alone (e.g. buyer and seller interactions), but to understand and manage *all* the networks of relationships and interactions around the dyad. This leads to the conclusion that the essence of relationship marketing is an approach 'based on interactions, relationships and networks'.

2.2 Differences between transaction and relationship marketing

In the preceding discussion, no specific mention is made of how relationship 'markets' or types of relationships differ by industry. Is relationship marketing generic to all industries? Are the various types of relationships that may be developed, as discussed by Christopher *et al.* (1991), Bitner (1995), and Gummesson (1995), relevant to all types of firms, be they in the consumer product or industrial and service sectors? Before answering these questions it is useful to clarify further the specific differences between transaction and relationship marketing.

One underlying difference between the two types of marketing is that transaction marketing tends to focus on the outcome and value distribution surrounding the product, while relationship marketing tends to focus on service processes and value creation (Sheth *et al.* 1988; Grönroos 1990*b*, 1994). This suggests that transaction marketing may be more appropriate for product-based industries such as fast-moving consumer goods (FMCG), where a lesser amount of service is usually involved in the differentiation process, as compared with firms in the industrial goods or services markets (see Fig. 22.2).

This distinction between product and service is also evident in the work of Christopher *et al.* (1991), whose seven dimensions are used to distinguish between transaction and relationship marketing (see Box 22.1). In a similar manner,

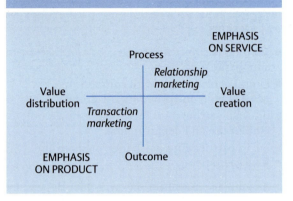

Figure 22.2 **Transaction versus relationship marketing**

Box 22.1 **Seven dimensions distinguishing transaction and relationship marketing**

Dimension	Transaction marketing	Relationship marketing
Focus	Single sale	Customer retention
Orientation	Product features	Product benefits
Time scale	Short term	Long term
Customer service	Limited	High
Customer commitment	Limited	High
Customer contact	Moderate	High
Quality	Production's concern	All employees' concern

Source: Chistopher *et al.* (1991: 9).

Grönroos (1990*b*) has identified eight dimensions, as shown in Box 22.2. It is important to note, however, that the distinction between product and service is less apparent in this categorization. Although Grönroos implies a product/service difference in the discussion surrounding 'dominating quality', the characteristics distinguishing transaction from relationship marketing are more focused on the dimensions of the relationship *per se*.

While each of the above schemata offers the opportunity to compare transaction and relation-

Box 22.2 **Eight dimensions distinguishing transaction and relationship marketing**

Dimension	Transaction marketing	Relationship marketing
Time perspective	Short-term focus	Long-term focus
Dominating marketing function	Marketing mix	Interactive marketing (supported by marketing mix activities)
Price elasticity	Customers tend to be more sensitive to price	Customers tend to be less sensitive to price
Dominating quality	Quality of output (technical quality) becomes dominating	Quality of interactions (functional quality dimension) grows in importance and may become dominating
Measurement of customer satisfaction	Monitoring market share (indirect approach)	Managing the customer database (direct approach)
Customer information system	*Ad hoc* customer satisfaction surveys	Real-time customer feedback system
Interdependency between marketing operations and personnel	Interface of no or limited strategic importance	Interface of substantial strategic importance
Role of internal marketing	Internal marketing of no or limited importance to success	Internal marketing of substantial strategic importance to success

Source: Grönroos (1990*b*).

ship marketing along key dimensions, they also imply that there are only two types of marketing (transaction and relationship), and that the differences between the two are categorical. A more comprehensive classification system has been developed by Coviello, Brodie, and Munro (1997), which suggests that the 'types' of marketing might be more complex than a simple dichotomy.

This classification system was developed from a detailed content analysis of the marketing literature, focusing on how researchers defined and used various terms associated with marketing practice. This review included the work of North Americans, Europeans, Australasians, and other writers. From the analysis, two common themes were found, and, within these, twelve dimensions were derived.

Seven of these dimensions were to do with *relational* aspects of business practice:

- the focus of the relational exchange;
- parties involved in the relational exchange;
- communication patterns between parties in the relational exchange;
- type of contact between parties;
- duration of the relational exchange;
- formality of the relational exchange;
- balance of power in the relational exchange.

Five of the dimensions had to do with *managerial* aspects of business practice:

- managerial intent regarding customers and other parties;
- managerial decision-making focus;
- types of marketing investment made by the firm;
- organizational level at which marketing decisions are implemented;
- managerial planning time frame.

Following the identification of the above dimensions, the source literature was reanalysed to define each dimension more clearly in the context of marketing practice. From this, two general marketing perspectives were identified, encompassing four distinct types of marketing practice. The first perspective is labelled *transactional marketing*, and the second *relational marketing*. However, the relational perspective encompasses three different types of marketing. Therefore, Coviello *et al.*'s (1997) framework describes the following:

- *transaction marketing*, using the marketing-mix approach to attract customers;
- *database marketing*, using technology-based tools to target and retain customers;

- *interaction marketing*, developing interpersonal relationships between individuals such as buyers and sellers;
- *network marketing*, positioning the firm in a connected set of inter-firm relationships.

Of note, the themes, dimensions, and resultant 'types' of marketing offered by Coviello *et al.* (1997) do not distinguish between product and service markets. Rather, the conceptual framework focuses on identifying potential types of marketing practice that might be universal. The question, therefore, becomes what types of marketing are actually in practice across various product-market types? This will be discussed in the following section.

3 Examining marketing practice

To gain a better understanding of contemporary marketing practice, this section discusses empirical research carried out in the second half of the 1990s describing major trends in marketing, the 'types' of marketing currently practised at the time, and managerial views on the future of marketing.

3.1 Major trends in marketing practice

To gain a perspective on the nature of marketing practice, a study was undertaken by Brodie, Coviello, Brookes, and Little (1997) of 135 New Zealand firms, using middle managers as respondents. As part of an ongoing research programme, the New Zealand sample size was then increased, and the study was also replicated in Canada, Sweden, and Finland, but this chapter presents only the results from the New Zealand study. The firms in all samples represent a range of FMCG, consumer durable (CD), industrial good, service, non-profit, and commodity product markets.

In one part of the study, managers were asked to identify any major trends affecting their industry or firm (see Box 22.3). 'Development of relationships' was the most frequent response, followed by trends relating to 'increased customer price sensitivity/price wars' and 'increased competition'. These results are perhaps not surprising if

| Box 22.3 | **Ranking of major marketing trends** |

Rank	Trend noted by respondents
1	Development of relationships with value-added services; technology and knowledge sharing; partnerships; relationships with mass markets; co-operating to add value; clients rely on us
2	Customers focused on cost, price; price sensitive; retail margins eroding; margin cuts to win accounts; price wars
3	Increased competition; fight for share; more new products, offerings
4	Increased use of technology for advertising and communication
5	Development of loyalty programmes; more direct marketing
6	Customers more knowledgeable, demanding

the emphasis on relationship development is in response to increasing competition and the 'fight for share' in a domestic market where customers are increasingly knowledgeable, price focused, and demanding.

At an industry-specific level, respondents from both the FMCG and CD sectors describe an increase in demanding, price-focused trade buyers and end-consumers. They also report increased competition through new/modified offerings, and, perhaps not surprisingly, price wars. Overall, managers from these sectors do not report a specific shift to 'relationship' development, particularly in comparison with industrial good and service managers.

The respondents were also asked about how marketing practice was changing in their organization (see Box 22.4). The aggregate results indicate that there is a tendency for firms to become more focused in their marketing practice, emphasizing 'relationship development' and 'customer targeting'.

Looking again at the FMCG and CD sectors, managers report an increased 'customer focus' in terms of becoming more customer oriented and targeting specific customers. This may be due to the reported trends of margin cuts/price wars, increased competition, and an increasingly demanding customer. Of note, however, the FMCG and CD managers in this study did not report development of one-to-one relationships and actively working with customers at a personal level.

3.2 Types of marketing in practice

Coviello *et al.*'s (1997) classification system was used to develop a series of questions to measure the extent to which each firm's marketing practice reflected either transaction marketing or the three types of relational marketing (i.e. database marketing, interaction marketing, and network marketing).

It was of particular interest to identify whether or not there were sectors (e.g. FMCG or CD) where one type of marketing practice was more dominant than others. Alternatively, were there sectors or types of firms where more than one type of marketing practice was dominant? Finally, were there firms where all four types of marketing were practised (i.e. transaction, database, interaction, and network marketing)?

For each of the 135 firms in the sample, index ratings were developed to indicate the extent to which each of the four types of marketing was practised. The frequency of firms in each category, by marketing type, is reported in Table 22.1. The table shows that the majority of organizations practise more than one type of marketing, if not all types. For example, 81 per cent of the organizations were rated as medium to high on the transaction-marketing index and 70 per cent rated at the same level on the database-marketing index. Similarly, 87 per cent rated medium or high on the interaction-marketing index, while 66 per cent were at the same level on the network marketing index.

Analysis of these patterns suggests that all types of firms practise all types of marketing. Further analysis of the results indicates, however, that certain types of marketing practice are more common in some sectors than others. For example, small, high-technology, service firms seem to emphasize interaction and network marketing. Conversely, larger, older consumer goods firms (often multinational subsidiaries) tend to score higher on the transaction-marketing index. At the same time, there is evidence of consumer product companies that scored very high on the relational-marketing indices.

Given that a combination of marketing types may be practised across firms, the question arises: which combinations are evident? Fig. 22.3 indicates some interesting combinations. For

---

Box 22.4 Ranking of major changes in marketing

Rank	Change noted by respondents
1	*Changing resources/structure*: more focused marketing resources and structure; changed structure, objectives; specific marketing person appointed
2	*Developing relational philosophy*: development of one-to-one relationships; alliances; working with customers; drive to a personal level
3	*Increased segmentation/niching*: more segmentation; customer targeting; value added to more important customers
4	*Changing market orientation*: more focused on customers; customer oriented
5	*Increased measurability/accountability*: increased reporting of sales and profit; more accountability in decision-making; more performance tracking; more planning
6	*Increased use of technology*: more technologically advanced; use of e-mail; new information system; more proactive on innovation and technology

---

Table 22.1 Comparison of index values by marketing type (%)

Index value	Transaction	Database	Interaction	Network
Low	19	30	13	34
Medium	55	49	37	35
High	26	21	50	31
Total	*100*	*100*	*100*	*100*

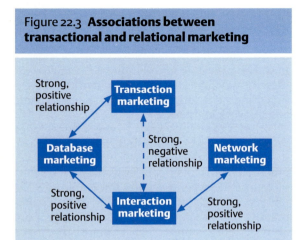

Figure 22.3 **Associations between transactional and relational marketing**

example, a firm practising interaction marketing is also likely to practise database and network marketing, but not transaction marketing. At the same time, a firm practising transaction marketing is likely to practise database marketing. Also of note, there is no clear relationship between either transaction and database marketing and/or network marketing.

These patterns may indicate that certain types of firms lie at the transactional end of a continuum of marketing practice, and, in fact, the findings of Brodie *et al.* (1997) suggest they are larger, well-established organizations. Conversely, other firms may be more relational in their approach, given the positive relationships between database and interaction marketing, and also between network and interaction marketing. Beyond this, however, the analysis fails clearly to identify specific types of firms that are dominated by more than one type of marketing practice, and simply highlights that all four types of marketing are in evidence and practised by most types of firms, to varying degrees. Further, a firm may have a portfolio of relationships, and thus will draw from a portfolio of marketing types (transaction, database, interaction, and network marketing) as and when appropriate.

For example, a large FMCG firm (e.g. soft drinks) may aggressively pursue its end-consumer market through traditional transaction-marketing activities: mass media promotion, price specials, intensive distribution, and brand extensions to reach various niches in the broad market. At the same time, this firm might also use database-marketing techniques by applying information technologies to target specific buyers through the Internet, interactive kiosks, etc. Further, in conjunction with the transaction approach, the firm might initiate a contest for its end-consumers, a contest requiring submission of the consumer's name, contact information, and other pertinent details. This information is compiled onto a database, and used for further target marketing efforts.

While this soft-drink firm might appear to be dominated by a mixture of transaction- and database-marketing activities, it also practises interaction marketing in the context of developing and managing its wholesaler, retailer, and supplier relationships. Some or all of these relationships may be part of an extended network of contacts. This network is also likely to involve other organizations with which the firm is strategically allied, such as restaurants and cinema chains. In some situations, the firm may also have sole supplier arrangements (e.g. a national fast-food restaurant chain). As such, network marketing is practised.

Similarly, a small software developer will actively work to establish network relationships to access markets and leverage the marketing capability of other firms (network marketing). Most of these relationships evolve from actively developed personal one-to-one relationships (interaction marketing). In the same way, the soft-drink firm may appear to be dominated by transaction and perhaps database marketing, the software firm may seem to be driven by interaction and network marketing. However, the software firm may have managers with specific responsibility for product/brand decisions related to product, pricing, promotion, and distribution (transaction marketing). These managers might also make active use of technology to 'get closer' to their customers, through e-mail, bulletin boards, and other information technology (IT) tools (database marketing).

Overall, the results of Brodie *et al.* (1997) indicate that both the transactional and relational marketing approaches can and do coexist. There is also evidence of a 'shift' in managerial thinking as well as practice. For example, there appears to be a movement within each sector towards increased customer orientation (at the very least), if not efforts to improve customer understanding, and develop synergistic relationships and partnerships.

Thus, it can be concluded that there is evidence to support the perspective that relationship marketing is increasingly practised, with the emphasis on getting closer to customers, and facilitating, building, and maintaining relationships over time. On the other hand, it is also important to recognize that this is not done at the expense of neglecting the transactional aspects of marketing activity.

3.3 Future marketing practice

The research of Brodie *et al.* (1997) also asked respondents to identify how their marketing practices might need to change in the future, given their industry dynamics. As in the previous sections, clear patterns can be identified for firms marketing consumer products when compared with those marketing industrial products and services.

3.3.1 Consumer products

Respondents suggest that changes to their marketing practice should include improved efforts to 'understand customer needs', 'listen more', and develop 'high-level contact with primary customers'. This might imply an effort to move beyond the emphasis on customer focus to a richer understanding of key customers (both trade and final consumers). Further, respondents see a need for improved quality of planning, with greater emphasis on formal planning rather than a reliance on intuition, or reacting to situations as they occur. As will be examined in more detail in Section 4.5, a major feature of consumer products, including consumer durables, is the growing concentration of retail power, and the increasing need for manufacturers to develop strategies, structures, and programmes specifically for these chains.

3.3.2 Industrial goods

Given the move to relationship development and loyalty programmes in the industrial-goods sector, most of the required changes relate to improving efforts in customer satisfaction, understanding the customer, and utilizing databases to target and service customers. As with the FMCG and CD respondents, additional suggestions relate to ongoing improvements in planning, systems, and performance measures.

☞ 'It is important for a relationship to continue if the partners are to derive the benefits that the relationship brings each of them.' (Chapter 23, p. 537)

3.3.3 Services

Similar to the patterns for consumer and industrial-goods firms, the major suggestions from managers in service firms involve 'listening more' to customers in an effort to develop customer intimacy. Other suggestions include developing high-level contact with primary customers, and targeting niche markets or specific clients. The trend to increased use of technology in this sector is also reflected in the suggestion that database tools (as well as other information system tools) be used to target, service, and profile customers. Finally, the service-firm respondents suggest that improvements to the quality of planning and business systems are necessary, but, additionally, suggest the need for a coordinated, cross-functional team approach. This latter suggestion is unique to the service sector.

Overall, it appears that, across sectors, respondents are consistent in their view towards developing a relational orientation, which supports the contention that relationship marketing is becoming pervasive. Although managers of consumer product firms may not perceive themselves as currently practising relationship marketing *per se*, the data suggest that it is becoming increasingly important to consumer products, in the same way that it is currently to industrial goods and services. Associated with this is the recognition of the need for improvements in planning and information systems.

4 The increasing importance of relationship marketing to consumer products

4.1 Future trends

The research about marketing practice has shown that the dominant trend in the organizations studied is to develop relationships. However, there is

---

considerable variation in the way relationship marketing is being practised (e.g. database, interaction, and network) and in most organizations aspects of both transaction and relationship marketing coexist. Further, managers of all types of organizations, including consumer products, report a need actively to get closer to and better to understand their customers. Thus, although consumer product firms may appear to be less relational than industrial and service firms, relationship marketing is in fact both practised in and relevant to them.

As previously discussed, there are a number of changes taking place in the practice of marketing. These include:

- changing resources/structure;
- developing a relational philosophy;
- increased segmentation and niche marketing;
- a changing market orientation;
- increased measurability/accountability;
- increased use of technology.

This section examines a number of compelling reasons why the relationship-marketing concept is increasing in importance to firms marketing consumer products. Five trends that are related to the findings of Brodie *et al.* (1997) are discussed, in the particular context of IT influences.

- *increasing service aspects of consumer products*—related to 'developing a relational philosophy' and 'increased segmentation and niche marketing';
- *financial accountability, loyalty, and customer value management*—related to 'increased measurability and accountability'.
- *organizational transformation*—related to 'changing resources/structure';
- *retailing and systemic relationships*—related to 'a changing market orientation';
- *interactive media and mass customization*—related to 'increased segmentation and niche marketing'.

All of these trends are highly interrelated, with IT being an underlying force behind the change. Of prime interest when examining the impact of these trends in the context of consumer products is the strategic use of IT in facilitating relationships, and, in particular, marketing relationships. Also important is the convergent nature of the technologies. For example, Porter and Millar (1985: 145) claim:

Information technology is more than just computers. Today, information technology must be conceived of broadly to encompass the information that businesses create and use as well as a wide spectrum of increasingly convergent and linked technologies that process the information. In addition to computers, then, data recognition equipment, communications technologies, factory automation, and other hardware and services are involved.

However, in examining the reasons for change, it is not that IT is new. What is new is the growing persuasiveness of IT into virtually every aspect of running an organization. Information technologies are transforming the nature of products, services, structures, functions, processes, and communications. In effect, IT has moved from the back end of the business systems to the front end in virtually all industries. That is, IT links companies and their suppliers, distributors, resellers, and customers into what might be termed a 'seamless' network of relationships and interactions throughout an industry's entire value system. This not only adds value to existing forms of products or services, but also creates new forms of value (Normann and Ramirez 1993).

4.2 Service aspects of consumer products

The service sector now dominates Western and other developing economies, and the service component of consumer products is increasingly used as the key point of differentiation or competitive advantage. This is happening to such an extent that it may be becoming arbitrary where one draws the line between what is a product and what is a service organization. Once a firm takes on a service orientation, then the management of both the internal and external relationships in an organization become increasingly important. Writers such as Heskett, Sasser, and Hart (1990) in their description of the service delivery system identify these relationships. An important aspect of this system is the management of internal communications and relationships, and the key performance indicator is employee motivation and satisfaction.

Examples of the blurring of the boundaries between a product and a service are increasingly being shown in consumer-goods companies. For example, a footwear company includes a protective spray on its shoes, which minimizes the amount of cleaning, while a producer of breakfast

Washing machines go online for long life and hassle-free maintenance

As part of its warranty agreement, when a white goods manufacturer installs a washing machine into a household, its latest machine may have the electronic capability of monitoring the ongoing usage of the machine. Suppose that several months after the machine has been installed, the household has a new child. If detergent dosage or load weight patterns begin to show that undue strains are beginning to be placed on the motor, the machine has the built-in communications capability automatically to page the manufacturer's service depot. The depot receives a message for a service representative to visit the household and adjust the machine before it becomes a major problem. In this way, while both the IT and the servicing component are largely unobtrusive to the household, they are nevertheless essential to maintaining customer satisfaction and potential loyalty. For example, during the preventative maintenance visit the service representative has been trained to advise the household as to the optimum methods of loading and washing, and to the best machine to suit that household's changed needs. If the warranty arrangements permit, the manufacturer may install a more suitable machine at no cost to the household other than the terms specified in the contract. Clearly, a relationship is developed with the customer for this consumer durable, using service as the lever for retention.

cereals includes an automatic seal to keep the cereal fresh after use. Often the facilitating factor is IT. An example is where consumer product companies include web page addresses that can be used to provide online help and further information about the product. Another example is where consumer products are becoming 'wired' back to the manufacture (see Insert).

4.3 Financial accountability, loyalty, and customer value management

As consumer product markets become more competitive, managers are being challenged to accept that an emphasis on a limited range of performance financial measures is now inadequate as a means of determining the overall well-being of a company and its brands. Increasingly, the argu-

ment is that 'what is required is a balanced presentation of both financial and operational measures' (Kaplan and Norton 1992: 71). One issue is how to put 'hard' values on what may be considered 'soft' measures. For example, in trying to improve their customer loyalty rates, some organizations are rethinking the 'service–profit chain' interconnections. Thus, measures are taken to show the impact of employee satisfaction and loyalty on the 'value' of the products they make and deliver. This is based on the premiss that these results might contribute to higher customer satisfaction and loyalty scores and, ultimately, greater 'lifetime value' results for the organization.

☞ 'Hence, it is wise to view customers *not as customers or clients only, but as customer relationships*.' (Chapter 21, p. 512)

☞ 'While habitual buying under low involvement looks quite like brand loyalty in a high involvement situation, it is actually quite different . . .' (Chapter 6, p. 115)

Kaplan and Norton (1992, 1993, 1996) argue for a management reporting system that brings together the disparate elements of a company's competitive and performance measures. These include measures of a variety of perspectives of the business:

- *customer:* a mix of measures that show how customers view the organization;
- *internal business:* the set of measures of what technologies, competencies, and processes a company must excel at internally to meet the expectations of its customers and to beat its competitors;
- *innovation and learning:* the range of measures that tell a company that its ability to innovate, improve, and learn will ensure long-term competitiveness and success;
- *financial performance:* the critical financial measures that track whether a firm's strategy, tactics, and processes are contributing to bottom-line improvement and other indicators of success required by shareholders, in particular.

The 'balanced scorecard' described by Kaplan and Norton puts vision and strategy, not control, at the centre of the organization's activities. As a result, the measures are intended to act as goals, so executives will take appropriate actions to realize these goals. A key factor to successfully

> **Bank uses balance scorecard to meet multiple objectives**
>
> A bank holds vast amounts of information about individual customers. The falling cost of data storage and increasing power and sophistication of data modelling and manipulation mean that the bank is now able to track, respond, and even predict changing customer characteristics and requirements. As a result, it can continually develop, and redevelop, financial offerings for specifically targeted individuals by searching through its database for customers with similar characteristics to those who have been most responsive to the bank's offerings. As suggested by Kaplan and Norton, the bank is attempting to meet its balanced scorecard of customer, internal business, innovation and learning, and financial performance objectives.

implement this approach issue is the management of the organization's *internal* and *external relationships*. Thus, as with service management, relationship marketing becomes a central activity, as illustrated by the banking industry (see Insert).

The white goods manufacturer and banking examples (see Inserts) have common characteristics that further highlight the importance of relationships. There are clear and focused objectives, programmes that offer value and reward loyalty, powerful systems that measure and monitor performance, and management structures and processes that support and refine the organization's activities. According to Mendonca and McCallum (1995), companies such as these now recognize that the heavy initial expense of acquiring a new customer makes it vital to maintain customer relationships as long as possible; indeed, excellent marketers view profitability on an individual customer lifetime basis.

4.4 Organizational transformation

In claiming that we are entering a new era of information technology, Tapscott and Caston (1993) argue that, as computers have moved 'to the front line' of most organizations, control over the application of computers has shifted from the vendors or suppliers of computers to the users. This has lead Tapscott and Caston (1993) to identify three critical shifts that are transforming organizations

and are having important implications for relationship management and marketing.

- *From personal to work-group computing.* At the local, work-group, level of the firm, standalone personal computers have been linked to each other. Such networking systems allow for greater streamlining of work processes and hence the possibility of both faster turnaround times and a reduction in errors.

- *From system islands to integrated systems.* The local 'islands of technology' are linked electronically. That this was not the case earlier was the result of any number of reasons. For example, the existence of both functional 'chimneys' in the firm's value chain—R&D, purchasing, manufacturing, logistics and warehousing, marketing, servicing, etc.—and corporate-wide specialists—human resources, financial accounts, etc. These chimneys are now coming down, as companies downsize and flatten their structures to eliminate impediments to faster information flows, greater teamwork, and speedy decision-making. In the process, companies are building 'platforms' to allow the 'islands' to be linked electronically. They are also installing decision support systems that allow executives to access vital information in a range of forms: numbers, graphics, pictures, video clips, etc., from a variety of disparate systems. This occurs often in 'real-time' and, most critically, in a format tailor-made for that executive.

- *From internal to inter-enterprise computing.* Not only has the firm become 'wired' internally, but its computer systems are now stretching outwards to link them electronically with other players in the industry value system: suppliers, distribution channels, customers, and even competitors. The emerging information technologies, such as point-of-sale devices, shared databases, voice response systems, and electronic messaging, when combined with agreed standards, such as electronic data interchange (EDI), the computer-to-computer interchange of business documents, are all combining to improve the ways in which companies relate to each other.

By using technologies such as interactive communications, computer networks, and sophisticated software programmes, organizations are finding new ways to build *closer relationships* with both customers and suppliers (Rayport and Sviokla 1994). These new systems can strengthen customer loyalty and thus provide an organizational structure

Sharing knowledge through BP's virtual team network

Two important features of the old bureaucratic organization was that is that it connected the leaders of the corporation to their businesses, and it allowed businesses to exchange critical knowledge. Can these features be preserved in the newer flat, lean, and decentralized organizations? British Petroleum believes it can because of the advances in information technology. BP is amazingly flat and lean. Its revenues in 1996 were $US 70 billion, with 53,000 employees, and some 90 business units that span the globe. There is literally nobody between the general managers of the business units and the nine operating executives who oversee the businesses with the chief executive. In order to share knowledge about customers and the company's assets, BP has created virtual team networks, which are linked by computer technology. These networks aim to allow people to work cooperatively and share knowledge quickly and easily regardless of time, distance, and organizational boundaries.

that allows for the development of stronger relationships. British Petroleum is achieving this (see Insert).

4.5 Retailers and systemic relationships

Retailing and consumer products go hand in hand, and of particular interest to consumer product marketers are the relationships that exist between the firm and retailers. Growing retail power is a relatively recent phenomenon, whether it be automobile megadealers, consumer electronics outlets, grocery supermarket chains, home furnishing depots, or toy warehouses. It also has the potential to change the balance of power and the nature of the relationships between consumer-goods companies and retailers.

During the 1990s, in areas as diverse as Western Europe, North America, and parts of the Pacific Basin, a small number of supermarket chains began to dominate their respective markets. In doing this they were becoming increasingly competent and sophisticated in the development of their marketing strategies including own-branding. This is leading to retailers becoming dominant in their relationships with what they term their 'suppliers'. For example, in a study of

major supermarket groups in the UK, Brookes (1995) identified several major shifts by leading chains such as J. Sainsbury, Marks & Spencer, and Tesco, and their impact on fresh-produce suppliers.

Retailers are also seeking to build long-term 'co-operative partnerships' as opposed to 'adversarial relationships' with their suppliers (Buzzell and Ortmeyer 1995). In order to ensure continuous supply, 'programme' buying on a global scale is now the norm for many leading retail groups. To ensure 'transparency' of suppliers' trading terms, retailers expect to probe their suppliers' cost structures and are likely to suggest ways of reducing costs, and then ask for the savings to be passed on to them. Retailers expect to be kept regularly informed, and are often involved in all stages of quality assurance and therefore impose standards at every stage from when the particular produce is planted to when it is placed onto supermarket shelves. They may want direct involvement with their suppliers' R&D activities, and they may ask for exclusive rights to new products when it suits their purpose.

☞ 'The customer's [the retailer's] objective is to secure or improve his position through his purchasing strategy.' (Chapter 7, p. 137)

In effect, some retail groups now have the capability to impose what may be termed their 'systemic power' over their suppliers, where systemic power is defined as the power that one party has to effect the whole 'system' of the other (Brookes 1995). Systemic power can be seen as either coercive or cooperative in nature. In practice it is likely to be a combination of the two. The belief in the strategic importance of systemic power is consistent with the argument that effective supply-chain management (Davis 1993), and in particular the logistics component (Fuller et al. 1994), is essential to the success of an organization. That is, they reduce costs (Shapiro, et al. 1992; Davis 1993), while still benefiting both parties (Bowersox 1990).

To ensure systemic relationships actually work, retailers now 'reach back' into their suppliers' research and development, production and processing, logistics and distribution, merchandising, and marketing and servicing processes and systems, in order to ensure their compatibility and compliance. A key to this integration is the sharing of data and the modelling. This provides both partners with 'learning loops' that aid in progressively lowering costs throughout the value system. By using IT this way, both partners are adopting what Haeckel and Nolan (1993) describe as 'managing by wire'. Those suppliers who can thus meet their major retailer customer's systemic requirements, by regarding expertise in IT as part of their core capabilities (Stalk *et al.* 1992), are also likely to achieve preferred-supplier status. As a result, consumer-goods companies now need to focus increasing attention on capabilities to do with category, account, and trade promotion management (De Vincentis and Kotcher 1995).

While consumer-goods manufacturers are redeveloping their relationships with major retailers, they are also building closer relationships with their end-consumers. Information technologies are at the forefront of this building process as well. For example, packaged goods companies are setting up home pages and cooperating with retailers through Internet home shopping. In this case the manufacturers are developing closer relationships with the retailers, so that they can participate in the 'one-to-one' dialogue that is taking place via the Internet.

4.6 Interactive media and mass customization

The application of IT is having a major impact on marketing communications in consumer product markets, where the emphasis is on building individual relationships through electronic interaction. These include:

- new interactive possibilities, from local CD-ROM kiosks to the global Internet;
- constantly increasing computer processing power at ever-reducing costs;
- developments in master databases and complex decision support systems;
- expanding collaborative networking arrangements with suppliers and other stakeholders.

Electronic retailing, such as the Amazon bookstore, offers a glimpse of the future of the relationship marketing via the intersection of interactive media and mass customization of operations. In New Zealand, an equivalent is the Great New Zealand Shopping Mall, a joint venture between Woolworth's (the country's second largest supermarket group), Courier Post (a division of New Zealand Post), and Ad Pacifica (a local software firm) (see Box 22.5).

IT-based interactivity is seen as a means by which firms continually update their learning about customers changing perceptions of value (Deighton 1996). Interactivity has several crucial characteristics: the ability to address an individual, the ability to gather and remember the response of the individual, and the ability to address the individual once more in a way that takes into account his or her particular response. When interactive communications are matched to agile operations and manufacturing (Bylinsky 1994; A. Taylor 1994; Kotha 1995), one effect is that organ-

---

Box 22.5 **Interactive home shopping**

Upon registration to the Great New Zealand Shopping Mall via the Internet, a subscriber downloads the necessary software and fills out a direct-debit form. When a shopper has done his or her shopping and passes through the on-screen checkout, a simple clicking of 'okay' authorizes a debit to the shopper's account. The groceries are packed and dispatched from a central city facility and delivered by courier at a time to suit each customer. A commission on the fee for packing and delivery of the groceries is automatically deducted on behalf of the software development firm. Since the service is in real time, prices are constantly adjusted, and if stocks at the central depot run out, they are automatically deleted from the electronic shelves as well.

The research, modelling, and individual customer relationship building possibilities of Woolworth's electronic home shopping mall are limited only by the firm's internal resources, goals, and imagination, and its capacity to process and use the vast amounts of continuous data that will become available to it and its consortium partners. For example, while a customer is in the process of shopping online, various in-store promotions may be presented, such as an electronic coupon on a discount for an item that the modelling had shown was likely to be purchased by a given customer with certain characteristics and buying patterns. Under these circumstances, the added value to customers of shopping electronically is bound into the combination of products and services that are being offered simultaneously.

izations create the possibility of *anything, in any way, at any time, and anywhere* (McKenna 1991). In the process, firms become two things: one-to-one marketers, whereby information is elicited from each customer with respect to individual needs, preferences and other characteristics; and mass customizers, whereby the customer is provided with individually customized goods or services (Pine *et al.* 1995).

Web-based troubleshooting

'Motive has developed software that can engage remote devices in two-way dialogues over the Internet, diagnosing and often correcting problems in their software and hardware.'

Source: *Information Strategy* (Nov. 1988).

👉 'By late 1996 Tesco had analysed its customer database and identified 5,000 different segments . . .' (Chapter 8, p. 169)

Rather than continuing to mass produce and mass market for increasingly elusive 'average' consumers, or segments of 'average' consumers, some consumer goods manufacturers are now starting to target individual customers. This involves using their new-found agile research, manufacturing, and marketing capabilities to design, develop, build, deliver, and service products, services, and messages to 'fit' the specific requirements of individual customers (see Insert). A feature of this agile manufacturing and marketing is that the flexibility moves the centre of value away from the hardware technology (the product and service). What becomes more important are the combined networking, interactions, and relationship building processes (Normann and Ramirez 1993; Rayport and Sviokla 1994).

Box 22.6 **Key future trends for consumer markets and the underlying relationship marketing characteristics**

Trend	Transactional marketing characteristics	Relationship marketing characteristics
Service Aspects of Consumer Products	■ Emphasis on product or service benefits ■ Focus on managing and improving product/service uses and experiences	■ Emphasis on product–service interdependencies ■ Emphasis on managing and improving product–service uses, experiences, and relationships with supplier
Financial accountability, loyalty, and customer value management	■ Focus on measures of financial control in particular ■ Focus on internal measures	■ Focus on a balanced set of strategic, operational, and organizational measures of performance, advantage, and improvement, in particular ■ Focus on both internal and external measures
Organizational transformation	■ Focus on internal functional specializations and coordination	■ Focus on internal and external 'boundaryless' processes of interdependencies
Retailers and systemic relationships	■ Mainly adversarial interactions between retailer and suppliers ■ Issue of power	■ Increasingly 'systemic' relationship building and long-term mutual interdependencies throughout industry value system, facilitated by pervasive use of IT
Interactive media and mass customization	■ Focus on one-way communication to aggregates of target customer	■ Focus on integration of interactive communications with individual customers and the mass customization possibilities in operations and/or manufacturing

5 Summary and a glimpse into the future

THE purpose of this chapter has been to examine the nature of relationship marketing and its relevance to consumer-product marketing. While relationship marketing may originally have been more prevalent in industrial and service markets, it is becoming pervasive to all types of businesses, including consumer products. However, the shift to relationship marketing is not at the exclusion of traditional transaction marketing. The research on marketing practice has shown that most organizations practise a combination of transaction marketing and relationship marketing. The type of relationship marketing practised varies between a database approach (using technology-based tools to target and retain customers), to an interaction-based approach (developing interpersonal relationships between individual buyers and sellers), to a network approach (positioning the firm in a connected set of inter-firm relationships).

Section 4 discussed five future trends that highlight the increasing importance of relationship marketing to consumer product marketing in the next decade. A driving force behind all of these trends is information technology. The effects of these trends are summarized in Box 22.6, which shows that these trends impact not only on relationship marketing but also on transactional marketing. This further strengthens the conclusion that the shift to relationship marketing is not at the exclusion of traditional transaction marketing and that most organizations are likely to practise a combination of transaction marketing and relationship marketing.

Further reading

Achrol, R. S. (1991), 'Evolution of the Marketing Organization: New Forms for Turbulent Environments', *Journal of Marketing*, 55/3 (Oct.), 77–93.

Doyle, P. (1995), 'Marketing in the New Millennium', *European Journal of Marketing*, 29/13: 23–41.

Ford, D. (1998) (ed.), *Managing Business Relationships* (Chichester: John Wiley & Sons).

George, M., Freeling, A., and Court, D. (1994), 'Reinventing the Marketing Organization', *The McKinsey Quarterly*, 4: 43–62.

Grönroos, C. (1994), 'From Marketing Mix to Relationship Marketing: Towards a Paradigm Shift in Marketing', *Asia–Australia Marketing Journal*, 2/1: 9–29.

Iacobucci, D., and Ostrom, A. (1996), 'Commercial and Interpersonal Relationships', *International Journal of Research in Marketing*, 13: 53–72.

Sheth, J. N. (1994), 'The Domain of Relationship Marketing', unpublished paper, Second Research Conference on Relationship Marketing, Centre for Relationship Marketing, Emory University, Atlanta, Georgia.

Discussion questions

1 What factors have provided the impetus for the increased interest in relationship marketing?

2 Under what conditions might it be inappropriate for a consumer-goods supplier to attempt to build relationships with its customers?

3 What are the factors that limit the development of relationship marketing?

4 Many professional firms (such as solicitors) have traditionally maintained very close relationships with their major clients—knowing their business well, socializing with their managers, constantly considering how new legal developments might impact on their activities, and so on. Are such firms practising relationship marketing?

5 Do the recent developments in technology that enable firms to manufacture very small batches at an economic cost encourage the development of relationship marketing?

Integrating the five trends: Relationship marketing in the car industry

The case starts with a driver wishing to replace her vehicle. Using promotional information received through television and magazine advertising, the customer accesses an online search service from a home computer and pulls down comparative information on a number of competitive makes. A complete listing of local dealers selling the make considered most appropriate is requested, and the nearest dealer is e-mailed for a car to be delivered to the customer's home for a test drive.

Assuming that the test drive is satisfactory, the customer then visits the dealer to discuss the financial arrangements and the specific requirements of the vehicle. This negotiating process could also be done electronically. The sales consultant electronically orders the car to the customer's requirements and confirms the exact date and time when the car will be built and delivered to the customer's home. All the components are ordered electronically from the factory's preferred suppliers and they arrive just in time for assembly. The car is built and delivered exactly as promised.

When the car is delivered, the customer is issued with a 'smart' card that contains information about both the car and the driver. At various times the customer may access an electronic forum set up on the Internet by the manufacturer, and from which the customer may request information or assistance. Using this same forum, and with the approval of the customer, at regular interviews she may be asked for details of satisfaction and dissatisfaction. Car and driver details are thus 'tracked' and emerging patterns are determined and assessed by the manufacturer. Potential problems may be pre-empted by the manufacturer having the dealer send an e-mail message that informs the customer when preventative maintenance work is due. When paying for any repair work, the customer uses her major credit cards, which have been issued in conjunction with the automobile manufacturer.

At some stage (perhaps in three or four years, time, at some specific mileage level, or as the car's financing term nears its end), the customer is personally invited by either the dealer or the manufacturer to trade in the car for a new one. The new vehicle may be better suited to the customer's changed personal, household, or lifestyle characteristics and driving requirements (all of which are identified though the 'tracking process').

In this case, the customer is impacted at an early stage by traditional media advertising (*transaction marketing*). She then enters an electronic relationship (created by investment in *database marketing*), and may visit the dealership to negotiate contractual details (initiating *interaction marketing*). Over time, the dealer and/or manufacturer may target her, both personally and electronically, building an ongoing interaction-based relationship. This relationship is developed in the context of the network of relationships that exist between the manufacturer, dealer, and other partners. Such partners include the financial service organization managing the customer's credit card relationship. Thus, *network marketing* also impacts on the customer. Overall, this is but one example of how *both* transaction and relationship marketing might be practised in a consumer product market.

Discussion questions

1 Identify how the five trends that have been discussed in Section 4 of this chapter are impacting on the car industry.

2 Choose another industry that you are familiar with and discuss the relevance of the changes discussed in this case.

3 Elaborate on how transaction marketing and relationship marketing are practised together in this case.

Chapter 23

Relationship Marketing in Organizational Markets: From Competition to Cooperation

Dave Wilson

Objectives

The objectives of this chapter are:

1 to describe the development of a more cooperative approach to the management of relationships between business customers and their suppliers;

2 to consider how good partners can be identified;

3 to set out a model of business relationship marketing;

4 to describe a practical approach to business relationship marketing that has been developed in America;

5 to consider the factors that will affect the future development of business relationship marketing.

1 Introduction

ONCE upon a time buyers and sellers worked in an adversarial atmosphere. The basic paradigm was one in which a buyer would have several potential sellers whom he or she would play against each other, trying for the lowest price. The game was to offer larger shares of the buyer's business to the supplier that would give the best price or perhaps give a better deal on inventory, hold inventory for the buyer, or do some other special service. The goal was to extract the best value from the relationship by playing one supplier against another. A buyer would create a competitive environment between the suppliers and at times an adversarial environment between the buyer and the seller. Over time, this paradigm lost its potency, as American and European businesses became less competitive in relationship to Asian firms. These businesses moved to increase their competitiveness by improving the quality of their products and lowering the costs of creating the products. To be effective in improving quality and reducing costs, they needed to work more closely with their suppliers. The adversarial form of competition required a large base of suppliers who would be played against each other. When they moved to a buying model with the goals of improving quality and cost reduction, close relationships became necessary to reach the goals. It became very difficult to manage multiple suppliers in this new environment with its demands of working together, as quality improvement required both the buyer and the seller to work very closely together and coordinate their activities. To achieve quality improvement, the buyer and seller had to change the basic paradigm from one of competition to one of cooperation, so that both parties would gain in the relationship. The supplier base was reduced and the buyers focused on a limited number of suppliers with whom they developed deep and meaningful relationships as both parties gained in such an environment.

☞ 'Price has typically become less crucial in supplier–manufacturer relatioships, where long-term partnership, relationship marketing, and single sourcing are now key elements.' (Chapter 10, p. 221)

This change from 'a competitive to a cooperative' relationship does not mean that buyers and sellers did not have good personal relationships under the old model. These personal relationships allowed a supplier to gain small advantages over his or her competitor. The supplier with good personal relationships with the buyer would also gain, as sometimes there was a shortage or, in the event of the supplier making an error, the buyer would pull out all the stops to help the supplier. Nevertheless, the basic atmosphere was one of adversarial negotiation when it came to price setting and to gaining concessions on the size of orders and volume. A very competitive environment existed.

In Chapter 7 you had an opportunity to understand how buyers and sellers interacted under the more traditional adversarial model. In this chapter we are going to examine how relationships evolve and develop and what are the key variables that must be managed as one develops a relationship. We will also examine value creation, core capabilities, and how relationships merge together to lead us into developing value-creating networks or value chains. These value networks are the next major areas of competition in the next century. We will briefly discuss these with an example as we conclude the chapter. Electronic commerce and its impact upon value networks conclude the chapter.

2 How do we pick partners?

NOT every business transaction is worthy of a deep relationship. The problem is sorting through the myriad of transactions that the firm must conduct to be able to do business. Fig. 23.1 provides a simple 2 × 2 matrix that helps organize and classify potential partners. The X axis describes the value added to the buyer's product by the seller, ranging from low to high. The Y axis shows the amount of operating risk associated with doing business with the seller, which ranges from high to low. The upper-right quadrant represents those partnerships where the potential partner adds a lot of value to the buyer's product and has a very low risk associated in doing business with the seller. We call these relationships *integrative*, because they work towards integrating the two firms into a free-flowing exchange between the firms, resulting in a lower cost of doing busi-

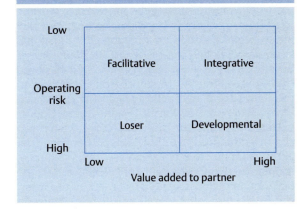

Figure 23.1 **Evaluation of potential partners**

ness. The upper-left quadrant involves those firms that add very little value but are low-risk partners and therefore make doing business very easy. We call relationship with these firms *facilitative*, because they facilitate transactions at a low cost. The lower-right quadrant shows *developmental* relationships, because the potential seller can offer a high value to the buyer, but the buyer must invest in the seller to help it improve its ability to deliver a product and lower its operating risk. The lower-left quadrant features firms that we call *losers* because they neither provide low operating risk in doing business nor add significant value to the product of the seller. We will focus our efforts on describing relationship that fall into the *facilitative* and *integrative* categories, as developing a relationship in both cases has many variables in common. The difference between the two types of relationships is the intensity of some of the variables.

3 Empirical models of buyer–seller relationships

THE early work in relationships was done by the Industrial Marketing and Purchasing (IMP) group (Hakansson 1982). Using an ethnographic methodology, the members of the group developed an interaction approach to describe the relationship between buyers and sellers. They interviewed 878 buyers and sellers from 318 firms in France, Italy, West Germany, Sweden, and the UK to determine how these individuals worked with their partners in buying or selling. The IMP group began its research studying the traditional adversarial model. But, as it did its fieldwork, it developed a model of cooperation, as it believed that a cooperative model better represented the data that it had collected. It conceptualized buyer–seller interaction as dyadic interaction at both the firm and the individual level, with interaction influenced by the climate between the firms. Climate reflects the power, independence, cooperation, expectation, and closeness of the parties and the business environment of the interaction (Hakansson 1982; Turnbull and Paliwoda 1986). The IMP group views interaction as a series of short-term social and task interactions between buyers and sellers within the context of a long-term business process that holds the firms together.

Many scholars have studied buyer–seller relationships in business markets and the channel relationships. Wilson and Möller (1988) developed a summary list of variables that had been successfully used in modelling different relationship situations. The key variables from the Wilson and Möller list are discussed below.

3.1 Reputation

Companies, like people, have reputations. They can be based on very sweeping evaluations, such as 'they're a good supplier'. Alternatively a reputation may relate only to specific aspects of behaviour, so that a customer might be described as slow to pay but totally honest. When a firm starts a business a relationship with a new customer or supplier, the reputation of that other organization will be very important. If it has a 'good' reputation, it will be assumed that it will wish to maintain that reputation. If it has a poor reputation, then the new partner at least has some warning of what problems might arise.

3.2 Performance satisfaction

The essential activity of a business relationship is in the delivery of the product or service that the buyer is buying. A relationship cannot succeed if firm's and buyer's basic needs are not met. Satisfaction is defined as the degree to which business transactions meet the business performance expectations of the partner. Performance satisfaction includes both product-specific performance and non-product attribute performance.

3.3 Trust

Trust is the essential ingredient that holds relationships together. It allows the parties to make investments, to share secrets, and to be able to work together in a way that will generate the value inherent within the relationship. Without trust, the relationship is doomed to failure. Definitions of trust generally involve a belief that one relationship partner will act in the best interest of the other partner.

3.4 Social bonds

Social bonds are really a fancy name for good personal relationships between the partners. Personal relationships help hold a relationship together, as good personal relations facilitate communications between the partners.

☞ 'While the contact between different parties is often referred to as that of business to business, the practical reality suggests that it is driven by interpersonal contact between individuals.' (Chapter 11, p. 252)

3.5 Comparison level of alternatives

Anderson and Narus (1990), drawing upon the work of Thibault and Kelley (1959), defined the comparison level of the alternatives (CL_{alt}) as the quality of the outcome available from the best available relationship partner. The concept of CL_{alt} is important, because, when there are many equivalent alternatives, the desire to stay in the partnership is weakened. On the other hand, if there are very few visible alternatives, the desire to stay in the partnership is strengthened, and hence CL_{alt} has a direct effect upon commitment to the relationship.

3.6 Mutual goals

Mutual goals are the degree to which partners share goals that can be accomplished only through joint action and the maintenance of the relationship. Mutual goals encourage both mutuality of interest and stewardship behaviour that will support the achievement of these goals.

3.7 Interdependence and power

The power of the buyer or seller is closely aligned to the interdependence of the partners in a relationship. Power and balance are the degree to which one partner's dependence upon the other partner is able to influence the partner to take action it otherwise would not take. The building of a relationship where one is dependent upon another partner is one of the most difficult tasks that business people must deal with in creating relationships. By nature, business people are independent operators and find it very difficult to give up some portion of their independence to place themselves in the hands of a partner. Nevertheless, this is a critical step in the formation of a relationship and is obviously closely related to trust.

3.8 Shared technology

Shared technology is the degree to which one partner values the technology contributed by the other partner to the relationship. Shared technology is closely linked to core capabilities and, as such, is highly valued within relationships.

3.9 Non-retrievable investments

Non-retrievable investments are defined as the relationship-specific commitment of resources that a partner invests in the relationship. These non-retrievable investments (training and equipment, capital improvements) cannot be recovered if the relationship terminates. Since non-retrievable investments cannot be recovered when the relationship ends, they act as an impediment to ending the relationship. They are highly correlated with the partners' commitment level.

3.10 Adaptation

Adaptation happens when one party in a relationship changes its process or modifies the item exchanged to accommodate the other party (Hakansson 1982). Both buyers and sellers make adaptations for each other. The partners expect that over time each partner will make changes to accommodate the other partner.

3.11 Structural bonds

Structural bonds develop over time with the investment that each partner makes in the relationship, the sharing of technology, and the adapting of processes to suit the partner's mode of doing business. These strong bonds hold the partnership together, because the cost of leaving the partnership becomes too high and the best alternative is to make the partnership work. Once a firm has a high level of structural bonds, it also tends to become very committed to maintaining the relationship. Structural bonds often emerge without either partner realizing that they are developing these strong ties to the partnership.

3.12 Cooperation

Anderson and Narus (1990: 45) defined cooperation as 'similar or complimentary coordinated action taken by firms in interdependent relationships to achieve mutual outcomes or singular outcomes with expected reciprocation over time'. Interaction of cooperation and commitment results in cooperative behaviour, allowing the partnerships to work and ensuring that both parties receive the benefits of the relationship.

3.13 Commitment

Commitment is the most common dependent variable used in buyer–seller relationship studies. Commitment is important in discriminating between those people who stay or leave the relationship. Commitment represents the desire to continue the relationship and to work to ensure its long-term success. It is important for a relationship to continue if the partners are to derive the benefits that the relationship brings each of them. Regardless of how we measure relationship commitment, in most instances only time generates the profitability of a relationship.

The variables we have just discussed are the basic elements and descriptions of relationships. If you think about these variables as a set of building blocks, you can construct various definitions of relationships. It is possible to add other variables not on the list—for example, situational factors such as culture and national values.

In the next section we will discuss the process of building a relationship.

4 Relationship building process

WHEN a firm decides to change its mode of operation from one of competition to one of cooperation, the task is to create new relationships. The easiest path is to select your best supplier and then build a new relationship with that supplier. Obviously both parties have to change their attitudes towards how they do business, because an adversarial view is not compatible with a competitive view. Entrenched methods, policies, and beliefs need to be changed. For example, how the partner firms reward buyers and sellers has to be changed to make a relationship work. If buyers are rewarded for lower prices, they will continue to threaten sellers, which does not support the need for close cooperation.

There will be situations in which there is no clear partner and the firm must go out and seek a new partner. The process described in Box 23.1 is a relationship development model with five stages. Partner selection, defining purpose, boundary definition, creating relationship value, and relationship maintenance represent the five basic stages one goes through in creating a new relationship. Box 23.1 shows how the variables discussed in Section 4 relate to each of the stages. It is assumed that not all variables are salient at the same time in the relationship. Variables are important at different stages, but after being considered some variables may become latent. For example, trust is very important in the early stages, but once it has been established one does not have to deal with it every day. It becomes latent and only when trust is impinged upon does it again become a salient variable.

4.1 Partner selection

The first stage in the five-stage model is to find an appropriate partner. The partner's reputation is critical in the search for a partner. The early search focus is upon the trustworthiness of potential partners. Without trust it becomes very difficult to move forward in the process.

Box 23.1 **Integrating the relationship variables and the relationship development process**

Variable	STAGE IN RELATIONSHIP DEVELOPMENT				
	Partner selection	Defining purpose	Boundary definition	Creating relationship value	Relationship maintenance
Reputation	▬▬▬	– – –	– – –	– – –	– – –
Performance Satisfaction	▬▬▬	– – –	– – –	– – –	– – –
Trust	▬▬	– – –	– – –	– – –	– – –
Social Bonds	▬▬▬	– – –	– – –	– – –	– – –
Comparison level of alternatives (CL$_{ALT}$)	▬▬▬	– – –	– – –	– – –	– – –
Mutual Goals					
Interdependence and power	▬▬▬▬▬▬				
Shared technology	▬▬▬▬▬▬▬▬▬▬				
Non-retrievable Investments				▬▬▬▬▬	
Adaptation				▬▬▬▬▬	
Structural bonds				▬▬▬	
Cooperation				▬▬▬	
Commitment				▬▬▬	

Personal social interaction is very important in getting to know the individuals within the partnering firm. It is at this stage that social interaction, reputation, and one's gut feelings about the partnering firm help assess whether it is trustworthy or not. Developing a good interaction with the partnering firm's individuals and investing the time to get to know each other form an important step in creating strong social bonds that will help improve communication and understand the values of the partner, thus establishing trust.

4.2 Defining purpose

Defining the purpose of the relationship will help the partners to clarify their mutual goals as well as their individual goals. If the balance of individual goals and mutual goals is biased towards individual goals, it is likely that a relationship will suffer from this imbalance. The partners together are trying to establish the general purpose of the relationship—what they hope to achieve and how they intend to achieve their goals—and in addition they must also convince others within their own organizations of the importance of the purpose of the relationship. Relationships fail many times because they have not been sold inside the partnering firms. If the two groups developing the relationship are convinced that it is a good thing to do, but fail to achieve the support from their internal team, then the relationship will flounder. Defining the purpose or scope of the shared goals is a critical decision. If the relationship is too broadly defined, there may not be enough detail to make decisions between issues. If it is too narrowly defined, it may not be of interest to senior management. It is best to start with a narrowly defined purpose and let success broaden the goals of the relationship.

4.3 Boundary definition

Boundary definition answers the question where does each partner's organization end and the hybrid begin? The next question is what is the hybrid's legitimate claim upon the resources of the partners? Relationships have no clear legal definition and seldom have legal structures that define the boundaries of the relationship. Relationships may be considered as a hybrid relationship between the two partners that is informal and that develops a governance structure that draws

upon, but it is not governed by, the structure of the parent organization. Boundary definition defines the degree to which each partner penetrates the other organization and achieves joint action.

4.4 Creating relationship value

Value creation is the process by which the competitive abilities of the hybrid and the partners are enhanced by being in the relationship. It is their joint effort founded on this hybrid structure that has evolved in the earlier stages that creates value (see Insert). Value comes from the synergistic combination of the partner's strengths, capabilities, market position, and resources. Unfortunately, not all relationships are symmetrical. But, for the relationship to flourish, each partner needs to see some benefit beyond working independently or in an adversarial model. It is the coming-together of the partnership that creates value beyond what individual firms can create. It is this value creation, which cannot be achieved in a competitive model, that is the driving force for moving to a model of cooperation.

Doing marketing *with* customers not *to* them

'In many firms people on the front-line identify and resolve problems with customers without the need for instructions from a central marketing department. This changes the nature of the value the organization generates. Instead of being embedded in a stand-alone product or service, value emerges from the interaction between firm and customer.'

Source: Mitchel (1998).

Value sharing is usually a function of the interdependence and power relationship modified by the degree of structural bonding present in the relationship—in other words, how each partner is able to exert influence in proportion to its contribution to the value creation process. Being locked into the relationship through structural bonds modifies a firm's share of the value created. If one cannot leave the relationship, then one must make the best of the relationship. That generally means trying to work towards a cooperative working atmosphere, which may mean a firm does not fully exploit its ability to extract value equal to its contribution.

4.5 Relationship maintenance

Once the relationship has been established, the unglamorous but essential task of making the relationship work on a day-to-day basis begins. Communication, trust, and attitude towards co-operation are important variables in maintaining the relationship. Early in the relationship, individuals are learning about the other firm's culture and business rhythm. It is easy to misunderstand a partner and read incorrectly the signal that is being sent, it is particularly easy for individuals who may be new to the relationship, either because they have been hired recently or because they have been transferred into the group, to misconstrue the relationship and how it operates. Activities that enhance communication improve the relationship. Texas Instruments asks individuals from each side of the partnership to list their perception of the buying firm's needs. The two lists are used as the agenda for a meeting to clarify the customer needs. As the lists seldom match, the discussion about the customer's needs and how the suppliers came to develop their list helps improve the communication between the teams. It aligns efforts to address the important issues in the partnership.

Other buyer and seller teams may do team-building activities together, such as an Outward Bound programme to create team morale and communication. These types of activities help solidify trust and communication. Nevertheless, in any complex relationships there are bound to be rough spots. Having a procedure in place to mediate problems before they occur is very useful. The energy goes towards solving the problem, without the distraction of how the problem will be resolved.

Trust is like a bank account in that in troubled times it can be drawn upon by individuals to help the team through a difficult problem. Even the best relationships have unforeseen events that stress the relationship. For example, a supplier of plastic containers needed in the production of speakers had an accident on the shop floor when a worker dropped and cracked a critical die that formed the speaker box. While the buying partner was distressed, as it had to curtail production, it knew that the supplier was working twenty-four hours a day to correct the problem. The history of trust and forthright communication built over time helped the partners to work through the situation. Nasty words may have been exchanged in

frustration, but the 'bank account' of goodwill, trust, and personal relationships helped the partnership to survive.

All relationships will have problems sooner or later. There are just too many people and activities involved in complex relationships for all of the events to work smoothly all of the time. Careful selection of the individuals who manage the interface between the partners is important. Relationship managers should have good interpersonal skills, a knowledge of the business skills needed to do the key tasks, a flexible mind, and an ability to handle difficult tasks under conditions of uncertainty. They need a positive attitude towards cooperation as a business model. In many firms, there is latent suspicion that we are 'sleeping with the enemy' when the firm enters a relationship. If this is the case, the first problem that occurs brings out all of the latent hostility and may break up the partnership. In the early stages of a relationship success or failure is determined by the personal individuals involved, as in the early stages the relationship is more vulnerable to the human factors. Later in relationships, when strong structural bonds have developed, the cost of ending the relationship is a powerful force in encouraging the partners to make the relationship work. Management may tell the individuals involved to make the relationship work or the management will find a team that is able to make it work.

One of the strengths of a JIT II style of relationship, which is described in the next section, lies in the intimate relationship between the buyer and seller when the seller's personnel live in the buyer's firm. Communication, trust, and positive attitudes are more likely to emerge in the JIT II environment than in a more arm's-length arrangement. Working closely together each day on a common problem creates deep relationships.

5 JIT II: An example of integrative relationships

JIT II is the concept where the selling firm places an individual within the buying firm to act as the purchasing and product-planning person for the firm's own product. The buying firm moves the purchasing person to another job and the selling firm provides the person to perform the planning and buying tasks within the firm. JIT II is an example of an integrative relationship, because the buyer now works for the seller and is dedicated to making the buying task operate as smoothly as possible. He or she has the power to go back into his or her own firm to ensure that the buying firm is completely satisfied not only with the product but also with the process of exchange. As the two firms work more closely together, they develop ways of reducing and removing redundancies in the purchasing transaction process. This helps lower costs and makes the system work much more smoothly. The selling firm gains because it gets 100 per cent of the product category on an evergreen contract and is now able to help smooth its production process as its own person is supplying the input to the forecast. Working within the buying firm, the representative of the selling firm is able to get early warning of changes in production schedules, is part of the planning team within the buying firm, and translates this information into actions that smooth the production process within his or her own firm.

The selling firm is able to plan more efficiently, gains the additional volumes, and has the opportunity to shape new product development to fit its production process. The seller's representative within the buying firm is called an 'in-plant' person. This in-plant person has the opportunity to work with the buyer's engineers and designers on new product development and can influence the design in a way that makes it easier for his or her plant to manufacture. This helps lower the cost for all concerned. The buyer gains through lower prices and reduction of redundant activities between the partners and thereby lower costs. The seller gains through larger volumes, smoother production, designs that best fit its equipment and reduction of operating costs by removing of redundancies. How these cost savings are shared is a negotiated process, but in most instances both parties gain. It is a classic win–win situation.

👉 'In the business-to-business sphere, because purchases tend to be more rational and problem based, ideas from customers in the form of *specific problems and requests* is the most common source [of new product ideas]. Increasingly, developers emphasize long-term relationships with customers . . . when they develop pioneering industrial products.' (Chapter 24, p. 554)

> ### If this is where you work, who do you work for?'
>
> 'We read about supplier–customer relationships so intimate that, of 1,000 workers in an auto manufacturing plant, only 200 of those are employed by the manufacturer. The remaining 800 are contractors' employees. A supplier's employees can be on site and authorized to issue purchase release orders for the materials under contract with that supplier.'
>
> *Source*: Cushman (1997).

Many firms operate a similar system, although not calling it JIT II. Working closely together is the key element in achieving cost savings (see Insert). At the Bose factory where JIT II was developed, there is a logistical team that represents the key functions necessary for import and export of products. Many of Bose's key customers are located overseas. If General Motors sells more Cadillacs than it had originally planned to sell, GM expects Bose to be able to meet the new production schedule. Bose, through working with its logistical partners—trucking, sea transportation, and custom bonding—is able to locate the needed parts by using its integrated computer systems to locate inventory anywhere in the world. Any inventory that is not at sea can be accessed and air shipped to move it to a production line. This ability treats inventory located in logistical process as available inventory to Bose. Finding and rerouting inventory would not normally be easy to do, as the communication lags between the firms would make it much more difficult to assemble the needed inventory smoothly under a time constraint. The BOSE example in the case study illustrates how the logistical team manages international inventory.

6 Future of relationships

RELATIONSHIPS are evolving from a firm-to-firm basis towards a network of firms competing against a network of firms. Products using multiple technologies increase the need for firms to have multiple core capabilities or core competencies to be leading competitors. However, the complexity and rapid changes of technology make it difficult for any one firm to be master of all of the capabilities necessary to deliver high-tech products. To build products that deliver value, it is often necessary for buying firms to form partnerships with firms that bring to the relationship core capabilities that the buying firms do not possess. For example, a modern automobile has a number of computer chips in it that makes it a major computing machine. An automobile firm is not able to be on the cutting edge of electronics and chip technology and at the same time be an expert on paint and coating for the automobile. To be able to provide the high level of performance on the myriad of technologies that combine to create the modern automobile, a major automobile producer must form alliances with a number of firms (see Insert). Therefore, we see a set of alliances at General Motors—the Oldsmobile division, for example—competing against a set of

Fellow travellers not followers

It has been predicted that by 2003 there will be only about twenty-five global car component manufacturers. These companies will become part of the network of car manufacturing. As they expand their manufacturing bases into new territories, the car manufacturers will invite these firms to set up manufacturing plants next to their own.

alliances at Ford Automotive, Toyota, or Volkswagen.

Core competencies/core capabilities are at the heart of building these value-creating networks. Understanding value creation and having the ability to create and manage relationships are core capabilities. How a firm builds this set of relationships and forms its value-creation network or, as it is sometimes called, a value chain is a critical, strategic task. Figs. 23.2 and 23.3 are simple examples of a complex process, but they illustrate how Compaq Computer and the Dell Computer Corporation have built their value networks. Both of these firms are major players in the computer market. You will note that Compaq serves a wide range of markets through a number of channels. Dell has a more focused view of the market, aiming at business, education, and sophisticated consumers. The interesting difference is that Dell markets before it manufactures. The majority of the Dell computers are made to customer specifications, and therefore are sold before they are built. Compaq, because of its distribution strategy, manufactures for inventory, which puts a financial burden on the firm to hold and carry the inventory. Computers have a very short technology life and anything not sold is losing value as price decreases may overrun its cost. The risk of the two models is quite different. Dell is able to operate with a much lower working capital than Compaq.

Figure 23.2 Building towards enacted value chain: Compaq Computer

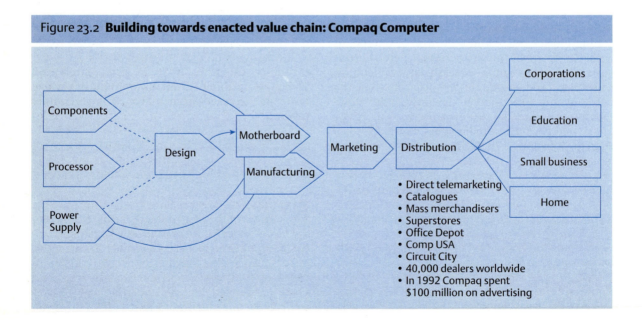

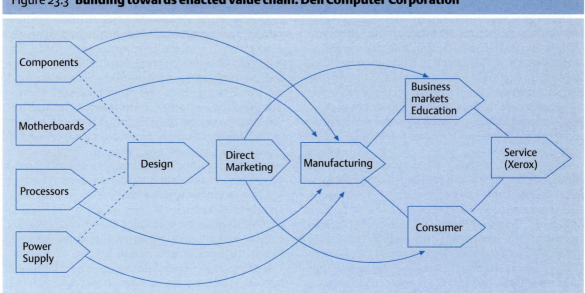

Figure 23.3 **Building towards enacted value chain: Dell Computer Corporation**

The result has been a movement on the part of other computer firms to adapt the Dell model of building after selling to their own systems. Compaq is now moving to authorize its partners in the distribution channel to assemble computers that will reduce some of the market-side risk. Compaq can address markets where the customer wants to purchase from a retail outlet. These two value networks have different business models underlying them. The ultimate test of the value networks will be in the marketplace.

This very simple example of how relationships, capabilities, and value creation come together to create a value-creating network or value chain illustrates the importance of understanding the total market structure. At the end of the 1990s business was moving in a vigorous manner to develop value-chain/value-network analysis (see Insert). The structure of the partnership network affects a firm's ability to go to market and its competitive position. Developing, maintaining, and managing relationships will be a core capability for many firms. Being able to be a value-creating partner within the value network will cause a firm to be sought after by partners.

6.1 Electronic commerce

As value networks or value chains emerge, one of the great forces shaping value networks is elec-

Ford's Amazon in Brazil

In 1998 Ford started to build a plant in Brazil to manufacture two subcompact cars. Between ten and fifteen primary suppliers (about a tenth of the normal number), who will together contribute $1 billion to the cost of the plant, will serve the plant. They will produce their modules (that is, entire subassemblies) on site, thus reducing transportation and storage costs.

tronic commerce (e-commerce). Dell is reported to be selling about three million dollars per day or over a billion dollars a year of computer equipment over the Internet. The cost of Web sales is significantly lower than the cost of sales made either through the direct sales force calling on large organizations or through individuals talking to other individuals on the telephone. The ultimate force in redefining value networks or value chains will be e-commerce. E-commerce has the potential to redefine marketplaces as it changes value networks. The benefits of e-commerce are many, beginning with the ability to broaden the reach of the firm and offer a larger potential customer base. Geographic boundaries no longer exist and the e-commerce site, depending upon the software and hardware behind the web site, can operate twenty-four hours a day, 365 days per year.

The Web opens a new channel to service current customers and build sales with new customers. Business-to-business marketers should be natural users of e-commerce, as they have a customer base that has computers and are likely to be connected to the Web. Payment systems and delivery systems are in place and management control can be established through control of who is authorized to buy and where the product may be shipped.

E-commerce makes it possible to reduce the costs associated with holding large physical inventories as the time gained in order processing reduces the need for holding inventories in branch locations. The value network can be connected electronically; improving the responsiveness of the system and reducing inventory.

The costs of serving a customer who specifies his or her needs and places an order over the Web are significantly less than making a sales call or using a telephone sales system. Faster customer response is accomplished with twenty-four-hour access. Customers with questions are able to access directly centrally maintained current information. Customers can see the status of their orders and shipment information. It is possible to have a 'hot' button that will connect a customer to a twenty-four-hour sales operation.

In some circumstances, new products can be developed working with lead users over the Net as they respond to prototypes. Launching a new or revised product is fast, as product specifications and prices can quickly be added to the Web server and made available to the customer base.

Customer relationships exist at a different level from traditional relationships. Since e-commerce may offer the buyer a choice of how to connect with the company—either through a salesperson, over the Web, or a combination—customers will be able to build the type of relationship that they prefer. A customer profile can be developed for each customer by running a data collection program in the background. These data can be used as input for new product development, target marketing, and gaining better understanding of the customer.

The Web delivers images, text, voice, and video organized on hyperlinked HTML pages. Interesting multimedia presentations can make the shopping experience an educational and compelling buying experience.

A database marketing system as shown in Fig. 23.4 is the heart of Web marketing. The data warehouse is built upon operational data such as customer descriptions, sales histories, billing and accounting records, responses to promotions, and a myriad of other internal records. External overlays are purchased, such as credit ratings, usage of the product category, and other relevant data that describe the customer. Data marts of specialized data are extracted from the warehouse to be used by marketing analysts to create new products or marketing programmes. The marketing action and support module implements the marketing programmes developed by the analysts. The Web contact point is unique in that it is a two-way communication, as the customer inputs data to the warehouse by searching for product, placing orders, and responding to programmes designed to elicit the customer's needs.

E-commerce will not replace traditional business-to-business relationships but will become an important extension as to how business is conducted. E-commerce will be a potent force in redefining value networks. Channel members, such as distributors, may be the firms most at risk, as their functions may be eroded as firms go direct to their customers. The term 'disintermediated' was coined to explain the removal of middlemen in the world of e-commerce. Dell is an example of a firm that chose to bypass channels of distribution and go direct to its markets. Dell is precluded from consumer markets that require a salesperson to help the customer understand its needs and options. However, once the consumer becomes knowledgeable about computers, then Dell becomes a potential supplier. Within the computer market, alternative value networks compete for customers. Web-based buying systems change the economics of serving market segments generally in favour of the Web-based system.

Looking into the future, it is possible to visualize a Web-based customer system that would elicit customer needs from a technology buyer and then create a product to meet those needs. The buyer would then be able to manipulate the product and make a trade-off between different levels of engineering performance and price. The system could even provide comparisons in performance and price between off-the-shelf products and the custom product. The buyer could be informed as to when the product could be manufactured and the delivery date. The hardware and

Figure 23.4 **Major components of a database marketing system**

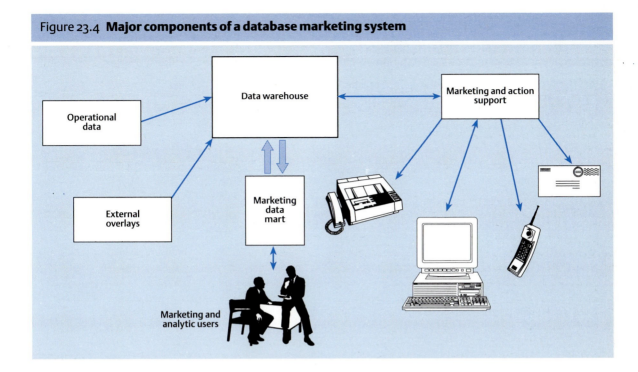

software are currently available to build such a system.

6.2 Strategic implications

We began the chapter by looking at the change from a competitive to a cooperative paradigm. We conclude by looking to the future, where cooperation will drive value-creating networks and their ability to compete with other value-creating networks. Buyer and seller relationships are continuing to evolve, as partners start to understand their respective roles within value-creating networks. What was originally a relationship between two individuals, a buyer and a seller, who traded products for money has developed into a strategic vision of how two or more firms can fit into and play a role in value-creating networks.

Further reading

Child, J., and Faulkner, D. (1998), *Strategies of Cooperation* (Oxford: Oxford University Press).

Domberger, S. (1998), *The Contracting Organization* (Oxford: Oxford University Press).

Ford, D. (1998) (ed.), *Managing Business Relationships* (Chichester: Wiley).

Gemunden, H. G., Ritter, T., and Walter, A. (1998), *Relationships and Networks in International Markets* (Oxford: Elsevier Science).

Möller, K., and Wilson, D. (1995) (eds.), *Business Marketing: An Interaction and Network Perspective* (Norwell, Mass.: Kluwer Academic Publishers).

Discussion questions

1 Suggest a way in which a supplier can categorize its customers into those where a cooperative supply relationship should be sought and those where each transaction should be treated as essentially an isolated case.

2 Do all customers want close relationships with their suppliers?

3 It is often implied that, if a salesperson is physically based in customer's organization, there is a risk that he will become closely identified with the customer's point of view. Is this a desirable situation from the supplier's point of view?

4 It is often suggested that a supplier should demonstrate its commitment to those customers with which it wants to develop a close relationship. How can a service organization demonstrate such commitment?

5 Does the development of a situation where supplier and customers are more closely committed to each other (as in the JIT II situation) indicate a need for a supplier to develop a customer profitability analysis?

BOSE Corporation has extended the concept of JIT II to its inbound and outbound transportation operation. It previously operated a traditional operation, with each carrier calling on BOSE to sell its services and a support person located at the carrier's location. Fig. 23.5 illustrates the traditional mode of operation. JIT II combines the carrier inside and outside roles at the BOSE location under the control of the BOSE's manager, which creates a powerful operating structure (see Fig. 23.6).

The transportation 'in-plant' employee is responsible for ensuring the on-time delivery of a damage-free JIT service to BOSE. Using electronic data interchange (EDI), the in-plant tracks and, expedites when necessary all of the freight moving within the system. The in-plant may assume such duties as ensuring proper routing, auditing the financial performance, and tracking and reporting carrier performance.

Figure 23.5 Traditional transportation relationship

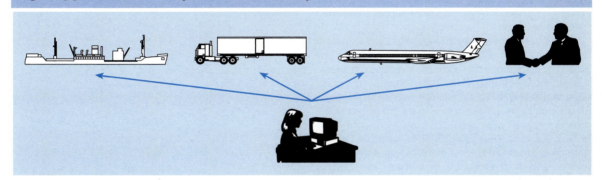

Figure 23.6 JIT II transportation system

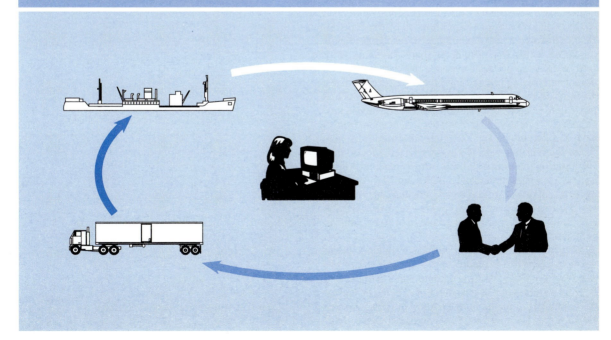

The JIT II system is particularly effective in crisis situations. In the old model the BOSE person had to coordinate the key players at their location via telephone; now they sit around a table or video console and work together to solve a problem. For example, suppose a plant needs a key part number 44,376 because a major auto customer has sold more cars than forecast. The part is made in Taiwan and is shipped via boat to San Francisco and trucked to BOSE. The EDI system can locate the part as it moves through the transportation system. In this case, it finds one shipment in the middle of the ocean and another just about to be loaded on a truck for shipment to BOSE. The trucking in-plant arranges for the parts to be pulled off the transport truck and delivered to the airport for delivery in twelve hours to BOSE. If the part was on the dock in Taiwan, the in-plant team would combine to arrange air shipping and custom clearing to have the parts delivered in the shortest time.

The ability to access inventory anywhere in the system but at sea has been called total material control (TMC) by BOSE. The system operates with the in-plants representing each mode of transport (air, land, sea, export/import) working together using supplier EDI systems to integrate information to track the position of all the goods in the transportation system. BOSE controls all freight from its shipping point. TMC allows BOSE to locate and obtain material days or even weeks before its arrival date. It is a flexible system of inventory in motion. The cost of crisis expediting is significantly less than carrying buffer inventory.

Beyond the day-to-day management of the system the transportation team works to reduce costs and improve the performance of the transportation system. Working in a JIT II relationship has changed how all of the firms involved do business. The time it takes to resolve problems is reduced as the key individuals share the same work space so they can just walk over and talk with each other rather than playing phone tag between their old offices. The firms develop closer working arrangements, which in turn lead to cost savings. For example, the sea freight firm is the first to receive shipment documentation from a BOSE supplier in the Far East. This information is now shared immediately with the import/export broker firm, which sets up its custom file before the ship departs. If the parts are needed immediately, BOSE can have them air freighted and the customs files are already prepared. This level of integration of activities could be set up in the traditional buyer–seller model, but would be much harder to implement.

The day-to-day interaction between the individuals makes it easier to see opportunities for improving the overall system. They share the common goal of improving the total system, not just their piece of it. Being inside the plant helps the in-plants to understand BOSE's problems and they can work with BOSE personnel to solve these problems. For example, the sea shipping in-plant working with BOSE production and transportation planning people developed a series of process improvements that yielded a saving of one-third of the transit time for goods. This saving reduced the in-process inventory cost significantly and benefited the shipper by releasing containers for use by BOSE or other customers. These improvements were not evident when each party was optimizing its part of the system, but became evident in the JIT II operating system.

Discussion question

What challenges do developments such as that described in BOSE pose for firms trying to enter an industry?

Chapter 24

Designing and Marketing New Products and Services

Ulrike de Brentani

Objectives

The objectives of this chapter are:

1 to explain what new product development is;

2 to discuss the strategic importance of new product development;

3 to consider the new product development processes and the features which lead to new product success;

4 to describe the distinctive issues of developing new services.

1 Introduction

How, at the beginning of the twenty-first century, do companies continue to prosper in such a rapidly changing market and technological environment? We have learned, among other things, that understanding customers is a basic requirement so that we can respond to their ever-expanding needs and changing wants. Maintaining a highly competitive product or service offering is also essential if we are to position our products such that they gain customer preference and achieve a differential advantage in the marketplace. And seeking market opportunities—that is, approaching more diversified market or product segments and expanding on the international scene—has increasingly become a fundamental condition for continued growth and profitability. These are just a few of the concerns we have as marketers to ensure the continued success of our organizations. Although diverse, what all these strategies have in common is that they are concerned with new product development. In all cases, marketers must assess their organization's strategy and determine in what ways the company's goods and services can or should be changed in order to achieve the planned performance objectives.

2 What is new product development?

NEW-PRODUCT development deals with creating, designing, and marketing new goods and services. 'New' products can involve highly original, *new-to-the-world*, products or services, such as when fax machines or automated teller banking services were first introduced. Or, as is much more common, they can involve changes to existing offerings, in the form of *improvements* so that the products work better, or in the form of *adaptations* so that they respond more explicitly to the needs of specific customer groups. For example, PC software developers regularly improve their products so that they work faster, perform more functions, and are more user-friendly; in other instances, the software is modified or adapted to answer the needs of specific research or industrial applications. Many other 'new' products entail the development of *new brands* that are either direct imitations of existing products or incorporate adjustments in the form of ingredient mix, packaging, image, positioning, or price. Hence, new-product or service development involves a broad array of strategies and activities for the firm. In all cases, such efforts are or should be directed at enhancing the short- or long-term performance of the organization.

3 New product strategy

ORGANIZATIONS can decide to use either a reactive or a proactive approach to new-product development. Either strategy is appropriate depending on the set of conditions in the particular market and firm.

3.1 Reactive strategy

When companies use a *reactive* new-product development strategy, they respond to conditions as they occur in the marketplace. For example, Microsoft's announcement in the late 1990s that it was to undertake research towards creating Java-based office software—Java is a computer language that allows programs to work on any type of operating system—can be seen as a move to *defend* or protect the 80 per cent (US) market share held by its Windows-based office software. Other reactive strategies include product *imitation* and *second but better*. In both of these cases, the company waits for a competitor to develop a new product and then either quickly introduces a 'me-too' version or incorporates improvements that offer unique benefits for a particular market niche. With this type of strategy, firms can avoid the high risks associated with introducing new-to-the-world products that can result from an incomplete understanding of the technology or market wants, design errors, or slow product adoption by consumers. But late market entry comes with its own set of risks, since it usually means that the firm does not gain the significant rewards that come with being first to market, such as high market share, above average profits due to greater experience, production and market economies, and a leadership image.

In the business-to-business market, companies typically use a *responsive* approach, since they must generally react to specific customer problems or requests when they develop new products or services. This makes sense, since organizational clients typically do not buy products unless these respond to a specific purpose in their operations (von Hippel 1978). It is important to note, however, that reactive does not necessarily mean passive. For example, business firms who successfully bid on industrial contracts have usually established a system that ensures timely and accurate information flows from users in their field of operation. Such firms make sure that they are knowledgeable about key technology and competitive trends in their product and market arenas, so that they can respond quickly and effectively.

3.2 Proactive strategy

A *proactive* new-product development strategy is one in which the selling organization initiates the change. Companies do so by explicitly assigning resources to take advantage of key opportunities or to pre-empt future threats in the environment. In the aforementioned example of the Java-based office software (that allowed programs to transcend any type of computer operating system), the Corel Corporation had taken the initiative to *undertake R&D* to incorporate a technology that was still in its infancy into its WordPerfect office software in the hope of prying customers loose from its chief rival, Microsoft Word. Another commonly used proactive approach involves a more entrepreneurial stance, where an individual or small group of persons in the organization undertakes certain actions to make an idea happen. CN Rail, one of Canada's two large railways, undertook such a project in the mid-1990s. In a collaborative venture with Ultramar—a relatively small Canadian oil company that depended exclusively on water transportation for its limited shipping needs (approximately 250 kilometres along a main river route from its refinery to its primary market—CN Rail took the initiative to redesign and patent a high-tech version of an interconnected tank-car train that created a veritable 'pipeline on wheels'. This 'super' tank-train included a fleet of cars that travelled in sixteen-unit string formations, with loading and unloading connections at one end of each string and with product pumped through the cars in succession. This project was highly proactive and risky for both firms. For the client (Ultramar), it represented a contradiction to all traditions in the industry, but it offered a way substantially to reduce shipping costs, to expand market reach, and to deal with the increasingly demanding requirements of the environmental community (e.g. oil spills on inland water routes). For CN Rail, the project represented a new and proactive approach to gain access to a major market segment, to make use of its underused railway capacity, and to achieve growth by developing an image as a transportation 'pioneer' in what was generally viewed to be a mature and not very innovative industry.

Which strategy—*reactive* or *proactive*—should firms follow when developing new products? Clearly, this depends on the specific product and market circumstances, as well as on the characteristics and resources of the company in question. Particularly in situations where it is important to defend existing products and markets, where competitive imitation is extensive, where innovations are difficult to protect against competition, or where the firm lacks the resources (human, capital, and expertise) to become the dominant innovator, a reactive strategy is more appropriate. Moreover, in the industrial market, responding to new needs or problems identified by customers is the norm. In contrast, a proactive new product strategy is necessary when the company wants to gain a measure of control in the marketplace. Achieving above average sales and profit growth, entering new markets, attaining pioneer status in an industry or a technology, and blocking competition from imitating or improving on a successful product offering all call for a more proactive strategy. Needless to say, companies who select this strategy must have the resources, the opportunities, and the commitment to succeed in such ventures.

☞ 'New products are often co-developed, which results in a very early integration of the suppliers in the technical platform of their customers.' (Chapter 7, p. 142)

4 Importance of new-product development

NEW-PRODUCT development is both important and risky for firms. As shown in the above examples, it is important because it is a primary in-

gredient in the corporate and marketing strategies that ensure continued prosperity. However, having a winning product line today does not guarantee the long-term well-being of the organization. Without successful new-product efforts, companies risk their very survival. The average life of products is becoming shorter, as customers continue to demand novel and better products, and as competitors, armed with new and rapidly advancing technologies, are faster in devising improvements, replacements, and pioneering innovations. In computer software, for example, new products are usually obsolete by the time they are introduced to the market. Companies that want to survive in this field must continually innovate not only through regular upgrades and improvements but also through pioneering efforts that shift the product to a new plane and can thus create a competitive advantage for the firm.

Apart from the dangers of *not* innovating, companies face the added risk that comes with the potential for failure when they do undertake new-product development. New products fail at a disconcerting rate and companies can incur huge losses, not only in immediate monetary terms when they fail to recover their development and marketing costs (see Insert), but also in terms of future potential when a new-product failure negatively impacts on the reputation or image of the firm. In the services sector, in particular, while the visible monetary costs associated with developing a new service are frequently relatively low (for example, there is no unsold inventory), the opportunity costs that can result from a loss of reputation and client trust when a newly introduced service performs poorly can be substantial. For example, when a new corporate debit-card service—which was guaranteed to cover all business travel and entertainment expenses—did not function as

The billion dollar shave

It cost Gillette an estimated $1 billion to develop and launch its Mach 3 razor. Given that it is essentially a new-product development of limited complexity in comparison with, say, a new drug, this is a staggering figure. Interestingly, approximately 75 per cent of the cost is believed to have been spent on developing 200 new pieces of production equipment that will enable Gillette to produce the razor three times faster than any of its other razors.

promised for the VP of a major corporation, the service provider not only lost this debit-card account, but was not considered seriously by this firm as a provider for any future financial service.

Researchers in Europe and North America estimate that between 33 and 60 per cent of all new products fail either in the marketplace or after substantial resources have already been invested in development (Crawford 1997). Clearly, learning about product innovation is important, both because it is a key ingredient in the marketing strategies that ensure corporate survival and success, and because we must better understand how to reduce the rate and the cost of failure.

5 New-product success and failure

WHY do some new products succeed while others fail? Researchers have looked at this question for goods and for services in both the industrial and consumer sector. Most often, new-product *failure* has been associated with overestimated market potential; poor product design—that is, designs that do not work well, are incompatible with customer preferences or systems, or cost too much; poorly planned marketing programmes—that is, incorrect positioning, poor advertising, inadequate training, or too high a price; high cost of development; ignoring market research findings; and development problems and costs that went far beyond initial expectations.

Although it is important to understand what factors cause new-product failure, avoiding these does not necessarily ensure success. By comparing large numbers of successful products with failures, several studies have shown that the characteristics that are shared by high performers are different from the reasons for failure. There are certain key *success* factors that have been shown to be strongly linked to winning new products (Cooper 1984, 1996), including:

■ *unique, superior product*: the new product that delivers unique benefits and superior value to customers; it is competitively differentiated in terms of quality and meeting user needs;

■ *strong market orientation*: strong focus on customer needs and wants, the competitive situation,

and the nature of the market; customer input throughout the new product process;

■ *sharp, early product definition*: up-front market and product assessment clearly specifying the target market, descriptions of the product concept and benefits to be delivered, the positioning strategy, and prioritized product features, attributes, requirements, and specifications;

■ *high quality of execution*: a complete, consistent, and planned new-product development process with high-quality performance throughout by an empowered, multifunctional team;

■ *attractive market environment*: a large, high-growth market with a positive and innovative economic climate;

■ *project synergy*: a strong fit between the needs of the new-product project and the company's unique resources, competencies, and experiences—in effect, a 2 + 2 = 5 scenario.

6 The new-product development process

ON reviewing the factors that lead to new-product success and failure, it becomes clear that most of these factors are linked to the process companies use for planning, designing, and marketing new products. Thus, essential to eliminating the causes for failure and to increasing the chances for success is a good understanding of the new-product development process. This process, as presented in this chapter, assumes that companies undertake new product development as part of a *proactive* innovation strategy. Moreover, because innovation in goods and in services has many things in common, the process is first described in more generic, product, terms. Section 8 deals more specifically with new-service development.

Proactive new-product development is driven by the corporate and marketing strategy of the firm (see Insert). Organizations need to have clearly established *objectives* about sales and profit growth and about the degree to which these are expected to come from new-product development. In addition, based on an in-depth analysis of the organization's resources, distinctive competencies and weaknesses, and the business and technological environments, managers should

Why another new chocolate bar?

When Cadburys launched 'Fuse' in 1996 it had two objectives. First, to increase the market for chocolate confectionery. Second, to increase its share of the snacking sector that was dominated by brands with ingredients such as: fruit, nuts, and cereal. The second objective was based on a market research of consumers' snacking habits that had identified both the growth of 'snacking' and a gap in the market for a more chocolatey snack.

Box 24.1 **Stages of the new product development process**

STAGE 1
IDEA GENERATION
Use external and internal sources to identify opportunities for new products and services

STAGE 2
IDEA SCREENING
Assess new-product ideas using required and preference criteria; first 'go/no-go' decision

STAGE 3
CONCEPT EVALUATION
Develop core benefit propositions; assess customer reactions re benefits, price and quality, competitive superiority, positioning

STAGE 4
THE BUSINESS CASE
Assess financial viability of project; based on market study, sales/cost projections, product protocol, and marketing and production plans

STAGE 5
PRODUCT DEVELOPMENT and TESTING
Develop alternative designs; prototype tests in-house and with customers

STAGE 6
MARKET TESTING and VALIDATION
Test new product and marketing strategy under actual/controlled/simulated market conditions; pre-launch business analysis

STAGE 7
MARKET LAUNCH
Undertake full or roll-out new-product commercialization; track launch programme; recover product or service failures

have a clear idea of the specific new-product and market arenas in which their firm wants to operate.

New-product development involves a series of stages, beginning with the identification of potential opportunities and ending with the commercialization and post-launch evaluation of new products. Ideally, the process is designed in the form of a 'stage-gate' system where each stage of activity is followed by an evaluation 'gate' where projects are assessed or reassessed in terms of a set of benchmark criteria that determine the 'go', 'kill', 'hold', or 'recycle' decision for the new product (Cooper 1990). The process, which is depicted in Box 24.1, includes seven basic activity stages, which are described below.

6.1 Stage 1: Idea generation

New-product development starts with the search for new-product ideas. Ideas can come from many sources—both *external* and *internal* to the firm—and several techniques, ranging from formal to highly informal, can be used by companies to identify potential opportunities. The key to a successful idea-generation phase is not to depend on chance but to work within an established system that will furnish an ample volume and variety of the right types of new-product ideas.

6.1.1 External sources

External sources of new-product ideas include customers, competitors, channel members, trade associations and shows, and inventors.

■ Consumer-goods firms frequently use formal *consumer surveys* in order to learn about changes in customer needs and wants, or to pinpoint problems consumers have with particular types of products.

- *Perceptual* and *preference mapping* techniques can also be used to identify what product attributes are important to buyers and what gaps exist in the product offerings of competitors. Both approaches can lead to important ideas for new products.

- On a less formal level, companies can use *focused group discussions* with small groups of customers to gain insights about their likes, dislikes, and attitudes, or they may encourage *customer feedback letters* that provide suggestions, preferences, and complaints.

- In the business-to-business sphere, because purchases tend to be more rational and problem based, ideas from customers in the form of *specific problems and requests* are the most common source.

- Increasingly, developers emphasize long-term relationships with customers ('relationship marketing') and attempt to work in collaboration with 'lead users' (von Hippel 1986)—that is, user firms that are at the leading edge of the trend in the types of problems they face and/ or the types of solutions they seek—when they develop pioneering industrial products. For example, the first industrial users of computer aided design (CAD) techniques were lead customers of an information technology (IT) technique that has become the norm in a broad mix of industries.

- *Competitors* are also extremely important as a source of new-product ideas. Companies should have an *extensive information system*—with up-to-date reports from both internal and external sources—keeping them informed about what current and potential competitors are up to. In addition, many firms actively examine their competitors' products (e.g. reverse engineering) in order to imitate or improve on them.

- *Channel members*, including distributors and suppliers, can also play a role in providing new-product ideas. Companies who *survey* or have *regular contact* with retailers and industrial distributors can learn about customer needs and trends, about competitive products, and about potential new-product forms, through the lens of these market and product specialists.

6.1.2 Internal sources

Companies who undertake proactive new-product development typically do not rely exclusively on external sources for new-product ideas. They establish idea-generation systems within their own firm. In this way, they can reduce the element of chance in finding enough good ideas and take full advantage of their known resources and specialized capabilities. Internal sources include R&D and design laboratories, marketing, production, new-product idea committees, employee suggestion programmes, and also senior management.

- Companies whose business is of a technological nature—e.g. pharmaceutical, computer software, or aerospace firms—or firms that want to gain/maintain a competitive edge or that want to be seen as pioneers in their field invest substantial resources in both *pure and applied research* in order to come up with ideas for new products.

- Ideas for product improvements and completely new products also often come from within the firm—for example, from *employees* who have regular contact with customers, production people, or marketing personnel. Some firms establish an internal culture that actively encourages this source of ideas by running suggestion schemes, seriously considering all submissions, and presenting prizes for the better ideas.

- An *idea-generation committee* is another popular approach to creating pools of new-product ideas. Small groups, from within marketing or comprising personnel from different functional areas, often use a technique called *brainstorming* in order to come up with creative proposals. Brainstorming counts on an informal and relaxed, anything-goes, kind of setting. By adhering to certain operating guidelines—that is, a group leader who provides encouragement, who disallows negative criticism, and who ensures that all ideas are examined and recorded—the process can be particularly successful in stimulating creativity.

- *Senior managers* can also play an important idea-generation role particularly in smaller, entrepreneurial firms. It is usually through the creativeness and entrepreneurial spirit of these senior people that the firm was originally established and became successful. In many successful firms, these managers continue to play a role in the product development process, not only up-front in establishing strategy and objectives, and in creating an innovative culture within the firm, but by staying intimately involved with the company's creative side.

The objective of idea generation is to create an ample pool of new-product ideas that complement the firm's preferred strategic arenas. Although in some cases this stage can be quite costly (for example, pure biotech research or aerospace research), on average the cost of generating an idea is incredibly low compared to the eventual cost of developing and commercializing the resulting new product (Booz, Allen, and Hamilton 1982). Thus, every effort should be made to establish a system that generates an abundant volume of proposals.

6.2 Stage 2: Idea screening

Idea screening is the first 'gate' or 'go/no-go' decision in the new-product development process. Since the vast majority of new-product ideas generated will not be developed, the objective of screening is to eliminate most of the proposals so that scarce resources are spent only on those ideas that have the best potential for success. New-product ideas that get the 'go' decision should fit the organization's new-product strategy and show clear potential for achieving a competitive advantage. Because the number of ideas can be substantial, it is often efficient to use a two-stage screening system: in the first *culling* or pre-screening phase the ideas are assessed in terms of a small number of basic 'must-have' criteria; then in the second full-screening phase the ideas are evaluated in terms of a much broader set of 'would-like-to-haves' or preference criteria (Crawford 1997).

To undertake effective screening, it is necessary first to provide a short description of each idea in terms of a standardized set of elements including the product idea, the targeted customer group(s), and competitive brands or product forms, as well as rough estimates of market size, cost and time to develop, product cost and price, ROI, and likely payback period. A screening committee then uses a short checklist of *culling* criteria by which to assess (yes/no rating) whether or not the ideas are in line with basic corporate requirements. For example, if a basic tenet of the firm's new-product strategy is to become a major player in the global arena, then ideas that have only domestic-market potential would automatically be eliminated from the pool.

The surviving ideas are put through a *full-screening* process. In this phase, the screening committee uses a more extensive set of evaluation criteria that should reflect the organization's new-product objectives, its distinctive capabilities and resources, as well as a number of market- and project-related factors. The aim is to rate the ideas in terms of characteristics that are linked to the ultimate performance of new products. By using a weighted set of criteria—where the weights reflect the relative importance of each criterion (e.g. not important (=1) to very important (=10)) in determining success—each product idea is rated (e.g. very low (=1) to very high (=10)) on each factor; the factor rating is then multiplied by the weight, and the weighted ratings are finally summed to determine a project 'score'. (Since screening is typically performed by a committee of evaluators, the final project score is usually based on average factor ratings.) This permits a ranking of the proposals in terms of their overall potential for success. The committee's decision may be to accept only the highest rated ideas or only those that surpass a certain 'cut-off' score, which may be based on past 'go' decisions.

Such a screening model, however, is not only instrumental as a basis for making the early 'go/no-go' decision for new-product ideas, but can also be used as a diagnostic tool that reveals certain problem areas that need to be dealt with in products that do get the 'go' decision or for those that are put on 'hold' for recycling purposes. Box 24.2 presents an example of a screening model and describes how projects are scored and ranked.

Because screening is an evaluation 'gate' that comes very early in the new-product development process, when very little hard data are typically available about the project, it is a difficult decision to make well. Thus, much effort has gone into developing effective screening methods. Increasingly, firms are using more sophisticated decision models, where both the criteria and the weights used are based on actual research-based evidence of what factors are used by firms and linked to performance (Cooper 1984; de Brentani 1986).

Effective screening marks an essential *internal* evaluation point signalling those ideas that fit the firm's capabilities, resources, and new-product strategies, and that appear to show potential for success (see Insert on p. 557). A good decision model can go far in minimizing both the 'drop'

Box 24.2 **An idea screening model**

Evaluation Criterion	Importance Weight (A)	Mean Rating (B)	Weighted Rating (A × B)
I. Technical factors	(1–10)	(1–10)	
Technical difficulty			
R&D skills required			
Design complexity			
Availability of R&D resources			
Technical equipment required			
Rate of technological change			
Likelihood of technical superiority			
Patentability			
Relative cost of technical research/design			
■ TOTAL TECHNICAL SCORE			
II. Commerical factors			
Market-size potential			
Market-growth potential			
Market-share potential			
Competitive aggressiveness			
Strength of customer need			
Likelihood of distributor interest			
Product uniqueness (for user)			
Differentiated from competitive offerings			
Market launch effort required			
Probable profit			
Probable payback period			
■ TOTAL COMMERCIAL SCORE			
TOTAL PROJECT SCORE			

Project: _____ Evaluator: _____ Date: _____

error (eliminating potentially good ideas) and the 'go' error (moving forward product ideas that are likely to fail). In some cases, screening eliminates over 90 per cent of the new-product ideas that were conceived during idea generation. This is as it should be, since the costs of a project increase dramatically as it moves through the new-product development cycle (Booz, Allen, and Hamilton 1982). A good screening effort ensures that scarce resources are allocated to those new-product ideas that fit the firm's strategic objectives and capabili-

ties, and that seem to have the highest potential for success.

6.3 Stage 3: Concept evaluation

New-product ideas that pass internal screening should next be submitted to an *external* evaluation in order to get feedback from the marketplace. This is a critical step, but one that organizations often perform poorly or omit altogether. As a result, many new products fail. They fail because

---

Stage gates typically kill 87 per cent of all new-products projects

A gate's function is to assess new-product ideas and to distinguish potential 'winners' from 'losers'. Typically the likelihood that, at the start of the process, an idea will ultimately succeed has been found to be 13 per cent. Research shows that, on average, out of a total of seven new-product ideas, four reach the design stage, two are tested, and only one is actually launched in the marketplace. Thus, the stage-gate system ensures that, when the costs are at their highest, the company commits resources to only a very small number of high potential projects.

Sources: Booz, Allen, and Hamilton (1982); Cooper (1990).

---

they reflect only the preferences and capabilities of the company and do not adequately respond to customer needs or provide benefits that significantly distinguish them from competitive offerings.

During *concept evaluation*, each new-product idea is described in the form of one or more *core benefit propositions*, which are then presented to potential customers for their reactions. Each core benefit proposition relates to a specific market segment and expresses the product idea in terms of the unique benefit(s) it provides for customers, the planned quality and price level, as well as the benefits and attributes (physical and psychological) required to meet and surpass competition (see Box 24.3 for an example of a core benefit proposition). Companies then use research ranging from informal focus groups to broad market surveys, including product and brand positioning studies, to get feedback about: customer need level, perceived value, communicability and believability of the idea, comparison with competitive products, and purchase intentions. Firms should pay particular attention to results that suggest the ideas are *not* good for the firm (Urban and Hauser 1993).

What makes the concept evaluation stage of the new-product development process a challenge is that core benefit propositions are usually abstract in nature—this is particularly true for highly innovative ideas—and may be difficult for customers to conceptualize in realistic terms. This could lead to customer feedback that has little to do with eventual market reactions to the commercialized product. Consider, for example, when the fax

machine was first developed; consumers who took part in concept evaluation studies probably had a difficult time visualizing the ultimate product. Hence, efforts are often undertaken to make concepts more tangible through drawings, CAD, or, more recently, 'virtual reality'. In the business-to-business sector, the concept evaluation stage is somewhat easier, because customers tend to be more informed and to have a clearer, less emotional, understanding of their needs.

☞ 'Most information about new products, for example, would be incomprehensible unless the product category were already known . . .' (Chapter 6, p. 118)

6.4 Stage 4: The business case

The *business case* is the first in-depth evaluation of the financial viability of the project. It marks a critical phase in the new-product process since it makes or breaks the project. After testing the product concept (previous stage), the company must now develop a preliminary plan for developing, producing, and marketing the new product. This requires research on the *market size* and *competitive structure*, some preliminary *technical* analysis to provide a basis for the design and production approach, and also some *legal* and *patent* search where appropriate. This up-front research results in a business case that includes:

- the *product protocol*: a set of statements articulating the new product in terms of the target market, the product concept—that is, benefits and positioning—and the product design, including planned features and attributes, and distinct requirements and specifications;
- short- and long-term sales, cost, and profit projections;
- detailed development plan;
- preliminary marketing and production plan;
- defined project team.

The business case is the first full financial evaluation of the new-product project. It will undergo several revisions during the stages that follow, as more and better information becomes available. It marks a pivotal decision gate in the new product process, since it opens the door to full-scale development and this typically involves a significant increase in cost and investment (Cooper 1990).

Box 24.3 **Example of core benefit proposition**

Definition

A core benefit proposition is a simple concept statement of the unique benefits that the new product or service will provide to a specific target group of customers and by which it will meet or surpass competition.

Example: International Bankcard Cash Service in Key Business and Tourist Centres

Core benefit proposition: provide convenient, highly user-friendly, immediate, secure, and informed cash services to affluent cash/bank card-holders in high traffic business and tourist centres worldwide.

Target Customers: affluent local residents and shoppers, business people, and tourists.

Service Offering	*Competition*
Convenient	
■ several high-access locations where affluent locals, tourists, and business people convene and shop;	■ frequently not convenient
	■ location difficult to find, out-of-way
■ mix of currency notes (medium + large)	■ lower traffic locations
	■ often only large currency notes
User-friendly	
■ language of choice (5); high-tech touch screen	■ low-tech systems; only one language
■ simple-to-follow icons; easy to make corrections	■ unclear how to insert card
■ cannot forget card	■ can forget card in machine
Immediate	
■ never out of cash	■ often out of cash on week-ends;
■ fast, high-tech ATMs	■ slower ATMs
Secure	
■ well lit, highly public places; enter via card; glass environment	■ less 'safe' locations; no privacy
■ transaction record only if desired	■ always a transaction record
■ cannot forget card	■ easy to forget card
Informed	
■ information on cost of $HK in home currency of card	■ no exchange information
■ confirm final withdrawal decision	■ less informed decision
All cash/bank cards	
■ all local and international credit and money cards	■ only local banks (some)
■ account withdrawals and cash advances	■ only MC or VISA

6.5 Stage 5: Product development and testing

It is in the *product-development* phase that the new product takes on explicit and tangible (in the case of manufactured goods) form, as designers convert the conceptual and psychological attributes into a product that is both technically and commercially feasible. Development typically entails several cycles involving small-scale designs and/or prototype models. Technical, production, and marketing personnel must work closely together during this stage in the effort to translate the product's 'customer attributes' into 'engineering attributes', where the latter take into account the best trade-offs between customer preferences and product costs (and ultimately price) (Hauser and Clausing 1988).

☞ 'A number of highly successful firms deliberately seek to encourage interdepartmental cooperation. . . . Others, such as Procter & Gamble, always include somebody from the production and financial side of the organization when forming new product teams.' (Chapter 17, p. 435)

New techniques speed product development

Once the design of an aircraft is fixed different parts of the manufacturing process can now be tried on a computer. For example, a virtual pipe-bending machine makes sure that the fuel lines that have to snake their way around the airframe can be created without literally tying themselves in knots.

Depending on the product, the development phase can be very time-consuming and costly. But, increasingly, new products must be developed and brought to market quickly in order to meet customer wants in a timely manner and to stay ahead of competition. To this end, CAD, which creates computer-based prototypes and where the final product design is fed into a computer controlled manufacturing (CCM) system, has made tremendous contributions both in reducing costs and in speeding up the design process of manufactured goods (see Insert).

During development, companies typically employ two types of new-product *prototype tests*: technical and product-use tests. Both types of tests can lead to important revisions or even to the decision to abandon the product. In-house, *technical* prototype tests are used for eliminating bugs, improving the quality and reliability of the product, ensuring safety, and improving production economy and feasibility. In the industrial sphere, such tests are often referred to as *alpha tests*, where products are tested by the developing company's own personnel (for example, testing a new accounting software in the company's own accounting department).

In addition to in-house technical tests, *product-use* tests with customers help to determine whether the new product indeed captures the conceptual attributes that are defined in the protocol. For consumer products, tests can be both *in-lab* (for example, focus groups, product use on company premises) and in the *field*, providing feedback about how the product performs under 'normal' use conditions, product misuse, and customer excitement and preference. For example, a company that develops toys for young children might use several design stages and prototype tests. In-house technical tests would be carried out first to ensure the proper functioning, robustness, safety, and so on of the toy; in-house customer tests would follow to assess the toy's learning

and/or play value, as well as such aspects as the child's interest, attitude, frustration level during play, and misuse of the toy. In addition, testing the toy in the home or in the normal play environment would be important, not only because this is more realistic for the child but also because the parents would be involved and they have certain ideas about what benefits and attributes a toy should have (for example, it is a good 'babysitter', it does not provoke fights between siblings, and so on) (see Insert).

Tamagatchi skids on its 'virtual pet'

In the second half of the 1990s Tamagatchi, a large Japanese toy company, pioneered the idea of a 'virtual pet'—an electronic toy that, once activated, causes an alien 'pet' to be 'born'. This pet cries incessantly and eventually 'dies' unless its needs to be fed, changed, and played with are attended to. When testing the toy, it is unlikely that Tamagatchi took into account the dilemma faced by parents and schoolteachers when they attempted to silence these electronic pets without being responsible for their deaths.

For industrial products, testing specific applications of the new product at the customer site is referred to as *beta testing*. While this form of testing often provides important insights about user-related problems—such as difficulties with the equipment, user-friendliness, compatibility, and training needs—it does not give all of the real information that the product developer needs: that is, how the new product operates in solving whatever problems the customers may have and in whatever way the customers want to use it in their own working environment. As a result, large mainframe computer manufacturers and also software developers often go a step further and give their new products to certain organizations (for example, universities) for *gamma testing*, where the equipment/software is put through whatever applications, and abuse, are considered normal by the users (Crawford 1997).

6.6 Stage 6: Market testing and validation

New products that make it through the development stage are ready to be introduced to the market. But commercialization is the most costly and resource-intensive stage in the process and, so far, whenever customers have become involved in evaluating the new product, it has usually been under conditions that are not entirely realistic. *Market testing*, therefore, is an effort to expose prospective customers to both the new product and its marketing strategy under realistic or near-real purchase conditions, in order to determine if, and to what extent, they actually buy. Such a test not only provides the firm with experience in marketing the new product, but gives valuable feedback about the new product itself and its marketing programme—that is, about the positioning strategy, advertising, distribution, pricing, branding, and packaging issues. Market testing helps planners come up with more precise sales and market share forecasts, and provides diagnostic information about the planned marketing programme, so that revisions can be made prior to full launch of the new product.

6.6.1 How much testing?

An important question related to market testing is: how much is enough? The answer varies for each product. For some new products, there should be very limited or no market testing. This would be the case for durable products that have no (or a very long-term) repeat purchase cycle; in such cases, researchers would have to wait too long for any kind of result and this would only be about the initial trial of the product. Market testing is also contraindicated when the test would leak sensitive, advance information about the product or strategy, allowing competitors to pre-empt the pioneering effort of the firm. It is not uncommon for companies in the same industry to be working on similar product ideas and technologies—for example, in Canada two major national brewers (Molson and Labatt) introduced 'Dry' beer and 'Ice' beer within days of each other. In addition, it is important to remember that a key source of new-product ideas is the competition, and, particularly if the product is easy to imitate, market testing can be detrimental for a new-product pioneer. In certain other cases, the issue of timing may make market testing unfeasible. In the fashion or toy industry, for example, new products are not only highly competitive (imitation) but must have a novelty appeal at just the right time (pre-season or tangent to a particular event). Market testing is likely to compromise the surprise effect in such cases. Additionally, how much market testing is needed depends on the product's degree of newness. When L'Oreal, for example, adds yet another hair care product to its extensive line, less market testing is probably required. The company has an excellent understanding of its product line, its customers and distributors, and the marketing approach and risks associated with undertaking such a launch. In contrast, when firms are dealing with pioneering, high-cost ventures—for example, when mobile telephones were first introduced—substantial market testing is called for in order to ensure a successful strategy.

☞ 'Less and less frequently do companies enjoy long periods of competitive product advantage. A new product, even when a competitor is caught by surprise, can often be quickly duplicated, or a highly similar product soon introduced. To test a contemplated new product in the marketplace over a long period of time will alert competitors.' (Chapter 8, p. 157)

6.6.2 Market testing in consumer markets

Most test markets are carried out for new *consumer* products, with companies using one or more of three basic approaches: (1) full test market, (2) controlled test market, and (3) simulated test market. A *full test market* entails offering the new product for sale on a limited basis and using the planned marketing strategy in defined market areas. On average, such a test uses about three to four test cities that are representative of the markets in question, runs for about one year (depending on repeat purchase pattern and competitive reactions), and supplements basic sales information with store audits, consumer panels, and buyer surveys. Full test markets can easily cost close to $US1 million and in the 1990s were found to be less reliable, as the increasing speed at which markets and competitive environments changed conflicted with the time needed to carry out such tests. Moreover, finding a truly 'representative' test city is not really possible. To deal with these problems, companies have shifted to using several other market-testing techniques (including the 'roll-out' market launch strategy discussed in the next section, Stage 7).

To reduce time, cost, and potential information leakage to competition, companies are increasingly using *controlled test markets* as a way of getting pre-launch market data. Here, the company typically hires the services of a research firm that maintains a panel of stores that carry the new product. In addition to getting highly accurate electronic scanner data to track sales, the approach can be used to test alternative shelf strategies, or in-store displays and promotions, since the distribution of the product and the in-store strategy are 'controlled' by the research firm. The test can also incorporate alternative advertising appeals via the local cable television company. Controlled test markets are advantageous, because they involve less time and lower costs. Their drawbacks include: a less-than-normal marketing process, a non-representative sample of stores and customers, and the possibility of leaks to competition.

An approach that became quite popular in the late 1990s, particularly for relatively low-priced, packaged, consumer goods, was the *simulated test market*. Here, the new product and its marketing strategy stay completely out of the real-world environment and this serves substantially to reduce testing costs and to guard against competitive imitation. Using the A–T–R model, the idea is to get estimates of consumer awareness (A), trial (T), and repeat purchase (R) of the new product, which, together with factors that describe the planned marketing strategy (i.e. market segments, extent of distribution, and prices), can be used to forecast the sales of the new product. Typically, a market-research firm rents an area in a shopping mall, where it sets up a drug- or grocery-store aisle. The new product being tested is placed on the shelf in this 'simulated' store. Consumers are then approached, shown several advertisements (to create and test *awareness* of the new product), and provided with a small amount of money that they may use for shopping in this store (*trial*). Both the respondents who buy and those who do not buy the product under study get the product for trial and are given the opportunity to *repeat purchase* it later by phone one or more times ('sales waves'). Using the data collected about the advertising, trial, and repurchase behaviour, together with a computer model (for example, ASSESSOR (Urban and Katz 1983)) that is based on the simulated and actual sales of many similar products, has been found to be surprisingly successful in projecting the national sales for the new product. Typically, these tests can be carried out in 8–14 weeks, involve about 300 to 600 people, and cost between $US50,000 to $US250,000 (Urban and Hauser 1993). Companies can use it either as a

final market test or, in cases where there is a lot of uncertainty and a great deal at stake, as a *pre-test* to the full test market.

6.6.3 Market testing in industrial markets

In the *industrial* market, new-product developers also undertake market testing, but on a much smaller scale. Organizational customers are usually unwilling to spend time or incur potential production problems in order to help a supplier in testing a new product. So, one tactic that is sometimes used is the *speculative sale*, where salespeople, using prepared selling materials, a real product, and a veritable price list (including discounts, etc.), approach the customer and pretend to make a sale. What is being tested here is the customer's level of interest and excitement, willingness to ask for a sample, or state an intention to purchase if the product were available. In other cases, companies go a bit further. They introduce the product on an *informal sale* basis—either at a trade show or as part of a regular sales call—and attempt to make the actual sale. Even more realistic is a test of the new product in dealer display rooms, since this would represent a much more normal selling situation.

At the end of test marketing, but before moving on to what is usually the costliest stage in the new-product process—the market launch—companies frequently undertake one final *pre-commercialization business analysis*. This is the final 'go/kill' gate in the new-product process and is based on a critical review of all the test activities and results, a reappraisal or updated financials, and an approval of the final production and marketing plans. If the project passes this gate, it faces its first real moment of truth: it must now meet customer requirements and the firm's established benchmarks.

6.7 Stage 7: Market launch

At the *commercialization* or *launch* stage, the company is finally committed to producing the product and it is at this stage that costs increase dramatically. Substantial investments typically need to be made in facilities, training, inventory, and the launch programme. An important part of what determines the extent of the launch effort is the *launch goals* that the company has set for the new product. The size and breadth of market chosen, and the speed at which the organization hopes to achieve market share, are primary factors determining the launch strategy and the required level of resource commitment.

Companies can decide to undertake a full market launch or use a roll-out strategy when commercializing the new product. *Full market launch* may be essential in cases where developers want to gain the 'first mover advantage' and when the competition is not far behind. Being first in the most important markets usually translates into getting the best distributors, an image as a pioneer in the industry, and a larger long-term market share (Robinson and Fornell 1985; Robinson 1988). For example, in the introduction of the 'Dry' and the 'Ice' beer by Canada's two large breweries, a two-day lag by one of the firms in launching the new product to Canada's primary markets translated into a long-term market share difference of several points worth millions of dollars. But, a full market launch is also the riskiest and the most costly route, and has often led to failure when inadequate resources were assigned to the effort.

Companies can reduce the cost and risk associated with new-product commercialization by using a *roll-out* strategy. With this approach, the new product is introduced, one segment at a time, either geographically or by type of customer or by trade channel. For example, in 1998 the ING financial group (of Netherlands) recently entered the Canadian banking market with a new service—a no-fee, no minimum deposit, no branch (i.e. 'virtual' banking service) but high-interest savings account—by focusing first on Canada's largest industrial and financial centre, Toronto. Plans to enter other centres depended on what the company had learned from the Toronto experience. By using such a sequential approach, not only can those responsible for the launch learn from their mistakes (a form of market testing) and make timely adjustments, but successful efforts in one market arena can contribute to funding the launch in the next segment. The key is to choose those segments first that are the most likely to adopt the new product quickly (that is, lead users or early adopters), and who represent customer groups that provide the needed feedback when roll-out is used as a quasi market testing ground. But, roll-out can also present problems, particularly in cases where the new product is easily imitated. Frequently, while the pioneering firm moves slowly from niche to niche, a less risk-averse firm endowed with more extensive re-

sources copies the product and enters the broader market immediately, thus gaining the largest market share and a better-known reputation.

No matter how thorough the pre-launch research and how well planned the launch, for most new products there are still many unknowns when commercialization finally gets underway. For this reason, a *launch tracking* system is required whereby the firm can assess the new product's performance in the marketplace as soon as possible after launch. With an effective evaluation system in place—tracking sales and market reactions as well as production and service problems—management receives timely information about how well the product is doing (that is, whether it is meeting the benchmark objectives) and where its performance needs improvement.

7 Organizing for successful new-product development

HAVING a formal new-product development process in place and having the necessary technical capabilities and resources available to master each stage of the process are clearly essential for achieving the firm's new-product objectives. But there is at least one essential factor that has consistently been found to have an overriding impact on new-product success and that has to do with how the development process is organized and managed within the firm. Making certain that the right people are involved at the right time and in the right way will significantly affect the speed and the effectiveness of the process. Certain key factors have come to light:

The first is that there is a need for a 'seamless enterprise' (Dimancescu 1992) that combines the specialized resources of the firm—such as R&D, marketing, customer service, production, and design—into a viable cross-functional team. Such a team can be in the form of a *new-product committee*, where members maintain their regular jobs and become involved on a part-time basis at different stages of the process; or it could take the form of a *venture team*, where the group of individuals works together on a full-time basis for the entire project. Involving individuals from diverse functional areas ensures that the product ideas, core benefits, product positionings, product and process designs, customer reactions, and marketing strategies can always be analysed and handled from radically different points of view. But creating the seamless enterprise and the fully functioning *cross-functional team* takes many years of effort. Peoples' natural tendency is to operate within 'silos' of specialized knowledge (i.e. be among your own kind) rather than to interact and test out ideas in an open and creative—and potentially incongruous—setting. In organizations that have succeeded in moving in this direction, the move has been shown to lead to major leaps in creativity, to fewer and much less serious errors, and to real improvements in both the speed and the costs associated with new-product development (Gupta *et al.* 1987; Moenaert *et al.* 1992).

A second factor is a need for a market-driven process where customers and customer-related personnel become involved up-front as an important source of ideas and as a feedback mechanism throughout the new-product process. In fact, in the industrial sector, new-product development is increasingly occurring in close collaboration with customers to ensure that the product does indeed respond to their problems, systems, and needs. To get this market input, in addition to the project team that is responsible for a particular project, organizations often have a *new-product department*, whose function it is to generate new ideas, to get customer involvement, to ensure a successful interface between marketing and technical staff, and to monitor the stages of the new-product process and launch.

Thirdly, there is a need for *speed*. Speed yields competitive advantage, because being first with a unique idea is important. Speed yields higher profitability, because revenues are realized earlier and because being first-to-market leads to a larger market share. And speed means fewer surprises, because the market is less likely to have changed and competitors are less likely to have had the time to pre-empt or imitate your moves. Speeding up the new-product development process requires not only that firms organize around multifunctional teams (see above) but that they switch from using a sequential, stage-by-stage process—the process described in this chapter—to a *parallel process* where many of tasks are carried out concurrently and across functions. In other words, rather than running a relay race where one group sequentially passes on the baton to the next, the way the team operates is analogous to a rugby or football match where several members are running towards the goal—passing the ball back and forth—and simultaneously performing the different tasks (for example, designing the product, testing preliminary designs, developing the marketing plan, training the staff, testing launch approaches, and so on) that move the project forward to ultimate launch (Gehani 1992).

A fourth factor is that new products need a *project champion*—that is, an individual who is sold on the new-product idea, who takes ownership of the project, and who is charged with the responsibility of moving the project forward at a timely pace, particularly during periods of apparently insurmountable problems and/or low enthusiasm. A project champion is someone who is capable, empowered, and highly motivated to succeed. Early in the process, this person should probably be a more creative, inspiring type of leader, while more of a disciplinarian is typically called for during the later stages of the process (Crawford 1997).

Finally, there is a need for *senior management support* and involvement in new-product development. Top management has to be involved, not only up-front, in setting the new-product strategy and objectives of the firm, but also at the really critical assessment gates—such as pre-development and pre-launch evaluation—to ensure that all new products are actually in line with these long-term goals. But even more important is senior management's responsibility for creating an *innovative culture* within the firm, where both individualism and team effort are supported, where people are permitted to make mistakes, and where creativeness, risk-taking, and entrepreneurship are encouraged and rewarded.

8 New-service development

WHEN we speak about 'product' in marketing or in new-product development, we generally use the term generically, meaning goods *and/or* services. Often this makes sense, since much of what is true about developing and marketing physical goods also relates to services. Therefore, a great deal of what has been covered so far in this chapter—for example, the importance of having a formal new-product process, the need to develop and assess core benefit propositions prior to undertaking design, the value of input from potential customers and from a cross-functional team throughout the new-product process—is as critical for the successful development of new services as it is for manufactured goods. Indeed, research has borne this out. In a large Canadian study of new financial services, the primary factors that distinguished successes from failures were found to be largely similar to those that researchers had identified for new manufactured goods (Cooper and de Brentani 1991; Atuahene-Gima 1996).

Despite these similarities, however, we increasingly distinguish in marketing between goods and services. One important reason for this is that services make up an increasing part of most organizations' product portfolio. As was shown in Chapter 21 on marketing services, there are few 'pure' goods on the market and our entire economy is increasingly fuelled by the services sector. Another reason is that services *are* different from goods, and, by taking these differences into account, we can improve our performance in the marketplace. This too was an important finding in the major Canadian study of new service development; it showed that several of the factors that distinguish services from physical goods do impact or how organizations achieve new service success (de Brentani 1991; de Brentani and Ragot 1996). Service intangibility, for example, has the effect that the process used for designing services must be different, since pure services never take on physical form. Moreover, the fact that customers tend to be an integral part of the service production and delivery process (inseparability) means that firms have much less control over what is eventually launched on the market. These are just two examples of how some of the elements that distinguish services from physical goods can impact on new-product development in services (Easingwood 1986). Given the high cost and risk associated with new product failure, it makes sense to look in some depth at the issues that affect *new-service development*, and the impact of some of services' distinguishing features.

8.1 Impact of service intangibility

Services are primarily *intangible*, invisible entities that are not easily visualized or examined by customers prior to purchase. How does this distinguishing feature impact on the new-product process in services?

■ Because services create processes and experiences and often involve only limited up-front investments, they appear to be easy to develop and to modify. This often results in a new-product process that is quite haphazard, with firms introducing new services too quickly and leading to: *proliferation* of services, services that are *not differentiated* in any unique way, and *poor service design*, where little effort is committed to ensuring that the new service meets customer and functional specifications.

■ Intangible services are not patentable. This, together with ease of development, leads to faster imitation by competitors. As a result, developers often bypass the pre-launch testing phase, which can increase the risk of failure.

■ An idea for a new good eventually takes on physical form and this can be extremely useful in evaluating its functional, customer, and profit potential. New service ideas, in contrast, *remain conceptual* throughout the new-product development process, which means that uncertainty about the exact nature of the service and, therefore, its risk of failure remain high. To overcome this problem, companies should undertake detailed service *blueprinting*, or service mapping, during the design stage as a way of identifying and quantifying all component parts, distinguishing features, processes, and possible fail points (Shostack 1984).

■ Potential customers have greater difficulty visualizing new services, particularly those that are highly innovative and new-to-the-world, and in comparing newly launched competitive services. Therefore, when launching a new service, the firm must help clients to conceptualize and evaluate it by creating a strong *service image* and by linking its *corporate reputation* to the new service offering (i.e. the company *is* the service) (de Brentani and Ragot 1996). Moreover, by incorporating in the launch programme some form of *tangible evidence* (physical clues that describe the new service), the service can be made less abstract and less difficult to perceive and evaluate. For example, in 1998 the Fidelity Investment Corporation introduced a new mutual fund that was to invest in Canada's resource-based industries; it was called 'True North' and used a launch brochure featuring pictures of mountain ranges, fresh water, and unspoiled natural habitats as physical clues about its performance potential.

8.2 Effect of simultaneity

Because production and consumption in services occur more or less *simultaneously*, customer satisfaction and, therefore, ultimately the success of any new service are as much linked to its outcome (what the customer ends up with) as to the process by which it is produced, delivered, and consumed. What does this mean for new-service development?

■ When planning and designing a new service, both the outcome and the *service experience* become integral parts of the new service offering. Because developers must focus on both of these elements, this can lead to a new-service development process that is *more complex* and, therefore, more prone to error and to new-service failure. On the other hand, focus on both the service outcome and the customer experience offers marketers substantially greater potential for identifying attractive ideas for new services and for differentiating the offering from competitors.

■ *Customer involvement* is critical at each stage of the new-product process: that is, during idea generation, where complaints or needs about the service process often represent a rich pool of ideas for new services; during concept evaluation, where elements of the production/delivery process may embody core benefits or key differentiating features of the service; during service design, in order to test blueprints of alternate service processes (i.e. service prototypes); and during pre-launch testing, in order to test the actual production–delivery–consumption system under real-life conditions. In fact, in *industrial* services, because customers frequently play such an integral role in producing the service—for example, an executive training seminar—they often become close collaborators throughout the entire development process (de Brentani and Ragot 1996).

■ As with physical goods, the involvement of a cross-functional team from start to finish is essential. But, for services, of particular importance is a good interface between IT or *systems specialists* and *front-line personnel* whose often very different perceptions of processes and of customers are essential input for really creative, yet customer satisfying, solutions. All too often companies forget to include the front-line people who are closest to the market and who potentially have the greatest insights about what leads to customer satisfaction (de Brentani 1989; Easingwood and Storey 1993).

■ The interaction between client and service firm during service delivery puts a special onus on the front line in ensuring the success of a new-service launch. Front-line personnel need not only know the characteristics and features of the new service, but also be motivated to promote it to clients. Too often, front-line personnel view another service offering as simply added workload. Thus, a new-service launch programme requires both external and *internal marketing*. In other words, the launch programme must be aimed both at the potential client and at the personnel who will be responsible for delivering the new service offering.

8.3 Impact of service variability

Another important distinguishing feature is that services are *variable*, or heterogeneous, since, each time services are produced and consumed, the process, the outcome, and/or the customer experience are likely to vary. The degree of heterogeneity depends on whether the service is people or equipment based, the extent to which the company controls the variation in the service process, and what role the customer plays in producing/consuming the service. Service variability impacts on new-service development in several ways:

■ Firms can direct their new-service development efforts towards making services more or less heterogeneous (Shostack 1987). Especially with the rapid advancements in IT and computer technology, many new services are becoming more highly *standardized*. For example, the courier industry has radically reduced inconsistency and customer uncertainty by introducing mailing/shipping services that offer 100 per cent tracking (to determine exactly where the item is) and guaranteed on-time delivery. But standardization is not always appropriate. In many cases—particularly in business-to-business services—what makes a new service successful is that it closely meets the specific requirements of the customer (de Brentani 1995). This calls for service *customization*, something that is done much more easily, and at a much lower cost, for services than for physical goods precisely because heterogeneity is integral to services. Therefore, a good approach to take during idea generation is deliberately to focus on both standardization and customization as potential sources of new-service ideas. Interestingly, the increasing power of computer technology is permitting both more standardized (i.e. highly consistent) and more customized (i.e. customer-specific packages) services at very low costs.

■ Variability also plays a role during the design phase of the new-service development process. Clearly, much of the effort when *blueprinting* the potential new service goes into planning and controlling for the level of variation in the service outcome(s) and at various points in the service delivery process (for example, what degree of personalization to offer, extent of waiting time required, and so on) (Shostack 1984). This permits a much greater level of fine-tuning the new service both to customer needs and to provider resources, since different levels of service heterogeneity can be planned for different market segments and for different levels of provider capacity. In fact, the design stage in the new-service development process can overlap market testing by getting customer feedback to different 'blueprints'.

■ The variability and simultaneity factors, together, can have an important effect on reducing the cost and the risk of failure during new-service launch. By carefully tracking performance, and by training and empowering the front-line personnel to identify and respond to customer reactions, new services that do not fully perform as expected (for example, production bottlenecks, customer dissatisfaction or misunderstanding) can often be 'recovered' relatively easily even after the launch. In the case of manufactured goods, a newly launched product that has a flaw or does not meet customer requirements is usually impossible or certainly very costly to redeem (there are long delays, costly recalls, unsold inventory). In services, in contrast, problems or malfunctions are usually more obvious and quicker to recognize (because of simultaneity), and, because the service can be adjusted in much less time (heterogeneity), *service recovery* is a key element in the launch plan of a new service (Hart *et al.* 1990). This permits market testing and commercialization to be carried out simultaneously.

■ Two additional characteristics that distinguish services and that can impact a new-service development are service *perishability* and service *specialization*. Both factors affect the idea-generation phase to the extent that they point in certain directions for new-service ideas.

■ Because the demand for services often varies and since services cannot be produced to inventory (perishability), this creates overcapacity problems during purchase lulls, while potentially strapping the organization to capacity when demand is high. Firms often respond to this problem by looking for new-service ideas that are highly synergistic with *existing facilities* and resources (for the low demand periods) and/or that do a better job in accommodating peak-time demand with *essential-task* type of services (Berry 1980). Some large accounting firms, for example, have introduced financial consulting services in order to make use of some of their expert capacity, which is at a low usage level during some periods; during periods of high usage, such as the tax season, they often substitute essential task services for some of their regular accounting services.

■ Many services, both business and consumer, are of a professional nature, where clients look for and service providers attempt to deliver highly *specialized expertise* (for example, lawyers, planning consultants). This often has a limiting effect on what types of new services the firm can offer. For example, a recruitment firm specializing in attracting CEOs will find it difficult to expand its service line (for example, to middle managers or clerical staff), since this could negatively impact on the reputation that has been the basis for its success. In other words, for professional service providers, synergy with the firm's specialization and reputation is a key criterion when generating and screening new-service ideas (de Brentani and Ragot 1996).

9 Summary and the future

NEW-PRODUCT and new-service development is an essential concern for ensuring the success, indeed the continued viability, of firms. Meeting customers' continually expanding and changing requirements, keeping up with or surpassing competition, responding to advancements in technology, and adjusting to the shortening product life cycle all require that firms focus on the creation of new products and services as an integral and essential element of their corporate and marketing strategy. Most of the issues discussed in this chapter will be relevant in the future. Nevertheless, trends suggest that certain issues will be of particular significance in the future. These include the following.

■ Increasingly, firms must use *both* a proactive and reactive approach to new product development. As competition increases—because of the globalization of markets and firms, and the deregulation of entire industry sectors such as telecommunications and financial services—companies must not only try to be one step ahead of their rivals, but also be constantly aware of and respond to the creative solutions brought to the market by entirely new competitors.

■ The product life cycle will continue to shorten even in what may be considered mature or low-technology fields. In particular, the rate at which certain technologies—for example, information and computer technology—are advancing will serve to open all new-product fields to the onslaught of creative new-product development. Consider, for example, the 'virtual bank', which has been made possible through a combination of electronic, communications, computer, information, and Internet technologies. A much shorter product life will lead to several outcomes: companies will have even less time in which to recoup new-product development investments; even greater efforts will be required to speed up the new-product development process (see Insert); and attempts to improve, rejuvenate, and replace marketed products must be continual. Moreover, despite the efforts on the part of firms to improve the probability of new-product success—through better processes, market orientation, and cross-functional organizations—the rate of failure will also continue to appreciate because of increases in the required speed of development (leading to greater potential for error) and in environmental changes (leading to greater uncertainty).

■ In the future, when we speak of new-*product* development, more and more we will mean new-*service* development. Not only is our economy becoming more service oriented, but there are few products that do not have an important service component. This is of particular relevance in the industrial market and can be expected to increase. Hence, understanding how services differ from physical goods and how this impacts on new-service development will be essential.

■ Collaboration between firms—between competitors, producer–client, channel members, and so on—is likely to increase when it comes to new-product or new-service development. As markets become more global, and technologies more complex and costly to harness (frequently involving highly different but converging technologies), companies will increasingly collaborate with one another in order to access the knowledge, skills, and resources of the partner firms; increase the speed of product development; and reduce the likelihood of failure. Collaborating with customers in the business-to-business sector will be particularly important as a way to reduce risk by developing new products and services that more closely respond to customer needs and that are at the cutting edge of user trends.

Further reading

Cooper, R. G. (1996), 'Overhauling the New Product Process?', *Industrial Marketing Management*, 25/5: 465–82.

de Brentani, U. (1991), 'Success Factors in Developing New Business Services', *European Journal of Marketing*, 25/2 (Mar.–Apr.), 93–103.

de Brentani, U., and Ragot, E. (1996), 'Developing New Business-to-Business Professional Services: What Factors Impact Performance?', *Industrial Marketing Management*, 25/6 (Nov.), 517–30.

Hart, C. W. L., Heskett, J. L., and Sasser, W. E. Jr. (1990), 'The Profitable Art of Service Recovery', *Harvard Business Review*, 68/4 (July–Aug.), 148–56.

Hutlink, E. J., Griffin, A., and Hart, S. (1997), 'Industrial New Product Launch Strategies and Product Development Performance', *Journal of Product Innovation Management*, 14: 243–57.

Faster to market

Toyota's 1996 Annual Report stated that it could now bring a vehicle to market eighteen months after approving the design, compared with an average of twenty-seven months two years previously.

Moenaert, R. K., Deschoolmeester, D., De Meyer, A., and Souder, W. E. (1992), 'Information Styles of Marketing and R&G Personnel during Technological Innovation Projects', *R&D Management*, 22/1 (Jan.), 21–39.

Montoya-Weiss, M. M., and Calantone, R. (1994), 'Determinants of New Product Performance: A Review and Meta-Analysis', *Journal of Product Innovation Management*, 11/5 (Nov.), 397–417.

Discussion questions

1 Compare the new-product development process that is likely to be used for a pioneering venture involving a new-to-the-world product with that of a me-too product that is in the maturity stage of the product life cycle. For each stage of the new-product development process, consider the types of effort required, and the problems and risks involved.

2 The 'We-Imitate-You' Company has a straightforward new-product strategy. It carefully monitors its key competitors, identifies successful new-product launches, and then quickly copies these. Discuss why a firm might adopt such a philosophy. Critically evaluate this approach, taking into account potentially positive and negative as well as short- and long-term effects on the firm.

3 Pundits insist that involving a cross-functional team in all phases of the new-product development process substantially increases the likelihood of new-product success. What specific functional areas should compromise such a team and what input is each likely to have during the stages of the new-product development process?

4 Recently the president of one very successful high-tech company stated that the key to developing really successful, creative, new products is to keep the company's marketing personnel away from the R&D people. Suggest reasons why this might be true. How might such an attitude be justified in the light of a statement calling for a cross-functional team throughout the new-product development process?

5 Identify a recent new-service introduction and discuss how the four factors that distinguish services from physical goods are likely to have impacted on the stages of the new-product development process. Choose different types of new services—i.e. new-to-the-world, high tech service; service adaptation or modification; consumer versus industrial service—in order to obtain insights during these discussions.

6 Describe an example of an organization that primarily uses a 'proactive' new-product strategy; do the same for a 'reactive' strategy. Using examples, under what conditions would it make sense for a firm to use both strategies in its overall new-product approach?

7 Using an example of a recent new-product introduction (or one described in a case), attempt to link as many of the 'key' success and/or 'failure' factors described in the chapter to explain the performance of this new product/service.

8 Choose a firm (handled in a case/project) and, based on its overall strategy, objectives, and resources, choose a set of five 'culling' criteria that its screening committee should probably use during the pre-screening (culling) stage of the new-product process.

9 What might account for the fact that, even though the test market results for a given new product predicted an excellent outcome, the results of the actual launch were much less positive?

Mini Case
Eldonmat plc—a new coating
Keith Blois

Eldonmat plc specializes in the manufacturing of coatings for use in specialized industrial applications and its coatings are used in a wide range of applications. It had recently, in response to an approach from Cryptec, developed a new coating. In part of its production process Cryptec uses a machine that requires a coating to be applied to particular moving parts. The coating material currently utilized was causing problems and tended to 'lift off' the surface to which it was applied. When this happened, unless the machine was stopped almost immediately, it was often damaged. Unfortunately the location of these coated surfaces in the machine made regular inspection a problem. Furthermore, as there seemed to be no pattern to this 'lifting off', even regular inspections did not guarantee that the possibility of a failure would be identified.

In response to Cryptec drawing its attention to this particular difficulty, Eldonmat had evolved a new coating material, Corflan. The type of machine that Cryptec was using was manufactured by about five firms and was also used in a wide range of industries, so the potential market for this new material appeared to be quite substantial.

Eldonmat found that it was able to apply Corflan to one of Cryptec's machines in trials conducted by its R&D laboratory; but when it tried to develop an application procedure that could be used under normal production conditions, all sorts of difficulties arose. For example, the temperature of the material to be coated was quite critical to the effective application of Corflan. In fact, if the temperature was not kept to within a few degrees of a specified level, Corflan was at least as likely to lift off as the coating currently used in that application.

In addition, there was the problem that the equipment used to apply the existing coating could not handle Corflan. Eldonmat therefore approached Murphy, one of the firms that currently manufactured the coating applicators, and asked it to manufacture an applicator to handle Corflan. Murphy was not overenthusiastic about this request, as it had heard rumours that Corflan was not working well in one of the machines that Cryptec had allowed Eldonmat to try the new coating on. Eldonmat was convinced that this was a rumour based on the result of one of its early trials, when, at that stage in the Corflan's development, it had been unaware that the success of the application was very sensitive to the temperature of the material being coated. Eventually the only way Eldonmat could get Murphy to manufacture the new applicator was to agree to guarantee that, if fewer than 100 were sold in the first year, it would recompense Murphy for the costs incurred.

While it had been negotiating with Murphy, Eldonmat's salesforce had been approaching the manufacturers of the machinery that needed coating to explain to them the advantages that the new coating offered to their customers. The level of interest shown by the manufacturers was initially quite high, as they regularly received complaints, particularly from any new users of their machines who had had 'lift-off' problems. It seemed that those of their customers who had owned such machines before had come to accept that this surface coating was problematical and tried to cope by inspecting the relevant parts of the machinery more frequently. However, this additional inspection was clearly a cost to these firms and even regular inspections sometimes failed to note the first signs of lift-off.

During the twelve months that it took Murphy to complete the development of and make the first production batch of the new applicator, Eldonmat had been able to persuade one of the machinery manufacturers to experiment, using a prototype applicator, with the use of Corflan. It had done this and sold two machines with Corflan on them. The coating on one of the two machines had very quickly developed problems and, even more unfortunately, caused substantial damage to the machine before the problem had been identified. However, the other machine's performance had been completely satisfactory and, indeed, seemed to demonstrate an improved performance over that achieved before Corflan had been used.

Now, nearly four years after the initial formulation of Corflan, Eldonmat heard that the machinery manufacturers' sales staff were advising any customers who asked them about Corflan that it was an unreliable material.

Discussion question

Evaluate the effectiveness of Eldonmat's development of Corflan and the market for Corflan.

Chapter 25
Marketing in Small Firms

David Carson

Objectives

The objectives of this chapter are:

1 to identify the differences between small firms and large companies, and to consider how they impact upon decision-making, particularly with regards to resources, expertise, and market impact;

2 to discuss the characteristics of small-firm marketing decision-making and how they are different to conventional large company marketing;

3 to understand the critical role of entrepreneurial behaviour by reviewing closely linked entrepreneurial and marketing characteristics and assessing their impact on small-firms marketing;

4 to propose approaches to market research, customer focus, selling, delivery, and pricing that are appropriate for small firms.

1 Introduction

THIS chapter begins with a consideration of the *differences* between small firms and large companies, such as size (obviously), organization structures, and functional frameworks. These issues are considered in terms of how they impact upon decision-making, particularly with regards to resources, expertise, and market impact.

The chapter then discusses the *characteristics* of small-firm marketing decision-making and how they are different from conventional large-company marketing. An entrepreneurial influence is considered by reviewing closely linked entrepreneurial and marketing characteristics and assessing their impact on small-firm marketing.

Inherent influences on marketing are discussed, such as costs and budgets, industry infrastructures, experiential knowledge possessed and used by the small-firm owner manager, and the importance of market knowledge. Further discussion shows how these inherent influences impact upon small-firm marketing. Examples of small-firm marketing are presented as illustrations and as contrasts to much of the conventional marketing theories presented in the textbook literature. These examples consider an export development approach that outflanks the known 'barriers' to developing international markets. Also included are 'alternative' approaches to market research, customer focus, selling, delivery, and pricing. Finally, some 'solutions' are offered for improving the efficiency and sufficiency of small-firm marketing, focusing on the importance of marketing 'competencies' and 'networking' as the basis of improving marketing efficiency, overcoming deficiencies and outlining 'quality' improvements in small-firm marketing decision making.

Throughout the chapter, the term 'small firm' will be taken to encompass SME (small to medium-sized enterprise), and thus to mean anything from a self-employed individual to a company with several hundred employees but that still behaves more like a small enterprise than a large corporation. Similarly, the terms entrepreneur, entrepreneurial, and owner manager are considered as meaning largely the same in the context of marketing decision-making in small firms.

The author would like to thank Dr A. Gilmore, D. Cummins, and A. O'Donnell, University of Ulster, for their assistance.

2 Differences between small firms and large companies

2.1 Management and marketing decision-making in large companies

In large organizations decision-making is made within a highly structured and ordered framework. Decision-making has a clear hierarchy depending upon the scope and focus of a decision. There are clear boundaries of responsibility whereby decisions can be taken. In such a decision-making structure there will be close coordination and cooperation between the various decision-making domains. In addition, because of the diversity of decision-making and the number of decision-makers, time scales for decision-making are likely to be long. This inevitably introduces a planning element in large-company decision-making.

These are just a few of the characteristics of large-company decision-making, but they serve to highlight the context in which decisions are made, and indeed, the essence of such decision-making. Typical managerial tasks are based upon strong theoretical foundations. For example, there are well-founded managerial activities that have been developed and internalized in line with organizational structures and standard practices in terms of organizing for business. Thus managers work to known and practised procedures, using appropriate and accepted analysis and evaluation criteria. Decision-making processes are based on order and form, and customs and practice. Leadership is often derived from hierarchical power and authority. From this it can clearly be deduced that management decision-making is a distinct discipline.

Much of the literature surrounding decision-making in marketing is derived from the management literature in its style and frameworks. Naturally, marketing management—indeed, the function of marketing—will adhere to conventional management principles and structures. In general, conventional marketing management decision-making is inherently formal, sequential, structured, and disciplined. It is also systems oriented and considers issues in both short- and long-term time scales.

When considering the literature in relation to marketing motivations, there is a general consensus that the customer is the primary motivator for much of marketing. And, indeed, in just about every conventional marketing textbook, the literature is clear in stating that marketing should have a customer focus and that marketers should strive to create customer satisfaction and well-being. Marketers are expected to meet customer desires and expectations and to develop customer relations through good customer service. So marketing decision-making in large companies will have the clear focus of customer orientation as a primary motivator and will address this focus through established and structured frameworks derived from the management discipline.

2.2 Marketing/entrepreneurial decision-making in small firms

Small-firm decision-making processes are different from those of large companies. Most decisions originate with and flow through the entrepreneur or owner manager, who is likely to be involved in all aspects of his or her firm's activities. As the direction and control of the enterprise rest with this one individual, it is this individual's personality and style that shape the nature of decision-making. The entrepreneurial owner manager does not need structures and frameworks, but instead will intuitively coordinate and perform decision-making in a way that is 'natural' to him or her. Whilst much of what has been stated can be intuitively accepted, is there evidence to corroborate such a contention?

☞ 'In any organization, but clearly particularly in large ones, there is a difficulty in ensuring that the various parts of the organization know what the others are doing.' (Chapter 17, p. 414)

There is a substantial literature from the last thirty years or so of the twentieth century that attempted to define entrepreneurs and entrepreneurship in terms of inherent characteristics (Timmons 1978; Meredith et al. 1982). Definitional attempts stemmed from an intuitive perception that entrepreneurs are different in some way from managers, or at least perform tasks in such a way that distinguishes them from managers.

Obviously entrepreneurs must take decisions beyond a functional domain and their decisions involve the firm's survival and well-being as a whole. It is this dimension that dictates elements of entrepreneurship behaviour as opposed to simply taking decisions within known and defined frameworks and operational tasks.

Therefore, the conventional literature descriptions of entrepreneurs and entrepreneurship can be characterized by aspects such as follows:

■ *risk-taking*—in that they must take risks in order to be competitive or to grow the business;

■ *opportunistic*—in terms of seeking and identifying opportunities for future survival and success;

■ *innovative/creative*—because they need to do things differently in order to differentiate themselves from competitors or to develop something new;

■ *adaptive and change oriented*—because they are small and flexible and must react to and anticipate changes in their environment;

■ *visionary*—because they, more than most, need to see into the future;

■ *individualistic*—because they are constantly thinking about issues that are inherently personal, especially if it is their own business.

The literature on the motivations for entrepreneurs and entrepreneurship largely agrees that such individuals have strong motivations for being in business (Arens 1990; Osborne 1995). Indeed, such motivations are often founded in a need for growth. However, there are a number of widely recognized motivations for being in business. For example:

■ *independence*—such individuals prefer to be their own boss and like the freedom of taking their own decisions;

■ *personal satisfaction*—derived from the above, such individuals glean satisfaction from doing business for themselves and the challenges that this presents;

■ *employee well-being*—entrepreneurs are concerned with the well-being of their employees in an almost paternal sense;

■ *satisfying customers*—entrepreneurs are concerned with satisfying customers and devote considerable effort into ensuring that their customers get good service; they might often perceive this as part of their competitive advantage;

■ *integrity, morality, ethics*—such individuals perceive themselves as possessing all of these characteristics when doing business.

☞ '. . . successful entrepreneurs an traders have always accepted as a fundamental truth the fact that creating customer satisfaction is the only way to long-term business success.' (Chapter 2, p. 27)

There are, of course, many other characteristics and motivations describing entrepreneurs, but these lists are sufficient to make the point that entrepreneurs and entrepreneurship are distinguished as being 'different' by these and other characteristics. It must, of course, also be acknowledged that there are significant similarities between entrepreneurs and managers in performing tasks and it is easy to find a few, such as that both are task oriented, both are judgemental, both are directive, both are cost control conscious, and so on. However, it is the *differences* that are most striking. Hisrich and Peters (1995) offer a meaningful discussion of the differences between entrepreneurs and managers (Box 25.1). In considering, Hisrich and Peters, it is reasonable to deduce that, on a continuum of differences to similarities, there is a bias towards differences in characteristics in terms of a general style and emphasis in decision-making. If this is so, then there are significant implications for understanding the essence of small-firm marketing decision-making.

3 Entrepreneurship and marketing practice in small firms

3.1 Entrepreneurs in practice in small firms

There is no clear definition of who the entrepreneur is. Indeed, it can be argued that little is known about entrepreneurs, even though interest and publications on the subject abound. The literature on entrepreneurship generally is characterized by its diversity of findings and arguments. Manifold discussions have inspired much debate and created much confusion and, most writers

Box 25.1 **Differences between entrepreneurs' and managers' decision-making**

ENTREPRENEUR CHARACTERISTICS

- Perception of opportunity
- Commitment: revolutionary, with short duration
- Directive with colleagues
- Lacks control over environment—risk-taker
- Management: flat, with multiple informal networks
- Challenge to authority

MANAGER CHARACTERISTICS

- Need to control resources
- Commitment: evolutionary, with long duration
- Negotiates with colleagues
- Seeks control over environment—risk-reducer
- Management: works to budgeting and formal planning systems
- Seeks power, status, authority, and responsibility

Source: Hisrich and Peters (1995: 34–7).

would agree, have not advanced any specific generic definitions of the entrepreneur. Cunningham and Lischevan (1991), in seeking to dispel some of the confusion, present their interpretation of the literature in six schools of thought; the great person, the psychological, the classical, the management, the leadership, and the intrepreneurial schools of entrepreneurship. Key characteristics that emerge from this are that the entrepreneur is an agent for innovation and change, a calculating risk-taker, a 'goal-setter' and 'goal-getter', who, though domineering in management style, is inspirational in terms of his or her influence on associates. In addition to flexibility and creativity, vision is identified as being a key characteristic. As Kirzner (1973) states, 'The Entrepreneur perceives what others have not seen and acts upon that perception. The market is constantly sending signals to those alert enough to perceive them. The Entrepreneur is one who sees the future as no-one sees it.'

The entrepreneur values his or her personal networks and business freedom and is constantly on the look-out for opportunities to create wealth. This person has, it is argued, inborn character traits that differentiate him or her from other groups of individuals.

Whilst all of the above may indeed be important motivations for entrepreneurs, it must be recognized that there are several other immensely strong motivations that will drive entrepreneurs. There is a long-held view, shared by some academics and most practitioners, that entrepreneurs' primary motivation is 'profit'—a view supported here. Entrepreneurs are in business to make money; they strive to achieve security through having enough money to do business and to make profit. Allied to this motivation is a constant constraint and therefore concern surrounding lack of cash and cash flow.

If such a notion is accepted, then it is interesting to compare this primary 'in-practice' motivation with some of the literature characteristics and motivations supposedly possessed by entrepreneurs. For example:

- *Innovative/creative.* In practice, entrepreneurs will display these characteristics only if they have a need for new sources of money. They will often take on new work in the hope of success, and if this is forthcoming, then all is well; if not, then innovation stops.

- *Opportunistic.* In practice, entrepreneurs will display this characteristic in similar circumstances to the above, but only until a barrier occurs and risk is involved.

- *Risk-taker.* In practice, again, entrepreneurs will display this characteristic in similar circumstances to the above, but will take risks only until money is threatened.

- *Change oriented.* In practice, entrepreneurs display this characteristic only because the business is likely to be small, and, as it will always have to grow, change is unavoidable.

It can be argued that, when it comes to understanding good marketing practice by entrepreneurs, much more sensitivity to the unique characteristics of the entrepreneur is required (see Insert). Tried and tested perceptions, refined in a

What is an entrepreneur?

Typically, entrepreneurs are people who own and control their own enterprises. They are almost always focused upon the well-being, survival, and development of their enterprises. Their everyday activities are centred around doing business and simply running their enterprise.

If entrepreneurs are seen outside the premises of their enterprise, it is likely to be for a reason that concerns or impacts upon the enterprise. Thus, most typically, they will be seen with customers or potential customers. If they are seen at an 'event', it is likely that they are there in order to assess the threat or opportunity presented by the event. Even if they have been invited as 'all-expenses-paid' guests to an event, they are likely to take up such an invitation only if they see some potential gain as a result of attending.

Whilst entrepreneurs will display a wide range of traits and characteristics, in essence they are clever, highly focused, self-centred individuals whose primary concern is the well-being and development of their own enterprise.

big business environment, will not do. Characteristics in which small firms are uniquely different can be summarized as negative attitudes to marketing; the perception of marketing as a cost; distribution and selling treated as uncontrollable problems; and, possibly more significant, the belief that each case is so specific that it cannot be treated with general rules.

A definition of small-firm marketing characteristics would typically acknowledge limited resources, lack of specialist expertise, and limited impact on the market place' (Carson 1990). The need for the small-firm owner to seek a strategy for growth that is sensitive to his or her unique characteristics and circumstances is apparent. Some such 'alternative' approaches that take cognizance of the unique character of the small firm and of the entrepreneur are presented later in this chapter.

3.2 Marketing in practice in small firms

The literature descriptions of marketing decision-making, alluded to earlier, may not actually happen in practice. This notion is reinforced by a number of more recent studies. Greenley and

Bayus (1994) reviewed the results of several studies on the nature of marketing planning and found that the general tenor of the results was that few companies seem to adopt the prescriptions of marketing planning that are advocated in the literature. Piercy's (1990) studies also revealed that managers did not adhere to the textbook descriptions of 'rational' decision-making.

The views of Greenley and Bayus and of Piercy are reinforced by Carson's (1993) consideration of this issue in relation to marketing-decision-making in small firms. Various characteristics of marketing decision-making in practice can be identified. It is argued that much of marketing decision-making in practice resembles aspects of entrepreneurship. For example, small firm marketing decision-making in practice is:

- *simplistic and haphazard*—in that it is immediate and reactive to circumstances;
- *undisciplined and spontaneous*—perhaps because it is predominately intuitive;
- *unstructured*—mainly because of the above;
- *irrational*—partly because of the above and also because it is individualistic in nature;
- *short term*—because of all of the above (Carson 1993).

As with management and entrepreneurship characteristics, there is a bias towards differences with regard to marketing decision-making characteristics as depicted by the literature and that which happens in practice.

This divergence can be found also in the motivations for doing business. Marketers' primary motivation in practice is to gain increased sales and to make profit from increasing sales. This practical motivation is compounded by a marketer's greatest concern—that of declining sales and stronger competition. Of course, it can be argued that, by being customer focused, enterprises can achieve sales and profit even against strong competition. However, in reality, marketers will be customer focused *only* if this leads to sales increases and profits. The incompatibility between the theoretical literature and marketing in practice can be detected with regard to quality, price, and customer service in particular. Customers expect 'best' quality, whereas marketers will equate quality with profit; customers expect lowest prices, whereas marketers hope for higher prices. Consequently, good customer service and care often championed as having a customer focus may in fact provide a clandestine stimulation and exploitation of customers by marketers. These issues are revisited in more detail later in this chapter.

In this debate it is easy to appreciate that a significant commonality can be found between marketers and entrepreneurs, in that both have a primary focus on sales and money (cash), and the greatest concern of both is a decline in sales, which will result in a reduction in money, cash, and profits. Secondary to these factors will be a customer focus, although, in a public sense, the customer will always be championed as being most important to a company. That is to say, both entrepreneurs and marketers will extol the virtues of a customer focus and the importance of customer satisfaction when asked the question, 'What is the most important factor in your business?', but privately they will raise issues of cash and money, sales and profits, before concerning themselves with customer services and satisfaction.

From the discussion so far, it is clear that small-firm marketing decision-making is different from that which is depicted in conventional marketing literature. It has been argued here that not only is the conventional literature unhelpful to small firm owner managers, but also that there is a lack of true understanding of their behaviour and motivations. To underline this view, two brief illustrations are offered: one highlights the influence upon marketing decision-making of the industry in which a small firm exists; the other focuses on the difficulties and barriers faced by small firms in beginning to export and internationalize.

3.3 Industry norms

All enterprises exist within a market or industry. Such industries have evolved customs and practices over time to the point whereby they have actually established industry 'norms'. These customs and practices are known by the industry and the industry will expect that all business and trading conform to these customs and practices. Small firms in particular, because of their relative size, must comply with such industry norms, which will impact upon marketing in a variety of ways. For example, in the context of price, these customs and practices will be manifest as 'acceptable' and 'expected' mark-ups and margins. Such margins will be known, particularly where products have little differentiation. Each player in the supply chain will know 'who gets what' proportion of the overall price/cost structure. It is only when a new product or new service that has a high degree of differentiation is introduced that new cost structures can apply and these will quickly become established and set.

Similarly, the channels of distribution and the sequences and flows within these channels are invariably 'established'. All firms must conform to these set patterns, but small firms in particular have little other choice, simply because they do not have the resources to break away and do things differently. Also, customs and practice are often set, even dictated, by large competitors, whose influence is such that their way of doing business is the established norm for the whole industry.

3.4 Small firm exporting difficulties and barriers

Exporting is a crucial component of the well-being of any developed economy. Substantial government resources are devoted to encouraging exporting and much of this effort goes towards stimulating and helping small firms to export. However, it is recognized that it is difficult to get small firms to begin to export. Why should this be so? Box 25.2 considers some of the inherent issues behind a decision to begin exporting.

3.4.1 Influence of the entrepreneur

The owner manager in the small firm is the key decision-maker, who decides whether or not to internationalize his or her company's operations, to what extent to do so, and how best to exploit potential opportunities. The literature suggests that, for many small firms, the adoption and implementation of marketing are an innovation in themselves and that the decision to internationalize that marketing effort is no less entrepreneurial. The small-firm owner is encouraged by numerous influences to internationalize his or her company's activities, but, equally, the barriers to doing so are substantial and, for many firms, insurmountable.

The reasons for any company to consider exporting have been well researched in the literature and the key influences identified and listed. However, it is generally recognized that the key variable in small-business internationalization is the decision-maker of the firm. He or she is the one to decide starting, ending, and increasing

---

Box 25.2 Small-firm barriers to exporting

Why do small firms find it difficult to export? Some obvious reasons emerge when taking cognizance of small-firm and entrepreneur characteristics:

■ *Exporting is more expensive*: small firms have limited resources, therefore exporting costs can be prohibitive.

■ *Exporting needs longer-term gestation*: small firms are centred on short-term issues, which can often take precedence over longer-term export requirements.

■ *Exporting is relatively high risk*: small-firm entrepreneurs seek to reduce risk, therefore other activities will present a lower risk than exporting.

■ *Exporting involves many strange circumstances and uncertainties*: small-firm entrepreneurs prefer to know their market and business environment.

■ *SME entrepreneurs rely on business contacts and networks*: in exporting these are more difficult to find and establish in the short term.

■ *Engaging new export customers or export markets requires almost the same amount of time/energy/resources to develop every time*: small firms rely on additional sales at reduced costs and/or as a follow-on to existing business.

■ *Legal, political and trading regulations require additional or time-consuming resources*: small firms are unlikely to have these.

These aspects and many others serve as barriers to small-firm exporting.

---

international activities. He or she lays down the goals concerning exporting and determines the organizational commitment. A positive attitude to exporting, an aggressive and dynamic personality, flexibility and self-confidence, and clear entrepreneurial characteristics are often cited as being significant psychological factors distinguishing the potential exporter. Having broad multicultural horizons, competency in language, and being knowledgeable about export marketing practice come under the objective factors distinguishing the likely exporting company owner.

3.4.2 Motivations

It is suggested that the driving forces for either starting or exploiting export activities are that the firm wants to utilize and develop its resources in such a way that its short-run and/or long-run economic objectives are served. But to facilitate a fuller understanding of the nature of the decision to export as a particular internationalization strategy, export motives can be classified in a schematic form by distinguishing between internal and external and proactive and reactive dimensions of the process. The schema is reproduced in Fig. 25.1 as a classification of export development. Here it is sufficient to say that, from their research amongst over 650 Danish companies, Albaum and his colleagues identified a number of key motivating factors under each category, which had an influence on a company's

Figure 25.1 A classification of export motives

	INTERNAL	EXTERNAL
PROACTIVE	Managerial urge Growth and profit goals Marketing advantages Economies of scale Unique product/ technology competence	Foreign markets Change agents
REACTIVE	Risk diversification Extend sales of a seasonal product Excess capacity of resources	Unsolicited orders Small home market Stagnant or declining home market

decision to internationalize, amongst the most critical being growth and profit goals and risk diversification.

The entrepreneur is the key determinant of whether the operations of the small firm are internationalized and the desire for growth and profits appears to be the strongest prompt for wanting to do so. So what is to stop the small-firm owner from internationalizing his or her enterprise's activities?

3.4.3 **Difficulties**

There has been a great deal written in the literature about the difficulties that small firms have in *internationalizing* their commercial efforts. There is a varied mixture of agreement and disagreement as to what those difficulties are exactly, the circumstances when they prevail, and the impact they have on those internationalization efforts. The most frequently mentioned internal barriers to exporting are seen to be lack of information and problems with respect to capacity and distribution. External barriers appear to be perceived lack of demand from abroad, red tape, and the level of costs involved. Similarly, small-firm owner managers have listed the most serious problems in seeking to internationalize their activities as the level of risk, the complexity of procedures involved, and costs. Most significantly, lack of knowledge of export markets is especially important to small enterprises. Gathering knowledge about export markets is perceived by owner managers as costly, particularly in terms of the time required to gather it, interpret it, and make decisions on it. Information overload is quickly reached where the small-business owner will simply stop gathering the information and a decision to export will be either abandoned or confirmed on the basis of what he has got. But the quality of such decisions, made in circumstances of limited information and against a background of minimal margins for error, is bound to be suspect and a source of considerable stress and pressure for the small-firm owner. Such pressure forces the small-firm owner to focus on the immediate or short-term issues, where the risks and uncertainties are more controllable, and may discourage any long-term commitment to a planned approach to internationalizing the small firm's activities.

3.4.4 **Stages of internationalization**

The importance of the various problems facing the small-firm owner manager is a function of the export stage that the enterprise has reached. There is a general agreement in the literature that internationalization is best understood as a gradual process of several discernible steps. There is also a general agreement that exporting problems differ among the various stages of a firm's export development, which is mainly due to the issue that functions, practices, and managerial experiences vary accordingly at each stage. Of course, firm size is another important factor differentiating the nature and magnitude of exporting problems experienced. Internationalization has been divided into three phases: phase one suggesting an experimental involvement, phase two an active involvement, and phase three a more committed effort, where the company has become proactive in its internationalization activity. Bilkey and Tesar (1979) provide a more detailed framework for understanding the stages.

- *Stage one*: management is not interested in exporting, not even in filling an unsolicited order.
- *Stage two*: management would fill an unsolicited export order but is not interested in exploring the feasibility of exporting.
- *Stage three*: management is actively exploring the feasibility of exporting.
- *Stage four*: firm exports on an experimental basis to a psychologically close country.
- *Stage five*: firm now an experienced exporter to the psychologically close country.
- *Stage six*: management explores feasibility of exporting to additional countries that are psychologically further away.

3.4.5 **Short cuts**

Attempts to leapfrog these internationalization phases through joint ventures or 'piggy-backing' with larger, already internationalized, companies are seen by many writers as risky, particularly for the small firm in the very early stages of such activity when its lack of knowledge and experience places it at a decided disadvantage when negotiating contracts with larger more experienced partners. Small firms wanting to internationalize their activities may be unable to do so, because of what can be called a 'strategy gap', caused by a lack of resources generally but particularly by a lack of knowledge and networks. Many small-firm owners seek to bridge this gap by forming strategic alliances with larger companies. The risk, particularly in those early stages when the small-business owner lacks the knowledge and experience of international marketing, is one of losing control of its internationalization effort to larger, more experienced, and resource-richer partners.

The alternative approach is to go it alone, though lack of relevant knowledge and experience may make this avenue too troublesome and risky. The choice to adopt and implement one approach as opposed to the other depends on the small-firm owner's perception of the relative benefits of each, and this in turn will be a function of his or her level of experience in international business, knowledge of export marketing, and entrepreneurial character.

3.4.6 Overall barriers

All in all, exporting, particularly in the initial stages, is extremely difficult for small firms. To a small-firm owner manager the barriers to exporting are immense and indeed may be perceived as far outweighing the reasons and motivations for exporting. Conventional wisdom for developing export markets is in the main sound—that is, that a newly exporting firm should identify a suitable market and soundly research that market for potential customers. Once a foothold has been established, that market is potentially ripe for exploitation and development. Such an approach may have many trialists and some will succeed, it is, however, inappropriate for many more firms, as discussed earlier.

The reason for outlining the difficulties and barriers to export development by small firms is obvious. It is because of the huge importance exporting carries in the successful development of any economy and the recognition that much of the export development must stem from the small-firm sector. The emphasis on these barriers is designed to reinforce the need to ask such questions as: 'Is there another way to develop export markets?' 'What can be done to overcome the many barriers that many firms, particularly entrepreneurial-led firms, experience?' These questions are addressed later in this chapter as part of an alternative approach to exporting that is entirely compatible with small-firm characteristics.

4 Fundamental aspects of small-firm marketing

As noted above, one of the main barriers to exporting or indeed any market development is a lack of knowledge about an environment. On this aspect the marketing literature is clear: market knowledge is crucial to sound marketing decision-making. Of course, market knowledge is important, but the ability to interpret this knowledge in making sound marketing decisions is of equal if not more importance. How does a small-firm owner manager acquire such ability? What

are the inherent ingredients for sound marketing decision-making? What aspects are most important for SME marketing? It is argued here that there are two important aspects to sound SME marketing. These are the existence and use of personal-contact networks and the possession of fundamental marketing competencies. It is not the intention here to enter into a detailed description of either of these aspects, but to provide a brief summary description of each with regards to small-firm owner managers.

4.1 Personal-contact networks

With regards to personal-contact networks, it is sufficient to acknowledge that from an entrepreneur's perspective he or she is likely to be the focal person of a network of known individuals. These individuals will have a mutual appreciation and understanding of the entrepreneur's business and the relationships will be built on trust and effective communication (Aldrich and Zimmer 1986). The personal-contact network will, of course, have variations in terms of depth and breadth and most importantly purpose. For example, an entrepreneur's marketing network is likely to be made up of individuals from suppliers and competitors, professional bodies and business associates, as well as customers, friends, and acquaintances.

The importance of such a network to small-firm entrepreneurs is immense. Given the limitations of marketing resources inherent in small firms, it is the network that both helps to form and guide marketing decisions, but that is also the vehicle for performing marketing. The personal-contact network will be used by the entrepreneur owner manager to seek out sales opportunities and to glean actual sales on the back of wider information exchanges. The network will be used, often proactively but mainly intuitively, to create and maintain a high profile of the small firm within its market. The network will be expected to provide not just information, but actual sales enquiries and contacts.

☞ 'For example, small, high-technology, service firms seem to emphasize interaction and network marketing.' (Chapter 22, p. 523)

4.2 Marketing competencies

The importance of marketing competencies is not fully discussed in the literature and thus a little more time is taken here to explain this aspect. In management, and indeed business in general, a competency is both an attribute and a skill. There are many definitions of management competency. In a general sense, competencies can be described as underlying 'characteristics' combining knowledge, skills, and attributes important for job performance. In the context of management, skill implies an ability that can be developed, not necessarily inborn, and that is manifested in performance, not merely in potential (Carson *et al.* 1995*a*).

In understanding the term 'management competency' it is useful to review some of those management tasks and activities that require management characteristics in order to be performed. So, for example, a manager must be able to analyse and judge a circumstance in order to take a decision. Therefore, these aspects are indeed management competencies. Similarly, a manager must provide leadership, coordination, and motivation—again all management competencies. The list and range of such attributes (competencies) can be exhaustive. For example, a manager must have intelligence, foresight, and intuition and be a positive thinker; he or she must be able to communicate, possess vision and creativity, and be a lateral thinker. Undoubtedly, a manager must have knowledge and experience. These are only a few of the competencies that any manager, or for that matter business person, must possess in some form or other and that must be utilized in differing ways and with differing emphasis.

But if the above competencies are some of those that are required for any performance in management, which if any are more appropriate for marketing decision-making in small firms? The answer, no doubt, lies in the fact that all may be appropriate. However, it can be surmised that the characteristics and nature of marketing as a concept bring an inherent emphasis and requirement for certain competencies over others. For example, an SME marketer may require competencies of imagination and flair to add to creativity and vision. Similarly, a marketer may require specific selling skills coupled with resilience to add to communication competency. A marketer may need to be distinctly entrepreneurial in taking decisions and may also need numeracy in addition to analytical skills in dealing with sales and profits. What is clear here is that a marketer/entrepreneur must possess a spectrum of competencies that can be utilized and employed in a variety of ways. Of course, this spectrum does not consist of a list of unrelated components.

It is obvious from this discussion that marketing competencies are not possessed and indeed performed in isolation from other competencies. There is an inherent interrelationship between all competencies in a variety of ways. It is important to emphasize that a marketer/entrepreneur acknowledges such interrelationships by viewing competencies as inseparable. For example, the competency of knowledge alone will not achieve meaningful marketing performance. Equally, communication competency alone will be of little value without, for example, knowledge. Both of these competencies will be enhanced by experience and all will contribute to judgement ability. Together, these competencies, treated inseparably, will more likely achieve effective specific action.

Given that there are a wide variety of competencies, from a learning and education perspective it would be unrealistic to try to develop all such competencies. Is it possible to focus on a few competencies that might be deemed to be more appropriate for small-firm marketing? A core focal competency for marketing is deemed to be experiential knowledge. That is knowledge acquired through experience and developed as an accumulation of knowledge and experience built upon and from communication and judgement. Developed proactively, such experiential knowledge will allow effective specification to occur more rapidly than if competencies are viewed as isolated learning acquirements.

So far in this discussion, significant issues have been raised about the appropriateness of conventional marketing in the context of small firms. The rest of this chapter is devoted to outlining some alternative approaches to marketing that are deemed to be more appropriate for small firms. Inherent to all of the examples outlined below are the importance to small-firm marketing of personal-contact networks and marketing competencies. First, it is contended that one area in particular can benefit from the issues raised in this discussion—that is, in the export development of small firms. This issue is of particular importance because of the contribution that small-firm exporting can make to overall regional development in an economy. Following this example, further 'alternative' marketing approaches consider market research, customer focus, selling, distribution, and pricing. Finally, some criteria for analysing small-firm marketing performance are offered as an evaluation and assessment of sound marketing for small firms.

5 'Alternative' marketing for small firms

5.1 Alternative marketing 1: export marketing

The alternative approach to developing exporting offered here is designed to appeal to the entrepreneurial instincts of the small owner-managed firm that has never before exported but that may have been trading in a small-market niche within its home market.

The approach is based on the proposition that entrepreneurally led small firms can best develop export markets by first importing products into their home domestic market and, once having established a relationship with a foreign supplier, then beginning to use this supplier's network for exporting products. The fundamental foundations of this theoretical proposition stem from the following.

- *Local knowledge.* An entrepreneur has an intimate knowledge of the local home market. The entrepreneur knows the wants and needs of his or her market, the type of products that are most in demand, and has an intuitive feel for new potential products.

- *Differentiation of established products.* Consumers in today's developed economies know what they want, particularly in relation to standard everyday regular purchases such as basic food items or similar domestic products. Retailers, of course, pander to this comfort purchasing pattern by standardizing products and emphasizing strong brands. Thus, consumers are not overly receptive to entirely new products. They are, however, often curiously attracted to new variations of products they can easily recognize—that is, products that are differentiated through packaging or origin.

- Contact networks. Entrepreneurs will be more comfortable doing business with personal contacts with whom they have developed a good relationship. Such networks are strong in both buying-from and selling-to situations.

- Big-company–small-firm interfaces. Small firms are just as likely to do business with large companies as they do with other small firms. Such relationships can be one of either buying from or selling to, or even both, but in the initial stages the former may be preferred.

These fundamental foundations are more strongly biased, initially, towards *importing* than exporting. It might be argued that there is still a fundamental barrier in establishing the initial contact, but it is immeasurably easier to establish a contact when seeking to purchase than when trying to sell.

Having established a 'tentative' supplier contact, the entrepreneur can use his or her local knowledge to assess the potential of the supplier's products as appropriately differentiated but still easily recognizable products. The entrepreneur can now use his or her selling skills in developing the 'new' products in the local market. During this time the relationship between the entrepreneur and the supplier company personnel is growing and cementing. Both parties may make visits to each other's establishments as a natural progression of the trading relationship. It is during these visits that opportunities will arise for introducing the entrepreneur's products to the supplier. The supplier can be encouraged to 'introduce' the product to some of his or her own personal contacts in the 'foreign' market on the basis that they might be interested.

Thus the network begins to widen and new contacts are made. Most importantly the entrepreneur has begun to export in the most natural way possible—one that is wholly compatible with his or her inherent characteristics. The original supplier company is able to widen the contact network, or the entrepreneur is able to do so, as is the new buyer contact once exporting has begun.

The benefits for all parties in this alternative export development approach are clear. The entrepreneur utilizes a new and differentiated source of supply and gains additional sales in the local home market. The foreign supplier establishes a beachhead in a new market. Eventually the entrepreneur has the opportunity to begin exporting though the mechanism of the personal-contact network established as a result of the importing activities. The new foreign buyer, if different from the original supplier, is assured by the recommendation of a fellow countryman that the entrepreneur is trustworthy.

5.2 **Alternative marketing 2: customer versus profit orientation**

Textbook marketing theory in relation to the customer has acquired the status of a *missionary doctrine*. That is, the theoretical emphasis is on the customer as the *central focus* of all marketing activity; the zealous emphasis is on meeting customer wants and needs, anticipating these wants and needs in order to satisfy and meet customer expectations, and adapting to the flow of customers' changing desires. In adhering to this theory marketing educators have *indoctrinated* students with a generation of textbook messages built upon the 'missionary doctrine'. The literature has presented the customer as an idol: his or her every desire must be met and views sought before taking any decisions. The literature continues to compound and reinforce this focus by, for example, the 'new' philosophies of relationship marketing based on customer services and customer care.

It is contended here that there may be a dichotomy between marketing theory as presented by the literature and that which is practised by practitioners. This dichotomy has long been rec-

ognized by educators working with entrepreneurs and small-business owner managers. The central focus of marketing theory (the customer) is incompatible with the central focus of the marketing practitioner, which is, albeit implicit rather explicit, that of profit. Both the customer and the marketing practitioner have different agendas and objectives and more often these are incompatible. For example, the consumer will diligently seek to satisfy his or her own expectations and demands when making a purchase, whilst, on the other hand, a company will seek to make profits from the exchange that will serve to satisfy shareholder return on investment and employee salary increases. It might be expected that some compromise between these divergent objectives will prevail (see Fig. 25.2). What is the implication of this for marketing theory? An alternative approach to conventional customer orientation marketing might be to accept a new 'alternative philosophy', as presented, in Box 25.4.

Consider how such an alternative philosophy might appear in relation to two important and integral dimensions of marketing—quality and price. Generally, it can be assumed that con-

---

Box 25.3 **Two contrasting scenarios, one representing a customer focus and the other a sales/profit focus, as an illustration of customer versus sales/profit orientation**

Scenario One: A Customer Focus

A team talk led by a sales/marketing manager who has totally accepted the marketing philosophy and advocates that the customer is the central focus of the company's activities.

'OK, we are here to plan our campaign for the next three months. Our customers have given us a clear indication as to their preferences. So what have we got?

'There is the old-established product, which we know is being superseded by newer products, but we must recognize that there are still some of our most loyal customers out there who are accustomed to buying it. Let's not offend these people by discontinuing the line. We'll keep it available for those who demand it for as long as they desire it.

'Our leading product is obviously being well received by the bulk of our market. We are known for being the best value for money available in this area, so whatever the competition get up to we must still beat them on price.'

Scenario Two: A Sales/Profit Focus

A team talk led by a hard-bitten sales/marketing manager who has come up through the ranks of sales representation based on aggression and persistence.

'OK, we are coming into a period of heavy competition. We have competition leaning on us. We have a "dog" of an old product that some laggards still think is good. We also have a main product that thinks it's playing follow the leader around the market. So what are we going to do?

First, let us kill the "dog" and forget about loyalty. As for the so-called main product, I don't care what the competition do with their price, we are already low enough; any lower and we'll be giving it away. So I want some serious aggressive selling from you guys, don't give me any excuses. Promise these people the earth if you have too, as long as you get in before the competition. We will worry about customer reaction next period, but I want results.'

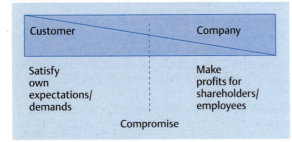

Figure 25.2 **Compromise of focus**

Figure 25.3 **Factors impacting upon quality/price from the company/customer perspectives**

Box 25.4 **A new 'alternative philosophy'**

1. Refocus the professional doctrine, not on the customer, but on the HONESTY–OPENNESS–FRANKNESS of the message.

2. Focus on 'Marketing for Profit'.

3. Treat the customer as a 'player' in the game of exchange and trade.

4. Recognize that the customer has his or her own agenda and objectives.

5. Focus the marketing message on 'WE WANT TO SELL YOU SOMETHING AND WE AIM TO PERSUADE YOU TO BUY IT'.

6. Recognize that the customer wants the best for him or herself and that the company wants the best for itself.

ophy alongside the missionary doctrine? It would appear to have more 'real-world' relevance than current conventional education. (A fuller description of this argument can be found in Carson *et al.* 1995*b*.)

5.3 **Alternative marketing 3: scientific versus natural marketing research**

Much of the foundation philosophy of marketing research stems from the rigour required by 'scientific' social-science research. A basic tenet is that, if research is to be considered valid, it must be carried out with a discipline and rigour that emphasize objectivity and validity, and show clearly cause and effect. As a consequence, much of the conventional literature focuses upon methodologies and how they must be performed 'correctly'. Similarly, an emphasis is placed upon the 'one best method' for a particular piece of research, even to the point of underlining the difficulties and complexities of using more than one method.

Consider for a moment the single aspect of questionnaire construction. Textbooks give instructions on devising appropriate questions that occur in a correct sequence and that have proper lead and follow-on questions. An emphasis is also given to the objectivity, construction, and sequence of 'forced-choice' questions and interpretation of answers to open-ended questions. Here again there may be a dichotomy between theory

sumers will seek the best quality at a minimum price, whereas companies will optimize quality and try to maximize price. Where the exchange occurs between these two extreme aims will depend upon the amount of negotiation, the strength of position, the depth of desire to trade, the alternatives and choice available, and the uniqueness of the product that exist between a company and its potential customers (Fig. 25.3).

The above new alternative philosophy is not too different from marketing in practice. Generally, naturally, and often subconsciously and implicitly, the manager/practitioner focus on the customer is on finding out, manipulating, assessing, exploiting, outflanking, surprising, and stimulating customers towards a meaningful sale for the company. Would it be better to accept this philos-

and practice. Although not in the strictest sense, market research as described above can be deemed to derive its origins and philosophy from 'scientific' social-science research.

☞ 'In smaller companies Aguilar (1967) found that top management *were* the main scanners but ... the information they generally scanned was somewhat narrow and too focused in nature to be considered a true environmental scan.' (Chapter 8, p. 167)

However, it is important to recognize that marketing practitioners and particularly entrepreneurs and owner managers of small firms do not carry out research in this way. Instead, they take a naturalistic, even artistic approach to gathering market information. 'Artistic' in this sense relates to the notion that a practitioner's research will be uniquely created by the individual and related only to his or her company. Interpretation of findings, gathered haphazardly, spontaneously, opportunistically, and personally, will be perceived, in terms of significance and meaning, uniquely by that individual. Just as in art, interpretation is individualistically in the 'eye of the beholder', whether this is the artist who created the piece or the viewer of the piece.

Practitioner market research will use any method at its disposal, regardless of correctness and compatibility. Typically, a practitioner will gather information from a variety of sources and in a variety of ways. The concepts of rigour and validity seldom enter into the mind frame. The practitioner will have a feel for the value and usefulness of information and its source and will intuitively accept or reject information as it is gathered. Much of the information gathering (note the use of the term 'information gathering' as opposed to market research), may well be semi-conscious.

How can marketing writers make research more practitioner 'real', whilst not rejecting the characteristics of 'scientific' social-science research, particularly in relation to its rigour and validity? Could textbooks accommodate the ethos of 'practitioner' research? 'Scientific' research fails to recognize that market information is of a unique value to an individual and his or her company. Interpretation of findings is an entirely personal thing for the purpose of understanding and this understanding is precisely personal. Equally, could writers not accept the approach of using and

or adopting any research methods with which the researcher is comfortable and which he or she chooses to use out of convenience or expediency?

5.4 Alternative marketing 4: small-firm selling

Conventional descriptions of selling in marketing textbooks primarily take a formal and sequential step approach whereby the process begins with prospecting and preparation behind a selling scenario. The sale itself begins with a formal 'opening' followed by presentation and demonstration. Guidance on how to deal with objections is often included before descriptions of how to 'close' the sale and subsequently to follow up after a suitable period. In addition to this formal selling approach, whole sections of the textbooks are devoted to the organization of the sales statistics and to the 'efficiencies' of managing a sales force.

Is this of value to small-firm owner managers? To some degree perhaps, particularly for some inexperienced entrepreneurs embarking upon a business venture for the first time. However, for the experienced entrepreneur it is of little value and help, primarily for two reasons. First, it follows a rigid, formal, and sequential approach that, as alluded to earlier, is alien to entrepreneurial practice and, secondly, and most significantly, an entrepreneur will sell on the basis of his or her own experiential knowledge (competency) built up over the everyday running of the business. Undoubtedly, there will have been much trial and error in building this experience, but mistakes will have been learned from and successes honed, practised, and refined. Often selling approaches will have been copied by observing competitors' successful activities and comments, and feedback from customers will be taken into account. The essence of small-firm selling can be deemed to be simply intuitively assessing the personality and mood of the buyer. This may involve getting to know the buyer and his or her circumstances over time. However, the entrepreneur's experiential knowledge of buying scenarios, coupled with knowledge of the industry and the individual in question, will all serve to enable the entrepreneur to assess the personality and mood of the individual. He or she will adapt the selling approach to suit the individual's personality or mood at any particular time. Any selling will be built around persuasion, and such persuasion is likely to be couched in befriending the individual. Clearly, experiential knowledge in its widest context is a meaningful competency for natural marketing. Also inherent in this natural selling will be networking dimensions, which are often the basis of the 'befriending' that is occurring naturally.

5.5 Alternative marketing 5: small-firm distribution

Similar to the conventional literature approaches in other aspects of marketing, distribution also adheres to a rigour and formality in its frameworks. Typical chapter headings in textbooks cover issues such as the nature and type of channels, behaviour, and function of channel intermediaries, and physical distribution management and systems. In reality, small-firm distribution is not concerned with elaborate distribution channel variations. Indeed, for most small firms distribution channels are predetermined by industry norms and practices that small firms most conform to in order to do business. As mentioned earlier in this chapter, most distribution channels will have been established over a lengthy period and a small firm, because of its size and position within an industry or market, is often forced to conform to the established practices.

Distribution delivery in small firms, when under control, is largely reactive to customer requirements. Planned delivery is often founded upon the need to maintain cash flows; thus the aim will often be to deliver immediately when stocks are available. Sometimes such a policy will lead to inefficiencies and lack of coordination. Often delivery is an uncontrolled dimension whereby deliveries are made just in time or involve fulfilling unrealistic promises, etc. Frequently, non-delivery or part delivery is blamed on suppliers' deficiencies rather than on those of the small firm. Generally, a small firm will seek to establish a pattern and routine for delivery that is regular and consistent, as it is in this way that the 'chaos' of delivery can be minimized.

5.6 Alternative marketing 6: small-firm pricing

Much of the conventional marketing literature of pricing as a marketing strategy indulges in elaborate positional justifications, ranging from premium pricing at one end of the spectrum, whereby firms are encouraged to charge high prices on the strength of some kind of distinctive differentiation, and, at the other extreme, discount pricing, whereby firms are encouraged to price below the competitive norms in order to secure more orders. In between lie a plethora of variable pricing strategies for all kinds of justifications and scenarios. In addition, the textbook literature counsels readers to take account of a huge variety of factors when determining price, such as value to customers, quality relationships, competitor and intermediary effects, to mention just a few.

Small-firm pricing does not adhere to any of these elaborate pricing descriptions. Indeed, where price is used as a marketing tool, it is often in the form of price reduction as a consequence of competitor pressure. Generally, small firms must again adhere to industry norms, which consist of known and expected margins, established and set over many years within a distribution channel. A small firm, or any company, for that matter, that prices significantly above or below an expected industry norm will raise major enquiries from the industry, not least from competitors. Similarly, consumers within any market are generally aware of price/value ranges, and this awareness often restricts, even dictates, the scope of pricing available to a small firm. The only exception to this is where a high (rare) marketing differentiation exists.

5.7 Alternative marketing 7: the small-firm marketing plan

The theoretical foundation stemming from conventional learning based on the textbook literature in relation to marketing planning advocates that the marketing manager carries out a situation analysis to arrive at a SWOT (strengths, weaknesses, opportunities, and threats) analysis. On the basis of this a text will often encourage consideration of radical change through the introduction of new products (immediately), entering new markets (immediately), more investment in promotion activity, and so on.

The problem here arises from 'encouraging radical change' out of a situation analysis. Such radical change almost inevitably ensues from such an exercise, principally because of two factors. First, textbooks often describe a circumstance in extreme 'black-or-white' solutions for the purposes of illustration; and marginal changes appear dull and unimpressive. Secondly, it is difficult to incorporate into a situation analysis the invariable company-specific nuances of internal cultures and decision-making practices unique to an individual company. Generally, because of these factors, writers fail to explain the importance of accommodating the views of existing management in incorporating situation-analysis outcomes. Writers do not recognize that managers generally do not like change, especially radical change. Also, most managers have a vested interest in the status quo and therefore may be unsettled by extensive change. Similarly, most managers/entrepreneurs cannot finance expensive solutions, and they need/want solutions that are simple and workable and that they understand and can support.

What is the issue here? It could be argued that there are many issues and indeed there are, and it may be that these issues are inherent in the understanding of the situation analysis process. However, there are some aspects that are not considered. For example, how does an existing management team (or an entrepreneur) think when it comes to making decisions? What constraints and pressures are they under that will allow them to take decisions or not? To increase relevance to small firms, textbooks might more realistically adhere to the following aspects when outlining such a study:

■ Do not advocate 'radical' change, instead recommend that any change should be introduced gradually in order to allow confidence to emerge.

■ Do not change the product and ways of doing things and recognize that managers do not want to change immediately and that they are probably more interested in securing sales/customers/profit. Consequently, most emphasis should centre on improving marketing communication.

■ Look for solutions within the firm's existing systems. Therefore, solutions should encourage the involvement of the company's managers and employees in working out problems and creating solutions.

■ Promote marketing without advocating heavy promotional expenditure and price reductions.

■ Emphasize marketing availability, suitability, value perception, and communication.

A marketing text that had to contend with these issues would appear radically different from the existing conventional texts' consideration of the 'situation analysis' as a topic.

Consider briefly another issue inherent in this area of marketing. What is the emphasis given in a textbook description of a marketing plan? Attention will focus on the comprehensiveness and sequentiality of the process, so a text will present a comprehensive situation analysis and SWOT analysis. But this is not what a company's management, especially an entrepreneur, wants to read. Managers with some years' experience will know as much as they need to know about their environment. They will be aware of the broad changes and trends, they will constantly monitor competitive activity, they will be aware of the latest marketing innovations, and so on. Therefore, what marketing managers, and owner managers want to learn about is ideas and solutions that are viable. As such, textbooks might focus on 'what to do' and show how this will work. They need not devote long tracts on describing the process of a situation analysis and SWOT analysis (unless the text is aimed at a 'first starter' market). In offering ideas and solutions they need not say 'should do'; instead they might say 'how to . . .'. This kind of emphasis will interest the small-firm owner manager much more than having to accept a perfectly correct procedure that deals with issues which he or she already knows about intuitively. In most cases an entrepreneur will seek to glean ideas and solutions to his or her own problems and will want to acquire such solutions quickly and without lengthy and elaborate procedure.

6 Assessment of the 'quality' of marketing decision-making in small firms

THE examples of small-firm marketing described above serve to illustrate the natural and intuitive way in which an entrepreneur owner manager will tend to do marketing. This approach to marketing decision-making is unlikely to conform to conventional literature descriptions of marketing. An entrepreneur is likely to perceive such descriptions as prescriptive and inappropriate for his or her business. However, small-firm owner managers do have a desire to assess the value of their decision-making. Generally, they are cautious about taking 'big' decisions for fear of a failure that will threaten their business. They also have a desire to know if what they are doing is working efficiently and effectively. It is with these issues in mind that this chapter concludes with an outline of criteria that will assess the 'quality' of marketing decision-making in small firms. The criteria offered below are designed to allow the entrepreneur to carry out an assessment in a way that is conducive to his or her own decision-making processes. It is primarily concerned with the use and value of marketing activity and how it is performed. The framework offered below assumes some level of awareness of conventional marketing theories. For example, entrepreneurs will be aware of concepts such as target-market segments and niche marketing.

The scope of the factors influencing qualitative marketing decision-making is, of course, broad and complex and may take account of all or as many of the factors of influence as possible in order to gain a complete picture of the marketing decision-making process. It is also possible to focus on a few or one specific aspect of influence in order both to gain insight into the degree of influence of this aspect and to understand the nature of the processes inherent in this aspect. In the broad and general sense, marketing decision-making can be deemed to involve decisions both that are about, and that are influenced by, factors that are internal to the enterprise and that are about external dimensions. Whilst it is recognized that external market factors are of significant importance to research in areas of marketing, especially in the context of small firms, which are influenced perhaps to a greater extent by market forces than larger organizations, it is nevertheless not taken into consideration in this assessment framework other than to acknowledge its existence and that most small firms will be inherently aware of their environment in order to survive. The rationalization for this is that any small firm that is growing is doing so on the basis of its current marketing activity and, since all marketing activity is inherently market based, the evidence of growth is an indication that such a firm is competing positively in its market environment. It is also recognized that competition is an inherent part of the small-firm market because all small firms exist in markets where there are other small firms and some larger competitors. Therefore, this discussion recognizes that growing small firms exist in dynamic and competitive market environments. This as-

sumption also serves to underline the importance of qualitative marketing decision-making factors, since the quality of such decisions are imperative if the small firm is to maintain growth.

So this discussion is concerned with internal marketing decision-making factors of a qualitative nature that contribute to an enterprise's growth. However, decision-making within a firm is also a highly complex domain. Strong influences on this decision-making are issues such as the culture belonging to the firm and the personality traits possessed by the owner manager. Whilst these are again undoubtedly important in understanding aspects of qualitative decision-making, they are nevertheless outside the focus of this discussion. Of course, they are inherent within the domain of the discussion and are recognized as influencers and contributors to decision-making outcomes, but it is the *managerial context* of decision-making that is of primary interest in this context. The quality of external dimensions can be assessed in terms of market knowledge, standing, profile, and image, as well as of the number of customers, whether they are long-standing or new, and the ratio of both.

'Good' marketing is manifest in the tangible dimensions of good/increased sales and profits. Whilst it is possible to recognize good examples of marketing activity, or, in other words, quality marketing, the question is one of whether this marketing activity can be assessed as being good quality in terms other than the tangible dimensions of sales and profits.

It is judged that quality in marketing can be assessed by evaluating the *use* of marketing—that is, assessing how marketing is performed. This assessment will determine a placement of marketing along a continuum between negative and positive extremes. For example, by using terms such as poor/excellent; inactive/active; reactive/proactive, and so on, assessing these on a continuum of extremes (see Fig. 25.4). On the basis of the above, it is possible to address the components of marketing activity and to assess these in terms of their *use* and *how they are performed*. Assessment of such quality dimensions will be from a 'holistic' perception for all marketing activity. While 'textbook' frameworks will be of help in assessing quality of marketing decision-making, these will serve as parameters of such dimensions. The strength of this assessment will come from enriching such parameters by actual performance criteria stemming directly from the firm's own

Figure 25.4 **Negative and positive extremes**

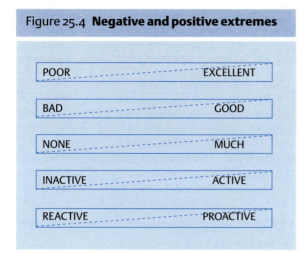

POOR	EXCELLENT
BAD	GOOD
NONE	MUCH
INACTIVE	ACTIVE
REACTIVE	PROACTIVE

marketing performance. As a consequence, analysis should go beyond the narrow decision-making frameworks of the traditional marketing domain of product, pricing, distribution, selling, and customer service. Although these represent the framework for the analysis criteria, they are simply that, a useful framework. Again the enrichment will come from how a small firm *uses* and *performs* marketing.

In assessing the quality of marketing and, indeed, in assessing how marketing is used and performed, it is useful to return to the underlying aspects of competency and networking. These aspects can be deemed to be the inherent foundations of good small-firm marketing. That is, it is judged that good small-firm marketing will have a foundation based upon the owner managers' 'competency' of experiential knowledge that has been acquired through the accumulation of knowledge and experience and the development of communication skills. The combination of these competencies allows entrepreneurs and owner managers to make sound judgemental decisions with regard to a variety of marketing aspects. Allied to experiential knowledge competency is the inherent ability of a small-firm owner manager to utilize effectively the personal and business network of contacts and influence. It is the network that enables the small-firm owner manager to exploit marketing circumstances that can be deemed to be uniquely small-firm oriented. An entrepreneur owner manager is unlikely to have the resources proactively to carry out a full range of marketing activities; with a comprehen-

sive and vibrant network, however, an entrepreneur will be able to compensate for any lack of resources. The combination of active networking and experiential knowledge provides the underpinnings that will allow an entrepreneur owner manager meaningfully to assess the quality of his or her marketing performance, for example, by recognizing the value and importance of the criteria presented in the examples below. Three aspects that mirror the alternative marketing scenarios are offered as illustration, these are pricing quality, delivery quality, and selling quality. The criteria are based on the integration and coordination of as many aspects of marketing activity that can be deemed necessary to perform good sound marketing in a small firm.

6.1 Marketing quality assessment: pricing quality

Qualitative marketing factors in pricing may be determined by the suitability, viability, and compatibility of price. This can be assessed in relation to price against the competition price, the quality of the product that price belongs to, and the overall image of the company. The extent of manipulation of price to aid marketing will also be important. Therefore, price can be assessed in terms of the product refinement/improvement/development processes. Assessment of price can also take account of issues such as the number/range/scope of products and the extent of 'targeting' towards a given market niche. 'Quality' may be deemed to exist if products and pricing are subjected to refinement, improvement, and so on, and if these adjustments have generated a compatible range of products at a variety of prices. In particular, quality pricing would involve using price and the mechanism for setting it as a tool integrated with other marketing activities.

6.2 Marketing quality assessment: delivery quality

Qualitative marketing factors in delivery may be assessed in terms of how the product/service is delivered and the quality and expertise of the person(s)/systems delivering it. In particular, how the delivery is managed relative to frequency and immediacy in relation to the type of product, customer requirements, and competitors' activity will also be important. Quality can also be assessed in terms of how the reliability of delivery is managed and ensured and how complete the delivery performance is perceived to be (by the owner manager). The interaction and communication between all parties before, during, and after the delivery process will contribute to the overall assessment of quality in delivery.

6.3 Marketing quality assessment: selling quality

Quality in selling may be assessed in terms of the ability to execute the whole sales process. Of particular importance are how salespeople do their selling and how they approach and communicate with customers—that is, the salespeoples' ability to create initial desire and need with the sales message, to stimulate sales, to manage customer contact in terms of frequency, reliability, and efficiency, and to contribute to the development of relationships between salespeople and customers.

The completion of a quality assessment of marketing activity would also expect to consider the quality of aspects such as communication, customer service, and any other aspects of marketing activity deemed to be important.

In summary, this discussion offers a definition of some important issues that may be expected to be inherent in how entrepreneurs *do* marketing. Because, the criteria put forward here suggest degrees of 'quality', it is possible, therefore, to determine this quality of marketing decision-making and, as such, how this 'quality' may contribute to growth of the enterprise.

There are some meaningful questions that emerge from the above that a small-firm owner manager should ask about his or her marketing. For example:

■ How much do you know about your market environment? Do you know your market position *vis-à-vis* competitors in terms of size, product/ company standing, price comparison, etc.? How strong/weak is your product(s) *vis-à-vis* competitor offerings?

■ Do you satisfy your customers completely? Are there potential customers that you do not reach and why?

■ Is your price competitive? Is your price compatible with your product quality and range?

■ Do you deliver on time, consistently, and reli-

ably? Can your delivery systems respond to specific customer requirements?

■ In selling, how well do you know your customer? In particular what messages and arguments do they most respond to?

In addition, other questions might be considered:

■ How good is your and your staff's communication with customers? How would you assess your overall communication package?

■ How would you rate your customer service over that of you nearest competitors? If it is poorer, why is this so and what could you do about it?

7 Summary

So what are the issues arising out of this discussion? It is argued in this chapter that there may be a dichotomy between literature theory and actual practice. Essentially, not only do entrepreneurs have different characteristics from managers, but these characteristics can also be found in practising marketing managers' decision-making as well as entrepreneurial decision-making and this decision-making is carried out in a different manner and is incompatible with the conventional literature descriptions of how marketing decision-making should be performed. In essence, the motivations and decision-making style of small-firm owner managers and marketing managers are in practice similar; and these motivations and decision-making styles are different from conventional literature descriptions pertaining to both. The issues raised by this notion are that a better understanding is needed of how small-firm marketing is performed. It has long been recognized that entrepreneurs and small-firm owner managers do not 'manage' according to the principles and techniques presented by the textbooks, and similarly it is recognized that they take decisions that stem from their unique characteristics rather than any textbook philosophy.

Perhaps some of the most innovative learning in marketing is based upon accumulated competencies combined with an inherent ability of the entrepreneur to use personal-contact networks to maximize marketing potentials. As an illustration of the application of these competencies and networks, some time has been taken in this chapter to offer an alternative approach to export marketing development. Following the 'alternative' theme, a number of examples of natural, entrepreneurial, small-firm marketing are offered as a contrast to conventional marketing theories stemming from the textbook literature. Finally, some criteria for assessing the quality of marketing in small firms have been outlined both as a means of allowing an entrepreneur owner manager to assess his or her own marketing and also as a further illustration of what is the essence of small-firm marketing.

Considerable emphasis has been placed upon the fact that conventional marketing literature is inappropriate for small-firm marketing. How relevant is this assertion? Increasingly, educators are raising the voice of doubt (Baker 1993, 1995; Brownlie *et al.* 1994; Brown *et al.* 1996). Key questions need to be addressed. Is marketing being taught correctly, regardless of the learning audience? Are teaching and learning methods appropriate? Is the subject of marketing as conventionally perceived still relevant to the issues and circumstances of today? If the answer is no to each, or any, of these questions, then what are the alternatives? It is incumbent upon educators to find acceptable solutions.

Discussion questions

1 How does small-firm marketing decision-making differ from large-company decision-making?

2 What are the characteristics of conventional marketing decision-making and how do these differ from decision-making in small firms?

3 In what ways are entrepreneurs and marketing practitioners similar?

4 How do small-firm entrepreneurs owner managers utilize competencies and networks to overcome marketing deficiencies?

Further reading

Carson, D., Cromie, S., McGowan, P., and Hill, J. (1995*a*), *Marketing and Entrepreneurship in SMEs: An Innovative Approach* (Hemel Hempsted: Prentice-Hall).

Hisrich, R. D., and Peters, M. P. (1995), *Entrepreneurship: Starting, Developing and Managing a New Enterprise* (3rd edn, Chicago: Irwin).

Levinson, J. C. (1984), *Guerrilla Marketing: Secrets for Making Big Profits from your Small Business* (Boston: Houghton Mifflin).

Prushan, V. H. (1997), *No-Nonsense Marketing: 101 Practical Ways to Win and Keep Customers* (New York: Wiley & Sons).

Smith, J. (1996), *Guide to Integrated Marketing* (Entrepreneur Magazine Series, USA; New York: Wiley & Sons).

UIC/AMA Marketing/Entrepreneurship Interface Symposium Proceedings 1987–1997 (available from University of Illinois at Chicago, Department of Entrepreneurship Studies).

Mini Case
Eaton and Caron (EC) Marketing

This case study describes the situation of a small agency firm, Eaton and Caron (EC) Marketing, doing business with the food distribution industry in Ireland. The entrepreneur Paul Eaton had established a network of relationships among all the major food buyers in Ireland. He had been selling a wide variety of food and related products to the food distribution industry for several years. He felt it was time to expand the business beyond its established but narrow parameters. He was stimulated by new developments in the European Union markets.

Paul's new venture emerged out of a visit to France and the Benelux countries with a friend. He travelled overland and purposefully called into a variety of supermarkets as he came upon them. He purchased a range of products and carefully recorded details of packaging, description, price, and source manufacturer or wholesale supplier. After several days it became obvious to Paul that Holland offered the best potential for sourcing products. His observations led him to a large general distributor that had its base in Holland, near Amsterdam. Paul was able to use his personal-contact network back home in Ireland to identify a name and obtain a letter of introduction to the Dutch company.

The Dutch company was happy to supply products to Paul's trading company, subject to normal trading and credit checks. It was agreed to run a trial on ten products that matched the profile of differentiated basic food products. The chosen products comprised a range of Dutch coffee and a selection of Belgium chocolate. Most of the ten products proved highly successful in the Irish market. Buyers were intrigued by the nonconformity of the products and consumers appeared to be attracted to the continental differentiation.

The relationship between Paul and the Dutch suppliers flourished, as might have been expected given the mutual benefits experienced by both parties. Within three months the product range had expanded to incorporate four new ranges: pasta, biscuits, savoury snacks, and beverages. The total number of individual products had expanded to sixty-five.

Towards the end of the first year of trading Paul was again in Holland—his third visit in eight months. The relationship had developed to a stage where Paul felt comfortable to raise the issue of selling his Irish products to the Dutch market. His Dutch partners were immediately enthusiastic and placed telephone calls to potential buyers extolling the merits of Paul and his company and organiz-

ing meetings for Paul, who, simply by extending his visit, was able to follow up immediately. Agreements were made with two Dutch buyers for some of Paul's products. Exporting had begun.

Currently, Paul's company continues to expand its export sales simply by servicing the agents in Holland. Sales of Dutch imported products continue to grow. Paul is expanding his activity into other European countries. He has visited major food exhibitions in France and Germany, with a view to buying other European products—that is, by importing first and using his new relationship to develop export sales.

Source: Carson, Cromie, McGowan, and Hill (1995a).

Discussion question

What lesson would you draw from Paul's experience if you were the owner of a small firm, with no previous experience of exporting, considering starting to export to another European country?

Chapter 26

Direct Marketing

Adrian Sargeant

Objectives

The objectives of this chapter are:

1 to introduce the role of direct marketing in the marketing process;

2 to explain the benefits of direct marketing;

3 to introduce the concept of customer lifetime value;

4 to distinguish between customer acquisition and customer retention activity, providing examples of each;

5 to consider the critical role of the customer database.

1 What is direct marketing?

BY this stage in the text you will already be familiar with a number of standard definitions of marketing. You will also have appreciated the centrality of customer requirements to the marketing management process and the necessity of satisfying those requirements better than the competition. The same basic principles apply in the realm of direct marketing. Indeed, direct marketing has much in common with the underlying philosophy of 'general' marketing; it is only the approach that is different.

Specifically, direct marketing is an approach to marketing that treats customers as individuals and characterizes them, not only by their individual characteristics, but also by how they have behaved in the past. Thus, for example, organizations engaged in direct marketing will tend not to view all 30–40-year-old customers as alike. They will endeavour to identify subtle differences in behaviour, each of which could potentially be used to inform the development of a uniquely tailored customer relationship. In short, database information about historic behaviours is integrated into the marketing decision-making process and utilized to ensure that all customers receive a marketing mix specifically adapted to their requirements.

☞ 'Direct marketing also offers marketers audience selectivity, since they can select those whom they wish to reach and observe the responses.' (Chapter 12, p. 282)

This contrasts sharply with the days of the traditional mass-marketing approach, when organizations treated all customers alike. A standard campaign was developed to address everyone, regardless of individual preferences or whether they had been a customer in past. Fortunately the death knell for this form of marketing was sounded when, in 1970, Alvin Toffler introduced the term *demassification* into marketing vocabulary, noting that mass markets were gradually eroding and with them the need for mass-marketing approaches. By the mid-1970s consumers had started to become more discerning, thoughtful, and individualist. Indeed, in the modern era consumers have come to expect greater choice and products/services that are ever more tailored to their own individual requirements. For evidence of the impact of this new thinking, Naisbitt (1982) reminds us of those not so distant days when bathtubs were white, telephones were black, and cheques were green. Marketing certainly came a long way in the last thirty years of the twentieth century.

This increasing consumer choice has also been reflected in the proliferation of communication channels. In the late 1940s it was possible to reach half the adult population of the UK with a single ad in the *Radio Times*. The early days of commercial television offered similar opportunities for mass marketing. Brands could be created almost instantaneously with high-profile campaigns and market shares could be doubled virtually overnight. With the onset of the new millennium and the proliferation of communication media, mass advertising is losing its appeal. Highly focused channels now exist that can reach a customer group much more cost effectively than would previously have been the case. Indeed, the profile of individuals using particular media can be carefully compared with the known profile of a particular organization's customers and the closest match identified. Media can now be selected with a high concentration of customers possessing very specific characteristics. Advances in targeting and database technology have greatly facilitated this process and media wastage is being rapidly eliminated.

One of the pioneers of mass marketing, William Hesketh Lever, famously remarked that he knew half the money he spent on advertising was wasted, but that he did not know which half. Even at the time he was making this comment one group of marketers had a pretty good idea how their advertising was working. For some time, early direct marketers had been testing customer responses to various media and using this information to tailor both their media selection and the creative approach employed. Direct marketing activity has the advantage of being infinitely measurable. Whilst marketers can only make educated guesses about the impact of a traditional advertising campaign, the customer response to most forms of direct marketing can be measured to two or even three decimal places. Opportunities for testing abound and direct marketers rolling out an expensive campaign are now in a position to predict with a high degree of accuracy the consumer response that will ultimately be achieved.

This characteristic of measurability is reflected in the Direct Marketing Association's definition of direct marketing: 'Direct marketing is an interactive system of marketing that uses one or more advertising media to effect a measurable response and/or transaction at any location.' Although this is a definition now widely supported by leading practitioners (e.g. Nash 1995; Stone 1996), it does perhaps lack an emphasis on the collection and manipulation of customer data that characterize so much direct-marketing activity. The definition developed by the UK's Institute of Direct Marketing makes this additional dimension clear. Direct marketing is: 'the planned recording, analysis and tracking of customers' direct response behaviour over time . . . in order to develop future marketing strategies for long-term customer loyalty and to ensure continued business growth'.

In the modern era, this process of recording, analysing, and tracking customer behaviour is greatly facilitated by database technology. Customer information can now be easily captured, processed, and used to inform the development of strategy. Advances in computing power have made it much easier for organizations to process vast quantities of information and hence to develop more personalized relationships with their customers. We will explore later in this chapter exactly how this might be achieved.

2 The development of a discipline

MANY people assume that direct marketing is a new phenomenon. This could not be further from the truth. Direct marketing has its roots in the mail-order industry and, as the chart in Box 26.1 makes clear, the basic ideas have been around for centuries. Indeed, those early pioneers would have adopted many of the same distinctions between categories of customer that are made today. Most, for example, would have recognized the distinction between active/lapsed customers and unconverted enquiries. Certainly from the middle of the nineteenth century a separate marketing approach would have been adopted for each distinct customer group.

Most of the organizations listed in Box 26.1

Box 26.1 The history of a discipline

1498	Aldus Manutius published the first book catalogue to appear with prices in Italy.
1667	William Lucas published the first gardening catalogue.
1727	Benjamin Franklin's mail-order library was established in Philadelphia.
1833	Antonio Fattorini established his mail-order watch club in Bradford (what was later to become Empire Stores).
1905	Freeman's established the first modern mail-order catalogue.
1926	Sherman and Sackheim launched their now famous Book of the Month Club in the USA.

constitute early examples of stand-alone direct marketing. In fact, this is only one of three categories of approach to direct marketing now commonly adopted: stand-alone, integrated, and peripheral. Each is briefly described below.

Stand-alone direct marketing In many ways this might best be regarded as the 'ultimate' direct-marketing approach. Organizations that employ stand-alone direct marketing employ no other means to manage the relationship with their customers. Organizations such as First Direct and Direct Line insurance clearly fall within this category. Customers are typically recruited via direct response press advertising and/or direct mail. Thereafter the relationship is managed by a combination of telephone and mail. Both organizations pride themselves on the degree of service provided and both maximize the benefit they can provide for their customers through a careful manipulation of their database.

Integrated direct marketing A second approach is to employ direct marketing as part of an integrated marketing mix. Here direct marketing may be viewed as complementing the other marketing activities undertaken. Organizations such as the AA, or a major charity such as Save the Children, can be classified as adopting this general approach. The AA, for example, recruits new customers through its kiosks at motorway service areas, press advertising, mass television advertising, and even direct mail. The organization has also a network of retail outlets situated in many high-street locations. Once customers are recruited, direct marketing is employed to develop

the value of these customers to the organization, perhaps through cross-selling other product lines, or even asking them to 'recommend a friend.' In such cases direct marketing is an integral part of a very broad mix.

Peripheral direct marketing The final category of direct-marketing activity embraces those organizations for which direct marketing is only an occasional tactical marketing tool. The customer database may be poorly developed and direct marketing is regarded as a peripheral activity. Indeed it may often be initiated as a knee-jerk response to falling sales, or a short-term response to competitive pressures. It will typically be employed for the purposes of customer recruitment and the second side of the equation—namely, customer retention and development—will be all but ignored.

3 The cornerstones of direct marketing

HOLDER (1998) argues that direct marketing comprises four components. These are continuity, interaction, targeting, and control. Continuity contrasts with the mass-marketing approach where the 'contact' with the customer is standardized and regarded merely as a series of one-off exchanges. All customers are treated alike and very simple 'product'-based messages are employed stressing the desirability of making a particular purchase. The emphasis lies in making a profit on each sale and budgets and communications strategy are developed accordingly.

In direct marketing, the goal is to use customer information to develop an ongoing relationship with each individual on the database. Direct marketers recognize that it is not essential that the organization makes a profit on each transaction with the customer, provided that over the full duration of their relationship a respectable return on investment (ROI) can be obtained. Thus the costs of recruitment are less of an issue for direct marketers, as they recognize the future potential (or lifetime value) that will accrue from each customer. Indeed, the concept of customer lifetime value lies at the core of successful direct-marketing activity and drives both what the organization is prepared to spend on recruiting each new customer and what it is prepared to spend on developing a relationship with a customer over time.

The interaction component emphasizes the fact that direct channels afford marketers numerous opportunities to engage the customer, with creative opportunities far superior to those that would be available through traditional channels. A Royal National Institute for the Deaf (RNID) Christmas mailing to its donors, for example, included a newsletter, a donation form, an audio cassette featuring a Christmas message from the charity's chief executive, and even a festive party whistle in keeping with the 'celebratory' nature of the season.

The concept of targeting stresses that direct-marketing activity is also characterized by a unique ability to target customers with relevant communications. Modern geodemographic and lifestyle lists make it possible to target consumers with increasingly relevant marketing offers (see Section 7). Once customers have been recruited, information in respect of past-purchase behaviour can be used to develop ever more refined communication strategies. Customers ordering baby clothes from a mail-order catalogue today, for example, are likely to be in the market for 'toddler toys' in 18–24 months. Database information can thus be used to ensure that they receive relevant product information at the appropriate time.

The control component draws attention to direct marketing's ability to pre-test almost every dimension of a direct communication. In the case of the RNID mailing, for example, the charity could conceivably have tested the impact of

- including, or not including, the cassette;
- including, or not including, the party whistle;
- the presence of a message on the envelope;
- the choice of colour(s) to appear in the newsletter;
- the impact of asking the donor for specific sums.

In practice perhaps three or four versions of a mailing might be developed and mailed to a small sample of the database. The pattern of response can then be assessed and the most effective version of the mailing rolled out to the remainder of the customer base. Not only does this allow an organization to select the most appropriate mailing; it also allows it to predict with a high degree of accuracy the performance of the overall campaign.

It is these four elements together that combine to make direct marketing a unique discipline within marketing. At its core, however, is the concept of customer lifetime value, since it is this that will shape the strategy to be adopted.

4 Customer lifetime value

BITRAN and Mondschein (1997: 109) define lifetime value (LTV) as 'the total net contribution that a customer generates during his/her lifetime on a house-list'. It is, therefore, a measure of the total worth to an organization of its relationship with a particular customer. To calculate it one has to estimate the costs and revenues that will be associated with managing the communication with that customer during each year of his/her relationship. If, for example, the relationship extends over a period of four years, one can subtract the likely costs of servicing the relationship with that customer (e.g. product costs, catalogues, newsletters, telephone calls, etc.) from the revenue so generated. In essence, the contribution each year to the organization's overheads can then be calculated. Of course, there is a certain amount of crystal-ball gazing involved, since it becomes increasingly more difficult to predict costs and revenues the further one looks into the future. To take account of this uncertainty and to reflect the fact that a £50 sale in four years' time will be worth in real terms much less than it would today, it is also important to discount the value of the future contribution streams that will be generated. After all, instead of investing the money in dealings with its customers, an organization could simply elect to place the money in an interest-bearing account at a building society. Unless the return from direct-marketing activity can be expected to match, or hopefully exceed, what could be generated by an interest-bearing account, it will clearly not be worthwhile. If this analysis is conducted right across the database, a key advantage accrues. Organizations can employ an LTV analysis to increase their overall profitability by getting rid of customers who will never be profitable and concentrating resources on recruiting and retaining those that will (Dwyer 1989; Jackson 1989).

4.1 Calculating the LTV of individual customers

The formula for calculating LTV in the case of an individual customer is as follows.

$$\text{LTV} = \sum_{i=1}^{n} C_i (1+d)^{-i}$$

where:

C = net contribution from each year's marketing activities

d = discount rate

i = the expected duration of the relationship (in years).

This somewhat complex-looking equation merely indicates that it is necessary to calculate the likely future contribution by a customer each year, discount these future contributions, and then add them all together. The grand total is the LTV of a given customer. Table 26.1 shows a worked example.

Suppose for the sake of argument that a customer has just been recruited. We know that she was recruited from a standard cold mailing and, from the details she supplied when she made her first purchase, that she is female, aged 45, living in a certain type of housing (identifiable from her postcode information), and interested in a very specific product category (e.g. classical music CDs). On the basis of a historical analysis of the database, the marketer can determine the future revenue that a person matching this profile would be likely to generate. On the basis of this information, coupled with projected costs, it is possible to produce the forecast given in Table 26.1 of the contribution that this customer will make to the organization over the duration of her predicted five-year relationship. As previously indicated, the value of the future contributions must be discounted and on this basis the predicted LTV of the customer is calculated to be £387. This information can be used to facilitate planning and to assign the customer to an appropriate pattern of communication.

Many organizations now employ this analysis. The Ford Motor Company estimates the LTV of a typical customer to be of the order of £100,000, whilst, in the USA, Domino Pizzas have calculated their average customer LTV to be $4,000. In this latter case, the knowledge that customers are actually worth such a substantial sum, instead of the few cents profit that might accrue from an individual sale, has had a considerable impact on the way the organization has developed its marketing activity.

4.2 The benefits of LTV analysis

LTV can be used to drive five management decisions:

- assigning acquisition allowances;
- choosing media for initial customer acquisition;
- setting selection criteria for retention marketing;
- investing in the reactivation of lapsed customers;
- Assigning an asset value to the marketing database.

Each of these will now be considered in turn.

Table 26.1 **Example LTV Analysis (£)**

Revenue and costs	Year 1	Year 2	Year 3	Year 4	Year 5	TOTAL
1 Total income	60	70	130	140	150	550
2 Total costs	9	9	10	17	18	63
3 Contribution (1–2)	51	61	120	123	132	487
4 Discounted value	51	55	99	92	90	387

Note: Discount rate of 10% per annum.

Forecasting is very difficult—especially about the future!

'Many companies that know average lifetime values still manage their customers on their past value rather than predicted lifetime value.'

Source: Stone (1997: 49).

4.2.1 Assigning acquisition allowances

An understanding of the LTV of an organization's customers can guide the determination of how much a particular organization may be willing to spend to recruit each new customer (Lewis 1995) (see Insert). As was highlighted earlier, many organizations conscientiously strive to achieve as close as possible a break-even position at the end of each of their recruitment campaigns. Whilst commendable, this is not at all necessary, so long as the future income stream from the customers being recruited is a healthy one. Organizations employing the LTV concept would, therefore, tend to assign somewhat higher acquisition allowances than those that do not. In financial terms this is simply because a marketer employing a traditional approach will calculate campaign ROI thus:

$$ROI = \frac{\text{immediate revenue generated}}{\text{cost of acquisition campaign}}$$

A direct marketer employing the LTV concept would, by contrast, calculate ROI as:

$$ROI = \frac{\begin{array}{c}\text{initial revenue} + \\ \text{(sum of all future} \\ \text{contributions less discount)}\end{array}}{\text{cost of acquisition campaign}}$$

where
ROI = return on customer acquisition investment
future contribution = estimated annual contribution to profit
discount = reduction in value of future pounds to today's rate (discounted cashflow).

4.2.2 Choosing media for initial customer acquisition

Marketers engaged in the perennial problem of customer acquisition are well versed in the necessity of asking questions such as

- Which media should I be using for my recruitment activity?
- What balance should I adopt between the media options that are available?
- On what basis should I select potential customers for target

The traditional approach to answering these questions would have been to consider the pattern of response typically received from each media in the past, calculate likely ROIs for each, and then select the most attractive option on this basis.

Such analyses, however, suggest suboptimal allocations of marketing resources, because they ignore certain known customer behaviours. Customers recruited from one medium may never buy again, whilst customers recruited by another medium exhibit much greater degrees of loyalty. The overall profitability from one relationship can, therefore, vary considerably from that of another. LTV analysis can be used to good effect as an aid to selection of recruitment media and to help focus marketing activity on those customers who are likely to have the highest value to the organization over time.

Of course, to be in a position to utilize LTV as a decision-making tool, an organization needs a considerable amount of historical transactional data. Successful forecasting of the LTV of a given individual, or (more usually) segment of the database, requires a detailed understanding of how similar individuals or segments have behaved in the past.

4.2.3 Setting selection criteria for retention marketing

LTV calculations can prove instructive for more than just recruitment planning. The information can be used to guide contact strategies for ongoing customer development. LTV analysis can be employed to identify customers with whom it will never be possible to conduct profitable business. In many cases it may cost an organization more to mail them with catalogues, product reminders, etc., than it could ever hope to recoup from an individual's pattern of purchase.

If an organization calculates a projected LTV for each customer on the database, customers can be assigned to specific segments, and contact strategies can be customized to raise LTV. Initially, this may involve simply recognizing the difference in contribution, so as to offer particularly high-value customers a differentiated pattern of care that reflects their status. Many of the airlines, for example, now offer 'membership' benefits to their frequent fliers, or those that they perceive will become frequent fliers in the future. As companies become more experienced in the use of LTV analysis, it will also be possible to associate the impact of differentiated standards of care, or forms of contact, upon the LTV for a given customer. As Peppers and Rogers (1995: 49) note: 'Instead of measuring the effectiveness of a marketing programme by how many sales transactions occur across an entire market during a particular period, the new marketer will gauge success by the projected increase or decrease in a customer's expected future value to the company.'

4.2.4 Investing in the reactivation of lapsed customers

Most organizations now recognize the value of their database. Few would question the established wisdom that existing customers will always be the most cost-effective source of additional sales. Few would also disagree with the notion that reactivating lapsed customers can be profitable. Having been sufficiently motivated to buy at least once in the past, with the proper encouragement it is eminently possible that such individuals will buy again. The problem, however, for many organizations lies in deciding which lapsed customers should be selected for contact. Whilst one could do this easily on the basis of the total amount spent, the size of the average purchase, or the length of time since the last purchase, it can be instructive to use projected LTV to inform the decision. With the right persuasion to respond, targeting those with a higher forecast LTV is likely to prove the most efficient use of resources. A 'reactivation allowance' can be built into the budget. How much an organization is prepared to commit to reactivating one customer would inform the nature and quality of the contact strategy employed.

4.2.5 Assigning an asset value to the marketing database

There are many competing demands upon the income of a typical company. Quite reasonably, expenditure on marketing is often perceived as a cost to be minimized. Whilst it is certainly true that marketing could be regarded as a cost, it should actually be seen as an investment. Using LTV analyses, organizations can explore the future behaviour of their database; this information can be used to place an overall value on customers as intangible assets. This can have a remarkably sobering impact on those responsible for the organization's financial management. The justification for customer recruitment activity suddenly becomes clear, and the rationale for doing more for customers than simply sending them catalogues is obvious.

5 Customer acquisition versus retention

As will already be clear from the previous section, direct marketers draw a firm distinction between customer-acquisition activity (that is, activity designed to attract new customers to the organization) and customer-retention activity (that is, activity designed to keep them loyal over time). It is estimated to cost up to five times as much to conduct business with a new customer than to conduct it with an existing one. An organization's cheapest source of custom will always be its existing customers. Existing customers have, after all, already demonstrated their interest in the available products/services by virtue of their past purchase and are therefore considerably more likely to purchase again. Thus, for example, a supplier of garden seeds is likely to generate a much higher response from mailings to its past customers than it will ever achieve using a cold list of prospects, because inevitably its catalogues could be sent to some individuals who have little/no interest in gardening, or who are perfectly happy buying from another supplier.

Indeed, in the case of direct mail, there is a world of difference in response rates between cold mailings (that is, those to prospective customers) and warm mailings (those to existing customers). It would be usual for the former to achieve a response rate of between 0.1 and 5 per cent, whilst response rates to the latter have been known to exceed even 50 per cent.

In practice, direct marketers draw a distinction between four distinct groups of customers, each possessing its own unique response characteristics. This is illustrated in Fig. 26.1. As one works along the continuum from repeat sales to the

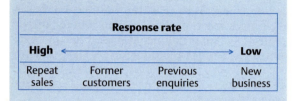

Figure 26.1 **Response rates by category of customer**

Response rate			
High ⟵		⟶	**Low**
Repeat sales	Former customers	Previous enquiries	New business

generation of completely new business, the attainable response rates worsen considerably.

It is not only response rates, though, that make targeting existing customers a particularly attractive option. Organizations generally know more about the needs and wants of their existing customers, if only by virtue of their purchase history. This makes it possible to tailor the market offerings more precisely to those customer needs, quite possibly allowing the organization to change a premium for the enhanced quality of service that results.

Existing customers can also be cross-sold different product lines and be encouraged to generate referrals of other individuals who might have a similarly enhanced interest in the organization's products. There is, therefore, a world of difference between the likely profitability of customer-acquisition activity and customer-retention activity. Indeed, many organizations expect to do little more than initially break even from acquisition activity, but are content in the knowledge that they will be able to cultivate quite profitable relationships with the customers they recruit over the full duration of their relationship with them.

In terms of the balance of resources, it makes sense to target the majority of the marketing resources at those customers that will be worth the most to an organization and generate the highest levels of profitability. Typically, therefore, in the

case of an established organization, customer-retention activity normally accounts for between 70 and 80 per cent of a direct-marketing budget, with a much smaller percentage being allocated to the more speculative customer-acquisition side of the business (see Insert). This balance will obviously vary dependent on the direct-marketing strategy adopted and may be different in the case of organizations setting themselves aggressive market-share targets, as the emphasis in such a case would be on building numbers in the database.

The use of direct marketing for both customer acquisition and customer retention will now be considered in turn.

6 Customer Acquisition

EVERY organization needs to consider ongoing customer acquisition. New customers will always be necessary to replace those that for one reason or another will stop doing business with an organization in a given year. Even if the service provided is excellent and levels of satisfaction are high, some customers will still terminate their relationship. In some markets this may be because they have outgrown the need for the product, their interests have changed, they no longer have the necessary moneys, or they may have died or moved away. Customer-acquisition activity is essential to preserve and if necessary enhance the overall number of customers on the database. It can also help to inject 'freshness' into a house list, because it is often the case that customers will be at their most profitable in the period immediately following their recruitment (Holder 1998).

In developing a customer-acquisition campaign there are seven stages that should normally be considered. These are illustrated in Fig. 26.2. Each of these steps will now be briefly reviewed in turn.

6.1 Objectives

The first step in developing a customer-acquisition programme is to decide on the objectives the organization wishes to achieve. Objectives are an important part of the plan, as they are the only mechanism by which its success can be measured. If a plan achieves its stated objectives, one might reasonably conclude that it has been a

Loyal customers are worth a fortune

'Good long-standing customers are worth so much that in some industries, reducing customer defections by as little as five points—from say 15% to 10% per year—can double profits.'

Source: Caulkin (1996: 9).

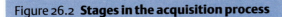
Figure 26.2 **Stages in the acquisition process**

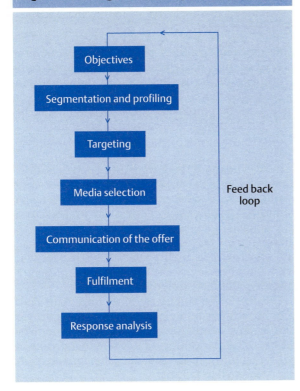

success. Without them, one can only speculate as to the planner's original intent and the effectiveness of the activities undertaken has no benchmark against which to be assessed. Valuable resources could be being wasted, but the organization would have no mechanism for identifying that was in fact the case.

Recruitment objectives would normally address the following issues.

- The target response rate that will be achieved.
- The number of new customers that will be attracted over a given time period or campaign. This is not the same as the previous point, since it takes into account the conversion rate of new customers. A large number of customers might respond to a press ad, requesting a brochure, for example, but ultimately only a few of these enquirers might actually make a purchase.
- The desired return on investment (ROI), although it is important to note that many recruitment campaigns are expected initially to operate at a loss.

- The desired LTV of the customers recruited. Organizations with an established database will already know the profile of their high-value customers. Newly recruited customers can be compared with this profile to assess their likely future potential. Objectives can, therefore, be couched in terms of the degree of 'match' obtained.
- The allowable cost per sale (i.e. how much is the organization prepared to spend to make each new sale?)

6.2 **Segmentation and profiling**

Having delineated recruitment objectives, the next stage is to determine which potential customers (or prospects) will be targeted. In essence there are two approaches, the appropriateness of which will be determined by the extent to which an organization has a prior knowledge of its markets. These methods can be categorized as being either *a priori* or cluster based and *post hoc*. An *a priori* approach is based on the notion that marketers decide in advance of any research which categories of customer they intend to target. Typically this might involve classifying customers into segments according to their demographic, geodemographic, or lifestyle characteristics. The marketer would then carry out research to identify the attractiveness of each segment and make a decision on the basis of the results as to which segment or segments to pursue.

☞ 'Geodemographic segmentation combines the use of location and demographic variables. Simply defined *geodemographics* is "the analysis of people by where they live" . . . ' (Chapter 16, p. 388)

Post hoc segmentation, by contrast, may be most appropriate where the marketer is already familiar with the market for a particular product/service and is perhaps in possession of a database of customers who are already purchasing the product category in question. It is now a comparatively simple matter to employ an analytical tool to develop a profile of the 'typical' customer. The level of detail an organization can achieve with this profile will clearly depend on the number of variables stored in the database, but most organizations should be able to develop a demographic and/or geodemographic profile of consumers who have typically responded well in the past.

Indeed, some organizations may be in a position to take this analysis one stage further. Consider Fig. 26.3. Organizations with larger databases will undoubtedly find that purchase patterns are not uniform. Individuals exhibit wildly different LTVs and this information can be employed to great effect in informing recruitment activity. Figure 26.3 shows an example of a database that has been profiled by customer LTV. At the bottom of the pyramid there is a large number of customers who will contribute very little to the organization over the duration of their lifetime. At the top there are a small number of individuals who will contribute a great deal.

There is no particular mystique about this pattern. It is commonly observed in database analysis and reflects what has come to be known as the Pareto Rule. It is often the case that 80 per cent of the contribution gained by an organization can be accounted for by 20 per cent of the organization's customers.

Whilst many organizations base their recruitment activity on the profile of a 'typical' customer, it is actually those individuals towards the top of the pyramid that should be of greatest interest. Ideally recruitment activity should, therefore, be based on a profile of the highest value customers and NOT on that of the database as a whole. It is, therefore, now common practice to divide a database into decile segments based on value and to use the profile of the top deciles to inform the nature of recruitment activity.

6.3 Targeting

This detailed customer profile can then be employed to inform the selection of appropriate recruitment media to reach other individuals in society who match these characteristics. If direct mail is to be employed, the information can be used to inform the criteria for the selection of appropriate prospects from commercially available lists.

In the late 1990s there were estimated to be over 4,000 such lists in existence in the UK alone. Navigating the range of alternatives can, therefore, be somewhat problematic, unless an organization has considerable past experience on which to draw. For this reason, many organizations engage the services of a highly specialized list broker, who can offer advice on the best lists to meet a specific set of recruitment requirements.

The list is the singularly most important concern in any customer-acquisition campaign. No matter how strong the creative activity—no matter how strong the offer—if it is sent to individuals with no interest in the product category, the mailing is doomed to failure.

Consumer lists fall broadly into the categories of geodemographic and lifestyle and a detailed profile of existing customers can greatly assist an organization in refining the criteria that will be used to select between the various options available.

6.3.1 Geodemographic lists

Geodemographics represent an attempt to categorize consumers by the type of housing they live in. The idea underlying the use of the approach is that 'birds of a feather will flock together'—in other words, that similar types of people will tend to live in similar types of housing, have similar interests, and be in the market for similar categories of product.

There are a variety of commercial geodemographic systems now available, each capable of supplying a list of consumers matching a certain set of characteristics. These include ACORN, MOSAIC, PINPOINT, and FINPIN.

The common point in all of these systems is their use of census data. In the UK, a detailed census of the population is conducted every ten years. The next census is due in 2001. The census consists

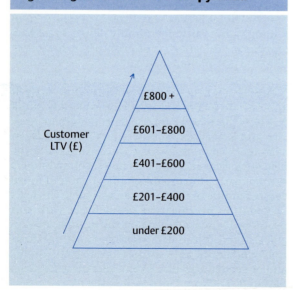

Figure 26.3 **The customer value pyramid**

Customer LTV (£)

£800 +

£601–£800

£401–£600

£201–£400

under £200

of a questionnaire sent to every household in the country, which gathers data on over 300 variables. The majority of households receive a standard census document, whilst a small percentage (15 per cent) receive a more detailed document for completion. In a typical census, over 96 per cent of the questionnaires will be completed.

Contrary to what many people believe, census information is not published at an individual level. Census information is available only at the level of the 'enumeration district', which typically contains ten postcodes (see Table 26.2). For direct marketers this poses something of a problem, because the most useful unit of analysis for marketing purposes is undoubtedly the postcode. Geodemographic systems such as ACORN have, therefore, to match census data from the enumeration district to the relevant bundle of postcodes. They achieve this match by employing the relevant map references for enumeration districts and postcodes. In practice this stage is the most common source of error in a geodemographic system, for the following reasons (Fairlie 1992).

■ The boundary for some enumeration districts can cut across a postcode. One postcode could thus include households in two different enumeration districts.

■ The map references for postcodes are often imprecise.

■ The only map references available outside London for enumeration districts (EDs) are those for the centroid of the ED. Since EDs do not have a regular shape, attempts to associate the relevant postcodes could introduce a substantial amount of error.

By this stage in the analysis, each postcode now has a mass of relevant census data associated with it. Geodemographic systems then employ a number of analytical processes that allow them to reduce the high number of census variables down to a more manageable number that is capable of explaining key differences in consumer behaviour. To develop market segments, a technique such as cluster analysis will then be utilized to identify groups of postcodes that appear to behave similarly in relation to this reduced number of variables. The aim is to group together postcodes with similar behaviours, whilst ensuring that the difference between these postcode groups is as large as possible.

All the major suppliers of geodemographic information employ slightly different sets of census data and employ differing statistical techniques to derive the final segments that will comprise their system. Typically this might include information in respect of:

■ age
■ marital status
■ household composition
■ household size
■ employment type
■ travel to work
■ unemployment
■ car ownership
■ housing tenure
■ amenities
■ housing type
■ socio-economic group

Table 26.2 UK postal units

Postal unit	Example	Number in UK	Number of households
Postal area	Reading (R)	121	200,000
Postal district	RG9	2,900	8,275
Postal sector	RG9 1	9,000	2,700
Enumeration district	Approx. ten postcodes	148,000	c.150
Postcode	RG9 1PD	1,600,000	10–15

Source: Royal Mail.

Some suppliers of geodemographic systems will enhance the utility of their system by conducting research with a representative sample of households from each segment. This allows the supplier to overlay information about the detailed purchasing behaviour of each group of customers. An example, drawn from the ACORN system, is depicted in Box 26.2.

The system has had a number of benefits for marketers, notably that, when a particular company has some knowledge of its customer base, it may profile it and obtain a geodemographic 'picture' of the typical target segment (or segments) that it is addressing. This information may then be utilized to target other individuals who exhibit similar characteristics, perhaps with direct mail. Wastage is minimized and response rates have been shown to be consistently higher than those achieved through the use of lists selected on the basis of geographical location alone.

Towards the end of the 1990s there were moves to create segmentation systems based on so-called fuzzy geodemographics. Instead of allocating households to one of a prescribed number of segments on the basis of their response to a combination of census variables, these new systems will be capable of identifying the *key* census variables that drive behaviour in relation to *a given product category*. Using consumer responses to these variables, the systems will then identify an appropriate number of market segments and allocate postcodes to these segments accordingly. What results is in essence a separate geodemographic classification system for every corporate use of the system. Hence, for one manufacturer, the fuzzy system might group postcodes into twenty segments that behave differently in relation to their product. For another manufacturer, in a different sector, it might identify sixty-three distinct segments of customer behaviour. These new systems will allow direct marketers much more flexibility to relate geodemographic analysis, specifically to their own unique needs.

6.3.2 Lifestyle lists

A plethora of lifestyle information is now available commercially. Lifestyle databases differ from geodemographic databases since they collect data at an individual level. Organizations offering this service draw on the results from large commercial surveys, or product registration cards, completed by individuals with a willingness to take part. Questionnaires are often very detailed, with a typical lifestyle survey containing over 200 questions. To facilitate completion respondents are often lured by the prospect of a prize draw, or a promotional premium that ensures that they derive some direct benefit in exchange for the time necessary to complete the instrument. A number of typical lifestyle products are presented in Table 26.3.

Four broad categories of data collected by lifestyle companies were identified by Reynolds (1993):

- names and addresses;
- data pertaining to product purchase patterns—or anticipated product purchase patterns;

Table 26.3 **Lifestyle products**

Supplier	Product Name	Description	Size (m. individuals)
CACI	Lifestyles UK	List and profiling tool, capable of tagging existing databases. Each individual may be selected by 300 different lifestyle attributes.	44
NDL	The Lifestyle Selector	Data collected from product registration guarantees; c. 4 million returned annually.	16
Claritas	Lifestyle Selector	Data collected from in-product questionnaires and satisfaction surveys.	12
ICD	Facts of Living Survey	Compiled by mailing members of the electoral roll.	8
Consumer Surveys Ltd.	Lifestyle Focus	Compiled by mailing 14 million households. Typically 200 lifestyle questions posed.	4

Box 26.2 **An illustration of an ACORN area**

Type 26 Mature Established Home Owning Areas

These comfortable, mature neighbourhoods have very low levels of recent home movers. The largely middle-aged population contains very many people who own their homes outright. ACORN Type 26 is found all over Britain, but the highest concentrations are in Norfolk, the Isle of Wight and North Yorkshire. Cleethorpes is a typical town with many areas of this Type.

Demographics

These neighbourhoods have a mature age profile. There are below average numbers of children, especially 0–4 year olds, and younger adults. The largest age group is the 45–64 year olds, of whom there are 35% more than average. The household structure is characterized by a high proportion of older couples, in the 55+ age group, with no dependent children. The proportion of adults who are married is 23% above average.

Socio-Economic Profile

The unemployment rate in these neighbourhoods is only half the national average. The proportion of retired people is 23% above average. Women in couples without children are much more likely to be working part time or not working than working full time. Of those in employment, 19% work in manufacturing, a proportion just above the national average, while 61% work in services (identical to the national average). The socio-economic profile peaks in the skilled, non-manual groupings. Whilst the proportion of people with degrees is 15% below average, the propor-

tion holding diplomas is nearly 30% above average.

Housing

44% of homes are owned outright—this is 84% higher than the average. A further 48% are being purchased by mortgage and so levels of rented housing are very low in these areas. Nearly 90% of the housing stock is either detached or semi-detached. In terms of house size, there is an average representation of very large homes (7+ rooms), but the majority are 3–6 rooms in size.

Food and Drink

Grocery shopping trips tend to be made by car and on a weekly or less frequent basis. Both freezer ownership and usage of freezer centres are average. Consumption of most food products, including frozen foods, is below average, partly as a result of small household sizes. A few products, however, are used heavily, notably flour and dog food. Beer consumption is well below average. Table

wine and, in particular, sherry are the favourite drinks.

Durables

Car ownership levels are above average, but not dramatically so. People in these neighbourhoods change their cars much less often than average, and the proportion of people who have owned their car for more than 5 years is over 30% higher than average. The proportion of large cars is relatively high. Purchase rates for most durables are low with the exception of video cameras and dishwashers, both of which are purchased at above average rates. The proportion of homes having replacement windows fitted is nearly 50% higher than average.

Financial

Financially, these are very comfortable areas. The income profile peaks in the £25–30,000 per annum band. Ownership of most financial products is above average, with the exception of hire purchase agreements. 59%

more people than average have National Savings Certificates. The rate of new savings account opening is 35% above average.

Media

These are areas where The Telegraph and The Mail have well above average readership levels. Amongst Sunday titles, The Sunday Telegraph, The Sunday Express and The Mail on Sunday are all read here by significantly more people than average. ITV viewing is medium, but commercial radio listening is light.

Leisure

The proportion of people taking holidays is above average, especially for winter and long holidays. Caravanning and camping are both more popular in this ACORN Type than on average. Gardening is a very popular activity: 70% more people than average have a greenhouse and garden expenditure is about 30% above average. People are more likely than average to eat out during the day and steakhouses are a very popular choice. These people are less active in terms of both sports and cultural pursuits. Activities which do show above average popularity are golf, rambling and visiting stately homes.

Atitudes

An interesting aspect of these people is that they do not have particularly strong views on anything. They are happy with their standard of living and less likely than average to budget carefully when shopping or to search for the lowest prices.

Source: CACI Ltd. 1999, all rights reserved. ACORN and CACI are registered trademarks of CACI Ltd.

- demographic and socio-economic information;
- values and lifestyle information.

There are many systems available commercially most of which work on a similar principle, although the variables utilized in each case are slightly different. It would, therefore, be advantageous prior to utilizing one of these systems to have carried out some initial market research to identify specifically which lifestyle variables are significant in a given market.

6.3.3 Choosing a list

Typically, 1,000 names and addresses may be purchased from a commercial list for between £80 and £150, a much lower cost than many people believe. In practice, the exact costs will be determined by the following factors.

- *The level of detail that is to be employed in prospect selection.* Some suppliers will charge less for a list of single males that they will for a list of single males who own their own homes, have a disposable income in excess of £30,000, and take an interest in rugby. In this latter example, it may take a supplier a little longer to extract the required individuals from their system and costs will vary accordingly.
- *Whether it is intended to purchase the list or merely rent it.* Most suppliers offer organizations a choice and lists can be purchased outright, or rented for a specified number of uses. Dummy addresses are often inserted to ensure that the list is used only on the number of occasions that was originally specified!
- *Whether the list can be bought 'off the shelf'.* Organizations can elect either to employ an existing list, or to pay to have one constructed specifically to meet their requirements. This would be more normal in industrial markets where a very specific set of criteria may often need to be met. This is an expensive option—because of the time required to conduct the necessary research—and charges may reach as high as £30 per name.

Given the plethora of available lists, it is always essential to evaluate the alternatives available. A number of the criteria that can be employed to assess lists for their suitability are given below.

- *The level of detail that can be supplied.* Lists vary considerably in terms of the sophistication they can offer marketers for targeting purposes.

- *The level and nature of previous usage.* It is important to clarify the extent to which prior use has been made of the list and in particular whether competitors have already employed the list to market their own goods and services. Lists can become 'tired' very quickly, and assessing the extent to which they have been previously employed can be a very significant issue.
- *Past results.* Suppliers can often give an indication of the response rates achieved by previous clients. Accepting that these might tend to fall as the list ages, such information can nevertheless prove invaluable in assessing the desirability of using a particular list.

There are also a number of tests that can be conducted in-house. Whilst most suppliers have a minimum order quantity, it should always be possible to obtain a small sample of the members of a list and ascertain response rates with a test mailing. Subsequent analysis of the response should allow an organization to predict with a high degree of accuracy the response it will achieve when the whole list is eventually mailed. If two competing lists are being evaluated, the pattern of response can be compared and the most appropriate option pursued.

6.3.4 Other sources of prospects

Throughout this chapter we have made numerous references to the use of cold lists for recruitment purposes. Whilst these do typically represent a common source of new customers, they are by no means the only source that may be employed. Indeed there are a number of sources of potential new customers. These are illustrated in Fig. 26.4. The diagram has been arranged as a pyramid to reflect both the number of prospects likely to be generated and the likely response rates that will be achieved by an approach. The most high-quality prospects any organization can hope to generate are those supplied by its own satisfied customers. So-called member-get-member (MGM) schemes have become increasingly popular. In essence, current customers are invited to introduce a friend or acquaintance to a company in return for a small gift or premium. When the newly introduced customer makes his or her first purchase, the premium is shipped. Such schemes have a high conversion rate, since those newly introduced individuals are often expecting to receive their first mailing and have been recom-

Figure 26.4 **The acquisition pyramid**

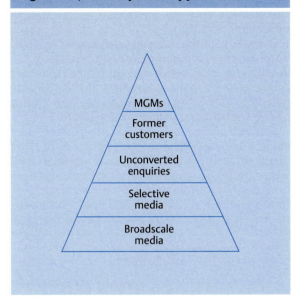

- MGMs
- Former customers
- Unconverted enquiries
- Selective media
- Broadscale media

mended because they already possess an interest in the products/services available.

At the next level down are an organization's former customers. Companies often neglect this group, feeling that perhaps they are no longer interested in the products/services available. Whilst this may be true, organizations will still achieve a higher response rate from the members of this group than they will by targeting any of the remaining three groups in the pyramid. This is simply because an interest in the product category clearly exists. The problem lies in incentivizing former customers to make a further purchase and an organization may wish to test a combination of different offers and creative ideas, to identify the campaign with the greatest reactivation potential.

Unconverted enquiries are also a good source of new customers. Again, such individuals must have had an interest in the broad product category available, but were unwilling or unable to make a purchase at the time the original enquiry was made. The enquirer's circumstances may change over time and a timely reminder may well pay dividends.

The remaining categories of selective and broadscale media are also available for recruitment purposes. Dell Computers, for example, could elect to advertise in either a selective media—for example, *Personal Computer World*—or a broadscale media—for example, the *Daily Mail*. The response to an advert in the former is likely to be much stronger, since all the readers of *Personal Computer World* have by definition an interest in personal computing. The same cannot be said of the readers of the *Daily Mail* and the relative levels of response will reflect this.

In attempting to meet recruitment objectives it would always be advisable to consider working down through the pyramid, progressing through each level, until such time as the recruitment objectives are met. Bearing in mind the likely response rates that will be obtained, it would be folly to progress immediately to broadscale media without first exhausting the possibility of reactivating former customers or generating sales from unconverted enquiries.

6.4 Media selection

A variety of media can be employed for the purposes of customer recruitment. These include direct mail, telemarketing, direct response press advertising (DRPA), door-to-door distribution, direct response television advertising (DRTV), inserts, and the Internet and electronic media, as well as, radio, in-house magazines, vending machines, and so on. The major recruitment media are described below.

6.4.1 Direct mail

The terms direct mail and direct marketing have become almost synonymous. A steadily increasing volume of items from 1.5 billion items in 1986 to well in excess of 3.5 billion items in 1997 has contributed to an increasing consumer awareness of the medium. It has suffered historically, though, from a poor image, with early, poorly targeted campaigns leading to a public perception of the medium as 'junk mail'. In fairness to the industry, however, improvements in targeting technology have greatly reduced the number of poorly targeted mailings and the majority of consumers now receive mailings that relate, at least in part, to their likely needs. It is also important to recognize that the label 'junk' is perhaps most fairly attributed to cold mailings, since once a customer has started doing business with an organization they are much less likely to be antagonized by its subsequent communications.

As a medium, direct mail has a number of

advantages. It is a genuinely one-to-one medium that facilitates the communication of a very distinct and targeted message. Mail-order companies can mail only those customers that they know will be interested in a given product category and those that they know can afford to purchase the range on offer. Organizations can also make use of the enhanced creative opportunities the medium offers.

The mailing illustrated in Fig. 26.5 was dispatched by Honda to those individuals on its database it thought might be interested (and financially able) to purchase its new CR-V vehicle. Each item was sent separately, with a few days between each mailing. As the car sponge, ice cube tray, and salt and pepper pot were sequentially dispatched, the only accompaniment to the mail-

ing was a sleeve surrounding each item proclaiming 'something for the glove compartment of the ultimate recreational vehicle'. There was no other clue as to the origin of each mailing. In the final mailing of the sequence, consumers received a storage case for a pair of Ray-Ban sunglasses. On opening the case, consumers discovered that they could collect a pair of Ray-Bans to fill the case when they arranged to test drive the new Honda CR-V—the ultimate recreational vehicle!

Mailings such as the one described engage consumers in a way that would be impossible in other media. Indeed, some mailings now appeal to a variety of different consumer senses. Some organizations now mail audio or video cassettes to get their message across. A leading cruise line, specializing in cruises to the Orient, even went so far as to

Figure 26.5 **Honda CR-V mailing**

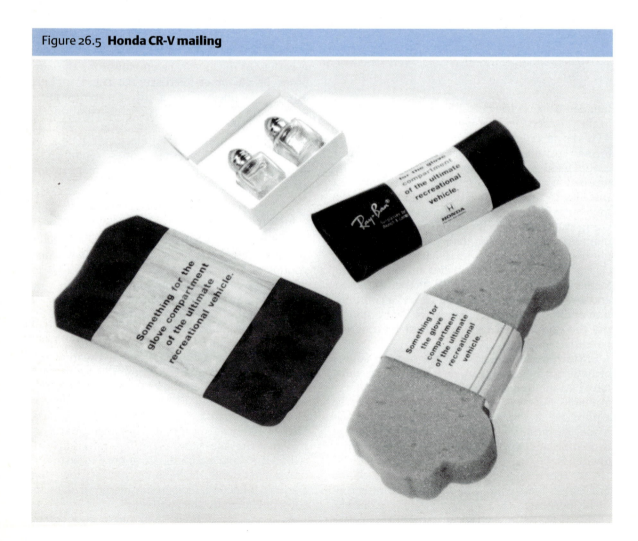

include a sachet of Jasmine tea with their brochure, so that consumers could experience the 'taste of the Orient' as they read through the details of the cruises on offer.

6.4.2 Telemarketing

Despite the commonly held perception that telemarketing is a relatively new medium, expenditure in this area in both the USA and UK now outstrips what is spent each year on direct mail. Telemarketing has been used to good effect for both 'inbound' and 'outbound' purposes.

In respect of the former, many organizations now offer their customers a convenient number to call the organization for information, or to place an order. On occasions the organization concerned will bear the full cost of the inbound call, whilst, on others, the consumer can call in for the cost of a local call, with the organization paying any balance that might be due directly to the telephone company. The earliest example of successful inbound telemarketing was the campaign in the USA to restore the Statue of Liberty. Consumers who wanted to make a donation were asked to call 1-800 THE LADY. Indeed, the increasing incidence of alphanumeric keypads has recently led to some particularly creative telemarketing approaches. During the 1990s in the USA, for example, if you wished to apply for an American Express Gold Card, you dialled 1-800 WEALTHIER.

The term 'outbound' telemarketing, by contrast, refers to telephone communications initiated by the organization. Early use of this medium by organizations selling double glazing and other home-improvement products was viewed as intrusive and the use of telemarketing for cold-customer recruitment has been much criticized. More acceptable, perhaps, are 'warm' uses of the technique, where customer interest in a product category has already been established and where the content of the call is thus more likely to be of interest.

Companies new to the use of telemarketing can either elect to employ their own telemarketing staff, or engage the services of a specialist agency, who will answer or initiate calls as if they were part of the client's organization. The use of such agencies can be particularly helpful, where it could prove difficult to anticipate the customer response. Not only can they offer guidance based on their experience, but the fact that they service a number of clients often means they have the necessary manpower to cover an especially large and perhaps unanticipated response.

6.4.3 Direct Response Press Advertising (DRPA)

DRPA differs from traditional press advertising in that the purpose of the ad is always to initiate a direct response. The ad will typically contain a high degree of information about the product/service and a response mechanism will be provided such as a coupon or an '0800' inbound telemarketing number. As with other forms of direct marketing, it is possible to track the response from particular ads. Telephone operators can be instructed to record the source of the enquiry and, in the case of coupons, a code can be printed on each coupon, uniquely identifying the nature and date of the publication. Replies can be carefully analysed and the most effective media identified.

6.4.4 Door-to-door distribution

Carriers such as the Royal Mail offer a service that allows a direct-marketing organization to concentrate its resources in particular geographical regions. Leaflets or fliers can be delivered with the mail to all the households in a specified area. It is clearly less targeted than direct mail, but has considerable advantages in terms of cost, since there are no postal charges to pay. For these reasons it is now common practice to employ door-to-door distribution in the case of those products/services with a fairly universal appeal (Bird 1989).

6.4.5 Direct Response Television Advertising (DRTV)

As with DRPA, the aim of this form of advertising is to engender a direct response. An increasing proportion of television advertising now contains a response number and may hence be classified under this general heading. The fragmentation of television channels means that advertisers can now reach highly specialized audiences with this form of communication (Young 1994). The birth of digital TV only served to increase the pace of fragmentation and, since highly specialized audiences are usually more willing to watch commercials that relate specifically to their needs, the duration of commercials will lengthen. In effect, television advertising has come 'full circle'. The earliest forms of television commercial were quite bland affairs, where the details of the product would be recounted in great detail. Indeed some commercials in the late 1940s were as long as thirty minutes in duration. Advertising carried by some specialist channels is now beginning to resemble these early approaches. Indeed, some channels (e.g. QVC) are now entirely given over to DRTV appeals.

6.4.6 Inserts

Inserts are loose-leaf or bound in cards inserted into many newspapers and magazines. Anyone buying a magazine in recent times will be familiar with the use of this medium, particularly if they have held the magazine upside down and shaken it. A flood of paper and card inserts will doubtless have assembled on the carpet. As a direct response media, these inserts would typically carry a response telephone number or a reply coupon. Indeed, many inserts are actually designed as response cards in themselves and on completion can be placed directly in the mail for return to the company.

Inserts are typically much more effective than press advertising and can often generate between four and six times the response of an equivalent press ad (Stone 1996). Inserts can also offer enhanced opportunities for testing, since several different versions of the insert can be printed, with no additional insertion costs being incurred, since the inserts are delivered *en masse* to the media owner. The principal drawback of inserts is the cost. The cost per thousand is usually four to five times that of the equivalent press advertising.

6.4.7 The internet and electronic media

Since the introduction of the World Wide Web in 1991, the use of the Internet has grown almost exponentially. By the late 1990s the Internet was attracting what has been described as a 'sophisticated consumer' demanding timely information and a prompt and personalized service. Research indicates that a typical internet user is male, aged 35 years, with an above-average level of education and household income (Nua What's New 1997). The gender gap is narrowing, though, and the profile continues to soften with each passing year, embracing ever more broader sections of society.

Not only is access to the Internet widening; users appear ever more likely to use the Internet to make product purchases, despite early concerns over the security of transmitting credit-card information over the Web. Indeed, between 20 and 30 per cent of users have made at least one purchase using this new electronic medium. Many organizations are, therefore, beginning to exploit the potential of the Internet for marketing purposes, and the proportion of sites offering visitors the capacity to purchase goods and services is increasing rapidly every year.

Davenport (1996) identifies four levels of internet presence.

- *Electronic brochure*. This is a site that provides only the most basic of information about the organization and its services.
- *electronic catalogue*. A detailed online catalogue enables customers to browse and if so desired, to place an order by using the phone or fax.
- *diret response without cash transactions*. This category is similar to the above, but the site permits online ordering. Payment must, however, be handled via conventional means.
- *Full direct response and payment*. Some sites permit all of the above, but in addition allow the user to pay for the goods ordered on line. To deal with concerns over the security of personal financial information, many sites now provide a data encryption facility to ensure that the link with them is secure.

The household penetration of Internet use is expected to increase dramatically with the advent of Web TV. The merging of traditional entertainment channels with the flexibility and information provision of the Web will represent a considerable marketing opportunity. Consumers exposed to DRTV will shortly be able to request further information direct from the manufacturer, seek wider information about other suppliers of a given product category, or even make a purchase direct from their own armchair at the simple press of a button. Web TV should also allow advertisers to target individuals with a known interest in particular products/services. The pattern of advertising to which we are all exposed will be made to vary at an individual level and will be driven by our unique needs and preferences.

This personalization is already prevalent on the Internet. Users visiting a web site for the first time are often asked to provide information about themselves that can be stored by the company for future reference. As a service to their customers, companies store basic information about each individual in a 'cookie' file on the customer's home (or office) pc. Most users are unaware that data are being stored on their computer in this way, but it can be a helpful facility, since the next time they call into the company's web site, the organization requests information from their cookie file and is able to identify them. The appearance of the site can then be made to vary by the individual's known preferences. The 'home page' of the Internet bookshop Amazon is presented in Box 26. 3. As you can see, although this is the first screen in the

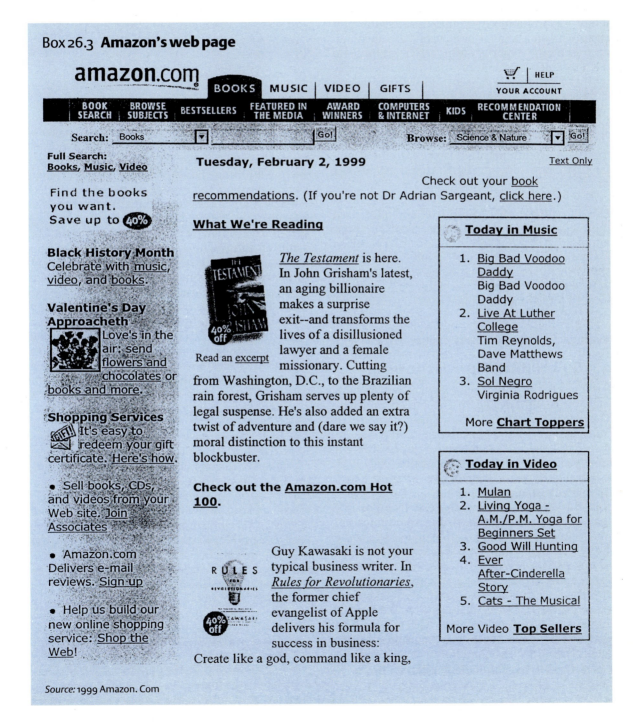

Box 26.3 **Amazon's web page**

Source: 1999 Amazon. Com

site I have visited, the organization has already recognized me, addressed me by name, and prepared a list of texts it believes I will find of interest.

Of course, web sites are not the only media opportunity offered by Internet technology. Electronic mail (e-mail) is increasing in popularity and many organizations now communicate with their customers on a regular basis using this medium. At present, the majority of this activity is inbound (i.e. customer initiated) or undertaken primarily with the customer's consent. Whilst it is technically possible for organizations to send out large numbers of unsolicited e-mails, or SPAM as it has come to be known in Internet jargon (reflecting the effect of a can of spam thrown into a fan), such forms of communication are extremely unpopular. Most organizations therefore respect the wishes of other Net users and avoid their use. When immigration lawyers Cantor and Siegel failed to observe this 'netiquette' and advertised their legal services through every available Internet discussion group, their organization received many thousands of hate-mail responses which resulted in the organization being thrown off the network. The lawyers have since claimed, however, that their tactics gained them over $100,000 worth of new business.

6.5 Communication of the offer

Having selected appropriate media, the offer can then be communicated to the target audience. There may typically be several different ways of framing the offer and incentivizing a response. Direct marketers will often test a series of different creative approaches and compare the likely ROIs achievable by offering a range of different incentives to engender a response.

In the direct-marketing context, it is possible that a multi-stage approach to communication may be planned. In the example in Box 26.4 there are several different approaches that may be used to engender a response. In general, the greater the number of stages in a communications strategy, the greater will be the ultimate response. It is, of course, a matter of balancing the cost of employing additional stages, with the return that will be generated by the additional investment. Past experience or additional research will often suggest the optimal number of stages to employ.

Box 26.4 Contact strategy: consumer

- Mail
- Mail → 0800
- Mail → Phone
- Press → 0800 → Mail follow-up
- Mail → 0800 → Mail follow-up → Phone

Source: Holder (1998).

6.6 Fulfilment

When the response from customers is received, the organization must then ensure that the order (or request for further information) is processed within the time frame promised in the original communication The response must be handled as efficiently and effectively as possible. This process is known as 'fulfilment'. Testing will have suggested the likely response rates that will be achieved and the organization can use this information to plan fulfilment resources accordingly. In many consumer markets, manufacturers will elect to outsource the fulfilment aspect of the campaign to ensure that an adequate level of service is provided. Fulfilment is a highly specialized operation and it will often be more economic for a manufacturer to rely on an external supplier than to have resources of its own standing idle between direct-marketing campaigns.

6.7 Response analysis

The final step in a recruitment campaign is perhaps the most critical. A detailed assessment of campaign performance can be invaluable in guiding future direct-marketing strategy and tactics. Performance can be compared against the objectives that were originally set for the campaign and against other campaigns that have been run in the past. The profile of responding customers can also be compared with the profile that was originally envisaged and any refinements necessary can be made to the targeting of future campaigns.

The most common financial criteria that are employed to assess recruitment campaigns are as follows:

- % response;
- % conversion (i.e. from enquiries to sales);
- £ cost per customer;

- £ revenue per customer;
- £ profit per customer;
- £ projected LTV per customer;
- ROI.

7 Building a customer database

As soon as new customers have been recruited, their details and purchase behaviour will be stored in the marketing database. This information can then be used to refine the targeting of additional customer-acquisition activity and it can also be used to inform the development of ongoing relationships with the individuals concerned.

☞ 'Marketing-database data become "information" when we identify the recency, frequency, and monetary value (RFM) of customer orders.' (Chapter 8, p. 169)

As Kotler (1994) notes: 'A marketing database is an organized collection of comprehensive data about individual customers, prospects or suspects that is current, accessible and actionable for such marketing purposes as lead generation, lead qualification, sale of a product or service, or maintenance of customer relationships.' Given Kotler's definition, the creation of a computerized database is the single most important investment that many organizations can make. As will already have become clear, the benefits a database can offer in terms of a more detailed understanding of consumer behaviour can lead to an infinitely more effective use of marketing resources.

Before taking the decision to invest in a database, however, an organization needs to be clear;

- what the primary purpose of the database will be;
- what secondary functions the database will be expected to fulfil;
- the other systems with which the database must interact—e.g. accounting;
- the categories of data it is intended to store;
- the volume of data it is intended to store;
- the forms of analysis and/or segmentation the database will be expected to accomplish;

- the forms of marketing it is intended to support;
- the range of outputs that will be expected.

7.1 Three ways of producing a database

An understanding of these issues should enable an organization to select between the various options open to it in the acquisition of appropriate database software. For a typical organization, these are likely to include the following.

- *Purchasing or leasing a commercially available software package*. There are a great many packages currently on the market and their number continues to grow on an almost daily basis. Packages will support many forms of direct-marketing activity, including direct mail and telemarketing. Other more sophisticated systems will aid in market research and even allow the development of geodemographic profiles of the customers on the system.

- *Using proprietary software*. This differs from packaged software in that it is usually developed by highly specialized third parties such as Marketing Computer Bureaux. These organisations usually lease the software and work with the users to help them carry out their marketing activity and analysis.

- *Designing a custom database*. This is clearly the most expensive of the three options and therefore beyond the reach of most smaller organizations. Moreover, one would need a very strong argument in favour of this alternative, since the range of proprietary or packaged software is likely to meet all but the most specialized of needs perfectly adequately. Circumstances that are likely to warrant this considerable investment include the necessity to link with a wide range of other systems, the desire for a particularly specialized function, and/or the sheer size of the database to be created.

7.2 What information should be stored?

Data in respect of customers are typically held in 'files' that usually require the user to follow a set format. Each variable that is stored (for example, age, gender, and so on) will have a specific 'field' into which such information must be entered.

More sophisticated packages also contain a number of user-definable fields, so that the database can to a certain extent be customized to the needs of the individual organization. Box 26.5 illustrates the information that would typically be stored in the case of both consumer and business-to-business contexts.

It is interesting to note that the collection of a customer's telephone number has taken on a new significance since telephone systems have been equipped with a facility known as caller recognition. This allows the system to recognize the person calling by his or her telephone number and to display the relevant customer file in front of an operator so that he or she can welcome the caller by name. Not only is this a more personal service, since the operator has immediate access to the customer record, but the time taken to process an enquiry is considerably shortened—something of benefit to both parties to the transaction. This facility is likely to become ever more powerful now that telephone users can be allocated their own unique telephone number, which they can then use for a lifetime, taking it with them when they move from house to house.

Box 26.5 Elements of a database

Consumer database	Business-to-business database
ID Number	ID Number
Title	Title of organization
Name	Names and titles of contacts
Gender	
Address	Addresses
Telephone number	Telephone numbers
Fax number	Fax numbers
E-mail	E-mail addresses
Recruitment source	Classification (SIC code)
Socio-economic group	Business size
Geodemographic coding	Geographic characteristics
Purchase history	Purchase history
Credit limit	Purchase channels
Communication history	Credit limit
Preferences	Communication history
Other information	Preferences
	Other information

8 Customer retention

THE role of the database for the purposes of recruitment has already been explained. It can also offer considerable utility, however, for customer development and retention. This is achieved by segmenting the database and developing a uniquely tailored service for each of the segments identified. Customers will thus receive communications that are relevant to them as individuals, with improvements in satisfaction and loyalty likely to result.

A number of criteria can be applied to segment a database and thus select individuals (or organizations) to receive a particular campaign. Variables such as age, gender, income, geographic location, geodemographic coding, occupation, lifestyle, and so on could all be used for this purpose. Communications with specific themes can be sent to those who experience suggests would be most receptive. In the context of database segmentation, there are, however, a number of other variables that could be utilized—namely:

- original recruitment media;
- amount of most recent purchase;
- product categories purchased;
- date of most recent purchase;
- frequency of purchase;
- nature of the desired relationship;
- LTV.

Each of these variables is considered below.

Original recruitment media Data in respect of the original recruitment media can be used to good effect, since all customers are unlikely to behave in the same way. Customers recruited by DRTV, for example, are notoriously poor responders to direct mail. There would, therefore, be little point in attempting to develop a relationship with this group by mail. An approach based on the telephone, however, may prove more productive.

Amount of most recent purchase Similarly, the amount of the most recent purchase (or average order value) can be used to develop a customer from a low-value category (say £30 per annum) to a higher-value category (say £100 per annum). As an organization starts to understand more about the interests of its customers, it can refine the content of communications accordingly. It can also frame the 'offer' to encourage the customer to spend ever greater amounts of money with the organization concerned—what direct marketers refer to as building 'share of the customer' (McDonald 1998). It is important to note that average order value can also be used to ensure that mailings containing the details of high-value products are not sent to those with insufficient resources to purchase.

Product categories purchased A knowledge of the product categories purchased can be employed to ensure not only that customers receive future mailings that are particularly pertinent to their interests, but also those concerning related products/services that are also likely to be of interest. This is known as cross-selling.

Some organizations will also use this information for a second purpose—what direct marketers refer to as 'up-selling'. Customers, for example, currently buying a car at the bottom of a manufacturer's range can be targeted to receive details of a slightly larger vehicle when they are considering repurchase. Recent purchasers of a Peugeot 106, for example, could be sent details of the 206 eighteen months after purchasing their previous vehicle.

Date of most recent purchase The date of most recent purchase can be used to control the timing of the next contact that an organization will have with a given customer. There are few things that irritate customers more than placing an order one day and then receiving another marketing communication a few days later for a similar product. Marketing communications should be timed at appropriate intervals, based on the record of previous correspondence and the customer's purchase history.

Information about the date of last order can also be used to identify customers who appear to have lapsed. On the basis of the value of their prior relationship, a decision can then be taken in respect of whether to delete them from the active portion of the database, or whether to attempt to reactivate them with a particularly attractive promotional offer.

Frequency of purchase Many organizations make the mistake of attempting to develop customers solely by order value. Mail-order catalogues, for example, often encourage their 'agents' to place ever larger orders through the provision of a series of financial and/or gift-related incentives. It is im-

portant to recognize though that customers can also be developed by the frequency with which they make an order. Persuading a customer who might typically make two purchases a year worth £40 to an organization to make a third will have the same effect on overall revenue as developing their average order value to £60. There are, therefore, two distinct alternatives.

Nature of the desired relationship Rather than manipulating the database to provide customers with the contact strategy the organization believes customers will find most appropriate, many organizations are now allowing customers to select for themselves whether and how they might wish to hear from an organization again. Increasingly customers are being offered a choice over the receipt of further communications, the product lines they wish to be kept informed about, and when and how often they would like these communications to be received. Some organizations even offer their customers choice over the media that will subsequently be employed (for example, mail, e-mail, telephone, fax, and so on).

LTV As was noted previously, the projected LTV of customers can be used to ensure that they receive a standard of care that reflects their value to the organization. Whilst losing any customer is regrettable, losing higher-value customers should be a matter of great concern. Database information can hence be employed to ensure that a particular effort is expended to retain and develop higher-value customers.

Data in respect of LTV can also be used periodically to clean the database. In almost every database there will be groups of customers with whom it will never be profitable to develop a relationship. Customers that make no contribution to the organization's profit, or who are actually costing the organization money to support, can be identified and deleted from the active portion of the database. In the author's experience, as much as 10 per cent of the active portion of a database can be made up of customers who will never be profitable.

9 The future

THE direct-marketing revolution has barely begun. As the pace of technological change quickens, opportunities for direct marketers to develop what *Business Week* has referred to as a 'silicon simulacrum' of the relationships that people used to have with tradesmen such as butchers, bakers, and so on will abound. Tailored approaches will become the norm and tailoring the approach to dealing with different categories of customers will no longer mean increasing marketing cost. Modern databases can greatly facilitate the identification of discrete customer segments and suggest contact strategies designed specifically to build customer value.

Whilst it is always difficult to speculate about the future, a number of trends can already be observed. These include:

Channel integration The need for households to own a separate hi-fi, television, video recorder, and home computer will shortly be ended. Integrated home entertainment and information systems are already in the development stage. A new generation of intelligent Web TVs, for example, will record user preferences and search for the programming and information that will be of most interest. Facilities will exist to download relevant audio, video, and printed information and users will be able to purchase most of the goods and services they require from the comfort of their own armchair. There can be little doubt that the fragmentation of the advertising media will continue, but that it will become increasingly easier to navigate the alternatives from one central point of access. Direct marketers of the future will hence find it easier to reach potential new customers, but perhaps more difficult to retain them, as information about alternative products becomes much easier to assemble.

Rise in integrated communications Marketers have been making increasing efforts to integrate direct-marketing activities within their overall communications mix. Organizations can no longer afford to manage each of these activities separately—opportunities for synergy have now to be exploited to have the maximum impact on the target market. When launching the new Peugeot 406, Peugeot was keen to integrate every aspect of its campaign. In the run-up to the launch, dealerships received packs of promotional material, including point of sale material featuring stills from the forthcoming television commercials, CDs with the music from the commercials for distribution to customers, and a range of full-colour brochures—again featuring scenes from the ads.

Past customers of Peugeot, likely to be interested in this category of vehicle, received 'teaser' mailings to generate an awareness of the launch, without giving anything away about the look of the car. These mailings were also designed to make the recipients feel special, as they were amongst the few individuals to be aware of the launch. The copy informed them of the timing of the first television commercial, when the details of the new car would finally be revealed. Press ads were also designed and placed in the broadscale media to draw attention to the launch. These featured the numbers 406 and the date and time the first commercial could be viewed.

The television commercial itself was aired after the national news and space was bought on every major television channel. Viewers to ITV, Channel 4, and the major satellite channels were all exposed to the first ad simultaneously—the first time in television history such an event had been orchestrated.

In this example, each of the direct channels was carefully integrated to build up consumer awareness of, and interest in, the television commercial, where all would finally be revealed about the look and style of the new car. Such integrated approaches are likely to become the norm in the future, as companies recognize that the impact of one media can be greatly enhanced by the synergistic impact of others.

Share of customer not share of market Much of this chapter has been concerned with the concept of customer LTV. Whilst this is a fundamental concept in direct marketing, organizations are only just starting to recognize the implications thereof. As database technology improves and companies are able to gather and store more information about their customer base, opportunities for a more meaningful analysis of LTV will abound. Until the second half of the 1990s, for example, the major airlines targeted their frequent flier programmes at the individuals who had historically flown most frequently with their airline. In other words, they were basing their approach on the *historic value* of a given group of customers. As airlines gained more knowledge about the flying behaviour of their customers, however, it soon became apparent that frequent fliers were only frequent fliers for a period of around four years. After that, the individual's job role would typically change and it was no longer necessary for him or her to travel on such a frequent basis.

The problem from the airline marketer's perspective was that it would typically take between eighteen months and two years to identify frequent fliers (on the basis of past purchases), which allowed the airline a small window of only two years in which to keep them loyal and develop a larger share of their custom.

At the end of the twentieth century the smarter airlines were in a position to profile the behaviour of their customers and to predict with a fair degree of accuracy those individuals who would *become* frequent fliers in the future. This maximized the airline's ability to keep the customers loyal throughout their most intensive period of travel.

Technology will thus allow organizations of the future to identify potentially high-value customers early in their relationship with a given organization and allow marketers to concentrate on developing a relationship that will generate an ever larger percentage of that customer's overall expenditure in a given product category. When Tesco's introduced its loyalty card, its purpose was largely to ensure that the customer had good reasons for conducting every weekly shop at the Tesco's store. The company was trying to attract a greater share of its existing customers' overall spend, rather than concentrating on bringing in ever greater numbers of customers. This is a change of emphasis that will continue to permeate many sectors in the future.

Ethical behaviours Mention has also been made in this chapter about consumer concerns over different forms of direct-marketing activity. Many traditional forms of direct marketing have been judged intrusive and an invasion of an individual's privacy. Organizations will need to become increasingly sensitive to such issues, as many of the new direct channels rely on the electronic transmission of data. Customer privacy and security will become an intrinsic consideration in any new media campaign (McDonald 1998). Organizations will need to educate consumers about how their data will be held and how, if at all, it will be used by them in the future. Changing regulatory frameworks will also give customers greater control over this process and companies will need to ensure that they have an appropriate infrastructure in place to respect the wishes of their individual customers (see Insert).

> **Guaranteeing privacy may be the differentiator**
>
> 'Businesses that use data to deliver better service to customers while also respecting their privacy will be the real winners in the direct marketing revolution.'
> *The Economist*, (9 Jan. 1999, p. 69)

10 Summary

IN this chapter we have provided a general overview of the subject of direct marketing. We have defined it as a unique discipline within marketing, the aim of which is to deal with customers on a one-to-one basis, through a careful analysis of information stored on an organization's database. It is this unique emphasis on the use of customer information that characterizes so much direct-marketing activity.

We have also explored in detail the role of the marketing database and explained its role in informing both customer-acquisition and customer-retention activity. The structure of a typical customer-acquisition plan was highlighted and a range of recruitment media was discussed.

The chapter concluded by speculating as to the likely direction the discipline will take. The rise of new electronic channels, improvements in technology and a general move towards media fragmentation look set to secure its future. Indeed it may not be long before all marketing activity can be legitimately classified under this one general heading.

Further reading

Introductory textbooks

McDonald, W. J. (1998), *Direct Marketing: An Integrated Approach* (Singapore: McGraw Hill).

Tapp, A. (1998), *Principles of Direct and Database Marketing* (London: Pitman/FT Publishing).

Practitioner texts

Baier, M. (1996), *How To Find and Cultivate Customers Through Direct Marketing* (Lincolnwood, Ill.: NTC Publications).

McCorkell, G. (1997), *Direct and Database Marketing* (London: Kogan Page).

Stone, M., Davies, D., and Bond, A. (1995), *Direct Hit: Direct Marketing with a Winning Edge* (London: Pitman Publishing).

Textbooks on specific aspects of direct marketing

King, J. M., Knight, P., and Mason, J. H. (1997), *Web Marketing Cookbook* (New York: John Wiley).

Lewis, H. G., and Nelson, C. (1995), *World's Greatest Direct Mail Sales Letters* (Lincolnwood, Ill.: NTC Publications).

Reitman, J. I. (1996), *Beyond 2000: The Future of Direct Marketing* (Lincolnwood, Ill.: NTC Publications).

Shaver, D. (1996), *The Next Step in Database Marketing: Consumer Guided Marketing* (New York: John Wiley).

Some useful journal articles

Evans, M., O'Malley, L., and Patterson, M. (1996), 'Direct Marketing Communications in the UK: A Study of Growth, Past, Present and Future', *Journal of Marketing Communications*, 2: 51–65.

Muranyi, N. R. (1995), 'Database Marketing in FMCGs: What is The State of the Art?', *Journal of Database Marketing*, 4/1: 13–20.

Thwaites, D., and Lee, S. C. I. (1994), 'Direct Marketing in the Financial Services Industry', *Journal of Marketing Management*, 10: 377–90.

Wang, P., and Petrison, J. (1993), 'Direct Marketing Activities and Personal Privacy', *Journal of Direct Marketing*, 7/1: 7–19.

Discussion questions

1 How would you characterize direct marketing? How does it differ from a mass-marketing approach?

2 Explain how a manufacturer of consumer goods might employ a knowledge of customer lifetime value to inform the development of its marketing strategy.

3 How might an organization typically generate a list of potential new customers to receive a recruitment campaign?

4 What are the key differences between lifestyle and geodemographic lists?

5 In your role as the fundraising director of the Royal National Lifeboat Institution (RNLI), develop a customer-acquisition plan to recruit 100,000 new donors to the organization.

6 A manufacturer of industrial fasteners is about to develop a customer database for the first time. What advice would you offer its marketing department? What information should be stored on the new database? How might it be used to inform marketing strategy?

7 What are the primary concerns that consumers have about the use of direct-marketing techniques? How might the direct-marketing industry counter these criticisms?

Benedictine liqueur: the repositioning of a brand

In the 1990s the drinks market was replete with attempts to move brands towards a younger target audience. Tia Maria and Harvey's Bristol Cream have both made successful and highly publicized attempts to reposition their brands. Other big names such as Southern Comfort have chosen to broaden their appeal, by moving away from the perception of an after-dinner drink towards that of an exotic cocktail mixer.

Against this background, Benedictine, too, has recognized the need for change. The brand has a 400-year-old history and has been around for long enough for drinkers to form a distinctive perception of the 'values' of the product. The organization recognized in 1996, however, that the perception was no longer one that was appropriate, given the competitive pressures in the market. The profile of drinkers was ageing and the brand was viewed as being rather staid and old-fashioned.

The marketing team, therefore, sought a way to reposition the brand, add some excitement, and build sales volumes, without alienating the existing and loyal customer base. The budget to achieve this goal was comparatively small. Whilst competitors such as Tia Maria or Southern Comfort were both able to consider the use of television advertising to assist in their repositioning, the Benedictine brand is small by comparison, with much smaller sums being available for the purposes of marketing. The marketing team, therefore, decided on a highly targeted direct-marketing approach—any other approach would have resulted in a high degree of wastage, which the team was keen to avoid.

An additional problem with television advertising was the likely timing thereof. In common with other alcoholic drinks, Christmas is a period of peak sales for the Benedictine brand. It would, therefore, have been logical to advertise in the period immediately prior to the holiday, but in so doing the brand would have had to compete with a concentration of other advertising messages from competitors with a larger share of the voice.

The decision to invest in direct marketing was triggered by the existence of a small but accurate database of existing customers that had been built in the past from on-bottle promotions, money-off vouchers, and an offer of free miniatures. This made it possible for Benedictine to have its customer base profiled against the *Target Group Index* (*TGI*) and for the lifestyle characteristics of its drinkers to be identified.

The results of the analysis revealed that the Benedictine drinker could be either male or female, was typically well educated, aged 35+ from socio-economic groups ABC1, and culturally aware. Drinkers appeared to enjoy leisure activities such as theatre visits, gardening, art, travel, and food. The Benedictine team decided to develop a campaign that would focus on these drinkers, developing lifetime value rather than attempting expensive customer acquisition. Direct mail was to be the chosen medium.

The TGI profile made it possible to identify that existing drinkers had a distinct set of interests and that these interests were generally related to sensory stimulation of one form or another. The marketing team soon recognized that customers would be likely to respond to an appeal designed, equally, to stimulate the senses. Customer mailings were hence given an 'awaken your senses' theme.

The Benedictine liqueur is made from a traditional (and secret) recipe in the Normandy region of France. This, together with its 400 years of history, combine to give the brand an interesting story to tell. The mailings Benedictine developed were designed to build on these characteristics and associate the brand with art, good food, and the beauties of the garden. Drinkers were offered recipes and cocktail mixes and given many different reasons for increasing their product usage. Mailings (which took place twice a year) also included money-off tokens and an opportunity to earn discounts for a second purchase. Take-up rates to these offers is usually very high and response rates of over 40 per cent have been reported.

Product packaging was also redesigned to include a new promotional sleeve, inviting drinkers to send in their details in return for entry to a promotional prize draw. As a consequence the organization's database grew from a mere 6,000 to well over 17,000 in just two years. These enhanced numbers and ongoing consumer response to new direct-marketing campaigns provided ever more detailed information for the organization about the nature of its customer group. As the organization continued to learn, the quality and targeting of its communications strategy continued to be refined.

Discussion question

1 Critically appraise Benedictine's strategy? Can you discern any weaknesses in the approach adopted?

2 In developing its retention programme, what controls would you expect the Benedictine team to have put in place?

3 How might the Benedictine team approach a customer-acquisition programme? What form might this take?

Case 5
Fieldstone Ltd

Keith Blois

If Peter Wyndham had not just retired, then Dave Marriott, Dunnans's Marketing and Sales Manager, would have been pretty certain what he should do. However, only two weeks ago Peter had retired from Fieldstone, where he had been Purchasing Manager, and had been replaced by Vincent Best, who had taken up the post the day after Peter's last day in the office at Fieldstone. Dave had so far had no opportunity to meet or even speak on the phone with Best. All that he knew about him was that he had previously been employed by Unwins, a company that, while it claimed to be firm but fair in its dealings with its suppliers, was regarded by its suppliers as taking an adversarial approach towards supply matters. So Dave was concerned that Best's arrival might lead to a change in the relationship that existed between Dunnans and Fieldstone, which had over a number of years developed into one where there was mutual trust and understanding between the two firms. His concern had been heightened a few days ago when John Bissett (Fieldstone's Assistant Purchasing Manager) had told him that in his first week at the company Best had issued a memo setting out his policy regarding the forms of entertainment that his staff might accept from suppliers. Bisset knew this to be basically a copy of an Unwin's document and said that it appeared to be a lengthy and bureaucratic way of saying 'None'.

Dunnans had been a supplier of specialized styrene resins to Fieldstone for many years. The relationship had grown steadily and now in an average year Fieldstone's purchases from Dunnans amounted to about £0.5 million. Dunnans had several competitors who were keen to get Fieldstone's business. However, by maintaining a high-quality service and offering a considerable amount of technical and research support, Dunnans had consistently obtained the major share of Fieldstone's orders, even though its prices were always fractionally higher than its competitors. More than one of Dunnans's competitors thought that Dunnans's relationship with Fieldstone was 'a bit cosy', and about a year ago Fieldstone's Managing Director, having heard of this view, had challenged Peter to justify the situation. Peter had as a consequence then arranged a meeting between the Managing Director, himself, and Dave, during which a frank discussion of the

companies' relationship had taken place. Dave had agreed that Dunnans's prices were consistently marginally above those quoted by the competition but pointed out that it provided Fieldstone with a more extensive and comprehensive technical service than any of the competitors did or could offer. He was also able to point out that on a number of occasions Dunnans had responded at not inconsiderable cost to itself but at no charge to Fieldstone to significant short-term changes in demand from Fieldstone. Dave had also made the point that it would not be sensible for Dunnans to charge Fieldstone too much, as this would inevitably affect Fieldstone's competitiveness and this could not be in Dunnans's own interest in the long term. At the end of the discussion Fieldstone's Managing Director indicated that, as long as the prices quoted by Dunnans remained only marginally higher than those of the competitors, he felt that the situation was acceptable.

Both Dave and Forsyth, his Deputy, had got on well with Peter and John Bissett. Having known and worked with each other over a large number of years, their relationship had developed to the point where frequent face-to-face contact was unnecessary. Instead, much of their interaction was by phone, and indeed they were on the phone to each other several times a month. They were welcome to visit each other's factory at any time and they granted each other as much open contact as was possible. Their secretaries knew that they would always accept phone calls from each other. When they did have meetings, they usually had lunch together, but they never met for purely social reasons. The exception to this was that Peter, like Dave, enjoyed a day at the horse races from time to time. So, about once a year (but not every year), Peter had invited Dave and his wife to join him and his partner in the box that Dunnans hired at one of the smaller Ascot race meetings. On such occasions they had made it a strict rule never to discuss work, not least because Mrs Wyndham— who was a bit of a dragon—did not like it.

The market in which Fieldstone operated, though expanding steadily, had recently become extremely competitive. Its growth in the UK compared with a reduced level of activity on the Continent had attracted the attention of some overseas companies and in the last year two new companies had opened factories in the UK. Given that the minimum economic size of this type of factory was equivalent to about 10 per cent of the current UK market, the effect had been to create excess capacity in the UK market, which it was felt would take about four years to absorb. For some of the established companies, such as Fieldstone, whose plants were old, the arrival of this additional capacity had presented a real problem, as their factories were less efficient than those of the newcomers. This meant that their costs were higher and the new entrants had been able and willing to set about 'buying' market share with low prices. Indeed, the competition had become fairly aggressive, with rumours of what were described as 'dirty tricks' being played. Although nobody was too explicit as to what these tricks were, there was no doubt that the atmosphere within the industry had become quite hostile. Indeed, both its suppliers and customers had become aware of the change.

Six weeks ago Pickens, one of Fieldstone's long-standing customers, had asked for quotes for what it described as 'a one-off order' for the type of product that Fieldstone supplied. In fact, it was the biggest single contract for this type of material to be placed on the market for several years. It was known that it was connected with a large order that Pickens had obtained from abroad following a serious fire in an overseas plant and that it was quite separate from Pickens's regular business.

Pickens was a large and successful manufacturer and was often cited in the press as a company that demonstrated that taking a responsible long-term view of its relationship with its employees, customers, and suppliers was good business practice. The management at Fieldstone had always regarded this publicity with some amusement. As Peter had pointed out to Dave, 'Yes, they are responsible customers. But if they do you a favour, it's always remembered and traded in sometime. Frankly, I don't think they are any different from us—we try to see our suppliers as partners. Remember, though, it's easier to adopt this philosophy when business is good. I'm not sure what we would be like if times got really tough.'

The Pickens contract was unusual, not just for its size but also because of a requirement that deliveries should both start within a week of the order being placed and be completed as soon as possible but definitely within four weeks. In spite of the intense competition for this contract, Fieldstone had been tipped off that it had won it. It had, therefore, four weeks ago, placed a large order with Dunnans for delivery of resin to start as soon as possible and to be completed within three weeks. It made this request, as it wanted to be in a position to commence manufacturing the moment the Pickens order had been received. In fact, Fieldstone had wanted, and Dunnans had managed to supply, the whole order in two weeks. Even though the order was for a type of resin that Fieldstone regularly used, meeting the delivery requirement for such a large quantity at such short notice had caused Dunnans a lot of difficulty. However, Peter had met Dave and given him a full briefing of the situation. He had explained that it was not just the size of the contract that made it so important but the fear that, if one of the two newcomers won it, they would use this as a foot in the door to get at the regular business. He also felt that, if Fieldstone could successfully meet the demanding delivery requirements, this would impress Pickens's management in terms both of its production capabilities and also of its relationships with its suppliers. Apparently recently one of Pickens's buyers had made some adverse comparisons between Fieldstone's plant and the quality of the plant used by the newcomers. Peter had also stressed that the fact that Fieldstone had placed the order should be treated as confidential. Dave could not see that it would be a very profitable order, because of the disruption that would be caused by fitting it into an already full production schedule, but accepted it because he felt obliged to assist an old customer.

In fact, Blanc, one of the two newcomers to the UK industry, was awarded the Pickens contract, this being the first time they had obtained any business from Pickens. Fieldstone's management was furious, 'stuff business loyalty' being one of the politer phrases emanating from their board room. The concern was that the awarding of this contract to Blanc confirmed the view that some of Pickens's management did see Fieldstone as weak relative to the newcomers with their modern plants.

Peter, in his last contact before retiring, had thanked Dave for Dunnans's help in supplying the material for the Pickens contract—not least because he was aware that producing the material under such conditions must have pushed costs up. He said that, as a token of its appreciation, Fieldstone, instead of taking the normal thirty days' credit, would pay for the deliveries at once and retain the material, using it up over a period of months. Unfortunately, of course, he pointed out that Fieldstone would not now require all of the deliveries from Dunnan that it had already scheduled for its regular production.

Dunnans had managed to obtain some business from both Blanc and Butot—the two new entrants to the business—a fact that was well known in the industry. However, in the case of Blanc, it seemed that Dunnans was regarded as the second-string supplier, and, indeed, Dave had never been able to obtain a meeting with anybody other than Blanc's Deputy Purchasing Manager. Dave had, therefore, been surprised to be asked to attend an urgent meeting with Blanc's Managing Director. At this meeting he was asked if he could supply 'at once' a very large volume of the same resin that he had just delivered to Fieldstone. In the discussion it rapidly became apparent that, having obtained the order from Pickens, Blanc could not fulfil the delivery conditions because apparently its main supplier was having production problems. Dave promised to let Blanc know within twenty-four hours if he could help. Blanc's Managing Director had indicated at the close of the meeting that, if Dunnans could help, this would be remembered when contracts were being placed in the future.

As he drove back to his office Dave thought the matter through. He was very keen to get into a stronger position with Blanc, as it was the company running the most modern plant in the UK. It was also reputed to have a strong management team, with ambitious plans for developing its share of the UK market. There seemed to be little doubt in the industry that before long it was likely to become the UK market leader in its field. However, Dave knew that Dunnans was still recovering from the disruption caused by meeting Fieldstone's urgent request. The only way he believed that Dunnans could meet Blanc's requirement would be if he could buy back some of the excess resin that Fieldstone currently held.

When he got back to his office, Dave learnt two things. First that morning the Production Manager had reported that one of his machines had developed a fault that required about a week's maintenance and this would affect the firm's ability to keep up with some existing orders. Secondly, Forsyth had been talking with Bisset, who had told him that Best had been in a very good mood that day because he understood that 'Blanc was having trouble with the big contract it had "stolen" from Fieldstone and that Blanc would never get another contract from Pickens if it let it down now.'

As Dave said to Forsyth, he knew what he would have done if Peter had still been at Fieldstone—he would have phoned him up and explained the situation. His guess is that Peter would have agreed to let him buy the material back. However, with Peter gone, he wondered what he should do now. Should he try to buy the material back without disclosing why he wanted it—it was, after all, known that there was a market shortage. Should he be quite frank as to why he wanted it? Alternatively might it be wiser, given what he had heard about him, not even to raise the matter with Best?

Discussion question

What advice would you give Dave?

Glossary

advertising any paid form of non-personal presentation and promotion of a product or organization by an identified sponsor

attitudes enduring systems of positive or negative evaluations of, or emotional feelings towards, an object

augmented product the core product plus any additional services and benefits that may be supplied

backward integration obtaining ownership or increased control of an organization's supply systems (see also *forward integration* and *vertical integration*)

billings the total charges for advertising space or time, production, and other services provided by an advertising agency to its client

bottom-up planning designing, developing, and implementing of programmes by middle-level and lower-level managers and other personnel who work out the details and follow through on them (see also *top-down planning*)

brand a name, term, sign, symbol, design, or combination of these that seeks to identify the product of an organization and differentiate it from those of competitors

brand mark that part of the brand which, while it can be recognized, cannot be uttered; it might be a symbol or even the product's shape

branding the process of creating, assigning, and publicizing a brand name, term, sign, symbol, etc., to one or more products

break-even the volume of sales necessary, at a specific price, for a seller to recover all relevant costs of a product

burst a large number of advertisements for a product placed in the media over a short period of time

buying centre all those people who play some role in an organization's purchasing decisions

cannibalization the erosion of sales of an existing product by a new product marketed by the same firm

cash cow a product in the mature or declining stage of the product life cycle that can be 'milked' for as much profit as possible

catchment area the geographic region or area from which the bulk of an organization's customers are drawn

category this is a distinct group of goods and services that consumers believe to be interrelated and/or substitutable in meeting a consumer need

category management the group of cross-functional retail managers assigned to manage a category

centralized management the dispersion of decision-making authority to staff at lower levels in an organization

chain store one of a group of centrally owned retail stores of similar type with some degree of centralized control over operations

channels of distribution see *distribution or delivery system*

cognitive dissonance perceived inconsistency within an individual's own beliefs or attitudes or between these and their behaviour; a person's attempt to reduce the dissonance through changes in either behaviour or cognition

commodity a generic product category or product that cannot be distinguished by a potential customer from similar products offered by competitors

communication the transmission of a message from a sender (or source) to a receiver (or recipient)

communication medium the channel through which a message is transmitted to an audience or individual (see also *message*)

communication mix the combination of elements (Personal selling, media advertising, public relations, publicity, and on-site display) used by an organization to communicate its message(s) to its target market(s)

comparative advertising advertising messages that make specific brand comparisons using actual product names (sometimes referred to as 'knocking copy'); the comparisons are usually unfavourable

concentrated marketing strategy the focusing on one target group, in a segmented market, and the designing of a marketing strategy specifically to reach that group, rather than trying to be all things to all people

concept testing testing a new concept to establish the reaction of a sample of typical potential consumers to the concept

consumer goods goods purchased by individuals and households for consumption

consumers individuals or households or organizations that are current or prospective purchasers or users of goods and services

contingency plans plans, prepared in advance, outlining a course of action to deal with situations that might potentially arise

contribution (or gross contribution) the monetary difference between total sales revenues (gross income) and variable expenses (see also *margin*)

convenience products products that consumers usually purchase frequently, immediately, and with a minimal effort in comparison and shopping (see also *shopping products* and *speciality products*)

convenience store a small store with a limited stock of grocery and household products, that remains open for long hours

copy testing a preliminary test of alternative advertising copy appeals or selling messages to assess their relative effectiveness for specific audiences

core product the central elements of a product that serves a basic consumer or societal need (see also *product*)

cost centre an organizational unit whose costs are clearly identifiable

cost per thousand the cost of advertising for each 1,000 homes reached by TV or radio, or for each 1,000 circulated copies of a publication (often abbreviated CPM)

cost-plus pricing establishing a price by adding a standard mark-up to the estimated cost of the product

coupons certificates that are mailed, handed out, or incorporated in print advertising that entitle the bearer to a specified monetary savings on a purchase of a specific product

cross-sectional data or study research information gathered from a whole population (or a representative sample of that population at a single point in time) (see also *longitudinal data*)

cumulative audience the radio or TV audience (having allowed for the effect of duplicate viewing) delivered by a specific programme in a particular time slot over a measured period of time usually one to four weeks

customer service a term that describes all the supplementary services provided by an organization to satisfy customers, and combat competitors, such as technical assistance and information, order taking, complaint handling, refunds, or substitutions

decentralized management the result of the dispersion of decision-making power to relevant personnel at lower levels within an organization (see also *centralized management*)

decision-making unit (DMU) an individual or group of individuals involved in making decisions on the purchase of a specific product

demographic segmentation categorizing or differentiating people based on demographic variables such as age, sex, religion, race, occupation, etc.

differentiated marketing strategy developing different products and/or marketing programmes for each market segment that the organization plans to serve

direct competitor an organization offering a product that meets similar consumer needs and is broadly similar in substance or process to one's own product

direct selling selling to the end-user by the producer without use of retail or wholesale intermediaries

discount a price reduction offered by a seller either to encourage the buyer to adapt its behaviour (e.g. a quantity discount) or to compensate for activities undertaken on behalf of the seller (e.g. a functional discount)

discretionary income what is left out of an individual's or household's disposable income after paying for necessities (see *disposable income*)

disposable income personal (or household) income remaining after deduction of income taxes and compulsory payments such as social security

dissonance see *cognitive dissonance*

distribution or delivery system the combination of internal organizational resources and external intermediaries employed to move a product from the point of production or creation to the final consumer; goods necessarily move through physical distribution channels, involving transportation, storage, and display; services may be delivered to the customer directly at the production site, or, in certain instances, transmitted electronically

diversification the process of entering new markets with one or more products that are new to the organization

dogs low-growth, low-market-share businesses that only generate sufficient cash to keep themselves from declining

drip the placing of an advertisement in the media at fairly long intervals

durable goods goods such as appliances, furniture, and automobiles that are expected to last several years or more

ECR (efficient consumer response) a strategy in which retailers and suppliers work closely together to maximize consumer satisfaction and minimize cost

EDI (electronic data interchange) a system that processes invoices automatically and triggers stock transfers once certain pre-agreed criteria are met

EFTPOS electronic fund transfer at point of sale

elasticity of demand (to price) the responsiveness of sales volume to a change in price: demand is said to be *price inelastic* when raising (or lowering) price by a certain percentage has a proportionately smaller impact on sales volume, and *price elastic* when the impact on volume is proportionately greater than the price change

EPOS electronic point of sale

evoked set the array of specific brands for a product category consciously considered by a consumer when making a purchase decision

experiment an attempt to measure cause-and-effect relationships under controlled or natural conditions

fixed costs costs that remain unchanged in total for a given time period despite wide fluctuations in the organization's activity levels; these would include: property taxes, executive salaries, rent insurance, and depreciation (see also *variable costs*)

focus-group interviews a small group discussion method of obtaining qualitative information from individuals who are broadly representative of the target market

forward integration obtaining ownership or increased control of the means by which an organization distributes its products to endusers (see also *backward integration* and *vertical integration*)

franchise the licensing of a production and distribution business, dealership, or complete business format where one organization authorizes a number of independent outlets to market a product or service and engage in a business using the franchiser's trade names and methods of operation

frequency the number of times an accumulated audience has the opportunity to be exposed to the same advertising messages within a measured period of time

FTC act federal trade commission act

generic competitor an organization offering a product that, while possibly different in substance or process, is capable of satisfying the same general consumer needs as one's own product (see also *direct competitor*)

going-rate pricing setting prices on the basis of competitors' pricing policies

gross rating points a measurement of advertising impact derived by multiplying the number of persons exposed to an advertisement by the average number of exposures per person (see also *reach* and *frequency*)

horizontal integration the process of obtaining ownership or increased control of one's competitors (see also *vertical integration*)

impulse purchase a purchase decision made on the spur of the moment without prior planning

industrial marketing selling technical goods and services to corporate purchasers as opposed to individuals and households

intensive distribution stocking a product in as many outlets in a defined geographical area as possible

intermediary an organization or individual that serves as a go-between, or facilitator, between producer, marketer, and customer

knocking copy see *comparative advertising*

lifestyle a person's living pattern as presented by his or her activities, interests, and opinions

list price the price shown on the marketer's sales list and used as the basis for computing discounts

longitudinal data or study research information gathered over time (usually at regular intervals) from the same population or sample; this allows the researcher to monitor individual changes among participants in the study

loss leaders a product of known or accepted quality whose price is set at a level where a loss or no profit is made with the intent of attracting consumers in the hope that they will then also purchase other products

manufacturer's agent/representative an intermediary who handles non-competing but related lines of goods, usually within an exclusive territory

margin the difference between the selling price of a product and its production cost (for a manufacturer or service provider) or purchase cost (for a wholesaler or retailer); the margin may be expressed in monetary units or as a percentage of the selling price

mark-down a reduction in the originally established price of a product

market the set of all current and potential consumers of a particular product

marker aggregation see *undifferentiated marketing strategy*

market definition an attempt by the organization to determine which segment of the market its operations are or should be serving

market development an organization's marketing of its current line of products to new markets or segments

market niche a segment of a market where there is demand for a product with specific attributes distinguishing it from competing offerings

market penetration an organization's attempt to increase consumption of its current products in its current markets

market potential a calculation of maximum possible sales (in units or currency values) or usage opportunities in a defined territorial area for all marketers of a product during a stated period of time

market segment a homogeneous subset of the target market that may require a marketing plan tailored to the segment's distinctive characteristics

market segmentation the process of identifying distinctive submarkets or segments within the target market

market share the ratio of an organization's sales volume for a particular product category to total market volume on either an actual or a potential basis

marketing audit a systematic, critical, unbiased, and comprehensive review and appraisal of an organization's or subunit's marketing objectives, strategies, policies, and activities

marketing concept the management approach that seeks to make the firms do what is in the interest of the customer and not the customer do what is in the interest of the firm

marketing orientation the implementation of the marketing concept by creating a customer focus within the firm

marketing mix the basic ingredients (or elements) in a marketing programme that influence consumers' decisions on whether or not to patronize the organization

marketing planning the tasks of setting up objectives for marketing activity and of determining and scheduling the steps necessary to achieve such objectives

marketing research the systematic gathering, recording, and analysing of data to provide information for marketing decision-making

mark-up the amount by which a seller increases the selling price of a product over its original purchase price; mark-up is generally computed as a percentage of the final selling price rather than of the original price

mass media informational networks, reaching large numbers of people, that carry news, features, editorial opinion, and advertising—specifically newspapers, magazines, radio, and television; the term can also be applied to other communication vehicles, such as billboards, poster sites, and mail service, that can be used to convey marketing messages to large numbers of people

merchandising selecting, displaying, and promoting products in a retail store or other distribution outlet

message a spoken or written communication

national account a customer operating over extended geographic areas whose service and sales needs are typically coordinated out of a head office

niche market a specific (usually small) market segment that allows a firm to aim a given brand at only a portion of the total market

noise (or clutter) conflicting, counter, or unrelated communications that detract from an advertiser's ability to communicate a specific message to members of a target audience

non-durable goods consumer goods such as food, health and beauty aids, and items that are consumed or otherwise used up relatively quickly (see also *durable goods*)

opinion leader an individual who influences other people's purchase and consumption behaviour

opportunity cost the maximum benefit forgone by using scarce resources (e.g. money, management time, physical facilities) for one purpose instead of the next best alternative

OTS (opportunity to see) the number of opportunities that an average member of the target audience will have to see an advertisement

own-label brands brands owned by retailers or other channel intermediaries, as distinct from manufacturers' brands (also known as *private label*)

penetration strategy an aggressive marketing strategy, based upon low price and heavy advertising and promotional expenditures, that is designed to gain quickly a large share of the market for a specific product

perceived value pricing setting prices on estimates of the value that customers perceive the product to possess

point-of-sale advertising promotional displays used by retailers within stores to promote specific products (also known as point-of-purchase advertising)

positioning positioning is the choice of target-market segments that determines where and how the company competes, aiming to help customers recognize the differences between competing products

price defined narrowly as the monetary cost to the purchaser of obtaining a product; more broadly, it includes other monetary outlays associated with purchasing and using the product, as well as all non-monetary costs associated with purchase and use of a good or service (or adoption of a social behaviour), such as time and physical and psychological effort

price elasticity see *elasticity of demand*

price leader a firm whose pricing policies are followed by other companies in the same industry

pricing strategy the mix of monetary price level charged to the final purchaser, terms and methods of payment (e.g. cheques, credit cards, exact change), and discounts offered to both intermediaries and final purchasers

primary data information the researcher collects through observation, experimentation, or survey research (see also *secondary data*)

primary demand the current level of demand for all sources for the entire product class in question

prime time the evening hours of broadcasting, when audience size is usually the largest and advertising rates are highest

private-label brands brands owned by retailers or other channel intermediaries, as distinct from manufacturers' brands (also known as *own label*)

proactive selling actively seeking out prospective customers (see also *reactive selling*)

product what the organization offers to prospective customers for their acquisition, use, consumption, or adoption; the term includes physical goods, services, and social behaviours or causes (such as driving safely, giving blood, etc.)

product class a group of products that serves the same general function or fulfils the same basic need

product development the process of developing or acquiring new or improved products for an organization's current market (see also *diversification*)

product differentiation creating and communicating product attributes that cause consumers to perceive the product as being different from the other offerings on the market

product life cycle the movement of a product from market introduction through growth, maturity, and decline stages to eventual termination; each of these phases requires a distinctive marketing strategy

product line all the products marketed by a given organization, sometimes subdivided into sets of product lines

product mix the complete set of all goods and services that a seller offers to the market

product portfolio mix of products offered by an organization, grouped with reference to market share, cash flow, and growth characteristics

product recall retrieval by the manufacturer of products (usually defective) that are already in the hands of customers and/or channel intermediaries

profit centre an organizational unit whose revenues and costs are clearly identifiable and whose management is held responsible for controlling both costs and revenues

promotional activities various non-recurrent selling efforts, often of a short-term nature, such as contests, discount coupons, special displays, and introductory offers

public relations the managing of public perceptions of an organization and its products by making available news about the organization to the media, or by interacting directly with opinion leaders

publicity the end result of the staging and publicizing of special events and activities to attract community attention, often via the news media.

pull strategy a marketing strategy based upon heavy advertising by the manufacturer to potential end-users, with the objective of 'pulling' the product through the channels or distribution (see also *push strategy*)

push strategy a marketing strategy in which the channels of distribution take major responsibility for promotional and personal selling efforts to end-users, designed to 'push' the product out of the store (see also *pull strategy*)

reach the number (or percentage) of target-audience members who are exposed to an advertising campaign at least once

reactive selling letting customers take the initiative in seeking out the vendor, who then tries to complete the transaction (see also *proactive selling*)

roll-out the process of extending distribution and advertising/promotion for a new product from a limited geographic area to a wider (or national) area

secondary data existing information in an accessible form that can be used to provide insights for management decision-making or serve as inputs to new primary data-collection efforts (see also *primary data*)

shopping products products that the consumer, when deciding which to purchase, will usually compare on bases such as suitability, quality, price, and style (see also *convenience products* and *speciality products*)

speciality products products with unique characteristics and/or brand identification for which a significant group of buyers are habitually willing to make a special purchasing effort (see also *convenience products* and *shopping products*)

spot advertising the purchase of TV or radio time on a station-by-station or market-by-market basis rather than network wide

stars high-growth, high-market-share companies or products that often require substantial financing to maintain their growth

SKU (stock-keeping unit) the lowest level of disaggregation at which a product can be ordered; it reflects size, style, colour, and other distinctive variations

store audit retail and wholesale audits that track the movement of goods through the distribution channel to provide manufacturers with sales and market share data (see also *marketing audit*)

strategic business (management) unit (SBU/SMU) a unit within a larger organization that is essentially treated as a separate entity and established as an independent profit centre, usually with a distinct mission, objective, competitive environment, and managerial requirements (see also *profit centre*)

target market the portion of the total market that the organization has decided to supply

target marketing focusing the marketing efforts on specific segments within the total market

telemarketing use of the telephone as a tool for marketing communication (e.g. sales and advertising) and as a channel for proactive account management

test marketing evaluating customer response to a new product by putting it on the market in a limited geographic area

time-series data see *longitudinal data*

top-down planning designing programmes to be implemented by top-level management; participation filters down to the lower levels (see also *bottom-up planning*)

trademark a brand or part of a brand that is given legal protection and that may be used only by its owner or with the owner's permission

trading up encouraging current or prospective customers to purchase a more expensive version of a given product

undifferentiated marketing strategy a plan whereby the organization treats the market as an aggregate and designs its products and marketing programme to appeal to the greatest number of consumers possible

segmentation subdividing the total consumer market on the basis of where, when, why, and in what quantities the product is used

value pricing establishing price levels on the basis of how the buyer perceives the value of the product rather than on the basis of the costs to be recovered by the seller

variable costs costs that change in direct proportion to changes in activity, such as materials and parts, sales commissions, and certain labour and supplies (see also *fixed costs*)

vertical integration the process of purchasing or acquiring control over one's suppliers (see *backward integration*), or one's distributors (see *forward integration* and *horizontal integration*), or both

wholesaler a business unit in the channel of distribution that buys goods or services from producers and resells them to other merchants or to institutional purchasers but not to household consumers

References

Aaker, D. A. (1982), 'Positioning your Product', *Business Horizon*, 25/3: 56–62.

——(1988, 1992, and 1995), *Strategic Market Management* (2nd, 3rd, and 4th, edns.; New York: Wiley).

——(1991), *Managing Brand Equity* (New York: Free Press).

Achrol, R. S. (1991), 'Evolution of the Marketing Organization: New Forms for Turbulent Environments', *Journal of Marketing*, 55/3 (Oct.), 77–93.

Aguilar, F. J. (1967), *Scanning the Business Environment* (New York: Macmillan).

Ajzen, I. (1985), 'From Intentions to Actions: A Theory of Planned Behaviour', in J. Kuhl and J. Beckmann (eds.), *Action Control: From Cognition to Behavior* (Berlin: Springer), 11–39.

Albers, S. (1986), 'Controlling Independent Manufacturer Representatives by Using Commission Rate Functions Depending on Achieved Sales Volume', in K. Backhaus and D. T. Wilson (eds.), *Industrial Marketing: A German–American Perspective* (Berlin: Springer-Verlag), 88–112.

——(1989), *Decision Support Systems for Salesforce Management* (in German) (Berlin: Duncker & Humblot).

——(1996*a*), 'Optimisation Models for Salesforce Compensation', *European Journal of Operational Research*, 89: 1–17.

——(1996*b*), 'CAPPLAN: A Decision Support System for Planning the Pricing and Sales Effort Policy of a Salesforce', *European Journal of Marketing*, 30/7: 68–82.

——(1997), 'Rules for the Allocation of a Marketing Budget across Products or Market Segments', in D. Arnott *et al.* (eds.), *Marketing: Progress, Prospects, Perspectives: Proceedings of the 26th EMAC Conference, 20th–23rd May 1997* (Warwick Business School), 1–17.

Aldenderfer, M. S., and Blashfield, R. K. (1984), *Cluster Analysis* (Beverly Hills, Calif.: Sage Publications).

Alderson, W. (1954), 'Factors Governing the Development of Marketing Channels', in R. M. V. Clewett (ed.), *Marketing Channels for Manufactured Products* (Homewood, Ill.: Irwin).

——(1965), *Dynamic Marketing Behavior* (Homewood, Ill.: Irwin).

Aldrich, H., and Zimmer, C. (1986), 'Entrepreneurship through Social Networks', in D. A. Sexton and R. W. Smilor (eds.), *The Art and Science of Entrepreneurship* (Cambridge, Mass.: Ballenger).

Alexander, R. S. (1980), *Marketing Definitions: A Glossary of Marketing Terms* (Chicago: American Marketing Association).

Alpert, F., Wilson, B., and Elliott, M. T. (1993), 'Price Signaling: Does it Ever Work?', *Journal of Consumer Marketing*, 10/4: 4–14.

American Marketing Association (1960), 'Report of the Definitions Committee' (Chicago: American Marketing Association).

Ames, B. C. (1968), 'Marketing Planning for Industrial Products', *Harvard Business Review*, 46 (Sept.–Oct.), 100–12.

Anderson, J. C., and Narus, J. A. (1990), 'A Model of Distributor Firm and Manufacturing Firm Working Partnerships', *Journal of Marketing*, 54: 42–58.

——Hakansson, H., and Johanson, J. (1994), 'Dyadic Business Relationships within a Business Network Context', *Journal of Marketing*, 58 (Oct.), 1–15.

Anderson, P. F., and Chambers, T. M. (1985), 'A Reward/Measurement Model of Organizational Buying Behavior', *Journal of Marketing*, 49: 7–23.

Anderson, R. E. (1996), 'Personal Selling and Sales Management in the New Millennium', *Journal of Personal Selling and Sales Management*, 6/4: 17–32.

Anderson, W. T., and Golden, L. L. (1984), 'Life Style and Psychographics: A Critical Review and Recommendation', in T. C. Kinnear (ed.), *Advances in Consumer Research*, 11 (Provo, Ut.: Association for Consumer Research), 405–11.

Andrews, K. (1965), *The Concept of Corporate Strategy* (Homewood, Ill.: Dow-Jones–Irwin).

Annual Abstract of Statistics (London: HMSO).

Ansoff, H. I. (1965), *Corporate Strategy* (New York, McGraw-Hill).

——(1987), *Corporate Strategy* (Harmondsworth: Penguin).

Antonides, G., and van Raaij, W. F. (1998), *Consumer Behaviour: A European Perspective* (Chichester, UK: Wiley).

——(1990), *Implanting Strategic Management* (Englewood Cliffs, NJ: Prentice Hall).

Archer, B. (1998), 'NPD Blues', *Marketing Business* (May), 50–4.

Arens, S. (1990), 'The Entrepreneurial Lifestyle: Could It Be For You?', *Communication World*, 7/3: 27–31.

Arndt, J. (1979), 'Towards a Concept of Domesticated Markets', *Journal of Marketing*, 43/4: 69–75.

Arthur, W. (1996), 'Increasing Returns and the New World of Business', *Harvard Business Review* (July–Aug.), 100–9.

Assael, H. (1992), *Consumer Behavior and Marketing Action* (4th edn.; Boston, Mass.: Kent).

Atuahene-Gima, K. (1996), 'Differential Potency of Factors Affecting Innovation Performance in Manufacturing and Services Firms in Australia', *Journal of Product Innovation Management*, 13/1 (Feb.), 35–52.

Avlonitis, G. J. (1984), 'Industrial Product Elimination: Major Factors to Consider', *Industrial Marketing Management*, 13/1: 77–85.

——(1985), 'Product Elimination Decision-Making: Does Formality Matter?', *Journal of Marketing*, 49/1 (Winter), 41–52.

——(1986), 'The Management of the Product Elimination Function: Theoretical and Empirical Analysis', in

A. G. Woodside (ed.), *Advances in Business Marketing* (Greenwich, Conn.: JAI Press), 1–66.

Avlonitis, G. J. (1987), 'Linking Different Types of Product Elimination Decisions to their Performance Outcome', *International Journal of Research in Marketing*, 4/1: 43–57.

——(1990), 'Project Dropstrat: Product Elimination and the Product Life Cycle Concept', *European Journal of Marketing*, 24/9: 55–67.

——(1993), 'Project Dropstrat: What Factors do Managers Consider in Deciding Whether to Drop a Product?', *European Journal of Marketing*, 27/4: 35–57.

——and James, B. G. S. (1982), 'Some Dangerous Axioms of Product Elimination Decision-Making', *European Journal of Marketing*, 16/1: 36–48.

——and Karayianni, D. (1996), 'The Impact of Internet on the Marketing Strategies of Business-to-Business Companies', Working Paper, Athens University of Economics and Business.

Axelsson, B., and Easton, G. (1992), *Industrial Networks: A New View of Reality* (London: Routledge).

Badaracco, J. L. (1991), *The Knowledge Link* (Boston: Harvard Business School Press).

Baier, M. (1996), *How to Find and Cultivate Customers through Direct Marketing* (Lincolnwood, Ill.: NTC Publications).

Bailey, A., and Johnson G. (1994), 'The Process of Strategy Development', Cranfield School of Management Research Paper.

Bainbridge, J. (1998), '2010 Vision', *Marketing*, 4th June, 18–19.

Baker, M. J. (1985), *Marketing Strategy and Management* (London: Macmillan).

——(1991), *The Marketing Book* (Oxford: Butterworth-Heinemann).

——(1993), 'Editorial', *Journal of Marketing Management*, 9/2: 101–3.

——(1995), 'Special Issue on the Commodification of Marketing Knowledge', *Journal of Marketing Management*, 11/7: 619–750.

Bamossy, G. S. (1988), in P. S. H. Leeflang (ed.), *Probleemgebied Marketing* (Holland: Stenfert Kroese).

Barksdale, H., and Darden, B. (1971), 'Marketers Attitude toward the Marketing Concept', *Journal of Marketing*, 35/4 (Oct.), 29–36.

Barrell, R., and Pain, N. (1997), 'The Growth of Foreign Direct Investment in Europe', *National Institute Economic Review*, 160 (Apr.), 63–75.

Barrett, P. (1997), 'Service Takes Wheel at BMW', *Marketing*, 6 Nov., 1.

Bartels, R. (1962), *History of Marketing Thought* (Homewood, Ill.: Irwin).

Barwise, P., Higson, C., Likierman, A., and Marsh, P. R. (1989), *Accounting for Brands* (London Business School: for the Institute of Chartered Accountants in England and Wales).

——Marsh, P. R., and Wensley, R. (1989), 'Must Finance and Marketing Clash?', *Harvard Business Review* (Sept.–Oct.), 85–90.

Basu, A. K., and Mazumdar, T. (1995), 'Using a Menu of Geographic Pricing Plans: A Theoretical Investigation', *Journal of Retailing*, 71/2: 173–202.

Bateson, J. (1995), *Managing Services Marketing* (Orlando, Fla.: Dryden Press).

Batra, R., Myers, J. G., and Aaker, D. A. (1996), *Advertising Management* (5th edn.; Englewood Cliffs, NJ: Prentice Hall).

Baumol, J., Panzar, J. C., and Willig, R. D. (1982), *Contestable Markets and the Theory of Industry Structure* (New York: Harcourt Brace Jovanovich).

Beane, T. P., and Ennis, D. M. (1987), 'Market Segmentation: A Review', *European Journal of Marketing*, 21/5 (Oct.), 20–42.

Beem, E., and Schaffer, R. H. (1981), *Triggers to Action: Some Elements in a Theory of Promotional Inducement* (Report 81-106; Cambridge, Mass.: Marketing Science Institute).

Belch, G. E., and Belch, M. A. (1995), *Introduction to Advertising and Promotion—An Integrated Marketing Communications Perspective* (3rd. edn.; Homewood, Ill.: Irwin).

Bellizzi, J. A., and McVey, P. (1983), 'How Valid is the Buy-Grid Model?', *Industrial Marketing Management*, 12: 57–62.

Benady, D. (1996), 'Soft Targets', *Marketing Week*, 19 Jan.

Bennett, Peter D. (1988) (ed.), *Dictionary of Marketing Terms* (Chicago, Ill.: American Marketing Association).

Berkowitz, N. E., Kerin, R. A., and Rudelius, W. (1989), *Marketing* (Homewood, Ill.: Irwin).

Berry, L. L. (1980), 'Services Marketing is Different', *Business*, 30 (May–June), 24–9.

——(1981), 'The Employee as Customer', *Journal of Retail Banking*, 3/1: 33–41.

——and Parasuraman, A. (1993), 'Building a New Academic Field—The Case of Services Marketing', *Journal of Retailing*, 69/1: 13–60.

————(1995), *Marketing Services: Competing through Quality.* (New York: Wiley).

Bettman, J. R. (1979), *An Information Processing Theory of Consumer Choice* (Reading, Mass.: Addison-Wesley).

——and Park, C. W. (1980), 'Effect of Prior Knowledge and Experience and Phase of the Choice Process on Consumer Decision Processes: A Protocol Analysis', *Journal of Consumer Research*, 7: 234–48.

Bilkey, W. J., and Tesar, G. (1979), 'The Export Behaviour of Small Sized Manufacturing Firms', *Journal of International Business Studies*, 9 (Spring–Summer), 93–8.

Bilsen, R., van Waterschoot, W., and Lagasse, L. (1997), *Marketingbeleid: Theorie en Praktijk* (7th edn.; Antwerpen: Standaard Uitgeverij).

Bird, D. (1989), *Commonsense Direct Marketing* (London: Kogan Page).

Bitner, M. J. (1995), 'Building Service Relationships: It's All About Promises', *Journal of the Academy of Marketing Science*, 23/4: 246–51.

Bitran, G., and Mondschein S. (1997), 'A Comparative Analysis of Decision Making Procedures in the Catalog

Sales Industry', *European Management Journal*, 15(2): 105–16.

Blattberg, R. C., and Neslin, S. A. (1989), 'Sales Promotions: The Long and the Short of It', *Marketing Letters*, 1/1: 81–97.

—— and Sen, S. K. (1976), 'Market Segments and Stochastic Brand Choice Models', *Journal of Marketing Research*, 13/1 (Feb.), 34–45.

—— Briesch, R., and Fox, E. J. (1995), 'How Promotions Work', *Marketing Science*, 14, Pt. 2/3: G122–G132.

Bleackly, M., and Williamson, P. (1997), 'The Nature and Extent of Corporate Restructuring within Europe's Single Market', *European Management Journal*, 15/5: 484–97.

Bleek, J., and Ernst, D. (1993), *Collaborating to Compete: Using Strategic Alliances and Acquisitions in the Global Marketplace* (New York: Wiley).

Blois, K. J. (1978), 'Market Structure and Marketing Policies', *European Journal of Marketing*, 12/8: 571–8.

—— (1988), 'Automated Manufacturing Creates Market Opportunities', *Journal of General Management*, 13/4: 57–73.

—— (1991), 'Product Augmentation and Competitive Advantage', *Journal of General Management*, 16/3: 29–38.

—— and Cowell, D. W. (1973), *Short Cases in Marketing Management* (Aylesbury: International Textbook Co. Ltd.).

Bonoma, T., and Shapiro, B. P. (1983), *Segmenting the Industrial Market* (Lexington, Mass.: Lexington Books).

Booz, Allen, and Hamilton (1982), *New Products Management for the 1980s* (New York: Booz, Allen and Hamilton).

Borden, N. (1964), 'The Concept of the Marketing Mix', *Journal of Advertising Research* (June), 2–7.

Borys, B., and Jemison, D. B. (1989), 'Hybrid Arrangements as Strategic Alliances: Theoretical Issues in Organizational Combinations', *Academy of Management Review*, 14 (Feb.), 234–49.

Bovée, C. L., Thill, V., Dovel, G. P., and Wood, M. B. (1995), *Advertising Excellence* (New York: McGraw-Hill).

Bowersox, D. J. (1990), 'The Strategic Benefits of Logistics Alliances', *Harvard Business Review* (July–Aug.), 36–45.

Bradley, F. (1995), *Marketing Management: Providing, Communicating and Delivering Value* (London: Prentice Hall).

Brassington, F., and Pettitt, S. (1997), *Principles of Marketing* (London: Pitman Publishing).

Britt, S. H. (1969), 'Are So-Called Successful Advertising Campaigns Really Successful?', *Journal of Advertising Research*, 9/2: 3–9.

Brockhoff, K. (1967), 'A Test for the Product Life Cycle', *Econometrica* (July–Oct.), 472–84.

Brodie, R. J., Bonfer, A., and Cutler, J. (1996), 'Do Managers Overreact to Each Other's Promotional Activity?', *International Journal of Research in Marketing*, 13/4: 379–87.

—— Coviello, N. E., Brookes, R. W., and Little, V. (1997), 'Towards a Paradigm Shift in Marketing? An Examination of Current Marketing Practices', *Journal of Marketing Management*, 13/5: 383–406.

Brookes, R. W. (1995), 'Recent Changes in the Retailing of Fresh Produce: Strategic Implications for Fresh Produce Suppliers', *Journal of Business Research*, 32/2 (Feb.), 149–61.

Brown, H. E., Shivishankar, R., and Brucker, R. W. (1989), 'Requirements Driven Market Segmentation', *Industrial Marketing Management*, 18/2: 105–12.

Brown, J. J., and Reingen, P. H. (1987), 'Social Ties and Word-of-Mouth Referral Behaviour', *Journal of Consumer Research*, 14: 350–62.

Brown, R. (1993), *Market Focus* (Oxford: Butterworth-Heinemann).

Brown, S., Bell, J., and Carson, D. (1996) (eds.), *Marketing Apocalypse: Eschatology Escapology and the Illusion of the End* (London: Routledge).

Brownlie, D., Saren, M., Whittington, R., and Wensley, R. (1994) (eds.), 'Special Issue: "The New Marketing Myopia: Critical Perspectives on Theory and Research in Marketing"', *European Journal of Marketing*, 28/3: 1–84.

Bruijniks, H. (1996), 'Category Management', *ECR Europe*, Newsletter (Jan.), 10.

Brunsø, K., Grunert, K. G., and Bredahl, L. (1996), 'An Analysis of National and Cross-National Consumer Segments Using the Food-Related Lifestyle Instrument in Denmark, France, Germany and the United Kingdom', MAPP working paper no. 35 (Aarhus: Aarhus School of Business).

Buell, V. (1975), 'The Changing Role of the Product Manager in Consumer Goods Companies', *Journal of Marketing*, 39/3 (July), 3–11.

Buisson, D. H. (1995), 'Commodity Marketing', in M. J. Baker (ed.), *Companion Encyclopedia of Marketing* (London: Routledge).

Buttle, F. (1996), *Relationship Marketing: Theory and Practice* (London: Paul Chapman).

Buzzell, R. D. (1966), 'Competitive Behaviour and Product Life Cycles', in J. S. Wright and J. L. Goldstucker (eds.), *New Ideas for Successful Marketing* (Proceedings of the American Marketing Association; Chicago, Ill., Spring), 46–8.

—— and Gale, B. (1987), *The PIMS Principles: Linking Strategy to Performance* (New York: Free Press).

—— and Ortmeyer, G. (1995), 'Channel Partnerships Streamline Distribution', *Sloan Management Review*, 36 (Spring), 85–96.

Bylinsky, G. (1994), 'The Digital Factory', *Fortune*, 14 Nov., 56–65.

Calantone, R. J., and Cooper, R. G. (1979), 'A Discriminant Model for Identifying Scenarios of Industrial New Product Failure', *Journal of the Academy of Marketing Science*, 7/3: 163–83.

Calonius, H. (1988), 'A Buying Process Model', in K. Blois and S. Parkinson (eds.), *Innovative Marketing—A European Perspective* (Proceedings of the XVIIth Annual Conference of the European Marketing Academy, University of Bradford, England).

Camillus, J. C. (1975), 'Evaluating the Benefits of Formal Planning Systems', *Long Range Planning*, 8/3: 33–40.

Cannon, T. (1996), *Basic Marketing: Principles and Practice* (London: Cassell).

Carlzon, J. (1987), *Moments of Truth* (Cambridge, Mass.: Ballinger).

Carson, D. (1990), 'Some Exploratory Models for Assessing Small Firms' Marketing Performance: A Qualitative Approach', *European Journal of Marketing*, 24/11: 2–49.

——(1993), 'A Philosophy for Marketing Education in Small Firms', *Journal of Marketing Management*, 9/2 (Apr.), 189–204.

——Cromie, S., McGowan, P., and Hill, J. (1995a), *Marketing and Entrepreneurship in SMEs: An Innovative Approach* (Hemel Hempsted: Prentice Hall).

——Gilmore, A., and McLaran, P. (1995b), 'To Hell with the Customer, Where's the Profit', in S. Brown, J. Bell, and D. Carson (eds.), *Proceedings of the Marketing Eschatology Retreat* (University of Ulster), 22–24 September 72–83.

Caulkin, S. (1996), 'Is Congenital Short-Termism Driving Customers Away?', in *Customer* (Leeds: Ventura Marketing Communications).

Caves, R. E., and Porter, M. E. (1977), 'From Entry Barriers to Mobility Barriers: Conjectural Decisions and Deterrence to New Competition', *Quarterly Journal of Economics*, 91: 241–62.

Chakravarthy, B. (1997), 'A New Strategy Framework for Coping with Turbulence', *Sloan Management Review*, 38 (Winter), 69–82.

Chamberlin, E. H. (1933), *The Theory of Monopolistic Competition* (Cambridge, Mass.: Harvard University Press).

——(1957), *Towards a More General Theory of Value* (Oxford: Oxford University Press).

Channon, D. (1996), 'Direct Line Insurance PLC', in C. Baden-Fuller and M. Pitt (eds.), *Strategic Innovation* (London: Routledge), 55–74.

Chevalier, M., and Zumino, D. (1948), 'Product Line Strategy', *Management Decision*, 12/3: 127–8.

Child, J., and Faulkner, D. (1998), *Strategies of Cooperation* (Oxford: Oxford University Press).

Choffray, J.-M., and Lilien, G. L. (1978), 'A New Approach to Industrial Market Segmentation', *Sloan Management Review*, 19/3 (Spring), 17–29.

Christopher, M., Payne, A., and Ballantyne, D. (1991), *Relationship Marketing: Bringing Quality, Customer Service, and Marketing Together* (Oxford: Butterworth-Heinemann).

Chu, W., Gerstner, E., and Hess, J. D. (1995), 'Costs and Benefits of Hard-Sell', *Journal of Marketing Research*, 32/1: 97–102.

Churchill, G. A., Ford, N. M., and Walker, O. C. (1993), *Sales Force Management* (Homewood, Ill.: Irwin).

Clark, H. H., and Haviland, S. E. (1974), 'Psychological Processes in Linguistic Explanation', in D. Cohen (eds.), *Explaining Linguistic Phenomena* (Washington: Hemisphere), 91–124.

Clegg, A. (1996), 'Colour Blind', *Marketing Week*, 21 June, 38–40.

Coeyman, M. (1994), 'DuPont, Tioxide Plan Capacity Hike', *Chemical Week*, 19 Oct., 14.

Coles, G. J., and Culley, J. D. (1986), 'Not all Prospects are Created Equal', *Business Marketing*, 71/5 (May), 52–8.

Collins, A. (1991), *Competitive Retail Marketing* (Maidenhead: McGraw-Hill).

Cooper, G. (1996), 'Lazy Car Salesmen Give Customers a Raw Deal', *Independent*, 30 July.

Cooper, R. (1995), 'Olympus Optical Company (A)', Harvard Business School Series 9-195-072.

Cooper, R. G. (1984), 'New Product Strategies: What Distinguishes the Top Performers', *Journal of Product Innovation Management*, 1/3 (Sept.), 93–103.

——(1990), 'Stage-Gate Systems: A New Tool for Managing New Products', *Business Horizons*, 33/3 (May–June), 44–54.

——(1996), 'Overhauling the New Product Process', *Industrial Marketing Management*, 25/5: 465–82.

——and de Brentani, U. (1991), 'New Industrial Financial Services: What Distinguishes the Winners', *Journal of Product Innovation Management*, 8/3 (June), 75–90.

Coopers & Lybrand (1993), *Building Customer Loyalty in Grocery Retailing* (London: Coca-Cola Retail Research Group).

——(1996a), *Annual Review* (London).

——(1996b), *European ECR Study* (London).

Copeland, M. J. (1923), 'The Relations of Consumer Buying Habits to Marketing Methods', *Harvard Business Review*, 1/2 (Apr.), 282–9.

Corstjens, J., and Corstjens, M. (1995), *Store Wars: The Battle for Mindspace and Shelfspace* (Chichester: Wiley).

Cort, S. G., Stith, R. M., and Lahoti, D. (1997), 'Industrial Distribution, Survival of the Smartest', *Business Economics*, 32/4 (Oct.), 55–8.

Cova, B., and Holstius, K. (1993), 'How to Create Competitive Advantage in Project Business', *Journal of Marketing Management*, 9: 105–21.

——and Salle, R. (1991), 'Buying Behaviour in European and American Industry: Contrasts', *European Management Journal*, 9/4: 433–6.

—— ——(1992), 'L'Évolution de la modélisation du comportement d'achat industriel: Panorama des nouveaux courants de recherche', *Recherche et Applications en Marketing*, 7/2: 83–106.

Coviello, N. E., Brodie, R. J., and Munro, H. J. (1997), 'Understanding Contemporary Marketing: Development of a Classification Scheme', *Journal of Marketing Management*, 13/6: 501–22.

Cox, D. F. (1967), 'The Sorting Rule Model of the Consumer Product Evaluation Process', in D. F. Cox (ed.), *Risk Taking and Information Handling in Consumer Behavior* (Boston: Graduate School of Business Administration, Harvard University), 324–69.

Cravens, D. W., Hills, G. E., and Woodruff, R. B. (1980), *Marketing Decision Making: Concepts and Strategy* (Homewood, Ill.: Irwin).

Crawford, M. (1997), *New Products Management* (Chicago: Irwin).

Crompton, F., George, W. R., Grönroos, C., and Karvinen, M. (1987), 'Internal Marketing', in J. A. Czepiel et al. (eds.), *The Service Challenge: Integrating for Competitive Advantage* (Chicago: American Marketing Association).

Cronin, J. J., Jr., and Taylor, S. A. (1994), 'SERVPERF versus SERVQUAL: Reconciling Performance-Based and Perceptions-Minus-Expectations Measurement of Service Quality', *Journal of Marketing*, 58 (Jan.), 125–31.

Cunningham, J., and Lischevan, J. (1991), 'Defining Entrepreneurship', *Journal of Small Business Management*, 29/1: 45–61.

Cunningham, M. J. (1969), 'The Application of Product Life Cycles to Corporate Strategy', *British Journal of Marketing* (Spring), 32–44.

Cushman, C. (1997), 'Which Hat are you Wearing?', *Purchasing Today*, 8/3: 20–1.

Dahringer, L. D., and Mülbacher, H. (1991), *International Marketing: A Global Perspective* (Reading, Mass.: Addison-Wesley).

Dale, B., and Powley, R. (1985), 'Purchasing Practices in the United Kingdom: A Case Study', *Journal of Purchasing and Materials Management* (Spring), 23–6.

Dalgic, T. (1992), 'Euromarketing: "Charting the map for globalization" ', *International Marketing Review*, 9/5: 31–43.

——(1994a), ' "Niche" Marketing Principles—Guerrillas vs. Gorillas', *Journal of Segmentation in Marketing*, 2/1: 5–16.

——(1994b), 'International Marketing and Market Orientation—An Early Attempt at Integration', *Advances in International Marketing*, 6: 69–82.

——(1998), ' "Niche" Marketing Principles—Guerrillas vs. Gorillas', *Journal of Segmentation in Marketing*, 2/1: 5–16.

——and Maarten, L. (1994), ' "Niche" Marketing Revisited: Concept, Applications and Some European Cases', *European Journal of Marketing*, 28/4: 39–55.

——and van der Weijden, A. (1994), 'Market Orientation in the High-Tech Industry of the Benelux Countries', in J. G. Groeneveld (ed.), *Benelux Electronics Market* (Dutch Industrial Electronics Organization—Het Instrument, Industriele Elektronica—and Belgian Trade Association of Producers and Importers of Electronic Materials), 43–70.

Davenport, H. (1996), 'Marketing on the Internet', *Journal of Targeting, Measurement and Analysis for Marketing*, 4(3): 61–9.

Davidson, H. (1972), *Offensive Marketing* (London: Penguin).

——(1998), *Even More Offensive Marketing* (London: Penguin).

Davies, G. (1993), *Trade Marketing Strategy* (London: Paul Chapman).

——(1997), 'Loyalty is a Gift that Can't be Bought', *Admap* (July–Aug.), 26–30.

——and Brooks, I. M. (1989), *Positioning Strategy in Retailing* (London: Paul Chapman).

Davies, R. L. (1995) (ed.), *Retail Planning Policies in Western Europe* (London: Routledge).

——and Finney, M. (1997), *Shopping for New Markets: Retailers' Expansion across Europe's Borders* (Oxford/London: OXIRM/Jones Lang Wootton).

Davies, S., and Lyons, B. (1996), *Industrial Organization in the European Union* (Oxford: Oxford University Press).

Davis, T. (1993), 'Effective Supply Chain Management', *Sloan Management Review*, 34 (Summer), 35–46.

Dawson, J. A. (1996), 'Retail Change in the European Community', in R. L. Davies (ed.), *Retail Planning Policies in Western Europe* (London: Routledge).

Day, G. S. (1990), *Market Driven Strategy: Processes for Creating Value* (New York: Free Press).

——(1993), 'The Capabilities of Market-Driven Organizations', (Report No. 93–123; Cambridge, Mass.: Marketing Science Institute).

——(1994), 'The Capabilites of Market-Driven Organizations', *Journal of Marketing*, 58/4: 37–52.

——(1997), 'Maintaining the Competitive Edge', in G. S. Day and D. J. Reibstein (eds.), *Wharton on Dynamic Competitive Strategy* (New York: Wiley), 48–75.

——Shocker, A. D., and Srivastava, R. K. (1979), 'Customer-Oriented Approaches to Identifying Product-Markets', *Journal of Marketing*, 43/4: 8–19.

——and Wensley, R. (1988), 'Assessing Advantage: A Framework for Diagnosing Competitive Superiority', *Journal of Marketing*, 52/2 (Apr.), 1–20.

de Almeida, P. M. (1980), 'A Review of Group Discussion Methodology', *European Research*, 3/8: 114–20

de Brentani, U. (1986), 'Do Firms Need a Custom Designed New Product Screening Model?', *Journal of Product Innovation Management*, 3/2: 108–19.

——(1989), 'Success and Failure in New Industrial Services', *Journal of Product Innovation Management*, 6/4 (Dec.), 239–58.

——(1991), 'Success Factors in Developing New Business Services', *European Journal of Marketing*, 25/2 (Mar.–Apr.), 93–103.

——(1995), 'New Industrial Service Development: Scenarios for Success and Failure', *Journal of Business Research*, 32/2: 93–103.

——and Ragot, E. (1996), 'Developing New Business-to-Business Professional Services: What Factors Impact Performance?', *Industrial Marketing Management*, 25/6 (Nov.), 517–30.

de Chernatony, L. (1992), *Creating Powerful Brands* (Oxford: Butterworth-Heinemann).

——and McDonald, M. (1998), *Creating Powerful Brands in Consumer, Service and Industrial Markets* (2nd edn., Oxford: Butterworth-Heinemann).

De Pauw, F. (1997), 'Pompeï bedreigd door nieuwe ramp', *De Standaard*, 27 Aug.

De Vincentis, J. R., and Kotcher, L. K. (1995), 'Packaged Goods Salesforce—Beyond Efficiency', *McKinsey Quarterly*, 1: 72–85.

Deighton, J. (1996), 'The Future of Interactive Marketing', *Harvard Business Review*, (Nov.–Dec.), 151–62.

Deshpande, R., Farley, J. U., and Webster, F. E. (1990), 'Corporate Culture, Customer Orientation and Innovation', *Journal of Marketing*, 57/1: 23-38.

Dhalla, N. K., and Yuspeh, J. (1976), 'Forget the Product Life Cycle Concept', *Harvard Business Review*, (Jan.–Feb.), 102-10.

Dheeden, H. (1996), 'Swàtchchchchch . . . !', *De Standaard*, 21 June.

Diamantopoulos, A., and Schlegelmilch, B. B. (1997), *Taking the Fear out of Data Analysis* (London: Dryden Press).

Dibb, S. (1997), 'How Marketing Planning Builds Internal Networks', *Long Range Planning*, 30/19: 53-63.

—— and Simkin, L. (1996), *The Market Segmentation Workbook: Target Marketing for Marketing Managers* (London: ITBP).

—— —— (1997), 'A Program for Implementing Market Segmentation', *Journal of Business and Industrial Marketing*, 12/1: 51-65.

—— —— Pride, W., and Ferrell, O. C. (1997), *Marketing: Concepts and Strategies* (Boston: Houghton Mifflin).

Dickson, P., and Sawyer, A. G. (1990), 'The Price Knowledge and Search of Supermarket Shoppers', *Journal of Marketing*, 54/3 (July), 42-53.

Dimancescu, D. (1992), *The Seamless Enterprise: Making Cross Functional Management Work* (New York: Harper Business).

Dolan, R., and Neslin, S. A. (1990), *Sales Promotion: Concepts, Methods and Strategies* (Englewood Cliffs, NJ: Prentice Hall).

Domberger, S. (1998), *The Contracting Organization* (Oxford: Oxford University Press).

Dougherty, D. (1992), 'Interpretative Barriers to Successful Product Innovation in Large Firms', *Organization Science*, 3 (May), 179-202.

Doyle, P. (1976), 'The Realities of Product Life Cycle', *Quarterly Review of Marketing*, 1/4 (Summer), 1-6.

—— (1994), *Marketing Management and Strategy* (London: Prentice Hall).

—— (1995), 'Marketing in the New Millennium', *European Journal of Marketing*, 29/13: 23-41.

—— (1998), 'Radical Strategies for Profitable Growth', *European Management Journal*, 16/3: 253-61.

—— Law, P., Wienberg, C., and Simmonds, K. (1974), *Analytical Marketing Management* (London: Harper & Row).

—— Woodside, A. G., and Mitchell, P. (1979), 'Organizations Buying in New-Task and Rebuy Situations', *Industrial Marketing Management*, 8: 7-11.

—— Saunders, J., and Wong, V. (1986), 'A Comparative Study of Japanese Marketing Strategies in the British Market', *Journal of International Business Studies*, 17/1: 27-46.

DRI Europe Ltd. (1997), *The Single Market Review—Price Competition and Price Convergence*, Subseries V, 1 (Office for Official Publications of the European Communities, Kogan Page-Earthscan).

Drucker, P. (1954), *The Practice of Management* (New York: Harper & Row).

—— (1968), *The Practice of Management* (London: Pan Books).

Dunning, J. R., (1995), *Multinational Enterprises and the Global Economy Workplace* (Reading, Mass.: Addison-Wesley).

Dwyer, F. R. (1989), 'Customer Lifetime Valuation to Support Marketing Decision-Making', *Journal of Direct Marketing*, 3/4: 8-15.

Easingwood, G. J. (1986), 'New Product Development for Services', *Journal of Product Innovation Management*, 3/4: 264-75.

—— and Storey, C. (1993), 'Marketplace Success Factors for New Financial Services', *Journal of Services Marketing*, 7/1: 41-54.

—— —— (1996), 'The Value of Multi-Channel Distribution Systems in the Financial Services Sector', *Service Industries Journal*, 16/2: 223-41.

The Economist (1999), 'Direct Hit', 9 Jan., 69.

Edquist, C., and Jacobsson, S. (1988), *Flexible Automation* (Oxford: Basil Blackwell).

Eiglier, P., and Langeard, E. (1976), 'Principle politique pour les enterprises des services', working paper, Aix-en Provance Institut d'Administration des Entreprises Université d'Aix-Marseille.

—— —— (1981), 'A Conceptual Approach of the Service Offering', in H. Larsen, and S. Heede (eds.), *Proceedings of the EAARM Xth Annual Conference* (Copenhagen School of Economics and Business Administration, Denmark).

Engel, J. F., Fiorillo, H. F., and Cayley, M. A. (1972), *Market Segmentation: Concepts and Applications* (New York: Holt, Rinehart, & Winston).

—— Blackwell, R. D., and Kollat, D. T. (1978), *Consumer Behavior* (New York: Holt, Rinehart, & Winston).

England, L. (1980), 'Is Research a Waste of Time?', *Marketing*, 16 Apr., 5-7.

Esslemont, D. (1996), 'Segmentation and Targeting', *Elmar Internet Discussion Group*, University of South Carolina (elmar@sc.edu), 29 Aug., 16.35.

Eurobarometer (1994), *20th Anniversary Trends, 1973-1993* (Luxembourg: European Commission, May).

European Commission (1990), *Eurobarometer*, 33/2 (June).

—— (1996), 'Economic Evaluation of the Internal Market', *European Economy*, 4.

—— (1997), 'Annual Economic Report for 1997'. *European Economy*, 63.

Eurostat (1992), *Basic Statistics of the Community* (29th edn.; Brussels).

—— (1996), *Enterprises in Europe, Fourth Report* (Luxembourg: European Commission).

—— (1997a), *The Single Market Review—Results of the business Survey* (Luxembourg: Office for Official Publications of the European Communities, Kogan Page-Earthscan).

—— (1997b), *Panorama of EU Industry* (Luxembourg: European Commission).

—— (1998), *European Economy*, Supplement B (June).

Evans, M., O'Malley, L., and Patterson, M. (1996), 'Direct Mail and Consumer Response: An Empirical Study of

Consumer Experiences of Direct Mail'. *Journal of Database Marketing*, 3/3: 250–61.

Fairly, P. (1995), 'Tioxide Grows Material Group', *Chemical Week*, 5 July, 18.

Fairlie, R. (1992), 'Making the Most of Geodemographic and Psychographic Profiles', in *Practitioners' Guide to Direct Marketing* (Teddington, Richmond-upon-Thames: IDM).

Farhangmehr, M., and Veiga, P. (1995), 'The Changing Consumer in Portugal', *International Journal of Research in Marketing*, 12: 485–502.

Farley, J. U. (1964), 'An Optimal Plan for Salesmen's Compensation', *Journal of Marketing Research*, 1/2: 39–43.

Farquhar, C. Dibb, S., and Simkin, L. (1994), *The Marketing Casebook* (London: Routledge).

Felton, A. (1959), 'Making the Marketing Concept Work', *Harvard Business Review*, 37/4 (July–Aug.), 55–65.

Fernie, J. (1990), (ed.) *Retail Distribution Management* (London: Kogan Page).

Fildes, R., and Lofthouse, S. (1975), 'Market Share Strategy and the Product Life Cycle: A Comment', *Journal of Marketing*, 39/4 (Oct.), 57–60.

Financial Times (1997), *FT 500* (London: Pitman).

——(1998), 'Dealing with the Dealers', 4 Mar.

Fishbein, M. (1963), 'An investigation of the Relationships between Beliefs about an Object and the Attitude toward that Object', *Human Relations*, 16: 233–9.

——and Ajzen, I. (1975), *'Belief, Attitude, Intention and Behavior'* (Reading, Mass.: Addison-Wesley).

Fisher, R. J., Maltz, E., and Jaworski, B. J. (1997), 'Enhancing Communication between Marketing and Engineering', *Journal of Marketing*, 61/3: 54–70.

Fisk, R. P., Brown, S. W., and Bitner, M. J. (1993), 'The Evolution of the Services Marketing Literature', *Journal of Retailing*, 69 (Spring), 61–103.

Fletcher, K., and Peters, L. (1996), 'Issues in Consumer Information Management', *Journal of the Market Research Society*, 38/2: 145–60.

Folkes, V., and Wheat, R. D. (1995), 'Consumers' Price Perceptions of Promoted Products', *Journal of Retailing*, 71/3: 317–28.

Ford, D. (1997) (ed.), *Understanding Business Markets* (2nd edn., London: Dryden Press).

——(1998) (ed.), *Managing Business Relationships* (Chichester: Wiley).

Forrester Research (1997), *Business Marketing* (May).

Frank, R. E., Massy, W. F., and Wind, Y. (1972), *Market Segmentation* (Englewood Cliffs, NJ: Prentice Hall).

Franwick, G. L., James, C. W., Hutt, M. D., and Reingen, P. H. (1994), 'Evolving Patterns of Organizational Beliefs in the Formation of Strategy', *Journal of Marketing*, 58 (Apr.), 96–110.

Frazer, C. (1983), 'Creative Strategy: A Management Perspective', *Journal of Advertising*, 12/4: 36–41.

Fry, A. (1987), 'The Post-It Note: An Entrepreneurial Success', SAM *Advanced Management Journal* (Summer), 4–9.

Fudge, W. K., and Lodish, L. M. (1977), 'Evaluation of the Effectiveness of a Model Based Salesman's Planning System by Field Experimentation', *Interfaces*, 8/1, Pt. 2: 97–106.

Fukuyama, F. (1995), *Trust: The Social Virtues and the Creation of Prosperity* (London: Hamish Hamilton).

Fuller, J. B., O'Connor, J., and Rawlinson, R. (1994), 'Tailored Logistics: The Next Advantage', *Harvard Business Review* (May–June), 87–98.

Gabbott, M., and Hogg, G. (1997), *Services Marketing Management: A Reader* (Orlando, Fla.: Dryden Press).

Gain, B. (1996), 'Natural Products Gain Favor', *Chemical Week*, 158/48 (11 Dec.), 35–7.

Ganbegyan, A. (1989), *Moving the Mountain* (London: Bantam Press).

Gattorna, J. L., and Walters, D. W. (1996), *Managing the Supply Chain: A Strategic Perspective* (London: Macmillan Business Books).

GEA Consulenti Associata di Gestione Aziendale (1994), *Supplier–Retailer Collaboration in Supply Chain Management: Project V* (London: Coca-Cola Retail Research Group).

Gehani, R. R. (1992), 'Concurrent Product Development for Fast-Track Corporations', *Long Range Planning*, 25/6: 40–7.

Gemunden, H. G., Ritter, T., and Walter, A. (1998), *Relationships and Networks in International Markets* (Oxford; Elsevier Science).

George, M., Freeling, A., and Court, D. (1994), 'Reinventing the Marketing Organization', *McKinsey Quarterly*, 4: 43–62.

George, W. R. (1986), 'Internal Communications Programs as a Mechanism for Doing Internal Marketing', in V. Venkatesan *et al.* (eds.), *Creativity in Services Marketing* (Chicago: American Marketing Association).

Gerstner, E., and Hess, J. D. (1995), 'Pull Promotions and Channel Coordination', *Marketing Science*, 14/1: 43–60.

Gijsbrechts, E., Swinnen, G., and van Waterschoot, W. (1995), 'The Changing Consumer in Belgium', *International Journal of Research in Marketing*, 12: 389–403.

Glazer, R. (1991), 'Marketing in Information Intensive Environments: Strategic Implications of Knowledge as an Asset', *Journal of Marketing*, 55/4 (Oct.), 1–19.

Gonik, J. (1978), 'Tie Salesmen's Bonuses to their Forecasts', *Harvard Business Review*, 56/3 (May–June), 116–23.

Gopal, C., and Cypress, H. (1993), *Integrated Distribution Management* (Homewood, Ill.: Business One Irwin).

Gordon, W. (1991), 'Accessing the Brand through Research', in D. Cowley (ed.), *Understanding Brands* (London: Kogan Page).

Gould, R. A. (1969), *Yiwara: Foragers of the Australian Desert* (London: Collins).

Grant, R. M. (1995), *Contemporary Strategy Analysis* (2nd edn.; Oxford: Basil Blackwell).

Gray, R. (1995), 'A Green and Pleasant Brand', *Marketing*, 20 July.

Green, P. E. (1977), 'A New Approach to Market Segmentation', *Business Horizons*, 20/1: 61–73.

Greenleaf, E. A. (1995), 'The Impact of Reference Price Effects on the Profitability of Price Promotions', *Marketing Science*, 14/1: 82–104.

Greenley, G. E., and Bayus, B. L. (1994), 'Marketing Planning in UK and US Companies', *Journal of Strategic Marketing*, 2/2: 140–54.

Greenway, E. (1999), 'Undergoing Analysis', *Marketing Business* (May), 58.

Grewal, D., and Baker, J. (1994), 'Do Retail Store Environmental Factors Affect Consumers' Price Acceptability? An Empirical Examination', *International Journal of Research in Marketing*, 11/2: 107–15.

Griffin, A., and Hauser, J. R. (1996), 'Integrating R&D and Marketing', *Journal of Product Innovation Management*, 13/3: 191–215.

Grönroos, C. (1979), *Marknadsföring av tjänster. En analys av marknadsföringsfunktionen i tjänsteföretag* (The Marketing of Services. An Analysis of the Marketing Function of Service Firms) (in Swedish) (Stockholm: Akademilitteratur).

——(1982a), 'An Applied Service Marketing Theory', *European Journal of Marketing*, 16 (Jan.–Feb.), 30–41.

——(1982b), *Strategic Management and Marketing in the Service Sector* (Helsingfors: Swedish School of Economics and Business Administration, published in 1983 in the UK by Chartwell-Bratt and in the USA by Marketing Science Institute).

——(1983), *Service Management and Marketing* (Lexington, Mass.: Lexington Books).

——(1984), 'A Service Quality Model and its Marketing Implications', *European Journal of Marketing*, 18/4: 36–44.

——(1989), 'Defining Marketing: A Market-Oriented Approach', *European Journal of Marketing*, 23/1: 52–60.

——(1990a), *Service Management and Marketing: Managing the Moments of Truth in Service Competition* (Lexington, Mass.: Lexington Books).

——(1990b), 'The Marketing Strategy Continuum: Towards a Marketing Concept for the 1990s', *Management Decision*, 29/1: 9.

——(1994), 'From Marketing Mix to Relationship Marketing: Towards a Paradigm Shift in Marketing', *Asia–Australia Marketing Journal*, 2/1: 9–29.

——(1998), 'Marketing Services: A Case of a Missing Product', *Journal of Business and Industrial Marketing*, 13/4.

—— and Gummesson, E. (1985), 'The Nordic School of Service Marketing', in C. Grönroos and E. Gummesson (eds.), *Service Marketing—Nordic School Perspectives* (Stockholm: Stockholm University), 6–11.

Gross, A. C., Banting, P. M., Meredith, L. N., and Ford, I. D. (1993), *Business Marketing* (Boston: Houghton Mifflin).

Grunert, K. G. (1996), 'Automatic and Strategic Processes in Advertising Effects', *Journal of Marketing*, 60/4: 88–101.

—— Grunert, S. C., Glatzer, W., and Imkamp, H. (1995), 'The Changing Consumer in Germany', *International Journal of Research in Marketing*, 12: 417–33.

Grunert, S. C., and Juhl, H. J. (1995), 'Values, Environmental Attitudes, and Buying Organic Foods', *Journal of Economic Psychology*, 16/1: 39–62.

Guiltinan, J. P., and Gundlach, G. T. (1996), 'Aggressive and Predatory Pricing: A Framework for Analysis', *Journal of Marketing*, 60/3 (July), 87–102.

Gummesson, E. (1977), *Marknadsföring och försäljning av konsulttjänster* (Stockholm: Akademilitteratur).

——(1987), 'The New Marketing: Developing Long-Term Interactive Relationships', *Long-Range Planning*, 20/4: 10–20.

——(1990), *The Part-Time Marketer* (Center for Service Research, University of Karlstad, Sweden).

——(1991), 'Marketing Revisited: The Crucial Role of the Part-Time Marketers', *European Journal of Marketing*, 25/2: 60–7.

——(1994a), 'Broadening and Specifying Relationship Marketing', *Asia–Australia Marketing Journal*, 2/1: 31–43.

——(1994b), 'Making Relationship Marketing Operational', *International Journal of Service Industry Management*, 5/5 (Nov.), 5–20.

——(1995), *Relationsmarknadsfoering: Fraan 4P till 30R* (Malmo: Liber-Hermods).

Gupta, A. K., and Wilemon, D. (1988), 'Why R&D Resists Marketing Information', *Research Technology Management*, 36/6: 36–41.

—— Raj, S. P., and Wilemon, D. L. (1987), 'Managing the R&D–Marketing Interface', *Research Management*, 30/2: 38–43.

Gutman, J. (1982), 'A Means-End Chain Model Based on Consumer Categorization Processes', *Journal of Marketing*, 46/2: 60–72.

Haas, R. W. (1992), *Business Marketing Management: An Organizational Approach* (Boston: PWS-Kent).

Haeckel, S. H., and Nolan, R. L. (1993), 'Managing by Wire', *Harvard Business Review*, (Sept.–Oct.), 122–32.

Hakansson H. (1982) (ed.), *International Marketing and Purchasing of Industrial Goods—An Interaction Approach* (New York: Wiley).

—— and Snehota, I. (1995), *Developing Relationships in Business Networks* (London: Routledge).

—— Johanson, J., and Wootz, B. (1976), 'Influence Tactics in Buyer–Seller Processes', *Industrial Marketing Management*, 4/6: 319–32.

Haley, R. I. (1968), 'Benefit Segmentation: A Decision Oriented Research Tool', *Journal of Marketing*, 32/3 (July), 30–5.

——(1984), 'Benefit Segmentation—20 Years Later', *Journal of Consumer Marketing*, 1/2: 5–13.

Hall, R. W., and Partyka, J. G. (1997), 'On the Road to Efficiency', *OR/MS Today*, 24/3: 38–47.

Hallén, L., Johanson, J., and Seyed-Mohamed, N. (1991), 'Inter-Firm Adaptation in Business Relationships', *Journal of Marketing*, 55 (Apr.), 29–37.

Hamel, G., and Prahalad, C. K. (1994a), 'Seeing the Future First', *Fortune*, 130/5 (5 Sept.), 64–8.

—— —— (1994b), *Competing for the Future* (Boston: Harvard Business School Press).

Hankinson, G., and Cowking, P. (1993), *Branding in Action* (Hemel Hempstead: McGraw-Hill).

—— —— (1996), *The Reality of Global Brands* (Hemel Hempstead: McGraw-Hill).

—— —— (1997), 'Branding in Practice: The Profile and Role of Brand Managers in the UK', *Journal of Marketing Management*, 13: 239–64.

Hanmer-Lloyd, S. (1993), 'Relationship Appraisal: A Route to Improved Reseller Channel Performance', 9th IMP Conference Proceedings, Bath, September.

Harris, D., and Walters, D. (1992), *Retail Operations Management* (Hemel Hempstead: Prentice Hall).

Hart, C. W. L., Heskett, J. L., and Sasser, W. E., Jr. (1990), 'The Profitable Art of Service Recovery', *Harvard Business Review*, 68/4 (July–Aug.), 148–56.

Hart, S. (1989), 'The Analysis and Revitalisation of Problem Products', in G. J. Avlonitis, N. K. Papavasiliou, and A. G. Kouremenos (eds.), *Marketing Thought and Practice in the 1990s* (Proceedings of the 18th Annual Conference of the European Marketing Academy, Athens), 1125–50.

Hauser, J. R., and Clausing, D. (1988), 'The House of Quality', *Harvard Business Review*, 66/3 (May–June), 63–73.

Hayes-Roth, B. (1982), 'Opportunism in Consumer Behavior', in A. A. Mitchell (ed.), *Advances in Consumer Research* 9 (Provo, ut.: Association for Consumer Research), 132–5.

Haywood, C. D. (1997), 'An Analysis of the Market potential for Electric Vehicles in the United Kingdom', dissertation (University of Warwick).

Heller, R. (1990), *Signposts for Management* (London: Rank Xerox).

Helfferich, E., Hinfelaar, M., and Kasper, H. (1997), 'Towards a Clear Terminology on International Retailing', *International Review of Retail, Distribution and Consumer Research*, 7/3: 287–307.

Henley Centre for Forecasting Ltd. (1995), *Dataculture 2000* (London: Henley Centre).

Herbig, P., and O'Hara, B. S. (1994), 'Industrial distributors in the Twenty-First Century', *Industrial Marketing Management*, 23/3: 199–203.

Heskett, J. L., Sasser, W. E., and Hart, C. W. L. (1990), 'Service Breakthroughs: Changing the Rules of the Game' (New York: Free Press).

Hill, T., Nicholson, A., and Westbork, R. (1997), 'Strategic Management of the Operations Function', *London Business School Papers: Mastering Management*, 11/5: 322–6.

Hilton, R. W. (1994), *Managerial Accounting* (2nd edn.; New York: McGraw-Hill).

Hisrich, R. D., and Peters, M. P. (1995), *Entrepreneurship: Starting, Developing and Managing a New Enterprise* (3rd edn.; Chicago: Irwin).

Hoffman, D., and Novak, T. (1996), 'Marketing in Hypermedia Computer Mediated Environments: Conceptual Foundations', *Journal of Marketing*, 60/3 (July), 50–68.

Holbrook, M. B., and Howard, J. A. (1976), 'Frequently Purchased Nondurable Goods and Services', in R. Ferber (ed.), *Selected Aspects of Consumer Behaviour* (Washington: National Science Foundation), 189–222.

Holder, D. (1998), *IDM Diploma Course Material* (Teddington, Richmond-upon-Thames: Institute of Direct Marketing).

Hollander, S. C., and LaFrancis, K. M. (1993), 'Balkanization of America: Lessons from the Interstate Trade Barrier Experience', *Contemporary Marketing History* (Proceedings of the Sixth Conference on Historical Research in Marketing and Marketing Thought, Atlanta, Ga.).

Hollister J. (1958), 'Marketing Behaviour of Small and Medium Firms in the Netherlands, unpublished research report (Delft: RVB).

Hooley, G. J. (1980), 'The Multivariate Jungle: The Academic's Playground but the Manager's Minefield', *European Journal of Marketing*, 14/7: 379–86.

—— (1984), *Marketing in the UK: A Survey of Current Practice and Performance* (Maidenhead: Chartered Institute of Marketing).

—— and Saunders, J. (1993), *Competitive Positioning: The Key to Market Success* (Hemel Hempstead: Prentice Hall).

Hopkins, D. S. (1981), 'The Marketing Plan', *Research Report*, 801 (New York: Conference Board).

Houston, F. (1986), 'The Marketing Concept—What It Is and What It Is Not', *Journal of Marketing*, 50/2 (Apr.), 81–7.

—— and Gassenheimer, J. B. (1987), 'Marketing and Exchange', *Journal of Marketing*, 51/4 (Oct.), 3–18.

—— Gassenheimer, J. B., and Maskulka, J. M. (1992), *Marketing Exchange, Transactions, and Relationships* (Westport, Calif.: Quorum Books).

Howard, D. G., Savins, D. M., Howell, W., and Ryans, J. K., Jr. (1991), 'The Evolution of Marketing Theory in the United States and Europe', *European Journal of Marketing*, 25/2: 7–16.

Hoy, F. (1994), 'The Dark Side of Franchising or Appreciating Flaws in an Imperfect World', *International Small Business Journal*, 12/2: 26–38.

Hubbard, P. (1998), 'Dell and E-Commerce—A Perfect Match', paper presented at Traditional & New Distribution Channels—Strategy, Selection and Management Conference, Horwood House Conference Centre, Milton Keynes, Mar.

Humby, C. (1996a), 'Opening the Information Warehouse', *Marketing*, 18 Sept., 34–7.

—— (1996b), 'Digging for Information', *Marketing*, 21 Nov., 41–2.

Hunt, S. D., and Morgan, R. M. (1995), 'The Comparative Advantage Theory of Competition', *Journal of Marketing*, 59/2: 1–15.

Hutlink, E. J., Griffin, A., and Hart, S. (1997), 'Industrial New Product Launch Strategies and Product Development Performance', *Journal of Product Innovation Management*, 14: 243–57.

Hutt, M. D., and Speh, T. W. (1998), *Business Marketing Management* (6th edn.; Fort Worth, Tex.: Dryden Press).

Iacobucci, D. (1996) (ed.), *Networks in Marketing* (Thousand Oaks, Calif.: Sage Publications).

——and Ostrom, A. (1996), 'Commercial and Interpersonal Relationships', *International Journal of Research in Marketing*, 13: 53–72.

IMF (1997), *World Economic Outlook* (May).

Ind, R. (1997), *The Corporate Brand* (London: Macmillan).

Ingram, T. N., Schwepker, G. H., and Hutson, D. (1992), 'Why Salespersons Fail', *Industrial Marketing Management*, 21/3: 225–31.

Institute for Grocery Distribution (1995), *The Category Management Revolution* (Letchmore Heath: IGD Business Publications).

Irons, K. (1991), *Managing Service Companies* (London: Economist Intelligence Unit).

——(1994), *Managing Service Companies* (Wokingham: Addison-Wesley).

Jackson, D. (1989), 'Determining a Customer's Lifetime Value', *Direct Marketing* (Mar.), 60–123.

——(1992), 'In Quest of the Grail: Breaking the Barriers to Customer Valuation', *Direct Marketing* (Mar.), 44–7.

Jackson, R., and Pride, W. (1986), 'The Use of Approved Vendor Lists', *Industrial Marketing Management*, 15: 165–9.

Jaikumar, R. (1986), 'Postindustrial Manufacturing', *Harvard Business Review* (Nov.–Dec.), 69–76.

Jain, S. C. (1981), *Marketing Planning and Strategy* (Cincinnati, Oh.: South Western Publishing).

Janiszewski, C. (1993), 'Preattentive Mere Exposure Effects', *Journal of Consumer Research*, 20: 376–93.

Jaworski, B., and Kohli, A. (1993), 'Market Orientation: Antecedents and Consequences', *Journal of Marketing*, 57/3 (July), 53–70.

Jeffreys, J. B. (1954), *Retail Trading in Britain, 1850–1950* (Cambridge: Cambridge University Press).

Jennings, R. G., and Plank, R.E. (1995), 'When the Purchasing Agent Is a Committee: Implications for Industrial Marketing', *Industrial Marketing Management*, 24: 411–19.

Jensen, J. M. (1991), 'Family Purchase Decisions: A Buying Center Approach', in K. D. Frankenberg, H. H. Larsen, F. Hansen, M. Friestad, and G. S. Albaum (eds.), *Proceedings of the 5th Biannual International Conference of the Academy of Marketing Science* (Copenhagen: Copenhagen Business School), 332–7.

Jobber, D. (1995), *Principles and Practice of Marketing* (London: McGraw-Hill).

Johnson, G., and Scholes, K. (1984), *Exploring Corporate Strategy* (Englewood Cliffs, NJ: Prentice Hall).

Johnston, M. (1998), 'No Gambling at this Casino', *Information Strategy*, 3/2: 17–19.

Johnston, W. J., and Bonoma, T. V. (1981), 'Purchase Process for Capital Equipment and Services', *Industrial Marketing Management*, 10: 253–64.

——and Lewin, E. L. (1994), 'A Review and Integration on Organizational Buying Behavior', Marketing Science Institute, Report Number 94-111, July.

——and Lewin, J. E. (1996), 'Organizational Buying Behavior: Toward an Integrative Framework', *Journal of Business Research*, 35: 1–15.

Joseph, W. B., Gardner, J. T., Thach, S., and Vernon, F. (1995), 'How Industrial Distributors View Distributor—Supplier Partnership Arrangements', *Industrial Marketing Management*, 24: 27–36.

Kaas, K. P. (1982), 'Consumer Habit Forming, Information Acquisition, and Buying Behavior', *Journal of Business Research*, 10: 3–15.

Kahn, R. L., and Cannel, C. F. (1968), 'Interviewing', *International Encyclopaedia of the Social Sciences*, 2/2: 118–35.

Kalyanam, K. (1996), 'Pricing Decisions under Demand Uncertainty: A Bayesian Mixture Model Approach', *Marketing Science*, 15/3: 207–21.

Kalyanaram, G., and Little, J. D. C. (1994), 'An Empirical Analysis of Latitude of Price Acceptance in Consumer Package Goods', *Journal of Consumer Research*, 21/2 (Dec.), 408–18.

Kalwani, M. U., and Narayandas, N. (1995), 'Long-Term Manufacturer–Supplier Relationships: Do They Pay Off for Supplier Firms?', *Journal of Marketing*, 59/1: 1–16.

Kanter, R. M. (1989), 'The New Managerial Work', *Harvard Business Review*, 67 (Nov.–Dec.), 85–92.

Kapferer, J.-N. (1986), 'Beyond Positioning: retailer's identity', *Retail Strategies for Profit and Growth*, (Amsterdam: ESOMAR).

Kaplan, R., and Norton, D. (1992), 'The Balanced Scorecard: Measures that Drive Performance', *Harvard Business Review* (Jan.–Feb.), 71–9.

————(1993), 'Putting the Balanced Scorecard to Work', *Harvard Business Review* (Sept.–Oct.), 134–42.

————(1996), 'Using the Balanced Scorecard as a Strategic Management System', *Harvard Business Review* (Jan.–Feb.), 75–85.

Kapoor, V., and Gupta, A. (1997), 'Agressive Sourcing: A Free-Market Approach', *Sloan Management Review*, 21–3.

Katona, G. (1975), *Psychological Economics* (New York: Elsevier).

Kaufman, P. J., Smith, N. C., and Ortmeyer, G. K. (1994), 'Deception in Retailer High-Low Pricing', *Journal of Retailing*, 70/2: 115–138.

Kaul, A., and Wittink, D. R. (1995), 'Empirical Generalizations about the Impact of Advertising on Price Sensitivity and Price', *Marketing Science*, 14, pt. 2/3: G151–G160.

Kay, J. (1996), *The Business of Economics* (Oxford: Oxford University Press).

Keegan, W. (1995), *Global Marketing Management* (Englewood Cliffs, NJ: Prentice Hall).

Kench, R., and Evans, M. J. (1991), 'IT: The Information-Technology Dichotomy', *Marketing Intelligence & Planning*, 9/5: 16–22.

Kirchler, E. (1995), 'Studying Economic Decisions within Private Households: A Critical Review and Design for a "Couple Experiences Diary"', *Journal of Economic Psychology*, 16: 393–420.

Kirzner, I. M. (1973), *Competition and Entrepreneurship* (Chicago: Chicago University Press).

Kohli, A. A., and Jaworski, B. (1990), 'Market Orientation: The Construct, Research Propositions and Managerial Implications', *Journal of Marketing*, 54/2 (Apr.), 2–18.

——Jaworski, E. J., and Kumar, A. (1993), 'MARKOR: A Measure of Market Orientation', *Journal of Marketing Research*, 30/4: 467–78.

Kotha, S. (1995), 'Mass Customization: Implementing the Emerging Paradigm for Competitive Advantage', *Strategic Management Journal*, 16: 21–42.

Kotler, P. (1965), 'Phasing out weak products', *Harvard Business Review*, 43/2 (Mar.–Apr.), 107–18.

——(1967, 1984, 1991, 1994, 1997), *Marketing Management* (various edns.; Englewood Cliffs, NJ: Prentice Hall).

——(1972), 'A Generic Concept of Marketing', *Journal of Marketing*, 36/2 (Apr.), 46–54.

——(1973), 'The Major Tasks of Marketing Management', *Journal of Marketing*, 37/4 (Sept.–Oct.), 42–9.

——(1974), 'Marketing during Periods of Shortage', *Journal of Marketing*, 38/3 (July–Aug.), 20–9.

——(1977), 'From Sales Obsession to Marketing Effectiveness', *Harvard Business Review*, 55/6 (Nov.–Dec.), 67–75.

——(1986), 'Megamarketing', *Harvard Business Review*, 64/2 (Mar.–Apr.), 117–24.

——and Levy, S. J. (1971), 'Demarketing, Yes, Demarketing', *Harvard Business Review*, 49/6 (Nov.–Dec.), 74–80.

——Armstrong, G., Saunders, J., and Wong, V. (1996), *Principles of Marketing* (Hemel Hempstead: Prentice Hall).

Kotter, J. P., and Heskett, J. L. (1992), *Corporate Culture and Performance* (New York: Free Press).

Kouremenos, A., and Avlonitis, G. J. (1995), 'The Changing Consumer in Greece', *International Journal of Research in Marketing*, 12: 435–48.

Krafft, M. (1995), *Salesforce Compensation in the Light of the New Institutional Theories* (in German) (Wiesbaden: Gabler Verlag).

Krajlic, P. (1983), 'Purchasing Must Become Supply Management', *Harvard Business Review* (Sept.–Oct.), 109–17.

Kraushar, P. (1972), 'Death Defying Products', *Marketing* (Dec.).

Kroeber-Riel, W. (1984), 'Emotional Product Differentiation by Classical Conditioning', in T. C. Kinnear (ed.), *Advances in Consumer Research*, 11 (Provo, Ut.: Association for Consumer Research), 538–43.

Krugman, P. (1994), *The Age of Diminished Expectations* (Cambridge, Mass.: MIT Press).

——(1995), *Peddling Prosperity* (Cambridge, Mass.: MIT Press).

——and Venables, T. (1993), 'Integration, Specialisation and Adjustment', CEPR Discussion Paper, No. 886 CEPR.

Kucmarski, T. D. (1988), *Managing New Products* (Englewood Cliffs, NJ: Prentice Hall).

Kuhlmann, E. (1983), 'Consumer Socialization of Children and Adolescents: A Review of Current Approaches', *Journal of Consumer Policy*, 6: 397–418.

Laaksonen, H., and Reynolds, J. (1994), 'Own Brands in Food Retailing across Europe', *Journal of Brand Management*, 2/1: 37–46.

Laaksonen, P., Laaksonen, M., and Moller, K. (1998), 'The Changing Consumer in Finland', *International Journal of Research in Marketing*, 15: 169–80.

Laforet, S., and Sounders, J. (1994), 'The Use of Portfolios of Brands: A Study of Major Grocery Manufacturers', in J. Bloemer, J. Lemmink, and H. Kasper (eds.), *Marketing: Its Dynamics and Challenges* (Proceedings of the 23rd Annual Conference of the European Marketing Academy, Maastricht, The Netherlands), 549–65.

Lal, R., and Padmanabhan, V. (1995), 'Competitive Response and Equilibria', *Marketing Science*, 14, pt. 2/3: G101–G108.

——and Rao, R. (1997), 'Supermarket Competition: The Case of Every Day Low Pricing', *Marketing Science*, 16/1: 60–80.

——Little, J. D. C., and Villas-Boas, J. M. (1996), 'A Theory of Forward Buying, Merchandising, and Trade Deals', *Marketing Science*, 15/1: 21–37.

Lambkin, M. (1993), *The Irish Consumer Market: A Guidebook for Marketing Managers* (Dublin: Marketing Society).

——and Bradley, F. (1995), 'The Changing Consumer in Ireland', *International Journal of Research in Marketing*, 12: 449–66.

Lamey, J. (1996), *Supply Chain Management: Best Practice and the Impact for New Partnerships.* (London: Financial Times Management Report, FT Retail and Consumer Publishing).

Lastovicka, J. L., and Joachimsthaler, E. A. (1988), 'Improving the Detection of Personality-Behavior Relationships in Consumer Research', *Journal of Consumer Research*, 14/4 (Mar.), 583–7.

Laurent, G., and Kapferer, J.-N. (1985), 'Measuring Consumer Involvement Profiles', *Journal of Marketing Research*, 22: 41–53.

Lear, Robert W. (1963), 'No Easy Road to Market Orientation', *Harvard Business Review*, 41/5 (Sept.–Oct.), 53–60.

Leeflang, P. S. H. (1988) (ed.), *Probleemgebied Marketing* (Holland: Steafert Kroese).

——and Wittink, D. R. (1996), 'Competitive Reaction versus Consumer Response: Do Managers Overreact?', *International Journal of Research in Marketing*, 13/2: 103–19.

——and Pahud de Mortanges, C. (1993), 'The Internal European Market and Strategic Marketing Planning: Implications and Expectations', *Journal of International Consumer Marketing*, 6/2: 7–23.

——and Van Raaij, W. F. (1993), 'The Netherlands: Recent Changes in Environmental Variables and their Consequences for Future Consumption and Marketing', *International Journal of Research in Marketing*, 10/4: 345–63.

————(1995), 'The Changing Consumer in the European Union: A Meta-Analysis', *International Journal of Research in Marketing*, 12: 373–87.

Leenders M., and Blenkhorn D. (1988), *Reverse Marketing: The New Buyer-Seller Relationship.* New York: The Free Press.

Lefebvre, L. A., Lefebvre, E., and Harvey, J. (1996), 'Intangible Assets as Determinants of Advanced Manufacturing Technology Adoption in SMEs', *IEEE Transactions on Engineering Management*, 43/3: 307–22.

Lehman, D. R., and Jocz, K. E. (1997) (eds.), *Reflections of the Futures of Marketing* (Cambridge, Mass.: Marketing Science Institute).

Lehtinen, J. R. (1983), *Asiakasohjautuva palveluyritys* (Espoo, Finland: Weilin+Göös).

Lei, D., Hitt, M. A., and Goldhar, J. D. (1996), 'Advanced Manufacturing Technology: Organizational Design and Strategic Flexibility', *Organization Studies*, 17/3: 501–23.

Leith, A., and Riley, N. (1998), 'Understanding Need States and their Role in Developing Successful Marketing Strategies', *Journal of the Market Research Society*, 40/1: 25–32.

Leppard, J. (1987), 'A Reappraisal of the Role of Marketing Planning', *Quarterly Review of Marketing*, 12 (Autumn), 1–7.

Levitt, T. (1960), 'Marketing Myopia', *Harvard Business Review*, 38/4 (July–Aug.), 45–56.

——(1965), 'Exploit the Product Life Cycle', *Harvard Business Review*, 43/6 (Nov.–Dec.), 81–94.

——(1969), *The Marketing Mode* (New York: McGraw-Hill).

——(1980), 'Marketing Success through Differentiation—of Anything', *Harvard Business Review*, 58/1 (Jan.–Feb.), 83–91.

——(1983a), 'After the sale is over . . . ', *Harvard Business Review*, 61/4 (Sept.–Oct.), 87–93.

——(1983b), *The Marketing Imagination* (New York: Free Press).

——(1983c), 'The Globalization of Markets', *Harvard Business Review*, 6/1: 92–102.

Levy, M., and Weitz, B. (1995), *Retailing Management* (Chicago, Ill.: Irwin).

Lewis, R. J. (1993), *Activity-Based Costing for Marketing and Manufacturing* (Westport, Conn.: Quorum Books).

Lewis, T. (1995), 'Using Data-Driven Marketing to Enhance Acquisition Performance', *Journal of Database Marketing*, 311: 13–23.

Liander, B. (1967), *Comparative Analysis for International Marketing* (Boston: Allyn & Bacon).

Lichtenthal, D. J., and Wilson, D. T. (1992), 'Becoming Market Oriented', *Journal of Business Research*, 24: 191–207.

Lichtenstein, D. R., Ridgway, N. M., and Netemeyer, R. G. (1993), 'Price Perceptions and Consumer Shopping Behavior: A Field Study', *Journal of Marketing Research*, 30/2 (May), 234–45.

Lilien, G. L., and Kotler, P. (1983), *Marketing Decision Making: A Model-building Approach* (New York: Harper & Row).

——and Rangaswamy, A. (1998), *Marketing Engineering* (Reading, Mass.: Addison-Wesley).

——Kotler, P., and Moorthy, K. S. (1992), *Marketing Models* (Englewood Cliffs, NJ: Prentice Hall).

Liljander, V. (1995), '*Comparison Standards in Perceived Service Quality*' Research report A: 63, CERS Center for Relationship Marketing and Service Management, Swedish School of Economics and Business Administration, Helsingfors, Finland.

——and Strandvik, T. (1995), 'The Nature of Customer Relationships in Services', in T. A. Swartz, D. A. Bowen, and S. W. Brown (eds.), *Advances in Services Marketing and Management*, 4.

Link, J., and Hildebrand, V. (1993), *Database Marketing and Computer Aided Selling* (in German) (Munich: Vahlen Verlag).

Littler, D. (1992), 'Market Segmentation', in M. J. Baker (ed.), *Marketing Strategy and Management* (London: Macmillan), 90–103.

Liu, Hong, *et al.* (1992), 'Market Effect, Control Effect and Market Orientation', working paper, University of Warwick.

Lodish, L. M. (1971), 'CALLPLAN: An Interactive Salesman's Call Planning System', *Management Science*, 18: 25–40.

——Curtis, E., Ness, M., and Simpson, M. K. (1988), 'Sales Force Sizing and Deployment Using a Decision Calculus Model at Syntex Laboratories', *Interfaces*, 18/1: 5–20.

Lovelock, C. (1992), *Managing Services* (Englewood Cliffs, NJ: Prentice Hall).

Low, G., and Fullerton, R. (1994), 'Brands, Brand Management and the Brand Management System: A Critical-Historical Evaluation', *Journal of Marketing Research*, 31 (May), 173–90.

Lusch, R. F., and Laczniak, G. R. (1987), 'The Evolving Marketing Concept, Competitive Intensity and Organisational Performance', *Journal of Academy of Marketing Science*, 15/3 (Fall), 1–11.

Lutz, R. J., and Bettman, J. R. (1977), 'Multiattribute Models in Marketing: A Bicentennial Review', in A. G. Woodside, J. N. Sheth, and P. D. Bennett (eds.), *Consumer and Industrial Buying Behavior* (New York: Elsevier), 137–49.

Lyons, V. (1996), 'Just a Stereotype', *Marketing Week*, 21 June, 40–1.

McCarthy, E. J. (1960), *Basic Marketing* (Homewood; Ill.: Irwin).

——and Perreault, W. D. (1997), *Basic Marketing: A Managerial Approach* (Homewood, Ill.: Irwin).

——and William, P., Jr. (1990), *Basic Marketing* (Homewood, Ill.: Irwin).

McDonald, M. H. B. (1982), 'The Theory and Practice of Marketing Planning for Industrial Goods in International Markets', Ph.D. thesis (Cranfield).

——(1995), *Marketing Plans* (Oxford: Butterworth-Heinemann).

——(1997), 'Exploiting Technique Interrelationships', paper presented at the AMA Conference, Manchester Metropolitan University Conference, July.

——and Dunbar, I. (1995), *Market Segmentation* (Basingstoke: Macmillan).

McDonald, W. J. (1998), *Direct Marketing: An Integrated Approach* (Singapore: McGraw-Hill).

McGee, L. W., and Spiro, R. L. (1988), 'The Marketing Concept in Perspective', *Business Horizons*, 31/3: 40–6.

McGoldrick, P. J. (1990), *Retail Marketing* (London: McGraw-Hill).

——(1994), (ed.), *Cases in Retail Management* (London: Pitman).

McGugan, G. (1997), 'By Firing Humans, France Finally Masters Good Service', *Canadian Business* (Aug.), 79–80.

McHenry, R. (1993). (ed.), *The New Encyclopaedia Britannica* (15th edn.; Chicago: Encyclopaedia Britannica Inc.).

McKenna, R. (1991), 'Marketing is Everything', *Harvard Business Review*, 69/1 (Jan.–Feb.), 65–79.

McKitterick, J. B. (1957), 'What is the Marketing Management Concept?' in F. M. Bass (ed.), *The Frontiers of Marketing Thought and Science* (New York: American Marketing Association).

McNamara, C. (1972), 'The Present Status of the Marketing Concept', *Journal of Marketing*, 36/1: 50–7.

McTaggart, J. M., Kontes, P. W., and Mankins, M. C. (1994), *The Value Imperative* (New York: Free Press).

McVey, P. (1960), 'Are Channels of Distribution What the Textbooks Say?', *Journal of Marketing* (Jan.), 61–4.

Magrath, A. J., and Hardy, K. G. (1987), 'Avoiding the Pitfalls in Managing Distribution Channels', *Business Horizons* (Sept.–Oct.), 29–33.

Maier, J., and Saunders, J. (1990), 'The Implementation of Segmentation in Sales Management', *Journal of Personal Selling and Sales Management*, 10/1: 39–48.

Marcel, C., and Nassoy, B. (1984), *Stratégie marketing de l'achat industriel* (Paris: CDAF).

Marketing Business (1998), 'Sir Richard Greenbury: A Broad View of M & S', *Marketing Business* (Apr.), 8.

Marketing Forum (1994), 'Say Yes to Market-Oriented Culture', *Management Review* (Mar.).

Market Research Society (1994), *The Opinion Polls and the 1992 General Election* (London).

——(1997), *Proposed Revised Code of Conduct* (London).

Marketing News (1985), 'AMA Board Approves New Marketing Definition', 1 Mar. 1.

Marketing Science Institute (1990), *Research Priorities 1990–1992: A Guide to MSI Research Programs and Procedures* (Cambridge, Mass.: Marketing Science Institute).

Markusen, J. R. (1995), 'The Boundaries of Multinational Enterprises and the Theory of International Trade', *Journal of Economic Perspectives*, 9/2: 169–89.

Mars Group Recruitment Literature (1997).

Marshall, M., and Siegler, F. (1993), 'Selecting the Right Rep Firm', *Sales and Marketing Management* (Jan.), 46–50.

Martin, J. (1995), 'Ignore your Customer', *Fortune* (European edn.) 131/8 (1 May), 83–6.

Maslow, A. H. (1954), *Motivation and Personality* (New York: Harper & Row).

Mason, J. L. (1965), 'The Low Prestige of Personal Selling', *Journal of Marketing*, 29/4: 7–10.

Mathur, S. S., and Kenyon, A. (1998), *Creating Value: Shaping Tomorrow's Business* (paperback edn.; Oxford: Butterworth-Heinemann).

Mendonca, L., and McCallum, G. D. (1995), 'Battling for the Wallet', *McKinsey Quarterly*, 2: 76–92.

Meredith, G. G., Nelson, R. E., and Neck, P. A. (1982), *The Practice of Entrepreneurship* (Geneva: International Labour Office).

Michman, R. D. (1990), 'Managing Structural Changes in Marketing Channels', *Journal of Business and Industrial Marketing*, 5/2 (Summer–Autumn), 5–14.

Midler, C. (1993), *La Voiture qui n'existait pas: Management des projets et transformation de l'entreprise* (Paris: Interéditions).

Millward, M. (1987), 'How to Get Better Value from your Research Budget', *AMSO Handbook and Guide to Buying Market Research in the UK*, 6–10.

Mintel International Group (1998), *2010: Marketing to Tomorrow's Consumers* (London).

Mintzberg, H., and Waters, J. A. (1985), 'Of Strategy: Deliberate and Emergent', *Strategic Management Journal*, 6/3: 257–73.

Mitchel, A. (1998), *Marketing Business*, 69 (May), 16.

Mitchell, A. (1997), *Efficient Consumer Response: A New Paradigm for the European FMCG Sector* (London: Financial Times Retail and Consumer Publishing).

Moenaert, A., and Souder, W. E. (1996), 'Content and Antecedents of Information Utility at the R&D/Marketing Interface', *Management Science*, 42/11: 1592–1607.

Moenaert, R. K., Deschoolmeester, D., De Meyer, A., and Souder, W. E. (1992), 'Information Styles of Marketing and R&G Personnel during Technological Innovation Projects', *R&D Management*, 22/1 (Jan.), 21–39.

Möller, K. (1986), 'Buying Behavior of Industrial Components: Inductive Approach for Descriptive Model Building', in P. Turnbull and S. Paliwoda (eds.), *Research in International Marketing* (London: Croom Helm), 79–132.

——(1992), 'Research Traditions in Marketing: Theoretical Notes', in *Economics and Marketing Essays in Honour of Goesta Mickwitz* (Helsinki: Multiprint), 197–218.

——and Wilson, D. T. (1995), 'Business Relationships: An Interaction Perspective', in K. Moller and D. Wilson (eds.), *Business Marketing: An Interaction and Network Perspective* (Norwell: Kluwer).

Monroe, K. (1990), *Pricing: Making Profitable Decisions* (New York: McGraw-Hill).

Montoya-Weiss, M. M., and Calantone, R. (1994), 'Determinants of New Product Performance: A Review and Meta-Analysis', *Journal of Product Innovation Management*, 11/5: 397–417.

Morden, A. (1987), *Elements of Marketing* (London: DPP Publications).

Morgan, R. M., and Hunt, S. D. (1994), 'The Commitment-Trust Theory of Relationship Marketing', *Journal of Marketing*, 58/3: 20–38.

Morita, A. (1987), *Made in Japan* (London: Collins).

Morris, M. H., and Calantone, R. J. (1990), 'Four Components of Effective Pricing', *Industrial Marketing Management*, 19/4: 321–9.

Morrison, A., and Wensley, R. (1991), 'Boxing Up or Boxed In?: A Short History of the Boston Consulting Group Share/Growth Matrix', *Journal of Marketing Management*, 7/2: 105–29.

MSI Review (1997), 'A Conversation with Carl Gustin, Kodak's Chief Marketing Officer' (Fall), 5–8.

Moutinho, L., and Evans, M. J. (1992), *Applied Marketing Research* (Reading, Mass.: Addison-Wesley).

Muhlbacher, H., Botschen, M., and Beutelmeyer, W. (1997), 'The Changing Consumer in Austria', *International Journal of Research in Marketing*, 14: 309–19.

Munkelt, I. (1992), 'Offers by Sales Trainers' (in German), *Absatzwirtschaft*, 7: 64–81.

Murphy, P. E., and Enis, B. M. (1986), 'Classifying Products Strategically', *Journal of Marketing*, 50/3 (July), 24–42.

——and Staples, W. A. (1979), 'A Modernized Family Life Cycle', *Journal of Consumer Research*, 6/1: 12–22.

Myers, K. H., Jr., and Smalley, O. A. (1959), 'Marketing History and Economic Development', *Business History Review*, 33 (Summer): 387–400.

Naert, Ph. N., and Leeflang, P. S. H. (1978), *Building Implementable Marketing Models* (Leiden: Martinus Nijhoff).

Nagle, T. T., and Holden, R. K. (1995), *The Strategy and Tactics of Pricing: A Guide to Profitable Decision Making* (Englewood Cliffs, NJ: Prentice Hall).

Naisbitt, J. (1982), *Megatrends* (New York: Warner Books).

Narus, J. A., and Anderson, J. C. (1987), 'Distribution and Contributions to Partnerships with Manufacturers', *Business Horizons* (Sept.–Oct.), 34–42.

Narver, J. C., and Slater, S. F. (1990a), 'The Effect of a Market Orientation on Business Profitability', *Journal of Marketing*, 54/4: 20–35.

————(1990b), 'Relative Emphasis in a Market Orientation and its Effects on Business Profitability', *Journal of Marketing* (AMA Summer Educators Conference Proceedings; Chicago: American Marketing Association).

Nash, E. (1995), *Direct Marketing Strategy: Planning, Execution* (3rd edn.; New York: McGraw-Hill).

Nelson, R. R., and Winter, S. G. (1982), *An Evolutionary Theory of Economic Change* (Cambridge, Mass.: Harvard University Press).

Nilsson, O. S., and Solgaard, H. S. (1995), 'The Changing Consumer in Denmark', *International Journal of Research in Marketing*, 12: 405–16.

Norman, D. A. (1968), 'Toward a Theory of Memory and Attention', *Psychological Review*, 75: 522–36.

Normann, R. (1984), *Service Management* (New York: Wiley).

——and Ramirez, R. (1993), 'From Value Chain to Value Constellation: Designing Interactive Strategy', *Harvard Business Review* (July–Aug.), 65–77.

Nua What's New (1997), 'Nua Internet Surveys What's New' (Mar.–Apr.) Online, *WWW. URL: [www.nua.ie/surveys/WhatsNew.html#March]*.

Nuefio, J. L., and Bennett, H. (1997), 'The Changing Span-ish Consumer', *International Journal of Research in Marketing*, 14: 19–33.

O'Brien, L., and Jones, C. (1995), 'Do Rewards Really Create Loyalty', *Harvard Business Review* (May–June), 75–82.

O'Connor, D. (1997), 'Retail Concentration and Multinational Expansion: Two Important Retail Trends', *Discount Merchandiser* (May), 67–70.

OECD (1996a), *Labour Force Statistics* (Paris).

——(1996b), *Labour Force Statistics 1974–1994* (Paris).

——(1996c), *Country Surveys* (Paris).

——(1997), *National Accounts* (Paris).

Ohmae, K. (1983a), *The Mind of the Strategist* (London: Penguin).

——(1983b), 'The Strategic Triangle and Business Unit Strategy', *McKinsey Quarterly* (Winter), 9–24.

——(1990), *The Borderless World: Power and Strategy in the International Economy* (London: Collins).

Oliver, R. L. (1980), 'A Cognitive Model of the Antecedents and Consequences of Satisfaction Decisions', *Journal of Marketing Research*, 17: 460–9.

——(1996), 'A Conceptual Model of Service Quality and Service Satisfaction: Compatible Goals, Different Concepts', T. A. Swartz, D. A. Bowen, and S. W. Brown (eds.), in *Advances in Services Marketing and Management 2* (Greenwich, Conn.: JAI Press).

O'Malley, L., Patterson, M., and Evans, M., 'Intimacy or Intrusion? The Privacy Dilemma for Relationship Marketing in Consumer Markets', *Journal of Marketing Management*, 13/6: 541–61.

O'Reilly, B. (1997), 'The Secrets of America's Most Admired Corporations: New Ideas; New Products', *Fortune*, 135/4 (3 Mar.), 62.

O'Shaughnessy, J. (1995), *Competitive Marketing* (3rd edn.; London: Routledge).

Osborne, R. L. (1995), 'The Essence of Entrepreneurial Success', *Management Decision*, 33/7: 4–9.

Ourusoff, A. (1994), 'Brands: What's Hot. What's Not', *Financial World*, 2 Aug., 40–54.

Padmanabhan, V., and Bass, F. M. (1993), 'Optimal Pricing of Successive Generations of Product Advances', *International Journal of Research in Marketing*, 10/2: 185–207.

Page, A. (1993), 'Assessing New Product Development and Performance: Establishing Crucial Norms', *Journal of Product Innovation Management*, 10/4 (Sept.), 273–90.

Page, M. J., Pitt, L. F., and Berthon, P. R. (1996), 'Before They Leave Switch on the Light: Knowing the Value of Keeping Customers', *Journal of Targeting Measurement and Analysis for Marketing*, 5/3: 232–46.

Pain, N., and Lansbury, M. (1997), 'Regional Economic Integration and Foreign Direct Investment: The Case of German Investment in Europe' *National Institute Economic Review*, 160 (Apr.).

Parasuraman, A., Zeithaml, V. A., and Berry, L. L. (1985), 'A Conceptual Model of Service Quality and its Implications for Further Research', *Journal of Marketing*, 49 (Fall), 41–50.

——————(1988), 'SERVQUAL: A Multiple-Item Scale

for Measuring Consumer Perceptions of Service Quality', *Journal of Retailing*, 64/1: 12–37.

Parker, P. M. (1995), 'Sweet Lemons: Illusory Quality, Self-Deceivers, Advertising and Price', *Journal of Marketing Research*, 32 (Aug.), 291–307.

——and Neelamegham, R. (1997), 'Price Elasticity Dynamics over the Product Life Cycle: A Study of Consumer Durables', *Marketing Letters*, 8/2: 205–16.

Parkinson, S. (1991), 'Customer Orientation', *Manager Update*, 3/2: 13–20.

Pascale, R. (1990), *Managing on the Edge* (London: Viking Books).

Patterson, M., Evans, M., and O'Malley, L. (1996), 'The Growth of Direct Marketing and Consumer Attitudinal Response to the Privacy Issue', *Journal of Targeting, Measurement and Analysis for Marketing*, 4/3: 201–13.

Payne, F. A. (1988), 'Developing a Marketing-Oriented Organisation', *Business Horizons*, 31/3 (May–June), 46–53.

Peppers, D., and Rogers, M. (1993), *One-to-One Future: Building Relationships One Customer at a Time* (New York: Currency/Doubleday).

——(1995), 'A New Marketing Paradigm: Share of Customer not Market Share', *Managing Service Quality*, 5/3: 48–51.

Peter, J. P., Olson, J. C., and Grunert, K. G. (in press), *Consumer Behaviour and Marketing Strategy* (European edn.; Maidenhead: McGraw-Hill).

Peteraf, M. A. (1993), 'The Cornerstones of Competitive Advantage: A Resource-Based View', *Strategic Management Journal*, 14/3: 179–91.

Peters, T. J., and Waterman, R. H. (1982), *In Search of Excellence* (London: Harper & Row).

Petty, R. E., Cacioppo, J. T., and Schumann, D. (1983), 'Central and Peripheral Routes to Advertising Effectiveness: The Moderating Role of Involvement', *Journal of Consumer Research*, 10: 135–46.

Phelps, N. A. (1996), *Multinationals and European Integration* (London: Jessica King Publishers).

Phillips, C., Doole, I., and Lowe, R. (1994), *International Marketing Strategy* (London: Routledge).

Piercy, N. (1985), *Marketing Organisation: An Analysis of Information Processing, Power and Politics* (London: Allen & Unwin).

——(1989), 'The Role of the Marketing Department in the UK Retail Organisations', *International Journal of Retailing*, 4/2: 46–65.

——(1990), 'Marketing Concepts and Actions: Implementing Marketing-Led Strategic Change', *European Journal of Marketing*, 24/2: 24–42.

——(1991), *Market-Led Strategic Change: Making Marketing Happen in Your Organisation* (London: Thorsons).

——(1998), 'Marketing Implementation: The Implications of Marketing Paradigm Weakness for the Strategy Execution Process', *Journal of the Academy of Marketing Science*, 26/3: 22–36.

——and Alexander, N. (1988), 'The Status Quo of the Marketing Organisation in UK Retailing', *Service Industries Journal*, 8/2: 155–76.

——and Evans, M. J. (1983), *Managing Marketing Information* (London: Croom Helm).

——and Morgan, N. (1989), 'Marketing Organisation in the UK Financial Service Industry', *Journal of Bank Marketing*, 7/4: 3–10.

————(1991), 'Internal Marketing—The Missing Half of the Marketing Programme', *Long-Range Planning*, 24/2: 82–92.

————(1993), 'Strategic and Operational Market Segmentation: A Managerial Analysis', *Journal of Strategic Marketing*, 1/4: 123–40.

Pierson, G. J. (1993), 'Business Orientation: Cliché or Substance?', *Journal of Marketing Management*, 9/3: 233–43.

Pine, B. J. (1992), *Mass Customization: The New Frontier in Business Competition* (Boston: Harvard Business School Press).

——Peppers, D., and Rogers, M. (1995), 'Do you want to Keep your Customers Forever?', *Harvard Business Review* (Mar.–Apr.), 103–14.

Plank, R. E. (1985), 'A Critical Review of Industrial Market Segmentation', *Industrial Marketing Management*, 14/2: 79–91.

Plummer, J. (1974), 'The Concept and Application of Life Style Segmentation', *Journal of Marketing*, 38/1 (Jan.), 33–7.

Polli, P., and Cook, V. (1969), 'Validity of the Product Life Cycle', *Journal of Business*, 42/4 (Oct.), 385–400.

Porter, J. L., and Renforth, W. (1978), 'Franchise Arrangements: Spotting the Important Legal Flaws', *Journal of Small Business Management* (Oct.), 27–31.

Porter, M. E. (1980), *Competitive Strategy* (New York: Macmillan).

——(1985), *Competitive Advantage: Creating and Sustaining Superior Advantage* (New York: Free Press).

——and Millar, V. E. (1985), 'How Information Gives You Competitive Advantage', *Harvard Business Review* (July–Aug.), 149–60.

Pride, M. W., and Ferrell, O. C. (1989), *Marketing: Concepts and Strategies* (Boston: Houghton Mifflin).

Prahalad, C. K., and Hamel, G. (1994), 'Strategy as a Field of Study: Why Search for a New Paradigm', *Strategic Management Journal*, 15 (special issue), 5–16.

Proctor, T. (1996), *Marketing Management: Integrating Theory and Practice* (London: ITBP).

Quelch, A. J., and Klein, R. L. (1996), 'The Internet and International Marketing', *Sloan Management Review*, 37/3 (Spring), 60–75.

Quelch, J. A., Kashiani, H., and Vandermerwe, S. (1994), *European Cases in Marketing Management* (Homewood, Ill.: Irwin).

Rappaport, A. (1986), *Creating Shareholder Value* (New York: Free Press).

RaStaschs, R. C. (1975), 'The Shifting Role of the Product Manager', *Harvard Business Review*, 53/1 (Jan.–Feb.), 65–73.

Rathmell, J. M. (1974), *Marketing in the Service Sector* (Cambridge, Mass.: Winthrop Publishers).

Ray, D. (1997), 'Annual Survey of Promotional Practices

Documents Industry Trends', *Direct Marketing*, 60/3: 24–5.

Rayport, J. F., and Sviokla, J. J. (1994), 'Managing in the Marketspace', *Harvard Business Review* (Nov.–Dec.), 141–50.

——— (1995), 'Exploiting the Virtual Value Chain', *Harvard Business Review*, 73/6: 75.

Reeder, R. R., Brierty, E. G., and Reeder, B. H. (1991), *Industrial Marketing* (Englewood Cliffs, NJ: Prentice Hall).

Reich, R. (1991), *The Work of Nations: Preparing Ourselves for 21st Century Capitalism* (London: Simon & Schuster).

Reynolds, J. (1993), 'Lifestyle Databases, Strategic Marketing Tools', *Journal of Targeting Measurement and Analysis for Marketing*, 2/1: 23–36.

——— (1997), *Home Shopping across Europe* (London: KPMG).

Ries, A., and Trout, J. (1986), *Positioning: The Battle for your Mind* (New York: McGraw-Hill).

Rijkens, R. (1992), *European Advertising Strategies* (London: Cassell).

Ringbakk, K. A. (1971), 'Why Planning Fails', *European Business*, 29 (Spring), 15–16.

Robbins, S. P. (1992), *Essentials of Organizational Behaviour* (Englewood Cliffs, NJ: Prentice Hall).

Robinson, J. (1933), *The Economics of Imperfect Competition* (London: Macmillan).

Robinson, P. J., Faris, C. W., and Wind, Y. (1967), *Industrial Buying and Creative Marketing* (Boston: Allyn & Bacon).

Robinson, W. T. (1988), 'Sources of Market Pioneer Advantages: The Case of Industrial Goods Industries', *Journal of Marketing Research*, 25/1 (Feb.), 87–94.

——— and Fornell, C. (1985), 'The Sources of Market Pioneer Advantages in Consumer Goods Industries', *Journal of Marketing Research*, 22/3 (Aug.), 297–304.

Rosen, B., Boddewyn, J., and Lewis, E. (1989), 'US Brands Abroad: An Empirical Study of Global Branding', *International Marketing Review*, 6/1: 7–21.

Rowthorn, R., and Ramswamy, R. (1997), 'Deindustrialization: Causes and Implications', IMF Working Paper WP/97/42.

Rubin, P. (1978), 'The Theory of the Firm and the Structure of the Franchise Contract', *Journal of Law and Economics*, 23: 223–33.

Rumelt, R. P. (1984), 'Towards a Strategic Theory of the Firm', in R. B. Lamb (ed.), *Competitive Strategic Management* (Englewood Cliffs, NJ: Prentice Hall).

——— (1991), 'How Much does Industry Matter?', *Strategic Management Journal*, 12/3: 167–85.

Saddick, S. M. A. (1966), 'Marketing in the Wood, Textile, Machinery and Clothing Industry', Ph.D. thesis (Bradford).

Salle, R., and Silvestre, H. (1992), *Vendre à l'industrie— Approche stratégique de la relation Business to Business* (Paris: Liaisons).

Sanchez, R. (1995), 'Strategic Flexibility in Product Competition', *Strategic Management Journal*, 16 (summer special issue), 135–59.

Sarkar, M. B., Butler, B., and Seinfeld, C. (1996), 'Intermediaries and Cybermediaries: A Continuing Role for Mediating Players in the Electronic Marketplace', *Journal of Computer-Mediated Communication*.

Sashittal, S., and Wilemon, L. (1994), 'Integrating Technology and Marketing: Implications for Improving Customer Responsiveness', *International Journal of Technology Management*, 9/5–7: 691–708.

Saunders, J. (1995), 'Quantitative Methods in Marketing', in M. J. Baker (ed.), *Companion Encyclopedia of Marketing* (London: Routledge).

——— and Saker, J. (1994), 'The Changing Consumer in the UK', *International Journal of Research in Marketing*, 11: 477–89.

Saxe, R., and Weitz, B. A. (1982), 'The SOCO Scale: A Measure of the Customer Orientation of Salespeople', *Journal of Marketing Research*, 19: 343–51.

Schwartz, S. H. (1992), 'Universals in the Content and Structure of Values: Theoretical Advances and Empirical Tests in 20 Countries', in M. P. Zanna (ed.), *Advances in Experimental Social Psychology 25* (San Diego, Calif.: Academic Press), 1–65.

——— and Bilsky, W. (1987), 'Toward a Universal Psychological Structure of Human Values', *Journal of Personality and Social Psychology*, 53: 550–62.

Sellers, P. (1989), 'The ABC's of Marketing to Kids', *Fortune*, 8 May, 115.

Shapiro, B. P. (1988), 'What the Hell is Marketing Oriented?', *Harvard Business Review*, 66/6 (Nov.–Dec.), 119–25.

——— Rangan, V. K., and Sviokla, J. J. (1992), 'Staple Yourself to an Order', *Harvard Business Review* (July–Aug.), 113–22.

Sharp, B. (1991), 'Marketing Orientation: More than Just Customer Focus', *International Marketing Review*, 8/4: 20–5.

——— (1995), 'Business Orientation and Corporate Success: A Correspondence Analysis of Wong and Saunders' Findings', *Journal of Strategic Marketing*, 3/3: 205–14.

Shearer, B. (1995), 'TiO$_2$ Producers Mull New Plants', *Chemical Marketing Reporter*, 247/2 (9 Jan.), 3, 19.

Sheppard, B. H., Hartwick, J., and Warshaw, P. R. (1988), 'The Theory of Reasoned Action: A Meta-Analysis of Past Research with Recommendations for Modifications and Future Research', *Journal of Consumer Research*, 15: 325–43.

Sheth, J. N. (1973), 'A Model of Industrial Buyer Behavior', *Journal of Marketing*, 37: 50–6.

——— (1994), 'The Domain of Relationship Marketing', unpublished paper, Second Research Conference on Relationship Marketing, Centre for Relationship Marketing, Emory University, Atlanta, Ga.

——— Gardner, D. M., and Garrett, D. E. (1988), *Marketing Theory: Evolution and Evaluation* (New York: Wiley).

Shostack, G. L. (1977), 'Breaking Free from Product Marketing', *Journal of Marketing*, 41 (Apr.), 73–80.

——— (1984), 'Designing Services that Deliver', *Harvard Business Review*, 62/1 (Jan.–Feb.), 133–9.

——(1987), 'Service Positioning through Structural Change', *Journal of Marketing*, 51/1 (Jan.), 34–43 (*http://shum.huji.ac.il/jcmc/vol1/issue3/vol1no3.html*).

Simon H. A. (1952), 'A Formal Theory of Interaction in Social Group', *American Sociological Review*, 17: 77–84.

——(1956), 'Rational choice and the structure of the environment', *Psychological Review*, 63: 129–38.

——(1989), *Price Management* (Amsterdam: Elsevier Science Publishers).

Skiera, B., and Albers, S. (1998), 'COSTA: Contribution Optimizing Sales Territory Alignment', *Marketing Science*, 17/3: 196–213.

Skinner, J. S. (1990), *Marketing* (Boston: Houghton Mifflin).

Slater, F. S., and Narver, C. J. (1995), 'Market Orientation and Learning Organization', *Journal of Marketing*, 59/3: 63–75.

Sleight, P. (1997), *Targeting Customers* (2nd edn.; Henley on Thames: NTC Publications Ltd.).

Smallwood, J. E. (1973), 'The Product Life Cycle: A Key to Strategic Marketing Planning', *MSU Business Topics* (Winter), 29–35.

Smith, M., and Dikolli, S. (1995), 'Customer Profitablity Analysis: An Activity-Based Costing Approach', *Managerial Auditing Journal*, 10/7: 3–7.

Smith, W. R. (1956), 'Product Differentiation and Market Segmentation as Alternative Marketing Strategies', *Journal of Marketing*, 21/3 (July), 3–8.

Social Trends (1996) (London: HMSO).

Song, X. M., Montoya-Weiss, M. M., and Schmidt, J. B. (1997), 'Antecedents and Consequences of Cross-Functional Cooperation: A Comparison of R&D, Manufacturing and Marketing Perspectives', *Journal of Product Innovation Management*, 14/1: 35–47.

Souder, W. E. (1988), 'Managing Relations between R&D and Marketing in New Product Development Projects', *Journal of Product Innovation Management*, 5/1: 6–19.

Spreng, R. A., and Mackoy, R. D. (1996), 'An Empirical Examination of a Model of Perceived Service Quality and Satisfaction', *Journal of Retailing*, 72/2: 201–14.

Stalk, G., Evans, P., and Schulman, L. E. (1992), 'Competing on Capabilities: The New Rules of Corporate Strategy', *Harvard Business Review* (Mar.–Apr.), 57–69.

Stanton, W. J. (1997), *Fundamentals of Marketing* (New York: McGraw-Hill).

Stanworth, J. (1995), 'A European Perspective on the Success of the Franchise Relationship', paper presented at the 9th Annual Conference of the Society of Franchising, San Juan, Puerto Rico, 21–22 Jan.

Stasch, S. F., and Lanktree, B. (1980), 'Can your Marketing Planning Procedures be Improved?', *Journal of Marketing*, 4/3: 79–90.

Stephenson, P. R., Cron, W. L., and Frazier, G. L. (1979), 'Delegating Pricing Authority to the Sales Force: The Effects on Sales and Profit Performance', *Journal of Marketing*, 43/2: 21–8.

Stern, A. (1986), 'The Strategic Value of Price Structure', *Journal of Business Strategy*, 7 (Autumn), 22–31.

Stern, L. W., Sturdivant, F. D., and Getz, G. A. (1993), 'Accomplishing Channel Change: Paths and Pitfalls', *European Management Journal*, 11/1: 3–8.

Stiving, M., and Winer, R. S. (1997), 'An Empirical Analysis of Price Endings with Scanner Data', *Journal of Consumer Research*, 24/1 (June), 57–67.

Stone, B. (1996), *Successful Direct Marketing Methods* (5th edn.; Chicago: NTC Business Books).

Stone, M. (1997), 'Chance of a Lifetime', *Direct Response* (Sept.), 49.

Street, R. (1998), 'Traditional and New Channels—Changing Routes to Market', *Traditional and New Distribution Channels—Selection, Strategy and Management Conference* (Milton Keynes: National Materials Handling Centre, Mar.).

Tapp, A. (1998), *Principles of Direct and Database Marketing* (London: Pitman/FT Publishing).

Tapscott, D., and Caston, A. (1993), *Paradigm Shift: The New Promise of Information Technology* (New York: McGraw-Hill).

Taylor, A. (1994), 'The Golden Age of Autos', *Fortune*, 4 Apr., 40–50.

Taylor, F. W. (1947), *The Principles of Scientific Management* (New York: Harper).

Taylor, T. C. (1985), 'Xerox's Sales Force Learns a New Game', *Sales & Marketing Management*, 1 July, 48–51.

Teas, R. K. (1993), 'Expectations, Performance Evaluation, and Consumers' Perception of Quality', *Journal of Marketing*, 57 (Oct.), 18–34.

Tellis, G. J. (1986), 'Beyond the Many Faces of Price: An Integration of Pricing Strategies', *Journal of Marketing*, 50/4 (Oct.), 146–60.

——(1988), 'The Price Elasticity of Selective Demand: A Meta Analysis of Econometric Models of Sale', *Journal of Marketing Research*, 25/4 (Nov.), 331–41.

——and Zufryden, F. S. (1995), 'Tackling the Retailer Decision Maze: Which Brands to Discount, How Much, When and Why?', *Marketing Science*, 14, part 2/3: 271–99.

Thaler, R. (1985), 'Mental Accounting and Consumer Choice', *Marketing Science*, 4/3: 199–214.

Thompson, H. (1998), 'Marketing Strategies: What do your Customers Really Want?', *Journal of Business Strategy*, 19/4: 16–22.

Thompson, H. U. (1962), *Product Strategy* (London: Business Publications Ltd.).

Thorelli, H. B., and Burnett, S. C. (1981), 'The Nature of Product Life Cycles for Industrial Goods Business', *Journal of Marketing*, 45/4: 97–108.

Timmons, J. A. (1978), 'Characteristics and Role Demands of Entrepreneurship', *American Journal of Small Business*, 3: 5–17.

Townsend, R. (1971), *Up the Organization* (New York: Holder Fawcett).

Toyne, B., and Walters, P. G. P. (1993), *Global Marketing Management: A Strategic Perspective* (Englewood Cliffs, NJ: Prentice Hall).

Treacy, M., and Wiersema, F. (1993), 'Customer Intimacy

and Other Value Disciplines', *Harvard Business Review*, 71/1 (Jan.–Feb.), 84–93.

Triffin, R. (1940), *Monopolistic Competition and General Equilibrium Theory* (Boston: Harvard University Press).

Trout, J., and Rivkin, S. (1996), *The New Positioning: The Latest on the World's Number 1 Business Strategy* (New York: McGraw-Hill).

Turnbull, P. W., and Paliwoda, S. J. (1986) (eds.), *Research in International Marketing* (London: Croom Helm).

Tzokas, N., Saren, M., and Brownlie, D. (1997), 'Generating Marketing Resources by Means of R&D Activities in High Technology Firms', *Industrial Marketing Management*, 26/4: 331–40.

Udell, J. G. (1968), 'Towards a Theory of Marketing Strategy', *British Journal of Marketing* (Winter), 298–303.

UNCTAD (1996), *World Investment Report 1966* (Geneva: Investment, Trade and International Policy Arrangements).

Uncles, M., and Ellis, D. (1989), 'The Buying of Own-Labels', *European Journal of Marketing*, 23/3: 57–70.

Unger, L. (1981), 'Consumer Marketing Trends in the 1980s when Growth Slows', *European Research*, 9/2: 69–74.

Urban, G. L., and Hauser, J. R. (1993), *Design and Marketing of New Products* (Englewood Cliffs, NJ: Prentice-Hall).

——and Katz, G. M. (1983), 'Pre-Test-Market Models: Validation and Managerial Implications', *Journal of Marketing Research*, 20/3 (Aug.), 221–34.

van Dam, Y., and van Trijp, H. L. M. (1993), 'Consumer Perceptions of and Pretences for Product Packaging', in J. Chias and J. Sureda (eds.), *Marketing for the New Europe: Dealing with Complexity* (Proceedings of the 22nd Annual Conference of the European Marketing Academy, Barcelona, 25–28 May), 1469–85.

Vanden Bergh, B., Alder, K., and Oliver, K. (1987), 'Linguistic Distinction among Top Brand Names', *Institute of Advertising Research* (Aug.–Sept.).

Van den Bulte, C. (1991), *The Concept of the Marketing Mix Revisited: A Case Analysis of Methaphor in Marketing Theory and Management* (Ghent: Vlerick School of Management).

van der Hart, H. (1990), 'Government Organisations and their Customers in the Netherlands: Strategy, Tactics and Operations', *European Journal of Marketing*, 24/7: 31–42.

van Everdingen, Y. M., and van Raaij, W. F. (1998), 'The Dutch People and the Euro: A Structural Equations Analysis Relating National Identity and Economic Expectations to Attitude towards the Euro', *Journal of Economic Psychology*, 19/6: 721–40.

van Raaij, W. F., and Eilander, G. (1983), 'Consumer Economizing Tactics for Ten Product Categories', *Advances in Consumer Research*, 10: 169–74.

——and Gianotten, H. J. (1990), 'Consumer Confidence, Expenditure, Saving and Credit', *Journal of Economic Psychology*, 11: 269–90.

van Waterschoot, W. (1995), 'The Marketing Mix', in M. J. Baker (ed.), *Companion Encyclopedia of Marketing* (London: Routledge).

——and Van den Bulte, C. (1992), 'The 4P Classification of the Marketing Mix Revisited', *Journal of Marketing*, 56/4 (Oct.), 83–93.

Varaldo, R., and Marbach, G. (1995), 'The Changing Consumer in Italy', *International Journal of Research in Marketing*, 12: 467–83.

Venkatesh, R., and Mahajan, V. (1993), 'A Probabilistic Approach to Pricing a Bundle of Products or Services', *Journal of Marketing Research*, 30 (Nov.), 494–508.

von Hippel, E. (1978), 'Successful Industrial Products from Customer Ideas: Presentation of a New Customer-Active Paradigm with Evidence and Implications', *Journal of Marketing*, 42/1 (Jan.), 39–49.

——(1986), 'Lead Users: A Source of Novel Product Concepts', *Management Science*, 32/7 (July), 791–805.

Waldo, C. N. (1973), 'What's Bothering Marketing Chiefs Most? Segmenting', *Advertising Age*, 4 June, 77.

Walters, R. G., and McKenzie, S. B. (1988), 'A Structural Equations Analysis of the Impact of Price Promotions on Store Performance', *Journal of Marketing Research*, 25 (Feb.), 51–63.

Warren, K., Moriarty, S., and Duncan, T. (1992), *Marketing* (Englewood Cliffs, NJ: Prentice Hall).

Wasson, C. R. (1971), *Product Management: Product Life Cycles and Competitive Marketing Strategy* (St Charles, Ill.: Challenge Books).

——(1976), 'The Importance of the Product Life Cycle to the Industrial Marketer', *Industrial Marketing Management*, 5/6: 299–308.

Webster, F. E., Jr. (1979), *Industrial Marketing Strategy* (New York: Wiley).

——(1988), 'The Rediscovery of the Marketing Concept', *Business Horizons*, 31 (May–June), 29–39.

——(1992), 'The Changing Role of Marketing in the Corporation', *Journal of Marketing*, 56/4: 1–17.

——(1994), 'Executing the New Marketing Concept', *Marketing Management*, 31: 8–18.

——and Wind, Y. (1972), 'A General Model of Organizational Buying Behavior', *Journal of Marketing*, 36: 12–19.

Weichmann, W. E., and Pringle, L. E. (1979), 'Problems that Plague Multinational Marketers', *Harvard Business Review* (July–Aug.), 118–24.

Weinstein, A. (1987), *Market Segmentation* (Chicago: Probus Publishing Company).

——(1994), *Market Segmentation: Using Demographics, Psychographics and Other Niche Marketing Techniques to Predict and Model Consumer Behaviour* (Chicago: Probus Publishing Company).

Wells, W. D., and Gubar, G. (1966), 'Life-Cycle Concepts in Marketing Research', *Journal of Marketing Research*, 6: 355–63.

Wikstrom, S. R. (1997), 'The Changing Consumer in Sweden', *International Journal of Research in Marketing*, 14: 261–74.

Wilkinson, I. A., and Young, L. C. (1994), 'Business Dancing—The Nature and Role of Interfirm Relationships in Business Strategy', *Asia–Australia Marketing Journal*, 2/1: 67–79.

Williamson, O. E. (1975), *Markets and Hierarchies: Analysis and Antitrust Implications* (New York: Free Press).

——(1985), *The Economic Institutions of Capitalism* (New York: Free Press).

——(1991), 'Comparative Economic Organizations: The Analysis of Discrete Structural Alternatives', *Administrative Science Quarterly*, 36: 269–96.

Wilson, A. (1972), *The Marketing of Professional Services* (London: McGraw-Hill).

Wilson, D. T. (1995), 'An Integrated Model of Buyer–Seller Relationships', *Journal of the Academy of Marketing Science*, 23/4: 335–45.

—— and Möller, K. E. (1988), 'Buyer–Seller Relationships: Alternative Conceptualizations', Report 10-1988, Institute for the Study of Business Markets, Pennsylvania State University.

—— and Mummalaneni, V. (1986), 'Bonding and Commitment in Supplier Relationship: A Preliminary Conceptualization', *Industrial Marketing and Purchasing*, 1/3: 44–58.

Wind, Y. (1978), 'Issues and Advances in Segmentation Research', *Journal of Marketing Research*, 18: 317–37.

——(1980), 'Going to Market: New Twist for some Old Tricks', *Wharton Magazine*, 4.

——(1995), 'Market Segmentation', in M. J. Baker (ed.), *Companion Encyclopaedia of Marketing* (London: Routledge).

—— and Cardozo, R. N. (1974), 'Industrial Marketing Segmentation', *Industrial Marketing Management*, 3: 153–66.

Winkler, J. (1990), 'Marketing Guide: Pricing', *Marketing*, 9 Aug., 17–20.

Woodside, A. G., and Vyas, N. (1987), *Industrial Purchasing Strategies* (Lexington, Mass.: Lexington Books).

Workman, J. P. (1995), ' "Engineering's" Interactions with Marketing Groups in an Engineering-Driven Organization', *IEEE Transactions on Engineering Management*, 42/2: 129–39.

World Values Study Group (1990), *World Values Survey* (Ann Arbor: Institute for Social Research, University of Michigan).

Wrigley, N. (1988), 'Retail Restructuring and Retail Analysis', in N. Wrigley (ed.), *Store Choice, Store Location and Market Analysis* (London: Routledge).

Young, M. (1994), 'Direct Response Television', *Journal of Targeting Measurement and Analysis for Marketing*, 2/2: 125–38.

Zeithaml, V. A. (1988), 'Consumer Perceptions of Price, Quality and Value', *Journal of Marketing*, 52/3: 2–23.

—— and Bitner, M. J. (1996), *Services Marketing* (New York: McGraw-Hill).

—— Berry, L. L., and Parasuraman, A. (1988), 'Communication and Control Processes in the Delivery of Service Quality', *Journal of Marketing*, 52 (Apr.), 35–48.

Index